Get Ahead of the Curve

Problem Solving for Students.

Automatically graded assignments (and the ability to get the highest possible grade by reworking the same assignments with new problems) motivate students to solve a lot more problems.

Instant feedback, including detailed tutorial instruction (complete solutions, step-by-step explanations, links to book material, etc.), provides instant gratification and immediate learning.

Graphing tools and questions integrated into assignments enable students to manipulate and even draw graphs that are automatically graded.

Solving Problems for Professors.

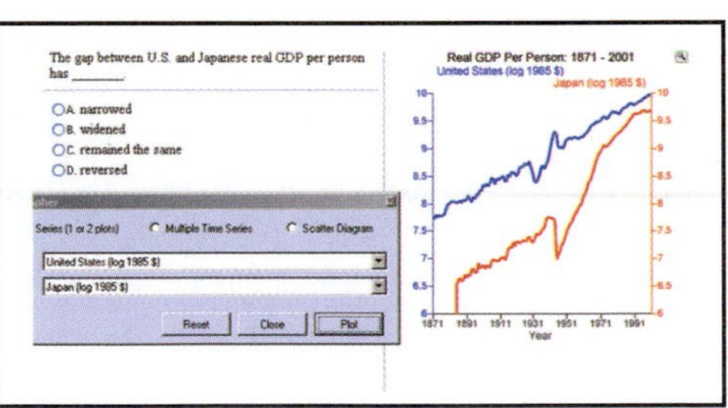

Easily create, assign, and automatically grade homework, quizzes, and tests.

Assign problems and exercises based on the actual end-of-chapter materials in the text book. Many have algorithmic versions for variety and extra practice.

Track students' progress through one easy-to-view, automatically populated grade book.

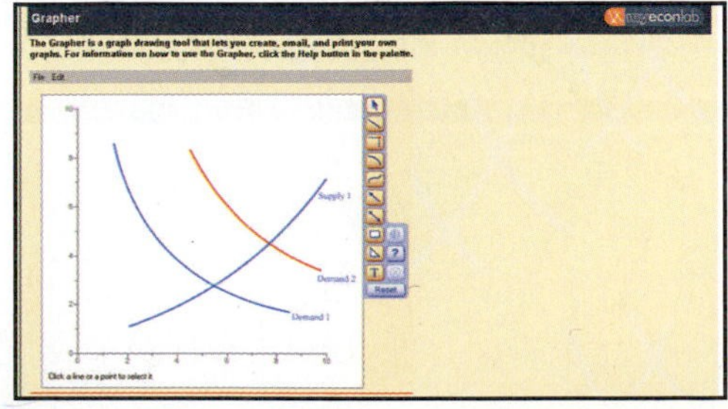

Get supplementary problems and teaching resources (like test banks and lecture slides) all in one place.

These features, plus personalized study plans for students, full etext options, practice tests, eStudy guides, and more, are all available in MyEconLab.

www.myeconlab.com

essentials of economics

R. Glenn Hubbard

Library of Congress Cataloging-in-Publication Data

Hubbard, R. Glenn.
Essentials of economics / R. Glenn Hubbard, Anthony Patrick O'Brien.
p. cm.
Includes bibliographical reference and index.
ISBN 0-13-230924-6
1. Economics I. O'Brien, Anthony Patrick. II. Title.
HB171.H83 2006
330—dc22

2006019451

AVP/Executive Editor: David Alexander
VP/Editorial Director: Jeff Shelstad
Manager, Product Development: Pamela Hersperger
Project Manager: Mary Kate Murray
Editorial Assistant: Michael Dittamo
Senior Development Editor: Lena Buonanno
Sr. Media Project Manager: Peter Snell
AVP/Executive Marketing Manager: Sharon Koch
Marketing Assistant: Patrick Barbera
Associate Director, Production Editorial: Judy Leale
Senior Managing Editor: Cynthia Regan
Senior Production Editor: Anne Graydon
Permissions Coordinator: Charles Morris
Associate Director, Manufacturing: Vincent Scelta
Senior Manufacturing Buyer: Diane Peirano
Design/Composition Manager: Christy Mahon
Composition Liaison: Suzanne Duda
Senior Art Director: Pat Smythe
Interior Design: Liz Harasymczuk
Cover Design: Pat Smythe
Illustration (Interior): ElectraGraphics, Inc.
Infographics: Ray Cruz
Manager, Photo Rights and Permissions: Zina Arabia
Image Permission Coordinator: Cynthia Vincenti
Photo Researcher: Diane Austin
Composition/Full-Service Project Management: Carlisle Publishing Services
Printer/Binder: Quebecor
Typeface: 10.5/12 Minion

Credits and acknowledgments borrowed from other sources and reproduced, with permission, in this textbook appear on page C-1.

Pearson Education LTD.
Pearson Education Singapore, Pte. Ltd
Pearson Education, Canada, Ltd
Pearson Education–Japan
Pearson Education Australia PTY, Limited
Pearson Education North Asia Ltd
Pearson Educación de Mexico, S.A. de C.V.
Pearson Education Malaysia, Pte. Ltd.

10 9 8 7 6 5 4 3 2 1
ISBN: 0-13-230924-6

For Constance, Raph, and Will

—R. Glenn Hubbard

To my mother and the memory of my father

—Anthony Patrick O'Brien

AUTHORSHIP

Glenn Hubbard policymaker, professor, and researcher. R. Glenn Hubbard is the Dean and Russell L. Carson Professor of Finance and Economics in the Graduate School of Business at Columbia University and Professor of Economics in Columbia's Faculty of Arts and Sciences. He is also a research associate of the National Bureau of Economic Research and a director of Automatic Data Processing, Black Rock Closed-End Funds, R. H. Donnelly, Inc., Duke Realty, KKR Financial Corporation, and Ripplewood Holdings. He received his Ph.D. in economics from Harvard University in 1983. From 2001–2003, he served as Chairman of the White House Council of Economic Advisers, and from 1991–1993, he was Deputy Assistant Secretary of the U.S. Treasury Department. Glenn Hubbard's fields of specialization are public economics, financial markets and institutions, corporate finance, macroeconomics, industrial organization, and public policy. He is the author of more than 90 articles in leading journals, including the *American Economic Review, Journal of Finance, Journal of Financial Economics, Journal of Political Economy, Journal of Public Economics, Quarterly Journal of Economics, RAND Journal of Economics,* and *Review of Economics and Statistics.* His research has been supported by grants from the National Science Foundation, the National Bureau of Economic Research, and numerous private foundations.

Tony O'Brien award-winning professor and researcher. Anthony Patrick O'Brien is a professor of economics at Lehigh University. He received his Ph.D. from the University of California, Berkeley, in 1987. He has taught principles of economics for more than 15 years, in both large sections and small honors classes. He received the Lehigh University Award for Distinguished Teaching. He was formerly the director of the Diamond Center for Economic Education and was named a Dana Foundation Faculty Fellow and Lehigh Class of 1961 Professor of Economics. He has been a visiting professor at the University of California, Santa Barbara, and the Graduate School of Industrial Administration at Carnegie Mellon University. Anthony O'Brien's research has dealt with such issues as the evolution of the U.S. automobile industry, the sources of U.S. economic competitiveness, the development of U.S. trade policy, the causes of the Great Depression, and the causes of black–white income differences. His research has been published in leading journals, including the *American Economic Review,* the *Quarterly Journal of Economics,* the *Journal of Money, Credit, and Banking, Industrial Relations,* and the *Journal of Economic History.* His research has been supported by grants from government agencies and private foundations. In addition to teaching and writing, Anthony O'Brien also serves on the editorial board of the *Journal of Socio-economics.*

CONTEXTUAL LEARNING

We are convinced that students learn to apply economic principles best if they are taught in a familiar context. Whether they open an art studio, do social work, trade on Wall Street, work for the government, or tend bar, students must understand the economic forces behind their work. And though business students will have many opportunities to see economic principles in action in various courses, liberal arts students may not. We therefore use many diverse real-world business and policy examples to illustrate economic concepts and to develop educated consumers, voters, and citizens.

Here are several examples of our approach:

- *A strong set of introductory chapters.* Our introductory chapters provide students with a solid foundation in the basics. We emphasize the key ideas of marginal analysis and economic efficiency. In Chapter 4, "Market Efficiency and Market Failure," we use the concepts of consumer surplus and producer surplus to measure the economic effects of price ceilings and price floors as they relate to the familiar examples of rental properties and the minimum wage. (We revisit consumer surplus and producer surplus in Chapter 18, "Comparative Advantage, International Trade, and Exchange Rates," where we discuss outsourcing and analyze government policies that affect trade, and in Chapter 9, "Monopoly and Antitrust Policy," where we examine the effect of market power on economic efficiency.) In Chapter 5, "Firms, the Stock Market, and Corporate Governance," we provide students with a basic understanding of how firms are organized, how they raise funds, and how they provide information to investors. We also illustrate how in a market system entrepreneurs meet consumer wants and efficiently organize production. To explore how government policy affects business, we cover the WorldCom and Enron business scandals and the objectives of the 2002 Sarbanes-Oxley Act.
- *Early coverage of policy issues.* To pique interest and expose students to policy issues early in the course, we discuss outsourcing in Chapter 1, rent control, the minimum wage, air pollution, and global warming in Chapter 4, and government policy towards illegal drugs in Chapter 6, "Consumer Choice and Elasticity."
- *A broad discussion of macro statistics.* Many students pay some attention to the financial news and know that the release of stastitics by federal agencies can cause movements in stock and bond prices. A background in macroeconomic statistics helps clarify some of the policy issues encountered in later chapters. In Chapter 11, "GDP: Measuring Total Production and Income," and Chapter 12, "Unemployment and Inflation," we provide students with an understanding of the uses and potential shortcomings of the key macroeconomic statistics, without getting bogged down in the minutiae of how the statistics are constructed. So, for instance, we discuss the important differences between the payroll survey and the household survey for understanding conditions in the labor market. We explain why the financial markets react more strongly to news from the payroll survey.

CONTEXTUAL LEARNING

- *Coverage of long-run topics.* We place key macroeconomic issues in their long-run context in Chapter 13, "Economic Growth, the Financial System, and Business Cycles." This chapter puts the business cycle in the context of underlying long-run growth. We discuss what actually happens during the phases of the business cycle, which we believe is important material if students are to have the understanding of business cycles they will need to interpret economic events. Yet this material is often discussed only briefly or omitted entirely in other books. This chapter also provides an overview of the financial system and an explanation of the sources of long-run economic growth.
- *A dynamic model of aggregate demand and aggregate supply.* We take a fresh approach to the standard aggregate demand-aggregate supply model. We realize there is no good, simple alternative to using the *AD-AS* model when explaining movements in the price level and in real GDP. But we know that more instructors are dissatisfied with the *AD-AS* model than with any other aspect of introductory macroeconomics. The key problem, of course, is that *AD-AS* is a static model that attempts to account for dynamic changes in real GDP and the price level. Our approach retains the basics of the *AD-AS* model, but makes it more accurate and useful by making it more dynamic. We emphasize two points: First, changes in the position of the short-run (upward-sloping) aggregate supply curve depend mainly on the state of expectations of the inflation rate. Second, the existence of growth in the economy means that the long-run (vertical) aggregate supply curve shifts to the right every year. This "dynamic" *AD-AS* model provides students with a more accurate understanding of the causes and consequences of fluctuations in real GDP and the price level. We introduce this model in Chapter 14, "Aggregate Demand and Aggregate Supply Analysis," and use it to discuss monetary policy in Chapter 16 and fiscal policy in Chapter 17.
- *Coverage of both the demand side and supply side effects of fiscal policy.* Our discussion of fiscal policy in Chapter 17 carefully distinguishes between automatic stabilizers and discretionary fiscal policy. We also have significant coverage of the supply-side effects of fiscal policy.

When George Lucas was asked why he made *Star Wars,* he replied, "It's the kind of movie I like to see, but no one seemed to be making them. So, I decided to make one." We realized that no one seemed to be writing the kind of textbook we wanted to use in our classes. So, after years of supplementing texts with fresh, lively, real-world examples from newspapers, magazines, and professional journals, we decided to write an economics text that delivered complete economics coverage with many real-world business examples. Our goal was to keep our classes "widget free."

We believe the course is a success if students can apply what they have learned in both personal and business settings, and if they have developed the analytical skills to understand what they read in the media. That's why we explain economic concepts by using many real-world business examples and applications. Here are a few examples:

Did Abercrombie and Fitch narrow its target market too much? (Chapter 10)

Which category of unemployment applies to optical engineers at Lucent? (Chapter 12)

How do exchange rates affect Caterpillar, Inc.'s sales? (Chapter 14)

Each CHAPTER-OPENING CASE sets a real-world context for learning, sparks students' interest in economics, and gives the chapter a unifying theme.

Each chapter opener covers a real-world situation faced by companies such as Cisco, Ford Motor Company, and the homebuilder Toll Brothers, Inc. The company is integrated in the narrative, graphs, and pedagogical features of the chapter. Many of the chapter openers focus on the role of the entrepreneur in developing new products and bringing them to the market. Here are a few examples of topics we explore:

Why was the Google IPO so successful, and how can we track the stock? (Chapter 5)

How did a tariff on sugar affect candy manufacturers? (Chapter 18)

How does Starbuck's grow through product differentiation? (Chapter 10)

How did fluctuations in GDP affect hiring at Freightliner, a commercial truck manufacturer based in Portland, Oregon? (Chapter 11)

How Hewlett-Packard Manages the Demand for Printers

In early 2005 the board of directors at Hewlett-Packard (H-P) ousted chief executive officer Carly Fiorina and replaced her with Mark Hurd, then the chief executive officer of NCR Corporation. What happened?.

Carly Fiorina had been a business celebrity for many years. In July 1999 she became H-P's chief executive officer, which made her the first woman to head one of the 100 largest firms in the United States. In

with Compaq had failed to improve H-P's performance in the personal computer market.

Printers, and not personal computers, are H-P's most successful product. Although printers account for only about 30 percent of the firm's sales, they account for 70 percent of its profits. In fact, as *An Inside Look* at the end of this chapter discusses, to increase the demand for printers the firm is will-

example, Carly Fiorina announced that sales of H-P printers had declined sharply in the first half of that year compared to the first half of 2000. Two events caused this decline: First, m small busines decided not to u computers to fas ful machines. Pu are a key part of ers. Second, t

POLICY EXAMPLES

AN INSIDE LOOK shows students how to apply the concepts of a chapter to the analysis of a newspaper article.

Reading the newspaper and other periodicals is an important part of understanding the current business climate. At the end of each chapter, a two-page periodical feature consists of an excerpt of an article, analysis of the article, graph(s), and critical thinking questions.

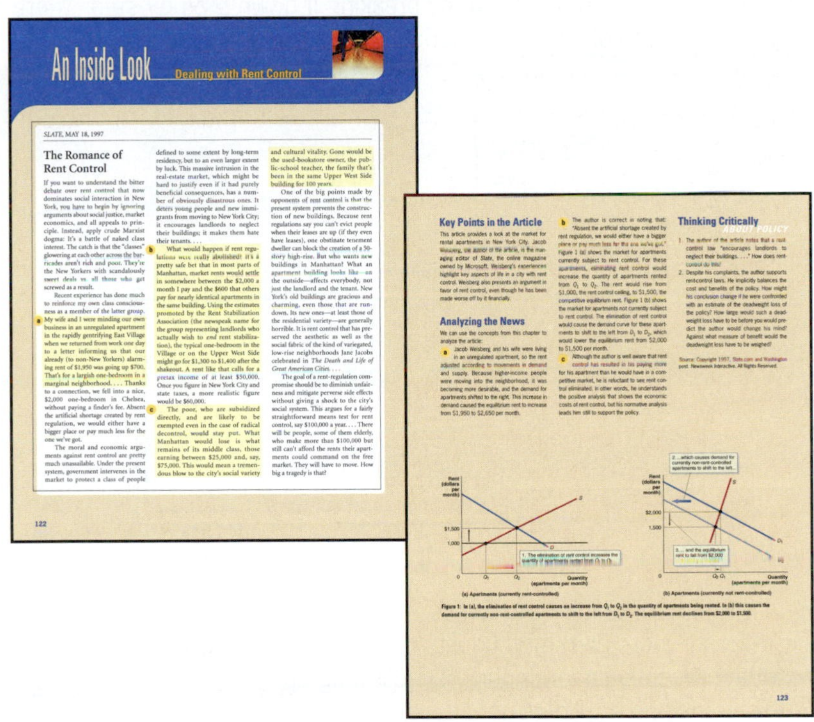

MAKING THE CONNECTION between concepts and the real world.

In each chapter, between two and four "Making the Connection" features present relevant, stimulating, and provocative news stories, primarily about business.

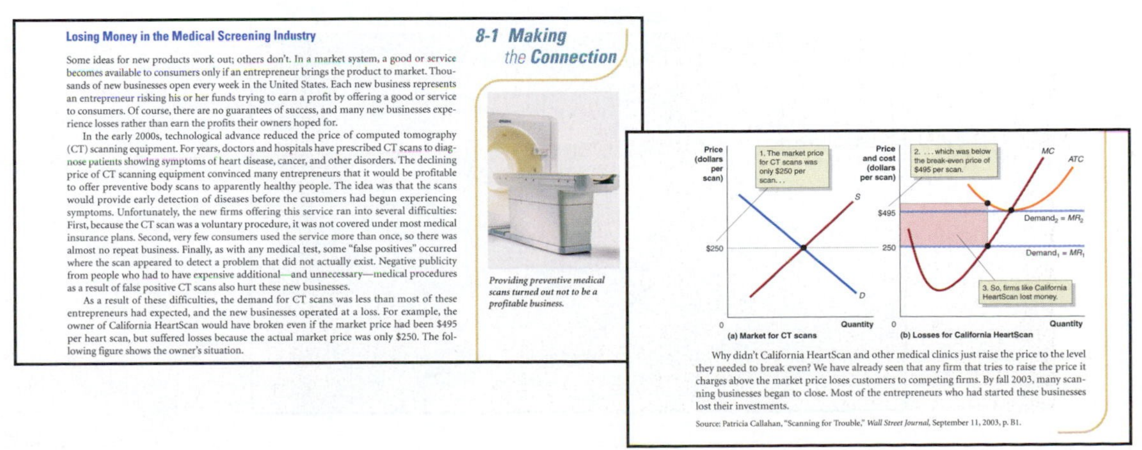

Losing Money in the Medical Screening Industry

8-1 Making the Connection

Some ideas for new products work out; others don't. In a market system, a good or service becomes available to consumers only if an entrepreneur brings the product to market. Thousands of new businesses open every week in the United States. Each new business represents an entrepreneur risking his or her funds trying to earn a profit by offering a good or service to consumers. Of course, there are no guarantees of success, and many new businesses experience losses rather than earn the profits their owners hoped for.

In the early 2000s, technological advance reduced the price of computed tomography (CT) scanning equipment. For years, doctors and hospitals have prescribed CT scans to diagnose patients showing symptoms of heart disease, cancer, and other disorders. The declining price of CT scanning equipment convinced many entrepreneurs that it would be profitable to offer preventive body scans to apparently healthy people. The idea was that the scans would provide early detection of diseases before the customers had begun experiencing symptoms. Unfortunately, the new firms offering this service ran into several difficulties: First, because the CT scan was a voluntary procedure, it was not covered under most medical insurance plans. Second, very few consumers used the service more than once, so there was almost no repeat business. Finally, as with any medical test, some "false positives" occurred where the scan appeared to detect a problem that did not actually exist. Negative publicity from people who had to have expensive additional—and unnecessary—medical procedures as a result of false positive CT scans also hurt these new businesses.

As a result of these difficulties, the demand for CT scans was less than most of these entrepreneurs had expected, and the new businesses operated at a loss. For example, the owner of California HeartScan would have broken even if the market price had been $495 per heart scan, but suffered losses because the actual market price was only $250. The following figure shows the owner's situation.

Providing preventive medical scans turned out not to be a profitable business.

Why didn't California HeartScan and other medical clinics just raise the price to the level they needed to break even? We have already seen that any firm that tries to raise the price it charges above the market price loses customers to competing firms. By fall 2003, many scanning businesses began to close. Most of the entrepreneurs who had started these businesses lost their investments.

Source: Patricia Callahan, "Scanning for Trouble," *Wall Street Journal*, September 11, 2003, p. B1.

SOLVED PROBLEMS

SOLVED PROBLEMS offer a hands-on approach to learning.

As we all know, many students have great difficulty handling applied economics problems. We help students overcome this hurdle by including two or three worked-out problems tied to select chapter-opening learning objectives and the associated quantitative information. Our goals are to keep students focused on the main ideas of each chapter and to give students a model of how to solve an economic problem by breaking it down step by step. There are additional exercises in the end-of-chapter materials tied to every Solved Problem.

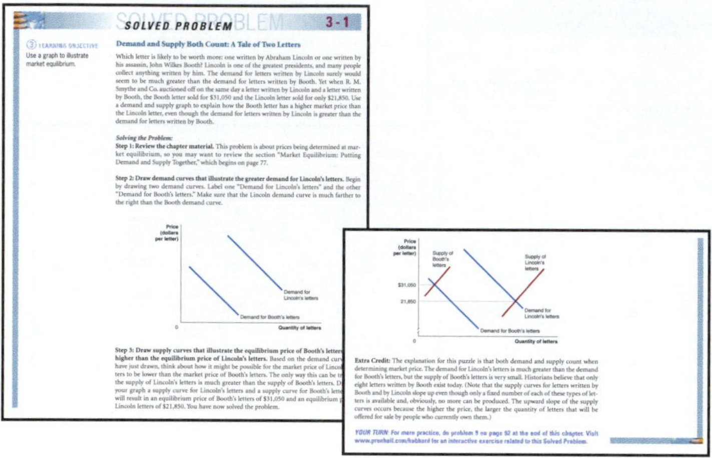

SOLVED PROBLEM 3-1

③ LEARNING OBJECTIVE
Use a graph to illustrate market equilibrium.

Demand and Supply Both Count: A Tale of Two Letters

Which letter is likely to be worth more: one written by Abraham Lincoln or one written by his assassin, John Wilkes Booth? Lincoln is one of the greatest presidents, and many people collect anything written by him. The demand for letters written by Lincoln surely would seem to be much greater than the demand for letters written by Booth. Yet when R. M. Smythe and Co. auctioned off on the same day a letter written by Lincoln and a letter written by Booth, the Booth letter sold for $31,050 and the Lincoln letter sold for only $21,850. Use a demand and supply graph to explain how the Booth letter has a higher market price than the Lincoln letter, even though the demand for letters written by Lincoln is greater than the demand for letters written by Booth.

Solving the Problem:

Step 1: Review the chapter material. This problem is about prices being determined at market equilibrium, so you may want to review the section "Market Equilibrium: Putting Demand and Supply Together," which begins on page 77.

Step 2: Draw demand curves that illustrate the greater demand for Lincoln's letters. Begin by drawing two demand curves. Label one "Demand for Lincoln's letters" and the other "Demand for Booth's letters." Make sure that the Lincoln demand curve is much farther to the right than the Booth demand curve.

Step 3: Draw supply curves that illustrate the equilibrium price of Booth's letters higher than the equilibrium price of Lincoln's letters. Based on the demand cur have just drawn, think about how it might be possible for the market price of Linco ters to be lower than the market price of Booth's letters. The only way this can be tr the supply of Lincoln's letters is much greater than the supply of Booth's letters. D your graph a supply curve for Lincoln's letters and a supply curve for Booth's lette will result in an equilibrium price of Booth's letters of $31,050 and an equilibrium Lincoln letters of $21,850. You have now solved the problem.

Extra Credit: The explanation for this puzzle is that both demand and supply count when determining market price. The demand for Lincoln's letters is much greater than the demand for Booth's letters, but the supply of Booth's letters is very small. Historians believe that only eight letters written by Booth exist today. (Note that the supply curves for letters written by Booth and by Lincoln slope up even though only a fixed number of each of these types of letters is available and, obviously, no more can be produced. The upward slope of the supply curves occurs because the higher the price, the larger the quantity of letters that will be offered for sale by people who currently own them.)

YOUR TURN: For more practice, do problem 9 on page 92 at the end of this chapter. Visit www.prenhall.com/hubbard for an interactive exercise related to this Solved Problem.

Don't Let This Happen To You!

We know from many years of teaching which concepts students find most difficult. Each chapter contains a box feature alerting students to the most common pitfalls in that chapter's material. We test the students' understanding by following up with a related question in the end-of-chapter "Problems and Applications" section.

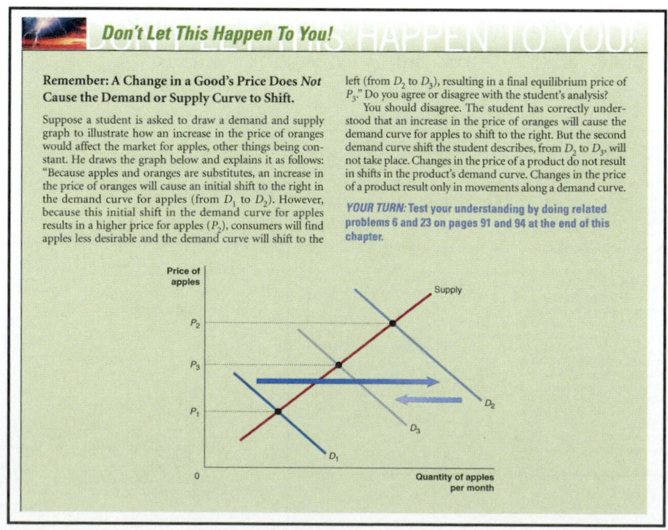

Don't Let This Happen To You!

Remember: A Change in a Good's Price Does *Not* Cause the Demand or Supply Curve to Shift.

Suppose a student is asked to draw a demand and supply graph to illustrate how an increase in the price of oranges would affect the market for apples, other things being constant. He draws the graph below and explains it as follows: "Because apples and oranges are substitutes, an increase in the price of oranges will cause an initial shift to the right in the demand curve for apples (from D_1 to D_2). However, because this initial shift in the demand curve for apples results in a higher price for apples (P_2), consumers will find apples less desirable and the demand curve will shift to the left (from D_2 to D_3), resulting in a final equilibrium price of P_3." Do you agree or disagree with the student's analysis?

You should disagree. The student has correctly understood that an increase in the price of oranges will cause the demand curve for apples to shift to the right. But the second demand curve shift the student describes, from D_2 to D_3, will not take place. Changes in the price of a product do not result in shifts in the product's demand curve. Changes in the price of a product result only in movements along a demand curve.

YOUR TURN: Test your understanding by doing related problems 6 and 23 on pages 91 and 94 at the end of this chapter.

GRAPHS AND SUMMARY TABLES

Graphs

Graphs are an indispensable part of the principles of economics course but are a major stumbling block for many students. Every chapter (except Chapter 1) includes end-of-chapter problems that require students to draw, read, and interpret graphs. Interactive graphing exercises can be found on the book's supporting Web site. We use four devices to help students read and interpret graphs:

1. Captions
2. Boxed Notes
3. Color-Coded Curves

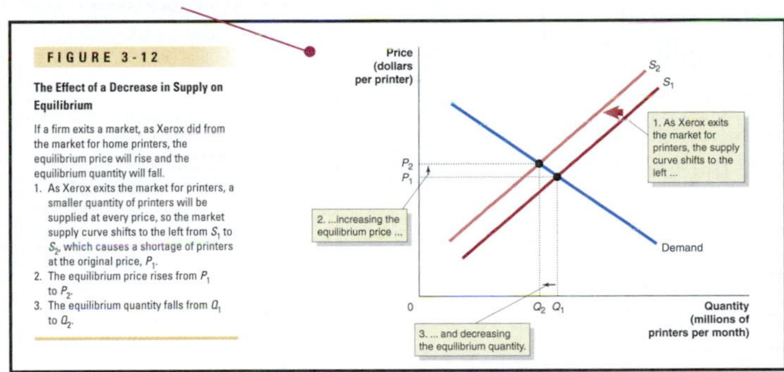

FIGURE 3-12

The Effect of a Decrease in Supply on Equilibrium

If a firm exits a market, as Xerox did from the market for home printers, the equilibrium price will rise and the equilibrium quantity will fall.

1. As Xerox exits the market for printers, a smaller quantity of printers will be supplied at every price, so the market supply curve shifts to the left from S_1 to S_2, which causes a shortage of printers at the original price, P_1.
2. The equilibrium price rises from P_1 to P_2.
3. The equilibrium quantity falls from Q_1 to Q_2.

4. Summary Tables with Graphs

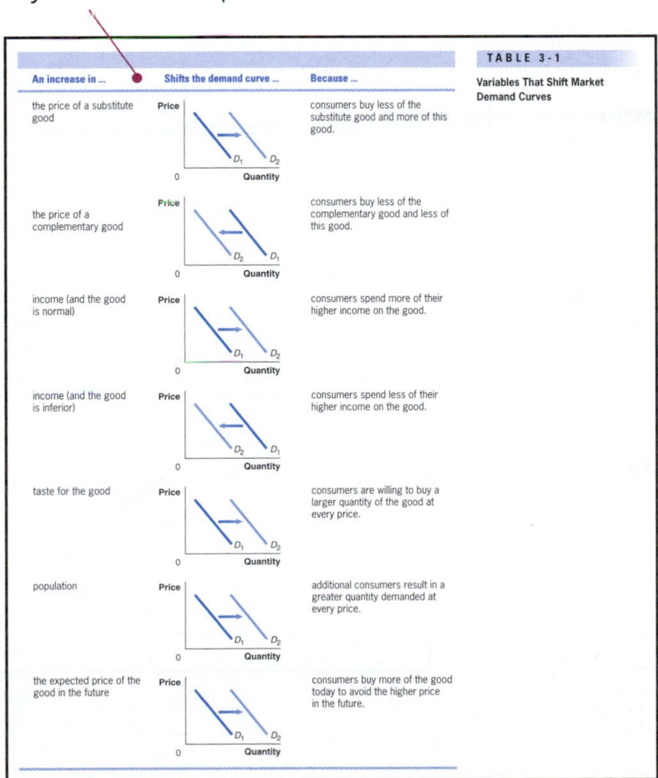

TABLE 3-1

Variables That Shift Market Demand Curves

An increase in ...	Shifts the demand curve ...	Because ...
the price of a substitute good	Price, 0, Quantity, D_1, D_2	consumers buy less of the substitute good and more of this good.
the price of a complementary good	Price, 0, Quantity, D_2, D_1	consumers buy less of the complementary good and less of this good.
income (and the good is normal)	Price, 0, Quantity, D_1, D_2	consumers spend more of their higher income on the good.
income (and the good is inferior)	Price, 0, Quantity, D_2, D_1	consumers spend less of their higher income on the good.
taste for the good	Price, 0, Quantity, D_1, D_2	consumers are willing to buy a larger quantity of the good at every price.
population	Price, 0, Quantity, D_1, D_2	additional consumers result in a greater quantity demanded at every price.
the expected price of the good in the future	Price, 0, Quantity, D_1, D_2	consumers buy more of the good today to avoid the higher price in the future.

INTEGRATED RESOURCES

Integrated Resources

The authors and Prentice Hall have worked together to integrate all text, print, and media resources to make teaching and learning easier.

Integration Benefits Students and Instructors

All textbooks have supporting resources, but not all textbooks have supporting resources that are seamlessly integrated with each other and the text. One of the driving forces behind the development of this resource package is our belief that concepts are grasped more easily in a familiar setting. That's why we decided to integrate the features of the text with the print and media resources for both students and instructors. And we did more than "integrate." We also enhanced the lecture materials by including additional examples in the Instructor's Manual.

Everything works together for a unified, efficient teaching and learning experience. Here's one example:

On this page is a "Solved Problem" that appears in the text. The facing page shows you how we integrate that Solved Problem—as well as the "Don't Let This Happen To You!" feature—in the end-of-chapter problems. Additional Solved Problems appear in the Instructor's Manual and Study Guide. See the pages that follow for more about supplements.

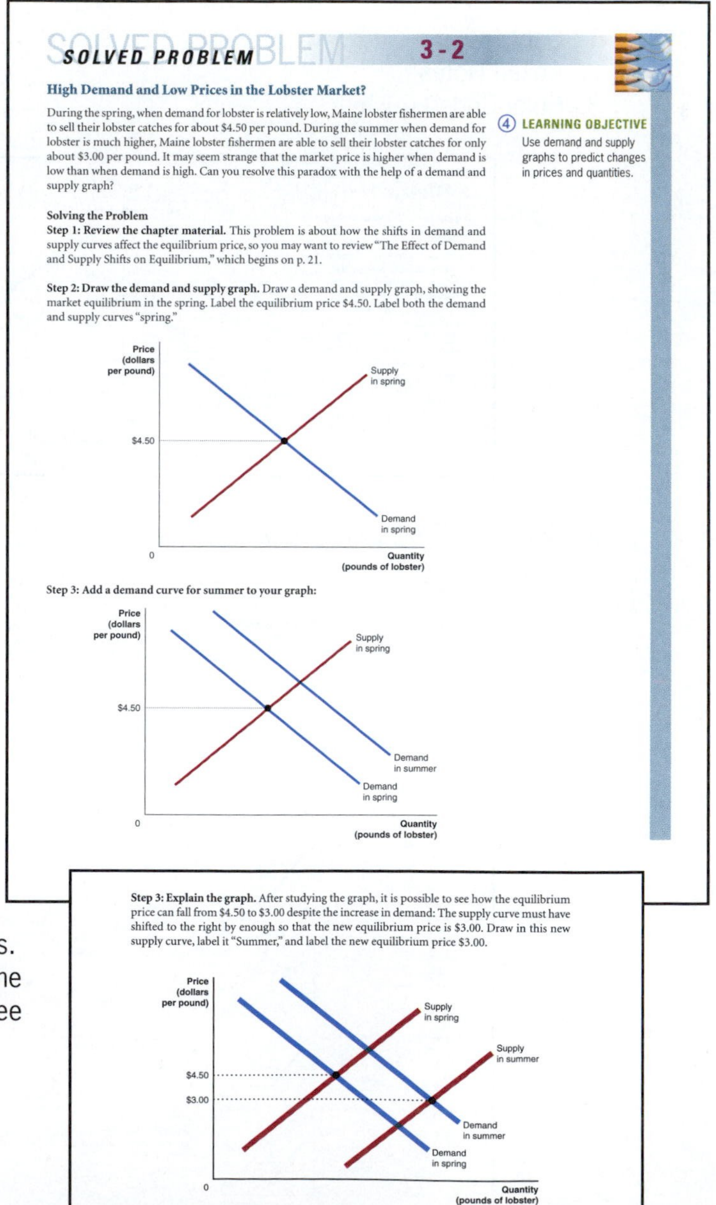

SOLVED PROBLEM 3-2

High Demand and Low Prices in the Lobster Market?

During the spring, when demand for lobster is relatively low, Maine lobster fishermen are able to sell their lobster catches for about $4.50 per pound. During the summer when demand for lobster is much higher, Maine lobster fishermen are able to sell their lobster catches for only about $3.00 per pound. It may seem strange that the market price is higher when demand is low than when demand is high. Can you resolve this paradox with the help of a demand and supply graph?

④ **LEARNING OBJECTIVE**
Use demand and supply graphs to predict changes in prices and quantities.

Solving the Problem

Step 1: Review the chapter material. This problem is about how the shifts in demand and supply curves affect the equilibrium price, so you may want to review "The Effect of Demand and Supply Shifts on Equilibrium," which begins on p. 21.

Step 2: Draw the demand and supply graph. Draw a demand and supply graph, showing the market equilibrium in the spring. Label the equilibrium price $4.50. Label both the demand and supply curves "spring."

Step 3: Add a demand curve for summer to your graph:

Step 3: Explain the graph. After studying the graph, it is possible to see how the equilibrium price can fall from $4.50 to $3.00 despite the increase in demand: The supply curve must have shifted to the right by enough so that the new equilibrium price is $3.00. Draw in this new supply curve, label it "Summer," and label the new equilibrium price $3.00.

Solved Problems appear in the chapters. Additional Solved Problems appear in the following areas:

- End-of-Chapter "Problems and Applications" section
- Instructor's Manual
- PowerPoint Slides
- Print Study Guide
- Test Item File

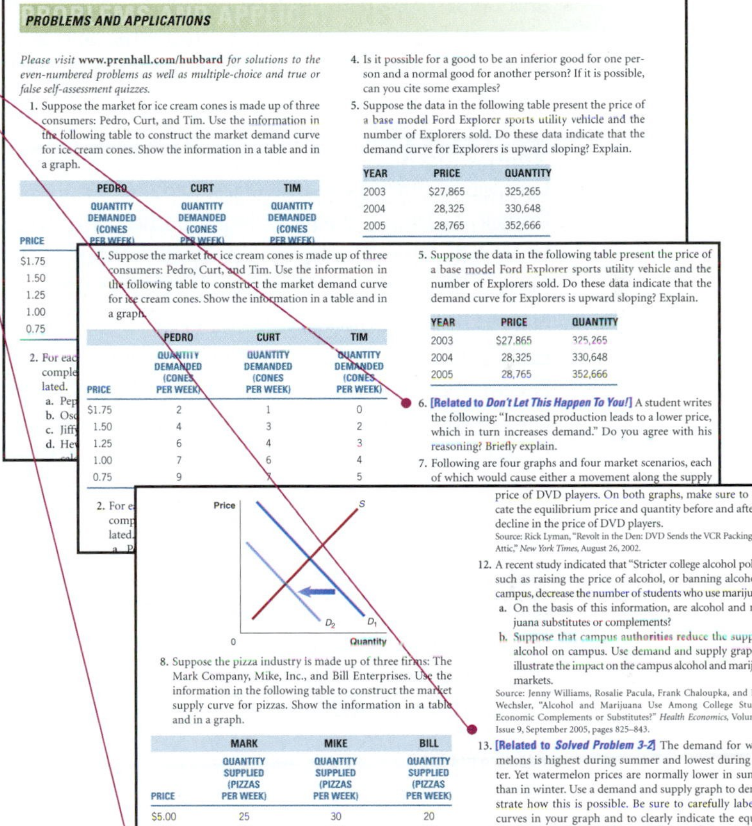

PROBLEMS AND APPLICATIONS

Please visit **www.prenhall.com/hubbard** *for solutions to the even-numbered problems as well as multiple-choice and true or false self-assessment quizzes.*

1. Suppose the market for ice cream cones is made up of three consumers: Pedro, Curt, and Tim. Use the information in the following table to construct the market demand curve for ice cream cones. Show the information in a table and in a graph.

PRICE	PEDRO QUANTITY DEMANDED (CONES PER WEEK)	CURT QUANTITY DEMANDED (CONES PER WEEK)	TIM QUANTITY DEMANDED (CONES PER WEEK)
$1.75	2	1	0
1.50	4	3	2
1.25	6	4	3
1.00	7	6	4
0.75	9	7	5

2. For eac... comple... lated.
   a. Pep...
   b. Osc...
   c. Jiff...
   d. He...

4. Is it possible for a good to be an inferior good for one person and a normal good for another person? If it is possible, can you cite some examples?
5. Suppose the data in the following table present the price of a base model Ford Explorer sports utility vehicle and the number of Explorers sold. Do these data indicate that the demand curve for Explorers is upward sloping? Explain.

YEAR	PRICE	QUANTITY
2003	$27,865	325,265
2004	28,325	330,648
2005	28,765	352,666

6. **[Related to *Don't Let This Happen To You!*]** A student writes the following: "Increased production leads to a lower price, which in turn increases demand." Do you agree with his reasoning? Briefly explain.
7. Following are four graphs and four market scenarios, each of which would cause either a movement along the supply

8. Suppose the pizza industry is made up of three firms: The Mark Company, Mike, Inc., and Bill Enterprises. Use the information in the following table to construct the market supply curve for pizzas. Show the information in a table and in a graph.

PRICE	MARK QUANTITY SUPPLIED (PIZZAS PER WEEK)	MIKE QUANTITY SUPPLIED (PIZZAS PER WEEK)	BILL QUANTITY SUPPLIED (PIZZAS PER WEEK)
$5.00	25	30	20
5.50	30	40	25
5.75	35	50	30
6.00	40	60	35
6.25	45	70	40

9. **[Related to *Solved Problem 3–1*]** In *The Wealth of Nations*, Adam Smith discussed what has come to be known as the "diamond and water paradox":

price of DVD players. On both graphs, make sure to indicate the equilibrium price and quantity before and after the decline in the price of DVD players.
Source: Rick Lyman, "Revolt in the Den: DVD Sends the VCR Packing to the Attic," *New York Times*, August 26, 2002.

12. A recent study indicated that "Stricter college alcohol policies, such as raising the price of alcohol, or banning alcohol on campus, decrease the number of students who use marijuana."
    a. On the basis of this information, are alcohol and marijuana substitutes or complements?
    b. Suppose that campus authorities reduce the supply of alcohol on campus. Use demand and supply graphs to illustrate the impact on the campus alcohol and marijuana markets.

    Source: Jenny Williams, Rosalie Pacula, Frank Chaloupka, and Henry Wechsler, "Alcohol and Marijuana Use Among College Students: Economic Complements or Substitutes?" *Health Economics*, Volume 13, Issue 9, September 2005, pages 825–843.
13. **[Related to *Solved Problem 3-2*]** The demand for watermelons is highest during summer and lowest during winter. Yet watermelon prices are normally lower in summer than in winter. Use a demand and supply graph to demonstrate how this is possible. Be sure to carefully label the curves in your graph and to clearly indicate the equilibrium summer price and the equilibrium winter price.
14. The following appeared in the *Wall Street Journal*: "U.S. farmers are headed for the lowest corn harvest since 1997, but the soybean crop is expected to reach an all-time high. Prices for both crops are expected to rise." Draw demand and supply graphs illustrating the market for corn and the market for soybeans. Show the impact of a larger soybean crop on the equilibrium price in each market. Holding

Please visit www.prenhall.com/hubbard

SUPPLEMENTS

Resources for the Instructor

Instructor's Manual

Edward Scahill of the University of Scranton prepared the microeconomics chapters of the Instructor's Manual, and Iordanis Petsas of the University of Scranton prepared the macroeconomics chapters. The Instructor's Manual includes chapter-by-chapter summaries, learning objectives, extended examples and class exercises, teaching outlines incorporating key terms and definitions, teaching tips, topics for class discussion, *new* Solved Problems, and solutions to all review questions and problems in the book. The Instructor's Manual is available in print and for download from the Instructor's Resource Center.

Test Bank

Cathleen Leue of the University of Oregon organized the test item file with contributions from Ratha Ramoo of Diablo Valley College, James Swofford of the University of Alabama, Robert Gillette of the University of Kentucky, and Kelly Blanchard of Purdue University. The test bank includes multiple-choice, true/false, short-answer, and graphing questions. The test bank was accuracy checked by Harold Elder of the University of Alabama; Solina Lindahl of California Polytechnic State University, San Luis Obispo; Brian Rosario of the University of California–Davis; Joseph Santos of South Dakota State University; Nora Underwood of the University of Central Florida; Kristin Vangaasbeck of California State University, Sacramento; Robert Whaples of Wake Forest University; and Anthony Zambelli of Cuyamaca College.

TestGen

This computerized package allows instructors to customize, save, and generate classroom tests. The test program permits instructors to edit, add, or delete questions from the test bank; edit existing graphics and create new graphics; analyze test results; and organize a database of tests and student results. This software allows for extensive flexibility and ease of use. It provides many options for organizing and displaying tests, along with search and sort features. The software and the test bank can be downloaded from the Instructor's Resource Center (**www.prenhall.com/hubbard**).

Acetates

All figures and tables from the text are reproduced and provided as full-page, four-color acetates.

PowerPoint® Lecture Presentation

There are two sets of PowerPoint® slides for professors to use prepared by Fernando and Yvonn Quijano:

1. A comprehensive set of PowerPoint® slides that can be used by instructors for class presentations or by students for lecture preview or review. The presentation includes all the graphs, tables, and equations in the textbook. It displays figures in a step-by-step, automated mode, using a single click per slide.
2. A comprehensive set of PowerPoint® slides with CRS (Classroom Response Systems) questions built in so instructors can incorporate CRS "clickers" into their classroom lectures. For more information on Prentice Hall's partnership with CRS, see the facing page.

Instructors may download these PowerPoint® presentations from the Instructor's Resource Center (**www.prenhall.com/hubbard**).

Instructor's Resource CD-ROM

The Instructor's Resource CD-ROM contains all faculty and student resources that support this text. Instructors have the ability to access and edit the Instructor's Manual, test bank, and PowerPoint® presentations. By simply clicking on a chapter or searching for a keyword, faculty can access an interactive library of resources. Faculty can pick and choose from the various supplements and export them to their hard drive.

Classroom Response Systems

Classroom Response Systems (CRS) is an exciting new wireless polling technology that makes large and small classrooms even more interactive because it enables instructors to pose questions to their students, record results, and display those results instantly. Students can answer questions easily using compact remote-control transmitters. Prentice Hall has partnerships with leading classroom response systems providers and can show you everything you need to know about setting up and using a CRS system. We'll provide the classroom hardware, text-specific PowerPoint® slides, software, and support, and we'll also show you how your students can benefit! Learn more at **www.prenhall.com/crs.**

Blackboard and WebCT Course Content

Prentice Hall offers fully customizable course content for the Bb and WebCT Course Management Systems.

Resources for the Student

Study Guide

Edward Scahill of the University of Scranton and Nicholas Noble of Miami University prepared the Study Guide. Tony Lima of California State University, Hayward, accuracy checked it. The Study Guide reinforces the textbook and provides students with the following:

- Chapter summary
- Discussion of each learning objective
- Section-by-section review of the concepts presented
- Helpful study hints
- Additional Solved Problems to supplement those in the text
- Key Terms with definitions
- Self-Test including 40 multiple-choice questions, plus a number of short-answer and true/false questions, with accompanying answers and explanations

Companion Website.

This free Web site, **www.prenhall.com/hubbard**, gives students access to select solutions to end-of-chapter problems, an interactive study guide with instant feedback, economics updates, student PowerPoint® slides, and many other resources to promote success in the principles of economics course.

PowerPoint® Slides

For student use as a study aide or note-taking guide, these PowerPoint® slides, prepared by Fernando and Yvonn Quijano, may be downloaded from the Companion Website at **www.prenhall.com/hubbard**. The slides include:

- All graphs, tables, and equations in the text
- Figures in step-by-step, automated mode, using a single click per slide
- End-of-chapter key terms with hyperlinks to relevant slides

SafariX WebBooks

SafariX WebBooks (online versions of the printed texts) will be available for students to purchase in lieu of a standard print text, without any modifications needed to how the instructor or professor teaches the course.

Learn more at **www.prenhall.com/safariX**.

Get Ahead of the Curve

Problem Solving for Students.

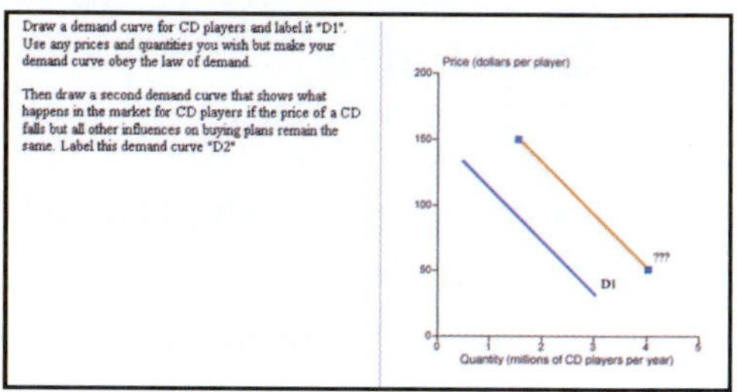

Automatically graded assignments (and the ability to get the highest possible grade by reworking the same assignments with new problems) motivate students to solve a lot more problems.

Instant feedback, including detailed tutorial instruction (complete solutions, step-by-step explanations, links to book material, etc.), provides instant gratification and immediate learning.

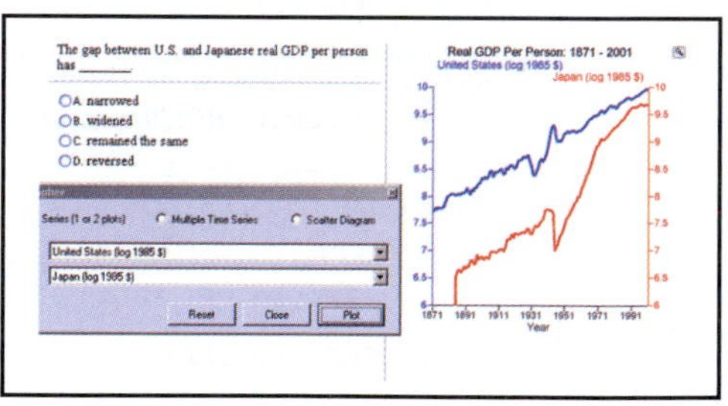

Graphing tools and questions integrated into assignments enable students to manipulate and even draw graphs that are automatically graded.

Solving Problems for Professors.

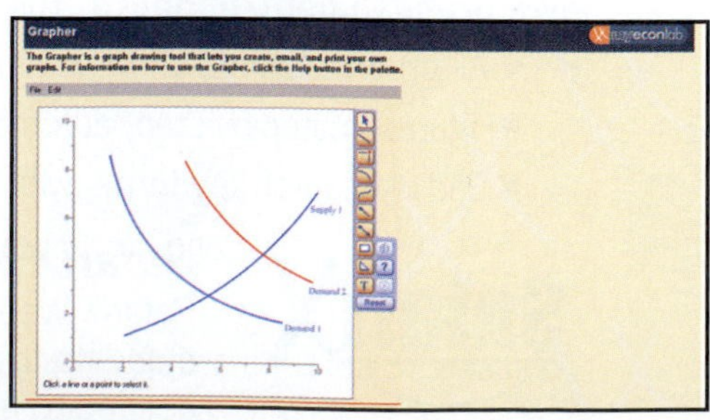

Easily create, assign, and automatically grade homework, quizzes, and tests.

Assign problems and exercises based on the actual end-of-chapter materials in the text book. Many have algorithmic versions for variety and extra practice.

Track students' progress through one easy-to-view, automatically populated grade book.

Get supplementary problems and teaching resources (like test banks and lecture slides) all in one place.

These features, plus personalized study plans for students, full etext options, practice tests, eStudy guides, and more, are all available in MyEconLab.

www.myeconlab.com

CLASS TESTERS, ACCURACY REVIEWERS, AND CONSULTANTS

Class Testers

We are grateful to both the professors who class tested manuscript and their students for providing clear-cut recommendations on how to make chapters interesting, relevant, and comprehensive.

Charles A. Bennett, Gannon University
Anne E. Bresnock, University of California–Los Angeles and California State Polytechnic University–Pomona
Linda Childs-Leatherbury, Lincoln University, Pennsylvania
John Eastwood, Northern Arizona University
David Eaton, Murray State University
Paul Elgatian, St. Ambrose University
Patricia A. Freeman, Jackson State University
Robert Godby, University of Wyoming
Frank Gunter, Lehigh University
Ahmed Ispahani, University of LaVerne
Brendan Kennelly, Lehigh University and National University of Ireland–Galway
Ernest Massie, Franklin University
Carol McDonough, University of Massachusetts–Lowell
Shah Mehrabi, Montgomery College
Sharon Ryan, University of Missouri–Columbia
Bruce G. Webb, Gordon College
Madelyn Young, Converse College
Susan Zumas, Lehigh University

Accuracy Review Board

Our accuracy checkers did a particularly painstaking and thorough job of helping us proof the graphs, equations, and features of the book in page proof stages. We are grateful for their time and commitment to the book and supplements:

Kelly Hunt Blanchard, Purdue University
Harold Elder, University of Alabama
Marc Fusaro, East Carolina University
Robert Gillette, University of Kentucky
William L. Goffe, State University of New York–Oswego
Travis Hayes, University of Tennessee–Chattanooga
Anisul M. Islam, University of Houston–Downtown
Faik A. Koray, Louisiana State University
Tony Lima, California State University–Hayward
James A. Moreno, Blinn College
Matthew Rafferty, Quinnipiac University
Jeff Reynolds, Northern Illinois University
Brian Rosario, University of California–Davis
Joseph M. Santos, South Dakota State University
Edward Scahill, University of Scranton
Robert Whaples, Wake Forest University

Consultant Board

We received guidance at several critical junctures from a dedicated Consultant Board. We relied on the Board for input on content, figure treatment, and design.

Susan Dadres, Southern Methodist University
Harry Ellis, Jr., University of North Texas
Robert Godby, University of Wyoming
William L. Goffe, State University of New York–Oswego
Donn M. Johnson, Quinnipiac University
Mark Karscig, Central Missouri State University
Jenny Minier, University of Kentucky
Nicholas Noble, Miami University
Matthew Rafferty, Quinnipiac University
Helen Roberts, University of Illinois–Chicago
Robert Rosenman, Washington State University
Joseph M. Santos, South Dakota State University
Martin C. Spechler, Indiana University–Purdue University Indianapolis
Robert Whaples–Wake Forest University

REVIEWERS

Reviewers

The guidance and recommendations of the following professors helped us shape the manuscript over the course of three years. We extend special thanks to Joseph Santos of South Dakota State University for helping prepare some of the Inside Look features, and Robert Gillette of the University of Kentucky, Robert Whaples of Wake Forest University, Nicholas Noble of Miami University, and Lee Craig of North Carolina State University for reviewing and preparing some of the review questions and problems and applications that appear at the ends of chapters.

ALABAMA Doris Bennett, Jacksonville State University • Harold W. Elder, University of Alabama–Tuscaloosa • James L. Swofford, University of Southern Alabama **ARIZONA** Doug Conway, Mesa Community College • John Eastwood, Northern Arizona University • Price Fishback, University of Arizona **CALIFORNIA** Renatte Adler, San Diego State University • Robert Bise, Orange Coast Community College • Victor Brajer, California State University–Fullerton • Anne E. Bresnock, University of California–Los Angeles and California State Polytechnic University–Pomona • David Brownstone, University of California–Irvine • Maureen Burton, California State Polytechnic University–Pomona • James G. Devine, Loyola Marymount University • Roger Frantz, San Diego State University • Andrew Gill, California State University–Fullerton • Amihai Glazier, University of California—Irvine • Lisa Grobar, California State University–Long Beach • Steve Hamilton, California Polytechnic State University–San Louis Obispo • Ahmed Ispahani, University of LaVerne • George A. Jouganatos, California State University–Sacramento • Philip King, San Francisco State University–Chico • Don Leet, California State University–Fresno • Rose LeMont, Modesto Junior College • Solina Lindahl, California Polytechnic State University–San Luis Obispo • Kristen Monaco, California State University–Long Beach • W. Douglas Morgan, University of California–Santa Barbara • Joseph M. Pogodzinksi, San Jose State University • Michael J. Potepan, San Francisco State University • Ratha Ramoo, Diablo Valley College • Ariane Schauer, Marymount College • Frederica Shockley, California State University–Chico • Mark Siegler, California State University–Sacramento • Lisa Simon, California Polytechnic State University–San Louis Obispo • Rodney B. Swanson, University of California–Los Angeles • Rodney B. Swanson, University of California–Los Angeles • Kristin A. Van Gaasbeck, California State University–Sacramento • Mike Visser, Sonoma State University • Anthony Zambelli, Cuyamaca College **COLORADO** Rhonda Corman, University of Northern Colorado • Dale DeBoer, University of Colorado–Colorado Springs • Murat Iyigun, University of Colorado at Boulder • Nancy Jianakoplos, Colorado State University • Jay Kaplan, University of Colorado–Boulder • Stephen Weiler, Colorado State University **CONNECTICUT** Christopher P. Ball, Quinnipiac University • Donn M. Johnson, Quinnipiac University • Judith Mills, Southern Connecticut State University • Matthew Rafferty, Quinnipiac University **DELAWARE** Fatma Abdel-Raouf, Goldey-Beacom College • Andrew T. Hill, University of Delaware **FLORIDA** Herm Baine, Broward Community College–Central • Al DeCook, Broward Community College • Martine Duchatelet, Barry University • Hadley Hartman, Santa Fe Community College • Richard Hawkins, University of West Florida • Barbara Moore, University of Central Florida • Augustine Nelson, University of Miami • Jamie Ortiz, Florida Atlantic University • Robert Pennington, University of Central Florida • Jerry Schwartz, Broward Community College–North • William Stronge, Florida Atlantic University • Nora Underwood, University of Central Florida **IDAHO** Don Holley, Boise State University **ILLINOIS** Teshome Abebe, Eastern Illinois University • Ali Akarca, University of Illinois–Chicago • James Bruehler, Eastern Illinois University • Louis Cain, Loyola University Chicago and Northwestern University • Rik Hafer, Southern Illinois

University–Edwardsville • Alla A. Melkumian, Western Illinois University • Christopher Mushrush, Illinois State University • Jeff Reynolds, Northern Illinois University • Helen Roberts, University of Illinois–Chicago • Eric Schulz, Northwestern University • Charles Sicotte, Rock Valley Community College • Neil T. Skaggs, Illinois State University • Mark Witte, Northwestern University • Laurie Wolff, Southern Illinois University–Carbondale • Paula Worthington, Northwestern University **INDIANA** Kelly Blanchard, Purdue University • Cecil Bohanon, Ball State University • Thomas Gresik, University of Notre Dame • Fred Herschede, Indiana University–South Bend • James K. Self, Indiana University–Bloomington • Esther-Mirjam Sent, University of Notre Dame • Virginia Shingleton, Valparaiso University • Martin C. Spechler, Indiana University–Purdue University–Indianapolis • Geetha Suresh, Purdue University–West Lafayette • Willard Witte, Indiana University-Bloomington **IOWA** Terry Alexander, Iowa State University • Paul Elgatian, St. Ambrose University • Jonathan Warner, Dordt College **KANSAS** Jodi Messer Pelkowski, Wichita State University • Joel Potter, Kansas State University • Josh Rosenbloom, University of Kansas • Bhavneet Walia, Kansas State University **KENTUCKY** Tom Cate, Northern Kentucky University • Nan-Ting Chou, University of Louisville • David Eaton, Murray State University • Robert Gillette, University of Kentucky • Hak Youn Kim, Western Kentucky University • Jenny Minier, University of Kentucky • John Vahaly, University of Louisville **LOUISIANA** Faik Koray, Louisiana State University • Paul Nelson, University of Louisiana–Monroe • Tammy Parker, University of Louisiana–Monroe • Wesley A. Payne, Delgado Community College **MASSACHUSETTS** William L. Casey, Jr., Babson College • Arthur Schiller Casimir, Western New England College • Michael Enz, Western New England College • Todd Idson, Boston University • Russell A. Janis, University of Massachussetts–Amherst • Anthony Laramie, Merrimack College • Carol McDonough, University of Massachusetts–Lowell • William O'Brien, Worcester State College • Gregory H. Wassall, Northeastern University • Bruce G. Webb, Gordon College • Gilbert Wolpe, Newbury College **MARYLAND** Carey Borkoski, Anne Arundel Community College • Kathleen A. Carroll, University of Maryland–Baltimore County • Dustin Chambers, Salisbury University • Shah Mehrabi, Montgomery College • David Mitch, University of Maryland–Baltimore County • John Neri, University of Maryland • Henry Terrell, University of Maryland **MICHIGAN** John Nader, Grand Valley State University • Robert J. Rossana, Wayne State University • Mark Wheeler, Western Michigan University **MISSOURI** Jo Durr, Southwest Missouri State University • Julie H. Gallaway, Southwest Missouri State University • Terrel Galloway, Southwest Missouri State University • Mark Karscig, Central Missouri State University • Steven T. Petty, College of the Ozarks • Sharon Ryan, University of Missouri–Columbia • Ben Young, University of Missouri–Kansas City **MINNESOTA** Monica Hartman, University of St. Thomas **MISSISSIPPI** Randall Campbell, Mississippi State University • Patricia A. Freeman, Jackson State University **NEBRASKA** James Knudsen, Creighton University • Craig MacPhee, University of Nebraska–Lincoln • Mark E. Wohar, University of Nebraska–Omaha **NEW HAMPSHIRE** Evelyn Gick, Dartmouth College • Neil Niman, University of New Hampshire **NEW JERSEY** Len Anyanwu, Union County College • Maharukh Bhiladwalla, Rutgers University–New Brunswick • Gary Gigliotti, Rutgers University–New Brunswick • John Graham, Rutgers University–Newark • Berch Haroian, William Paterson University • Paul Harris, Camden County College **NEW MEXICO** Donald Coes, University of New Mexico **NEW YORK** Erol Balkan, Hamilton College • Ranjit S. Dighe, State University of New York–Oswego • William L. Goffe, State University of New York–Oswego • Wayne A. Grove, LeMoyne College • Christopher Inya, Monroe Community College • Clifford Kern, State University of New York–Binghampton • Mary Lesser, Iona College • Howard Ross, Baruch College

• Leonie Stone, State University of New York–Geneseo • Ganti Subrahmanyam, University of Buffalo • Jogindar S. Uppal, State University of New York–Albany • Susan Wolcott, Binghamton University **NORTH CAROLINA** Otilia Boldea, North Carolina State University • Robert Burrus, University of North Carolina–Wilmington • Lee A. Craig, North Carolina State University • Kathleen Dorsainvil, Winston-Salem State University • Marc Fusaro, East Carolina University • Salih Hakeem, North Carolina Central University • Haiyong Liu, East Carolina University • Kosmas Marinakis, North Carolina State University • Todd McFall, Wake Forest University • Shahriar Mostashari, Campbell University • Peter Schuhmann, University of North Carolina–Wilmington • Carol Stivender, University of North Carolina–Charlotte • Vera Tabakova, East Carolina University • Robert Whaples, Wake Forest University • Gary W. Zinn, East Carolina University **OHIO** John P. Blair, Wright State University • Kyongwook Choi, Ohio University–Main Campus • Darlene DeVera, Miami University • Tim Fuerst, Bowling Green State University • Kenneth Kuttner, Oberlin College • Ernest Massie, Franklin University • Mike Nelson, University of Akron • Nicholas Noble, Miami University • Rochelle Ruffer, Youngstown State University • Kate Sheppard, University of Akron • Steve Szheghi, Wilmington College • Melissa Thomasson, Miami University • Yaqin Wang, Youngstown State University • Sourushe Zandvakili, University of Cincinnati **OKLAHOMA** David Hudgins, University of Oklahoma **OREGON** Bill Burrows, Lane Community College • Tom Carroll, Central Oregon Community College • Larry Singell, University of Oregon • Ayca Tekin-Koru, Oregon State University **PENNSYLVANIA** Gustavo Barboza, Mercyhurst College • Charles A. Bennett, Gannon University • Howard Bodenhorn, Lafayette College • Milica Bookman, St. Joseph's University • Robert Brooker, Gannon University • Linda Childs-Leatherbury, Lincoln University • Satyajit Ghosh, University of Scranton • Mehdi Haririan, Bloomsburg University • Joseph Jozefowicz, Indiana University of Pennsylvania • Nicholas Karatjas, Indiana University of Pennsylvania • Brendan Kennelly, Lehigh University • Iordanis Petsas, University of Scranton • Adam Renhoff, Drexel University • Edward Scahill, University of Scranton • Rajeev Sooreea, Pennsylvania State University–Altoona • Sandra Trejos, Clarion University • Peter Zaleski, Villanova University • Susan Zumas, Lehigh University **SOUTH CAROLINA** Calvin Blackwell, College of Charleston • Chad Turner, Clemson University • Madelyn Young, Converse College **SOUTH DAKOTA** Joseph M. Santos, South Dakota State University • Jason Zimmerman, South Dakota State University **TENNESSEE** Bichaka Fayissa, Middle Tennessee State University • Travis Hayes, University of Tennessee–Chattanooga • Christopher C. Klein, Middle Tennessee State University • Millicent Sites, Carson-Newman College **TEXAS** Rashid Al-Hmoud, Texas Tech University • Mike Cohick, Collin County Community College • Cesar Corredor, Texas A&M University • Susan Dadres, Southern Methodist University • Harry Ellis, Jr., University of North Texas • Paul Emberton, Texas State University • Diego Escobari, Texas A&M University • Nicholas Feltovich, University of Houston–Main • Charles Harold Fifield, Baylor University • Richard Gosselin, Houston Community College–Central • Sheila Amin Gutierrez de Pineres, University of Texas–Dallas • James

W. Henderson, Baylor University • Ansul Islam, University of Houston–Downtown • Kathy Kelly, University of Texas–Arlington • Thomas Kemp, Tarrant County College–Northwest • Akbar Marvasti, University of Houston–Downtown • James Mbata, Houston Community College • Carl Montano, Lamar University • James Moreno, Blinn College • John Pisciotta, Baylor University • Sara Saderion, Houston Community College–Southwest • Ivan Tasic, Texas A&M University • Rebecca Thornton, University of Houston • Chris Wreh, North Central Texas College **UTAH** Lowell Glenn, Utah Valley State College • Aric Krause, Westminster College • Arden Pope, Brigham Young University **VIRGINIA** Lee Badgett, Virginia Military Institute • Lee A. Coppock, University of Virginia • Carrie Meyer, George Mason University • James Roberts, Tidewater Community College–Virginia Beach • Araine A. Schauer, Mary Mount College • Sarah Stafford, The College of William & Mary • Michelle Vachris, Christopher Newport University • James Wetzel, Virginia Commonwealth University **WASHINGTON** Robert Rosenman, Washington State University **WASHINGTON, DC** Leon Battista, American Enterprise Institute **WISCONSIN** • Pascal Ngoboka, University of Wisconsin–River Falls • Kevin Quinn, St. Norbert College • John R. Stoll, University of Wisconsin–Green Bay **WYOMING** Robert Godby, University of Wyoming

A Word of Thanks

We benefited greatly from the dedication and professionalism of the Prentice Hall team. Executive Editor David Alexander's energy and support were indispensable. David helped mold the presentation and provided words of encouragement whenever our energy flagged. Developmental Editor Lena Buonanno worked tirelessly to ensure this text was as good as it could be. We are literally astonished at the amount of time, energy, and unfailing good humor she brought to this project. Director of Key Markets David Theisen provided invaluable insight into how best to structure a principles text. His advice helped shape nearly every chapter. Executive Marketing Manager Sharon Koch and Marketing Development Manager Kathleen McLellan helped develop a unique and innovative marketing plan. Steve Deitmer, Director of Development, brought sound judgment to the many decisions required to create this book. Mike Dittamo, Editorial Assistant, was involved in many aspects of the book including coordinating the review program and assisting with the supplements. Karen Misler coordinated the extensive supplement package that accompanies the book. Mike Reynolds, Pat Smythe, and Maria Lange turned our manuscript pages into a beautiful published book. Photo researcher Diane Austin located photographs that captured the essence of key concepts. We also thank Jason Hockenberry at Lehigh University who provided research assistance.

A good part of the burden of a project of this magnitude is borne by our families. We appreciate the patience, support, and encouragement of our wives and children. We extend special thanks to Constance Hubbard for her diligent reading of page proofs.

BRIEF CONTENTS

CONTENTS

Part 4: Market Structure and Firm Strategy

Part 6: Long-Run Growth and Short Run Fluctuations

Part 7: Monetary and Fiscal Policy

We use business examples to explain economic concepts. The table that follows highlights the topic and real-world company introduced in the chapter-opening vignette and revisited throughout the chapter. This table also lists the companies that appear in our *Making the Connection* and *An Inside Look* features.

Chapter Title	Chapter Opener	Making the Connection	An Inside Look
CHAPTER 1			
Economics: Foundations and Models	What Happens When U.S. Firms Move to China?	When Economists Disagree: A Debate over Outsourcing	How Does Economic Growth in China Affect Other Countries? Source: Economist
CHAPTER 2			
Trade-offs, Comparative Advantage, and the Market System	Managers Making Choices at BMW	Trade-offs and Tsunami Relief • Story of the Market System in Action, "I, Pencil" • Property Rights in Cyberspace: Napster, Kazaa, and iTunes	Choosing the Production Mix at BMW Source: WSJ
CHAPTER 3			
Where Prices Come From: The Interaction of Demand and Supply	How Hewlett-Packard Manages the Demand for Printers	Why Supermarkets Need to Understand Substitutes and Complements • Companies Respond to a Growing Hispanic Population • Estimating the Demand for Printers at Hewlett-Packard • The Falling Price of Large Flat-Screen Televisions	Hewlett-Packard Cuts PC Prices to Sell More Printers Source: WSJ
CHAPTER 4			
Market Efficiency and Market Failure	Should the Government Control Apartment Rents?	The Consumer Surplus from Satellite Television • Price Floors in Labor Markets: The Minimum Wage • Does Holiday Gift Giving Have a Deadweight Loss? • The Reduction in Infant Mortality Due to the Clean Air Act • Can Tradeable Permits Reduce Global Warmimg?	Dealing with Rent Control Source: Slate
CHAPTER 5			
Firms, the Stock Market, and Corporate Governance	Google: From Dorm Room to Wall Street	What's in a "Name"? Lloyd's of London Learns about Unlimited Liability the Hard Way • Following General Electric's Stock and Bond Prices in the Financial Pages • A Bull in China's Financial Shop	Google's Initial Public Offering Source: WSJ
CHAPTER 6			
Consumer Choice and Elasticity	Can LeBron James Get You to Drink Powerade?	Why Do Firms Pay Tiger Woods to Endorse Their Products? • Professor Krueger Goes to the Super Bowl • Why Don't Students Study More? • The Price Elasticity of Demand for Breakfast Cereal	Can Whoopi Goldberg Get You to Buy Slim-Fast? Source: Boston Globe

Chapter Title	Chapter Opener	Making the Connection	An Inside Look
CHAPTER 7			
Technology, Production, and Costs	Sony Uses a Cost Curve to Determine the Price of Radios	Improving Inventory Control at Wal-Mart • Fixed Costs in the Publishing Industry • Adam Smith's Famous Account of the Division of Labor in a Pin Factory • The Colossal River Rouge: Diseconomies of Scale at the Ford Motor Company • The Changing Input Mix in Walt Disney Film Animation	Using Long-Run Average Cost Curves to Analyze Expansion at Sony and Samsung Source: FT
CHAPTER 8			
Firms in Perfectly Competitive Markets	Perfect Competition in the Market for Organic Apples	Losing Money in the Medical Screening Industry • When to Close a Laundry • The Decline of Apple Production in New York State	The United States and Australia Reduce Trade Barriers Source: San Francisco Chronicle
CHAPTER 9			
Monopoly and Antitrust Policy	Time Warner Rules Manhattan	Is Xbox a Close Substitute for Playstation 2? • The End of the Christmas Plant Monopoly • Are Diamond (Profits) Forever? The De Beers Diamond Monopoly • The Antitrust Case Against Microsoft	A "Monopoly Mindset" in the Cable Industry? Source: WSJ
CHAPTER 10			
Monopolistic Competition and Oligopoly	Starbucks: Growth through Product Differentiation	The Rise and Fall of Apple's Macintosh Computer • Staying One Step Ahead of the Competition: Eugène Schueller and L'Oréal • Abercrombie and Fitch: Can the Product Be Too Differentiated? • A Beautiful Mind: Game Theory Goes to the Movies	Starbucks and McDonald's Cater to Insomniacs Source: WSJ
CHAPTER 11			
GDP: Measuring Total Production and Income	Increases in GDP Spur Hiring at Freightliner	Exchange Rates in the Financial Spending on Homeland Security • How the Underground Economy Hurts Developing Countries • Did World War II Bring Prosperity? • How Freightliner Uses Forecasts of GDP	Distorted Price Signals Nurture Movements in Canadian GDP Source: WSJ
CHAPTER 12			
Unemployment and Inflation	Lucent Technologies Deals with Unemployment and Inflation	What Explains the Increase in "Kramers"? • How Should We Categorize the Unemployment at Lucent Technologies? • Why Did Henry Ford Pay His Workers Twice as Much as Other Car Manufacturers? • Why a Lower Inflation Rate Is Like a Tax Cut for Lucent's Bondholders	Managers and Workers at Boeing Negotiate Wages Source: Wichita Eagle

Chapter Title	Chapter Opener	Making the Connection	An Inside Look
CHAPTER 13			
Economic Growth, the Financial System, and Business Cycles	Growth and the Business Cycle at the Ford Motor Company	The Connection between Economic Prosperity and Health • What Explains Rapid Economic Growth in Botswana? • Ebenezer Scrooge: Accidental Promoter of Economic Growth? • Who Decides If the Economy Is in a Recession?	Growth and the Chinese Automobile Industry Source: Business Week Online
CHAPTER 14			
Aggregate Demand and Aggregate Supply Analysis	Caterpillar Recovers Slowly from the 2001 Recession	The Effect of Exchange Rates on Caterpillar's Sales • Does Rising Productivity Growth Reduce Employment? • Karl Marx: Capitalism's Severest Critic	Construction Company Komatsu Benefits from Exports to China Source: FT
CHAPTER 15			
Money, Banks, and the Federal Reserve System	McDonald's Money Problems in Argentina	Money in a World War II Prisoner-of-War Camp • Money without a Government? The Strange Case of the Iraqi Dinar • The 2001 Bank Panic in Argentina • The German Hyperinflation of the Early 1920s	Does Using the Dollar Destabilize Latin American Countries? Source: WSJ
CHAPTER 16			
Monetary Policy	Why Did Homebuilder Toll Brothers, Inc., Prosper during the 2001 Recession?	Was There a Housing Market "Bubble" in the Early 2000s? • The Fed Responds to the Terrorist Attacks of September 11, 2001 • Why Was Monetary Policy Ineffective in Japan? • Why Does Wall Street Care about Monetary Policy?	Monetary Policy Spurs Housing Boom Source: WSJ
CHAPTER 17			
Fiscal Policy	A Boon for H&R Block	The Future of Social Security and Medicare • Limits to Fiscal Policy: Japan in the Late 1990s • Did Fiscal Policy Fail during the Great Depression? • Should the United States Adopt the "Flat Tax"?	Tax Receipts Increase in 2005, but Deficit Still Looms Large Source: The Economist
CHAPTER 18			
Comparative Advantage, International Trade, and Exchange Rates	Sugar Quota Drives U.S. Candy Manufacturers Overseas	Has Outsourcing Hurt the U.S. Economy? • Why Is Dalton, Georgia, the Carpet-Making Capital of the World? • The Unintended Consequences of Banning Goods Made with Child Labor • Has NAFTA Helped or Hurt the U.S. Economy?	The United States and Australia Reduce Trade Barriers Source: San Francisco Chronicle

chapter one

Economics: Foundations and Models

What Happens When U.S. Firms Move to China?

➤ You have probably seen the words "Made in China" on a variety of the products you own, including running shoes, clothing, towels, and sheets. It may not be surprising that relatively simple products are manufactured in China, where workers receive much lower wages than in the United States. Until recently, though, most people would not have expected sophisticated, high-technology products to be designed and manufactured in China. That is why an announcement by Massachusetts-based 3Com Corporation in late 2004 was so surprising. 3Com is a leading high-technology firm with 2,000 employees and annual sales of $700 million. The firm introduced a new network switch for corporate computer systems that not only was manufactured in China but had been designed by Chinese engineers.

3Com's price for the switch was $183,000. 3Com's even larger rival, Cisco Systems—which is based in San Jose, California, with 34,000 employees and annual sales of more than $30 billion—charged $245,000 for a comparable switch, designed and manufactured in the United States. The difference in price showed that even when producing some high-technology goods, it was cheaper for U.S. firms to operate in China. Because the salaries of engineers are so much lower in China, 3Com was able to use four times as many engineers to design its switch, which it claimed had twice the capacity of Cisco's switch. The cost to manufacture the switch was also much lower in China, where the average factory worker earns only $0.64 per hour, including benefits, compared with about $22.00 per hour earned by the average factory worker in the United States.

Many U.S., Japanese, and European firms have been moving the production of goods and services to other countries. This process of firms producing goods and services outside of their home country is called *outsourcing* (sometimes also referred to as *off-shoring*). U.S. firms have been outsourcing for decades, but some of the recently outsourced jobs require high skill levels, as was true of the jobs 3Com moved from the United States to China. To cite another example that has received much publicity, Dun & Bradstreet (now known as D&B), a

business information firm founded in New York in 1841, has begun purchasing much of its software engineering services from a firm in Bangalore, India, because Indian software engineers typically receive salaries 75 percent lower than do software engineers in the United States.

Articles on outsourcing appear frequently in business magazines and the financial pages of newspapers, and the issue has also been the subject of heated debate among political commentators, policymakers, and presidential candidates. The focus of the debate has been the question: "Has outsourcing been good or bad for the U.S. economy?" This question is one of many that cannot be answered without using economics. In this chapter, and the remainder of this book, we will see how economics helps in answering important questions about outsourcing, as well as many other issues. Economics provides us with tools for understanding why outsourcing has increased, why some firms are more likely to move production to other countries, and what the effects of outsourcing will be on the wages of U.S. workers, the profits of U.S. firms, and the overall ability of the U.S. economy to produce more and better goods and services. *An Inside Look* on page 16 discusses the effects of economic growth in China on jobs and wages in the United States and Europe.

Source: Pete Engardio and Dexter Roberts, "The China Price," *Business Week*, December 6, 2004.

LEARNING OBJECTIVES

After studying this chapter, you should be able to:

① Discuss these three important economic ideas: *People are rational. People respond to incentives. Optimal decisions are made at the margin.*

② Discuss how an economy answers these questions: *What* goods and services will be produced? *How* will the goods and services be produced? *Who* will receive the goods and services?

③ Understand the role of models in economic analysis.

④ Distinguish between microeconomics and macroeconomics.

⑤ Become familiar with important economic terms.

In this book, we use economics to answer questions such as the following:

- How are the prices of goods and services determined?
- How does pollution affect the economy, and how should government policy deal with these effects?
- Why do firms engage in international trade, and how do government policies affect international trade?
- Why does government control the prices of some goods and services, and what are the effects of those controls?

Economists do not always agree on the answers to every question. In fact, as we will see, economists engage in lively debates on some issues. Economics is a dynamic field in which new questions are constantly arising, and new methods of analyzing and answering those questions are being developed.

Scarcity The situation in which unlimited wants exceed the limited resources available to fulfill those wants.

All the questions we discuss in this book reflect a basic fact of life: People must make choices as they try to attain their goals. The choices reflect the trade-offs people face because we live in a world of **scarcity,** which means that although our wants are unlimited, the resources available to fulfill those wants are limited. You might like to have a 60-inch plasma television in every room of your home, but unless you are a close relative of Bill Gates, you probably lack the money to purchase them. Every day you must make choices about how to spend your limited income on the many goods and services available. The finite amount of time available to you also limits your ability to attain your goals. If you spend an hour studying for your economics midterm, you have one less hour available to study for your history midterm. Firms and the government are in the same situation you are: They have limited resources available to them as they attempt to attain their goals. **Economics** is the study of the choices consumers, business managers, and government officials make to attain their goals, given their scarce resources.

Economics The study of the choices people make to attain their goals, given their scarce resources.

We begin this chapter by discussing three important economic ideas that we will return to many times in the book: *People are rational. People respond to incentives. Optimal decisions are made at the margin.* Then we consider the three fundamental questions that any economy must answer: *What* goods and services will be produced? *How* will the goods and services be produced? *Who* will receive the goods and services? Next we consider the role of *economic models* in helping us to analyze the many issues presented throughout this book. **Economic models** are simplified versions of reality used to analyze real-world economic situations. Later in this chapter, we explore why economists use models and how they construct them. Finally, we discuss the difference between microeconomics and macroeconomics, and we preview some important economic terms.

Economic model Simplified versions of reality used to analyze real-world economic situations.

Building a Foundation: Economics and Individual Decisions

① LEARNING OBJECTIVE

Discuss these three important economic ideas: *People are rational. People respond to incentives. Optimal decisions are made at the margin.*

As you try to achieve your goals, whether they are buying a new computer or finding a part-time job, you will interact with other people in *markets*. A **market** is a group of buyers and sellers of a good or service and the institution or arrangement by which they come together to trade. Most of economics involves analyzing what happens in markets. Throughout this book, as we study how people make choices and interact in markets, we will return to three important ideas:

Market A group of buyers and sellers of a good or service and the institution or arrangement by which they come together to trade

1. People are rational.
2. People respond to economic incentives.
3. Optimal decisions are made at the margin.

People Are Rational

Economists generally assume that people are rational. This assumption does *not* mean that economists believe everyone knows everything or always makes the "best" decision. It does mean that economists assume that consumers and firms use all available information as they act to achieve their goals. Rational individuals weigh the benefits and costs of each action, and they choose an action only if the benefits outweigh the costs. For example, if Microsoft charges a price of $239 for a copy of Windows, economists assume that the managers at Microsoft have estimated that a price of $239 will earn Microsoft the most profit. The managers may be wrong; perhaps a price of $265 would be more profitable, but economists assume that the managers at Microsoft have acted rationally on the basis of the information available to them in choosing the price. Of course, not everyone behaves rationally all the time. Still, the assumption of rational behavior is very useful in explaining most of the choices that people make.

People Respond to Economic Incentives

Human beings act from a variety of motives, including religious belief, envy, and compassion. Economists emphasize that consumers and firms consistently respond to *economic* incentives. This fact may seem obvious, but it is often overlooked. For example, according to an article in the *Wall Street Journal*, the FBI couldn't understand why banks were not taking steps to improve security in the face of an increase in robberies: "FBI officials suggest that banks place uniformed, armed guards outside their doors and install bullet-resistant plastic, known as a 'bandit barrier,' in front of teller windows." FBI officials were surprised that few banks took their advice. But the article also reported that installing bullet-resistant plastic costs $10,000 to $20,000 and a well-trained security guard receives $50,000 per year in salary and benefits. The average loss in a bank robbery is only about $1,200. The economic incentive to banks is clear: It is less costly to put up with bank robberies than to take additional security measures. That banks respond as they do to the threat of robberies may be surprising to the FBI—but not to economists.

Optimal Decisions Are Made at the Margin

Some decisions are "all or nothing": An entrepreneur decides whether or not to open a new restaurant. She either starts the new restaurant or she doesn't. You decide whether to enter graduate school or to take a job. You either enter graduate school or you don't. But most decisions in life are not all or nothing. Instead, most decisions involve doing a little more or a little less. If you are trying to decrease your spending and increase your saving, the decision is not really a choice between saving every dollar you earn or spending it all. The choice is actually between buying a caffè mocha at Starbucks every day or cutting back to three times per week.

Economists use the word *marginal* to mean an extra or additional benefit or cost of a decision. Should you watch another hour of TV or spend that hour studying? The *marginal benefit* (or, in symbols, *MB*) of watching more TV is the additional enjoyment you receive. The *marginal cost* (or *MC*) is the lower grade you receive from having studied a little less. Should Apple Computer produce an additional 300,000 iPods? Firms receive *revenue* from selling goods. Apple's marginal benefit is the additional revenue it receives from selling 300,000 more iPods. Apple's marginal cost is the additional cost—for wages, parts, and so forth—of producing 300,000 more iPods. *Economists reason that the optimal decision is to continue any activity up to the point where the marginal benefit equals the marginal cost—in symbols, where* MB = MC. Often we apply this rule without consciously thinking about it. Usually you will know whether the additional enjoyment from watching a television program is worth the additional cost involved in not spending that hour studying, without giving it a lot of thought. In business situations, however, firms often have to make careful calculations to determine, for example, whether the additional revenue received from increasing production is greater or less than the additional cost of the production. Economists refer to analysis that involves comparing marginal benefits and marginal costs as **marginal analysis.**

Marginal analysis Analysis that involves comparing marginal benefits and marginal costs.

In each chapter of this book, you will see a special feature entitled "Solved Problem." This feature will increase your understanding of the material by leading you through the steps of solving an applied economic problem. After reading the problem, you can test your understanding by working the related problems that appear at the end of the chapter and in the study guide that accompanies this book.

SOLVED PROBLEM 1-1

① LEARNING OBJECTIVE

Discuss these three important economic ideas: *People are rational. People respond to incentives. Optimal decisions are made at the margin.*

Apple Computer Makes a Decision at the Margin

Suppose Apple is currently selling 3,000,000 iPods per year. Managers at Apple are considering whether to raise production to 3,300,000 iPods per year. One manager argues, "Increasing production from 3,000,000 to 3,300,000 is a good idea because we will make a total profit of $100 million if we produce 3,300,000." Do you agree with her reasoning? What, if any, additional information do you need to decide whether Apple should produce the additional 300,000 iPods?

Solving the Problem:

Step 1: Review the chapter material. The problem is about making decisions, so you may want to review the section "Optimal Decisions Are Made at the Margin," which begins on page 5. Remember to think "marginal" whenever you see the word "additional" in economics.

Step 2: Explain whether you agree with the manager's reasoning. We have seen that any activity should be continued to the point where the marginal benefit is equal to the marginal cost. In this case, that involves continuing to produce iPods up to the point where the additional revenue Apple receives from selling more iPods is equal to the marginal cost of producing them. The Apple manager has not done a marginal analysis, so you should not agree with her reasoning. Her statement about the *total* profit of producing 3,300,000 iPods is not relevant to the decision whether or not to produce the last 300,000 iPods.

Step 3: Explain what additional information you need. You will need additional information to make a correct decision. You will need to know the additional revenue Apple would earn from selling 300,000 more iPods and the additional cost of producing them.

YOUR TURN: **For more practice, do related problems 4, 5, and 6 on page 19 at the end of this chapter.**

The Economic Problem That Every Society Must Solve

② LEARNING OBJECTIVE

Discuss how an economy answers these questions: *What* goods and services will be produced? *How* will the goods and services be produced? *Who* will receive the goods and services?

We have already noted the important fact that we live in a world of scarcity. As a result, any society faces the economic problem that it has only a limited amount of economic resources—such as workers, machines, and natural resources—and therefore can produce only a limited amount of goods and services. Therefore, society faces **trade-offs:** Producing more of one good or service means producing less of another good or service. Trade-offs force society to make choices, particularly when answering the following three fundamental questions:

Trade-off The idea that because of scarcity, producing more of one good or service means producing less of another good or service.

1. *What* goods and services will be produced?
2. *How* will the goods and services be produced?
3. *Who* will receive the goods and services produced?

Throughout this book, we will return to these questions many times. For now, we can briefly introduce each question.

What Goods and Services Will Be Produced?

How will society decide whether to produce more economics textbooks or more DVD players? More day care facilities or more football stadiums? Of course, "society" does not make decisions; only individuals make decisions. The answer to the question of what will be produced is determined by the choices made by consumers, firms, and the government. Every day you help to decide which goods and services will be produced when you choose to buy an iPod rather than a DVD player, or a caffè mocha rather than a chai tea. Similarly, Apple must choose whether to devote its scarce resources to making more iPods or more iBook laptop computers. The federal government must also choose whether to spend more of its limited budget on breast cancer research or on homeland security. In each case, consumers, firms, and the government face the problem of scarcity by trading off one good for another.

How Will the Goods and Services Be Produced?

Firms choose how to produce the goods and services they sell. In many cases, firms face a trade-off between using more workers or using more machines. For example, a local service station has to choose whether to provide car repair services using more diagnostic computers and fewer auto mechanics or more auto mechanics and fewer diagnostic computers. Similarly, movie studios have to choose whether to produce animated films using highly skilled animators to draw them by hand or fewer animators and more computers. In deciding whether to move production offshore to China, firms are often choosing between a production method in the United States that uses fewer workers and more machines or a production method in China that uses more workers and fewer machines.

Who Will Receive the Goods and Services Produced?

In the United States, who receives the goods and services produced depends largely on how income is distributed. Those individuals with the highest income have the ability to buy the most goods and services. Often, people are willing to give up some of their income—and, therefore, some of their ability to purchase goods and services—by donating to charities to increase the incomes of poorer people. In 2004, Americans donated $241 billion to charity, or an average donation of $2,100 for each household in the country. An important policy question, however, is whether the government should intervene to make the distribution of income more equal. Such intervention already occurs in the United States, because people with higher incomes pay a larger fraction of their incomes in taxes and because the government makes payments to people with low incomes. There is disagreement over whether the current attempts to redistribute income are sufficient or whether there should be more or less redistribution.

Centrally Planned Economies versus Market Economies

Centrally planned economy An economy in which the government decides how economic resources will be allocated.

Market economy An economy in which the decisions of households and firms interacting in markets allocate economic resources.

Societies organize their economies in two main ways to answer the three questions of what, how, and who. A society can have a **centrally planned economy** in which the government decides how economic resources will be allocated. Or a society can have a **market economy** in which the decisions of households and firms interacting in markets allocate economic resources.

From 1917 to 1991, the most important centrally planned economy in the world was that of the Soviet Union, which was established when V. I. Lenin and his Communist Party staged a revolution and took over the Russian Empire. In the Soviet Union, the government decided what goods to produce, how to produce them, and who would receive them. Government employees managed factories and stores. The objective of these managers was to follow the government's orders, rather than to satisfy the wants of consumers. Centrally planned economies like the Soviet Union have not been successful in producing low-cost, high-quality goods and services. As a result, the standard of living of the average person in a centrally planned economy tends to be quite low. All centrally planned economies have also been political dictatorships. Dissatisfaction with low living standards and political repression finally led to the collapse of the Soviet Union in 1991. Today, only a few small countries, such as Cuba and North Korea, still have completely centrally planned economies.

All the high-income democracies, such as the United States, Canada, Japan, and the countries of Western Europe, are market economies. Market economies rely primarily on privately owned firms to produce goods and services and to decide how to produce them. Markets, rather than the government, determine who receives the goods and services produced. In a market economy, firms must produce goods and services that meet the wants of consumers, or the firms will go out of business. In that sense, it is ultimately consumers who decide what goods and services will be produced. Because firms in a market economy compete to offer the highest-quality products at the lowest price, they are under pressure to use the lowest-cost methods of production. For example, in the past 10 years some U.S. firms, particularly in the electronics and furniture industries, have been under pressure to reduce their costs to meet those of Chinese firms.

In a market economy, the income of an individual is determined by the payments he receives for what he has to sell. If he is a civil engineer and firms are willing to pay a salary of $85,000 per year for engineers with his training and skills, that is the amount of income he will have to purchase goods and services. If the engineer also owns a house that he rents out, his income will be even higher. One of the attractive features of markets is that they reward hard work. Generally, the more extensive the training a person has received and the longer the hours the person works, the higher the person's income will be. Of course, luck—both good and bad—also plays a role here, as elsewhere in life. We can conclude that market economies answer the question "Who receives the goods and services produced?" with the answer "Those who are most willing and able to buy them."

The Modern "Mixed" Economy

In the nineteenth and early twentieth centuries, the U.S. government engaged in relatively little regulation of markets for goods and services. Beginning in the middle of the twentieth century, government intervention in the economy dramatically increased in the United States and other market economies. This increase was primarily caused by the high rates of unemployment and business bankruptcies during the Great Depression of the 1930s. Some government intervention was also intended to raise the incomes of the elderly, the sick, and people with limited skills. For example, in the 1930s, the United States established the Social Security system, which provides government payments to retired and disabled workers, and minimum wage legislation, which sets a floor on the wages employers can pay in many occupations. In more recent years, government intervention in the economy has also expanded to meet such goals as protection of the environment and the promotion of civil rights.

Some economists argue that the extent of government intervention makes it no longer accurate to refer to the U.S., Canadian, Japanese, and Western European economies as market economies. Instead, they should be referred to as *mixed economies.* In a **mixed economy,** most economic decisions result from the interaction of buyers and sellers in markets, but the government plays a significant role in the allocation of resources. As we will see in later chapters, economists continue to debate the role government should play in a market economy.

Mixed economy An economy in which most economic decisions result from the interaction of buyers and sellers in markets, but in which the government plays a significant role in the allocation of resources.

One of the most important developments in the international economy in recent years has been the movement of China from being a centrally planned economy to being a more mixed economy. The Chinese economy had suffered decades of economic stagnation following the takeover of the government by Mao Zedong and the Communist Party in 1949. Although China remains a political dictatorship, production of most goods and services is now determined in the market, rather than by the government. The result has been rapid economic growth that in the near future may lead to total production of goods and services in China surpassing total production in the United States.

Efficiency and Equity

Market economies tend to be more efficient than centrally planned economies. There are two types of efficiency: *productive efficiency* and *allocative efficiency.* **Productive efficiency** occurs when a good or service is produced at the lowest possible cost. **Allocative efficiency** occurs when production reflects consumer preferences. Markets tend to be efficient because they promote competition and facilitate *voluntary exchange.* **Voluntary exchange** refers to the situation in which both the buyer and seller of a product are made better off by the transaction. We know that the buyer and seller are both made better off, because otherwise the buyer would not have agreed to buy the product or the seller would not have agreed to sell it. Productive efficiency is achieved when competition among firms in markets forces the firms to produce goods and services at the lowest cost. Allocative efficiency is achieved when the combination of competition among firms and voluntary exchange between firms and consumers results in firms producing the mix of goods and services that consumers prefer most. Competition will force firms to continue producing and selling goods and services as long as the additional benefit to consumers is greater than the additional cost of production. In this way, the mix of goods and services produced will reflect consumer preferences.

Productive efficiency The situation in which a good or service is produced at the lowest possible cost.

Allocative efficiency A state of the economy in which production reflects consumer preferences; in particular, every good or service is produced up to the point where the last unit provides a marginal benefit to consumers equal to the marginal cost of producing it.

Voluntary exchange The situation that occurs in markets when both the buyer and seller of a product are made better off by the transaction.

Although markets promote efficiency, they don't guarantee it. Inefficiency can arise from various sources. To begin with, it may take some time to achieve an efficient outcome. When DVD players were introduced, for example, productive efficiency was not achieved instantly. It took several years for firms to discover the lowest-cost method of producing this good. As we will discuss in Chapter 4, governments sometimes reduce efficiency by interfering with voluntary exchange in markets. For example, many governments limit the imports of some goods from foreign countries. This limitation reduces efficiency by keeping goods from being produced at the lowest cost. The production of some goods damages the environment. In this case, government intervention can increase efficiency, because without such intervention firms may ignore the costs of environmental damage, and thereby fail to produce the goods at the lowest possible cost.

Just because an economic outcome is efficient does not necessarily mean that society finds it desirable. Many people prefer economic outcomes that they consider fair or equitable, even if these outcomes are less efficient. **Equity** is harder to define than efficiency, but it usually involves a fair distribution of economic benefits. For some people, equity involves a more equal distribution of economic benefits than would result from an emphasis on efficiency alone. For example, some people support taxing people with higher incomes to provide the funds for programs that aid the poor. Although equity may be increased by reducing the incomes of high-income people and increasing the incomes of the poor, efficiency may be reduced. People have less incentive to open new businesses, to supply labor, and to save if the government takes a significant

Equity The fair distribution of economic benefits.

amount of the income they earn from working or saving. The result is that fewer goods and services are produced and less saving takes place. As this example illustrates, *there is often a trade-off between efficiency and equity.* In this case, the total amount of goods and services produced falls, although the distribution of the income to buy those goods and services is made more equal. Government policymakers often confront this trade-off.

③ LEARNING OBJECTIVE
Understand the role of models in economic analysis.

Economic Models

Economists rely on economic theories or *models* (the words "theory" and "model" are used interchangeably) to analyze real-world issues, such as the economic effects of outsourcing. As mentioned earlier, economic models are simplified versions of reality used to analyze real-world economic situations. Economists are certainly not alone in relying on models: An engineer may use a computer model of a bridge to help test whether it will withstand high winds, or a biologist may make a physical model of a nucleic acid to better understand its properties. One purpose of economic models is to make economic ideas sufficiently explicit and concrete to be used for decision making by individuals, firms, or the government. For example, we will see in Chapter 3 that the model of demand and supply is a simplified version of how the prices of products are determined by the interactions among buyers and sellers in markets.

Economists use economic models to answer questions. For example, consider the question from the opening of this chapter: Has outsourcing been good or bad for the U.S. economy? For a complicated question such as the effects of outsourcing, economists often use several models to examine different aspects of the issue. For example, a model of how wages are determined might be used to analyze how outsourcing affects wages in particular industries. A model of international trade might be used to analyze how outsourcing affects income growth in the countries involved. Sometimes economists use an existing model to analyze an issue, but in other cases economists must develop a new model. To develop a model, economists generally follow these steps:

1. Decide on the assumptions to be used in developing the model.
2. Formulate a testable hypothesis.
3. Use economic data to test the hypothesis.
4. Revise the model if it fails to explain well the economic data.
5. Retain the revised model to help answer similar economic questions in the future.

The Role of Assumptions in Economic Models

Any model is based on making assumptions because models have to be simplified to be useful. We cannot analyze an economic issue unless we reduce its complexity. For example, economic models make *behavioral assumptions* about the motives of consumers and firms. Economists assume that consumers will buy those goods and services that will maximize their well-being or their satisfaction. Similarly, economists assume that firms act to maximize their profits. These assumptions are simplifications because they do not describe the motives of every consumer and every firm. How can we know if the assumptions in a model are too simplified or too limiting? We discover this when we form hypotheses based on these assumptions and test these hypotheses using real-world information.

Forming and Testing Hypotheses in Economic Models

Economic variable Something measurable that can have different values, such as the wages of software programmers.

A *hypothesis* in an economic model is a statement that may be either correct or incorrect about an *economic variable.* An **economic variable** is something measurable that can have different values, such as the wages paid to software programmers. An example of a hypothesis in an economic model is the statement that outsourcing by U.S. firms reduces wages paid to software programmers in the United States. An economic hypothesis is usually about a *causal relationship;* in this case, the hypothesis states that outsourcing causes, or leads to, lower wages for software programmers.

Before accepting a hypothesis, we must test it. To test a hypothesis we must analyze statistics on the relevant economic variables. In this case, we must gather statistics on the wages paid to software programmers, and perhaps on other variables as well. Testing a hypothesis can be tricky. For example, showing that the wages paid to software programmers fell at a time when outsourcing was increasing would not be enough to demonstrate that outsourcing *caused* the wage fall. Just because two things are *correlated*—that is, they happen at the same time—does not mean that one caused the other. For example, suppose that the number of workers trained as software engineers greatly increased at the same time that outsourcing was increasing. In that case, the fall in wages paid to software engineers might have been caused by the increased competition among workers for these jobs, rather than by the effects of relocating programming jobs from the United States to India or China. Over a period of time, many economic variables will be changing, which complicates testing hypotheses. In fact, when economists disagree about a hypothesis, such as the effect of outsourcing on wages, it is often because of disagreements over interpreting the statistical analysis used to test the hypothesis.

Note that hypotheses must be statements that could in principle turn out to be incorrect. Statements such as "Outsourcing is good" or "Outsourcing is bad" are value judgments, rather than hypotheses, because it is not possible to disprove them.

Economists accept and use an economic model if it leads to hypotheses that are confirmed by statistical analysis. In many cases, the acceptance is tentative, however, pending the gathering of new data or further statistical analysis. In fact, economists often refer to a hypothesis having been "not rejected," rather than being "accepted," by statistical analysis. But what if statistical analysis clearly rejects a hypothesis? For example, what if the model leads to a hypothesis that outsourcing by U.S. firms lowers wages of U.S. software programmers, but this hypothesis is rejected by the data? In that case, the model must be reconsidered. It may be that an assumption used in the model was too simplified or too limiting. For example, perhaps the model we used to determine the effect of outsourcing on wages paid to software programmers assumed that software programmers in China and India had the same training and experience as software programmers in the United States. If, in fact, U.S. software programmers have more training and experience than Chinese and Indian programmers, this difference may explain why our hypothesis was rejected by the economic statistics.

The process of developing models, testing hypotheses, and revising models occurs not just in economics but also in disciplines such as physics, chemistry, and biology. It is often referred to as the *scientific method.* Economics is a *social science* because it applies the scientific method to the study of the interactions among individuals.

In each chapter, the feature entitled "Making the Connection" discusses a business news story, or other application, related to the chapter material. Read Making the Connection 1-1 for two viewpoints about outsourcing.

1-1 Making the Connection

When Economists Disagree: A Debate over Outsourcing

There is an old saying in the newspaper business that it's not news when a dog bites a man, but it is news when a man bites a dog. In 2004, many newspapers ran a "man bites dog" story concerning economics.

Most economists believe that international trade—including the trade that results when firms move production offshore—increases economic efficiency and raises incomes. It was news, then, when MIT economist Paul Samuelson, a winner of the Nobel Prize in Economics, wrote an article in the *Journal of Economic Perspectives* questioning whether incomes in the United States will be higher as a result of the outsourcing of jobs to India and China. Samuelson presented a model of the effects of outsourcing that can be illustrated with the following hypothetical case: Suppose a bank in New York has been using a company in South Dakota to handle its telephone customer service. It then switches to using a company in Bangalore, India that pays its workers much lower wages. Samuelson argued that even when the workers fired by the

Does outsourcing by U.S. firms raise or lower incomes in the United States?

South Dakota firm eventually find new jobs, these may pay lower wages. If outsourcing becomes widespread enough, Samuelson argued, it may result in a significant decline in U.S. incomes.

Many economists objected to Samuelson's argument. One economist who wrote a rebuttal to Samuelson was Jagdish Bhagwati, a former student of Samuelson's and a professor of economics at Columbia University. Bhagwati argued that in Samuelson's example the wages of South Dakota call center workers were reduced by outsourcing, but the costs to the bank were also reduced, which would allow the bank to reduce the prices it charged its customers. In Bhagwati's model, these gains to consumers from lower prices more than offset the loss to workers from lower wages, so the United States experiences a net gain from outsourcing. Samuelson argued, though, that if the United States exports the product—in this case banking services—to other countries, the lower price hurts the exporting firms. In that case, the United States might still be hurt by outsourcing.

This brief summary does not do full justice to the models of Samuelson and Bhagwati, which are too complicated for us to cover in this chapter. We can, however, discuss the sources of the disagreement between these two economists. We have seen that economists sometimes differ about the assumptions that should be used in building a model. That is not the case here: Samuelson and Bhagwati basically agree on the model and the assumptions to be used. Instead, they disagree over how to interpret the relevant economic statistics. Bhagwati argues that the number of U.S. jobs moving to other countries has been relatively small, amounting to about 1 percent of the jobs created in the U.S. economy each year. He also argues that the jobs lost to outsourcing tend to be low-wage jobs, such as telephone customer service or data entry, and are likely to be replaced by higher-wage jobs. Samuelson argues that the impact of outsourcing is greater than Bhagwati believes, and he is less optimistic that newly created jobs in the United States will pay higher wages than the jobs lost to outsourcing.

The debate between Samuelson and Bhagwati demonstrates that economics is an evolving discipline. New models are continually being introduced, and new hypotheses are being formulated and tested. We can expect the debate over the economic impact of outsourcing to continue to be lively.

Sources: Paul A. Samuelson, "Where Ricardo and Mill Rebut and Confirm Arguments of Mainstream Economists Supporting Globalization," *Journal of Economic Perspectives*, Vol. 18, No. 3, Summer 2004, pp. 135–146; Jagdish Bhagwati, Arvind Panagariya, and T. N. Srinivasan, "The Muddles Over Outsourcing," *Journal of Economic Perspectives*, Vol. 18, No. 4, Fall 2004, pp. 93–114; and Steve Lohr, "An Elder Challenges Outsourcing's Orthodoxy," *New York Times*, September 9, 2004, p. C1.

Normative and Positive Analysis

Throughout this book as we build economic models and use them to answer questions, we need to bear in mind the distinction between *positive analysis* and *normative analysis.*

Positive analysis is concerned with *what is* and **normative analysis** is concerned with *what ought to be.* Economics is about positive analysis, which measures the costs and benefits of different courses of action.

Positive analysis Analysis concerned with what is.

Normative analysis Analysis concerned with what ought to be.

We can use the federal government's minimum wage law to compare positive and normative analysis. In 2005 under this law, it was illegal for an employer to hire a worker at a wage less than $5.15 per hour. Without the minimum wage law, some firms and some workers would voluntarily agree to a lower wage. Because of the minimum wage law, some workers have difficulty finding jobs and some firms end up paying more for labor than they otherwise would have. A positive analysis of the federal minimum wage law uses an economic model to estimate how many workers have lost their jobs because of the law, its impact on the costs and profits of businesses, and the gains to workers receiving the minimum wage. After economists complete this positive analysis, the decision as to whether the minimum wage law is a good idea or a bad idea is a normative one and depends on how people assess the trade-off involved. Supporters of the law believe that the losses to employers and to workers who are unemployed as a result of the law are more than offset by the gains to those workers who receive higher wages than they would have without the law. Opponents of the law believe the losses are greater than the gains. The assessment by any individual would depend, in part, on that person's values and political views. The positive analysis provided by an economist would play a role in the decision but can't by itself decide the issue one way or the other.

In each chapter you will see a "Don't Let This Happen To You!" box like the one below. The goal of these boxes is to alert you to common pitfalls in thinking about economic ideas. After reading the box, test your understanding by working the related problem that appears at the end of the chapter.

LEARNING OBJECTIVE

Distinguish between microeconomics and macroeconomics.

Microeconomics and Macroeconomics

Economic models can be used to analyze decision making in many areas. We group some of these areas together as *microeconomics* and others as *macroeconomics.* **Microeconomics** is the study of how households and firms make choices, how they interact in markets, and how the government attempts to influence their choices. Microeconomic issues include explaining how consumers react to changes in product prices and how firms decide what prices to charge. Microeconomics also involves policy issues, such as analyzing the most efficient way to reduce teenage smoking, analyzing the costs and

Microeconomics The study of how households and firms make choices, how they interact in markets, and how the government attempts to influence their choices.

Don't Let This Happen To You!

Don't Confuse Positive Analysis with Normative Analysis

"Economic analysis has shown that the minimum wage law is a bad idea because it causes unemployment." Is this statement accurate? As of 2005, the federal minimum wage law prevents employers from hiring workers at a wage of less than $5.15 per hour. This wage is higher than some employers are willing to pay some workers. If there were no minimum wage law, some workers who currently cannot find any firm willing to hire them at $5.15 per hour would be able to find employment at a lower wage. Therefore, positive economic analysis indicates that the minimum wage law causes unemployment (although economists disagree about how much unemployment is caused by the minimum wage). *But,* those workers who still have jobs benefit from the minimum wage because they are paid a higher wage than they otherwise would be. In other words, the minimum wage law creates both losers (the workers who become unemployed and the firms that have to pay higher wages) and winners (the workers who receive higher wages).

Do the gains to the winners more than offset the losses to the losers? The answer to that question involves normative analysis. Positive economic analysis can only show the consequences of a particular policy; it cannot tell us whether the policy is "good" or "bad." So, the statement at the beginning of this box is inaccurate.

YOUR TURN: **Test your understanding by doing related problem 16 on page 20 at the end of this chapter.**

benefits of approving the sale of a new prescription drug, and analyzing the most efficient way to reduce air pollution.

Macroeconomics The study of the economy as a whole, including topics such as inflation, unemployment, and economic growth.

Macroeconomics is the study of the economy as a whole, including topics such as inflation, unemployment, and economic growth. Macroeconomic issues include explaining why economies experience periods of recession and increasing unemployment and why over the long run some economies have grown much faster than others. Macroeconomics also involves policy issues, such as whether government intervention is capable of reducing the severity of recessions.

The division between microeconomics and macroeconomics is not hard and fast. Many economic situations have *both* a microeconomic and a macroeconomic aspect. For example, the level of total investment by firms in new machinery and equipment helps to determine how rapidly the economy grows—which is a macroeconomic issue. But to understand how much new machinery and equipment firms decide to purchase, we have to analyze the incentives individual firms face—which is a microeconomic issue.

(5) LEARNING OBJECTIVE

Become familiar with important economic terms.

A Preview of Important Economic Terms

In the following chapters you will encounter certain important terms again and again. Becoming familiar with these terms is a necessary step in learning economics. Here we provide a brief introduction to some of these terms. We will discuss them all in greater depth in later chapters:

- ***Entrepreneur.*** An entrepreneur is someone who operates a business. In a market system it is entrepreneurs who decide what goods and services to produce and how to produce them. An entrepreneur starting a new business puts his or her own funds at risk. If an entrepreneur is wrong about what consumers want or about the best way to produce goods and services, the entrepreneur's funds can be lost. This is not an unusual occurrence: In the United States, about half of new businesses close within four years. Without entrepreneurs willing to assume the risk of starting and operating businesses, economic progress would be impossible in a market system.
- ***Innovation.*** There is a distinction between an *invention* and *innovation.* An invention is the development of a new good or a new process for making a good. An innovation is the practical application of an invention. (Innovation also may be used more broadly to refer to any significant improvement in a good or in the means of producing a good.) Much time often passes between the appearance of a new idea and its development to the point where it can be widely used. For example, the Wright Brothers first achieved self-propelled flight at Kitty Hawk, North Carolina, in 1903, but the Wright Brothers' plane was very crude, and it wasn't until the introduction of the DC-3 by Douglas Aircraft in 1936 that regularly scheduled intercity airline flights became common in the United States. Similarly, the first digital electronic computer—the ENIAC—was developed in 1945, but the first IBM personal computer was not introduced until 1981 and widespread use of computers did not have a significant effect on the productivity of American business until the 1990s.
- ***Technology.*** A firm's technology is the processes it uses to produce goods and services. In the economic sense, a firm's technology depends on many factors, such as the skill of its managers, the training of its workers, and the speed and efficiency of its machinery and equipment.
- ***Firm, company, or business.*** A firm is an organization that produces a good or service for profit. Economists use the words "firm," "company," and "business" interchangeably.
- ***Goods.*** Goods are tangible merchandise, such as books, computers, or DVD players.
- ***Services.*** Services are activities done for others, such as providing haircuts or investment advice.
- ***Revenue.*** A firm's revenue is the total amount received for selling a good or service. It is calculated by multiplying the price per unit by the number of units sold.

➤ ***Opportunity cost.*** The concept of opportunity cost is one of the most important in economics. The opportunity cost of any activity is the highest-valued alternative that must be given up to engage in that activity. Consider the example of an entrepreneur who could receive a salary of $80,000 per year working as a manager at a firm but opens her own firm instead. In that case, the opportunity cost of her entrepreneurial services to her own firm is $80,000, even though she does not pay herself an explicit salary.

➤ ***Profit.*** A firm's profit is the difference between its revenue and its costs. Economists distinguish between *accounting profit* and *economic profit.* Accounting profit excludes the cost of some economic resources that the firm does not pay for explicitly. Economic profit includes the opportunity cost of all resources used by the firm. When we refer to profit in this book, we mean economic profit. It is important not to confuse *profit* with *revenue.*

➤ ***Household.*** A household consists of all persons occupying a home. Households are suppliers of factors of production—particularly labor—used by firms to make goods and services. Households also demand goods and services produced by firms and governments.

➤ ***Factors of production or economic resources.*** Firms use factors of production to produce goods and services. The main factors of production are labor, capital, human capital, natural resources—including land—and entrepreneurial ability. Households earn income by supplying the factors of production to firms.

➤ ***Capital.*** The word "capital" can refer to *financial capital* or to *physical capital.* Financial capital includes stocks and bonds issued by firms, bank accounts, and holdings of money. In economics, though, "capital" refers to physical capital, which includes manufactured goods that are used to produce other goods and services. Examples of physical capital are computers, factory buildings, machine tools, warehouses, and trucks. The total amount of physical capital available in a country is referred to as the country's *capital stock.*

➤ ***Human capital.*** Human capital refers to the accumulated training and skills that workers possess. For example, workers with a college education generally have more skills and are more productive than workers who have only a high school degree.

Conclusion

The best way to think of economics is as a group of useful ideas about how individuals make choices. Economists have put these ideas into practice by developing economic models. Consumers, business managers, and government officials use these models every day to help them make choices. In this book, we explore many key economic models and give examples of how they can be applied in the real world.

Most students taking an introductory economics course do not major in economics or become professional economists. Whatever your major may be, the economic principles you will learn in this book will improve your ability to make choices in many aspects of your life. These principles will also improve your understanding of how decisions are made in business and government.

Reading the newspaper and other periodicals is an important part of understanding the current business climate and learning how to apply economic concepts to a variety of real-world events. At the end of each chapter, you will see a two-page periodical feature entitled *An Inside Look.* This feature consists of an excerpt of an article that relates to the company we introduced at the start of the chapter and also to the concepts we have discussed throughout the chapter. A summary and analysis and supporting graphs highlight the economic key points of the article. Test your understanding by answering the *Thinking Critically* questions. Read *An Inside Look* on the next page to learn why some economists argue that fears about outsourcing to China are unjustified.

An Inside Look How Does Economic Growth in China Affect Other Countries?

ECONOMIST, SEPTEMBER 30, 2004

The Halo Effect

"WHAT you cannot avoid, welcome," says an old Chinese proverb. The world would be wise to bear that in mind in its dealings with China. The country's global integration will have a bigger impact on the world economy than that of any previous emerging economy. Fortunately, though, it will be mostly a force for good, boosting overall prosperity.

China's ascent will affect the outside world more than Japan's did in its time. . . .

The idea that China may become the world's biggest economy, with an enormous army of cheap workers, fills many in the rich western world with dread. Yet China's combination of rapid growth, vast size and openness could deliver a big boost to incomes outside China as well as at home. Rather like America when it entered the world economy in the late 19th century, China will be giving a huge boost to both global demand and supply. . . .

a Jobs will be lost in manufacturing in the developed world, but new jobs will be created, largely because most of the money that China earns from exports is being spent on imports from rich economies. Sustained growth in income and jobs relies on a continuous shift of resources to higher-value industries. A frozen job market with no hiring or firing would be in nobody's interest.

Individual countries can maximise their gains from Chinese integration and minimise their losses by making their own economies more flexible, increasing mobility between sectors and improving education. A study by the McKinsey Global Institute looked at what happened to workers who lost their jobs because of firms moving their production to low-wage countries such as China or India. McKinsey estimates that in America 70% of them find new work within six months, but in Germany only 40% do, partly because of a generous benefit system as well as strict hiring and firing laws. . . .

b In flexible labour markets, many of the workers who lose their jobs will eventually be re-employed in more productive industries. It is ironic, therefore, that American politicians and businessmen have been complaining most loudly about China stealing their country's jobs. With its flexible economy, America should adjust more easily than Europe. Fears about the threat from China stem from a series of widely held myths.

American business lobbies and trade unions claim that offshoring has cost their country [3 million] manufacturing jobs in the past three years. But most of those job losses were likelier to have been caused by the recession or by labour-saving IT investment. . . .

Moreover, even if outsourcing does export jobs to China, part of the income created there flows back as increased demand for American goods and services. Work by Matthew Slaughter, an economist at the Tuck School of Business at Dartmouth College, finds that outsourcing also creates new jobs back home for engineers, finance and marketing experts to supply services or hi-tech components to foreign affiliates. In a study of 2,500 American multinational firms in the ten years to 2001, Mr. Slaughter found that the number of jobs in their foreign subsidiaries rose by 2.9 [million], but in America itself by as much as 5.5 [million]. Moreover, these firms' domestic employment increased faster than jobs in purely domestic firms. . . .

c Fears that Chinese exports are growing at the expense of other countries are based on a fixed-lump-of-trade fallacy. In fact, trade is a positive-sum game: the more participants there are, the more opportunities arise, allowing countries to produce more with the same amount of labour and to obtain goods and services more cheaply. China's expansion will hugely add to those opportunities.

Key Points in the Article

This article discusses the effect of economic growth in China on jobs and wages in the United States and Europe. The article notes that many people fear that a rapid growth in China will reduce incomes and economic growth in the United States and Europe. The article argues these fears are unjustified. It also provides advice on the types of policies countries should pursue to increase their gains from China's integration into the world economy.

Analyzing the News

a Figure 1 shows that for several countries, including the United States, China has become an increasingly important market for exports. We noted previously in this chapter that markets tend to be efficient because they involve *voluntary exchange*. With voluntary exchange both the buyer and the seller are made better off. This insight applies to international trade between the United States and China as much as to domestic trade within the United States. One strength of a market system is that it facilitates shifting of resources from declining industries to expanding industries, as noted in the article.

b Making the Connection 1-1 presented the debate between economists Paul Samuelson and Jagdish Bhagwati over whether outsourcing has helped or hurt the U.S. economy. One key aspect of the debate concerned whether workers who lose their jobs because of outsourcing are eventually likely to find comparable or better jobs. The article makes the argument that when labor markets are flexible—meaning that there are few restrictions on workers moving between jobs—it is more likely that displaced workers will find good replacement jobs.

c We have seen in this chapter that economists use models to analyze economic issues such as the effects of outsourcing. One advantage of economic models is that they make explicit the assumptions that are being made. Models also generate hypotheses that can be tested against the real world. According to the article, people who fear that an increase in exports from China must come at the expense of other countries also are using a model, but it is a model that is not explicitly stated. The article refers to this model as the "fixed-lump-of-trade fallacy." We know the model is a fallacy because the evidence shows that many countries can increase their exports at the same time.

Thinking Critically

1. The article argues that outsourcing to China will make the global economy and the U.S. economy more prosperous and efficient. What impact does the article suggest outsourcing will have on equity?
2. What evidence from the article suggests that positive analysis of the impact of outsourcing will be difficult, even among people using the same economic model?

Source: "The Halo Effect: How China's Expansion Will Affect Jobs and Growth Elsewhere," *Economist*, September 30, 2004. www.economist.com

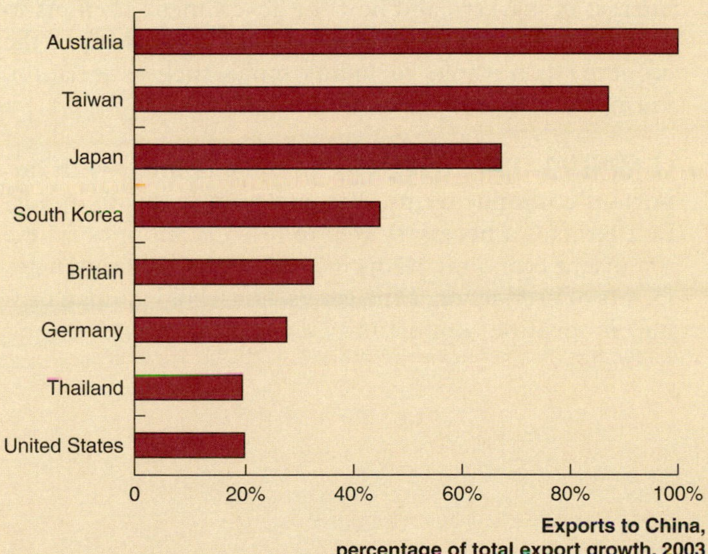

Figure 1: Many countries, including the United States, have experienced rapidly increasing exports to China.

Source: Thomson Datastream: national statistics.

SUMMARY

LEARNING OBJECTIVE ① Discuss these three important economic ideas: People are rational. People respond to incentives. Optimal decisions are made at the margin. Economists assume people are rational in the sense that consumers and firms use all available information as they take actions intended to achieve their goals. Rational individuals weigh the benefits and costs of each action, and choose an action only if the benefits outweigh the costs. Although people act from a variety of motives, ample evidence indicates that they respond to economic incentives. Economists use the word "marginal" to mean extra or additional. The optimal decision is to continue any activity up to the point where the marginal benefit equals the marginal cost.

LEARNING OBJECTIVE ② Discuss how an economy answers these questions: *What* goods and services will be produced? *How* will the goods and services be produced? *Who* will receive the goods and services? The choices of consumers, firms, and governments determine what goods and services will be produced. Firms choose how to produce the goods and services they sell. In the United States, who receives the goods and services produced depends largely on how income is distributed in the marketplace. In a centrally planned economy, most economic decisions are made by the government. In a market economy, most economic decisions are made by consumers and firms. Most economies, including that of the United States, are mixed economies in which most economic decisions are made by consumers and firms, but in which the government also plays a significant role. There are two types of efficiency: *productive efficiency* and *allocative efficiency.* Productive efficiency occurs when a good or service is produced at the lowest possible cost. Allocative efficiency occurs when production reflects consumer preferences. *Equity* is harder to define than efficiency, but it usually involves a fair distribution of economic benefits. Government policymakers often face a trade-off between equity and efficiency.

LEARNING OBJECTIVE ③ Understand the role of models in economic analysis. Economists rely on economic models when they apply economic ideas to real-world problems. *Economic models* are simplified versions of reality used to analyze real-world economic situations. Economists accept and use an economic model if it leads to hypotheses that are confirmed by statistical analysis. In many cases, the acceptance is tentative, however, pending the gathering of new data or further statistical analysis. Economics is a *social science* because it applies the scientific method to the study of the interactions among individuals. Economics is concerned with positive analysis rather than normative analysis. Positive analysis is concerned with what is. Normative analysis is concerned with what ought to be.

LEARNING OBJECTIVE ④ Distinguish between microeconomics and macroeconomics. *Microeconomics* is the study of how households and firms make choices, how they interact in markets, and how the government attempts to influence their choices. *Macroeconomics* is the study of the economy as a whole, including topics such as inflation, unemployment, and economic growth.

LEARNING OBJECTIVE ⑤ Become familiar with important economic terms. Becoming familiar with important terms is a necessary step to learn economics. These important economic terms include capital, entrepreneur, factors of production, firm, goods, household, human capital, innovation, opportunity cost, profit, revenue, and technology.

KEY TERMS

REVIEW QUESTIONS

1. What is scarcity? Why is scarcity central to the study of economics?
2. Briefly discuss each of the following economic ideas: People are rational. People respond to incentives. Optimal decisions are made at the margin.
3. What are the three economic questions that every society must answer? Briefly discuss the differences in how centrally planned, market, and mixed economies answer these questions.
4. What is the difference between productive efficiency and allocative efficiency?
5. What is the difference between efficiency and equity? Why do government policymakers often face a trade-off between efficiency and equity?
6. Why do economists use models? How are economic data used to test models?
7. Describe the five steps by which economists arrive at a useful economic model.
8. What is the difference between normative analysis and positive analysis? Is economics concerned mainly with normative analysis or mainly with positive analysis? Briefly explain.
9. Briefly discuss the difference between microeconomics and macroeconomics.

PROBLEMS AND APPLICATIONS

Please visit **www.prenhall.com/hubbard** *for solutions to the even-numbered problems as well as multiple-choice and true or false self-assessment quizzes.*

1. In a column in the *Wall Street Journal,* Robert McTeer Jr., former president of the Federal Reserve Bank of Dallas, wrote, "My take on training in economics is that it becomes increasingly valuable as you move up the career ladder. I can't think of a better major for corporate CEO's [chief executive officers], congressmen or American presidents." Why might studying economics be particularly good preparation for being the top manager of a corporation or a leader in government?

   Source: Robert D. McTeer Jr., "The Dismal Science? Hardly!" *Wall Street Journal,* June 4, 2003.
2. Does Bill Gates, the richest person in the world, face scarcity? Does everyone? Are there any exceptions?
3. Do you agree or disagree with the following assertion: "The problem with economics is that it assumes consumers and firms always make the correct decision. But we know everyone's human, and we all make mistakes."
4. **[Related to *Solved Problem 1-1*]** Suppose Dell is currently selling 250,000 Pentium 4 laptops per month. A manager at Dell argues, "The last 10,000 laptops we produced increased our revenue by $8.5 million and our costs by $8.9 million. However, because we are making a substantial total profit of $25 million from producing 250,000 laptops, I think we are producing the optimal number of laptops." Briefly explain whether you agree with the manager's reasoning.
5. **[Related to *Solved Problem 1-1*]** Two students are discussing Solved Problem 1-1.

   Joe: "I think the key additional information you need to know in deciding whether to produce 300,000 more iPods is the amount of profit you currently are making while producing 3,000,000. Then you can compare the profit earned from selling 3,300,000 iPods with the profit earned from selling 3,000,000. This information is more important than the additional revenue and additional cost of the last 300,000 iPods produced."

   Jill: "Actually, Joe, knowing how much profits change when you sell 300,000 more iPods is exactly the same as knowing the additional revenue and the additional cost."

   Briefly evaluate their arguments.
6. **[Related to *Solved Problem 1-1*]** Late in the semester a friend tells you, "I was going to drop my psychology course so I could concentrate on my other courses, but I had already put so much time into the course that I decided not to drop it." What do you think of your friend's reasoning? Would it make a difference to your answer if your friend has to pass the psychology course at some point to graduate? Briefly explain.
7. In the first six months of 2003, branches of Commerce Bank in New York City were robbed 14 times. The New York City Police recommended steps the bank could take to deter robberies, including the installation of plastic barriers called "bandit barriers." The police were surprised the bank did not take their advice. According to a deputy

commissioner of police, "Commerce does very little of what we recommend. They've told our detectives they have no interest in ever putting in the barriers." Wouldn't Commerce Bank have a strong incentive to install bandit barriers to deter robberies? Why, then, wouldn't they do it?
Source: Dan Barry, "Friendly Bank Makes It Easy for Robbers," *New York Times*, July 5, 2003.

8. In 1838, the U.S. Army was given the job of moving the Cherokees, Creeks, Choctaws, and Seminoles from the eastern United States to Oklahoma. Contractors were given $65 per person (about $1,270 in today's money) to provide food and medicine for the Indians during the 1,000-mile forced march. Many of the contractors provided scanty food portions, bad meat, and no medicine. As a result, approximately one-quarter of these Indians perished along the way. How could the incentives have been changed so that the death rates would have been lower?
9. Suppose an economist develops an economic model and finds that "it works great in theory, but it fails in practice." What should the economist do next?
10. Dr. Strangelove's theory is that the price of mushrooms is determined by the activity of subatomic particles that exist in another universe parallel to ours. When the subatomic particles are emitted in profusion, the price of mushrooms is high. When subatomic particle emissions are low, the price of mushrooms also is low. How would you go about testing Dr. Strangelove's theory? Discuss whether or not this theory is useful.
11. Would you expect the new and better machinery and equipment to be adopted more rapidly in a market economy or in a centrally planned economy? Briefly explain.
12. Centrally planned economies have been less efficient than market economies.
    a. Has this happened by chance or is there some underlying reason?
    b. If market economies are more economically efficient than centrally planned economies, would there ever be a reason to prefer having a centrally planned economy rather than a market economy?
13. Thomas Sowell, an economist at the Hoover Institution at Stanford University, has written that "All economic systems not only provide people with goods and services, but also restrict or prevent them from getting as much of these goods and services as they wish."

    Why is it necessary for all economic systems to do this? How does a market system prevent people from getting as many goods and services as they wish?
    Source: Thomas Sowell, *Applied Economics: Thinking Beyond Stage One*, New York: Basic Books, 2004, p. 16.
14. Suppose that your local police department recovers 100 tickets to a big NASCAR race in a drug raid. It decides to distribute these to residents and announces that tickets will be given away at 10 A.M., Monday morning at City Hall.
    a. What groups of people will be most likely to try to get the tickets? Think of specific examples and then generalize.
    b. What is the opportunity cost of distributing the tickets this way?
    c. Productive efficiency occurs when a good or service (such as the distribution of tickets) is produced at the lowest possible cost. Is this an efficient way to distribute the tickets? If possible, think of a more efficient method of distributing the tickets.
    d. Is this an equitable way to distribute the tickets? Explain.
15. Many large firms have begun outsourcing work to China.
    a. Why have they done this?
    b. Is outsourcing work to low-wage Chinese workers a risk-free proposition for large firms?
16. **[Related to *Don't Let This Happen To You!*]** Explain which of the following statements represent positive analysis and which represent normative analysis:
    a. A 50-cent-per-pack tax on cigarettes will reduce smoking by teenagers by 12 percent.
    b. The federal government should spend more on AIDS research.
    c. Rising paper prices will increase textbook prices.
    d. The price of coffee at Starbucks is too high.
17. Briefly explain whether each of the following is primarily a microeconomic issue or a macroeconomic issue:
    a. The effect of higher cigarette taxes on the quantity of cigarettes sold
    b. The effect of higher income taxes on the total amount of consumer spending
    c. The reasons for the economies of East Asian countries growing faster than the economies of sub-Saharan African countries
    d. The reasons for low rates of profit in the airline industry
18. The American Bar Association has proposed a law that would prohibit anyone except lawyers from giving legal advice. Under the proposal, income tax preparers, real estate agents, hospitals, labor unions, and anyone else who offered legal advice would be penalized. One critic of the proposal argued that the proposal would protect attorneys more than it would protect consumers.
    a. How might the proposal protect consumers?
    b. Why did the critic of the proposal argue that it would protect attorneys more than it would protect consumers?
    c. Briefly discuss whether you consider the proposed law to be a good idea.

    Source: Adam Liptak, "U.S. Opposes Proposal to Limit Who May Give Legal Advice," *New York Times*, February 3, 2003.

Appendix

Using Graphs and Formulas

Graphs are used to illustrate key economics ideas. Graphs appear not just in economics textbooks but also in newspaper and magazine articles that discuss business and economic ideas. Why the heavy use of graphs? Because they serve two useful purposes: (1) They simplify economic ideas, and (2) They make the ideas more concrete so they can be applied to real-world problems. Economic and business issues can be complicated, but a graph can help cut through complications and highlight the key relationships needed to understand a business issue. In that sense, a graph can be like a street map.

For example, suppose you take a bus to New York City to see the Empire State Building. After arriving at the Port Authority Bus Terminal, you will probably use a map similar to the one shown below to find your way to the Empire State Building.

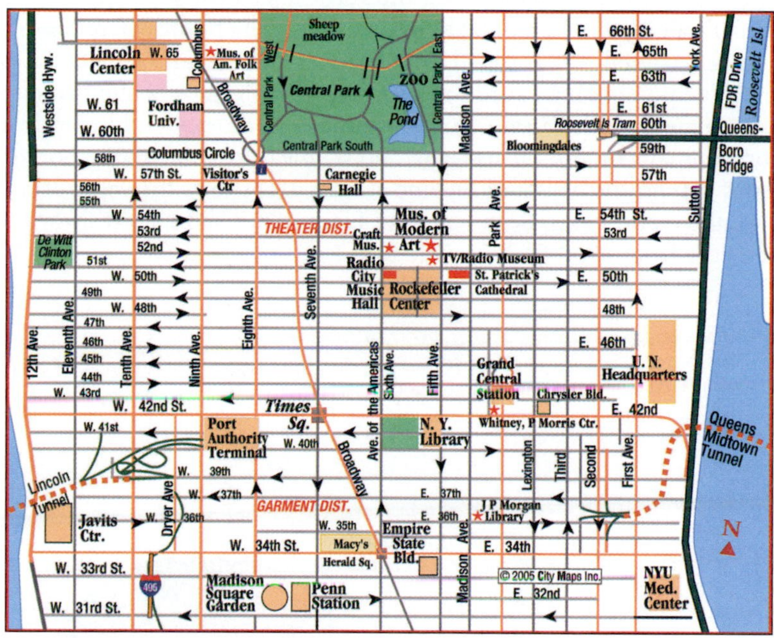

Maps are very familiar to just about everyone, so we don't usually think of them as being simplified versions of reality, but they are. This map does not show much more than the streets in this part of New York City and some of the most important buildings. The names, addresses, and telephone numbers of the people who live and work in the area aren't given. Almost none of the stores and buildings those people work and live in are shown either. It doesn't tell you which streets allow curbside parking and which don't. In fact, the map tells you almost nothing about the messy reality of life in this section of New York City, except how the streets are laid out, which is the essential information you need to get from the Port Authority to the Empire State Building.

Think about someone who says, "I know how to get around in the city, but I just can't figure out how to read a map." It certainly is possible to find your destination in a city without a map, but it's a lot easier with one. The same is true of using graphs in economics. It is possible to arrive at a solution to a real-world problem in economics and business without using graphs, but it is usually a lot easier if you do use them.

Often the difficulty students have with graphs and formulas is just a lack of familiarity. With practice, all the graphs and formulas in this text will become familiar to you. Once you are familiar with them, you will be able to use them to analyze problems that would otherwise seem very difficult. What follows is a brief review of how graphs and formulas are used.

Graphs of One Variable

Figure 1A-1 displays values for *market shares* in the U.S. automobile market using two common types of graphs. Market shares show the percentage of industry sales accounted for by different firms. In this case, the information is for groups of firms: the "Big Three"—Ford, General Motors, and DiamlerChrysler—as well as Japanese firms, European firms, and Korean firms. Panel (a) displays the information on market shares as a *bar graph,* where the market share of each group of firms is represented by the height of its bar. Panel (b) displays the same information as a *pie chart,* with the market share of each group of firms represented by the size of its slice of the pie.

Information on economic variables is also often displayed in *time-series graphs.* Time-series graphs are displayed on a coordinate grid. In a coordinate grid we can measure the value of one variable along the vertical axis (or *y*-axis), and the value of another variable along the horizontal axis (or *x*-axis). The point where the vertical axis intersects the horizontal axis is called the *origin.* At the origin the value of both variables is zero. The points on a coordinate grid represent values of the two variables. In Figure 1A-2 we measure the number of automobiles and trucks sold worldwide by the Ford Motor Company on the vertical axis, and we measure time on the horizontal axis. In time-series graphs, the height of the line at each date shows the value of the variable measured on the vertical axis. Both panels of Figure 1A-2 show Ford's worldwide sales during each year from 1999 to 2003. The difference between panel (a) and panel (b)

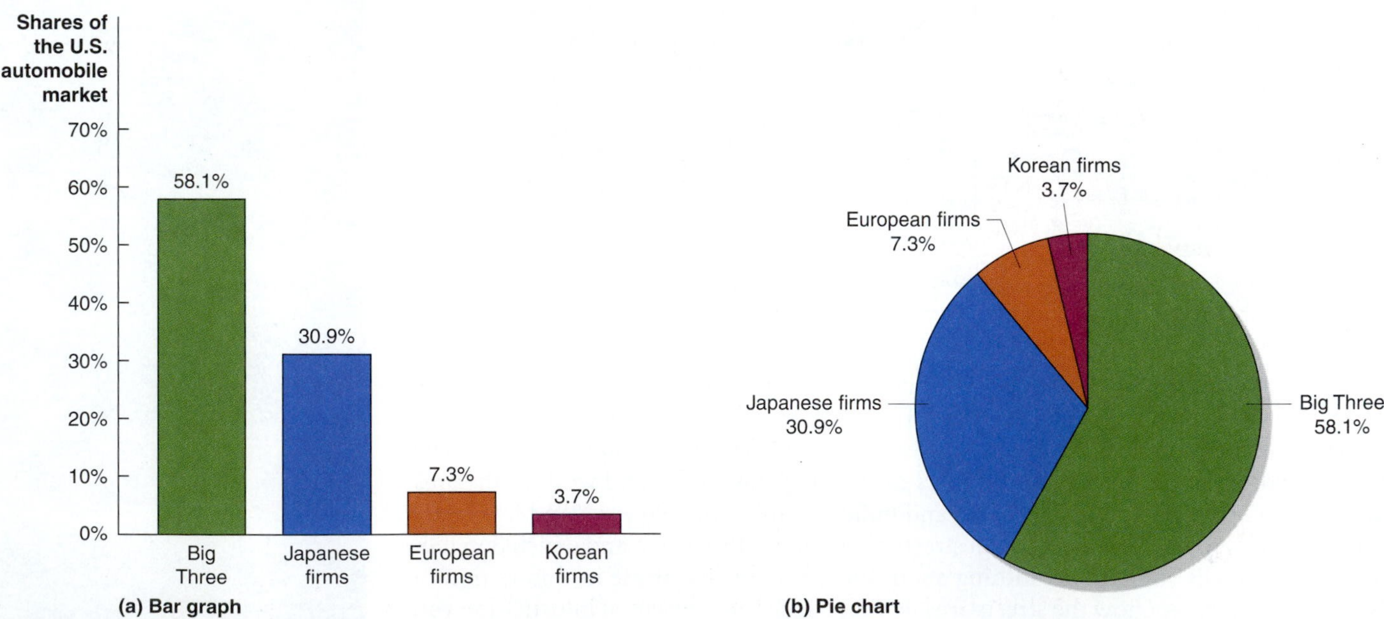

FIGURE 1A-1 Bar Graphs and Pie Charts

Values for an economic variable are often displayed as a bar graph or as a pie chart. In this case, panel (a) shows market share data for the U.S. automobile industry as a *bar graph,* where the market share of each group of firms is represented by the height of its bar. Panel (b) displays the same information as a *pie chart,* with the market share of each group of firms represented by the size of its slice of the pie.

Source: Ann Keeton, "December U.S. Auto Rise; GM's Decline," *Wall Street Journal,* January 5, 2005, p. A2.

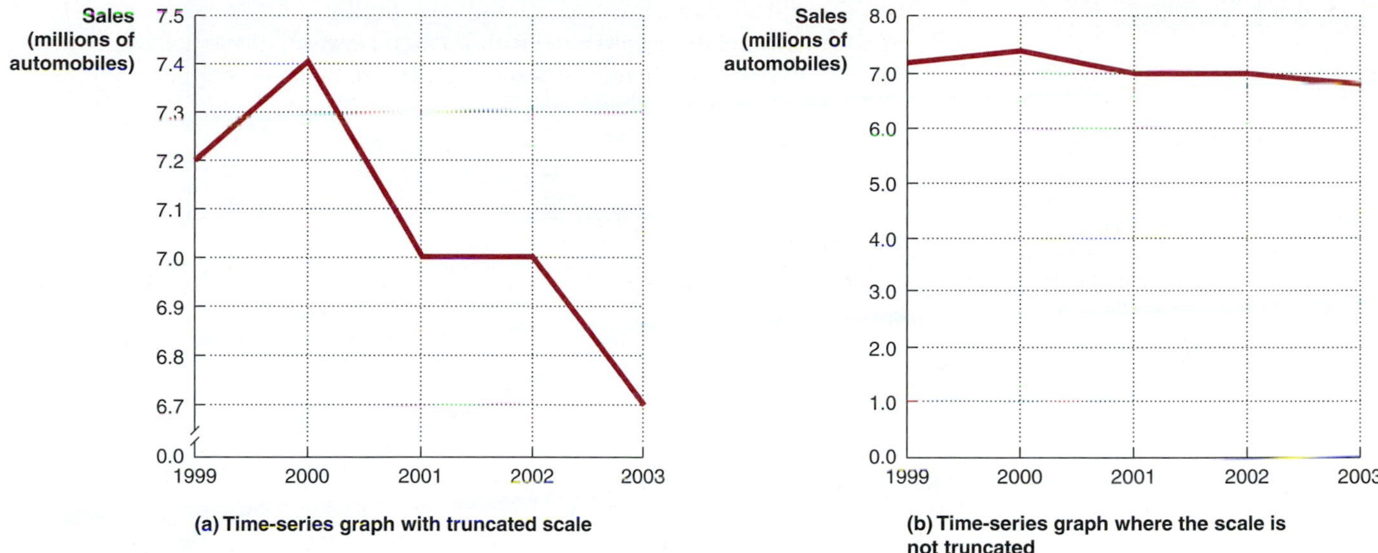

FIGURE 1A-2 Time-Series Graphs

Both panels present time-series graphs of Ford Motor Company's worldwide sales during each year from 1999 to 2003. Panel (a) has a truncated scale on the vertical axis, while panel (b) does not. As a result, the fluctuations in Ford's sales appear smaller in panel (b) than in panel (a).

Source: Ford Motor Company, *Annual Report*, various years.

illustrates the importance of the scale used in a time-series graph. In panel (a), the scale on the vertical axis is truncated, which means that it does not start with zero. The slashes (//) near the bottom of the axis indicate that the scale is truncated. In panel (b), the scale is not truncated. In panel (b) the fluctuations in Ford's sales appear smaller than in panel (a). (Technically, the horizontal axis is also truncated because we start with the year 1999, not the year 0.)

Graphs of Two Variables

We often use graphs to show the relationship between two variables. For example, suppose you are interested in the relationship between the price of a pepperoni pizza and the quantity of pizzas sold per week in the small town of Bryan, Texas. A graph showing the relationship between the price of a good and the quantity of the good demanded at each price is called a *demand curve.* (As we will discuss later, in drawing a demand curve for a good we have to hold constant any variables other than price that might affect the willingness of consumers to buy the good.) Figure 1A-3 shows the data you have collected on price and quantity. The figure shows a two-dimensional grid on which we measure the price of pizza along the *y*-axis and the quantity of pizza sold per week along the *x*-axis. Each point on the grid represents one of the price and quantity combinations listed in the table. We can connect the points to form the demand curve for pizza in Bryan, Texas. Notice that the scales on both axes in the graph are truncated. In this case, truncating the axes allows the graph to illustrate more clearly the relationship between price and quantity by excluding low prices and quantities.

Slopes of Lines

Once you have plotted the data in Figure 1A-3, you may be interested in how much the quantity of pizza sold increases as the price decreases. The *slope* of a line tells us how

FIGURE 1A-3

Plotting Price and Quantity Points in a Graph

The figure shows a two-dimensional grid on which we measure the price of pizza along the vertical axis (or y-axis) and the quantity of pizza sold per week along the horizontal axis (or x-axis). Each point on the grid represents one of the price and quantity combinations listed in the table. By connecting the points by a line, we can better illustrate the relationship between the two variables.

Price (dollars per pizza)	Quantity (pizzas per week)	Points
$15	50	*A*
14	55	*B*
13	60	*C*
12	65	*D*
11	70	*E*

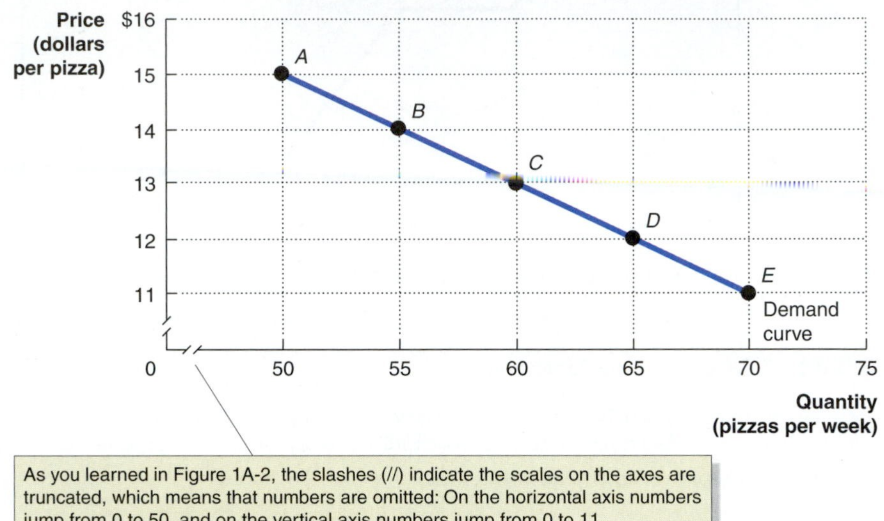

much the variable we are measuring on the y-axis changes as the variable we are measuring on the x-axis changes. We can use the Greek letter delta (Δ) to stand for the change in a variable. The slope is sometimes referred to as the rise over the run. So, we have several ways of expressing slope:

$$\text{Slope} = \frac{\text{Change in value on the vertical axis}}{\text{Change in value on the horizontal axis}} = \frac{\Delta y}{\Delta x} = \frac{\text{Rise}}{\text{Run}}.$$

Figure 1A-4 reproduces the graph from Figure 1A-3. Because the slope of a straight line is the same at any point, we can use any two points in the figure to calculate the slope of the line. For example, when the price of pizza decreases from $14 to $12, the quantity of pizza sold increases from 55 per week to 65 per week. Therefore, the slope is:

$$\text{Slope} = \frac{\Delta\text{Price of pizza}}{\Delta\text{Quantity of pizza}} = \frac{(\$12 - \$14)}{(65 - 55)} = \frac{-2}{10} = -0.2.$$

The slope of this line gives us some insight into how responsive consumers in Bryan, Texas are to changes in the price of pizza. The larger the value of the slope (ignoring the negative sign), the steeper the line will be, which indicates that not many additional pizzas are sold when the price falls. The smaller the value of the slope, the flatter the line will be, which indicates a greater increase in pizzas sold when the price falls.

Taking Into Account More Than Two Variables on a Graph

The demand curve graph in Figure 1A-4 shows the relationship between the price of pizza and the quantity of pizza sold, but we know that the quantity of any good sold depends on more than just the price of the good. For example, the quantity of pizza sold in a given week in Bryan, Texas can be affected by such other variables as the price of hamburgers, whether an advertising campaign by local pizza parlors has begun that week, and so on. Allowing the values of any other variables to change will cause the position of the demand curve in the graph to change.

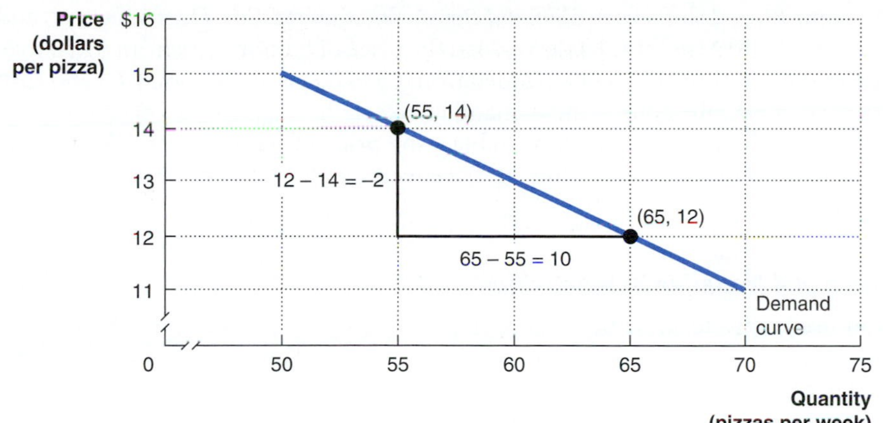

FIGURE 1A-4

Calculating the Slope of a Line

We can calculate the slope of a line as the change in the value of the variable on the *y*-axis divided by the change in the value of the variable on the *x*-axis. Because the slope of a straight line is constant, we can use any two points in the figure to calculate the slope of the line. For example, when the price of pizza decreases from $14 to $12, the quantity of pizza demanded increases from 55 per week to 65 per week. So, the slope of this line equals −2 divided by 10, or −0.2.

Suppose, for example, that the demand curve in Figure 1A-4 was drawn holding the price of hamburgers constant at $1.50. If the price of hamburgers rises to $2.00, then some consumers will switch from buying hamburgers to buying pizza, and more pizzas will be sold at every price. The result on the graph will be to shift the line representing the demand curve to the right. Similarly, if the price of hamburgers falls from $1.50 to $1.00, some consumers will switch from buying pizza to buying hamburgers, and fewer pizzas will be sold at every price. The result on the graph will be to shift the line representing the demand curve to the left.

The table in Figure 1A-5 shows the effect of a change in the price of hamburgers on the quantity of pizza demanded. For example, suppose at first we are on the line labeled *Demand curve*$_1$. If the price of pizza is $14 (point *A*), an increase in the price of hamburgers from $1.50 to $2.00 increases the quantity of pizza demanded from 55 to 60 per

	Quantity (pizzas per week)		
Price (dollars per pizza)	When the Price of Hamburgers = $1.00	When the Price of Hamburgers = $1.50	When the Price of Hamburgers = $2.00
$15	45	50	55
14	50	55	60
13	55	60	65
12	60	65	70
11	65	70	75

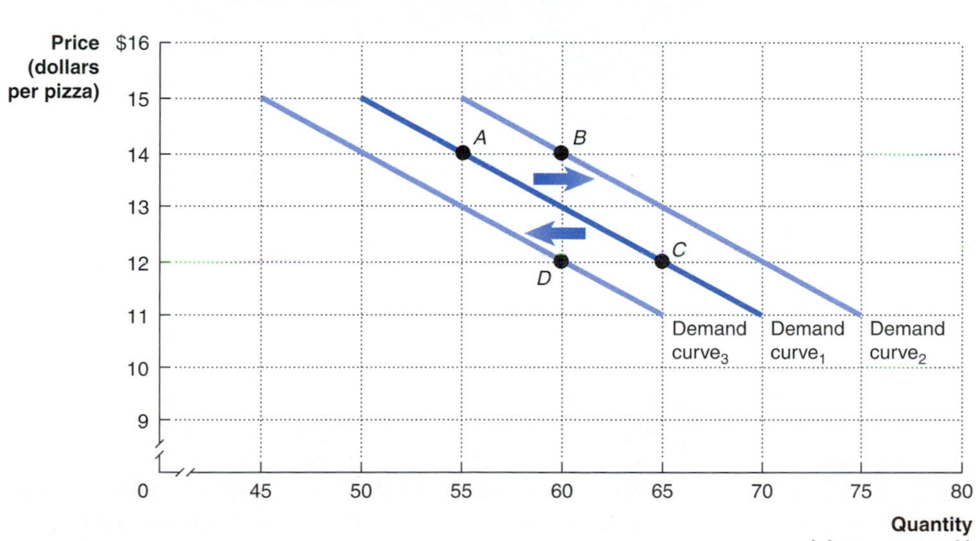

FIGURE 1A-5

Showing Three Variables on a Graph

The demand curve for pizza shows the relationship between the price of pizzas and the quantity of pizza demanded, *holding constant other factors that might affect the willingness of consumers to buy pizza.* If the price of pizza is $14 (point *A*), an increase in the price of hamburgers from $1.50 to $2.00 increases the quantity of pizza demanded from 55 to 60 per week (point *B*) and shifts us to Demand curve$_2$. Or, if we start on Demand curve$_1$ and the price of pizza is $12 (point *C*), a decrease in the price of hamburgers from $1.50 to $1.00 decreases the quantity of pizza demanded from 65 to 60 per week (point *D*), and shifts us to *Demand curve*$_3$.

week (point *B*), and shifts us to *Demand curve*$_2$. Or, if we start on *Demand curve*$_1$ and the price of pizza is $12 (point *C*), a decrease in the price of hamburgers from $1.50 to $1.00 decreases the quantity of pizza demanded from 65 to 60 per week (point *D*) and shifts us to *Demand curve*$_3$. By shifting the demand curve, we have taken into account the effect of changes in the value of a third variable—the price of hamburgers. We will use this technique of shifting curves to allow for the effects of additional variables many times in this book.

Positive and Negative Relationships

We can use graphs to show the relationships between any two variables. Sometimes the relationship between the variables is *negative*, meaning that as one variable increases in value the other variable decreases in value. This was the case with the price of pizza and the quantity of pizza demanded. The relationship between two variables can also be *positive*, meaning that the values of both variables increase together. This positive co-movement is the case, for example, with the level of total income—or *disposable personal income*—received by households in the United States and the level of total *consumption spending*, which is spending by households on all types of goods and services, apart from houses. The table in Figure 1A-6 shows the values for income and consumption spending for the years 2001–2004 (the values are in billions of dollars). The graph plots the data from the table, with national income measured along the horizontal axis and consumption spending measured along the vertical axis. Notice that the four points do not all fall exactly on the line. This is often the case with real-world data. To examine the relationship between two variables, economists often use the straight line that best fits the data.

Slopes of Nonlinear Curves

The relationship between some economic variables cannot be represented accurately by a straight line. For example, panel (a) of Figure 1A-7 shows the hypothetical relationship between Apple's total cost of producing iPods and the quantity of iPods produced. The relationship is curved, rather than linear. In this case, the cost of production is increasing at an increasing rate, which often happens in manufacturing. Put a different way, as we move up the curve, its slope becomes larger. To see this effect, first remember that we calculate the slope of a curve by dividing the change in the variable on the *y*-axis by the

FIGURE 1A-6

Graphing the Positive Relationship between Income and Consumption

In a positive relationship between two economic variables, as one variable increases, the other variable also increases. This figure shows the positive relationship between disposable personal income and consumption spending. As disposable personal income in the United States has increased, so has consumption spending.

Source: U.S. Department of Commerce, Bureau of Economic Analysis.

Year	Disposable Personal Income (billions of dollars)	Consumption Spending (billions of dollars)
2001	$7,486	$7,055
2002	7,827	7,376
2003	8,159	7,760
2004	8,632	8,229

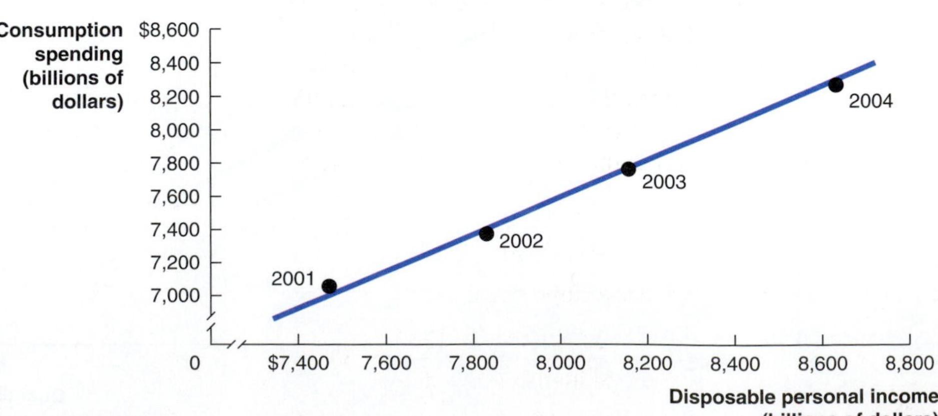

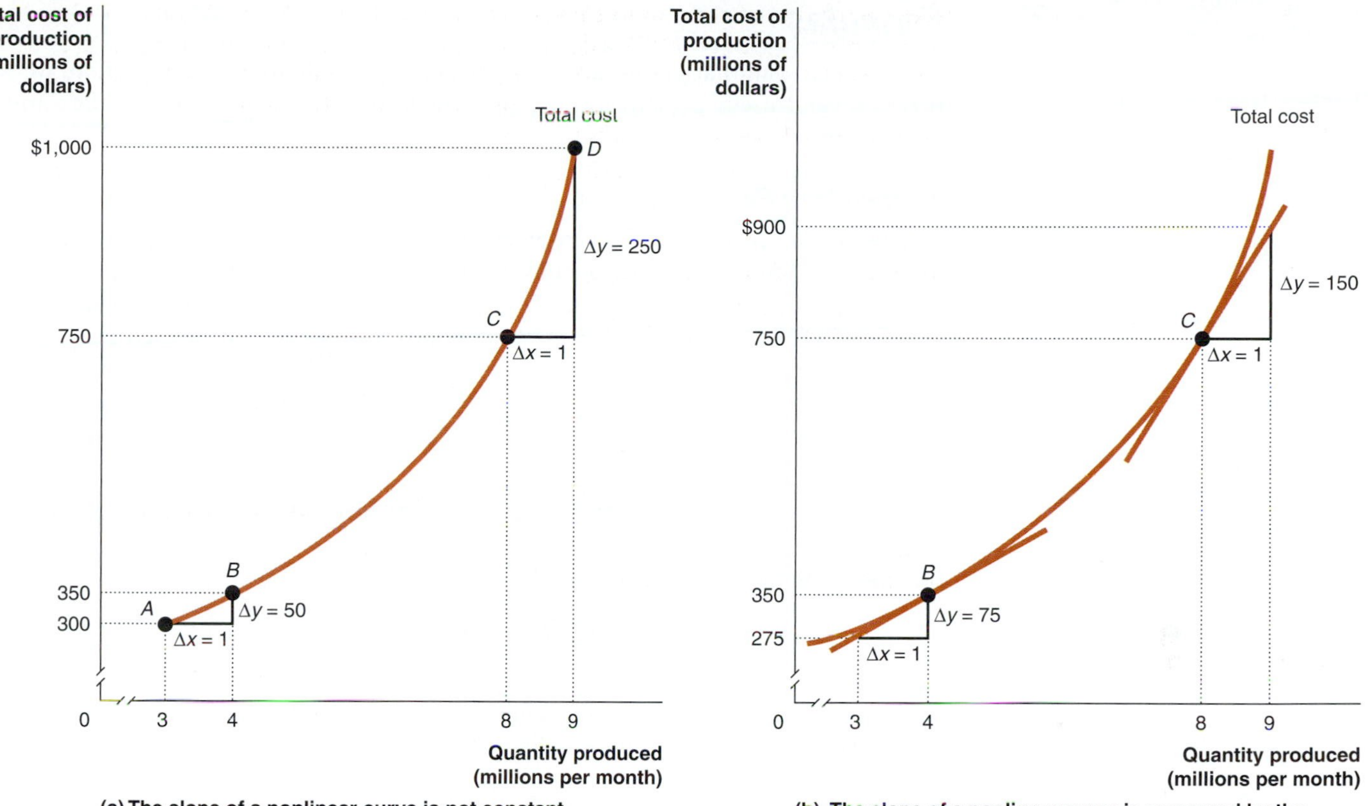

(a) The slope of a nonlinear curve is not constant

(b) The slope of a nonlinear curve is measured by the slope of the tangent line

FIGURE 1A-7 The Slope of a Nonlinear Curve

The relationship between the quantity of iPods produced and the total cost of production is curved, rather than linear. In panel (a), in moving from point *A* to point *B*, the quantity produced increases by 1 million iPods, while the total cost of production increases by $50 million. Farther up the curve, as we move from point *C* to point *D*, the change in quantity is the same—1 million iPods—but the change in the total cost of production is now much larger: $250 million. Because the change in the *y* variable has increased, while the change in the *x* variable has remained the same, we know that the slope has increased. In panel (b), we measure the slope of the cuve at a particular point by the slope of the tangent line. The slope of the tangent line at point *B* is 75, and the slope of the tangent line at point *C* is 150.

change in the variable on the *x*-axis. In moving from point *A* to point *B*, the quantity produced increases by 1 million iPods, while the total cost of production increases by $50 million. Farther up the curve, as we move from point *C* to point *D*, the change in quantity is the same—1 million iPods—but the change in the total cost of production is now much larger: $250 million. Because the change in the *y* variable has increased, while the change in the *x* variable has remained the same, we know that the slope has increased.

To measure the slope of a nonlinear curve at a particular point, we must measure the slope of the *tangent line* to the curve at that point. A tangent line will only touch the curve at that point. We can measure the slope of the tangent line just as we would the slope of any straight line. In panel (b), the tangent line at point *B* has a slope equal to

$$\frac{\Delta\text{Cost}}{\Delta\text{Quantity}} = \frac{75}{1} = 75.$$

The tangent line at point *C* has a slope equal to

$$\frac{\Delta\text{Cost}}{\Delta\text{Quantity}} = \frac{150}{1} = 150.$$

Once again we see that the slope of the curve is larger at point *C* than at point *B*.

Formulas

We have just seen that graphs are an important economic tool. In this section, we will review several useful formulas and show how to use them to summarize data and to calculate important relationships.

Formula for a Percentage Change

One important formula is the *percentage change*. The percentage change is the change in some economic variable, usually from one period to the next, expressed as a percentage. An important macroeconomic measure is the real *Gross Domestic Product* or GDP. GDP is the value of all the final goods and services produced in a country during a year. "Real" GDP is corrected for the effects of inflation. When economists say that the U.S. economy grew 4.4 percent during 2004, they mean that real GDP was 4.4 percent higher in 2004 than it was in 2003. The formula for making this calculation is:

$$\left(\frac{\text{GDP}_{2004} - \text{GDP}_{2003}}{\text{GDP}_{2003}}\right) \times 100$$

or, more generally for any two periods:

$$\text{Percentage change} = \left(\frac{\text{Value in the second period} - \text{Value in the first period}}{\text{Value in the first period}}\right) \times 100.$$

In this case, real GDP was \$10,381 billion in 2003 and \$10,842 billion in 2004. So, the growth rate of the U.S. economy during 2004 was:

$$\left(\frac{\$10{,}842 - \$10{,}381}{\$10{,}381}\right) \times 100 = 4.4\%.$$

Notice that it didn't matter that in using the formula we ignored the fact that GDP is measured in billions of dollars. In fact, when calculating percentage changes, *the units don't matter*. The percentage increase from \$10,381 billion to \$10,842 billion is exactly the same as the percentage increase from \$10,381 to \$10,842.

Formulas for the Areas of a Rectangle and a Triangle

Areas that form rectangles and triangles on graphs can have important economic meaning. For example, Figure 1A-8 shows the demand curve for Pepsi. Suppose that the price is currently \$2.00 and that 125,000 bottles of Pepsi are sold at that price. A firm's *total revenue* is equal to the amount it receives from selling its product, or the price times the quantity sold. In this case, total revenue will equal \$2.00 per bottle times 125,000 bottles, or \$250,000.

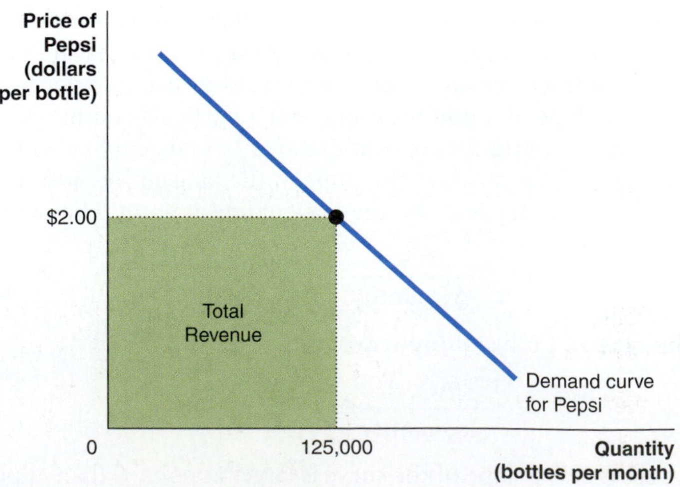

FIGURE 1A-8

Showing a Firm's Total Revenue on a Graph

The area of a rectangle is equal to its base multiplied by its height. Total revenue is equal to price multiplied by quantity. Here, total revenue is equal to the price of \$2.00 per bottle times 125,000 bottles, or \$250,000. The area of the green-shaded rectangle shows the firm's total revenue.

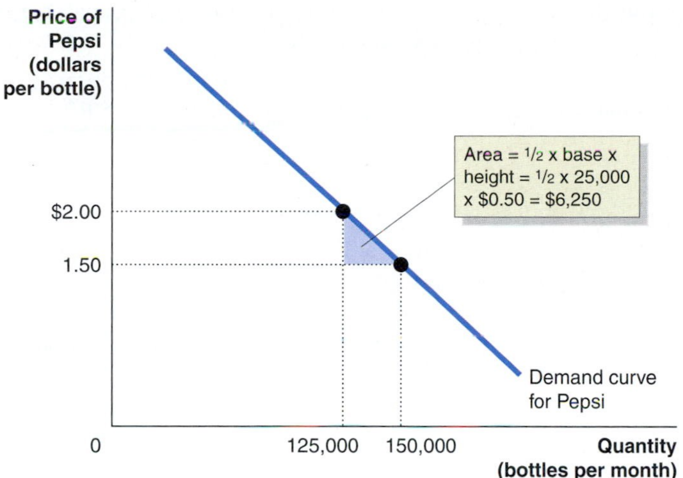

FIGURE 1A-9

The Area of a Triangle

The area of a triangle is equal to ½ multiplied by its base multiplied by its height. The area of the blue-shaded triangle has a base equal to 150,000 − 125,000, or 25,000 and a height equal to \$2.00 − \$1.50, or \$0.50. Therefore, its area equals ½ × 25,000 × \$0.50, or \$6,250.

The formula for the area of a rectangle is:

$$\text{Area of a rectangle} = \text{base} \times \text{height}.$$

In Figure 1A-8, the green-shaded rectangle also represents the firm's total revenue because its area is given by the base of 125,000 bottles multiplied by the price of \$2.00 per bottle.

We will see in later chapters that areas that are triangles can also have economic significance. The formula for the area of a triangle is:

$$\text{Area of a triangle} = \tfrac{1}{2} \times \text{base} \times \text{height}.$$

The blue-shaded area in Figure 1A-9 is a triangle. The base equals 150,000 − 125,000, or 25,000. Its height equals \$2.00 − \$1.50, or \$0.50. Therefore its area equals ½ × 25,000 × \$0.50, or \$6,250. Notice that the blue area is only a triangle if the demand curve is a straight line, or linear. Not all demand curves are linear. However, the formula for the area of a triangle will usually still give us a good approximation, even if the demand curve is not linear.

Summary of Using Formulas

You will encounter several other formulas in this book. Whenever you must use a formula, you should follow these steps:

1. Make sure you understand the economic concept that the formula represents.
2. Make sure that you are using the correct formula for the problem you are solving.
3. Make sure that the number you calculate using the formula is economically reasonable. For example, if you are using a formula to calculate a firm's revenue and your answer is a negative number, you know you made a mistake somewhere.

PROBLEMS AND APPLICATIONS

Please visit **www.prenhall.com/hubbard** *for solutions to the even-numbered problems as well as multiple-choice and true or false self-assessment quizzes.*

1. The following table gives the relationship between the price of custard pies and the number of pies Jacob buys per week.

PRICE	QUANTITY OF PIES	WEEK
\$3.00	6	July 2
2.00	7	July 9
5.00	4	July 16
6.00	3	July 23
1.00	8	July 30
4.00	5	August 6

a. Is the relationship between the price of pies and the number of pies Jacob buys a positive relationship or a negative relationship?
b. Plot the data from the table on a graph similar to Figure 1A-3. Draw a straight line that best fits the points.
c. Calculate the slope of the line.

2. The following table gives information on the quantity of lemonade demanded on sunny and overcast days. Plot the data from the table on a graph similar to Figure 1A-5. Draw two straight lines representing the two demand curves—one for sunny days, the other for overcast days.

PRICE (DOLLARS PER GLASS)	QUANTITY (GLASSES OF LEMONADE PER DAY)	WEATHER
$0.80	30	Sunny
0.80	10	Overcast
0.70	40	Sunny
0.70	20	Overcast
0.60	50	Sunny
0.60	30	Overcast
0.50	60	Sunny
0.50	40	Overcast

3. Using the information in Figure 1A-2, calculate the percentage change in auto sales from one year to the next. Between which years did sales fall at the fastest rate?

4. Real GDP in 1981 was $5,292 billion. Real GDP in 1982 was $5,189 billion. What was the percentage change in real GDP from 1981 to 1982? What do economists call the percentage change in real GDP from one year to the next?

5. Assume the demand curve for Pepsi passes through the following two points:

PRICE PER BOTTLE OF PEPSI	NUMBER OF BOTTLES OF PEPSI SOLD
$2.50	100,000
1.25	200,000

a. Draw a graph with a linear demand curve that passes through these two points.
b. Show on the graph the areas representing total revenue at each price. Give the value for total revenue at each price.

6. What is the area of the blue triangle shown in the following figure?

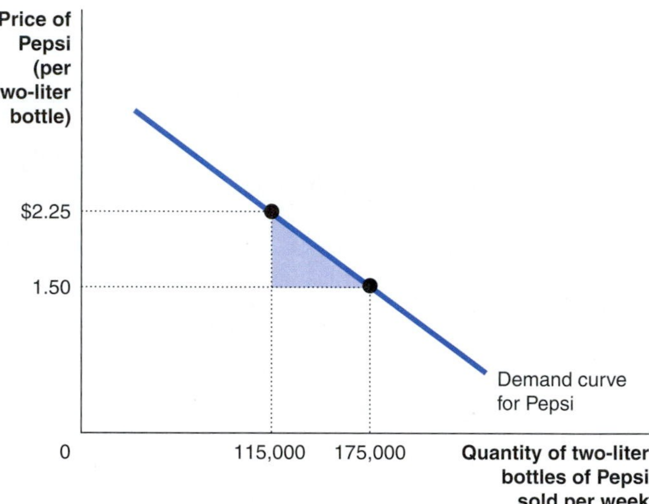

chapter two

Trade-offs, Comparative Advantage, and the Market System

Managers Making Choices at BMW

When you think of cars that combine fine engineering, high performance, and cutting-edge styling, you are likely to think of BMW. The Bayerische Motoren Werke, or Bavarian Motor Works, was founded in Germany in 1916 as a company devoted to manufacturing aircraft engines. In the early 1920s, BMW began to make motorcycles. In 1928 it produced its first car. Today, BMW employs nearly 100,000 workers in 23 factories in 15 countries to produce eight car models. In 2004, it had worldwide sales of about $70 billion.

To compete in the automobile market, the managers of BMW must make many strategic decisions, such as whether to introduce a new car model. In 2004, for example, BMW introduced the 1-Series, a hatchback that is significantly smaller than most other BMW models. Some BMW managers had opposed developing the 1-Series because they believed that it was inconsistent with the company's image of producing more expensive, higher-performance models. But other managers argued that the company needed a model that would appeal to younger drivers and could compete with the Volkswagen Golf and the Audi A3. Another strategic decision faced by BMW's managers is where to focus their advertising. In the late 1990s, for example, some of BMW's managers opposed advertising in China because they were skeptical about the country's sales potential. Other managers, however, argued that rising incomes were rapidly increasing the size of the Chinese market. BMW decided to advertise in China, and by 2004 it had become the company's eighth-largest market.

Over the years, BMW's managers have also faced the strategic decision of whether to concentrate production in factories in Germany or to build new factories in its overseas markets. Keeping production in Germany makes it easier for BMW's managers to supervise production and to employ German workers, who generally have high levels of technical training. Building factories in other countries, however, has two benefits. First, the lower wages paid to workers in other countries reduce the

LEARNING OBJECTIVES

After studying this chapter, you should be able to:

1. Use a production possibilities frontier to analyze opportunity costs and trade-offs.
2. Understand comparative advantage and explain how it is the basis for trade.
3. Explain the basic idea of how a market system works.

cost of manufacturing vehicles. Second, BMW can reduce political friction by producing vehicles in the same country in which they sell them. In 2003, BMW opened a plant at Shenyang, in northeast China, to build its 3-Series and 5-Series cars. Previously, in 1995, BMW opened a U.S. factory in Spartanburg, South Carolina, which currently produces the Z4 roadster and X5 sports utility vehicle (SUV).

Managers also face smaller scale—or tactical—business decisions. For instance, for many years, BMW used two workers to attach the gearbox to the engine in each car. In 2002, an alternative method of attaching the gearbox using a robot, rather than workers, was developed. In choosing which method to use, managers at BMW faced a trade-off because the robot method had a higher cost, but installed the gearbox in exactly the correct position, which reduces engine noise when the car is driven. Ultimately, the managers decided to adopt the robot method. A similar type of tactical business decision must be made in scheduling production at BMW's Spartanburg, South Carolina, plant. The plant produces both the Z4 and the X5 models, and a decision must be made each month as to the quantity of each model that should be produced. *An Inside Look* on page 54 discusses a similar decision BMW has to make at its Munich, Germany, plant.

Scarcity The situation in which unlimited wants exceed the limited resources available to fulfill those wants.

➤ In a market system, managers at most firms must make decisions like those made by BMW's managers. The decisions managers face reflect the key fact of economic life: ***Scarcity*** *requires trade-offs.* Scarcity exists because we have unlimited wants but only limited resources available to fulfill those wants. Goods and services are scarce. So, too, are the economic resources, or *factors of production*—workers, capital, natural resources, and entrepreneurial ability—used to make them. Your time is scarce, which means you face trade-offs: If you spend an hour studying for an economics exam, you have one less hour to spend studying for a psychology exam or going to the movies. If your university decides to use some of its scarce budget funds to buy new computers for the computer labs, those funds will not be available to buy new books for the library or to resurface the student parking lot. If BMW decides to devote some of the scarce workers and machinery in its Spartanburg assembly plant to producing more Z4 roadsters, those resources will not be available to produce more X5 SUVs.

Many of the decisions of households and firms are made in markets. One key activity that takes place in markets is trade. By engaging in trade, people can raise their standard of living. Trade involves the decisions of millions of households and firms spread around the world. In this chapter, we provide an overview of how the market system coordinates the independent decisions of these millions of households and firms. We begin our analysis of the economic consequences of scarcity and the working of the market system by introducing an important economic model: the *production possibilities frontier.*

1 LEARNING OBJECTIVE

Use a production possibilities frontier to analyze opportunity costs and trade-offs.

Production Possibilities Frontiers and Real-World Trade-offs

As we saw in the opening to this chapter, BMW operates an automobile factory in Spartanburg, South Carolina, where it assembles Z4 roadsters and X5 sports utility vehicles. Because the firm's resources—workers, machinery, materials, and entrepreneurial skills—are limited, BMW faces a trade-off: Resources devoted to producing Z4s are not available for producing X5s, and vice versa. Chapter 1 explained that economic models can be useful in analyzing many questions. We can use a simple model called the *production possibilities frontier* to analyze the trade-offs BMW faces in its Spartanburg plant. A **production possibilities frontier** is a curve showing the maximum attainable combinations of two products that may be produced with available resources. In BMW's case, the two products are Z4 roadsters and X5 sports utility vehicles, and the resources are BMW's workers, materials, robots, and other machinery.

Production possibilities frontier A curve showing the maximum attainable combinations of two products that may be produced with available resources.

Graphing the Production Possibilities Frontier

Figure 2-1 uses a production possibilities frontier to illustrate the trade-offs facing BMW. The numbers from the table are plotted in the graph. The line in the graph is BMW's production possibilities frontier. If BMW uses all its resources to produce roadsters, it can produce 800 per day—point *A* at one end of the production possibilities frontier. If BMW uses all its resources to produce SUVs, it can produce 800 per day—point *E* at the other end of the production possibilities frontier. If BMW devotes resources to producing both vehicles, it could be at a point like *B,* where it produces 600 roadsters and 200 SUVs.

BMW's Production Choices at Its Spartanburg Plant		
Choice	Quantity of Roadsters Produced	Quantity of SUVs Produced
A	800	0
B	600	200
C	400	400
D	200	600
E	0	800

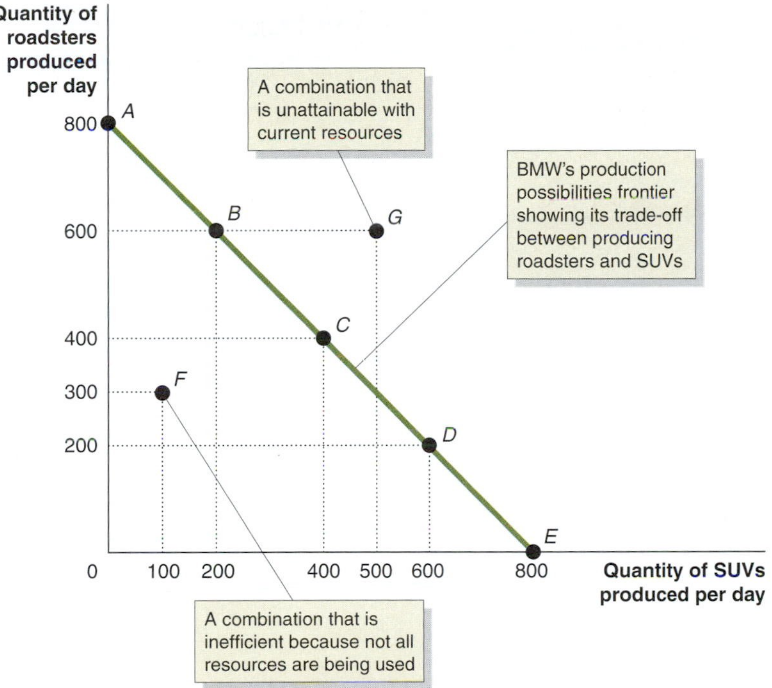

FIGURE 2-1

BMW's Production Possibilities Frontier

BMW faces a trade-off: To build one more roadster, it must build one less SUV. The production possibilities frontier illustrates the trade-off BMW faces. Combinations on the production possibilities frontier—like points *A, B, C, D,* and *E*—are *technically efficient* because the maximum output is being obtained from the available resources. Combinations inside the frontier—like point *F*—are *inefficient* because some resources are not being used. Combinations outside the frontier—like point *G*—are *unattainable* with current resources.

All the combinations either on the frontier—like *A, B, C, D,* and *E*—or inside the frontier—like point *F*—are *attainable* with the resources available. Combinations on the frontier are *efficient* because all available resources are being fully utilized, and the fewest possible resources are being used to produce a given amount of output. Combinations inside the frontier—like point *F*—are *inefficient* because maximum output is not being obtained from the available resources—perhaps because the assembly line is not operating at capacity. BMW might like to be beyond the frontier—at a point like *G* where it would be producing 600 roadsters and 500 SUVs—but points beyond the production possibilities frontier are *unattainable* given the firm's current resources. To produce the combination at *G*, BMW would need more machines or more workers.

Notice that if BMW is producing efficiently and is on the production possibilities frontier, the only way to produce more of one vehicle is to produce less of the other vehicle. Recall from Chapter 1 that the **opportunity cost** of any activity is the highest valued alternative that must be given up to engage in that activity. For BMW, the opportunity cost of producing one SUV is the number of roadsters the company will not be able to produce because it has already devoted those resources to producing SUVs. For example, in moving from point *B* to point *C*, the opportunity cost of producing 200 more SUVs per day is the 200 fewer roadsters that can be produced.

Opportunity cost The highest-valued alternative that must be given up to engage in an activity.

What point on the production possibilities frontier is best? We can't tell without further information. If consumer demand for SUVs is greater than demand for roadsters, the company is likely to choose a point closer to *E*. If demand for roadsters is greater than demand for SUVs, the company is likely to choose a point closer to *A*.

SOLVED PROBLEM 2-1

Drawing a Production Possibilities Frontier for Rosie's Boston Bakery

① LEARNING OBJECTIVE

Use a production possibilities frontier to analyze opportunity costs and trade-offs.

Rosie's Boston Bakery specializes in cakes and pies. Rosie has 5 hours per day to devote to baking. In 1 hour, Rosie can prepare 2 pies or 1 cake.

a. Use the information given to complete the following table:

	HOURS SPENT MAKING		QUANTITY MADE	
CHOICE	CAKES	PIES	CAKES	PIES
A	5	0		
B	4	1		
C	3	2		
D	2	3		
E	1	4		
F	0	5		

b. Use the data in the table to draw a production possibilities frontier graph illustrating Rosie's trade-offs between making cakes and making pies. Label the vertical axis "Quantity of cakes made." Label the horizontal axis "Quantity of pies made." Make sure to label the values where Rosie's production possibilities frontier intersects the vertical and horizontal axes.

c. Label the points representing choice *D* and choice *E*. If Rosie is at choice *D*, what is her opportunity cost of making more pies?

Solving the Problem:

Step 1: Review the chapter material. This problem is about using production possibilities frontiers to analyze trade-offs, so you may want to review the section "Graphing the Production Possibilities Frontier," which begins on page 34.

Step 2: Answer question (a) by filling in the table. If Rosie can produce 1 cake in 1 hour, then with choice *A* she will make 5 cakes and 0 pies. Because she can produce 2 pies in 1 hour, with choice *B* she will make 4 cakes and 2 pies. By similar reasoning, you can fill in the remaining cells in the following table:

	HOURS SPENT MAKING		QUANTITY MADE	
CHOICE	CAKES	PIES	CAKES	PIES
A	5	0	5	0
B	4	1	4	2
C	3	2	3	4
D	2	3	2	6
E	1	4	1	8
F	0	5	0	10

Step 3: Answer question (b) by drawing the production possibilities frontier graph. Using the data in the table in question (a), you should draw a graph that looks like this:

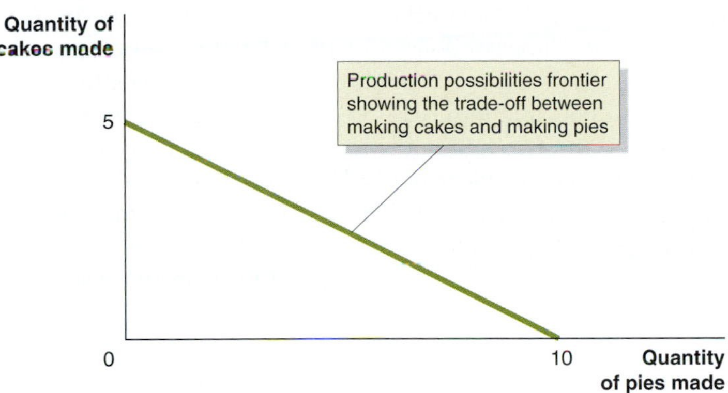

If Rosie devotes all 5 hours to making cakes, she will make 5 cakes. Therefore, her production possibilities frontier will intersect the vertical axis at 5 cakes made. If Rosie devotes all 5 hours to making pies, she will make 10 pies. Therefore, her production possibilities frontier will intersect the horizontal axis at 10 pies made.

Step 4: Answer question (c) by showing choices *D* and *E* on your graph. The points for choices *D* and *E* can be plotted using the information from the table:

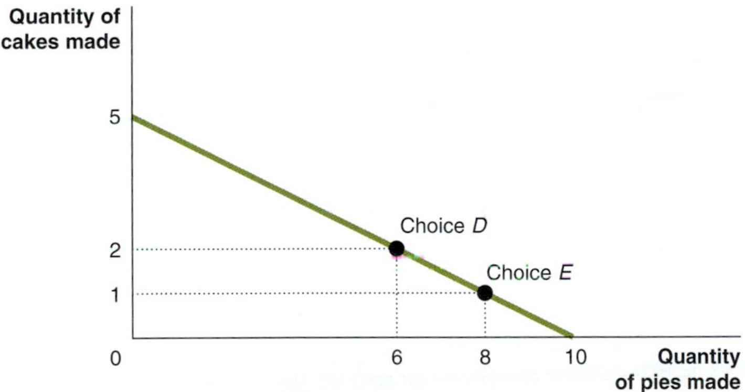

Moving from choice *D* to choice *E* increases Rosie's production of pies by 2 but lowers her production of cakes by 1. Therefore, her opportunity cost of making 2 more pies is making 1 less cake.

YOUR TURN: **For more practice, do related problem 6 on page 58 at the end of this chapter.**

2-1 Making the Connection

Trade-offs and Tsunami Relief

In December 2004, an earthquake caused a tidal wave—or tsunami—to flood coastal areas of Indonesia, Thailand, Sri Lanka, and other countries bordering the Indian Ocean. Over 280,000 people died, and billions of dollars worth of property was destroyed. Governments and individuals around the world moved quickly to donate to relief efforts. The U.S. government donated $950 million, and individual U.S. citizens donated more than an additional $500 million. Both governments and individuals face limited budgets, however, and funds used for one purpose are unavailable to be used for another purpose. Although governments and individuals did increase their total charitable giving following the tsunami disaster, much of the funds spent on tsunami relief appear to have been diverted from other uses. A difficult trade-off resulted: Giving funds to victims of the tsunami meant fewer funds were available to aid other good causes.

For example, some of the funds provided by the U.S. government for reconstruction in the tsunami-devastated areas came from existing aid programs. As a result, spending on other aid projects in the region declined. Similarly, nonprofit organizations in New York City reported sharp declines in donations to the homeless and the poor, as donors gave funds for tsunami relief instead. According to a report in the newspaper *Crain's New York Business,* "Some groups such as Bailey House, which helps homeless people who have AIDS, have even started receiving letters from longtime donors warning that this year's gifts are being redirected to the tsunami relief effort." As one commentator observed, "The milk of human kindness is probably flowing at the usual rate in the United States. It's just getting channeled in different directions."

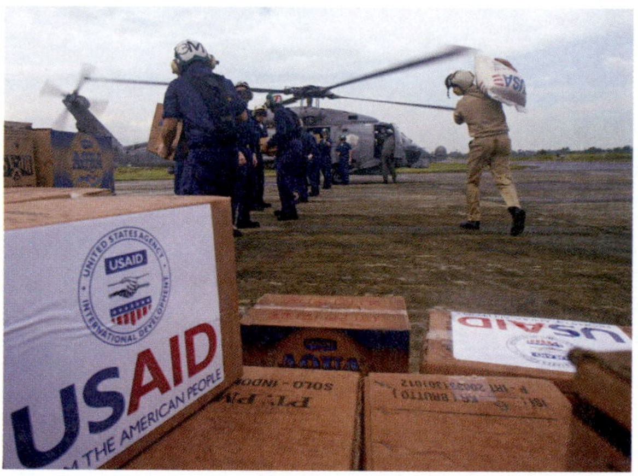

More funds for tsunami relief meant less funds for other charities.

Governments in the area also faced a trade-off in considering whether to spend funds to install tsunami warning systems, similar to existing systems in the Pacific Ocean. Tsunamis are fairly common in the Pacific Ocean but quite rare in the Indian Ocean. Records dating back to the early 1500s indicate that the tsunami of 2004 was by far the worst in the last 500 years. Funds that governments in poor countries, such as Indonesia, would spend on tsunami warning systems would have to be diverted from spending on health, education, or other programs.

Source: Daniel Gross, "Zero-Sum Charity," *Slate,* January 20, 2005.

Increasing Marginal Opportunity Costs

We can also use the production possibilities frontier to explore issues related to the economy as a whole. For example, suppose we divide all the many goods and services produced in the economy into just two types: military goods and civilian goods. In Figure 2-2, we let tanks represent military goods and automobiles represent civilian goods. If all the country's resources are devoted to producing military goods, 400 tanks can be produced in one year. If all resources are devoted to producing civilian goods, 500 automobiles can be produced in one year. Devoting resources to producing both goods results in the economy being at other points along the production possibilities frontier.

Notice that this production possibilities frontier is bowed outward, rather than being a straight line. Because the curve is bowed out, the opportunity cost of automobiles in terms of tanks depends upon where the economy currently is on the production

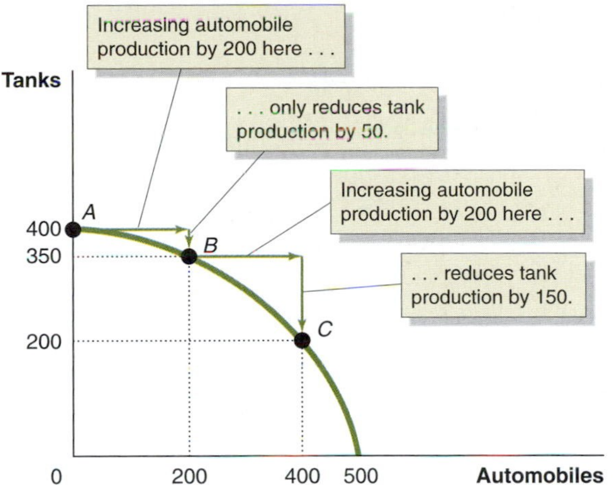

FIGURE 2-2

Increasing Marginal Opportunity Cost

As the economy moves down the production possibilities frontier, it experiences *increasing marginal opportunity costs* because increasing automobile production by a given quantity requires larger and larger decreases in tank production. For example, to increase automobile production from 0 to 200—moving from point *A* to point *B*—the economy only has to give up 50 tanks. But to increase automobile production by another 200 vehicles—moving from point *B* to point *C*—the economy has to give up 150 tanks.

possibilities frontier. For example, to increase automobile production from zero to 200—moving from point *A* to point *B*—the economy only has to give up 50 tanks. But to increase automobile production by another 200 vehicles—moving from point *B* to point *C*—the economy has to give up 150 tanks.

As the economy moves down the production possibilities frontier, it experiences *increasing marginal opportunity costs* because increasing automobile production by a given quantity requires larger and larger decreases in tank production. Increasing marginal opportunity costs occur because some workers, machines, and other resources are better suited to one use than to another. At point *A* some resources that are well suited to producing automobiles are being forced to produce tanks. Shifting these resources into producing automobiles by moving from point *A* to point *B* allows a substantial increase in automobile production, without much loss of tank production. But as the economy moves down the production possibilities frontier, more and more resources that are better suited to tank production are switched into automobile production. As a result, the increases in automobile production become increasingly smaller while the decreases in tank production become increasingly larger. We would expect in most situations that production possibilities frontiers will be bowed outward, rather than linear as in the BMW example we discussed earlier.

The idea of increasing marginal opportunity costs illustrates an important economic concept: *The more resources already devoted to any activity, the smaller the payoff to devoting additional resources to that activity.* The more hours you have already spent studying economics, the smaller the increase in your test grade from each additional hour you spend—and the greater the opportunity cost of using the hour in that way. The more funds a firm has devoted to research and development during a given year, the smaller the amount of useful knowledge it receives from each additional dollar—and the greater the opportunity cost of using the funds in that way. The more funds the federal government spends cleaning up the environment during a given year, the smaller the reduction in pollution from each additional dollar—and, once again, the greater the opportunity cost of using the funds in that way.

Economic Growth

At any given time, the total resources available to any economy are fixed. Therefore, if the United States produces more automobiles, it must produce less of something else—tanks in our example. Over time, though, the resources available to an economy may increase. For example, both the labor force and the capital stock—the amount of physical capital available in the country—may increase. The increase in the available labor force and the capital stock shifts the production possibilities frontier outward for the U.S. economy and makes it possible to produce both more automobiles and more tanks.

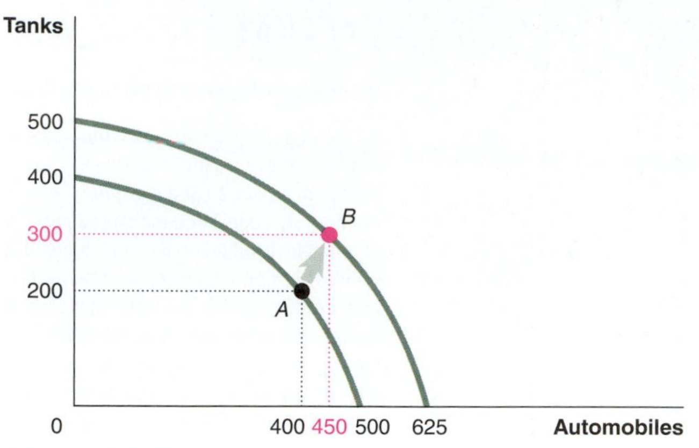

(a) Shifting out the production possibilities frontier

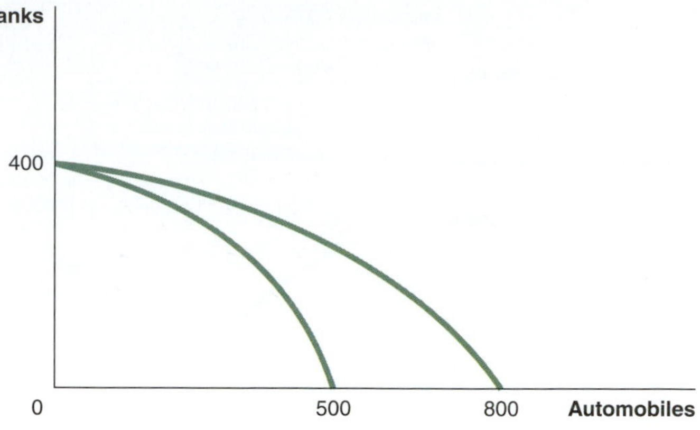

(b) Technological change in the automobile industry

FIGURE 2-3 **Economic Growth**

Panel (a) shows that as more economic resources become available and technological change occurs, the economy can move from point *A* to point *B*, producing more tanks and more automobiles.

Panel (b) shows the results of technological advance in the automobile industry that increases the quantity of vehicles workers can produce per year, while leaving the maximum quantity of tanks that can be produced unchanged. Shifts in the production possibilities frontier represent *economic growth.*

Panel (a) of Figure 2-3 shows that the economy can move from point *A* to point *B*, producing more tanks and more automobiles.

Similarly, technological advance makes it possible to produce more goods with the same amount of workers and machinery, which also shifts the production possibilities frontier outward. Technological advance need not affect all sectors equally. Panel (b) of Figure 2-3 shows the results of technological advance in the automobile industry that increases the quantity of vehicles workers can produce per year, while leaving unchanged the quantity of tanks that can be produced.

Economic growth The ability of the economy to produce increasing quantities of goods and services.

Shifts in the production possibilities frontier represent **economic growth** because they allow the economy to increase the production of goods and services, which ultimately raises the standard of living. In the United States and other high-income countries, the market system has aided the process of economic growth, which over the past two hundred years has greatly increased the health and well-being of the average person.

② LEARNING OBJECTIVE

Understand comparative advantage and explain how it is the basis for trade.

Trade

Trade The act of buying or selling.

Having discussed the important ideas of production possibilities frontiers and opportunity costs, we can use them to understand the basic economic activity of *trade.* Markets are fundamentally about **trade,** which is the act of buying and selling. Many of the trades in which we engage take place indirectly: We sell our labor services as, say, an accountant, salesperson, or nurse for money, and then use the money to buy goods and services. Ultimately an accountant, salesperson, or nurse is trading his or her services for food, clothing, and other goods and services. One of the great benefits to trade is that it makes it possible for people to become better off by increasing both their production and their consumption.

Specialization and Gains from Trade

Consider the following situation: You and your neighbor both have fruit trees on your property. Initially, suppose that you have only apple trees and your neighbor has only cherry trees. In this situation, if you both like apples and cherries there is an obvious opportunity for both of you to gain from trade: You trade some of your apples for some of your neighbor's cherries, making you both better off. But what if there are apple and

	You		Your Neighbor	
	Apples	Cherries	Apples	Cherries
All time devoted to picking apples	20 pounds	0 pounds	30 pounds	0 pounds
All time devoted to picking cherries	0 pounds	20 pounds	0 pounds	60 pounds

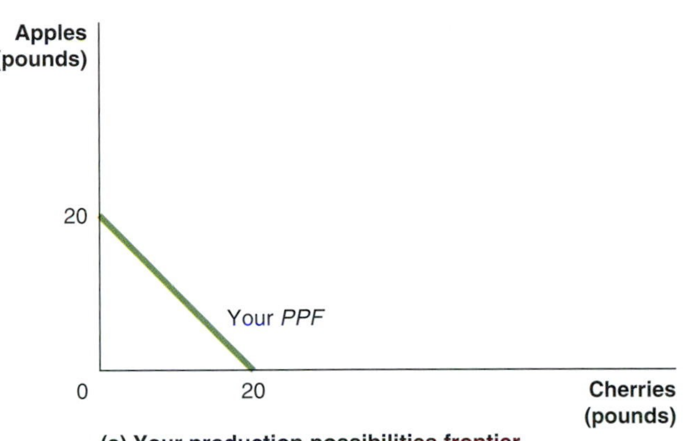

(a) Your production possibilities frontier

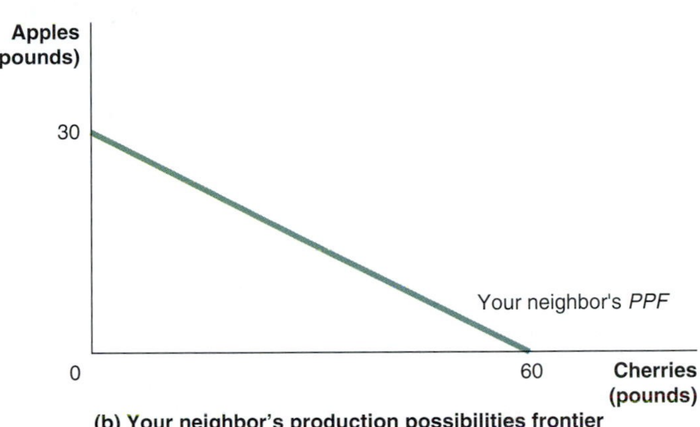

(b) Your neighbor's production possibilities frontier

FIGURE 2-4 Production Possibilities for You and Your Neighbor, without Trade

The table in Figure 2-4 shows how many pounds of apples and how many pounds of cherries you and your neighbor can each pick in one month. The graphs in the figure use the data from the table to construct production possibilities frontiers (*PPFs*) for you and your neighbor. Panel (a) shows your *PPF.* If you devote all of your time to picking apples and none of your time to picking cherries, you can pick 20 pounds. If you devote all of your time to picking cherries, you can pick 20 pounds. Panel (b) shows that if your neighbor devotes all of her time to picking apples, she can pick 30 pounds. If she devotes all of her time to picking cherries, she can pick 60 pounds.

cherry trees growing on both of your properties? In that case there can still be gains from trade. For example, your neighbor might be very good at picking apples and you might be very good at picking cherries. In that case, it makes sense that both can benefit if your neighbor concentrates on picking apples and you concentrate on picking cherries. You can then trade some of your cherries for some of your neighbor's apples. But what if your neighbor is actually better at picking both apples and cherries than you are? It might not seem that in this case your neighbor has anything to gain from trading with you, but in fact she does.

We can use production possibilities frontiers (*PPFs*) to show how your neighbor can benefit from trading with you even though she is better than you are at picking both apples and cherries. (For simplicity, and because it will not have any effect on the conclusions we draw, we will assume that the *PPFs* in this example are straight lines.) The table in Figure 2-4 shows how many apples and how many cherries you and your neighbor can pick in one month. The graph in the figure uses the data from the table to construct *PPFs* for you and your neighbor. Panel (a) shows your *PPF.* If you devote all your time to picking apples and none of your time to picking cherries, you can pick 20 pounds of apples per month. If you devote all your time to picking cherries, you can pick 20 pounds per month. Panel (b) shows that if your neighbor devotes all her time to picking apples, she can pick 30 pounds. If she devotes all her time to picking cherries, she can pick 60 pounds.

The production possibilities frontiers in Figure 2-4 show the opportunities you and your neighbor have to consume apples and cherries, *without trade.* Suppose that when you don't trade with your neighbor, you pick and consume 8 pounds of apples and 12 pounds of cherries per month. This combination of apples and cherries is represented by point *A* in panel (a) of Figure 2-5. When she doesn't trade with you, your neighbor picks and consumes 9 pounds of apples and 42 pounds of cherries per

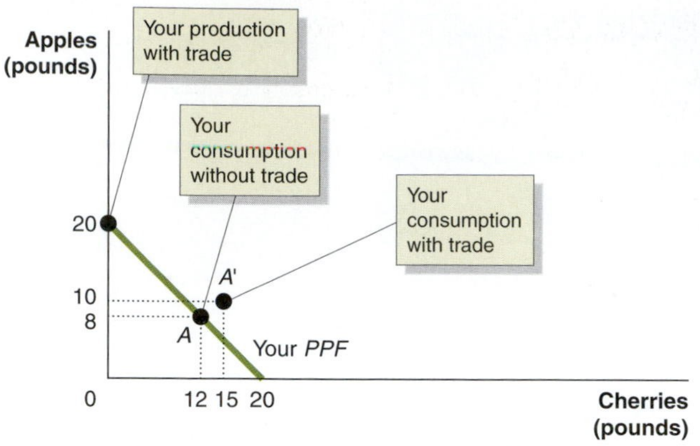

(a) Your production and consumption after trade

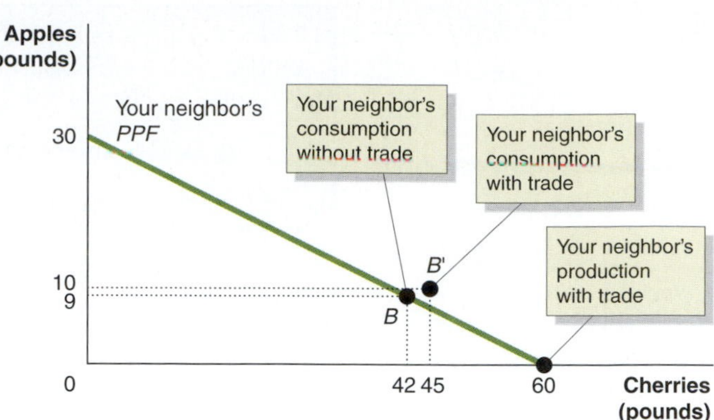

(b) Your neighbor's production and consumption with trade

FIGURE 2-5 Gains from Trade

When you don't trade with your neighbor, you pick and consume 8 pounds of apples and 12 pounds of cherries per month—point *A* in panel (a). When your neighbor doesn't trade with you, she picks and consumes 9 pounds of apples and 42 pounds of cherries per month—point *B* in panel (b). If you specialize in picking apples, you can pick 20 pounds. If your neighbor specializes in picking cherries, she can pick 60 pounds. If you trade 10 pounds of your apples for 15 pounds of your neighbor's cherries, you will be able to consume 10 pounds of apples and 15 pounds of cherries—point *A'* in panel (a). Your neighbor can now consume 10 pounds of apples and 45 pounds of cherries—point *B'* in panel (b). You and your neighbor are both better off as a result of trade.

month. This combination of apples and cherries is represented by point *B* in panel (b) of Figure 2-5.

After years of picking and consuming your own apples and cherries, suppose your neighbor comes to you one day with the following proposition: She offers next month to trade you 15 pounds of her cherries for 10 pounds of your apples. Should you accept this offer? You will have more apples and more cherries to consume if you do. To take advantage of her offer, first, rather than splitting your time between picking apples and picking cherries, you should specialize in picking only apples. We know this will allow you to pick 20 pounds of apples. You can trade 10 of those 20 pounds of apples to your neighbor for 15 pounds of her cherries. The result is you will be able to consume 10 pounds of apples and 15 pounds of cherries (point *A'* in panel (a) of Figure 2-5). You are clearly better off as a result of trading with your neighbor: You now can consume 2 more pounds of apples and 3 more pounds of cherries than you were consuming without trading. You have moved beyond your *PPF!*

Your neighbor has also benefited. By specializing in picking only cherries, she can pick 60 pounds. She trades 15 pounds of cherries to you for 10 pounds of apples. The result is she can consume 10 pounds of apples and 45 pounds of cherries (point *B'* in panel (b) of Figure 2-5). This is 1 more pound of apples and 3 more pounds of cherries than she was consuming before trading with you. She also has moved beyond her *PPF.* Table 2-1 summarizes the changes in production and consumption that result from your trade with your neighbor.

Absolute Advantage versus Comparative Advantage

Absolute advantage The ability of an individual, firm, or country to produce more of a good or service than competitors using the same amount of resources.

Perhaps the most remarkable aspect of the preceding example is that your neighbor benefits from trading with you even though she is better at picking both apples and cherries than you are. **Absolute advantage** is the ability to produce more of a good or service than competitors using the same amount of resources. Your neighbor has an absolute advantage over you in producing both apples and cherries because she can pick more of each fruit than you can in the same amount of time. This observation seems to suggest that your neighbor should pick her own apples *and* her own cherries. We have just seen, however, that she is better off if she specializes in cherry picking and leaves the apple picking to you.

TABLE 2-1

A Summary of the Gains from Trade

	YOU		YOUR NEIGHBOR	
	APPLES (IN POUNDS)	CHERRIES (IN POUNDS)	APPLES (IN POUNDS)	CHERRIES (IN POUNDS)
Production *and* consumption *without* trade	8	12	9	42
Production *with* trade	20	0	0	60
Consumption *with* trade	10	15	10	45
Gains from trade (increased consumption)	2	3	1	3

We can consider further why both you and your neighbor benefit from specializing in picking only one fruit. First, think about the opportunity cost to each of you of picking the two fruits. We saw from the *PPF* in Figure 2-4 that if you devoted all your time to picking apples, you would be able to pick 20 pounds of apples per month. As you move down your *PPF* and shift time away from picking apples to picking cherries, you have to give up 1 pound of apples for each pound of cherries you pick (the slope of your *PPF* is −1—for a review of calculating slopes, see the appendix to Chapter 1). Therefore, your opportunity cost of picking 1 pound of cherries is 1 pound of apples. By the same reasoning, your opportunity cost of picking 1 pound of apples is 1 pound of cherries. Your neighbor's *PPF* has a different slope, and so she faces a different trade-off. As she shifts time from picking apples to picking cherries, she has to give up 0.5 pound of apples for every 1 pound of cherries she picks (the slope of your neighbor's *PPF* is −0.5). As she shifts time from picking cherries to picking apples, she gives up 2 pounds of cherries for every 1 pound of apples she picks. Therefore, her opportunity cost of picking 1 pound of apples is 2 pounds of cherries, and her opportunity cost of picking 1 pound of cherries is 0.5 pound of apples.

Table 2-2 summarizes the opportunity costs for you and your neighbor of picking apples and cherries. Note that even though your neighbor can pick more apples in a month than you can, the *opportunity cost* of picking apples is higher for her than for you because when she picks apples she gives up more cherries than you do. So, even though she has an absolute advantage over you in picking apples, it is more costly for her to pick apples than it is for you. The table also shows us that her opportunity cost of picking cherries is lower than your opportunity cost of picking cherries. **Comparative advantage** is the ability of an individual, firm, or country to produce a good or service at a lower opportunity cost than other producers. In apple picking, your neighbor has an *absolute advantage* over you, but you have a *comparative advantage* over her. Your neighbor has both an absolute and a comparative advantage over you in picking cherries. As we have seen, you are better off specializing in picking apples, and your neighbor is better off specializing in picking cherries. Another way of thinking about why it would be costly for your neighbor to spend time picking apples is that even though she can pick 1.5 times as many apples in a month as you can—30 pounds per month for her versus 20 pounds per month for you—she can pick 3 times as many cherries—60 pounds per month for her versus 20 pounds for you. So, by specializing in picking cherries she is spending her time in the activity where her absolute advantage over you is the greatest.

Comparative advantage The ability of an individual, firm, or country to produce a good or service at a lower opportunity cost than other producers.

TABLE 2-2

Opportunity Costs of Picking Apples and Cherries

	OPPORTUNITY COST OF PICKING 1 POUND OF APPLES	OPPORTUNITY COST OF PICKING 1 POUND OF CHERRIES
You	1 pound of cherries	1 pound of apples
Your neighbor	2 pounds of cherries	0.5 pound of apples

Don't Let This Happen To You!

Don't Confuse Absolute Advantage and Comparative Advantage

First, make sure you know the definitions:

- *Absolute advantage:* The ability of an individual, firm, or country to produce more of a good or service than competitors using the same amount of resources. In our example, your neighbor has an absolute advantage over you both in picking apples and in picking cherries.
- *Comparative advantage:* The ability of an individual, firm, or country to produce a good or service at a lower opportunity cost than other producers. In our example, your neighbor has a comparative advantage in picking cherries, but you have a comparative advantage in picking apples.

Keep these two key points in mind:

1. It is possible to have an absolute advantage in producing a good or service without having a comparative advantage. This would be the case with your neighbor picking apples.
2. It is possible to have a comparative advantage in producing a good or service without having an absolute advantage. This would be the case with you picking apples.

***YOUR TURN:* Test your understanding by doing related problem 14 on page 59 at the end of this chapter.**

Comparative Advantage and the Gains from Trade

We have just derived an important economic principle: *The basis for trade is comparative advantage, not absolute advantage.* The fastest apple pickers do not necessarily do much apple picking. If the fastest apple pickers have a comparative advantage in some other activity—picking cherries, playing major league baseball, or being industrial engineers—they are better off specializing in that other activity. Individuals, firms, and countries are better off if they specialize in producing goods and services for which they have a comparative advantage and obtain the other goods and services they need by trading. We will return to the important concept of comparative advantage in Chapter 8, which is devoted to the subject of international trade.

SOLVED PROBLEM 2-2

② LEARNING OBJECTIVE

Understand comparative advantage and explain how it is the basis for trade.

Comparative Advantage and the Gains from Trade

We will see in Chapter 8 the important role that comparative advantage plays in analyzing international trade. For now, consider this simple problem. Suppose that Canada and the United States both produce maple syrup and honey. These are the combinations of the two goods that each country can produce in one day:

CANADA		UNITED STATES	
HONEY (IN TONS)	MAPLE SYRUP (IN TONS)	HONEY (IN TONS)	MAPLE SYRUP (IN TONS)
0	60	0	50
10	45	10	40
20	30	20	30
30	15	30	20
40	0	40	10
		50	0

a. Who has a comparative advantage in producing maple syrup? Who has a comparative advantage in producing honey?

b. Suppose that Canada is currently producing 30 tons of honey and 15 tons of maple syrup and the United States is currently producing 10 tons of honey and 40 tons of maple syrup. Demonstrate that Canada and the United States can both be better off if they specialize in producing only one good and then engage in trade.

c. Illustrate your answer to question (b) by drawing a *PPF* for the United States and a *PPF* for Canada. Show on your *PPF*s the combinations of honey and maple syrup produced and consumed in each country before and after trade.

Solving the Problem:

Step 1: Review the chapter material. This problem concerns comparative advantage, so you may want to review the section "Absolute Advantage versus Comparative Advantage," which begins on page 42.

Step 2: Answer question (a) by calculating who has a comparative advantage in each activity. Remember that a country has a comparative advantage in producing a good if it can produce the good at the lowest opportunity cost. When Canada produces 1 more ton of honey, it produces 1.5 fewer tons of maple syrup. On the one hand, when the United States produces 1 more ton of honey, it produces 1 less ton of maple syrup. Therefore, the United States's opportunity cost of producing honey—1 ton of maple syrup—is lower than Canada's—1.5 tons of maple syrup. On the other hand, when Canada produces 1 more ton of maple syrup, it produces ⅔ less of a ton of honey. When the United States produces 1 more ton of maple syrup, it produces 1 less ton of honey. Therefore, Canada's opportunity cost of producing maple syrup—⅔ of a ton of honey—is lower than that of the United States—1 ton of honey. We can conclude that the United States has a comparative advantage in the production of honey and Canada has a comparative advantage in the production of maple syrup.

Step 3: Answer question (b) by showing that specialization makes Canada and the United States better off. We know that Canada should specialize where it has a comparative advantage and the United States should specialize where it has a comparative advantage. If both countries specialize, Canada will produce 60 tons of maple syrup and 0 tons of honey, and the United States will produce 0 tons of maple syrup and 50 tons of honey. After both countries specialize, the United States could then trade 30 tons of honey to Canada in exchange for 40 tons of maple syrup (other mutually beneficial trades are possible as well). We can summarize the results in a table:

	BEFORE TRADE		AFTER TRADE	
	HONEY (IN TONS)	MAPLE SYRUP (IN TONS)	HONEY (IN TONS)	MAPLE SYRUP (IN TONS)
Canada	30	15	30	20
United States	10	40	20	40

The United States is better off after trade because it can consume the same amount of maple syrup and 10 more tons of honey. Canada is better off after trade because it can consume the same amount of honey and 5 more tons of maple syrup.

Step 4: Answer question (c) by drawing the *PPF*s.

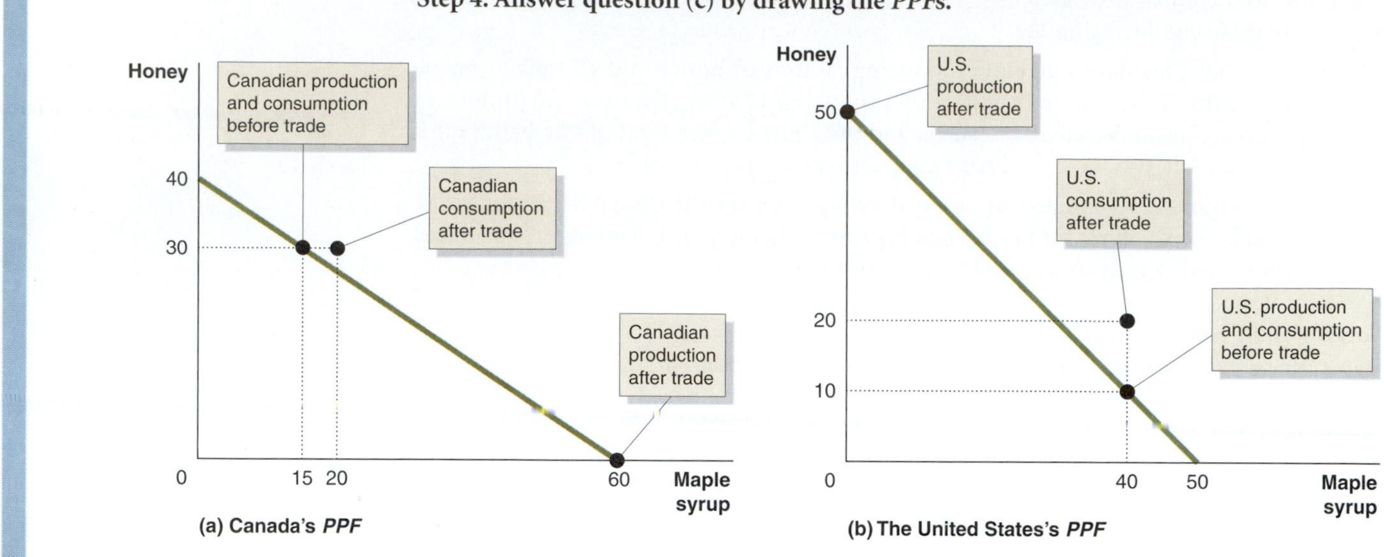

(a) Canada's *PPF*

(b) The United States's *PPF*

YOUR TURN: **For more practice, do related problems 12 and 13 on page 59 at the end of this chapter.**

③ **LEARNING OBJECTIVE**

Explain the basic idea of how a market system works.

The Market System

We have seen that households, firms, and the government face trade-offs and incur opportunity costs because of the scarcity of resources. We have also seen that trade allows people to specialize according to their comparative advantage. By engaging in trade, people can raise their standard of living. Of course, trade in the modern world is much more complex than the examples we have considered so far. Trade today involves the decisions of millions of people spread around the world. But how does an economy make trade possible, and how are the decisions of these millions of people coordinated? In the United States and most other countries, trade is carried out in markets. Markets also determine the answers to the three fundamental questions discussed in Chapter 1: *What* goods and services will be produced? *How* will the goods and services be produced? *Who* will receive the goods and services?

Market A group of buyers and sellers of a good or service and the institution or arrangement by which they come together to trade.

Product markets Markets for goods—such as computers—and services—such as medical treatment.

Factor markets Markets for the factors of production, such as labor, capital, natural resources, and entrepreneurial ability.

Recall that the definition of a **market** is a group of buyers and sellers of a good or service and the institution or arrangement by which they come together to trade. Markets take many forms: They can be physical places, like the local pizza parlor or the New York Stock Exchange, or virtual places, like eBay. In a market, the buyers are demanders of goods or services, and the sellers are suppliers of goods or services. Households and firms interact in two types of markets: *product markets* and *factor markets.* **Product markets** are markets for goods—such as computers—and services—such as medical treatment. In product markets, households are demanders and firms are suppliers. **Factor markets** are markets for the *factors of production,* such as labor, capital, natural resources, and entrepreneurial ability. In factor markets, households are suppliers and firms are demanders. Most people earn most of their income by selling their labor services to firms in the labor market.

The Circular Flow of Income

Two key groups participate in markets:

- A *household* consists of all the individuals in a home. Households are suppliers of factors of production—particularly labor—used by firms to make goods and services. Households use the income they receive from selling the factors of production to purchase the goods and services supplied by firms.

- *Firms* are suppliers of goods and services. Firms use the funds they receive from selling goods and services to buy the factors of production needed to make the goods and services.

We can use a simple economic model called a **circular-flow diagram** to see how participants in markets are linked. Figure 2-6 shows that in factor markets households supply labor and other factors of production in exchange for wages and other payments from firms. In product markets, households use the payments they earn in factor markets to purchase the goods and services supplied by firms. Firms produce these goods and services using the factors of production supplied by households. In the figure, the

Circular-flow diagram A model that illustrates how participants in markets are linked.

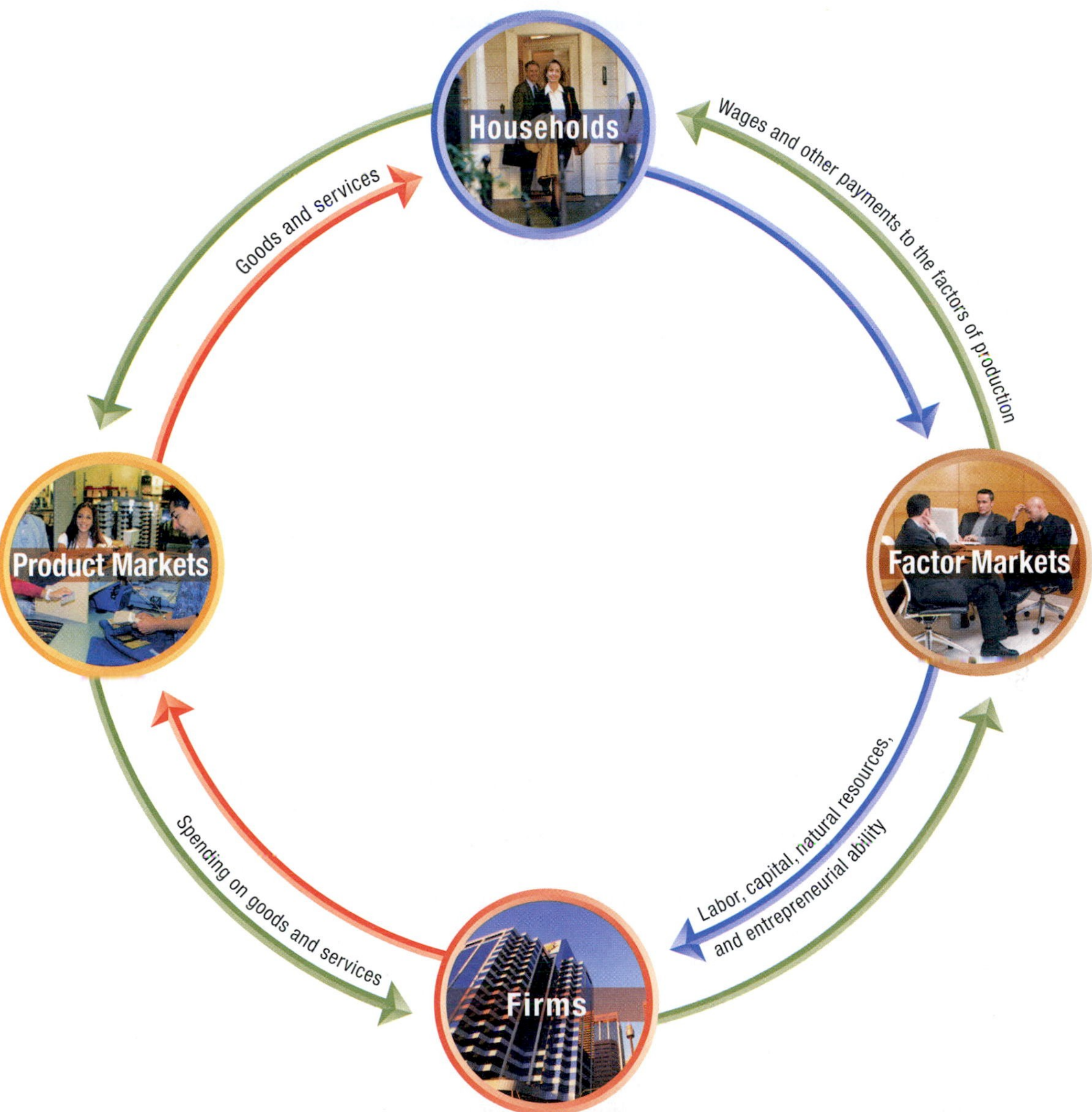

FIGURE 2-6 **The Circular-Flow Diagram**

Households and firms are linked together in a circular flow of production, income, and spending. The blue arrows show the flow of the factors of production. In factor markets, households supply labor, entrepreneurial ability, and other factors of production to firms. Firms use these factors of production to make goods and services that they supply to households in product markets. The red arrows show the flow of goods and services from firms to households. The green arrows show the flow of funds. In factor markets, households receive wages and other payments from firms in exchange for supplying the factors of production. Households use these wages and other payments to purchase goods and services from firms in product markets. Firms sell goods and services to households in product markets, and they use the funds to purchase the factors of production from households in factor markets.

blue arrows show the flow of factors of production from households through factor markets to firms. The red arrow shows the flow of goods and services from firms through product markets to households. The green arrows show the flow of funds from firms through factor markets to households, and the flow of spending from households through product markets to firms.

Like all economic models, the circular-flow diagram is a simplified version of reality. For example, Figure 2-6 leaves out the important role played by government in buying goods from firms and in making payments, such as Social Security or unemployment insurance payments, to households. The figure also leaves out the role played by banks, the stock and bond markets, and other parts of the *financial system* in aiding the flow of funds from lenders to borrowers. Finally, the figure does not show that some goods and services purchased by domestic households are produced in foreign countries, and some goods and services produced by domestic firms are sold to foreign households. The government, the financial system, and the international sector are explored further in later chapters. Despite these simplifications, the circular-flow diagram in Figure 2-6 is useful in seeing how product markets, factor markets, and their participants are linked together. One of the great mysteries of the market system is that it manages successfully to coordinate the independent activities of so many households and firms.

The Gains from Free Markets

Free market A market with few government restrictions on how a good or service can be produced or sold, or on how a factor of production can be employed.

A **free market** exists when the government places few restrictions on how a good or a service can be produced or sold, or on how a factor of production can be employed. Governments in all modern economies intervene more than is consistent with a fully free market. In that sense, we can think of the free market as being a benchmark against which we can judge actual economies. Relatively few government restrictions are placed on economic activity in the United States, Canada, the countries of Western Europe, Hong Kong, Singapore, and Estonia. So these countries come close to the free market benchmark. In countries such as Cuba and North Korea, the free market system has been rejected in favor of centrally planned economies with extensive government control over product and factor markets. Countries that come closest to the free market benchmark have been more successful than countries with centrally planned economies in providing their people with rising living standards.

The Scottish philosopher Adam Smith is considered the father of modern economics because one of his books, *An Inquiry into the Nature and Causes of the Wealth of Nations,* published in 1776, was an early and very influential argument for the free market system. Smith was writing at a time when extensive government restrictions on markets were still very common. In many parts of Europe the *guild system* still prevailed. Under this system, governments would give guilds, or organizations of producers, the authority to control the production of a good. For example, the shoemakers' guild controlled who was allowed to produce shoes, how many shoes they could produce, and what price they could charge. In France, the cloth makers' guild even dictated the number of threads that were allowed in the weave of the cloth.

Smith argued that such restrictions reduced the income or wealth of a country and its people by restricting the quantity of goods produced. Some people at the time supported the restrictions of the guild system because it was in their financial interest to do so. If you were a member of a guild, the restrictions served to reduce the competition you would face. But other people sincerely believed that the alternative to the guild system was economic chaos. Smith argued that these people were wrong and that a country could enjoy a smoothly functioning economic system if firms were freed from guild restrictions.

The Market Mechanism

In Smith's day, defenders of the guild system worried that if, for instance, the shoemakers' guild did not control shoe production, either too many or too few shoes would be produced. Smith argued that prices would do a better job of coordinating the activities of buyers and sellers than the guilds could. A key to understanding Smith's argument is the assumption that *individuals usually act in a rational, self-interested way.* In particular, individuals take those actions most likely to make themselves better off financially. This assumption of rational, self-interested behavior underlies nearly all economic analysis. In fact, economics can be distinguished from other fields that study human behavior—such as sociology and psychology—by its emphasis on the assumption of self-interested behavior. Adam Smith understood—as economists today understand—that people's motives can be complex. But in analyzing people in the act of buying and selling, the motivation of financial reward usually provides the best explanation for the actions people take.

For example, suppose that a significant number of consumers switch from buying cars to buying SUVs, as in fact happened in the United States during the 1990s. Firms will find that they can charge higher prices for SUVs than they can for cars. The self-interest of these firms will lead them to respond to consumers' wishes by producing more SUVs and fewer cars. Or suppose that consumers decide that they want to eat less bread, pasta, and other foods high in carbohydrates, as many did following the increase in popularity of the Atkins and South Beach diets. Then the prices firms can charge for bread and pasta will fall. The self-interest of firms will lead them to produce less bread and pasta, which in fact is what happened.

In the case where consumers want more of a product, and in the case where they want less of a product, the market system responds without a guild or anyone else giving orders about how much to produce or what price to charge. In a famous phrase, Smith said that firms would be led by the "invisible hand" of the market to provide consumers with what they wanted. Firms would respond to changes in prices by making decisions that ended up satisfying the wants of consumers.

Story of the Market System in Action: "I, Pencil"

2-2 Making the Connection

The pencil seems like a very simple product. In fact, its production requires the coordinated activities of many different people, spread around the world. The economist Leonard Read showed how markets achieve this coordination by writing an "autobiography" of a pencil sold by the Eberhard Faber Pencil Company of California. It is one of the most famous accounts of how the market system works. The pencil writes that:

> My family tree begins with a [cedar] tree that grows in Northern California and Oregon. Now contemplate all the saws and trucks and rope and the countless other gear used in harvesting and carting the cedar logs to the railroad siding. . . .
>
> The logs are shipped to a mill in San Leandro, California. . . . The cedar logs are cut into small, pencil-length slats less than one-fourth of an inch in thickness. . . . Once in the pencil factory . . . each slat is given eight grooves by a complex machine, after which another machine lays leads in every other slat. . . .
>
> My "lead" itself—it contains no lead at all—is complex. The graphite is mined in Ceylon . . . [and] is mixed with clay from Mississippi in which ammonium hydroxide is used in the refining process. . . . To increase their strength and smoothness the leads are then treated with a hot mixture which includes candelilla wax from Mexico, paraffin wax, and hydrogenated natural fats.
>
> My cedar receives six coats of lacquer. Do you know all the ingredients of lacquer? Who would think that the growers of castor beans and the refiners of castor oil are a part of it? They are.
>
> My bit of metal–the ferrule–is brass. Think of all the persons who mine zinc and copper and those who have the skills to make shiny sheet brass from these products of nature.
>
> Then there's my crowning glory . . . the part man uses to erase the errors he makes with me. . . . It is a rubber-like product made by reacting rape-seed oil from the Dutch

The market coordinates the activities of the many people spread around the world who contribute to the making of a pencil.

East Indies with sulfur chloride. . . . Then, too, there are numerous vulcanizing and accelerating agents. The pumice comes from Italy; and the pigment which gives [the eraser] its color is cadmium sulfide.

[M]illions of human beings have had a hand in my creation, no one of whom even knows more than a very few of the others. . . . There isn't a single person in all these millions, including the president of the pencil company, who contributes more than a tiny, infinitesimal bit of know-how. . . .

There is a fact still more astounding: the absence of a master mind, of anyone dictating or forcibly directing these countless actions which bring me into being. No trace of such a person can be found. Instead, we find the Invisible Hand at work.

Source: Leonard E. Read, *"I, Pencil,"* Irvington-on-Hudson, NY: Foundation for Economic Education, Inc. 1999. Used with permission of Foundation for Economic Education, Inc. Available online at www.econlib.org/library/Essays/rdPncl1.html.

The Role of the Entrepreneur

Entrepreneur Someone who operates a business, bringing together the factors of production—labor, capital, and natural resources—to produce goods and services.

Entrepreneurs are central to the working of the market system. An **entrepreneur** is someone who operates a business. Entrepreneurs must first determine what goods and services they believe consumers want, and then decide how those goods and services might be produced most profitably. Entrepreneurs bring together the factors of production—labor, capital, and natural resources—to produce goods and services. They put their own funds at risk when they start businesses. If they are wrong about what consumers want or about the best way to produce goods and services, they can lose those funds. In fact, it is not unusual for entrepreneurs who eventually achieve great success to fail at first. For instance, early in their careers both Henry Ford and Sakichi Toyoda, whose company eventually became the Toyota Motor Corporation, started companies that quickly failed.

The Legal Basis of a Successful Market System

In a free market, government does not restrict how firms produce and sell goods and services, or how they employ factors of production, but the absence of government intervention is not enough for a market system to work well. Government has to provide secure rights to private property for a market system to work at all. In addition, government can aid the working of the market by enforcing contracts between private individuals through an independent court system. Many economists would also say the government has a role in facilitating the development of an efficient financial system as well as systems of education, transportation, and communication. The protection of private property and the existence of an independent court system to impartially enforce the law provide a *legal environment* that will allow a market system to succeed.

PROTECTION OF PRIVATE PROPERTY For a market system to work well, individuals must be willing to take risks. Someone with $250,000 can be cautious and keep it safely in a bank—or even in cash, if the person doesn't trust the banking system. But the market system won't work unless a significant number of people are willing to risk their funds by investing them in businesses. Investing in businesses is risky in any country. Many businesses fail every year in the United States and other high-income countries. But in the high-income countries, someone who starts a new business or invests in an existing business doesn't have to worry that the government, the military, or criminal gangs might decide to seize the business or demand payments for not destroying the business. Unfortunately, in many poor countries owners of businesses are not well protected from having their businesses seized by the government or from having their profits taken by criminals. Where these problems exist, opening a business can be extremely risky. Cash can be concealed easily, but a business is difficult to conceal and difficult to move.

Property rights refer to the rights individuals or firms have to the exclusive use of their property, including the right to buy or sell it. Property can be tangible, physical property, such as a store or factory. Property can also be intangible, such as the right to an idea.

Property rights The rights individuals or firms have to the exclusive use of their property, including the right to buy or sell it.

Two amendments to the U.S. Constitution guarantee property rights: The 5th Amendment states that the federal government shall not deprive any person "of life, liberty, or property, without due process of law." The 14th Amendment extends this guarantee to the actions of state governments: "No state . . . shall deprive any person of life, liberty, or property, without due process of law." Similar guarantees exist in every high-income country. Unfortunately, in many developing countries such guarantees do not exist or are poorly enforced.

In any modern economy, *intellectual property rights* are very important. Intellectual property includes books, films, software, and ideas for new products or new ways of producing products. To protect intellectual property, the federal government will grant a *patent* that gives an inventor—which is often a firm—the exclusive right to produce and sell a new product for a period of 20 years from the date the product was invented. For instance, because Microsoft has a patent on the Windows operating system, other firms cannot sell their own versions of Windows. The government grants patents to encourage firms to spend money on the research and development necessary to create new products. If other companies could freely copy Windows, Microsoft would not have spent the funds necessary to develop it. Just as a new product or a new method of making a product receives patent protection, books, films, and software receive *copyright* protection. Under U.S. law, the creator of a book, film, or piece of music has the exclusive right to use the creation during the creator's lifetime. The creator's heirs retain this exclusive right for 50 years.

Property Rights in Cyberspace: Napster, Kazaa, and iTunes

2-3 Making the Connection

The development of the Internet has led to new problems in protecting intellectual property rights. Songs, newspaper and magazine articles, and even entire motion pictures can be copied and e-mailed from one computer to another. Controlling unauthorized copying is harder today than it was when "copying" meant making a printed copy. The problem of unauthorized copying of music became particularly severe in 1999 when Napster, a small firm in San Mateo, California, created software that allowed people to download music from the Web without the authorization of the copyright holders. Needless to say, this was not good news for record companies. An article in *Newsweek* quoted a high-school student in Falls Church, Virginia: "I haven't purchased a CD in quite some time." Another student said, "Napster's the best thing ever created. I don't have to spend any money." In fact, a sharp decline in music CD sales occurred in the early 2000s.

The record companies and some artists—including the heavy metal band Metallica—sued Napster for copyright infringement. In spring 2001, a federal court ruled that Napster was violating the copyrights on the songs it allowed to be downloaded and ordered the firm to stop allowing users to swap copyrighted material. Unfortunately for the record companies, a new service called Kazaa quickly replaced Napster. Legal action against Kazaa proved

Metallica sued to stop copyright infringement of their songs on the Internet.

difficult because it was harder to determine the names of people using the service and because the developers of Kazaa live outside the United States and have proved difficult to sue in U.S. courts.

Music companies have attempted to combat free downloads of music by offering inexpensive legal downloads. Some of these legal Web sites, such as Apple's iTunes and Sony's Connect, have been successful. During 2004, legal music downloads increased more than ten times over the previous year. But legal Internet sales still represented only about 1 percent of total music sales worldwide. Not surprisingly, overall music sales were still declining. The failure to give full protection of property rights in music continued to reduce the willingness of music companies to offer as many CDs for sale. The reduction in the quantity of CDs that would be produced if property rights were fully enforced represents a loss of efficiency to the economy.

Sources: Steven Levy, "The Noisy War Over Napster," *Newsweek*, June 5, 2000; "Skype: Catch Us If You Can," *Fortune*, January 26, 2004; Eric Pfanner, "More People Paying for Online Music," *International Herald Tribune*, January 20, 2005.

ENFORCEMENT OF CONTRACTS AND PROPERTY RIGHTS Much business activity involves someone agreeing to carry out some action in the future. For example, you may borrow $20,000 to buy a car and promise the bank—by signing a loan contract—that you will pay back the money over the next five years. Or Microsoft may sign a licensing agreement with a small technology company, agreeing to use that company's technology for a period of several years in return for a fee. Usually these agreements take the form of legal contracts. For a market system to work, businesses and individuals have to rely on these contracts being carried out. If one party to a legal contract does not fulfill its obligations—perhaps the small company had promised Microsoft exclusive use of its technology, but then began licensing it to other companies—the other party can go to court to have the agreement enforced. Similarly, if a property owners in the United States believes that the federal or state government has violated their rights under the 5th or 14th Amendments, they can go to court to have their rights enforced.

But going to court to enforce a contract or private property rights will only be successful if the court system is independent and judges are able to make impartial decisions on the basis of the law. In the United States and other high-income countries, the court systems have enough independence from other parts of the government and enough protection from intimidation by outside forces—such as criminal gangs—that they are able to make their decisions based on the law. In many developing countries, the court systems lack this independence and will not provide a remedy if the government violates private property rights or if a person with powerful political connections decides to violate a business contract.

If property rights are not well enforced, the production of goods and services will be reduced. This reduces economic efficiency, leaving the economy inside its production possibilities frontier.

Conclusion

We have seen that by trading in markets, people are able to specialize and pursue their comparative advantage. Trading on the basis of comparative advantage makes all participants in trade better off. The key role of markets is to facilitate trade. In fact, the market system is a very effective means of coordinating the decisions of millions of consumers, workers, and firms. At the center of the market system is the consumer. To be successful, firms must respond to the desires of consumers. These desires are communicated to firms through prices. To explore how markets work, we must study the behavior of consumers and firms. We continue this exploration of markets in Chapter 3 when we develop the model of demand and supply.

Before moving on to Chapter 3, read *An Inside Look* on the next page to learn how BMW allocates its scarce resources in its Munich plant.

An Inside Look

Choosing the Production Mix at BMW

WALL STREET JOURNAL, MAY 6, 2004

BMW's Net Profit Rises 2.5% As New Models Benefit Sales

Bayerische Motoren Werke AG posted a 2.5% increase in first-quarter net profit, as the launches of the 6-Series coupe and X3 sport-utility vehicle boosted sales.

The luxury-car manufacturer, which sells the BMW, Mini and Rolls-Royce brands, benefited from new products that allowed it to outpace rival Mercedes, a unit of Daimler-Chrysler AG, in terms of vehicle sales in the year's first three months.

BMW's net profit rose to €523 million ($632.3 million) from €510 million a year earlier. Revenue climbed 4.9% to €10.8 billion from €10.3 billion. The rise in revenue outpaced the gain in car sales, which climbed 3.2% to 269,973 vehicles from 261,573.

a The company, based in Munich, got off to a slow start in 2004 as renovation work at its Munich plant through the end of January slowed production of the 3-Series. The second quarter began well, as the company sold 9% more cars in April compared with a year earlier, Chief Executive Helmut Panke said.

That jump in car sales suggests that a stronger earnings rise is in store for the current quarter. Mr. Panke said he expects earnings growth to roughly track a projected rise in car sales.

b The company repeated a forecast for record 2004 earnings, aiming to top 2002's net profit of €2.02 billion. "What's encouraging is that they still expect to achieve record earnings," said Michael Raab, an analyst at Sal. Oppenheim.

BMW's first-quarter performance was enough for the company to overtake Mercedes as the world's leading maker of premium cars—at least for now. BMW's car sales exceeded those of Mercedes, although Mercedes had the upper hand in revenue terms.

"BMW is definitely faring way better than Mercedes, but the two companies are in different stages in their product cycles," said Thomas Ryard, an analyst with forecaster World Markets Research Centre. "I'm not sure it's going to be a long-lasting trend. By 2005, Mercedes should come back."

Last year, BMW launched its flagship 5-Series. This year, it is rolling out the 6-Series, X3, Mini convertible and 1-Series compact. Most of the development expenses for these models have already been booked.

By contrast, Mercedes is at the beginning of the biggest product offensive in its history. It launched a redesigned C-Class in March and is bringing out new versions of its compact A-Class this fall. In 2005, Mercedes expects to introduce two sport-utility vehicles, a redesign of the company's luxury S-Class, and a crossover family, known as the R-Class.

But Mercedes, which produces the Mercedes-Benz, Smart and Maybach brands, won't realize the benefits of these new models until later this year and in 2005.

Mercedes's first-quarter car sales declined 9% to 266,000 vehicles, burdened by the new-model program. But the Mercedes-Benz brand still topped BMW's core brand, selling 246,000 cars during the first quarter, compared with the BMW brand's 222,000.

Key Points in the Article

The article discusses the strong performance of BMW during the first months of 2004. The firm's sales rose sufficiently for it to overtake Mercedes for the lead in production of high-priced, or "premium," cars. The article spotlights the strong sales of the X3 SUV, which along with the Z8 roadster, is assembled at the company's plant in Munich, Germany. Renovations of the Munich plant reduced production of the X3 at the beginning of the year. BMW had been introducing new models and also increasing its capacity to produce existing models.

Analyzing the News

a We can use the economic model of production possibilities frontiers to analyze this news article. First, note that the renovations at the Munich plant meant that initially the company was operating inside its production possibilities frontier at this plant. This is shown in Figure 1, where production in early 2004 is represented by point *A*. Moving to the frontier makes it possible for BMW to produce more roadsters and more SUVs.

b The strong demand for the X3 SUV has caused BMW to allocate more workers and machines to producing this model. Once BMW is on the production possibilities frontier at the Munich plant, its opportunity cost of producing more X3 SUVs is the reduction in the quantity of Z8 roadsters produced. (Actually, we are simplifying a little here, because at various times BMW has produced other models in the Munich plant as well. We could show this by drawing a production possibilities frontier with the quantity of X3 SUVs on the horizontal axis and the quantity of all other models produced in the plant on the vertical axis. But the point would be the same: Once BMW is on the production possibilities frontier for this plant, it can only produce more X3s by producing less of something else.) In Figure 2 the popularity of the X3 causes BMW to move from point *B* to point *C*.

Thinking Critically ABOUT POLICY

1. Launching the 6-Series coupe and the X3 SUV boosted BMW's sales in early 2004. If launching new products boosts sales, should BMW launch a new line of cars *every* year? Every month? Explain.
2. Some BMW's are made in Germany, some in South Carolina, some in other places. Should the U.S. government encourage the domestic production of BMW's by banning imports of BMWs?

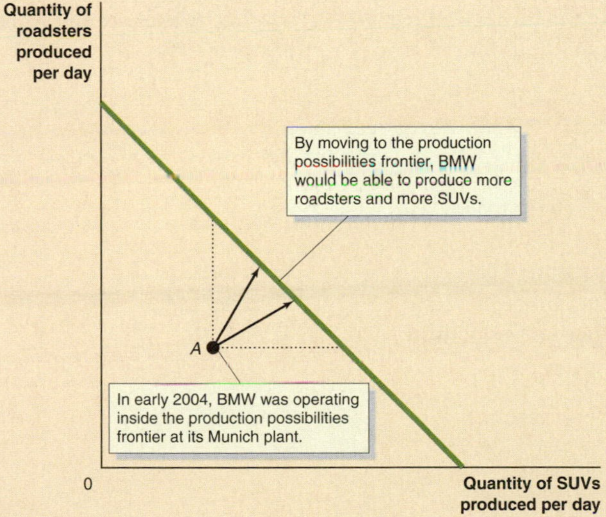

Figure 1: BMW was operating inside the Munich plant's production possibilities frontier in early 2004.

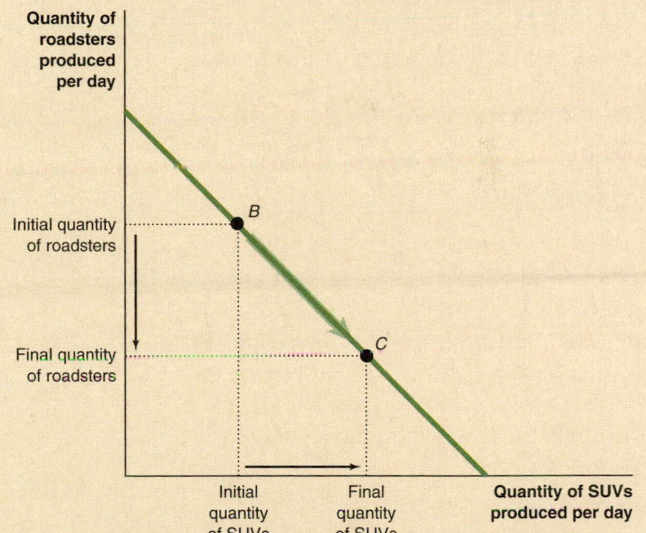

Figure 2: Once BMW is on the production possibilities frontier in its Munich plant, a larger quantity of X3 SUVs produced is only possible if a smaller quantity of Z8 roadsters is produced.

SUMMARY

LEARNING OBJECTIVE ① Use a production possibilities frontier to analyze opportunity costs and trade-offs. The production possibilities frontier is a curve showing the maximum attainable combinations of two products that may be produced with available resources. It is used to illustrate the trade-offs that arise from scarcity. Points on the frontier are technically efficient. Points inside the frontier are inefficient and points outside the frontier are unattainable. Because of increasing marginal opportunity costs, production possibilities frontiers are usually bowed-out, or concave, rather than straight lines. This illustrates the important economic concept that the more resources that are already devoted to any activity, the smaller the payoff to devoting additional resources to that activity is likely to be.

LEARNING OBJECTIVE ② Understand comparative advantage and explain how it is the basis for trade. Fundamentally, markets are about *trade,* which is the act of buying or selling. People trade on the basis of *comparative advantage.* An individual, firm, or country has a comparative advantage in producing a good or service if it can produce the good or service at the lowest opportunity cost. People are usually better off specializing in the activity for which they have a comparative advantage and trading for the other goods and services they need. It is important not to confuse comparative advantage with *absolute advantage.* An individual, firm, or country has an *absolute advantage* in producing a good or service if it can produce more of that good or service from the same amount of resources. It is possible to have an absolute advantage in producing a good or service without having a comparative advantage.

LEARNING OBJECTIVE ③ Explain the basic idea of how a market system works. A *market* is a group of buyers and sellers of a good or service and the institution or arrangement by which they come together to trade. *Product markets* are markets for goods and services, such as computers and medical treatment. *Factor markets* are markets for the factors of production, such as labor, capital, natural resources, and entrepreneurial ability. Adam Smith argued in his 1776 book, *The Wealth of Nations,* that in a free market where the government does not control the production of goods and services, changes in prices lead firms to produce the goods and services most desired by consumers. If consumers demand more of a good, its price will rise. Firms respond to rising prices by increasing production. If consumers demand less of a good, its price will fall. Firms respond to falling prices by producing less of a good. A market system will only work well if there is protection for *property rights,* which are the rights of individuals and firms to use their property.

KEY TERMS

REVIEW QUESTIONS

1. What do economists mean by scarcity? Can you think of anything that is not scarce according to the economic definition?
2. What is a production possibilities frontier? How can we show economic efficiency on a production possibilities frontier? How can we show inefficiency? What causes a production possibilities frontier to shift outward?
3. What does increasing marginal opportunity costs mean? What are the implications of this idea for the shape of the production possibilities frontier?
4. What is absolute advantage? What is comparative advantage? Is it possible for a country to have a comparative advantage in producing a good without also having an absolute advantage? Briefly explain.
5. What is the basis for trade? What advantages are there to specialization?
6. What is the circular-flow diagram, and what does it demonstrate?

7. What are the two main categories of participants in markets? Which participants are of greatest importance in determining what goods and services are produced?
8. What is a free market? In what ways does a free market economy differ from a centrally planned economy?
9. What is an entrepreneur? Why do entrepreneurs play a key role in a market system?
10. Under what circumstances are firms likely to produce more of a good or service? Under what circumstances are firms likely to produce less of a good or service?
11. What are private property rights? What role do they play in the working of a market system? Why are independent courts important for a well-functioning economy?

PROBLEMS AND APPLICATIONS

Please visit **www.prenhall.com/hubbard** *for solutions to the even-numbered problems as well as multiple-choice and true or false self-assessment quizzes.*

1. Draw a production possibilities frontier showing the trade-off between the production of cotton and the production of soybeans.
   a. Show the effect that a prolonged drought would have on the initial production possibilities frontier.
   b. Suppose genetic modification makes soybeans resistant to insects, allowing yields to double. Show the effect of this technological change on the initial production possibilities frontier.
2. **[Related to the *Chapter Opener*]** One of the trade-offs faced by BMW is between safety and gas mileage. For example, adding steel to a car makes it safer but also heavier, which results in lower gas mileage. Draw a hypothetical production possibilities frontier facing BMW engineers that shows this trade-off.
3. Suppose you win free tickets to a movie plus all you can eat at the snack bar for free. Would there be a cost to you to attend this movie? Explain.
4. Suppose we can divide all the goods produced by an economy into two types: consumption goods and capital goods. Capital goods, such as machinery, equipment, and computers, are goods used to produce other goods.
   a. Use a production possibilities frontier graph to illustrate the trade-off to an economy between producing consumption goods and producing capital goods. Is it likely that the production possibilities frontier in this situation would be a straight line (as in Figure 2-1) or concave (as in Figure 2-2)? Briefly explain.
   b. Suppose that technological advance occurs that affects the production of capital goods but not consumption goods. Show the effect on the production possibilities frontier.
   c. Suppose that country A and country B currently have identical production possibilities frontiers, but that country A devotes only 5 percent of its resources to producing capital goods over each of the next 10 years, whereas country B devotes 30 percent. Which country is likely to experience more rapid economic growth in the future? Illustrate using a production possibilities frontier graph. Your graph should include production possibilities frontiers for country A today and in 10 years, and for country B today and in 10 years.
5. Use the following production possibilities frontier for a country to answer the questions:

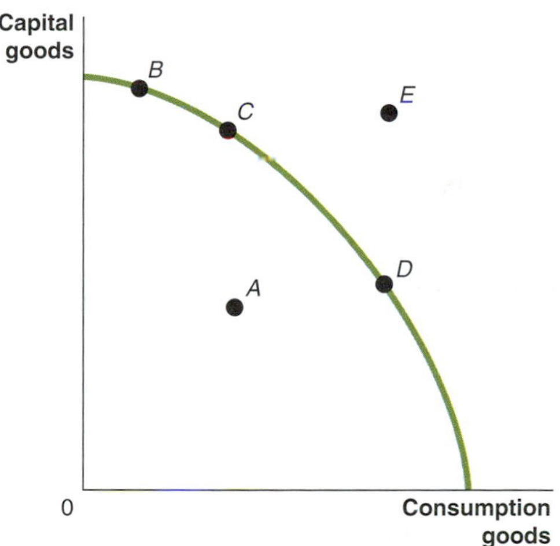

   a. Which point(s) are unattainable? Briefly explain why.
   b. Which point(s) are efficient? Briefly explain why.
   c. Which point(s) are inefficient? Briefly explain why.
   d. At which point is the country's future growth rate likely to be the highest? Briefly explain why.

6. **[Related to *Solved Problem 2-1*]** You have exams in economics and chemistry coming up and 5 hours available for studying. The table shows the trade-offs you face in allocating the time you will spend in studying each subject.

	HOURS SPENT STUDYING		MIDTERM SCORE	
CHOICE	ECONOMICS	CHEMISTRY	ECONOMICS	CHEMISTRY
A	5	0	95	70
B	4	1	93	78
C	3	2	90	84
D	2	3	86	88
E	1	4	81	90
F	0	5	75	91

   a. Use the data in the table to draw a production possibilities frontier graph. Label your vertical axis "Score on economics exam" and label your horizontal axis "Score on chemistry exam." Make sure to label the values where your production possibilities frontier intersects the vertical and horizontal axes.
   b. Label the points representing choice *C* and choice *D*. If you are at choice *C*, what is your opportunity cost of increasing your chemistry score?
   c. Under what circumstances would *A* be a sensible choice?

7. Suppose the president is attempting to decide whether the federal government should spend more on research to find a cure for heart disease. He asks you, one of his economic advisors, to prepare a report discussing the relevant factors he should consider. Discuss the main issues you would deal with in your report.

8. Congress has given the Environmental Protection Agency (EPA) the authority to write regulations to implement the provisions of the Clean Air Act, a law aimed at reducing air pollution. According to the Clean Air Act, the EPA is not to consider the cost of complying with the regulations. Why do you suppose Congress would have constrained the EPA in this way? Do you agree that costs should not be taken into account when drafting environmental regulations?

9. Lawrence Summers was a professor of economics at Harvard and served as Secretary of the Treasury in the Clinton administration before becoming president of Harvard. He has been quoted as giving the following moral defense of the economic approach:

> There is nothing morally unattractive about saying: We need to analyze which way of spending money on health care will produce more benefit and which less, and using our money as efficiently as we can. I don't think there is anything immoral about seeking to achieve environmental benefits at the lowest possible costs.

   Would it be more moral to reduce pollution without worrying about the cost or by taking the cost into account? Briefly explain.

   Source: David Wessel, "Precepts from Professor Summers," *Wall Street Journal*, October 17, 2002.

10. In *The Wonderful Wizard of Oz* and his other books about the Land of Oz, L. Frank Baum observed that if people's wants were modest enough, most goods would not be scarce. According to Baum, this was the case in Oz:

> There were no poor people in the Land of Oz, because there was no such thing as money. . . . Each person was given freely by his neighbors whatever he required for his use, which is as much as anyone may reasonably desire. Some tilled the lands and raised great crops of grain, which was divided equally among the whole population, so that all had enough. There were many tailors and dressmakers and shoemakers and the like, who made things that any who desired them might wear. Likewise there were jewelers who made ornaments for the person, which pleased and beautified the people, and these ornaments also were free to those who asked for them. Each man and woman, no matter what he or she produced for the good of the community, was supplied by the neighbors with food and clothing and a house and furniture and ornaments and games. If by chance the supply ever ran short, more was taken from the great storehouses of the Ruler, which were afterward filled up again when there was more of any article than people needed. . . .
>
> You will know, by what I have told you here, that the Land of Oz was a remarkable country. I do not suppose such an arrangement would be practical with us.

   Do you agree with Baum that the economic system in Oz wouldn't work in the contemporary United States? Briefly explain why or why not.

   Source: L. Frank Baum, *The Emerald City of Oz*, pp. 30–31. First edition published in 1910.

11. Using the same amount of resources, the United States and Canada can both produce lumberjack shirts and lumberjack boots as shown in the following production possibilities frontiers:

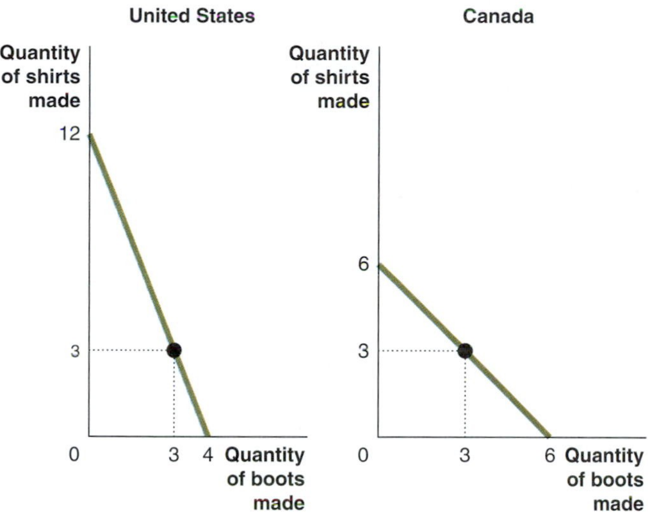

a. Who has a comparative advantage in producing lumberjack boots? Who has a comparative advantage in producing lumberjack shirts? Explain your reasoning.
b. Does either country have an absolute advantage in producing both goods? Explain.
c. Suppose that both countries are currently producing three pairs of boots and three shirts. Show that both can be better off if they specialize in producing one good and then engage in trade.

12. **[Related to *Solved Problem 2-2*]** Suppose Iran and Iraq both produce oil and olive oil. The table shows combinations of both goods that each country can produce in a day, measured in thousands of barrels.

IRAQ		IRAN	
OIL	OLIVE OIL	OIL	OLIVE OIL
0	8	0	4
2	6	1	3
4	4	2	2
6	2	3	1
8	0	4	0

a. Who has the comparative advantage in producing oil? Explain.
b. Can these two countries gain from trading oil and olive oil? Explain.

13. **[Related to *Solved Problem 2-2*]** Suppose that France and Germany both produce schnitzel and wine. The following table shows combinations of the goods that each country can produce in a day:

FRANCE		GERMANY	
WINE (BOTTLES)	SCHNITZEL (POUNDS)	WINE (BOTTLES)	SCHNITZEL (POUNDS)
0	8	0	15
1	6	1	12
2	4	2	9
3	2	3	6
4	0	4	3
		5	0

a. Who has a comparative advantage in producing wine? Who has a comparative advantage in producing schnitzel?
b. Suppose that France is currently producing 1 bottle of wine and 6 pounds of schnitzel and Germany is currently producing 3 bottles of wine and 6 pounds of schnitzel. Demonstrate that France and Germany can both be better off if they specialize in producing only one good and then engage in trade.

14. **[Related to *Don't Let This Happen To You!*]** In the 1950s, the economist Bela Balassa compared 28 manufacturing industries in the United States and Britain. In every one of the 28 industries, Balassa found that the United States had an absolute advantage. In these circumstances, would there have been any gain to the United States from importing any of these products from Britain? Explain.

15. Identify whether each of the following transactions will take place in the factor market or in the product market, and whether households or firms are supplying the good or service, or demanding the good or service:
a. George buys a BMW X5 SUV.
b. BMW increases employment at its Spartanburg plant.
c. George works 20 hours per week at McDonald's.
d. George sells land he owns to McDonald's so it can build a new restaurant.

16. In *The Wealth of Nations,* Adam Smith wrote the following (Book I, Chapter II):

> It is not from the benevolence of the butcher, the brewer, or the baker, that we expect our dinner, but from their regard to their own interest.

Briefly discuss what he meant by this.

17. In a commencement address to economics graduates at the University of Texas, Robert McTeer Jr., who was then the president of the Federal Reserve Bank of Dallas, argued, "For my money, Adam Smith's invisible hand is the most important thing you've learned by studying economics." What's so important about the idea of the invisible hand?
Source: Robert D. McTeer Jr., "The Dismal Science? Hardly!" *Wall Street Journal,* June 4, 2003.

18. Evaluate the following argument: "Adam Smith's analysis is based on a fundamental flaw: He assumes that people are motivated by self-interest. But this isn't true. I'm not selfish, and most people I know aren't selfish."

19. Writing in the *New York Times,* Michael Lewis argued that "a market economy is premised on a system of incentives designed to encourage an ignoble human trait: self-interest." Do you agree that self-interest is an "ignoble human trait"? What incentives does a market system provide to encourage self-interest?
Source: Michael Lewis, "In Defense of the Boom," *New York Times,* October 27, 2002.

20. An editorial in *Business Week* magazine offered this opinion:

> Economies should be judged on a simple measure: their ability to generate a rising standard of living for all members of society, including people at the bottom.

Briefly discuss whether or not you agree.
Source: "Poverty: The Bigger Picture," *Business Week,* October 7, 2002.

21. An estimated 400 million to 600 million people worldwide are squatters who live on land to which they have no legal title, usually on the outskirts of cities in less-developed countries. Economist Hernando de Soto persuaded Peru's government to undertake a program to make it cheap and easy for these squatters to obtain a title to the land they had been occupying. How would this creation of property rights be likely to affect the economic opportunities available to these squatters?
Source: Alan B. Krueger, "A Study Looks at Squatters and Land Title in Peru," *New York Times,* January 9, 2003.

22. In colonial America, the population was spread thinly over a large area and transportation costs were very high because it was difficult to ship products by road for more than short distances. As a result, most of the free population lived on small farms where they not only grew their own food but also usually made their own clothes and very rarely bought or sold anything for money. Explain why the incomes of these farmers were likely to rise as transportation costs fell. Use the concept of comparative advantage in your answer.

23. During the 1928 presidential election campaign, Herbert Hoover, the Republican candidate, argued that the United States should only import those products that could not be produced here. Do you believe that this would be a good policy? Explain.

chapter three

Where Prices Come From: The Interaction of Demand and Supply

How Hewlett-Packard Manages the Demand for Printers

In early 2005 the board of directors at Hewlett-Packard (H-P) ousted chief executive officer Carly Fiorina and replaced her with Mark Hurd, then the chief executive officer of NCR Corporation. What happened?

Carly Fiorina had been a business celebrity for many years. In July 1999 she became H-P's chief executive officer, which made her the first woman to head one of the 100 largest firms in the United States. In 2002, she brought about the largest merger of two technology firms in U.S. history when H-P purchased Compaq Computer Corporation. By 2004, she presided over a firm that employed 150,000 workers and had total sales of $80 billion. Fiorina's ouster in 2005 from H-P reflected the relatively weak performance of the firm during her time as chief executive officer. In particular, the merger with Compaq had failed to improve H-P's performance in the personal computer market.

Printers, and not personal computers, are H-P's most successful product. Although printers account for only about 30 percent of the firm's sales, they account for 70 percent of its profits. In fact, as *An Inside Look* at the end of this chapter discusses, to increase the demand for printers the firm is willing to sell its personal computers at low prices.

Hewlett-Packard's success, like that of any firm, depends on its ability to analyze changes in demand and supply. Because of the importance of printers to H-P, the firm devotes significant resources to monitoring and forecasting consumer demand. Its forecasts of demand, however, are not always successful. In 2001, for example, Carly Fiorina announced that sales of H-P printers had declined sharply in the first half of that year compared to the first half of 2000. Two events caused this decline: First, many individuals and small businesses unexpectedly decided not to upgrade their existing computers to faster and more powerful machines. Purchasers of new PCs are a key part of the market for printers. Second, the U.S. economy moved into recession, lowering the incomes of many consumers and reducing the profits of many businesses. Fiorina admitted she had been taken by surprise by this decline in sales: "Stuff happens that you're not able to see even with a ton of information, and the downturn in the economy was a clear case of that. Everybody had loads of information, and everybody missed it."

H-P did a better job anticipating changes in the types of printers con-

sumers would demand. For example, increasing sales of digital cameras have had an important impact on the market for printers. During 2003, 50 million digital cameras were sold, and many people bought both a camera and a new printer designed to print digital photos. Printers aimed at the digital photo market usually include a slot for memory cards from the cameras, and an LCD (liquid crystal display) screen for previews of photos. Many of these printers are multifunction devices (MFD) that combine printing, scanning, copying, and faxing. These MFDs sell for higher prices—and are more profitable—than basic printers. In 2004, H-P had a 58 percent share of the MFD market in the United States. Lexmark was second but far behind with a 21 percent share.

Unfortunately for Carly Fiorina, H-P's success with MFDs was not matched by success with personal computers. Some members of the firm's board of directors were particularly concerned that H-P had relied too heavily on selling personal computers in retail stores, rather than building up direct sales to consumers through the Internet as Dell Computer had done so successfully. The board gave Mark Hurd, the new chief executive officer, the responsibility of increasing the firm's competitiveness in the personal computer market. *An Inside Look* on page 88 discusses HP's strategy for competing with Dell.

Sources: Olga Kharif, "Printing a Record of Growth," Business Week Online, February 17, 2004; Pui-Wing Tam, "Copy Machine: H-P, Post-Compaq, Looks Like Its Old Self," Wall Street Journal, May 7, 2004; quote from Carly Fiorina: "A Conversation with Carly Fiorina—Forbes 5th Annual CIO Forum," December 2, 2003, Dallas, Texas.

LEARNING OBJECTIVES

After studying this chapter, you should be able to:

1. Discuss the variables that influence demand.
2. Discuss the variables that influence supply.
3. Use a graph to illustrate market equilibrium.
4. Use demand and supply graphs to predict changes in prices and quantities.

In Chapter 1, we learned how economists use models to predict human behavior. In Chapter 2, we used the model of production possibilities frontiers to analyze scarcity and trade-offs. In this chapter and the next, we explore the model of demand and supply, which is the most powerful tool in economics, and use it to explain how prices are determined. We begin by discussing consumers and the demand side of the market, then we turn to firms and the supply side. As you will see, we will apply the model of demand and supply again and again throughout this book to understand business and the economy.

1 LEARNING OBJECTIVE
Discuss the variables that influence demand.

The Demand Side of the Market

Chapter 2 explained that in a market system consumers ultimately determine which goods and services will be produced. The most successful businesses are the ones that respond best to consumer demand. But what determines consumer demand for a product? Certainly, many factors influence the willingness of consumers to buy a particular product. For example, consumers who are considering buying a printer will make their decisions based on, among other factors, the income they have available to spend, whether they have recently purchased a personal computer or digital camera, and the effectiveness of the advertising campaigns of the companies that sell printers. The main factor in consumer decisions, though, will be the price of the printers. Thus, it makes sense to begin with price when analyzing the decisions of consumers to buy a product. It is important to note that when we discuss demand, we are considering not what a consumer *wants* to buy, but what the consumer is both willing and *able* to buy.

The Demand of an Individual Buyer

Households, firms, and government agencies all buy printers. Suppose the Prudential Insurance Company intends to purchase printers for a number of its employees. We might determine the relationship between the price of printers and the number of printers the company would be willing to buy during a particular period of time by asking Kate, the company's purchasing manager, "If the price of a printer were $125, how many printers would you be willing to buy over the next month?"

Suppose Kate responds that she would be willing to purchase 5 printers over the next month at a price of $125 each. The amount of a good or a service that a consumer is willing and able to purchase at a particular price is referred to as the **quantity demanded**. Figure 3-1 shows Kate's quantity demanded at a price of $125. On the vertical axis, we measure the price of printers, and on the horizontal axis we measure the number of printers demanded during the next month.

Quantity demanded The amount of a good or service that a consumer is willing and able to purchase at a given price.

Demand Schedules and Demand Curves

We can repeat our question using different prices. The table in Figure 3-2 shows the number of printers Kate would be willing to buy at five different prices. Tables that show the relationship between the price of a product and the quantity of the product demanded are called **demand schedules**. The graph in Figure 3-2 plots the numbers from the table as a **demand curve**, a curve that shows the relationship between the price of a product and the quantity of a product demanded.

Although we have asked Kate only about her willingness to buy printers at five different prices, we can connect the points in Figure 3-2 to form a continuous downward-sloping demand curve. The demand curve slopes downward because Kate

Demand schedule A table showing the relationship between the price of a product and the quantity of the product demanded.

Demand curve A curve that shows the relationship between the price of a product and the quantity of the product demanded.

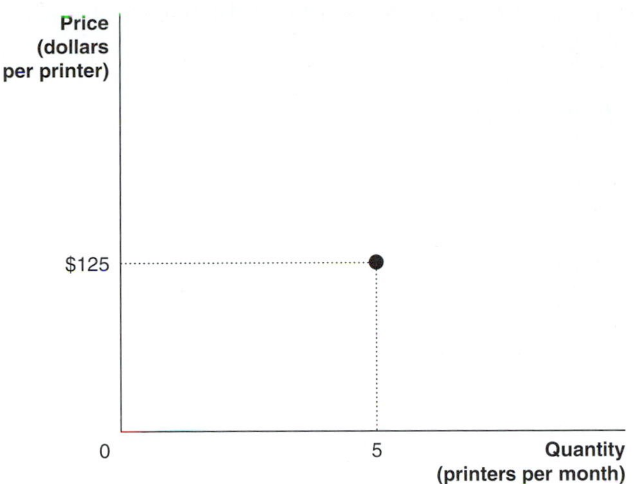

FIGURE 3-1

Plotting a Price–Quantity Combination on a Graph

At a price of $125 per printer, Kate, the purchasing manager for the Prudential Insurance Company, will be willing to buy 5 printers in the next month.

will buy more printers as the price falls. When the price of a printer is $175, Kate buys 3 printers. When the price of a printer falls to $150, Kate buys 4 printers. Buyers demand a larger quantity of a product as the price falls because the product becomes cheaper relative to other products and because they can afford to buy more at a lower price.

Individual Demand and Market Demand

Figure 3-2 shows an individual demand curve. To understand how a market works, however, we need to examine **market demand**, or the demand by all the consumers of a given good or service. We can determine market demand by asking additional consumers how many printers they would purchase at various prices. Ordinarily, the market that we would be interested in would include at least all of the consumers of the product in a city and might include all of the consumers in the world. To keep things simple, let's assume that the market for printers consists of Kate from the Prudential Insurance Company and two individual consumers: Sam and Paul. Figure 3-3 shows that we can find the market demand for printers by adding the number of printers demanded by Kate, Sam, and Paul at each price. The table shows the demand schedules for printers of these three consumers. We plot the numbers from the demand schedule in graphs 3-3(a), 3-3(b), and 3-3(c).

Market demand The demand by all the consumers of a given good or service.

Demand Schedule	
Price (dollars per printer)	Quantity (printers per month)
$175	3
150	4
125	5
100	6
75	7

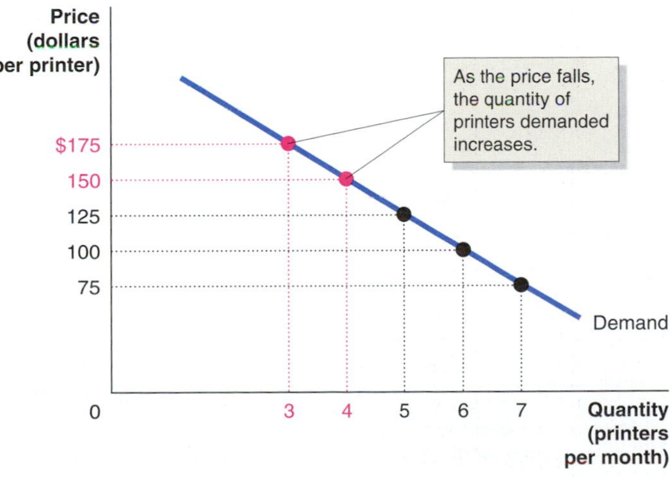

FIGURE 3-2

Kate's Demand Schedule and Demand Curve

As the price changes, Kate changes the quantity of printers she is willing to buy. We can show this as a *demand schedule* in a table, or as a *demand curve* on a graph. The table and graph both show that as the price of printers falls, the quantity demanded rises. When the price of a printer is $175, Kate buys 3 printers. When the price of a printer drops to $150, Kate buys 4 printers. Therefore, Kate's demand curve is downward sloping.

Figure 3-3(d) on page 67 shows the market demand curve for printers. The market demand curve tells us how many units of the product consumers in this market would be willing to buy at each price during a certain period of time. For instance, consumers in this market would be willing to buy a total of 26 printers during the next month at a price of $100 per printer: Kate is willing to buy 6, Sam is willing to buy 11, and Paul is willing to buy 9.

The Law of Demand

Law of demand Holding everything else constant, when the price of a product falls, the quantity demanded of the product will increase, and when the price of a product rises, the quantity demanded of the product will decrease.

The market demand curve for printers shown in Figure 3-3(d) is downward sloping: As the price of printers falls, the quantity of printers demanded increases. The inverse relationship between the price of a product and the quantity of the product demanded is known as the **law of demand**: Holding everything else constant, when the price of a product falls, the quantity demanded of the product will increase, and when the price of a product rises, the quantity demanded of the product will decrease. The law of demand holds for any market demand curve. Economists have never found an exception to it. In fact, Nobel Prize–winning economist Paul Samuelson once remarked that the surest way for an economist to become famous would be to discover a market demand curve that sloped upward rather than downward.

What Explains the Law of Demand?

It makes sense that consumers will buy more of a good when the price falls and less of a good when the price rises, but let's look more closely at why this is true. When the price of printers falls, consumers buy a larger quantity of printers because of the *substitution effect* and the *income effect.*

FIGURE 3-3 Deriving the Market Demand Curve from Individual Demand Curves

The table shows that the total quantity demanded in a market is the sum of the quantities demanded by each buyer at each price. We find the market demand curve by adding horizontally the individual demand curves in parts (a), (b), and (c). At a price of $100, Kate demands 6 printers, Sam demands 11 printers, and Paul demands 9 printers. Therefore, part (d) shows that a price of $100 and a quantity demanded of 26 is a point on the market demand curve.

	Quantity (printers per month)			
Price (dollars per printer)	Kate	Sam	Paul	Market
$175	3	5	6	14
150	4	7	7	18
125	5	9	8	22
100	6	11	9	26
75	7	13	10	30

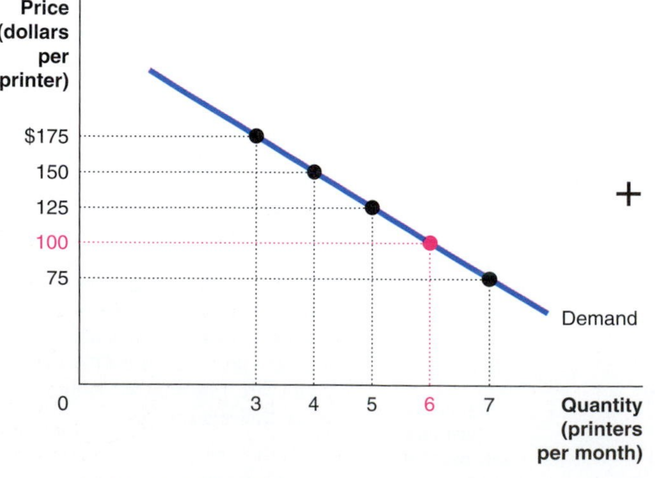

(a) Kate's demand curve

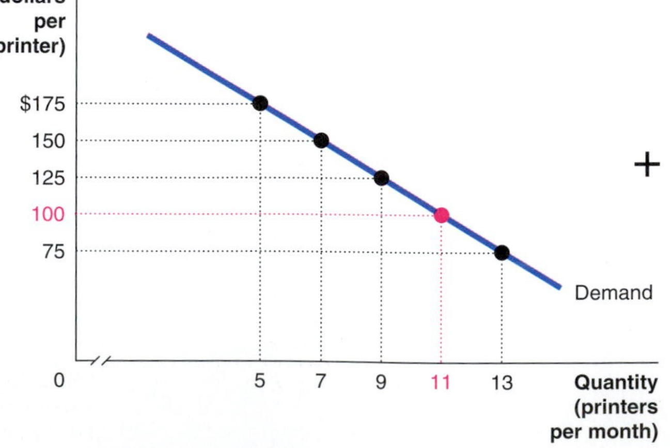

(b) Sam's demand curve

SUBSTITUTION EFFECT The **substitution effect** of a price change refers to the fact that a fall in price makes a good less expensive *relative* to other goods that are *substitutes.* This change leads consumers to buy more of a good when its price falls—or less of a good when its price rises. When the price of printers falls, consumers will substitute buying printers for buying other goods or services. For example, a consumer who has digital camera pictures printed at Wal-Mart might instead buy a printer if the price of printers falls.

Substitution effect The change in the quantity demanded of a good that results from a change in price making the good more or less expensive relative to other goods that are substitutes.

THE INCOME EFFECT The **income effect** of a price change refers to the change in the quantity demanded of a good that results from the effect of a change in the good's price on consumers' purchasing power. Purchasing power refers to the quantity of goods that can be bought with a fixed amount of income. When the price of a good falls, the increased purchasing power of consumers' incomes will usually lead them to purchase a larger quantity of the good. When the price of a good rises, the decreased purchasing power of consumers' incomes will usually lead them to purchase a smaller quantity of the good.

Income effect The change in the quantity demanded of a good that results from the effect of a change in the good's price on consumer purchasing power.

Thus, a fall in the price of printers leads consumers to buy more printers, both because they are now cheaper relative to substitute products and because the purchasing power of the consumers' incomes has increased.

Holding Everything Else Constant: The Ceteris Paribus *Condition*

Notice that the definition of the law of demand contains the phrase "holding everything else constant." In constructing the market demand curve for printers, we focused only on the effect that changes in the price of printers would have on the quantity of printers consumers would be willing and able to buy. We were holding constant other variables that might affect the willingness of consumers to buy printers. Economists refer to the necessity of holding all variables other than price constant in constructing a demand curve as the ***ceteris paribus*** condition—*ceteris paribus* is Latin for "all else equal."

Ceteris paribus ("all else equal") The requirement that when analyzing the relationship between two variables—such as price and quantity demanded—other variables must be held constant.

What would happen if we allowed a variable—other than price—to change that might affect the willingness of consumers to buy printers? Consumers would then change the quantity they demand at each price. We can illustrate this by shifting the market demand curve. A shift of a demand curve is *an increase or decrease in demand.* A movement along a demand curve is *an increase or decrease in the quantity demanded.* As

FIGURE 3-3 continued

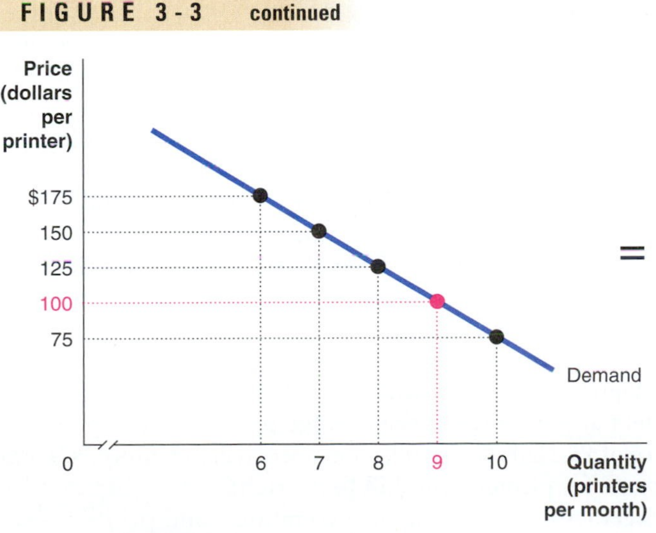

(c) Paul's demand curve

=

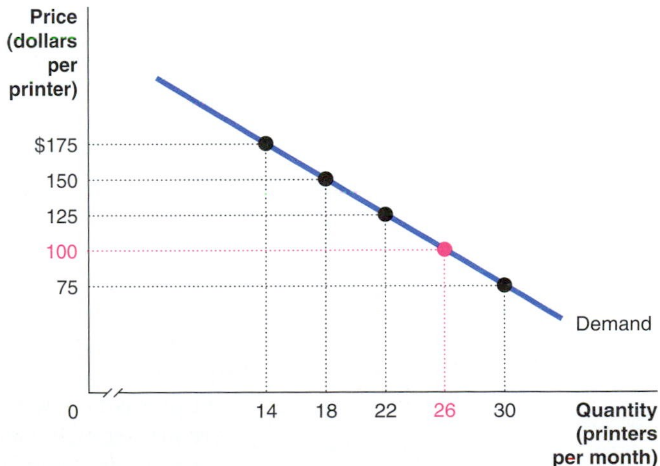

(d) Market demand curve

FIGURE 3-4

Shifting the Demand Curve

When consumers increase the quantity of a product they wish to buy at a given price, the market demand curve shifts to the right from D_1 to D_2. When consumers decrease the quantity of a product they wish to buy at any given price, the demand curve shifts to the left from D_1 to D_3.

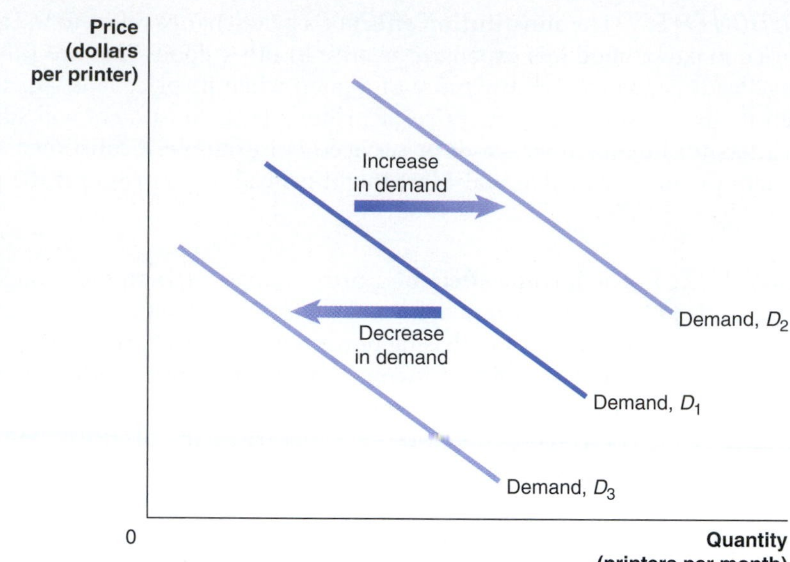

Figure 3-4 shows, we shift the demand curve to the right if consumers decide to buy more of the good at each price, and we shift the demand curve to the left if consumers decide to buy less.

Variables That Shift Market Demand

Many variables other than price can influence market demand. These five are the most important:

- Prices of related goods
- Income
- Tastes
- Population and demographics
- Expected future prices

We can discuss how changes in each of these variables affects the market demand curve for printers.

PRICES OF RELATED GOODS Consider again the market demand curve for printers. Suppose that the market demand curve in Figure 3-3(d) represents the willingness and ability of consumers to buy printers during a period when Wal-Mart charges $0.50 to print one digital photo. If Wal-Mart lowers the price to $0.25 per photo, how will the market demand for printers change? Fewer printers will be demanded at every price. We show this by shifting the demand curve for printers to the left.

Substitutes Goods and services that can be used for the same purpose.

Goods and services that can be used for the same purpose—like printers and having digital photos printed at stores—are **substitutes.** When two goods are substitutes, the more you buy of one, the less you will buy of the other. A decrease in the price of a substitute causes the demand curve for a good to shift to the left. An increase in the price of a substitute causes the demand curve for a good to shift to the right.

Many consumers purchase a new printer when they buy a new computer. Suppose the market demand curve in Figure 3-3(d) represents the willingness of consumers to buy Hewlett-Packard's printers at a time when the average price of a new personal computer is $1,300. If the price of PCs falls to $1,100, consumers will buy more PCs *and* more printers: The demand curve for printers will shift to the right.

Complements Goods that are used together.

Products that are used together—such as personal computers and printers—are **complements.** When two goods are complements, the more you buy of one, the more you will buy of the other. A decrease in the price of a complement causes the demand curve for a good to shift to the right. An increase in the price of a complement causes the demand curve for a good to shift to the left.

Why Supermarkets Need to Understand Substitutes and Complements

3-1 Making the Connection

Supermarkets sell what sometimes seems like a bewildering variety of goods. The first row of the following table shows the varieties of eight products stocked by five Chicago supermarkets.

	COFFEE	FROZEN PIZZA	HOT DOGS	ICE CREAM	POTATO CHIPS	REGULAR CEREAL	SPAGHETTI SAUCE	YOGURT
Varieties in Five Chicago Supermarkets	391	337	128	421	285	242	194	288
Varieties Introduced in a 2-Year Period	113	109	47	129	93	114	70	107
Varieties Removed in a 2-Year Period	135	86	32	118	77	75	36	51

Source: Juin-Kuan Chong, Teck-Hua Ho, and Christopher S. Tang, "A Modeling Framework for Category Assortment Planning," *Manufacturing & Service Operations Management*, 2001, Vol. 3, No. 3, pp. 191–210.

A supermarket shouldn't remove a slow-selling soup from its shelves without researching whether shoppers use that soup as a substitute or a complement for another soup.

Supermarkets are also constantly adding new varieties of goods to their shelves and removing old varieties. The second row of the table shows that these five Chicago supermarkets added 113 new varieties of coffee over a two-year period, while the third row shows they eliminated 135 existing varieties. How do supermarkets decide which varieties to add and which to remove?

Christopher Tang is a professor at the Anderson Graduate School of Management at the University of California, Los Angeles (UCLA). In an interview with the *Baltimore Sun*, Tang argues that supermarkets should not necessarily remove the slowest-selling goods from their shelves but should consider the relationships among the goods. In particular, they should consider whether the goods being removed are substitutes or complements with the remaining goods. A lobster bisque soup, for example, could be a relatively slow seller but might be a complement to other soups because it can be used with them to make a sauce. In that case, removing the lobster bisque would hurt sales of some of the remaining soups. Tang suggests the supermarket would be better off removing a slow-selling soup that is a substitute for another soup. For example, the supermarket might want to remove one of two brands of cream of chicken soup.

Source: Lobster bisque example from Lorraine Mirabella, "Shelf Science in Supermarkets," *Baltimore Sun*, March 17, 2002, p. 16.

INCOME In addition to the prices of other goods, the income that consumers have available to spend also affects their willingness and ability to buy a good. Suppose that the market demand curve in Figure 3-3(d) reflects the willingness of consumers to buy printers when average household income is $43,000. If household income rises to $45,000, the demand for printers will increase, which we show by shifting the demand curve to the right. A good is a **normal good** when demand increases following an increase in income and decreases following a decrease in income. Most goods are normal goods, but the demand for some goods falls when income rises, and rises when income falls. For instance, as your income rises you might buy less canned tuna fish or fewer hot dogs, and buy more prime rib or shrimp. A good is an **inferior good** when demand decreases following an increase in income and increases following a decrease in income. So, hot dogs and tuna fish would be examples of inferior goods, not because they are of low quality, but because you buy less of them as your income increases.

Normal good A good for which the demand increases as income rises and decreases as income falls.

Inferior good A good for which the demand increases as income falls, and decreases as income rises.

TASTES Consumers can also be influenced by an advertising campaign for a product. If Hewlett-Packard and other companies begin to heavily advertise their printers on television and in magazines, consumers are more likely to buy them at every price and the demand curve will shift to the right. An economist would say that the advertising campaign has affected consumers' *taste* for printers. Taste is a catchall category that refers to the many subjective elements that can enter into a consumer's decision to buy a product. A consumer's taste for a product can change for many reasons. Sometimes trends play a substantial role. For example, the popularity of low-carbohydrate diets caused a decline in demand for some goods, such as bread and donuts, and an increase in demand for beef. In general, when consumers' taste for a product increases, the demand curve will shift to the right, and when consumers' taste for a product decreases, the demand curve for the product will shift to the left.

Demographics The characteristics of a population with respect to age, race, and gender.

POPULATION AND DEMOGRAPHICS Population and demographic factors can affect the demand for a product. As the population of the United States increases, so will the number of consumers, and the demand for most products will increase. The **demographics** of a population refers to its characteristics, with respect to age, race, and gender. As the demographics of a country or region change, the demand for particular goods will increase or decrease because different categories of people tend to have different preferences for those goods. For instance, the demand for baby food will be greatest when the fraction of the population under the age of two is the greatest.

3-2 Making the Connection

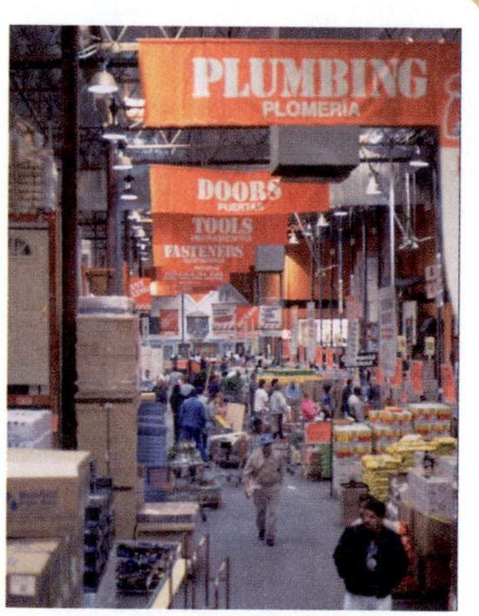

Firms are responding to the tastes of a growing Hispanic population. Some Home Depot stores, for example, include signs in both English and Spanish.

Companies Respond to a Growing Hispanic Population

In the fall of 2002, Blockbuster Video began stocking more than 1,000 videos and DVDs that had been dubbed in Spanish. Kmart began selling a clothing line named after Thalia, a Mexican singer. The Ford Motor Company hired Mexican actress and singer Salma Hayek to appear in commercials. A used car dealer in Pennsylvania displayed a sign stating "Salga Manejando Hoy Mismo" (or "Drive Out Today" in English). These companies were responding to the rising spending power of Hispanic Americans. The increase in spending by Hispanic households was due partly to increased population growth and partly to rising incomes. By 2020, the Hispanic share of the U.S. consumer market is expected to grow to more than 13 percent—almost twice what it had been in 2000. The Selig Center for Economic Growth at the University of Georgia has forecast that the incomes of Hispanic households will increase more than twice as fast between 2003 and 2007 as the incomes of non-Hispanic households.

As the demand for goods purchased by Hispanic households increases, more can be sold at every price. Not surprisingly, companies have responded by devoting more resources to serving this demographic group.

Source: Eduardo Porter, "Buying Power of Hispanics Is Set to Soar," *Wall Street Journal*, April 18, 2003, p. B1.

EXPECTED FUTURE PRICES Consumers choose not only which products to buy but also when to buy them. On the one hand, if enough consumers become convinced that printers will be selling for lower prices three months from now, the demand for printers will decrease now, as consumers postpone their purchases to wait for the expected price decrease. On the other hand, if enough consumers become convinced that the price of printers will be higher three months from now, the demand for printers will increase now, as consumers try to beat the expected price increase.

Table 3-1 summarizes the most important variables that cause market demand curves to shift. You should note that the table shows the shift in the demand curve that results from an *increase* in each of the variables. A *decrease* in these variables would cause the demand curve to shift in the opposite direction.

TABLE 3-1

Variables That Shift Market Demand Curves

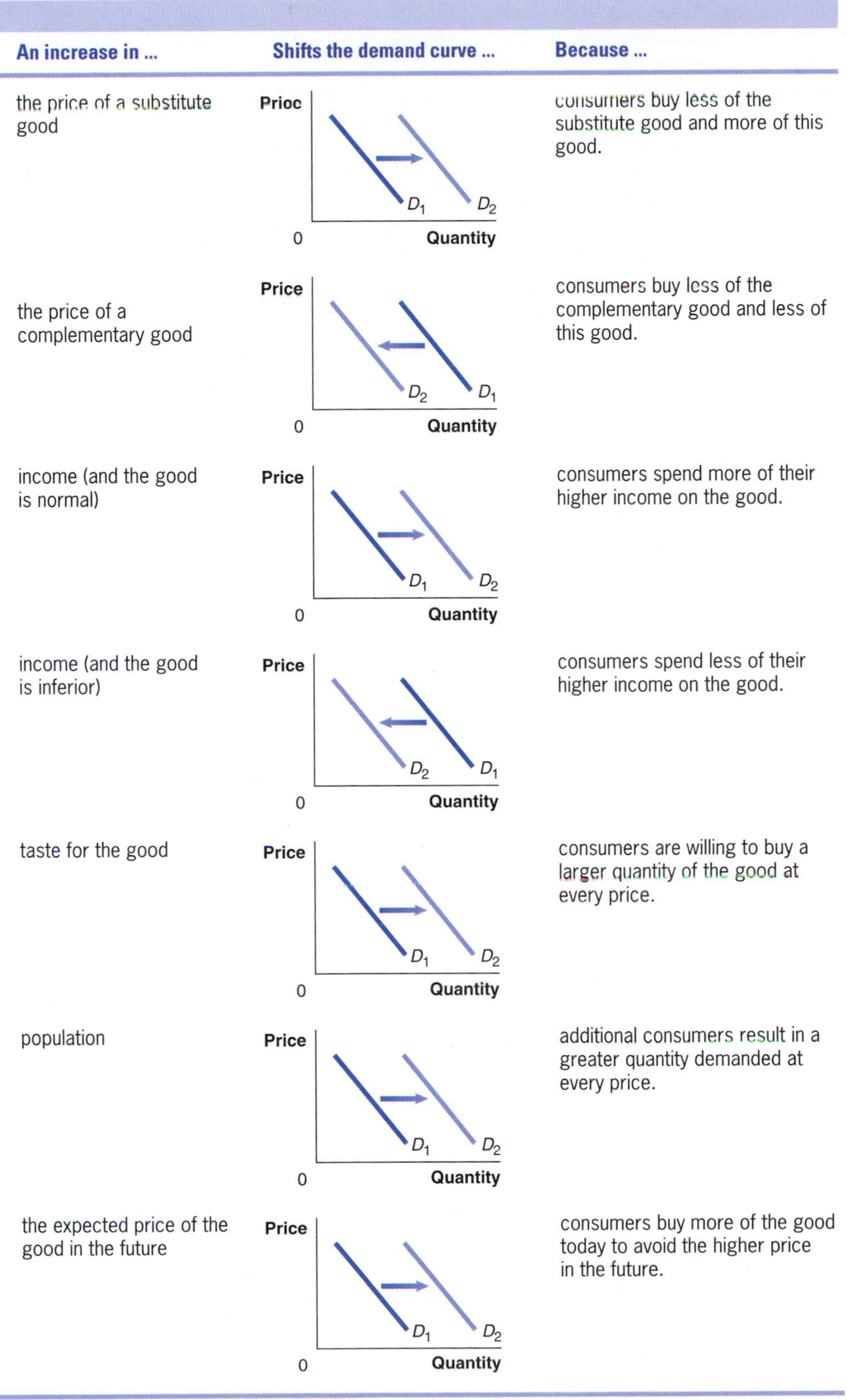

An increase in ...	Shifts the demand curve ...	Because ...
the price of a substitute good		consumers buy less of the substitute good and more of this good.
the price of a complementary good		consumers buy less of the complementary good and less of this good.
income (and the good is normal)		consumers spend more of their higher income on the good.
income (and the good is inferior)		consumers spend less of their higher income on the good.
taste for the good		consumers are willing to buy a larger quantity of the good at every price.
population		additional consumers result in a greater quantity demanded at every price.
the expected price of the good in the future		consumers buy more of the good today to avoid the higher price in the future.

FIGURE 3-5

A Change in Demand versus a Change in the Quantity Demanded

If the price of printers falls from \$175 to \$150, the result will be a movement along the demand curve from point *A* to point *B*—an increase in quantity demanded from 50,000 to 60,000. If consumers' income increases, or another factor changes that makes consumers want more of the product at every price, the demand curve will shift to the right—an increase in demand. In this case, the increase in demand from D_1 to D_2 causes the quantity of printers demanded at a price of \$175 to increase from 50,000 at point *A* to 70,000 at point *C*.

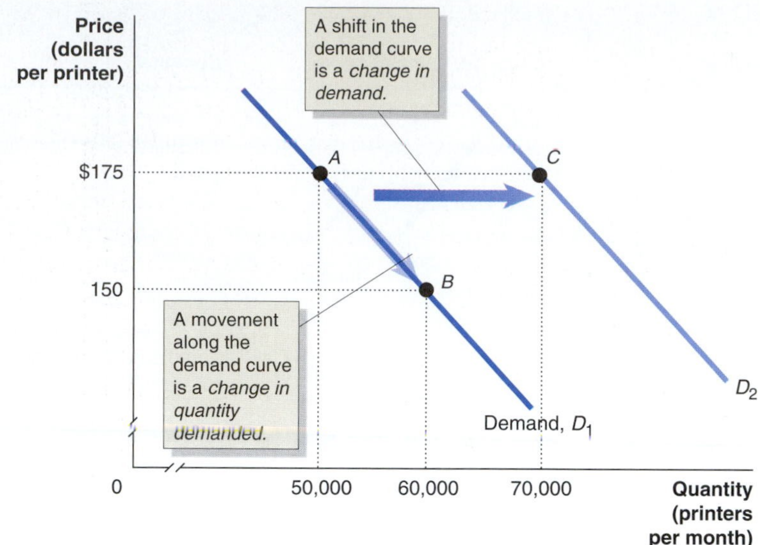

A Change in Demand versus a Change in Quantity Demanded

It is important to understand the difference between a *change in demand* and a *change in quantity demanded.* A change in demand refers to a shift of the demand curve. A shift occurs if there is a change in one of the variables, *other than the price of the product,* that affects the willingness of consumers to buy the product. A change in quantity demanded refers to a movement along the demand curve as a result of a change in the product's price. Figure 3-5 illustrates this important distinction. If the price of printers falls from \$175 to \$150, the result will be a movement along the demand curve from point *A* to point *B*—an increase in quantity demanded from 50,000 to 60,000. If consumers' incomes increase, or another factor changes that makes consumers want more of the product at every price, the demand curve will shift to the right—an increase in demand. In this case, the increase in demand from D_1 to D_2 causes the quantity of printers demanded at a price of \$175 to increase from 50,000 at point *A* to 70,000 at point *C*.

3-3 Making the Connection

Estimating the Demand for Printers at Hewlett-Packard

Conceptually, it is easy to sum up individual demand curves to construct the market demand curve, as we did in Figure 3-3(d). In practice, though, economists usually estimate market demand curves directly, without estimating individual demand curves first. The most detailed information on the relationship between price and quantity demanded can be obtained from statistically estimating demand curves. The use of statistical methods to estimate economic relationships is called *econometrics.*

Forecasters at Hewlett-Packard statistically estimate demand curves using data on the quantity of printers sold, the price of printers, advertising expenditures, and other variables that can affect sales. Because characteristics of printers change very rapidly, the forecasters specifically control for shifts of the demand curve to the right as a result of improvements to the printers being offered for sale. Throughout the 1990s, Hewlett-Packard had great success with its forecasting techniques. During the 1999 Christmas season, many companies selling products on the Internet were taken by surprise by the volume of orders they received and disappointed many customers when they couldn't fill their orders. Hewlett-Packard's forecasting system, however, allowed them to avoid this problem.

Unfortunately for Hewlett-Packard, their forecasters were less successful in 2001. During the first half of that year, the demand for printers was much lower than had been forecast and the company was stuck with large numbers of unsold printers. Two events caused the shift to the left of the demand curve for printers in the first half of 2001. The first was the surprising decline in personal computer sales for use in homes and small offices, resulting from the unexpected decisions by many families and small businesses not to upgrade their existing computers. The drop in PC sales caused a drop in printer sales, because printers are a complementary good. The second event was the U.S. economy moving into recession, lowering the incomes of many consumers and reducing the profits of many businesses. As Hewlett-Packard's experiences in 2001 show, forecasting demand can greatly aid the planning of business managers but can never be perfectly accurate.

Sources: Joel Bryant and Kim Jensen, "Forecasting Inkjet Printers at Hewlett-Packard Company," *Journal of Business Forecasting*, Summer 1994; and Scott Culbertson, Jim Burruss, and Lee Buddress, "Control System Approach to E-Commerce Fulfillment: Hewlett-Packard's Experience," *Journal of Business Forecasting*, Winter 2000–2001.

Inaccurate forecasts in 2001 caused Hewlett-Packard to produce more printers than they could sell.

The Supply Side of the Market

② LEARNING OBJECTIVE

Discuss the variables that influence supply.

Just as many variables influence the willingness and ability of consumers to buy a particular good or service, many variables also influence the willingness and ability of firms to sell a good or service. The most important of these variables is price. The amount of a good or service that a firm is willing and able to supply at a given price is the **quantity supplied.** Holding other variables constant, when the price of a good rises, producing the good is more profitable and the quantity supplied will increase. When the price of a good falls, the good is less profitable and the quantity supplied will decrease.

Quantity supplied The amount of a good or service that a firm is willing and able to supply at a given price.

Supply Schedules and Supply Curves

A **supply schedule** is a table that shows the relationship between the price of a product and the quantity of the product supplied. The table in Figure 3-6 is a supply schedule showing the quantity of printers that Hewlett-Packard would be willing to supply per month at different prices. The graph in Figure 3-6 plots the numbers from the supply schedule as a *supply curve.* A **supply curve** shows the relationship between the price of a product and the quantity of the product supplied. The supply schedule and supply curve both show that as the price of printers rises, Hewlett-Packard will increase the quantity it supplies. At a price of $150 per printer, H-P will supply 9.5 million printers. At the higher price of $175, it will supply 10 million.

Supply schedule A table that shows the relationship between the price of a product and the quantity of the product supplied.

Supply curve A curve that shows the relationship between the price of a product and the quantity of the product supplied.

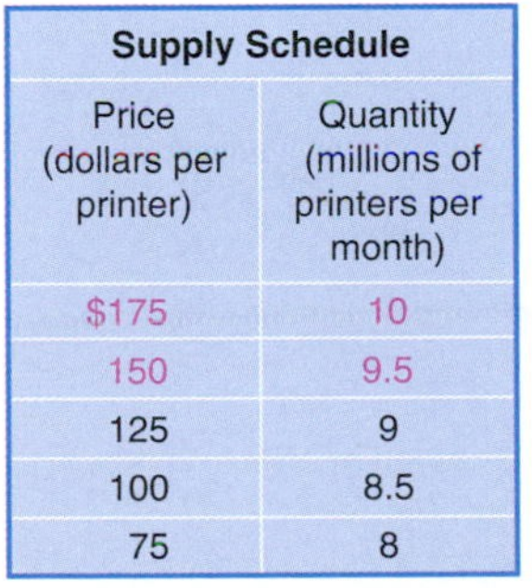

Supply Schedule	
Price (dollars per printer)	Quantity (millions of printers per month)
$175	10
150	9.5
125	9
100	8.5
75	8

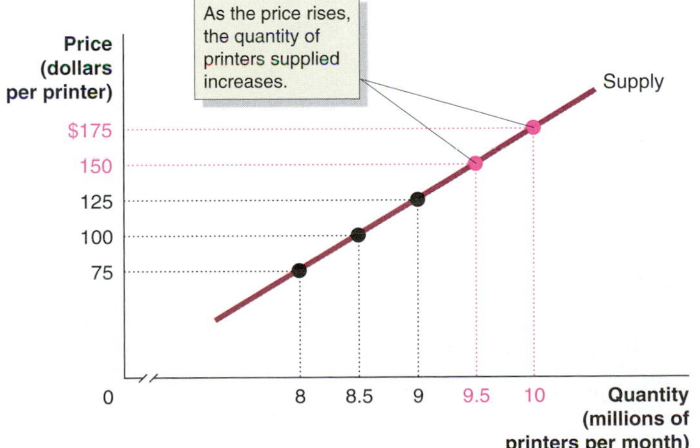

FIGURE 3-6

Hewlett-Packard's Supply Schedule and Supply Curve

As the price changes, Hewlett-Packard changes the quantity of printers it is willing to supply. We can show this as a *supply schedule* in a table, or as a *supply curve* on a graph. The supply schedule and supply curve both show that as the price of printers rises, Hewlett-Packard will increase the quantity it supplies. At a price of $150 per printer, H-P will supply 9.5 million printers. At a price of $175, it will supply 10 million.

Individual Supply and Market Supply

To construct the *market supply curve* for printers, we add the number of printers supplied at each price by each company producing printers. To keep things simple, suppose that Lexmark and Epson are the only other companies producing printers. Figure 3-7 shows that we can find the market supply curve by adding the number of printers supplied by Hewlett-Packard, Lexmark, and Epson at each price. Figure 3-7(d) at the bottom of page 75 shows the market supply curve for printers. For example, at a price of $125, Epson supplies 5 million printers, Lexmark supplies 7.5 million printers, and Hewlett-Packard supplies 9 million printers. Therefore, the quantity supplied in the market at a price of $125 is 21.5 million printers.

The Law of Supply

Law of supply Holding everything else constant, increases in price cause increases in the quantity supplied, and decreases in price cause decreases in the quantity supplied.

The market supply curve in Figure 3-7(d) is upward sloping. This pattern reflects the **law of supply**, which states that, holding everything else constant, increases in price cause increases in the quantity supplied, and decreases in price cause decreases in the quantity supplied. Notice that the definition of the law of supply—like the definition of the law of demand—contains the phrase "holding everything else constant." If only the price of the product changes, there is a movement along the supply curve, which is *an increase or decrease in the quantity supplied.* As Figure 3-8 shows, if any other variable that affects the willingness of firms to supply a good changes, the supply curve will shift, *which is an increase or decrease in supply.* When firms increase the quantity of a product they wish to sell at a given price, the supply curve shifts to the right. The shift from S_1 to S_3 represents an *increase in supply.* When firms decrease the quantity of a product they wish to sell at a given price, the supply curve shifts to the left. The shift from S_1 to S_2 represents a *decrease in supply.*

FIGURE 3-7 Deriving the Market Supply Curve from the Individual Supply Curves

The table shows that the total quantity supplied in a market is the sum of the quantities supplied by each seller. We can find the market supply curve by adding horizontally the individual supply curves. For example, at a price of $125, Epson supplies 5 million printers, Lexmark supplies 7.5 million printers, and Hewlett-Packard supplies 9 million printers. Therefore, the quantity supplied in the market at a price of $125 is 21.5 million printers.

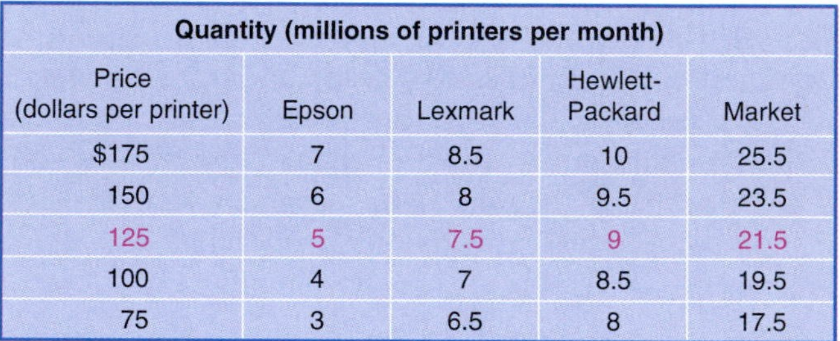

Price (dollars per printer)	Quantity (millions of printers per month)			
	Epson	Lexmark	Hewlett-Packard	Market
$175	7	8.5	10	25.5
150	6	8	9.5	23.5
125	5	7.5	9	21.5
100	4	7	8.5	19.5
75	3	6.5	8	17.5

(a) Epson's supply curve

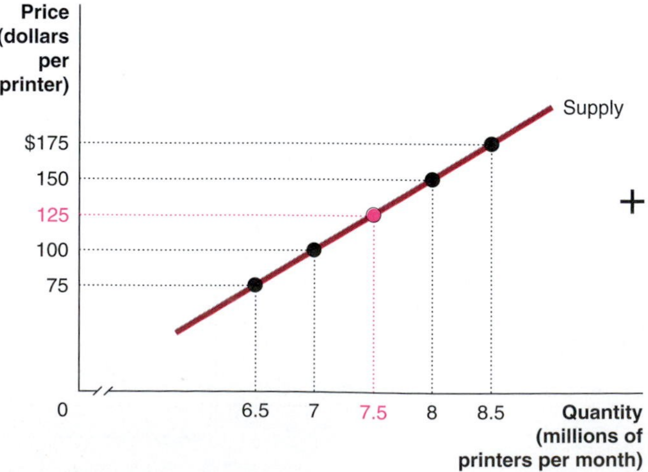

(b) Lexmark's supply curve

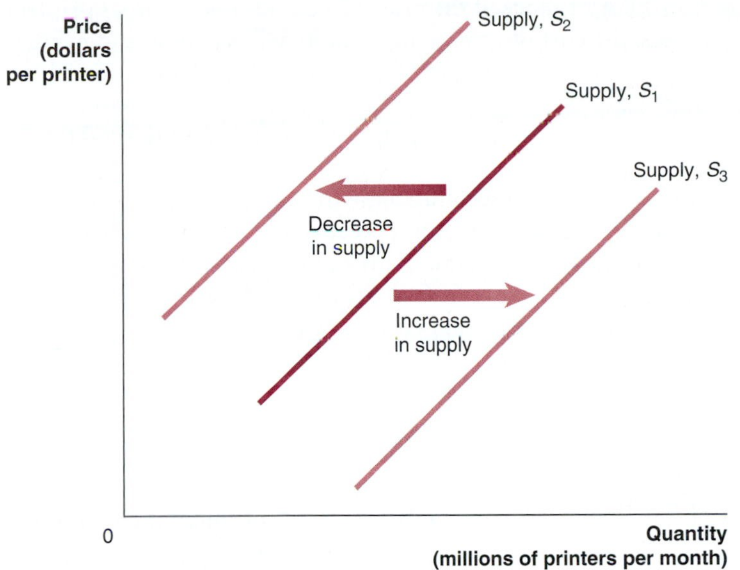

FIGURE 3-8

Shifting the Supply Curve

When firms increase the quantity of a product they wish to sell at a given price, the supply curve shifts to the right. The shift from S_1 to S_3 represents an *increase in supply.* When firms decrease the quantity of a product they wish to sell at a given price, the supply curve shifts to the left. The shift from S_1 to S_2 represents a *decrease in supply.*

Variables That Shift Supply

The following are the most important variables that shift supply:

- Prices of inputs
- Technological change
- Prices of substitutes in production
- Expected future prices
- Number of firms in the market

We can discuss how each of these variables affects the supply of printers.

PRICES OF INPUTS The factor most likely to cause the supply curve for a product to shift is a change in the price of an *input.* (An *input* is anything used in the production of

FIGURE 3-7 continued

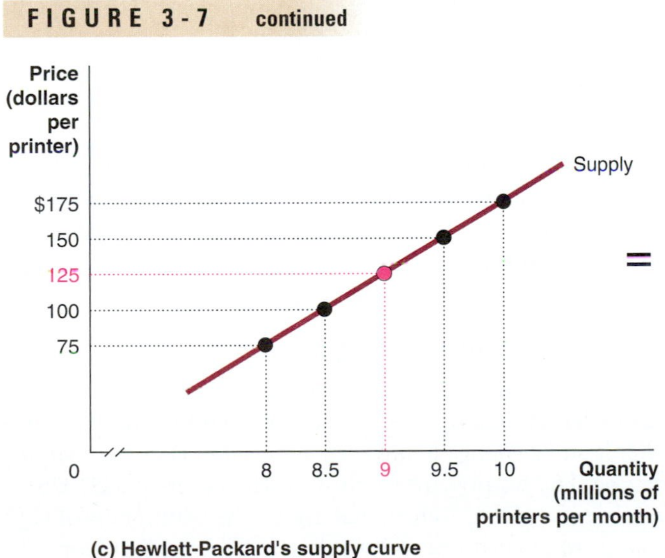

(c) Hewlett-Packard's supply curve

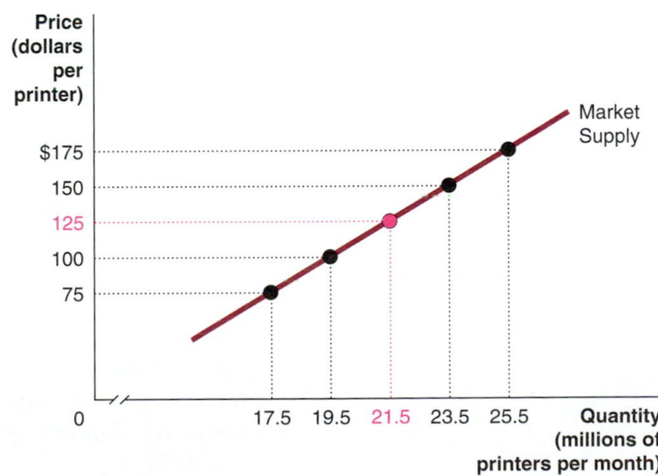

(d) Market supply curve

a good or service.) For instance, if the price of a component of laser printers, such as the laser scanner, rises, the cost of producing printers will increase and printers will be less profitable at every price. The supply of printers will decline, and the market supply curve for printers will shift to the left. Similarly, if the price of an input declines, the supply of printers will increase, and the supply curve will shift to the right.

Technological change Change in the ability of a firm to produce a given level of output with a given quantity of inputs.

TECHNOLOGICAL CHANGE A second factor that causes a change in supply is *technological change.* **Technological change** is a positive or negative change in the ability of a firm to produce a given level of output with a given quantity of inputs. Positive technological change occurs whenever a firm is able to produce more output using the same amount of inputs. This shift will happen when the *productivity* of workers or machines increases. If a firm can produce more output with the same amount of inputs, its costs will be lower and the good will be more profitable to produce at any given price. As a result, when positive technological change occurs, the firm will increase the quantity supplied at every price and its supply curve will shift to the right. Normally, we expect technological change to have a positive impact on a firm's willingness to supply a product. Negative technological change is relatively rare, although it could result from a natural disaster or a war that reduces the ability of a firm to supply as much output with a given amount of inputs. Negative technological change will raise a firm's costs, and the good will be less profitable to produce. Therefore, negative technological change causes a firm's supply curve to shift to the left.

PRICES OF SUBSTITUTES IN PRODUCTION Firms often choose which good or service they will produce. Alternative products that a firm could produce are called *substitutes in production.* For instance, if the price of color printers increases, color printers will become more profitable and Hewlett-Packard, Lexmark, and the other printer companies will shift some of their productive capacity away from black-and-white printers toward color printers. They will offer fewer black-and-white printers for sale at every price, so the supply curve for black-and-white printers will shift to the left.

EXPECTED FUTURE PRICES If a firm expects that the price of its product will be higher in the future than it is today, it has an incentive to decrease supply now and increase it in the future. For instance, if Hewlett-Packard believes that printer prices are temporarily low–perhaps because of a price war among firms making printers—it may store some of its production today to sell tomorrow when it expects prices will be higher.

NUMBER OF FIRMS IN THE MARKET Finally, a change in the number of firms in the market will change supply. When new firms *enter* a market, the supply curve shifts to the right, and when existing firms leave, or *exit,* a market, the supply curve shifts to the left. For instance, when Xerox decided that it would no longer produce printers for home use, the market supply curve shifted to the left.

Table 3-2 summarizes the most important variables that cause market supply curves to shift. You should note that the table shows the shift in the supply curve that results from an *increase* in each of the variables. A *decrease* in these variables would cause the supply curve to shift in the opposite direction.

A Change in Supply versus a Change in Quantity Supplied

We noted earlier that it is important to understand the difference between a change in demand and a change in quantity demanded. It is also important to understand the difference between a *change in supply* and a *change in quantity supplied.* A change in supply refers to a shift of the supply curve. The supply curve will shift when there is a change in one of the variables, *other than the price of the product,* that affects the willingness of suppliers to sell the product. A change in quantity supplied refers to a movement along the

TABLE 3-2

Variables That Shift Market Supply Curves

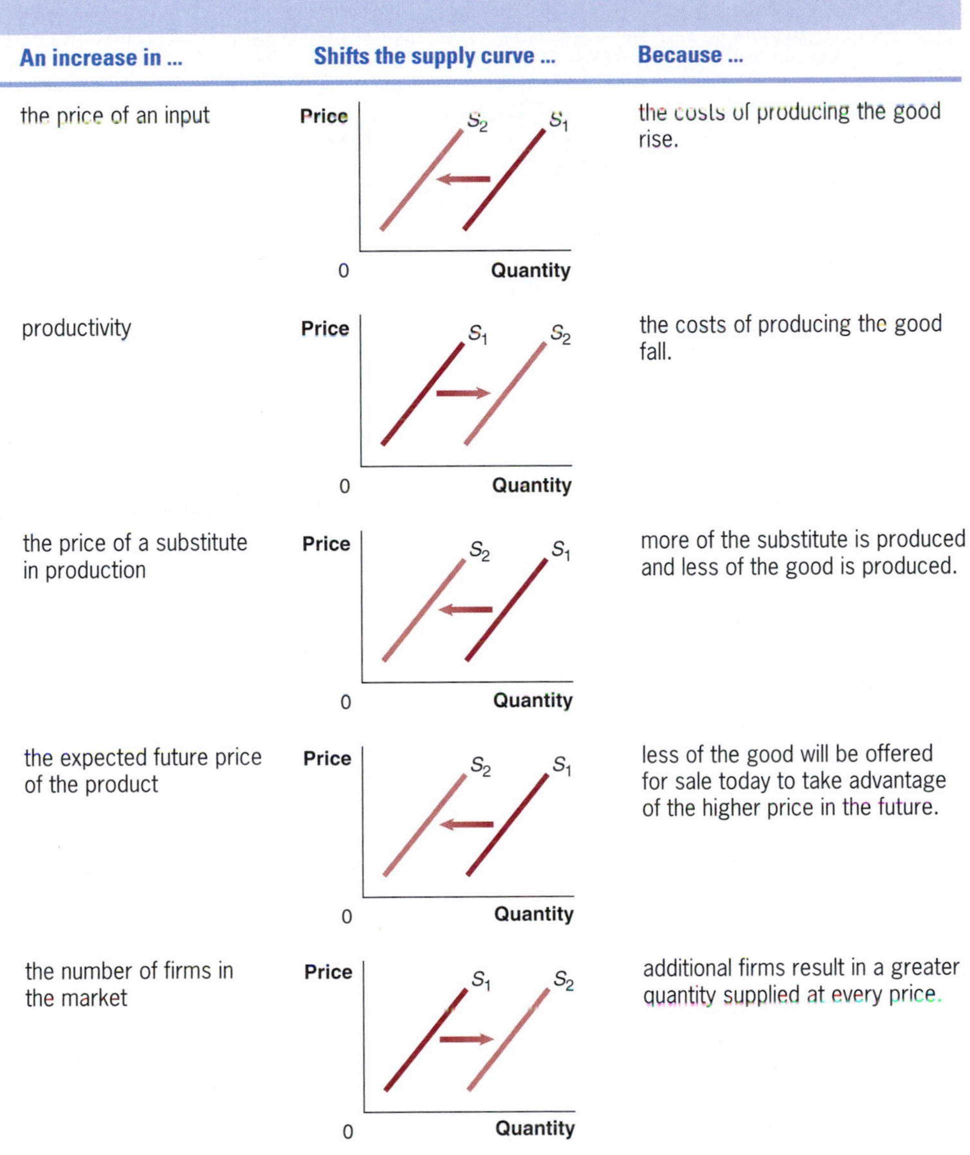

An increase in ...	Shifts the supply curve ...	Because ...
the price of an input	Price, S_2, S_1, 0, Quantity	the costs of producing the good rise.
productivity	Price, S_1, S_2, 0, Quantity	the costs of producing the good fall.
the price of a substitute in production	Price, S_2, S_1, 0, Quantity	more of the substitute is produced and less of the good is produced.
the expected future price of the product	Price, S_2, S_1, 0, Quantity	less of the good will be offered for sale today to take advantage of the higher price in the future.
the number of firms in the market	Price, S_1, S_2, 0, Quantity	additional firms result in a greater quantity supplied at every price.

supply curve as a result of a change in the product's price. Figure 3-9 illustrates this important distinction. If the price of printers rises from \$125 to \$150, the result will be a movement up the supply curve from point *A* to point *B*—an increase in quantity supplied from 21.5 million to 23.5 million. If the price of an input decreases or another factor makes sellers supply more of the product at every price change, the supply curve will shift to the right—an increase in supply. In this case, the increase in supply from S_1 to S_2 causes the quantity of printers supplied at a price of \$150 to increase from 23.5 million at point *B* to 27.0 million at point *C*.

Market Equilibrium: Putting Demand and Supply Together

③ **LEARNING OBJECTIVE**

Use a graph to illustrate market equilibrium.

The purpose of markets is to bring buyers and sellers together. As we saw in Chapter 2, instead of being chaotic and disorderly, the interaction of buyers and sellers in markets ultimately results in firms being led to produce those goods and services most desired by consumers. To understand how this process happens, we first need to see how markets manage to reconcile the plans of buyers and sellers.

FIGURE 3-9

A Change in Supply versus a Change in the Quantity Supplied

If the price of printers rises from $125 to $150, the result will be a movement up the supply curve from point *A* to point *B*—an increase in quantity supplied from 21.5 million to 23.5 million. If the price of an input decreases or another factor changes that makes sellers supply more of the product at every price, the supply curve will shift to the right—an increase in supply. In this case, the increase in supply from S_1 to S_2 causes the quantity of printers supplied at a price of $150 to increase from 23.5 million at point *B* to 27.0 million at point *C*.

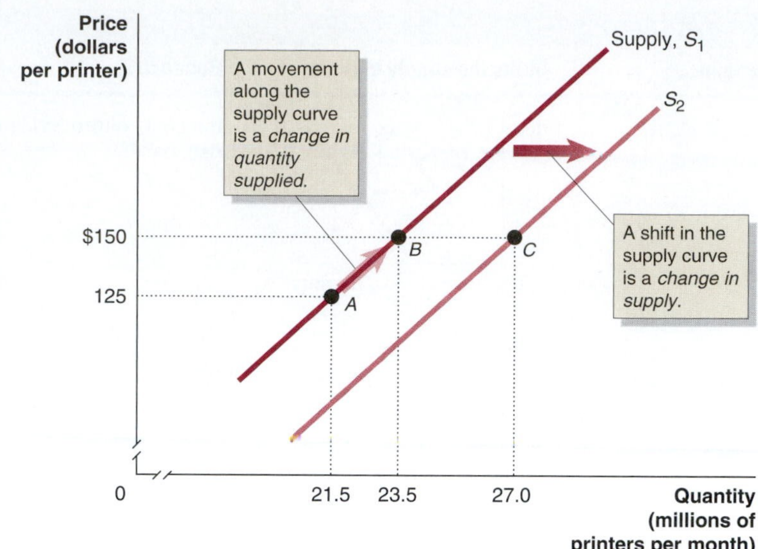

Market equilibrium A situation in which quantity demanded equals quantity supplied.

Competitive market equilibrium A market equilibrium with many buyers and many sellers.

In Figure 3-10, we bring together the market demand curve for printers and the market supply curve. Notice that the demand curve crosses the supply curve at only one point. This point represents a price of $100 and a quantity of 19.5 million printers. Only at this point is the quantity of printers consumers are willing to buy equal to the quantity of printers firms are willing to sell. This is the point of **market equilibrium.** Only at market equilibrium will the quantity demanded equal the quantity supplied. In this case, the *equilibrium price* is $100 and the *equilibrium quantity* is 19.5 million. Markets that have many buyers and many sellers are *competitive markets,* and equilibrium in these markets is a **competitive market equilibrium.**

How Markets Eliminate Surpluses and Shortages

A market that is not in equilibrium moves toward equilibrium. Once a market is in equilibrium, it remains in equilibrium. To see why, consider what happens if a market is not

FIGURE 3-10

Market Equilibrium

Where the demand curve crosses the supply curve determines market equilibrium. In this case, the demand curve for printers crosses the supply curve at a price of $100 and a quantity of 19.5 million. Only at this point is the quantity of printers consumers are willing to buy equal to the quantity of printers firms are willing to sell: The quantity demanded is equal to the quantity supplied.

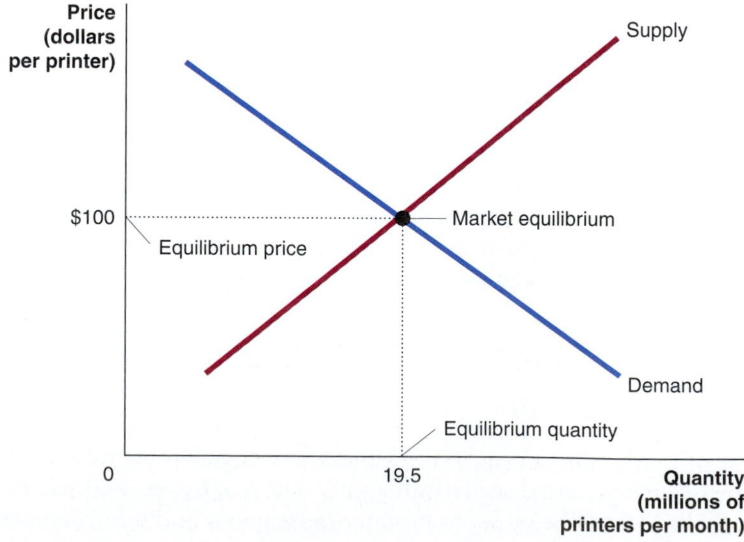

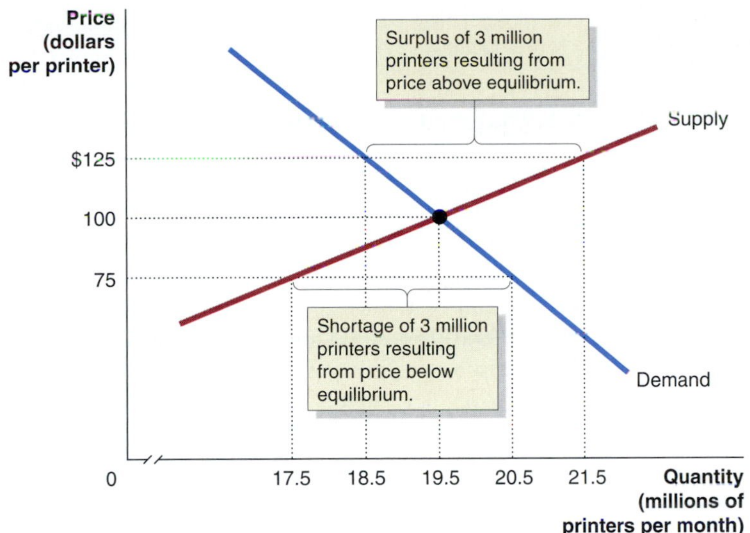

FIGURE 3-11

The Effect of Surpluses and Shortages on the Market Price

When the market price is above equilibrium, there will be a *surplus*. In the figure, a price of $125 for printers results in 21.5 million being supplied, but only 18.5 million being demanded, or a surplus of 3 million. As firms cut the price to dispose of the surplus, the price will fall to the equilibrium of $100. When the market price is below equilibrium, there will be a *shortage*. A price of $75 results in 20.5 million printers being demanded, but only 17.5 million being supplied, or a shortage of 3 million. As consumers who are unable to buy a printer offer to pay higher prices, the price will rise to the equilibrium of $100.

in equilibrium. For instance, suppose that the price in the printer market was $125, rather than the equilibrium price of $100. As Figure 3-11 shows, at a price of $125, the quantity of printers supplied would be 21.5 million and the quantity of printers demanded would be 18.5 million. When the quantity supplied is greater than the quantity demanded, there is a **surplus** in the market. In this case, the surplus is equal to 3 million printers (21.5 million − 18.5 million = 3 million). When there is a surplus, firms have unsold goods piling up, which gives them an incentive to increase their sales by cutting the price. Cutting the price will simultaneously increase the quantity demanded and decrease the quantity supplied. This adjustment will reduce the surplus, but as long as the price is above $100, there will be a surplus and downward pressure on the price will continue. Only when the price has fallen to $100 will the market be in equilibrium.

Surplus A situation in which the quantity supplied is greater than the quantity demanded.

If, however, the price were $75, the quantity supplied would be 17.5 million and the quantity demanded would be 20.5 million, as shown in Figure 3-11. When the quantity demanded is greater than the quantity supplied, there is a **shortage** in the market. In this case, the shortage is equal to 3 million printers (20.5 million − 17.5 million = 3 million). When a shortage occurs, some consumers will be unable to obtain the product and will have an incentive to offer to buy the product at a higher price. A higher price will simultaneously increase the quantity supplied and decrease the quantity demanded. This adjustment will reduce the shortage, but as long as the price is below $100, there will be a shortage and upward pressure on the price will continue. Only when the price has risen to $100 will the market be in equilibrium.

Shortage A situation in which the quantity demanded is greater than the quantity supplied.

At a competitive market equilibrium, all consumers willing to pay the market price will be able to buy as much of the product as they want, and all firms willing to accept the market price will be able to sell as much of the product as they want. As a result, there will be no reason for the price to change unless either the demand curve or the supply curve shifts.

Demand and Supply Both Count

Always keep in mind that it is the interaction of demand and supply that determines the equilibrium price. Neither consumers nor firms can dictate what the equilibrium price will be. No firm can sell anything at any price unless it can find a willing buyer, and no consumer can buy anything at any price without finding a willing seller.

SOLVED PROBLEM 3-1

③ **LEARNING OBJECTIVE**

Use a graph to illustrate market equilibrium.

Demand and Supply Both Count: A Tale of Two Letters–

Which letter is likely to be worth more: one written by Abraham Lincoln or one written by his assassin, John Wilkes Booth? Lincoln is one of the greatest presidents, and many people collect anything written by him. The demand for letters written by Lincoln surely would seem to be much greater than the demand for letters written by Booth. Yet when R. M. Smythe and Co. auctioned off on the same day a letter written by Lincoln and a letter written by Booth, the Booth letter sold for $31,050 and the Lincoln letter sold for only $21,850. Use a demand and supply graph to explain how the Booth letter has a higher market price than the Lincoln letter, even though the demand for letters written by Lincoln is greater than the demand for letters written by Booth.

Solving the Problem:

Step 1: Review the chapter material. This problem is about prices being determined at market equilibrium, so you may want to review the section "Market Equilibrium: Putting Demand and Supply Together," which begins on page 77.

Step 2: Draw demand curves that illustrate the greater demand for Lincoln's letters. Begin by drawing two demand curves. Label one "Demand for Lincoln's letters" and the other "Demand for Booth's letters." Make sure that the Lincoln demand curve is much farther to the right than the Booth demand curve.

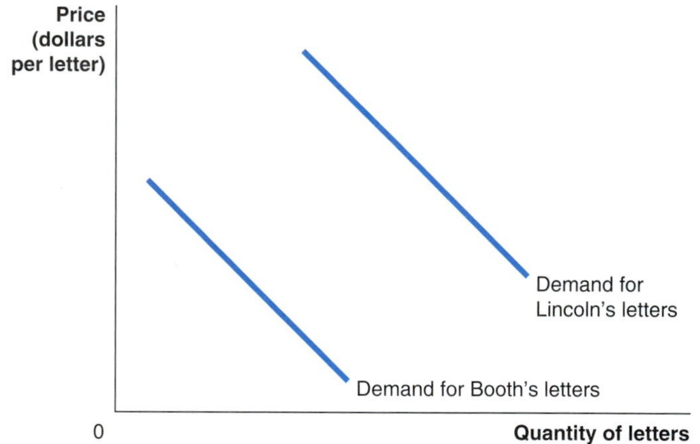

Step 3: Draw supply curves that illustrate the equilibrium price of Booth's letters being higher than the equilibrium price of Lincoln's letters. Based on the demand curves you have just drawn, think about how it might be possible for the market price of Lincoln's letters to be lower than the market price of Booth's letters. The only way this can be true is if the supply of Lincoln's letters is much greater than the supply of Booth's letters. Draw on your graph a supply curve for Lincoln's letters and a supply curve for Booth's letters that will result in an equilibrium price of Booth's letters of $31,050 and an equilibrium price of Lincoln letters of $21,850. You have now solved the problem.

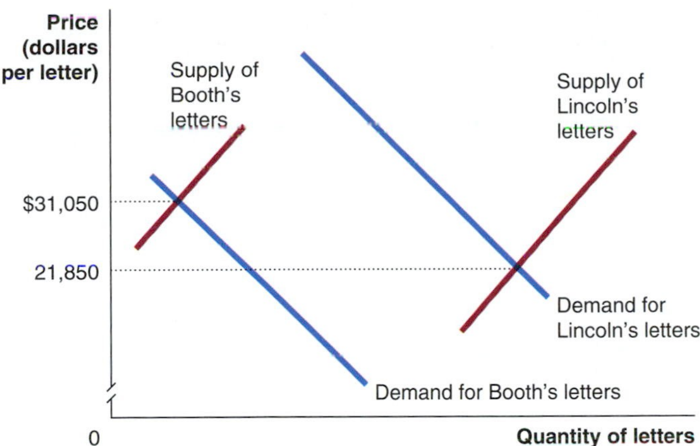

Extra Credit: The explanation for this puzzle is that both demand and supply count when determining market price. The demand for Lincoln's letters is much greater than the demand for Booth's letters, but the supply of Booth's letters is very small. Historians believe that only eight letters written by Booth exist today. (Note that the supply curves for letters written by Booth and by Lincoln slope up even though only a fixed number of each of these types of letters is available and, obviously, no more can be produced. The upward slope of the supply curves occurs because the higher the price, the larger the quantity of letters that will be offered for sale by people who currently own them.)

YOUR TURN: **For more practice, do related problem 9 on page 92 at the end of this chapter.**

The Effect of Demand and Supply Shifts on Equilibrium

④ **LEARNING OBJECTIVE**

Use demand and supply graphs to predict changes in prices and quantities.

We have seen that the interaction of demand and supply in markets determines the quantity of a good that is produced and the price at which it sells. We have also seen that several variables cause demand curves to shift, and other variables cause supply curves to shift. As a result, demand and supply curves in most markets are constantly shifting, and the prices and quantities that represent equilibrium are constantly changing. In this section, we see how shifts in demand and supply curves affect equilibrium price and quantity.

The Effect of Shifts in Supply on Equilibrium

When Xerox decided to stop producing printers for the home market, the market supply curve for printers shifted to the left. Figure 3-12 shows the supply curve shifting from S_1 to S_2. This caused a shortage of printers at the original equilibrium price, P_1. The shortage was eliminated as the equilibrium price of printers rose to P_2, and the equilibrium quantity fell from Q_1 to Q_2. If new firms enter the printer market, the supply curve will shift to the right, causing the equilibrium price to fall and the equilibrium quantity to rise.

FIGURE 3-12

The Effect of a Decrease in Supply on Equilibrium

If a firm exits a market, as Xerox did from the market for home printers, the equilibrium price will rise and the equilibrium quantity will fall.

1. As Xerox exits the market for printers, a smaller quantity of printers will be supplied at every price, so the market supply curve shifts to the left from S_1 to S_2, which causes a shortage of printers at the original price, P_1.
2. The equilibrium price rises from P_1 to P_2.
3. The equilibrium quantity falls from Q_1 to Q_2.

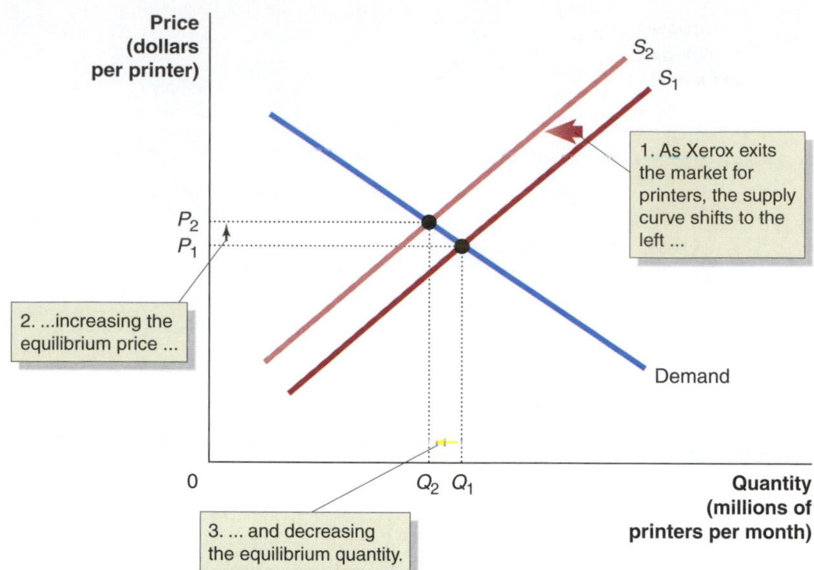

3-4 Making the Connection

The Falling Price of Large Flat-Screen Televisions

Research on flat-screen televisions using liquid crystal displays (LCDs) began in the 1960s. However, it was surprisingly difficult to use this research to produce a television priced low enough for many consumers to purchase. One researcher noted, "In the 1960s, we used to say 'In ten years, we're going to have the TV on the wall.' We said the same thing in the seventies and then in the eighties." A key technical problem in manufacturing LCD televisions was making glass sheets large enough, thin enough, and clean enough to be used as LCD screens. Finally, in 1999, Corning, Inc., developed a process to manufacture glass less than 1 millimeter thick that was very clean because it was produced without being touched by machinery.

Corning's breakthrough led to what the *Wall Street Journal* described as a "race to build new, better factories." The firms producing the flat screens are all located in Taiwan, South Korea, and Japan. The leading firms are Korea's Samsung Electronics and LG Phillips LCD, Taiwan's AU Optronics, and Japan's Sharp Corporation. In 2004, AU Optronics opened a new factory with 2.4 million square feet of clean room in which the LCD screens are manufactured. This factory is nearly five times as large as the largest factory in which Intel makes computer chips. In all, 10 new factories manufacturing LCD screens were scheduled to come into operation between late 2004 and late 2005. The figure shows that this increase in supply was expected to drive the

Corning's breakthrough spurred the manufacture of LCD televisions in Taiwan, South Korea, and Japan, and an eventual decline in price.

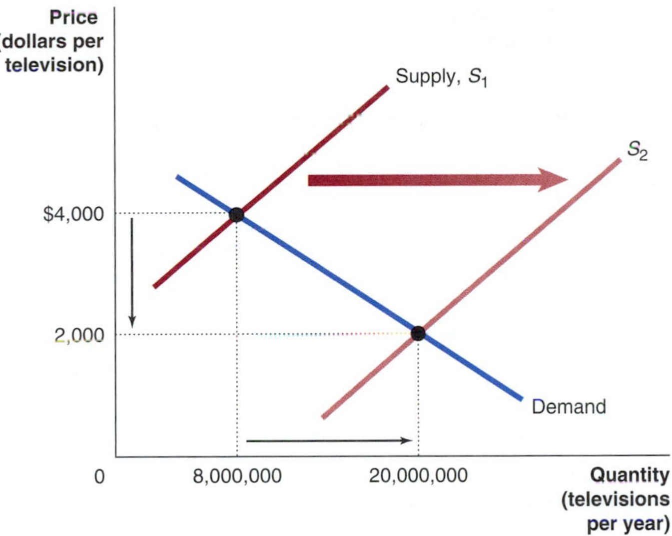

price of a typical large LCD television from $4,000 in the fall of 2004 to $2,000 in 2006, increasing the quantity demanded worldwide from 8,000,000 to 20,000,000.

Sources: Evan Ramstad, "Big Display: Once a Footnote, Flat Screens Grow into Huge Industry," *Wall Street Journal*, August 30, 2004, p. A1; and Michael Schuman, "Flat Chance: Prices on Cool TVs Are Dropping as New Factories Come on Line," *Time*, October 18, 2004, pp. 64–66.

The Effect of Shifts in Demand on Equilibrium

When population growth and income growth occur, the market demand for printers shifts to the right. Figure 3-13 shows the effect of a demand curve shifting to the right from D_1 to D_2. This shift causes a shortage at the original equilibrium price, P_1. To eliminate the shortage, the equilibrium price rises to P_2, and the equilibrium quantity rises from Q_1 to Q_2. However, if the price of a complementary good, such as personal computers, were to rise, the demand for printers would decrease. This change would cause the demand curve for printers to shift to the left, and the equilibrium price and quantity would both decrease.

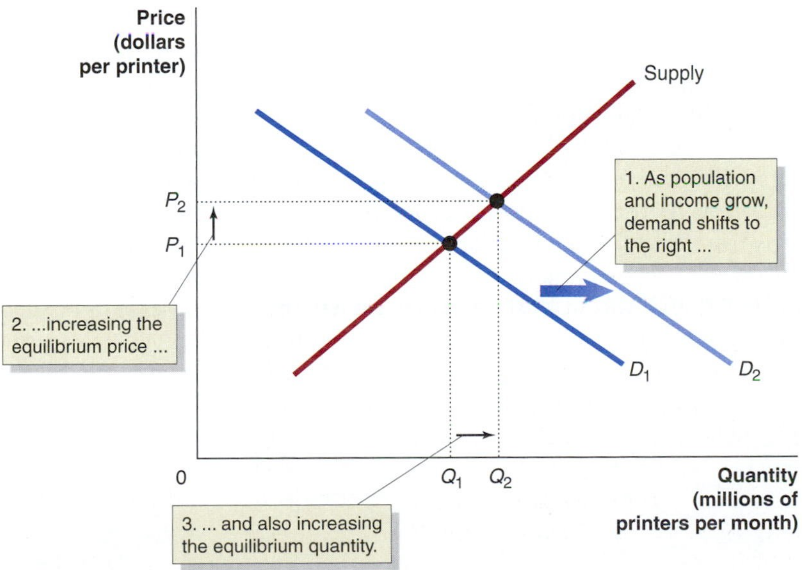

FIGURE 3-13

The Effect of an Increase in Demand on Equilibrium

Increases in income and population will cause the equilibrium price and quantity to rise.

1. As population and income grow, the quantity demanded increases at every price, and the market demand curve shifts to the right from D_1 to D_2, which causes a shortage of printers at the original price, P_1.
2. The equilibrium price rises from P_1 to P_2.
3. The equilibrium quantity rises from Q_1 to Q_2.

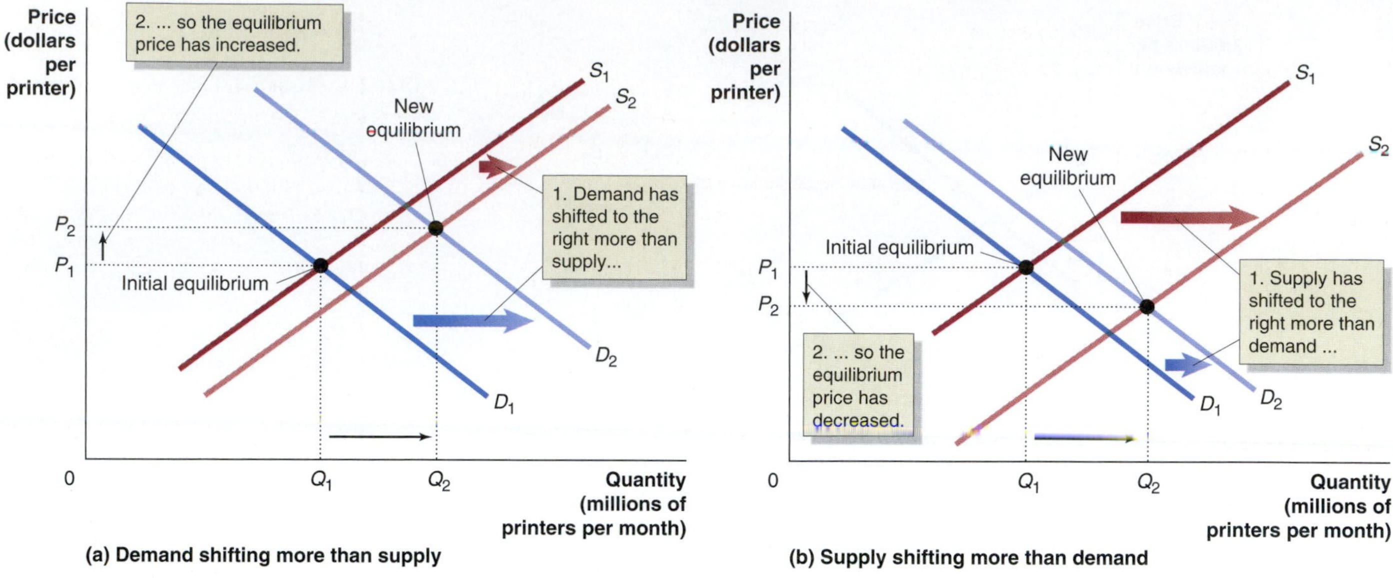

FIGURE 3-14 Shifts in Demand and Supply over Time

Whether the price of a product rises or falls over time depends on whether or not demand shifts to the right more than supply.

In panel (a), demand shifts to the right more than supply and the equilibrium price rises.

1. Demand shifts to the right more than supply.
2. Equilibrium price rises from P_1 to P_2.

In panel (b), supply shifts to the right more than demand and the equilibrium price falls.

1. Supply shifts to the right more than demand.
2. Equilibrium price falls from P_1 to P_2.

The Effect of Shifts in Demand and Supply over Time

Whenever only demand or only supply shifts, we can easily predict the effect on equilibrium price and quantity. But what happens if *both* curves shift? For instance, in many markets, the demand curve shifts to the right over time, as population and income grow. The supply curve also often shifts to the right as new firms enter the market and positive technological change occurs. Whether the equilibrium price in a market rises or falls over time usually depends on whether demand shifts to the right more than does supply. Panel (a) of Figure 3-14 shows that when demand shifts to the right more than supply, the equilibrium price rises. But, as panel (b) shows, when supply shifts to the right more than demand, the equilibrium price falls.

For instance, during the 1990s the demand for chicken increased rapidly, as many consumers attempted to avoid the potential health problems associated with eating too much red meat. At the same time, according to a U.S. Department of Agriculture report, positive technological change occurred in the "feed, hatchery, processing, and breeding stages" of producing chickens. Whether the retail price of chicken would be higher in 2000 than it was in 1991 depended on whether the increase in the demand for chicken was greater or smaller than the increase in the supply. Figure 3-15 shows that, in fact, demand shifted farther to the right than did supply, and the retail price of chicken rose from an average of \$0.88 per pound in 1991 to an average of \$1.07 per pound in 2000.

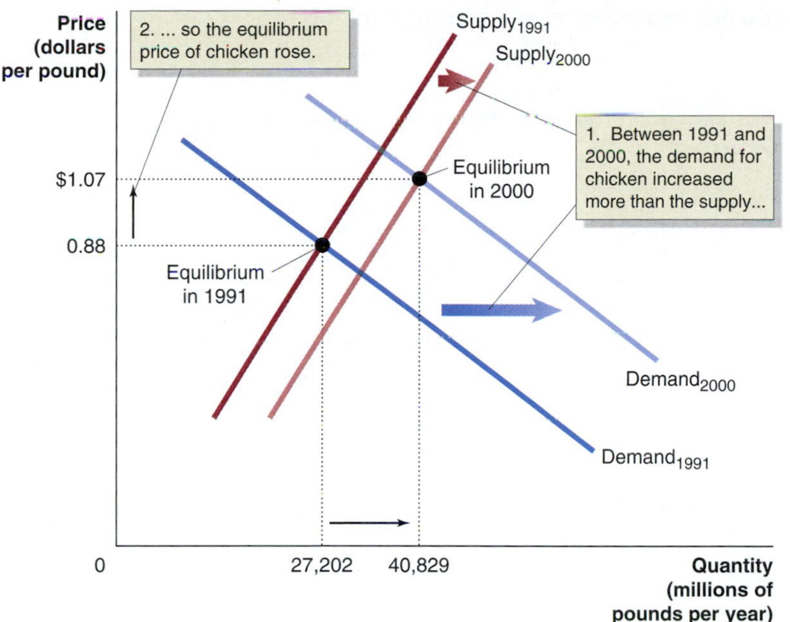

FIGURE 3-15

The Demand for Chicken Has Increased More Than the Supply

The supply of chicken increased rapidly during the 1990s, but the demand increased even faster. The result was that the equilibrium price of chicken rose. (The prices have been adjusted for the effects of inflation.)

1. Between 1991 and 2000, the demand for chicken shifted to the right more than supply.
2. The equilibrium price of chicken rose from $0.88 per pound in 1991 to $1.07 per pound in 2000.

SOLVED PROBLEM 3-2

High Demand and Low Prices in the Lobster Market?

④ **LEARNING OBJECTIVE**

Use demand and supply graphs to predict changes in prices and quantities.

During the spring when demand for lobster is relatively low, Maine lobster fishermen are able to sell their lobster catches for about $4.50 per pound. During the summer when demand for lobster is much higher, Maine lobster fishermen are able to sell their lobster catches for only about $3.00 per pound. It may seem strange that the market price is higher when demand is low than when demand is high. Can you resolve this paradox with the help of a demand and supply graph?

Solving the Problem:

Step 1: Review the chapter material. This problem is about how shifts in demand and supply curves affect the equilibrium price, so you may want to review the section "The Effects of Shifts in Demand and Supply over Time," which begins on page 84.

Step 2: Draw the demand and supply graph. Draw a demand and supply graph, showing the market equilibrium in the spring. Label the equilibrium price $4.50. Label both the demand and supply curves "spring."

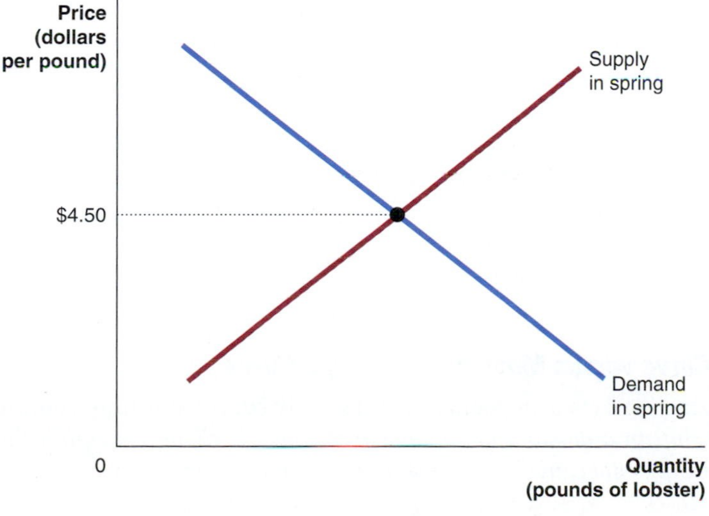

Step 3: Add a demand curve for summer to your graph.

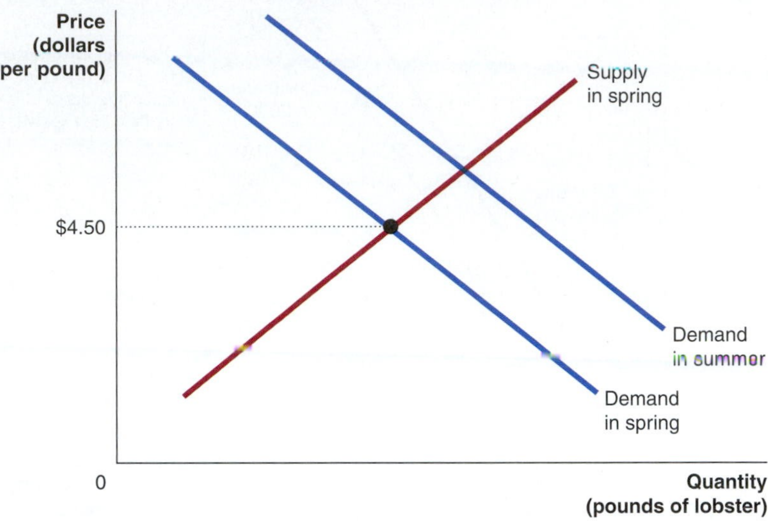

Step 4: Explain the graph. After studying the graph, it is possible to see how the equilibrium price can fall from $4.50 to $3.00 despite the increase in demand: The supply curve must have shifted to the right by enough so that the new equilibrium price is $3.00. Draw in this new supply curve, label it "summer," and label the new equilibrium price $3.00. The demand for lobster does increase in summer compared with the spring. But the increase in the supply of lobster between spring and summer is even greater. So, the equilibrium price falls.

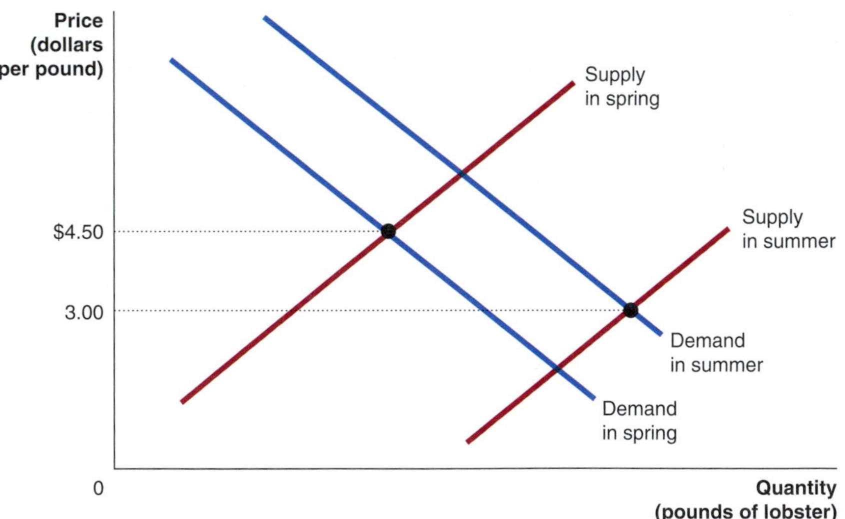

Source: Carey Goldberg, "Down East, the Lobster Hauls Are Up Big," *New York Times*, May 31, 2001.

YOUR TURN: **For more practice, do related problem 13 on page 92 at the end of this chapter.**

Shifts in a Curve versus Movements along a Curve

When analyzing markets using demand and supply curves, it is important to remember that *when a shift in a demand or supply curve causes a change in equilibrium price, the change in price does not cause a further shift in demand or supply.* For instance, suppose an

Don't Let This Happen To You!

Remember: A Change in a Good's Price Does *Not* Cause the Demand or Supply Curve to Shift.

Suppose a student is asked to draw a demand and supply graph to illustrate how an increase in the price of oranges would affect the market for apples, other things being constant. He draws the graph below and explains it as follows: "Because apples and oranges are substitutes, an increase in the price of oranges will cause an initial shift to the right in the demand curve for apples from D_1 to D_2. However, because this initial shift in the demand curve for apples results in a higher price for apples, P_2, consumers will find apples less desirable and the demand curve will shift to the left from D_2 to D_3, resulting in a final equilibrium price of P_3." Do you agree or disagree with the student's analysis?

You should disagree. The student has correctly understood that an increase in the price of oranges will cause the demand curve for apples to shift to the right. But the second demand curve shift the student describes, from D_2 to D_3, will not take place. Changes in the price of a product do not result in shifts in the product's demand curve. Changes in the price of a product result only in movements along a demand curve.

***YOUR TURN:* Test your understanding by doing related problems 6 and 23 on pages 91 and 94 at the end of this chapter.**

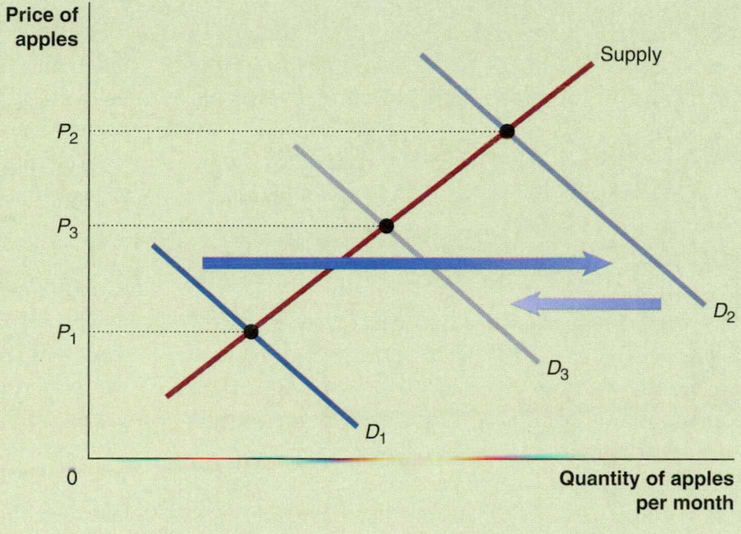

increase in supply causes the price of a good to fall, while everything else that affects the willingness of consumers to buy the good is constant. The result will be an increase in the quantity demanded, but not an increase in demand. For demand to increase, the whole curve must shift. The point is the same for supply: If the price of the good falls, but everything else that affects the willingness of sellers to supply the good is constant, the quantity supplied decreases but not the supply. For supply to decrease, the whole curve must shift.

Conclusion

The interaction of demand and supply determines market equilibrium. When many buyers and many sellers participate in the market, the result is a competitive market equilibrium. In a competitive market equilibrium, all consumers willing to pay the market price will be able to buy as much of the good as they want, and all firms willing to accept the market price will be able to sell as much of the product as they want. The model of demand and supply provides us with a powerful tool for predicting how changes in the actions of consumers and firms will cause changes in equilibrium prices and quantities. We will use the model of demand and supply in the next chapter to evaluate consumer surplus, producer surplus, price floors, and price ceilings. Before moving on, read *An Inside Look* on the next page to learn about H-P's strategy for competing with Dell.

An Inside Look Hewlett-Packard Cuts PC Prices to Sell More Printers

WALL STREET JOURNAL, MAY 12, 2004

Picking a Big Fight with Dell, H-P Cuts PC Profits Razor-Thin

In the past decade, Dell Inc. has surpassed International Business Machines Corp., Gateway Inc., and Compaq Computer Corp., riding direct sales and ruthless efficiency to become the world's largest seller of personal computers.

Two years ago, Hewlett-Packard Co. looked like the next victim. Instead, H-P is fighting back, briefly overtaking Dell in PC sales late last year, and drawing Dell into a bloody war of attrition in which consumers are the big winners.

a H-P's radical strategy for challenging Dell: selling PCs without worrying about profit.

"We think the PC business is strategic," says Chief Executive Carly Fiorina. She says she is willing to allow the company's $22 billion computer division to do little more than break even because PC sales help H-P make money on printers, consulting and consumer electronics. . . .

The result is the biggest threat yet to Dell, the PC industry's most profitable company. Having acquired Compaq in 2002, H-P is using its size to slash prices, in an attempt to undercut Dell's formula for gleaning profits in one of the nation's most competitive markets.

Still, for H-P, the strategy is a serious gamble. By cutting prices, the company earns less on each sale, leaving it with less of a cushion to absorb the inevitable shocks that roil competitive markets. H-P's profit margins in its PC division haven't exceeded 1% since the merger.

Dell continues to post solid profits; its operating profit margins of more than 8% are the widest in the industry. But its executives are complaining that H-P is subsidizing its PC business with earnings from other divisions, which to some suggests Dell is beginning to feel H-P's heat.

b The subsidies impair "the economics of the overall industry," adds Michael S. Dell, the company's founder and chairman. "It's not a healthy process."

It is healthy for customers. Personal-computer prices industry-wide fell by 9% during the first three quarters of 2003, according to Dell, compared with 4.5% a year earlier. Laptop prices fell even faster.

Corporate customers are exploiting the competition. Late last year, Getty Images, the Seattle photo distributor, asked H-P and Dell to compete for a sale of 500 desktop computers and 165 laptops. Kenneth Stringer, Getty's vice president of technical operations, specified how much he expected to pay for each computer.

"They both said, 'OK, we're ready to go there,' " Mr. Stringer says. But then H-P offered free advice for improving Getty's disaster-recovery plan and creating a digital archive of more than 70,000 film clips.

With $73 billion in annual sales, H-P offers a broader line of goods and services than Dell, with $41 billion in sales. And H-P isn't shy about tapping other parts of its empire to help sell PCs. Its credit arm offers generous financing terms. The consulting unit advises customers on how to save money on their technology operations . . .

c Only a few years ago . . . neither H-P nor Compaq could match Dell's mastery of the computer industry's central dynamic: falling prices. Most PCs are assembled from standard parts that all manufacturers buy at similar prices. Technological advances continually shrink the cost of disk drives, display screens and computer chips. . . .

Beginning in the mid-1990s, Dell turned this to its advantage. It flourished by building computers to order and selling them directly to consumers and businesses over the telephone and the Internet. Dell PCs are built only after a sale is made, with components procured at the cheapest prices available . . .

As Dell was thriving, executives from H-P and Compaq mapped out plans to take the company on, even before H-P's $19 billion acquisition of Compaq became final.

The team made plans to stop losing money in the soon-to-be-combined PC units of the two companies, agreeing to cut costs and close weak businesses as soon as the deal closed in May 2002.

Within months, H-P had shaved an average of $26 from the cost of building a PC, compared with Compaq's pre-merger costs, according to an H-P executive.

The result: H-P cut losses in the PC unit by roughly two-thirds in the fiscal year ended October 2002. . . .

In the fourth quarter of last year, H-P sold more computers than Dell . . .

But the victory would soon be reversed, as Dell retook the lead in the first quarter of 2004. . . .

Key Points in the Article

The article discusses the rivalry between Dell and Hewlett-Packard. Hewlett-Packard is willing to sell PCs for a little or no profit, because selling PCs increases demand for complementary products, such as printers. The article also notes that personal computer prices fell during 2003, as they have every year since 1981. These price declines result from positive technological change that reduces the cost of making PCs, and shifts the market supply curve to the right.

Analyzing the News

a Hewlett-Packard management sees PCs playing a strategic role in their plan to maximize profits for Hewlett-Packard as a whole. Printers, consulting provided to firms purchasing PCs, and consumer electronics are all complementary goods to PCs. We can use the economic model of demand and supply developed in this chapter to analyze this strategy.

Because PCs and printers are complementary goods, a decrease in the price of PCs will cause an increase in the demand for printers. This pattern is shown in Figure 1, where the demand curve for printers shifts from D_1 to D_2. This causes a shortage of printers at the original price, P_1. To eliminate the shortage, the equilibrium price increases from P_1 to P_2, and the equilibrium quantity increases from Q_1 to Q_2.

b Hewlett-Packard's strategy of increasing printer sales by reducing PC prices has no guarantee of success. Because Dell's own profits are made primarily from selling PCs, rather than related products, it is unlikely to pursue a strategy similar to H-P's. When Michael Dell complains that H-P's strategy is hurting "the economics of the overall industry," he means that the low prices H-P is charging for PCs hurts the profits of all PC makers. In fact, as discussed in the opener to this chapter, one of the reasons that Carly Fiorina was ousted as chief executive officer in 2005 was that H-P's board of directors became dissatisfied with the inability of the firm to earn significant profits from selling personal computers.

c Positive technological change reduces the cost of making PCs. The article notes that: "Technological advances continually shrink the cost of disk drives, display screens and computer chips." Reductions in cost make PCs more profitable to produce at every price. This causes the supply of PCs to increase, or shift to the right. This pattern is shown in Figure 2, where the supply curve for PCs shifts from S_1 to S_2. This causes a surplus of PCs at the original price, P_1. To eliminate the surplus, the equilibrium price decreases from P_1 to P_2, and the equilibrium quantity increases from Q_1 to Q_2.

Thinking Critically

1. Suppose Dell Inc., IBM, and *Gateway* Inc., simply refused to cut their prices as a result of Hewlett-Packard's strategy. What would happen to the quantity of computers sold by these companies?
2. Further suppose that one manufacturer's computers were not particularly good substitutes for another's. How would that affect your answer to the previous question?

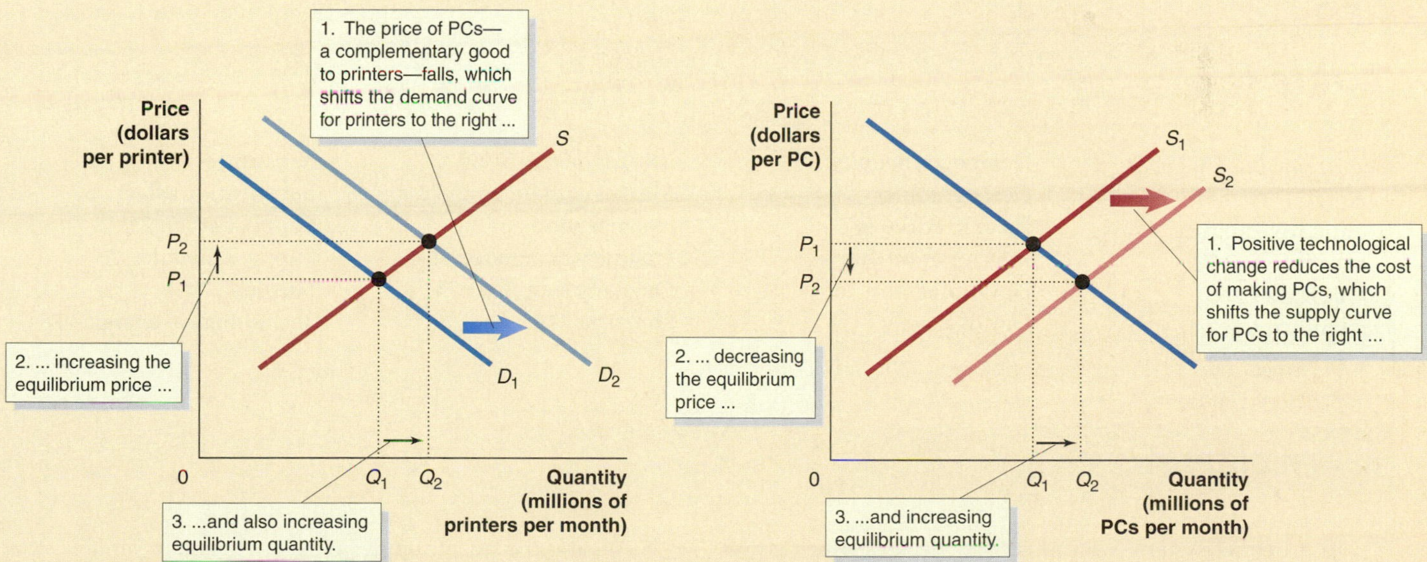

Figure 1: The fall in the price of PCs causes the demand for printers to shift to the right.

Figure 2: A fall in the cost of PCs shifts the supply curve for PCs to the right.

SUMMARY

LEARNING OBJECTIVE ① Discuss the variables that influence demand. The types and quantities of goods and services produced ultimately depend on the desires of consumers. A *demand curve* is a graph showing the relationship between the price of a good and the quantity of the good consumers are willing and able to buy over a period of time. We can find the market demand curve by adding horizontally the individual demand curves of each buyer. The *law of demand* states that *ceteris paribus*—holding everything else constant—the quantity of a product demanded increases when the price falls and decreases when the price rises. Changes in the prices of related goods, income, tastes, population and demographics, and expected future prices all cause the demand curve to shift. Demand curves always slope downward. A *change in demand* refers to a shift of the demand curve. A *change in quantity demanded* refers to a movement along the demand curve as a result of a change in the product's price.

LEARNING OBJECTIVE ② Discuss the variables that influence supply. When the price of a product rises, producing the product is more profitable and a greater amount will be supplied. The *law of supply* states that, holding everything else constant, the quantity of a product supplied increases when the price rises and decreases when the price falls. Changes in the prices of inputs, technology, the prices of substitutes in production, expected future prices, and the number of firms in a market all cause the supply curve to shift. A *change in supply* refers to a shift of the supply curve. A *change in quantity supplied* refers to a movement along the supply curve as a result of a change in the product's price.

LEARNING OBJECTIVE ③ Use a graph to illustrate market equilibrium. *Market equilibrium* occurs where the supply curve intersects the demand curve. Only at this point is the quantity supplied equal to the quantity demanded. Prices above equilibrium result in *surpluses*, which cause the market price to fall. Prices below equilibrium result in *shortages*, which cause the market price to rise.

LEARNING OBJECTIVE ④ Use demand and supply graphs to predict changes in prices and quantities. In most markets, demand and supply curves shift frequently, causing changes in equilibrium prices and quantities. Over time, if demand increases more than supply, equilibrium price will rise. If supply increases more than demand, equilibrium price will fall.

KEY TERMS

Ceteris paribus ("all else equal") 67
Competitive market equilibrium 78
Complements 68
Demand curve 64
Demand schedule 64
Demographics 70
Income effect 67
Inferior good 69
Law of demand 66
Law of supply 74
Market demand 65
Market equilibrium 78
Normal good 69
Quantity demanded 64
Quantity supplied 73
Shortage 79
Substitutes 68
Substitution effect 67
Supply curve 73
Supply schedule 73
Surplus 79
Technological change 76

REVIEW QUESTIONS

1. In a market system, who ultimately decides which goods and services will be produced?
2. What do economists mean when they use the Latin expression *ceteris paribus*?
3. What is the difference between a change in demand and a change in quantity demanded?
4. What is the law of demand? What are the main variables that will cause the demand curve to shift? Give an example of each.
5. What is the law of supply? What are the main variables that will cause a supply curve to shift? Give an example of each.
6. What do economists mean by "market equilibrium"? What will happen in a market if the current price is above the equilibrium price? What will happen if the current price is below the equilibrium price?
7. What happens to the equilibrium price in a market if the demand curve shifts to the right? Draw a demand and supply graph to illustrate your answer.

8. What happens to the equilibrium price in a market if the supply curve shifts to the left? Draw a demand and supply graph to illustrate your answer.
9. If, over time, the demand curve for a product shifts to the right more than the supply curve does, what will happen to the equilibrium price? What will happen to the equilibrium price if the supply curve shifts to the right more than the demand curve? For each case, draw a demand and supply graph to illustrate your answer.

PROBLEMS AND APPLICATIONS

Please visit **www.prenhall.com/hubbard** *for solutions to the even-numbered problems as well as multiple-choice and true or false self-assessment quizzes.*

1. Suppose the market for ice cream cones is made up of three consumers: Pedro, Curt, and Tim. Use the information in the following table to construct the market demand curve for ice cream cones. Show the information in a table and in a graph.

	PEDRO	CURT	TIM
PRICE	QUANTITY DEMANDED (CONES PER WEEK)	QUANTITY DEMANDED (CONES PER WEEK)	QUANTITY DEMANDED (CONES PER WEEK)
$1.75	2	1	0
1.50	4	3	2
1.25	6	4	3
1.00	7	6	4
0.75	9	7	5

2. For each of the following pairs of products, state which are complements, which are substitutes, and which are unrelated.
   a. Pepsi and Coke
   b. Oscar Mayer hot dogs and Wonder hot dog buns
   c. Jiffy peanut butter and Smucker's strawberry jam
   d. Hewlett-Packard printers and Texas Instruments hand calculators
3. State whether each of the following events will result in a movement along the demand curve for McDonald's Big Mac hamburgers or whether it will cause the curve to shift. If the demand curve shifts, indicate whether it will shift to the left or to the right and draw a graph to illustrate the shift.
   a. The price of Burger King's Whopper hamburger declines.
   b. McDonald's distributes coupons for $1.00 off on a purchase of a Big Mac.
   c. Because of a shortage of potatoes, the price of French fries increases.
   d. Kentucky Fried Chicken raises the price of a bucket of fried chicken.
4. Is it possible for a good to be an inferior good for one person and a normal good for another person? If it is possible, can you cite some examples?
5. Suppose the data in the following table present the price of a base model Ford Explorer sports utility vehicle and the number of Explorers sold. Do these data indicate that the demand curve for Explorers is upward sloping? Explain.

YEAR	PRICE	QUANTITY
2003	$27,865	325,265
2004	28,325	330,648
2005	28,765	352,666

6. **[Related to *Don't Let This Happen To You!*]** A student writes the following: "Increased production leads to a lower price, which in turn increases demand." Do you agree with his reasoning? Briefly explain.
7. Following are four graphs and four market scenarios, each of which would cause either a movement along the supply curve for Pepsi or a shift of the supply curve. Match each scenario with the appropriate diagram.
   a. A decrease in the supply of Coke
   b. Average household income in the United States drops from $42,000 to $41,000
   c. An improvement in soft-drink bottling technology
   d. An increase in the price of sugar

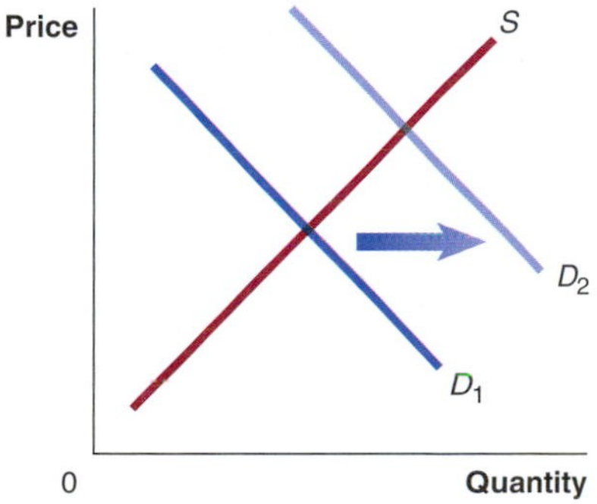

8. Suppose the pizza industry is made up of three firms: The Mark Company, Mike, Inc., and Bill Enterprises. Use the information in the following table to construct the market supply curve for pizzas. Show the information in a table and in a graph.

	MARK	MIKE	BILL
PRICE	QUANTITY SUPPLIED (PIZZAS PER WEEK)	QUANTITY SUPPLIED (PIZZAS PER WEEK)	QUANTITY SUPPLIED (PIZZAS PER WEEK)
$5.00	25	30	20
5.50	30	40	25
5.75	35	50	30
6.00	40	60	35
6.25	45	70	40

9. **[Related to *Solved Problem 3-1*]** In *The Wealth of Nations,* Adam Smith discussed what has come to be known as the "diamond and water paradox":

> Nothing is more useful than water: but it will purchase scarce anything; scarce anything can be had in exchange for it. A diamond, on the contrary, has scarce any value in use; but a very great quantity of other goods may frequently be had in exchange for it.

Graph the market for diamonds and the market for water. Show how it is possible for the price of water to be much lower than the price of diamonds, even though the demand for water is much greater than the demand for diamonds.

10. Briefly explain under what conditions zero would be the equilibrium quantity.

11. According to an article in the *New York Times,* "Sales of DVD's in the United States have risen dramatically since the discs first went on the market in 1997, thanks in part to a drop in the price of DVD players." Draw a demand and supply graph for the DVD market and use it to show the effect on this market of a decline in the price of DVD players. Now draw a demand and supply graph for the VCR market and use it to show the effect on this market of a decline in the price of DVD players. On both graphs, make sure to indicate the equilibrium price and quantity before and after the decline in the price of DVD players.
Source: Rick Lyman, "Revolt in the Den: DVD Sends the VCR Packing to the Attic," *New York Times,* August 26, 2002.

12. A recent study indicated that "Stricter college alcohol policies, such as raising the price of alcohol, or banning alcohol on campus, decrease the number of students who use marijuana."
    a. On the basis of this information, are alcohol and marijuana substitutes or complements?
    b. Suppose that campus authorities reduce the supply of alcohol on campus. Use demand and supply graphs to illustrate the impact on the campus alcohol and marijuana markets.

Source: Jenny Williams, Rosalie Pacula, Frank Chaloupka, and Henry Wechsler, "Alcohol and Marijuana Use Among College Students: Economic Complements or Substitutes?" *Health Economics,* Volume 13, Issue 9, September 2005, pages 825–843.

13. **[Related to *Solved Problem 3-2*]** The demand for watermelons is highest during summer and lowest during winter. Yet watermelon prices are normally lower in summer than in winter. Use a demand and supply graph to demonstrate how this is possible. Be sure to carefully label the curves in your graph and to clearly indicate the equilibrium summer price and the equilibrium winter price.

14. The following appeared in the *Wall Street Journal:* "U.S. farmers are headed for the lowest corn harvest since 1997, but the soybean crop is expected to reach an all-time high. Prices for both crops are expected to rise." Draw demand and supply graphs illustrating the market for corn and the market for soybeans. Show the impact of a larger soybean crop on the equilibrium price in each market. Holding

everything else constant, what must be happening to the demand for soybeans for the equilibrium price of soybeans to rise?

15. According to an article in the *Wall Street Journal*, the price of flat-screen televisions fell between 2001 and 2004 from more than $8,000 to about $3,000. During that period Sharp, Matsushita Electric Industrial, and Samsung all began producing flat-screen televisions. Use a demand and supply graph to explain what happened to the quantity of flat-screen televisions sold during this period.
Source: Evan Ramstad and Gary McWilliams, "Flat-TV Prices Are Falling," *Wall Street Journal*, November 3, 2004, p. 81.

16. According to an article in the *New York Times*, during the summer of 2001 in San Francisco the quantity supplied of commercial real estate space—such as space in office buildings—was four million square feet more than the quantity of commercial real estate space demanded. Draw a demand and supply graph illustrating the San Francisco commercial real estate market. Predict what was likely to happen to rents for office space in San Francisco.
Source: Matt Richtel, "A City Takes a Breath after the Dot-Com Crash," *New York Times*, July 24, 2001.

17. During the late 1990s many consumers were having their vision problems corrected by laser surgery. An article in the *Wall Street Journal* in early 2001 noted two developments in the market for laser eye surgery. The first was about increasing concerns related to side effects from the surgery, including blurred vision and, occasionally, blindness. The second development was that the companies renting eye-surgery machinery to doctors had reduced their charges. One large company had cut its charge from $250 per patient to $100. Use a demand and supply graph to illustrate the effects of these two developments on the market for laser eye surgery.
Source: Laura Johannes and James Bandler, "Slowing Economy, Safety Concerns Zap Growth in Laser Eye Surgery," *Wall Street Journal*, January 8, 2001, p. B1.

18. Following the September 11, 2001, terrorist attacks, automobile companies became worried that the demand for new cars would decline. To maintain their sales, they reduced the prices of new cars. The following chart shows the effect this had on the prices of some *used* cars:

VEHICLE	PERCENTAGE CHANGE IN PRICE, JULY TO NOVEMBER
2000 Cadillac de Ville	−11.3%
1998 Lexus LS540	−12.2
1999 BMW 3231	−11.3
1999 Chevrolet Tahoe	−14.0
2000 Ford Explorer	−15.9
2000 Ford F-Series	−11.4

Explain why the prices of used cars fell in these circumstances. Use a demand and supply graph of the used car market to illustrate your answer.

19. The market for autographs, including letters or other documents signed by famous people, is subject to frequent large price changes, as are markets for most collectibles. The following table is adapted from one originally appearing in an article in the *Wall Street Journal*. It gives the 1997 price for an autograph, the 2001 price, and a brief comment by the *Wall Street Journal* reporter. Use the information contained in the Comment Column of the table to draw a demand and supply graph for each of the three autographs listed that can account for the change in its market price from 1997 to 2001.

AUTOGRAPH	1997 PRICE	2001 PRICE	COMMENT
The Beatles	$2,500	$7,475	"As boomers get rich, so do prices for pieces . . . signed by the Fab Four."
Princess Diana	14,000	2,000	"Demand rose after her death in 1997, but now the market's full of items like her signed Christmas cards."
Robert E. Lee	200,000	100,000	"The Civil War's out."

Source: Brooks Barnes, "Signature Market: Hard to Read," *Wall Street Journal*, July 13, 2001.

20. Historically, the production of many perishable foods, such as dairy products, was highly seasonal. Thus, as the supply of those products fluctuated, prices tended to fluctuate tremendously—typically by 25 to 50 percent or more—over the course of the year. One impact of mechanical refrigeration, which was commercialized on a large scale in the last decade of the nineteenth century, was that suppliers could store perishables from one season to the next. Economists have estimated that as a result of refrigerated storage, wholesale prices rose by roughly 10 percent during peak supply periods, while they fell by almost the same amount during the off season. Use a demand and supply graph for each season to illustrate how refrigeration affected the market for perishable food.
Source: Lee A. Craig, Barry Goodwin, and Thomas Grennes, "The Effect of Mechanical Refrigeration on Nutrition in the U.S.," *Social Science History*, Vol. 28, No. 2 (Summer 2004), pp. 327–328.

21. Briefly explain whether each of the following statements is true or false.
    a. If the demand and supply for a product both increase, the equilibrium quantity of the product must also increase.
    b. If the demand and supply for a product both increase, the equilibrium price of the product must also increase.

c. If the demand for a product decreases and the supply of the product increases, the equilibrium price of the product may increase or decrease, depending upon whether supply or demand has shifted by more.

22. According to an article in the *Wall Street Journal,* "Online auctioneers like eBay are having a huge impact on the price of fame. After Cal Ripken Jr. announced his retirement from baseball . . . dozens of Ripken-autographed game jerseys, baseball cards and Wheaties boxes flooded the online bazaar." Use a demand and supply graph to illustrate the impact of eBay on the equilibrium price of Cal Ripken memorabilia.

23. **[Related to *Don't Let This Happen To You!*]** A student was asked to draw a demand and supply graph to illustrate the effect on the personal computer market of a fall in the price of computer hard drives, *ceteris paribus.* She drew the graph below and explained it as follows:

> Hard drives are an input to personal computers, so a fall in the price of hard drives will cause the supply curve for personal computers to shift to the right (from S_1 to S_2). Because this shift in the supply curve results in a lower price (P_2), consumers will want to buy more personal computers and the demand curve will shift to the right (from D_1 to D_2). We know that more personal computers will be sold, but we can't be sure whether the price of personal computers will rise or fall. That depends on whether the supply curve or the demand curve has shifted farther to the right. I assume that the effect on supply is greater than the effect on demand, so I show the final equilibrium price (P_3) as being lower than the initial equilibrium price (P_1).

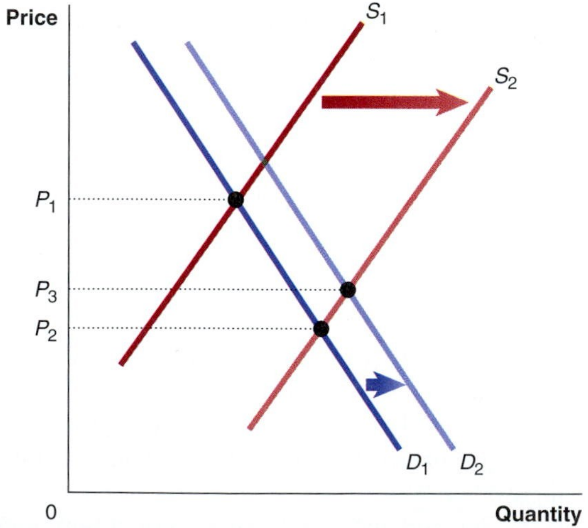

Explain whether you agree or disagree with the student's analysis. Be careful to explain exactly what—if anything—you find wrong with her analysis.

24. David Surdam, an economist at Loyola University of Chicago, makes the following observation of the world cotton market at the beginning of the Civil War:

> [A]s the supply of American-grown raw cotton decreased and the price of raw cotton increased, there would be a *movement along* the supply curve of non-American raw cotton suppliers and the quantity supplied by these producers would increase.

Illustrate this observation with one demand and supply graph for the market for American-grown cotton and another demand and supply graph for the market for non-American cotton. Make sure that your graphs clearly show: (1) the initial equilibrium before the decrease in the supply of American-grown cotton and (2) the final equilibrium. Also clearly show any shifts in the demand and supply curves for each market.

Source: David G. Surdam, "King Cotton: Monarch or Pretender? The State of the Market for Raw Cotton on the Eve of the American Civil War," *The Economic History Review,* Vol. 51, No. 1 (February 1998), p. 116.

25. Proposals have been made to increase government regulation of childcare businesses by, for instance, setting education requirements for childcare workers. Suppose that these regulations increase the quality of childcare and cause the demand for childcare services to increase. At the same time, assume that complying with the new government regulations increases the costs of childcare businesses. Draw a demand and supply graph to illustrate the effects of these changes in the market for childcare services. Briefly explain whether the total quantity of childcare services purchased will increase or decrease as a result of regulation.

26. Below are the supply and demand functions for two markets. One of the markets is for BMW automobiles, and the other is for a cancer-fighting drug, without which lung cancer patients will die. Briefly explain which diagram most likely represents which market.

chapter four

Market Efficiency and Market Failure

Should the Government Control Apartment Rents?

Robert F. Moss owns one apartment building in New York City. He deals with more government red tape than the average businessperson. Unlike most business owners, for example, he is not free to charge the prices he would like for the service he offers. In New York, San Francisco, Los Angeles, and nearly 200 smaller cities, apartments are subject to rent control by the local government. Rent control puts a ceiling on the maximum rent that landlords can charge for an apartment.

About one million of New York City's two million apartments are subject to rent control. The other one million apartments have their rents determined in the market by the demand and supply for apartments. Mr. Moss's building includes apartments that are rent controlled and apartments that are not. The market-determined rents are usually far above the controlled rents. The government regulations that determine what rent Mr. Moss can charge for a rent-controlled apartment are very complex. The following is Mr. Moss's description:

> [W]hen [an apartment] is vacated state rent laws entitle landlords to raise rents in three primary ways: a vacancy increase of 20 percent for a new tenant's two-year lease (a bit less for a one-year lease); one-fortieth per month of the cost of any improvements, and a "longevity bonus" for longtime residents (calculated at six-tenths of 1 percent times the tenant's last legal rent multiplied by the number of years of residency beyond eight) . . . (Apartments renting for $2,000 a month are automatically deregulated if they are vacant. Occupied apartments whose rent reaches that figure can be deregulated if the income of the tenants has been $175,000 or more for two years.)

Needless to say, a businessperson who earns a living by renting out apartments in one or two buildings in New York has to deal with much more complex government regulation of prices than a businessperson who owns, say, a McDonald's restaurant.

Larger companies also struggle with the complexity of rent-control regulations. This was the case for several companies that built multiple apartment buildings in New York during the 1970s. In exchange for renting apartments to moderate- and low-income tenants at controlled rents, the companies were allowed to charge market rents after 20 years. Unfortunately for the companies, when the 20 years were over, attempts to start charging market rents were often met with lawsuits from unhappy tenants. In 2004, New York Mayor Michael Bloomberg proposed that the law be changed to keep many of these apartment buildings under rent control.

Tenants in rent-controlled apartments in New York are very reluctant to see rent control end because rents for rent-controlled apartments are much lower than rents for apartments that aren't rent controlled. It turns out, however, that rent control actually drives up the rents of apartments that aren't rent controlled. *An Inside Look* on page 122 shows how a magazine reporter and his family ended up paying a higher rent for an apartment in New York than they would have if there had been no rent control.

Rent control is one way in which the government intervenes in the economy. Some government intervention occurs when there is *market failure,* which is a situation where the market fails to produce the efficient level of output. For example, government environmental policies are intended to remedy market failures resulting from pollution.

Source: Robert F. Moss, "A Landlord's Lot Is Sometimes Not an Easy One," *New York Times,* August 3, 2003, Section 11, p. 1.

After studying this chapter, you should be able to:

① Understand the concepts of consumer surplus and producer surplus.

② Understand the concept of economic efficiency, and use a graph to illustrate how economic efficiency is reduced when a market is not in competitive equilibrium.

③ Use demand and supply graphs to analyze the economic impact of price ceilings and price floors.

④ Identify examples of positive and negative externalities and use graphs to show how externalities affect economic efficiency.

⑤ Analyze government policies to achieve economic efficiency in a market with an externality.

We saw in Chapter 3 that, in a competitive market, the price adjusts to ensure that the quantity demanded equals the quantity supplied. Stated another way, in equilibrium, every consumer willing to pay the market price is able to buy as much of the product as the consumer wants and every firm willing to accept the market price can sell as much as it wants. Despite this, consumers would naturally prefer to pay a lower price, and sellers would prefer to receive a higher price. Normally, consumers and firms have no choice but to accept the equilibrium price if they wish to participate in the market. Occasionally, however, consumers succeed in having the government impose a **price ceiling,** which is a legally determined maximum price that sellers may charge. Rent control is an example of a price ceiling. Firms also sometimes succeed in having the government impose a **price floor,** which is a legally determined minimum price that sellers may receive. In markets for farm products such as milk, the government has been setting price floors that are above the equilibrium market price since the 1930s.

Price ceiling A legally determined maximum price that sellers may charge.

Price floor A legally determined minimum price that sellers may receive.

The government will also sometimes intervene in markets where there is an *externality.* An **externality** is a benefit or cost that affects someone who is not directly involved in the production or consumption of a good or service. Air pollution is just one example of an externality. In the case of air pollution, there is a *negative externality* because, for example, people with asthma may bear a cost even though they were not involved in the buying or selling of the electricity that caused the pollution. *Positive externalities* are also possible. For instance, medical research can provide a positive externality because people who are not directly involved in producing it or paying for it can benefit. A competitive market usually does a good job of producing the economically efficient amount of a good or service. This may not be true, though, if there is an externality in the market. When there is a negative externality, the market may produce a quantity of the good that is greater than the efficient amount. When there is a positive externality, the market may produce a quantity that is less than the efficient amount.

Externality A benefit or cost that affects someone who is not directly involved in the production or consumption of a good or service.

Unfortunately, whenever the government imposes a price ceiling or a price floor, or implements a policy to deal with an externality, there are economic consequences. It is important for government policymakers and for voters to understand these consequences when evaluating the effects of these policies. Economists have developed the concepts of *consumer surplus, producer surplus,* and *economic surplus,* which we discuss in the next section. In the following sections we use these concepts to analyze the economic effects of price ceilings, price floors, and government policies towards externalities.

1 LEARNING OBJECTIVE

Understand the concepts of consumer surplus and producer surplus.

Consumer Surplus and Producer Surplus

We can analyze the effects of government interventions in markets, such as imposing price ceilings and price floors, using the concepts of consumer surplus, producer surplus, and economic surplus. Consumer surplus measures the dollar benefit consumers receive from buying goods or services in a particular market. Producer surplus measures the dollar benefit firms receive from selling goods or services in a particular market. Economic surplus in a market is the sum of consumer surplus plus producer surplus. As we will see, *when the government imposes a price ceiling or a price floor, the amount of economic surplus in a market is reduced*—in other words, price ceilings and price floors reduce the total benefit to consumers and firms from buying and selling in a market. To understand why this is true, we need to understand how consumer surplus and producer surplus are determined.

Consumer Surplus

Demand curves show the willingness of consumers to purchase a product at different prices. For instance, Figure 4-1 shows Joe Irvin's demand curve for chai tea. If the price is $3.00 per cup, Joe will buy 4 cups per week. If the price is $2.00 per cup, Joe will buy 5 cups per week. The fact that Joe is willing to pay $3.00 for the fourth cup means that the marginal benefit to him from that cup is $3.00. Similarly, the fact that Joe is willing to pay $2.00 for the fifth cup means that the marginal benefit to him from that cup is $2.00. The **marginal benefit** is the additional benefit to a consumer from consuming one more unit of a good or service. In fact, we can think of Joe's demand curve as representing his marginal benefit curve for chai tea.

Marginal benefit The additional benefit to a consumer from consuming one more unit of a good or service.

Suppose that the market price for chai tea is $2.00 per cup. In this case, for the fifth cup Joe buys in a week, his marginal benefit is equal to the price. For the other 4 cups he buys in a week, however, his marginal benefit is greater than the price he pays. In other words, for the first 4 cups of tea Joe buys in a week, he is paying less than the maximum price he would have been willing to pay, as shown by his marginal benefit. The difference between the highest price a consumer is willing to pay and the price the consumer actually pays is called **consumer surplus.**

Consumer surplus The difference between the highest price a consumer is willing to pay and the price the consumer actually pays.

Figure 4-2 shows the market demand curve for chai tea. In the figure, the quantity demanded at a price of $2.00 is 15,000 cups per week. An important point to understand is that nearly all consumers in this market receive some consumer surplus from their purchases because the marginal benefit they receive is greater than the price they pay. The only consumers who receive no consumer surplus are those who would not have purchased any chai tea if the price had been higher than $2.00. We can calculate total consumer surplus in the market by adding up the consumer surplus received on each unit purchased. Because the demand curve measures the marginal benefit received by consumers, we can draw the following important conclusion: *The total amount of consumer surplus in a market is equal to the area below the demand curve and above the market price.* Consumer surplus is shown as the blue area in Figure 4-2, and represents the benefit to consumers in excess of the price they paid to purchase the product—in this case, chai tea.

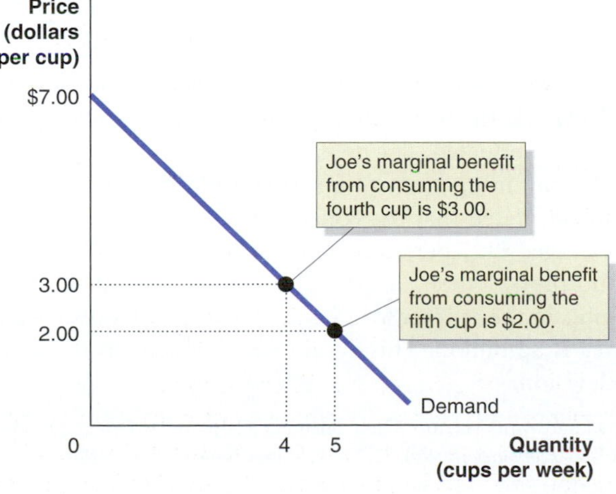

FIGURE 4-1

The Demand Curve Is Also the Marginal Benefit Curve

The demand curve shows a consumer's willingness to purchase a product at various prices. In this case, we know that Joe's willingness to pay $3.00 to purchase 4 cups of chai tea per week means that his *marginal benefit* from consuming the fourth cup is $3.00. Similarly, his willingness to pay $2.00 to purchase 5 cups of tea per week means that his marginal benefit from consuming the fifth cup is $2.00. So, the demand curve is also a marginal benefit curve.

FIGURE 4-2

Total Consumer Surplus in the Market for Chai Tea

The demand curve tells us that most buyers of chai tea would have been willing to pay more than the market price of $2.00. For each buyer, consumer surplus is equal to the difference between the highest price he or she is willing to pay and the market price actually paid. Therefore, the total amount of consumer surplus in the market for chai tea is equal to the area below the demand curve and above the market price. Consumer surplus represents the benefit to consumers in excess of the price they paid to purchase the product.

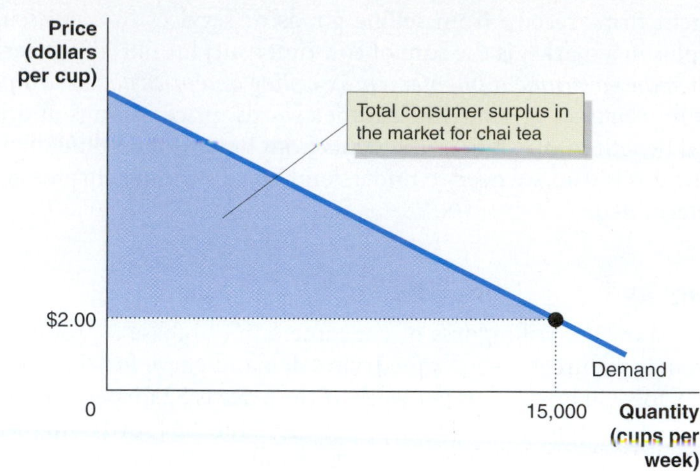

4-1 Making the Connection

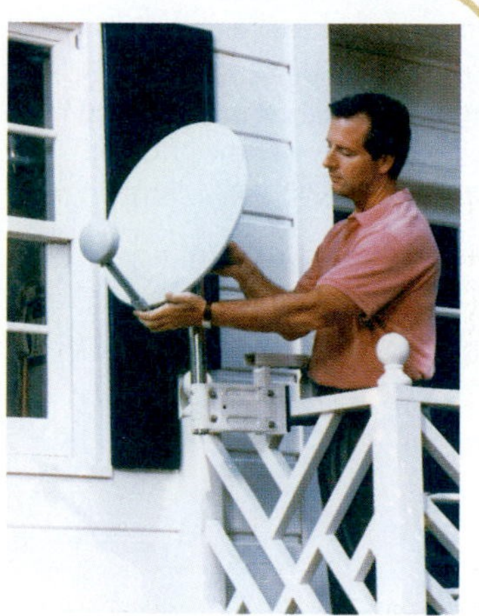

How much consumer surplus will the owner of this satellite dish receive?

The Consumer Surplus from Satellite Television

Consumer surplus allows us to measure the benefit consumers receive in excess of the price they paid to purchase the product. Recently, Austan Goolsbee and Amil Petrin, economists at the Graduate School of Business at the University of Chicago, have estimated the consumer surplus that households receive from subscribing to satellite television. To do this, they estimated the demand curve for satellite television and then computed the shaded area shown in the graph.

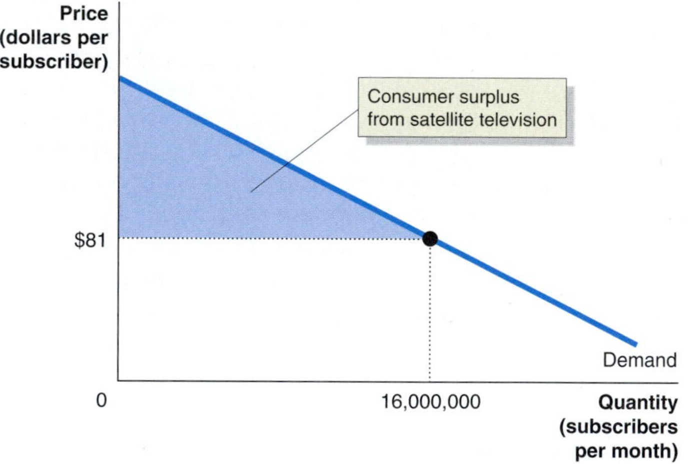

Sixteen million consumers paid an average price of $81 per month to subscribe to DirectTV or DISH Network, the two main providers of satellite television in 2001, the year for which the study was conducted. The demand curve shows that many consumers would have been willing to pay more than $81 rather than do without satellite television. Goolsbee and Petrin calculated that the consumer surplus for households subscribing to satellite television averaged $127 per month, which is the difference between the price they would have paid, and the $81 they did pay. The shaded area on the graph represents the total consumer surplus in the market for satellite television. Goolsbee and Petrin estimate the value of this area is $2 billion. This is one year's benefit to the consumers who subscribe to satellite television.

Source: Austan Goolsbee and Amil Petrin, "The Consumer Gains from Direct Broadcast Satellites and the Competition with Cable TV," *Econometrica*, Vol. 72, No. 2, March 2004, pp. 351–381.

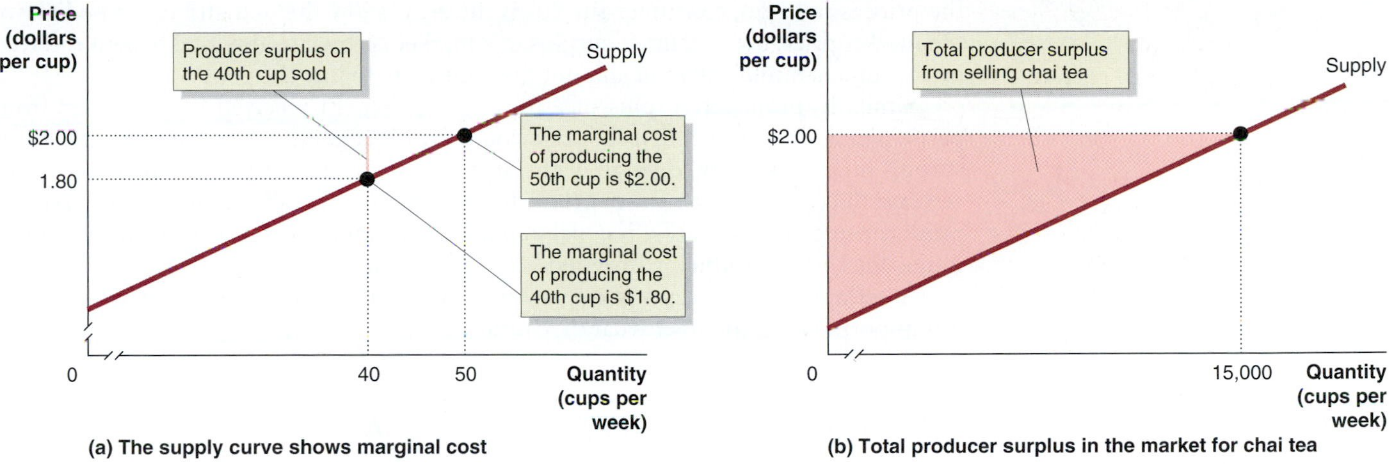

(a) The supply curve shows marginal cost

(b) Total producer surplus in the market for chai tea

FIGURE 4-3 Producer Surplus

The supply curve shows a firm's willingness to supply a product at various prices. In panel (a), we know that Heavenly Tea's willingness to supply 40 cups of chai tea at a price of $1.80 per cup means that the *marginal cost* of producing the 40th cup is $1.80. Similarly, the firm's willingness to supply 50 cups at a price of $2.00 per cup means its marginal cost of producing the 50th cup is $2.00. Producer surplus on the 40th cup sold is the difference between the $2.00 market price of the cup and $1.80, which is the lowest price tea sellers would have been willing to accept. In panel (b), the total amount of producer surplus tea sellers receive from selling chai tea can be calculated by adding up for the entire market the producer surplus received on each cup sold. In the figure, this is equal to the area above the supply curve and below the market price, shown in red.

Producer Surplus

Supply curves show the willingness of firms to supply a product at different prices. The willingness to supply a product depends on the cost of producing it. Firms will supply an additional unit of a product only if they receive a price equal to the additional cost of producing that unit. **Marginal cost** is the additional cost to a firm of producing one more unit of a good or service. In Figure 4-3(a), we know that because Heavenly Tea is willing to supply 50 cups of chai tea at a price of $2.00 per cup, the 50th cup must have a marginal cost of $2.00. The supply curve also shows us that Heavenly Tea would be willing to supply 40 cups at a price of $1.80 per cup. So, the marginal cost of the 40th cup is $1.80. The supply curve, then, is also a marginal cost curve.

Marginal cost The additional cost to a firm of producing one more unit of a good or service.

Notice, though, that if the market price of chai tea is $2.00, Heavenly Tea is able to sell the 40th cup for $0.20 more than the lowest price—$1.80—it would have been willing to accept. This $0.20 is the *producer surplus* on that particular cup of tea. **Producer surplus** is the difference between the lowest price a firm would have been willing to accept and the price it actually receives. The supply curve shows us that Heavenly Tea receives some producer surplus on nearly every cup of chai tea supplied. The marginal cost of the 50th cup is $2.00, and Heavenly Tea receives a price of $2.00, so it receives no producer surplus on that cup. The total amount of producer surplus tea sellers receive from selling chai tea can be calculated by adding up the producer surplus received on each cup sold. Therefore, *the total amount of producer surplus in a market is equal to the area above the market supply curve and below the market price.* The total producer surplus tea sellers receive from selling chai tea is shown as the red area in Figure 4-3(b).

Producer surplus The difference between the lowest price a firm would have been willing to accept and the price it actually receives.

What Consumer Surplus and Producer Surplus Measure

We have seen that consumer surplus measures the benefit to consumers from participating in a market, and producer surplus measures the benefit to producers from participating in a market. It is important, however, to be clear what we mean by this. In a sense, consumer surplus is measuring the *net* benefit to consumers from participating in a market, rather than the *total* benefit. That is, if the price of a product were zero, then the consumer surplus in a market would be all of the area under the demand curve. When the price is not zero, consumer surplus is the area below the demand curve and above the market price. So, consumer surplus in a market is equal to the total benefit received by consumers minus the total amount they must pay to buy the good.

Similarly, producer surplus measures the net benefit received by producers from participating in a market. If producers could supply a good at zero cost, the producer surplus in a market would be all of the area below the market price. When cost is not zero, producer surplus is the area below the market price and above the supply curve. So, producer surplus in a market is equal to the total amount firms receive from consumers minus the cost of producing the good.

As we apply the concepts of consumer surplus and producer surplus in this chapter, it is important to remember what they measure.

(2) LEARNING OBJECTIVE

Understand the concept of economic efficiency, and use a graph to illustrate how economic efficiency is reduced when a market is not in competitive equilibrium.

The Efficiency of Competitive Markets

In Chapter 3, we defined a *competitive market* as a market with many buyers and many sellers. An important advantage of the market system is that it results in efficient economic outcomes. But what do we mean by economic efficiency? The concepts we have developed so far in this chapter give us two ways to think about the economic efficiency of competitive markets. We can think in terms of marginal benefit and marginal cost. We can also think in terms of consumer surplus and producer surplus. As we will see, these two approaches lead to the same outcome, but using both can increase our understanding of economic efficiency.

Marginal Benefit Equals Marginal Cost in Competitive Equilibrium

Figure 4-4 again shows the market for chai tea. Recall that the demand curve shows the marginal benefit received by consumers, and the supply curve shows the marginal cost of production. To achieve economic efficiency in this market, the marginal benefit from the last unit sold should equal the marginal cost of production. The figure shows that this equality occurs at competitive equilibrium where 15,000 cups per week are produced, and marginal benefit and marginal cost are both equal to $2.00. Why is this outcome economically efficient? Because every cup of chai tea has been produced where the marginal benefit to buyers is greater than or equal to the marginal cost to producers.

Another way to see why the level of output at competitive equilibrium is efficient is to consider what would be true if output were at a different level. For instance, suppose that output of chai tea were 14,000 cups per week. Figure 4-4 shows that at this level of output, the marginal benefit from the last cup sold is $2.20, whereas the marginal cost is

FIGURE 4-4

Marginal Benefit Equals Marginal Cost Only at Competitive Equilibrium

In a competitive market, equilibrium occurs at a quantity of 15,000 cups and a price of $2.00 per cup, where marginal benefit equals marginal cost. This is the economically efficient level of output because every cup has been produced where the marginal benefit to buyers is greater than or equal to the marginal cost to producers.

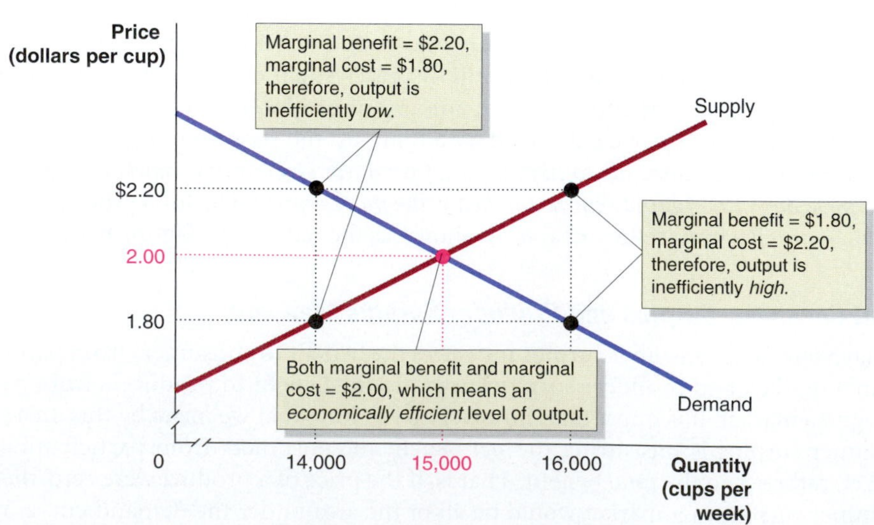

only $1.80. This level of output is not efficient because 1,000 more cups could be produced for which the additional benefit to consumers is greater than the additional cost of production. Consumers would willingly purchase those cups, and tea sellers would willingly supply them, making both consumers and sellers better off. Similarly, if the output of chai tea were 16,000 cups per week, the marginal cost of the 16,000th cup is $2.20, whereas the marginal benefit is only $1.80. Tea sellers would only be willing to supply this cup at a price of $2.20, which is $0.40 higher than consumers would be willing to pay. In fact, consumers would not be willing to pay the price tea sellers would need to receive for any cup beyond the 15,000th.

To summarize, we can say this: *Equilibrium in a competitive market results in the economically efficient level of output, where marginal benefit equals marginal cost.*

Economic Surplus

Economic surplus in a market is the sum of consumer surplus and producer surplus. In a competitive market, with many buyers and sellers and no government restrictions, economic surplus is at a maximum when the market is in equilibrium. To see this, let's look one more time at the market for chai tea, which is shown in Figure 4-5. The consumer surplus in this market is the blue area below the demand curve and above the line indicating the equilibrium price of $2.00. The producer surplus is the red area above the supply curve and below the price line.

Economic surplus The sum of consumer surplus and producer surplus.

Deadweight Loss

To show that economic surplus is maximized at equilibrium, consider the situation when the price of chai tea is *above* the equilibrium price, as shown in Figure 4-6. At a price of $2.20 per cup, the number of cups consumers are willing to buy per week drops from 15,000 to 14,000. At competitive equilibrium, consumer surplus is equal to the sum of areas *A*, *B*, and *C*. At a price of $2.20, fewer cups are sold at a higher price, so consumer surplus declines to just the area of *A*. At competitive equilibrium, producer surplus is equal to the sum of areas *D* and *E*. At the higher price of $2.20, producer surplus changes to be equal to the sum of areas *B* and *D*. The sum of consumer and producer surplus—economic surplus—has been reduced to the sum of areas *A*, *B*, and *D*. Notice that this is less than the original economic surplus by an amount equal to areas *C* and *E*. Economic surplus has declined because at a price of $2.20, all the cups between the 14,000th and the 15,000th, which would have been produced in competitive equilibrium, are not being produced. These "missing" cups are not providing any consumer or producer surplus, so economic surplus has declined. The reduction in economic surplus resulting from a market not being in competitive equilibrium is called the **deadweight loss.** In the figure, it is equal to the sum of areas *C* and *E*.

Deadweight loss The reduction in economic surplus resulting from a market not being in competitive equilibrium.

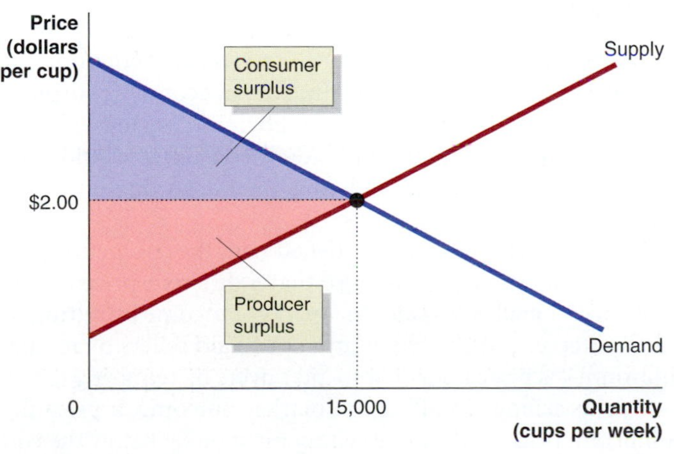

FIGURE 4-5

Economic Surplus Equals the Sum of Consumer Surplus and Producer Surplus

The economic surplus in a market is the sum of the blue area representing consumer surplus and the red area representing producer surplus.

FIGURE 4-6

When a Market Is Not in Equilibrium There Is a Deadweight Loss

Economic surplus is maximized when a market is in competitive equilibrium. When a market is not in equilibrium, there is a deadweight loss. When the price of chai tea is $2.20, instead of $2.00, consumer surplus declines from an amount equal to the sum of areas *A, B,* and *C*, to just area *A*. Producer surplus increases from the sum of areas *D* and *E*, to the sum of areas *B* and *D*. At competitive equilibrium, there is no deadweight loss. At a price of $2.20, there is a deadweight loss equal to the sum of areas *C* and *E*.

	At Competitive Equilibrium	At a Price of $2.20
Consumer Surplus	*A* + *B* + *C*	*A*
Producer Surplus	*D* + *E*	*B* + *D*
Deadweight Loss	None	*C* + *E*

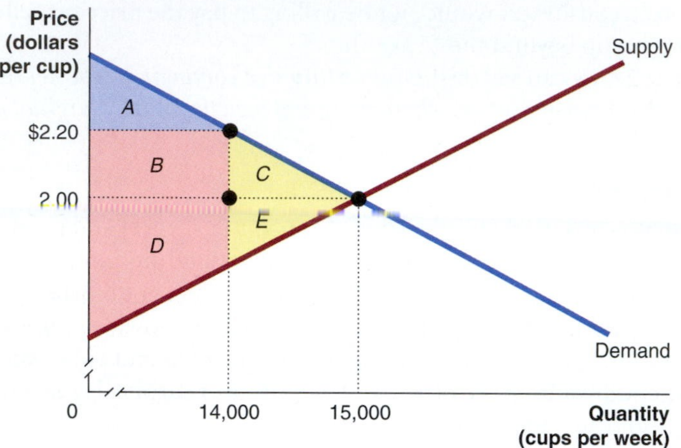

Economic Surplus and Economic Efficiency

Consumer surplus measures the benefit to consumers from buying a particular product, such as chai tea. Producer surplus measures the benefit to firms from selling a particular product. Therefore, economic surplus—which is the sum of the benefit to firms plus the benefit to consumers—is the best measure we have of the benefit to society from the production of a particular good or service. This gives us a second way of characterizing the economic efficiency of a competitive market: *Equilibrium in a competitive market results in the greatest amount of economic surplus, or total net benefit to society, from the production of a good or service.* Anything that causes the market for a good or service not to be in competitive equilibrium reduces the total benefit to society from the production of that good or service.

Economic efficiency A market outcome in which the marginal benefit to consumers of the last unit produced is equal to its marginal cost of production, and in which the sum of consumer surplus and producer surplus is at a maximum.

Now we can give a more general definition of *economic efficiency* in terms of our two approaches: **Economic efficiency** is a market outcome in which the marginal benefit to consumers of the last unit produced is equal to its marginal cost of production, and in which the sum of consumer surplus and producer surplus is at a maximum.

(3) LEARNING OBJECTIVE

Use demand and supply graphs to analyze the economic impact of price ceilings and price floors.

Government Intervention in the Market: Price Floors and Price Ceilings

Notice that we have *not* concluded that every *individual* is better off if a market is at its competitive equilibrium. We have only concluded that economic surplus, or the *total* net benefit to society, is greatest at competitive equilibrium. Any individual producer would rather charge a higher price, and any individual consumer would rather pay a lower price, but usually producers can sell and consumers can buy only at the competitive equilibrium price.

Producers or consumers who are dissatisfied with the competitive equilibrium price can lobby the government to legally require that a different price be charged. The U.S. government only occasionally overrides the market outcome by setting prices. When the government does intervene, it can either attempt to aid sellers by requiring that a price be above equilibrium—a price floor—or to aid buyers by requiring that a price be below equilibrium—a price ceiling. To affect the market outcome, a price floor must be set above the equilibrium price, and a price ceiling must be set below the equilibrium price.

Otherwise, the price ceiling or price floor will not be *binding* on buyers and sellers. The preceding section demonstrates that moving away from competitive equilibrium will reduce economic efficiency. We can use the concepts of producer and consumer surplus and deadweight loss to see more clearly the economic inefficiency of binding price floors and price ceilings.

Price Floors: The Example of Agricultural Markets

The Great Depression of the 1930s was the greatest economic disaster in U.S. history, affecting every sector of the U.S. economy. Many farmers were unable to sell their products or could sell them only at very low prices. Farmers were able to convince the federal government to intervene to raise prices by setting price floors for many agricultural products. Government intervention in agriculture—often referred to as the "farm program"—has continued ever since. To see how a price floor in an agricultural market works, suppose that the equilibrium price in the wheat market is \$3.00 per bushel but the government decides to set a price floor of \$3.50 per bushel. As Figure 4-7 shows, the price of wheat rises from \$3.00 to \$3.50 and the quantity of wheat sold falls from 2.0 billion bushels per year to 1.8 billion. Suppose, initially, that production of wheat also falls to 1.8 billion bushels.

Just as we saw in the earlier example of the market for chai tea (see Figure 4-6), the producer surplus received by wheat farmers increases by an amount equal to the area of the red rectangle *A* and falls by an amount equal to the area of the yellow triangle *C*. The area of the red rectangle *A* represents a transfer from consumer surplus to producer surplus. The total fall in consumer surplus is equal to the area of the red rectangle *A* plus the area of the yellow triangle *B*. Wheat farmers benefit from this program, but consumers lose. There is also a deadweight loss equal to the areas of the yellow triangles *B* and *C*, which represents the decline in economic efficiency due to the price floor. There is a deadweight loss because the price floor has reduced the amount of economic surplus in the market for wheat. Or, looked at another way, the price floor has caused the marginal benefit of the last bushel of wheat to be greater than the marginal cost of producing it. We can conclude that a price floor reduces economic efficiency.

The actual federal government farm programs have been more complicated than just legally requiring farmers not to sell their output below a minimum price. We assumed initially that farmers reduce their production of wheat to the amount

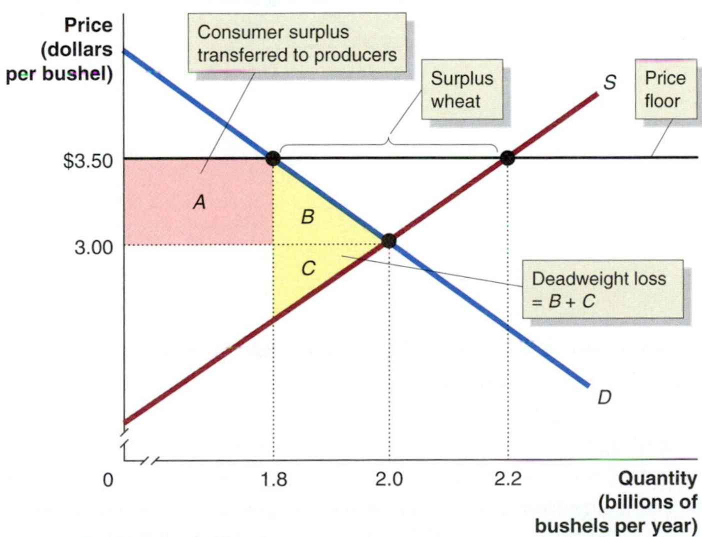

FIGURE 4-7

The Economic Effect of a Price Floor in the Wheat Market

If wheat farmers convince the government to impose a price floor of \$3.50 per bushel, the amount of wheat sold will fall from 2.0 billion bushels per year to 1.8 billion. If we assume that farmers produce 1.8 billion bushels, producer surplus then increases by the red rectangle *A*—which is transferred from consumer surplus—and falls by the yellow triangle *C*. Consumer surplus declines by the red rectangle *A* plus the yellow triangle *B*. There is a deadweight loss equal to the yellow triangles *B* and *C*, representing the decline in economic efficiency due to the price floor. In reality, a price floor of \$3.50 per bushel will cause farmers to expand their production from 2.0 billion to 2.2 billion bushels, resulting in a surplus of wheat.

consumers are willing to buy. In fact, as Figure 4-7 shows, a price floor will cause the quantity of wheat that farmers want to supply to increase from 2.0 billion to 2.2 billion bushels. Because the higher price also reduces the amount of wheat consumers wish to buy, the result is a surplus of 0.4 billion bushels of wheat (the 2.2 billion bushels supplied minus the 1.8 billion demanded).

The federal government's farm programs often have resulted in large surpluses of wheat and other agricultural products. The government has usually either bought the surplus food or paid farmers to restrict supply by taking some land out of cultivation. Because both of these options are expensive, Congress passed the Freedom to Farm Act of 1996. The intent of the act was to phase out price floors and government purchases of surpluses and return to a free market in agriculture. To allow farmers time to adjust, the federal government began paying farmers subsidies, or cash payments based on the number of acres planted. Although the *subsidies* were originally scheduled to be phased out, Congress has continued to pay them.

4-2 Making the Connection

Many economists believe there are better policies than the minimum wage for raising the incomes of low-skilled workers.

Price Floors in Labor Markets: The Minimum Wage

The minimum wage may be the most controversial "price floor." Supporters see the minimum wage as a way of raising the incomes of low-skilled workers. Opponents argue that it results in fewer jobs and imposes large costs on small businesses.

Congress has set a national minimum wage of $5.15 per hour for most occupations. It is illegal for an employer to pay less than this wage in those occupations. For most workers, the minimum wage is irrelevant because it is well below the wage employers are voluntarily willing to pay them. But for low-skilled workers—such as workers in fast-food restaurants—the minimum wage is above the wage they would otherwise receive. The figure below shows the effect of the minimum wage on employment in the market for low-skilled labor.

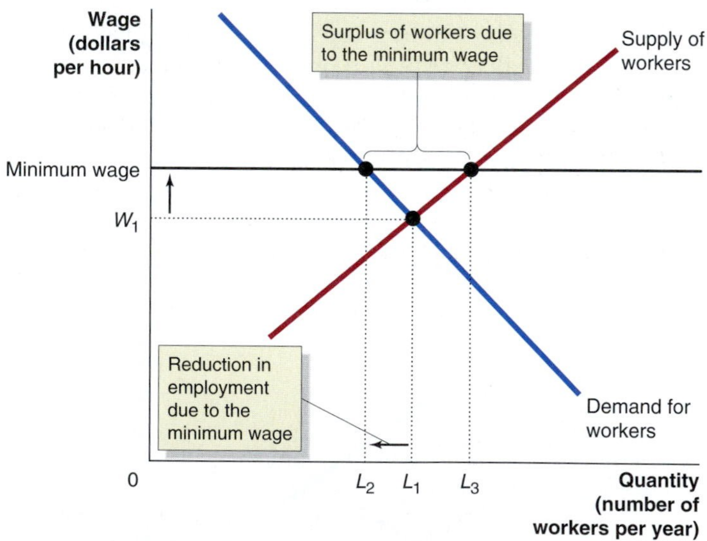

Without a minimum wage, the equilibrium wage would be W_1, and the number of workers hired would be L_1. With a minimum wage set above the equilibrium wage, the quantity of workers demanded by employers declines from L_1 to L_2 and the quantity of labor supplied increases to L_3, leading to a surplus of workers unable to find jobs equal to $L_3 - L_2$. The quantity of labor supplied increases because the higher wage attracts more people to work. For instance, some teenagers may decide that working after school is worthwhile at the minimum wage of $5.15 per hour, but would not have been worthwhile at a lower wage.

This analysis is very similar to our analysis of the wheat market in Figure 4-7. Just as a price floor in the wheat market leads to less wheat consumed, a price floor in the labor market should lead to fewer workers hired. Views differ sharply among economists, however, concerning how large a reduction in employment the minimum wage causes. For instance, David Card of the University of California, Berkeley, and Alan Krueger of Princeton University conducted a study of fast-food restaurants in New Jersey and Pennsylvania that indicates the effect of minimum wage increases on employment is very small. Card and Krueger's study has been very controversial, however. Other economists have examined similar data and have come to the different conclusion that the minimum wage does lead to a significant decrease in employment.

Whatever the extent of employment losses from the minimum wage, because it is a price floor, it will cause a deadweight loss, just as a price floor in the wheat market does. Therefore, many economists favor alternative policies for attaining the goal of raising the incomes of low-skilled workers. One policy many economists support is the *earned income tax credit*. The earned income tax credit reduces the amount of tax that low-income wage earners would otherwise pay to the federal government. Workers with very low incomes who do not owe any tax receive a payment from the government. Compared with the minimum wage, the earned income tax credit can increase the incomes of low-skilled workers without reducing employment. The earned income tax credit also places a lesser burden on the small businesses that employ many low-skilled workers, and it might cause a smaller loss of economic efficiency.

Sources: David Card and Alan B. Krueger, *Myth and Measurement: The New Economics of the Minimum Wage*, Princeton, NJ: Princeton University Press, 1995; David Neumark and William Wascher, "Minimum Wages and Employment: A Case Study of the Fast-Food Industry in New Jersey and Pennsylvania: Comment," *American Economic Review*, Vol. 90, No. 5, December 2000, pp. 1,362–1,396; and David Card and Alan B. Krueger, "Minimum Wages and Employment: A Case Study of the Fast-Food Industry in New Jersey and Pennsylvania: Reply," *American Economic Review*, Vol. 90, No. 5, December 2000, pp. 1,397–1,420.

Price Ceilings: The Example of Rent Controls

Support for governments setting price floors typically comes from sellers, but support for governments setting price ceilings typically comes from consumers. For example, when there is a sharp increase in gasoline prices, there will often be proposals for the government to impose a price ceiling on the market for gasoline. As we saw in the opening to this chapter, New York is one of the cities that imposes rent controls, which put a ceiling on the maximum rent that landlords can charge for an apartment. Figure 4-8 shows the market for apartments in a city that has rent controls.

Without rent control, the equilibrium rent would be $1,500 per month and 2,000,000 apartments would be rented. With a maximum legal rent of $1,000 per month, landlords reduce the quantity of apartments supplied to 1,900,000. The fall in the quantity of apartments supplied is the result of some apartments being converted to offices or sold off as condominiums, some small apartment buildings being

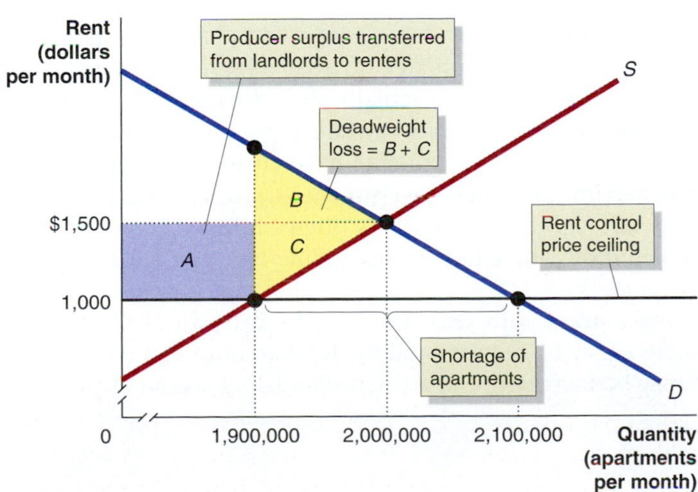

FIGURE 4-8

The Economic Effect of a Rent Ceiling

Without rent control, the equilibrium rent is $1,500 per month. At that price, 2,000,000 apartments would be rented. If the government imposes a rent ceiling of $1,000, the quantity of apartments supplied falls to 1,900,000, while the quantity of apartments demanded increases to 2,100,000, resulting in a shortage of 200,000 apartments. Producer surplus equal to the area of the blue rectangle *A* is transferred from landlords to renters, and there is a deadweight loss equal to the areas of the yellow triangles *B* and *C*.

Don't Let This Happen To You!

Don't Confuse "Scarcity" with a "Shortage"

At first glance, the following statement seems correct: "There is a shortage of every good that is scarce." In everyday conversation, we describe a good as "scarce" if we have trouble finding it. For instance, if you are looking for a present for a child, you might call the latest hot toy "scarce" if you are willing to buy it at its listed price but can't find it online or in any store. But recall from Chapter 2 that economists have a broad definition of *scarce*. In the economic sense, almost everything—except undesirable things like garbage—is scarce. A shortage of a good occurs only if the quantity demanded is greater than the quantity supplied at the current price. Therefore, the preceding statement—"There is a shortage of every good that is scarce"—is incorrect. In fact, there is no shortage of most scarce goods.

***YOUR TURN:* Test your understanding by doing related problem 7 on page 127 at the end of this chapter.**

converted to single-family homes, and, over time, some apartment buildings being abandoned. In New York City, rent control has resulted in whole city blocks being abandoned by landlords who were unable to cover their costs with the rents they were allowed to charge. In London, when rent controls were applied to rooms and apartments located in a landlord's own home, the quantity of these apartments supplied dropped by 75 percent.

In Figure 4-8, with the rent ceiling of $1,000, the quantity of apartments demanded rises to 2,100,000. There is a shortage of 200,000 apartments. Consumer surplus increases by rectangle *A* and falls by triangle *B*. Rectangle *A* would have been part of producer surplus if rent control were not in place. With rent control, it is part of consumer surplus. Rent control causes the producer surplus received by landlords to fall by rectangle *A* plus triangle *C*. Triangles *B* and *C* represent the deadweight loss. There is a deadweight loss because rent control has reduced the amount of economic surplus in the market for apartments. Rent control has caused the marginal benefit of the last apartment rented to be greater than the marginal cost of supplying it. We can conclude that a price ceiling, such as rent control, reduces economic efficiency.

Renters as a group benefit from rent controls—total consumer surplus is larger—but landlords lose. Because of the deadweight loss, the total loss to landlords is greater than the gain to renters. Notice also that although renters as a group benefit, the number of renters is reduced, so some renters are made worse off by rent controls because they are unable to find an apartment at the legal rent.

Black Markets

To this point, our analysis of rent controls is incomplete. In practice, renters may be worse off and landlords may be better off than Figure 4-8 makes it seem. We have assumed that renters and landlords actually abide by the price ceiling, but sometimes they don't. Because rent control leads to a shortage of apartments, renters who would otherwise not be able to find apartments have an incentive to offer landlords rents above the legal maximum. When governments try to control prices by setting price ceilings or price floors, buyers and sellers often find a way around the controls. The result is a **black market** where buying and selling take place at prices that violate government price regulations.

Black market Buying and selling at prices that violate government price regulations.

In a housing market with rent controls, the total amount of consumer surplus received by renters may be reduced and the total amount of producer surplus received by landlords may be increased if apartments are being rented at prices above the legal price ceiling.

SOLVED PROBLEM 4-1

What's the Economic Effect of a "Black Market" for Apartments?

③ **LEARNING OBJECTIVE**

Use demand and supply graphs to analyze the economic impact of price ceilings and price floors.

In many cities with rent controls, the actual rents paid can be much higher than the legal maximum. Because rent controls cause a shortage of apartments, desperate tenants will often be willing to pay landlords rents that are higher than the law allows, perhaps by writing a check for the legally allowed rent and paying an additional amount in cash. Look again at Figure 4-8. Suppose that competition among tenants results in the black market rent rising to $2,000 per month. At this rent, tenants demand 1,900,000 apartments. Use a graph showing the market for apartments to compare this situation with the one shown in Figure 4-8. Be sure to note any differences in consumer surplus, producer surplus, and deadweight loss.

Solving the Problem:

Step 1: Review the chapter material. This problem is about price controls in the market for apartments, so you may want to review the section "Price Ceilings: The Example of Rent Controls," which begins on page 107.

Step 2: Draw a graph similar to Figure 4-8, with the addition of the black market price.

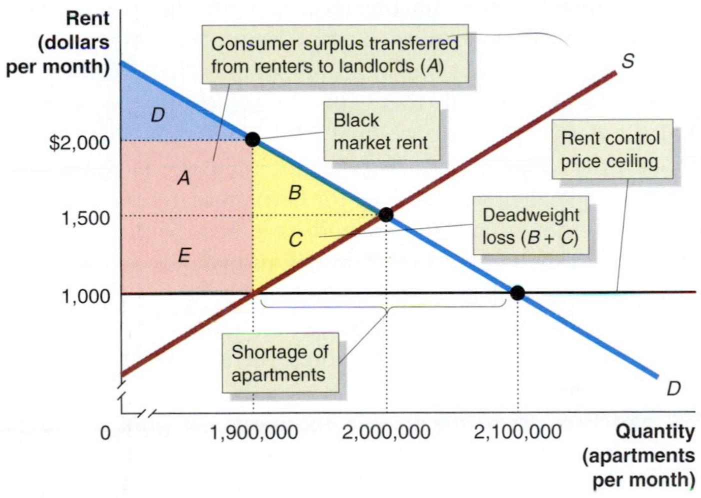

Step 3: Analyze the changes from Figure 4-8. Because the black market rent is now $2,000—even higher than the original competitive equilibrium rent of $1,500—compared with Figure 4-8, consumer surplus declines by an amount equal to the red rectangle *A* plus the red rectangle *E*. The remaining consumer surplus is the blue triangle *D*. Note that the rectangle *A*, which would have been part of consumer surplus without rent control, represents a transfer from renters to landlords. Compared with the situation shown in Figure 4-8, producer surplus has increased by an amount equal to rectangles *A* and *E*, and consumer surplus has declined by the same amount. Deadweight loss is equal to triangles *B* and *C*, the same as in Figure 4-8.

Extra Credit: This analysis leads to a surprising result: With an active black market in apartments, rent control may leave renters as a group worse off—with less consumer surplus—than if there were no rent control. There is one more possibility to consider, however. If enough landlords become convinced that they can get away with charging rents above the legal ceiling, the quantity of apartments supplied will increase. Eventually, the market could even end up at the competitive equilibrium with an equilibrium rent of $1,500 and equilibrium quantity of 2,000,000 apartments. In that case the rent control price ceiling becomes nonbinding, not because it was set below the equilibrium price, but because it was not legally enforced.

YOUR TURN: For more practice, do related problem 6 on page 126 and problem 9 on page 127 at the end of this chapter.

Rent controls can also lead to an increase in racial and other types of discrimination. With rent controls, more renters will be looking for apartments than there are apartments to rent. Landlords can afford to indulge their prejudices by refusing to rent to people they don't like. In cities without rent controls, landlords face more competition, which makes it more difficult to turn down tenants on the basis of irrelevant characteristics, such as race.

4-3 Making the Connection

Does Holiday Gift Giving Have a Deadweight Loss?

The deadweight loss that results from rent control occurs, in part, because consumers rent fewer apartments than they would in a competitive equilibrium. Their choices are *constrained* by government. When someone receives a gift, she is also constrained because the person who gave the gift has already chosen the product. In many cases, the recipient would have chosen a different gift for herself. Economist Joel Waldfogel of the University of Pennsylvania points out that gift giving results in a deadweight loss. The amount of the deadweight loss is equal to the difference between the gift's price and the dollar value the recipient places on the gift. Waldfogel surveyed his students, asking them to list every gift they had received for Christmas, to estimate the retail price of each gift, and to state how much they would have been willing to pay for each gift. Waldfogel's students estimated that their families and friends had paid $438 on average on the students' gifts. The students themselves, however, would have been willing to pay only $313 to buy the presents. If the deadweight losses experienced by Waldfogel's students were extrapolated to the whole population, the deadweight loss of Christmas gift giving could be as much as $13 billion.

If the gifts had been cash, the people receiving the gifts would not have been constrained by the gift givers' choices, and there would have been no deadweight loss. If your sister had given you cash instead of that sweater you didn't like, you could have bought whatever you wanted. Why then do people continue giving presents rather than cash? One answer is that most people receive more satisfaction from giving a present than from giving cash. If we take this satisfaction into account, the deadweight loss from gift giving will be lower than in Waldfogel's calculations.

Caution: Gift giving may lead to deadweight loss.

Source: Joel Waldfogel, "The Deadweight Loss of Christmas," *American Economic Review*, Vol. 83, No. 4, December 1993, pp. 328–336.

The Results of Government Controls on Prices: Winners, Losers, and Inefficiency

When the government imposes price floors or price ceilings, three important results occur:

- Some people win.
- Some people lose.
- There is a loss of economic efficiency.

The winners with rent control are the people who are paying less for rent because they live in rent-controlled apartments. Landlords may also gain if they break the law by charging rents above the legal maximum for their rent-controlled apartments, provided these illegal rents are higher than the competitive equilibrium rents would have been. The losers from rent control are the landlords of rent-controlled apartments who abide by the law, and renters who are unable to find apartments to rent at the controlled price. Rent control reduces economic efficiency because fewer apartments are rented than would be in a competitive market (refer again to Figure 4-8). The resulting deadweight loss measures the decrease in economic efficiency.

Positive and Normative Analysis of Price Ceilings and Price Floors

Are rent controls, government farm programs, and other price ceilings and price floors bad? As we saw in Chapter 1, questions of this type have no right or wrong answers. Economists are generally skeptical of government attempts to interfere with competitive market equilibrium. Economists know the role competitive markets have played in raising the average person's standard of living. They also know that too much government intervention has the potential to reduce the ability of the market system to produce similar increases in living standards in the future.

But recall from Chapter 1 the difference between positive and normative analysis. Positive analysis is concerned with *what is,* and normative analysis is concerned with *what should be.* Our analysis of rent control and of the federal farm programs in this chapter is positive analysis. We discussed what the economic results of these programs are. Whether these programs are desirable or undesirable is a normative question. Whether the gains to the winners more than make up for the losses to the losers and for the decline in economic efficiency is a matter of judgment and not strictly an economic question. Price ceilings and price floors continue to exist partly because they are supported by people who understand their downside but still believe they are good policies. They also persist because many people do not understand their downside, because they are unfamiliar with the economic analysis we have used in this chapter.

Externalities and Efficiency

4 LEARNING OBJECTIVE

Identify examples of positive and negative externalities and use graphs to show how externalities affect economic efficiency.

When you consume a Big Mac, only you benefit, but when you consume a college education, other people will also benefit. College-educated people are less likely to commit crimes and, by being better informed voters, more likely to contribute to better government policies. So, although you capture most of the benefits of your college education, you do not capture all of them.

When you buy a Big Mac, the price you pay covers all of McDonald's costs of producing the Big Mac. When you buy electricity from a utility that burns coal and generates acid rain, the price you pay for the electricity does not cover the cost of the damage caused by the acid rain.

So, there is a *positive externality* in the production of college educations, because people who do not pay for college educations will nonetheless benefit from them. There is a *negative externality* in the generation of electricity because, for example, people with homes on a lake from which fish and wildlife have disappeared because of acid rain have incurred a cost, even though they might not have bought their electricity from the polluting utility.

The Effect of Externalities

Externalities interfere with the *economic efficiency* of a market equilibrium. We have seen that a competitive market achieves economic efficiency by maximizing the sum of consumer surplus and producer surplus. *But that result only holds if there are no externalities in production or consumption.* An externality causes a difference between the *private cost* of production and the *social cost,* or the *private benefit* from consumption and the *social benefit.* The **private cost** is the cost borne by the producer of a good or service. The **social cost** is the private cost plus any external cost resulting from production, such as the cost of pollution. Unless there is an externality, the private cost and the social cost will be equal. The **private benefit** is the benefit received by the consumer of a good or service. The **social benefit** is the private benefit plus any external benefit, such as the benefit to others resulting from your college education. Unless there is an externality, the private benefit and the social benefit will be equal.

Private cost The cost borne by the producer of a good or service.

Social cost The total cost of producing a good, including both the private cost and any external cost.

Private benefit The benefit received by the consumer of a good or service.

Social benefit The total benefit from consuming a good, including both the private benefit and any external benefit.

HOW A NEGATIVE EXTERNALITY IN PRODUCTION REDUCES ECONOMIC EFFICIENCY

Consider first how a negative externality in production affects economic efficiency. Up until now, we have assumed that the producer of a good or service must bear all of the costs of production. We now know that this observation is not always true. In producing electricity, some private costs are borne by the utility, but some external costs of acid rain are borne by farmers, fishermen, and the general public. The social cost of producing electricity is the sum of the private cost plus the external cost. Figure 4-9 shows the effect on the market for electricity of a negative externality in production.

S_1 is the market supply curve and reflects only the private costs that utilities have to bear in generating electricity. If utilities also had to bear the cost of acid rain, the supply curve would be S_2, which reflects the true social cost of generating electricity. The equilibrium with a price P_2 and quantity Q_2 is efficient. The equilibrium with a price P_1 and quantity Q_1 is not efficient. To see why, remember that an equilibrium is economically efficient if economic surplus—which is the sum of consumer surplus plus producer surplus—is at a maximum. When economic surplus is at a maximum, the net benefit to society from the production of the good or service is at a maximum. With an equilibrium quantity of Q_2, economic surplus is at a maximum, so this equilibrium is efficient. But with an equilibrium quantity of Q_1, economic surplus is reduced by the deadweight loss, shown in Figure 4-9 by the yellow triangle, and the equilibrium is not efficient. The deadweight loss occurs because the supply curve is above the demand curve for the production of the units of electricity between Q_2 and Q_1. That is, the additional cost—including the external cost—of producing these units is greater than the marginal

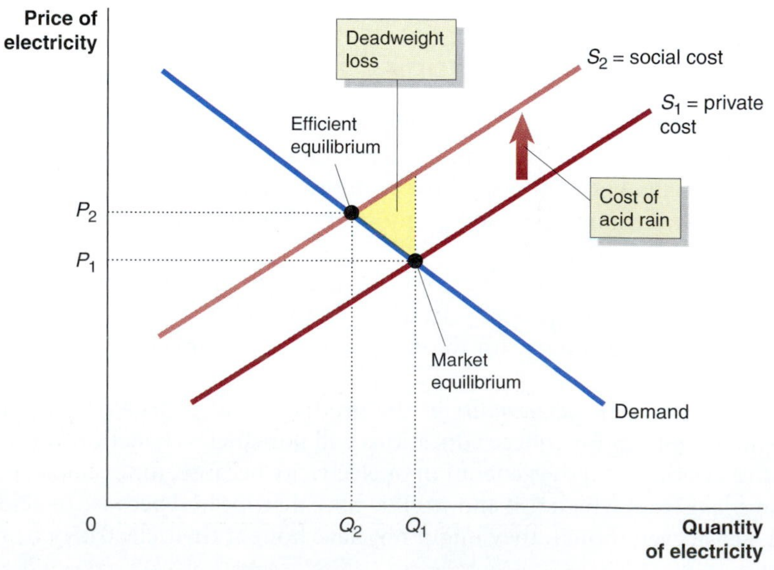

FIGURE 4-9

The Effect of Pollution on Economic Efficiency

Because utilities do not bear the cost of acid rain, they produce electricity beyond the economically efficient level. Supply curve S_1 represents just the private cost that the utility has to pay. Supply curve S_2 represents the social cost, which includes the costs to those affected by acid rain. The figure shows that if the supply curve were S_2, rather than S_1, market equilibrium would occur at a price of P_2 and a quantity of Q_2, the economically efficient level of output. But when the supply curve is S_1, the market equilibrium occurs at a price of P_1 and a quantity of Q_1 where there is a deadweight loss equal to the area of the yellow triangle. Because of the deadweight loss, this equilibrium is not efficient.

benefit to consumers. In other words, because of the cost of the acid rain, economic efficiency would be improved if less electricity were produced.

We can conclude the following: *When there is a negative externality in producing a good or service, too much of the good or service will be produced at market equilibrium.*

HOW A POSITIVE EXTERNALITY IN CONSUMPTION REDUCES ECONOMIC EFFICIENCY

We have seen that a negative externality interferes with achieving economic efficiency. The same holds true for a positive externality. Up until now, we have assumed that the demand curve reflects all the benefits that come from consuming a good. But we have seen that a college education generates benefits that are not captured by the student receiving the education and so will not be reflected in the market demand curve for college education. Figure 4-10 shows the effect of a positive externality in consumption on the market for a college education.

If students receiving a college education could capture all its benefits, the demand curve would be D_2, which reflects the social benefits. The actual demand curve is D_1, however, reflecting only the private benefits received by students. The efficient equilibrium would come at price P_2 and quantity Q_2. At this equilibrium, economic surplus is maximized. The market equilibrium, at price P_1 and quantity Q_1, will not be efficient because the demand curve is above the supply curve for production of the units between Q_1 and Q_2. That is, the additional benefit—including the external benefit—for producing these units is greater than the marginal cost. As a result, there is a deadweight loss equal to the area of the yellow triangle. Because of the positive externality, economic efficiency would be improved if more college educations were produced. We can conclude the following: *When there is a positive externality in consuming a good or service, too little of the good or service will be produced at market equilibrium.*

Externalities Can Result in Market Failure

We have seen that because of externalities, the efficient level of output may not occur in either the market for electricity or the market for college educations. These are examples of **market failure**: situations in which the market fails to produce the efficient level of output. Later we will discuss possible solutions to problems of externalities. But first we need to consider why externalities occur.

Market failure Situations in which the market fails to produce the efficient level of output.

What Causes Externalities?

We saw in Chapter 2 that governments need to guarantee *property rights* for a market system to function well. **Property rights** refer to the rights individuals or businesses

Property rights The rights individuals or businesses have to the exclusive use of their property, including the right to buy or sell it.

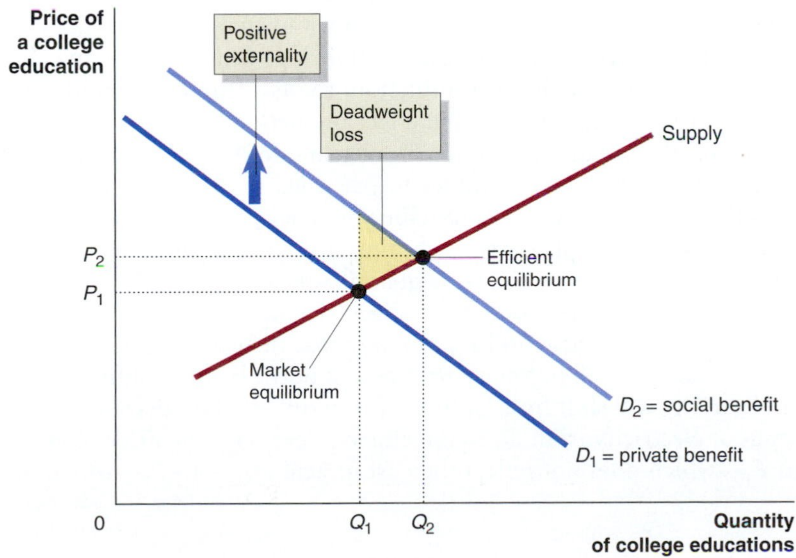

FIGURE 4-10

The Effect of a Positive Externality on Efficiency

People who do not consume college educations can still benefit from them. As a result, the social benefit from a college education is greater than the private benefit as seen by college students. Because only the private benefit is reflected in the market demand curve D_1, the quantity of college educations produced, Q_1, is too low. If the market demand curve were D_2 instead of D_1, the level of college educations produced would be Q_2, which is the efficient level. At the market equilibrium of Q_1, there is a deadweight loss equal to the area of the yellow triangle.

have to the exclusive use of their property, including the right to buy or sell it. Property can be tangible, physical property, such as a store or factory. Property can also be intangible, such as the right to an idea. Most of the time, the U.S. government and the governments of other high-income countries do a good job of enforcing property rights, but in certain situations property rights do not exist or cannot be legally enforced.

Consider the following situation: Lee owns land that includes a lake. A paper company wants to lease some of Lee's land to build a pulp and paper mill. The paper mill will discharge pollutants into Lee's lake. Because Lee owns the lake, he can charge the paper company the cost of cleaning up the pollutants. The result is that the cost of the pollution is a private cost to the paper company and is reflected in the price of the paper it sells. There is no externality, the efficient level of paper is produced, and there is no market failure.

Now suppose that the paper company builds its paper mill on privately owned land on the banks of a lake that is owned by the state. In the absence of any government regulations, the company will be free to discharge pollutants into the lake. The cost of the pollution will be external to the company because it doesn't have to pay the cost of cleaning it up. More than the economically efficient level of paper will be produced, and a market failure will occur. Or, suppose that Lee owns the lake, but the pollution is caused by acid rain generated by an electric utility hundreds of miles away. The law does not allow Lee to charge the utility for the damage caused by the acid rain. Even though someone is damaging Lee's property, the law does not allow him to enforce his property rights in this situation. Once again, there is an externality, and the market failure will result in too much electricity being produced.

Similarly, if you buy a house, the government will protect your right to exclusive use of that house. No one else can use the house without your permission. Because of your property rights in the house, your private benefit from the house and the social benefit are the same. When you buy a college education, however, other people are, in effect, able to benefit from your college education. You have no property right that will enable you to prevent them from benefiting or to charge them for the benefits they receive. As a result, there is a positive externality and the market failure will result in too few college educations being supplied.

We can conclude the following: *Externalities and market failures result from incomplete property rights or from the difficulty of enforcing property rights in certain situations.*

5 LEARNING OBJECTIVE

Analyze government policies to achieve economic efficiency in a market with an externality.

Government Solutions to Externalities

When property rights are incomplete or when property rights are difficult to enforce, should the government intervene in a market? If the government does intervene in a market, what will be the effects? The first economist to analyze market failure systematically was A. C. Pigou, a British economist at Cambridge University. Pigou argued that to deal with a negative externality in production, the government should impose a tax equal to the cost of the externality. The effect of such a tax is shown in Figure 4-11, which reproduces the negative externality from acid rain shown in Figure 4-9. If the federal government requires electric utilites to pay a tax on each unit of electricity produced, then the utilities per unit cost of selling electricity will increase by the amount of the tax. This causes the supply curve to shift up from S_1 to S_2 becasue utilities will now require a higher price to supply the same quantity of electricity.

By imposing a tax on the production of electricity equal to the cost of acid rain, the government will cause electric utilities to *internalize* the externality. As a consequence, the cost of the acid rain will become a private cost borne by the utilities, and the supply curve for electricity will shift from S_1 to S_2. The result will be a decrease in the equilibrium output of electricity from Q_1 to the efficient level Q_2. The price of electricity will rise from P_1—which does not reflect the cost of acid rain—to P_2—which does reflect the cost.

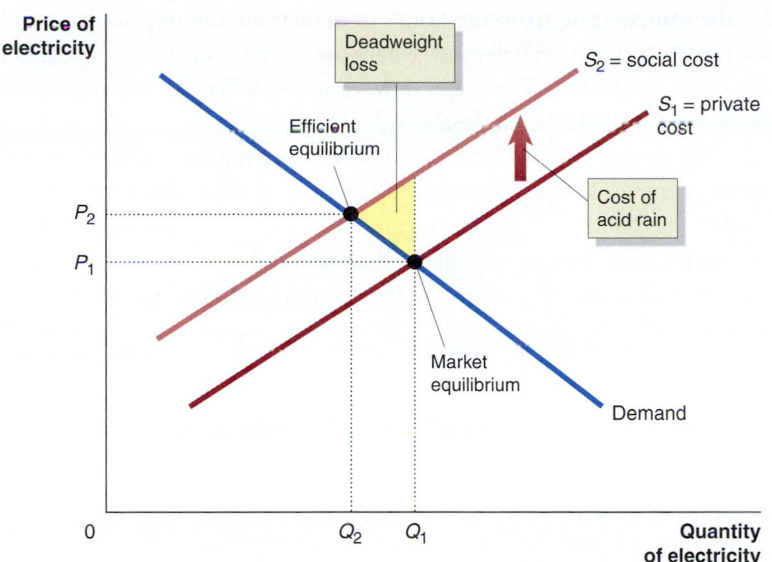

FIGURE 4-11

When There is a Negative Externality, a Tax Can Bring about the Efficient Level of Output

Because utilities do not bear the cost of acid rain, they produce electricity beyond the economically efficient level. If the government imposes a tax equal to the cost of acid rain, the utilities will internalize the externality. As a consequence, the supply curve will shift up from S_1 to S_2. As a result, market equilibrium changes from Q_1, where an inefficiently high level of electricity is produced, to Q_2, the economically efficient equilibrium. The price of electricity will rise from P_1—which does not reflect the cost of acid rain—to P_2—which does reflect the cost.

SOLVED PROBLEM 4-2

Using a Tax to Deal with a Negative Externality

Companies producing toilet paper bleach the paper to make it white. The bleach is discharged into rivers and lakes and causes substantial environmental damage. Suppose the following graph illustrates the situation in the toilet paper market:

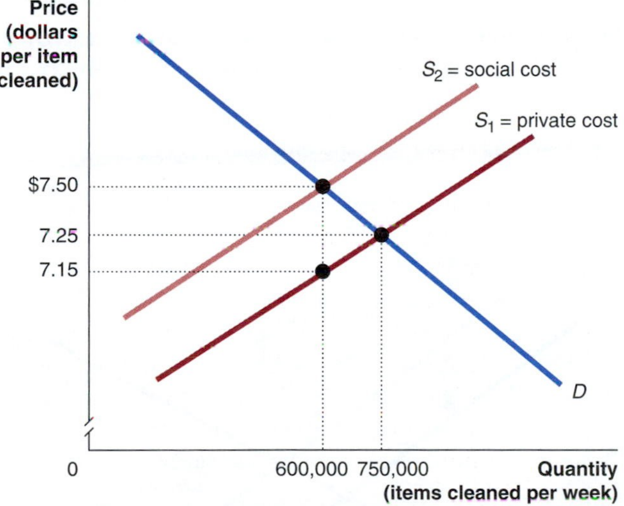

Explain how the federal government can use a tax on toilet paper to bring about the efficient level of production. What should the value of the tax be?

Solving the Problem:

Step 1: Review the chapter material. This problem is about the government using a tax to deal with a negative externality in production, so you may want to review the section "Government Solutions to Externalities," which begins on page 114.

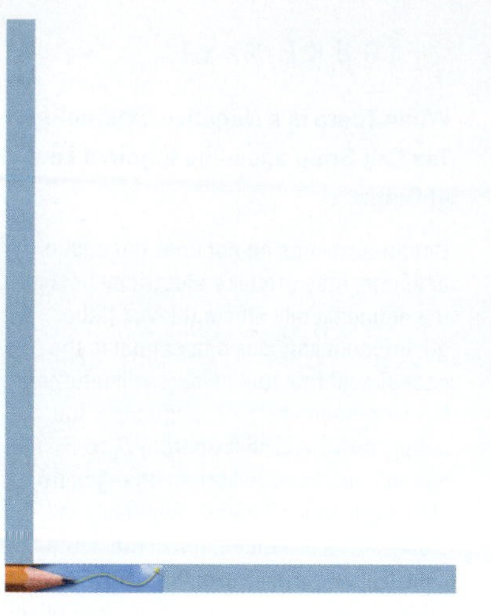

Step 2: Use the information from the graph to determine the necessary tax. The efficient level of toilet paper production will occur where the price of toilet paper is equal to the marginal social cost of production. The graph shows that this will occur at a price of $150 per ton and production of 350,000 tons. In the absence of government intervention, the price will be $125 per ton and production will be 450,000 tons. It is tempting—but incorrect!—to think that the government could bring about the efficient level of production by imposing a per-ton tax equal to the difference between the price when production is at its optimal level and the current market price. But this would be a tax of only $25. The diagram shows that at the optimal level of production, the difference between the marginal private cost and the marginal social cost is $50. Therefore, a tax of $50 per ton is required to shift the supply curve up from S_1 to S_2.

YOUR TURN: **For more practice, do related problem 23 on page 128 at the end of this chapter.**

Pigou also argued that the government can deal with a positive externality in consumption by giving consumers a subsidy, or payment, equal to the value of the externality. The effect of the subsidy is shown in Figure 4-12, which reproduces the positive externality from college education shown in Figure 4-10.

By paying college students a subsidy equal to the external benefit from a college education, the government will cause students to *internalize* the externality. That is, the external benefit from a college education will become a private benefit received by college students, and the demand curve for college educations will shift from D_1 to D_2. The equilibrium number of college educations supplied will increase from Q_1 to the efficient level Q_2. In fact, the government does heavily subsidize college educations. All states have government-operated universities that charge tuitions well below the cost of providing the education. The state and federal governments also provide students with grants and low-interest loans that subsidize college educations. The economic justification for these programs is that college educations provide an external benefit to society.

Because using government taxes and subsidies to deal with externalities was first proposed by A. C. Pigou, they are sometimes referred to as **Pigovian taxes and subsidies.**

Pigovian taxes and subsidies Government taxes and subsidies intended to bring about an efficient level of output in the presence of externalities.

FIGURE 4-12

When There is a Positive Externality, a Subsidy Can Bring about the Efficient Level of Output

People who do not consume college educations can still benefit from them. As a result, the social benefit from a college education is greater than the private benefit seen by college students. If the government pays a subsidy equal to the external benefit, students will internalize the externality. The subsidy will cause the demand curve to shift up from D_1 to D_2. The result will be that market equilibrium shifts from Q_1, where an inefficiently low level of college educations is supplied, to Q_2, the economically efficient equilibrium.

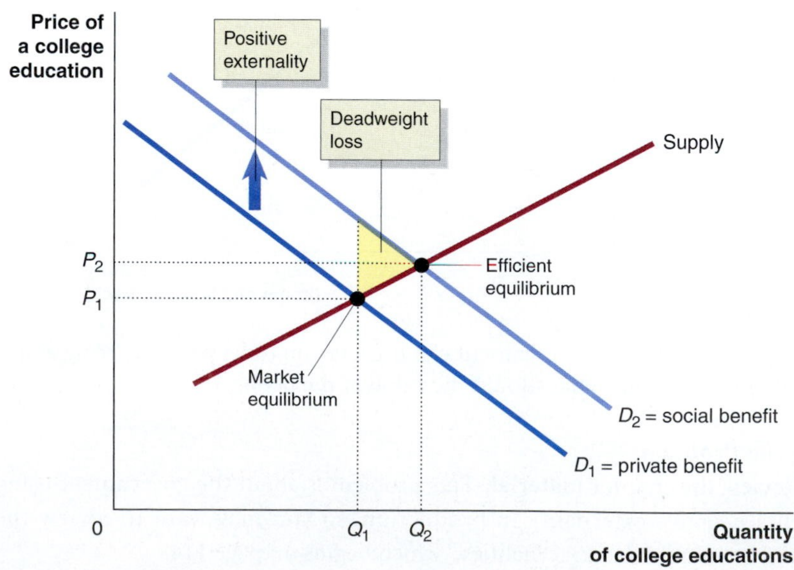

The Reduction in Infant Mortality Due to the Clean Air Act

4-4 Making the Connection

The following bar graph shows that tremendous progress has been made in the United States in reducing air pollution since the Clean Air Act was passed by Congress in 1970: Emissions of the six main air pollutants have fallen by almost half. Over the same period, real U.S. gross domestic product—which measures the value, corrected for inflation, of all the final goods and services produced in the country—increased 175 percent, energy consumption increased 42 percent, and the number of miles traveled by all vehicles increased 155 percent.

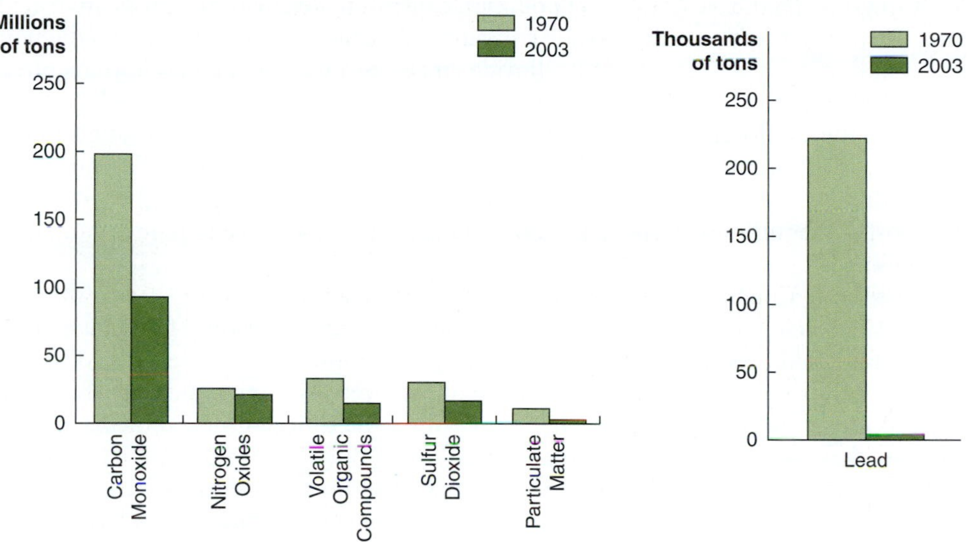

As we have seen, when levels of pollution are high, the marginal benefit of reducing pollution also is high. We would expect, then, that the benefit of reducing air pollution in 1970 was much higher than the benefit from a proportional reduction in air pollution would be today, when the level of pollution is much lower. Kenneth Y. Chay of the University of California, Berkeley, and Michael Greenstone of MIT have shown that the benefits from the air pollution reductions that occurred in the period immediately after passage of the Clean Air Act were indeed high. Chay and Greenstone argue that the exposure of pregnant women to high levels of air pollution can be damaging to their unborn fetuses, possibly by retarding lung functioning. This damage would increase the chance that the infant would die in the first weeks after being born. In the two years following passage of the Clean Air Act, there was a sharp reduction in air pollution and also a reduction in infant mortality. The decline in infant mortality mainly was due to a reduction in deaths within one month of birth. Of course, other factors also may have been responsible for the decline in infant mortality, but Chay and Greenstone use statistical analysis to isolate the effect of the decline in air pollution. They conclude that "1,300 fewer infants died in 1972 than would have in the absence of the Clean Air Act."

Reduction in air pollution has been linked to a decline in infant mortality.

Source: Kenneth Y. Chay and Michael Greenstone, "Air Quality, Infant Mortality, and the Clean Air Act of 1970," NBER Working Paper 10053, October 2003.

Command and Control versus Tradeable Emissions Allowances

Command and control approach Government-imposed quantitative limits on the amount of pollution firms are allowed to generate, or government-required installation by firms of specific pollution control devices.

Although the federal government has sometimes used taxes and subsidies to deal with externalities, in dealing with pollution it has traditionally used a *command and control approach* with firms that pollute. A **command and control approach** to reducing pollution involves the government imposing quantitative limits on the amount of pollution firms are allowed to generate, or requiring that firms install specific pollution control devices. For example, in 1983, the federal government required the installation of catalytic converters to reduce auto emissions on all new automobiles.

Congress could have used direct pollution controls to deal with the problem of acid rain, which is caused by sulfur dioxide emissions. To achieve its objective of a reduction of 8.5 million tons per year in sulfur dioxide emissions by 2010, it could have required every electric utility to reduce sulfur dioxide emissions by the same specified amount. However, this approach would not have been an economically efficient solution to the problem. Utilities can have very different costs of reducing sulfur dioxide emissions. Some utilities that already use low-sulfur coal can reduce emissions further only at a high cost. Other utilities, particularly those in the Midwest, are able to reduce emissions at a lower cost.

As a result, Congress decided to use a market-based approach by setting up a system of tradeable emissions allowances to reduce sulfur dioxide emissions. The federal government gave utilities allowances equal to the total amount of allowable emissions. The utilities were then free to buy and sell the allowances. An active market where the allowances can be bought and sold is conducted on the Chicago Mercantile Exchange. Utilities that could reduce emissions at low cost did so and sold their allowances. Utilities that could only reduce emissions at high cost bought allowances. Using tradeable emissions allowances to reduce acid rain has been a great success and has made it possible for utilities to meet Congress's emissions goal at a much lower cost than expected. As Figure 4-13 shows, just before Congress enacted the allowances program in

FIGURE 4-13

Estimated Cost of the Acid Rain Program in 2010

The Edison Electric Institute estimated in 1989 that the program to reduce acid rain pollution would cost utilities a total of $7.4 billion by 2010. The system of tradeable emissions allowances used in the program resulted in the bulk of the reduction in pollution being carried out by the utilities that could do it at the lowest cost. As a result, the program is likely to cost $870 million, which is almost 90 percent less than the original estimate.

Note: To correct for the effect of inflation, the costs are measured in dollars of 1990 purchasing power.

Source: Environmental Protection Agency, *Progress Report on the EPA Acid Rain Program*, November 1999, Figure 2.

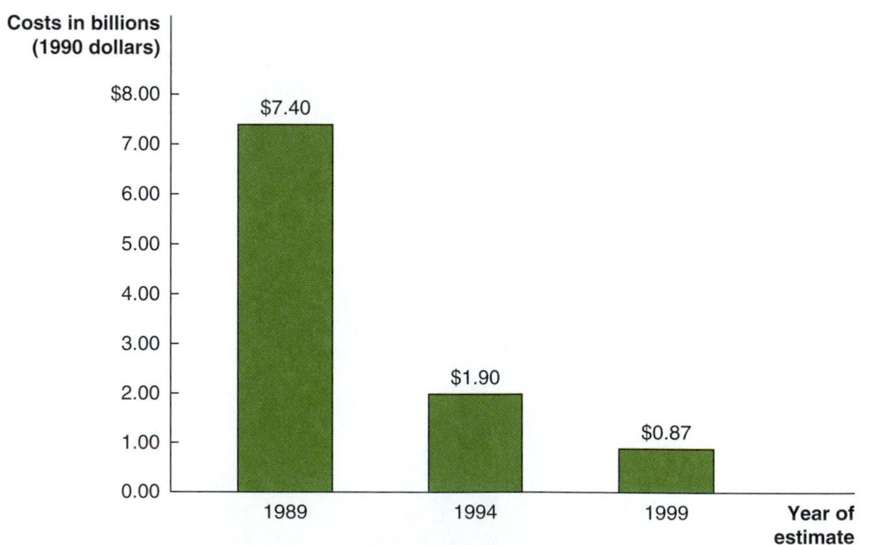

1990, the Edison Electrical Institute estimated that the cost to utilities of complying with the program would be $7.4 billion by 2010. By 1994, the federal government's General Accounting Office estimated the cost would be less than $2 billion. In practice, the cost appears likely to be almost 90 percent less than the initial estimate, or only about $870 *million*.

Licenses to Pollute?

Some environmentalists have criticized tradeable emissions allowances, labeling them "licenses to pollute." They argue that just as the government does not issue licenses to rob banks or to drive drunk, it should not issue licenses to pollute. But this criticism ignores one of the central lessons of economics: Resources are scarce and trade-offs exist. Resources that are spent reducing one type of pollution are not available to reduce other types of pollution or for any other use. Because reducing acid rain using tradeable emissions allowances cost utilities $870 million, rather than $7.4 billion as originally estimated, society saved more than $6.5 billion.

Can Tradeable Permits Reduce Global Warming?

4-5 Making the Connection

In the past 25 years, the global surface temperature has increased about three-quarters of 1 degree Fahrenheit (or four-tenths of 1 degree Centigrade) compared with the average for the previous 30 years. The following graph shows changes in temperature over the years since 1880.

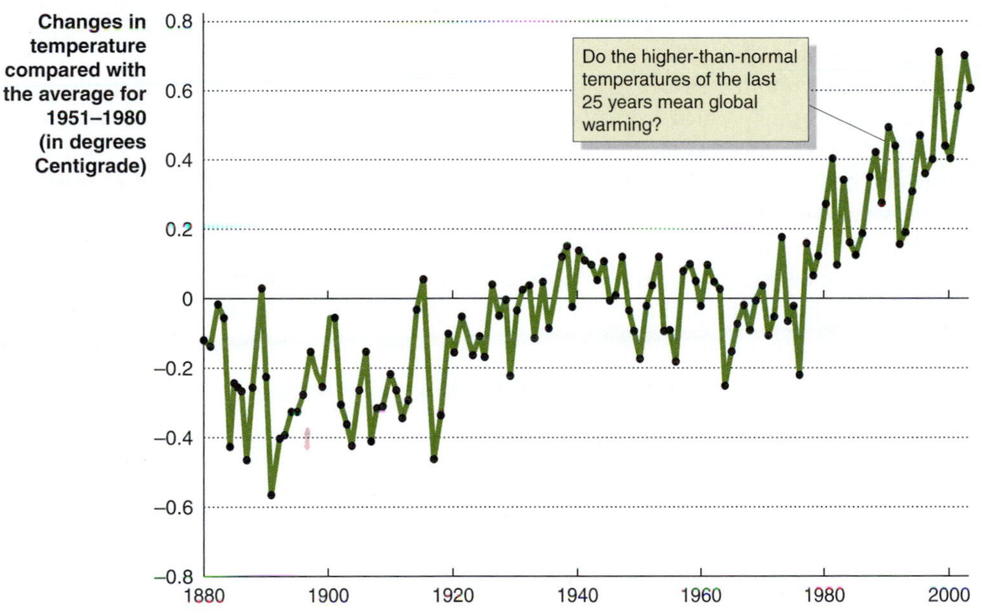

Global temperatures have gone through many periods of warming and cooling. In fact, the below-normal temperatures that prevailed before 1970 led some scientists to predict the eventual arrival of a new ice age. Nevertheless, many scientists are convinced that the recent warming is not part of the natural fluctuations in temperature but is instead due to the burning of fossil fuels, such as coal, natural gas, and petroleum. Burning these fuels releases CO_2 (carbon dioxide), which accumulates in the atmosphere as a "greenhouse gas."

Rapid growth in India has led to rapid increases in CO_2 emissions.

Greenhouse gases cause some of the heat released from the earth to be reflected back, increasing temperatures.

If greenhouse gases continue to accumulate in the atmosphere, according to some estimates, global temperatures could increase by 3 degrees Fahrenheit or more during the next 100 years. Such increases in temperature could lead to significant changes in climate, which might result in more storms and flooding as well as other problems. By 1995, a number of nations had concluded that the threat of global warming was significant enough to take steps toward reducing emissions of CO_2 and other greenhouse gases. The result was the 1997 Kyoto Treaty, which, if accepted, would have required the high-income countries to reduce their CO_2 emissions by more than 5 percent compared with their 1990 levels. However, President George W. Bush was not willing to commit the United States to the treaty. He argued that the costs to the United States of complying with the treaty were too high, particularly because some scientists were still skeptical that CO_2 emissions actually were causing the increase in temperature. Even scientists who believed that CO_2 emissions contribute to rising temperatures were skeptical that the Kyoto Treaty would have much effect on global warming. President Bush also argued that developing countries should be included in any agreement. Some developing countries, such as China and India, are experiencing rapid economic growth, which in turn has led to rapid increases in CO_2 emissions.

The mechanism by which reductions in CO_2 emissions would occur has also been in dispute. The United States has favored a global system of tradeable emission permits for CO_2 that would be similar to the system for sulfur dioxide we discussed earlier in this chapter. As we have seen, this type of system has the potential to reduce CO_2 emissions at the lowest cost. Most European countries, however, have been reluctant to give full acceptance to such a system, preferring instead to require that each country reduce emissions by a specified amount. It seems unlikely that the debate over the costs and benefits of reducing CO_2 emissions will be resolved any time soon.

Source for data in graph: NASA, Goddard Institute for Space Studies, www.giss.nasa.gov/data/update/gistemp/graphs.

Conclusion

The model of demand and supply introduced in Chapter 3 showed that markets free from government intervention eliminate surpluses and shortages, and do a good job of responding to the wants of consumers. We have seen in this chapter that both consumers and firms sometimes try to use the government to change market outcomes in their favor. The concepts of consumer and producer surplus and deadweight loss allow us to measure the benefits consumers and producers receive from competitive market equilibrium. They also allow us to measure the effects of government price floors and price ceilings.

In this chapter, we have also seen that the government has an indispensable role to play in the economy when the absence of well-defined and enforceable property rights keeps the market from operating efficiently. Because no one has a property right for clean air, in the absence of government intervention, firms will produce too great a quantity of products that generate air pollution.

Read *An Inside Look* on the next page to learn how rent control affects people looking for apartments in New York City.

An Inside Look

Dealing with Rent Control

SLATE, MAY 18, 1997

The Romance of Rent Control

If you want to understand the bitter debate over rent control that now dominates social interaction in New York, you have to begin by ignoring arguments about social justice, market economics, and all appeals to principle. Instead, apply crude Marxist dogma: It's a battle of naked class interest. The catch is that the "classes" glowering at each other across the barricades aren't rich and poor. They're the New Yorkers with scandalously sweet deals vs. all those who get screwed as a result.

Recent experience has done much to reinforce my own class consciousness as a member of the latter group. **a** My wife and I were minding our own business in an unregulated apartment in the rapidly gentrifying East Village when we returned from work one day to a letter informing us that our already (to non-New Yorkers) alarming rent of $1,950 was going up $700. That's for a largish one-bedroom in a marginal neighborhood. . . . Thanks to a connection, we fell into a nice, $2,000 one-bedroom in Chelsea, without paying a finder's fee. Absent the artificial shortage created by rent regulation, we would either have a bigger place or pay much less for the one we've got.

The moral and economic arguments against rent control are pretty much unassailable. Under the present system, government intervenes in the market to protect a class of people defined to some extent by long-term residency, but to an even larger extent by luck. This massive intrusion in the real-estate market, which might be hard to justify even if it had purely beneficial consequences, has a number of obviously disastrous ones. It deters young people and new immigrants from moving to New York City; it encourages landlords to neglect their buildings; it makes them hate their tenants. . . .

b What would happen if rent regulations were really abolished? It's a pretty safe bet that in most parts of Manhattan, market rents would settle in somewhere between the $2,000 a month I pay and the $600 that others pay for nearly identical apartments in the same building. Using the estimates promoted by the Rent Stabilization Association (the newspeak name for the group representing landlords who actually wish to *end* rent stabilization), the typical one-bedroom in the Village or on the Upper West Side might go for $1,300 to $1,400 after the shakeout. A rent like that calls for a pretax income of at least $50,000. Once you figure in New York City and state taxes, a more realistic figure would be $60,000.

c The poor, who are subsidized directly, and are likely to be exempted even in the case of radical decontrol, would stay put. What Manhattan would lose is what remains of its middle class, those earning between $25,000 and, say, $75,000. This would mean a tremendous blow to the city's social variety and cultural vitality. Gone would be the used-bookstore owner, the public-school teacher, the family that's been in the same Upper West Side building for 100 years.

One of the big points made by opponents of rent control is that the present system prevents the construction of new buildings. Because rent regulations say you can't evict people when their leases are up (if they even have leases), one obstinate tenement dweller can block the creation of a 50-story high-rise. But who wants new buildings in Manhattan? What an apartment building looks like—on the outside—affects everybody, not just the landlord and the tenant. New York's old buildings are gracious and charming, even those that are rundown. Its new ones—at least those of the residential variety—are generally horrible. It is rent control that has preserved the aesthetic as well as the social fabric of the kind of variegated, low-rise neighborhoods Jane Jacobs celebrated in *The Death and Life of Great American Cities*. . . .

The goal of a rent-regulation compromise should be to diminish unfairness and mitigate perverse side effects without giving a shock to the city's social system. This argues for a fairly straightforward means test for rent control, say $100,000 a year. . . . There will be people, some of them elderly, who make more than $100,000 but still can't afford the rents their apartments could command on the free market. They will have to move. How big a tragedy is that?

Key Points in the Article

This article provides a look at the market for rental apartments in New York City. Jacob Weisberg, the author of the article, is the managing editor of *Slate*, the online magazine owned by Microsoft. Weisberg's experiences highlight key aspects of life in a city with rent control. Weisberg also presents an argument in favor of rent control, even though he has been made worse off by it financially.

Analyzing the News

We can use the concepts from this chapter to analyze the article:

a Jacob Weisberg and his wife were living in an unregulated apartment, so the rent adjusted according to movements in demand and supply. Because higher-income people were moving into the neighborhood, it was becoming more desirable, and the demand for apartments shifted to the right. This increase in demand caused the equilibrium rent to increase from $1,950 to $2,650 per month.

b The author is correct in noting that: "Absent the artificial shortage created by rent regulation, we would either have a bigger place or pay much less for the one we've got." Figure 1 (a) shows the market for apartments currently subject to rent control. For these apartments, eliminating rent control would increase the quantity of apartments rented from Q_1 to Q_2. The rent would rise from $1,000, the rent control ceiling, to $1,500, the competitive equilibrium rent. Figure 1 (b) shows the market for apartments not currently subject to rent control. The elimination of rent control would cause the demand curve for these apartments to shift to the left from D_1 to D_2, which would lower the equilibrium rent from $2,000 to $1,500 per month.

c Although the author is well aware that rent control has resulted in his paying more for his apartment than he would have in a competitive market, he is reluctant to see rent control eliminated. In other words, he understands the positive analysis that shows the economic costs of rent control, but his normative analysis leads him still to support the policy.

Thinking Critically ABOUT POLICY

1. The author of the article notes that a rent-control law "encourages landlords to neglect their buildings. . . ." How does rent-control do this?
2. Despite his complaints, the author supports rent-control laws. He implicitly balances the cost and benefits of the policy. How might his conclusion change if he were confronted with an estimate of the deadweight loss of the policy? How large would such a deadweight loss have to be before you would predict the author would change his mind? Against what measure of benefit would the deadweight loss have to be weighed?

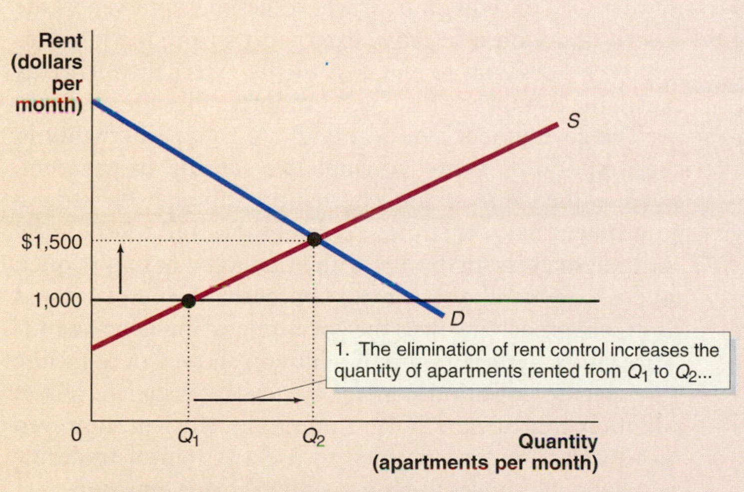

(a) Apartments (currently rent-controlled)

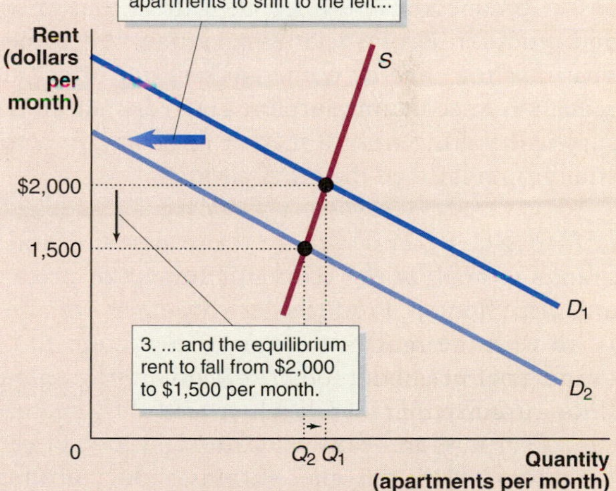

(b) Apartments (currently not rent-controlled)

Figure 1: In (a), the elimination of rent control causes an increase from Q_1 to Q_2 in the quantity of apartments being rented. In (b) this causes the demand for currently non-rent-controlled apartments to shift to the left from D_1 to D_2. The equilibrium rent declines from $2,000 to $1,500.

SUMMARY

LEARNING OBJECTIVE ① Understand the concepts of consumer surplus and producer surplus. *Marginal benefit* is the additional benefit to a consumer from consuming one more unit of a good or service. The demand curve is also a marginal benefit curve. *Consumer surplus* is the difference between the highest price a consumer is willing to pay for a product and the price the consumer actually pays. The total amount of consumer surplus in a market is equal to the area below the demand curve and above the market price. *Marginal cost* is the additional cost to a firm of producing one more unit of a good or service. The supply curve is also a marginal cost curve. *Producer surplus* is the difference between the lowest price a firm is willing to accept and the price it actually receives. The total amount of producer surplus in a market is equal to the area above the supply curve and below the market price.

LEARNING OBJECTIVE ② Understand the concept of economic efficiency, and use a graph to illustrate how economic efficiency is reduced when a market is not in competitive equilibrium. Equilibrium in a competitive market is *economically efficient. Economic surplus* is the sum of consumer surplus and producer surplus. Economic efficiency is a market outcome in which the marginal benefit to consumers from the last unit produced is equal to the marginal cost of production, and where the sum of consumer surplus and producer surplus is at a maximum. When the market price is above or below the equilibrium price, there is a reduction in economic surplus. The reduction in economic surplus resulting from a market not being in competitive equilibrium is called the *deadweight loss.*

LEARNING OBJECTIVE ③ Use demand and supply graphs to analyze the economic impact of price ceilings and price floors. Producers or consumers who are dissatisfied with the market outcome can attempt to convince the government to impose *price floors* or *price ceilings.* Price floors usually increase producer surplus, decrease consumer surplus, and cause a deadweight loss. Price ceilings usually increase consumer surplus, reduce producer surplus, and cause a deadweight loss. The results of the government imposing price ceilings and prices floors are that some people win, some people lose, and a loss of economic efficiency occurs. Positive analysis is concerned with what is, and normative analysis is concerned with what should be. Positive analysis shows that price ceilings and price floors cause deadweight losses. Whether these policies are desirable or undesirable, though, is a normative question.

LEARNING OBJECTIVE ④ Identify examples of positive and negative externalities and use graphs to show how externalities affect economic efficiency. An *externality* is a benefit or cost to parties who are not involved in a transaction. Pollution and other externalities in production cause a difference between the private cost borne by the producer of a good or service and the *social cost,* which includes any external cost, such as the cost of pollution. An externality in consumption causes a difference between the *private benefit* received by the consumer and the *social benefit,* which includes any external benefit. If externalities exist in production or consumption, the market will not produce the optimal level of a good or service. This outcome is referred to as *market failure.*

LEARNING OBJECTIVE ⑤ Analyze government policies to achieve economic efficiency in a market with an externality. When private solutions to externalities are unworkable, the government will sometimes intervene. One way to deal with a negative externality in production is to impose a tax equal to the cost of the externality. The tax causes the producer of the good to internalize the externality. The government can deal with a positive externality in consumption by giving consumers a subsidy, or payment, equal to the value of the externality. Although the federal government has sometimes used subsidies and taxes to deal with externalities, in dealing with pollution it has more often used a "command and control approach." A command and control approach involves the government imposing quantitative limits on the amount of pollution allowed or requiring that specific pollution control devices be installed. Direct pollution controls are not economically efficient, however. As a result, Congress decided to use a system of tradeable emissions allowances to reduce sulfur dioxide emissions.

KEY TERMS

Black market 108
Command and control approach 118
Consumer surplus 99
Deadweight loss 103
Economic efficiency 104
Economic surplus 103
Externality 98
Marginal benefit 99
Marginal cost 101
Market failure 113
Pigovian taxes and subsidies 116
Price ceiling 98
Price floor 98
Private benefit 112
Private cost 112
Producer surplus 101
Property rights 113
Social benefit 112
Social cost 112

REVIEW QUESTIONS

1. What is marginal benefit? Why is the demand curve referred to as a marginal benefit curve? What is marginal cost? Why is the supply curve referred to as a marginal cost curve?
2. What is consumer surplus? How does consumer surplus change as the equilibrium price of a good rises or falls?
3. What is producer surplus? How does producer surplus change as the equilibrium price of a good rises or falls?
4. What is economic efficiency? Why do economists define efficiency in this way?
5. Why would some consumers tend to favor price controls, while others would be against them?
6. Do producers tend to favor price floors or price ceilings? Why?
7. What is an externality? Give an example of a positive externality and of a negative externality.
8. When will the private cost of producing a good differ from the social cost? Give an example. When will the private benefit from consuming a good differ from the social benefit? Give an example.
9. How do externalities affect the economic efficiency of a market equilibrium?
10. What is market failure? When is market failure likely to arise?
11. What is a Pigovian tax? At what level must a Pigovian tax be set to achieve efficiency?
12. Why do most economists favor tradeable emissions allowances to the command and control approach to pollution?

PROBLEMS AND APPLICATIONS

Please visit **www.prenhall.com/hubbard** *for solutions to the even-numbered problems as well as multiple-choice and true or false self-assessment quizzes.*

1. The figure below illustrates the market for apples in which the government has imposed a price floor of $10 per crate.

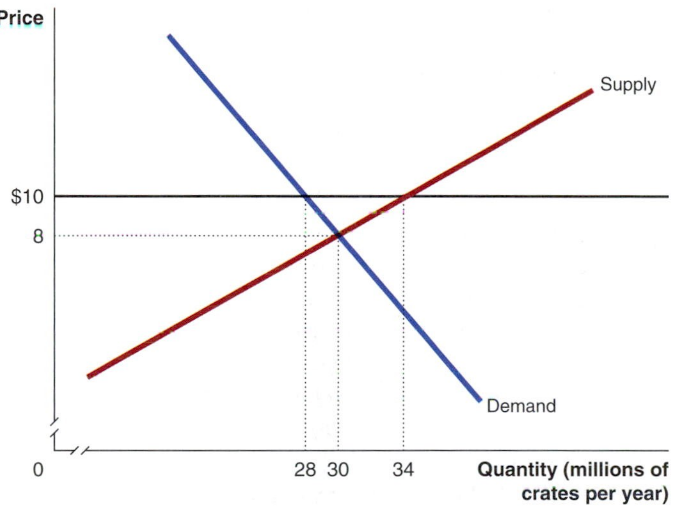

a. How many crates of apples will be sold after the price floor has been imposed?
b. Will there be a shortage or a surplus? If there is a shortage or a surplus, how large will it be?
c. Will apple producers benefit from the price floor? If so, explain how they will benefit.

2. Use the information on the kumquat market in the following table to answer the questions.

PRICE (PER CRATE)	QUANTITY DEMANDED (MILLIONS OF CRATES PER YEAR)	QUANTITY SUPPLIED (MILLIONS OF CRATES PER YEAR)
$10	120	20
15	110	60
20	100	100
25	90	140
30	80	180
35	70	220

a. What are the equilibrium price and quantity? How much revenue do kumquat producers receive when the market is in equilibrium? Draw a graph showing the market equilibrium and the area representing the revenue received by kumquat producers.
b. Suppose the federal government decides to impose a price floor of $30 per crate. Now how many crates of kumquats will consumers purchase? How much revenue will kumquat producers receive? Assume that the government does not purchase any surplus kumquats. On your graph from question (a), show the price floor,

the change in the quantity of kumquats purchased, and the revenue received by kumquat producers after the price floor is imposed.

c. Suppose the government imposes a price floor of $30 per crate and purchases any surplus kumquats from producers. Now how much revenue will kumquat producers receive? How much will the government spend purchasing surplus kumquats? On your graph from question (a), show the area representing the amount the government spends to purchase the surplus kumquats.

3. Suppose that the government sets a price floor for milk that is above the competitive equilibrium price.
   a. Draw a graph showing this situation. Be sure that your graph shows the competitive equilibrium price, the price floor, the quantity that would be sold in competitive equilibrium, and the quantity that is sold with the price floor.
   b. Compare the economic surplus in this market when there is a price floor and when there is no price floor.

4. Suppose that the government restricts the number of dairy farmers, which results in the supply curve for milk shifting to the left. Briefly explain whether each of the following will increase or decrease.
   a. Consumer surplus
   b. Producer surplus
   c. Economic surplus

   Using a demand and supply graph, illustrate your answer in each case.

5. To drive a taxicab legally in New York City, you must have a medallion issued by the city government. Only 12,187 medallions have been issued. Let's assume this puts an absolute limit on the number of taxi rides that can be supplied in New York City on any day, because no one breaks the law by driving a taxi without a medallion. Let's also assume that each taxi can provide 6 trips per day. In that case, the supply of taxi rides is fixed at 73,122 (or 6 rides per taxi × 12,187 taxis). We show this in the following graph with a vertical line at this quantity. *Assume that there are no government controls on the prices that drivers can charge for rides.* Use the figure at the top of the next column to answer the following questions.
   a. What would the equilibrium price and quantity be in this market if there were no medallion requirement?
   b. What are the price and quantity with the medallion requirement?
   c. Indicate on the graph the areas representing consumer surplus and producer surplus if there were no medallion requirement.
   d. Indicate on the graph the areas representing consumer surplus, producer surplus, and deadweight loss with the medallion requirement.

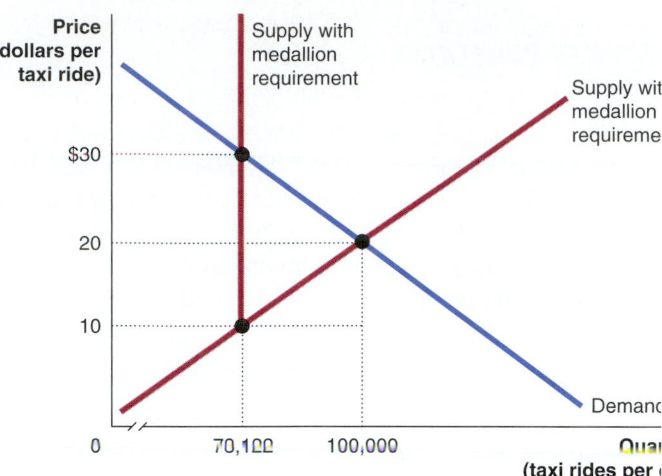

6. **[Related to *Solved Problem 4-1*]** Use the information in the following table on the market for apartments in Bay City to answer the following questions.

RENT	QUANTITY DEMANDED	QUANTITY SUPPLIED
$500	375,000	225,000
600	350,000	250,000
700	325,000	275,000
800	300,000	300,000
900	275,000	325,000
1,000	250,000	350,000

   a. In the absence of rent control, what is the equilibrium rent and what is the equilibrium quantity of apartments rented? Draw a demand and supply graph of the market for apartments to illustrate your answer. In equilibrium, will there be any renters who are unable to find an apartment to rent or any landlords who are unable to find a renter for an apartment?
   b. Suppose the government sets a ceiling on rents of $600 per month. What is the quantity of apartments demanded, and what is the quantity of apartments supplied?
   c. Assume that all landlords abide by the law. Use a demand and supply graph to illustrate the impact of this price ceiling on the market for apartments. Be sure to indicate on your diagram each of the following: (i) the area representing consumer surplus after the price ceiling has been imposed, (ii) the area representing producer surplus after the price ceiling has been imposed, and (iii) the area representing the deadweight loss after the ceiling has been imposed.
   d. Assume that the quantity of apartments supplied is the same as you determined in (b). But now assume that landlords ignore the law and rent this quantity of

apartments for the highest rent they can get. Briefly explain what this rent will be.

7. **[Related to *Don't Let This Happen To You!*]** Briefly explain whether you agree or disagree with the following statement: "If there is a shortage of a good it must be scarce, but there is not a shortage of every scarce good."
8. A student makes the following argument:

   > A price floor reduces the amount of a product that consumers buy, because it keeps the price above the competitive market equilibrium. A price ceiling, on the other hand, increases the amount of a product that consumers buy, because it keeps the price below the competitive market equilibrium.

   Do you agree with the student's reasoning? Use a demand and supply graph to illustrate your answer.
9. **[Related to *Solved Problem 4-1*]** Suppose that initially the gasoline market is in equilibrium at a price of $2.00 per gallon and a quantity of 45 million gallons per month. Then a war in the Middle East disrupts imports of oil into the United States, shifting the supply curve for gasoline from S_1 to S_2. The price of gasoline begins to rise and consumers protest. The federal government responds by setting a price ceiling of $2.00 per gallon. Use the graph to answer the following questions.

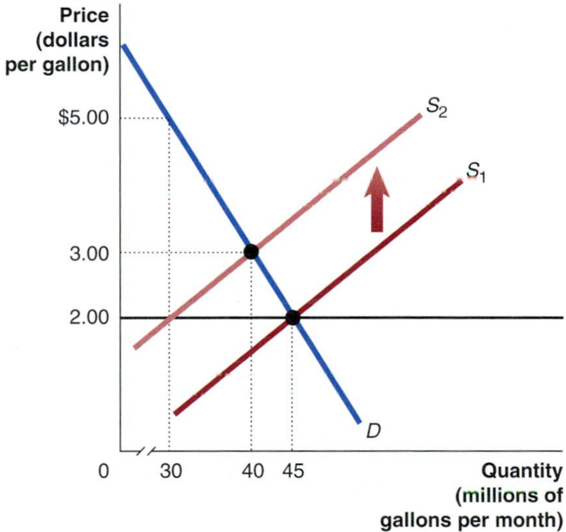

   a. If there were no price ceiling, what would be the equilibrium price of gasoline, the quantity of gasoline demanded, and the quantity of gasoline supplied? Now assume that the price ceiling is imposed and that there is no black market in gasoline. What are the price of gasoline, the quantity of gasoline demanded, and the quantity of gasoline supplied? How large is the shortage of gasoline?
   b. Assume that the price ceiling is imposed and there is no black market in gasoline. Show on the graph the areas representing consumer surplus, producer surplus, and deadweight loss.
   c. Now assume there is a black market and the price of gasoline rises to the maximum that consumers are willing to pay for the amount supplied by producers at $2.00 per gallon. Show on the graph the areas representing producer surplus, consumer surplus, and deadweight loss.
   d. Are consumers made better off by the price ceiling? Briefly explain.
10. **[Related to the *Chapter Opener*]** Rent controls were first imposed in New York City in the early 1940s during a housing shortage brought on by World War II. Why do you think that, once established, rent controls continued in New York City for many decades?
11. An advocate of medical care system reform makes the following argument:

   > The 15,000 kidneys that are transplanted in the United States each year are received free from organ donors. Despite this, because of hospital and doctor's fees, the average price of a kidney transplant is $250,000. As a result, only rich people or people with very good health insurance can afford these transplants. The government should put a ceiling of $100,000 on the price of kidney transplants. That way, middle-income people will be able to afford them, the demand for kidney transplants will increase, and more kidney transplants will take place.

   Do you agree with the advocate's reasoning? Use a demand and supply graph to illustrate your answer.
12. In the United States, Amazon.com, BarnesandNoble.com, and many other retailers sell books, DVDs, and music CDs for less than the price marked on the package. In Japan, retailers are not allowed to discount prices in this way. Who benefits and who loses from this Japanese law?
13. Most family businesses in the United States receive little direct support from the federal government. However, family farms have been receiving support from the federal government since the 1930s. Why do you suppose family farms have been singled out as meriting special support from the government?
14. The competitive equilibrium rent in the city of Lowell is currently $1,000 per month. The government decides to enact rent control and to establish a price ceiling for apartments of $750 per month. Briefly explain whether rent control is likely to make you personally better or worse off if you are:
   a. someone currently renting an apartment in Lowell.
   b. someone who will be moving to Lowell next year and who intends to rent an apartment.

c. a landlord who intends to abide by the rent-control law.
d. a landlord who intends to ignore the law and illegally charge the highest rent you can for your apartments.

15. The chapter states that your consuming a Big Mac does not create an externality. But suppose you arrive at your favorite McDonald's at lunchtime and get in a long line to be served. By the time you reach the counter, there are 10 people in line behind you. Because you decided to have a Big Mac for lunch—instead of, say, a pizza—each of those 10 people must wait in line an additional 2 minutes. Or suppose that after a lifetime of consuming Big Macs you develop heart disease. Because you are now over age 65, the government must pay most of your medical bills through the Medicare system. Is it still correct to say that your consuming a Big Mac created no externalities? Might there be a justification here for the government to intervene in the market for Big Macs? Explain.

16. The chapter discusses the cases of consumption generating a positive externality and production generating a negative externality. Is it possible for consumption to generate a negative externality? If so, give an example. Is it possible for production to generate a positive externality? If so, give an example.

17. If the marginal cost of reducing a certain type of pollution is zero, should all of that pollution be eliminated? Briefly explain.

18. Discuss the factors that determine the marginal cost of reducing crime. Discuss the factors that determine the marginal benefit of reducing crime. Would it be economically efficient to reduce the amount of crime to zero? Briefly explain.

19. A columnist for the *Wall Street Journal* observes:

> No one collects money from those who benefit from the flood control a wetland provides, or the nutrient recycling a forest does. . . . In a nutshell, market failures help drive habitat loss.

What does she mean by market failures? What does she mean by habitat loss? Explain why she believes one is causing the other. Illustrate your argument with a graph showing the market for land to be used for development.
Source: Sharon Begley, "Furry Math? Market Has Failed to Capture True Value of Nature," *Wall Street Journal*, August 9, 2002, p. B1.

20. In discussing cleaning up oil spills, Gary Shigenka of the National Oceonographic and Atmospheric Agency observed that "The first 90% of any cleanup comes easy. But the tradeoffs for the remaining bits are brutal." He estimates that the last 1 percent of oil removed can cost seven times as much as the first 99 percent. Why should it be any more costly to clean up the last 1 percent of an oil spill than to clean up the first 1 percent? What trade-offs do you think Shigenka was referring to?
Source: Keith Johnson and Gautam Naik, "For Spain, Exxon Valdez Offers Some Surprising Lessons," *Wall Street Journal*, November 22, 2002.

21. We saw in this chapter that market failure occurs when firms ignore the costs generated by pollution in deciding how much to produce. Government intervention usually is necessary to bring about a more efficient level of production. Before 1989, the Communist governments of Eastern Europe directly controlled the production of most goods and were free to choose how much of each good would be produced and what production process would be used. When these Communist governments collapsed, it was revealed that the countries of Eastern Europe suffered from very high levels of pollution, much higher than had existed in the United States and other high-income countries even before there was government antipollution legislation. Discuss reasons why the nonmarket Communist system generated more pollution than market economies.

22. Bjorn Lomborg, director of the Environmental Assessment Institute in Denmark, argued in a column in the *New York Times:*

> Traditionally, the developed nations of the West have shown a greater concern for environmental sustainability, while the third world countries have a stronger desire for economic development.

Recall the definition of a normal good given in Chapter 3. Is environmental protection a normal good? If so, is there any connection between this fact and Lomborg's observation? Briefly explain. How do the marginal cost and marginal benefit of environmental protection change with economic development?
Source: Bjorn Lomborg, "The Environmentalists Are Wrong," *New York Times*, August 26, 2002.

23. **[Related to *Solved Problem 4-2*]** The fumes from dry cleaners can contribute to air pollution. Suppose the figure on the next page illustrates the situation in the dry cleaning market:
a. Explain how a government can use a tax on dry cleaning to bring about the efficient level of production. What should the value of the tax be?
b. How large is the deadweight loss (in dollars) from excessive dry cleaning, according to the figure?

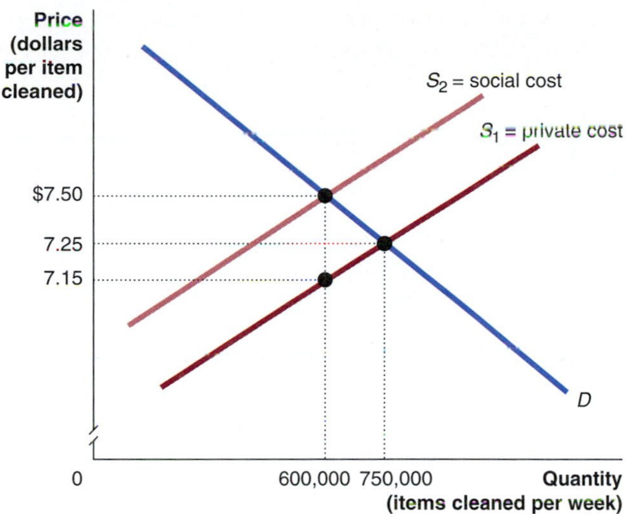

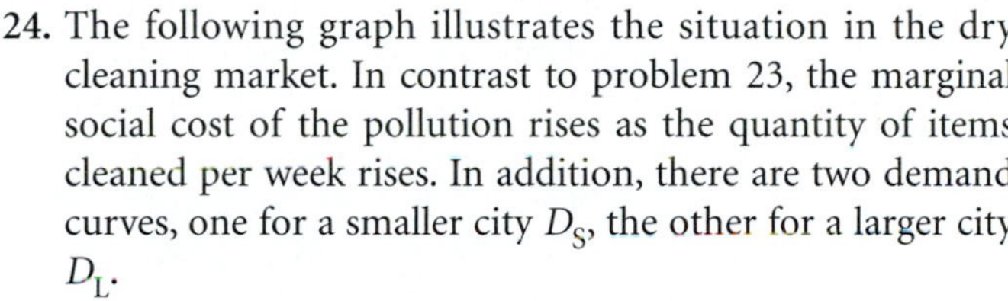
24. The following graph illustrates the situation in the dry cleaning market. In contrast to problem 23, the marginal social cost of the pollution rises as the quantity of items cleaned per week rises. In addition, there are two demand curves, one for a smaller city D_S, the other for a larger city D_L.

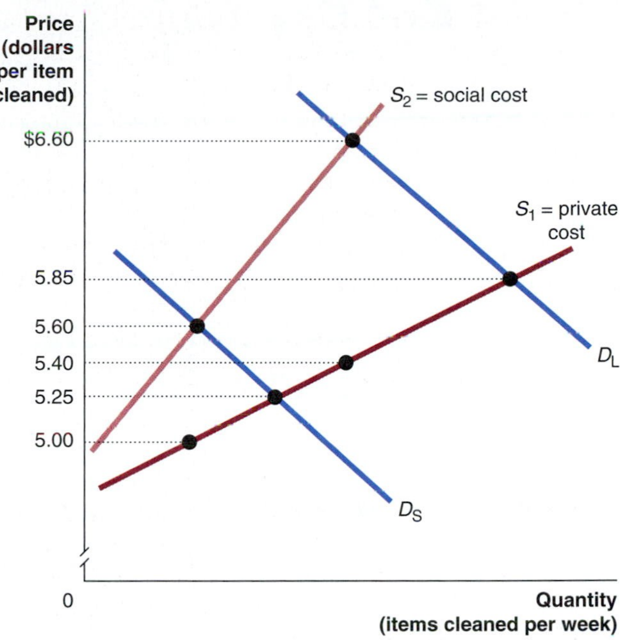

a. Explain why the social cost curve has a different slope than the private cost curve.

b. What tax rate per item cleaned will achieve economic efficiency in the smaller city? In the larger city? Explain why the tax rate differs from one city to the next.

chapter five

Firms, the Stock Market, and Corporate Governance

Google: From Dorm Room to Wall Street

There could be no question that Google was cool. The world's most widely used Internet search engine, Google had become the essence of cool as a way to research information stored on Web sites. Founded in 1998 by Larry Page and Sergey Brin, Google grew quickly. In 2005, Google employed 3,000 people and earned $3.2 billion in revenue. Google's founders had transformed the Internet search engine and brought value to users through a combination of intellect, technology, and the talents of many employees. Google's key advantage over competitors such as A9 and Ask Jeeves was its search algorithms that allowed users to find easily Web sites most relevant to a subject. Google had other advantages as well, such as its automatic foreign-language translation. Google had become so dominant that other major Web sites, such as AOL and Yahoo, were using it as their search engine. And "Google" had even become a verb: "I couldn't remember the name of the founder of Microsoft, so I googled it." Google's huge popularity allowed it to do what most other Internet sites could not: make money selling advertising.

And Google was hot. In 2004, Google sold part of the firm to outside investors by offering stock—and partial ownership—to the public. This stock offering vaulted Larry Page and Sergey Brin to the ranks of the super-rich. Google's stock offering also gained significant press attention, as the firm bypassed conventional financial practice and used an automated online auction to help set the share price and determine who should receive stock. The offering's size grabbed attention, too: It was the most anticipated stock sale since the 1995 launch of Netscape, a deal that sparked the late-1990s Internet gold rush on Wall Street. *An Inside Look* on page 146 discusses movements in Google's stock price in the months following the firm's first sale of stock in August 2004.

A business like Google is more than a black box, transforming inputs into outputs. As the firm grew larger, it was less the informal organization put together by the founders and more a complex organization with greater need for management and funds to grow. Indeed, Google's offering of stock to outside investors provided the firm with a major inflow of funds for growth.

Once a firm grows very large, its owners often do not continue to manage it. The large modern corporation is owned by millions of individual investors who have purchased the firm's stock. With ownership so dispersed, the top managers who actually run the firm have the opportunity to make decisions that are in the managers' best interests, but that may not be in the best interests of the stockholders who own the firm.

Against this backdrop, Google faced significant costs associated with selling stock to the public. High-profile corporate accounting scandals in 2001 and 2002 at major U.S. firms, such as Enron, WorldCom, and Tyco, led to the passage of stronger—and more costly—securities regulation under the Sarbanes-Oxley Act, enacted by Congress in 2002. Google's growth prospects and the health of the financial system were intertwined.

LEARNING OBJECTIVES

After studying this chapter, you should be able to:

1. Categorize the major types of business in the United States.
2. Describe the typical management structure of corporations and understand the concepts of separation of ownership from control and the principal-agent problem.
3. Explain how firms obtain the funds they need to operate and expand.
4. Understand the information provided in firms' financial statements.
5. Understand the business accounting scandals of 2002, as well as the role of government in corporate governance.

In this chapter, we look at the firm: how it is organized, how it raises funds, and the information it provides to investors. As we have already discussed, in a market system, firms are responsible for organizing the factors of production to produce goods and services. Firms are the vehicles entrepreneurs use to earn profits by responding to consumer wants as expressed in the market. To succeed, entrepreneurs must meet consumer wants by producing new or better goods and services, or by finding ways of producing existing goods and services at a lower cost so they can be sold at a lower price. Entrepreneurs also need access to sufficient funds, and they must be able to efficiently organize production. As the typical firm in many industries has become larger during the past hundred years, the task of efficiently organizing production has become more difficult. The problem of successfully coordinating the activities of large firms is one of the causes of the recent business scandals in the United States. Toward the end of this chapter, we look at why these scandals occurred and at the steps businesses and the government have taken to avoid similar problems in the future.

1 LEARNING OBJECTIVE

Categorize the major types of business in the United States.

Types of Firms

In studying a market economy, it is important to understand the basics of how firms operate. In the United States, there are three legal categories of firms: *sole proprietorships, partnerships,* and *corporations.* A **sole proprietorship** is a firm owned by a single individual. Although most sole proprietorships are small, some are quite large in terms of sales, number of persons employed, and profits earned. **Partnerships** are firms owned jointly by two or more—sometimes many—persons. Most law and accounting firms are partnerships. The famous Lloyd's of London insurance company is a partnership. Although some partnerships, such as Lloyd's, can be quite large, most large firms are organized as *corporations.* A **corporation** is a legal form of business that provides the owners with limited liability.

Sole proprietorship A firm owned by a single individual and not organized as a corporation.

Partnership A firm owned jointly by two or more persons and not organized as a corporation.

Corporation A legal form of business that provides the owners with limited liability.

Who Is Liable? Limited and Unlimited Liability

A key distinction among these three types of firms is that the owners of sole proprietorships and partnerships have unlimited liability. Unlimited liability means there is no legal distinction between the personal assets of the owners of the firm and the assets of the firm. An **asset** is anything of value owned by a person or a firm. If a sole proprietorship or a partnership owes a lot of money to the firm's suppliers or employees, the suppliers and employees have a legal right to sue the firm for payment, even if this requires the firm's owners to sell some of their personal assets, such as stocks or bonds. In other words, with sole proprietorships and partnerships, the owners are not legally distinct from the firms they own.

Asset Anything of value owned by a person or a firm.

It may seem only fair that the owners of a firm be responsible for a firm's debts. But early in the nineteenth century it became clear to many state legislatures in the United States that unlimited liability was a significant problem for any firm that was attempting to raise funds from large numbers of investors. An investor might be interested in making a relatively small investment in a firm but be unwilling to become a partner in the firm for fear of placing at risk all of his or her personal assets if the firm were to fail. To get around this problem, state legislatures began to pass *general incorporation laws,* which allowed firms to be organized as corporations. Under the corporate form of business, the owners of a firm have **limited liability,** which means that if the firm fails, the owners can never lose more than the amount they had invested in the firm. The personal assets of the owners of the firm are not affected by the failure of the firm. In fact, in the eyes of the law, a corporation is a legal "person" separate from its owners. Limited liabil-

Limited liability The legal provision that shields owners of a corporation from losing more than they have invested in the firm.

TABLE 5-1

Differences among Business Organizations

	SOLE PROPRIETORSHIP	PARTNERSHIP	CORPORATION
Advantages	• Control by owner	• Ability to share work	• Limited personal liability
	• No layers of management	• Ability to share risks	• Greater ability to raise funds
Disadvantages	• Unlimited personal liability	• Unlimited personal liability	• Costly to organize
	• Limited ability to raise funds	• Limited ability to raise funds	• Possible double taxation of income

ity has made it possible for corporations to raise funds by issuing shares of stock to large numbers of investors. For example, if you buy a share of Google stock, you are part owner of the firm, but even if Google were to go bankrupt, you would not be personally responsible for any of Google's debts. Therefore, you could not lose more than the amount you had paid for the stock.

Corporate organizations also have some disadvantages. In the United States, corporate profits are taxed twice—once at the corporate level and again when investors receive a share of corporate profits. Corporations, because they generally are larger than sole proprietorships and partnerships, also are more difficult to organize and harder to run. Table 5-1 reviews the advantages and disadvantages of different forms of business organization.

5-1 Making the Connection

What's in a "Name"? Lloyd's of London Learns about Unlimited Liability the Hard Way

The world-famous insurance company Lloyd's of London got its start in Edward Lloyd's coffeehouse in London in the late 1600s. Ship owners would come to the coffeehouse looking for someone to insure (or "underwrite") their ships and cargos in exchange for a flat fee (or "premium"). The customers of the coffeehouse, themselves merchants or ship owners, who agreed to insure ships or cargos would have to make payment from their personal funds if an insured ship were lost at sea. By the late 1700s the system had become more formal: Each underwriter would recruit investors, known as "Names," and use the funds raised to back insurance policies sold to a wide variety of clients. In the twentieth century Lloyd's became famous for some of its unusual insurance policies. It issued an insurance policy on the legs of Betty Grable, a 1940s movie star. One man bought an insurance policy against seeing a ghost.

Investors in Lloyd's of London lost billions of dollars during the 1980s and 1990s.

By the late 1980s, 34,000 persons around the world had invested in Lloyd's as Names. A series of disasters in the late 1980s and early 1990s—including the *Exxon Valdez* oil spill in Alaska, Hurricane Hugo in South Carolina, and an earthquake in San Francisco—resulted in huge payments on insurance policies written by Lloyd's. In 1989, Lloyd's lost \$3.85 billion. In 1990 it lost an additional \$4.4 billion. It then became clear to many of the Names that Lloyd's was not a corporation and that the Names did not have the limited liability enjoyed by corporate shareholders. On the contrary, the Names were personally responsible for paying the losses on the insurance policies. Many Names lost far more than they had invested. Some investors, such as Charles Schwab, the discount stockbroker, were wealthy enough that their losses were sustainable, but others were less fortunate. One California investor ended up living in poverty after having to sell his \$1 million house to pay his share of the losses. Another Name, Sir Richard Fitch, a British admiral, committed suicide after most of his wealth was wiped out. As many as 30 Names may have committed suicide as a result of their losses.

By 2004, only 2,500 Names—undoubtedly sadder but wiser—remained as investors in Lloyd's. New rules have allowed insurance companies to underwrite Lloyd's policies for the first time. Today, Names provide only about 20 percent of Lloyd's funds.

Sources: Charles Fleming, "The Master of Disaster Is Trying to Avoid One," *Wall Street Journal*, November 17, 2003 and "Lloyd's of London: Insuring for the Future," *Economist*, September 16, 2004.

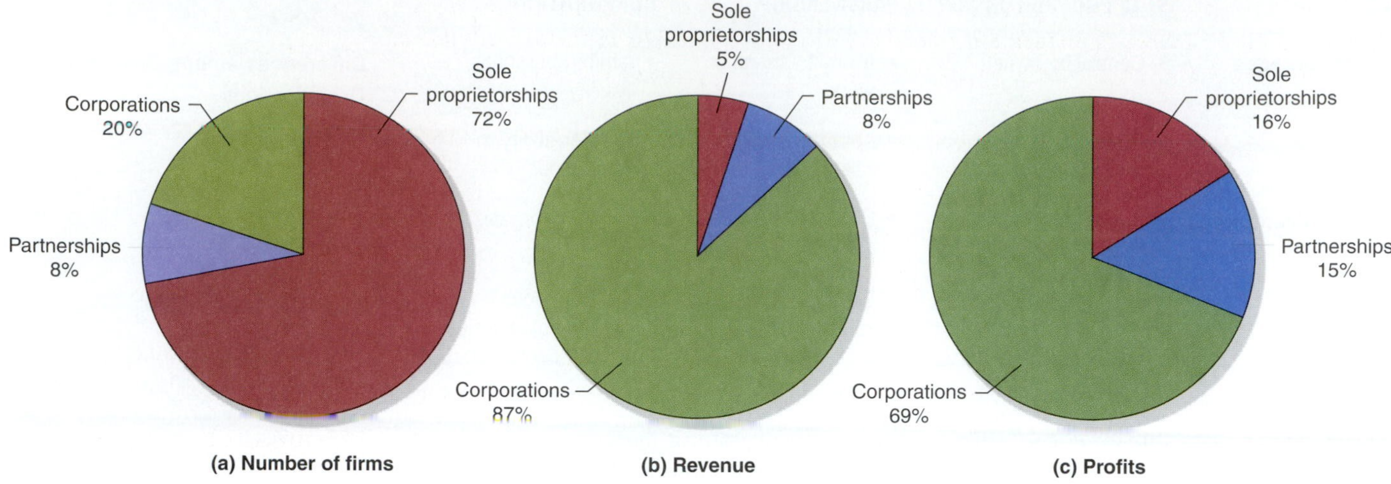

FIGURE 5-1 Business Organizations: Sole Proprietorships, Partnerships, and Corporations

The three types of firms in the United States are sole proprietorships, partnerships, and corporations. Panel (a) shows that only 20 percent of all firms are corporations. Yet, as panels (b) and (c) show, corporations account for a majority of the total revenue and profits earned by all firms.

Source: Statistical Abstract of the United States, 2004–2005.

Corporations Earn the Majority of Revenue and Profits

Figure 5-1 gives basic statistics on the three types of business organizations. Panel (a) shows that almost three-quarters of all firms are sole proprietorships. Panels (b) and (c) show that although only 20 percent of all firms are corporations, corporations account for the majority of revenue and profits earned by all firms. *Profit* is the difference between revenue and the total cost to the firm of producing the goods and services it offers for sale.

There are nearly 5 million corporations in the United States, but only 22,000 have annual revenues of more than $50 million. We can think of these 22,000 firms—including Microsoft, General Electric, and Exxon Mobil—as representing "big business." These large firms account for more than four-fifths of all U.S. corporate profits.

② LEARNING OBJECTIVE

Describe the typical management structure of corporations and understand the concepts of separation of ownership from control and the principal-agent problem.

The Structure of Corporations and the Principal-Agent Problem

Because large corporations account for most sales and profits in the economy, it is important to know how they are managed. Most large corporations have a similar management structure. This structure can lead to problems on the scale of the 2002 business scandals, which we will discuss later. The way in which a corporation is structured and the impact a corporation's structure has on the firm's behavior is referred to as **corporate governance.**

Corporate governance The way in which a corporation is structured and the impact a corporation's structure has on the firm's behavior.

Corporate Structure and Corporate Governance

Corporations are legally owned by their *shareholders,* the owners of the corporation's stock. Unlike founder-dominated businesses, such as family businesses, a corporation's shareholders, although they are the firm's owners, do not manage the firm directly. Instead, they elect a *board of directors* to represent their interests. The board of directors appoints a *chief executive officer* (CEO) to run the day-to-day operations of the corporation. Sometimes the board of directors will also appoint other members of *top management,* such as the *chief financial officer* (CFO). At other times the CEO appoints other members of top management. Members of top management, including the CEO and CFO, will often serve on the board of directors. Members of management serving on the board of directors are referred to as *inside directors*. Members of the board of directors who do not have a direct management role in the firm are referred to as *outside directors*. The outside directors are intended to act as checks on the decisions of top managers, but the distinction between an outside director and an inside director is not always clear. For example, the CEO of a firm that sells a good or service to a large corporation may sit on the board of directors of that corporation. Although an outside director, this person may be reluctant to displease the top managers because the top managers have the power to stop purchasing from his firm. In some instances, top managers have effectively controlled their firms' boards of directors.

Unlike founder-dominated businesses, the top management of large corporations does not generally own a large share of the firm's stock, so large corporations have a **separation of ownership from control.** Although the shareholders actually own the firm, top management controls the day-to-day operations of the firm. Because top managers do not own the entire firm, they may have an incentive to decrease the firm's profits by spending money to purchase private jets or schedule management meetings at luxurious resorts. Economists refer to the conflict between the interests of shareholders and the interests of top management as a **principal-agent problem.** This problem occurs when agents—in this case, a firm's top management—pursue their own interests rather than the interests of the principal who hired them—in this case, the shareholders of the corporation. To reduce the impact of the principal-agent problem, in the 1990s, many boards of directors began to tie the salaries of top managers to the profits of the firm or to the price of the firm's stock. They hoped this would give top managers an incentive to make the firm as profitable as possible, thereby benefiting its shareholders.

Separation of ownership from control In many large corporations the top management, rather than the shareholders, control day-to-day operations.

Principal-agent problem A problem caused by an agent pursuing his own interests rather than the interests of the principal who hired him.

SOLVED PROBLEM 5-1

Does the Principal-Agent Problem Also Apply to the Relationship between Managers and Workers?

(2) LEARNING OBJECTIVE
Describe the typical management structure of corporations and understand the concepts of separation of ownership from control and the principal-agent problem.

Briefly explain whether you agree or disagree with the following argument: "The principal-agent problem applies not just to the relationship between shareholders and top managers. It also applies to the relationship between managers and workers. Just as shareholders have trouble monitoring whether top managers are earning as much profit as possible, managers have trouble monitoring whether workers are working as hard as possible."

Solving the Problem:

Step 1: Review the chapter material. This problem concerns the principal-agent problem, so you may want to review the section "Corporate Structure and Corporate Governance," which begins on page 134.

Step 2: Evaluate the argument. You should agree with the argument. A corporation's shareholders have difficulty monitoring the activities of top managers. In practice, they attempt to do so indirectly through the corporation's board of directors. But a board of directors may be influenced heavily by—or even controlled by—the firm's top managers. Even if a board of directors is not controlled by top management, it may be difficult for the board to know whether actions taken by top managers—say, opening a branch office in Paris—will increase the profitability of the firm or just increase the enjoyment of the top managers.

To answer the problem, we must extend this analysis to the relationship between managers and workers: Managers would like workers to work as hard as possible. Workers would often rather not work hard, particularly if they do not see a direct financial reward for doing so. Managers can have trouble monitoring whether workers are working hard or goofing off. Is that worker in his cubicle diligently staring at a computer screen because he is hard at

work on a report or because he is surfing the Web for sports scores or writing a long e-mail to his girlfriend? Thus, the principal-agent problem does apply to the relationship between managers and workers.

Extra Credit: Boards of directors try to reduce the principal-agent problem by designing compensation policies for top managers that give them financial incentives to increase profits. (Although, as we will see later in this chapter, these plans can sometimes backfire.) Similarly, managers try to reduce the principal-agent problem by designing compensation policies that give workers an incentive to work harder. For example, some manufacturers pay factory workers on the basis of how much they produce, rather than on the basis of how many hours they work.

YOUR TURN: **For more practice, do related problems 6 and 7 on page 149 at the end of this chapter.**

③ **LEARNING OBJECTIVE**

Explain how firms obtain the funds they need to operate and expand.

How Firms Raise Funds

Owners and managers of firms try to earn a profit. To earn a profit, a firm must raise funds to pay for its operations, including paying its employees and buying machines. Indeed, a central challenge for anyone running a firm, whether that person is a sole proprietor or a top manager of a large corporation, is raising the funds needed to operate and expand the business. Suppose you decide to open an online trading service using $100,000 you have saved in a bank. You use the $100,000 to rent a building for your firm, to buy computers, and to pay other start-up expenses. Your firm is a great success and you decide to expand by moving to a larger building and buying more computers. You can obtain the funds for this expansion in three ways:

1. If you are making a profit, you could reinvest the profits back into your firm. Profits that are reinvested in a firm, rather than taken out of a firm and paid to the firm's owners, are *retained earnings.*
2. You could also obtain funds by taking on one or more partners who would invest in the firm. This arrangement would increase the firm's *financial capital.*
3. Finally, you could borrow the funds from relatives, friends, or a bank.

Sources of External Funds

Unless firms rely on retained earnings, they have to obtain the *external funds* they need from others who have funds available to invest. It is the role of an economy's *financial system* to transfer funds from savers to borrowers—directly through financial markets or indirectly through financial intermediaries such as banks.

Firms can raise external funds in two distinct ways. The first relies on financial intermediaries such as banks and is called **indirect finance.** If you put $1,000 in a checking account or a savings account, or if you buy a $1,000 certificate of deposit (CD), the bank will loan most of those funds to borrowers. The bank will combine your funds with those of other depositors and, for example, make a $100,000 loan to a local business.

Indirect finance A flow of funds from savers to borrowers through financial intermediaries such as banks. Intermediaries raise funds from savers to lend to firms (and other borrowers).

The second way for firms to acquire external funds is through *financial markets.* Raising funds in these markets, such as the New York Stock Exchange on Wall Street in New York, is called **direct finance.** Direct finance usually takes the form of the borrower selling the lender a *financial security.* A financial security is a document—sometimes in electronic form—that states the terms under which the funds have passed from the buyer of the security—who is lending funds—to the borrower. *Bonds* and *stocks* are the two main types of financial securities.

Direct finance A flow of funds from savers to firms through financial markets.

BONDS **Bonds** are financial securities that represent promises to repay a fixed amount of funds. When General Electric (GE) sells a bond to raise funds, it promises to pay the purchaser of the bond an interest payment each year for the term of the bond, as well as a final payment of the amount of the loan, or the *principal*, at the end of the term. GE may need to raise many millions of dollars to build a factory, but each individual bond has a principal or *face value*, of $1,000, which is the amount each bond purchaser is lending GE. So, GE must sell many bonds to raise all the funds it needs. Suppose GE promises it will pay interest of $60 per year to anyone who will buy one of its bonds. The interest payments on a bond are referred to as **coupon payments.** The **interest rate** is the cost of borrowing funds, usually expressed as a percentage of the amount borrowed. If we express the coupon as a percentage of the face value of the bond, we have the interest rate on the bond, called the *coupon rate*. In this case the interest rate is

Bond A financial security that represents a promise to repay a fixed amount of funds.

Coupon payment Interest payment on a bond.

Interest rate The cost of borrowing funds, usually expressed as a percentage of the amount borrowed.

$$\frac{\$60}{\$1{,}000} = 0.06, \text{ or } 6\%.$$

Many bonds issued by corporations have terms, or *maturities*, of 30 years. If you bought a bond from GE, GE would pay you $60 per year for 30 years, and at the end of the thirtieth year GE would pay you back the $1,000 principal.

STOCKS When you buy a newly issued bond from a firm, you are lending funds to that firm. When you buy **stock** issued by a firm, you are actually buying part ownership of the firm. When a corporation sells stock, it is doing the same thing the owner of a small business does when she takes on a partner: The firm is increasing its financial capital by bringing additional owners into the firm. Any individual shareholder usually owns only a small fraction of the total shares of stock issued by a corporation. As we discussed earlier, corporations are run by their top managers who answer to the corporation's board of directors, which is elected by the shareholders. Although some individuals may own enough of a firm's stock to influence the actions of the firm, the average shareholder does not.

Stock A financial security that represents partial ownership of a firm.

A shareholder is entitled to a share of the corporation's profits, if there are any. Corporations generally keep some of their profits—known as retained earnings—to finance future expansion. The remaining profits are paid to shareholders as **dividends.** If investors expect the firm to earn economic profits on its retained earnings, the firm's share price will rise, providing a *capital gain* for investors. If a corporation is unable to make a profit, it usually will not pay a dividend. Under the law, corporations must make payments on any debt they have before making payments to their owners. That is, the corporation must make promised payments to bondholders before it may make any dividend payments to shareholders. In addition, when firms sell stock, they acquire from investors an open-ended commitment of funds to the firm. Therefore, unlike bonds, stocks do not have a maturity date, so the firm is not obliged to return the investor's funds at any particular date.

Dividends Payments by a corporation to its shareholders.

Stock and Bond Markets Provide Capital—and Information

The original purchasers of stocks and bonds may resell them to other investors. In fact, most of the buying and selling of stocks and bonds that takes place each day is investors reselling existing stocks and bonds to each other, rather than corporations selling new stocks and bonds to investors. The buyers and sellers of stocks and bonds together make up the *stock and bond markets*. There is no single place where stocks and bonds are bought and sold. Some trading of stocks and bonds takes place in buildings known as *exchanges*, such as the New York Stock Exchange or Tokyo Stock Exchange. In the United States, the stocks and bonds of the largest corporations are traded on the New York Stock Exchange. The development of computer technology has spread the trading of stocks and bonds outside of exchanges to *securities dealers* linked by computers. These

Don't Let This Happen To You!

When Google Shares Change Hands, Google Doesn't Get the Money

If Google becomes a popular investment, with shares changing hands often as views about the firm's valuation shift, that's great for Google, right? Think of all that money flowing into Google's coffers as shares change hands and the stock price goes up. *Wrong.* Google raises funds in a primary market, but shares change hands in a secondary market. Those trades don't put money into Google's hands, but they do give important information to the firm's managers. Let's see why.

Primary markets are those in which newly issued claims are sold to initial buyers by the issuer. Businesses can raise funds in a primary financial market in two ways—by borrowing or by selling shares—which result in different types of claims on the borrower's future income. Although you hear about the stock market fluctuations each night on the evening news, debt instruments actually account for more of the funds raised by borrowers. In mid-2005, the value of debt instruments in the United States was about $25 trillion compared to $12 trillion for equities.

In *secondary markets,* claims that have already been issued are sold by one investor to another. If Google sells shares to the public, it is turning to a primary market for new funds. Once Google shares are issued, investors trade the shares in the secondary market. The founders of Google do not receive any new funds when Google shares are traded on secondary markets. The initial seller of a financial instrument raises funds from a lender only in the primary market. Secondary markets convey information to firms' managers and to investors by determining the price of financial instruments. For example, a major increase in Google's stock price conveys the market's good feelings about the firm, and the firm may decide to raise funds to expand. Hence, secondary markets are valuable sources of information for corporations that are considering raising funds.

Primary and secondary markets are both important, but they play different roles. As an investor, you principally will trade financial instruments in a secondary market. As a corporate manager, you may help decide how to raise new funds to expand the firm where you work.

YOUR TURN: Test your understanding by doing related problem 14 on page 150 at the end of this chapter.

dealers comprise the *over-the-counter market.* The stocks of many computer and other high-technology firms—including Microsoft and Intel—are traded in the most important of the over-the-counter markets, the *National Association of Securities Dealers' Automated Quotation System,* which is referred to by its acronym, NASDAQ.

Shares of stock represent claims on the profits of the firms that issue them. Therefore, as the fortunes of the firms change and they earn more or less profit, the prices of the stock the firms have issued should also change. Similarly, bonds represent claims to receive coupon payments and one final payment of principal. Therefore, a particular bond that was issued in the past may have its price go up or down depending upon whether the coupon payments being offered on newly issued bonds are higher or lower than on existing bonds. If you hold a bond with a coupon of $80 per year and newly issued bonds have coupons of $100 per year, the price of your bond will fall because it is less attractive to investors. The price of a bond will be affected by changes in investors' perceptions of the issuing firm's ability to make the coupon payments. For example, if investors begin to believe that a firm may soon go out of business and stop making coupon payments to its bondholders, the price of the firm's bonds will fall to very low levels.

Changes in the value of a firm's stocks and bonds offer important information for a firm's managers, as well as for investors. An increase in the stock price means that investors are more optimistic about the firm's profit prospects, and the firm's managers may wish to expand the firm's operations as a result. By contrast, a decrease in the firm's stock price indicates that investors are less optimistic about the firms' profit prospects, so that management may want to shrink the firm's operations. Likewise, changes in the value of the firm's bonds imply changes in the cost of external funds to finance the firm's investment in research and development or in new factories. A higher bond price indicates a lower cost of new external funds, while a lower bond price indicates a higher cost of new external funds.

5-2 Making the Connection

Following General Electric's Stock and Bond Prices in the Financial Pages

If you read the stock and bond listings in your local paper or the *Wall Street Journal*, you will notice that newspapers manage to pack into a small space a lot of information about what happened to stocks and bonds during the previous day's trading. The following figure reproduces a section from one page of the stock quotations from the *Wall Street Journal*. Let's focus on the highlighted listing for General Electric, and examine the information in each column.

- The first column (YLD %CHG) gives the percentage change in the price of the stock from the beginning of the year to date. In this case, the price of GE's stock had fallen 1.1 percent since the beginning of 2005.
- The second column (52-WEEK HI) and the third column (52-WEEK LO) give the highest price GE stock has traded for and the lowest price GE has traded for during the previous year. These numbers tell you how *volatile* the stock price is—that is, how much it fluctuates over the course of the year.
- The fourth column (STOCK (SYM)) gives a compact version of the firm's name followed by the firm's "ticker" symbol, which you may have seen scrolling along the bottom of the screen on cable financial news channels.
- The fifth column (DIV) gives the dividend expressed in dollars. In this case, .88 means that GE paid a dividend of $0.88 per share.
- The sixth column (YLD %) gives the *dividend yield*, which is calculated by dividing the dividend by the *closing price* of the stock—that is, the price at which GE stock last sold before the close of trading on the previous day.
- The seventh column (PE) gives the *P-E ratio* (or price-earnings ratio), which is calculated by dividing the price of the firm's stock by its earnings per share (remember that because firms retain some earnings, earnings per share is not necessarily the same as dividends per share). GE's P-E ratio was 22, meaning that its price per share was 22 times its earnings per share. You would have to pay $22 to buy $1 of GE earnings.
- The eighth column (VOL 100s) gives the number of shares of stock traded on the previous day (in hundreds of shares). So, 26,135,600 shares of GE stock were traded the previous day on the New York Stock Exchange.
- The ninth column (CLOSE) is the price the stock sold for the last time it was traded before the close of trading on the previous day, which in this case was $36.10.
- The tenth and final column (NET CHG) gives the amount by which the closing price changed from the closing price the day before. In this case, the price of GE's stock had fallen by $0.15 per share from its closing price the day before. Changes in GE's stock price give the firm's managers a signal that they may want to expand or contract the firm's operations.

YTD % CHG	52-WEEK HI	LO	STOCK (SYM)	DIV	YLD %	PE	VOL 100s	CLOSE	NET CHG
–14.9	14.10	6.79	GenlCbl BGC		...	51	2066	11.79	–0.26
0.9	109.98	90.61	GenDynam GD	1.60F	1.5	16	7304	105.57	0.06
–1.1	37.75	29.55	GenElec GE	.88	2.4	22	261356	36.10	–0.15
3.8	39.30	24.31	GenGrthProp GGP	1.44	3.8	31	21099	37.53	–0.86
11.7	53.98	17.75	GenMaritime GMR	1.77p	...	6	5522	44.64	–0.46

Now we can look at the listings for corporate bonds. As with stocks, to understand the information printed on bonds, you must understand the conventions used. Look at the highlighted Ford bond, and once again we examine the information in each column of the listing.

- The first column (COMPANY (TICKER)) gives the firm name and ticker symbol.
- The second column (COUPON) gives the coupon rate. It is always expressed as a percentage of $1,000. So, this corporate bond pays a coupon of $50.00 per year and has a coupon rate of 5.00%.

Stock and bond tables in local newspapers help investors track a firm's prospects.

- The third column (MATURITY) gives the date on which the bond matures, when the investor will receive a payment of the face value, or principle, of $1,000.
- The fourth column (LAST PRICE) gives the price that the bond sold for the last time it was traded before the close of trading the previous day. (Because this listing is from the paper of May 4, the listed price is for May 3.) The price is expressed as a percentage of $1,000. So, the price was 101.666 percent of $1,000, or $1,016.66.
- The fifth column (LAST YIELD) shows the interest rate on the bond if an investor purchased the bond at its current price. The yield of 4.739% is lower than the coupon rate of 5.00% because the bond is currently selling for a price greater than $1,000.
- The sixth column (EST SPREAD) and seventh column (UST) allow an investor to compare the interest rate on this bond to the interest rate on a corresponding bond issued by the United States Treasury. The spread is quoted in *basis points,* with 100 basis points equal to one percentage point. The 10 under UST indicates that the spread is calculated relative to the interest rate on a 10-year Treasury note. Therefore, we know that the interest rate on the Treasury note must have been 4.739% − 0.54% = 4.199%.
- Finally, the eighth column (EST $ VOL) gives the dollar value of the bonds traded the previous day in thousands of dollars. In this case, $53,979,000 worth of these GE bonds were traded.

	COUPON	MATURITY	LAST PRICE	LAST YIELD	*EST SPREAD	UST†	EST $ VOL (000's)
Morgan Stanley	5.300	May 01, 2013	102.064	4.977	78	10	57,739
Clear Channel Communications Inc. (CCU)	4.900	May 15, 2015	89.270	6.364	220	10	55,270
General Electric (GE)	5.000	Feb 01, 2013	101.666	4.739	54	10	53,979
Clear Channel Communications Inc. (CCU)	5.500	Sep 15, 2014	94.359	6.306	214	10	53,535
May Department Stores (MAY)	5.750	Jul 15, 2014	103.837	5.218	105	10	53,200

4 LEARNING OBJECTIVE

Understand the information provided in firms' financial statements.

Using Financial Statements to Evaluate a Corporation

To raise funds, a firm's managers must persuade financial intermediaries or buyers of its bonds or stock that it will be profitable. Before a firm can sell new issues of stock or bonds, it must first provide investors and financial regulators with information about its finances. To borrow from a bank or other financial intermediary, the firm must disclose financial information to the lender as well.

In most high-income countries, government agencies set requirements for information disclosure for firms that desire to sell securities in financial markets. In the United States, the Securities and Exchange Commission requires publicly owned firms to report their performance in financial statements prepared using standard accounting methods, often referred to as *generally accepted accounting principles.* Such disclosure reduces information costs, but it doesn't eliminate them, for two reasons. First, some firms may be too young to have much information for potential investors to evaluate. Second, managers may try to present the required information in the best possible light so that investors will overvalue their securities.

Private firms also collect information on business borrowers and sell the information to lenders and investors. As long as the information-gathering firm does a good job, lenders and investors purchasing the information will be better able to judge the quality of borrowing firms. Firms specializing in information—including Moody's Investor Service, Standard & Poor's Corporation, Value Line, and Dun and Bradstreet—collect information from businesses and sell it to subscribers. Buyers include individual investors, libraries, and financial intermediaries. You can find some of these publications in your college library or through online information services.

A Bull in China's Financial Shop

5-3 Making the Connection

Prospects for Sichuan Changhong Electric Co., manufacturer of plasma televisions and liquid crystal displays, looked excellent in 2004, with rapidly growing output, employment, and profits earned from trade in the world economy. And Changhong was not alone. In the early 2000s the Chinese economy was sizzling. China's output grew by 9.5 percent during 2004, dominated by an astonishing 26 percent growth in investment in plant and equipment. The Chinese economic juggernaut caught the attention of the global business community—and charged onto the U.S. political stage, as China's growth fueled concerns about job losses in the United States.

Yet at the same time many economists and financial commentators worried that the Chinese expansion—which was fueling rising living standards in a rapidly developing economy with 1.3 billion people—would come to an end. Indeed, the debate seemed to be over whether China's boom would have a "soft landing" (with gradually declining growth) or a "hard landing" (possibly leading to an economic financial crisis).

Why? Although China's saving rate was estimated to be a very high 40 percent of GDP, the financial system was doing a poor job of allocating capital. Excessive expansion in office construction and factories was fueled less by careful financial analysis than by the directions of national and local government officials trying to encourage growth. With nonperforming loans—where the borrower cannot make promised payments to lenders—at unheard-of levels, China's banks were in financial trouble. Worse still, they continued to lend to weak, politically connected borrowers.

China's prospects for long-term economic growth depend importantly on a better developed financial system to generate information for borrowers and lenders. Many economists have urged Chinese officials to improve accounting transparency and information disclosure so that stock and bond markets can flourish. In the absence of well-functioning financial markets, banks are crucial allocators of capital. There, too, information disclosure and less government direction of lending will help oil the Chinese growth machine in the long run.

Chinese firms, like Changhong, may well play a major role on the world's economic stage. For Chinese firms to add enough value to raise the standard of living for Chinese workers over the long run, though, China's creaky financial system needs repair.

Will China's weak financial system derail economic growth?

What kind of information do investors and firm managers need? A firm must answer three basic questions: what to produce, how to produce it, and what price to charge. To answer these questions, a firm's managers need two pieces of information: The first is the firm's revenues and costs, and the second is the value of the property and other assets the firm owns and the firm's debts, or other **liabilities,** that it owes to other persons and firms. Potential investors in the firm also need this information to decide whether to buy the firm's stocks or bonds. Managers and investors find this information in the firm's *financial statements,* principally its

Liability Anything owed by a person or a firm.

income statement and balance sheet. We discuss each of these statements and then use them to understand the business scandals of 2002 we mentioned at the beginning of this chapter.

The Income Statement

Income statement A financial statement that sums up a firm's revenues, costs, and profit over a period of time.

A firm's **income statement** sums up its revenues, costs, and profit over a period of time. Corporations issue annual income statements, although the 12-month *fiscal year* covered may be different from the calendar year to reflect the seasonal pattern of the business better. We explore an income statement in greater detail in the appendix to this chapter.

Accounting profit A firm's net income measured by revenue less operating expenses and taxes paid.

GETTING TO ACCOUNTING PROFIT The income statement shows a firm's revenue, costs, and profit for the firm's fiscal year. To determine profitability, the income statement starts with the firm's revenue and subtracts its operating expenses and taxes paid. The remainder, *net income,* is the **accounting profit** of the firm.

Opportunity cost The highest-valued alternative that must be given up to engage in an activity.

Explicit cost A cost that involves spending money.

Implicit cost A nonmonetary opportunity cost.

. . . AND ECONOMIC PROFIT Accounting profit is not the ideal measure of a firm's profits because it neglects some of the firm's costs. Remember that economists always measure cost as *opportunity cost.* The **opportunity cost** of any activity is the highest-valued alternative that must be given up to engage in that activity. Costs are either *explicit* or *implicit.* When the firm spends money, an **explicit cost** results. If the firm incurs an opportunity cost but does not spend money, an **implicit cost** results. For example, firms pay explicit labor costs to employees. They have many other explicit costs as well, such as the cost of the electricity used to light their office buildings.

Some costs are implicit, however. The most important of these is the opportunity cost to investors of the funds they have invested in the firm. Economists refer to the minimum amount that investors must earn on the funds they invest in a firm, expressed as a percentage of the amount invested, as a *normal rate of return.* If a firm fails to provide investors with at least a normal rate of return, it will not be able to remain in business over the long run because investors will not continue to invest their funds in the firm. For example, Bethlehem Steel was once the second-leading producer of steel in the United States and a very profitable firm with stock that sold for more than $50 per share. By 2002, investors became convinced that the firm's uncompetitive labor costs in world markets meant that the firm would never be able to provide investors with a normal rate of return. Many investors expected the firm would eventually have to declare bankruptcy, and as a result, the price of Bethlehem Steel's stock plummeted to $1 per share. Shortly thereafter the firm declared bankruptcy, and its remaining assets were sold off to a competing steel firm. The return (in dollars) that investors require to continue investing in the firm is a true cost to the firm and should be subtracted from the firm's revenues to calculate its profits.

The necessary rate of return that investors must receive to continue investing in a firm varies from firm to firm. If the investment is risky—as would be the case with a biotechnology start-up—investors will require a high rate of return to compensate them for the risk. Investors in firms in more established industries, such as electric utilities, may require lower rates of return. With respect to any particular firm, the exact rate of return required by investors is difficult to calculate, which also makes it difficult to include in an income statement. Firms have other implicit costs besides the return required by investors that can also be difficult to calculate. As a result, the rules of accounting generally require that only explicit costs be recognized for purposes of keeping the firm's financial records and for paying taxes. *Economic costs* include both explicit costs *and* implicit costs. **Economic profit** is equal to the firm's revenues minus all of its costs, implicit and explicit. Because accounting profit excludes some implicit costs, it will be larger than economic profit.

Economic profit A firm's revenues minus all of its costs, implicit and explicit.

The Balance Sheet

A firm's **balance sheet** sums up its financial position on a particular day, usually the end of a quarter or a year. We analyze a balance sheet in detail in the appendix to this chapter. Recall that an asset is anything of value that the firm owns, and a liability is a debt or obligation owed by the firm. Subtracting the value of a firm's liabilities from the value of its assets leaves its *net worth*. We can think of the net worth as what the firm's owners would be left with if the firm were closed, its assets were sold, and its liabilities were paid off. Investors can determine a firm's net worth by inspecting its balance sheet.

Balance sheet A financial statement that sums up a firm's financial position on a particular day, usually the end of a quarter or a year.

Understanding the Business Scandals of 2002

5 LEARNING OBJECTIVE

Understand the business accounting scandals of 2002, as well as the role of government in corporate governance.

A firm's financial statements provide important information on the firm's ability to add value for investors and the economy. Accurate and easy-to-understand financial statements are inputs for decisions by the firm's managers and investors. Indeed, the information in accounting statements helps guide resource allocation in the economy.

Firms disclose financial statements in periodic filings to the federal government and in *annual reports* to shareholders. An investor is more likely to buy a firm's stock if the firm's income statement shows a large after-tax profit and if its balance sheet shows a large net worth. The top management of a firm has at least two reasons to attract investors and keep the firm's stock price high. First, a higher stock price increases the funds the firm can raise when it sells a given amount of stock. Second, to reduce the principal-agent problem, boards of directors will often tie the salaries of top managers to the firm's stock price or to the profitability of the firm.

Top managers clearly have an incentive to maximize the profits reported on the income statement and the net worth reported on the balance sheet. If top managers make good decisions, the firm's profits will be high, and the firm's assets will be large relative to its liabilities. The business scandals that came to light in 2002 revealed, however, that some top managers inflated profits and hid liabilities that should have been listed on their balance sheets.

At Enron, an energy trading firm, chief financial officer Andrew Fastow was accused of creating partnerships that were supposedly independent of Enron, but in fact were owned by the firm. He was accused of transferring large amounts of Enron's debts to these partnerships, which reduced the liabilities on Enron's balance sheet, thereby increasing the firm's net worth. Falstow's deception made Enron more attractive to investors, increasing its stock price—and Fastow's compensation. In 2001, however, Enron was forced into bankruptcy. The firm's shareholders lost billions of dollars, and many employees lost their jobs. In 2004, Fastow pleaded guilty to conspiracy and was sentenced to 10 years in federal prison.

At WorldCom, a telecommunications firm, David Myers, the firm's controller, pleaded guilty to falsifying "WorldCom's books, to reduce WorldCom's reported actual costs and therefore increase WorldCom's reported earnings." Myers's actions caused WorldCom's income statement to overstate the firm's profits by more than $10 billion. The scandals at Enron and WorldCom were the largest cases of corporate fraud in U.S. history.

How was it possible for corporations such as Enron and WorldCom to falsify their financial statements? The federal government does regulate how financial statements are prepared, but this regulation cannot by itself guarantee the accuracy of the statements. All firms that issue stock to the public have their statements *audited* by a certified public accountant. The accountant is an employee of an accounting firm, *not* of the firm being audited. The audit is intended to provide investors with an independent opinion as to whether the firm's financial statements fairly reflect the true financial condition of the firm. Unfortunately, as the Enron and WorldCom scandals revealed, top managers who are determined to deceive investors about the true financial condition of their firms also can deceive outside auditors.

The private sector's response to the corporate scandals was almost immediate. In addition to the reexamination of corporate governance practices at many corporations, the New York Stock Exchange and the NASDAQ put forth initiatives to ensure the accuracy and accessibility of information.

To guard against future scandals, new federal legislation was enacted in 2002. The landmark *Sarbanes-Oxley Act* of 2002 requires that corporate directors have a certain level of expertise with financial information and mandates that chief executive officers personally certify the accuracy of financial statements. The Sarbanes-Oxley Act also requires that financial analysts and auditors disclose whether any conflicts of interest might exist that would limit their independence in evaluating a firm's financial condition. The purpose of this provision is to ensure that analysts and auditors are acting in the best interests of shareholders. The Act promotes management accountability by specifying the responsibilities of corporate officers and by increasing penalties (including long jail sentences) for managers who do not meet their responsibilities.

Perhaps the most noticeable corporate governance reform under the Sarbanes-Oxley Act is the creation of the Public Company Accounting Oversight Board, a special national board to oversee the auditing of public companies' financial reports. The board's mission is to promote the independence of auditors to ensure they disclose accurate information. On balance, most observers acknowledge that the Sarbanes-Oxley Act brought back confidence in the U.S. corporate governance system, though questions remain for the future about whether the Act may chill legitimate business risk-taking by diverting management attention from the core business toward regulatory compliance. And the high accounting costs of implementing Sarbanes-Oxley are borne by all shareholders.

Outside the United States, the European Commission released plans in 2003 to tighten corporate governance rules, and Japan has debated such reforms as well. The challenge of ensuring the accurate reporting of firms' economic profits is a global one.

SOLVED PROBLEM 5-2

(5) LEARNING OBJECTIVE
Understand the business accounting scandals of 2002, as well as the role of government in corporate governance.

What Makes a Good Board of Directors?

Business Week magazine has listed 3M Company as having one of the best boards of directors of any U.S. corporation:

> With just one insider on its nine-member board, the company gets high marks for independence. Outside directors include the CEOs of Lockheed-Martin, Allstate, and Amgen. . . . No directors have business ties to the company.

a. What is an "insider" on a board of directors?
b. Why might having too many insiders be a problem?
c. Why would having outside directors who are CEOs of large firms be a good thing?
d. Why would directors not having business ties to the firm be a good thing?

Source: "The Best Boards and the Worst Boards," *Business Week*, October 7, 2002, p. 107.

Solving the Problem:

Step 1: Review the chapter material. The context of this problem is the business scandals of 2002 and the underlying principal-agent problem that arises because of the separation of ownership from control in large corporations, so you may want to review the section "Understanding the Business Scandals of 2002," which begins on page 143.

Step 2: Answer question (a) by defining "insiders." "Insiders" are members of top management who also serve on the board of directors.

Step 3: Answer question (b) by explaining why having too many insiders on a board may be a problem. Having members of top management on the board of directors provides the board with information about the firm that only top managers possess. Having too many insiders on a board, however, means that top managers may end up controlling the board rather than the other way around. A corporation's board of directors is supposed to provide the monitoring and control of top managers that shareholders cannot provide directly.

Step 4: Answer question (c) by explaining why having directors who are CEOs of large firms may be a good thing. Members of boards of directors are sometimes retired politicians, academics, or philanthropists. Although these people may be well intentioned and hard working, some of them may lack the knowledge and experience to successfully monitor top managers. CEOs of other large corporations, on the other hand, do have the experience to judge better whether top managers are making decisions in the best interests of the firm.

Step 5: Answer question (d) by stating why directors should not have business ties to the firm. If a CEO of Firm 1 sits on the board of directors of Firm 2, she is an outside director, but if her company does a significant amount of business with Firm 2, she may be reluctant to do anything to displease the top managers because the top managers have the power to stop doing business with her firm.

YOUR TURN: **For more practice, do related problems 16 and 17 on page 150 at the end of this chapter.**

Conclusion

In a market system, firms make independent decisions about which goods and services to produce, how to produce them, and what prices to charge. In modern high-income countries, such as the United States, large corporations account for a majority of the sales and profits earned by firms. Generally, the managers of these corporations do a good job of representing the interests of stockholders, while providing the goods and services demanded by consumers. As the business scandals of 2002 showed, however, some top managers enriched themselves at the expense of stockholders and consumers by manipulating financial statements. Legislative strengthening of financial regulation in the Sarbanes-Oxley Act of 2002 and greater financial market scrutiny of financial statements have helped restore investor and management confidence in firms' financial statements.

Read *An Inside Look* on the next page about Google's initial pubic offering (IPO) for a discussion of the role expectations of future profits play in determining stock prices.

An Inside Look

Google's Initial Public Offering

WALL STREET JOURNAL, JANUARY 3, 2005

Technology Shares Slip, But Google Passes $200

a Google shares soared past $200 Monday, with an upbeat note from Goldman Sachs buoying Web search stocks as the broader technology market fell. Goldman Sachs raised its earnings and revenue estimates for Google and Yahoo, sending Google shares up $9.92, or 5.1%, to $202.71 on the Nasdaq Stock Market. It was the company's highest close since its initial public offering, and marked the first time the search giant's shares finished above the $200 mark.

Search companies fared well last year, helped by Google's high-profile IPO in August. Since then, the company's shares have more than doubled. Goldman raised its fourth-quarter revenue estimate for Google to $592 million from $579 million. The firm also increased its earnings-per-share forecast to 76 cents from 74 cents.

The Goldman note helped push other search stocks higher. Yahoo climbed 50 cents to $38.18 on Nasdaq as Goldman increased its fourth-quarter sales estimate for the company to $773 million from $747 million.

b The note also lifted search rival Ask Jeeves $1.07, or 4%, to $27.82 on Nasdaq.

But the broader tech market didn't fare as well, with lackluster manufacturing numbers for December and the onset of jitters ahead of this month's slew of earnings news. The Nasdaq Composite Index shed 23.29, or 1.1%, to close at 2152.15 in the first session of the new year. The tech heavy index gained 8.6% last year.

Morgan Stanley's high-tech index declined 5.17 to 502.50, and the Nasdaq 100 Index of nonfinancial stocks fell 17.61 to 1603.51.

Among some individual stocks, Sun Microsystems lost 28 cents, or 5.2%, to $5.11 on Nasdaq after Sanford Bernstein cut the network giant's shares to "underperform" from "market perform." The firm says the company's calendar fourth quarter didn't experience a material acceleration, and that it doesn't see upside to its revenue expectations for the fiscal second-quarter of 2005.

Shares of Corning eased 6 cents to $11.71 on the Big Board after the technology giant announced that the Chinese Ministry of Commerce found Saturday that the company had not dumped standard single-mode optical fiber into the Chinese market.

c Nortel Networks rose 6 cents to $3.55 on the New York Stock Exchange. The telecommunications-equipment supplier said the Big Board has granted it an additional three months to file its 2003 annual report with the Securities and Exchange Commission. The exchange will allow Nortel to continue listing while the company continues to sort through accounting irregularities in 2003.

Shares of Tellabs gained 59 cents, or 6.9%, to $9.18 on Nasdaq after Robert W. Baird upgraded the maker of telecom equipment to "outperform" from "neutral." Analysts expect solid bookings due to improved international and fiber-to-the-premises business.

Key Points in the Article

The Money and Investing section (or C section) of the *Wall Street Journal* is devoted to analyzing the stock and bond markets. Because technology stocks, such as Google, have been an important part of the stock market, the *Wall Street Journal* prints an article each day called "Tech Stocks." This particular article discusses price changes in the stocks of Google, Ask Jeeves, Nortel, and several other companies. In each case, the author attempts to explain why the prices of the stocks changed as they did.

Analyzing the News

a Buying a share of stock in Google, or any other firm, means buying part ownership of the firm. As a part owner, you have a claim to your share of the firm's profits. Therefore, firms that earn large profits have high stock prices. Investors are always searching for new information on the future profitability of firms. In the instance discussed here, an analyst for Goldman Sachs, an investment firm, issued a "research note" that forecast higher profits for Google than most investors had been expecting. Apparently, enough investors believed the Goldman Sachs analyst was correct, because demand for Google's shares increased, raising the price per share by almost $10 during the day.

Google sold stock to the public for the first time on August 19, 2004. This *initial public offering*, or IPO, was unusual because the firm used an Internet auction to determine the price and who would receive the shares. Most firms use investment bankers to handle their IPOs, with the result that small investors sometimes have difficulty buying shares on the day they are first issued. Figure 1 shows movements in the price of Google's stock from the time of the IPO through mid-January 2005.

b As discussed earlier in this chapter, the stocks of many computer and other high-technology firms, including Google, are traded on NASDAQ. The NASDAQ Composite Index declined during the day discussed in the article. The NASDAQ Composite Index converts the stock prices of all the stocks that are traded on Nasdaq into a single index number. This index makes it possible for investors to gauge the overall performance of these stocks. Although the stocks of some firms, such as Google and Ask Jeeves, rose during the day, investors at that time were worried about the profitability of high-technology firms, so on average, the prices of NASDAQ stocks declined.

c In the chapter, we discussed some of the accounting problems that had plagued many firms. For a firm's stock to be traded on the New York Stock Exchange—the "Big Board"—the firm needs to meet certain requirements, including the filing of accurate financial statements with the Securities and Exchange Commission. Failure to meet these requirements can cause a firm to be "delisted," which means its stock can no longer be traded on the Big Board. Being delisted makes it extremely difficult for a firm to continue selling stock. Nortel, which is based in Ontario, Canada, and manufactures telecommunications equipment, had failed to file its 2003 annual report with the Securities and Exchange Commission because the firm had discovered accounting irregularities that resulted in its reported profits being higher than its actual profits. The firm had fired ten executives and finance officials. Several of the executives gave back $8.6 million in salary bonuses they had received on the basis of the firm's profits being overstated.

Thinking Critically ABOUT POLICY

1. According to Figure 1, on October 22, 2004, Google's stock was selling for about $150 per share, then Google reported its net profit at $52 million and the stock's price jumped to over $175 per share.
   a. Did investors as a group expect the stock to jump by over $25 per share before the company announced its net profit?
   b. Do stocks' prices always jump upward when companies announce that they've earned a profit? Explain.
2. Someone who knew that Google was about to announce a big profit—for example, someone in Google's top management—could have earned a bundle quickly by buying Google stock at $150 per share and then selling it at $175 per share a day or so later. Such "insider trading" is illegal, however. Do you think that "insider trading" should be illegal? What are the benefits associated with it? What are the problems associated with it?

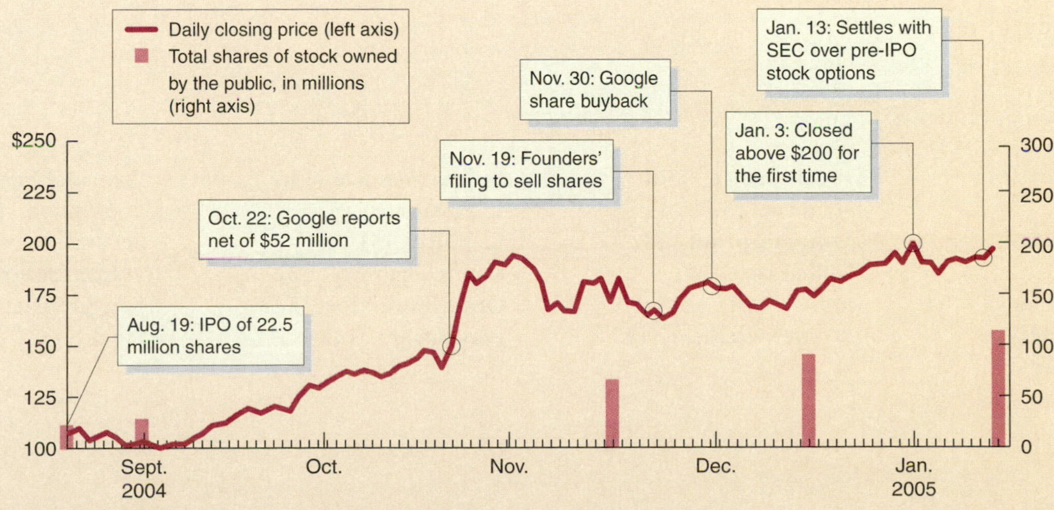

Figure 1: Movements in Google's stock price, August 2004–January 2005.

SUMMARY

LEARNING OBJECTIVE ① Categorize the major types of business in the United States. There are three types of firms: *sole proprietorships, partnerships,* and *corporations.* The owners of sole proprietorships and partners have *unlimited liability,* which means there is no legal distinction between the personal assets of the owners of the business and the assets of the business. The owners of corporations have *limited liability,* which means they can never lose more than their investment in the firm. Although only 20 percent of firms are corporations, they account for the majority of revenue and profit earned by all firms.

LEARNING OBJECTIVE ② Describe the typical management structure of corporations and understand the concepts of separation of ownership from control and the principal-agent problem. Most corporations have a similar management structure: The shareholders elect a board of directors that appoints the corporation's top managers, such as the chief executive officer. Because the top management often does not own a large fraction of the stock in the corporation, large corporations have a *separation of ownership from control.* Because top managers have less incentive to increase the corporation's profits than to increase their own salaries and their own enjoyment, corporations can suffer from a *principal-agent problem.* A principal-agent problem exists when the principals—in this case, the shareholders of the corporation—have difficulty in getting the agent—the corporation's top management—to carry out their wishes.

LEARNING OBJECTIVE ③ Explain how firms obtain the funds they need to operate and expand. Firms rely on *retained earnings*—which are profits retained by the firm and not paid out to the firm's owners—or on using the savings of households for the funds they need to operate and expand. The savings of households flow directly to businesses when investors buy stocks and bonds in financial markets. Savings flow indirectly to businesses when households deposit money in saving and checking accounts in banks and the banks lend these funds to businesses. Federal, state, and local governments also sell bonds in financial markets and households also borrow funds from banks. When a firm sells a bond, it is borrowing money from the buyer of the bond. When a firm sells stock, it is selling part ownership of the firm to the buyer of the stock. The original purchasers of stocks and bonds may resell them in stock and bond markets, such as the New York Stock Exchange.

LEARNING OBJECTIVE ④ Understand the information provided in firms' financial statements. A firm's *income statement* sums up its revenues, costs, and profit over a period of time. A firm's *balance sheet* sums up its financial position on a particular day, usually the end of a quarter or year. Firms report their *accounting profit* on their income statements. Because accounting profit excludes some implicit costs, it is larger than *economic profit.*

LEARNING OBJECTIVE ⑤ Understand the business accounting scandals of 2002, as well as the role of government in corporate governance. Because their compensation often rises with the profitability of the corporation, top managers have an incentive to overstate the profits reported on their firm's income statements. During 2002, it became clear that the top managers of several large corporations had done this, even though intentionally falsifying financial statements is illegal. The *Sarbanes-Oxley Act* of 2002 and greater scrutiny of financial statements have helped to restore investor and management confidence in firm's financial statements.

KEY TERMS

Accounting profit 142
Asset 132
Balance sheet 143
Bond 137
Corporate governance 134
Corporation 132
Coupon payment 137
Direct finance 136
Dividends 137
Economic profit 142
Explicit cost 142
Implicit cost 142
Income statement 142
Indirect finance 136
Interest rate 137
Liability 141
Limited liability 132
Opportunity cost 142
Partnership 132
Principal-agent problem 135
Separation of ownership from control 135
Sole proprietorship 132
Stock 137

REVIEW QUESTIONS

1. What are the three major types of business in the United States? Briefly discuss the most important characteristics of each type.
2. What is limited liability? Why are owners of corporations granted limited liability by the government?
3. What do we mean by the separation of ownership from control in large corporations? How is this related to the principal-agent problem?
4. What is the difference between direct finance and indirect finance? If you borrow money from a bank to buy a new car, are you using direct finance or indirect finance?
5. Why is a bond considered to be a loan but a share of stock is not? Why do corporations issue both bonds and shares of stock?
6. How do the stock and bond markets provide information to businesses? Why do stock and bond prices change over time?
7. What is the Sarbanes-Oxley Act? Why was it passed?

PROBLEMS AND APPLICATIONS

Please visit **www.prenhall.com/hubbard** *for solutions to the even-numbered problems as well as multiple-choice and true or false self-assessment quizzes.*

1. Suppose that shortly after graduating from college you decide to start your own business. Will you organize the business as a sole proprietorship, a partnership, or a corporation? Explain your reasoning.
2. In a May 10, 2003, opinion piece in the *New York Times*, sociologist Dalton Conley proposed the *elimination* of limited liability to corporate shareholders. Do you think that corporations should be granted limited liability? What are the benefits of limited liability? What is its downside? Would you be more willing to buy bonds from a company with limited liability? Would you be more willing to buy the stock of a company with limited liability?
3. Suppose that a firm in which you have invested is losing money. Would you rather own the firm's stock or the firm's bonds? Explain.
4. Suppose you originally invested in a firm when it was small and unprofitable. Now the firm has grown considerably and is large and profitable. Would you be better off if you had bought the firm's stock or the firm's bonds? Explain.
5. The principal-agent problem arises almost everywhere in the business world—but it also crops up even closer to home. Discuss the principal-agent problem that exists in the college classroom. Who is the principal? Who is the agent? What is the problem between this principal and this agent?
6. **[Related to *Solved Problem 5-1*]** Briefly explain whether you agree or disagree with the following argument: "The separation of ownership from control in large corporations and the principal-agent problem means that top managers can work short days, take long vacations, and otherwise slack off."
7. **[Related to *Solved Problem 5-1*]** An economic consultant gives the board of directors of a firm the following advice: "You can increase the profitability of the firm if you change your method of compensating top management. Instead of paying your top management a straight salary, you should pay them a salary plus give them the right to buy the firm's stock in the future at a price above the stock's current market price." Explain the consultant's reasoning. To what difficulties might this compensation scheme lead?
8. The following is from an article in the *New York Times:*

   > In theory, boards [of directors] design pay packages to attract and inspire good chief executives and to align their interests with those of shareholders. . . . But what kind of pay packages are appropriate at companies still run by the founding family?

   The article quotes one expert as arguing: "There is little or no justification for treating an owner-manager in exactly the same way as a standard CEO."

   What does the article mean by saying that pay packages should "align [chief executives'] interests with those of shareholders"? What kind of pay packages would achieve this objective? Do you agree that an "owner-manager" should have a pay package different from that of a CEO who is not a member of the family that started the firm? Briefly explain.

   Source: Diana B. Henriques, "What's Fair Pay for Running the Family Store?," *New York Times*, January 12, 2003.

9. If you deposit $20,000 in a savings account at a bank, you might earn 3 percent interest per year. Someone who borrows $20,000 from a bank to buy a new car might have to pay an interest rate of 8 percent per year on the loan. Knowing this, why don't you just lend your money directly to the car buyer, cutting out the bank?

10. **[Related to the *Chapter Opener*]** When Google's owners wanted to raise funds for expansion in 2004, they decided to sell stock in their company rather than to borrow the money. Why do some companies fund their expansion by borrowing, while others fund expansion by issuing new stock?

11. The following listing for a corporate bond issued by Sara Lee Corporation appeared in the *Wall Street Journal* on May 4, 2005:

COUPON	MATURITY	LAST PRICE	LAST YIELD	EST SPREAD	UST	EST $ VOL (000s)
3.875	June 15, 2013	91.047	5.244	108	10	84,860

   a. If you bought this bond, what is the total coupon payment you would receive during the next year (in dollars)?
   b. For what price did this bond sell at the close of trading on May 3?
   c. What was the yield on a 30-year U.S. Treasury bond on May 3?

12. Consider again the information for the Sara Lee bond in problem 11. Why weren't investors willing to pay $1,000 for this bond, which has a face value of $1,000?

13. In 2005, the French government began issuing bonds with 50-year maturities. Would this bond be purchased only by very young investors who expect to still be alive when the bond matures? Briefly explain.

14. **[Related to *Don't Let This Happen To You!*]** Briefly explain whether you agree or disagree with the following statement: "The total value of the shares of Microsoft stock traded on the NASDAQ last week was $250 million, so the firm actually received more revenue from stock sales than from selling software."

15. Loans from banks are the most important external source of funds to businesses because most businesses are too small to borrow in financial markets by issuing stocks or bonds. Most investors are reluctant to buy the stocks or bonds of small businesses because of the difficulty of gathering accurate information on the financial strength and profitability of the businesses. Nevertheless, news about the stock market is included in nearly every network news program and is often the lead story in the business section of most newspapers. Is there a contradiction here? Why is the average viewer of TV news or the average reader of a newspaper interested in the fluctuations in prices in the stock market?

16. **[Related to *Solved Problem 5-2*]** In the fall of 2002, Buford Yates, director of accounting at WorldCom, pleaded guilty to fraud. In federal court he said that top managers at WorldCom ordered him to make certain adjustments to the firm's financial statements.

> I came to believe that the adjustments I was being directed to make in WorldCom's financial statements had no justification and contravened generally accepted accounting principles. I concluded that the purpose of these adjustments was to incorrectly inflate WorldCom's reported earnings.

What are "generally accepted accounting principles"? How would the "adjustments" Yates was ordered to make benefit top managers at WorldCom? Would these adjustments also benefit WorldCom's stockholders? Briefly explain.

Source: Devlin Barrett, "Ex-WorldCom Exec Pleads Guilty," Associated Press, October 8, 2002.

17. **[Related to *Solved Problem 5-2*]** In 2002, *Business Week* listed Apple Computer as having one of the worst boards of directors:

> Founder Steve Jobs owns just two shares in the company. . . . The CEO of Micro Warehouse, which accounted for nearly 2.9% of Apple's net sales in 2001, sits on the compensation committee. . . . There is an interlocking directorship—with Gap CEO Mickey Drexler and Jobs sitting on each other's boards.

Why might investors be concerned that a top manager like Steve Jobs owns only two shares in the firm? Why might investors be concerned if a member of the board of directors also has a business relationship with the firm? What is an "interlocking directorship"? Why is it a bad thing?

Source: "The Best Boards and the Worst Boards," *Business Week*, October 7, 2002, p. 107.

18. The following is from a *Business Week* editorial:

> Welcome to the revolution. After years of paying lip service to reform, Enron Corp. and the ensuing wave of business scandal has finally produced a dramatic change in corporate governance. . . . [I]nvestors are rewarding companies with good governance and punishing those without it.

How are investors able to reward or punish firms? What impact will these rewards and punishments have on boards of directors and top managers?

Source: "Boardrooms Are Starting to Wake Up," *Business Week*, October 7, 2002, p. 107.

19. Dane decides to give up a job earning $100,000 per year as a corporate lawyer and converts the duplex that he owns into a UFO museum. (He had been renting out the duplex for $20,000 a year.) His direct expenses include $50,000 per year paid to his assistants and $10,000 per year for utilities. Fans flock to the museum to see his collection of extraterrestrial paraphernalia, which he easily could sell on eBay for $1,000,000. Over the course of the year, the museum brings in revenues of $100,000.
    a. How much is Dane's accounting profit for the year?
    b. Is he earning an economic profit? Explain.

20. **[Related to the *Chapter Opener*]** What impact would these events be likely to have on the price of Google's stock?
    a. A competitor launches a search engine that's just as good as Google's.
    b. The corporate income tax is abolished.
    c. Google's board of directors becomes dominated by close friends and relatives of its top management.
    d. The price of wireless Internet connections unexpectedly drops, so more and more people use the Internet.
    e. Google announces a huge profit of $1 billion, but everybody anticipated that Google would earn a huge profit of $1 billion.

Appendix

Tools to Analyze Firms' Financial Information

As we saw in the chapter, modern business organizations are not just "black boxes" transforming inputs into output. Most business revenues and profits are earned by large corporations. Unlike founder-dominated firms, the typical large corporation is run by managers who generally do not own a controlling interest in the firm. Large firms raise funds from outside investors, and outside investors seek information on firms and the assurance that the managers of firms will act in the interests of the investors.

This chapter showed how corporations raise funds by issuing stocks and bonds. This appendix provides more detail to support that discussion. We begin by analyzing *present value* as a key concept in determining the prices of financial securities. We then provide greater information on *financial statements* issued by corporations, using Google as an example.

Using Present Value to Make Investment Decisions

Firms raise funds equity (stock) and debt (bonds and loans) to investors and lenders. If you own shares of stock or a bond, you will receive payments in the form of dividends or coupons over a number of years. Most people value funds they already have more highly than funds they will not receive until some time in the future. For example, you would probably not trade $1,000 you already have for $1,000 you will not receive for one year. The longer you will have to wait to receive a payment, the less value it will have for you. One thousand dollars you will not receive for two years is worth less to you than $1,000 you will receive after one year. The value you give today to money you will receive in the future is called the future payment's **present value.** The present value of $1,000 you will receive in one year will be less than $1,000.

Why is this true? Why is the $1,000 you will not receive for one year less valuable to you than the $1,000 you already have? The most important reason is that if you have $1,000 today, you can use that $1,000 today. You can buy goods and services with the money and receive enjoyment from them. The $1,000 you receive in one year does not have direct use to you now.

Also, prices likely will rise during the year you are waiting to receive your $1,000. So, when you finally do receive the $1,000 in one year you will not be able to buy as much with it as you could with $1,000 today. Finally, there is some risk that you will not receive the $1,000 in one year. The risk may be very great if an unreliable friend borrows $1,000 from you and vaguely promises to pay you back in one year. The risk may be very small when you lend money to the federal government by buying a United States Treasury bond. In either case, there is at least some risk that you will not receive the funds promised.

When someone lends money, the lender expects to be paid back both the amount of the loan and some additional interest. If you decide that to be willing to lend your $1,000 today and you must be paid back $1,100 one year from now, you are charging $100/$1,000 = 0.10 or 10 percent interest on the funds you have loaned. Economists would say that you value $1,000 today as equivalent to the $1,100 to be received one year in the future.

Notice that $1,100 can be written as $1,000 (1 + 0.10). That is, the value of money received in the future is equal to the value of money in the present multiplied by 1 plus the interest rate, with the interest rate expressed as a decimal. Or,

Present value The value in today's dollars of funds to be paid or received in the future.

$$\$1{,}100 - 1{,}000\ (1 + 0.10).$$

Notice, also, that if we divide both sides by (1 + 0.10), we can rewrite this formula as:

$$\$1{,}000 = \frac{\$1{,}100}{(1+0.10)}.$$

The rewritten formula states that the present value is equal to the future value to be received in one year divided by one plus the interest rate. This formula is an important one because it can be used to convert any amount to be received in one year into its present value. Writing the formula generally, we have:

$$\text{Present Value} = \frac{\text{Future Value}_1}{(1+i)}.$$

The present value of funds to be received in one year—Future Value$_1$—can be calculated by dividing the amount of those funds to be received by 1 plus the interest rate. With an interest rate of 10 percent, the present value of $1,000,000 to be received one year from now is:

$$\frac{\$1{,}000{,}000}{(1+0.10)} = \$909{,}090.91.$$

This method is a very useful way of calculating the value today of funds that won't be received for one year. But financial securities such as stocks and bonds involve promises to pay funds over many years. Therefore, it would be even more useful if we could expand this formula to calculate the present value of funds to be received more than one year in the future.

This expansion is easy to do. Go back to the original example where we assumed you were willing to loan out your $1,000 for one year, provided you received 10 percent interest. Suppose you are asked to lend the funds for two years and that you are promised 10 percent interest per year for each year of the loan. That is, you are lending $1,000, which at 10 percent interest will grow to $1,100 after one year, and you are agreeing to loan that $1,100 out for a second year at 10 percent interest. So, after two years you will be paid back $1,100 (1 + 0.10) or $1,210. Or,

$$\$1{,}210 = \$1{,}000\ (1 + 0.10)(1 + 0.10)$$

or,

$$\$1{,}210 = \$1{,}000\ (1 + 0.10)^2.$$

This formula can also be rewritten as:

$$\$1{,}000 = \frac{\$1{,}210}{(1+0.10)^2}.$$

To put the formula in words, the $1,210 you receive two years from now has a present value equal to $1,210 divided by the quantity 1 plus the interest rate squared. If you were to agree to lend out your $1,000 for three years at 10 percent interest, you would receive:

$$\$1{,}331 = \$1{,}000\ (1 + 0.10)^3.$$

Notice, again, that:

$$\$1{,}000 = \frac{\$1{,}331}{(1+0.10)^3}.$$

You can probably see a pattern here. We can generalize the concept to say that the present value of funds to be received n years in the future—whether n is 1, 20, or 85 does not matter—equals the amount of the funds to be received divided by the quantity 1 plus the interest rate raised to the nth power. For instance, with an interest rate of 10 percent, the value of $1,000,000 to be received 25 years in the future is:

$$\text{Present Value} = \frac{\$1{,}000{,}000}{(1+0.10)^{25}} = \$92{,}296.$$

Or, more generally:

$$\text{Present Value} = \frac{\text{Future Value}_n}{(1+i)^n},$$

where Future Value_n represents funds that will be received in n years.

SOLVED PROBLEM 5A-1

How to Receive Your Contest Winnings

Suppose you win a contest and are given the choice of the following prizes:

Prize 1: $50,000 to be received right away, with four additional payments of $50,000 to be received each year for the next four years
Prize 2: $175,000 to be received right away

Explain which prize you would choose and the basis for your decision.

Solving the Problem:
Step 1: Review the material. This problem involves applying the concept of present value, so you may want to review the section "Using Present Value to Make Investment Decisions," which begins on page 152.

Step 2: Explain the basis for choosing the prize. Unless you need immediate cash, you should choose the prize with the highest present value.

Step 3: Calculate the present value of each prize. Prize 2 consists of one payment of $175,000 received right away, so its present value is $175,000. Prize 1 consists of five payments spread out over time. To find the present value of the prize, we must find the present value of each of these payments and add them together. To calculate present value we must use an interest rate. Let's assume an interest rate of 10 percent. In that case the present value of Prize 1 is:

$$\$50{,}000 + \frac{\$50{,}000}{(1+0.10)} + \frac{\$50{,}000}{(1+0.10)^2} + \frac{\$50{,}000}{(1+0.10)^3} + \frac{\$50{,}000}{(1+0.10)^4} =$$

$$\$50{,}000 + \$45{,}454.55 + \$41{,}322.31 + \$37{,}565.74 + \$34{,}150.67 = \$208{,}493.$$

Step 4: State your conclusion. Prize 1 has the greater present value, so you should choose it rather than Prize 2.

YOUR TURN: **For more practice, do related problems 1, 3, 4, and 5 on page 160 at the end of this appendix.**

Using Present Value to Calculate Bond Prices

Anyone who buys a financial asset, such as shares of stock or a bond, is really buying a promise to receive certain payments—dividends in the case of shares of stock or coupons in the case of a bond. The price investors are willing to pay for a financial asset should be equal to the value of the payments they will receive as a result of owning the asset. Because most of the coupon or dividend payments will be received in the future, it is their present value that matters. Put another way, we have the following important idea: *The price of a financial asset should be equal to the present value of the payments to be received from owning that asset.*

Let's consider an example. Suppose that in 1980 General Electric issued a bond with an $80 coupon that will mature in 2010. It is now 2008 and that bond has been bought and sold by investors many times. You are considering buying it. If you buy the bond, you will receive two years of coupon payments plus a final payment of the bond's principal or face value of $1,000. Suppose, once again, that you need an interest rate of 10 percent to invest your funds. If the bond has a coupon of $80, the present value of the payments you receive from owning the bond—and, therefore, the present value of the bond—will be:

$$\text{Present Value} = \frac{\$80}{(1+0.10)} + \frac{\$80}{(1+0.10)^2} + \frac{\$1{,}000}{(1+0.10)^2} = \$965.29.$$

That is, the present value of the bond will equal the present value of the three payments you will receive during the two years you own the bond. You should, therefore, be willing to pay $965.29 to own this bond and have the right to receive these payments from GE. This process of calculating present values of future payments is used to determine bond prices, with one qualification. The relevant interest rate used by investors in the bond market to calculate the present value and, therefore, the price of an existing bond is usually the coupon rate on comparable newly issued bonds. Therefore, the general formula for the price of a bond is:

$$\text{Bond Price} = \frac{\text{Coupon}_1}{(1+i)} + \frac{\text{Coupon}_2}{(1+i)^2} + \ldots + \frac{\text{Coupon}_n}{(1+i)^n} + \frac{\text{Face Value}}{(1+i)^n},$$

where Coupon_1 is the coupon payment to be received after one year, Coupon_2 is the coupon payment to be received after two years, up to Coupon_n, which is the coupon payment received in the year the bond matures. The ellipsis takes the place of the coupon payments—if any—received between the second year and the year the bond matures. Face Value is the face value of the bond, to be received when the bond matures. The interest rate on comparable newly issued bonds is i.

Using Present Value to Calculate Stock Prices

When you own a firm's stock, you are legally entitled to your share of the firm's profits. Remember that the profits a firm pays out to its shareholders are referred to as dividends. The price of a share of stock should be equal to the present value of the dividends investors expect to receive as a result of owning that stock. Therefore, the general formula for the price of a stock is:

$$\text{Stock Price} = \frac{\text{Dividend}_1}{(1+i)} + \frac{\text{Dividend}_2}{(1+i)^2} + \ldots$$

Notice that this formula looks very similar to the one we used to calculate the price of a bond, with a couple of important differences. First, unlike a bond, stock has no maturity date, so we have to calculate the present value of an infinite number of dividend payments. At first, it may seem that the stock's price must be infinite as well, but remember that dollars you don't receive for many years are worth very little today. For instance, a dividend payment of $10 that will be received 40 years in the future is worth only a little more than $0.20 today at a 10 percent interest rate. The second difference between the stock price formula and the bond price formula is that whereas the coupon payments you receive from owning the bond are known with certainty—they are written on the bond and cannot be changed—you don't know for sure what the dividend payments from owning a stock will be. How large a dividend payment you will receive depends upon how profitable the company will be in the future.

Although it is possible to forecast the future profitability of a company, this cannot be done with perfect accuracy. To emphasize this point, some economists rewrite the basic stock price formula by adding a superscript *e* to each Dividend term to emphasize that these are *expected* dividend payments. Because the future profitability of companies is often very difficult to forecast, it is not surprising that differences of opinion exist over what the price of a particular stock should be. Some investors will be very optimistic about the future profitability of a company and will, therefore, believe that the company's stock should have a high price. Other investors might be very pessimistic and believe that the company's stock should have a low price.

A Simple Formula for Calculating Stock Prices

It is possible to simplify the formula for determining the price of a stock, if we assume that dividends will grow at a constant rate:

$$\text{Stock Price} = \frac{\text{Dividend}}{(i - \text{Growth Rate})},$$

where Dividend is the dividend being received currently and Growth Rate is the rate at which those dividends are expected to grow. If a company currently is paying a dividend of $1 per share and Growth Rate is 10 percent, the company is expected to pay a dividend of $1.10 next year, $1.21 the year after that, and so on.

Now suppose that IBM currently is paying a dividend of $5 per share, the consensus of investors is that these dividends will increase at a rate of 5 percent per year for the indefinite future, and the interest rate is 10 percent. Then the price of IBM's stock should be:

$$\text{Stock Price} = \frac{\$5.00}{(0.10 - 0.05)} = \$100.00.$$

Particularly during the years 1999 and 2000, there was much discussion of whether the high prices of many Internet stocks—such as the stock of Amazon.com—were justified given that many of these companies had not made any profit yet and so had not paid any dividends. Is there any way that a rational investor would pay a high price for the stock of a company currently not earning profits? The formula for determining stock prices shows that it is possible, provided the investor's assumptions are optimistic enough! For example, during 1999, one stock analyst predicted that Amazon.com would soon be earning $10 per share of stock. That is, Amazon.com's total earnings divided by the number of shares of its stock outstanding would be $10. Suppose Amazon.com pays out that $10 in dividends and that the $10 will grow rapidly over the years, by, say, 7 percent per year. Then our formula indicates that the price of Amazon.com stock should be:

$$\text{Stock Price} = \frac{\$10.00}{(0.10 - 0.07)} = \$333.33.$$

If you are sufficiently optimistic about the future prospects of a company, a high stock price can be justified even if the company currently is not earning a profit. But investors in growth stocks must be careful. Suppose that investors believe that growth prospects for Amazon are only 4 percent per year instead of 7 percent because the firm turns out not to be as profitable as initially believed. Then our formula indicates that the price of Amazon.com stock should be:

$$\text{Stock Price} = \frac{\$10.00}{(0.10 - 0.04)} = \$166.67,$$

or only half the value assuming a more optimistic growth rage. Hence investors use information about firms' profitability and growth prospects to determine what the firm is worth.

Going Deeper into Financial Statements

Corporations disclose substantial information about their business operations and financial position to actual and potential investors. Some of this information meets the demands of participants in financial markets and of information-collection agencies, such as Moody's Investors Service, which develops credit ratings that help investors judge the riskiness of corporate bonds. Other information meets the requirements of the U.S. Securities and Exchange Commission.

Key sources of information about a corporation's profitability and financial position are its principal financial statements—the *income statement* and the *balance sheet.* These important information sources were first introduced in the chapter. Here we go into more detail, using recent data for Google as an example.

Analyzing Income Statements

As discussed in the chapter, a firm's income statement summarizes its revenues, costs, and profit over a period of time. Figure 5A-1 shows Google's income statement for 2004.

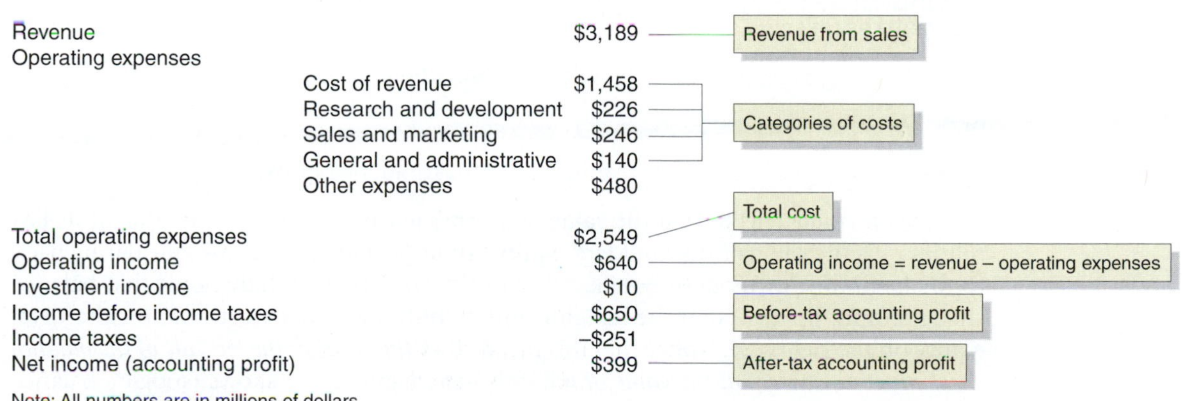

FIGURE 5A-1

Google's Income Statement for 2004

Google's income statement shows the company's revenue, costs, and profit for 2004. The difference between its revenue ($3,189 million) and its operating expenses ($2,549 million) is its operating income ($640 million). Most corporations also have investments, such as government or corporate bonds, that generate some income for them. In this case, Google earned $10 million, giving the firm an income before taxes of $650 million. After paying taxes of $251 million, Google was left with a net income, or accounting profit, of $399 million for the year.

Source: Google's Income Statement for 2004. Google Inc. "Consolidated Statements of Income," February 1, 2005. Used with permission of Google, Inc.

Google's income statement presents the results of the company's operations during the year. Listed first are the revenues it earned, largely from selling advertising on its Web site, from January 1, 2004 to December 31, 2004: $3,189 million. Listed next are Google's operating expenses, the most important of which is its *cost of revenue*—which is commonly known as *cost of sales* or *cost of goods sold:* $1,458 million. Cost of revenue is the direct cost of producing the products sold, including in this case the salaries of the computer programmers Google hires to write the software for its Web site. Google also has substantial costs for researching and developing its products ($226 million) and for advertising and marketing them ($246 million). General and administrative expenses ($140 million) includes costs such as the salaries of top managers.

The difference between a firm's revenue and its costs is its profit. "Profit" shows up in several forms on an income statement. A firm's *operating income* is the difference between its revenue and its operating expenses. Most corporations, including Google, also have investments, such as government and corporate bonds, that normally generate some income for them. In this case, Google earned $10 million on its investments, which increased its *income before taxes* to $650 million. The federal government taxes the profits of corporations. During 2004, Google paid $251 million—or about 39 percent of its profits—in taxes. *Net income* after taxes was $399 million. The net income that firms report on their income statements is referred to as their after-tax *accounting profit.*

Analyzing Balance Sheets

As discussed in the chapter, whereas a firm's income statement reports a firm's activities for a period of time, a firm's balance sheet summarizes its financial position on a particular day, usually the end of a quarter or a year. To understand how a balance sheet is organized, first recall that an asset is anything of value that the firm owns and a liability is a debt or obligation owed by the firm. Subtracting the value of a firm's liabilities from the value of its assets leaves its *net worth.* Because a corporation's stockholders are its owners, net worth is often listed as **stockholders' equity** on a balance sheet. Using these definitions, we can state the balance sheet equation (also called the basic accounting equation) as follows:

Stockholders' equity The difference between the value of a corporation's assets and the value of its liabilities; also known as net worth.

$$\text{Assets} - \text{Liabilities} = \text{Stockholders' Equity}$$

or,

$$\text{Assets} = \text{Liabilities} + \text{Stockholders' Equity.}$$

This formula tells us that the value of a firm's assets must equal the value of its liabilities plus the value of stockholders' equity. An important accounting rule dating back to the beginning of modern bookkeeping in fifteenth-century Italy holds that balance sheets should list assets on the left side and liabilities and net worth or stockholders' equity on the right side. Notice that this means that *the value of the left side of the balance sheet must always equal the value of the right side.* Figure 5A-2 shows Google's balance sheet as of December 31, 2004.

A couple of the entries on the asset side of the balance sheet may be unfamiliar: *Current assets* are assets that the firm could convert into cash quickly, such as the balance in its checking account or its accounts receivable, which is money currently owed to the firm for products that have been delivered but not yet paid for. *Goodwill* represents the difference between the purchase price of a company and the market value of its assets. It represents the ability of a business to earn an economic profit from its assets. For example, if you buy a restaurant that is located on a busy intersec-

ASSETS		LIABILITIES AND STOCKHOLDERS' EQUITY	
Current assets	$2,693	Current liabilities	$340
Property and equipment	379	Long-term liabilities	44
Investments	71	Total liabilities	384
Goodwill	123	Stockholders' equity	2,929
Other long-term assets	47		
Total assets	3,313	Total liabilities and stockholders' equity	3,313

FIGURE 5A-2

Google's Balance Sheet as of December 31, 2004

Corporations list their assets on the left of their balance sheets and their liabilities on the right. The difference between the value of the firm's assets and the value of its liabilities equals the net worth of the firm, or stockholders' equity. Stockholders' equity is listed on the right side of the balance sheet. Therefore, the value of the left side of the balance sheet must always equal the value of the right side.

Note: All numbers are in millions of dollars.

Source: Google's Balance Sheet as of December 31, 2004, source: Google, Inc., "Consolidated Balance Sheets," February 1, 2004. Used with permission of Google, Inc.

tion and you employ a chef with a reputation for preparing delicious food, you may pay more than the market value of the tables, chairs, ovens, and other assets. This additional amount you pay will be entered on the asset side of your balance sheet as goodwill.

Current liabilities are short-term debts such as accounts payable, which is money owed to suppliers for goods received but not yet paid for, or bank loans that will be paid back in less than one year. Long-term bank loans and the value of outstanding corporate bonds are *long-term liabilities.*

KEY TERMS

Present value 153

Stockholders' equity 158

REVIEW QUESTIONS

1. Why is money you receive at some future date worth less than money you receive today? If the interest rate rises, what effect does this have on the present value of payments you receive in the future?
2. Give the formula for calculating the present value of a bond that will pay a coupon of $100 per year for 10 years and that has a face value of $1,000.
3. Compare the formula for calculating the present value of the payments you will receive from owning a bond to the formula for calculating the present value of the payments you will receive from owning a stock. What are the key similarities? What are the key differences?
4. How is operating income calculated? How does operating income differ from net income? How does net income differ from accounting profit?
5. What's the key difference between a firm's income statement and its balance sheet? What is listed on the left side of a balance sheet? What is listed on the right side?

PROBLEMS AND APPLICATIONS

Please visit **www.prenhall.com/hubbard** *for solutions to the even-numbered problems as well as multiple-choice and true or false self-assessment quizzes.*

1. **[Related to *Solved Problem 5A-1*]** If the interest rate is 10 percent, what is the present value of a bond that matures in two years, pays $85 one year from now, and pays $1,085 two years from now?
2. The following is from an Associated Press story on the contract of baseball star Carlos Beltran:

   > Beltran's contract calls for his $11 million signing bonus to be paid in four installments: $5 million upon approval and $2 million each this June 15, 2005, and on Jan. 15, 2006, and Jan. 15, 2007. He gets a $10 million salary this year, $12 million in each of the following two seasons and $18.5 million in each of the final four seasons, with $8.5 million deferred annually from 2008–11. The players' association calculated the present day value of the contract at $115,726,946, using a 6 percent discount rate (the prime rate [which is the interest rate banks charge on loans to their best customers] plus 1 percent, rounded to the nearest whole number). For purposes of baseball's luxury tax, which currently uses a 3.62 percent discount rate, the contract is valued at $116,695,898.

   Briefly explain why the present value of Beltran's contract is lower if a higher interest is used to make the calculation than if a lower interest rate is used.

   Source: "Like Pedro, Beltran Gets Suite on Road," Associated Press, January 18, 2005.
3. **[Related to *Solved Problem 5A-1*]** Before the 2005 season pitcher Armando Benitez signed a contract with the San Francisco Giants baseball team that would pay him the following amounts: $4.1 million in 2005, $6.6 million in 2006, $7.6 million in 2007, $1.6 million in 2008, and $1.6 million in 2009. Assume that he receives each payment as a lump sum at the end of the season and that he received his 2005 payment one year after he signed the contract.
   a. Some newspaper reports described Benitez as having signed a "$21.5 million contract" with the Giants. Do you agree that $21.5 million was the value of this contract? Briefly explain.
   b. What was the present value of Benitez's contract at the time he signed it (assume an interest rate of 10 percent)?
   c. If you use an interest rate of 5 percent, what was the present value of his contract?
4. **[Related to *Solved Problem 5A-1*]** A winner of the Pennsylvania Lottery was given the choice of receiving $18 million at once or $1,440,000 per year for 25 years.
   a. If the winner had opted for the 25 annual payments, how much in total would she have received?
   b. At an interest rate of 10 percent, what would be the present value of the 25 payments?
   c. At an interest rate of 5 percent, what would be the present value of the 25 payments?
   d. What interest rate would make the present value of the 25 payments equal to the one payment of $18 million? (This question is difficult and requires the use of a financial calculator or a spreadsheet. *Hint:* If you are familiar with the Excel spreadsheet program, use the RATE function. Questions b and c can be answered by using the Excel NPV—Net Present Value—function.)
5. **[Related to *Solved Problem 5A-1*]** Before the start of the 2000 baseball season, the New York Mets decided they didn't want Bobby Bonilla playing for them any longer. But Bonilla had a contract with the Mets for the 2000 season that would have obliged the Mets to pay him $5.9 million. When the Mets released Bonilla, he agreed to take the following payments in lieu of the $5.9 million the Mets would have paid him in the year 2000: He will receive 25 equal payments of $1,193,248.20 each July 1 from 2011 to 2035. If you were Bobby Bonilla, which would you rather have had, the lump sum $5.9 million or the 25 payments beginning in 2011? Explain the basis for your decision.
6. Suppose that eLake, an online auction site, is paying a dividend of $2.00 per share. You expect this dividend to grow 2 percent per year, and the interest rate is 10 percent. What is the most you would be willing to pay for a share of stock in eLake? If the interest rate is 5 percent, what is the most you would be willing to pay? When interest rates in the economy decline, would you expect stock prices in general to rise or fall? Explain.
7. Suppose you buy the bond of a large corporation at a time when the inflation rate is very low. If the inflation rate increases during the time you hold the bond, what is likely to happen to the price of the bond?

8. Use the information in the following table for calendar year 2004 to prepare the McDonald's Corporation's income statement. Be sure to include entries for operating income and net income.

Revenue from company restaurants	$14,224 million
Revenue from franchised restaurants	4,841 million
Cost of operating company-owned restaurants	12,100 million
Income taxes	924 million
Interest expense	338 million
General and administrative cost	1,980 million
Cost of restaurant leases	1,003 million
Other operating costs	441 million

Source: McDonald's Corporation, *Consolidated Statement of Income, 2004*, January 28, 2005.

9. Use the information in the following table on the financial situation of Starbucks Corporation as of October 3, 2004, to prepare the firm's balance sheet. Be sure to include an entry for stockholders' equity.

Current assets	$1,359 million
Current liabilities	774 million
Property and equipment	1,471 million
Long-term liabilities	58 million
Goodwill	69 million
Other assets	419 million

Source: Starbucks Corporation, *Annual Report, 2004*.

10. The *current ratio* is equal to a firm's current assets divided by its current liabilities. Use the information in Figure 5A-2 to calculate Google's current ratio on December 31, 2004. Investors generally prefer that a firm's current ratio is greater than 1.5. What problems might a firm encounter if the value of its current assets is low relative to the value of its current liabilities?

chapter six

Consumer Choice and Elasticity

Can LeBron James Get You to Drink Powerade?

When Coca-Cola hired LeBron James to endorse its Powerade drink, it announced that he would create his own flavor—Flava23—and that DC Comics had been hired by the company to create a LeBron James comic book. Celebrity endorsements of this type are very common, of course. Over the years, Coca-Cola has used other celebrities, including Lance Armstrong, Paula Abdul, and Ray Charles, to advertise its products. Nor is Coca-Cola alone in using celebrity endorsements. From Britney Spears and Sean "P. Diddy" Combs endorsing Pepsi to Michael Jordan endorsing Nike basketball shoes to Oprah Winfrey endorsing Pontiac cars, celebrities appear constantly in radio, television, and magazine advertising. What do firms hope to gain from celebrity endorsements? The obvious answer is that firms expect celebrity advertising will increase sales of their products. But why should consumers buy more of a product just because it is endorsed by a celebrity?

In this chapter, we will examine how consumers make decisions about which products to buy. Firms must understand consumer behavior to determine whether strategies such as using celebrities in their advertising are likely to be effective. Coca-Cola has been a leader in innovative advertising, including the use of celebrity endorsements.

Firms have been advertising for centuries. Josiah Wedgwood, who manufactured dishes and other dinnerware in England in the late 1700s, was probably the first to use celebrity endorsements. He sold fine china to prominent people of the time, including Catherine the Great of Russia, at reduced prices, hoping that the publicity from these sales would increase his sales to the general public. However, true modern advertising campaigns with firms spending large amounts year in and year out only began in the late nineteenth and early twentieth centuries. Coca-Cola was founded in Atlanta, Georgia, in 1886 by John Styth Pemberton. After Asa G. Candler bought the company in 1891, Coke began to be sold nationally, first primarily in drugstore soda fountains. The firm's advertising in magazines, newspapers, billboards, and calendars featured pictures of attractive young women drinking Coke—instead of emphasizing the taste or other qualities of the cola. According to one business historian these young women

> presented an ideal of femininity. Young women aspired to be like

the girls in the advertisements; young men aspired to date them. And these girls drank Coca-Cola.

By the 1910s, Coca-Cola had moved from using unnamed women in its advertising to using movie stars. The attempt to associate Coke with celebrities in the minds of consumers continued through the following decades. Even Santa Claus was pressed into service. The modern image of Santa Claus as cheerful, chubby, and with a full white beard was actually created in 1931 by artist Haddon Sundblom for a Coke advertisement. From the 1950s on, Coke's television commercials often featured popular singers or sports figures of the time, including the Supremes, the Moody Blues, Ray Charles, and football star "Mean" Joe Greene.

Firms' attempts to distinguish their products in the minds of consumers from the products of rival firms will be an important theme in several of the following chapters. Advertising is one way in which firms try to distinguish their products. *An Inside Look* on page 192 shows that celebrity endorsements can sometimes be a risky form of advertising.

As firms analyze consumer demand, one key factor they study is how changes in the price of a product affect the quantity of the product consumers are willing to purchase. In this chapter we will see how to measure the responsiveness of the quantity demanded of a product to a change in its price.

Source: Richard S. Tedlow, *New and Improved: The Story of Mass Marketing in America*, New York: Basic Books, 1990, p. 48.

After completing this chapter, you should be able to:

① Define utility and explain how consumers choose goods and services to maximize their utility.

② Explain how social influences can affect consumption choices.

③ Describe how people can improve their decision making by taking into account nonmonetary opportunity costs, ignoring sunk costs, and being more realistic about their future behavior.

④ Define the price elasticity of demand and understand how to calculate it.

⑤ Understand the determinants of the price elasticity of demand.

⑥ Understand the relationship between the price elasticity of demand and total revenue.

We begin this chapter by exploring how consumers make decisions. In Chapter 2, we saw that economists usually assume that people act in a rational, self-interested way. In explaining consumer behavior, this means economists believe consumers make choices that will leave them as satisfied as possible, given their *tastes*, their *incomes*, and the *prices* of the goods and services available to them. We will see how the downward-sloping demand curves we encountered in Chapters 3 and 4 result from the economic model of consumer behavior. We will also see that in certain situations, knowing the best decision to make can be difficult. In these cases, economic reasoning provides a powerful tool for consumers to improve their decision making. Finally, we will see that *experimental economics* has shown that factors such as social pressure and notions of fairness can affect consumer behavior. We will look at how businesses take these factors into account when setting prices.

Whether you are managing a publishing company, bookstore, or coffee shop, you need to know how an increase or decrease in the price of your products will affect the quantity consumers are willing to buy. We saw in Chapter 3 that cutting the price of a good increases the quantity demanded, and that raising the price reduces the quantity demanded. But the critical question is this: *How much* will the quantity demanded change as a result of a price increase or decrease? Economists use the concept of **elasticity** to measure how one economic variable—such as the quantity demanded—responds to changes in another economic variable—such as the price. For example, the responsiveness of the quantity demanded of a good to changes in its price is called the *price elasticity of demand*. Knowing the price elasticity of demand allows you to compute the effect of a price change on the quantity demanded.

Elasticity A measure of how much one economic variable responds to changes in another economic variable.

1 LEARNING OBJECTIVE

Define utility and explain how consumers choose goods and services to maximize their utility.

Utility and Consumer Decision Making

We saw in Chapter 3 that the model of demand and supply is a powerful tool for analyzing how prices and quantities are determined. We also saw in Chapter 3 that, according to the *law of demand*, whenever the price of a good falls, the quantity demanded increases. Now we will show how the economic model of consumer behavior leads to the law of demand.

The Economic Model of Consumer Behavior in a Nutshell

Imagine walking through a shopping mall trying to decide how to spend your clothing budget. If you had an unlimited budget, your decision would be easy: Just buy as much of everything as you want. Given that you have a limited budget, what do you do? Economists assume that consumers act so as to make themselves as well off as possible. Therefore, you should choose among those combinations of clothes that you can afford, the one combination that makes you as well off as possible. Stated more generally, the economic model of consumer behavior predicts that consumers will choose to buy the combination of goods and services that makes them as well off as possible from among all the combinations that their budgets allow them to buy.

This prediction may seem obvious and not particularly useful. But as we explore the implication of this prediction, we will see that it leads to conclusions that are both useful and not obvious.

Utility

Ultimately, how well off you are from consuming a particular combination of goods and services depends upon your tastes, or preferences. There is an old saying—"There's no accounting for tastes"—and economists don't try to. If you buy Powerade instead of Gatorade, even though Gatorade has a lower price, you must receive more enjoyment or satisfaction from drinking Powerade. Economists refer to the enjoyment or satisfaction people receive from consuming goods and services as **utility**. So we can say that the goal of a consumer is to spend available income so as to maximize utility. But utility is a difficult concept to measure, because there is no way of knowing exactly how much enjoyment or satisfaction a consumer receives from consuming a product. Similarly, it is not possible to compare utility across consumers. There is no way of knowing for sure whether Jill receives more or less satisfaction than Jack from drinking a bottle of Powerade.

Utility The enjoyment or satisfaction people receive from consuming goods and services.

Two hundred years ago, economists had hoped it would be possible to measure utility in units called "utils." The util would be an objective measure in the same way that temperature is. If it is 70 degrees in New York and 70 degrees in Los Angeles, it is just as warm in both cities. These economists hoped it would be possible to say that if Jack's utility from eating a hamburger is 10 utils and Jill's utility is 5 utils, then Jack receives exactly twice the satisfaction from eating a hamburger that Jill does. In fact, it is not possible to measure utility across people. It turns out that none of the important conclusions of the economic model of consumer behavior depend on utility being directly measurable. Nevertheless, the economic model of consumer behavior is easier to understand if we assume that utility is something directly measurable, like temperature.

The Principle of Diminishing Marginal Utility

To make the model of consumer behavior more concrete, let's see how a consumer makes decisions in a case involving just two products: pepperoni pizza and Coke. To begin, consider how the utility you receive from consuming a good changes with the amount of the good you consume. For example, suppose that you have just arrived at a Super Bowl party where the hosts are serving pepperoni pizza, and you are very hungry. In this situation, you are likely to receive quite a lot of enjoyment, or utility, from consuming the first slice of pizza. Suppose this satisfaction is measurable and is equal to 20. After eating the first slice, you decide to have a second slice. Because you are no longer as hungry, the satisfaction you receive from eating the second slice of pizza will be less than the satisfaction you received from eating the first slice. Consuming the second slice would increase your utility by only an *additional* 16, which would raise your *total* utility from eating the two slices to 36. If you continue eating slices, each additional slice will give you less and less additional satisfaction.

The table in Figure 6-1 shows the relationship between the number of slices of pizza you consume while watching the Super Bowl and the amount of utility you receive. The second column in the table shows the total utility you receive from eating a particular number of slices. The third column shows the additional utility or **marginal utility (*MU*)** you receive from consuming one additional slice. (Remember that in economics "marginal" means additional.) For example, as you increase your consumption from 2 slices to 3 slices, your total utility increases from 36 to 46, so your marginal utility from consuming the third slice is 10. As the table shows, by the time you eat the fifth slice of pizza that evening, your marginal utility will be very low: only 2. If you were to eat a sixth slice, we will assume that you would become slightly nauseous and your marginal utility would actually be a *negative* 3.

Marginal utility (*MU*) The change in total utility a person receives from consuming one additional unit of a good or service.

Figure 6-1 also plots the numbers from the table as graphs. Panel (a) shows how your total utility rises as you eat the first five slices of pizza, and then falls as you eat the sixth slice. Panel (b) shows how your marginal utility declines with each additional slice you eat and finally becomes negative when you eat the sixth slice. The height of the marginal utility line at any quantity of pizza in panel (b) represents the change in

FIGURE 6-1

Total and Marginal Utility from Eating Pizza on Super Bowl Sunday

The table shows that for the first 5 slices of pizza, the more you eat, the more your total satisfaction or utility will increase. If you eat the sixth slice, you will start to feel ill from eating too much pizza, and your total utility will fall. Each additional slice increases your utility by less than the previous slice, so your marginal utility from each slice is less than the one before. Panel (a) shows your total utility rising as you eat the first 5 slices, and falling with the sixth slice. Panel (b) shows your marginal utility falling with each additional slice you eat, and becoming negative with the sixth slice. The height of the marginal utility line at any quantity of pizza in panel (b) represents the change in utility as a result of consuming that additional slice. For example, the change in utility as a result of consuming 4 slices instead of 3 is 6, so the height of the marginal utility line in panel (b) for the fourth slice is 6.

Number of Slices	Total Utility from Eating Pizza	Marginal Utility from the Last Slice Eaten
0	0	—
1	20	20
2	36	16
3	46	10
4	52	6
5	54	2
6	51	–3

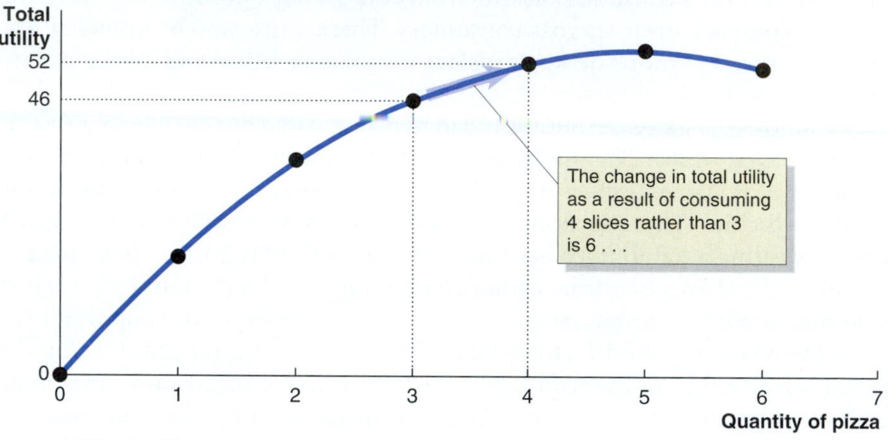

(a) Total utility

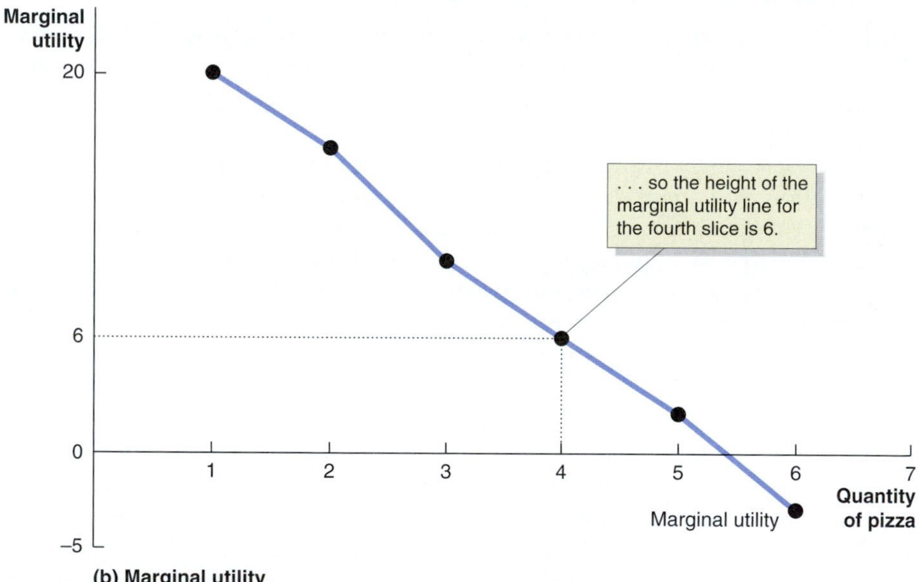

(b) Marginal utility

utility as a result of consuming that additional slice. For example, the change in utility as a result of consuming 4 slices instead of 3 is 6, so the height of the marginal utility line in panel (b) is 6.

Law of diminishing marginal utility Consumers experience diminishing additional satisfaction as they consume more of a good or service during a given period of time.

The relationship illustrated in Figure 6-1 between consuming additional units of a product during a period of time and the marginal utility received from consuming each additional unit is referred to as the **law of diminishing marginal utility.** For nearly every good or service, the more you consume during a period of time, the less you increase your total satisfaction from each additional unit you consume.

The Rule of Equal Marginal Utility per Dollar Spent

The key challenge for consumers is to decide how to allocate their limited incomes among all the products they wish to buy. Every consumer has to make trade-offs: If you have $100 to spend on entertainment for the month, then the more DVDs you buy, the fewer movies you can see in the theater. Economists refer to the limited amount of income you have available to spend on goods and services as your **budget constraint**. The principle of diminishing marginal utility helps us understand how consumers can best spend their limited incomes on the products available to them.

Budget constraint The limited amount of income available to consumers to spend on goods and services.

Suppose you attend a Super Bowl party at a restaurant and you have $10 to spend on refreshments. Pizza is selling for $2 per slice and Coke is selling for $1 per cup. Table 6-1 shows the relationship between the amount of pizza you eat, the amount of Coke you drink, and the amount of satisfaction or utility you receive. The values for pizza are repeated from the table in Figure 6-1. The values for Coke also follow the principle of diminishing marginal utility.

How many slices of pizza and how many cups of Coke do you buy if you want to maximize your utility? If you did not have a budget constraint, you would buy 5 slices of pizza and 5 cups of Coke, because that would give you total utility of 107 (54 + 53), which is the maximum utility you can achieve. Eating another slice of pizza or drinking another cup of Coke during the evening would lower your utility. Unfortunately, you do have a budget constraint: You have only $10 to spend. To buy 5 slices of pizza (at $2 per slice) and 5 cups of Coke (at $1 per cup), you would need $15.

To select the best way to spend your $10, remember this key economic principle: *Optimal decisions are made at the margin.* That is, most of the time economic decision makers—consumers, firms, and the government—are faced with decisions about whether to do a little more of one thing or a little more of an alternative. In this case, you are choosing between a little more pizza or a little more Coke. BMW chooses between manufacturing more roadsters or more SUVs in its South Carolina factory. Congress and the president choose between spending more dollars for research on heart disease or more dollars for research on breast cancer. Every economic decision maker faces a budget constraint, and every economic decision maker faces trade-offs.

The key to making the best consumption decision is to maximize utility by following the *rule of equal marginal utility per dollar:* As you decide how to spend your income, you should buy pizza and Coke up to the point where the last slice of pizza purchased and the last cup of Coke purchased give you equal increases in utility *per dollar*. By doing this, you will have maximized your total utility.

TABLE 6-1 Total Utility and Marginal Utility from Eating Pizza and Drinking Coke

NUMBER OF SLICES OF PIZZA	TOTAL UTILITY FROM EATING PIZZA	MARGINAL UTILITY FROM THE LAST SLICE	NUMBER OF CUPS OF COKE	TOTAL UTILITY FROM DRINKING COKE	MARGINAL UTILITY FROM THE LAST CUP
0	0		0	0	
1	20	20	1	20	20
2	36	16	2	35	15
3	46	10	3	45	10
4	52	6	4	50	5
5	54	2	5	53	3
6	51	−3	6	52	−1

TABLE 6-2 Converting Marginal Utility to Marginal Utility per Dollar

(1) SLICES OF PIZZA	(2) MARGINAL UTILITY (MU_{Pizza})	(3) MARGINAL UTILITY PER DOLLAR $\left(\frac{MU_{Pizza}}{P_{Pizza}}\right)$	(4) CUPS OF COKE	(5) MARGINAL UTILITY (MU_{Coke})	(6) MARGINAL UTILITY PER DOLLAR $\left(\frac{MU_{Coke}}{P_{Coke}}\right)$
1	20	10	1	20	20
2	16	8	2	15	15
3	10	5	3	10	10
4	6	3	4	5	5
5	2	1	5	3	3
6	−3	–	6	−1	–

It is important to remember that to follow this rule you must equalize your marginal utility per dollar spent, *not* your marginal utility from each good. Buying season tickets for your favorite NFL team or for the opera, or buying a BMW may give you a lot more satisfaction than drinking a cup of Coke, but the NFL tickets may well give you less satisfaction *per dollar* spent. To decide how many slices of pizza and how many cups of Coke to buy you must take the values for marginal utility in Table 6-1 and convert them to marginal utility per dollar. You can do this by dividing marginal utility by the price of each good, as shown in Table 6-2.

In column (3), we calculate marginal utility per dollar spent on pizza. Because the price of pizza is $2 per slice, the marginal utility per dollar from eating one slice of pizza equals 20 divided by $2, or 10 units of utility per dollar. Similarly, we show in column (6) that because the price of Coke is $1 per cup, the marginal utility per dollar from drinking 1 cup of Coke equals 20 divided by $1, or 20 units of utility per dollar. To maximize the total utility you receive, you must make sure that the utility per dollar of pizza for the last slice of pizza is equal to the utility per dollar of Coke for the last cup of Coke. Table 6-2 shows that there are three combinations of slices of pizza and cups of Coke where marginal utility per dollar is equalized. Table 6-3 lists these combinations, along with the total amount of money needed to buy each combination, and the total utility received from consuming each combination.

If you buy 4 slices of pizza, the last slice gives you 3 units of utility per dollar. If you buy 5 cups of Coke, the last cup also gives you 3 units of utility per dollar, so you have equalized your marginal utility per dollar. Unfortunately, as the third column in the table shows, to buy 4 slices and 5 cups, you would need $13 and you have only $10. You could also equalize your marginal utility per dollar by buying 1 slice and 3 cups, but that

TABLE 6-3 Equalizing Marginal Utility per Dollar Spent

COMBINATIONS OF PIZZA AND COKE WITH EQUAL MARGINAL UTILITIES PER DOLLAR	MARGINAL UTILITY PER DOLLAR (MARGINAL UTILITY/PRICE)	TOTAL SPENDING	TOTAL UTILITY
1 Slice of Pizza and 3 Cups of Coke	10	$2 + $3 = $5	20 + 45 = 65
3 Slices of Pizza and 4 Cups of Coke	5	$6 + $4 = $10	46 + 50 = 96
4 Slices of Pizza and 5 Cups of Coke	3	$8 + $5 = $13	52 + 53 = 105

would cost just $5, leaving you with $5 to spend. Only when you buy 3 three slices and 4 cups have you equalized your marginal utility per dollar and spent neither more nor less than the $10 available.

We can compactly summarize the two conditions for maximizing utility as follows:

1. $\dfrac{MU_{Pizza}}{P_{Pizza}} = \dfrac{MU_{Coke}}{P_{Coke}}$

2. Spending on pizza + Spending on Coke = Amount available to be spent

The first condition shows that the marginal utility per dollar spent must be the same for both goods. The second condition is the budget constraint, which states that total spending on both goods must equal the amount available to be spent. Of course, these conditions for maximizing utility apply not just to pizza and Coke, but to any two pairs of goods.

SOLVED PROBLEM 6-1

Finding the Optimal Level of Consumption

① LEARNING OBJECTIVE

Define utility and explain how consumers choose goods and services to maximize their utility.

The following table shows Lee's utility from consuming ice cream cones and cans of Lime Fizz Soda:

NUMBER OF ICE CREAM CONES	TOTAL UTILITY FROM ICE CREAM CONES	MARGINAL UTILITY FROM LAST CONE	NUMBER OF CANS OF LIME FIZZ	TOTAL UTILITY FROM CANS OF LIME FIZZ	MARGINAL UTILITY FROM LAST CAN
0	0	–	0	0	–
1	30	30	1	40	40
2	55	25	2	75	35
3	75	20	3	101	26
4	90	15	4	119	18
5	100	10	5	134	15
6	105	5	6	141	7

a. Ed inspects this table and says to Travis, "Lee's optimal choice would be to consume 4 ice cream cones and 5 cans of Lime Fizz, because with that combination his marginal utility from ice cream cones is equal to his marginal utility from Lime Fizz." Do you agree with Ed's reasoning? Briefly explain.

b. Suppose that Lee has an unlimited budget to spend on ice cream cones and cans of Lime Fizz. Under these circumstances, how many ice cream cones and how many cans of Lime Fizz will he consume?

c. Suppose Lee has $7 per week to spend on ice cream cones and Lime Fizz. The price of an ice cream cone is $2 and the price of a can of Lime Fizz is $1. If Lee wants to maximize his utility, how many ice cream cones and how many cans of Lime Fizz should he buy?

Solving the Problem:

Step 1: Review the chapter material. This problem involves finding the optimal consumption of two goods, so you may want to review the section "The Rule of Equal Marginal Utility per Dollar Spent," which begins on page 167.

Step 2: Answer question (a) by analyzing Ed's reasoning. Ed's reasoning is incorrect. To maximize utility, Lee needs to equalize marginal utility per dollar for the two goods.

Step 3: Answer question (b) by determining how Lee would maximize utility with an unlimited budget. With an unlimited budget, consumers maximize utility by continuing to buy each good as long as their utility is increasing. In this case, Lee will maximize utility by buying 6 ice cream cones and 6 cans of Lime Fizz.

Step 4: Answer question (c) by determining Lee's optimal combination of ice cream cones and cans of Lime Fizz. Lee will maximize his utility if he spends his $7 per week so that the marginal utility of ice cream cones divided by the price of ice cream cones is equal to the marginal utility of Lime Fizz divided by the price of Lime Fizz. We can use the following table to solve this part of the problem:

	ICE CREAM CONES		CANS OF LIME FIZZ	
QUANTITY	*MU*	$\frac{MU}{P}$	*MU*	$\frac{MU}{P}$
1	30	15	40	40
2	25	12.5	35	35
3	20	10	26	26
4	15	7.5	18	18
5	10	5	15	15
6	5	2.5	7	7

Lee will maximize utility by buying 1 ice cream cone and 5 cans of Lime Fizz. At this combination, the marginal utility of each good divided by its price equals 15. He has also spent all of his $7.

YOUR TURN: **For more practice, do related problems 2 and 3 on page 196 at the end of this chapter.**

What If the Rule of Equal Marginal Utility per Dollar Does Not Hold?

The idea of getting the maximum utility by equalizing the ratio of marginal utility to price for the goods you are buying can be difficult to grasp, so it is worth thinking about in another way. Suppose that instead of buying 3 slices of pizza and 4 cups of Coke, you buy 4 slices and 2 cups. Four slices and 2 cups cost $10, so you would meet your budget constraint by spending all the money available to you, but would you have gotten the maximum amount of utility? No, you wouldn't have. From the information in Table 6-1, we can list the additional utility per dollar you are getting from the last slice and the last cup and the total utility from consuming 4 slices and 2 cups:

Marginal utility per dollar for the fourth slice of pizza = 3 units of utility per dollar

Marginal utility per dollar for the second cup of Coke = 15 units of utility per dollar

Total utility from 4 slices of pizza and 2 cups of Coke = 87

Obviously, the marginal utilities per dollar are not equal. The last cup of Coke gave you considerably more satisfaction per dollar than did the last slice of pizza. You could raise your total utility by buying less pizza and more Coke. Buying 1 less slice of pizza frees up $2 that will allow you to buy 2 more cups of Coke. Eating 1 less slice of pizza reduces your utility by 6, but drinking 2 additional cups of Coke raises your utility by 15 (make sure you see this), for a net increase of 9. You end up equalizing your marginal utility per dollar (5 units of utility per dollar for both the last slice and the last cup) and raising your total utility from 87 to 96.

Where Demand Curves Come From

We saw in Chapter 3 that, according to the *law of demand*, whenever the price of a product falls, the quantity demanded increases. Now that we have covered the concepts of total utility, marginal utility, and the budget constraint, we can look more closely at why the law of demand holds.

In our example of optimal consumption of pizza and Coke at the Super Bowl party, we found the following:

Price of pizza = \$2 per slice ⇒ Quantity of pizza demanded = 3 slices

Price of pizza = \$1.50 per slice ⇒ Quantity of pizza demanded = 4 slices

In panel (a) of Figure 6-2, we plot the two points showing the optimal number of pizza slices you choose to consume at each price. In panel (b) of Figure 6-2, we draw a line connecting the two points. This downward-sloping line represents your demand curve for pizza. We could find more points on the line by changing the price of pizza and using the information in Table 6-2 to find the new optimal number of slices of pizza you would demand at each price.

Remember that according to the law of demand, demand curves always slope downward. We saw in Chapter 3 that the **income** and **substitution effects** of a fall in price cause consumers to increase the quantity of the good they demand. (Recall that the substitution effect is the change in the quantity demanded of a good that results from a change in price making the good more or less expensive relative to other goods that are substitutes. And the income effect is the change in quantity demanded of a good that results from the effect of a change in the good's price on consumer purchasing power.) There is a complicating factor, however: Only for normal goods will the income effect result in consumers increasing the quantity of the good they demand when the price falls. If the good is an inferior good, then the income effect leads consumers to *decrease* the quantity of the good they demand. The substitution effect, on the other hand, results in consumers increasing the quantity they demand of both normal and inferior goods when the price falls. So, when the price of an inferior good falls,

Income effect The change in the quantity demanded of a good that results from the effect of a change in price on consumer purchasing power, holding all other factors constant.

Substitution effect The change in the quantity demanded of a good that results from a change in price making the good more or less expensive relative to other goods, holding constant the effect of the price change on consumer purchasing power.

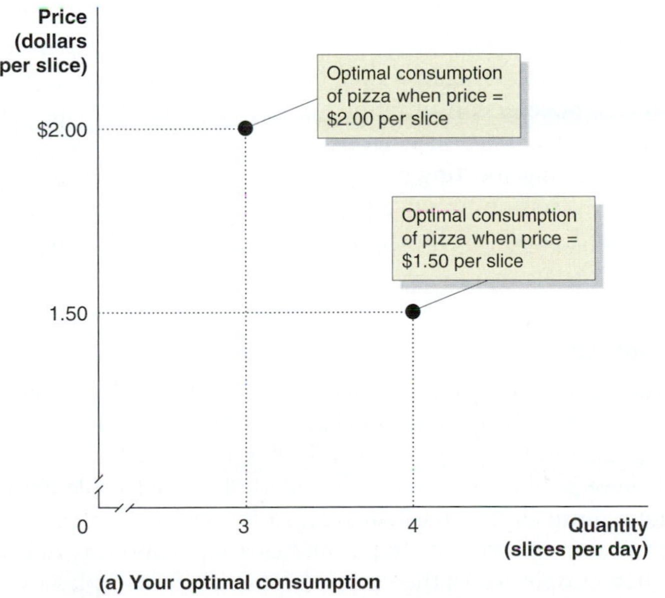

(a) Your optimal consumption

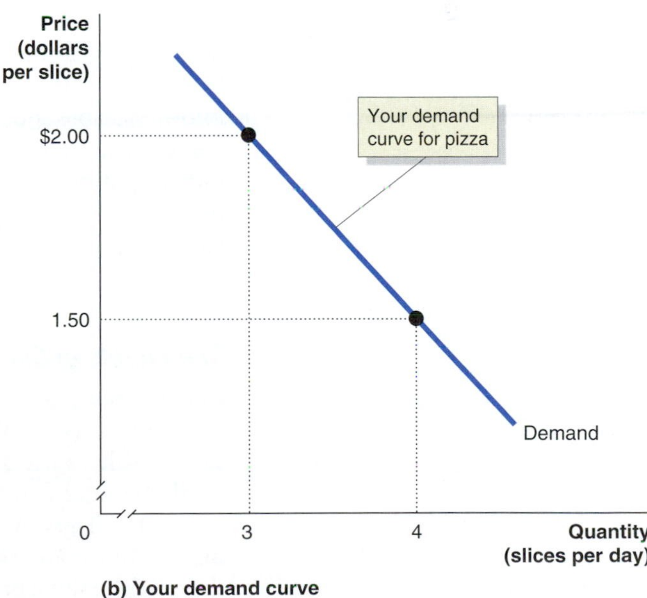

(b) Your demand curve

FIGURE 6-2 Deriving the Demand Curve for Pizza

A consumer responds optimally to the fall in the price of a product by consuming more of that product. In panel (a), the price of pizza falls from \$2 per slice to \$1.50, and optimal quantity of slices consumed rises from 3 to 4. When we graph this result in panel (b), we have the consumer's demand curve.

the income and substitution effects work in opposite directions: The income effect causes consumers to decrease the quantity of the good they demand, whereas the substitution effect causes consumers to increase the quantity of the good they demand. Is it possible, then, that consumers might actually buy less of a good when the price falls? If this happened, the demand curve would be upward-sloping. (Be sure you see why this would be true.)

For a demand curve to be upward-sloping, the good would have to be an inferior good, and the income effect would have to be larger than the substitution effect. Goods that have both these characteristics are called *Giffen goods.* Although we can conceive of there being Giffen goods, none has ever been discovered because for all actual goods the substitution effect is larger than the income effect. Therefore, even for an inferior good, a fall in price leads to an increase in quantity demanded and a rise in price leads to a decrease in the quantity demanded.

② **LEARNING OBJECTIVE**

Explain how social influences can affect consumption choices.

Social Influences on Decision Making

Sociologists and anthropologists have argued that social factors such as culture, customs, and religion are very important in explaining the choices consumers make. Economists have traditionally seen such factors as being relatively unimportant, if they take them into consideration at all. Recently, however, some economists have begun to study how social factors influence consumer choice.

For example, people seem to receive more utility from consuming goods they believe are popular. As the economists Kevin Murphy and Gary Becker, winner of the Nobel Prize in Economics, put it:

> The utility from drugs, crime, going bowling, owning a Rolex watch, voting Democratic, dressing informally at work, or keeping a neat lawn depends on whether friends and neighbors take drugs, commit crimes, go bowling, own Rolex watches, vote Democratic, dress informally, or keep their lawns neat.

This reasoning can help to explain why one restaurant is packed, while another restaurant that serves essentially the same food and has a similar décor has many fewer customers. Consumers decide which restaurant to go to partly on the basis of food and décor, but also on the basis of the restaurant's popularity. People receive utility from being seen eating at a popular restaurant because they believe it makes them appear knowledgeable and fashionable. Whenever consumption takes place publicly, many consumers will base their purchasing decisions on what other consumers buy. Examples include eating in restaurants, attending sporting events, wearing clothes or jewelry, or driving cars. In all these cases, the decision to buy a product will depend partly on the characteristics of the product and partly on how many other people are buying the product.

The Effects of Celebrity Endorsements

In many cases, it is not just the number of people who use a product that makes it desirable, but the types of people who use it. If consumers believe that movie stars or professional athletes use a product, demand for the product will often increase. This may be partly because consumers believe public figures are particularly knowledgeable about products: "Tiger Woods knows more about cars than I do, so I'll buy the same car he drives." But many consumers also feel more fashionable and closer to famous people if they use the same products these people do. All these considerations help to explain why companies are willing to pay millions of dollars to have celebrities endorse their products. As we saw at the beginning of this chapter, Coca-Cola has been using celebrities in its advertising for decades.

6-1 Making the Connection

Why Do Firms Pay Tiger Woods to Endorse Their Products?

Tiger Woods may be the best golfer who ever lived. In his first five years as a professional, he won 27 tournaments on the Professional Golfers Association (PGA) Tour. When he won the Masters Tournament in 2001, he became the first golfer ever to hold all four major professional golf championships at the same time. Even though Tiger Woods is a great golfer, should consumers care what products he uses? A number of major companies apparently believe consumers do care. The Nike, Titleist, American Express, Buick, and Rolex companies collectively pay him more than $50 million per year to endorse their products.

There seems little doubt that consumers do care what products Tiger uses, but *why* do they care? It might be that they believe Tiger has better information than they do about the products he endorses. The average weekend golfer might believe that if Tiger endorses Titleist golf clubs, maybe Titleist clubs are better than other golf clubs. But it seems more likely that people buy products associated with Tiger Woods or other celebrities because using these products makes them feel closer to the celebrity endorser or because it makes them appear to be fashionable.

When consumers buy the same products as celebrities, they feel fashionable and closer to the celebrities.

Network Externalities

Technology can also play a role in explaining why consumers buy products that many other consumers are already buying. There are **network externalities** in the consumption of a product if the usefulness of the product increases with the number of consumers who use it. For example, if you owned the only telephone in the world, it would not be very useful. The usefulness of telephones increases with the number of people who own them and use them. Similarly, your willingness to buy a DVD player will depend in part on the number of other people who have DVD players. The more people who have DVD players, the more movies that will be available in DVD format and the more useful a DVD player is to you.

Network externalities Network externalities exist when the usefulness of a product increases with the number of consumers who use it.

Some economists have raised the possibility that network externalities may have a significant downside because they might result in consumers buying products that contain inferior technologies. This outcome could occur because network externalities can create significant *switching costs* to changing products. Therefore, once a product becomes established, consumers may find it too costly to switch to a new product that contains a better technology. The selection of products may be *path dependent.* That means that because of switching costs, the technology that was first available may have advantages over better technologies that were developed later—in other words, the path along which the economy has developed in the past is important.

One possible example of path dependency and the use of an inferior technology is computers with QWERTY keyboards. QWERTY refers to the order of the letters along the top row of most keyboards. This order first became widespread when manual typewriters were developed in the late nineteenth century. The metal keys on these typewriters would stick together if a user typed too fast. Some economists have argued that the QWERTY keyboard was designed actually to slow down typists. With computers, the problem that QWERTY was developed to solve no longer exists, so keyboards could be changed easily to have letters in a more efficient layout. But because the overwhelming majority of people have learned to use keyboards with the QWERTY layout, there might be significant costs to them from switching even if a new layout ultimately made them faster typists.

Other products that supposedly embodied inferior technologies are VHS video recorders—supposedly inferior to Sony Betamax recorders—and the Windows computer operating system—supposedly inferior to the Macintosh operating system. Some economists have argued that because of path dependence and switching costs, network externalities can result in *market failures.* As we saw in Chapter 4, a market failure is a situation in which the market fails to produce the efficient level of output. If network externalities result in market failure, government intervention in these markets might improve economic efficiency. Many economists are skeptical, however, that network externalities really do lead to consumers being locked into products with inferior technologies. In particular, economists Stan Leibowitz of the University of Texas, Dallas, and Stephen Margolis of North Carolina State University have argued that in practice the gains from using a superior technology are larger than the losses due to switching costs. After carefully studying the cases of the QWERTY keyboard, VHS video recorders, and the Windows computer operating system, they have concluded that there is no good evidence that the alternative technologies were actually superior. The implications of network externalities for economic efficiency remain controversial among economists.

Does Fairness Matter?

If people were only interested in making themselves as well off as possible in a material sense, they would not be concerned with fairness. There is a great deal of evidence, however, that people like to be treated fairly and that they usually attempt to treat others fairly, even if doing so makes them worse off financially. Tipping servers in restaurants is an example. Diners in restaurants typically add 15 percent to their food bills as tips to their servers. Tips are not *required,* but most people see it as very unfair not to tip, unless the service has been exceptionally bad. You could argue that people leave tips not to be fair but because they are afraid that if they don't leave a tip, the next time they visit the restaurant they will receive poor service. Studies have shown, however, that most people leave tips at restaurants even while on vacation or in other circumstances where they are unlikely to visit the restaurant again.

There are many other examples where people willingly part with money when they are not required to do so and when they receive nothing material in return. The most obvious example is making donations to charity. Apparently donating money to charity or leaving tips in restaurants that they will never visit again gives people more utility than they would receive from keeping the money and spending it on themselves.

A TEST OF FAIRNESS IN THE ECONOMIC LABORATORY: THE ULTIMATUM GAME EXPERIMENT Economists have used experiments to increase their understanding of the role that fairness plays in consumer decision making. Experimental economics has been widely used during the last two decades, and a number of experimental economics laboratories exist in the United States and Europe. Economists Maurice Allais, Reinhard Selten, and Vernon Smith were awarded the Nobel Prize in Economics in part because of their contributions to experimental economics. Experiments make it possible to focus on a single aspect of consumer behavior. The *ultimatum game,* first popularized by Werner Güth of the Max Planck Institute of Economics, is an experiment that tests whether fairness is important in consumer decision making. Various economists have conducted the ultimatum game experiment under slightly different conditions, but with generally the same result. In this game, a group of volunteers—often college students—are divided into pairs. One member of each pair is the "allocator" and the other member of the pair is the "recipient."

Each pair is given an amount of money, say $20. The allocator decides how much of the $20 each member of the pair will get. There are no restrictions on how the allocator divides up the money. He or she could keep it all, give it all to the recipient, or anything in between. The recipient must then decide whether to accept the allocation or reject it. If the recipient decides to accept the allocation, each member of the pair gets to keep his or her share. If the recipient decides to reject the allocation, both members of the pair receive nothing.

If neither the allocator nor the recipient cared about fairness, optimal play in the ultimatum game is straightforward: The allocator should propose a division of the money in which the allocator receives $19.99 and the recipient receives $0.01. The allocator has maximized his or her gain. The recipient should accept the division, because the alternative is to reject the division and receive nothing at all: Even a penny is better than nothing.

In fact, when the ultimatum game experiment is carried out, both allocators and recipients act as if fairness is important. Allocators usually offer recipients at least a 40 percent share of the money, and recipients almost always reject offers of less than a 10 percent share. Why do allocators offer recipients more than a negligible amount? It might be that allocators do not care about fairness but fear that recipients do care and will reject offers they consider unfair. This possibility was tested in an experiment known as the *dictator game* carried out by Daniel Kahneman (a psychologist who shared the Nobel Prize in Economics in 2002), Jack Knetsch, and Richard Thaler using students at Cornell University. In this experiment, the allocators were given only two possible divisions of $20: either $18 for themselves and $2 for the recipient, or an even division of $10 for themselves and $10 for the recipient. One important difference from the ultimatum game was that *the recipient was not allowed to reject the division.* Of the 161 allocators, 122 chose the even division of the $20. Because there was no possibility of the $18/$2 split being rejected, the allocators must have chosen the even split because they valued acting fairly.

Why would recipients in the ultimatum game ever reject any division of the money in which they receive even a very small amount, given that even a small amount of money is better than nothing? Apparently, most people value fairness enough that they will refuse to participate in transactions they consider unfair, even if they are worse off financially as a result.

BUSINESS IMPLICATIONS OF FAIRNESS If consumers value fairness, how does that affect firms? One consequence is that firms will sometimes not raise prices of goods and services, even when there is a large increase in demand, because they are afraid their customers will consider the price increases unfair and may buy elsewhere.

For example, the Broadway play *The Producers* was extremely popular during its first year in production. Even though ticket prices were an average of $75, on most nights many more people wanted to buy tickets at that price than could be accommodated in the St. James Theater, where the play was running. Figure 6-3 illustrates this situation.

Notice that the supply curve in Figure 6-3 is a vertical line, which indicates that the capacity of the St. James Theater is fixed at 1,644 seats. At a price of $75 per ticket, there was a shortage of more than 400 tickets. Why didn't the theater raise ticket prices to $125, where the quantity supplied would equal the quantity demanded?

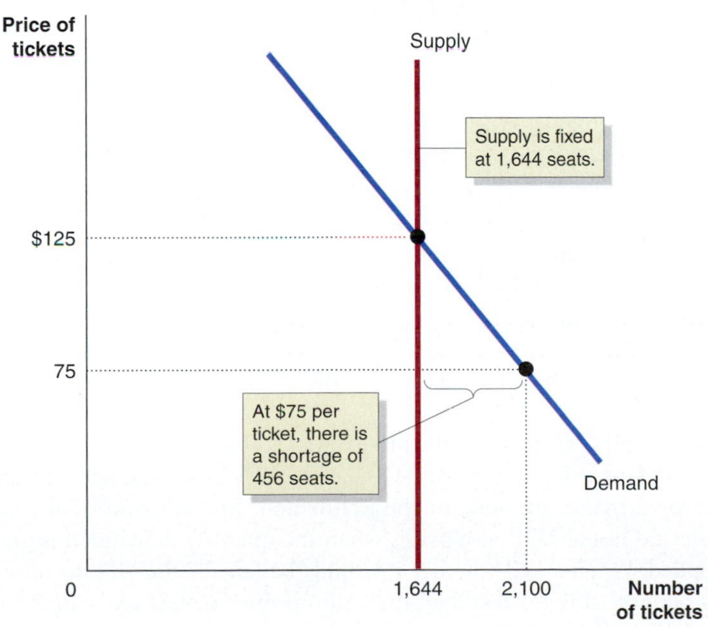

FIGURE 6-3

The Market for Tickets to *The Producers*

The St. James Theater could have raised prices for the Broadway musical *The Producers* to $125 per ticket and still sold all of the 1,644 tickets available. Instead, the theater kept the price of tickets at $75, even though the result was a shortage of more than 400 seats. Is it possible that this strategy maximized profits?

The following are two other examples in which it seems that businesses could increase their profits by raising prices: Each year many more people would like to buy tickets to see the Super Bowl than there are tickets for them to buy at the price the National Football League charges. Why doesn't the National Football League raise prices? At popular restaurants, there are often long lines of people waiting to be served. Some of the people will wait hours to be served, and some won't be served at all before the restaurant closes. Why doesn't the restaurant raise prices high enough to eliminate the lines?

In each of these cases, it appears that a firm could increase its profits by raising prices. The seller would be selling the same quantity—of seats in a theater or a football stadium or meals in a restaurant—at a higher price, so profits should increase. Economists have provided two explanations why firms will sometimes not raise prices in these situations. Gary Becker has suggested that the products involved—theatrical plays, football games, rock concerts, or restaurant meals—are all products that buyers consume together with other buyers. In those situations, the amount consumers wish to buy may be related to how much of the product other people are consuming. People like to consume, and be seen consuming, a popular product. In this case, a popular restaurant that increased its prices enough to eliminate lines might find that it had also eliminated its popularity.

Daniel Kahneman, Jack Knetsch, and Richard Thaler have offered another explanation for why firms don't always raise prices when doing so would seem to increase their profits. In surveys of consumers, these researchers found that most people considered it fair for firms to raise their prices following an increase in costs but unfair to raise prices following an increase in demand. For example, Kahneman, Knetsch, and Thaler conducted a survey in which people were asked their opinion of the following situation: "A hardware store has been selling snow shovels for $15. The morning after a large snowstorm, the store raises the price to $20." Eighty-two percent of those surveyed responded that they considered the hardware store's actions to be unfair. Kahneman, Knetsch, and Thaler have concluded that firms may sometimes not raise their prices even when the quantity demanded of their product is greater than the quantity supplied out of fear that in the long run they will lose customers who believe the price increases were unfair.

These explanations share the same basic idea: Sometimes firms will give up some profits in the short run to keep their customers happy and increase their profits in the long run.

6-2 Making the Connection

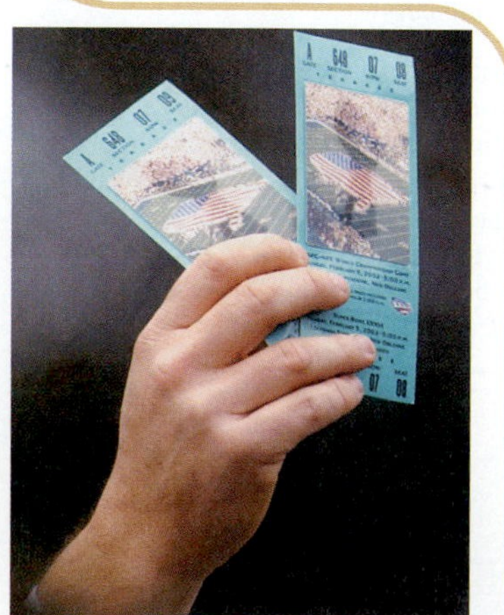

Should the NFL raise the price of Super Bowl tickets?

Professor Krueger Goes to the Super Bowl

Economist Alan Krueger of Princeton University has studied the question of why the National Football League does not charge a price for Super Bowl tickets that is high enough to make the quantity of tickets demanded equal to the quantity of tickets available. The prices may seem high—$400 for the best seats, $325 for the rest—but the quantity demanded still greatly exceeds the quantity supplied. Most Super Bowl tickets are allocated to the two teams playing in the game or to the league's corporate sponsors. To give ordinary fans a chance to attend the game, in 2001 the NFL set aside 500 pairs of tickets. They held a lottery for the opportunity to buy these tickets, and more than 36,000 people applied. Some fans were willing to pay as much as $5,000 to buy a ticket from ticket scalpers. (Scalpers buy tickets at their face value and then resell them at much higher prices, even though in Florida, where the 2001 Super Bowl was held, ticket scalping is illegal.)

Why didn't the NFL simply raise the price of tickets to clear the market? Krueger decided to survey football fans attending the game to see if their views could help explain this puzzle. Krueger's survey provides support for the Kahneman, Knetsch, and Thaler explanation of why companies do not always raise prices when the quantity demanded is greater than the quantity supplied. When asked whether it would "be fair for the NFL to raise the [price of tickets] to $1,500 if that is still less than the amount most people are willing to pay for tickets," 92 percent of the fans surveyed answered "no." Even 83 percent of the fans who had paid more than $1,500 for their tickets answered "no." Krueger concluded that whatever the NFL might gain in the short run from raising ticket prices, it would more than lose in the long run from alienating football fans.

Source: Alan B. Krueger, "Supply and Demand: An Economist Goes to the Super Bowl," *The Milken Institute Review*, Second Quarter 2001.

Behavioral Economics: Do People Make Their Choices Rationally?

③ LEARNING OBJECTIVE

Describe how people can improve their decision making by taking into account nonmonetary opportunity costs, ignoring sunk costs, and being more realistic about their future behavior.

When economists say that consumers and firms are behaving "rationally," they mean that consumers and firms are taking actions that are appropriate to reach their goals, given the information available to them. In recent years, some economists have begun studying situations in which people do not appear to be making choices that are economically rational. This new area of economics is called **behavioral economics**. Why might consumers or businesses not act rationally? The most obvious reason would be that they do not realize that their actions are inconsistent with their goals. As we discussed in Chapter 1, one of the goals of economics is to suggest ways to make better decisions. In this section, we discuss ways in which consumers can improve their decisions by avoiding some common pitfalls.

Behavioral economics The study of situations in which people act in ways that are not economically rational.

Consumers commonly commit the following three mistakes when making decisions:

- They take into account monetary costs but ignore nonmonetary opportunity costs.
- They fail to ignore sunk costs.
- They are overly optimistic about their future behavior.

Ignoring Nonmonetary Opportunity Costs

Remember from Chapter 2 that the **opportunity cost** of any activity is the highest-valued alternative that must be given up to engage in that activity. For example, if you own something you could sell, using it yourself involves an opportunity cost. It is often difficult for people to think of opportunity costs in these terms.

Opportunity cost The highest-valued alternative that must be given up to engage in an activity.

Consider the following example: Some of the fans at the 2001 Super Bowl had participated in a lottery run by the National Football League that allowed the winners to purchase tickets at their face value, which was either $325 or $400, depending on where in the stadium the seats were. Economist Alan Krueger of Princeton University surveyed the lottery winners (see Making the Connection 6-2 on p. 176), asking them two questions:

Question 1: If you had not won the lottery, would you have been willing to pay $3,000 for your ticket?

Question 2: If after winning your ticket (and before arriving in Florida for the Super Bowl) someone had offered you $3,000 for your ticket, would you have sold it?

In answer to the first question, 94 percent said that if they had not won the lottery they would not have paid $3,000 for a ticket. In answer to the second question, 92 percent said they would not have sold their ticket for $3,000. But these answers are contradictory! If someone offers you $3,000 for your ticket, then by using the ticket rather than selling it you incur an opportunity cost of $3,000. There really is a $3,000 cost involved in using that ticket, even though you do not pay $3,000 in cash. The alternatives of either paying $3,000 or not receiving $3,000 amount to exactly the same thing.

If the ticket is really not worth $3,000 to you, you should sell it. If it is worth $3,000 to you, you should be willing to pay $3,000 in cash to buy it. Not being willing to sell a ticket you already own for $3,000, while at the same time not being willing to buy a ticket for $3,000 if you didn't already own one, is inconsistent behavior. The

Endowment effect The tendency of people to be unwilling to sell something they already own even if they are offered a price that is greater than the price they would be willing to pay to buy the good if they didn't already own it.

inconsistency comes from a failure to take into account nonmonetary opportunity costs. Behavioral economists believe this inconsistency is caused by the **endowment effect**, which is the tendency of people to be unwilling to sell a good they already own even if they are offered a price that is greater than the price they would be willing to pay to buy the good if they didn't already own it.

The failure to take into account opportunity costs is a very common error in decision making. Suppose, for example, that a friend is in a hurry to have his room cleaned—it's the Friday before Parents Weekend—and he offers you $50 to do it for him. You turn him down and spend the time cleaning your own room, even though you know somebody down the hall who would be willing to clean your room for $20. Leave aside complicating details—the guy who asked you to clean his room is a real slob, or you don't want the person who offered to clean your room for $20 to go through your stuff—and you should see the point being made here. The opportunity cost of cleaning your own room is $50—the amount your friend offered to pay you to clean his room. It is inconsistent to turn down an offer from someone else to clean your room for $20 when you are doing it for yourself at a cost of $50. The key point here is this: *Nonmonetary opportunity costs are just as real as monetary costs and should be taken into account when making decisions.*

Business Implications of Consumers Ignoring Nonmonetary Opportunity Costs

Behavioral economist Richard Thaler has studied several examples of how businesses make use of consumers' failure to take into account opportunity costs. Whenever you buy something with a credit card, the credit card company charges the merchant a fee to process the bill. Credit card companies generally do not allow stores to charge higher prices to customers who use credit cards. A bill was introduced in Congress that would have made it illegal for credit card companies to enforce this rule. The credit card industry was afraid that if this law passed, credit card usage would drop because stores might begin charging a fee to credit card users. They attempted to have the law amended so that stores would be allowed to give a cash discount to people not using credit cards but would not be allowed to charge a fee to people using credit cards. There really is no difference in opportunity-cost terms between being charged a fee and not receiving a discount. The credit card industry was relying on the fact that *not* receiving a discount is a nonmonetary opportunity cost—and, therefore, likely to be ignored by consumers—but a fee is a monetary cost that people do take into account.

Film processing companies provide another example. Many of these companies have a policy of printing every picture on a roll of film, even if the picture is very fuzzy. Customers are allowed to ask for refunds on pictures they don't like. Once again, the companies are relying on the fact that passing up a refund once you have already paid for a picture is a nonmonetary opportunity cost, rather than a direct monetary cost. In fact, customers rarely ask for refunds.

Failing to Ignore Sunk Costs

Sunk cost A cost that has already been paid and cannot be recovered.

A **sunk cost** is a cost that has already been paid and cannot be recovered. Once you have paid money and can't get it back, you should ignore that money in any later decisions you make. Consider the following two situations:

Situation 1: You have paid $75 to buy a ticket to a play. The ticket is nonrefundable and must be used on Tuesday night, which is the only night the play will be performed. On Monday a friend calls and invites you to a local comedy club to see a comedian you both like who is appearing only on Tuesday night. Your friend offers to pay the cost of going to the club.

Situation 2: It's Monday night and you are about to buy a ticket for the Tuesday night performance of the same play as in situation 1. As you are leaving to buy the ticket, your friend calls and invites you to the comedy club.

Would your decision to go to the play or to the comedy club be different in situation 1 than in situation 2? Most people would say that in situation 1 they would go to the play, because otherwise they would lose the $75 they had paid for the ticket. In fact, though, the $75 is "lost" no matter what you do, because the ticket is not refundable. The only real issue for you to decide is whether you would prefer to see the play or prefer to go with your friend to the comedy club. If you would prefer to go to the club, the fact that you have already paid $75 for the ticket to the play is irrelevant. Your decision should be the same in situation 1 and situation 2.

Psychologists Daniel Kahneman and Amos Tversky explored the tendency of consumers not to ignore sunk costs by asking a sample of people the following questions:

Question 1: "Imagine that you have decided to see a play and have paid the admission price of $10 per ticket. As you enter the theater, you discover that you have lost the ticket. The seat was not marked and the ticket cannot be recovered. Would you pay $10 for another ticket?" Of those asked, 46 percent answered "yes" and 54 percent answered "no."

Question 2: A different sample of people was asked the following question: "Imagine that you have decided to see a play where admission is $10 per ticket. As you enter the theater, you discover that you have lost a $10 bill. Would you still pay $10 for a ticket to the play?" Of those asked, 88 percent answered "yes" and 12 percent answered "no."

The situations presented in the two questions are actually the same and should have received the same fraction of yes and no responses. Many people, though, have trouble seeing that in question 1 when deciding whether to see the play they should ignore the $10 already paid for a ticket because it is a sunk cost.

Being Unrealistic about Future Behavior

Studies have shown that a majority of adults in the United States are overweight. Why do many people choose to eat too much? One possibility is that they receive more utility from eating too much than they would from being thin. A more likely explanation, however, is that many people eat a lot today because they expect to eat less tomorrow. But they never do eat less, and so they end up overweight. (Of course, some people also suffer from medical problems that lead to weight gain.) Similarly, some people continue smoking today because they expect to be able to give it up sometime in the future. Unfortunately, for many people that time never comes and they suffer the health consequences of prolonged smoking. In both of these cases, people are overvaluing the utility from current choices—eating chocolate cake or smoking—and undervaluing the utility to be received in the future from being thin or not getting lung cancer.

Economists who have studied this question argue that many people have preferences that are not consistent over time. In the long run, you would like to be thin or give up smoking or achieve some other goal, but each day you make decisions to eat too much or to smoke that are not consistent with this long-run goal. Because you are unrealistic about your future behavior, you underestimate the costs of choices—like overeating or smoking—that you make today. A key way of avoiding this problem is to be realistic about your future behavior.

Why Don't Students Study More?

6-3 Making the Connection

Government statistics show that students who do well in college earn at least $10,000 more per year than students who fail to graduate or who graduate with low grades. So, over the course of a career of 40 years or more, students who do well in college will have earned upwards of $400,000 more than students who failed to graduate or who received low grades. Most colleges advise that students study at least two hours outside of class for every hour they spend in class. Surveys show that students often ignore this advice.

If the payoff to studying is so high, why don't students study more?

If the opportunity cost of not studying is so high, why do many students choose to study relatively little? Some students have work or family commitments that limit the amount of time they can study. But many other students study less than they would if they were more realistic about their future behavior. On any given night, a student has to choose between studying and other activities—like watching television, going to the movies, or going to a party—that may seem to provide higher utility in the short run. Many students choose one of these activities over studying because they expect to study tomorrow or the next day, but tomorrow they face the same choices and make similar decisions. As a result they do not study enough to meet their long-run goal of graduating with high grades. If they were more realistic about their future behavior, they would not make the mistake of overvaluing the utility from activities like watching television or partying because they would realize that those activities can endanger their long-run goal of graduating with honors.

Taking into account nonmonetary opportunity costs, ignoring sunk costs, and being more realistic about future behavior are three ways in which consumers are able to improve the decisions they make.

④ **LEARNING OBJECTIVE**

Define the price elasticity of demand and understand how to calculate it.

The Price Elasticity of Demand and Its Measurement

As firms analyze the demand for their products, a key factor they focus on is how responsiveness consumer demand is to a change in price. We know from the law of demand that when the price of a product falls, the quantity demanded of the product increases. But the law of demand tells firms only that the demand curves for their products slope downward. More useful is a measure of the responsiveness of the quantity demanded to a change in price. This measure is called the **price elasticity of demand**.

Price elasticity of demand The responsiveness of the quantity demanded to a change in price, measured by dividing the percentage change in the quantity demanded of a product by the percentage change in the product's price.

Measuring the Price Elasticity of Demand

We might measure the price elasticity of demand using the slope of the demand curve, because the slope of the demand curve tells us how much quantity changes as price changes. Using the slope of the demand curve to measure price elasticity has a drawback, however: The measurement of slope is sensitive to the units chosen for quantity and price. For example, suppose a \$1 decrease in the price of wheat leads to an increase in the quantity of wheat demanded from 1.1 billion bushels to 1.2 billion bushels. The change in quantity is 0.1 billion bushels and the change in price is $-\$1$, so the slope is $0.1/-1 = -0.1$. But if we measure price in cents, rather than dollars, the slope is $0.1/-100 = -0.001$. If we measure price in dollars, and wheat in millions of bushels, the slope is: $100/-1 = -100$. Clearly the value we compute for the slope can change dramatically depending on the units we use for quantity and price.

To avoid this confusion over units, economists use *percentage changes* when measuring the price elasticity of demand. Percentage changes are not dependent on units. (For a review of calculating percentage changes, see the Appendix to Chapter 1.) No matter what units we use to measure the quantity of wheat, 10 percent more wheat is 10 percent more wheat. Therefore, the price elasticity of demand is measured by dividing the percentage change in the quantity demanded by the percentage change in the price. Or,

$$\text{Price elasticity of demand} = \frac{\text{Percentage change in quantity demanded}}{\text{Percentage change in price}}.$$

It's important to remember that *the price elasticity of demand is not the same as the slope of the demand curve.*

If we calculate the price elasticity of demand for a price cut, the percentage change in price will be negative and the percentage change in quantity demanded will be positive. Similarly, if we calculate the price elasticity of demand for a price increase, the percentage change in price will be positive and the percentage change in quantity will be negative. Therefore, the price elasticity of demand is always negative. In comparing elasticities, though, we are usually interested in their relative size. So, we often drop the minus sign and compare their absolute values. In other words, although -3 is actually a smaller number than -2, a price elasticity of -3 is larger than a price elasticity of -2.

Elastic Demand and Inelastic Demand

If the quantity demanded is responsive to changes in price, the percentage change in quantity demanded will be *greater* than the percentage change in price, and the price elasticity of demand will be greater than 1 in absolute value. In this case, demand is **elastic**. For example, if a 10 percent fall in the price of bagels results in a 20 percent increase in the quantity of bagels demanded, then

$$\text{Price elasticity of demand} = \frac{20\%}{-10\%} = -2,$$

and we can conclude that the price of bagels is *elastic.*

Elastic demand Demand is elastic when the percentage change in quantity demanded is *greater* than the percentage change in price, so the price elasticity is *greater* than 1 in absolute value.

When the quantity demanded is not very responsive to price, however, the percentage change in quantity demanded will be *less* than the percentage change in price, and the price elasticity of demand will be less than 1 in absolute value. In this case demand is **inelastic**. For example, if a 10 percent fall in the price of wheat results in a 5 percent increase in the quantity of wheat demanded, then

$$\text{Price elasticity of demand} = \frac{5\%}{-10\%} = -0.5,$$

and we can conclude that the demand for wheat is *inelastic.*

Inelastic demand Demand is inelastic when the percentage change in quantity demanded is *less* than the percentage change in price, so the price elasticity is *less* than 1 in absolute value.

In the special case in which the percentage change in the quantity demanded is equal to the percentage change in price, the price elasticity of demand equals -1 (or 1 in absolute value). In this case, demand is **unit-elastic**.

Unit-elastic demand Demand is unit-elastic when the percentage change in quantity demanded is *equal to* the percentage change in price, so the price elasticity is *equal to* 1 in absolute value.

An Example of Computing Price Elasticities

Suppose you own a small bookstore and you are trying to decide whether to cut the price you are charging for the new John Grisham mystery novel. You are currently at point *A* in Figure 6-4: selling 16 copies of the novel per day at a price of \$30 per copy. How many more copies you will sell by cutting the price to \$20 depends on the price elasticity of demand for this novel. Let's consider two possibilities: If D_1 is the demand curve for this novel in your store, your sales will increase to 28 copies per day, point *B*. But if D_2 is your demand curve, your sales will increase only to 20 copies per day, point *C*. We might expect—correctly, as we will see—that between these points demand curve D_1 is elastic and demand curve D_2 is *inelastic.*

To confirm that D_1 is elastic between these points and that D_2 is inelastic, we need to calculate the price elasticity of demand for each curve. In calculating price elasticity between two points on a demand curve, though, we run into a problem because we get a

FIGURE 6-4

Elastic and Inelastic Demand Curves

Along D_1, demand is elastic between point *A* and point *B*, so cutting the price from $30 to $20 increases the number of copies sold from 16 per day to 28 per day. Along D_2, demand is inelastic between point *A* and point *C*, so cutting the price from $30 to $20 increases the number of copies sold from 16 per day to only 20 per day.

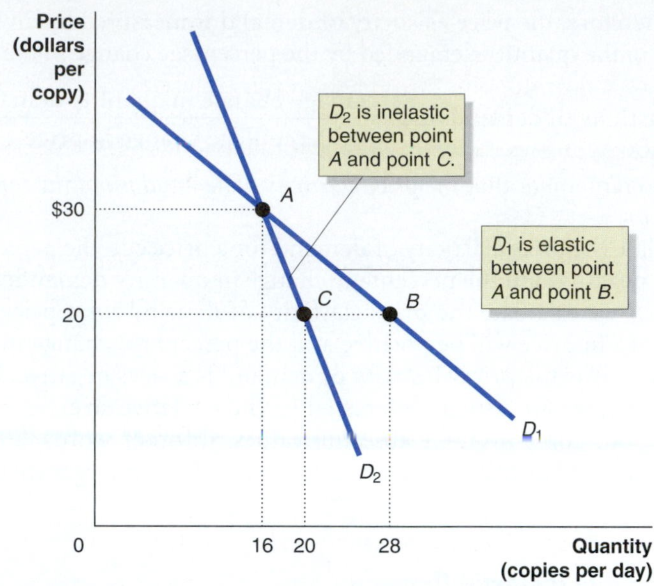

different value for price increases than for price decreases. For example, suppose we calculate the price elasticity for D_2 as the price is cut from $30 to $20. This reduction is a 33 percent price cut that increases the quantity demanded from 16 books to 20 books, or by 25 percent. Therefore, the price elasticity of demand between points *A* and *C* is 25/−33 = −0.8. Now let's calculate the price elasticity for D_2 as the price is *increased* from $20 to $30. This is a 50 percent price increase that decreases the quantity demanded from 20 books to 16 books, or by 20 percent. So, now our measure of the price elasticity of demand between points *A* and *C* is −20/50 = −0.4. It is not very satisfactory to have different values for the price elasticity of demand between the same two points on the same demand curve.

The Midpoint Formula

We can use the *midpoint formula* to ensure that we have only one value of the price elasticity of demand between the same two points on the same demand curve. The midpoint formula uses the *average* of the initial and final quantity and the initial and final price. If Q_1 and P_1 are the initial quantity and price and Q_2 and P_2 are the final quantity and price, the midpoint formula is:

$$\text{Price elasticity of demand} = \frac{(Q_2 - Q_1)}{\left(\frac{Q_1 + Q_2}{2}\right)} \div \frac{(P_2 - P_1)}{\left(\frac{P_1 + P_2}{2}\right)}.$$

The midpoint formula may seem challenging at first, but the numerator is just the change in quantity divided by the average of the initial and final quantities, and the denominator is just the change in price divided by the average of the initial and final prices.

Let's apply the formula to calculating the price elasticity of D_2 in Figure 6-4. Between point *A* and point *C* on D_2, the change in quantity is 4, and the average of the two quantities is 18. Therefore, there is a 22.2 percent change in quantity. The change in price is −$10, and the average of the two prices is $25. Therefore, there is a −40 percent change in price. So, the price elasticity of demand is 22.2/−40.0 = −0.6. Notice these three results from calculating the price elasticity of demand using the midpoint formula: First, as we suspected from examining Figure 6-4, demand curve D_2 is inelastic between points *A* and *C*. Second, our value for the price elasticity calculated using the midpoint formula is between the two values we calculated earlier. Third, the midpoint formula will give us the same value whether we are moving from the higher price to the lower price, or from the lower price to the higher price.

We can also use the midpoint formula to calculate the elasticity of demand between point *A* and point *B* on D_1. In this case, there is a 54.5 percent change in quantity and a −40 percent change in price. So, the elasticity of demand is 54.5/−40.0 = −1.4. Once again, as we suspected, demand curve D_1 is price elastic between points *A* and *B*.

When Demand Curves Intersect, the Flatter Curve Is More Elastic

Remember that elasticity is not the same thing as slope. Slope is calculated using changes in quantity and price, whereas elasticity is calculated using percentage changes. But it *is* true that when two demand curves intersect, the one with the smaller slope (in absolute value)—the flatter demand curve—is more elastic, and the one with the larger slope (in absolute value)—the steeper demand curve—is less elastic. In Figure 6-1, demand curve D_1 is more elastic than demand curve D_2.

Polar Cases of Perfectly Elastic and Perfectly Inelastic Demand

Although they do not occur frequently, you should be aware of the extreme, or polar, cases of price elasticity. If a demand curve is a vertical line, it is **perfectly inelastic**. In this case, the quantity demanded is completely unresponsive to price, and the price elasticity of demand equals zero. However much price may increase or decrease, the quantity remains the same. For only a very few products will the quantity demanded be

Perfectly inelastic demand Demand is perfectly inelastic when a change in price results in no change in quantity demanded.

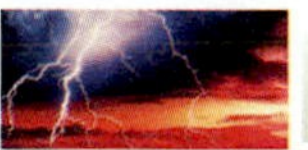

Don't Let This Happen To You!

Don't Confuse Inelastic with *Perfectly* Inelastic

You may be tempted to simplify the concept of elasticity by assuming that any demand curve described as being inelastic is *perfectly* inelastic. You should never assume this because perfectly inelastic demand curves are rare. For example, consider the following problem: "Use a demand and supply graph to show how a decrease in supply affects the equilibrium quantity of gasoline. Assume that the demand for gasoline is inelastic."

The following graph would be an *incorrect* answer to this problem:

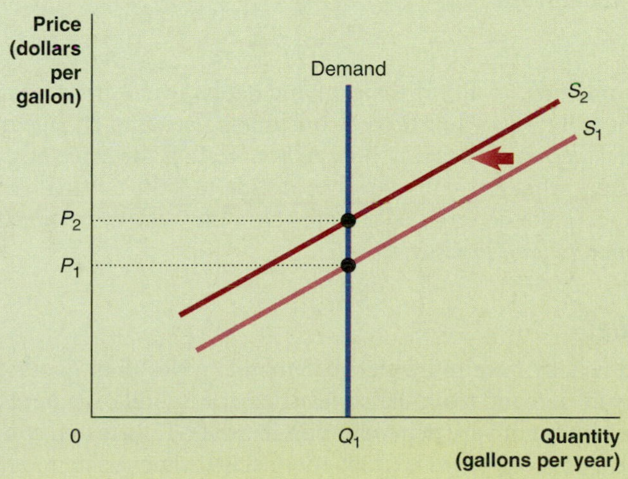

The demand for gasoline is inelastic, but it is not *perfectly* inelastic. When the price of gasoline rises, the quantity demanded falls. So, the graph that would be the correct answer to this problem would show a normal downward-sloping demand curve, rather than a vertical demand curve:

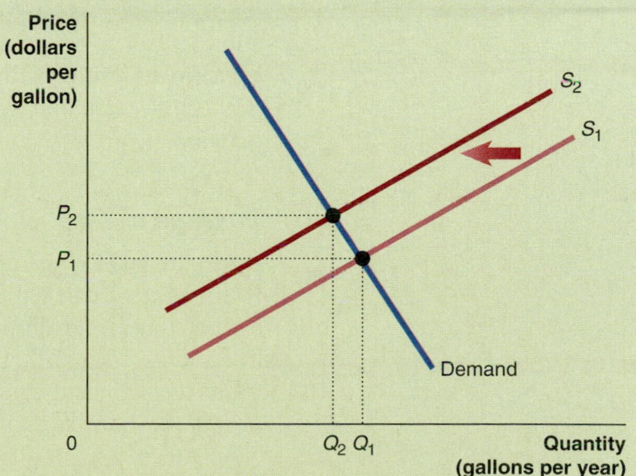

YOUR TURN: **Test your understanding by doing related problem 21 on page 198 at the end of this chapter.**

completely unresponsive to the price, making the demand curve a vertical line. The drug insulin is an example. Diabetics must take a certain amount of insulin each day. If the price of insulin declines, it will not affect the required dose and thus will not increase the quantity demanded. Similarly, a price increase will not affect the required dose or decrease the quantity demanded. (Of course, some diabetics will not be able to afford insulin at a higher price. If so, even in this case the demand curve may not be completely vertical and, therefore, not perfectly inelastic.)

Perfectly elastic demand Demand is perfectly elastic when a change in price results in an infinite change in quantity demanded.

If a demand curve is a horizontal line, it is **perfectly elastic**. In this case, the quantity demanded would be infinitely responsive to price, and the price elasticity of demand equals infinity. If a demand curve is perfectly elastic, an increase in price causes the quantity demanded to fall to zero. Once again, perfectly elastic demand curves are rare and it is important not to confuse elastic with perfectly elastic. Table 6-4 summarizes the different price elasticities of demand.

5 LEARNING OBJECTIVE

Understand the determinants of the price elasticity of demand.

What Determines the Price Elasticity of Demand for a Product?

We have seen that the demand for some products may be elastic, while the demand for other products may be inelastic. In this section, we examine why price elasticities differ among products. The key determinants of the price elasticity of demand are as follows:

- Availability of close substitutes
- Passage of time
- Necessities versus luxuries
- Definition of the market
- Share of the good in the consumer's budget

Availability of Close Substitutes

The availability of substitutes is the most important determinant of price elasticity of demand because how consumers react to a change in the price of a product depends on what alternatives they have. When the price of gasoline rises, consumers have few alternatives, so the quantity demanded falls only a little. But if Domino's raises the price of pizza, consumers have many alternatives, so the quantity demanded is likely to fall quite a lot. In fact, a key constraint on a firm's pricing policies is how many close substitutes exist for its product. In general, *if a product has more substitutes available, it will have more elastic demand. If a product has fewer substitutes available, it will have less elastic demand.*

Passage of Time

It usually takes consumers some time to adjust their buying habits when prices change. If the price of chicken falls, it will take a while before consumers decide to change from eating chicken for dinner once per week to eating it twice per week. If the price of gasoline increases, it will also take a while for consumers to decide to shift toward buying more fuel-efficient cars, reducing the quantity of gasoline they buy. *The more time that passes, the more elastic the demand for a product becomes.*

Luxuries versus Necessities

Goods that are luxuries will usually have more elastic demand curves than goods that are necessities. For example, the demand for milk is inelastic because milk is a necessity and the quantity that people buy is not very dependent on its price. Tickets to a concert are a luxury, so the demand for concert tickets is much more elastic than the demand for milk. *The demand curve for a luxury is more elastic than the demand curve for a necessity.*

TABLE 6-4

Summary of the Price Elasticities of Demand

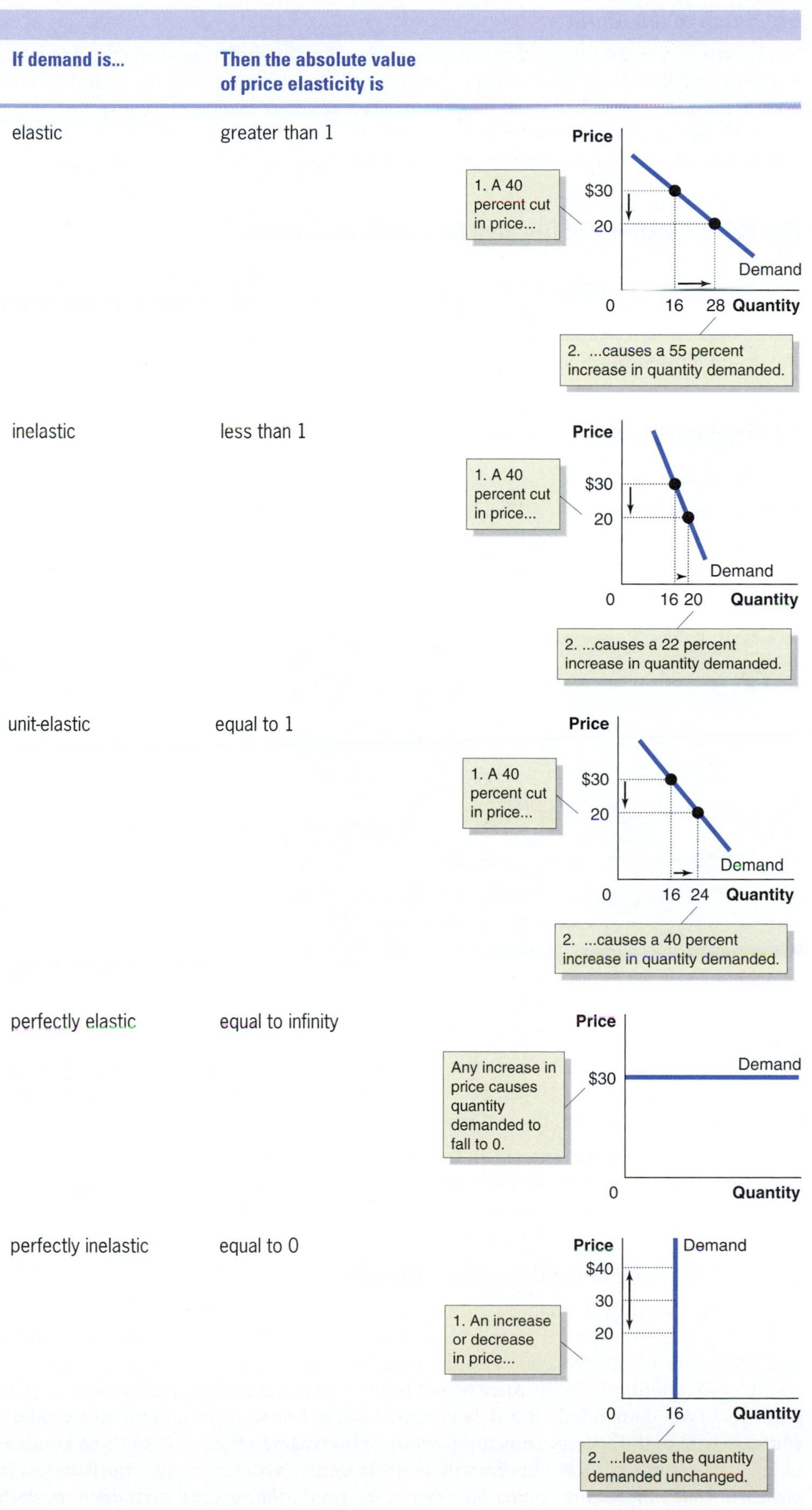

If demand is...	Then the absolute value of price elasticity is
elastic	greater than 1
inelastic	less than 1
unit-elastic	equal to 1
perfectly elastic	equal to infinity
perfectly inelastic	equal to 0

Definition of the Market

In a narrowly defined market, consumers will have more substitutes available. If the price of Kellogg's Raisin Bran rises, many consumers will start buying another brand of raisin bran. If the prices of all brands of raisin bran rise, the responsiveness of consumers will be lower. If the prices of all breakfast cereals rise, the responsiveness of consumers will be even lower. *The more narrowly we define a market, the more elastic demand will be.*

6-4 Making the Connection

The Price Elasticity of Demand for Breakfast Cereal

MIT economist Jerry Hausman has estimated the price elasticity of demand for breakfast cereal. He divided breakfast cereals into three categories: children's cereals, such as Trix or Froot Loops; adult cereals, such as Special K or Grape-Nuts; and family cereals, such as Corn Flakes and Raisin Bran. Some of the results of his estimates are given in the following table.

CEREAL	PRICE ELASTICITY OF DEMAND
Post Raisin Bran	−2.5
All family breakfast cereals	−1.8
All types of breakfast cereals	−0.9

Source: Jerry A. Hausman, "The Price Elasticity of Demand for Breakfast Cereal" in *The Economics of New Goods*, TF Bresnahan & RJ Gordon, eds. Used with permission of The University of Chicago Press.

What happens when the price of cereal rises?

Just as we would expect, the price elasticity for a particular brand of raisin bran was larger in absolute value than the elasticity for all family cereals, and the elasticity for all family cereals was larger than the elasticity for all types of breakfast cereals. If Post increases the price of its Raisin Bran by 10 percent, sales will decline by 25 percent, as many consumers switch to another brand of raisin bran. If the prices of all family breakfast cereals rise by 10 percent, sales will drop by 18 percent, as consumers switch to child or adult cereals. In both of these cases, demand is elastic. But if the prices of all types of breakfast cereals rise by 10 percent, sales will only decline by 9 percent. Demand for all breakfast cereals is inelastic.

Source: Jerry A. Hausman, "Valuation of New Goods under Perfect and Imperfect Competition," in Timothy F. Bresnahan and Robert J. Gordon, eds., *The Economics of New Goods*, Chicago and London: University of Chicago Press, 1997.

Share of the Good in the Consumer's Budget

Goods that take only a small fraction of a consumer's budget tend to have less elastic demand. For example, most people buy salt infrequently and in relatively small quantities. The share of the average consumer's budget that is spent on salt is very low. As a result, even a doubling of the price of salt is likely to result in only a small decline in the quantity of salt demanded. "Big-ticket items," such as houses, cars, and furniture, take up a larger share in the average consumer's budget. Increases in the prices of these goods are likely to result in significant declines in quantity demanded. In general, *the demand for a good will be less elastic the smaller the share of the good in the average consumer's budget.*

The Relationship between Price Elasticity and Total Revenue

6 LEARNING OBJECTIVE

Understand the relationship between the price elasticity of demand and total revenue.

Total revenue The total amount of funds received by a seller of a good or service, calculated by multiplying price per unit by number of units sold.

A firm is interested in price elasticity because it allows the firm to calculate how changes in price will affect its **total revenue**, which is the total amount of funds it receives from selling a good or service. Total revenue is calculated by multiplying price per unit by the number of units sold. When demand is inelastic, price and total revenue move in the same direction: An increase in price raises total revenue, and a decrease in price reduces total revenue. When demand is elastic, price and total revenue move inversely: An increase in price reduces total revenue, and a decrease in price raises total revenue.

To understand the relationship between price elasticity and total revenue, consider Figure 6-5. Panel (a) shows a demand curve for a John Grisham novel (as in Figure 6-4). This demand curve is inelastic between point *A* and point *B*. The total revenue received by a bookseller at point *A* equals the price of $30 multiplied by the 16 copies sold, or $480. This amount equals the areas of the rectangles *C* and *D* in the figure, because together the rectangles have a height of $30 and a base of 16 copies. Because this demand curve is inelastic between point *A* and point *B* (it was demand curve D_2 in Figure 6-4), cutting the price to $20 (point *B*) reduces total revenue. The new total revenue is shown by the areas of rectangles *D* and *E*, and it is equal to $20 multiplied by 20 copies, or $400. Total revenue falls because the increase in the quantity demanded is not large enough to make up for the decrease in price. As a result, the $80 increase in revenue gained as a result of the price cut—dark-green rectangle *E*—is less than the $160 in revenue lost—light-green rectangle *C*.

Panel (b) of Figure 6-5 shows a demand curve that is elastic between point *A* and point *B* (it was demand curve D_1 in Figure 6-4). In this case, cutting the price increases total revenue. At point *A*, the areas of rectangles *C* and *D* are still equal to $480, but at

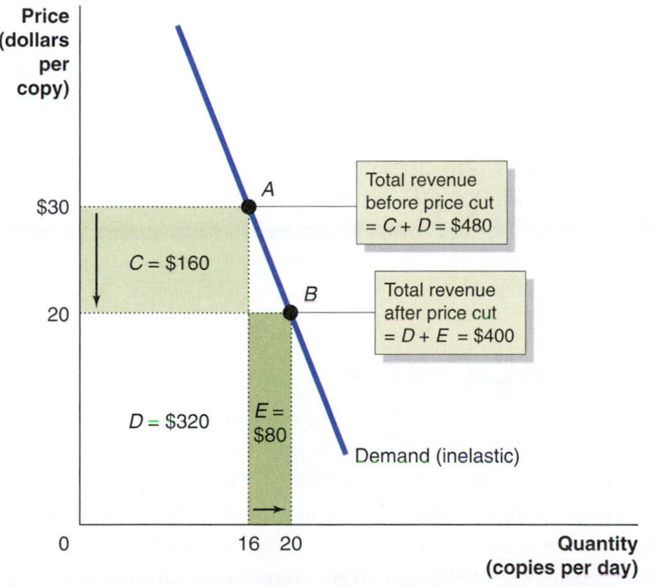

(a) Cutting price when demand is inelastic reduces total revenue.

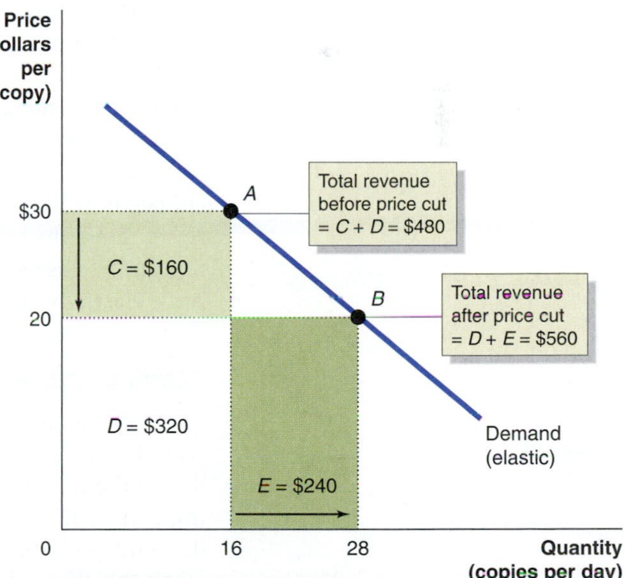

(b) Cutting price when demand is elastic increases total revenue.

FIGURE 6-5 The Relationship between Price Elasticity and Total Revenue

When demand is inelastic, a cut in price will decrease total revenue. In panel (a), at point *A* the price is $30, 16 copies are sold, and total revenue received by the bookseller equals $30 × 16 copies, or $480. At point *B*, cutting price to $20 increases the quantity demanded to 20 copies, but the fall in price more than offsets the increase in quantity. As a result, revenue falls to $20 × 20 copies, or $400. When demand is elastic, a cut in price will increase total revenue. In panel (b), at point *A* the area of rectangles *C* and *D* is still equal to $480. But at point *B* the area of rectangles *D* and *E* is equal to $20 × 28 copies, or $560. In this case, the increase in the quantity demanded is large enough to offset the fall in price, so total revenue increases.

TABLE 6-5

The Relationship between Price Elasticity and Revenue

IF DEMAND IS . . .	THEN . . .	BECAUSE . . .
elastic	an increase in price reduces revenue	the decrease in quantity demanded is proportionally *greater* than the increase in price.
elastic	a decrease in price increases revenue	the increase in quantity demanded is proportionally *greater* than the decrease in price.
inelastic	an increase in price increases revenue	the decrease in quantity demanded is proportionally *smaller* than the increase in price.
inelastic	a decrease in price reduces revenue	the increase in quantity demanded is proportionally *smaller* than the decrease in price.
unit-elastic	an increase in price does not affect revenue	the decrease in quantity demanded is proportionally *the same as* the increase in price.
unit-elastic	a decrease in price does not affect revenue	the increase in quantity demanded is proportionally *the same as* the decrease in price.

point *B*, the areas of rectangles *D* and *E* are equal to $20 multiplied by 28 copies, or $560. Here, total revenue rises because the increase in the quantity demanded is large enough to offset the lower price. As a result, the $240 increase in revenue gained as a result of the price cut—dark-green rectangle *E*—is greater than the $160 in revenue lost—light-green rectangle *C*.

The third, less common possibility is that demand is unit-elastic. In that case, a change in price is exactly offset by a proportional change in quantity demanded, leaving revenue unaffected. Therefore, when demand is unit-elastic, neither a decrease in price nor an increase in price affects revenue. Table 6-5 summarizes the relationship between price elasticity and revenue.

Elasticity and Revenue with a Linear Demand Curve

Along most demand curves, elasticity is not constant at every point. For example, a straight-line, or linear, demand curve for DVDs is shown in panel (a) of Figure 6-6. The demand curve shows that when the price falls by $1, consumers always respond by buying 2 more DVDs per month. When the price is high and the quantity demanded is low, demand is elastic. This is true because a $1 fall in price is a smaller percentage change when the price is high, and an increase of 2 DVDs is a larger percentage change when the quantity of DVDs is small. By similar reasoning, we can see why Jill's demand is inelastic when the price is low and the quantity demanded is high.

As panel (b) in Figure 6-6 shows, because over the price range from $8 to $4 demand is elastic, total revenue will increase as price falls. For example, as price falls from $7 to $6, total revenue increases from $14 to $24. Over the price range from $4 to zero, demand is inelastic, so total revenue will decrease as price falls. For example, as price falls from $3 to $2, total revenue decreases from $30 to $24.

Price	Quantity Demanded	Total Revenue
$8	0	$0
7	2	14
6	4	24
5	6	30
4	8	32
3	10	30
2	12	24
1	14	14
0	16	0

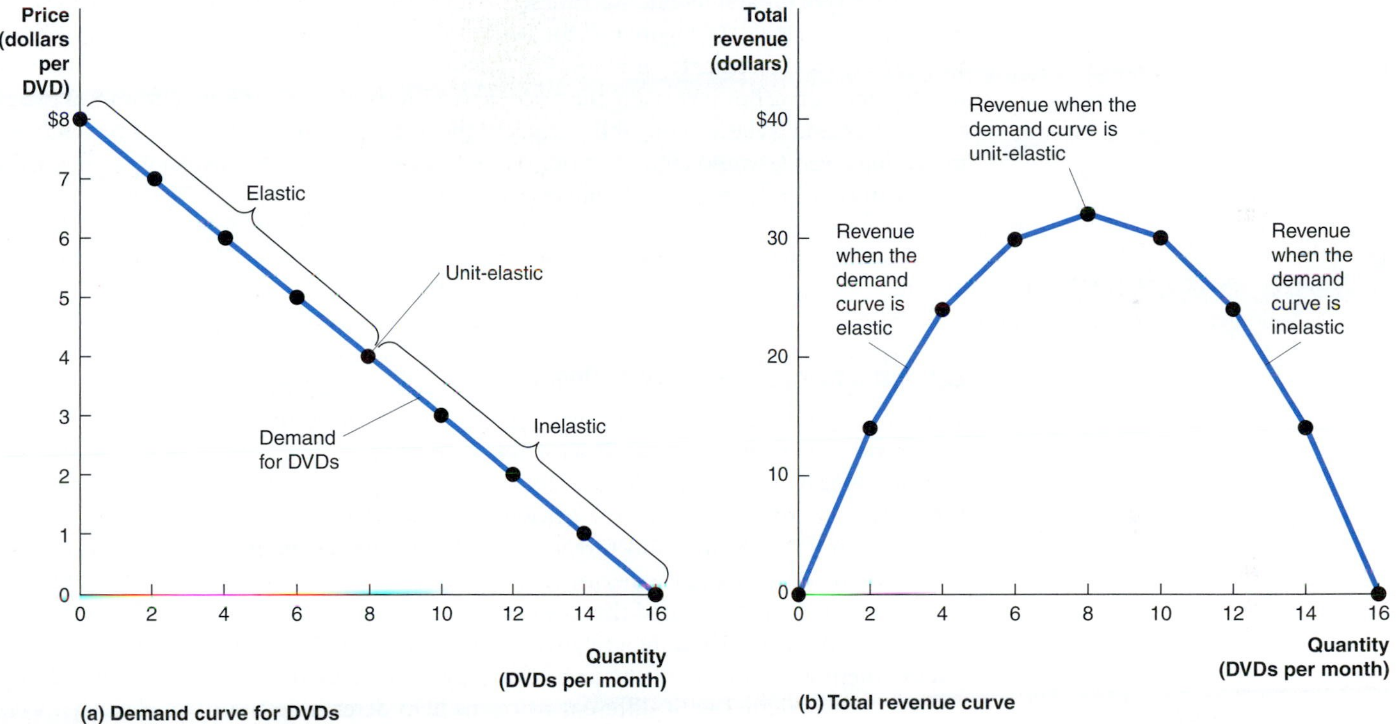

FIGURE 6-6 Elasticity Is Not Constant Along a Linear Demand Curve

The data from the table are plotted in the graphs. Panel (a) shows that as we move down the demand curve for DVDs, the price elasticity of demand declines. In other words, at higher prices demand is elastic and at lower prices demand is inelastic. Panel (b) shows that as the quantity of DVDs sold increases from zero, revenue will increase until it reaches a maximum of $32 when 8 DVDs are sold. As sales increase beyond 8 DVDs, revenue falls because demand is inelastic on this portion of the demand curve.

SOLVED PROBLEM 6-2

⑥ LEARNING OBJECTIVE
Understand the relationship between the price elasticity of demand and total revenue.

Price and Revenue Don't Always Move in the Same Direction

Briefly explain whether you agree or disagree with the following statement: "The only way to increase the revenue from selling a product is to increase the product's price."

Solving the Problem:

Step 1: Review the chapter material. This problem deals with the effect of a price change on a firm's revenue, so you may want to review the section "The Relationship between Price Elasticity and Total Revenue," which begins on page 187.

Step 2: Analyze the statement. We have seen that a price increase will increase revenue only if demand is inelastic. In Figure 6-6, for example, increasing the rental price of DVDs from $1 to $2 *increases* revenue from $14 to $24 because demand is inelastic along this portion of the demand curve. But increasing the price from $5 to $6 *decreases* revenue from $30 to $24 because demand is elastic along this portion of the demand curve. If the price is currently $5, increasing revenue would require a price *cut*, not a price increase. As this example shows, the statement is incorrect and you should disagree with it.

YOUR TURN: **For more practice, do related problem 20 on page 198 at the end of this chapter.**

Estimating Price Elasticity of Demand

To estimate the price elasticity of demand, economists need to know the demand curve for a product. In Chapter 3, we briefly discussed the fact that economists often use statistical methods to estimate the demand curve for a product. Economists generally use the same methods to estimate the price elasticity of demand. When trying to calculate the price elasticity of demand for new products, however, firms often rely on market experiments. With market experiments, firms will try different prices and observe the change in quantity demanded that results.

For example, DVDs were a relatively new product in 2001. The movie studios producing them were unsure of the price elasticity of the demand curves they were facing, so they experimented with different prices to help determine the price elasticity. VHS tapes had been on the market for many years, and the studios had determined their pricing strategies, given their estimates of the price elasticity of demand. As a result, the prices of VHS tapes of different movies were usually very similar.

At that time, the prices of DVDs were much less standardized because the studios were unsure of their price elasticities. Tom Adams, the head of Adams Market Research, a company that does research on the home video market, summed up the situation: "The studios have different views of the market, so they are setting different suggested retail prices, and the stores are discounting those prices to different degrees."

After several years of market experiments, the movie studios had more accurate estimates of the price elasticity of DVDs and the prices of most DVDs became similar. For instance, in the summer of 2006 nearly all newly released movie DVDs had a list price of about $29, which was often discounted to about $17 when they were sold online or in many stores.

Conclusion

In a market system, consumers are in the driver's seat. Goods are produced only if consumers want them to be. Therefore, how consumers make their decisions is an important area for economists to study, a fact that was highlighted when Daniel Kahneman—whose research was mentioned several times in this chapter—shared the 2002 Nobel Prize in Economics. Economists expect that consumers will spend their incomes so that the last dollar spent on each good provides them with equal additional amounts of satisfaction, or utility. In practice, there are significant social influences on consumer decision making, particularly when a good or service is consumed in public. Fairness also seems to be an important consideration for most consumers. Many consumers could improve the decisions they make if they would take into account non-monetary opportunity costs and ignore sunk costs.

In this chapter, we also explored the important concept of elasticity. Computing elasticities is important in economics because it allows us to measure how one variable changes in response to changes in another variable. For example, by calculating the price elasticity of demand for its product, a firm can make a numerical estimate of the effect of a price change on the revenue it receives.

This chapter has been devoted to studying consumers' choices. In the next several chapters, we will study firms' choices. Before moving on to the next chapter, read *An Inside Look* on the next page to learn how firms respond when celebrities they hired to endorse their products offend rather than attract consumers.

An Inside Look Can Whoopi Goldberg Get You to Buy Slim-Fast?

BOSTON GLOBE, JULY 20, 2004

A Celebrity Endorser Who Doesn't Offend? Slim Chance

Somewhere out there, a celebrity is doing or saying something unfortunate, and Madison Avenue is getting very nervous.

a A famous face is getting pulled over for erratic driving, checking into rehab, or making a statement either too impolitic or too political. In a few days, perhaps even a few hours, some ad executive, trembling in his $500 loafers, will learn a very old lesson about the perils of connecting a product with a well-known personality.

Last week, Whoopi Goldberg became the latest celebrity dumped for behavior deemed detrimental to the image of the product she was endorsing. Slim-Fast execs kicked Goldberg to the curb after her appearance at a recent star-studded fundraiser for Democratic presidential candidate John Kerry, where she made several off-color remarks about President George W. Bush.

b In severing ties with Goldberg, Terry Olson, Slim-Fast's vice president of marketing, said in a statement, "We are disappointed by the manner in which Ms. Goldberg chose to express herself, and sincerely regret that her recent remarks offended some of our consumers. Ads featuring Ms. Goldberg will no longer air."

Also taking a hit recently were sisters Mary-Kate and Ashley Olsen, who were dropped from the "Got Milk?" campaign after Mary-Kate sought help for what reportedly is an eating disorder. Officials from the Milk Processor Education Program said they yanked the magazine ads "out of sensitivity for her situation." And while that may be true, it's more likely that the company didn't want their product, promoted as a cornerstone of a nutritious diet, associated with someone struggling with eating issues.

c It costs millions of dollars to launch advertising campaigns, so it's a safe bet that companies don't shut these things down without a lot of hand-wringing and teeth-gnashing. Of course, it also raises questions as to why corporations are so eager to swoon for celebrity endorsers in the first place.

Presumably, companies hire some rappers, athletes, and actors for their edgy personas, in hopes that an accessible version of that attitude will magically transfer to their products. . . .

Personally, I've never understood the point—either consumers want a product or they don't. I'm hard pressed to believe that simply because Catherine Zeta-Jones smiles pretty and bats her big brown eyes I'm going to switch my cellphone service. There's always been something absurd in the idea that consumers will buy something simply because a famous face tells them to do so.

Key Points in the Article

This article discusses the problems firms may encounter when they use celebrity endorsements in their advertising. Whoopi Goldberg was dropped as an endorser by Slim-Fast after she made critical and vulgar comments about President George W. Bush. Mary-Kate and Ashley Olson were dropped from the "Got Milk?" campaign after Mary-Kate was reportedly hospitalized with an eating disorder. The author of the article argues that firms run the risk of negative publicity whenever they use celebrity endorsers. The author is also skeptical that celebrity endorsements really do have a significant effect on consumer choice.

Analyzing the News

a We saw in Chapter 3 that when consumers' taste for a product increases, the demand curve will shift to the right, and when consumers' taste for a product decreases, the demand curve for the product will shift to the left. When a firm hires a celebrity to endorse its products, it is hoping to increase consumers' taste for its product. If the endorsement is successful in increasing consumers' taste for the product, the result is shown in Figure 1. The figure shows the demand curve for Slim-Fast shifting from D_1 to D_2. The increase in demand allows the firm to sell more cans at every price. For example, at a price of P_1 it could sell Q_1 cans without the endorsement but Q_2 cans with the endorsement.

b As the author points out, if a celebrity generates negative publicity, consumers' taste for the product may decrease. Presumably, this is what Slim-Fast was afraid was happening with Whoopi Goldberg. The result is shown in Figure 2, where the demand curve shifts to the left and fewer cans of Slim-Fast are sold at every price.

c Advertising increases a firm's costs and—if it is successful—the demand for the firm's product, and, therefore, its revenues. If, because of some of the problems mentioned in this article, an advertising campaign reduces the demand for a product, the firm's profits will decline. But does a "successful" advertising campaign always increase a firm's profits? In fact, a firm's profits will increase only if the additional revenue the firm receives from selling a larger quantity of the product is greater than the additional cost resulting from the advertising campaign.

Thinking Critically ABOUT POLICY

1. The article's author says, "It costs millions of dollars to launch advertising campaigns, so it's a safe bet that companies don't shut these things down without a lot of hand-wringing and teeth-gnashing." Should a company whose celebrity endorser was just arrested base its decision about whether or not to cancel its ad campaign based on the amount it has already poured into making the ads? Should they do more "hand-wringing and teeth-gnashing" if creating the ad campaign costs an extra million dollars? Explain.

2. Some critics argue that advertising using celebrity endorsements serves no useful social purpose and should be banned or discouraged by the government. Do you agree? Explain.

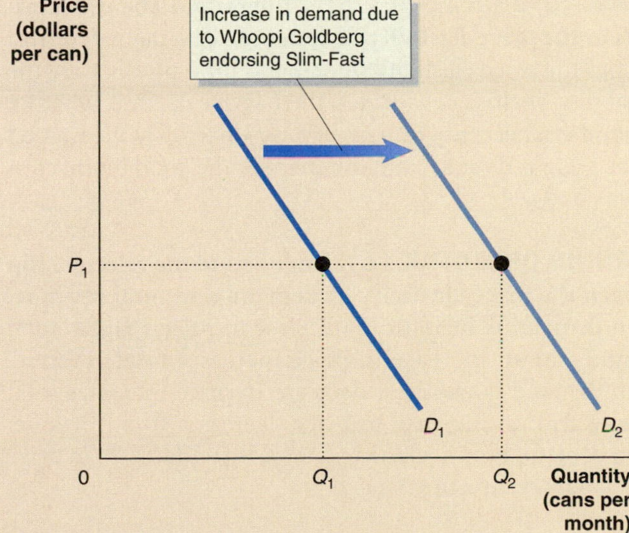

Figure 1: When successful, a celebrity endorsement can shift the demand curve for a product to the right, from D_1 to D_2.

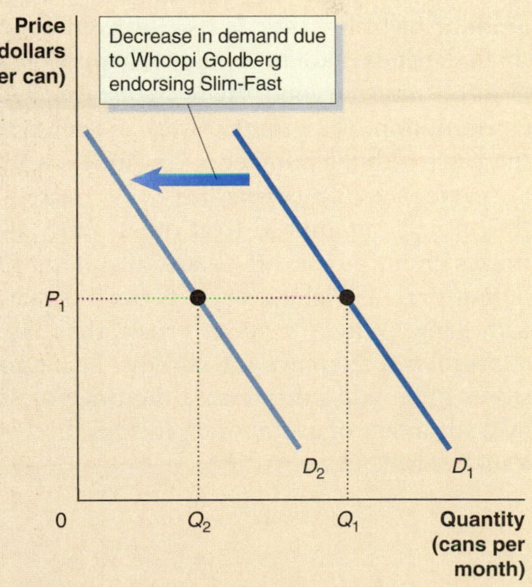

Figure 2: If a celebrity endorsing a product generates bad publicity, the demand curve for the product may shift to the left, from D_1 to D_2.

SUMMARY

LEARNING OBJECTIVE ① Define utility and explain how consumers choose goods and services to maximize their utility. *Utility* is the enjoyment or satisfaction that people receive from consuming goods and services. The goal of a consumer is to spend available income so as to maximize utility. The *law of diminishing marginal utility* states that consumers receive diminishing additional satisfaction as they consume more of a good or service during a given period of time. The *budget constraint* is the amount of income consumers have available to spend on goods and services. To maximize utility, consumers should make sure they spend their income so that the last dollar spent on each product gives them the same marginal utility. The *income effect* is the change in the quantity demanded of a good that results from the effect of a change in the price on consumer purchasing power. The *substitution effect* is the change in the quantity demanded of a good that results from a change in price making the good more or less expensive relative to other goods, holding constant the effect of the price change on consumer purchasing power. When the price of a good declines, the ratio of the marginal utility to the price rises, leading consumers to buy more of that good. As a result, whenever the price of a product falls, the quantity demanded increases. We saw in Chapter 3 that this is known as the *law of demand.*

LEARNING OBJECTIVE ② Explain how social influences can affect consumption choices. Social factors can have an influence on consumption. For example, the amount of utility people receive from consuming a good often depends upon how many other people they know who also consume the good. There are *network externalities* in the consumption of a product if the usefulness of the product increases with the number of consumers who use it. There is also evidence that people like to be treated fairly and that they usually attempt to treat others fairly, even if doing so makes them worse off financially. This result has been demonstrated in laboratory experiments, such as the ultimatum game. When firms set prices, they take into account consumers' preference for fairness. For example, hardware stores often will not increase the price of snow shovels to take advantage of a temporary increase in demand following a snowstorm.

LEARNING OBJECTIVE ③ Describe how people can improve their decision making by taking into account nonmonetary opportunity costs, ignoring sunk costs, and being more realistic about their future behavior. *Behavioral economics* is the study of situations in which people act in ways that are not economically rational. People would improve their decision making if they took into account nonmonetary opportunity costs, ignored sunk costs, and were more realistic about their future behavior.

LEARNING OBJECTIVE ④ Define the price elasticity of demand and understand how to calculate it. The *price elasticity of demand* measures how responsive quantity demanded is to changes in price. The price elasticity of demand is equal to the percentage change in quantity demanded divided by the percentage change in price. If the quantity demanded changes more than proportionally when price changes, the price elasticity of demand is greater than 1 in absolute value and demand is *elastic.* If the quantity demanded changes less than proportionally when price changes, the price elasticity of demand is less than 1 in absolute value and demand is *inelastic.* If the quantity demanded changes proportionally when price changes, the price elasticity of demand is equal to 1 in absolute value and demand is *unit-elastic.* Perfectly inelastic demand curves are vertical lines and perfectly elastic demand curves are horizontal lines. Relatively few products have perfectly elastic or perfectly inelastic demand curves.

LEARNING OBJECTIVE ⑤ Understand the determinants of the price elasticity of demand. The main determinants of the price elasticity of demand for a product are the availability of close substitutes, the passage of time, whether the good is a necessity or a luxury, how narrowly the market for the good is defined, and the share of the good in the consumer's budget.

LEARNING OBJECTIVE ⑥ Understand the relationship between the price elasticity of demand and total revenue. When demand is inelastic, a decrease in price reduces total revenue and an increase in price increases total revenue. When demand is elastic, a decrease in price increases total revenue and an increase in price decreases total revenue. When demand is unit-elastic, an increase or decrease in price leaves total revenue unchanged.

KEY TERMS

Behavioral economics 177
Budget constraint 167
Elastic demand 181
Elasticity 164
Endowment effect 178
Income effect 171
Inelastic demand 181
Law of diminishing marginal utility 166
Marginal utility (*MU*) 165
Network externalities 173
Opportunity cost 177
Perfectly elastic demand 184
Perfectly inelastic demand 183
Price elasticity of demand 180
Substitution effect 171
Sunk cost 178
Total revenue 187
Unit-elastic demand 181
Utility 165

REVIEW QUESTIONS

1. What is the economic definition of utility? Is utility measurable?
2. What is the definition of marginal utility? What is the law of diminishing marginal utility? Why is marginal utility more useful than total utility in consumer decision making?
3. What is meant by a consumer's budget constraint? What is the rule of equal marginal utility per dollar?
4. Explain how a downward-sloping demand curve results from consumers adjusting their consumption choices to changes in price.
5. Why do consumers pay attention to celebrity endorsements of products?
6. What are network externalities? For what types of products are network externalities likely to be important? What is path dependence?
7. What does it mean to be economically rational? Define behavioral economics, and give an example of three common mistakes that consumers often make.
8. Write the formula for the price elasticity of demand. Why isn't elasticity just measured by the slope of the demand curve?
9. If a 10 percent increase in the price of Cap'n Crunch cereal causes a 25 percent reduction in the number of boxes of cereal demanded, what is the price elasticity of demand for Cap'n Crunch cereal? Is demand for Cap'n Crunch elastic or inelastic?
10. What are the key determinants of the price elasticity of demand for a product? Which determinant is the most important?
11. If the demand for orange juice is inelastic, will an increase in the price of orange juice increase or decrease the revenue received by orange juice sellers?

PROBLEMS AND APPLICATIONS

Please visit **www.prenhall.com/hubbard** *for solutions to the even-numbered problems as well as multiple-choice and true or false self-assessment quizzes.*

1. You have 6 hours to study for 2 exams tomorrow. The relationship between hours of study and test scores is as follows:

ECONOMICS		PSYCHOLOGY	
HOURS	SCORE	HOURS	SCORE
0	54	0	54
1	62	1	60
2	69	2	65
3	75	3	69
4	80	4	72
5	84	5	74
6	87	6	75

a. Use the rule for determining optimal purchases to decide how many hours you should study each subject. Treat each point on an exam like 1 unit of utility and assume you are equally interested in doing well in economics and psychology.

b. Suppose now that you are a psychology major and that you value each point you earn on a psychology exam as being worth three times as much as each point you earn on an economics exam. Now how many hours will you study each subject?

2. **[Related to *Solved Problem 6-1*]** Joe has $16 to spend on Twinkies and Ho-Hos. Twinkies have a price of $1 per pack and Ho-Hos have a price of $2 per pack. Use the information in the following graphs to determine the number of Twinkies packs and the number of Ho-Hos packs Joe should buy to maximize his utility. Briefly explain your reasoning.

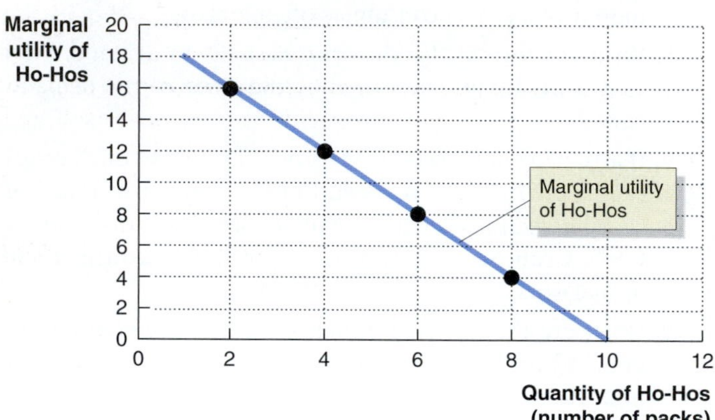

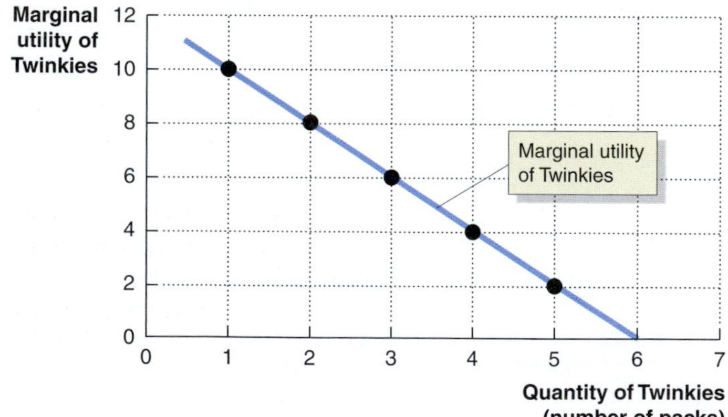

3. **[Related to *Solved Problem 6-1*]** Joe has $55 to spend on apples and oranges. Given the information in the following table, is Joe maximizing utility? Briefly explain.

PRODUCT	PRICE	QUANTITY	TOTAL UTILITY	MARGINAL UTILITY OF LAST UNIT
Apples	$0.50	50	1,000	20
Oranges	$0.75	40	500	30

4. Mary is buying corn chips and soda. She has 4 bags of corn chips and 5 bottles of soda in her shopping cart. The marginal utility of the fourth bag of corn chips is 10, and the marginal utility of the sixth bottle of soda is also 10. Is Mary maximizing utility? Briefly explain.

5. Which of the following products are most likely to have significant network externalities? Explain.
   a. Fax machines
   b. Dog food
   c. Board games
   d. Conventional (CRT) television sets
   e. Plasma television sets

6. Linux is a computer operating system that is an alternative to Microsoft's Windows system. According to a newspaper article:

> The dominance of the Windows operating system, which runs 95 percent of the world's PCs, is coming under greater attack in Asia than in any other part of the world, analysts say. Linux for PCs sold three times as many copies in Asia as in the US last year. . . . "In emerging markets such as India and China, where PC growth rates are the highest, Linux's momentum seems to be accelerating," said Robert Stimson, a Bank of America analyst in San Francisco.

If network externalities are important in choosing a computer operating system, why might Linux be more successful in Asia than in the United States?

Source: "Gates Blitzes Asia to Stem Linux Threat," *New Zealand Herald*, June 29, 2004.

7. Suppose your little brother tells you on Tuesday that one of his friends offered him $20 for his Barry Bonds rookie baseball card, but your brother decided not to sell the card. On Wednesday your brother loses the card. Your parents feel sorry for him and give him $20 to make up the loss. Instead of buying another Barry Bonds card with the money (which we will assume he could have done), your brother uses the money to go to the movies. Explain your brother's actions by using the concepts in this chapter.

8. Economist Richard Thaler has argued that the behavior of professional football teams during the college draft is an example of the endowment effect. Professional football teams take turns drafting eligible college players. Suppose that it's the New England Patriots' turn to pick, and the best college player not yet drafted is a quarterback. Suppose also that the Patriots already have a great quarterback and don't need another one. What should they do? Their optimal choice would appear to be to draft the quarterback and then trade him to another team that needs a quarterback. The Patriots could then receive in return a player from the other team who plays a position for which the Patriots need help. In fact, teams very rarely draft a college player and immediately trade him. Explain how the endowment effect could be involved here. (*Hint:* Consider the potential reaction of a team's fans to the team drafting a star college player and immediately trading him.)
   Source: Richard Thaler, *Quasi Rational Economics*, New York: Russell Sage Foundation, 1991, p. 10.
9. Suppose that *Spider-Man 3* comes out and hundreds of people arrive at the Cineplex only to discover that the movie is already sold out. Meanwhile, the Cineplex is also showing a boring movie in its third week of release in a mostly empty theater. Why would this firm charge the same $7.50 for a ticket to either movie, when the quantity of tickets demanded is much greater than the quantity supplied for one movie, and the quantity of tickets demanded is much less than the quantity supplied for the other?
10. You have tickets to see Bruce Springsteen in concert at a stadium 50 miles away. A severe thunderstorm on the night of the concert makes driving hazardous. Will your decision to attend the concert be different if you paid $70 for the tickets than if you received the tickets for free? Explain your answer.
11. Rob Neyer is a baseball writer for ESPN.com. He described attending a Red Sox game at Fenway Park in Boston and having a seat in the sun on a hot, humid day:

    > Granted, I could have moved under the overhang and enjoyed today's contest from a nice, cool, shady seat. But when you paid forty-five dollars for a ticket in the fourth row, it's tough to move back to the twenty-fourth [row].

    Evaluate Neyer's reasoning.
    Source: Rob Neyer, *Feeding the Green Monster*, New York: iPublish.com, 2001, p. 50.
12. After owning a used car for two years, you start having problems with it. You take it into the shop and are told that it will cost $4,000 to repair it. What factors will you take into account in deciding whether to have the repairs done or to junk the car and buy another one? Will the price you paid for the car be one of those factors? Briefly explain.
13. **[Related to the *Chapter Opener*]** Think of some businesses that don't use celebrities to endorse their products. Why do some firms, like Coca-Cola, use celebrity endorsers, while these other firms don't?
14. A newspaper story on the effect of higher milk prices on the market for ice cream contained the following:

    > As a result [of the increase in milk prices], retail prices for ice cream are up 4 percent from last year. And ice cream consumption is down 3 percent.

    Given this information, compute the price elasticity of demand for ice cream. Will the revenue received by ice cream suppliers have increased or decreased following the price increase? Briefly explain.
    Source: John Curran, "Ice Cream, They Scream: Milk Fat Costs Drive Up Ice Cream Prices," Associated Press, July 23, 2001.
15. The price elasticity of demand for cocaine has been estimated as equal to –0.28. Suppose that a successful war on illegal drugs reduces the supply of cocaine in the United States enough to result in a 20 percent increase in its price. What will be the percentage reduction in the quantity of cocaine demanded?
    Source: Henry Saffer and Frank Chaloupka, "The Demand for Illicit Drugs," *Economic Inquiry*, Vol. 37, No. 3, July 1999, pp. 401–411.
16. A study of the price elasticities of products sold in supermarkets contained the following data:

PRODUCT	PRICE ELASTICITY OF DEMAND
Soft drinks	−3.18
Canned soup	−1.62
Cheese	−0.72
Toothpaste	−0.45

    a. The demand which products is inelastic? Discuss reasons why the demand for each product is either elastic or inelastic.
    b. Use the information in the table to predict the change in the quantity demanded for each product following a 10 percent price increase.

    Source: Stephen J. Hoch, Byung-do Kim, Alan L. Montgomery, and Peter E. Rossi, "Determinants of Store-Level Price Elasticity," *Journal of Marketing Research*, Vol. 32, February 1995, pp. 17–29.
17. On most days the price of a rose is $1 and 8,000 roses are purchased. On Valentine's Day, the price of a rose jumps to $2 and 30,000 roses are purchased.
    a. Draw a supply and demand diagram showing why the price jumps.
    b. Based on this information, what do we know about the price elasticity of demand for roses? Calculate a value for the price elasticity of demand or explain why you can't calculate a value.

18. According to an article in the *Wall Street Journal:*

> Unlike airlines, even elite hotels don't have sophisticated systems that can react quickly to changes in demand. Even if they could, many hoteliers say people don't respond that much to lower rates. "We've tested this, cutting our rates by $50 [per night], and we didn't see an appreciable response in occupancy," says Jim Schultenover, a vice president for Ritz-Carlton.

On the basis of this information, would you conclude that the demand for hotel rooms is elastic or inelastic? Briefly explain.

Source: Jesse Drucker, "In Times of Belt-Tightening, We Seek Reasonable Rates," *Wall Street Journal*, April 6, 2001.

19. Use the following graph for Yolanda's Frozen Yogurt Stand to answer the questions that follow:

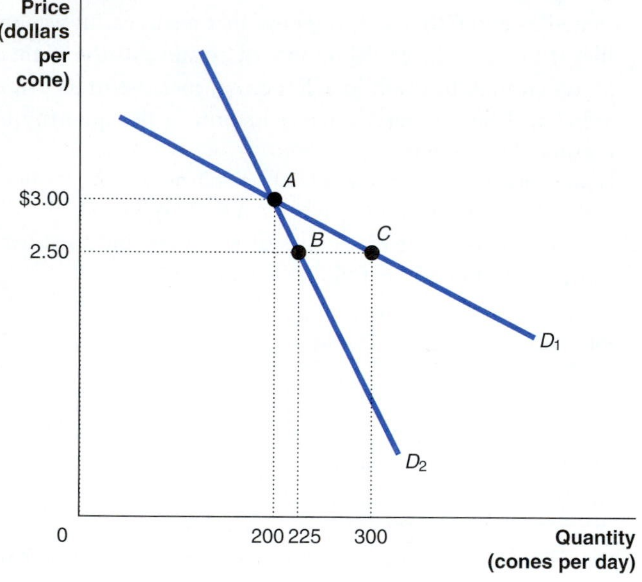

a. Use the midpoint formula to calculate the price elasticity of demand for D_1 between point *A* and point *C*, and the price elasticity of demand for D_2 between point *A* and point *B*. Which demand curve is more elastic, D_1 or D_2? Briefly explain.

b. Suppose Yolanda is initially selling 200 cones per day at a price of $3.00 per cone. If she cuts her price to $2.50 per cone and her demand curve is D_1, what will be the change in her revenue? What will be the change in her revenue if her demand curve is D_2?

20. **[Related to *Solved Problem 6-2*]** Briefly explain whether you agree or disagree with Manager 2's reasoning:

Manager 1: "The only way we can increase the revenue we receive from selling our frozen pizzas is by cutting the price."

Manager 2: "Cutting the price of a product never increases the amount of revenue you receive. If we want to increase revenue, we have to increase price."

21. **[Related to *Don't Let This Happen To You!*]** The publisher of a magazine gives his staff the following information:

Current price	$2.00 per issue
Current sales	150,000 copies per month
Current total costs	$450,000 per month

He tells them, "Our costs are currently $150,000 more than our revenues each month. I propose to eliminate this problem by raising the price of the magazine to $3.00 per issue. This will result in our revenue being exactly equal to our cost." Do you agree with the publisher's analysis? Explain.

chapter seven

Technology, Production, and Costs

Sony Uses a Cost Curve to Determine the Price of Radios

In early 2005, a high-profile management shake-up at Sony Corporation resulted in Howard Stringer being named the firm's first non-Japanese chairman and chief executive officer. The Tokyo-based firm remains a giant of the international economy, manufacturing televisions, computers, satellite systems, semiconductors, telephones, and LCDs, among other products. It is the third-largest manufacturing firm in Japan, after Toyota and Hitachi, and the thirtieth-largest firm in the world. In a survey of top business managers and financial analysts, Sony was the third most admired non-U.S. company in the world behind only Nokia, the Finnish cell phone manufacturer, and Toyota. In 2005, Sony employed more than 160,000 workers and had revenue of more than $72 billion. Like most firms, Sony started small. Its early success resulted from the vision and energy of two young entrepreneurs, Akio Morita and Masaru Ibuka. Sony was founded in 1945, and its first product was a rice cooker. Soon Morita and Ibuka decided to concentrate on manufacturing electronic goods. Their first successful product was a tape recorder.

In 1953, Sony purchased a license that allowed it to use transistor technology developed in the United States at Western Electric's Bell Laboratories. Sony used the technology to develop a transistor radio that was small enough to fit in a shirt pocket and far smaller than any other radio then available. At that time, hearing aids were the only consumer products that used transistors. In 1955, Morita, Sony's chairman, arrived in New York hoping to convince one of the U.S. department store chains to carry the Sony radios.

Morita offered to sell one department store chain 5,000 radios at a price of $29.95 each. If the chain wanted more than 5,000 radios, the price would change. As Morita described it later:

> I sat down and drew a curve that looked something like a lopsided letter U. The price for five thousand would be our regular price. That would be the beginning of the curve. For ten thousand there would be a discount, and that was at the bottom of the curve. For thirty thousand the price would begin to climb. For fifty thousand the price per unit would be higher than for five thousand, and for one hundred t[illegible]d units the price per un[illegible]

have to be much higher than for the first five thousand.

Why would the prices Morita offered the department store follow a U-shape? Because Sony's cost per unit, or *average cost*, of manufacturing the radios would have the same shape. Curves that show the relationship between the level of output and per unit cost are called *average total cost curves.* Average total cost curves typically have the U-shape of Morita's curve. As we explore the relationship between production and costs in this chapter, we will see why average total cost curves have this shape.

Today, Sony is one of the largest electronics firms in the world, but more than 50 years ago, when it was a small, struggling company, Akio Morita used a simple economic tool—the average cost curve—to help make an important business decision. Every day, in companies large and small, managers use economic tools to make decisions. *An Inside Look* on page 222 discusses the cost analysis underlying Sony's joint venture with Samsung to build a large factory to manufacture LCD panels for televisions and computers. In this chapter, we will focus on the relationship between a firm's technology and its production costs. In Chapter 8, we will see how firms use information about costs of production and about demand to determine how much to produce and what price to charge.

Source: Akio Morita, with Edwin M. Reingold and Mitsuko Shimomura, *Made in Japan: Akio Morita and Sony,* New York: Signet Books, 1986, p. 94.

LEARNING OBJECTIVES

After studying this chapter, you should be able to:

1. Define technology and give examples of technological change.
2. Distinguish between the economic short run and the economic long run.
3. Understand the relationship between the marginal product of labor and the average product of labor.
4. Explain and illustrate the relationship between marginal cost and average total cost.
5. Graph average total cost, average variable cost, average fixed cost, and marginal cost.
6. Understand how firms use the long-run average cost curve to plan.

In Chapter 6, we looked behind the demand curve to understand consumer decision making better. In this chapter, we look behind the supply curve to understand firm decision making better. Earlier chapters showed that supply curves are upward sloping because marginal cost increases as firms increase the quantity they supply of a good. In this chapter, we look more closely at why this is true. Once we have a good understanding of production and cost, we can proceed in the following chapters to understand how firms decide what level of output to produce and what price to charge.

Technology: An Economic Definition

1 LEARNING OBJECTIVE

Define technology and give examples of technological change.

Technology The processes a firm uses to turn inputs into outputs of goods and services.

The basic activity of a firm is to use *inputs,* such as workers, machines, and natural resources, to produce *outputs* of goods and services. A pizza parlor, for example, uses inputs such as pizza dough, pizza sauce, cooks, and ovens to produce pizza. A firm's **technology** is the processes it uses to turn inputs into outputs of goods and services. Notice that this economic definition of technology is broader than the everyday definition. In everyday language, "technology" is often used to mean only the development of new products. In the economic sense, a firm's technology depends on many factors, such as the skill of its managers, the training of its workers, and the speed and efficiency of its machinery and equipment. The technology of pizza production, for example, includes not only the capacity of the pizza ovens and how quickly they bake the pizza, but also how quickly the cooks can prepare the pizza for baking, how well the manager motivates the workers to work hard, and how well the manager has arranged the facilities to allow the cooks to quickly prepare the pizzas and get them in the ovens.

Technological change A change in the ability of a firm to produce a given level of output with a given quantity of inputs.

Whenever a firm experiences positive **technological change,** it is able to produce more output using the same inputs, or the same output using fewer inputs. Positive technological change can come from many sources. The firm's managers may rearrange the factory floor or the layout of a retail store, thereby increasing production and sales. The firm's workers may go through a training program. The firm may install faster or more reliable machinery or equipment. It is also possible for a firm to experience negative technological change. If a firm hires less-skilled workers or if its facilities are damaged during a hurricane or other natural disaster, the quantity of output it can produce from a given quantity of inputs may decline.

7-1 Making the Connection

Improving Inventory Control at Wal-Mart

Inventories are goods that have been produced but not yet sold. For a retailer such as Wal-Mart, inventories at any point in time include the goods on the store shelves, as well as goods in warehouses. Inventories are an input into Wal-Mart's output of goods sold to consumers. Holding inventories is costly, so firms have an incentive to hold as few inventories as possible and to *turn over* their inventories as rapidly as possible by ensuring that goods do not remain on the shelves long. Holding too few inventories, however, results in *stockouts,* where sales are lost because the goods were not on the shelf for customers to buy.

Improvements in inventory control meet the economic definition of positive technological change because they allow firms to produce the same output with fewer inputs. In recent years, many firms have adopted *just-in-time* inventory systems in which firms accept shipments from suppliers as close as possible to the time they will be needed. The just-in-time system was pioneered by Toyota, which used it to reduce the inventories of parts in its automobile assembly plants. Wal-Mart has been a pioneer in using similar inventory control systems in its stores.

Wal-Mart actively manages its *supply chain* stretching from the manufacturers of the goods it sells to its retail stores. Entrepreneur Sam Walton, the company founder, built a series of distribution centers spread across the country to supply goods to the retail stores. As goods are sold in the stores, this *point-of-sale* information is sent electronically to the firm's distribution centers. The information on sales is used to determine what products will be shipped to each store. Depending on a store's location relative to a distribution center, goods may be shipped overnight, using Wal-Mart's own trucks. This distribution system allows Wal-Mart to minimize its inventory holdings without running the risk of many stockouts. Because Wal-Mart sells 15 percent to 25 percent of all the toothpaste, disposable diapers, dog food, and many other products sold in the United States, it has been able to involve many manufacturers closely in its supply chain. For example, a company such as Procter & Gamble, which is one of the world's largest manufacturers of toothpaste, laundry detergent, toilet paper, and other products, receives Wal-Mart's point-of-sale and inventory information electronically. Procter & Gamble uses this information to help determine its production schedules and the quantities it should ship to Wal-Mart's distribution centers.

Technological change has been a key to Wal-Mart's becoming the largest firm in the United States, with 1.7 million employees and revenue of more than $285 billion in 2004.

Better inventory controls have helped reduce firms' costs.

The Short Run and the Long Run

② LEARNING OBJECTIVE

Distinguish between the economic short run and the economic long run.

When firms analyze the relationship between their level of production and their costs, they separate the time period involved into the short run and the long run. In the **short run,** at least one of the firm's inputs is fixed. In particular, in the short run the firm's technology and the size of its physical plant–its factory, store, or office—are both fixed, while the number of workers the firm hires is variable. In the **long run,** the firm is able to vary all of its inputs, and can adopt new technology and increase or decrease the size of its physical plant. Of course, the actual length of calendar time in the short run will be different from firm to firm. A pizza parlor may be able to increase its physical plant by adding another pizza oven and some tables and chairs in just a few weeks. BMW, in contrast, may take more than a year to increase the capacity of one of its automobile assembly plants by installing new equipment.

Short run The period of time during which at least one of the firm's inputs is fixed.

Long run A period of time long enough to allow a firm to vary all of its inputs, to adopt new technology, and to increase or decrease the size of its physical plant.

The Difference between Fixed Costs and Variable Costs

Total cost is the cost of all the inputs a firm uses in production. We have just seen that in the short run some inputs are fixed and others are variable. The costs of the fixed inputs are *fixed costs,* and the costs of the variable inputs are *variable costs.* We can also think of **variable costs** as the costs that change as output changes. Similarly, **fixed costs** are costs that remain constant as output changes. A typical firm's variable costs include its labor costs, its raw material costs, and its costs of electricity and other utilities. Typical fixed costs include lease payments for factory or retail space, payments for fire insurance, and payments for newspaper and television advertising. All of a firm's costs are either fixed or variable, so we can state the following:

Total cost The cost of all the inputs a firm uses in production.

Variable costs Costs that change as output changes.

Fixed costs Costs that remain constant as output changes.

$$\text{Total Cost} = \text{Fixed Cost} + \text{Variable Cost}$$

or, using symbols:

$$TC = FC + VC$$

7-2 Making the Connection

The salaries of editors are considered a fixed cost by publishers.

Fixed Costs in the Publishing Industry

An editor at Cambridge University Press gives the following estimates of the annual fixed cost for a medium-size academic book publisher:

COST	AMOUNT
Salaries and Benefits	$437,500
Rent	$75,000
Utilities	$20,000
Supplies	$6,000
Postage	$4,000
Travel	$8,000
Subscriptions, etc.	$4,000
Miscellaneous	$5,000
Total	$559,500

Academic book publishers hire editors, designers, and production and marketing managers who help prepare books for publication. Because these employees work on several books simultaneously, the number of people the company hires will not go up and down with the quantity of books the company publishes during any particular year. Publishing companies therefore consider the salaries and benefits of people in these job categories as fixed costs.

In contrast, for a company that *prints* books, the quantity of workers will vary with the quantity of books printed. The wages and benefits of the workers operating the printing presses, for example, would be a variable cost.

The other costs listed in the preceding table are typical of fixed costs at many firms.

Source: Beth Luey, *Handbook for Academic Authors,* 4th ed., Cambridge: Cambridge University Press, 2002, p. 244.

Implicit Costs versus Explicit Costs

Opportunity cost The highest-valued alternative that must be given up to engage in an activity.

Explicit cost A cost that involves spending money.

Implicit cost A nonmonetary opportunity cost.

It is important to remember that economists always measure costs as *opportunity costs.* The **opportunity cost** of any activity is the highest-valued alternative that must be given up to engage in that activity. As we saw in Chapter 5, costs are either *explicit* or *implicit.* When a firm spends money, it incurs an **explicit cost**. When a firm experiences a nonmonetary opportunity cost, it incurs an **implicit cost.**

For example, suppose that Jill Johnson owns a copy store. In operating her store, Jill has explicit costs, such as the wages she pays her workers and the payments she makes for electricity and paper. But some of Jill's most important costs are implicit. Before opening her own store, Jill earned a salary of $30,000 per year managing a store for someone else. To start her store, Jill quit her job, withdrew $50,000 from her bank account—where it earned her interest of $3,000 per year—and used the funds to equip her store with tables, shelves, a cash register, and other equipment. To open her store, Jill had to give up the $30,000 salary and the $3,000 in interest. This $33,000 is a cost to Jill of running her store. It is an implicit cost because it does not represent payments that Jill has to make. All the same, giving up that $33,000 per year is a real cost to Jill. In addition, during the course of the year, the $50,000 worth of equipment in Jill's store will lose some of its value due partly to wear and tear and partly to better equipment becoming available. *Economic depreciation* is the difference between what Jill paid for the equipment at the beginning of the year, and what she could sell the equipment for at the end of the year. If Jill's equipment could be sold for $40,000 at the end of the year, then the $10,000 in economic depreciation represents another implicit cost. (Note that the whole $50,000 she spent on the equipment is not a cost, because she still has the equipment at the end of the year, although it is now worth only $40,000.)

Table 7-1 lists Jill's costs. The entries in red are explicit costs and the entries in blue are implicit costs. As we saw in Chapter 5, the rules of accounting generally require that

TABLE 7-1

Jill Johnson's Costs per Year

Paper	$20,000
Wages	48,000
Lease payment for copy machines	10,000
Electricity	6,000
Lease payment for store	24,000
Foregone salary	30,000
Foregone interest	3,000
Economic depreciation	10,000
Total	151,000

only explicit costs be recognized for purposes of keeping the company's financial records and for paying taxes. Therefore, explicit costs are sometimes called *accounting costs. Economic costs* include both accounting costs and implicit costs.

The Production Function

Let's look at the relationship between the level of production and costs in the short run for Jill Johnson's copy store. To keep things simple, let's assume that Jill uses only labor—workers—and capital—machines—to produce a single good: photocopies. Many firms use more than two inputs and produce more than one good, but we can understand the relationship between output and cost more easily by focusing on the case of a firm using only two inputs and producing only one good. In the short run, Jill doesn't have time to build a larger store, bring in additional copy machines, or redesign the layout of her store. So, in the short run, she can increase or decrease the quantity of photocopies she produces only by increasing or decreasing the quantity of workers she employs.

The first three columns of Table 7-2 show the relationship between the quantity of workers and machines Jill uses each day and the quantity of copies she can produce. The relationship between the inputs employed by a firm and the maximum output it can produce with those inputs is called the firm's **production function.** Because a firm's technology is the processes it uses to turn inputs into output, the production function represents the firm's technology. In this case, Table 7-2 shows Jill's *short-run*

Production function The relationship between the inputs employed by the firm and the maximum output it can produce with those inputs.

TABLE 7-2 **Short-Run Production and Cost at Jill Johnson's Copy Store**

QUANTITY OF WORKERS	QUANTITY OF COPY MACHINES	QUANTITY OF COPIES	COST OF COPY MACHINES (FIXED COST)	COST OF WORKERS (VARIABLE COST)	TOTAL COST OF COPIES	COST PER COPY (AVERAGE TOTAL COST)
0	2	0	$30	$0	$30	—
1	2	625	30	50	80	$0.13
2	2	1325	30	100	130	0.10
3	2	2200	30	150	180	0.08
4	2	2600	30	200	230	0.09
5	2	2900	30	250	280	0.10
6	2	3100	30	300	330	0.11

production function because we are assuming the time period is too short for Jill to increase or decrease the quantity of copy machines she is using.

A First Look at the Relationship between Production and Cost

Table 7-2 also gives us information on Jill's costs. We can determine the total cost of producing a given quantity of copies if we know how many workers and machines are required to produce that quantity of copies and what Jill has to pay for those workers and machines. Suppose Jill leases 2 copy machines for $15 each per day. Therefore, her fixed costs will be $30 per day. If Jill pays $50 per day to each worker she hires, her variable costs will depend on how many workers she hires. In the short run, Jill can increase the quantity of copies she produces only by hiring more workers. The table shows that if she hires 1 worker she produces 625 copies during the day; if she hires 2 workers she produces 1,325 copies; and so on. On a particular day, Jill's total cost of producing copies is equal to the $30 she pays to lease the copy machines plus the amount she pays to hire workers. If Jill decides to hire 4 workers and produce 2,600 copies, her total cost will be $230: $30 to lease the copy machines and $200 to hire the workers. Her cost per copy is equal to her total cost of producing copies divided by the quantity of copies produced. If she produces 2,600 copies at a total cost of $230, her cost per copy, or **average total cost,** is $230/2,600 = $0.09.

Average total cost Total cost divided by the quantity of output produced.

Panel (a) of Figure 7-1 uses the numbers in the next-to-last column of Table 7-2 to graph Jill's total cost. Panel (b) uses the numbers in the last column to graph her average total cost. Notice in panel (b) that Jill's average cost roughly has the same U-shape as the

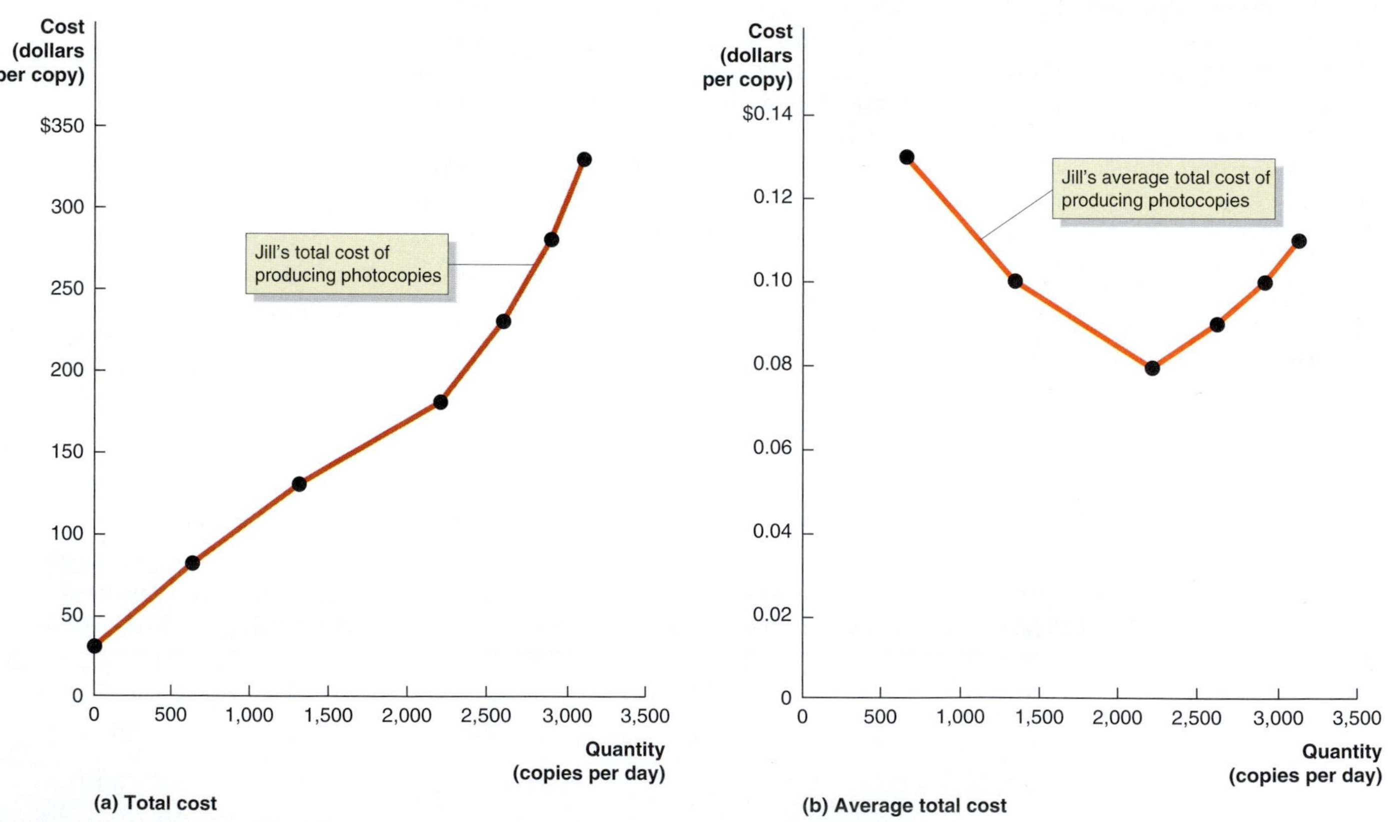

FIGURE 7-1 Graphing Total Cost and Average Total Cost at Jill Johnson's Copy Store

We can use the information from Table 7-2 to graph the relationship between the quantity of photocopies Jill produces and her total cost and average total cost. Panel (a) shows that total cost increases as the level of production increases. In panel (b), we see that average total cost is roughly U-shaped: As production increases from low levels, average cost falls before rising at higher levels of production. To understand why average cost has this shape, we must look more closely at the technology of producing photocopies, as shown by the production function.

average cost curve we saw Akio Morita calculate for Sony transistor radios at the beginning of this chapter. As production increases from low levels, average cost falls. Average cost then becomes fairly flat before rising at higher levels of production. To understand why average cost has this U-shape, we first need to look more closely at the technology of producing photocopies, as shown by the production function for Jill's store. Then we need to look at how this technology determines the relationship between production and cost.

The Marginal Product of Labor and the Average Product of Labor

③ **LEARNING OBJECTIVE**

Understand the relationship between the marginal product of labor and the average product of labor.

To have a better understand of the choices Jill faces given the technology available to her, think first about the situation in her store if she hires only one worker. That one worker will have to perform several different activities, including receiving orders from customers, answering customers' questions, running the copying jobs on the two copy machines, and ringing up sales on the cash registrar. If Jill hires two workers, some of these activities can be divided up: One worker could be assigned to the copy machines, and one worker could be assigned to take orders and work the cash register. With this division of tasks, Jill will find that hiring two workers actually allows her to produce more than twice as many copies as she could produce with just one worker.

The additional output produced by a firm as a result of hiring one more worker is called the **marginal product of labor.** We can calculate the marginal product of labor by determining how much total output increases as each additional worker is hired. We do this for Jill's copy store in Table 7-3.

Marginal product of labor The additional output a firm produces as a result of hiring one more worker.

When Jill hires only one worker, she produces 625 copies per day. When she hires two workers, she produces 1,325 copies per day. Hiring the second worker increases her production by 700 copies per day. So, the marginal product of labor for one worker is 625 copies. For two workers, the marginal product of labor rises to 700 copies. If Jill hires a third worker, total output rises to 2,200, an increase of 875 copies. So, the marginal product of labor for three workers rises to 875. These increases in marginal product result from the *division of labor* and from *specialization*. By dividing the tasks to be performed—the division of labor—Jill reduces the time workers lose moving from one activity to the next. She also allows them to become more specialized at their tasks. For example, a worker who concentrates on operating a copy machine will become skilled at using it quickly and efficiently.

The Law of Diminishing Returns

In the short run, the quantity of copy machines Jill leases is fixed, so as she hires more workers the marginal product of labor eventually begins to decline. This happens

TABLE 7-3

The Marginal Product of Labor at Jill Johnson's Copy Store

QUANTITY OF WORKERS	QUANTITY OF COPY MACHINES	QUANTITY OF COPIES	MARGINAL PRODUCT OF LABOR
0	2	0	—
1	2	625	625
2	2	1,325	700
3	2	2,200	875
4	2	2,600	400
5	2	2,900	300
6	2	3,100	200

Law of diminishing returns The principle that, at some point, adding more of a variable input, such as labor, to the same amount of a fixed input, such as capital, will cause the marginal product of the variable input to decline.

because at some point Jill uses up all the gains from the division of labor and from specialization and starts to experience the effects of the **law of diminishing returns.** This law states that adding more of a variable input, such as labor, to the same amount of a fixed input, such as capital, will eventually cause the marginal product of the variable input to decline. For Jill, this happens when she hires the fourth worker. Hiring four workers raises the quantity of copies she produces from 2,200 per day to 2,600. But the increase in the quantity of copies—400—is less than the increase when she hired the third worker—875.

If Jill kept adding more and more workers to the same quantity of machines, eventually workers would begin to get in each other's way and the marginal product of labor would actually become negative. When the marginal product is negative, the level of total output declines. No firm actually would hire so many workers as to experience a negative marginal product of labor and falling total output.

Graphing Production

Average product of labor The total output produced by a firm divided by the quantity of workers.

Panel (a) in Figure 7-2 shows the relationship between the quantity of workers Jill hires and her total output of photocopies, using the numbers from Table 7-3. Panel (b) shows the marginal product of labor. In panel (a), output increases as more workers are hired, but the increase in output does not occur at a constant rate. Because of specialization and the division of labor, output will at first increase at an increasing rate, with each additional worker hired causing production to increase by a *greater* amount than did the hiring of the previous worker. But after the third worker has been hired, hiring more workers while keeping the amount of machinery constant results in diminishing returns. Once the point of diminishing returns has been reached, production increases at a decreasing rate. Each additional worker hired after the third worker causes production to increase by a *smaller* amount than did the hiring of the previous worker. In panel (b), the marginal product of labor curve rises initially because of the effects of specialization and division of labor, and then falls due to the effects of diminishing returns.

7-3 Making the Connection

Adam Smith's Famous Account of the Division of Labor in a Pin Factory

The gains from division of labor and specialization are as important to firms today as they were in the eighteenth century when Adam Smith first discussed them.

In *The Wealth of Nations,* Adam Smith uses production in a pin factory as an example of the gains in output resulting from the division of labor. The following is an excerpt from his account of how pin making was divided into a series of tasks:

> One man draws out the wire, another straightens it, a third cuts it, a fourth points it, a fifth grinds it at the top for receiving the head; to make the head requires two or three distinct operations; to put it on is a [distinct operation], to whiten the pins is another; it is even a trade by itself to put them into the paper; and the important business of making a pin is, in this manner, divided into eighteen distinct operations.

Because the labor of pin making was divided up in this way, the average worker was able to produce about 4,800 pins per day. Smith speculated that a single worker using the pin-making machinery alone would make only about 20 pins per day. This lesson from more than 225 years ago showing the tremendous gains from division of labor and specialization remains relevant to most business situations today.

Source: Adam Smith, *An Inquiry into the Nature and Causes of the Wealth of Nations,* Vol. I, Oxford University Press edition, 1976, pp. 14–15.

The Relationship between Marginal and Average Product

The marginal product of labor tells us how much total output changes as the quantity of workers hired changes. We can also calculate how many copies workers produce on average. The **average product of labor** is the total output produced divided by the quantity of workers. For example, using the numbers in Table 7-3, if Jill hires four workers to produce 2,600 copies, the average product of labor is 2,600/4 = 650.

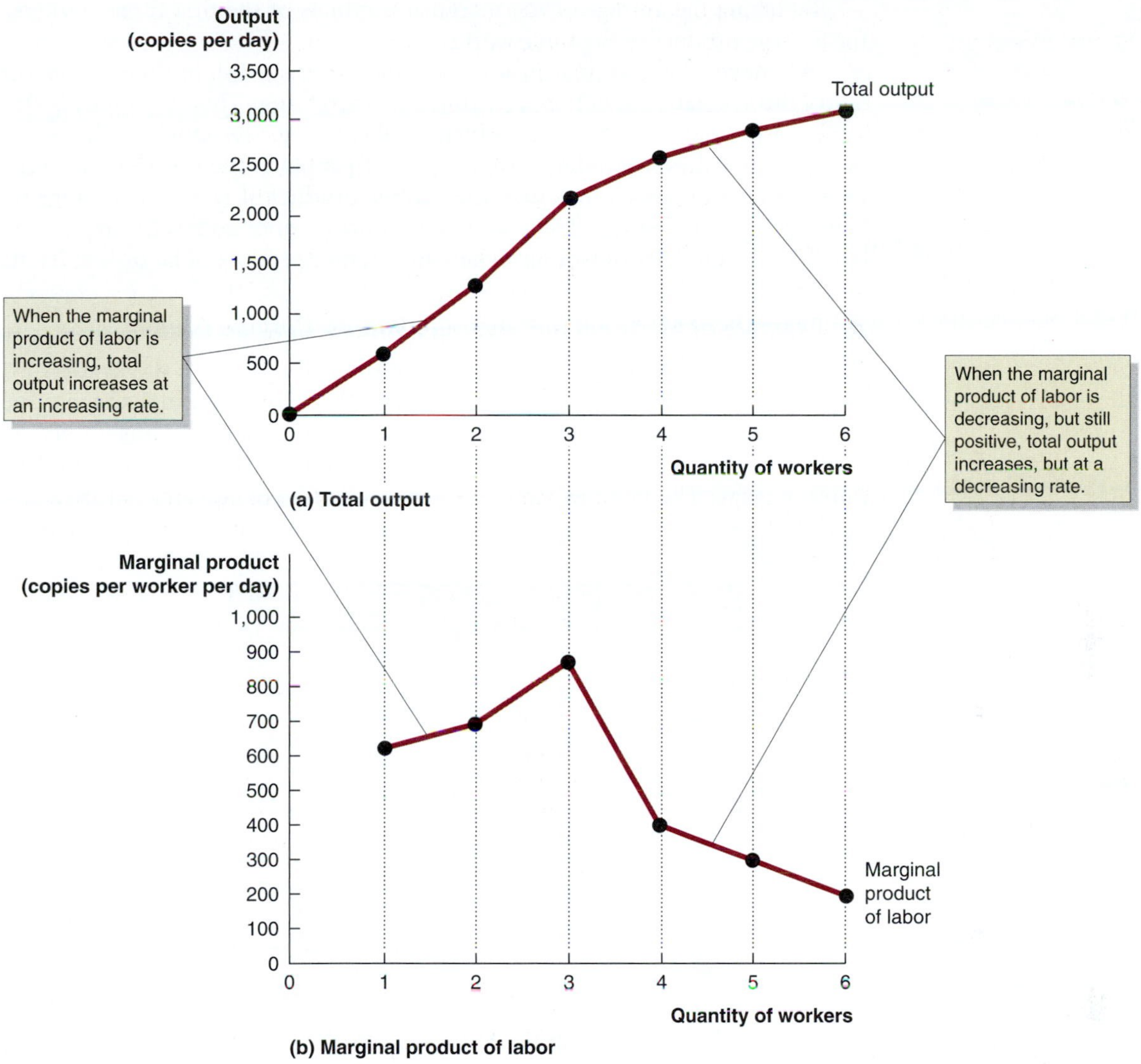

Output (copies per day)

When the marginal product of labor is increasing, total output increases at an increasing rate.

When the marginal product of labor is decreasing, but still positive, total output increases, but at a decreasing rate.

Total output

Quantity of workers

(a) Total output

Marginal product (copies per worker per day)

Marginal product of labor

Quantity of workers

(b) Marginal product of labor

FIGURE 7-2 Total Output and the Marginal Product of Labor

In panel (a), output increases as more workers are hired, but the increase in output does not occur at a constant rate. Because of specialization and the division of labor, output will at first increase at an increasing rate, with each additional worker hired causing production to increase by a *greater* amount than did the hiring of the previous worker. After the third worker has been hired, hiring more workers while keeping the amount of machinery constant results in diminishing returns. Once the point of diminishing returns has been reached, production increases at a decreasing rate. Each additional worker hired after the third worker causes production to increase by a *smaller* amount than did the hiring of the previous worker. In panel (b), the *marginal product of labor* is the additional output produced as a result of hiring one more worker. The marginal product of labor rises initially because of the effects of specialization and division of labor, and then falls due to the effects of diminishing returns.

We can state the relationship between the marginal and average products of labor this way: *The average product of labor is the average of the marginal products of labor.* For example, the numbers from Table 7-3 show that the marginal product of the first worker Jill hires is 625, the marginal product of the second worker is 700, and the marginal product of the third worker is 875. Therefore, the average product of labor for three workers is 733.3:

$$733.3 = (625 + 700 + 875) / 3$$

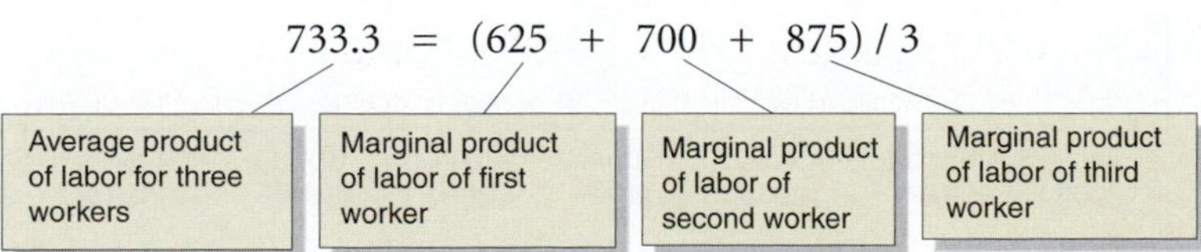

By taking the average of the marginal products of the first three workers, we have the average product of the three workers.

Whenever the marginal product of labor is greater than the average product of labor, the average product of labor must be increasing. This statement is true for the same reason that a person 6 feet, 2 inches tall entering a room where the average height is 5 feet, 10 inches raises the average height of people in the room. Whenever the marginal product of labor is less than the average product of labor, the average product of labor must be decreasing. The marginal product of labor equals the average product of labor for the quantity of workers where the average product of labor is at its maximum.

An Example of Marginal and Average Values: College Grades

The relationship between the marginal product of labor and the average product of labor is the same as the relationship between the marginal and average values of any variable. To see this more clearly, think about the familiar relationship between a student's grade point average (GPA) in one semester and his overall, or cumulative, grade point average. The table in Figure 7-3 shows Paul's college grades for each semester,

FIGURE 7-3

Marginal and Average GPAs

The relationship between marginal and average values for a variable can be illustrated using grade point averages (GPAs). We can calculate the GPA Paul earns in a particular semester (his "marginal GPA"), and we can calculate his cumulative GPA for all the semesters he has completed so far (his "average GPA"). Paul's GPA is only 1.50 in the fall semester of his freshman year. In each following semester through fall of his junior year, his GPA for the semester increases—raising his cumulative GPA. In Paul's junior year, even though his semester GPA declines from fall to spring, his cumulative GPA rises. Only in the fall of his senior year, when his semester GPA drops below his cumulative GPA, does his cumulative GPA decline.

	Semester GPA (Marginal) GPA	Cumulative GPA (Average) GPA
Freshman Year		
Fall	1.50	1.50
Spring	2.00	1.75
Sophomore Year		
Fall	2.20	1.90
Spring	3.00	2.18
Junior Year		
Fall	3.20	2.38
Spring	3.00	2.48
Senior Year		
Fall	2.40	2.47
Spring	2.00	2.41

Average GPA continues to rise, although marginal GPA falls.

With the marginal GPA below the average, the average GPA falls.

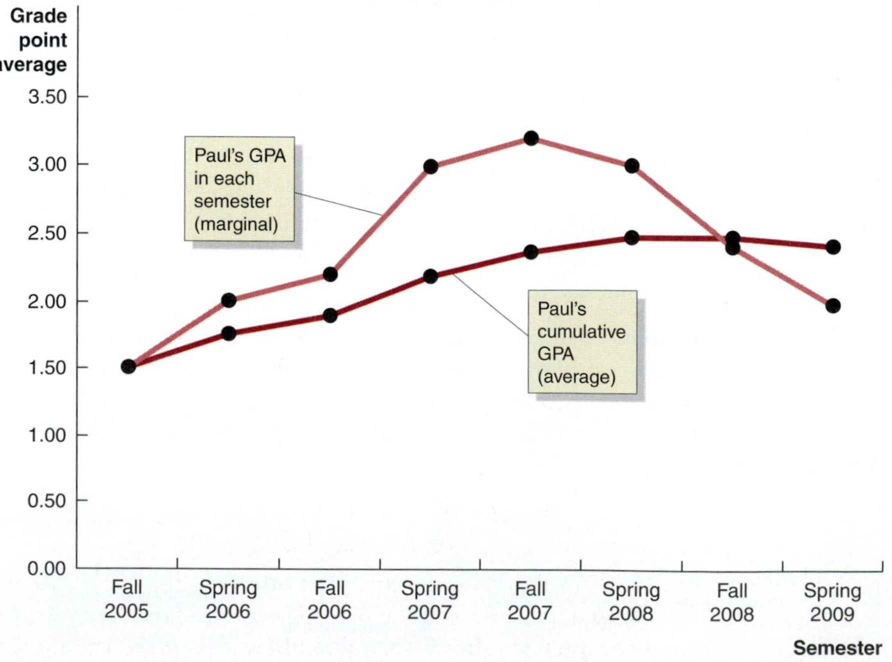

beginning with fall 2005. The graph in Figure 7-3 plots the grades from the table. Just as each additional worker hired adds to a firm's total production, each additional semester adds to Paul's total grade points. We can calculate what each individual worker hired adds to total production (marginal product), and we can calculate the average production of the workers hired so far (average product).

Similarly, we can calculate the GPA Paul earns in a particular semester (his "marginal GPA"), and we can calculate his cumulative GPA for all the semesters he has completed so far (his "average GPA"). As the table shows, Paul gets off to a weak start in college with only a 1.50 GPA in the fall semester of his freshman year. In each subsequent semester through the fall of his junior year, his GPA for the semester increases from the previous semester—raising his cumulative GPA. As the graph shows, however, his cumulative GPA does not increase as rapidly as his semester-by-semester GPA, because his cumulative GPA is held back by the low GPAs of his first few semesters. Notice that in Paul's junior year, even though his semester GPA declines from fall to spring, his cumulative GPA rises. Only in the fall of his senior year, when his semester GPA drops below his cumulative GPA, does his cumulative GPA decline.

The Relationship between Short-Run Production and Short-Run Cost

Explain and illustrate the relationship between marginal cost and average total cost.

We have seen that technology determines the values of the marginal product of labor and the average product of labor. In turn, the marginal and average products of labor will affect the firm's costs. Keep in mind that the relationships we are discussing are *short-run* relationships: We are assuming the time period is too short for the firm to change its technology or the size of its plant.

At the beginning of this chapter, we saw how Akio Morita used an average total cost curve to determine the price of radios. The average total cost curve Morita used and the average total cost curve in Figure 7-1 for Jill Johnson's copy store both have a U-shape. As we will soon see, the U-shape of the average total cost curve is determined by the shape of the curve that shows the relationship between *marginal cost* and the level of production.

Marginal Cost

As we saw in Chapter 1, one of the key ideas in economics is that optimal decisions are made at the margin. Consumers, firms, and government officials usually make decisions about doing a little more or a little less. As Jill Johnson considers whether to hire additional workers to produce additional photocopies, she needs to consider how much she will add to her total cost by producing the additional copies. **Marginal cost** is the change in a firm's total cost from producing one more unit of a good or service. We can calculate marginal cost for a particular increase in output by dividing the change in cost by the change in output. Expressing this idea mathematically (remembering that the Greek letter delta, Δ, means "change in") we can write:

Marginal cost The change in a firm's total cost from producing one more unit of a good or service.

$$MC = \frac{\Delta TC}{\Delta Q}.$$

In the table in Figure 7-4, we use this equation to calculate Jill's marginal cost of producing copies.

Why Are the Marginal and Average Cost Curves U-Shaped?

Notice in the graph in Figure 7-4 that Jill's marginal cost of producing copies declines at first and then increases, giving the marginal cost curve a U-shape. The table in Figure 7-4 also shows the marginal product of labor. This table allows us to see the important

FIGURE 7-4

Jill Johnson's Marginal Cost and Average Total Cost of Producing Copies

Quantity of Workers	Quantity of Copies	Marginal Product of Labor	Total Cost of Copies	Marginal Cost of Copies	Average Total Cost of Copies
0	0	—	$30	—	—
1	625	625	80	$0.08	$0.13
2	1,325	700	130	0.07	0.10
3	2,200	875	180	0.06	0.08
4	2,600	400	230	0.13	0.09
5	2,900	300	280	0.17	0.10
6	3,100	200	330	0.25	0.11

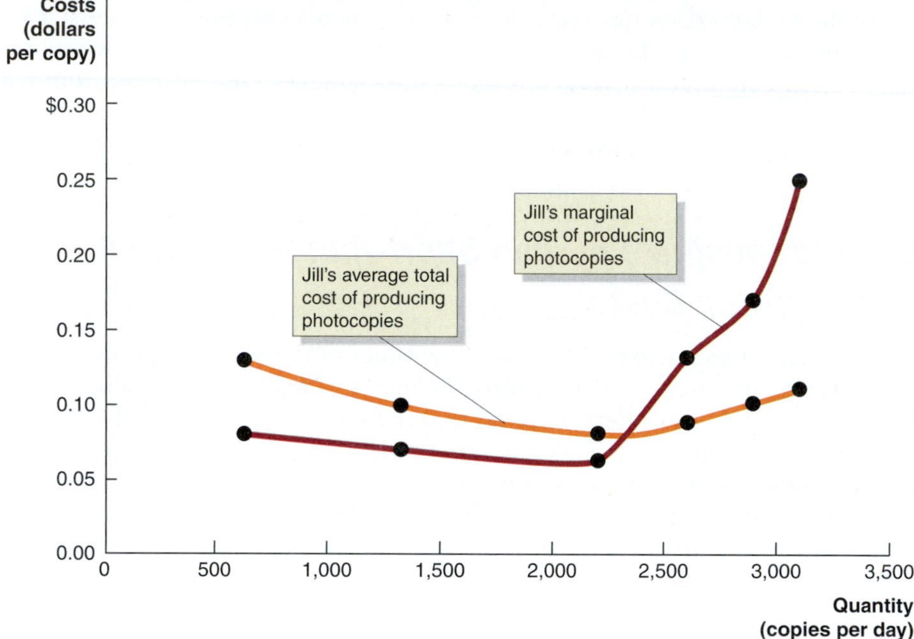

We can use the information in the table to calculate Jill's marginal cost and average total cost of producing copies. For the first three workers hired, the marginal product of labor is increasing. This increase causes the marginal cost of production to fall. For the last three workers hired, the marginal product of labor is falling. This causes the marginal cost of production to increase. Therefore, the marginal cost curve falls and then rises—has a U-shape—because the marginal product of labor rises and then falls. As long as marginal cost is below average total cost, average total cost will be falling. When marginal cost is above average total cost, average total cost will be rising. The relationship between marginal cost and average total cost explains why the average total cost curve also has a U-shape.

relationship between the marginal product of labor and the marginal cost of production: The marginal product of labor is *rising* for the first three workers, but the marginal cost of the copies produced by these workers is *falling*. The marginal product of labor is *falling* for the last three workers, but the marginal cost of copies produced by these workers is *rising*. To summarize this point: *When the marginal product of labor is rising, the marginal cost of output will be falling. When the marginal product of labor is falling, the marginal cost of production will be rising.*

One way to understand why this point is true is first to notice that the only additional cost to Jill from producing more copies is the additional wages she pays to hire more workers. She pays each new worker the same $50 per day. So the marginal cost of the additional copies each worker makes depends upon that worker's additional output, or marginal product. As long as the additional output from each new worker is rising, the marginal cost of that output will be falling. Once the additional output from each new worker is falling, the marginal cost of that output will be rising. *We can conclude that the marginal cost of production falls and then rises—a U-shape—because the marginal product of labor rises and then falls.*

The relationship between marginal cost and average total cost follows the usual relationship between marginal and average values. As long as marginal cost is below average total cost, average total cost will fall. When marginal cost is above average total cost, average total cost will rise. Marginal cost will equal average total cost when average total cost is at its lowest point. Therefore, the average total cost curve has a U-shape because the marginal cost curve has a U-shape.

SOLVED PROBLEM 7-1

The Relationship between Marginal Cost and Average Cost

④ LEARNING OBJECTIVE

Explain and illustrate the relationship between marginal cost and average total cost.

Is Jill Johnson right or wrong when she says the following? "I am currently producing 10,000 copies per day at a total cost of $500.00. If I produce 10,001 copies my total cost will rise to $500.11. Therefore, my marginal cost of producing copies must be increasing." Draw a graph to illustrate your answer.

Solving the Problem:

Step 1: Review the chapter material. This problem requires understanding the relationship between marginal and average cost, so you may want to review the section "Why Are the Marginal and Average Cost Curves U-Shaped?" which begins on page 211.

Step 2: Calculate average total cost and marginal cost. Average total cost is total cost divided by total output. In this case, average total cost is $500.11/10,001 = $0.05. Marginal cost is the change in total cost divided by the change in output. In this case, marginal cost is $0.11/1 = $0.11.

Step 3: Use the relationship between marginal cost and average total cost to answer the question. When marginal cost is greater than average total cost, marginal cost must be increasing. You have shown in step 2 that marginal cost is greater than average total cost. Therefore, Jill is right: Her marginal cost of producing copies must be increasing.

Step 4: Draw the graph.

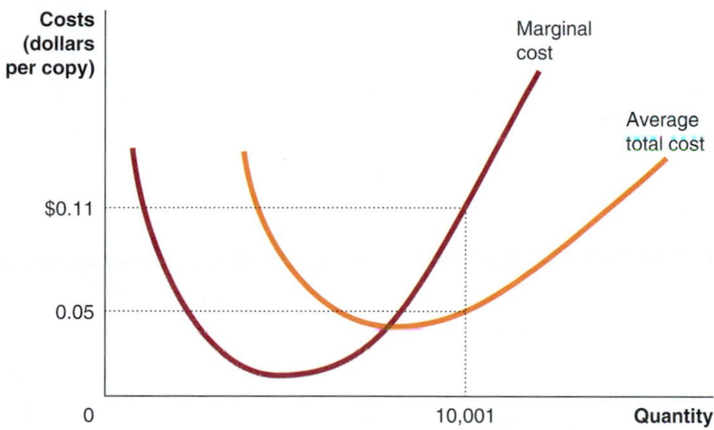

YOUR TURN: For more practice, do related problems 11, 15, 17, and 29 on pages 226, 227, and 229 at the end of this chapter.

Graphing Cost Curves

⑤ LEARNING OBJECTIVE

Graph average total cost, average variable cost, average fixed cost, and marginal cost.

We have seen that we calculate average total cost by dividing total cost by the quantity of output produced. Similarly, we can calculate **average fixed cost** by dividing fixed cost by the quantity of output produced. And we can calculate **average variable cost** by dividing variable cost by the quantity of output produced. Or, mathematically, with Q being the level of output, we have:

$$\text{Average total cost} = ATC = \frac{TC}{Q}$$

Average fixed cost Fixed cost divided by the quantity of output produced.

Average variable cost Variable cost divided by the quantity of units produced.

$$\text{Average fixed cost} = AFC = \frac{FC}{Q}$$

$$\text{Average variable cost} = AVC = \frac{VC}{Q}.$$

Finally, notice that average total cost is just the sum of average fixed cost plus average variable cost:

$$ATC = AFC + AVC.$$

The only fixed cost Jill incurs in operating her copy store is the $30 per day she pays to lease two copy machines. Her variable costs are the wages she pays her workers. The table and graph in Figure 7-5 show Jill's costs.

We will use graphs like the one in Figure 7-5 in the next several chapters to analyze how firms decide the level of output to produce and the price to charge. Before going further, be sure you understand the following three key facts about Figure 7-5:

FIGURE 7-5

Costs at Jill Johnson's Copy Store

Jill's costs of making copies are shown in the table and plotted in the graph. Notice three important facts about the graph: (1) The marginal cost (*MC*), average total cost (*ATC*), and average variable cost (*AVC*) curves are all U-shaped, and the marginal cost curve intersects both the average variable cost curve and average total cost curve at their minimum points. (2) As output increases, average fixed cost (*AFC*) gets smaller and smaller. (3) As output increases, the difference between average total cost and average variable cost decreases. Make sure you can explain why each of these three facts is true. You should spend time becoming familiar with this graph, because it is one of the most important graphs in microeconomics.

Quantity of Workers	Quantity of Copy Machines	Quantity of Copies	Cost of Copy Machines (Fixed Cost)	Cost of Workers (Variable Cost)	Total Cost of Copies	*ATC*	*AFC*	*AVC*	*MC*
0	2	0	$30	0	$30	—	—	—	—
1	2	625	30	$50	80	$0.13	$0.05	$0.08	$0.08
2	2	1,325	30	100	130	0.10	0.02	0.08	0.07
3	2	2,200	30	150	180	0.08	0.01	0.07	0.06
4	2	2,600	30	200	230	0.09	0.01	0.08	0.13
5	2	2,900	30	250	280	0.10	0.01	0.09	0.17
6	2	3,100	30	300	330	0.11	0.01	0.10	0.25

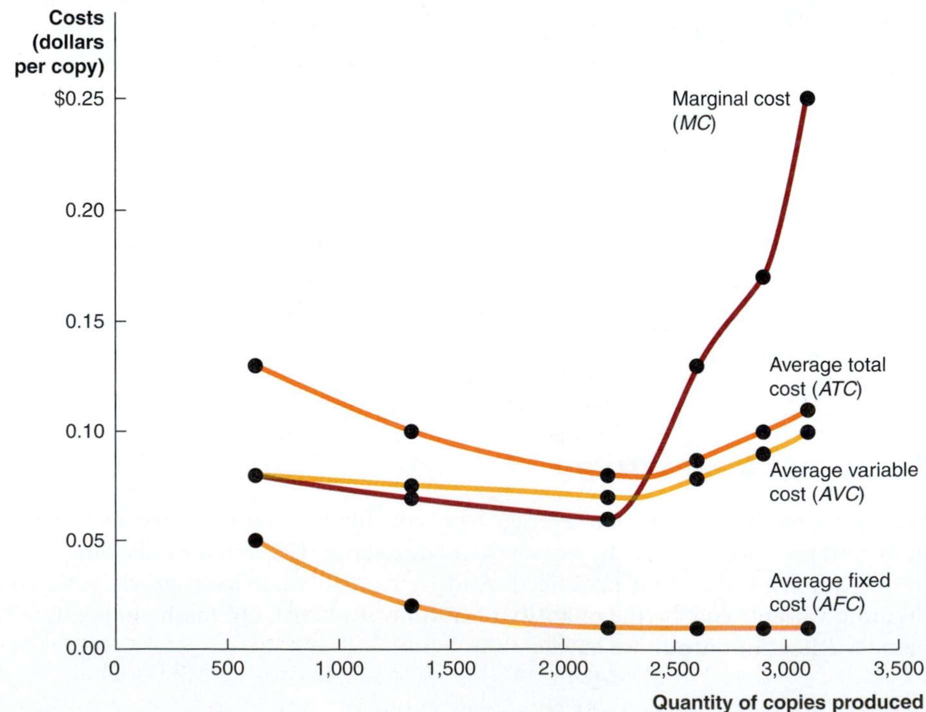

1. The marginal cost (MC), average total cost (ATC), and average variable cost (AVC) curves are all U-shaped, and the marginal cost curve intersects the average variable cost and average total cost curves at their minimum points. When marginal cost is less than either average variable cost or average total cost, it causes them to decrease. When marginal cost is above average variable cost or average total cost, it causes them to increase. Therefore, when marginal cost equals average variable cost or average total cost, they must be at their minimum points.
2. As output increases, average fixed cost gets smaller and smaller. This happens because in calculating average fixed cost we are dividing something that gets larger and larger—output—into something that remains constant—fixed cost. Firms often refer to this process of lowering average fixed cost by selling more output as "spreading the overhead." By "overhead" they mean fixed costs.
3. As output increases, the difference between average total cost and average variable cost decreases. This happens because the difference between average total cost and average variable cost is average fixed cost, which gets smaller as output increases.

Costs in the Long Run

(6) **LEARNING OBJECTIVE**

Understand how firms use the long-run average cost curve to plan.

The distinction between fixed cost and variable cost that we just discussed applies to the short run but *not* to the long run. For example, in the short run, Jill Johnson has fixed costs of $30 a day because she has signed an agreement to lease two copy machines for six months. When the six months are over, that cost becomes variable because Jill can choose whether or not to sign another agreement. The same would be true of any other fixed costs a company like Jill's might have. Once a company has purchased a fire insurance policy, the cost of the policy is fixed. But when the policy expires, the company must decide whether or not to renew it and the cost becomes variable. The important point here is that: *In the long run all costs are variable. There are no fixed costs in the long run.* In other words, in the long run, total cost equals variable cost and average total cost equals average variable cost.

Managers of successful companies simultaneously consider how they can most profitably run their current store, factory, or office and also whether in the long run they would be more profitable if they became larger or, possibly, smaller. Jill must consider how to run her current store, which has only two copy machines, but she also must plan what to do when her current lease agreements end. Should she lease more copy machines? Should she lease a larger store?

Economies of Scale

Short-run average cost curves represent the costs a firm faces when some input, such as the quantity of machines it uses, is fixed. The **long-run average cost curve** shows the lowest cost at which the firm is able to produce a given level of output in the long run, when no inputs are fixed. Many firms experience **economies of scale,** which means the firm's long-run average costs fall as it increases the quantity of output it produces. We can illustrate the effects of economies of scale in Figure 7-6, which shows the relationship between short-run and long-run average cost curves. Managers can use long-run average cost curves for planning because they show the effect on cost of expanding output by, for example, building a larger factory or store.

Long-run average cost curve A curve showing the lowest cost at which the firm is able to produce a given quantity of output in the long run, when no inputs are fixed.

Economies of scale Exist when a firm's long-run average costs fall as it increases output.

Long-Run Average Total Cost Curves for Bookstores

Figure 7-6 shows long-run average cost in the retail bookstore industry. If a bookstore expects to be able to sell only 1,000 books per month, the small store represented by the ATC curve on the left of the figure will allow it to sell this quantity of books at the lowest average cost. A much larger bookstore, such as one run by a national chain like Barnes &

FIGURE 7-6

The Relationship between Short-Run Average Cost and Long-Run Average Cost

If a bookstore expects to sell only 1,000 books per month, the small store represented by the *ATC* curve on the left of the figure will allow it to sell this quantity of books at the lowest average cost, which would be $22 per book. A larger bookstore will be able to sell 20,000 books per month at a lower cost of $18 per book. A bookstore selling 20,000 books per month and a bookstore selling 40,000 books per month will experience constant returns to scale and have the same average cost. A bookstore selling 20,000 books per month will have reached minimum efficient scale. Very large bookstores will experience diseconomies of scale, and their average costs will rise as sales increase beyond 40,000 books per month.

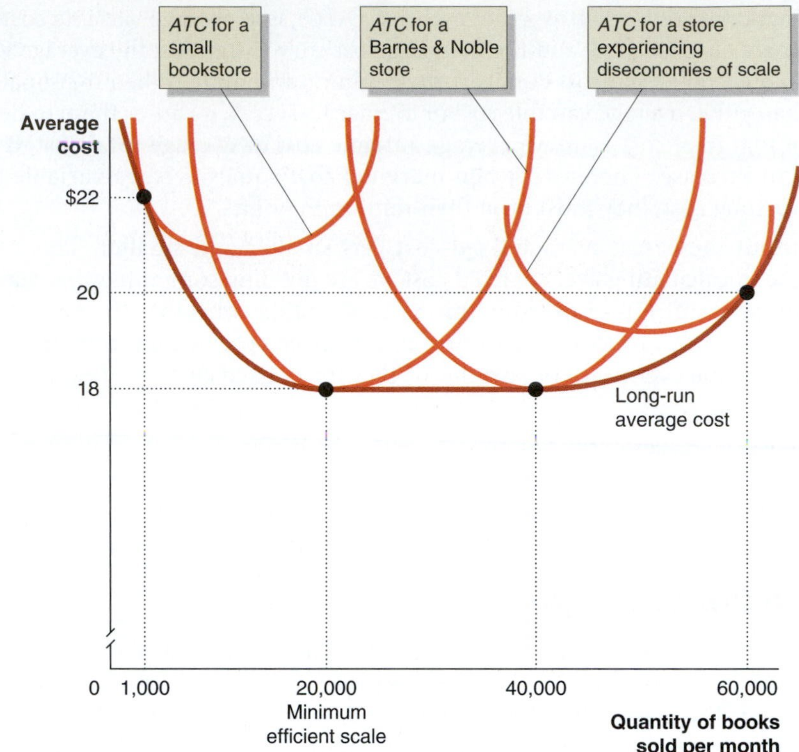

Noble, will be able to sell 20,000 books per month at a much lower average cost. For the small bookstore, the average total cost of selling 1,000 books per month would be $22 per book. For a Barnes & Noble store, the average total cost of selling 20,000 books would be only $18 per book. This decline in average cost represents the economies of scale that exist in bookselling. Why would the larger bookstore have lower average costs? One important reason is that the Barnes & Noble store is selling 20 times as many books per month as the small store but might need only six times as many workers. This saving in labor cost would reduce Barnes & Noble's average cost of selling books.

Firms may encounter economies of scale for several reasons. First, as with the case of Barnes & Noble, the firm's technology may make it possible to increase production with a smaller proportional increase in at least one input. Second, both workers and managers can become more specialized, enabling them to become more productive, as output expands. Third, large firms, like Barnes & Noble, Wal-Mart, and General Motors, may be able to purchase inputs at lower costs than smaller competitors. In fact, as Wal-Mart expanded, its bargaining power with respect to its suppliers increased and its average costs fell. Finally, as a firm expands it may be able to borrow money more cheaply, thereby lowering its costs.

Economies of scale do not continue forever. The long-run average cost curve in most industries has a flat segment that often stretches over a substantial range of output. As Figure 7-6 shows, a bookstore selling 20,000 books per month and a bookstore selling 40,000 books per month will have the same average cost. Over this range of output, firms in the industry will experience **constant returns to scale.** As these firms increase their output, they will have to increase their inputs, such as the size of the store and the quantity of workers, proportionally. The level of output at which all economies of scale have been exhausted is known as **minimum efficient scale.** A bookstore selling 20,000 books per month has reached minimum efficient scale.

Constant returns to scale Exist when a firm's long-run average costs remain unchanged as it increases output.

Minimum efficient scale The level of output at which all economies of scale have been exhausted.

Very large bookstores will experience increasing average costs as managers begin to have difficulty coordinating the operation of the store. Figure 7-6 shows that for sales above 40,000 books per month, firms in the industry will experience **diseconomies of scale.** Toyota ran into diseconomies of scale in 2004. The firm found that as it expanded production at its Georgetown, Kentucky, plant and its plants in China, its managers had difficulty keeping costs from rising. The president of Toyota's Georgetown plant was quoted as saying, "Demand for . . . high volumes saps your energy. Over a period of time, it eroded our focus . . . [and] thinned out the expertise and knowledge we painstakingly built up over the years." One analysis of the problems Toyota faced in expanding production concluded: "It is the kind of paradox many highly successful companies face: Getting bigger doesn't always mean getting better."

Diseconomies of scale Exist when a firm's long-run average costs rise as it increases output.

SOLVED PROBLEM 7-2

Using Long-Run Average Cost Curves to Understand Business Strategy

6 LEARNING OBJECTIVE

Understand how firms use the long-run average cost curve to plan.

In the fall of 2002, Motorola and Siemens were each manufacturing both mobile phone handsets and wireless infrastruture—the base stations needed to operate a wireless communications network. The firms discussed the following arrangement: Motorola would give Siemens its wireless infrastructure business in exchange for Siemens giving Motorola its mobile phone handsets business. The main factor motivating the trade was the hope of taking advantage of economies of scale in each business. Use long-run average total cost curves to explain why this trade might make sense for Motorola and Siemens.

Solving the Problem:

Step 1: Review the chapter material. This problem is about the long-run average cost curve, so you may want to review the material in the section "Costs in the Long Run," which begins on page 215.

Step 2: Draw long-run average cost graphs for Motorola and Siemens. The question does not provide us with the details of the quantity of each product each company is producing before the trade or their average costs of production. If economies of scale were an important reason for the trade, we can assume that Motorola and Siemens were not yet at minimum efficient scale in the wireless infrastructure and phone handset businesses. Therefore, we can draw the following graphs:

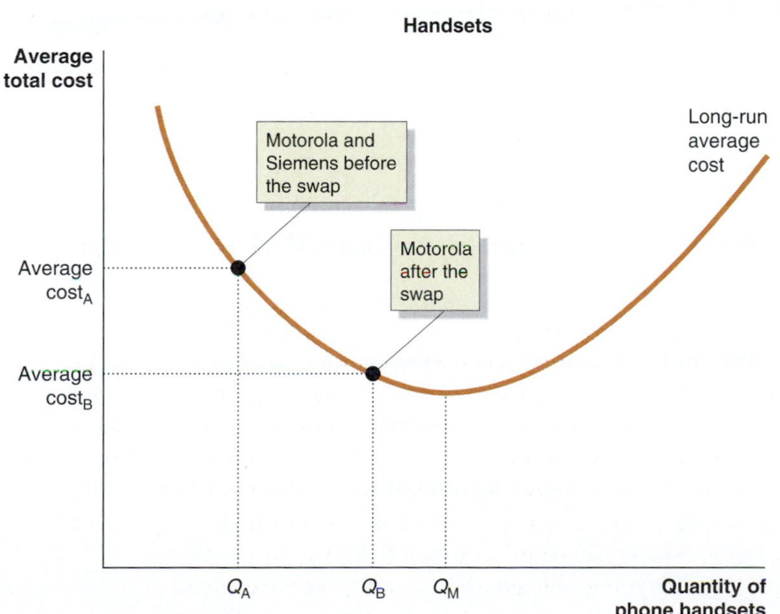

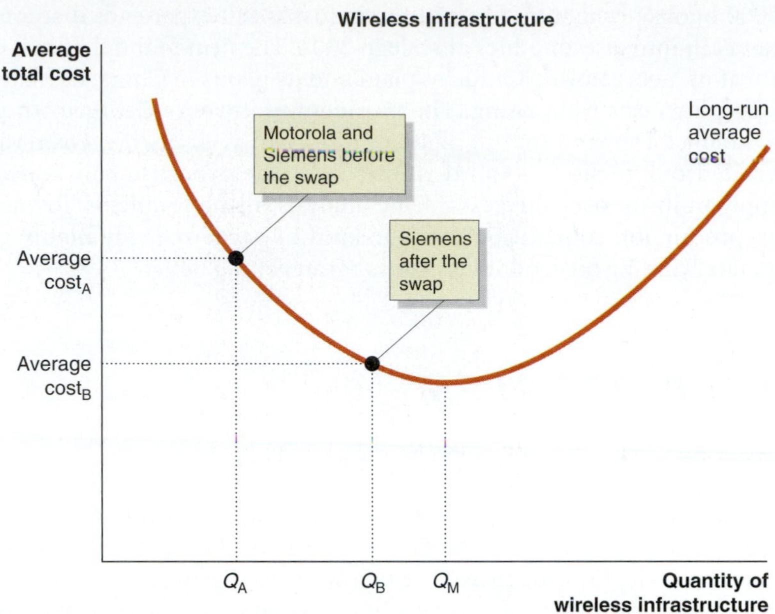

Step 3: Explain the curves in the graphs. Before the proposed trade, Motorola and Siemens are producing both products at less than the minimum efficient scale, which is Q_M in both graphs. After the trade, Motorola's production of handsets will increase, moving it from Q_A to Q_B in the first graph. This increase in production allows it to take advantage of economies of scale and reduce its average cost from Average Cost$_A$ to Average Cost$_B$. Similarly, production of wireless infrastructure by Siemens will increase from Q_A to Q_B, lowering its average cost from Average Cost$_A$ to Average Cost$_B$. As drawn, the graphs show that both firms will still be short of minimum efficient scale after the trade, although their average costs have fallen.

Extra Credit: These were new technologies at the time the trade was being discussed. As a result, companies making these products were only beginning to understand how large minimum efficient scale was. To survive in the industry, the managements of both companies wanted to lower their costs by taking advantage of economies of scale. As one industry analyst put it:

> Motorola and Siemens may be driven by the conviction that they have little choice. Most observers believe consolidation in both the [wireless] networking and handset areas is inevitable.

Source for quote: Ray Hegarty, "Rumored Motorola–Siemens Business Unit Swap? A Compelling M&A Story," www.thefeature.com.

***YOUR TURN:* For more practice, do related problems 14, 18, 19, 24, and 25 on pages 226, 227, and 228 at the end of this chapter.**

Over time, most firms in an industry will build factories or stores that are at least as large as the minimum efficient scale but not so large that diseconomies of scale occur. In the bookstore industry, stores will sell between 20,000 and 40,000 books per month. However, firms often do not know the exact shape of their long-run average cost curves. As a result, they may mistakenly build factories or stores that are either too large or too small.

The Colossal River Rouge: Diseconomies of Scale at the Ford Motor Company

7-4 Making the Connection

Is it possible for a factory to be too big?

When Henry Ford started the Ford Motor Company in 1903, automobile companies produced cars in small workshops using highly skilled workers. Ford introduced two new ideas that allowed him to take advantage of economies of scale. First, Ford used identical—or, interchangeable—parts so that unskilled workers could be used to assemble the cars. Second, instead of having groups of workers moving from one stationary automobile to the next, he had the workers remain stationary while the automobiles moved along an assembly line. Ford built a large factory at Highland Park, outside of Detroit, where he used these ideas to produce the famous Model T at an average cost well below what his competitors could match using older production methods in smaller factories.

Ford believed that he could produce automobiles at an even lower average cost by building a still larger plant along the River Rouge. Unfortunately, Ford's River Rouge plant was too large and suffered from diseconomies of scale. Ford's managers had great difficulty coordinating the production of automobiles in such a large plant. The following description of the River Rouge comes from the biography of Ford by Allan Nevins and Frank Ernest Hill:

> A total of 93 separate structures stood on the [River Rouge] site. . . . Railroad trackage covered 93 miles, conveyors 27 [miles]. About 75,000 men worked in the great plant. A force of 5000 did nothing but keep it clean, wearing out 5000 mops and 3000 brooms a month, and using 86 tons of soap on the floors, walls, and 330 acres of windows. The Rouge was an industrial city, immense, concentrated, packed with power. . . . By its very massiveness and complexity, it denied men at the top contact with and understanding of those beneath, and gave those beneath a sense of being lost in inexorable immensity and power.

Beginning in 1927, Ford produced the Model A—its only car model at that time—at the River Rouge plant. Ford failed to achieve economies of scale, and actually *lost money* on each of the four Model A body styles.

Ford could not raise the price of the Model A to make it profitable, because at a higher price the car could not compete with similar models produced by competitors such as General Motors and Chrysler. He eventually reduced the cost of making the Model A by constructing smaller factories spread out across the country. These smaller factories produced the Model A at a lower average cost than was possible at the River Rouge plant.

Sources: Quote from Allan Nevins and Frank Ernest Hill, *Ford: Expansion and Challenge, 1915–1933,* New York: Charles Scribner's Sons, 1957, pp. 293, 295.

Don't Let This Happen To You!

Don't Confuse Diminishing Returns with Diseconomies of Scale

The concepts of diminishing returns and diseconomies of scale may seem similar, but, in fact, they are unrelated. Diminishing returns applies only to the short run, when at least one of the firm's inputs, such as the quantity of machinery it uses, is fixed. The law of diminishing returns tells us that in the short run hiring more workers will, at some point, result in less additional output. Diminishing returns explains why marginal cost curves eventually slope upward. Diseconomies of scale apply only in the long run, when the firm is free to vary all its inputs, can adopt new technology, and can vary the amount of machinery it uses and the size of its facility. Diseconomies of scale explain why long-run average cost curves eventually slope upward.

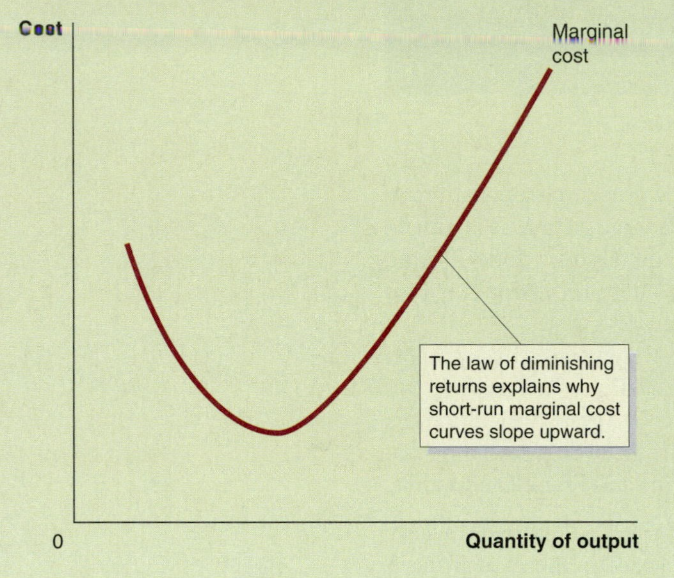

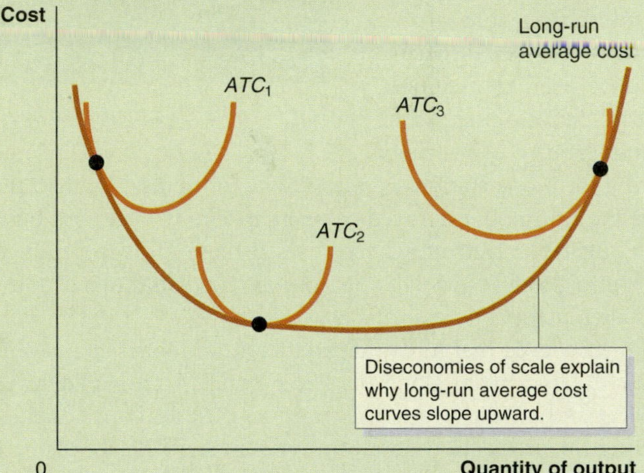

YOUR TURN: Test your understanding by doing related problem 21 on page 228 at the end of this chapter.

Conclusion

In this chapter, we discussed the relationship between a firm's technology, its production, and its costs. During the discussion, we encountered a number of definitions of costs. Because we will use these definitions in later chapters, it is useful to bring them together in Table 7-4 for you to review.

We have seen the important relationship between a firm's level of production and its costs. Just as this information was vital to Akio Morita in deciding which price to charge for his transistor radios, so it remains vital today to all firms as they attempt to decide the optimal level of production and the optimal prices to charge for their products. We will explore this point further in Chapter 8. Before moving on to that chapter, read *An Inside Look* on pages 222–223 to see how we can use long-run average cost curves to understand the motives behind the joint venture between Sony and Samsung.

TABLE 7-4

A Summary of Definitions of Cost

TERM	DEFINITION	SYMBOLS AND EQUATIONS
Total cost	Value of all the inputs used by a firm	TC
Fixed cost	Costs that remain constant when a firm's level of output changes	FC
Variable cost	Costs that change when the firm's level of output changes	VC
Marginal cost	Increase in total cost resulting from producing another unit of output	$MC = \frac{\Delta TC}{\Delta Q}$
Average total cost	Total cost divided by the quantity of units produced	$ATC = \frac{TC}{Q}$
Average fixed cost	Fixed cost divided by the quantity of units produced	$AFC = \frac{FC}{Q}$
Average variable cost	Variable cost divided by the quantity of units produced	$AVC = \frac{VC}{Q}$
Implicit cost	A nonmonetary opportunity cost	—
Explicit cost	A cost that involves spending money	—

An Inside Look

Using Long-Run Average Cost Curves to Analyze Expansion at Sony and Samsung

FINANCIAL TIMES, JULY 16, 2004

It's 'Win-Win' as Samsung, Sony Join on Flat Screens

It was a handshake that brought together the world's largest television-maker with the biggest producer of liquid crystal displays to create what they hope will be a new force in the flat-screen market. Nobuyuki Idei, chairman of Sony, and Yun Jong-yong, chief executive of Samsung Electronics, were marking the launch of S-LCD, the two companies' display-making joint-venture, at a sprawling new technology park in Asan, South Korea, yesterday. . . .

a By joining forces, Sony and Samsung have pitted themselves against LG Electronics of South Korea and Philips of the Netherlands. . . . Together with Sharp and a handful of Taiwanese manufacturers, S-LCD and LG Philips are investing billions of dollars in plants to make flat panel displays. The companies are anticipating years of rapid growth in the sector as households and offices replace bulky cathode ray tube TVs and computer monitors with slimmer LCD models. . . .

In addition to producing flat panel displays, Samsung, Sony, Sharp, LG and Philips are also among the world's biggest makers of TVs and monitors. That means they must seek a balance between keeping LCD prices high enough to make profits but low enough to attract consumers. Samsung and Sony are each investing [1,050 billion Korean won or $902 million] in S-LCD to build a so-called seventh-generation plant that will churn out 60,000 panels a month, starting in the first half of next year.

b The facility will produce bigger glass panels than the sixth-generation plants recently opened by Sharp and planned by LG Philips. This will allow S-LCD to make larger-sized TVs and cut more screens from each panel, reducing costs. By focusing on large-sized TVs, up to 46-inches in width, Samsung and Sony are aiming for potentially the most profitable part of the LCD market, in contrast to lower-margin small TVs and monitors.

Each company will be entitled to half the plant's output to feed their rival TV businesses and Samsung is building a second seventh-generation plant by itself. Keiji Nakazawa, the Sony-appointed chief finance officer of S-LCD, said the two companies would decide in the future whether to build more facilities together. . . .

The joint-venture with Samsung marks a first foray into LCD manufacturing for Sony. The Japanese company has fallen behind Sharp in the flat screen TV market and needed a reliable source of LCDs to catch up. In the first quarter of this year, Sharp made 26.5 per cent of global LCD TV sales, while Samsung and Sony each commanded 11.9 per cent, followed by Philips, LG and Toshiba.

Key Points in the Article

This article discusses the joint venture between Sony and Samsung to build a new plant to manufacture liquid crystal displays (LCDs) for flat-screen television sets. The joint venture will be known as "S-LCD." Sony, which manufacturers both television sets and computers that use LCDs, had previously purchased the LCDs it needed from other firms. Sony and Samsung expect output will expand as consumers and firms switch from televisions and computer monitors that use bulky cathode-ray tubes to thinner models that use LCDs. The plant will be a "seventh-generation" facility that will produce larger glass panels. Because it will be possible to cut more screens from each panel, costs will be lower than in existing plants.

Analyzing the News

a We can use the idea of long-run average cost from this chapter to analyze this article. We have seen that firms can use the concepts that underlie the long-run average cost curve to plan for future expansion. In this case, Sony and Samsung expect that they will be able to sell a larger output of flat-screen, LCD televisions and computer monitors as consumers and businesses switch away from bulky cathode-ray tube technology. In the new "seventh-generation" facility, the firms will be able to produce larger glass panels from which more television and computer screens can be cut. This change will reduce their average cost of production.

b Figure 1 shows the effects of the new technology used in the seventh-generation LCD plant. $LRAC_1$ is the long-run average cost curve for plants that use sixth-generation technology. ATC_1 is the optimal size plant using this technology. $LRAC_2$ is the long-run average cost curve for plants that use seventh-generation technology. ATC_2 is the optimal size plant using this technology. Notice that the average cost of producing LCDs is lower when the firm produces Q_3 in a seventh-generation plant (ATC_2) than when it produces Q_1 in a sixth-generation plant (ATC_1). Also notice, though, that if the demand for LCD panels results in output of less than Q_2 screens per month, a sixth-generation plant will actually allow production at lower average cost. Sony and Samsung expect that output will exceed Q_2, so they can lower their average cost of production by building a seventh-generation plant.

Thinking Critically

1. The figure below shows the *LRAC* curves for sixth- and seventh-generation factories. What is an eighth-generation factory's *LRAC* likely to look like? Explain.
2. The educational systems of South Korea and Japan are geared toward training in math, science, and engineering. For example, 5 percent of bachelor's degrees in the United States are in engineering, while this figure is 27 percent in South Korea and 19 percent in Japan. How are increases in these countries' engineering skills likely to affect the *LRAC* of producing LCD screens?

Source: Andrew Ward, "It's 'Win-Win' as Samsung, Sony Join on Flat Screens," *Financial Times*, July 16, 2004. Used with permission of Financial Times.

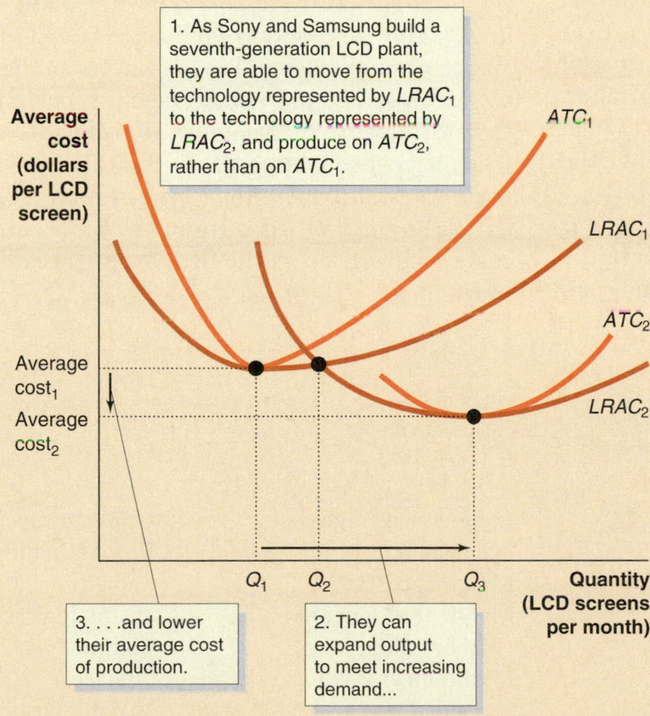

Figure 1: Seventh-generation LCD factories have lower average costs than sixth-generation factories.

SUMMARY

LEARNING OBJECTIVE 1 Define technology and give examples of technological change. The basic activity of a firm is to use inputs, such as workers, machines, and natural resources, to produce goods and services. The firm's *technology* is the processes it uses to turn inputs into goods and services.

LEARNING OBJECTIVE 2 Distinguish between the economic short run and the economic long run. In the *short run*, the firm's technology and the size of its factory, store, or office are fixed. In the *long run*, the firm is able to adopt new technology and to increase or decrease the size of its physical plant. The relationship between the inputs employed by the firm and the maximum output it can produce with those inputs is called the firm's *production function*.

LEARNING OBJECTIVE 3 Understand the relationship between the marginal product of labor and the average product of labor. The *marginal product of labor* is the additional output produced by a firm as a result of hiring one more worker. Specialization and division of labor cause the marginal product of labor to rise for the first few workers hired. Eventually, the *law of diminishing returns* causes the marginal product of labor to decline. The *average product of labor* is the total amount of output produced by a firm divided by the quantity of workers hired. When the marginal product of labor is greater than the average product of labor, the average product of labor increases. When the marginal product of labor is less than the average product of labor, the average product of labor decreases.

LEARNING OBJECTIVE 4 Explain and illustrate the relationship between marginal cost and average total cost. The *marginal cost* of production is the increase in total cost resulting from producing another unit of output. The marginal cost curve has a U-shape, because when the marginal product of labor is rising, the marginal cost of output will be falling. When the marginal product of labor is falling, the marginal cost of output will be rising. When marginal cost is less than average total cost, average total cost falls. When marginal cost is greater than average total cost, average total cost rises.

LEARNING OBJECTIVE 5 Graph average total cost, average variable cost, average fixed cost, and marginal cost. *Variable costs* are costs that change when the firm's level of output changes. *Fixed costs* are costs that remain constant when the firm's level of output changes. *Average total cost* is equal to total cost divided by the level of output. Average fixed cost is equal to fixed cost divided by the level of output. Average variable cost is equal to variable cost divided by the level of output. Figure 7-5 shows the relationship among marginal cost, average total cost, average variable cost, and average fixed cost. It is one of the most important graphs in microeconomics.

LEARNING OBJECTIVE 6 Understand how firms use the long-run average cost curve to plan. The *long-run average cost curve* shows the lowest cost at which a firm is able to produce a given level of output in the long run. For many firms, the long-run average cost curve falls as output expands because of *economies of scale*. After economies of scale have been exhausted, firms experience *constant returns to scale*, where their long-run average cost curve is flat. At high levels of output, the long-run average cost curve will turn up as the firm experiences *diseconomies of scale*.

KEY TERMS

Average fixed cost 214
Average product of labor 208
Average total cost 206
Average variable cost 214
Constant returns to scale 216
Diseconomies of scale 217
Economies of scale 215
Explicit cost 204
Fixed costs 203
Implicit cost 204
Law of diminishing returns 208
Long run 203
Long-run average cost curve 215
Marginal cost 211
Marginal product of labor 207
Minimum efficient scale 216
Opportunity cost 204
Production function 205
Short run 203
Technological change 202
Technology 202
Total cost 203
Variable costs 203

REVIEW QUESTIONS

1. What is the difference between technology and technological change? Is it possible for technological change to be negative? If so, give an example.
2. What is the difference between the short run and the long run? Is the amount of time that separates the short run from the long run the same for every firm?
3. What are implicit costs? How are they different from explicit costs?
4. Draw a graph showing the usual relationship between the marginal product of labor and the average product of labor. Why do the marginal product of labor and the average product of labor have the shapes you drew?
5. What is the law of diminishing returns? Does it apply in the long run?
6. Is a firm likely to stop hiring if the marginal product of the last worker hired is greater than the marginal product of the next-to-last worker hired? Explain.
7. Explain why the marginal cost curve intersects the average variable cost curve at the level of output where average variable cost is at a minimum.
8. What is the difference between total cost and variable cost in the long run?
9. What is minimum efficient scale? What is likely to happen in the long run to firms that do not reach minimum efficient scale?
10. What are economies of scale? What are diseconomies of scale? What is the main reason that firms eventually encounter diseconomies of scale as they keep increasing the size of their store or factory?

PROBLEMS AND APPLICATIONS

Please visit **www.prenhall.com/hubbard** *for solutions to the even-numbered problems as well as multiple-choice and true or false self-assessment quizzes.*

1. Which of the following are examples of a firm experiencing positive technological change?
   a. The firm is able to cut each worker's wage rate by 10 percent and still produce the same level of output.
   b. A training program makes the firm's workers more productive.
   c. An exercise program makes the firm's workers more healthy and productive.
   d. The firm cuts its workforce and is able to maintain its initial level of output.
   e. The firm rearranges the layout of its factory and finds that by using its initial set of inputs it can produce exactly as much as before.
2. Fill in the missing values in the following table:

QUANTITY OF WORKERS	TOTAL OUTPUT	MARGINAL PRODUCT OF LABOR	AVERAGE PRODUCT OF LABOR
0	0		
1	400		
2	900		
3	1,500		
4	1,900		
5	2,200		
6	2,400		
7	2,300		

3. Use the numbers from problem 2 to draw one graph showing how total output increases with the quantity of workers hired and a second graph showing the marginal product of labor and the average product of labor.
4. Suppose the total cost of producing 10,000 tennis balls is $30,000 and the fixed cost is $10,000.
   a. What is the variable cost?
   b. When output is 10,000, what are the average variable cost and the average fixed cost?
   c. Assuming that the cost curves have the usual shape, is the dollar difference between the average total cost and the average variable cost greater when the output is 10,000 tennis balls or when the output is 30,000 tennis balls? Explain.
5. A student looks at the data in Table 7-3 and draws this conclusion: "The marginal product of labor is increasing for the first 3 workers hired, then it declines for the next 3 workers. I guess each of the first 3 workers must have been hard workers. Then Jill must have had to settle for increasingly poor workers." Do you agree with the student's analysis? Briefly explain.
6. Sally looks at her college transcript and says to Sam, "How is this possible? My grade point average for this semester's courses is higher than my grade point average for last semester's courses, but my cumulative grade point average still went down from last semester to this semester." Explain to Sally how this is possible.

7. Is it possible for a firm to experience a technological change that would increase the marginal product of labor while leaving the average product of labor unchanged? Explain.
8. Jill Johnson operates her copy business in a building she owns in the center of the city. Similar buildings in the neighborhood rent for $4,000 per month. Jill is considering selling her building and renting space in the suburbs for $3,000 per month. Jill decides not to make the move. She reasons, "I would like to have a store in the suburbs, but I pay no rent for my store now and I don't want to see my costs rise by $3,000 per month." What do you think of Jill's reasoning?
9. When the DuPont chemical company first attempted to enter the paint business, it was not successful. According to a company report, in one year it "lost nearly $500,000 in actual cash in addition to an expected return on investment of nearly $500,000, which made a total loss of income to the company of nearly a million." Why did this report include as part of the company's loss the amount it had expected to earn—but didn't—on its investment in manufacturing paint?
   Source: Alfred D. Chandler Jr., Thomas K. McCraw, and Richard Tedlow, *Management Past and Present,* Cincinnati: South-Western, 2000, pp. 3–92.
10. An account of Benjamin Franklin's life notes that he started his career as a printer and publisher of the newspaper the *Pennsylvania Gazette.* He also opened a store where he sold stationery, books, and food. According to this account, "He could without expense apprise the public of items on hand by advertisements in his *Gazette.*" Is the author correct that Franklin did not incur a cost when he used space in his newspaper to run advertisements for his store? Briefly explain.
    Source: Richard Tedlow, "Benjamin Franklin and the Definition of American Values," in Alfred D. Chandler Jr., Thomas K. McCaw, and Richard S. Tedlow, *Management Past and Present: A Casebook on the History of American Business,* Cincinnati: South-Western College Publishing, 2000.
11. **[Related to *Solved Problem 7-1*]** Is Jill Johnson right or wrong when she says the following: "Currently, I am producing 20,000 copies per day at a total cost of $750.00. If I produce 20,001 copies my total cost will rise to $750.02, therefore my marginal cost of producing copies must be increasing." Illustrate your answer with a graph.
12. One description of the costs of operating a railroad makes the following observation: "The fixed . . . expenses which attach to the operation of railroads . . . are in the nature of a tax upon the business of the road; the smaller the [amount of] business, the larger the tax." Briefly explain why fixed costs are like a tax. In what sense is this tax smaller when the amount of business is larger?
    Source: Quoted in Alfred D. Chandler, Jr., Thomas K. McCraw, and Richard Tedlow, *Management Past and Present,* Cincinnati: South-Western, 2000, pp. 2–27.
13. In the ancient world, a book could be produced either on a scroll or as a codex, which was made of folded sheets glued together, something like a modern book. One scholar has estimated the following variable costs (in Greek drachmas) of the two methods:

	SCROLL	CODEX
Cost of writing (wage of a scribe)	11.33 drachmas	11.33 drachmas
Cost of paper	16.50 drachmas	9.25 drachmas

Another scholar points out that a significant fixed cost was involved in producing a codex:

> In order to copy a codex . . . the amount of text and the layout of each page had to be carefully calculated in advance to determine the exact number of sheets . . . needed. No doubt, this is more time-consuming and calls for more experimentation than the production of a scroll would. But for the next copy these calculations would be used again.

   a. Suppose that the fixed cost of preparing a codex was 58 drachmas and that there was no similar fixed cost for a scroll. Would an ancient book publisher who intended to sell 5 copies of a book be likely to publish it as a scroll or as a codex? What if he intended to sell 10 copies? Briefly explain.
   b. Although most books were published as scrolls in the first century A.D., by the third century most were published as codices. Considering only the factors mentioned in this problem, explain why this changeover may have taken place.

   Sources: T. C. Skeat, "The Length of the Standard Papyrus Roll and the Cost-Advantage of the Codex," *Zeitschrift fur Papyrologie and Epigraphik,* 1982, p. 175; and David Trobisch, *The First Edition of the New Testament,* New York: Oxford University Press, 2000, p. 73.
14. **[Related to *Solved Problem 7-2*]** Suppose that Jill Johnson has to choose between building a smaller store or a larger store. In the following graph, the relationship between costs and output for the smaller store is represented by the curve ATC_1 and the relationship between costs and output for the larger store is represented by the curve ATC_2.

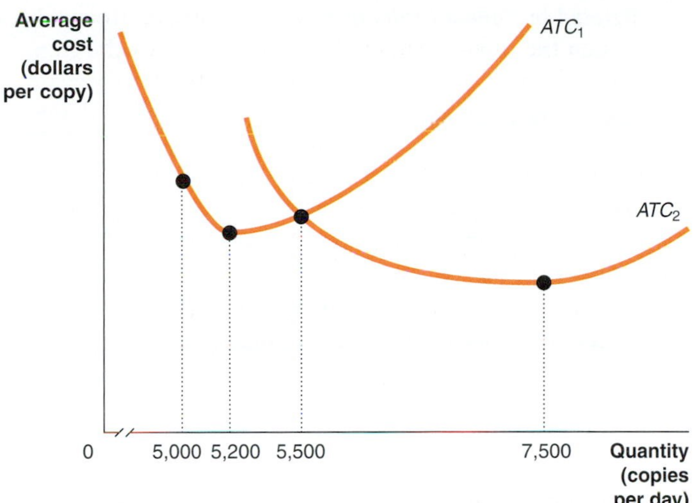

a. If Jill expects to produce 5,100 copies per day, should she build a smaller store or a larger store? Briefly explain.
b. If Jill expects to produce 6,000 copies per day, should she build a smaller store or a larger store? Briefly explain.
c. A student asks, "If the average cost of producing copies is lower in the larger store when Jill produces 7,500 copies per day, why isn't it also lower when Jill produces 5,200 copies per day?" Give a brief answer to the student's question.

15. **[Related to *Solved Problem 7-1*]** Use the information in the following graph to find the values for the following at an output level of 1,000:
    a. Marginal cost
    b. Total cost
    c. Variable cost
    d. Fixed cost

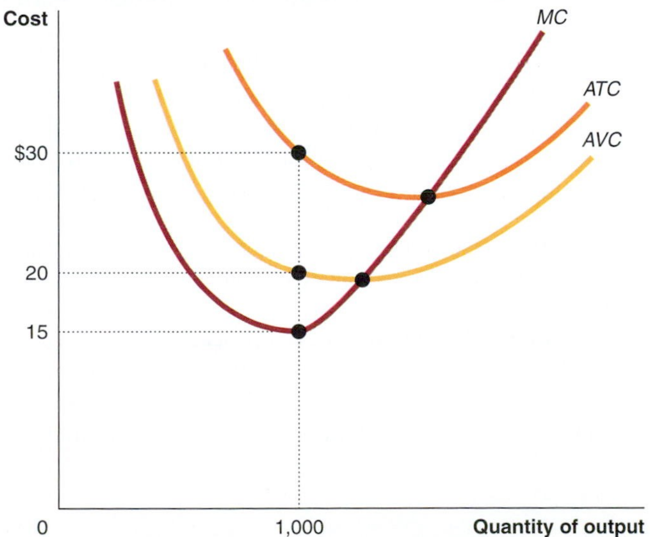

16. List the errors in the following graph. Carefully explain why the curves drawn this way are wrong. In other words, why can't these curves be as they are shown in the graph?

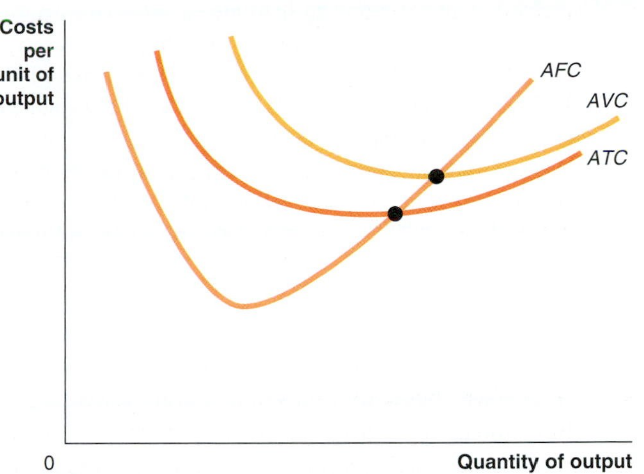

17. **[Related to *Solved Problem 7-1*]** Explain how the listed events (a–d) would affect the following at the Ford Motor Company:
    i. marginal cost
    ii. average variable cost
    iii. average fixed cost
    iv. average total cost
    a. Ford signs a new contract with the United Automobile Workers Union that requires the company to pay higher wages.
    b. The federal government starts to levy a $1,500 per vehicle tax on sport utility vehicles.
    c. The company decides to give its senior executives a one-time $100,000 bonus.
    d. Ford decides to increase the amount it spends on designing new car models.
18. **[Related to *Solved Problem 7-2*]** Suppose that Henry Ford had continued to experience increasing returns to scale no matter how large an automobile factory he built. Discuss what the implications of this would have been for the automobile industry.
19. **[Related to *Solved Problem 7-2*]** Read the following description of U.S. manufacturing in the late nineteenth century:

    > [W]hen . . . Standard Oil . . . reorganized its refinery capacity in 1883 and concentrated almost two-fifths of the nation's refinery production in three huge refineries, the unit cost dropped from 1.5 cents a gallon to 0.5 cents. A comparable concentration of two-fifths of the nation's output of textiles or shoes in three plants would have been impossible, and in any

case would have brought huge diseconomies of scale and consequently higher prices.

a. Use this information to draw a long-run average cost curve for an oil-refining firm and a long-run average cost curve for a firm manufacturing shoes.
b. Is it likely that there were more oil refineries in the United States in the late nineteenth century or more shoe factories? Briefly explain.
c. Why would concentrating two-fifths of total shoe output in three factories have led to higher shoe prices?

Source: Alfred D. Chandler Jr., Thomas K. McCraw, and Richard Tedlow, *Management Past and Present,* Cincinnati: South-Western, 2000, pp. 4–53.

20. One scholar has made the following comment on the publishing industry:

> If publishers were able to determine exactly what sells a book, they all would feature fewer titles and produce them in larger numbers.

What must be true about the costs of publishing books for this statement to be correct? Briefly explain.

Source: David Trobisch, *The First Edition of the New Testament,* New York: Oxford University Press, 2000, p. 75.

21. **[Related to *Don't Let This Happen To You!*]** Explain whether you agree or disagree with the following statement: "Henry Ford expected to be able to produce cars at a lower average cost at his River Rouge plant. Unfortunately, because of diminishing returns, his costs were actually higher."

22. **[Related to the *Chapter Opener*]** Review the discussion at the beginning of the chapter of Akio Morita selling transistor radios in the United States. Suppose that Morita became convinced that Sony would be able to sell more than 75,000 transistor radios each year in the United States. What steps would he have taken?

23. TIAA-CREF is a retirement system for people who work at colleges and universities. For some years, TIAA-CREF also sold long-term care insurance before deciding to sell that business to MetLife, a large insurance company. TIAA-CREF's chairman and chief executive officer explained the decision this way (a "premium" is the price a buyer has to pay for an insurance policy):

> In recent years, the long-term care insurance market has experienced significant consolidation. A few large insurance companies now own most of the business. MetLife has 428,000 policies, for example—nearly 10 times the number we have—and can achieve economies of scale that we can't. Over time, we would have had difficulty holding down premium rates.

Briefly explain what economies of scale have to do with the premiums that insurance companies can charge for their policies.

Source: "Long-Term Care Sale in Best Interest of Policyholders," *Advance,* Spring 2004, p. 6.

24. **[Related to *Solved Problem 7-2*]** The company eToys sold toys on the Internet. In 1999, the total value of the company was about $7.7 billion, but by early 2001 the company was in deep financial trouble and it eventually closed. One of the company's key mistakes was the decision in 2000 to build a large distribution center from which it would ship toys throughout the United States. The following description of this decision appeared in an article in the *Wall Street Journal:*

> [eToys built] a giant automated distribution center in Virginia. . . . Although many analysts agreed that the costly move was a sound decision for the long run . . . [the] decision meant eToys needed to generate much higher sales to justify its costs. . . . Despite a spiffy TV ad campaign and an expanded line of goods, there weren't enough customers.

What does the author mean that eToys "needed to generate much higher sales to justify its costs"? Use a graph like Figure 7-6 to illustrate your answer.

Source: Lisa Bannon, "The eToys Saga: Costs Kept Rising but Sales Slowed," *Wall Street Journal,* January 22, 2001.

25. **[Related to *Solved Problem 7-2*]** In 2003, Time Warner and the Walt Disney Company discussed merging their news operations. Time Warner owns the Cable News Network (CNN) and Disney owns ABC News. After analyzing the situation, the companies decided that a combined news operation would have higher average costs than either CNN or ABC News had separately. Use a long-run average cost curve graph to illustrate why the companies did not merge their news operations.

Source: Martin Peers and Joe Flint, "AOL Calls Off CNN–ABC Deal, Seeing Operating Difficulties," *Wall Street Journal,* February 14, 2003.

26. According to one account of the problems DuPont had in entering the paint business, "the du Ponts had assumed that large volume would bring profits through lowering unit costs." In fact, according to one company report, "The more paint and varnish we sold, the more money we lost." Draw an average cost curve graph showing the relationship between paint output and average cost as DuPont expected it to be. Draw another graph that would explain the result that the more paint the company sold, the more money it lost.

Source: Alfred D. Chandler Jr., Thomas K. McCraw, and Richard Tedlow, *Management Past and Present,* Cincinnati: South-Western, 2000, pp. 3–88.

27. According to a study of chicken processing plants by the U.S. Department of Agriculture, the largest plants have average costs that are 20 percent lower than the smallest plants. The report concludes, "These cost differentials are

consistent with the near-disappearance of small plants." Briefly explain the reasoning behind this conclusion.

Source: Michael Ollinger, James MacDonald, and Milton Madison, "Structural Change in U.S. Chicken and Turkey Slaughter," Economic Research Service, U.S. Department of Agriculture, Agricultural Economic Report No. 787.

28. Michael Korda was for many years editor-in-chief at the Simon & Schuster book publishing company. He has described how during the 1980s many publishing companies merged together to form larger firms. He claims that publishers hoped to take advantage of economies of scale. But, he concludes, "sheer size did not make publishing necessarily more profitable, and most of these big publishing monoliths would continue to disappoint their corporate owners in terms of earnings." On the basis of this information, draw a long-run average cost curve for a publishing firm reflecting the economies of scale that were expected to result from the mergers. Draw another long-run average cost curve reflecting the actual results experienced by the new larger publishing firms.

Source: Michael Korda, *Making the List: A Cultural History of the American Bestseller, 1900–1999,* New York: Barnes & Noble Books, 2001, p. 166.

29. **[Related to *Solved Problem 7-1*]** The following problem is somewhat more advanced. Using symbols, we can write that the marginal product of labor is equal to $\Delta Q/\Delta L$. Marginal cost is equal to $\Delta TC/\Delta Q$. Because fixed costs by definition don't change, marginal cost is also equal to $\Delta VC/\Delta Q$. If Jill Johnson's only variable cost is labor cost, then her variable cost is just the wage times the quantity of workers hired, or wL.

a. If the wage Jill pays is constant, then what is ΔVC in terms of w and L?

b. Use your answer to question a. and the expressions given above for the marginal product of labor and the marginal cost of output to find an expression for marginal cost, $\Delta TC/\Delta Q$, in terms of the wage, w, and the marginal product of labor, $\Delta Q/\Delta L$.

c. Use your answer to question b to determine Jill's marginal cost of producing copies if the wage is $75 per day and the marginal product of labor is 15. If the wage falls to $60 per day, while the marginal product of labor is unchanged, what happens to Jill's marginal cost? If the wage is unchanged at $75 per day and the marginal product rises to 25, what happens to Jill's marginal cost?

chapter eight 8

Firms in Perfectly Competitive Markets

Perfect Competition in the Market for Organic Apples

The market for organically grown food has expanded rapidly in the United States. As recently as 15 years ago, organic food was sold primarily in small health food stores. Today, organic food makes up an increasing fraction of all the food sold in supermarkets. By 2001, more than two-thirds of U.S. consumers were buying at least some organic food, and 12 percent of consumers were buying organic food almost exclusively. In 2002, the U.S. Department of Agriculture (USDA) established standards for organic food labeling. The standards were intended to protect consumers from false and misleading claims and to make it easier for U.S. farmers to export to foreign countries whose governments also require organic food labeling. According to the USDA, a firm can label and advertise food as "organic" only if that food is "produced without using most conventional pesticides; fertilizers made with synthetic ingredients or sewage sludge; bioengineering; or ionizing radiation." The USDA inspects the farm where the food is grown and all firms that handle the food before it arrives at the supermarket or restaurant.

More organic fresh fruits and vegetables are sold than any other food category. Organically grown apples became popular with consumers during the late 1990s. Farmers growing apples organically use only organic fertilizers and control insects with sprays made from soil compounds. These growing methods add about 15 percent to the cost of growing apples. The Yakima Valley of Washington State is particularly suited to growing apples organically because of the absence of certain insects. In 2004, Washington State accounted for more than half of U.S. organic apple production. In 1997, Yakima Valley apple farmers were able to sell organically grown apples for a price 50 percent higher than the price of regular apples, more than offsetting the higher costs of organic growing methods. This price difference made organically grown apples considerably more profitable than apples grown using traditional methods.

Between 1997 and 2001, many apple farmers switched from tradi-

tional to organic growing methods, increasing production of organically grown apples from 1.2 million boxes per year to more than 3 million boxes. The additional supply of organically grown apples forced down prices and made them no more profitable than apples grown using traditional methods. As one farmer in the Yakima Valley put it, "It's like anything else in agriculture. If people see an economic opportunity, usually it only lasts for a few years."

What the organic apple farmer experienced is not unique to agriculture. Throughout the economy, entrepreneurs are continually introducing new products, which—when successful—enable them to earn economic profits in the short run. But in the long run, competition among firms forces prices to the level where they just cover the costs of production. This process of competition is at the heart of the market system and is the focus of this chapter. *An Inside Look* on page 256 discusses how the increasing demand for organic food has affected the sales of organic snacks.

Sources: USDA Web site: www.ams.usda.gov/nop/Consumers/brochure.html, "Organic Food Industry Taps Growing American Market," *Agricultural Outlook*, October 2002; Emily Green, "Study Gives Nod to Organic Apples, but It's Crunch Time for All State Growers," *Seattle Times*, April 19, 2001; quote from farmer from the NPR Web site: www.npr.org, National Public Radio, *All Things Considered*, April 18, 2001.

LEARNING OBJECTIVES

After studying this chapter, you should be able to:

1. Define a perfectly competitive market, and explain why a perfect competitor faces a horizontal demand curve.
2. Explain how a perfect competitor decides how much to produce.
3. Use graphs to show a firm's profit or loss.
4. Explain why firms may shut down temporarily.
5. Explain how entry and exit ensure that perfectly competitive firms earn zero economic profit in the long run.
6. Explain how perfect competition leads to economic efficiency.

- Organic apple growing is an example of a *perfectly competitive* industry. Firms in perfectly competitive industries are unable to control the prices of the products they sell and are unable to earn an economic profit in the long run. There are two main reasons for this result: (1) Firms in these industries sell identical products; and (2) It is easy for new firms to enter these industries. Studying how perfectly competitive industries operate is the best way to understand how markets answer the fundamental economic questions we discussed in Chapter 1:
- What goods and services will be produced?
- How will the goods and services be produced?
- Who will receive the goods and services produced?

In fact, though, most industries are not perfectly competitive. In most industries, firms do *not* produce identical products, and in some industries it may be difficult for new firms to enter. There are thousands of industries in the United States. Although in some ways each industry is unique, industries share enough similarities that economists group them into four market structures. In particular, any industry has three key characteristics:

- The number of firms in the industry
- The similarity of the good or service produced by the firms in the industry
- The ease with which new firms can enter the industry

Economists use these characteristics to classify industries into the four market structures listed in Table 8-1.

Many industries, including restaurants, hardware stores, and other retailers, have many firms selling products that are differentiated, rather than identical, and fall into the category of *monopolistic competition.* Some industries, such as computers and automobiles, have only a few firms and are *oligopolies.* Finally, a few industries, such as the delivery of first-class mail by the U.S. Postal Service, have only one firm and are *monopolies.* After discussing perfect competition in this chapter, we will devote a chapter to each of these other market structures.

TABLE 8-1 The Four Market Structures

	MARKET STRUCTURE			
CHARACTERISTIC	**PERFECT COMPETITION**	**MONOPOLISTIC COMPETITION**	**OLIGOPOLY**	**MONOPOLY**
Number of firms	Many	Many	Few	One
Type of product	Identical	Differentiated	Identical or differentiated	Unique
Ease of entry	High	High	Low	Entry blocked
Examples of industries	• Wheat • Apples	• Selling DVDs • Restaurants	• Manufacturing computers • Manufacturing automobiles	• First-class mail delivery • Tap water

Perfectly Competitive Markets

① LEARNING OBJECTIVE

Define a perfectly competitive market, and explain why a perfect competitor faces a horizontal demand curve.

Why are firms in a **perfectly competitive market** unable to control the prices of the goods they sell, and why are the owners of these firms unable to earn economic profits in the long run? We can begin our analysis by listing the three conditions that make a market perfectly competitive:

1. There must be many buyers and many firms, all of whom are small relative to the market.
2. The products sold by all firms in the market must be identical.
3. There must be no barriers to new firms entering the market.

Perfectly competitive market A market that meets the conditions of (1) many buyers and sellers, (2) all firms selling identical products, and (3) no barriers to new firms entering the market.

All three of these conditions hold in the market for organic apples. No single consumer or producer of organic apples buys or sells more than a tiny fraction of the total apple crop. The apples sold by each apple grower are identical, and there are no barriers to a new firm entering the organic apple market by purchasing land and planting apple trees. As we will see, it is the existence of many firms, all selling the same good, that keeps any single organic apple farmer from affecting the price of organic apples.

Although the market for organic apples meets the conditions for perfect competition, the markets for most goods and services do not. In particular, the second and third conditions are very restrictive. In most markets that have many buyers and sellers, firms do not sell identical products. For example, not all restaurant meals are the same, nor is all women's clothing the same. In Chapter 10, we will explore the common situation of monopolistic competition where many firms are selling similar but not identical products. In this chapter, we concentrate on perfectly competitive markets so we can use as a benchmark the situation in which firms are facing the maximum possible competition.

A Perfectly Competitive Firm Cannot Affect the Market Price

Prices in perfectly competitive markets are determined by the interaction of demand and supply. The actions of any single consumer or any single firm have no effect on the market price. Consumers and firms have to accept the market price if they want to buy and sell in a perfectly competitive market.

Because a firm in a perfectly competitive market is very small relative to the market and because it is selling exactly the same product as every other firm, it can sell as much as it wants without having to lower its price. But if a perfectly competitive firm tries to raise its price, it won't sell anything at all, because consumers will switch to buying from the firm's competitors. Therefore, the firm will be a **price taker,** and will have to charge the same price as every other firm in the market. Although we don't usually think of firms as being too small to affect the market price, consumers are often in the position of being price takers. For instance, suppose your local supermarket is selling bread for $1.50 per loaf. You can load up your shopping cart with 10 loaves of bread and the supermarket will gladly sell them all to you for $1.50 per loaf. But if you go to the cashier and offer to buy the bread for $1.49 per loaf, he or she will not sell it to you. As a buyer, you are too small relative to the bread market to have any effect on the equilibrium price. Whether you leave the supermarket and buy no bread or you buy 10 loaves, you are unable to change the market price of bread by even one cent.

Price taker A buyer or seller that is unable to affect the market price.

The situation you face as a bread buyer is the same one a wheat farmer faces as a wheat seller. More than 225,000 farmers grow wheat in the United States. The market price of wheat is determined not by any individual wheat farmer but by the interaction in the wheat market of all the buyers and all the sellers. If any one wheat farmer has the best crop the farmer has ever had, or if any one wheat farmer stops growing wheat altogether, the market price of wheat will not be affected *because the market supply curve for wheat will not shift by enough to change the equilibrium price by even one cent.*

FIGURE 8-1

A Perfectly Competitive Firm Faces a Horizontal Demand Curve

A firm in a perfectly competitive market is selling exactly the same product as many other firms. Therefore, it can sell as much as it wants at the current market price, but it cannot sell anything at all if it raises the price by even one cent. As a result, the demand curve for a perfectly competitive firm's output is a horizontal line. In the figure, whether the wheat farmer sells 3,000 bushels per year or 7,500 bushels has no effect on the market price of $4.

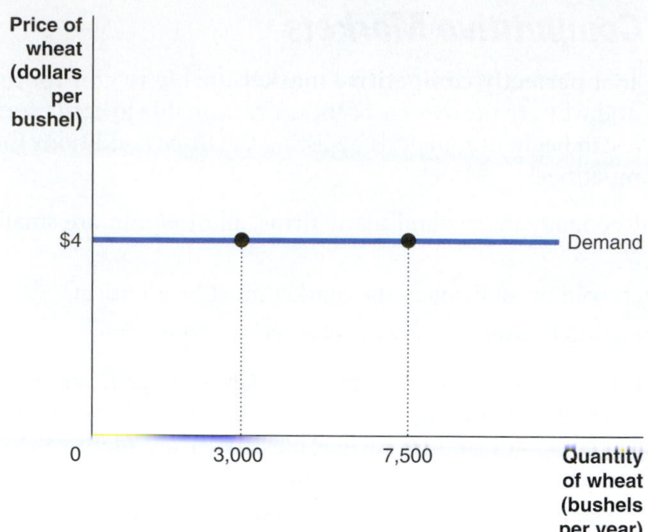

The Demand Curve for the Output of a Perfectly Competitive Firm

Suppose Robert Whaples grows wheat on a 250-acre farm in Washington State. Farmer Whaples is selling wheat in a perfectly competitive market, so he is a price taker. Because he can sell as much wheat as he chooses at the market price—but can't sell any wheat at all at a higher price—the demand curve for his wheat has an unusual shape: It is horizontal, as shown in Figure 8-1. With a horizontal demand curve, Farmer Whaples must accept the market price, which in this case is $4. Whether Farmer Whaples sells 3,000 bushels per year or 7,500 has no effect on the market price.

The demand curve for Farmer Whaples's wheat is very different from the market demand curve for wheat. Panel (a) of Figure 8-2 shows the market for wheat. The demand curve in panel (a) is the *market demand curve for wheat* and has the normal downward slope we are familiar with from the market demand curves in Chapter 3. Panel (b) of Figure 8-2 shows the demand curve for Farmer Whaples's wheat, which is a horizontal line. By viewing these graphs side by side, you can see that the price Farmer Whaples receives for his wheat in panel (b) is determined by the interaction of all sellers and all buyers of wheat in the wheat market in panel (a). Keep in mind, however, that the scales on the horizontal axes in the two panels are very different. In panel (a), the equilibrium quantity of wheat is 2 *billion* bushels. In panel (b), Farmer Whaples is producing only 7,500 bushels, or less than 0.0004 percent of market output. We need to use different scales in the two panels so we can display both of them on one page. Keep in mind the key point: Farmer Whaples's output of wheat is very small relative to the total market output.

② **LEARNING OBJECTIVE**

Explain how a perfect competitor decides how much to produce.

How a Firm Maximizes Profit in a Perfectly Competitive Market

We have seen that Farmer Whaples cannot control the price of his wheat. In this situation, how does he decide how much wheat to produce? We assume that Farmer Whaples's objective is to maximize profits. This is a reasonable assumption for most firms, most of the time. Remember that **profit** is the difference between total revenue (TR) and total cost (TC):

Profit Total revenue minus total cost.

$$\text{Profit} = TR - TC.$$

To maximize his profit, Farmer Whaples should produce the quantity of wheat where the difference between the total revenue he receives and his total cost is as large as possible.

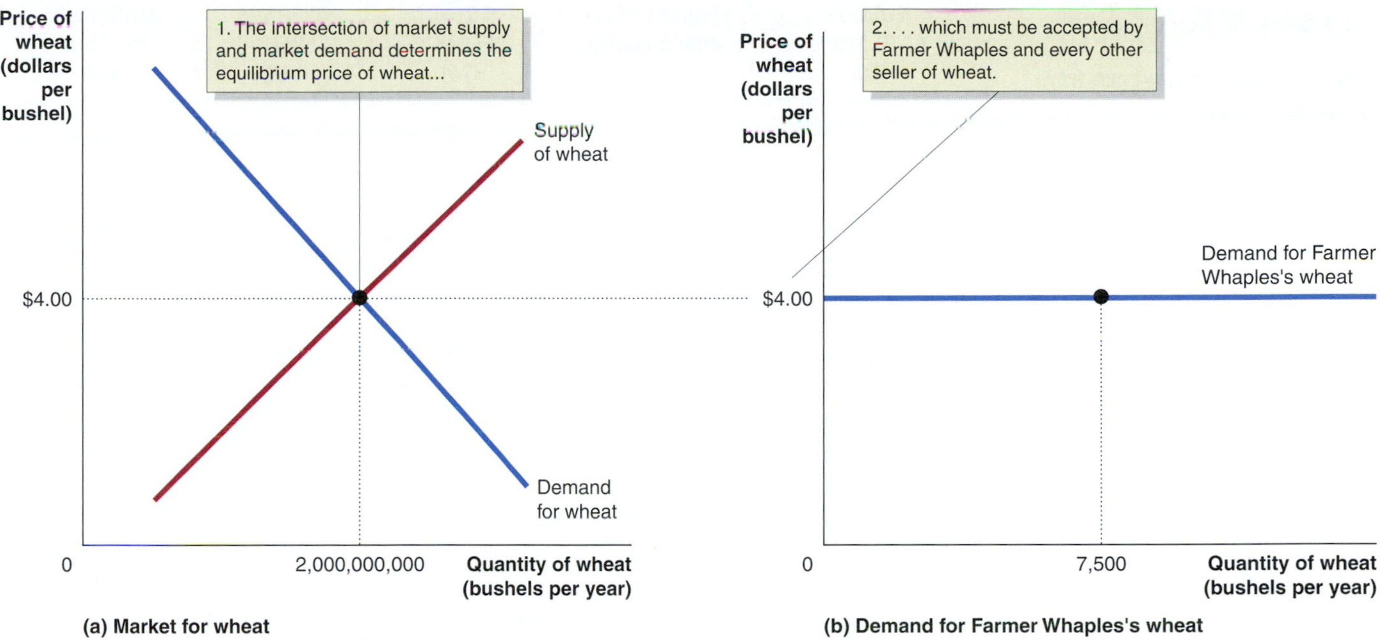

FIGURE 8-2 The Market Demand for Wheat versus the Demand for One Farmer's Wheat

In a perfectly competitive market, price is determined by the intersection of market demand and market supply. In panel (a), the demand and supply curves for wheat intersect at a price of $4 per bushel. An individual wheat farmer like Farmer Whaples has no ability to affect the market price for wheat. Therefore, as panel (b) shows, the demand curve for Farmer Whaples's wheat is a horizontal line. To understand this figure, it is important to notice that the scales on the horizontal axes in the two panels are very different. In panel (a), the equilibrium quantity of wheat is 2 *billion* bushels and in panel (b) Farmer Whaples is producing only 7,500 bushels of wheat.

Revenue for a Firm in a Perfectly Competitive Market

To understand how Farmer Whaples maximizes profits, let's first consider his revenue. To keep the numbers simple, we will assume that he owns a very small farm and produces at most 10 bushels of wheat per year. Table 8-2 shows the revenue Farmer Whaples will earn from selling various quantities of wheat if the market price for wheat is $4.

Don't Let This Happen To You!

Don't Confuse the Demand Curve for Farmer Whaples's Wheat with the Market Demand Curve for Wheat

The demand curve for wheat has the normal downward-sloping shape. If the price of wheat goes up, the quantity of wheat demanded goes down, and if the price of wheat goes down, the quantity of wheat demanded goes up. But the demand curve for the output of a single wheat farmer is *not* downward-sloping: It is a horizontal line. If an individual wheat farmer tries to increase the price he charges for his wheat, the quantity demanded falls to zero because buyers will purchase from one of the other 225,000 wheat farmers. But any one farmer can sell as much wheat as the farmer can produce without needing to cut the price. Both of these things are true because each wheat farmer is very small relative to the overall market for wheat.

When we draw graphs of the wheat market, we usually show the market equilibrium quantity in millions or billions of bushels. When we draw graphs of the demand for wheat produced by one farmer, we usually show the quantity produced in thousands of bushels. It is important to remember this difference in scale when interpreting these graphs.

Finally, it is not just wheat farmers who have horizontal demand curves for their products; any firm in a perfectly competitive market faces a horizontal demand curve.

***YOUR TURN:* Test your understanding by doing related problem 2 on page 259 at the end of this chapter.**

TABLE 8-2

Farmer Whaples's Revenue from Wheat Farming

NUMBER OF BUSHELS (*Q*)	MARKET PRICE (PER BUSHEL) (*P*)	TOTAL REVENUE (*TR*)	AVERAGE REVENUE (*AR*)	MARGINAL REVENUE (*MR*)
0	$4	$0	—	—
1	4	4	$4	$4
2	4	8	4	4
3	4	12	4	4
4	4	16	4	4
5	4	20	4	4
6	4	24	4	4
7	4	28	4	4
8	4	32	4	4
9	4	36	4	4
10	4	40	4	4

The third column in Table 8-2 shows that Farmer Whaples's *total revenue* rises by $4 for every additional bushel he sells because he can sell as many bushels as he wants at the market price of $4 per bushel. The fourth and fifth columns in the table show Farmer Whaples's *average revenue* and *marginal revenue* from selling wheat. His **average revenue (*AR*)** is his total revenue divided by the number of bushels he sells. For example, if he sells 5 bushels for a total of $20, his average revenue is $20/5 = $4. Notice that his average revenue is also equal to the market price of $4. In fact, for any level of output, a firm's average revenue is always equal to the market price. One way to see this is to note that total revenue equals price times quantity ($TR = P \times Q$), and average revenue equals total revenue divided by quantity ($AR = TR/Q$). So, $AR = TR/Q = (P \times Q)/Q = P$.

Average revenue (*AR*) Total revenue divided by the number of units sold.

Farmer Whaples's **marginal revenue (*MR*)** is the change in his total revenue from selling one more bushel:

Marginal revenue (*MR*) Change in total revenue from selling one more unit.

$$\text{Marginal Revenue} = \frac{\text{Change in total revenue}}{\text{Change in quantity}}, \text{ or } MR = \frac{\Delta TR}{\Delta Q}.$$

Because for each additional bushel sold he always adds $4 to his total revenue, his marginal revenue is $4. This outcome occurs because Farmer Whaples is selling wheat in a perfectly competitive market and can sell as much as he wants at the market price. In fact, Farmer Whaples's marginal revenue and average revenue are both equal to the market price. This is an important point: *For a firm in a perfectly competitive market, price is equal to both average revenue and marginal revenue.*

Determining the Profit-Maximizing Level of Output

To determine how Farmer Whaples can maximize profit, we have to consider his costs as well as his revenue. A wheat farmer will have many costs, including seed, fertilizer, and the wages of farm workers. In Table 8-3, we bring together the revenue data from Table 8-1 with cost data for Farmer Whaples's farm. Recall from Chapter 7 that a firm's *marginal cost* is the increase in total cost resulting from producing another unit of output.

Profit is shown in the fourth column and is calculated by subtracting total cost in the third column from total revenue in the second column. The fourth column shows that as long as Farmer Whaples produces between 2 and 9 bushels of wheat, he will earn a profit. His maximum profit is $9.00, which he will earn by producing 6 bushels of wheat. Producing more than 6 bushels reduces his profit. For example, if he produces

TABLE 8-3

Farmer Whaples's Profits from Wheat Farming

QUANTITY (BUSHELS) (*Q*)	TOTAL REVENUE (*TR*)	TOTAL COST (*TC*)	PROFIT (*TR* – *TC*)	MARGINAL REVENUE (*MR*)	MARGINAL COST (*MC*)
0	$0.00	$1.00	–$1.00	—	—
1	4.00	4.00	0.00	$4.00	$3.00
2	8.00	6.00	2.00	4.00	2.00
3	12.00	7.50	4.50	4.00	1.50
4	16.00	9.50	6.50	4.00	2.00
5	20.00	12.00	8.00	4.00	2.50
6	24.00	15.00	9.00	4.00	3.00
7	28.00	19.50	8.50	4.00	4.50
8	32.00	25.50	6.50	4.00	6.00
9	36.00	32.50	3.50	4.00	7.00
10	40.00	40.50	–0.50	4.00	8.00

7 bushels of wheat, his profit will decline from $9.00 to $8.50. The values for marginal cost given in the last column of the table help us understand why Farmer Whaples's profits will decline if he produces more than 6 bushels of wheat. After the sixth bushel of wheat, rising marginal cost causes Farmer Whaples's profits to fall.

In fact, we can use the values for marginal cost and marginal revenue given in the table to calculate Farmer Whaples's profits using a different method than comparing total cost and total revenue. To help compare the two methods of calculating profits, we illustrate one in panel (a) and one in panel (b) of Figure 8-3. Panel (a) shows Farmer Whaples's total revenue, total cost, and profit. Total revenue is a straight line on the graph because it increases at a constant rate of $4 for each additional bushel sold. Farmer Whaples's profits are maximized when the vertical distance between the line representing total revenue and the total cost curve is as large as possible. Just as we saw in Table 8-3, this occurs at an output of 6 bushels.

The last two columns of Table 8-3 provide information on the marginal revenue (*MR*) Farmer Whaples receives from selling another bushel of wheat and his marginal cost (*MC*) of producing another bushel of wheat. Panel (b) is a graph of Farmer Whaples's marginal revenue and marginal cost. Because marginal revenue is always equal to $4, it is a horizontal line at the market price. We have already seen that the demand curve for a perfectly competitive firm is also a horizontal line at the market price. *Therefore, the marginal revenue curve for a perfectly competitive firm is the same as its demand curve.* Farmer Whaples's marginal cost of producing wheat first falls and then rises, following the usual pattern we discussed in Chapter 7.

We know from panel (a) that profit is at a maximum at 6 bushels of wheat. In panel (b), profit is also at a maximum at 6 bushels of wheat. To understand why this result is true, remember a key economic principle that we discussed in Chapter 1: *Optimal decisions are made at the margin.* Firms use this principle to decide the quantity to produce. In deciding how much to produce, Farmer Whaples needs to compare the marginal revenue he earns from selling another bushel of wheat to the marginal cost of producing that bushel. The difference between the marginal revenue and the marginal cost is the additional profit (or loss) from producing one more bushel. As long as marginal revenue is greater than marginal cost, Farmer Whaples's profits are increasing and he will want to expand production. For example, he will not stop producing at 5 bushels of wheat because producing and selling the sixth bushel adds $4 to his revenue, but only $3 to his cost, so his profit increases by $1. He wants to continue producing until the marginal revenue he receives from selling another bushel is equal to the marginal cost of producing it. At that

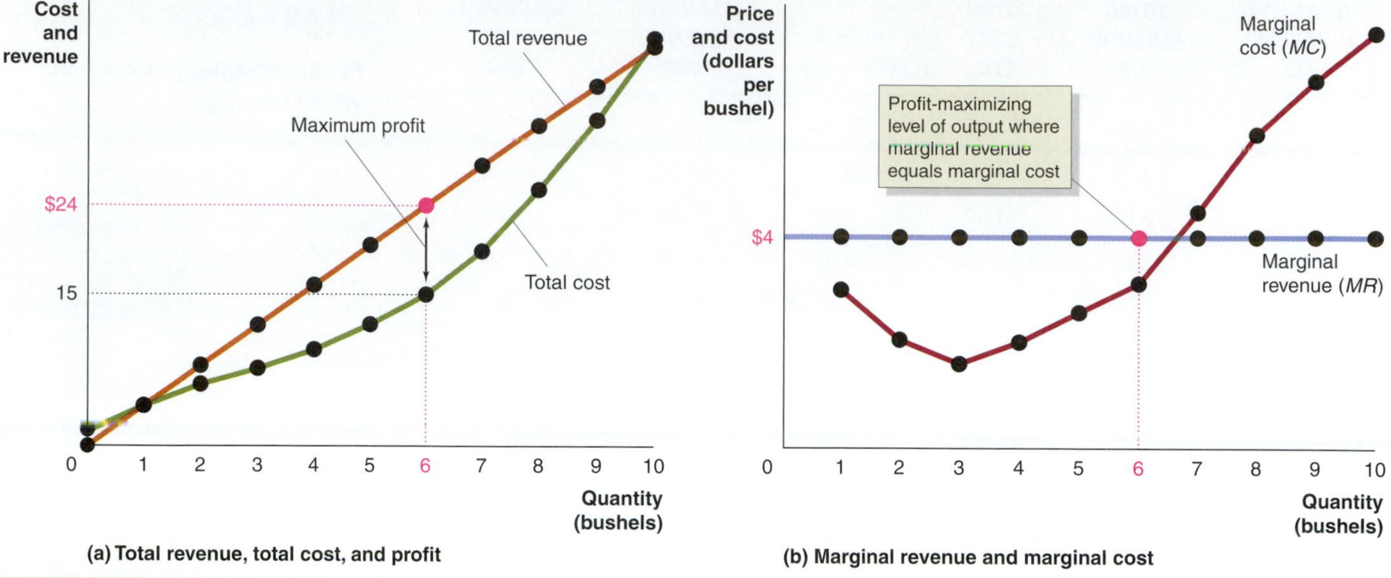

FIGURE 8-3 The Profit-Maximizing Level of Output

In panel (a), Farmer Whaples maximizes his profit where the vertical distance between total revenue and total cost is the largest. This happens at an output of 6 bushels. Panel (b) shows that Farmer Whaples's marginal revenue (*MR*) is equal to a constant $4 per bushel. Farmer Whaples maximizes profits by producing wheat up to the point where the marginal revenue of the last bushel produced is equal to its marginal cost, or *MR* = *MC*. In this case, at no level of output does marginal revenue exactly equal marginal cost. The closest Farmer Whaples can come is to produce 6 bushels of wheat. He will not want to continue to produce once marginal cost is greater than marginal revenue because this will reduce his profits. Panels (a) and (b) show alternative ways of thinking about how Farmer Whaples can determine the profit-maximizing quantity of wheat to produce.

level of output, he will make no *additional* profit by selling another bushel, so he will have maximized his profits.

Inspecting the table, we can see that at no level of output does marginal revenue exactly equal marginal cost. The closest Farmer Whaples can come is to produce 6 bushels of wheat. He will not want to continue to produce once marginal cost is greater than marginal revenue because this will reduce his profits. For example, the seventh bushel of wheat adds $4.50 to his cost, but only $4.00 to his revenue, so producing the seventh bushel *reduces* his profit by $0.50.

From the information in Table 8-3 and Figure 8-3, we can draw the following conclusions:

1. The profit-maximizing level of output is where the difference between total revenue and total cost is the greatest.
2. The profit-maximizing level of output is also where marginal revenue equals marginal cost, or *MR* = *MC*.

Both these conclusions are true for any firm, whether or not it is in a perfectly competitive industry. We can draw one other conclusion about profit maximization that is true only of firms in perfectly competitive industries: For a firm in a perfectly competitive industry, price is equal to marginal revenue, or *P* = *MR*. So, we can restate the *MR* = *MC* condition as *P* = *MC*.

③ **LEARNING OBJECTIVE**

Use graphs to show a firm's profit or loss.

Illustrating Profit or Loss on the Cost Curve Graph

We have seen that profit is the difference between total revenue and total cost. We can also express profit in terms of *average total cost* (*ATC*). This allows us to show profit on the cost curve graph we developed in Chapter 7.

To begin, we need to work through the several steps necessary to determine the relationship between profit and average total cost. Because profit is equal to total rev-

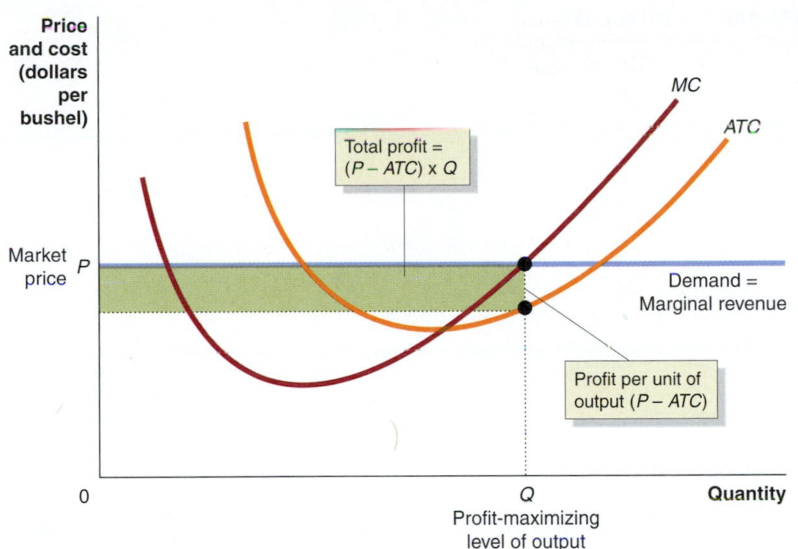

FIGURE 8-4

The Area of Maximum Profit

A firm maximizes profit at the level of output at which marginal revenue equals marginal cost. The difference between price and average total cost equals profit per unit of output. Total profit equals profit per unit multiplied by the number of units produced. Total profit is represented by the area of the green-shaded rectangle, which has a height equal to $(P - ATC)$ and a width equal to Q.

enue minus total cost (TC) and total revenue is price times quantity, we can write the following:

$$\text{Profit} = (P \times Q) - TC.$$

If we divide both sides of this equation by Q we have:

$$\frac{\text{Profit}}{Q} = \frac{(P \times Q)}{Q} - \frac{TC}{Q},$$

or

$$\frac{\text{Profit}}{Q} = P - ATC,$$

because TC/Q equals ATC. This equation tells us that profit per unit (or average profit) equals price minus average total cost. Finally, we obtain the expression for the relationship between total profit and average total cost by multiplying through again by Q:

$$\text{Profit} = (P - ATC) \times Q.$$

This expression tells us that a firm's total profit is equal to the quantity produced multiplied by the difference between price and average total cost.

Showing a Profit on the Graph

Figure 8-4 shows the relationship between a firm's average cost and its marginal cost that we discussed in Chapter 7. In this figure, we also show the firm's marginal revenue curve (which is the same as its demand curve) and the area representing total profit. Using the relationship between profit and average total cost that we just determined, we can say that the area representing total profit has a height equal to $(P - ATC)$ and a base equal to Q. This area is shown by the green-shaded rectangle.

SOLVED PROBLEM 8-1

Determining Profit-Maximizing Price and Quantity

③ **LEARNING OBJECTIVE**
Use graphs to show a firm's profit or loss.

Suppose that Andy sells basketballs in the perfectly competitive basketball market. His output per day and his costs are as follows:

OUTPUT PER DAY	TOTAL COST
0	$10.00
1	15.00
2	17.50
3	22.50
4	30.00
5	40.00
6	52.50
7	67.50
8	85.00
9	105.00

a. If the current equilibrium price in the basketball market is $12.50, to maximize profits how many basketballs will Andy produce, what price will he charge, and how much profit (or loss) will he make? Draw a graph to illustrate your answer. Your graph should be labeled clearly and should include Andy's demand, *ATC*, *AVC*, *MC*, and *MR* curves, the price he is charging, the quantity he is producing, and the area representing his profit (or loss).

b. Suppose the equilibrium price of basketballs falls to $5.00. Now how many basketballs will Andy produce, what price will he charge, and how much profit (or loss) will he make? Draw a graph to illustrate this situation, using the instructions in question (a).

Solving the Problem:

Step 1: Review the chapter material. This problem is about using cost curve graphs to analyze perfectly competitive firms, so you may want to review the section "Illustrating Profit or Loss on the Cost Curve Graph," which begins on page 238.

Step 2: Calculate Andy's marginal cost, average total cost, and average variable cost. To maximize profits, Andy will produce the level of output where marginal revenue is equal to marginal cost. We can calculate marginal cost from the information given in the table. We can also calculate average total cost and average variable cost, in order to draw the required graph. Average total cost *(ATC)* equals total cost *(TC)* divided by the level of output *(Q)*. Average variable cost *(AVC)* equals variable cost *(VC)* divided by output *(Q)*. To calculate variable cost, recall that total cost equals variable cost plus fixed cost. When output equals zero, total cost equals fixed cost. In this case fixed cost equals $10.00.

OUTPUT PER DAY (Q)	TOTAL COST (TC)	FIXED COST (FC)	VARIABLE COST (VC)	AVERAGE TOTAL COST (ATC)	AVERAGE VARIABLE COST (AVC)	MARGINAL COST (MC)
0	$ 10.00	$10.00	$ 0.00	—	—	—
1	15.00	10.00	5.00	$15.00	$ 5.00	$ 5.00
2	17.50	10.00	7.50	8.75	3.75	2.50
3	22.50	10.00	12.50	7.50	4.17	5.00
4	30.00	10.00	20.00	7.50	5.00	7.50
5	40.00	10.00	30.00	8.00	6.00	10.00
6	52.50	10.00	42.50	8.75	7.08	12.50
7	67.50	10.00	57.50	9.64	8.21	15.00
8	85.00	10.00	75.00	10.63	9.38	17.50
9	105.00	10.00	95.00	11.67	10.56	20.00

Step 3: Use the information from the table in Step 2 to calculate how many basketballs Andy will produce, what price he will charge, and how much profit he will earn if the market price of basketballs is $12.50. Andy's marginal revenue is equal to the market price of

$12.50. Marginal revenue equals marginal cost when Andy produces 6 basketballs per day. So, Andy will produce 6 basketballs per day and charge a price of $12.50 per basketball. Andy's profits are equal to his total revenue minus his total costs. His total revenue equals the 6 basketballs he sells multiplied by the $12.50 price, or $75.00. So, his profits equal $75.00 − $52.50 = $22.50.

Step 4: Use the information from the table in Step 2 to illustrate your answer to question (a) with a graph.

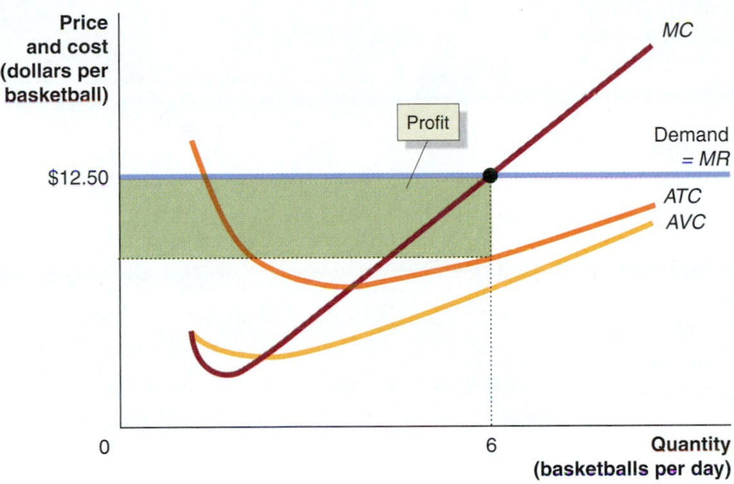

Step 5: Calculate how many basketballs Andy will produce, what price he will charge, and how much profit he will earn when the market price of basketballs is $5.00. Referring to the table in Step 2, we can see that marginal revenue equals marginal cost when Andy produces 3 basketballs per day. He charges the market price of $5.00 per basketball. His total revenue is only $15.00, while his total costs are $22.50, so he will have a loss of $7.50. (Can we be sure that Andy will continue to produce even though he is operating at a loss? We answer this question in the next section.)

Step 6: Illustrate your answer to question (b) with a graph.

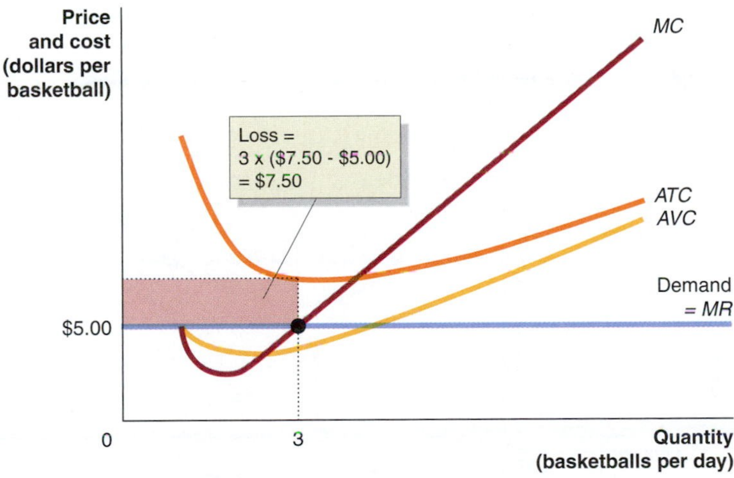

YOUR TURN: For more practice, do related problems 5 and 9 on pages 259 and 260 at the end of this chapter.

Illustrating When a Firm Is Breaking Even or Operating at a Loss

We have already seen that to maximize profits a firm produces the level of output where marginal revenue equals marginal cost. But will the firm actually make a profit at that

Don't Let This Happen To You!

Remember That Firms Maximize Total Profit, Not Profit per Unit

A student examines the following graph and argues, "I believe that a firm will want to produce at Q_1, not Q_2. At Q_1 the distance between price and average total cost is the greatest. Therefore, at Q_1 the firm will be maximizing its profits per unit." Briefly explain whether you agree with the student's argument.

The student's argument is incorrect because firms are interested in maximizing their *total* profits and not their profits per unit. We know that profits are not maximized at Q_1 because at that level of output marginal revenue is greater than marginal cost. A firm can always increase its profits by producing any unit that adds more to its revenue than it does to its costs. Only when the firm has expanded production to Q_2 will it have produced every unit for which marginal revenue is greater than marginal cost. At that point, it will have maximized profit.

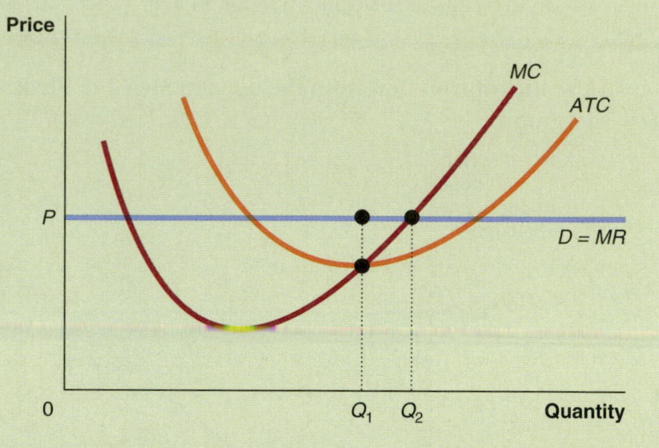

YOUR TURN: Test your understanding by doing related problem 12 on page 260 at the end of this chapter.

level of output? It depends on the relationship of price to average total cost. There are three possibilities:

1. $P > ATC$, which means the firm makes a profit.
2. $P = ATC$, which means the firm *breaks even* (its total cost equals its total revenue).
3. $P < ATC$, which means the firm experiences losses.

Figure 8-4 illustrated the first possibility, where the firm makes a profit. Panels (a) and (b) of Figure 8-5 show the situations where a firm experiences losses or breaks even.

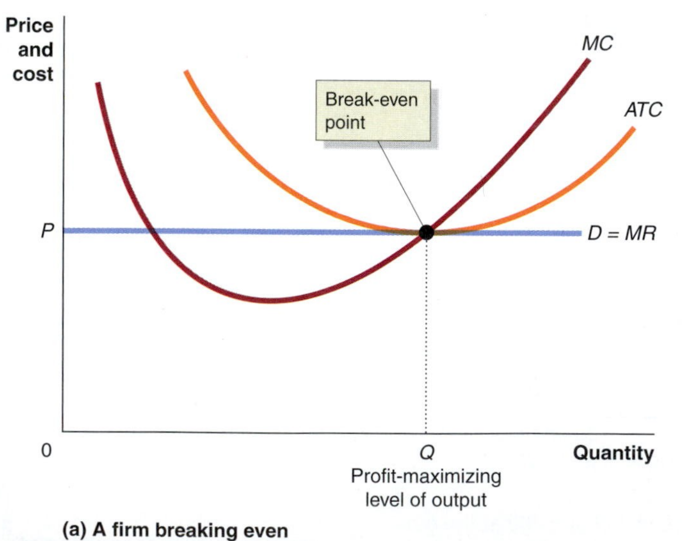

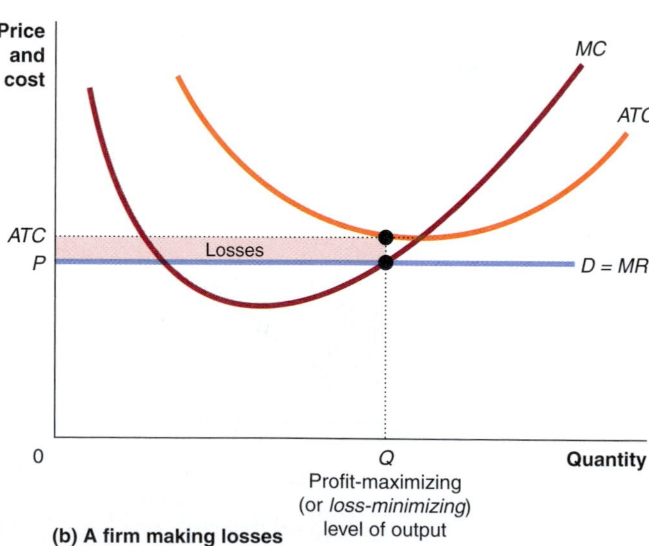

FIGURE 8-5 A Firm Breaking Even and a Firm Experiencing Losses

In panel (a), price equals average total cost and the firm breaks even because its total revenue will be equal to its total cost. In this situation, the firm makes zero economic profit. In panel (b), price is below average total cost and the firm experiences a loss. The loss is represented by the area of the red-shaded rectangle, which has a height equal to $(ATC - P)$ and a width equal to Q.

In panel (a) of Figure 8-5, at the level of output at which $MR = MC$, price is equal to average total cost. Therefore, total revenue is equal to total cost and the firm will break even, making zero economic profit. In panel (b), at the level of output at which $MR = MC$, price is less than average total cost. Therefore, total revenue is less than total cost and the firm has losses. In this case, maximizing profits amounts to *minimizing* losses.

Losing Money in the Medical Screening Industry

8-1 Making the Connection

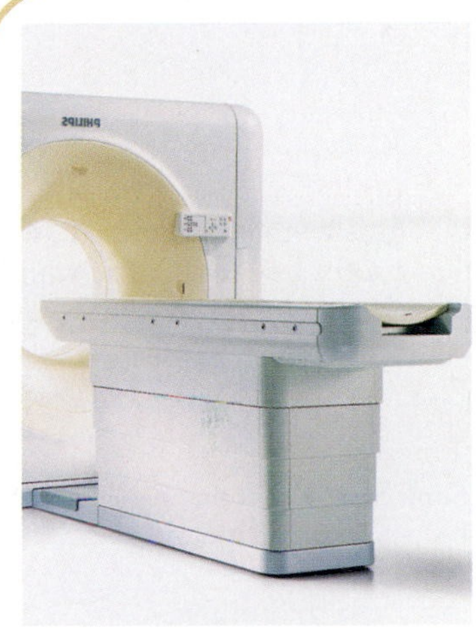

Providing preventive medical scans turned out not to be a profitable business.

Some ideas for new products work out; others don't. In a market system, a good or service becomes available to consumers only if an entrepreneur brings the product to market. Thousands of new businesses open every week in the United States. Each new business represents an entrepreneur risking his or her funds trying to earn a profit by offering a good or service to consumers. Of course, there are no guarantees of success, and many new businesses experience losses rather than earn the profits their owners hoped for.

In the early 2000s, technological advance reduced the price of computed tomography (CT) scanning equipment. For years, doctors and hospitals have prescribed CT scans to diagnose patients showing symptoms of heart disease, cancer, and other disorders. The declining price of CT scanning equipment convinced many entrepreneurs that it would be profitable to offer preventive body scans to apparently healthy people. The idea was that the scans would provide early detection of diseases before the customers had begun experiencing symptoms. Unfortunately, the new firms offering this service ran into several difficulties: First, because the CT scan was a voluntary procedure, it was not covered under most medical insurance plans. Second, very few consumers used the service more than once, so there was almost no repeat business. Finally, as with any medical test, some "false positives" occurred where the scan appeared to detect a problem that did not actually exist. Negative publicity from people who had to have expensive additional—and unnecessary—medical procedures as a result of false positive CT scans also hurt these new businesses.

As a result of these difficulties, the demand for CT scans was less than most of these entrepreneurs had expected, and the new businesses operated at a loss. For example, the owner of California HeartScan would have broken even if the market price had been \$495 per heart scan, but suffered losses because the actual market price was only \$250. The following figure shows the owner's situation.

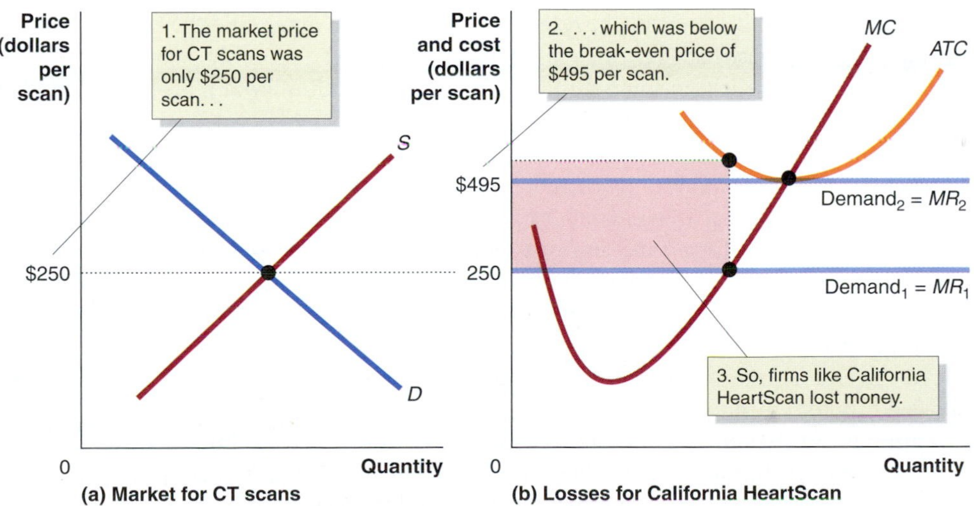

Why didn't California HeartScan and other medical clinics just raise the price to the level they needed to break even? We have already seen that any firm that tries to raise the price it charges above the market price loses customers to competing firms. By fall 2003, many scanning businesses began to close. Most of the entrepreneurs who had started these businesses lost their investments.

Source: Patricia Callahan, "Scanning for Trouble," *Wall Street Journal*, September 11, 2003, p. B1.

④ LEARNING OBJECTIVE

Explain why firms may shut down temporarily.

Deciding Whether to Produce or to Shut Down in the Short Run

In panel (b) of Figure 8-5, we assumed the firm would continue to produce, even though it was operating at a loss. In fact, in the short run a firm suffering losses has two choices:

1. Continue to produce
2. Stop production by shutting down temporarily

In many cases, a firm experiencing losses will consider stopping production temporarily. Even during a temporary shutdown a firm must still pay its fixed costs. For example, if the firm has signed a lease for its building, the landlord will expect to receive a monthly rent payment, even if the firm is not producing anything that month. Therefore, if a firm does not produce, it will suffer a loss equal to its fixed costs. This loss is the maximum the firm will accept. If, by producing, the firm would lose an amount greater than its fixed costs, it will shut down.

A firm may be able to reduce its loss below the amount of its total fixed cost by continuing to produce. This outcome will occur if the total revenue it receives is greater than its variable cost. The revenue over and above variable cost can be used to cover part of the firm's fixed cost. As a result, in this case the firm will have a smaller loss by continuing to produce than if it shut down.

Sunk cost A cost that has already been paid and that cannot be recovered.

In analyzing the firm's decision to shut down, we are assuming that its fixed costs are *sunk costs.* Remember from Chapter 6 that a **sunk cost** is a cost that has already been paid and cannot be recovered. We assume, as is usually the case, that the firm cannot recover its fixed costs by shutting down. Those funds have been spent and cannot be recovered, so the firm should treat its sunk costs as irrelevant to its decision making. Whether the firm's total revenue is greater or less than its variable costs is the key to deciding whether to shut down.

8-2 Making the Connection

Keeping a business open even when suffering losses can sometimes be the best decision in the short run.

When to Close a Laundry

An article in the *Wall Street Journal* describes what happened to Robert Kjelgaard when he quit his job writing software code at Microsoft and bought a laundry by paying the previous owner $80,000. For this payment, he received 76 washers and dryers and the existing lease on the building. The lease had six years remaining and required a monthly payment of $3,300. Unfortunately, Mr. Kjelgaard had difficulty operating the laundry at a profit. His explicit costs were $4,000 per month more than his revenue.

He tried to sell the laundry but was unable to do so. As he told a reporter, "It's hard to sell a business that's losing money." He considered closing the laundry, but as a sole proprietor he would be responsible for the remainder of the lease. At $3,300 per month for six years, he would be responsible for paying almost $200,000 out of his personal savings. Closing the laundry would still seem to be the better choice, because his $3,300 per month in sunk costs were less than the $4,000 per month plus the opportunity cost of his time, which he was losing from operating the laundry.

In the end he reorganized his business and hired a professional manager. This change allowed him to return to Microsoft and still reduce his losses to $2,000 per month. Because this amount was less than the $3,300 per month he would lose by shutting down, it made sense for him to continue to operate the laundry. But he was still suffering losses and, according to the article, his wife was "counting the days until the lease runs out."

Source: G. Pascal Zachary, "How a Success at Microsoft Washed Out at a Laundry," *Wall Street Journal,* May 30, 1995.

One option not available to a firm with losses in a perfectly competitive market is to raise its price. If the firm did raise its price, it would lose all its customers and its sales would drop to zero. For example, in a recent year the price of wheat in the United States was \$3.16 per bushel. At that price, the typical U.S. wheat farmer lost \$9,500. At a price of about \$4.25 per bushel, the typical wheat farmer would have broken even. But any wheat farmer who tried to raise his price to \$4.25 per bushel would have seen his sales quickly disappear because consumers could buy all the wheat they wanted at \$3.16 per bushel from the thousands of other wheat farmers.

The Supply Curve of the Firm in the Short Run

Remember that the supply curve for a firm tells us how many units of a product the firm is willing to sell at any given price. Notice that the marginal cost curve for a firm in a perfectly competitive market tells us the same thing. The firm will produce at the level of output where $MR = MC$. Because price equals marginal revenue for a firm in a perfectly competitive market, the firm will produce where $P = MC$. For any given price, we can determine from the marginal cost curve the quantity of output the firm will supply. *Therefore, the perfectly competitive firm's marginal cost curve also is its supply curve.* There is, however, an important qualification to this. We have seen that if a firm is experiencing losses, it will shut down if its total revenue is less than its variable cost:

$$\text{Total Revenue} < \text{Variable Cost},$$

or, in symbols:

$$P \times Q < VC.$$

If we divide both sides by Q, we have the result that the firm will shut down if:

$$P < AVC.$$

If the price drops below average variable cost, the firm will have a smaller loss if it shuts down and produces no output. *So, the firm's marginal cost curve is its supply curve only for prices at or above average variable cost.* The red line in Figure 8-6 shows the supply curve for the firm in the short run.

Recall that the marginal cost curve intersects the average variable cost where the average variable cost curve is at its minimum point. Therefore, the firm's supply curve is its marginal cost curve above the minimum point of the average variable cost curve. For prices below minimum average variable cost (P_{MIN}), the firm will shut down and its

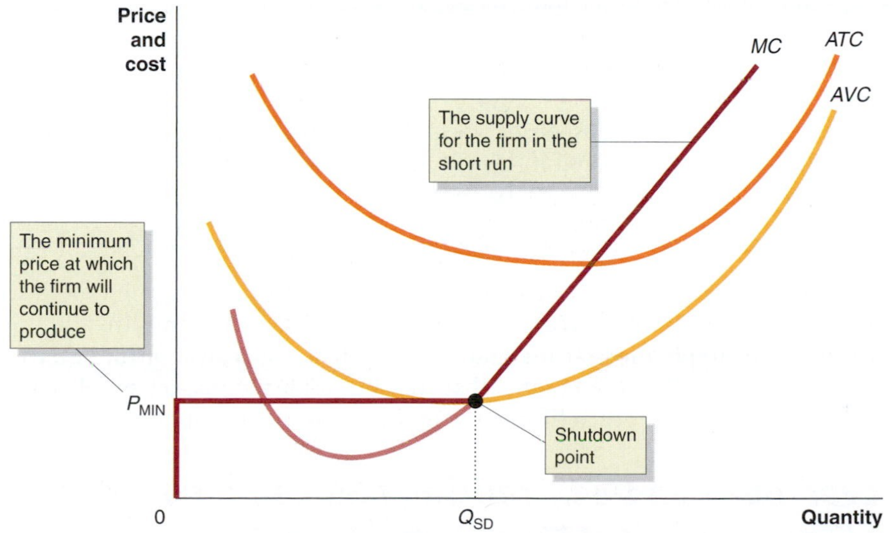

FIGURE 8-6

The Firm's Short-Run Supply Curve

The firm will produce at the level of output at which $MR = MC$. Because price equals marginal revenue for a firm in a perfectly competitive market, the firm will produce where $P = MC$. For any given price, we can determine the quantity of output the firm will supply from the marginal cost curve. In other words, the marginal cost curve is the firm's supply curve. But remember that the firm will shut down if the price falls below average variable cost. The marginal cost curve crosses the average variable cost at the firm's shutdown point. This point occurs at output level Q_{SD}. For prices below P_{MIN}, the supply curve is a vertical line along the price axis, which shows that the firm will supply zero output at those prices. The red line in the figure is the firm's short-run supply curve.

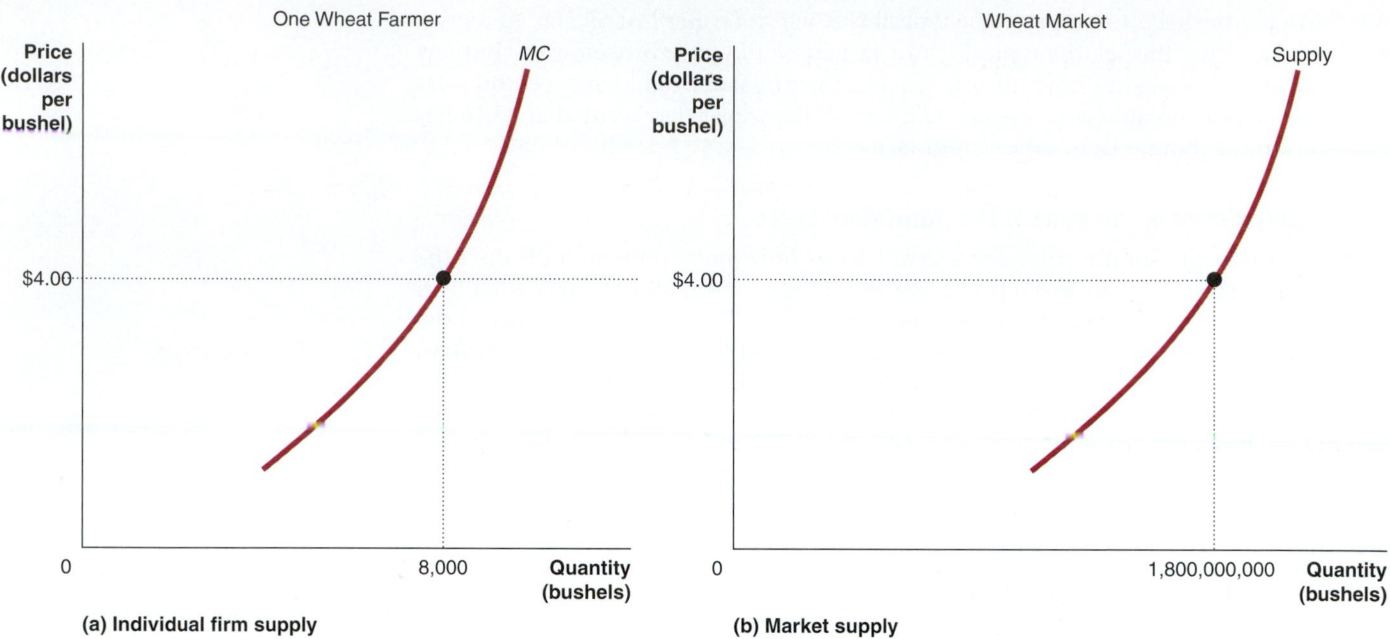

FIGURE 8-7 Firm Supply and Market Supply

We can derive the market supply curve by adding up the quantity that each firm in the market is willing to supply at each price. In panel (a), one wheat farmer is willing to supply 8,000 bushels of wheat at a price of $4 per bushel. If every wheat farmer supplies the same amount of wheat at this price and if there are 225,000 wheat farmers, the total amount of wheat supplied at a price of $4 will equal 8,000 bushels per farmer × 225,000 farmers = 1.8 billion bushels of wheat. This is one point on the market supply curve for wheat shown in panel (b). We can find the other points on the market supply curve by seeing how much wheat each farmer is willing to supply at each price.

output will fall to zero. The minimum point on the average variable cost curve is called the **shutdown point** and occurs in Figure 8-6 at output level Q_{SD}.

Shutdown point The minimum point on a firm's average variable cost curve; if the price falls below this point, the firm shuts down production in the short run.

The Market Supply Curve in a Perfectly Competitive Industry

We saw in Chapter 3 that the market supply curve is determined by adding up the quantity supplied by each firm in the industry at each price. Each firm's marginal cost curve tells us how much that firm will supply at each price. So, the market supply curve can be derived directly from the marginal cost curves of the firms in the industry. Panel (a) of Figure 8-7 shows the marginal cost curve for one wheat farmer. At a price of $4, this wheat farmer supplies 8,000 bushels of wheat. If every wheat farmer supplies the same amount of wheat at this price and if there are 225,000 wheat farmers, the total amount of wheat supplied at a price of $4 will be:

$$8{,}000 \text{ bushels per farmer} \times 225{,}000 \text{ farmers} = 1.8 \text{ billion bushels of wheat.}$$

Panel (b) shows a price of $4 and a quantity of 1.8 billion bushels as a point on the market supply curve for wheat. In reality, of course, not all wheat farms are alike. Some wheat farms will supply more at the market price than the typical farm; other wheat farms will supply less. The key point is that we can derive the market supply curve by adding up the quantity that each firm in the market is willing to supply at each price.

(5) LEARNING OBJECTIVE

Explain how entry and exit ensure that perfectly competitive firms earn zero economic profit in the long run.

"If Everyone Can Do It, You Can't Make Money at It"— The Entry and Exit of Firms in the Long Run

In the long run, unless a firm can cover all its costs, it will shut down and exit the industry. In a market system, firms continually enter and exit industries. In this section, we will see how profits and losses provide signals to firms that lead to entry and exit.

Economic Profit and the Entry or Exit Decision

To begin, let's look more closely at how economists characterize the profits earned by the owners of a firm. Suppose Anne Moreno decides to start her own business. After considering her interests and preparing a business plan, she decides to start an organic apple farm rather than open a restaurant or gift shop. After 10 years of effort, Anne has saved $100,000 and borrowed another $900,000 from a bank. With these funds, she has bought the land, apple trees, and farm equipment necessary to start her organic apple business. As we saw in Chapter 7, when someone invests her own funds in her firm, the opportunity cost to the firm is the return the funds would have earned in their best alternative use. If Farmer Moreno could have earned a 10 percent return on her $100,000 in savings in their best alternative use—which might have been, for example, to buy a small restaurant—then her apple business incurs a $10,000 opportunity cost. We can also think of this $10,000 as being the minimum amount that Farmer Moreno needs to earn on her $100,000 investment in her farm to remain in the industry in the long run.

Table 8-4 lists Farmer Moreno's costs. In addition to her explicit costs, we assume that she has two implicit costs: the $10,000, which represents the opportunity cost of the funds she invested in her farm, and the $30,000 salary she could have earned managing someone else's farm instead of her own. Her total costs are $125,000. If the market price of organic apples is $15 per box and Farmer Moreno sells 10,000 boxes, her total revenue will be $150,000 and her economic profit will be $25,000 (total revenue of $150,000 minus total costs of $125,000). Recall from Chapter 5 that **economic profit** equals a firm's revenues minus all of its costs, implicit and explicit. So, Farmer Moreno is covering the $10,000 opportunity cost of the funds invested in her firm, and she also is earning an additional $25,000 in economic profit.

Economic profit A firm's revenues minus all its costs, implicit and explicit.

ECONOMIC PROFIT LEADS TO ENTRY OF NEW FIRMS Unfortunately, Farmer Moreno is unlikely to earn an economic profit for very long. Suppose other apple farmers are just breaking even by growing apples using conventional methods. In that case, they will have an incentive to convert to organic growing methods so they can begin earning an economic profit. Remember that the more firms there are in an industry, the further to the right the market supply curve is. Panel (a) of Figure 8-8 shows that more farmers entering the market for organically grown apples will cause the market supply curve to shift to the right. Farmers will continue entering the market until the market supply curve has shifted from S_1 to S_2.

At that point, the market price will have fallen to $10 per box. Panel (b) shows the effect on Farmer Moreno, who we assume has the same costs as other organic apple

TABLE 8-4

Farmer Moreno's Costs per Year

EXPLICIT COSTS	
Water	$10,000
Wages	$15,000
Organic fertilizer	$10,000
Electricity	$5,000
Payment on bank loan	$45,000
IMPLICIT COSTS	
Foregone salary	$30,000
Opportunity cost of the $100,000 she has invested in her farm	$10,000
Total Cost	$125,000

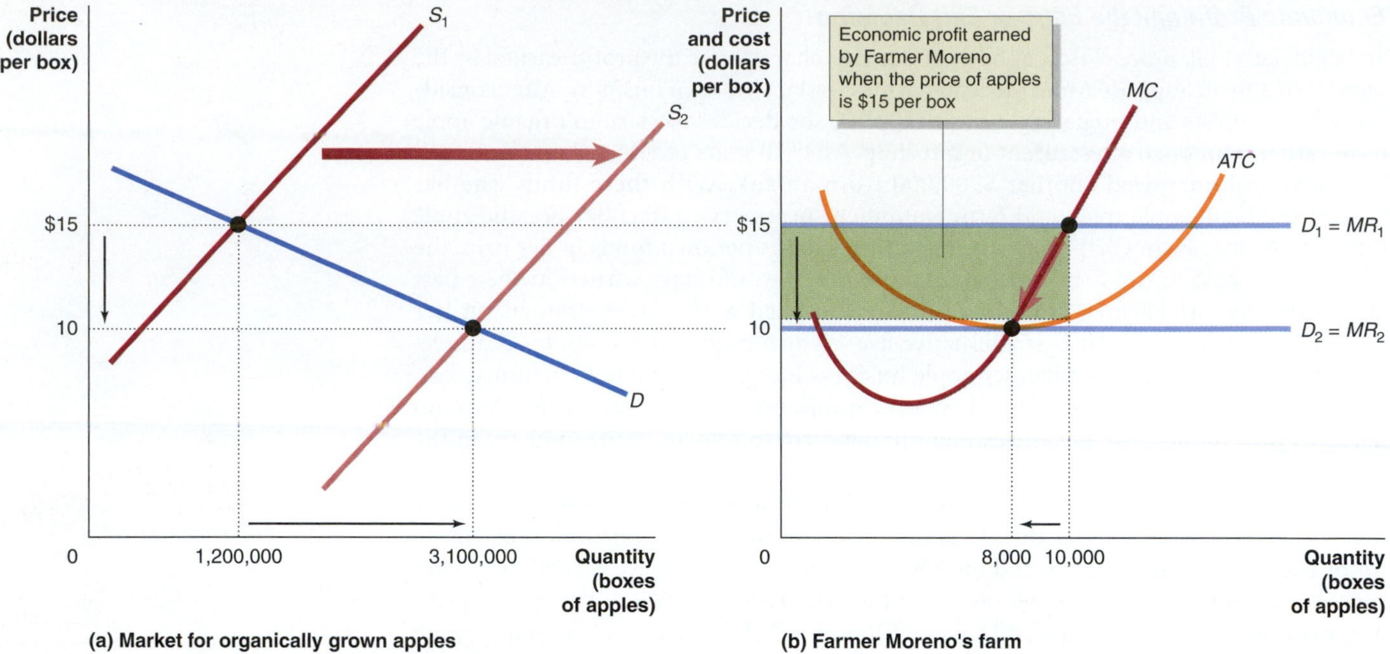

FIGURE 8-8 The Effect of Entry on Economic Profits

We assume that Farmer Moreno's costs are the same as the costs of other organic apple growers. Initially, she and other producers of organically grown apples are able to charge $15 per box and earn an economic profit. Farmer Moreno's economic profit is represented by the area of the green box. Panel (a) shows that as other farmers begin to grow apples using organic methods, the market supply curve shifts to the right from S_1 to S_2 and the market price drops to $10 per box. Panel (b) shows that the falling price causes Farmer Moreno's demand curve to shift down from D_1 to D_2, and she reduces her output from 10,000 boxes to 8,000. At the new market price of $10 per box, organic apple growers are just breaking even: Their total revenue is equal to their total cost, and they are earning zero economic profit. Notice the difference in scale between the graph in panel (a) and the graph in panel (b).

farmers. As the market price falls from $15 to $10 per box, Farmer Moreno's demand curve shifts down from D_1 to D_2. In the new equilibrium, Farmer Moreno is selling 8,000 boxes at a price of $10 per box. She and the other organic apple growers are no longer earning any economic profit. They are just breaking even, and the return on their investment is just covering the opportunity cost of these funds. New farmers will stop entering the market for organic apples because the rate of return is no better than they can earn elsewhere.

Will Farmer Moreno continue to grow organic apples even though she is just breaking even? She will because growing organic apples earns her as high a return on her investment as she could earn elsewhere. It may seem strange that new firms will continue to enter a market until all economic profits are eliminated and that established firms remain in a market despite not earning any economic profit. It only seems strange because we are used to thinking in terms of accounting profits, rather than *economic* profits. Remember that accounting rules generally require that only explicit costs be included on a firm's financial statements. The opportunity cost of the funds Farmer Moreno invested in her firm—$10,000—and her foregone salary—$30,000—are economic costs, but neither is an accounting cost. So, although an accountant would see Farmer Moreno as earning a profit of $40,000, an economist would see her as just breaking even. Farmer Moreno must pay attention to her accounting profit when preparing her financial statements and when paying her income tax. But because economic profit takes into account all her costs, it gives a truer indication of the financial health of her farm.

ECONOMIC LOSSES LEAD TO EXIT OF FIRMS Suppose some consumers decide there are no important benefits from eating organically grown apples and they switch back to buying conventionally grown apples. Panel (a) of Figure 8-9 shows that the demand

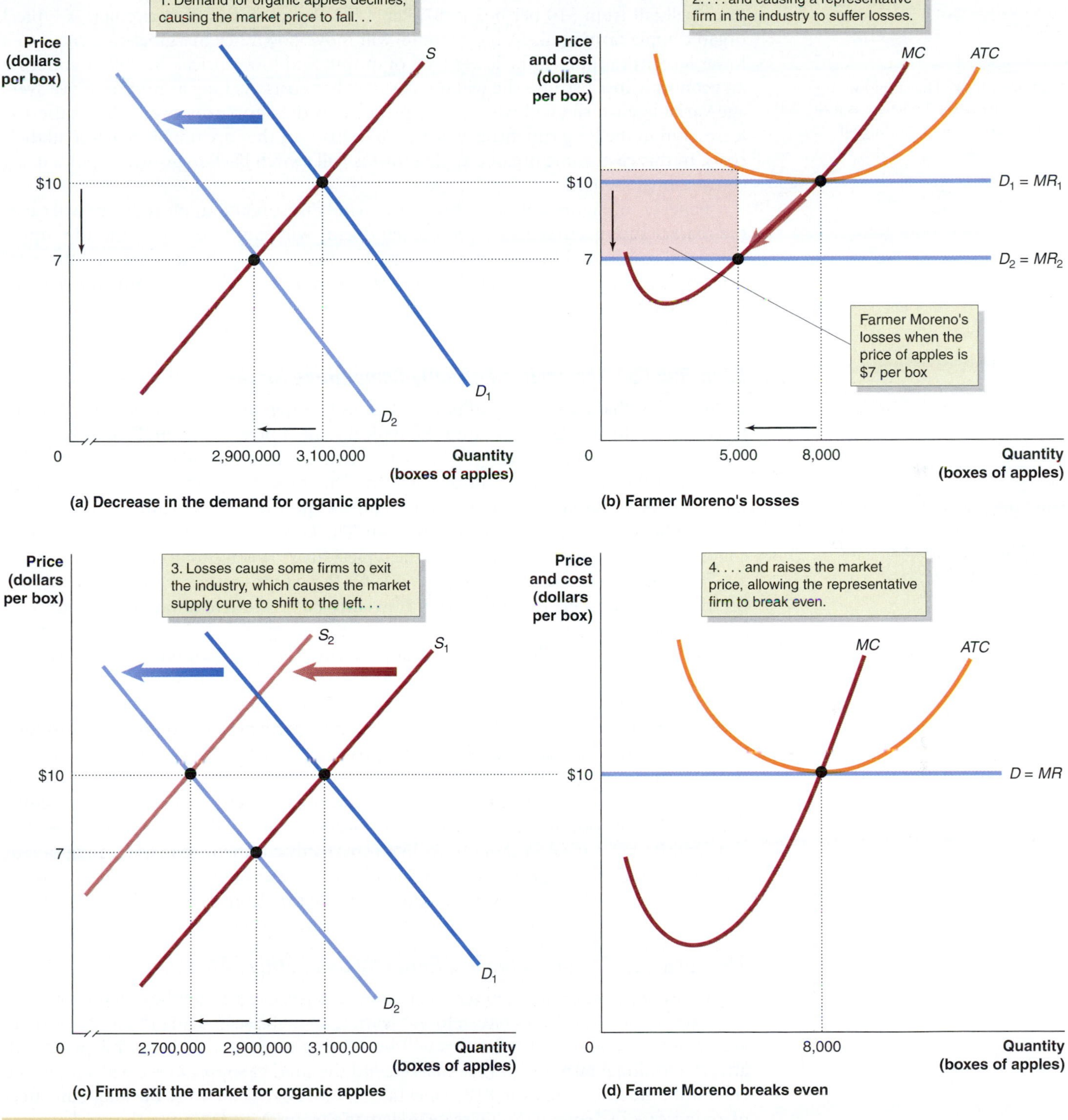

(a) Decrease in the demand for organic apples

(b) Farmer Moreno's losses

(c) Firms exit the market for organic apples

(d) Farmer Moreno breaks even

FIGURE 8-9 The Effect of Exit on Economic Losses

When the price of apples is $10 per box, Farmer Moreno and other producers of organically grown apples are breaking even. A total quantity of 3,100,000 boxes is sold in the market. She sells 8,000 boxes. Panel (a) shows a decline in the demand for organically grown apples from D_1 to D_2 that reduces the market price to $7 per box. Panel (b) shows that the falling price causes Farmer Moreno's demand curve to shift down from D_1 to D_2 and her output to fall from 8,000 to 5,000 boxes. At a market price of $7 per box, farmers have economic losses, represented by the area of the red box. As a result, some farmers will exit the market, which shifts the market supply curve to the left. Panel (c) shows that exit continues until the supply curve has shifted from S_1 to S_2 and the market price has risen from $7 back to $10. Panel (d) shows that with the price back at $10, Farmer Moreno will break even. In the new market equilibrium, total production of organic apples has fallen from 3,100,000 to 2,700,000 boxes.

curve for organically grown apples will shift to the left from D_1 to D_2, and the market price will fall from $10 per box to $7. Panel (b) shows that as the price falls, a typical organic apple farmer, like Anne Moreno, will move down her marginal cost curve to a lower level of output. At the lower level of output and lower price, she will be suffering an **economic loss** because she will not cover all her costs. As long as price is above average variable cost, she will continue to produce in the short run, even when suffering losses. But in the long run, firms will exit an industry if they are unable to cover all their costs. In this case, some organic apple growers will switch back to growing apples using conventional methods.

Economic loss The situation in which a firm's total revenue is less than its total cost, including all implicit costs.

Panel (c) of Figure 8-9 shows that firms exiting the organic apple industry will cause the market supply curve to shift to the left. Firms will continue to exit and the supply curve will continue shifting to the left until the price has risen back to $10 and the market supply curve is at S_2. Panel (d) shows that when the price is back to $10, the remaining firms in the industry will be breaking even.

Long-Run Equilibrium in a Perfectly Competitive Market

We have seen that economic profits attract firms to enter an industry. The entry of firms forces down the market price until the typical firm is breaking even. Economic losses cause firms to exit an industry. The exit of firms forces up the equilibrium market price until the typical firm is breaking even. This process of entry and exit results in *long-run competitive equilibrium.* In **long-run competitive equilibrium,** entry and exit have resulted in the typical firm breaking even. The *long-run equilibrium market price* is at a level equal to the minimum point on the typical firm's average total cost curve.

Long-run competitive equilibrium The situation in which the entry and exit of firms has resulted in the typical firm breaking even.

The long run in the organic apple market is three to four years, which is the amount of time it takes farmers to convert from conventional growing methods to organic growing methods. As discussed at the beginning of this chapter, only during the years from 1997 to 2001 was it possible for organic apple farmers to earn economic profits. By 2002 the entry of new firms had eliminated economic profits in the industry.

Firms in perfectly competitive markets are in a constant struggle to stay one step ahead of their competitors. They are always looking for new ways to provide a product, such as growing apples organically. It is possible for firms to find ways to earn an economic profit for a while, but to repeat the quote from a Yakima Valley organic apple farmer at the beginning of this chapter, "It's like anything else in agriculture. If people see an economic opportunity, usually it only lasts for a few years." There is no need to restrict this observation to agriculture. In any perfectly competitive market, an opportunity to make economic profits never lasts for long. As Sharon Oster, an economist at Yale University has put it, "If everyone can do it, you can't make money at it."

The Long-Run Supply Curve in a Perfectly Competitive Market

If the typical organic apple grower breaks even at a price of $10 per box, in the long run the market price will always return to this level. If an increase in demand causes the market price to rise above $10, farmers will be earning economic profits. This profit will attract additional farmers into the market, and the market supply curve will shift to the right until the price is back to $10. Panel (a) in Figure 8-10 illustrates the long-run effect of an increase in demand. An increase in demand from D_1 to D_2 causes the market price to temporarily rise from $10 per box to $15. At this price, farmers are making economic profits growing organic apples, but these profits attract entry of new farmers organic apples. The result is an increase in supply from S_1 to S_2, which forces the price back down to $10 per box and eliminates the economic profits.

Similarly, if a decrease in demand causes the market price to fall below $10, farmers will experience economic losses. These losses will cause some farmers to exit the market, the supply curve will shift to the left, and the price will return to $10. Panel (b)

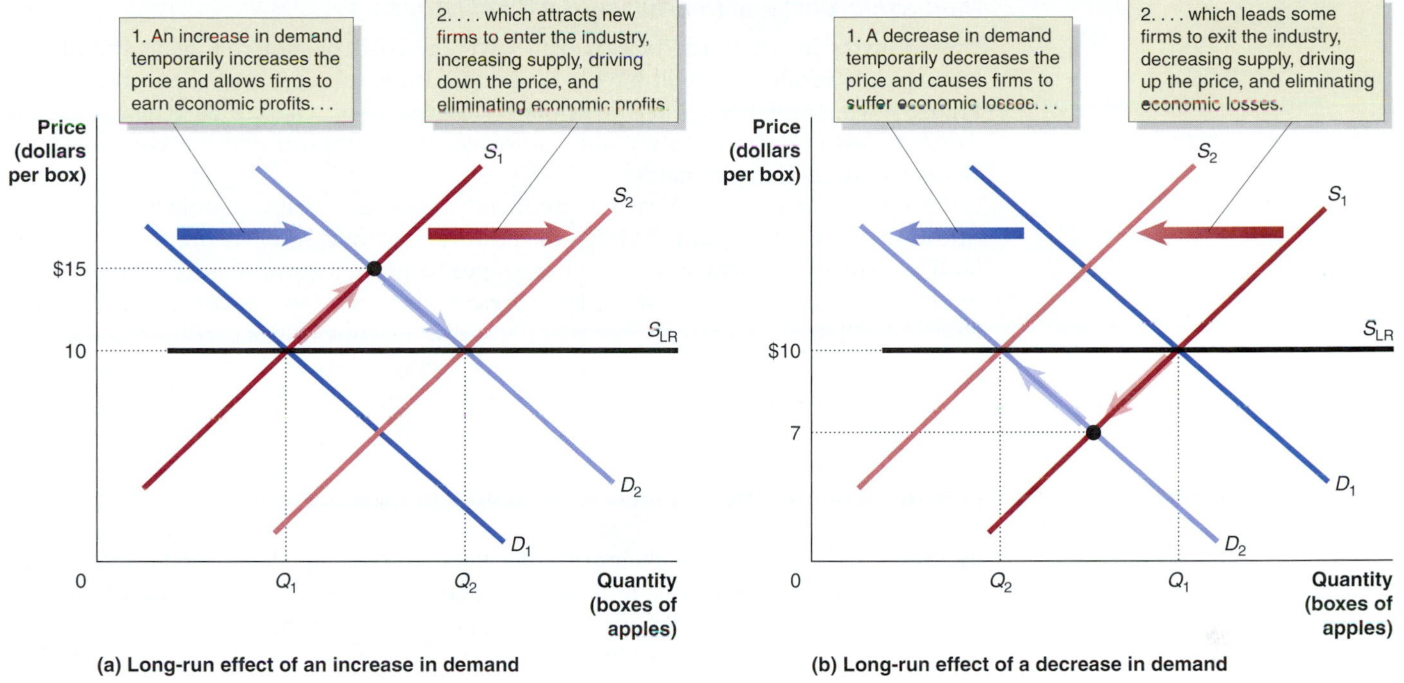

FIGURE 8-10 The Long-Run Supply Curve in a Perfectly Competitive Industry

Panel (a) shows that an increase in demand for organic apples will lead to a temporary increase in price from \$10 to \$15 per box, as the market demand curve shifts to the right from D_1 to D_2. The entry of new firms shifts the market supply curve to the right from S_1 to S_2, which will cause the price to fall back to its long-run level of \$10. Panel (b) shows that a decrease in demand will lead to a temporary decrease in price from \$10 to \$7 per box, as the market demand curve shifts to the left from D_1 to D_2. The exit of firms shifts the market supply curve to the left from S_1 to S_2, which causes the price to rise back to its long-run level of \$10. The long-run supply curve (S_{LR}) shows the relationship between market price and the quantity supplied in the long run. In this case, the long-run supply curve is a horizontal line.

in Figure 8-10 illustrates the long-run effect of a decrease in demand. A decrease in demand from D_1 to D_2 causes the market price to fall temporarily from \$10 per box to \$7. At this price, farmers are suffering economic losses growing organic apples, but these losses cause some farmers to exit the market for organic apples. The result is a decrease in supply from S_1 to S_2, which forces the price back up to \$10 per box and eliminates the losses.

Long-run supply curve A curve showing the relationship in the long run between market price and the quantity supplied.

The **long-run supply curve** shows the relationship in the long run between market price and the quantity supplied. In the long run, the price in the organic apple market will be \$10 per box, no matter how many boxes of apples are produced. So, as Figure 8-10 shows, the long-run supply curve (S_{LR}) for organic apples is a horizontal line at a price of \$10. Remember that the reason the price returns to \$10 in the long run is that this is the price at which the typical firm in the industry just breaks even. The typical firm breaks even at this price because it is at the minimum point on the firm's average total cost curve. We can draw the important conclusion that *in the long run, a perfectly competitive market will supply whatever amount of a good consumers demand at a price determined by the minimum point on the typical firm's average total cost curve.*

Because the position of the long-run supply curve is determined by the minimum point on the typical firm's average total cost curve, anything that raises or lowers the costs of the typical firm in the long run will cause the long-run supply curve to shift. For example, if a disease infects apple trees and the costs of treating the disease adds \$2 per box to the cost of producing apples, the long-run supply curve will shift up by \$2.

Increasing-Cost and Decreasing-Cost Industries

Any industry in which the typical firm's average costs do not change as the industry expands production will have a horizontal long-run cost curve, like the one in Figure 8-10. Industries, like the apple industry, where this holds true are called *constant-cost industries*. It's possible, however, for the typical firm's average costs to change as an industry expands.

For example, if an input used in producing a good is available in only limited quantities, the cost of the input will rise as the industry expands. If only a limited amount of land is available on which to grow the grapes to make a certain variety of wine, an increase in demand for wine made from these grapes will result in competition for the land and will drive up its price. As a result, more of the wine will be produced in the long run only if the price rises to cover the higher average costs of the typical firm. In this case, the long-run supply curve will slope upward. Industries with upward-sloping long-run supply curves are called *increasing-cost industries*.

Finally, in some cases the typical firm's costs may fall as the industry expands. Suppose that a new electronic product uses as an input a specialized memory chip that is currently produced only in small quantities. If demand for the electronic product increases, firms will increase their orders for the memory chip. We saw in Chapter 7 that if there are economies of scale in producing a good, its average cost will decline as output increases. If there are economies of scale in producing this memory chip, the average cost of producing it will fall, and competition will result in its price falling as well. This price decline, in turn, will lower the average cost of producing the new electronic product. In the long run, competition will force the price of the electronic product to fall to the level of the new lower average cost of the typical firm. In this case, the long-run supply curve will slope downward. Industries with downward-sloping long-run supply curves are called *decreasing-cost industries*.

⑥ LEARNING OBJECTIVE

Explain how perfect competition leads to economic efficiency.

Perfect Competition and Efficiency

Notice how powerful consumers are in a market system. If consumers want more organic apples, the market will supply them. This happens not because orders are given by a bureaucrat in a government office in Washington, DC, or by an official in an apple growers association. The additional apples are produced because an increase in demand results in higher prices and a higher rate of return on investments in organic growing techniques. Apple growers, trying to get the highest possible return on their investment, begin to switch from using conventional growing methods to using organic growing methods. If consumers lose their taste for organic apples and demand falls, the process works in reverse.

8-3 Making the Connection

The Decline of Apple Production in New York State

Although New York State is second only to Washington State in production of apples, production has been declining during the past 20 years. The decline has been particularly steep in counties close to New York City. In 1985, there were more than 11 thousand acres of apple orchards in Ulster County, which is 75 miles north of New York City. Today, fewer than five thousand acres remain. As it became difficult for apple growers in the county to compete with lower-cost producers elsewhere, the resources these entrepreneurs were using to produce apples—particularly land—became more valuable in other uses. Many farmers sold their land to housing developers. As one apple farmer put it, "Over the last ten years or so, [apple] prices have been stagnant or going down. I didn't see a return on the money, and I didn't want to continue."

In a market system, entrepreneurs will not continue to employ economic resources to produce a good or service unless consumers are willing to pay a price at least high enough for them to break even. Consumers were not willing to pay a high-enough price for apples for many New York State apple growers to break even on their investments. As a result, resources left apple production in that state.

When apple growers in New York State stopped breaking even, many sold their land to housing developers.

Sources: Lisa W. Foderaro, "Where Apples Don't Pay, Developers Will," *New York Times,* June 23, 2001; USDA, *2002 Census of Agriculture, Volume 1, Chapter 2,* New York County Level Data, Table 31.

Productive Efficiency

In the market system, consumers get as many apples as they want, produced at the lowest average cost possible. The forces of competition will drive the market price to the minimum average cost of the typical firm. **Productive efficiency** refers to the situation in which a good or service is produced at the lowest possible cost. As we have seen, perfect competition results in productive efficiency.

Productive efficiency The situation in which a good or service is produced at the lowest possible cost.

The managers of every firm strive to earn an economic profit by reducing costs. But in a perfectly competitive market, other firms quickly copy ways of reducing costs, so that in the long run, only the consumer benefits from cost reductions.

SOLVED PROBLEM 8-2

How Productive Efficiency Benefits Consumers

⑥ LEARNING OBJECTIVE

Explain how perfect competition leads to economic efficiency.

Writing in the *New York Times* on the technology boom of the late 1990s, Michael Lewis argues:

> The sad truth, for investors, seems to be that most of the benefits of new technologies are passed right through to consumers free of charge.

a. What do you think Lewis means by the benefits of new technology being "passed right through to consumers free of charge"? Use a graph like Figure 8-8 to illustrate your answer.

b. Explain why this result is a "sad truth" for investors.

Solving the Problem:

Step 1: Review the chapter material. This problem is about perfect competition and efficiency, so you may want to review the section "Perfect Competition and Efficiency," which begins on page 252.

Step 2: Explain what Lewis means using the concepts from this chapter. By "new technologies," Lewis means new products—like cell phones or DVD players—or lower-cost ways of producing existing products. In either case, new technologies will allow firms to earn economic profits for a while, but these profits will lead new firms to enter the market in the long run.

Step 3: Use a graph like Figure 8-8 to illustrate why the benefits of new technologies are "passed right through to consumers free of charge." Figure 8-8 shows the situation in which a firm is making economic profits in the short run but has these profits eliminated by entry in the long run. We can draw a similar graph to analyze what happens in the long run in the market for DVD players:

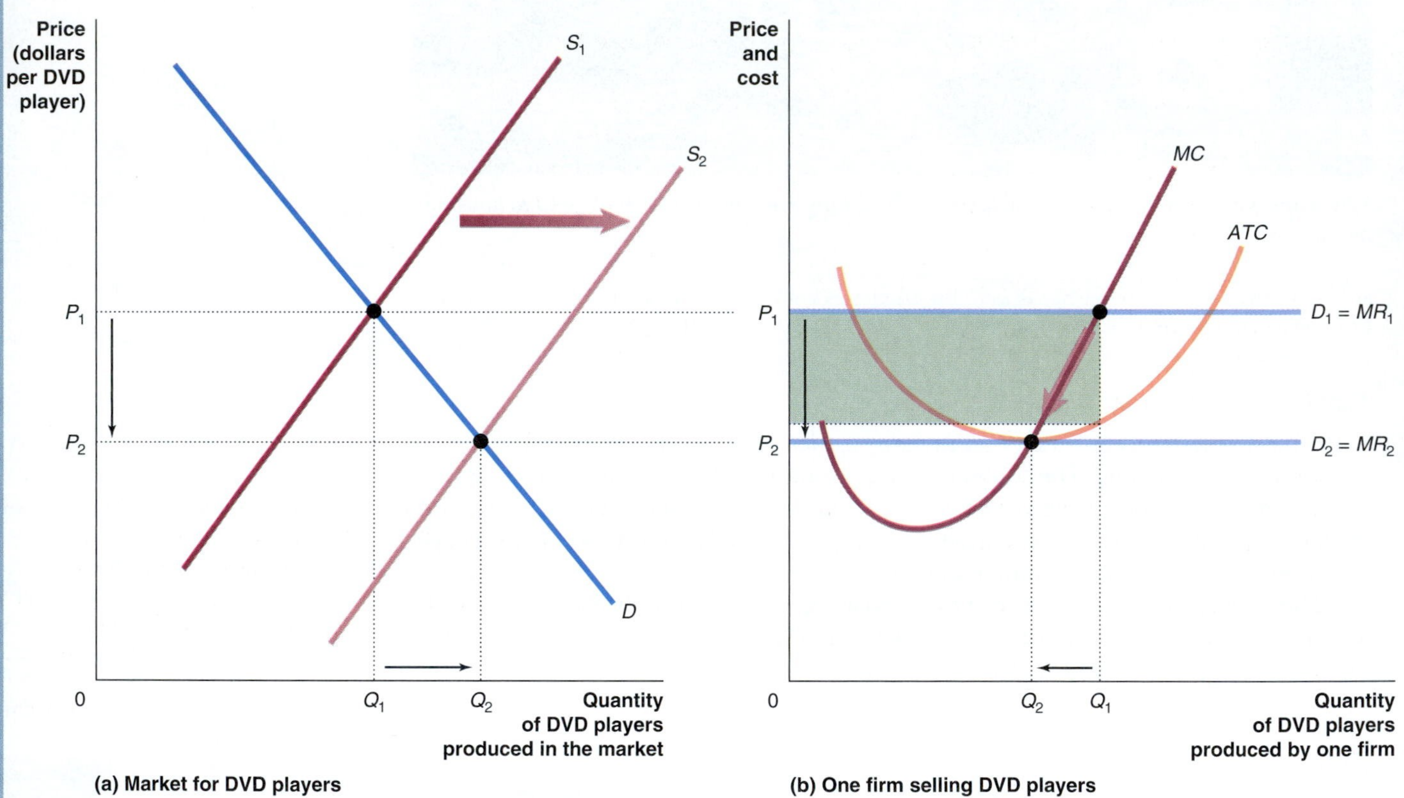

When DVD players were first introduced, prices were high and only a few firms were in the market. Panel (a) shows that the initial equilibrium price in the market for DVD players is P_1. Panel (b) shows that at this price the typical firm in the industry is earning an economic profit, which is shown by the green-shaded box. The economic profit attracts new firms into the industry. This entry shifts the market supply curve from S_1 to S_2 in panel (a) and lowers the equilibrium price from P_1 to P_2. Panel (b) shows that at the new market price P_2, the typical firm is breaking even. Therefore, DVD players are being produced at the lowest possible cost and productive efficiency is achieved. Consumers receive the new technology "free of charge" in the sense that they only have to pay a price equal to the lowest possible cost of production.

Step 4: Answer question (b) by explaining why the result in question (a) is a "sad truth" for investors. We have seen in answering question (a) that in the long run, firms only break even on their investment in producing high-technology goods. That result implies that investors in these firms are also unlikely to earn an economic profit in the long run.

Extra Credit: Lewis is using a key result from this chapter: In the long run, entry of new firms competes away economic profits. We should notice that, strictly speaking, the high-technology industries Lewis is discussing are not perfectly competitive. Cell phones or DVD players, for instance, are not identical and each cell phone company produces a quantity large enough to affect the market price. However, as we will see in Chapter 10, these deviations from perfect competition do not change the important conclusion that the entry of new firms benefits consumers by forcing prices down to the level of average cost. In fact, the price of DVD players dropped by more than 95 percent within five years of their first becoming available.

Source: Michael Lewis, "In Defense of the Boom," *New York Times,* October 27, 2002.

***YOUR TURN:* For more practice, do related problems 18 and 19 on page 261 at the end of this chapter.**

Allocative Efficiency

Not only do perfectly competitive firms produce goods and services at the lowest possible cost, they also produce the goods and services that consumers value most. Firms will produce a good up to the point where the marginal cost of producing another unit is equal to the marginal benefit consumers receive from consuming that unit. In other words, firms will supply all those goods that provide consumers with a marginal benefit at least as great as the marginal cost of producing them. We know this is true because:

1. The price of a good represents the marginal benefit consumers receive from consuming the last unit of the good sold.
2. Perfectly competitive firms produce up to the point where the price of the good equals the marginal cost of producing the last unit.
3. Therefore, firms produce up to the point where the last unit provides a marginal benefit to consumers equal to the marginal cost of producing it.

These statements are another way of saying that entrepreneurs in a market system efficiently *allocate* labor, machinery, and other inputs to produce the goods and services that best satisfy consumer wants. In this sense, perfect competition achieves **allocative efficiency.** As we will explore in the next few chapters, many goods and services sold in the U.S. economy are not produced in perfectly competitive markets. Nevertheless, productive efficiency and allocative efficiency are useful benchmarks against which to compare the actual performance of the economy.

Allocative efficiency A state of the economy in which production reflects consumer preferences; in particular, every good or service is produced up to the point where the last unit provides a marginal benefit to consumers equal to the marginal cost of producing it.

Conclusion

The competitive forces of the market impose relentless pressure on firms to produce new and better goods and services at the lowest possible cost. Firms that fail to adequately anticipate changes in consumer tastes or that fail to adopt the latest and most efficient technology do not survive in the long run. In the nineteenth century, the biologist Charles Darwin developed a theory of evolution based on the idea of the "survival of the fittest." Only those plants and animals that were best able to adapt to the demands of their environment were able to survive. Darwin wrote that he first realized the important role that the struggle for existence plays in the natural world after reading early nineteenth-century economists discuss the role it plays in the economic world. Just as "survival of the fittest" is the rule in nature, so it is in the economic world.

At the start of this chapter, we saw that there are four market structures: perfect competition, monopolistic competition, oligopoly, and monopoly. Now that we have studied perfect competition, in the following chapters we move on to the other three market structures. Before turning to those chapters, read *An Inside Look* on the next page to learn how firms are rushing to enter the market for organic snacks.

An Inside Look Firms Crank Out Organic Snacks

USA TODAY, JUNE 17, 2004

Organic Food Trend Chips Out a Niche in Snack Food Aisle

Organic food is breaking out of the produce section to a spot few anticipated: the snack aisle. Forget stereotypes of pristine strawberries or zucchinis untouched by preservatives, pesticides, hormones or antibiotics. It's sales of organic snacks, also produced in accordance with government rules to be labeled "organic," that are on fire.

a Sales of organic chips, nuts, nutrition bars and candy jumped 29.6% last year. That was outpaced only by organic meats (including poultry and fish), reports the Organic Trade Association.

All the good things about the $23 billion organic food industry are being processed by foodmakers at a near-frenetic pace into convenient snack foods. Organics are Frito-Lay's fastest-growing line. In a year, Frito-Lay has emerged as the No. 1 seller of organic snacks. It recently introduced organic Tostitos chips. Now, it's working on an organic Doritos line; perhaps, someday, potato chips.

"There's a perception that the organic consumer is living in a commune somewhere," says Stephen Quinn, marketing chief at Frito-Lay. "She's not. She's my wife."

Adding to the trend: more snacking of all kinds. For many time-pressed, two-worker families, a stream of snacks has replaced family meal time. That's one reason a record 120 organic snacks are scheduled to be introduced this year, up 40% from last year, estimates Lynn Dornblaser, director of consulting services at Mintel, a research firm. For some consumers, there's a who'd-a-thunk-it factor to organics' growth in snacks. "It seems to be a disconnect," says Dornblaser.

Nor are nutritionists overjoyed. "These are all dead, processed foods," laments Cynthia Lair, author of *Feeding the Whole Family.* "Organic or not, they won't make you healthier or give you more vitality. It's better to eat an apple." Organic snacks are late to the party, says Peter Meehan, CEO of Newman's Own Organics. "Things like organic produce and dairy have all grown years ahead of them."

Perhaps that's why sales of Garden of Eden's organic tortilla chips grew 41% in the past year. The company's organic snack business has grown more than 20% in the past year, says Ellen Deutsch, chief growth officer at parent company Hain Celestial Group.

b Such numbers have even some organic specialty companies that don't make processed snacks trying to squeeze into the snacking arena. Take Earthbound Farm, the biggest producer of organic produce, including those familiar bags of baby carrots. "My snack as a kid was a Twinkie," says Larry Hamwey, head of marketing. "But my three kids all know they have to have healthy snacks."

Key Points in the Article

At the beginning of this chapter, we discussed the increase in production of organically grown apples. This article discusses how the increasing demand for organic food has led to sales of organic snacks being "on fire." Large firms, such as Frito-Lay, are entering the market, with organic versions of Tostitos and Doritos. Medium-sized firms, such as Garden of Eden and Newman's Own Organics, are also entering the market. Even firms, such as Earthbound Farm, that don't currently produce snacks are planning to "squeeze into the snacking arena."

Analyzing the News

a One of the key points of this chapter is that, ultimately, it is *consumers* who decide which goods should be produced. If consumers increase their demand for organic snacks, then firms will redirect workers, machines, and natural resources toward producing those goods. In early 2003, an industry analyst (not quoted in the article) observed, "Organic is a niche, but a very profitable niche. Give consumers what they truly want/need and they will dig deeply into their pockets."

In fact, it is those profits that signal to entrepreneurs that demand for organic foods has increased. We know from the analysis in this chapter, though, that these profits will not persist in the long run. Figure 1 shows the short-run result of an increase in demand for organic snacks. The increased consumer demand for organic snacks raises the price of organic snacks from P_1 to P_2, which results in the typical firm earning economic profits.

b Figure 2 shows the long-run result. The economic profit earned by producing organic snacks will attract additional firms—such as Earthbound Farm, mentioned in the article—to enter the industry. This causes the market price to fall back to P_1. At a price of P_1, the typical firm is once again breaking even. The increase in consumer demand for organic snacks results in the quantity supplied rising in the long run, as new firms enter the industry, but the typical firm does not make an economic profit.

Thinking Critically ABOUT POLICY

1. Show, using a demand and supply graph and a cost-curve graph, what would happen if the government tightened its regulations, making it more difficult for the snacks mentioned in the article to be labeled as organic.
2. Show, using a demand and supply graph and a cost-curve graph, why organic snacks are likely to be more expensive than non-organic snacks.

Source: "Organic Food Trend Chips Out a Niche in Snack Food Aisle," by Bruce Horovitz, *USA Today*, June 17, 2004. Reprinted with permission.

Source for quote: Jerry Dryer, "Market Trends: Organic Lessons," *Prepared Foods*, January 2003.

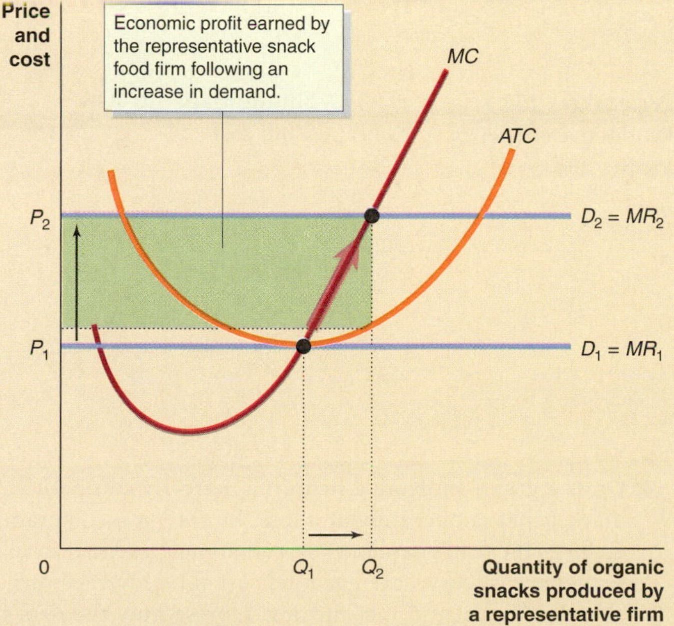

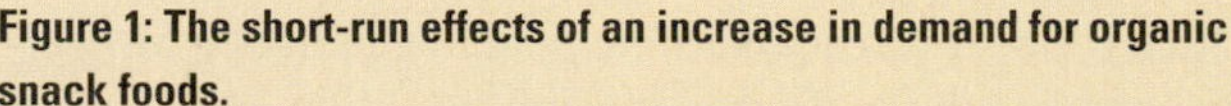
Figure 1: The short-run effects of an increase in demand for organic snack foods.

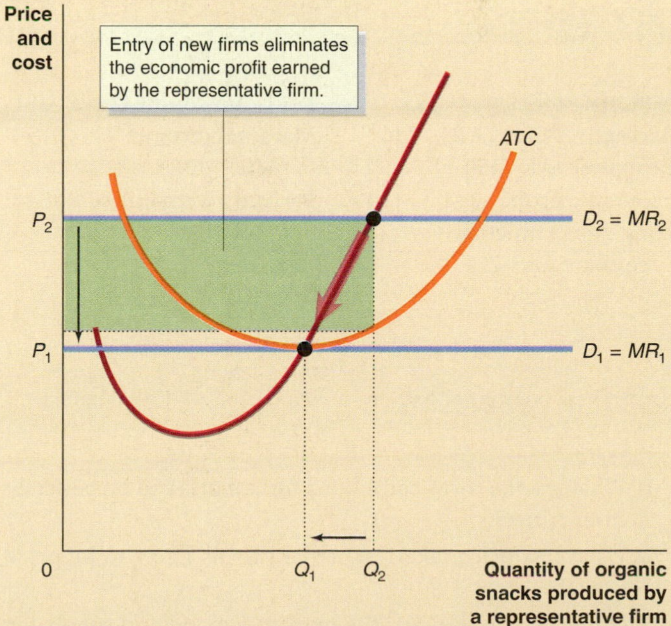

Figure 2: The long-run effects of an increase in demand for organic snack foods.

SUMMARY

LEARNING OBJECTIVE ① Define a perfectly competitive market, and explain why a perfect competitor faces a horizontal demand curve. A *perfectly competitive market* must have many buyers and sellers, firms must be producing identical products, and there must be no barriers to entry of new firms. The demand for a good or service produced in a perfectly competitive market will be downward-sloping, but the demand curve for the output of one firm in a perfectly competitive market will be a horizontal line at the market price. Firms in perfectly competitive markets are *price takers* and will see their sales drop to zero if they attempt to charge more than the market price.

LEARNING OBJECTIVE ② Explain how a perfect competitor decides how much to produce. A firm maximizes profit by producing the level of output where the difference between revenue and cost is the greatest. This is the same level of output where marginal revenue is equal to marginal cost.

LEARNING OBJECTIVE ③ Use graphs to show a firm's profit or loss. On a cost-curve graph, the area of profit or loss is a box with a height equal to price minus average total cost (for profit) or average total cost minus price (for loss) and a base equal to the level of output.

LEARNING OBJECTIVE ④ Explain why firms may shut down temporarily. In the short run, a firm will continue to produce as long as its price is at least equal to its average variable cost. If price falls below average variable cost, the firm will shut down. In the long run, a firm will shut down if price falls below average total cost.

LEARNING OBJECTIVE ⑤ Explain how entry and exit ensure that perfectly competitive firms earn zero economic profit in the long run. If firms make economic profits in the short run, new firms will enter the industry until the market price has fallen enough to wipe out the profits. If firms make economic losses, firms will exit the industry until the market price has risen enough to wipe out the losses. In the long run, firms in perfectly competitive markets break even.

LEARNING OBJECTIVE ⑥ Explain how perfect competition leads to economic efficiency. Perfect competition results in *productive efficiency,* which means that goods and services are produced at the lowest possible cost. Perfect competition also results in *allocative efficiency,* which means that the goods and services are produced up to the point where the last unit provides a marginal benefit to consumers equal to the marginal cost of producing it.

KEY TERMS

Allocative efficiency 255
Average revenue (*AR*) 236
Economic loss 250
Economic profit 247
Long-run competitive equilibrium 250
Long-run supply curve 251
Marginal revenue (*MR*) 236
Perfectly competitive market 233
Price taker 233
Productive efficiency 253
Profit 234
Shutdown point 246
Sunk cost 244

REVIEW QUESTIONS

1. What are the three conditions for a market to be perfectly competitive?
2. What is a price taker? When are firms likely to be price takers?
3. Draw a graph showing the market demand and supply for corn and the demand for the corn produced by one corn farmer. Be sure to indicate the market price and the price received by the corn farmer.
4. Draw a graph showing a firm in a perfectly competitive market that is operating at a loss. Be sure your diagram includes the firm's demand curve, marginal revenue curve, marginal cost curve, average total cost curve, average variable cost curve, and that the area representing the firm's losses is indicated.
5. Discuss why it is true that for a firm in a perfectly competitive market, the profit-maximizing condition $MR = MC$ is equivalent to the condition $P = MC$.

6. What is the difference between the firm's shutdown point in the short run and in the long run? Why are firms willing to accept losses in the short run but not in the long run?
7. When are firms likely to enter an industry? When are they likely to exit an industry?
8. Would a firm earning zero economic profit continue to produce, even in the long run?
9. Discuss the shape of the long-run supply curve in a perfectly competitive market. Suppose that a perfectly competitive market is initially at long-run equilibrium and then there is a permanent decrease in the demand for the product. Draw a graph showing how the market adjusts in the long run.
10. What is meant by allocative efficiency? What is meant by productive efficiency? Briefly discuss the difference between these two concepts.

PROBLEMS AND APPLICATIONS

Please visit ***www.prenhall.com/hubbard*** *for solutions to the even-numbered problems as well as multiple-choice and true or false self-assessment quizzes.*

1. Explain whether each of the following is a perfectly competitive market. For each market that is not perfectly competitive explain why it is not.
   a. Corn farming
   b. Retail bookselling
   c. Manufacturing automobiles
   d. Constructing new homes
2. **[Related to *Don't Let This Happen To You!*]** Explain whether you agree or disagree with the following remark: "According to the model of perfectly competitive markets, the demand for wheat should be a horizontal line. But this can't be true: When the price of wheat rises, the quantity of wheat demanded falls, and when the price of wheat falls, the quantity of wheat demanded rises. Therefore, the demand for wheat is not a horizontal line."
3. Suppose an assistant professor of economics is earning a salary of $65,000 per year. One day she quits her job, sells $100,000 worth of bonds that had been earning 5 percent per year, and uses the funds to open a bookstore. At the end of the year she shows an accounting profit of $80,000 on her income tax return. What is her economic profit?
4. Suppose that you and your sister both decide to open copy stores. Your parents always liked your sister better than you, so they purchase and give to her free of charge the three copiers she needs to operate her store. You, however, have to rent your copiers for $1,500 per month each. Does your sister have lower costs in operating her copier store than you have in operating your copier store because of this? Explain.
5. **[Related to *Solved Problem 8-1*]** Frances sells earrings in the perfectly competitive earring market. Her output per day and costs are as follows:

OUTPUT PER DAY	TOTAL COST
0	$1.00
1	2.50
2	3.50
3	4.20
4	4.50
5	5.20
6	6.80
7	8.70
8	10.70
9	13.00

   a. If the current equilibrium price in the earring market is $1.80, how many earrings will Frances produce, what price will she charge, and how much profit (or loss) will she make? Draw a graph to illustrate your answer. Your graph should be clearly labeled and should include Frances's demand, *ATC*, *AVC*, *MC*, and *MR* curves, the price she is charging, the quantity she is producing, and the area representing her profit (or loss).
   b. Suppose the equilibrium price of earrings falls to $1.00. Now how many earrings will Frances produce, what price will she charge, and how much profit (or loss) will she make? Show your work. Draw a graph to illustrate this situation, using the instructions in question a.
   c. Suppose the equilibrium price of earrings falls to $0.25. Now how many earrings will Frances produce, what price will she charge, and how much profit (or loss) will she make?

6. The financial writer Andrew Tobias has described an incident when he was a student at the Harvard Business School: Each student in the class was given large amounts of information about a particular firm and asked to determine a pricing strategy for the firm. Most of the students spent hours preparing their answers and came to class carrying many sheets of paper with their calculations. Tobias came up with the correct answer after just a few minutes and without having made any calculations. When his professor called on him in class for an answer, Tobias stated, "The case said the XYZ Company was in a very competitive industry . . . and the case said that the company had all the business it could handle." Given this information, what price do you think Tobias argued the company should charge? Briefly explain. (Tobias says the class greeted his answer with "thunderous applause.")
Source: Andrew Tobias, *The Only Investment Guide You'll Ever Need,* San Diego: Harcourt, 2002, pp. 6–8.

7. Harry Ellis produces table lamps in the perfectly competitive desk lamp market.
   a. Fill in the missing values in the table.

OUTPUT PER WEEK	TOTAL COSTS	*AFC*	*AVC*	*ATC*	*MC*
0	$100				
1	150				
2	175				
3	190				
4	210				
5	240				
6	280				
7	330				
8	390				
9	460				
10	540				

   b. Suppose the equilibrium price in the desk lamp market is $50. How many table lamps should Harry produce, and how much profit will he make?
   c. If next week the equilibrium price of desk lamps drops to $30, should Harry shut down? Explain.

8. The following graph represents the situation of a perfectly competitive firm. Indicate on the graph the areas that represent:
   a. Total cost
   b. Total revenue
   c. Variable cost
   d. Profit or loss

   Briefly explain whether the firm will continue to produce in the short run.

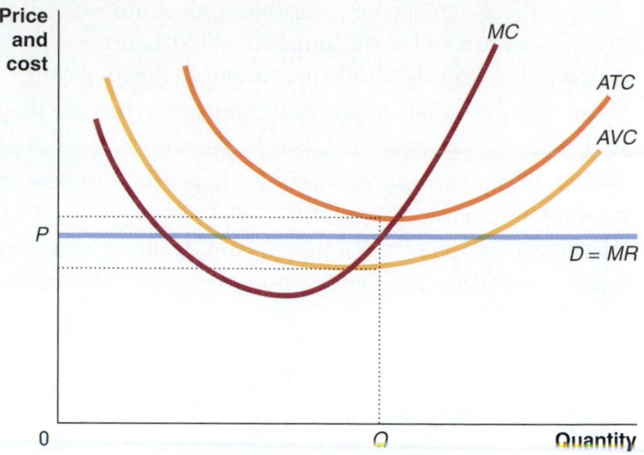

9. **[Related to *Solved Problem 8-1*]** Review Solved Problem 11-1, and then answer the following: Suppose the equilibrium price of basketballs falls to $2.50. Now how many basketballs will Andy produce? What price will he charge? How much profit (or loss) will he make?

10. Do you agree or disagree with the following statement? "The products for which demand is the greatest will also be the products that are most profitable to produce." Explain.

11. In panel (b) of Figure 8-9, Anne Moreno reduces her output from 8,000 to 5,000 boxes of apples when the price falls to $7. At this price and this output level she is operating at a loss. Why doesn't she just continue charging the original $10 and continue producing 8,000 boxes of apples?

12. **[Related to *Don't Let This Happen To You!*]** A student examines the following graph and argues, "I believe that a firm will want to produce at Q_1, not Q_2. At Q_1, the distance between price and marginal cost is the greatest. Therefore, at Q_1, the firm will be maximizing its profits." Briefly explain whether you agree with the student's argument.

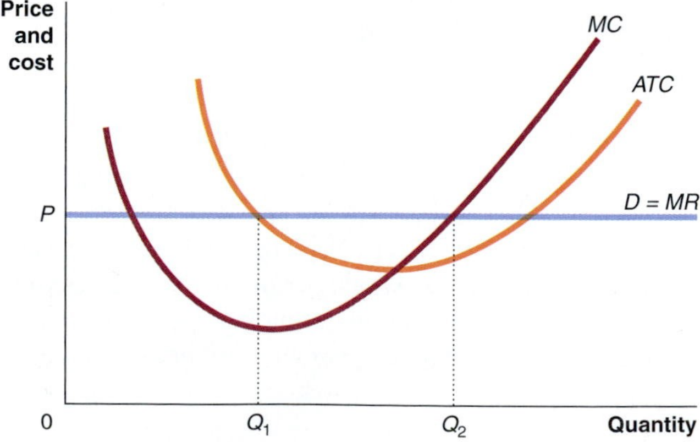

13. According to a report in the *Wall Street Journal,* during the fourth quarter of 2003 the profits of British Airways rose to 83 million pounds from 13 million pounds one year earlier. At the same time "the average amount the airline makes on each paying passenger fell 0.8%." If profit per passenger fell, how could total profits rise? Illustrate your answer with a graph. Be sure to indicate profit per passenger and total profit on the graph.
Source: Emma Blake, "British Airways Reports Sharp Jump in Net Profits," *Wall Street Journal,* February 9, 2004.

14. The following is from an article in the *Los Angeles Times:*

> Gerald Lasseigne, a 53-year-old information systems technician in Donaldsonville, La., lost his job last month when steep natural gas prices forced Triad Nitrogen to shut down its fertilizer plant on the banks of the Mississippi River.

Draw a graph showing the Triad Nitrogen company earning a profit from its fertilizer plant before the increase in the price of natural gas. Draw a second graph showing why Triad Nitrogen shuts down the plant following the increase in the price of natural gas.
Source: Warren Vieth and Aparna Kumar, "Higher Oil Prices Ooze into Economy," *Los Angeles Times,* March 25, 2003, p. C1.

15. Suppose you decide to open a copy store. You rent store space (signing a one-year lease), and you take out a loan at a local bank and use the money to purchase 10 copiers. Six months later a large chain opens a copy store two blocks away from yours. As a result, the revenue you receive from your copy store, while sufficient to cover the wages of your employees, and the costs of paper and utilities, doesn't cover all of your rent and the interest and repayment costs on the loan you took out to purchase the copiers. Should you continue operating your business?

16. The following statement appeared in a Congressional analysis of the airline industry: "In lean times, airlines can operate for extended periods of time [while making losses] . . . because revenues will cover a large part of their costs (Pan Am lost money for about a decade before finally closing down)." Why would Pan Am—or any airline—continue losing money for 10 years, rather than shut down immediately? In the statement "revenues will cover a large part of their costs," does it matter if the costs being referred to are fixed costs or variable costs? Briefly explain.
Source: Joint Economic Committee, Democratic Staff, *Assessing Losses for the Airline Industry and Its Workers in the Aftermath of the Terrorist Attacks,* October 3, 2001.

17. Club Mediterranee operates 120 Club Med resorts around the world. Following the September 11, 2001, terrorist attacks on the United States, many American tourists were reluctant to travel to foreign resorts. As a result, the prices Club Med could charge visitors to its resorts declined. In November 2001, Club Med decided to temporarily shut down 15 of its resorts. Analyze possible reasons for Club Med's decision. Be sure to discuss the likely relationship between the revenue Club Med received from operating these resorts and the resorts' fixed and variable costs.
Source: Rafer Guzmán, "Club Med Plans to Temporarily Close 15 Resorts," *Wall Street Journal,* November 9, 2001, p. B1.

18. **[Related to *Solved Problem 8-2*]** Discuss the following statement: "In a perfectly competitive market, in the long run consumers benefit from reductions in costs, but firms don't." Don't firms also benefit from cost reductions because they are able to earn greater profits?

19. **[Related to *Solved Problem 8-2*]** Suppose you read the following item in a newspaper article under the headline, "Price Gouging Alleged in Pencil Market:"

> Consumer advocacy groups charged at a press conference yesterday that there is widespread price gouging in the sale of pencils. They released a study showing that whereas the average retail price of pencils was $1.00, the average cost of producing pencils was only $0.50. "Pencils can be produced without complicated machinery or highly skilled workers, so there is no justification for companies charging a price that is twice what it costs them to produce the product. Pencils are too important in the life of every American for us to tolerate this sort of price gouging any longer," said George Grommet, chief spokesperson for the consumer groups. The consumer groups advocate passage of a law that would allow companies selling pencils to charge a price no more than 20 percent greater than their average cost of production.

Do you believe such a law would be advisable in a situation like this? Explain.

20. A student in a principles of economics course makes the following remark: "The economic model of perfectly competitive markets is fine in theory but not very realistic. It predicts that in the long run a firm in a perfectly competitive market will earn no profits. No firm in the real world would stay in business if it earned zero profits." Do you agree with this remark?

21. The following is an excerpt from a newspaper story on the state of the lettuce market in the spring of 2002:

> The shortage [of lettuce] began with freezing weather that cut per-acre yields by more than half in parts of California, where more than half of the nation's supply is grown. At the same time, many farmers grew less lettuce, fearing a drop in demand after Sept. 11 [2001] because many people dined out less. The result has been high prices. In some parts of the country, iceberg lettuce has topped $3 per head at grocery stores, up from the regular $1 to $2.

> Prices are expected to drop to their usual levels in the next two to three weeks as new supplies catch up to demand, said Ashraf Zaki, a market price reporter for the Agriculture Department in Forest Park, Ga.

Use a demand-and-supply graph to illustrate the changes in the lettuce market described in this story. Briefly explain any shifts of the demand and supply curves in your graph. Why was the market price reporter for the Agriculture Department confident that prices would drop "to their usual levels"?

Source: Justin Bachman, "Light on Lettuce at the Salad Bar," Associated Press, March 29, 2002.

22. Suppose that the laptop computer industry is perfectly competitive and that the firms that assemble laptops do not also make the displays for them. Suppose that the laptop display industry is perfectly competitive. Suppose that because the demand for laptop displays is currently relatively small, firms in the laptop display industry have not been able to take advantage of all the economies of scale in laptop display production. Use a graph of the laptop computer market to illustrate the long-run effects on equilibrium price and quantity in the laptop computer market of a substantial and sustained increase in the demand for laptop computers. Use another graph to show the impact on the cost curves of a typical firm in the laptop computer industry. Briefly explain your graphs. Do your graphs indicate that the laptop computer industry is a constant-cost industry, an increasing-cost industry, or a decreasing-cost industry?
23. **[Related to the *Chapter Opener*]** If in the long run apple growers who use organic methods of cultivation make no greater rate of return on their investment than apple growers who use conventional methods, why did a significant number of apple growers switch from conventional to organic methods in the first place?

chapter nine

Monopoly and Antitrust Policy

Time Warner Rules Manhattan

Today most people can hardly imagine life without cable television. In fact, almost 80 percent of U.S. homes have cable television: a larger fraction than have clothes dryers, dishwashers, air conditioning, or personal computers, and almost as many as have washing machines. The first cable systems were established in the 1940s in cities that were too small to support broadcast stations. Those systems consisted of large antennas set up on hills to receive broadcasts from television stations within range. The signals were then transmitted by cable to individual houses.

The cable industry grew slowly because the technology did not exist to rebroadcast the signals of distant stations, so cable systems offered few stations. By 1970 only about 7 percent of households had cable television. In addition, the Federal Communications Commission (FCC)—the federal government agency that regulates the television industry—placed restrictions on both rebroadcasting the signals of distant stations and on the fees that could be charged for "premium channels" that would show movies or sporting events. In the late 1970s two key developments occurred: First, satellite relay technology made it feasible for local cable systems to receive signals relayed via satellite from distant broadcast stations. Second, Congress loosened regulations on rebroadcasting distant stations and premium channels. The result of these developments was the growth of both "superstations," which are local broadcast stations in large cities—such as New York, Chicago, and Atlanta—whose programming is sent by satellite to cable systems around the country, and premium channels, such as Home Box Office (HBO).

One of the most successful of the superstations was WTBS, started by Atlanta entrepreneur Robert Edward "Ted" Turner III. Turner went on to found the Turner Broadcasting System (TBS), which included the Cable News Network (CNN), the first 24-hour news network. In 2001, Turner was involved in the largest merger of entertainment companies in history.

LEARNING OBJECTIVES

After studying this chapter, you should be able to:

① Define monopoly.

② Explain the four main reasons monopolies arise.

③ Explain how a monopoly chooses price and output.

④ Use a graph to illustrate how a monopoly affects economic surplus.

⑤ Explain how a firm can increase its profits through price discrimination.

⑥ Discuss government policies toward monopoly.

when AOL Time Warner was formed. The company—now known as Time Warner—was made up of leading firms from four segments of the entertainment industry: Warner Brothers (movie making), *Time* (magazine publishing), TBS (cable television), and AOL (Internet). Today, Time Warner operates cable systems in 22 states through Time Warner Cable.

A firm needs a license from the city government to enter a local cable television market. If you live in Manhattan and you want cable television, you have to purchase it from Time Warner Cable. Other cable companies could ask the New York City government for a license to compete against Time Warner Cable in Manhattan, but none has. This is not an unusual situation for a cable television system: Of the 10,000 markets for cable television in the United States, fewer than 400 have competing cable systems.

As the only provider of cable TV in Manhattan, Time Warner has a *monopoly*. Few firms in the United States are monopolies because in a market system whenever a firm earns economic profits, other firms will enter its market. Therefore, it is very difficult for a firm to remain the only provider of a good or service. In this chapter, we will develop an economic model of monopoly that can help us analyze how such firms affect the economy. *An Inside Look* on page 290 explores a cable executive's view of the industry.

Although few firms are monopolies, the economic model of monopoly can still be quite useful. As we saw in Chapter 8, even though perfectly competitive markets are rare, this market model provides a benchmark for how a firm acts in the most competitive situation possible: when it is in an industry with many firms that all supply the same product. Monopoly provides a benchmark for the other extreme, where a firm is the only one in its market and, therefore, faces no competition from other firms supplying its product. The monopoly model is also useful in analyzing situations where firms agree to *collude,* or not compete, and act together as if they were a monopoly. As we will discuss in this chapter, collusion is illegal in the United States, but it occasionally happens.

Monopolies also pose a dilemma for the government. Should the government allow monopolies to exist? Are there circumstances in which the government should actually promote the existence of monopolies? Should the government regulate the prices monopolies charge? If so, will such price regulation increase economic efficiency? In this chapter, we will also explore these public policy issues.

① LEARNING OBJECTIVE

Define monopoly.

Monopoly The only seller of a good or service that does not have a close substitute.

Is Any Firm Ever Really a Monopoly?

A **monopoly** is a firm that is the only seller of a good or service that does not have a close substitute. Because substitutes of some kind exist for just about every product, can any firm really be a monopoly? The answer is "yes," provided the substitutes are not "close" substitutes. But how do we decide whether a substitute is a close substitute? A narrow definition of monopoly used by some economists is that a firm has a monopoly if it can ignore the actions of all other firms. In other words, other firms must not be producing close substitutes if the monopolist can ignore other firms' prices. For example, candles are a substitute for electric lights, but your local electric company can ignore candle prices because however low the price of candles falls, almost no customers will give up using electric lights and switch to candles. Therefore, your local electric company is clearly a monopoly.

Many economists, however, use a broader definition of monopoly. For example, suppose Joe Santos owns the only pizza parlor in a small town (we will consider later the question of *why* a market may have only a single firm). Does Joe have a monopoly? Substitutes for pizzas certainly exist. If the price of pizza is too high, people will switch to hamburgers or fried chicken or some other food instead. People do not have to eat at Joe's or starve. Joe is in competition with the local McDonald's and Kentucky Fried Chicken, among other firms. So, Joe does not meet the narrow definition of a monopoly. But many economists would still argue that it is useful to think of Joe as having a monopoly.

Although hamburgers and fried chicken are substitutes for pizza, competition from firms selling them is not enough to keep Joe from earning economic profits. We saw in Chapter 8 that when firms earn economic profits, we can expect new firms to enter the industry, and in the long run the economic profits are competed away. This outcome will not happen to Joe as long as he is the *only* seller of pizza. Using the broader definition, Joe has a monopoly because there are no other firms selling a substitute close enough that his economic profits are competed away in the long run.

9-1 Making the Connection

Is Xbox a Close Substitute for PlayStation 2?

When Microsoft decided to develop a video-game console, it wanted to produce something very different from Nintendo's GameCube and Sony's PlayStation 2 (PS2). Unlike the competing systems, Microsoft's Xbox contains a hard disk and a version of the Windows computer

To many gamers, PlayStation 2 is a close substitute for Xbox.

operating system. As a result, the cost of producing it is much higher than the cost to Nintendo of producing the GameCube or the cost to Sony of producing the PS2. This change did not concern Microsoft because it believed it would be able to charge a higher price than Nintendo or Sony charged for their systems. After all, as Bruno Bonnell, the chairman of the French game maker Infogames Entertainment SA, put it, "The Xbox is a full-feature BMW, the PS2 is a Toyota."

Because consumers do not consider Toyotas to be close substitutes for BMWs, BMW can safely ignore competition from Toyota when setting the prices for its cars. Microsoft expected to be in a similar position. Unfortunately for Microsoft, consumers considered the Sony PS2 a close substitute for the Xbox. Microsoft was forced to charge the same price for the Xbox that Sony charged for the PS2. Although Sony was able to make a substantial profit at that price, Microsoft initially lost money on the Xbox because of its higher costs.

Source: *Wall Street Journal.* Eastern Edition [Staff Produced Copy Only] by Rebecca Buckman, Khanh T. L. tran, Robert. Copyright 2002 by Dow Jones & Co Inc. Reproduced with permission of Dow Jones & Co Inc in the format Textbook via Copyright Clearance Center.

Where Do Monopolies Come From?

LEARNING OBJECTIVE
Explain the four main reasons monopolies arise.

Because monopolies do not face competition, every firm would like to have a monopoly. But to have a monopoly, barriers to entering the market must be so high that no other firms can enter. *Barriers to entry* may be high enough to keep out competing firms for four main reasons:

1. Government blocks the entry of more than one firm into a market.
2. One firm has control of a key raw material necessary to produce a good.
3. There are important *network externalities* in supplying the good or service.
4. Economies of scale are so large that one firm has a *natural monopoly.*

Entry Blocked by Government Action

As we will discuss later in this chapter, governments ordinarily try to promote competition in markets, but sometimes governments take action to block entry into a market. In the United States, government blocks entry in two main ways:

1. By granting a *patent* or *copyright* to an individual or firm, which gives it the exclusive right to produce a product.
2. By granting a firm a *public franchise,* which makes it the exclusive legal provider of a good or service.

PATENTS AND COPYRIGHTS The U.S. government grants patents to firms that develop new products or new ways of making existing products. A **patent** gives a firm

Patent The exclusive right to a product for a period of 20 years from the date the product was invented.

the exclusive right to a new product for a period of 20 years from the date the product was invented. Because Microsoft has a patent on the Windows operating system, other firms cannot sell their own versions of Windows. The government grants patents to encourage firms to spend money on the research and development necessary to create new products. If other firms could have freely copied Windows, Microsoft is unlikely to have spent the money necessary to develop it. Sometimes firms are able to maintain a monopoly without patent protection, provided they can keep secret how the product is made.

Patent protection is of vital importance to pharmaceutical firms as they develop new prescription drugs. Pharmaceutical firms start research and development work on a new prescription drug an average of 12 years before the drug is available for sale. A firm applies for a patent about 10 years before it begins to sell the product. The average 10-year delay between the government granting a patent and the firm actually selling the drug is due to the federal Food and Drug Administration's requirements that the firm demonstrate that the drug is both safe and effective. Therefore, during the period before the drug can be sold, the firm will have substantial costs to develop and test the drug. If the drug does not make it successfully to market, the firm will have a substantial loss.

The profits the firm earns from the drug will increase throughout the period of patent protection—which is usually about 10 years—as the drug becomes more widely known to doctors and patients. After the patent has expired, other firms are free to legally produce chemically identical drugs called *generic drugs.* Gradually, competition from generic drugs will eliminate the profits the original firm had been earning. For example, when patent protection expired for Glucophage, a diabetes drug manufactured by Bristol-Myers Squibb, sales of the drug declined by more than $1.5 billion in the first year due to competition from 12 generic versions of the drug produced by other firms. When the patent expired on Prozac, an antidepressant drug manufactured by Eli Lilly, sales dropped by more than 80 percent. Most economic profits from selling a prescription drug have been eliminated 20 years after the drug was first offered for sale.

9-2 Making the Connection

The End of the Christmas Plant Monopoly

In December, the poinsettia plant seems to be almost everywhere, decorating stores, restaurants, and houses. Although it may seem strange that anyone can have a monopoly on the production of a plant, for many years the Paul Ecke Ranch in Encinitas, California, had a monopoly on poinsettias.

The poinsettia is a wildflower native to Mexico. It was almost unknown in the United States before Albert Ecke, a German immigrant, began selling it in the early twentieth century at his flower stand in Hollywood, California. Unlike almost every other flowering plant, the poinsettia blossoms in the winter. This timing, along with the plant's striking red and green colors, makes the Poinsettia ideal for Christmas decorating.

Albert Ecke's son, Paul, discovered that by grafting together two varieties of poinsettias it was possible to have multiple branches grow from one stem. The result was a plant that had more leaves and was much more colorful than conventional poinsettias. Paul Ecke did not attempt to patent his new technique for growing poinsettias. But because the Ecke family kept the technique secret for decades, it was able to maintain a monopoly on the commercial production of the plants. Unfortunately, for the Ecke family—but fortunately for consumers—a university researcher discovered the technique and published it in an academic journal.

New firms quickly entered the industry, and the price of poinsettias plummeted. Soon consumers could purchase them for as little as three for $10. At those prices, the firm was unable to earn economic profits. In late 2003, Paul Ecke III, the current owner of the company, decided to sell off more than half the firm's land to fund new state-of-the-art greenhouses and research into new varieties of plants that he hoped would earn the firm economic profits once again.

Sources: Cynthia Crossen, "Holiday's Ubiquitous Houseplant," *Wall Street Journal*, December 19, 2000; and Mike Freeman and David E. Graham, "Ecke Ranch Plans to Sell Most of Its Remaining Land," *San Diego Union-Tribune*, December 11, 2003.

At one time, the Ecke family had a monopoly on growing poinsettias, but many new firms entered the industry.

Just as a new product or a new method of making a product receives patent protection, books, films, and software receive **copyright** protection. U.S. law grants the creator of a book, film, or piece of music the exclusive right to use the creation during the creator's lifetime. The creator's heirs retain this exclusive right for 70 years after the creator's death. In effect, copyrights create monopolies for the copyrighted items. Without copyrights, however, individuals and firms would be less likely to invest in creating new books, films, and software.

Copyright A government-granted exclusive right to produce and sell a creation.

PUBLIC FRANCHISES The government will sometimes grant a firm a **public franchise** that allows it to be the only legal provider of a good or service. For example, state and local governments will often designate one company as the sole provider of electricity, natural gas, or water.

Public franchise A designation by the government that a firm is the only legal provider of a good or service.

Occasionally, the government will decide to provide certain services directly to consumers through a *public enterprise.* This is much more common in Europe than in the United States. For example, the governments in most European countries own the railroad systems. In the United States, many city governments provide water and sewage service themselves, rather than relying on private firms.

Control of a Key Resource

Another way for a firm to become a monopoly is by controlling a key resource. This happens infrequently because most resources, including raw materials such as oil or iron ore, are widely available from a variety of suppliers. There are, however, a few prominent examples of monopolies based on control of a key resource, such as the Aluminum Company of America (Alcoa) and the International Nickel Company of Canada.

For many years until the 1940s, Alcoa either owned or had long-term contracts to buy nearly all of the available bauxite, the mineral needed to produce aluminum. Without access to bauxite, competing firms had to use recycled aluminum, which limited the amount of aluminum they could produce. Similarly, the International Nickel Company of Canada controlled more than 90 percent of available nickel supplies. Competition in the nickel market increased when the Petsamo nickel fields in northern Russia were developed after World War II.

In the United States, a key resource for a professional sports team is a large stadium. The teams that make up the major professional sports leagues—Major League Baseball, the National Football League, and the National Basketball Association—usually have long-term leases with the stadiums in major cities. Control of these stadiums is a major barrier to new professional baseball, football, or basketball leagues forming.

Are Diamond (Profits) Forever? The De Beers Diamond Monopoly

9-3 Making the Connection

The most famous monopoly based on control of a raw material is the De Beers diamond mining and marketing company of South Africa. Before the 1860s, diamonds were extremely rare. Only a few pounds of diamonds were produced each year, primarily from Brazil and India. Then in 1870, enormous deposits of diamonds were discovered along the Orange River in South Africa. It became possible to produce thousands of pounds of diamonds per year,

De Beers promoted the sentimental value of diamonds as a way to maintain its position in the diamond market.

and the owners of the new mines feared that the price of diamonds would plummet. To avoid financial disaster, the mine owners decided in 1888 to merge and form De Beers Consolidated Mines, Ltd.

De Beers became one of the most profitable and longest-lived monopolies in history. The company has carefully controlled the supply of diamonds to keep prices high. As new diamond deposits were discovered in Russia and Zaire, De Beers was able to maintain prices by buying most of the new supplies.

Because diamonds are rarely destroyed, De Beers has always worried about competition from the resale of stones. Heavily promoting diamond engagement and wedding rings with the slogan "A Diamond Is Forever" was a way around this problem. Because engagement and wedding rings have great sentimental value, they are seldom resold, even by the heirs of the original recipients. De Beers advertising has been successful even in some countries, such as Japan, that have had no custom of giving diamond engagement rings. As the populations in De Beers's key markets age, its advertising in recent years has focused on middle-aged men presenting diamond rings to their wives as symbols of financial success and continuing love, and on professional women buying "right-hand rings" for themselves.

In the past few years, competition has finally come to the diamond business. By 2000, De Beers directly controlled only about 40 percent of world diamond production. The company became concerned about the amount it was spending to buy diamonds from other sources to keep them off the market. It decided to adopt a strategy of differentiating its diamonds by relying on its name recognition. Each De Beers diamond is now marked with a microscopic brand to reassure consumers of its high quality. Other firms, such as BHP Billiton, which owns mines in northern Canada, have followed suit by branding their diamonds. Sellers of Canadian diamonds stress that they are "mined under ethical, environmentally friendly conditions," as opposed to "blood diamonds," which are supposedly "mined under armed force in war-torn African countries and exported to finance military campaigns." Whether consumers will pay attention to brands on diamonds remains to be seen.

Sources: Edward Jay Epstein, "Have You Ever Tried to Sell a Diamond?" *Atlantic Monthly,* February 1982; Donna J. Bergenstock, Mary E. Deily, and Larry W. Taylor, "A Cartel's Response to Cheating: An Empirical Investigation of the De Beers Diamond Empire," Lehigh University Working Paper, January 2002; Bernard Simon, "Adding Brand Names to Nameless Stones," *New York Times,* June 27, 2002; Blythe Yee, "Ads Remind Women They Have Two Hands," *Wall Street Journal,* August 14, 2003; quote in last paragraph from Joel Baglole, "Political Correctness by the Carat," *Wall Street Journal,* April 17, 2003.

Network Externalities

Network externalities Exist when the usefulness of a product increases with the number of consumers who use it.

There are **network externalities** in the consumption of a product if the usefulness of the product increases with the number of people who use it. If you owned the only cell phone in the world, it would not be very valuable. The more cell phones in use, the more valuable they become to consumers.

Some economists argue that network externalities can serve as a barrier to entry. For example, in the early 1980s Microsoft gained an advantage over other software companies by developing MS-DOS, the operating system for the first IBM personal computers. Because IBM sold more computers than any other company, software developers wrote many application programs for MS-DOS. The more people who used MS-DOS-based programs, the greater the usefulness to a consumer from using an MS-DOS-based program. Today, Windows, the program Microsoft developed to succeed MS-DOS, has a 95 percent share in the market for personal computer operating systems (although Windows has a much lower share in the market for operating systems for servers). If another firm introduced a competing operating system, some economists argue that relatively few people would use it initially and few applications would run on it, which would limit the operating system's value to other consumers.

EBay was the first Internet site to attract a significant number of people to its online auctions. Once a large number of people began to use eBay to buy and sell collectibles, antiques, and many other products, it became a more valuable place to buy and sell. Yahoo.com, Amazon.com, and other Internet sites eventually started online auctions, but they found it difficult to attract buyers and sellers. On eBay, a buyer expects to find more sellers, and a seller expects to find more potential buyers than on Amazon or other auction sites.

As these examples show, network externalities can set off a *virtuous cycle:* If a firm can attract enough customers initially, it can attract additional customers because its product's value has been increased by more people using it, which attracts even more customers, and so on. With products like computer operating systems and online auctions, it might be difficult for new firms to enter the market and compete away the profits being earned by the first firm in the market.

Economists engage in considerable debate, however, about the extent to which network externalities are important barriers to entry in the business world. Some economists argue that the dominant positions of Microsoft and eBay reflect the efficiency of those firms in offering products that satisfy consumer preferences more than the effects of network externalities. In this view, the advantages existing firms gain from network externalities would not be enough to protect them from competing firms offering better products. In other words, a firm entering the operating system market with a program better than Windows, or a firm offering an Internet auction site better than eBay, would be successful despite the effects of network externalities.

Natural Monopoly

We saw in Chapter 7 that economies of scale exist when the firm's long-run average costs fall as it increases the quantity of output it produces. A **natural monopoly** occurs when economies of scale are so large that one firm can supply the entire market at a lower average total cost than two or more firms. In that case, there is really only "room" in the market for one firm.

Natural monopoly A situation in which economies of scale are so large that one firm can supply the entire market at a lower average total cost than can two or more firms.

Figure 9-1 shows the average total cost curve for a firm producing electricity and the total demand for electricity in the firm's market. Notice that the average total cost curve is still falling when it crosses the demand curve at point *A*. If the firm is a monopoly and produces 30 billion kilowatt-hours of electricity per year, its average total cost of production will be $0.04 per kilowatt-hour. Suppose instead that two firms are in the market, each producing half of the market output, or 15 billion kilowatt-hours per year. Assume that each firm has the same average total cost curve. The figure shows that producing 15 billion kilowatt-hours would move each firm back up its average cost curve, so that the average cost of producing electricity would rise to $0.06 per kilowatt-hour (point *B*). In this case, if one of the firms expands production, it will move down the average total cost curve. With lower average costs, it will be able to offer electricity at a lower price than the other firm can. Eventually, the other firm will be driven out of business and the remaining firm will have a monopoly. Because a monopoly would develop automatically—or *naturally*—in this market, it is a natural monopoly.

Natural monopolies are most likely to occur in markets where fixed costs are very large relative to variable costs. For example, a firm that produces electricity must make a

FIGURE 9-1

Average Total Cost Curve for a Natural Monopoly

With a natural monopoly, the average total cost curve is still falling when it crosses the demand curve (point *A*). If only one firm is producing electric power in the market and it produces where average cost intersects the demand curve, average total cost will equal $0.04 per kilowatt-hour of electricity produced. If the market is divided between two firms, each producing 15 billion kilowatt-hours, the average cost of producing electricity rises to $0.06 per kilowatt-hour (point *B*). In this case, if one firm expands production, it can move down the average total cost curve, lower its price, and drive the other firm out of business.

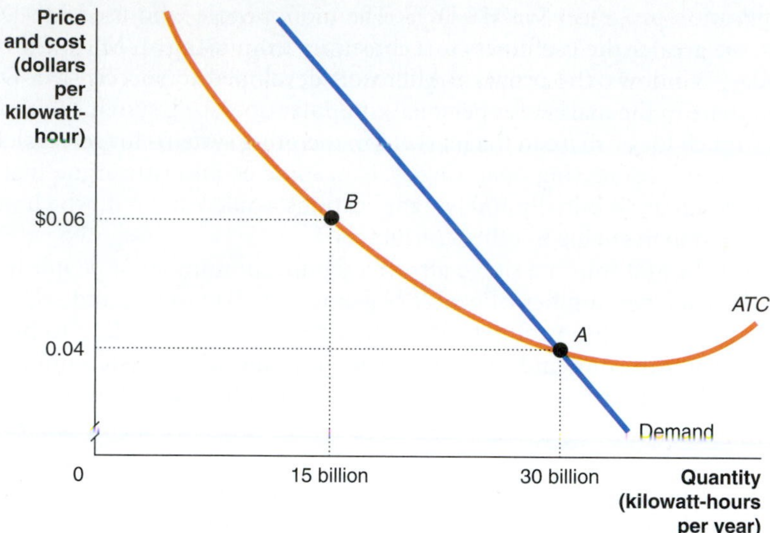

substantial investment in machinery and equipment necessary to generate the electricity and in wires and cables necessary to distribute it. Once the initial investment has been made, however, the marginal cost of producing another kilowatt-hour of electricity is relatively small.

SOLVED PROBLEM 9-1

② **LEARNING OBJECTIVE**

Explain the four main reasons monopolies arise.

Is the "Proxy Business" a Natural Monopoly?

A corporation is owned by its shareholders, who elect members of the corporation's board of directors and who also vote on particularly important issues of corporate policy. The shareholders of large corporations are spread around the country and relatively few of them are present at the annual meetings at which elections take place. Before each meeting, corporations must provide shareholders with annual reports and forms that allow them to vote by mail. Voting by mail is referred to as "proxy voting." Providing annual reports and ballots to shareholders is referred to on Wall Street as the "proxy business." Currently, one company, Automatic Data Processing, Inc. (ADP), controls almost all the proxy business.

According to the *Wall Street Journal*, Don Kittell of the Securities Industry Association has explained ADP's virtual monopoly by arguing that, "The economies of scale and the efficiencies achieved by ADP handling all the brokerage business—rather than multiple companies—resulted in savings to [corporations]."

a. Assuming Kittell is correct, draw a graph showing the market for handling proxy materials. Be sure that the graph contains the demand for proxy materials and ADP's average total cost curve. Explain why cost savings result from having the proxy business handled by a single firm.

b. According to a spokesman for ADP, the proxy business produces a profit rate of about 7 percent, which is lower than the profit rate the company receives from any of its other businesses. Does this information support or undermine Kittell's analysis? Explain.

Solving the Problem:

Step 1: Review the chapter material. This problem is about natural monopoly, so you may want to review the section "Natural Monopoly," which begins on page 271.

Step 2: Answer question (a) by drawing a natural monopoly graph and discussing the potential cost savings in this industry. Kittell is describing a situation of natural monopoly. Otherwise, the entry of another firm into the market would not raise average cost. Draw a natural monopoly graph, like the one in Figure 9-1:

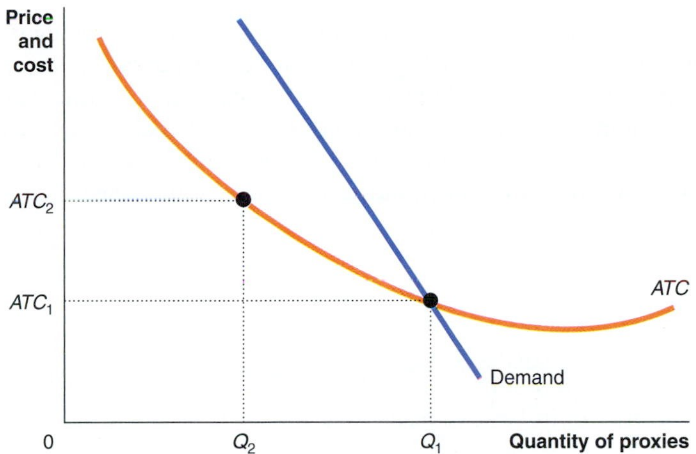

Make sure that your average total cost curve is still declining when it crosses the demand curve. If one firm can supply Q_1 proxies at an average total cost of ATC_1, then dividing the business equally between two firms each supplying Q_2 proxies would raise average total cost to ATC_2.

Step 3: Answer question (b) by discussing the implications of ADP's low profit rate in the proxy business. If ADP earns a low profit rate on its investment in this business even though it has a monopoly, Kittell probably is correct that the proxy business is a natural monopoly.

Extra Credit: Keep in mind that competition is not good for its own sake. It is good because it can lead to lower costs, lower prices, and better products. In certain markets, however, cost conditions are such that competition is likely to lead to higher costs and higher prices. These markets are natural monopolies that are best served by one firm.

Source: Phyllis Plitch, "Competition Remains Issue in Proxy-Mailing Costs," *Wall Street Journal*, January 16, 2002.

YOUR TURN: **For more practice, do related problem 12 on page 294 at the end of this chapter.**

How Does a Monopoly Choose Price and Output?

③ LEARNING OBJECTIVE

Explain how a monopoly chooses price and output.

Like every other firm, a monopoly maximizes profit by producing where marginal revenue equals marginal cost. A monopoly differs from other firms in that *a monopoly's demand curve is the same as the demand curve for the product.* We emphasized in Chapter 8 that the market demand curve for wheat was very different from the demand curve for the wheat produced by any one farmer. If, however, that farmer had a monopoly on wheat production, the two demand curves would be exactly the same.

Marginal Revenue Once Again

Recall from Chapter 8 that firms in perfectly competitive markets—such as a farmer in the wheat market—face horizontal demand curves. They are *price takers.* All other firms, including monopolies, are *price makers.* If price makers raise their prices, they will lose some, but not all, of their customers. Therefore, they face a downward-sloping demand curve and a downward-sloping marginal revenue curve as well. Let's examine why a firm's marginal revenue curve slopes downward if its demand curve slopes downward.

When a firm cuts the price of a product, one good thing and one bad thing happens:

- *The good thing:* It sells more units of the product.
- *The bad thing:* It receives less revenue from each unit than it would have received at the higher price.

For example, consider the table in Figure 9-2, which shows the demand curve for Time Warner Cable's basic cable package. For simplicity, we assume the market has only 10 potential subscribers, instead of the millions it actually has. If Time Warner charges a price of $60 per month, it won't have any subscribers. If it charges a price of $57, it sells 1 subscription. At $54, it sells 2, and so on. Time Warner's total revenue is equal to the number of subscriptions sold per month multiplied by the price. The firm's average revenue—or revenue per subscription sold—is equal to its total revenue divided by the quantity of subscriptions sold. Time Warner is particularly interested in marginal revenue because marginal revenue tells the firm how much revenue will increase if it cuts the price to sell one more subscription.

Notice that Time Warner's marginal revenue is less than the price for every subscription sold after the first subscription. To see why, think about what happens if Time Warner cuts the price of its basic cable package from $42 to $39, which increases its sub-

FIGURE 9-2

Calculating a Monopoly's Revenue

Time Warner Cable faces a downward-sloping demand curve for subscriptions to basic cable. To sell more subscriptions, it must cut the price. When this happens, it gains the revenue from selling more subscriptions but loses revenue from selling at a lower price the subscriptions that it could have sold at a higher price. The firm's marginal revenue is the change in revenue from selling another subscription. We can calculate marginal revenue by subtracting the revenue lost as a result of a price cut from the revenue gained. The table shows that Time Warner's marginal revenue is less than the price for every subscription sold after the first subscription. Therefore, Time Warner's marginal revenue curve will be below its demand curve.

Subscribers per Month (Q)	Price (P)	Total Revenue ($TR = P \times Q$)	Average Revenue ($AR = TR/Q$)	Marginal Revenue ($MR = \Delta TR/\Delta Q$)
0	$60	$0	—	—
1	57	57	$57	$57
2	54	108	54	51
3	51	153	51	45
4	48	192	48	39
5	45	225	45	33
6	42	252	42	27
7	39	273	39	21
8	36	288	36	15
9	33	297	33	9
10	30	300	30	3

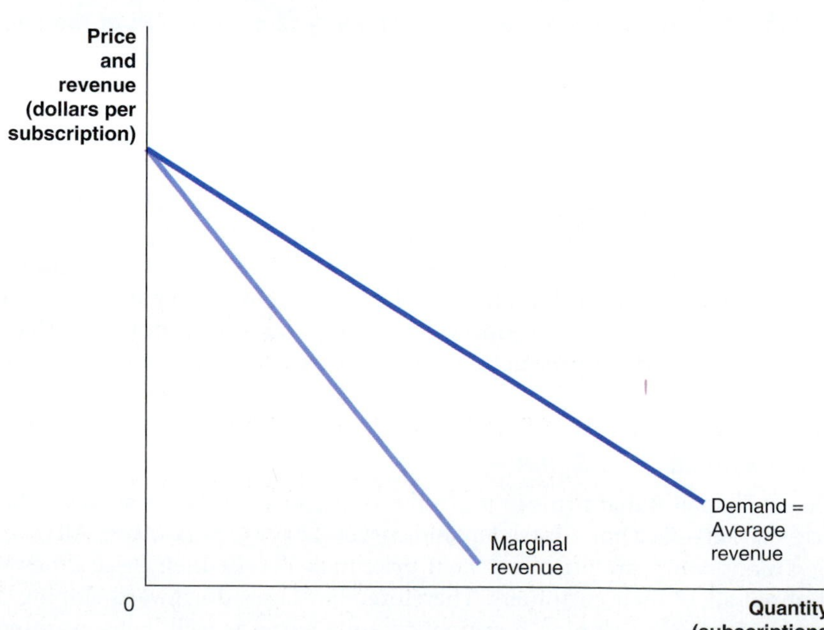

scriptions sold from 6 to 7. Time Warner increases its revenue by the $39 it receives for the seventh subscription. But it also loses revenue of $3 per subscription on the first 6 subscriptions because it could have sold them at the old price of $42. So, its marginal revenue on the seventh subscription is $39 − $18 = $21, which is the value shown in the table. The graph in Figure 9-2 plots Time Warner's demand and marginal revenue curves, based on the information given in the table.

Profit Maximization for a Monopolist

Figure 9-3 shows how Time Warner combines the information on demand and marginal revenue with information on average and marginal costs to decide how many subscriptions to sell and which price to charge. We assume that the firm's marginal cost and average total cost curves have the usual U-shapes we encountered in Chapters 7 and 8. In panel (a), we see how Time Warner can calculate its profit-maximizing quantity and price. As long as the marginal cost of selling one more subscription is less than the marginal revenue, the firm should sell additional subscriptions because it is adding to its profits. As Time Warner sells more cable subscriptions, rising marginal cost will eventually equal marginal revenue and the firm will be selling the profit-maximizing quantity of subscriptions. This happens with the sixth subscription, which adds $27 to the firm's costs and $27 to its revenues (point *A* in Figure 9-3 [a]). The demand curve tells us that Time Warner can sell 6 subscriptions for a price of $42 per month. We can conclude that Time Warner's profit-maximizing quantity of subscriptions is 6, and its profit-maximizing price is $42.

Panel (b) shows that the average total cost of 6 subscriptions is $30 and that Time Warner can sell 6 subscriptions at a price of $42 per month (point *B* on the demand curve). Time Warner is making a profit of $12 per subscription—the price of $42 minus the average cost of $30. Its total profit is $72 (6 subscriptions × $12 profit per subscription), which is shown by the area of the green-shaded rectangle in the figure.

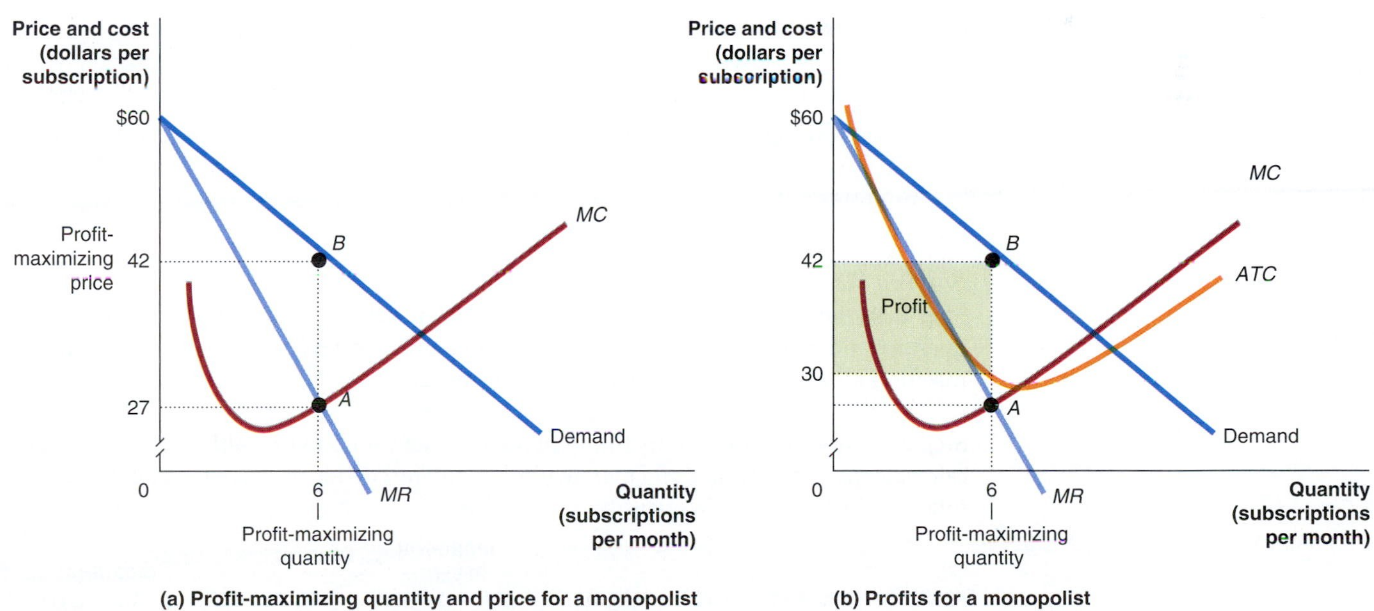

FIGURE 9-3 Profit-Maximizing Price and Output for a Monopoly

Panel (a) shows that to maximize profit, Time Warner should sell subscriptions up to the point that the marginal revenue from selling the last subscription equals its marginal cost (point *A*). In this case, the marginal revenue from selling the sixth subscription and the marginal cost are both $27. Time Warner maximizes profit by selling 6 subscriptions per month and charging a price of $42 (point *B*). In panel (b), the green box represents Time Warner's profits. The box has a height equal to $12, which is the price of $42 minus the average total cost of $30, and a base equal to the quantity of 6 cable subscriptions. Time Warner's profit equals $12 × 6 = $72.

We could also have calculated Time Warner's total profit as the difference between its total revenue and its total cost. Its total revenue from selling 6 subscriptions is \$252. Its total cost equals its average cost multiplied by the number of subscriptions sold or $\$30 \times 6 = \$180$. So, its profit is $\$252 - \$180 = \$72$.

It's important to note that even though Time Warner is earning economic profits, new firms will *not* enter the market. Because Time Warner has a monopoly, it will not face competition from other cable operators. Therefore, if other factors remain unchanged, Time Warner will be able to continue to earn economic profits, even in the long run.

SOLVED PROBLEM 9-2

③ LEARNING OBJECTIVE

Explain how a monopoly chooses price and output.

Finding Profit-Maximizing Price and Output for a Monopolist

Suppose that Comcast has a cable monopoly in Philadelphia. The following table gives Comcast's demand and costs per month for subscriptions to basic cable (for simplicity, we once again keep the number of subscribers artificially small):

PRICE	QUANTITY	TOTAL REVENUE	MARGINAL REVENUE ($MR = \Delta TR/\Delta Q$)	TOTAL COST	MARGINAL COST ($MC = \Delta TC/\Delta Q$)
\$17	3			\$56	
16	4			63	
15	5			71	
14	6			80	
13	7			90	
12	8			101	

a. Fill in the missing values in the table.

b. If Comcast wants to maximize profits, what price should it charge and how many cable subscriptions per month should it sell? How much profit will it make? Briefly explain.

c. Suppose the local government imposes a \$2.50 per month tax on cable companies. Now what price should Comcast charge, how many subscriptions should it sell, and what will its profits be?

Solving the Problem:

Step 1: Review the chapter material. This problem is about finding the profit-maximizing quantity and price for a monopolist, so you may want to review the section "Profit Maximization for a Monopolist," which begins on page 275.

Step 2: Answer question (a) by filling in the missing values in the table. Remember that to calculate marginal revenue and marginal cost, you must divide the change in total revenue or total cost by the change in quantity.

PRICE	QUANTITY	TOTAL REVENUE	MARGINAL REVENUE ($MR = \Delta TR/\Delta Q$)	TOTAL COST	MARGINAL COST ($MC = \Delta TC/\Delta Q$)
\$17	3	\$51	–	\$56	–
16	4	64	\$13	63	\$7
15	5	75	11	71	8
14	6	84	9	80	9
13	7	91	7	90	10
12	8	96	5	101	11

We don't have enough information from the table to fill in the values for marginal revenue or marginal cost in the first row.

Step 3: Answer question (b) by determining the profit-maximizing quantity and price. We know that Comcast will maximize profits by selling subscriptions up to the point where marginal cost equals marginal revenue. In this case, that means selling 6 subscriptions per month. From the information in the first two columns, we know Comcast can sell 6 subscriptions at a price of $14 each. Comcast's profits are equal to the difference between its total revenue and its total cost: Profit = $84 − $80 = $4 per month.

Step 4: Answer question (c) by analyzing the impact of the tax. This tax is a fixed cost to Comcast because it is a flat $2.50, no matter how many subscriptions it sells. Because the tax has no impact on Comcast's marginal revenue or marginal cost, the profit-maximizing level of output has not changed. So, Comcast will still sell 6 subscriptions per month at a price of $14, but its profits will fall by the amount of the tax from $4.00 per month to $1.50.

YOUR TURN: **For more practice, do related problems 13 and 14 on pages 295 and 294 at the end of this chapter.**

Don't Let This Happen To You!

Don't Assume That Charging a Higher Price Is Always More Profitable for a Monopolist

In answering question (c) of Solved Problem 9-2, it's tempting to argue that Comcast should increase its price to make up for the tax. After all, Comcast is a monopolist, so why can't it just pass along the tax to its customers? The reason it can't is that Comcast, like any other monopolist, must pay attention to demand. Comcast is not interested in charging high prices for the sake of charging high prices; it is interested in maximizing profits. Charging a price of $1,000 for a basic cable subscription sounds nice, but if no one will buy at that price, Comcast would hardly be maximizing profits.

To look at it another way, before the tax is imposed Comcast has already determined $14 is the price that will maximize its profits. After the tax is imposed, it must determine if $14 is still the profit-maximizing price. Because the tax has not affected Comcast's marginal revenue or marginal cost (or had any effect on consumer demand), $14 is still the profit-maximizing price, and Comcast should continue to charge it. The tax cuts into Comcast's profits but doesn't cause it to increase the price of cable subscriptions.

YOUR TURN: **Test your understanding by doing related problems 15 and 16 on page 295 at the end of this chapter.**

Does Monopoly Reduce Economic Efficiency?

LEARNING OBJECTIVE

Use a graph to illustrate how a monopoly affects economic surplus.

We saw in Chapter 8 that a perfectly competitive market is economically efficient. How would economic efficiency be affected if instead of being perfectly competitive, a market were a monopoly? In Chapter 4, we developed the idea of *economic surplus.* Economic surplus provides a way of characterizing the economic efficiency of a perfectly competitive market: *Equilibrium in a perfectly competitive market results in the greatest amount of economic surplus, or total benefit to society, from the production of a good or service.* What happens to economic surplus under monopoly? We can begin the analysis by considering the hypothetical case of what would happen if the television industry begins as perfectly competitive and then becomes a monopoly. (In reality the television industry is not perfectly competitive, but assuming that it is simplifies our analysis.)

Comparing Monopoly and Perfect Competition

Panel (a) in Figure 9-4 illustrates the situation if the market for televisions is perfectly competitive. Price and quantity are determined by the intersection of the demand and supply curves. Remember that none of the individual firms in a perfectly competitive

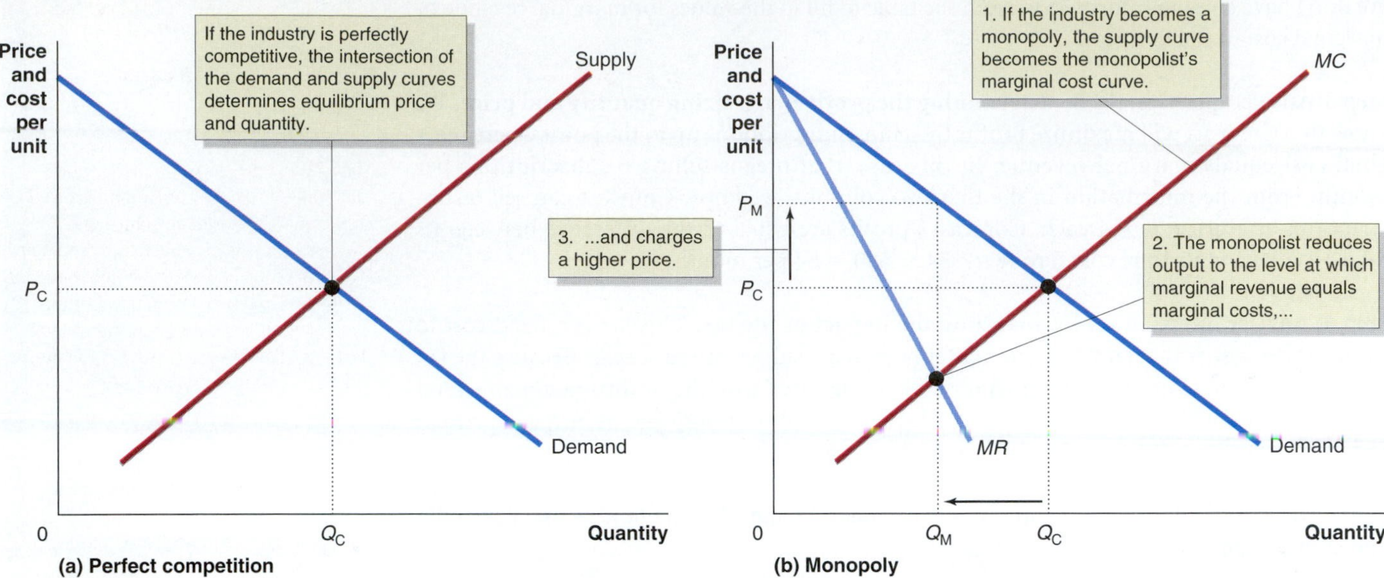

FIGURE 9-4 **What Happens If a Perfectly Competitive Industry Becomes a Monopoly?**

In panel (a), the television industry is perfectly competitive and price and quantity are determined by the intersection of the demand and supply curves. In panel (b), the perfectly competitive television industry became a monopoly. As a result, the equilibrium quantity falls, and the equilibrium price rises.

1. The industry supply curve becomes the monopolist's marginal cost curve.
2. The monopolist reduces output to where marginal revenue equals marginal cost, Q_M.
3. The monopolist raises the price from P_C to P_M.

industry has any control over price. Each firm must accept the price determined by the market. Panel (b) shows the consequences of the television industry becoming a monopoly. We know that the monopoly will maximize profits by producing where marginal revenue equals marginal cost. To do this, the monopoly reduces the quantity of televisions that would have been produced if the industry were perfectly competitive and increases the price. Panel (b) illustrates an important conclusion: *A monopoly will produce less and charge a higher price than would a perfectly competitive industry producing the same good.*

Measuring the Efficiency Losses from Monopoly

Figure 9-5 uses panel (b) from Figure 9-4 to illustrate how monopoly affects consumers, producers, and the efficiency of the economy. Recall from Chapter 4 that *consumer surplus* measures the net benefit received by consumers from purchasing a good or service. We measure consumer surplus as the area below the demand curve and above the market price. The higher the price, the smaller the consumer surplus. Because a monopoly raises the market price, it reduces consumer surplus. In Figure 9-5, the loss of consumer surplus is equal to rectangle *A* plus triangle *B*. Remember that *producer surplus* measures the net benefit to producers from selling a good or service. We measure producer surplus as the area above the supply curve and below the market price. The increase in price due to monopoly increases producer surplus by an amount equal to rectangle *A* and reduces it by an amount equal to triangle *C*. Because rectangle *A* is larger than triangle *C*, we know that a monopoly increases producer surplus compared with perfect competition.

Economic surplus is equal to the sum of consumer surplus plus producer surplus. By increasing price and reducing the quantity produced, the monopolist has reduced economic surplus by an amount equal to the areas of triangles *B* and *C*. This reduction in economic surplus is called *deadweight loss* and represents the loss of economic efficiency due to monopoly.

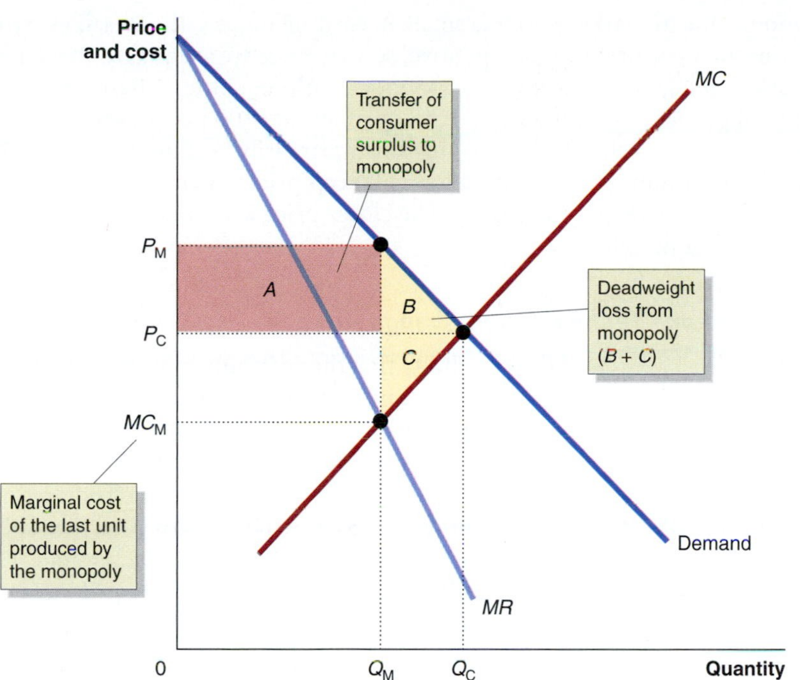

FIGURE 9-5

The Inefficiency of Monopoly

A monopoly charges a higher price, P_M, and produces a smaller quantity, Q_M, than a perfectly competitive industry, which charges a price of P_C and produces at Q_C. The higher price reduces consumer surplus by the area equal to the rectangle *A* and the triangle *B*. Some of the reduction in consumer surplus is captured by the monopoly as producer surplus and some becomes deadweight loss, which is the area equal to triangles *B* and *C*.

The best way to understand how a monopoly causes a loss of economic efficiency is to recall that price is equal to marginal cost in a perfectly competitive market. As a result, a consumer in a perfectly competitive market is always able to buy a good if she is willing to pay a price equal to the marginal cost of producing it. As Figure 9-5 shows, the monopolist stops producing at a point where the price is well above marginal cost. Consumers are unable to buy some units of the good for which they would be willing to pay a price greater than the marginal cost of producing them. Why doesn't the monopolist produce this additional output? Because the monopolist's profits are greater if it restricts output and forces up the price. A monopoly produces the profit-maximizing level of output, but fails to produce the efficient level of output from the point of view of society.

We can summarize the effects of monopoly as follows:

1. Monopoly causes a reduction in consumer surplus.
2. Monopoly causes an increase in producer surplus.
3. Monopoly causes a deadweight loss, which represents a reduction in economic efficiency.

How Large Are the Efficiency Losses Due to Monopoly?

We know that there are relatively few monopolies, so the loss of economic efficiency due to monopoly must be small. Many firms, though, have **market power,** which is the ability of a firm to charge a price greater than marginal cost. The analysis we just completed shows that some loss of economic efficiency will occur whenever a firm has market power and can charge a price greater than marginal cost, even if the firm is not a monopoly. The only firms that do *not* have market power are firms in perfectly competitive markets, who must charge a price equal to marginal cost. Because few markets are perfectly competitive, *some loss of economic efficiency occurs in the market for nearly every good or service.*

Market power The ability of a firm to charge a price greater than marginal cost.

Is the total loss of economic efficiency due to market power large or small? It is possible to put a dollar value on the loss of economic efficiency by estimating for every industry the size of the deadweight loss triangle, as in Figure 9-5. The first economist to do this was Arnold Harberger of the University of Chicago. His estimates—largely confirmed by later researchers—indicated that the total loss of economic efficiency in the

U.S. economy due to market power is small. According to his estimates, if every industry in the economy were perfectly competitive, so that price were equal to marginal cost in every market, the gain in economic efficiency would equal less than 1 percent of the value of total production in the United States, or about $300 per person.

The loss of economic efficiency is this small primarily because true monopolies are very rare. In most industries, competition will keep price much closer to marginal cost than would be the case in a monopoly. The closer price is to marginal cost, the smaller the size of the deadweight loss.

Market Power and Technological Change

Some economists have raised the possibility that the economy may actually benefit from firms having market power. This argument is most closely identified with Joseph Schumpeter, an Austrian economist who spent many years as a professor of economics at Harvard. Schumpeter argued that economic progress depended on technological change in the form of new products. For example, the replacement of horse-drawn carriages by automobiles, the replacement of ice boxes by refrigerators, or the replacement of mechanical calculators with electronic computers all represent technological changes that significantly raised living standards. In Schumpeter's view, new products unleash a "gale of creative destruction" in which older products—and, often, the firms that produced them—are driven out of the market. Schumpeter was unconcerned that firms with market power would charge higher prices than perfectly competitive firms:

> It is not that kind of [price] competition which counts but the competition from the new commodity, the new technology, the new source of supply, the new type of organization . . . competition which commands a decisive cost or quality advantage and which strikes not at the margins of the profits and outputs of the existing firms but at their foundations and their very lives.

Economists who support Schumpeter's view argue that the introduction of new products requires firms to spend funds on research and development. It is possible for firms to raise this money by borrowing from investors or from banks. But investors and banks are usually skeptical of ideas for new products that have not yet passed the test of consumer acceptance in the market. As a result, firms are often forced to rely on their profits to finance the research and development needed for new products. Because firms with market power are more likely to earn economic profits than are perfectly competitive firms, they are also more likely to carry out research and development and to introduce new products. In this view, the higher prices charged by firms with market power are unimportant compared with the benefits from the new products these firms introduce to the market.

Some economists disagree with Schumpeter's views. These economists point to the number of new products developed by smaller firms, including, for example, Steve Jobs and Steve Wozniak inventing the first Apple computer in Wozniak's garage, and Larry Page and Sergey Brin inventing the Google search engine as graduate students at Stanford. As we will see in the next section, government policymakers continue to struggle with the issue of whether, on balance, large firms with market power are good or bad for the economy.

5 LEARNING OBJECTIVE

Explain how a firm can increase its profits through price discrimination.

Price Discrimination: Charging Different Prices for the Same Product

Price discrimination Charging different prices to different customers for the same product when the price differences are not due to differences in cost.

One way firms can use their market power is by charging different prices for the same product. Charging different prices to different customers for the same good or service when the price differences are not due to differences in cost is called **price discrimination.** Not all firms are able to engage in price discrimination. In this section we examine the circumstances under which firms are able to use this pricing strategy,

The Requirements for Successful Price Discrimination

A successful strategy of price discrimination has three requirements:

1. A firm must possess market power.
2. Some consumers must have a greater willingness to pay for the product than other consumers, and the firm must be able to know what prices customers are willing to pay.
3. The firm must be able to divide up—or *segment*—the market for the product so that consumers who buy the product at a low price are not able to resell it at a high price. In other words, price discrimination will not work if arbitrage is possible.

Note that a firm selling in a perfectly competitive market cannot practice price discrimination because it can only charge the market price. But because most firms do not sell in perfectly competitive markets, they have market power and can set the price of the good they sell. Many firms may also be able to determine that some customers have a greater willingness to pay for the product than others. However, the third requirement—that markets be segmented so that customers buying at a low price will not be able to resell the product—can be difficult to fulfill. For example, some people really love Big Macs and would be willing to pay $10 rather than do without one. Other people would not be willing to pay a penny more than $1 for one. Even if McDonald's could identify differences in the willingness of its customers to pay for Big Macs, it would not be able to charge them different prices. Suppose McDonald's knows that Joe is willing to pay $10, whereas Jill will pay only $1. If McDonald's tries to charge Joe $10, he will just have Jill buy his Big Mac for him.

Only firms that can keep consumers from reselling a product are able to practice price discrimination. Because the product cannot be resold, the law of one price is not contradicted. For example, movie theaters know that many people are willing to pay more to see a movie at night than during the afternoon. As a result, theaters usually charge higher prices for tickets to night showings than for tickets to afternoon showings. They keep these markets separate by making the tickets to afternoon showings a different color or by having the time printed on them, and by having a ticket taker examine the tickets. That makes it difficult for someone to buy a lower-priced ticket in the afternoon and use the ticket to gain admission to an evening showing.

Figure 9-6 illustrates how the owners of movie theaters use price discrimination to increase their profits. The marginal cost to the movie theater owner from another person attending a showing is very small: a little more wear on a theater seat and a few more kernels of popcorn to be swept from the floor. In previous chapters, we have assumed that marginal cost has a U-shape. For our purposes here, we can simplify things by assuming that marginal cost is a constant $0.50, shown as a horizontal line in Figure 9-6. Panel (a) shows the demand for afternoon showings. In this segment of its market, the theater should maximize profit by selling the number of tickets for which marginal revenue equals marginal cost, or 350 tickets. We know from the demand curve that 450 tickets can be sold at a price of $4.50 per ticket. Panel (b) shows the demand for night showings. Notice that charging $4.50 per ticket would *not* be profit-maximizing in this market. At a price of $4.50, the theater sells 850 tickets, which is 225 more tickets than the profit-maximizing number of 625. By charging $4.50 for tickets to afternoon showings and $6.75 for tickets to night showings, the theater has maximized profits.

Figure 9-6 also illustrates another important point about price discrimination: When firms can price discriminate, they will charge customers who are less sensitive to price—those whose demand for the product is *less elastic*—a higher price and charge customers who are more sensitive to price—those whose demand is *more elastic*—a lower price. In this case, the demand for tickets to night showings is less elastic, so the price charged is higher, and the demand for tickets to afternoon showings is more elastic, so the price charged is lower.

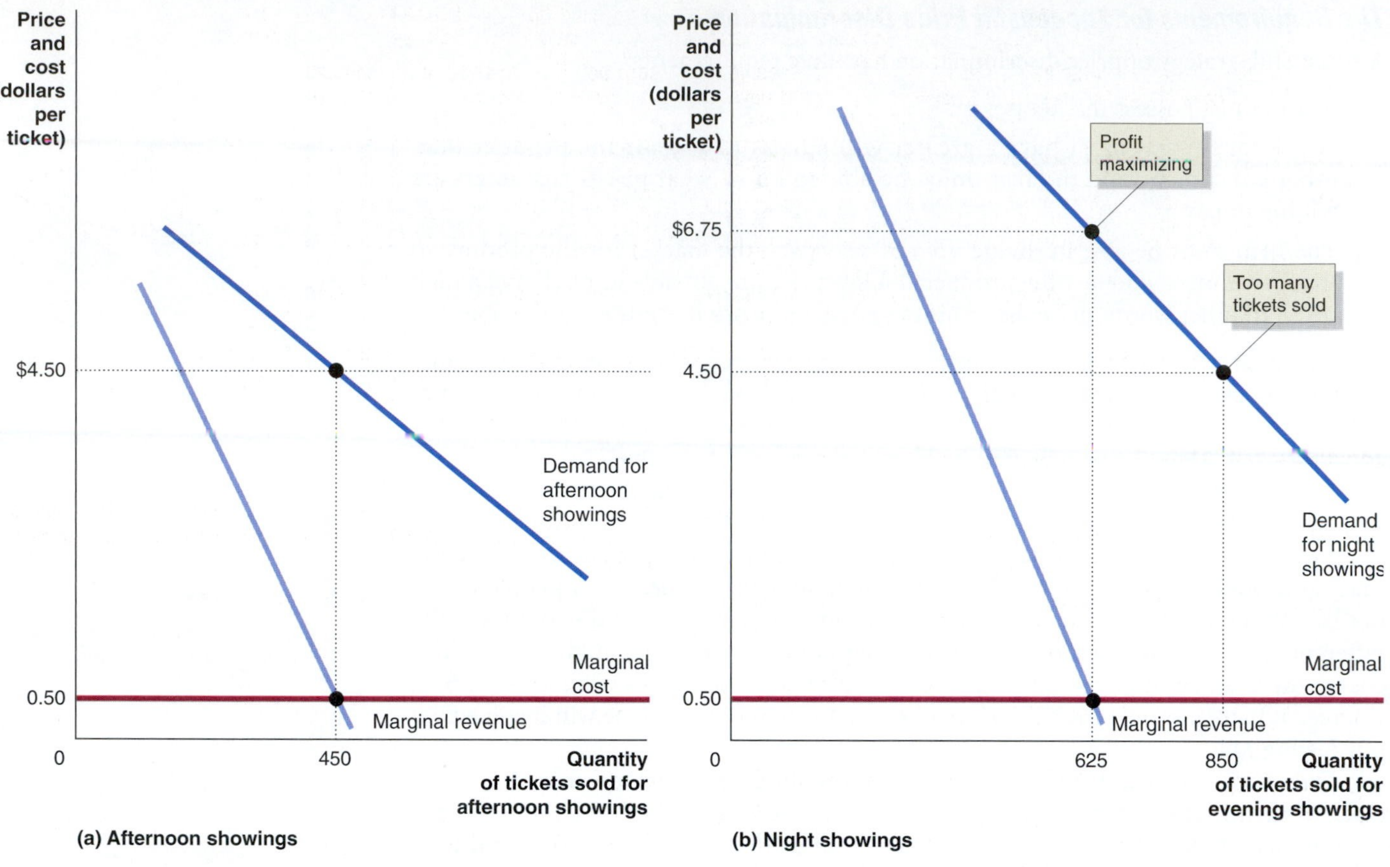

FIGURE 9-6 Price Discrimination by a Movie Theater

Fewer people want to go to the movies in the afternoon than in the evening. In panel (a), the profit-maximizing price for a ticket to an afternoon showing is $4.50. Charging this same price for night showings would not be profit-maximizing, as panel (b) shows. At a price of $4.50, 850 tickets would be sold to night showings, which is more than the profit-maximizing number of 625 tickets. To maximize profits, the theater should charge $6.75 for tickets to night showings.

Airlines: The Kings of Price Discrimination

Airline seats are a very perishable product. Once a plane has taken off from Chicago for Los Angeles, any seat that has not been sold on that particular flight will never be sold. In addition, the marginal cost of flying one additional passenger is low. This situation gives airlines a strong incentive to manage prices so that as many seats as possible are filled on each flight.

Airlines divide their customers into two main categories: business travelers and leisure travelers. Business travelers often have inflexible schedules, can't commit until the last minute to traveling on a particular day, and, most importantly, are not very sensitive to changes in price. The opposite is true for leisure travelers: They are flexible about when they travel, they are willing to buy their tickets well in advance, and they are sensitive to changes in price. Based on what we discussed earlier in this chapter, you can see that airlines will maximize profits by charging business travelers higher ticket prices than leisure travelers, but they need to determine who is a business traveler and who is a leisure traveler. Some airlines do this by requiring people who want to buy a ticket at the leisure price to buy 14 days in advance and to stay at their destination over a Saturday night. Anyone unable to meet these requirements must pay a much higher price. Because business travelers often cannot make their plans 14 days in advance of their flight and don't want to stay over a weekend, they end up paying the higher ticket price. The gap between leisure fares and business fares is often very substantial. For example, in April 2005, the price of a leisure-fare ticket between New

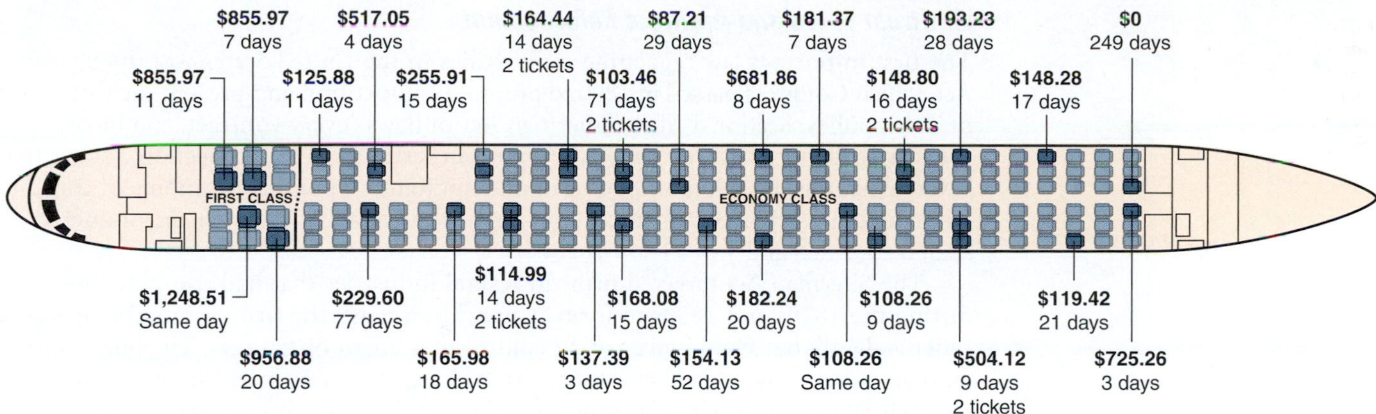

FIGURE 9-7 **33 Customers and 27 Different Prices**

To fill as many seats on a flight as possible, airlines charge many different ticket prices. The 33 passengers on this United Airlines flight from Chicago to Los Angeles paid 27 different prices for their tickets, including one passenger who used frequent flyer miles to obtain a free ticket. The first number in the figure is the price paid for the ticket; the second number is the number of days in advance that the ticket was purchased.

Source: Matthew L. Wald, "So, How Much Did You Pay for Your Ticket?" *New York Times,* April 12, 1998. Used with permission of New York Times Agency.

York and San Francisco on United Airlines was $363. The price of a business-fare ticket was $1,143.

The airlines go well beyond a single leisure fare and a single business fare in their pricing strategies. Although they ordinarily charge high prices for tickets sold only a few days in advance, they are willing to reduce prices for seats that they expect will not be sold at existing prices. Since the late 1980s, airlines have employed economists and mathematicians to construct computer models of the market for airline tickets. To calculate a suggested price each day for each seat, these models take into account factors that affect the demand for tickets, such as the season of the year, the length of the route, the day of the week, and whether the flight typically attracts primarily business or leisure travelers. This practice of continually adjusting prices to take into account fluctuations in demand is called *yield management.*

Since the late 1990s, Internet sites such as Priceline.com have helped the airlines to implement yield management. On Priceline.com, buyers commit to paying a price of their choosing for a ticket on a particular day and agree that they will fly at any time on that day. This gives airlines the opportunity to fill seats that otherwise would have gone empty, particularly on late night or early morning flights, even though the price may be well below the normal leisure fare. In 2001, several airlines combined to form the Internet site Orbitz, which became another means of filling seats at discount prices. In fact, in the last few years the chances that you paid the same price for your airline ticket as the person sitting next to you has become quite small. Figure 9-7 shows an actual United Airlines flight from Chicago to Los Angeles. The 33 passengers on the flight paid 27 different prices for their tickets, including one passenger who used frequent flyer miles to obtain a free ticket.

Government Policy toward Monopoly

⑥ **LEARNING OBJECTIVE**

Discuss government policies toward monopoly.

Because monopolies reduce consumer surplus and economic efficiency, most governments have policies that regulate their behavior. **Collusion** refers to an agreement among firms to charge the same price, or otherwise not to compete. In the United States, *antitrust laws* are government policies that deal with monopolies and collusion. These laws make illegal any attempts to form a monopoly or to collude. Governments also regulate firms that are natural monopolies, often by controlling the prices they charge.

Collusion An agreement among firms to charge the same price, or otherwise not to compete.

Antitrust Laws and Antitrust Enforcement

The first important law regulating monopolies in the United States was the Sherman Act, which Congress passed in 1890 to promote competition and prevent the formation of monopolies. Section 1 of the Sherman Act outlaws "every contract, combination in the form of trust or otherwise, or conspiracy in restraint of trade." Section 2 states that "every person who shall monopolize, or attempt to monopolize, or combine or conspire with any other person or persons, to monopolize any part of the trade or commerce . . . shall be deemed guilty of a felony."

The Sherman Act targeted firms in several industries that had combined together during the 1870s and 1880s to form "trusts." In a trust, the firms would be operated independently but would give voting control to a board of trustees. The board would enforce collusive agreements for the firms to charge the same price and not to compete for each other's customers. The most notorious of the trusts was the Standard Oil Trust, organized by John D. Rockefeller. After the Sherman Act was passed, trusts disappeared, but the term **antitrust laws** has lived on to refer to the laws aimed at eliminating collusion and promoting competition among firms.

Antitrust laws Laws aimed at eliminating collusion and promoting competition among firms.

The Sherman Act prohibited trusts and collusive agreements, but it left several loopholes. For example, it was not clear whether it would be legal for two or more firms to merge to form a new larger firm that would have substantial market power. A series of Supreme Court decisions interpreted the Sherman Act narrowly, and the result was a wave of mergers at the turn of the twentieth century. Included in these mergers was the United States Steel Corporation, which was formed from dozens of smaller companies. U.S. Steel, organized by J. P. Morgan, was the first billion-dollar corporation and controlled two-thirds of steel production in the United States. The Sherman Act also left unclear whether any business practices short of outright collusion were illegal.

To address the loopholes in the Sherman Act, in 1914 Congress passed the Clayton Act and the Federal Trade Commission Act. Under the Clayton Act, a merger was illegal if its effect was "substantially to lessen competition, or to tend to create a monopoly." The Federal Trade Commission Act set up the Federal Trade Commission (FTC), which was given the power to police unfair business practices. The FTC has brought lawsuits against firms employing a variety of business practices, including deceptive advertising. In setting up the FTC, however, Congress divided the authority to police mergers. Currently, both the Antitrust Division of the U.S. Department of Justice and the FTC are responsible for merger policy. Table 9-1 lists the most important U.S. antitrust laws and the purpose of each.

TABLE 9-1

Important U.S. Antitrust Laws

LAW	DATE	PURPOSE
Sherman Act	1890	Prohibited "restraint of trade," including price fixing and collusion. Also outlawed monopolization.
Clayton Act	1914	Prohibited firms from buying stock in competitors and from having directors serve on the boards of competing firms.
Federal Trade Commission Act	1914	Established the Federal Trade Commission (FTC) to help administer antitrust laws.
Robinson–Patman Act	1936	Prohibited charging buyers different prices if the result would reduce competition.
Cellar–Kefauver Act	1950	Toughened restrictions on mergers by prohibiting any mergers that would reduce competition.

Mergers: The Trade-off between Market Power and Efficiency

The federal government regulates business mergers because it knows that if firms gain market power by merging, they may use that market power to raise prices and reduce output. As a result, the government is most concerned with **horizontal mergers,** or mergers between firms in the same industry. Horizontal mergers are more likely to increase market power than **vertical mergers,** which are mergers between firms at different stages of the production of a good. An example of a vertical merger would be a merger between a company making personal computers and a company making computer hard drives.

Horizontal merger A merger between firms in the same industry.

Vertical merger A merger between firms at different stages of production of a good.

Regulating horizontal mergers can be complicated by two factors. First, the "market" that firms are in is not always clear. For example, if Hershey Foods wants to merge with Mars, Inc., makers of M&Ms, Snickers, and other candies, what is the relevant market? If the government looks just at the candy market, the newly merged company would have more than 70 percent of the market, a level at which the government would likely oppose the merger. What if the government looks at the broader market for "snacks"? In this market, Hershey and Mars compete with makers of potato chips, pretzels, peanuts, and, perhaps, even producers of fresh fruit. Of course, if the government looked at the very broad market for "food," then both Hershey and Mars have very small market shares and there would be no reason to oppose their merger. In practice, the government defines the relevant market on the basis of whether there are close substitutes for the products being made by the merging firms. In this case, potato chips and the other snack foods mentioned are not close substitutes for candy. So, the government would consider the candy market to be the relevant market and would oppose the merger on the grounds that the new firm would have too much market power.

The second factor that complicates merger policy is the possibility that the newly merged firm might be more efficient than the merging firms were individually. For example, one firm might have an excellent product but a poor distribution system for getting the product into the hands of consumers. A competing firm might have built a great distribution system but have an inferior product. Allowing these firms to merge might be good for both the firms and consumers. Or, two competing firms might each have an extensive system of warehouses that are only half full, but if the firms merged, they could consolidate their warehouses and significantly reduce their costs.

An example of the government dealing with the issue of greater efficiency versus reduced competition occurred in early 2000 when Time Warner, which as we have seen owns cable systems with more than 20 million subscribers, and America Online (AOL), which was the country's largest Internet Service Provider (ISP) with more than 26 million subscribers, announced plans to merge. The firms argued that the merger would speed the development of high-speed (or "broadband") Internet access and would lead to the more rapid growth of services such as interactive television. Some competing firms complained that the new firm created by the merger would have excessive market power. In particular, other ISPs were worried that they would be denied access to the cable systems owned by Time Warner. After more than a year of study, the FTC finally approved the merger, subject to certain conditions. One key condition was that Time Warner was required to allow AOL's competitors to offer their services over Time Warner's high-speed cable lines before AOL would be permitted to offer its services over those lines.

Most of the mergers that come under scrutiny by the Department of Justice and the FTC are between large firms. For simplicity, let's consider a case where all the firms in a perfectly competitive industry want to merge to form a monopoly. As we saw in Figure 9-5, as a result of this merger prices will rise and output will fall, leading to a decline in consumer surplus and economic efficiency. But what if the larger, newly merged firm actually is more efficient than the smaller firms had been? Figure 9-6 shows a possible result.

If costs are unaffected by the merger, we get the same result as in Figure 9-5: Price rises from P_C to P_M, quantity falls from Q_C to Q_M, consumer surplus is lower, and a loss

FIGURE 9-8

A Merger That Makes Consumers Better Off

This figure shows the result of all the firms in a perfectly competitive industry merging to form a monopoly. If costs are unaffected by the merger, the result is the same as in Figure 9-5: Price rises from P_C to P_M, quantity falls from Q_C to Q_M, consumer surplus declines, and a loss of economic efficiency results. If, however, the monopoly has lower costs than the perfectly competitive firms, it is possible the price will actually decline from P_0 to P_{Merge} and output will increase from Q_C to Q_{Merge} following the merger.

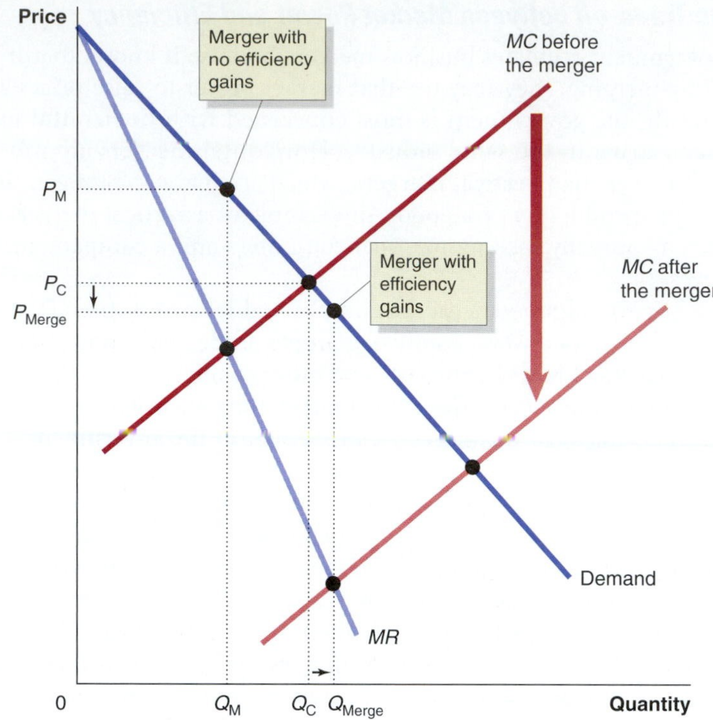

of economic efficiency results. If the monopoly has lower costs than the competitive firms, it is possible for price to decline and quantity to increase. In Figure 9-6, price declines after the merger from P_C to P_{Merge} and quantity increases from Q_C to Q_{Merge}. This leads to the following seemingly paradoxical result: *Although the newly merged firm has a great deal of market power, because it is more efficient, consumers are better off and economic efficiency is improved.* Of course, sometimes a merged firm will be more efficient and have lower costs, and other times it won't. Even if a merged firm is more efficient and has lower costs, this may not offset the increased market power of the firm enough to increase consumer surplus and economic efficiency.

As you might expect, whenever large firms propose a merger they claim that the newly merged firm will be more efficient and have lower costs. They realize that without these claims it is unlikely their merger will be approved. It is up to the Department of Justice and the FTC, along with the court system, to evaluate the merits of these claims.

The Department of Justice and the Federal Trade Commission Merger Guidelines

For many years after the passage of the Sherman Antitrust Act in 1890, lawyers from the Department of Justice enforced the antitrust laws. They rarely considered economic arguments, such as the possibility that consumers might be made better off by a merger if economic efficiency were significantly improved. This began to change in 1965 when Donald Turner became the first Ph.D. economist to head the Antitrust Division of the Department of Justice. Under Turner and his successors, antitrust policy was reshaped by economic analysis. In 1973, the Economics Section of the Antitrust Division was established and staffed with economists who evaluate the economic consquences of proposed mergers.

One of the fruits of this economic expertise was the joint development by the Department of Justice and the FTC of merger guidelines in 1982. The guidelines made it possible for economists and attorneys employed by firms considering a merger to understand whether the government was likely to allow the merger or to oppose it. The guidelines have three main parts:

1. Market definition
2. Measure of concentration
3. Merger standards

MARKET DEFINITION A market consists of all firms making products that consumers view as close substitutes. We can identify close substitutes by looking at the effect of a price increase. If our definition of a market is too narrow, a price increase will cause firms to experience a significant decline in sales—and profits—as consumers switch to buying close substitutes.

Identifying the relevant market involved in a proposed merger begins with a narrow definition of the industry. For the hypothetical merger of Hershey Foods and Mars, Inc. discussed previously in this chapter, we might start with the candy industry. If all firms in the candy industry increased price by 5 percent, would their profits increase or decrease? If profits would increase, the market is defined as being just these firms. If profits would decrease, we would try a broader definition—say, by adding in potato chips and other snacks. Would a price increase of 5 percent by all firms in the broader market raise profits? If profits increase, the relevant market has been identified. If profits decrease, we would consider a broader definition. We would continue this procedure until a market has been identified.

MEASURE OF CONCENTRATION A market is *concentrated* if a relatively small number of firms have a large share of total sales in the market. A merger between firms in a market that is already highly concentrated is very likely to increase market power. A merger between firms in an industry that has a very low concentration is unlikely to increase market power and can be ignored. The guidelines use the *Herfindahl-Hirschman Index (HHI)* of concentration, which adds together the squares of the market shares of each firm in the industry. The following are some examples of calculating a Herfindahl-Hirschman Index:

- 1 firm, with 100% market share (a monopoly):
  $\text{HHI} = 100^2 = 10{,}000$
- 2 firms, each with a 50% market share:
  $\text{HHI} = 50^2 + 50^2 = 5{,}000$
- 4 firms, with market shares of 30%, 30%, 20%, and 20%:
  $\text{HHI} = 30^2 + 30^2 + 20^2 + 20^2 = 2{,}600$
- 10 firms, each with market shares of 10%:
  $\text{HHI} = 10\,(10^2) = 1{,}000$

MERGER STANDARDS The HHI calculation for a market is then used to evaluate proposed horizontal mergers according to these standards:

- ***Post-Merger HHI below 1,000.***
  These markets are not concentrated, so mergers in them are not challenged.
- ***Post-Merger HHI between 1,000 and 1,800.***
  These markets are moderately concentrated. Mergers that raise the HHI by less than 100 probably will not be challenged. Mergers that raise the HHI by more than 100 may be challenged.
- ***Post-Merger HHI above 1,800.***
  These markets are highly concentrated. Mergers that increase the HHI by less than 50 points will not be challenged. Mergers that increase the HHI by 50 to 100 points may be challenged. Mergers that increase the HHI by more than 100 points will be challenged.

Increases in economic efficiency will be taken into account and can lead to approval of a merger that otherwise would be opposed, but the burden of showing that the efficiencies exist lies with the merging firms: "The merging firms must substantiate efficiency claims so that the [Department of Justice and the FTC] can verify by reasonable means the likelihood and magnitude of each asserted efficiency. . . . Efficiency claims will not be considered if they are vague or speculative or otherwise cannot be verified by reasonable means."

9-4 Making the Connection

Software pioneer, monopolist, or both?

The Antitrust Case against Microsoft

Microsoft was still a small company in 1981 when IBM chose it to provide the operating system for its personal computers. As other companies "cloned" the IBM PC, Microsoft's business increased. By 1992, it controlled more than 90 percent of the market for PC operating systems. Microsoft required computer manufacturers who installed Windows on any of their computers to pay Microsoft a royalty on every computer sold, whether or not the computer actually had Windows installed on it. The Department of Justice saw this as a potential violation of the antitrust laws because it made it more difficult for new firms to enter the market for operating systems. Any manufacturer of PCs who wanted to use Windows on any of its PCs would likely use it on all of its PCs, because if the manufacturer installed a non-Windows operating system on its PCs it would have to pay twice: once to Microsoft and once to the firm whose operating system it was actually using. To head off the investigation by the Justice Department, Microsoft agreed in 1994 to stop this practice. Thereafter, manufacturers of PCs would have to pay Microsoft only when a computer they sold actually had Windows installed on it.

Still, Microsoft's antitrust problems weren't over. In 1997, Microsoft tried to increase its share of the market for Internet browsers. At the time, the Netscape browser had the largest market share. When Microsoft released a new version of its Internet browser, Internet Explorer 4.0, it required PC firms to install it on all computers sold with Windows. The Justice Department decided that requiring PC firms using Windows to also install Internet Explorer violated Microsoft's 1994 agreement. In May 1998, the Justice Department filed a lawsuit charging that Microsoft had violated the Sherman Act. After a 78-day trial, Judge Thomas Penfield Jackson found that Microsoft had illegally monopolized the PC operating-system market and had illegally attempted to use this monopoly also to monopolize the browser market. Jackson ordered Microsoft to be broken into two companies: One company would produce the Windows operating system, and the other company would produce Microsoft's other software, including Internet Explorer.

Microsoft appealed the case, and the federal Court of Appeals ruled that Microsoft had taken actions to maintain a monopoly on PC operating systems, but it threw out Judge Jackson's order that the company be split up. The appeals court sent the case back to the district court for final resolution. In spring 2002, the Justice Department and Microsoft agreed on a settlement. As part of the settlement, Microsoft agreed to allow removal of the Internet Explorer icon from the Windows "desktop," and to allow computer manufacturers to include other companies' software icons on the desktop. Microsoft also agreed to make it easier for other operating systems to run on computers that had Windows installed on them. Nine states declined to go along with the settlement of the federal antitrust suit and pressed ahead with their own lawsuit.

The Microsoft case illustrates one of the key problems in enforcing the antitrust laws: the trade-off between efficiency and market power. Microsoft argues that embedding software such as Internet Explorer and a media player in Windows benefits consumers by improving the ease of using the software. At the same time, it may make it more difficult for makers of competing software to break into the market. The government has had little difficulty proving that Microsoft has market power, but as one observer puts it, "Proving that Microsoft's monopoly power harms consumers has always been a difficulty in the government's case against the company."

Sources: Last quote from Amy Harmon, "Why Gates Won't Apologize," *New York Times*, April 29, 2002; other material from Department of Justice Web site: www.usdoj.gov.

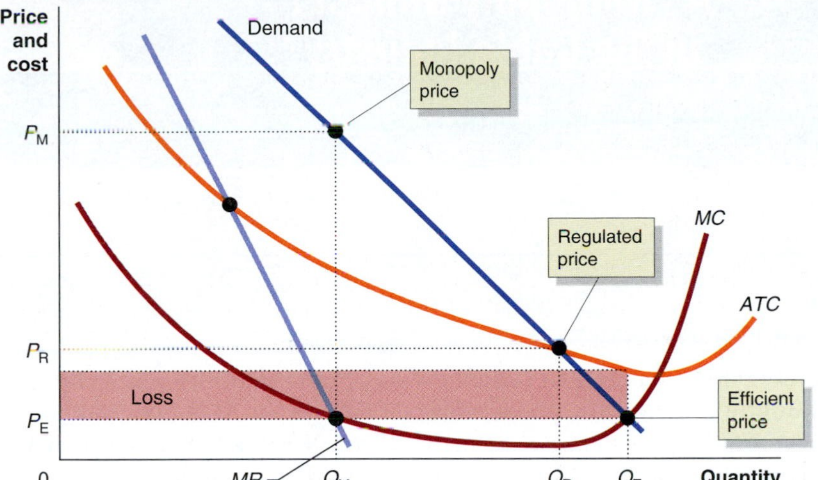

FIGURE 9-9

Regulating a Natural Monopoly

A natural monopoly that is not subject to government regulation will charge a price equal to P_M and produce Q_M. If government regulators want to achieve economic efficiency, they will set the regulated price equal to P_E and the monopoly will produce Q_E. Unfortunately, P_E is below average cost and the monopoly will suffer a loss shown by the shaded rectangle. Because the monopoly will not continue to produce in the long run if it suffers a loss, government regulators set a price equal to average cost, which is P_R in the figure.

Regulating Natural Monopolies

If a firm is a natural monopoly, competition from other firms will not play its usual role of forcing price down to the level where the company earns zero economic profit. As a result, local or state *regulatory commissions* usually set the prices for natural monopolies, such as firms selling natural gas or electricity. What price should these commissions set? Recall from Chapter 8 that economic efficiency requires the last unit of a good or service produced to provide an additional benefit to consumers equal to the additional cost of producing it. We can measure the additional benefit consumers receive by the price and the additional cost by marginal cost. Therefore, to achieve economic efficiency, regulators should require that the monopoly charge a price equal to its marginal cost. There is, however, an important drawback to doing so, which is illustrated in Figure 9-9. This figure shows the situation of a typical regulated natural monopoly.

Remember that with a natural monopoly the average total cost curve is still falling when it crosses the demand curve. If unregulated, the monopoly will charge a price equal to P_M and produce Q_M. To achieve economic efficiency, regulators should require the monopoly to charge a price equal to P_E. The monopoly will then produce Q_E. But here is the drawback: P_E is less than average total cost, so the monopoly will be suffering a loss, shown by the area of the red-shaded rectangle. In the long run, the owners of the monopoly will not continue in business if they are experiencing losses. Realizing this, most regulators will set the regulated price, P_R, equal to the level of average total cost at which the demand curve intersects the *ATC* curve. At that price, the owners of the monopoly are able to break even on their investment by producing the quantity Q_R.

Conclusion

The more intense the level of competition among firms, the better a market works. In this chapter we have seen that with monopoly—where competition is entirely absent—price is higher, output is lower, and consumer surplus and economic efficiency decline compared with perfect competition. Fortunately, true monopolies are rare. Even though most firms resemble monopolies in being able to charge a price above marginal cost, most markets have enough competition to keep the efficiency losses from market power quite low.

We've seen that barriers to entry are an important source of market power. Read *An Inside Look* on the next page to learn how cable companies use barriers to entry.

An Inside Look

A "Monopoly Mindset" in the Cable Industry?

WALL STREET JOURNAL, MAY 21, 2004

Why I'm Filing Chapter 11

Sometime in the next week or so, I anticipate that one of my companies, the cable, phone and video provider RCN, will file for what is known in the business as a consensual, pre-arranged Chapter 11 bankruptcy. That hardly makes me unique. Since 2000, nearly 70 major telecom companies have filed for bankruptcy. Hundreds, if not thousands, never even made it to Chapter 11 . . .

a Having built, bought, or started 10 telecom companies in the last 25 years, I think both Wall Street and Washington overlook the most persistent problem: The cable industry remains in the grip of a monopoly mindset. . . . [C]able rates have soared 40% and the industry giants continue to think in terms of how to dominate markets rather than of how to drive innovation. The bankruptcies that sidelined so many upstart cable providers have effectively spared the cable incumbents from facing competitive pressures—at least for the moment.

RCN was one of the "overbuilders" that started constructing a fiber pipeline in densely populated neighborhoods where competition was unknown. I believed—and still do—that a new infrastructure to the home was the critical step to creating a system that can bundle and deliver every type of service that consumers would want. Not just phone, cable and Internet, but home security, energy monitoring and even appliance diagnostics. . . .

b That idea of building a network that could attract multiple streams of revenue was drawn on the economics I learned as a freshman in college. Those economic principles dictated that if you have a network, you want to make it as expansive as possible and if you own content you want to deliver it over as big a network and to as many people as possible. Until 1996, the entire telecom industry operated on exactly the opposite principle. The incumbents depended on closed, proprietary systems guarded by regulations and old technology. The strategy was like building a road system that only goes to your store, or a railroad that only goes to your town.

[T]he major cable companies still divide-and-rule territory. When one company buys close to another, the rivals simply exchange geographic service areas, so that each side can expand their local fiefdoms—the same business model championed by Tony Soprano.

The cable companies have also relied on closed, proprietary technology to inhibit open competition. Rather than let customers go to Radio Shack and buy a standardized set-top box, they force you to rent their proprietary converter boxes. Over the last five years, RCN has had to spend nearly half a billion dollars replacing proprietary equipment each time a customer switched to our service. . . .

Comcast's recent bid to acquire Disney would have taken this anti-competitive approach one step further. Had the merger plan taken off—and if not this one, other, similar mergers will—then Disney's content would have been harder to get, more expensive, or less convenient to find for any consumer not part of the Comcast family.

Fortunately, the telecom story is not over. For many telecom companies—including my own—bankruptcy is not the end, but a new lease on life. I believe that the wave of bankruptcy filings will help launch a new era in telecom. Over the next year or two, I suspect we will see many companies re-emerging from bankruptcy, now in a much better position to compete without the dead weight of debt on their back. These may well be the companies that bring Voice-over-IP technology to the cable world, creating "Video-over-IP" competitors who change the way customers bring television into their homes. That possibility should worry today's cable giants who have been ignoring the logic of economics, the possibilities of technology and the interests of consumers for far too long.

Key Points in the Article

This article by David McCourt, the founder of cable television company RCN, discusses problems in the cable industry. He argues that many cable companies have a "monopoly mindset" that causes them to erect barriers to the entry of competing firms in order to make economic profits through high prices. McCourt argues that both the cable firms and the public would be better off if the firms concentrated on making profits through technological change and on being more responsive to consumers.

Analyzing the News

a McCourt argues that most cable companies are relying on barriers to entry to give them monopolies in local markets. Figure 1 shows the now-familiar graph of a monopoly firm making economic profits. The monopolist sells the quantity of subscriptions Q_M, where marginal revenue equals marginal cost, and charges the price P_M. The profits are shown by the area of the light-green rectangle.

b McCourt also argues that cable companies would be better off if they relied on expanding their markets—"If you have a network, you want to make it as expansive as possible"—and technological innovations—"a new infrastructure to the home was the critical step to creating a system that can bundle and deliver every type of service that consumers would want." Figure 2 shows that if McCourt's argument is correct, the new and better services and expanded market will shift out the demand curve the firm faces and increase its profits. Price rises from P_M^{Old} to P_M^{New}, quantity rises from Q_M^{Old} to Q_M^{New}, and profits increase from the area of the light-green rectangle to the area of the dark-green rectangle (which includes the smaller, light-green rectangle).

Thinking Critically ABOUT POLICY

1. If monopoly generally brings a loss of economic efficiency and consumer surplus, why would a local government give only *one* cable television company a license to enter its market? Should local governments continue this practice?
2. If you were one of the cable giants discussed by David McCourt, would you be willing to open up your network? Explain your answer.

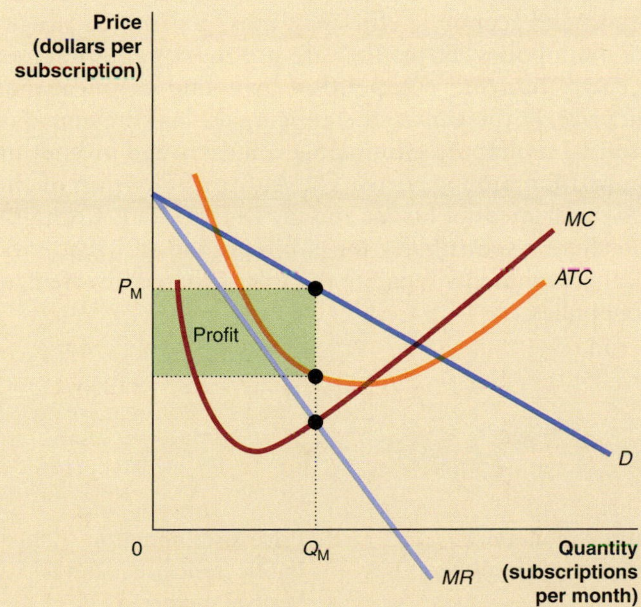

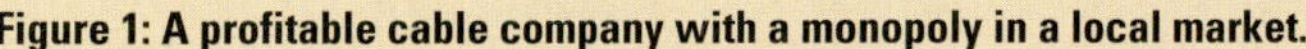

Figure 1: A profitable cable company with a monopoly in a local market.

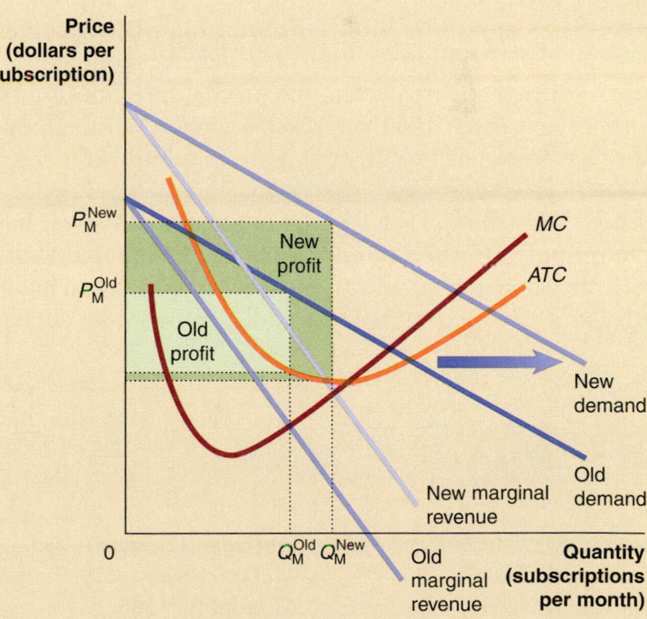

Figure 2: Better services and an expanded market increase firm profits.

SUMMARY

LEARNING OBJECTIVE ① Define monopoly. A *monopoly* exists only in the rare situation in which a firm is producing a good or service for which there are no close substitutes. A narrow definition of monopoly used by some economists is that a firm has a monopoly if it can ignore the actions of all other firms. Many economists favor a broader definition of monopoly. Under the broader definition, a firm has a monopoly if no other firms are selling a substitute close enough that the firm's economic profits are competed away in the long run.

LEARNING OBJECTIVE ② Explain the four main reasons monopolies arise. To have a monopoly, barriers to entering the market must be so high that no other firms can enter. *Barriers to entry* may be high enough to keep out competing firms for four main reasons: (1) government blocks the entry of more than one firm into a market by issuing a *patent* or giving a firm a *public franchise,* (2) one firm has control of a key raw material necessary to produce a good, (3) there are important *network externalities* in supplying the good or service, or (4) economies of scale are so large that one firm has a *natural monopoly.*

LEARNING OBJECTIVE ③ Explain how a monopoly chooses price and output. Monopolists face downward-sloping demand and marginal revenue curves and, like all other firms, maximize profit by producing where marginal revenue equals marginal cost. Unlike a perfect competitor, a monopolist that earns economic profits does not face the entry of new firms into the market. Therefore, a monopolist can earn economic profits, even in the long run.

LEARNING OBJECTIVE ④ Use a graph to illustrate how a monopoly affects economic surplus. Compared with a perfectly competitive industry, a monopoly charges a higher price and produces less, which reduces consumer surplus and economic efficiency. Some loss of economic efficiency will occur whenever firms have *market power* and can charge a price greater than marginal cost. The total loss of economic efficiency in the U.S. economy due to market power is small, however, because true monopolies are very rare. In most industries, competition will keep price much closer to marginal cost than would be the case in a monopoly.

LEARNING OBJECTIVE ⑤ Explain how a firm can increase its profits through price discrimination. *Price discrimination* occurs if a firm charges different prices for the same product when the price differences are not due to differences in cost. Three requirements must be met for a firm to successfully price discriminate: (1) A firm must possess market power. (2) Some consumers must have a greater willingness to pay for the product than other consumers, and firms must be able to know what customers are willing to pay. (3) Firms must be able to divide up—or, segment—the market for the product so that consumers who buy the product at a low price cannot resell it a high price. In the case of *perfect price discrimination,* each consumer pays a price equal to the consumer's willingness to pay.

LEARNING OBJECTIVE ⑥ Discuss government policies toward monopoly. Because monopolies reduce consumer surplus and economic efficiency, most governments regulate monopolies. Firms that are not monopolies have an incentive to avoid competition by colluding on output and price. In the United States, *antitrust laws* are aimed at deterring monopoly, eliminating collusion, and promoting competition among firms. The Antitrust Division of the U.S. Department of Justice and the Federal Trade Commission share responsibility for enforcing the antitrust laws. Local governments regulate the prices charged by natural monopolies.

KEY TERMS

Antitrust laws 284
Collusion 283
Copyright 269
Horizontal merger 285
Market power 279
Monopoly 266
Natural monopoly 271
Network externalities 270
Patent 267
Price discrimination 280
Public franchise 269
Vertical merger 285

REVIEW QUESTIONS

1. What is a monopoly? Can a firm be a monopoly if close substitutes for its product exist?
2. What are the four most important ways a firm becomes a monopoly?
3. What is "natural" about a natural monopoly?
4. If patents reduce competition, why does the federal government grant them?
5. What is a public franchise? Are all public franchises natural monopolies?
6. What is the relationship between a monopolist's demand curve and the market demand curve? What is the relationship between a monopolist's demand curve and its marginal revenue curve?
7. Draw a graph showing a monopolist that is earning a profit. Be sure your diagram includes the monopolist's demand, marginal revenue, average total cost, and marginal cost curves. Be sure to indicate the profit-maximizing level of output and price.
8. Suppose that a perfectly competitive industry becomes a monopoly. Describe the effects of this change on consumer surplus, producer surplus, and deadweight loss.
9. Explain why market power leads to a deadweight loss. Is the total deadweight loss from market power for the economy large or small?
10. What is price discrimination? Under what circumstances can a firm successfully practice price discrimination?
11 What is the purpose of the antitrust laws? Who is in charge of enforcing them?
12. What is the difference between a horizontal merger and a vertical merger? Which type of merger is more likely to increase the market power of the newly merged firm?
13. Why would it be economically efficient to require a natural monopoly to charge a price equal to marginal cost? Why do most regulatory agencies require natural monopolies to charge a price equal to average cost instead?

PROBLEMS AND APPLICATIONS

Please visit **www.prenhall.com/hubbard** *for solutions to the even-numbered problems as well as multiple-choice and true or false self-assessment quizzes.*

1. Is "monopoly" a good name for the game *Monopoly?* What aspects of the game involve monopoly? Explain briefly using the definition of monopoly.
2. The U.S. Postal Service (USPS) is a monopoly because the federal government has blocked entry into the market for delivering first-class mail. Is it also a natural monopoly? How can we tell? What would happen if the law preventing competition in this market were removed?
3. **[Related to the *Chapter Opener*]** Some observers say that changes in the past few years have eroded the monopoly power of local cable TV companies, even though no other cable firms have entered their markets. What are these changes? Do these "monopoly" firms still have monopoly power?
4. Patents are granted for 20 years, but pharmaceutical companies can't use their patent-guaranteed monopoly powers for anywhere near this long because it takes several years to acquire FDA approval of drugs. Should the life of drug patents be extended to 20 year *after* FDA approval? What would be the costs and benefits of this extension?
5. Just as a new product or a new method of making a product receives patent protection from the government, books, articles, and essays receive copyright protection. Under U.S. law, authors have the exclusive right to their writings during their lifetimes—unless they sell this right, as most authors do to their publishers—and their heirs retain this exclusive right for 50 years after their death. The historian Thomas Macaulay once described the copyright law as "a tax on readers to give a bounty to authors." In what sense does the existence of the copyright law impose a tax on readers? What "bounty" do copyright laws give authors? Discuss whether the government would be doing readers a favor by abolishing the copyright law.
Source of quotation from Macaulay: Thomas Mallon, *Stolen Words: The Classic Book on Plagiarism*, San Diego: Harcourt, 2001 (original ed. 1989), p. 59.
6. Before inexpensive pocket calculators were developed, many science and engineering students used slide rules to

make numerical calculations. Slide rules are no longer produced, which means nothing prevents you from establishing a monopoly in the slide rule market. Draw a graph showing the situation your slide rule firm would be in. Be sure to include on your graph your demand, marginal revenue, average total cost, and marginal cost curves. Indicate the price you would charge and the quantity you would produce. Are you likely to make a profit or a loss? Show this area on your diagram.

7. Are there any products for which there are no substitutes? Are these the only products for which it would be possible to have a monopoly? Briefly explain.

8. The German company Konig and Bauer has 90 percent of the world market for presses that print currency. Discuss the factors that would make it difficult for new companies to enter this market.

9. Does a monopolist have a supply curve? Briefly explain. (*Hint:* Look again at the definition of a supply curve in Chapter 3 and consider whether this applies to a monopolist.)

10. Use this diagram for a monopoly to answer the questions:

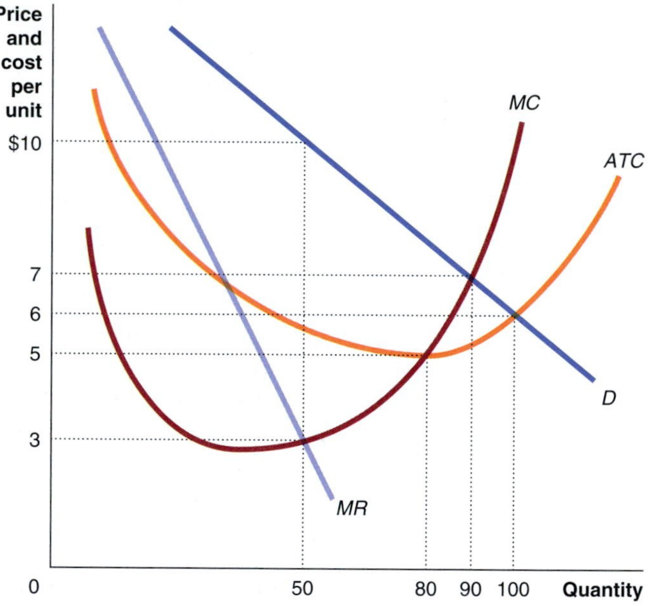

a. What quantity will the monopoly produce, and what price will the monopoly charge?
b. Suppose the monopoly is regulated. If the regulatory agency wants to achieve economic efficiency, what price should it require the monopoly to charge? How much output will the monopoly produce at this price? Will the monopoly make a profit if it charges this price? Briefly explain.

11. Use the following diagram for a monopoly to answer the questions:

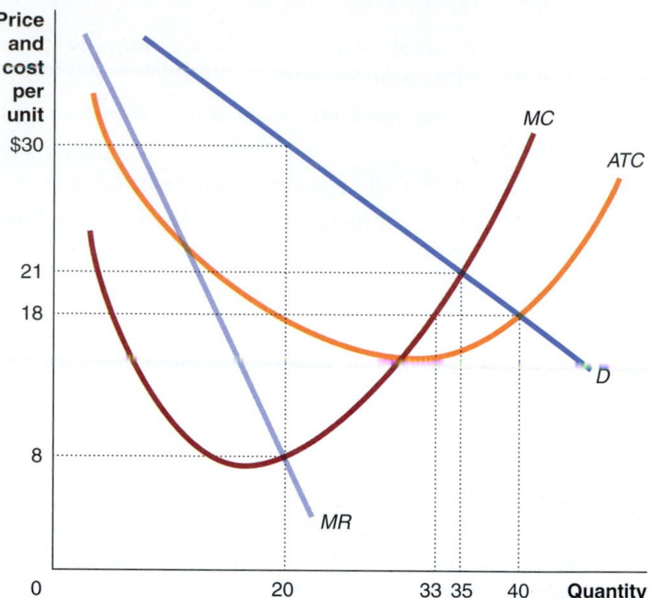

a. What quantity will the monopoly produce, and what price will the monopoly charge?
b. Suppose the government decides to regulate this monopoly and imposes a price ceiling of $18 (in other words, the monopoly can charge less than $18 but can't charge more). Now what quantity will the monopoly produce and what price will the monopoly charge? Will every consumer who is willing to pay this price be able to buy the product? Briefly explain.

12. **[Related to *Solved Problem 9-1*]** Suppose that the quantity demanded per day for a product is 90 when the price is $35. The following table shows costs for a firm with a monopoly in this market:

QUANTITY (PER DAY)	TOTAL COST
30	$1,200
40	1,400
50	2,250
60	3,000

Briefly explain whether this firm has a natural monopoly in this market.

13. **[Related to *Solved Problem 9-2*]** Ed Scahill has acquired a monopoly on the production of baseballs (don't ask how) and faces the demand and cost situation given in the table on the next page:

PRICE	QUANTITY (PER WEEK)	TOTAL REVENUE	MARGINAL REVENUE	TOTAL COST	MARGINAL COST
$20	15,000			$330,000	
19	20,000			365,000	
18	25,000			405,000	
17	30,000			450,000	
16	35,000			500,000	
15	40,000			555,000	

a. Fill in the remaining values in the table.
b. If Joe wants to maximize profits, what price should he charge and how many baseballs should he sell? How much profit will he make?
c. Suppose the government imposes a tax of $50,000 per week on baseball production. Now what price should Joe charge, how many baseballs should he sell, and what will his profits be?

14. **[Related to *Solved Problem 9-2*]** Use the information in Solved Problem 9-2 on pages 276–277 to answer the following questions:
   a. What will Comcast do if the tax is $6.00 per month, instead of $2.50? (*Hint:* Will its decision be different in the long run than in the short run?)
   b. Suppose that the flat per-month tax is replaced with a tax on the firm of $0.50 per cable subscriber. Now how many subscriptions should Comcast sell if it wants to maximize profit? What price does it charge? What are its profits? (Assume that Comcast will sell only the quantities listed in the table.)
15. **[Related to *Don't Let This Happen To You!*]** A student argues, "If a monopolist finds a way of producing a good at lower cost, he will not lower his price. Because he is a monopolist, he will keep the price and the quantity the same and just increase his profit." Do you agree? Use a graph to illustrate your answer.
16. **[Related to *Don't Let This Happen To You!*]** Discuss whether you agree or disagree with the following statement: "A monopolist maximizes profit by charging the highest price at which it can sell any of the good at all."
17. When home builders construct a new housing development, they will usually sell the rights to lay cable to a single cable television company. As a result, anyone buying a home in that development is not able to choose between competing cable companies. Some cities have begun to ban such exclusive agreements. Williams Township, Pennsylvania, decided to allow any cable company to lay cable in the utility trenches of new housing developments. The head of the township board of supervisors argued, "What I would like to see and do is give the consumers a choice. If there's no choice, then the price [of cable] is at the whim of the provider." In a situation in which the consumers in a housing development have only one cable company available, is the price really at the whim of the company? Would a company in this situation be likely to charge, say, $500 per month for basic cable services? Briefly explain why or why not.
   Source: Sam Kennedy, "Williams Township May Ban Exclusive Cable Provider Pacts," Allentown *Morning Call,* November 5, 2004, p. D1.
18. In a column in the *Wall Street Journal,* Walter Mossberg offered the following opinion:

   > There's a sucker in the software business today, and if you're in an average family with a couple of PCs, that sucker is you. . . . Families constitute the only significant customer group not getting a discount on [Microsoft] Office when upgrading multiple PCs. Big corporations, organizations and government agencies get a discount, called a "site license." College students get a discount. Small and medium-size businesses get a discount. But not families.

   Why might Microsoft charge families a higher price for Office than the other groups Mossberg mentions?
   Source: Walter Mossberg, "Microsoft Should Offer Families a Deal with Its Office Program," *Wall Street Journal,* July 18, 2002.
19. Sony will often sell electronic products at lower prices in the United States than in Japan. Does Sony consider the demand of U.S. consumers for these products to be more elastic or less elastic than the demand of Japanese consumers? Briefly explain.
20. An article in the *New York Times* observes that "On US Airways . . . a round-trip ticket between Washington and New Orleans could have been bought yesterday for as little as $198, while the cheapest unrestricted one-way fare was $638." Briefly discuss why this pricing strategy might be profit maximizing for US Airways.
   Source: Ian Ayers and Barry Nalebuff, "The Wrong Ticket to Ride," *New York Times,* March 24, 2004.
21. Political columnist Michael Kinsley writes, "The infuriating [airline] rules about Saturday night stayovers and so on are a crude alternative to administering truth serum and asking, 'So how much are you really willing to pay?' " Would a truth serum—or some other way of knowing how much people would be willing to pay for an airline ticket—really be all the airlines need to price discriminate? Briefly explain.
   Source: Michael Kinsley, "Consuming Gets More Complicated," *Slate,* November 21, 2001.

22. When a firm offers a rebate on a product, the buyer normally has to fill out a form and mail it in to receive a rebate check in the mail. A financial columnist argues:

    When a manufacturer offers a rebate, you needn't be too suspicious. The manufacturer wants to lower the price temporarily (to move an old product or combat a competitor's new low price), but doesn't have faith that the retailer will pass on the savings.

    But suppose that a manufacturer wants to engage in price discrimination. Would offering rebates be a way of doing this? Briefly explain.

    Source: Carol Vinzant, "The Great Rebate Scam," *Slate*, June 10, 2003.

23. The following phone call took place in February 1982 between Robert Crandall, the chief executive officer of American Airlines, and Howard Putnam, the chief executive officer of Braniff Airways. Although Crandall didn't know it, Putnam was recording the call:

    Crandall: I think it's dumb . . . to sit here and pound the (obscenity) out of each other and neither one of us making a (obscenity) dime . . .
    Putnam: Do you have a suggestion for me?
    Crandall: Yes, I have a suggestion for you. Raise your . . . fares 20 percent. I'll raise mine the next morning.
    Putnam: Robert, we . . .
    Crandall: You'll make more money and I will, too.
    Putnam: We can't talk about pricing.
    Crandall: Oh (obscenity), Howard. We can talk about any . . . thing we want to talk about.

    Who had a better understanding of antitrust law, Crandall or Putnam? Briefly explain.

    Source: Mark Potts, "American Airlines Charged with Seeking a Monopoly," *Washington Post*, February 24, 1983; "Blunt Talk on the Phone," *New York Times*, February 24, 1983; and Thomas Petzinger Jr., *Hard Landing: The Epic Contest for Power and Profits that Plunged the Airline Industry into Chaos*, New York: Random House, 1995, pp. 149–50.

24. Look again at the section "The Department of Justice and the Federal Trade Commission Merger Guidelines" that begins on page 286. Evaluate the following situations:
    a. A market initially has 20 firms, each with a 5 percent market share. Of the firms, 4 propose to merge, leaving a total of 16 firms in the industry. Are the Department of Justice and the Federal Trade Commission likely to oppose the merger? Briefly explain.
    b. A market initially has 5 firms, each with a 20 percent market share. Of the firms, 2 propose to merge, leaving a total of 4 firms in the industry. Are the Department of Justice and the Federal Trade Commission likely to oppose the merger? Briefly explain.

25. Industrial gases are used in the electronics industry. For example, nitrogen trifluoride is used for cleaning semiconductor wafers. The following table shows the market shares for the companies in this industry:

COMPANY	MARKET SHARE
Air Products	29%
Air Liquide	22
BOC Gases	21
Nippon Sanso	17
Praxzir	8
Other	3

    In 2000, Air Products discussed a merger with BOC Gases. Use the information in the section "The Department of Justice and the Federal Trade Commission Merger Guidelines" that begins on page 286 to predict whether the Department of Justice and the Federal Trade Commission opposed this merger. Assume that "Other" in the table consists of three firms, each of which has a 1 percent share of the market.

    Source for market share data: Graph in Dan Shope, "Air Products Turns a Corner," Allentown *Morning Call*, July 29, 2001.

26. The following table gives the market shares of the companies in the U.S. carbonated soft drink industry:

COMPANY	MARKET SHARE
Coca-Cola	37%
PepsiCo	35
Cadbury Schweppes	17
Other	11

    Use the information in the section "The Department of Justice and the Federal Trade Commission Merger Guidelines" that begins on page 286 to predict whether the Department of Justice and the Federal Trade Commission would be likely to approve a merger between any two of the first three companies listed. Does your answer depend on how many companies are included in the "Other" category? Briefly explain.

    Source: Pepsico *Annual Report, 2003.*

27. Most cities own the water system that provides water to homes and businesses. Some cities charge a flat monthly fee, while other cities charge by the gallon. Which method of pricing is more likely to result in economic efficiency in the water market? Be sure to refer to the definition of economic efficiency in your answer. Why do you think the same method of pricing isn't used by all cities?

28. Review the concept of externalities on page 98 in Chapter 4. If a market is a monopoly, will a negative externality in production always lead to production beyond the level of economic efficiency? Use a graph to illustrate your answer.

chapter ten

Monopolistic Competition and Oligopoly

Starbucks: Growth through Product Differentiation

Starbucks coffee shops seem to be everywhere—in malls, downtown shopping districts, airports, Barnes & Noble bookstores, and practically everywhere else you can imagine. By 2005, Starbucks operated 8,300 stores worldwide, with the company planning to eventually open 25,000. More than 25 million people visit a Starbucks each day.

Like many firms that are currently large, Starbucks started small. The first Starbucks was opened in Seattle in 1971 by entrepreneurs Gordon Bowker, Gerald Baldwin, and Zev Siegl. There were only five Starbucks stores in 1982 when Howard Schultz was hired to manage the firm's retail sales and marketing. Schultz, who would become chairman of the board and chief executive officer, was determined to make the company first a national chain, and then a worldwide chain. By 1993, Starbucks was opening stores on the East Coast, and in 1996 it opened its first store outside North America, in Tokyo, Japan.

Of course, fresh-brewed coffee has always been widely available in restaurants, diners, and donut shops. What Howard Schultz and the other Starbucks executives realized, however, was that a significant consumer demand existed for coffeehouses where customers could sit, relax, read the newspaper, and drink higher-quality coffee than was typically served in diners or donut shops. The espresso-based coffees served at Starbucks were relatively difficult to find elsewhere during the 1990s, as Starbucks expanded nationally.

Still, Starbucks is not unique: You probably know of three or more coffeehouses in your neighborhood. The coffeehouse market is competitive because it is inexpensive to open a new store by leasing store space and buying espresso machines. Hundreds of firms in the United States operate coffeehouses. Some firms are large nationwide chains, such as Diedrich Coffee, which has more than 2,400 stores in the United States and 10 foreign countries. Others are regional chains, such as Caribou Coffee, which operates 250 stores in nine states. Still others are small firms that operate only one store.

In Chapter 8, we discussed the situation of firms in perfectly competitive markets. These markets share three key characteristics:

1. There are many firms.
2. The products sold by all firms are identical.
3. There are no barriers to new firms entering the industry.

petitors. One journalist covering the computer industry has gone so far as to call the Macintosh "the most important consumer product of the last half of the twentieth century."

Microsoft produced the operating system known as MS-DOS (Microsoft Disk Operating System), which was used by almost all non-Apple computers. The financial success of the Macintosh led Microsoft to develop an operating system that would also use a mouse and icons. In 1992, Microsoft introduced the operating system Windows 3.1, which succeeded in reproducing many of the key features of the Macintosh. By August 1995, when Microsoft introduced Windows 95, non-Apple computers had become as easy to use as Macintosh computers. By that time, most personal computers operated in a way very similar to the Macintosh, and Apple was no longer able to charge prices that were significantly above those charged by its competitors. The Macintosh had lost its differentiation. Although the Macintosh continues to have a loyal following, particularly among graphic designers, today it has only a 3 percent share of the personal computer market.

Source: The quote in the first paragraph is from Steven Levy, *Insanely Great: The Life and Times of Macintosh, the Computer that Changed Everything*, New York: Viking, 1994, p. 7.

SOLVED PROBLEM 10-1

The Short Run and the Long Run for the Macintosh

③ **LEARNING OBJECTIVE**

Analyze the situation of a monopolistically competitive firm in the long run.

Use the information in Making the Connection 10-1 to draw a graph showing changes in the market for Macintosh computers between 1984 and 1995.

Solving the Problem:

Step 1: Review the chapter material. This problem is about how the entry of new firms affected the market for the Macintosh, so you may want to review the section "How Does the Entry of New Firms Affect the Profits of Existing Firms?" which begins on page 305.

Step 2: Draw the graph. Making the Connection 10-1 indicates that in 1984, when the Macintosh was first introduced, its differentiation from other computers allowed Apple to make a substantial economic profit. In 1995, the release of Windows 95 meant that non-Macintosh computers were as easy to use as Macintosh computers. Apple's product differentiation was eliminated, as was its ability to earn economic profits. The change over time in Apple's situation is shown in the following graph, which combines panels (a) and (b) from Figure 10-5 in one graph.

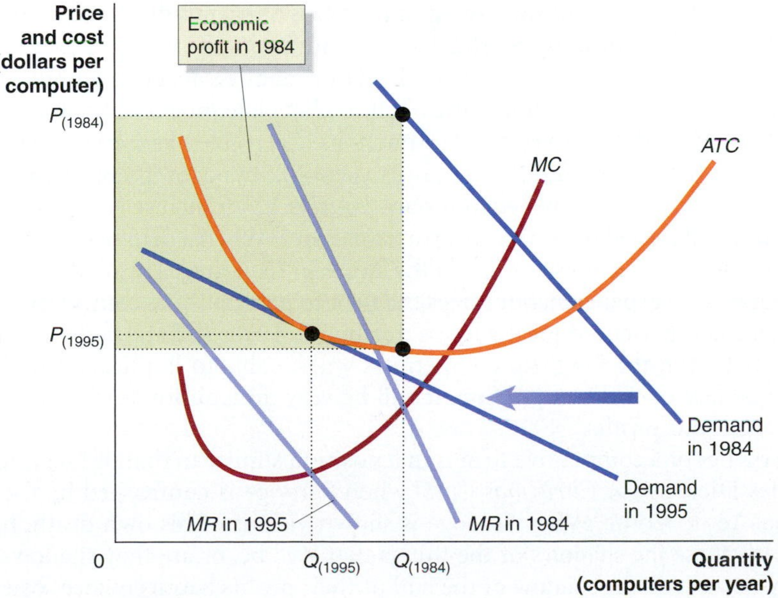

Between 1984 and 1995, Microsoft's development of the Windows operating system eliminated Macintosh's product differentiation. The demand curve for Macintoshes shifted to the left and became more elastic throughout the relevant range of prices.

Extra Credit: Note that this analysis is simplified. The Macintosh of 1995 was a different—and better—computer than the Macintosh of 1984. Apple has made changes to the Macintosh, such as the introduction of the colorful iMac computer in 1999, or the development of software in 2006 that made it possible to run Windows on the Macintosh, that have sometimes led to increases in sales. But the Macintosh has never been able to regain the high demand and premium prices it enjoyed from the mid-1980s to the early 1990s.

YOUR TURN: **For more practice, do related problem 10 on page 327 at the end of this chapter.**

Is Zero Economic Profit Inevitable in the Long Run?

The economic analysis of the long run shows the effects of market forces over time. In the case of Starbucks, the effect of market forces is to eliminate the economic profit earned by a monopolistically competitive firm. Owners of monopolistically competitive firms, of course, do not have to passively accept this long-run result. The key to earning economic profits is either to sell a differentiated product or to find a way of producing an existing product at a lower cost. If a monopolistically competitive firm selling a differentiated product is earning profits, these profits will attract the entry of additional firms and the entry of these firms eventually will eliminate the firm's profits. If a firm introduces new technology that allows it to sell a good or service at a lower cost, competing firms eventually will be able to duplicate this technology and eliminate the firm's profits. *But this result holds only if the firm stands still and fails to find new ways of differentiating its product or fails to find new ways of lowering the cost of producing its product.* Firms continually struggle to find new ways of differentiating their products as they try to stay one step ahead of other firms that are attempting to copy their success. As new coffeehouses enter the area served by the Starbucks coffeehouse, the owners can expect to see their economic profits competed away, unless they can find ways to differentiate their product.

In 2004, Howard Schultz, the chairman of Starbucks, was well aware of this fact. Although the firm had already opened 7,500 coffeehouses worldwide, he declared, "We are in the second inning of a nine-inning game. We are just beginning to tap into all sorts of new markets, new customers, and new products." In fact, Starbucks has used various strategies to differentiate itself from competing coffeehouses. Competitors have found it difficult to duplicate Starbucks's European espresso bar atmosphere, with its large, comfortable chairs, music playing, and groups of friends dropping in and out during the day. Most importantly, Starbucks has continued to be very responsive to its customers' preferences. As one observer put it, "How many retailers could put up with 'I'll have a grande low-fat triple-shot half-caf white-chocolate mocha, extra hot, easy on the whipped cream. And I'm in a rush'?" Starbucks has been able to maintain greater control over the operations of its coffeehouses, because unlike many of its competitors, all of its coffeehouses are company-owned; none are *franchises.* A franchise is a business with the legal right to sell a good or service in a particular area. When a firm uses franchises, local businesspeople are able to buy and run the stores in their area. This makes it easier for a firm to finance its expansion, but forces the firm to give up some control over its stores.

Starbucks experienced great success during the 1990s and the early 2000s, but history shows that in the long run competitors will be able to duplicate most of what it does. In the face of that competition, it will be very difficult for Starbucks to continue earning economic profits.

The owner of a competitive firm is in a position similar to that of Ebenezer Scrooge in Charles Dickens's *A Christmas Carol* when Scrooge is confronted by the Ghost of Christmas Yet to Come. When Scrooge is shown visions of his own death, he asks the Ghost, "Are these the shadows of the things that Will be, or are they shadows of things that May be, only?" The shadow of the end of their profits haunts owners of every firm.

Firms try to avoid losing profits by reducing costs, by improving their products, or by convincing consumers their products are indeed different from what competitors offer. To stay one step ahead of its competitors, a firm has to offer consumers goods or services that they perceive to have greater *value* than those offered by competing firms. Value can take the form of product differentiation that makes the good or service more suited to consumers' preferences, or it can take the form of a lower price.

10-2 Making the Connection

Staying One Step Ahead of the Competition: Eugène Schueller and L'Oréal

Today, L'Oréal, with headquarters in the Paris suburb of Clichy, is the largest seller of perfumes, cosmetics, and hair care products in the world. In addition to L'Oréal, its brands include Lancôme, Maybelline, Soft Sheen/Carson, Garnier, Redken, Ralph Lauren, and Matrix. Like most large firms, L'Oréal was started by an entrepreneur with an idea. Eugène Schueller was a French chemist who experimented in the evenings trying to find a safe and reliable hair coloring for women. In 1907, he founded the firm that became L'Oréal and began selling his hair coloring preparations to Paris hair salons. Schueller was able to take advantage of changes in fashion. In the early twentieth century, women began to cut their hair much shorter than had been typical in the nineteenth century, and it had become socially acceptable to spend time and money styling it. The number of hair salons in Europe and the United States increased rapidly. By the 1920s and 1930s, the international popularity of Hollywood films, many starring "platinum blonde bombshells" such as Jean Harlow, made it fashionable for women to color their hair. By the late 1920s, L'Oréal was selling its products throughout Europe, the United States, and Japan.

Unlike many monopolistically competitive firms, L'Oréal has earned economic profits for a very long time.

Perfumes, cosmetics, and hair coloring are all products that should be easy for rival firms to duplicate. We would expect, then, that the economic profits L'Oréal earned in its early years would have been competed away in the long run through the entry of new firms. In fact, though, the firm has remained profitable through the decades, following a strategy of developing new products, improving existing products, and expanding into new markets. For example, when French workers first received paid holidays during the 1930s, L'Oréal moved quickly to dominate the new market for suntan lotion. Today, the firm's SoftSheen brand is experiencing rapid sales increases in Africa. In early 2005, L'Oréal launched a new line of men's skin-care products, including shaving cream. As one observer put it, at L'Oréal "brands don't stay at home serving the same old clientele. They get spruced up, put in a new set of traveling clothes, and sent abroad to meet new customers." L'Oréal has maintained its ability to innovate by spending more on research and development than do competing firms. The firm has a research staff of more than 1,000.

One reason L'Oréal has been able to follow a focused strategy is that the firm has had only three chairmen in its nearly century of existence: founder Eugène Schueller, François Dalle, and Lindsay Owen-Jones, who became chairman in 1988. Owen-Jones has described the firm's strategy: "Each brand is positioned on a very precise [market] segment, which overlaps as little as possible with the others." The story of L'Oréal shows that it is possible for a firm to stay one step ahead of the competition, but it takes a top management committed to an entrepreneurial spirit of continually developing new products.

Source for quotes: Richard Tomlinson, "L'Oréal's Global Makeover," *Fortune*, September 30, 2002.

Comparing Perfect Competition and Monopolistic Competition

4 LEARNING OBJECTIVE

Compare the efficiency of monopolistic competition and perfect competition.

We have seen that monopolistic competition and perfect competition share the characteristic that in long-run equilibrium firms earn zero economic profits. As Figure 10-6 shows, however, there are two important differences between long-run equilibrium in the two markets.

- Monopolistically competitive firms charge a price greater than marginal cost.
- Monopolistically competitive firms do not produce at minimum average total cost.

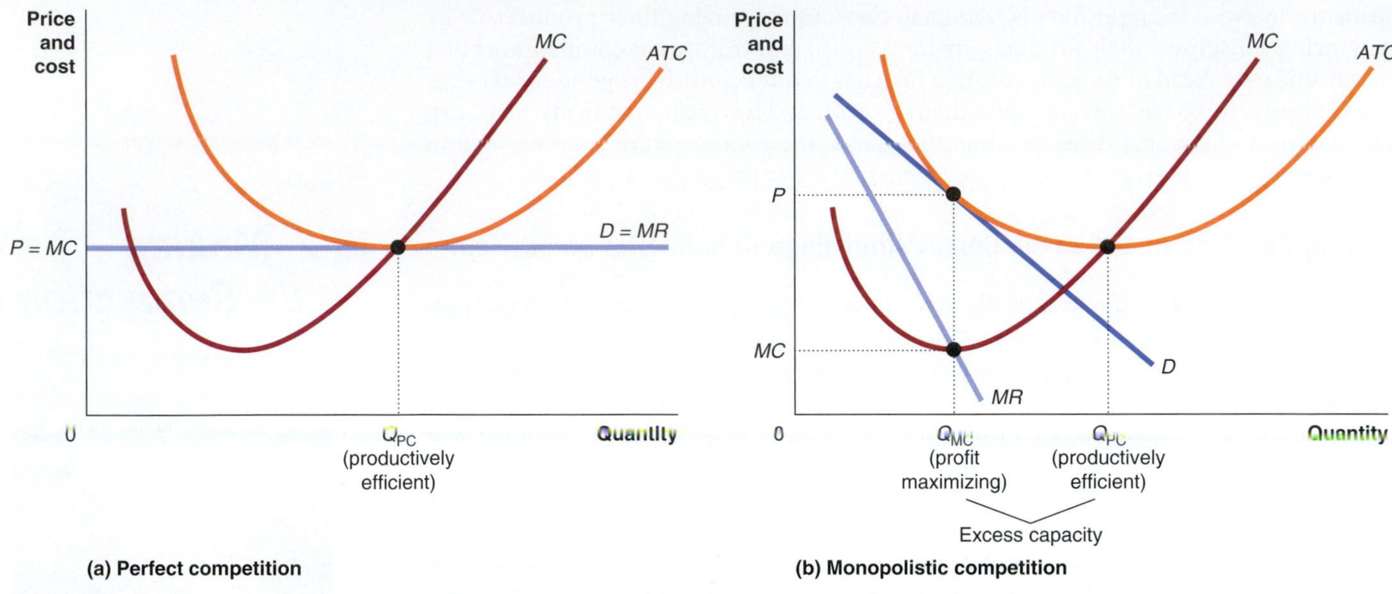

FIGURE 10-6 Comparing Long-Run Equilibrium under Perfect Competition and Monopolistic Competition

In panel (a), the perfectly competitive firm in long-run equilibrium produces at Q_{PC}, where price equals marginal cost and average total cost is at a minimum. The perfectly competitive firm is both allocatively efficient and productively efficient. In panel (b), the monopolistically competitive firm produces at Q_{MC}, where price is greater than marginal cost and average total cost is not at a minimum. As a result, the monopolistically competitive firm is neither allocatively efficient nor productively efficient. The monopolistically competitive firm has excess capacity equal to the difference between its profit-maximizing level of output and the productively efficient level of output.

Excess Capacity under Monopolistic Competition

Recall that a firm in a perfectly competitive market faces a perfectly elastic demand curve that is also its marginal revenue curve. Therefore, the firm maximizes profit by producing where price equals marginal cost. As panel (a) of Figure 10-6 shows, in long-run equilibrium, a perfectly competitive firm produces at the minimum point of its average total cost curve.

Panel (b) of Figure 10-6 shows that the profit-maximizing level of output for a monopolistically competitive firm comes at a level of output where price is greater than marginal cost and the firm is not at the minimum point of its average total cost curve. A monopolistically competitive firm has *excess capacity:* If it increased its output, it could produce at a lower average cost.

Is Monopolistic Competition Inefficient?

In Chapter 8, we discussed *productive efficiency* and *allocative efficiency.* Productive efficiency refers to the situation where a good is produced at the lowest possible cost. Allocative efficiency refers to the situation where every good or service is produced up to the point where the last unit provides a marginal benefit to consumers equal to the marginal cost of producing it. For productive efficiency to hold, firms must produce at the minimum point of average total cost. For allocative efficiency to hold, firms must charge a price equal to marginal cost. In a perfectly competitive market, both productive efficiency and allocative efficiency are achieved, but in a monopolistically competitive market, neither is achieved. Economists have debated whether the fact that monopolistically competitive markets are not productively or allocatively efficient means that there is a significant loss of well-being to society in these markets when compared with perfectly competitive markets.

How Consumers Benefit from Monopolistic Competition

Looking again at Figure 10-6, you can see that the only difference between the monopolistically competitive firm and the perfectly competitive firm is that the demand curve for the monopolistically competitive firm slopes downward, whereas the demand curve for the perfectly competitive firm is a horizontal line. The demand curve for the monopolistically competitive firm slopes downward because the good or service the firm is selling is differentiated from the goods or services being sold by competing firms. The perfectly competitive firm is selling a good or service identical to those being sold by its competitors. A key point to remember is that *firms differentiate their products to appeal to consumers.* When Starbucks coffeehouses begin offering new flavors of coffee, when Blockbuster stores begin carrying more DVDs and fewer VHS tapes, when General Mills introduces Apple-Cinnamon Cheerios, or when PepsiCo introduces caffeine-free Diet Pepsi, they are all attempting to attract and retain consumers through product differentiation. The success of these product differentiation strategies indicates that some consumers find these products preferable to the alternatives. Consumers, therefore, are better off than they would have been had these companies not differentiated their products.

We can conclude that consumers face a trade-off when buying the product of a monopolistically competitive firm: They are paying a price that is greater than marginal cost and the product is not being produced at minimum average cost, but they benefit from being able to purchase a product that is differentiated and more closely suited to their tastes.

10-3 Making the Connection

Abercrombie and Fitch: Can the Product Be Too Differentiated?

Did Abercrombie and Fitch narrow its target market too much?

Business managers often refer to differentiating their products as finding a "market niche." The larger the niche, the greater the potential profit but the more likely that other firms will be able to compete against you. Too small a niche, however, may reduce competition but also reduce profits. In 2004, some analysts believed that the market niche chosen by the managers of the Abercrombie and Fitch clothing stores was too small. Chief Executive Mike Jeffries was quoted as saying that his store's target customer was an "18-to-22 [year old] college guy who has a good body and is aspirational." He admitted that his was a narrow niche: "If I exclude people—absolutely. Delighted to do so."

But was A&F excluding too many people? One analyst argued "they've . . . pushed a lot of people out of the brand." A&F's sales results seemed to indicate that this analyst was correct. Managers of retail stores closely monitor "same-store sales," which measures how much sales have increased on average in the same stores from one year to the next. To offset the effects of inflation—or general increases in prices in the economy—same-store sales need to increase at least 2 percent to 3 percent each year. A firm whose strategy of product differentiation succeeds will experience increases in same-store sales of at least 5 percent to 6 percent each year. By 2004, A&F's 350 stores had experienced four consecutive years of *negative* same-store results. The company apparently had gone too far in narrowing its market niche.

Source: Shelly Branch, "Maybe Sex Doesn't Sell, A&F Is Discovering," *Wall Street Journal*, December 12, 2003.

(5) LEARNING OBJECTIVE

Show how barriers to entry explain the existence of oligopolies.

Oligopoly and Barriers to Entry

While in monopolistically competitive industries there are many firms, in oligopolies there are only a few firms. One measure of the extent of competition in an industry is the *concentration ratio*. Every five years, the U.S. Bureau of the Census publishes four-firm concentration ratios that state the fraction of each industry's sales accounted for by its four largest firms. Most economists believe that a four-firm concentration ratio of greater than 40 percent indicates that an industry is an oligopoly.

The concentration ratio has some flaws as a measure of the extent of competition in an industry. For example, concentration ratios do not include sales in the United States by foreign firms. Concentration ratios are also calculated for the national market, even though the competition in some industries, such as restaurants or college bookstores, is mainly local. Finally, competition sometimes exists between firms in different industries. For example, Wal-Mart is included in the discount department stores industry, but also competes with firms in the supermarket industry and the retail toy store industry. As we saw in Chapter 9, some economists prefer another measure of competition, known as the *Herfindahl-Hirschman Index*. Despite these shortcomings, concentration ratios can be useful in providing a general idea of the extent of competition in an industry.

Table 10-2 lists examples of oligopolies in manufacturing and retail trade. Notice that the "Discount Department Stores" industry that includes Wal-Mart is highly concentrated. Wal-Mart also operates Sam's Club stores, which are in the also heavily concentrated "Warehouse Clubs and Superstores" industry.

Barriers to Entry

Why do oligopolies exist? Why aren't there many more firms in the discount department store industry, the beer industry, or the automobile industry? We have seen that new firms will enter industries where existing firms are earning economic profits. But new firms often have difficulty entering an oligopoly. Anything that keeps new firms from entering an industry in which firms are earning economic profits is called a **barrier to entry.** Three barriers to entry are: economies of scale, ownership of a key input, and government-imposed barriers.

Barrier to entry Anything that keeps new firms from entering an industry in which firms are earning economic profits.

TABLE 10-2

Examples of Oligopolies in Retail Trade and Manufacturing

RETAIL TRADE		MANUFACTURING	
INDUSTRY	FOUR-FIRM CONCENTRATION RATIO	INDUSTRY	FOUR-FIRM CONCENTRATION RATIO
Discount Department Stores	95%	Cigarettes	99%
Warehouse Clubs and Supercenters	92%	Beer	90%
College Bookstores	71%	Aircraft	85%
Athletic Footwear Stores	70%	Automobiles	80%
Radio, Television, and Other Electronic Stores	69%	Breakfast Cereal	83%
Hobby, Toy, and Game Stores	64%	Dog and Cat Food	58%
Pharmacies and Drugstores	52%	Computers	45%

Source: For retail trade: U.S. Census Bureau, 2002 Census; for manufacturing: U.S. Census Bureau, 1997 Census.

Economies of Scale

The most important barrier to entry is economies of scale. Chapter 7 explained that **economies of scale** exist when a firm's long-run average costs fall as it increases output. The greater the economies of scale, the fewer the number of firms that will be in the industry. Figure 10-7 illustrates this point.

Economies of scale Economies of scale exist when a firm's long run average costs fall as it increases output.

If economies of scale are relatively unimportant in the industry, the typical firm's long-run average cost curve *(LRAC)* will reach a minimum at a level of output that is a small fraction of total industry sales—Q_1 in Figure 10-7. The industry will have room for a large number of firms and will be competitive. If economies of scale are significant, the typical firm will not reach the minimum point on its long-run average cost curve until it has produced a large fraction of industry sales—Q_2 in Figure 10-7. Then the industry will have room for only a few firms and will be an oligopoly.

Economies of scale can explain why there is much more competition in the restaurant industry than in the discount department store industry. Because very large restaurants do not have lower average costs than smaller restaurants, the restaurant industry has room for many firms. In contrast, large discount department stores, such as Wal-Mart, have much lower average costs than small discount department stores, in part because large department stores are able to buy in bulk directly from manufacturers. As a result, just four firms—Wal-Mart, Target, Kmart, and Costco—account for about 95 percent of all sales in this industry.

Ownership of a Key Input

If production of a good requires a particular input, then control of that input can be a barrier to entry. For many years, the Aluminum Company of America (Alcoa) controlled most of the world's supply of high-quality bauxite, the mineral needed to produce aluminum. The only way other firms could enter the industry to compete with Alcoa was to recycle aluminum. The De Beers Company of South Africa was able to block competition in the diamond market by controlling the output of most of the world's diamond mines. Until the 1990s, Ocean Spray had very little competition in the market for fresh and frozen cranberries because it controlled almost the entire supply of cranberries. Even today it controls about 80 percent of the cranberry crop.

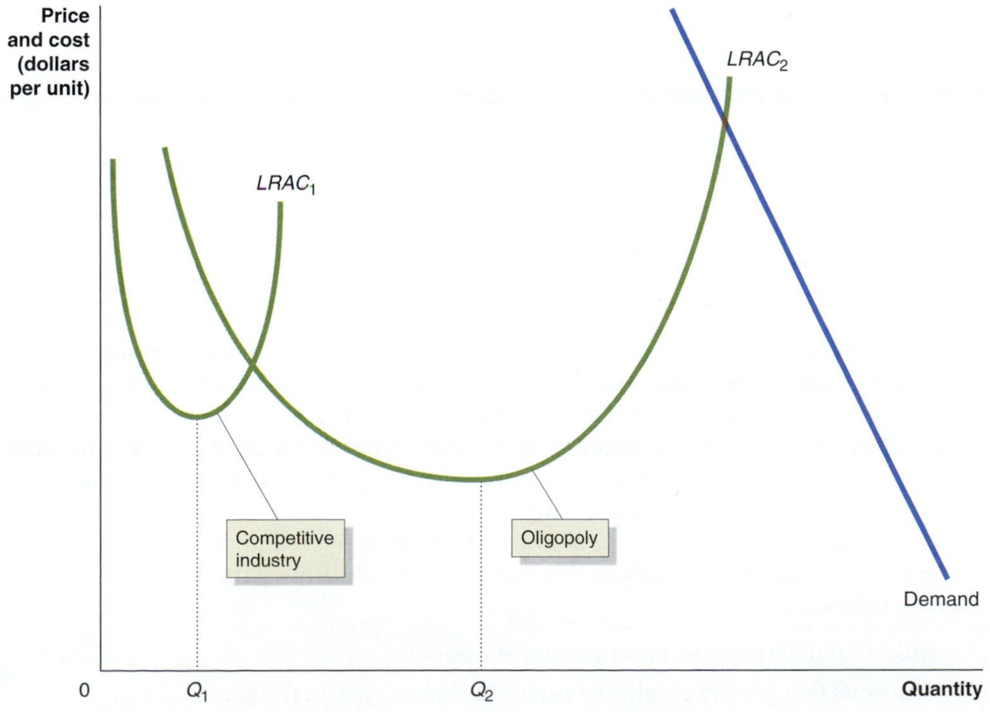

FIGURE 10-7

Economies of Scale Help Determine the Extent of Competition in an Industry

An industry will be competitive if the minimum point on the typical firm's long-run average cost curve ($LRAC_1$) occurs at a level of output that is a small fraction of total industry sales, like Q_1. The industry will be an oligopoly if the minimum point comes at a level of output that is a large fraction of industry sales, like Q_2.

Government-Imposed Barriers

Firms sometimes try to have the government impose barriers to entry. Many large firms employ *lobbyists* to convince state legislators and members of Congress to pass laws favorable to the economic interests of the firms. There are tens of thousands of lobbyists in Washington, DC alone. Top lobbyists command annual salaries of $300,000 or more, which indicates the value firms place on their activities. Examples of government-imposed barriers to entry are patents, licensing requirements, and barriers to international trade. Governments use patents to encourage firms to carry out research and development of new and better products and better ways of producing existing products. Output and living standards increase faster when firms devote resources to research and development, but a firm that spends money to develop a new product may not earn much profit if other firms can copy the product. For example, the pharmaceutical company Merck spends more than $3 billion per year to develop new prescription drugs. If rival companies could freely produce these new drugs as soon as Merck developed them, most of the firm's investment would be wasted. To avoid this problem, the federal government grants a **patent** that gives the firm the exclusive right to a new product for a period of 20 years from the date the product was invented. During the years the patent is in force, the firm can charge higher prices and make an economic profit on its successful innovation.

Patent The exclusive right to a product for a period of 20 years from the date the product was invented.

The government also restricts competition through occupational licensing. The United States currently has about 500 occupational licensing laws. For example, doctors and dentists in every state need licenses to practice. The justification for the laws is to protect the public from incompetent practitioners, but by restricting the number of people who can enter the licensed professions, the laws also raise prices. Studies have shown that states that make it harder to earn a dentist's license have prices for dental services that are about 15 percent higher than in other states. Similarly, states that require a license for out-of-state firms to sell contact lenses have higher prices for contact lenses. When state licenses are required for occupations like hair braiding, which was done several years ago in California, restricting competition is the main result.

Government also imposes barriers to entering some industries by imposing tariffs and quotas on foreign competition. For example, a quota on foreign sugar imports severely limits competition in the U.S. sugar market. As a result, U.S. sugar companies can charge prices that are more than twice as high as those charged by companies outside the United States.

In summary, to earn economic profits, all firms would like to charge a price well above average cost, but earning economic profits attracts new firms to enter the industry. Eventually the increased competition forces price down to average cost, and firms just break even. In an oligopoly, barriers to entry prevent—or at least slow down—entry, which allows firms to earn economic profits over a longer period.

⑥ LEARNING OBJECTIVE

Use game theory to analyze the actions of oligopolistic firms.

Using Game Theory to Analyze Oligopoly

As we noted at the beginning of the chapter, economists analyze oligopolies using *game theory*, which was developed during the 1940s by the mathematician John von Neumann and the economist Oskar Morgenstern. **Game theory** is the study of how people make decisions in situations where attaining their goals depends on their interactions with others. In oligopolies, the interactions among firms are crucial in determining profitability because the firms are large relative to the market.

Game theory The study of how people make decisions in situations where attaining their goals depends on their interactions with others; in economics, the study of the decisions of firms in industries where the profits of each firm depend on its interactions with other firms.

In all games—whether poker, chess, or Monopoly—the interactions among the players are crucial in determining the outcome. In addition, games share three key characteristics:

1. *Rules* that determine what actions are allowable.
2. *Strategies* that players employ to attain their objectives in the game.
3. *Payoffs* that are the results of the interaction among the players' strategies.

In business situations, the rules of the "game" include not just laws that a firm must obey, but also other matters beyond a firm's control—at least in the short run—such as its production function. A **business strategy** is a set of actions taken by a firm to achieve a goal, such as maximizing profits. The *payoffs* are the profits earned as a result of a firm's strategies interacting with the strategies of the other firms. The best way to understand the game theory approach is to look at an example.

Business strategy Actions taken by a firm to achieve a goal, such as maximizing profits.

A Duopoly Game: Price Competition between Two Firms

In the following simple example, we use game theory to analyze price competition in a *duopoly*—an oligopoly with two firms. Suppose that an isolated town in Alaska has only two stores: Wal-Mart and Target. Both stores sell the new Sony PlayStation 3. For simplicity, let's assume that no other stores stock PlayStation 3 and that consumers in the town can't buy it on the Internet or through mail-order catalogs. The manager of each store decides whether to charge \$150 or \$200 for the PlayStation. Which price will be more profitable depends on the price being charged by the other store. The decision regarding what price to charge is an example of a business strategy. In Figure 10-8 we organize the possible outcomes that result from the actions of the two firms into a *payoff matrix*. A **payoff matrix** is a table that shows the payoffs that each firm earns from every combination of strategies by the firms.

Payoff matrix A table that shows the payoffs that each firm earns from every combination of strategies by the firms.

Wal-Mart's profits are shown in blue and Target's profits are shown in red. If Wal-Mart and Target both charge \$200 for the PlayStation, each store will make a profit of \$10,000 per month from sales of the game console. If Wal-Mart charges the lower price of \$150, while Target charges \$200, Wal-Mart will gain many of Target's customers. Wal-Mart's profits will be \$15,000 and Target's will be only \$5,000. Similarly, if Wal-Mart charges \$200, while Target is charging \$150, Wal-Mart's profits will be only \$5,000, while Target's profits will be \$15,000. If both stores charge \$150, each will earn profits of \$7,500 per month.

Clearly, the stores will be better off if they both charge \$200 for the PlayStation. But will they both charge this price? One possibility is that the manager of the Wal-Mart and the manager of the Target will get together and *collude* by agreeing to charge the higher price. **Collusion** is an agreement among firms to charge the same price, or otherwise not to compete. Unfortunately, for Wal-Mart and Target—but fortunately for their customers—collusion is against the law in the United States. Companies that agree not to compete on price can be fined and the managers involved can be sent to jail.

Collusion An agreement among firms to charge the same price, or otherwise not to compete.

The manager of the Wal-Mart store legally can't discuss his pricing decision with the manager of the Target store, so he has to predict what he thinks the other manager will do. Suppose the Wal-Mart manager is convinced that the Target manager will charge \$200 for the PlayStation. In this case, the Wal-Mart manager will definitely charge \$150, because that will increase his profit from \$10,000 to \$15,000. But suppose instead the Wal-Mart manager is convinced that the Target manager will charge \$150. Then the Wal-Mart manager also definitely will charge \$150, because that will increase his profit from \$5,000 to \$7,500. In fact, whichever price the Target manager decides to charge, the

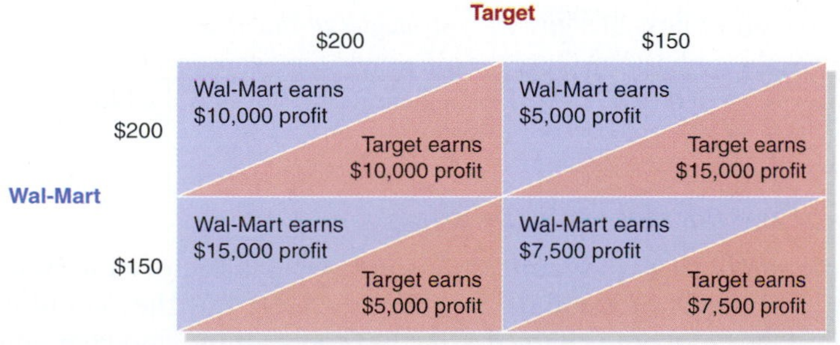

FIGURE 10-8

A Duopoly Game

Wal-Mart's profits are in blue, and Target's profits are in red. Wal-Mart and Target would each make profits of \$10,000 per month on sales of PlayStation 3 if they both charged \$200. However, each store manager has an incentive to undercut the other by charging a lower price. If both charge \$150, they would each make profits of only \$7,500 per month.

Wal-Mart manager is better off charging $150. So, we know that the Wal-Mart manager will choose a price of $150 for the PlayStation.

Now consider the situation of the Target manager. The Target manager is in the identical position to the Wal-Mart manager, so we can expect her to make the same decision to charge $150 for the PlayStation. In this situation each manager has a *dominant strategy.* A **dominant strategy** is the best strategy for a firm, no matter what strategies other firms use. The result is an equilibrium where both managers charge $150 for the PlayStation. This situation is an equilibrium because each manager is maximizing profits, *given the price chosen by the other manager.* In other words, neither firm can increase its profits by changing its price, given the price chosen by the other firm. An equilibrium where each firm chooses the best strategy, given the strategies chosen by other firms, is called a **Nash equilibrium,** named after Nobel Prize winner John Nash of Princeton University, a pioneer in the development of game theory.

Dominant strategy A strategy that is the best for the firm, no matter what strategy other firms use.

Nash equilibrium A situation where each firm chooses the best strategy, given the strategies chosen by other firms.

10-4 Making the Connection

A Beautiful Mind: Game Theory Goes to the Movies

In the film, A Beautiful Mind, *Russell Crowe played John Nash, winner of the Nobel Prize in Economics.*

John Nash is the most celebrated game theorist in the world, partly because of his achievements and partly because of his dramatic life. In 1948, at the age of 20, Nash received bachelor's and master's degrees in mathematics from the Carnegie Institute of Technology (now known as Carnegie Mellon University). Two years later he received a Ph.D. from Princeton for his 27-page dissertation on game theory. It was in this dissertation that he first discussed the concept that became known as the *Nash equilibrium.* Nash appeared to be on his way to a brilliant academic career until he developed schizophrenia in the 1950s. He spent decades in and out of mental hospitals. During these years he roamed the Princeton campus, covering blackboards in unused classrooms with indecipherable writings. He became known as the "Phantom of Fine Hall." In the 1970s, Nash gradually began to recover. In 1994, he shared the Nobel Prize in Economics with John Harsanyi of the University of California, Berkeley, and Reinhard Selten of Rheinische Friedrich–Wilhelms Universität, Germany, for his work on game theory.

In 1998, Sylvia Nasar of the *New York Times* wrote a biography of Nash, titled *A Beautiful Mind.* Three years later, the book was adapted into an award-winning film starring Russell Crowe. Unfortunately, the (fictitious) scene in the film that shows Nash discovering the idea of Nash equilibrium misstates the concept. In the scene, Nash is in a bar with several friends when four women with brown hair and one with blonde hair walk in. Nash and all of his friends prefer the blonde to the brunettes. One of Nash's friends points out that if they all compete for the blonde, they are unlikely to get her. In competing for the blonde, they will also insult the brunettes, with the result that none of them will end up with a date. Nash then gets a sudden insight. He suggests that they ignore the blonde and each approach one of the brunettes. That is the only way, he argues, that each of them will end up with a date.

Nash immediately claims that this is also an economic insight. He points out that Adam Smith had argued that the best result comes from everyone in the group doing what's best for himself. Nash argues, however, "The best result comes from everyone in the group doing what's best for himself *and* the group." But this is not an accurate description of the Nash equilibrium. As we have seen, in a Nash equilibrium each player uses a strategy that will make him as well off as possible, *given the strategies of the other players.* The bar situation would not be a Nash equilibrium. Once the other men have chosen a brunette, each man will have an incentive to switch from the brunette he initially chose to the blonde.

Firm Behavior and the Prisoners' Dilemma

Notice that the equilibrium in Figure 10-8 is not very satisfactory for either firm. The firms earn $7,500 profit each month by charging $150, but they could have earned $10,000 profit if they had both charged $200. By "cooperating" and charging the higher price they would have achieved a *cooperative equilibrium.* In a **cooperative equilibrium** players cooperate to increase their mutual payoff. We have seen, though, that the out-

Cooperative equilibrium An equilibrium in a game in which players cooperate to increase their mutual payoff.

come of this game is likely to be a **noncooperative equilibrium**, in which each firm pursues its own self-interest.

A situation like this, in which pursuing dominant strategies results in noncooperation that leaves everyone worse off, is called a **prisoners' dilemma.** The game gets its name from its similarity to the situation of two suspects arrested for a crime by the police. If the police lack other evidence, they may separate the suspects and offer each a reduced prison sentence in exchange for confessing to the crime and testifying against the other criminal. Because each suspect has a dominant strategy to confess to the crime, they will both confess and serve a jail term, even though they would have gone free if they had both remained silent.

Noncooperative equilibrium An equilibrium in a game in which players do not cooperate but pursue their own self-interest.

Prisoners' dilemma A game where pursuing dominant strategies results in noncooperation that leaves everyone worse off.

SOLVED PROBLEM 10-2

Is Advertising a Prisoners' Dilemma for Coca-Cola and Pepsi?

Coca-Cola and Pepsi both advertise aggressively, but would they be better off if they didn't? Their commercials are not designed to convey new information about the products. Instead, they are designed to capture each other's customers. Construct a payoff matrix using the following hypothetical information:

- *If neither firm advertises:* Coca-Cola and Pepsi both earn profits of $750 million per year.
- *If both firms advertise:* Coca-Cola and Pepsi both earn profits of $500 million per year.
- *If Coca-Cola advertises and Pepsi doesn't:* Coca-Cola earns profits of $900 million and Pepsi earns profits of $400 million.
- *If Pepsi advertises and Coca-Cola doesn't:* Pepsi earns profits of $900 million and Coca-Cola earns profits of $400 million.
  a. If Coca-Cola wants to maximize profit, will it advertise? Briefly explain.
  b. If Pepsi wants to maximize profit, will it advertise? Briefly explain.
  c. Is there a Nash equilibrium to this advertising game? If so, what is it?

Solving the Problem:

Step 1: Review the chapter material. This problem uses payoff matrixes to analyze a business situation, so you may want to review the section "A Duopoly Game: Price Competition between Two Firms," which begins on page 315.

Step 2: Construct the payoff matrix.

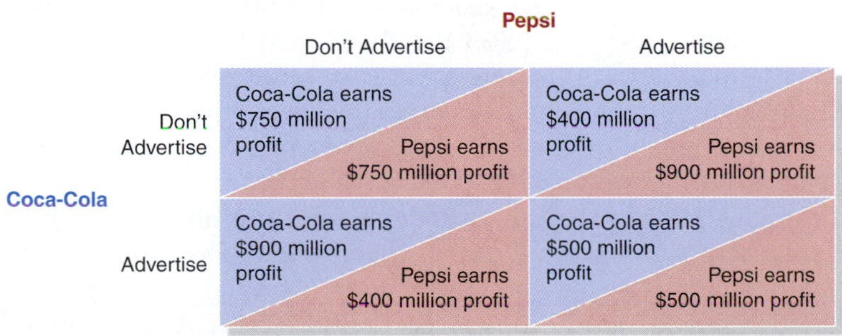

Step 3: Answer question (a) by showing that Coca-Cola has a dominant strategy of advertising. If Pepsi doesn't advertise, then Coca-Cola will make $900 million if it advertises, but only $750 million if it doesn't. If Pepsi advertises, then Coca-Cola will make $500 million if it advertises, but only $400 million if it doesn't. Therefore, advertising is a dominant strategy for Coca-Cola.

Step 4: Answer question (b) by showing that Pepsi has a dominant strategy of advertising. Pepsi is in the same position as Coca-Cola, so it also has a dominant strategy of advertising.

Step 5: Answer question (c) by showing that there is a Nash equilibrium for this game. Both firms advertising is a Nash equilibrium. Given that Pepsi is advertising, Coca-Cola's best strategy is to advertise. Given that Coca-Cola is advertising, Pepsi's best strategy is to advertise. Therefore, advertising is the optimal decision for both firms, *given the decision by the other firm.*

Extra Credit: This is another example of the prisoners' dilemma game. Coca-Cola and Pepsi would be more profitable if they both refrained from advertising, thereby saving the enormous expense of television and radio commercials and newspaper and magazine ads. Each firm's dominant strategy is to advertise, however, so they end up in an equilibrium where both advertise and their profits are reduced.

***YOUR TURN:* For more practice, do related problems 21 and 22 on page 328 at the end of this chapter.**

Can Firms Escape the Prisoners' Dilemma?

Although the prisoners' dilemma game seems to show that cooperative behavior always breaks down, we know that it doesn't. People often cooperate to achieve their goals, and firms find ways to cooperate by not competing on price. The reason the basic prisoners' dilemma story is not always applicable is that it assumes the game will be played only once. Most business situations, however, are repeated over and over. Each month the Target and Wal-Mart managers will decide again what price they will charge for PlayStation 3. In the language of game theory, the managers are playing a *repeated game.* In a repeated game, the losses from not cooperating are greater, and players can also employ *retaliation strategies* against those who don't cooperate. As a result, we are more likely to see cooperative behavior.

Figure 10-8 on page 315 shows that Wal-Mart and Target are earning $2,500 less per month by both charging $150 instead of $200 for the PlayStation. Every month that passes with both stores charging $150 increases the total amount lost: Two years of charging $150 will cause each store to lose $60,000 in profit. This lost profit increases the incentive for the store managers to cooperate by *implicitly* colluding. Remember that *explicit* collusion—such as the managers meeting and agreeing to charge $200—is illegal. But if the managers can find a way to signal each other that they will charge $200, they may be within the law.

Suppose, for example, that Wal-Mart and Target both advertise that they will match the lowest price offered by any competitor—in our simple example, they are each other's only competitor. These advertisements are signals to each other that they intend to charge $200 for the PlayStation. The signal is clear because each store knows that if it charges $150, the other store will automatically retaliate by also lowering its price to $150. The offer to match prices is a good *enforcement mechanism* because it guarantees that if either store fails to cooperate and charges the lower price it is automatically punished by having its competitor also charge the lower price. As Figure 10-9 shows, the stores have changed the payoff matrix they face.

With the original payoff matrix (a), there is no matching offer, and each store makes more profit if it charges $150 when the other charges $200. The matching offer changes the payoff matrix to (b). Now the stores can charge $200 and receive a profit of $10,000 per month, or they can charge $150 and receive a profit of $7,500 per month. The equilibrium shifts from the prisoners' dilemma result of both stores charging the low price and receiving low profits to a result where both stores charge the high price and receive high profits. An offer to match competitors' prices might seem to benefit consumers, but game theory shows that it actually may hurt consumers by helping to keep prices high.

Cartels: The Case of OPEC

In the United States, firms cannot legally meet to agree on what prices to charge and how much to produce. But suppose they could. Would this be enough to guarantee that their

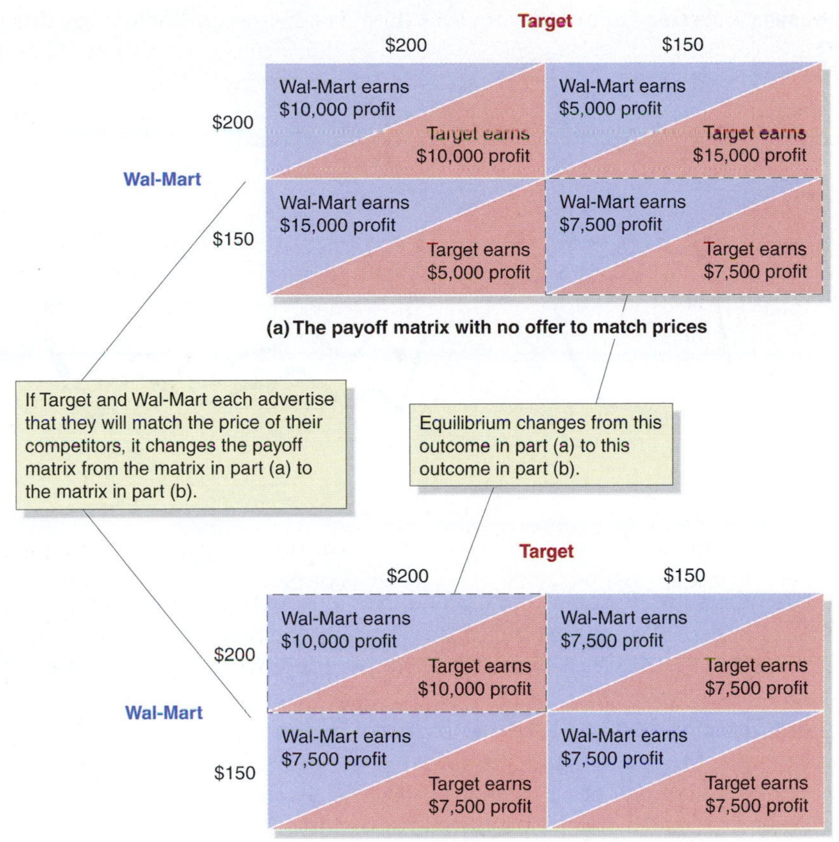

FIGURE 10-9

Changing the Payoff Matrix in a Repeated Game

Wal-Mart and Target can change the payoff matrix by advertising that they will match their competitor's price. This retaliation strategy provides a signal that one store charging a lower price will be met automatically by the other store charging a lower price. In payoff matrix (a), there is no matching offer and each store benefits if it charges $150 when the other charges $200. In payoff matrix (b), with the matching offer, the companies have only two choices: They can charge $200 and receive a profit of $10,000 per month, or they can charge $150 and receive a profit of $7,500 per month. The equilibrium shifts from the prisoners' dilemma result of both stores charging the low price and receiving low profits to both stores charging the high price and receiving high profits.

collusion would be successful? The example of the Organization of Petroleum Exporting Countries (OPEC) indicates that the answer to this question is "no." OPEC has 11 members, including Saudi Arabia, Kuwait, and other Arab countries, as well as Iran, Venezuela, Nigeria, and Indonesia. Together these countries own 75 percent of the world's proven oil reserves, although they pump a smaller share of the total oil sold each year. OPEC operates as a **cartel,** which is a group of firms that colludes to restrict output to increase prices and profits. The members of OPEC meet periodically and agree on *quotas,* quantities of oil that each country agrees to produce. The quotas are intended to reduce oil production well below the competitive level, to force up the price of oil, and to increase the profits of member countries.

Cartel A group of firms that colludes by agreeing to restrict output to increase prices and profits.

Figure 10-10 shows world oil prices from 1972 to 2004. The blue line shows the price of a barrel of oil in each year. Prices in general have risen since 1972, which has reduced the amount of goods and services that can be purchased with a dollar. The red line corrects for this by measuring oil prices in terms of the dollar's purchasing power in 2004. Although political unrest in the Middle East and other factors also affect the price of oil, the figure shows that OPEC had considerable success in raising the price of oil during the mid-1970s and early 1980s. Oil prices, which had been below $3 per barrel in 1972, rose to more than $35 per barrel in 1981, which was more than $70 measured in dollars of 2004 purchasing power. The figure also shows that OPEC has had difficulty sustaining the high prices of 1981 in later years, although in 2004 and 2005 oil prices rose in part due to increasing demand from China and India. Game theory helps us to understand why oil prices have fluctuated. If every member of OPEC cooperates and produces the low output level dictated by its quota, prices will be high and the cartel will earn large profits. Once the price has been driven up, however, each member has an incentive to stop cooperating and to earn even higher profits by increasing output beyond its quota. But if no country sticks to its quota, total oil output will increase and profits will decline. In other words, OPEC is caught in a prisoners' dilemma.

FIGURE 10-10

World Oil Prices, 1972–2004

The blue line shows the price of a barrel of oil in each year. The red line measures the price of a barrel of oil in terms of the purchasing price of the dollar in 2004. By reducing oil production, the Organization of Petroleum Exporting Countries (OPEC) was able to raise the world price of oil in the mid-1970s and early 1980s. Sustaining high prices has been difficult, however, because members often exceed their output quotas.

Source: U.S. Energy Information Agency, *Monthly Energy Review*, May 2005.

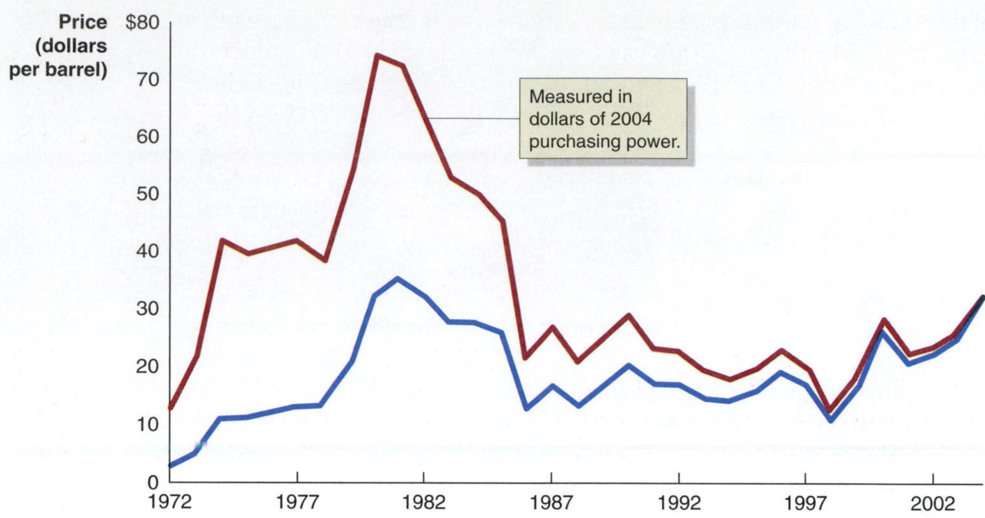

If the members of OPEC always exceeded their production quotas, the cartel would have no effect on world oil prices. In fact, periodically the members of OPEC meet and assign new quotas that, at least for a while, enable them to restrict output enough to raise prices. OPEC's occasional success at behaving as a cartel can be explained by two factors. First, the members of OPEC are participating in a repeated game. As we have seen, this increases the likelihood of a cooperative outcome. Second, Saudi Arabia has far larger oil reserves than any other member of OPEC. Therefore, it has the most to gain from high oil prices, and a greater incentive to cooperate. To see this, consider the payoff matrix shown in Figure 10-11. To keep things simple, let's assume that OPEC has only two members: Saudi Arabia and Nigeria. In Figure 10-11, "low output" corresponds to cooperating with the OPEC assigned output quota, and "high output" corresponds to producing at maximum capacity. The payoff matrix shows the profits received per day by each country.

We can see that Saudi Arabia has a strong incentive to cooperate and maintain its low output quota. By keeping output low, Saudi Arabia can by itself significantly raise the world price of oil, increasing its own profits, as well as those of other members of OPEC. Therefore, Saudi Arabia has a dominant strategy of cooperating with the quota

FIGURE 10-11

The OPEC Cartel with Unequal Members

Because Saudi Arabia can produce so much more oil than Nigeria, its output decisions have a much larger impact on the price of oil. In the figure, "low output" corresponds to cooperating with the OPEC-assigned output quota, and "high output" corresponds to producing at maximum capacity. Saudi Arabia has a dominant strategy to cooperate and produce a low output. Nigeria, on the other hand, has a dominant strategy not to cooperate and produce a high output. Therefore, the equilibrium of this game will occur with Saudi Arabia producing a low output and Nigeria producing a high output.

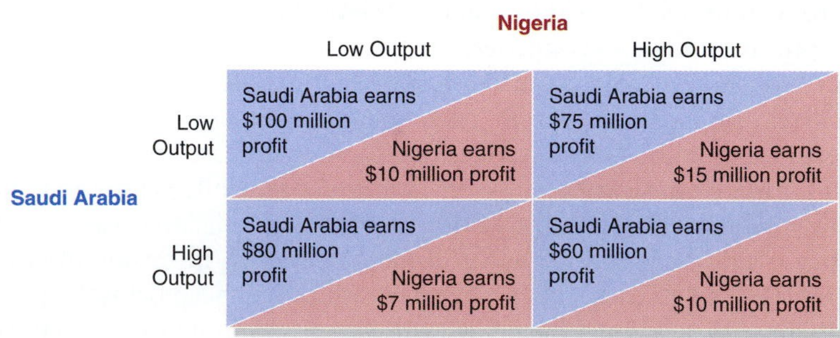

and producing a low output. Nigeria, however, cannot by itself have much impact on the price of oil. Therefore, Nigeria has a dominant strategy of not cooperating and producing a high output. The equilibrium of this game will occur with Saudi Arabia producing a low output and Nigeria producing a high output. In fact, OPEC often operates in just this way. Saudi Arabia will cooperate with the quota, while the other 10 members produce at capacity. Because this is a repeated game, however, Saudi Arabia will occasionally produce more oil than its quota to intentionally drive down the price and retaliate against the other members for not cooperating.

Conclusion

In this chapter, we have applied many of the ideas about competition we developed in Chapter 8 to the more common market structures of monopolistic competition and oligopoly. At the end of Chapter 8, we concluded that "The competitive forces of the market produce relentless pressure on firms to produce new and better goods and services, and to produce them at lower cost. Firms that fail to adequately anticipate changes in consumer tastes or that fail to adopt the latest and most efficient production techniques usually do not survive in the long run." These conclusions are as true for coffeehouses and firms in other monopolistically competitive markets as they are for wheat farmers or apple growers.

Even in the oligopolies discussed in this chapter, firms have difficulty earning economic profits in the long run. We have seen that firms attempt to avoid the effects of competition in various ways. For example, they can stake out a secure niche in the market, they can engage in implicit collusion with competing firms, or they can attempt to have the government impose barriers to entry.

This chapter concludes our discussion of microeconomics. Before moving on to macroeconomics, read *An Inside Look* on the next page to learn how some Starbucks and McDonald's locations differentiate themselves from competitors by extending their hours of operation.

An Inside Look

Starbucks and McDonald's Cater to Insomniacs

WALL STREET JOURNAL, JULY 15, 2004

Midnight Snack

SCHILLER PARK, Ill.— At about 3 a.m. recently, Michael Johnson sat at a table at a suburban Chicago McDonald's here eating lunch: Big Mac, with fries. This time of night, the 57-year-old truck driver says, few restaurants along his route from northern Indiana to western Illinois are open, and those that are tend to be far from the main highway.

Mr. Johnson eats in the middle of his 11 p.m. to 8 a.m. shift because, he says, "if you eat early, you come in sluggish, you're not as alert as you should be." So he's stopped at this highway rest stop regularly since it opened three weeks ago.

Having thoroughly squeezed the lunchtime market dry, the fast-food industry is chasing late-night customers like Mr. Johnson. Desperate for growth in a highly competitive business, chains from McDonald's Corp. to Wendy's International Inc. to Starbucks Corp. are keeping their doors open longer....

To cater to insomniacs, Starbucks has opened 41 all-night units in places such as Miami, Wheaton, Colo., Kenosha, Wis., and Atlanta, a striking departure for a company that generally closed at 6 p.m. just a few years ago.

Restaurants' impetus for rushing into the late-night market is clear: With more Americans working the overnight shift, society is increasingly operating around-the-clock. Wendy's, for instance, found that 25% of its late-night customers stop in on their way home from work, while 22% ducked out of the house for a snack or meal, and 19% were returning home from nightclubs, bars and other social venues.

"Americans are working later hours. Mom's working days. Dad's working nights, and the night shift people are looking for good meals," says Mike Roberts, president of McDonald's USA. "It's such an integral part of how many Americans are living today. It's going to be very important to our business."

A decade ago, Taco Bell, subsidiary of Yum! Brands Inc., led the fast-food charge into the late-night market once dominated by White Castle Management Co., Denny's Corp. and IHOP Corp. The company has invested millions of dollars in promoting its "Open 'Til Midnight or Later" slogan in television, print and radio ads, and many of its commercials end with a late-night shot. Still, only recently has competition followed....

a The six-hour traditional breakfast time, which is 5 a.m. to 11 a.m., accounted for 12% of all quick-service meals, compared with lunch, which was nearly half of all fast-food sales, and the dinner rush, which accounted for just over one-third. Several years ago, when franchisee Dennis Stabile started opening one of his suburban Chicago McDonald's restaurants earlier, at 5 a.m., sales between 7 a.m. and 8 a.m. grew by 50%. He saw similar results 9 p.m. to 11 p.m. after extending his hours past midnight. "Now that customers know you're open later, there's no question, 'Will McDonald's be open?,' because we always are," he says.

b Restaurant owners and executives say extending hours doesn't require developing a new menu. Overnight workers can transition the restaurant from the dinner to breakfast periods. And extended hours simply maximize use of space. "You're not paying any more taxes to be open 24 hours than you are by staying open 18 hours. The more profit you make, the more money you have to remodel," Mr. Stabile says.

Restaurants say security during late-night periods is of little concern, especially since many have invested heavily in such items as closed-circuit cameras within view of customers at cash registers. Others offer free meals to law-enforcement officials, hoping their presence will be a crime deterrent. Fast-food outlets with drive-thrus can close the unit and leave the drive-thru open, which provides safety for patrons and workers, says Dennis Lombardi, executive vice president at Technomic Inc., a food-consulting firm. The majority of McDonald's restaurants open for extended hours do so only with drive-thrus. Half of Starbucks's new 24-hour units are drive-thrus....

Key Points in the Article

This article discusses a new trend of restaurants staying open 24 hours per day. At one time, the market for late-night (or early-morning) meals was dominated by "family-style" restaurants, such as Denny's and the International House of Pancakes (IHOP). Recently, many other restaurants have begun to stay open 24 hours, including McDonald's, Wendy's, and Starbucks. Demand for late-night meals has increased as more U.S. workers are scheduled for night shifts, rather than the traditional 9-to-5 day shift.

Analyzing the News

a We saw in this chapter how important it is for firms to differentiate their products from those of their competitors. As a McDonald's owner asserted in this article, opening at 5:00 A.M. helped his normal 7:00 A.M. to 8:00 A.M. breakfast sales and being open after midnight helped his evening sales because "Now that customers know you're open later, there's no question, 'Will McDonald's be open?,' because we always are." In other words, by differentiating his product from that of other restaurants—that are not open early—the McDonald's owner is able to shift his firm's demand curve to the right. We show this in Figure 1, where the demand curve $D_{\text{open 24 hours}}$ is to the right of $D_{\text{open 16 hours}}$. Because price, $P_{\text{open 24 hours}}$, is above ATC, this strategy allows the McDonald's owner to earn economic profits, at least in the short run.

b As we saw in Chapter 7, business managers sometimes attempt to reduce their average fixed costs by "spreading the overhead." The article explains that for a restaurant "extended hours simply maximize use of space." Figure 2 shows that if staying open longer allows a restaurant to increase the quantity it sells from Q_1 to Q_2, its average fixed costs will decline from AFC_1 to AFC_2.

Thinking Critically ABOUT POLICY

1. Suppose that a law was passed banning restaurants from staying open past 10:00 P.M. Who would be harmed by this law? Would the law reduce profits in the fast-food market in the short run? In the long run? Use a graph like Figure 1 in your answer.
2. Suppose that a law was passed requiring fast-food firms to pay their night-shift employees twice as much as their daytime employees. What impact would this have on fast-food profits in the short run? In the long run? Use a graph like Figure 2 in your answer.

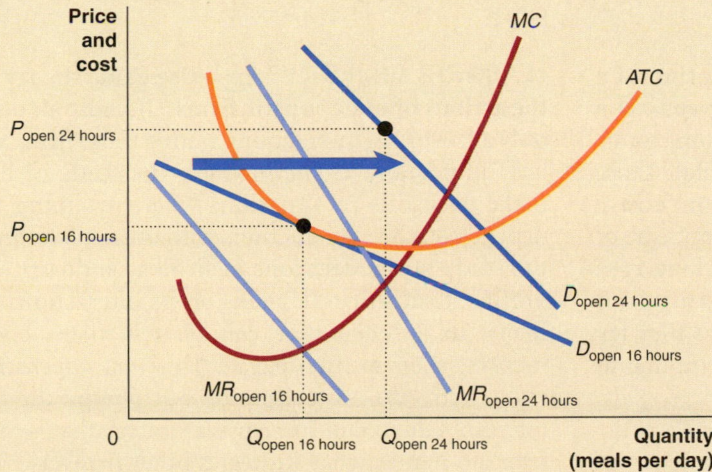

Figure 1: Product differentiation shifting the demand curve for a monopolistic competitor.

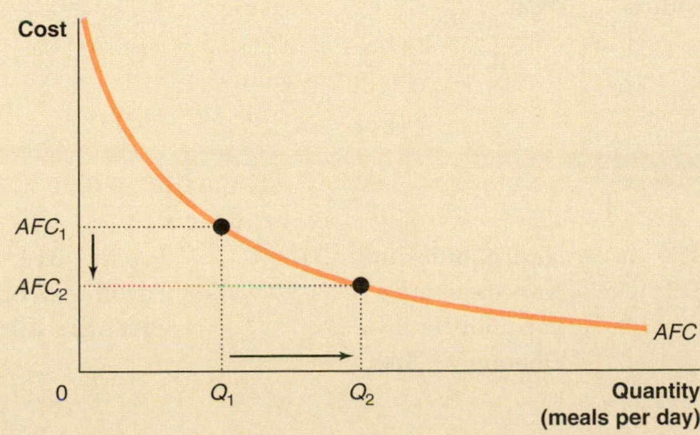

Figure 2: Spreading the overhead

SUMMARY

LEARNING OBJECTIVE ① Explain why a monopolistically competitive firm has a downward-sloping demand curve. A *monopolistically competitive* firm sells a differentiated product. Therefore, unlike a perfectly competitive firm, it faces a downward-sloping demand curve. When a monopolistically competitive firm cuts the price of its product, it sells more units, but must accept a lower price on the units it could have sold at the higher price. As a result, its marginal revenue curve is downward sloping.

LEARNING OBJECTIVE ② Explain how a monopolistically competitive firm decides the quantity to produce and the price to charge. A monopolistically competitive firm maximizes profits at the level of output where marginal revenue equals marginal cost. Price equals marginal revenue for a perfectly competitive firm, but price is greater than marginal revenue for a monopolistically competitive firm. Therefore, unlike a perfectly competitive firm, which produces where $P = MC$, a monopolistically competitive firm produces where $P > MC$.

LEARNING OBJECTIVE ③ Analyze the situation of a monopolistically competitive firm in the long run. If a monopolistically competitive firm is earning economic profits in the short run, entry of new firms will eliminate those profits in the long run. If a monopolistically competitive firm is suffering economic losses in the short run, exit of existing firms will eliminate those losses in the long run. Monopolistically competitive firms continually struggle to find new ways of differentiating their products as they try to stay one step ahead of other firms that are attempting to copy their success.

LEARNING OBJECTIVE ④ Compare the efficiency of monopolistic competition and perfect competition. Perfectly competitive firms produce where price equals marginal cost and at minimum average total cost. Perfectly competitive firms achieve both allocative and productive efficiency. Monopolistically competitive firms produce where price is greater than marginal cost and above minimum average total cost. Monopolistically competitive firms do not achieve either allocative or productive efficiency. Consumers face a trade-off when buying the product of a monopolistically competitive firm: They are paying a price that is greater than marginal cost and the product is not being produced at minimum average cost, but they benefit from being able to purchase a product that is differentiated and more closely suited to their tastes.

LEARNING OBJECTIVE ⑤ Show how barriers to entry explain the existence of oligopolies. An *oligopoly* is a market structure in which a small number of interdependent firms compete. *Barriers to entry* keep new firms from entering an industry. The three most important barriers to entry are economies of scale, ownership of a key input or raw material, and government barriers. Government barriers include patents, licensing, and barriers to international trade. Economies of scale are the most important barrier to entry.

LEARNING OBJECTIVE ⑥ Use game theory to analyze the actions of oligopolistic firms. Because an oligopoly has only a few firms, interactions among those firms are particularly important. *Game theory* is the study of how people make decisions in situations where attaining their goals depends on their interactions with others; in economics, it is the study of the decisions of firms in industries where the profits of each firm depends on its interactions with other firms. In a *cooperative equilibrium,* firms cooperate to increase their mutual payoff. In a *noncooperative equilibrium,* firms do not cooperate but pursue their own self-interest. A *dominant strategy* is a strategy that is the best for a firm, no matter what strategies other firms use. A situation where pursuing dominant strategies results in noncooperation that leaves everyone worse off is called a *prisoners' dilemma.* Because many business situations are repeated games, firms may end up implicitly colluding to keep prices high.

KEY TERMS

REVIEW QUESTIONS

1. What are the most important differences between perfectly competitive markets and monopolistically competitive markets? Give two examples of products sold in perfectly competitive markets and two examples of products sold in monopolistically competitive markets.
2. Why does the local McDonald's face a downward-sloping demand curve for Big Macs? If it raises the price it charges for Big Macs above the prices charged by other McDonald's, won't it lose all its customers?
3. Explain the differences between total revenue, average revenue, and marginal revenue.
4. Sally runs a McDonald's franchise. She is selling 350 Big Macs per week at a price of $3.25. If she lowers the price to $3.20, she will sell 351 Big Macs. What is the marginal revenue of the 351st Big Mac?
5. The text states, "Every firm that has the ability to affect the price of the good or service it sells will have a marginal revenue curve that is below its demand curve." Why is this true?
6. Does the fact that monopolistically competitive markets are not allocatively or productively efficient mean that there is a significant loss in economic well-being to society in these markets? In your answer, be sure to define what you mean by "economic well-being."
7. What is an oligopoly? Give three examples of oligopolistic industries in the United States.
8. What do barriers to entry have to do with the extent of competition, or lack thereof, in an industry? What are the most important barriers to entry?
9. Give brief definitions of the following concepts:
   a. game theory
   b. cooperative equilibrium
   c. noncooperative equilibrium
   d. dominant strategy
   e. Nash equilibrium
10. What is the difference between explicit collusion and implicit collusion? Give an example of each.
11. What is the prisoners' dilemma? How is the prisoners' dilemma result changed in a repeated game?

PROBLEMS AND APPLICATIONS

Please visit **www.prenhall.com/hubbard** *for solutions to the even-numbered problems as well as multiple-choice and true or false self-assessment quizzes.*

1. Complete the following table:

DVDs RENTED PER WEEK (Q)	PRICE (P)	TOTAL REVENUE ($TR = P \times Q$)	AVERAGE REVENUE ($AR = TR/Q$)	MARGINAL REVENUE ($MR = \Delta TR/\Delta Q$)
0	$8.00			
1	7.50			
2	7.00			
3	6.50			
4	6.00			
5	5.50			
6	5.00			
7	4.50			
8	4.00			

2. If Daniel sells 350 Big Macs at a price of $3.25 and his average cost of producing 350 Big Macs is $3.00, what is his profit?
3. Alicia manages a Hollywood Video store and has the following information on demand and costs:

DVDs RENTED PER WEEK (Q)	PRICE (P)	TOTAL COST (TC)
0	$6.00	$3.00
1	5.50	7.00
2	5.00	10.00
3	4.50	12.50
4	4.00	14.50
5	3.50	16.00
6	3.00	17.00
7	2.50	18.50
8	2.00	21.00

   a. To maximize profit, how many DVDs should Alicia rent, what price should she charge, and how much profit will she make?
   b. What is the marginal revenue received by renting the profit-maximizing DVD? What is the marginal cost of renting the profit-maximizing DVD?

4. A trucking company investigates the relationship between the gas mileage of its trucks and the average speed at which the trucks are driven on the highway. The company finds the relationship shown in the following graph:

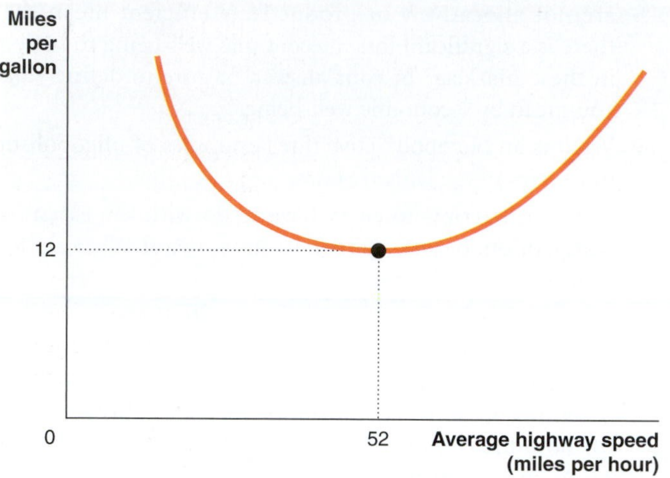

Will the firm maximize profits if it instructs its drivers to maintain an average speed of 52 miles per hour? Briefly explain.

5. Use the following graph to answer the questions.

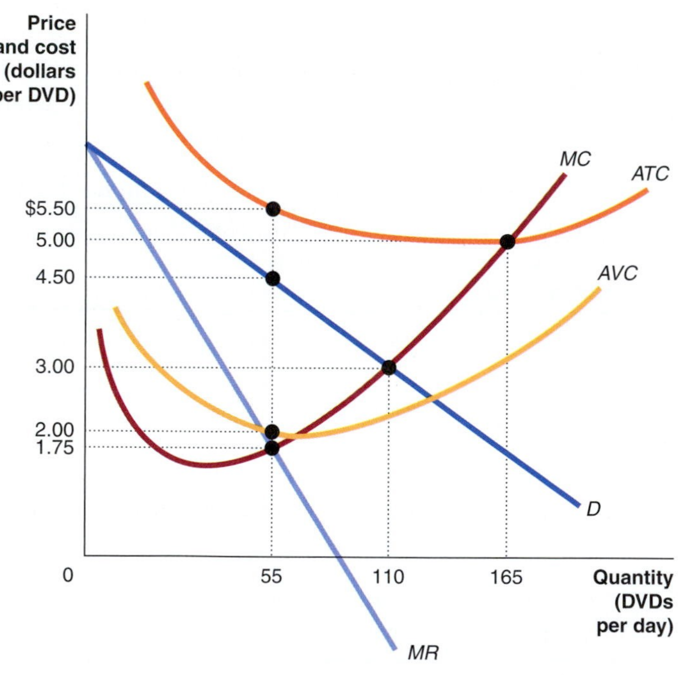

a. If the owner of this video store wants to maximize profits, how many DVDs should she rent per day and what rental price should she charge? Briefly explain your answer.
b. How much economic profit (or loss) is she making? Briefly explain.
c. Is the owner likely to continue renting this number of DVDs in the long run? Briefly explain.

6. During 2003, General Motors cut the prices of most of its car models. As a result, GM earned a profit of only $184 per car, compared to the profit of $555 per car it had earned in 2002. Does the decline in GM's profits per car indicate that cutting prices was not a profit-maximizing strategy? Briefly explain.
Source: Karen Lundergaard and Sholnn Freeman, "Detroit's Challenge: Weaning Buyers from Years of Deals," *Wall Street Journal*, January 6, 2004.

7. **[Related to *Don't Let This Happen To You!*]** A student remarks, "If firms in a monopolistically competitive industry are earning economic profits, new firms will enter the industry. Eventually, the representative firm will find its demand curve has shifted to the left until it is just tangent to its average cost curve and it is earning zero profit. Because firms are earning zero profit at that point, some firms will leave the industry and the representative firm will find its demand curve will shift to the right. In long-run equilibrium, price will be above average total cost by just enough so that each firm is just breaking even." Briefly explain whether you agree with this analysis.

8. The following excerpt is from an article in the *Wall Street Journal:*

> [Amazon.com], whose sales stagnated last year, increased revenue [this quarter] by 21 percent, to $806 million.... It attributed the increase to its price-cutting strategy: discounting books that cost more than $15 each and offering free shipping on orders of at least $49.

a. If Amazon.com's revenue increased after it cut the price of books, what must be true about the price elasticity of demand for ordering books online?
b. Suppose that before the price cut, Amazon.com was not selling the profit-maximizing quantity of books, but after the price cut it was. Draw a graph showing Amazon.com's situation before and after the price cut. (For simplicity, assume that Amazon charges the same price for all books.) Be sure your graph includes the price Amazon was charging and the quantity of books it was selling before the price cut; the price and quantity after the price cut; Amazon's demand, marginal revenue, average total cost, and marginal cost curves; and the areas representing its profits before and after the price cut.

Source: Saul Hansell, "Citing Its Price Strategy, Amazon Pares Loss," *Wall Street Journal*, July 24, 2002.

9. Before the fall of Communism, most basic consumer products in Eastern Europe and the Soviet Union were standardized. For example, government-run stores would offer for sale only one type of bar soap or one type of toothpaste. Soviet economists often argued that this system of standardizing basic consumer products avoided the waste associated with the differentiated goods and services produced in Western Europe and the United States. Do you agree with this argument?

10. **[Related to *Solved Problem 10-1*]** Michael Porter, an economist at the Harvard Business School, argues that firms in the U.S. commercial-printing industry have been "Investing heavily in the same new equipment, running their presses faster, and reducing crew sizes. But the resulting major productivity gains are being captured by customers and equipment suppliers, not retained in superior profitability." How would consumers gain from these productivity increases? Why haven't the productivity increases made the printing firms more profitable?
   Source: Michael E. Porter, "What Is Strategy?" *Harvard Business Review*, November–December 1996, p. 63.

11. According to an article in the *New York Times*, by 2003, "J. Crew, once a stylish powerhouse of preppy catalog retailing, had been floundering." Millard S. Drexler took over as chief executive officer and tried to restore the company's fortunes by offering new styles of clothes, "made of much more expensive materials: tight, military-style suede jackets, Shetland sweaters and sleek coats, designed in a range of colors—from pimento red to green the shade of a new-mown lawn." Drexler also raised the prices of most products the company sells. Use the model of monopolistic competition to analyze this situation.
   a. Draw a graph showing the impact Drexler hoped to have on J. Crew's profitability. For simplicity, your graph will be for a single J. Crew product and should include the demand curve, marginal cost, average total cost, the profit-maximizing price, and J. Crew's profits before and after Drexler changed the firm's strategy.
   b. Would Drexler's strategy likely be successful in increasing J. Crew's profits in the short run? Briefly explain. How about in the long run?
   Source: Tracie Rozhon, "Chief Seeks to Revive J. Crew's Preppy Heyday," *New York Times*, May 6, 2003.

12. 7-Eleven, Inc., operates more than 20,000 convenience stores worldwide. Edward Moneypenny, 7-Eleven's chief financial officer, was asked to name the biggest risk the company faced. He replied, "I would say that the biggest risk that 7-Eleven faces, like all retailers, is competition . . . because that is something that you've got to be aware of in this business." In what sense is competition a "risk" to a business? Why would a company in the retail business need to be particularly aware of competition?
   Source: Company Report, CEO Interview: Edward Moneypenny—7-Eleven, Inc., The Wall Street Transcript Corporation.

13. Michael Korda for many years was editor-in-chief at the Simon & Schuster book publishing company. He has described the many books that become bestsellers by promising to give readers financial advice that will make them wealthy, by, for example, buying and selling real estate. Korda is very skeptical about how useful the advice in these books is: "I have yet to meet anybody who got rich by buying a book, though quite a few people got rich by writing one." On the basis of the analysis in this chapter, discuss why it may be very difficult to become rich by following the advice found in a book.
   Source: Michael Korda, *Making the List: A Cultural History of the American Bestseller, 1900–1999*, New York: Barnes & Noble Books, 2001, p. 168.

14. **[Related to the *Chapter Opener*]** According to an article in *Fortune* magazine in early 2004, "The big question for [Starbucks's chairman Howard] Schultz is whether Starbucks can keep it up. There are those on Wall Street who say that Starbucks's game is almost over." What do you think the article means by "Starbucks's game is almost over"? Why would some people on Wall Street be making this prediction about a firm that in 2004 was making substantial economic profits?
   Source: Andy Serwer, "Hot Starbucks to Go," *Fortune*, January 12, 2004.

15. Thomas McCraw, a professor at the Harvard Business School, has written the following:

    > Throughout American history, entrepreneurs have tried, sometimes desperately, to create big businesses out of naturally small-scale operations. It has not worked.

   What advantage would entrepreneurs expect to gain from creating "big businesses"? Why would they be unsuccessful in doing so with "naturally small-scale operations"? Illustrate your answer with a graph showing long-run average costs.
   Source: Thomas K. McCraw, ed., *Creating Modern Capitalism*, Cambridge, MA: Harvard University Press, 1997, p. 323.

16. The figure below illustrates the average total cost curves for two automobile manufacturing firms: LittleAuto and BigAuto. Under which conditions would you expect to see the market composed of firms like LittleAuto and under which conditions would you expect to see the market dominated by firms like BigAuto?
    a. When the market demand curve intersects the quantity axis at less than 1,000 units
    b. When the market demand curve intersects the quantity axis at more than 1,000 units but less than 10,000 units
    c. When the market demand curve intersects the quantity axis at more than 10,000 units

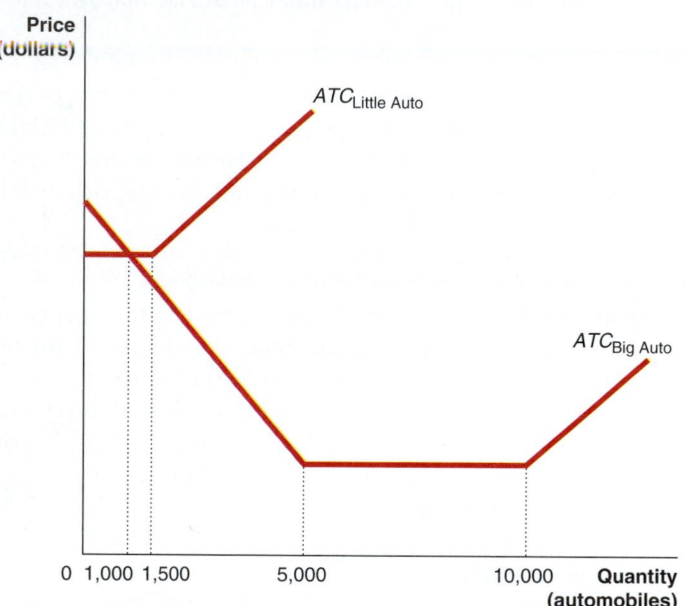

17. The figure below contains two long-run average cost curves. Briefly explain which cost curve would most likely be associated with an oligopoly and which would most likely be associated with a perfectly competitive industry.

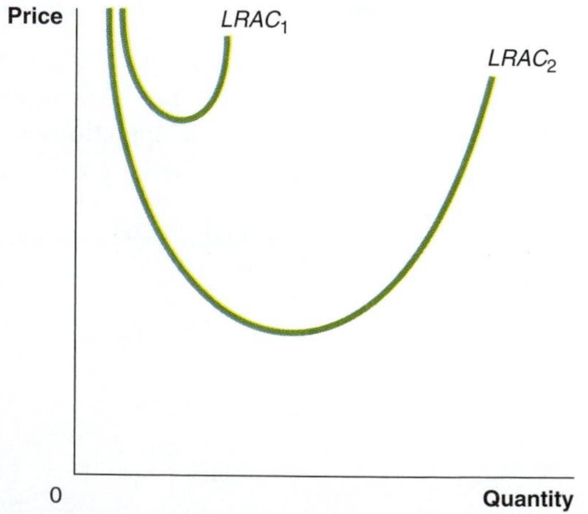

18. Consider the following two excerpts from articles in the *Wall Street Journal:*

    [From February 2003] An attempt by major airlines to raise fares $20 per round-trip ticket fell apart over the weekend as Northwest Airlines, the fourth-largest carrier, refused to go along.... By yesterday morning, all airlines had rolled back prices.

    [From August 2003] Northwest Airlines triggered a major round of discounting last week when it launched a fare sale for late summer and early fall travel—setting off a chain reaction in the industry. During the course of one day, airlines cut fares on nearly 35,881 routes.

    Briefly explain why airlines might be more likely to match price cuts than price increases.

    Sources: Scott McCartney and Susan Carey, "Airlines' Move to Raise Fares Falls Apart as Northwest Balks," *Wall Street Journal,* February 18, 2003; and Eleena De Lisser, "Fall Travel Deals Arrive Early," *Wall Street Journal,* August 14, 2003.

19. Bob and Tom are two criminals who have been arrested for burglary. The police put Tom and Bob in separate cells. They offer to let Bob go free if he confesses to the crime and testifies against Tom. Bob also is told that he will serve a 15-year sentence if he remains silent while Tom confesses. If he confesses and Tom also confesses, they will each serve a 10-year sentence. Separately, the police make the same offer to Tom. Assume that if Bob and Tom both remain silent, the police only have enough evidence to convict them of a lesser crime and they will serve 3-year sentences.
    a. Use this information to write a payoff matrix for Bob and Tom.
    b. Does Bob have a dominant strategy? If so, what is it?
    c. Does Tom have a dominant strategy? If so, what is it?
    d. What sentences do Bob and Tom serve? How might they have avoided this outcome?

20. Baseball players who hit the most home runs *relative to other players* usually receive the highest pay. Beginning in the mid-1990s, the typical baseball player became significantly stronger and more muscular. As one baseball announcer put it, "The players of 20 years ago look like stick figures compared with the players of today." As a result, the average number of home runs hit each year increased dramatically. Some of the increased strength gained by baseball players came from more weight training and better conditioning and diet. As some players admitted, though, some of the increased strength came from taking steroids and other illegal drugs. Taking steroids can significantly increase the risk of developing cancer and other medical problems.

a. In these circumstances, are baseball players in a prisoners' dilemma? Carefully explain.

b. Suppose that Major League Baseball begins testing players for steroids and firing players who are caught using them (or other illegal muscle-building drugs). Will this testing make baseball players as a group better off or worse off? Briefly explain.

21. **[Related to *Solved Problem 10-2*]** Beginning in 2003, the U.S. government spent billions of dollars rebuilding the Iraqi infrastructure that had been damaged by war. Much of the work was carried out by construction and engineering firms that had to bid for the business. Suppose, hypothetically, that only two companies—Bechtel and Halliburton—enter the bidding and that each firm is deciding whether to bid either $4 billion or $5 billion. (Remember that in this type of bidding, the winning bid is the *low* bid because the bid represents the amount the government will have to pay to have the work done.) Each firm will have costs of $2.5 billion to do the work. If they both make the same bid, they will both be hired and will split the work and the profits. If one makes a low bid and one makes a high bid, only the low bidder will be hired and it will receive all the profits. The result is the following payoff matrix:

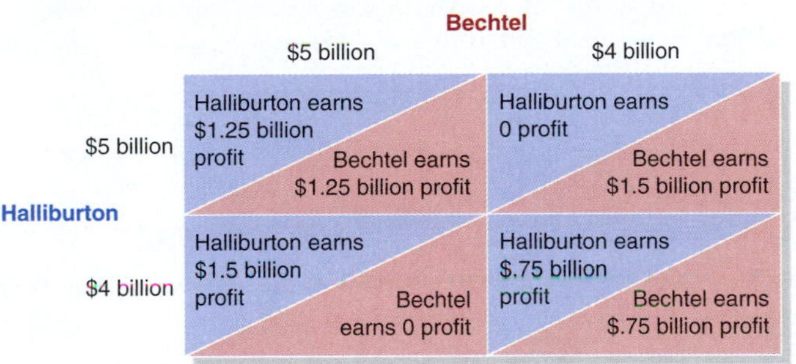

a. Is there a Nash equilibrium in this game? Briefly explain.

b. How might the situation be changed if the two companies expect to be bidding on many similar projects in future years?

22. **[Related to *Solved Problem 10-2*]** Suppose that Wal-Mart and Target are competing on whether to stick with barcodes or switch to radio frequency identification (RFID) tags to monitor the flow of products. Because many suppliers sell to both Wal-Mart and Target, it is much less costly for suppliers to use one system or the other, rather than to use both. The following payoff matrix shows the profits per year for each company resulting from the interaction of their strategies:

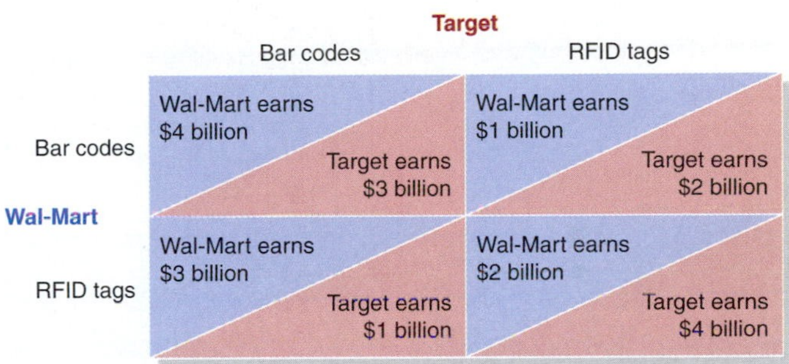

a. Briefly explain whether Wal-Mart has a dominant strategy.

b. Briefly explain whether Target has a dominant strategy.

c. Briefly explain whether there is a Nash equilibrium in this game.

chapter eleven

GDP: Measuring Total Production and Income

Increases in GDP Spur Hiring at Freightliner

Freightliner is the leading manufacturer of commercial vehicles in North America, producing more than 110,000 trucks and other vehicles in a typical year and exporting to more than 30 countries. The firm is owned by the DaimlerChrysler Corporation and is headquartered in Portland, Oregon. In the summer of 2004, Freightliner began hiring more workers in several of its manufacturing plants in North America. It added 700 workers at its plant near Portland, Oregon, 593 workers at its plant in Cleveland, North Carolina, 300 workers at its plant in St. Thomas, Ontario, Canada, and 165 workers at its plant in Gaffney, South Carolina. The firm's leading product is the Freightliner Class 8 heavy truck. It also manufactures American LaFrance fire trucks and emergency vehicles and Thomas Built Buses, along with other commercial vehicles.

Freightliner's increased hiring in the summer of 2004 was caused by an increase in demand for its trucks. This increase in demand was not the result of Freightliner's introducing innovative new products or starting an effective new marketing campaign. Instead, Freightliner was experiencing the effects of the *business cycle,* which refers to the alternating periods of economic expansion and recession that occur in the United States and other industrial economies. Production and employment increase during expansions and fall during recessions. In 2004, Freightliner was benefiting from the effects of an economic expansion, but just a few years earlier it had suffered from the effects of an economic recession. In fact, many of the workers hired in 2004 had previously been laid off by the firm. Rainer Schmüeckle, the president and chief executive officer (CEO) of Freightliner, explained the new hiring in terms of the business cycle: "The North American heavy-duty truck market continues its vigorous recovery and we have a positive outlook for further improvement. . . . Favorable economic conditions and customers' need to replace older equipment or expand their operations are driving a robust recovery of the North American Class 8 market."

Freightliner was not alone in experiencing an increase in demand during 2004. *An Inside Look* on page 350 discusses the increase in demand being experienced by Canadian firms during this period. As firms benefited from the economic expansion, they increased their hiring. This was good news for college graduates searching for work. In the summer of 2004, almost 150,000 fewer college graduates were unemployed than had been unemployed the previous summer. Although the job market had improved, it was still not as strong as in the late 1990s, when even fewer workers were unemployed.

Activities at companies like Freightliner can offer important insight into whether U.S. economic activity is surging or flagging. In 2001, as fears of recession in the United States intensified, the President's Council of Economic Advisers contacted economists in the trucking, airline, retailing, and financial services industries. In so doing, the government economists were able to collect and assess information on economic conditions before official data for the economy as a whole were tabulated. Individual firms like Freightliner must pay attention to developments in the overall economy. Macroeconomists and financial market participants also study economic developments at key firms to evaluate the current pace of economic activity.

Source: Robert Guy Matthews, "U.S. Recovery in Manufacturing Gains Momentum," *Wall Street Journal*, July 9, 2004, p. A2.

After studying this chapter, you should be able to:

① Explain how total production is measured.

② Discuss whether GDP is a good measure of economic well-being.

③ Discuss the difference between real variables and nominal variables.

④ Become familiar with other measures of total production and total income.

Microeconomics The study of how households and firms make choices, how they interact in markets, and how the government attempts to influence their choices.

Macroeconomics The study of the economy as a whole, including topics such as inflation, unemployment, and economic growth.

Business cycle Alternating periods of economic expansion and economic recession.

Expansion The period of a business cycle during which total production and total employment are increasing.

Recession The period of a business cycle during which total production and total employment are decreasing.

Economic growth The ability of an economy to produce increasing quantities of goods and services.

Inflation rate The percentage increase in the price level from one year to the next.

As we saw in Chapter 1, we can divide economics into the subfields of microeconomics and macroeconomics. **Microeconomics** is the study of how households and firms make choices, how they interact in markets, and how the government attempts to influence their choices. **Macroeconomics** is the study of the economy as a whole, including topics such as inflation, unemployment, and economic growth. In microeconomic analysis, economists generally study individual markets, such as the market for personal computers. In macroeconomic analysis, economists study factors that affect many markets at the same time. As we saw in the chapter opener, one important macroeconomic issue is the business cycle. The **business cycle** refers to the alternating periods of expansion and recession that the U.S. economy has experienced dating back at least to the early nineteenth century. A business cycle **expansion** is a period during which total production and total employment are increasing. A business cycle **recession** is a period during which total production and employment are decreasing. In the following chapters, we will discuss the causes of the business cycle and policies the government may use to reduce its effects.

Another important macroeconomic topic is **economic growth,** which refers to the ability of the economy to produce increasing quantities of goods and services. Economic growth is important because an economy that grows too slowly fails to raise living standards. In many countries in Africa, very little economic growth has occurred in the past 50 years, and many people remain in severe poverty. Macroeconomics analyzes both what determines the rate of economic growth within a country and the reasons why growth rates differ so greatly across countries.

Macroeconomics also analyzes what determines the total level of employment in an economy. As we will see, the level of employment is affected significantly by the business cycle, but other factors also help determine the level of employment in the long run. A related issue is why some economies are more successful than others in maintaining high levels of employment over time. Another important macroeconomic issue is what determines the **inflation rate,** or the percentage increase in the average level of prices from one year to the next. As with employment, inflation is affected both by the business cycle and by other long-run factors. Finally, macroeconomics is concerned with the linkages among economies: international trade and international finance.

Macroeconomic analysis provides information that consumers and firms need in order to understand current economic conditions and to help predict future conditions. A family may be reluctant to buy a house if employment in the economy is declining because some family members may be at risk of losing their jobs. Similarly, firms may be reluctant to invest in building new factories or to undertake major new expenditures on information technology if they expect that future sales may be weak. For example, in early 2003, DaimlerChrysler canceled plans to spend $1.2 billion to build a new factory in Windsor, Ontario, to manufacture Dodge pickup trucks. The decision was made because macroeconomic forecasts indicated that consumer demand for trucks and automobiles would be weak. Macroeconomic analysis can also aid the federal government in designing policies that help the U.S. economy perform more efficiently.

In this chapter and Chapter 12, we begin our study of macroeconomics by considering how best to measure key macroeconomic variables. As we will see, there are important issues involved in measuring macroeconomic variables. We start by considering measures of total production and total income in an economy.

Gross Domestic Product Measures Total Production

① LEARNING OBJECTIVE

Explain how total production is measured.

"Second Quarter [U.S.] GDP Data Show Economic Fundamentals Solid"

"Russian Government Cuts 2005 GDP Forecast to 5.8%"

"German Government Cuts 2005 GDP Forecast to 1.7% from 1.8%"

"Key Scandinavian Data: Danish Third Quarter GDP Growth Seen Easing"

"Chile's Third Quarter GDP Surges 6.8% on Year"

These headlines are from articles that appeared during one month in the *Wall Street Journal*. Why is GDP so often the focus of news stories? In this section, we explore what GDP is and how it is measured. We also explore why knowledge of GDP is important to consumers, firms, and government policymakers.

Measuring Total Production: Gross Domestic Product

Economists measure total production by **gross domestic product** or **GDP.** GDP is the market *value* of all *final* goods and services produced in a country during a period of time. In the United States, the Bureau of Economic Analysis (BEA) in the Department of Commerce compiles the data needed to calculate GDP. The BEA issues reports on the GDP every three months. GDP is a central concept in macroeconomics, so we need to consider its definition carefully.

Gross domestic product (GDP) The market value of all final goods and services produced in a country during a period of time.

GDP IS MEASURED USING MARKET VALUES, NOT QUANTITIES The word *value* is important in the definition of GDP. In microeconomics, we measure production in quantity terms: number of iPods produced by Apple, billions of tons of wheat grown by U.S. farmers, or number of trucks produced by Freightliner. When we measure total production in the economy, we can't just add together the quantities of every good and service because the result would be a meaningless jumble. Tons of wheat would be added to gallons of milk and numbers of trucks and so on. Instead, we measure production by taking the *value* in dollar terms of all the goods and services produced.

GDP INCLUDES ONLY THE MARKET VALUE OF FINAL GOODS In measuring GDP, we include only the value of **final goods and services.** A final good or service is one that is purchased by its final user and is not included in the production of any other good or service. A hamburger purchased by a consumer or a computer purchased by a business are final goods. Some goods and services, though, are used in the production of other goods and services. For example, Freightliner does not produce tires for its heavy trucks; it buys them from tire companies, such as Goodyear and Michelin. The tires are an **intermediate good,** whereas a Freightliner truck is a final good. In calculating GDP, we include the value of the Freightliner truck but not the value of the tire. If we included the value of the tire, we would be *double counting*. The value of the tire would be counted once when it was sold to Freightliner and a second time when Freightliner sold the truck that the tire was installed on to Federal Express or some other customer.

Final good or service A good or service purchased by a final user.

Intermediate good or service A good or service that is an input into another good or service, such as a tire on a truck.

GDP INCLUDES ONLY CURRENT PRODUCTION GDP includes only production that takes place during the indicated time period. For example, GDP in 2006 includes only the goods and services produced during that year. In particular, GDP does *not* include the value of used goods. If you buy a DVD of *The War of the Worlds* from Amazon.com, the purchase is included in GDP. If six months later you resell that DVD on eBay, that transaction is not included in GDP.

SOLVED PROBLEM 11-1

① LEARNING OBJECTIVE
Explain how total production is measured.

Calculating GDP

Suppose that a very simple economy produces only the following four goods and services: eye examinations, pizzas, textbooks, and paper. Assume that all of the paper in this economy is used in the production of textbooks. Use the information in the following table to compute GDP for the year 2007.

PRODUCTION AND PRICE STATISTICS FOR 2007

(1) PRODUCT	(2) QUANTITY	(3) PRICE PER UNIT
Eye examinations	100	$50.00
Pizzas	80	10.00
Textbooks	20	100.00
Paper	2,000	0.10

Solving the Problem:

Step 1: Review the chapter material. This problem is about gross domestic product, so you may want to review the section "Measuring Total Production: Gross Domestic Product," which begins on page 333.

Step 2: Determine which goods and services listed in the table should be included in the calculation of GDP. GDP is the value of all final goods and services. Therefore, we need to calculate the value of the final goods and services listed in the table. Eye examinations, pizzas, and textbooks are final goods. Paper would also be a final good if, for instance, a consumer bought it to use in a printer. However, here we are assuming that publishers purchase all the paper to use in manufacturing textbooks, so the paper is an intermediate good and its value is not included in GDP.

Step 3: Calculate the value of the three final goods and services listed in the table. Value is equal to the quantity produced multiplied by the price per unit, so we multiply the numbers in column (1) by the numbers in column (2):

PRODUCT	(1) QUANTITY	(2) PRICE PER UNIT	(3) VALUE
Eye examinations	100	$50	$5,000
Pizzas	80	10	800
Textbooks	20	100	2,000

Step 4: Add the value for each of the three final goods and services to find GDP.
GDP = Value of eye examinations produced + value of pizzas produced + value of textbooks produced = $5,000 + $800 + $2,000 = $7,800

YOUR TURN: **For more practice, do related problem 7 on page 353 at the end of this chapter.**

Production, Income, and the Circular Flow Diagram

When we measure the value of total production in the economy by calculating GDP, we are simultaneously measuring the value of total income. To see why the value of total production is equal to the value of total income, consider what happens to the money you spend on a single product. Suppose you buy an Apple iPod for $250 at a Best Buy store. *All* of that $250 must end up as someone's income. Apple and Best Buy will receive some of the $250 as profits, workers at Apple will receive some as wages, the salesperson who sold you the iPod will receive some as salary, the firms that sell parts to Apple will receive some as profits, the workers for these firms will receive some as wages, and so on: Every penny must end up as someone's income. (Note, though, that any sales tax on the iPod will be collected by the store and sent to the government without ending up as anyone's income.) Therefore, if we add up the value of every good and service sold in the economy, we must get a total that is exactly equal to the value of all of the income in the economy.

The circular-flow diagram in Figure 11-1 (page 336) was introduced in Chapter 2 to illustrate the interaction of firms and households in markets. We use it here to illustrate the flow of spending and money in the economy. Firms sell goods and services to three groups: domestic households, foreign firms and households, and the government. Expenditures by foreign firms and households (shown as the "Rest of the World" in the diagram) on domestically produced goods and services are called *exports.* For example, Freightliner sells 30 percent of its heavy trucks outside the United States. As we note at the bottom of Figure 11-1, we can measure GDP by adding up the total expenditures of these three groups on goods and services.

Firms use the *factors of production*—labor, capital, natural resources, and entrepreneurship—to produce goods and services. Households supply the factors of production to firms in exchange for income. We divide income into four categories: wages, interest, rent, and profit. Firms pay wages to households in exchange for labor services, interest for the use of capital, and rent for natural resources such as land. Profit is the income that remains after a firm has paid wages, interest, and rent. Profit is the return to entrepreneurs for organizing the other factors of production and for bearing the risk of producing and selling goods and services. As Figure 11-1 shows, federal, state, and local governments make payments of wages and interest to households in exchange for hiring workers and other factors of production. Governments also make *transfer payments* to households. **Transfer payments** include Social Security payments to retired and disabled people and unemployment insurance payments to unemployed workers. These payments are not included in GDP because they are not received in exchange for production of a new good or service. The sum of wages, interest, rent, and profit is total income in the economy. As we note at the top of Figure 11-1, we can measure GDP as the total income received by households.

Transfer payments Payments by the government to individuals for which the government does not receive a good or service in return.

The diagram also allows us to trace the ways that households use their income. Households spend some of their income on goods and services. Some of this spending is on domestically produced goods and services, and some is on foreign produced goods and services. Spending on foreign produced goods and services is known as *imports.* Households also use some of their income to pay taxes to the government. (Note that firms also pay taxes to the government.) Some of the income earned by households is not spent on goods and services or paid in taxes but is deposited in checking or savings accounts in banks or is used to buy stocks or bonds. Banks and stock and bond markets make up the *financial system.* The flow of funds from households into the financial system makes it possible for the government and firms to borrow. As we will see, the health of the financial system is of vital importance to an economy. Without the ability to borrow funds through the financial system, firms will have difficulty expanding and adopting new technologies. In fact, as we will discuss in Chapter 13, no country without a well-developed financial system has been able to sustain high levels of economic growth.

The circular flow diagram shows that we can measure GDP either by calculating the total value of expenditures on final goods and services or by calculating the value of total income. We get the same dollar amount of GDP whichever approach we take.

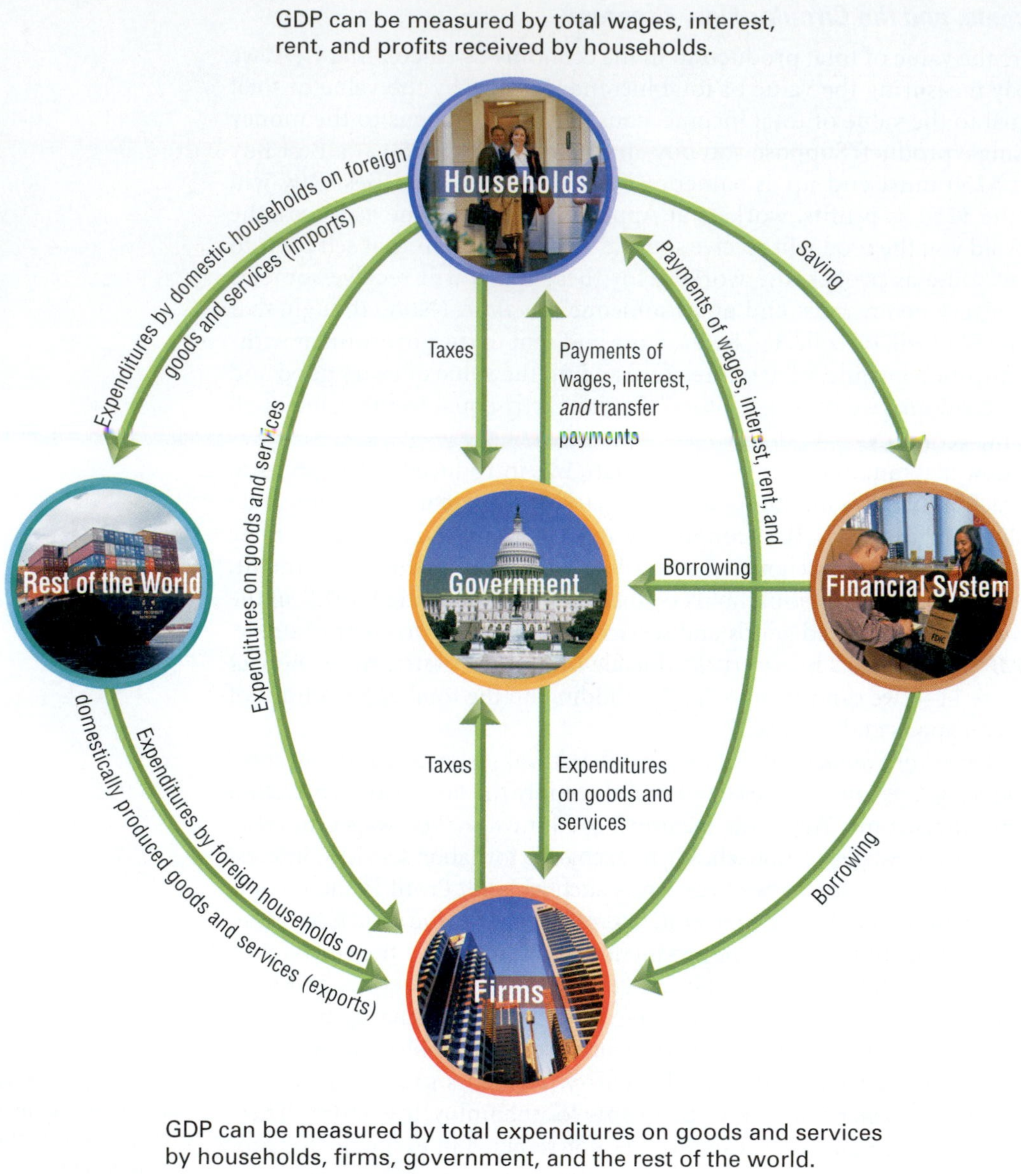

FIGURE 11-1 The Circular Flow and the Measurement of GDP

The circular-flow diagram illustrates the flow of spending and money in the economy. Firms sell goods and services to three groups: domestic households, foreign firms and households, and the government. To produce goods and services, firms use factors of production: labor, capital, natural resources, and entrepreneurship. Households supply the factors of production to firms in exchange for income in the form of wages, interest, profit, and rent. Firms make payments of wages and interest to households in exchange for hiring workers and other factors of production. The sum of wages, interest, rent, and profit is total income in the economy. We can measure GDP as the total income received by households. The diagram also shows that households use their income to purchase goods and services, pay taxes, and save. Firms and the government borrow the funds that flow from households into the financial system. We can measure GDP either by calculating the total value of expenditures on final goods and services or by calculating the value of total income.

Components of GDP

The Bureau of Economic Analysis (BEA) divides its statistics on GDP into four major categories of expenditures. Economists use these categories to understand why GDP fluctuates and to forecast future GDP.

Consumption Spending by households on goods and services, not including spending on new houses.

PERSONAL CONSUMPTION EXPENDITURES, OR "CONSUMPTION" **Consumption** expenditures are made by households and are divided into expenditures on *services*,

Don't Let This Happen To You!

Remember What Economists Mean by "Investment"

Notice that the definition of *investment* in this chapter is narrower than in everyday use. For example, people often say they are investing in the stock market or in rare coins. As we have seen, economists reserve the word *investment* for purchases of machinery, factories, and houses. Economists don't include purchases of stock or rare coins or deposits in savings accounts in the definition of investment because these activities don't result in the production of new goods. For example, a share of Microsoft stock represents part ownership of that company. When you buy a share of Microsoft stock, nothing new is produced—there is just a transfer in ownership. Similarly, buying a rare coin or putting $1,000 in a savings account does not result in an increase in production. GDP is not affected by any of these activities, so they are not included in the economic definition of investment.

YOUR TURN: **Test your understanding by doing related problem 9 on page 353 at the end of this chapter.**

such as medical care, education, and haircuts; expenditures on *nondurable goods,* such as food and clothing; and expenditures on *durable goods,* such as automobiles and furniture. The spending by households on new houses is not included in consumption. Instead, spending on new houses is included in the investment category, which we discuss next.

GROSS PRIVATE DOMESTIC INVESTMENT, OR "INVESTMENT" Spending on *gross private domestic investment,* or simply **investment** is divided into three categories: *Business fixed investment* is spending by firms on new factories, office buildings, and machinery used to produce other goods. *Residential investment* is spending by households on new housing. *Changes in business inventories* are also included in investment. Inventories are goods that have been produced, but not yet sold. If Freightliner has $200 million worth of unsold trucks at the beginning of the year and $350 million worth of unsold trucks at the end of the year, then the firm has spent $150 million on inventory investment during the year.

Investment Spending by firms on new factories, office buildings, machinery, and inventories, and spending by households on new houses.

GOVERNMENT CONSUMPTION AND GROSS INVESTMENT, OR "GOVERNMENT PURCHASES" **Government purchases** are spending by federal, state, and local governments on goods and services, such as teachers' salaries, highways, and aircraft carriers. Again, government spending on transfer payments is not included in government purchases because it does not result in the production of new goods and services.

Government purchases Spending by federal, state, and local governments on goods and services.

11-1 Making the Connection

Spending on Homeland Security

The federal government established the Department of Homeland Security after September 11, 2001, to guard against future terrorist attacks within the United States. Spending by this department is intended to increase the security of the nation's borders and transportation system, identify and arrest terrorists within the United States, and gather intelligence on potential terrorist threats.

Although the Department of Homeland Security has overall responsibility for homeland security, other federal agencies also have increased their spending on related programs. For example, the Department of Health and Human Services increased its spending on research to find new ways to combat the use of biological weapons from $300 million in 2001 to more than $4 billion in 2004. Several other federal agencies, such as the Department of Justice, the Department of Agriculture, and the Department of Transportation, increased their spending as well. In 2004, the total spending on homeland security by the Department of Homeland Security and other federal agencies was about $41.4 billion—about double the amount spent on these activities before 2001.

Government spending on homeland security more than doubled between 2001 and 2004.

Because the United States has a federal system of government, responsibility for some homeland security activities lies with state or local authorities. For example, spending to provide security for the Golden Gate Bridge is the responsibility of the state of California and the city of San Francisco. The Department of Homeland Security provides grants to help support this state and local spending. Of course, governments at all levels have limited budgets, so at some point spending more on homeland security requires them to spend less on other programs.

Sources: Congressional Budget Office, *Federal Funding for Homeland Security,* April 30, 2004; and Executive Office of the President, Office of Management and Budget, *Homeland Security.*

Net exports Exports minus imports.

NET EXPORTS OF GOODS AND SERVICES, OR "NET EXPORTS" **Net exports** is equal to *exports* minus *imports.* Exports are goods and services produced in the United States, but purchased by foreign firms, households, and governments. We add exports to our other categories of expenditures because otherwise we would not be including all spending on new goods and services produced in the United States. For example, if Freightliner sells $90 billion worth of trucks to firms in other countries, those exports are included in GDP because they represent production in the United States. Imports are goods and services produced in foreign countries, but purchased by U.S. firms, households, and governments. We subtract imports from total expenditures, because otherwise we would be including spending that does not result in production of new goods and services in the United States. For example, if U.S. consumers buy $150 billion worth of furniture manufactured in China, that spending is included in consumption expenditures. But the value of those imports is subtracted from GDP because the imports do not represent production in the United States.

An Equation for GDP and Some Actual Values

A simple equation sums up the components of GDP:

$$Y = C + I + G + NX.$$

The equation tells us that GDP (denoted as Y) equals consumption (C) plus investment (I) plus government purchases (G) plus net exports (NX). Figure 11-2 shows the values of the components of GDP for the year 2004. The graph in the figure highlights that consumption is by far the largest component of GDP. The table provides a more detailed breakdown and shows several interesting points:

- Consumer spending on services is greater than the sum of spending on durable and nondurable goods. This greater spending on services is reflected in the United States and other high-income countries by a continuing trend away from the production of goods and toward the production of services. As the populations of these countries have become, on average, both older and wealthier, their demand for services such as medical care and financial advice has increased faster than their demand for goods.

COMPONENTS OF GDP (billions of dollars)		
Consumption		$8,214
Durable Goods	$988	
Nondurable Goods	2,368	
Services	4,858	
Investment		1,928
Business Fixed Investment	1,199	
Residential Construction	674	
Change in Business Inventories	55	
Government Purchases		2,216
Federal	828	
State and Local	1,388	
Net Exports		–624
Exports	1,174	
Imports	1,798	
Total GDP		$11,734

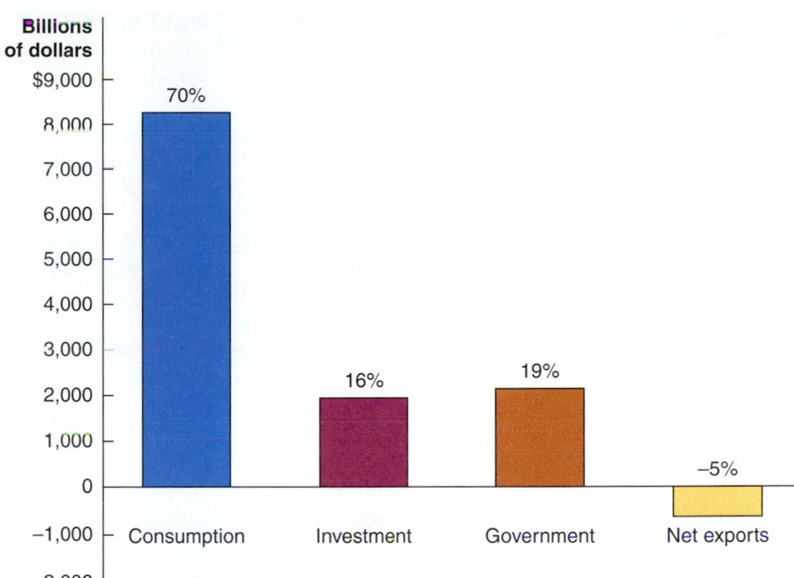

FIGURE 11-2 Components of GDP in 2004

Consumption accounts for 70 percent of GDP, far more than any of the other components. In recent years, net exports typically have been negative, which reduces GDP.

- Business fixed investment is the largest component of investment. As we will see in later chapters, spending by firms on new factories, computers, and machinery can fluctuate. For example, a decline in business fixed investment played an important role in causing the 2001 recession.
- Purchases made by state and local governments are greater than purchases made by the federal government. State and local government purchases are greater than federal government purchases because basic government activities, such as education and law enforcement, occur largely at the state and local levels.
- Imports are greater than exports, so net exports are negative. We will discuss in Chapter 18 why this pattern has been true typically for the U.S. economy.

Measuring GDP by the Value Added Method

We have seen that GDP can be calculated by adding together all expenditures on final goods and services. An alternative way of calculating GDP is the *value added method.* **Value added** refers to the additional market value a firm gives to a product and is equal to the difference between the price the firm sells a good for and the price it paid other firms for intermediate goods. Table 11-1 gives a hypothetical example of the value added by each firm involved in the production of a shirt offered for sale on L.L.Bean's Web site.

Value added The market value a firm adds to a product.

Suppose a cotton farmer sells $1.00 of raw cotton to a textile mill. If, for simplicity, we ignore any inputs the farmer may have purchased from other firms—such as cottonseed or fertilizer—then the farmer's value added is $1.00. The textile mill then weaves the raw cotton into cotton fabric, which it sells to a shirt company for $3.00. The textile mill's value added ($2.00) is the difference between the price it paid for the raw cotton ($1.00) and the price for which it can sell the cotton fabric ($3.00). Similarly, the shirt company's value added is the difference between the price it paid for the cotton fabric ($3.00) and the price it receives for the shirt from L.L.Bean ($15.00). L.L.Bean's value added is the difference between the price it pays for the shirt ($15.00) and the price it can sell the shirt for on its Web site ($35.00). Notice that *the price of the shirt on*

TABLE 11-1

Calculating Value Added

FIRM	VALUE OF PRODUCT	VALUE ADDED	
Cotton farmer	Value of raw cotton = $1.00	Value added by cotton farmer	= $1.00
Textile mill	Value of raw cotton woven into cotton fabric = $3.00	Value added by cotton textile mill = ($3.00 – $1.00)	= 2.00
Shirt company	Value of cotton fabric made into a shirt = $15.00	Value added by shirt manufacturer = ($15.00 –$3.00)	= 12.00
L.L.Bean	Value of shirt for sale on L.L. Bean's Web site = $35.00	Value added by L.L.Bean = ($35.00 – $15.00)	= 20.00
	Total Value Added		**= $35.00**

L.L.Bean's Web site is exactly equal to the sum of the value added by each firm involved in the production of the shirt. Therefore, we can calculate GDP by adding up the market value of every final good and service produced during a particular period. Or, we can arrive at the same value for GDP by adding up the value added of every firm involved in producing those final goods and services.

(2) LEARNING OBJECTIVE

Discuss whether GDP is a good measure of economic well-being.

Does GDP Measure What We Want It to Measure?

Economists use GDP to measure total production in the economy. For that purpose, we would like GDP to be as comprehensive as possible, not overlooking any significant production that takes place in the economy. Most economists believe that GDP does a good—but not flawless—job of measuring production. GDP is also sometimes used as a measure of well-being. Although it is generally true that the more goods and services people have, the better off they are, we will see that GDP provides only a rough measure of well-being.

Shortcomings in GDP as a Measure of Total Production

When the BEA calculates GDP, it does not include two types of production: production in the home and production in the underground economy.

HOUSEHOLD PRODUCTION With only a couple of exceptions, the U.S. Commerce Department does not attempt to estimate the value of goods and services that are not bought and sold in markets. If a carpenter makes and sells bookcases, the value of those bookcases will be counted in GDP. If the carpenter makes a bookcase for personal use, it will not be counted in GDP. *Household production* refers to goods and services people produce for themselves. The most important type of household production is the services a homemaker provides to the homemaker's family. If a person has been caring for children, cleaning house, and preparing the family meals, the value of such services is not included in GDP. If the person then decides to work outside the home, enrolls the children in day care, hires a cleaning service, and begins eating family meals in restaurants, the value of GDP will rise by the amount paid for day care, cleaning services, and restaurant meals, even though production of these services has not actually increased.

THE UNDERGROUND ECONOMY Individuals and firms sometimes conceal the buying and selling of goods and services, in which case their production won't be counted in GDP. Individuals and firms conceal what they buy and sell for three basic reasons: They are dealing in illegal goods and services, such as drugs or prostitution; they want to avoid paying taxes on the income they earn; or they want to avoid government regulations. This concealed buying and selling is referred to as the **underground economy.** Estimates of the size of the underground economy in the United States vary widely, but it may be as much as 10 percent of measured GDP, or more than $1 trillion. The underground economy in some poorer countries, such as Zimbabwe or Peru, may be more than half of measured GDP.

Underground economy Buying and selling of goods and services that is concealed from the government to avoid taxes or regulations or because the goods and services are illegal.

Is not counting household production or production in the underground economy a serious shortcoming of GDP? Most economists would answer "no" because the most important use of GDP is to measure changes in how the economy is performing over short periods of time, such as from one year to the next. For this purpose, omitting household production and production in the underground economy won't have much effect, because there is not likely to be much change in the amounts of these types of production from one year to the next.

We also use GDP statistics to measure how production of goods and services grows over fairly long periods of a decade or more. For this purpose, omitting household production and production in the underground economy may be more important. For example, beginning in the 1970s, the number of women working outside the home increased dramatically. Some of the goods and services—such as childcare and restaurant meals—produced in the following years were replacing what had been household production, rather than being true additions to total production.

How the Underground Economy Hurts Developing Countries

11-2 Making the Connection

Although few economists believe the underground economy in the United States amounts to more than 10 percent of measured GDP, the underground economy in some developing countries may be more than 50 percent of measured GDP. In developing countries, the underground economy is often referred to as the *informal sector,* as opposed to the *formal sector* in which output of goods and services is measured. Although it might not seem to matter whether production of goods and services is measured and included in GDP or unmeasured, a large informal sector can be a sign of government policies that are retarding economic growth.

In some developing countries, more than half the workers may be in the underground economy.

Because firms in the informal sector are acting illegally, they tend to be smaller and have less capital than firms acting legally. The entrepreneurs who start firms in the informal sector may be afraid their firms could someday be closed or confiscated by the government. Therefore, the entrepreneurs limit their investments in these firms. As a consequence, workers in these firms have less machinery and equipment to work with, and so can produce fewer goods and services. Entrepreneurs in the informal sector also have to pay the costs of avoiding government authorities. These costs can take the form of bribes to government officials. Construction firms operating in the informal sector in Brazil have to employ lookouts who can warn workers to hide when government inspectors come around. The informal sector is large in some developing economies because taxes are high and government regulations are extensive. For example, firms in Brazil pay 85 percent of all taxes collected, as compared with 41 percent in the United States. Not surprisingly, about half of all Brazilian workers are employed in the informal sector. In Zimbabwe and Peru, the fraction of workers in the informal sector may be as high as 60 or 70 percent.

Many economists believe taxes in developing countries are so high because these countries are attempting to pay for government sectors that are as large relative to their economies as the government sectors of industrial economies. Government spending in Brazil, for example, is 39 percent of measured GDP, compared to 31 percent in the United States. In the early twentieth century, when the United States was much poorer than it is today, government spending was only about 8 percent of GDP, so the tax burden on U.S. firms was much lower. In countries like Brazil, bringing firms into the formal sector from the informal sector may require reductions in government spending and taxes. In many developing countries, however, voters are very reluctant to see government services reduced.

Sources: Mary Anastasia O'Grady, "Why Brazil's Underground Economy Grows and Grows," *Wall Street Journal,* September 10, 2004, p. A13; and "In the Shadows," *Economist,* June 17, 2004.

Shortcomings of GDP as a Measure of Well-Being

The main purpose of GDP is to measure a country's total production. GDP is also frequently used, though, as a measure of well-being. For example, newspaper and magazine articles will show tables with levels of GDP per person in different countries, with the implication that people in the countries with higher levels of GDP are better off. Although increases in GDP often do lead to increases in the well-being of the population, it is important to be aware that GDP is not a perfect measure of well-being for several reasons.

THE VALUE OF LEISURE IS NOT INCLUDED IN GDP If an economic consultant decides to retire, GDP will decline even though the consultant may value increased leisure more than the income he or she was earning running a consulting firm. The consultant's well-being has increased, but GDP has decreased. In 1890, the typical American worked 60 hours per week. Today, the typical American works fewer than 40 hours per week. If Americans still worked 60-hour weeks, GDP would be much higher than it is, but the well-being of the typical person would be lower, because less time would be available for leisure activities.

GDP IS NOT ADJUSTED FOR POLLUTION OR OTHER NEGATIVE EFFECTS OF PRODUCTION When a dry cleaner cleans and presses clothes, the value of this service is included in GDP. If chemicals used by the dry cleaner pollute the air or water, GDP is not adjusted to compensate for the costs of the pollution. Similarly, the value of cigarettes produced is included in GDP with no adjustment made for the costs of the lung cancer that some smokers develop.

We should note, though, that increasing GDP often leads countries to devote more resources to pollution reduction. For example, in the United States between 1970 and 2004, as GDP was steadily increasing, emissions of the six main air pollutants declined by more than 50 percent. Developing countries often have higher levels of pollution than high-income countries because the lower GDPs of the developing countries make them more reluctant to spend resources on pollution reduction. Levels of pollution in China are much higher than in the United States, Japan, or the countries of Western Europe. According to the World Health Organization, seven of the ten most polluted cities in the world are in China, but as Chinese GDP continues to rise, it may devote more resources to reducing pollution.

GDP IS NOT ADJUSTED FOR CHANGES IN CRIME AND OTHER SOCIAL PROBLEMS An increase in crime will reduce well-being but may actually increase GDP if it leads to greater spending on police, security guards, and alarm systems. GDP is also not adjusted for changes in divorce rates, drug addiction, or other factors that may affect people's well-being.

To summarize, we can say that a person's well-being depends on many factors that are not taken into account in calculating GDP. Because GDP is designed to measure total production, it is perhaps not surprising that it does an imperfect job of measuring well-being.

11-3 Making the Connection

Did World War II Bring Prosperity?

The Great Depression of the 1930s was the worst economic downturn in U.S. history. GDP declined by more than 25 percent between 1929 and 1933 and did not reach its 1929 level again until 1938. The unemployment rate remained at very high levels of 10 percent or more through 1940. Then, in 1941 the United States entered World War II. The following graph shows that GDP rose dramatically during the war years of 1941 to 1945. (The graph shows values for real GDP, which as we will see in the next section, corrects measures of GDP for changes in the price level.) The unemployment rate also fell to very low levels—below 2 percent.

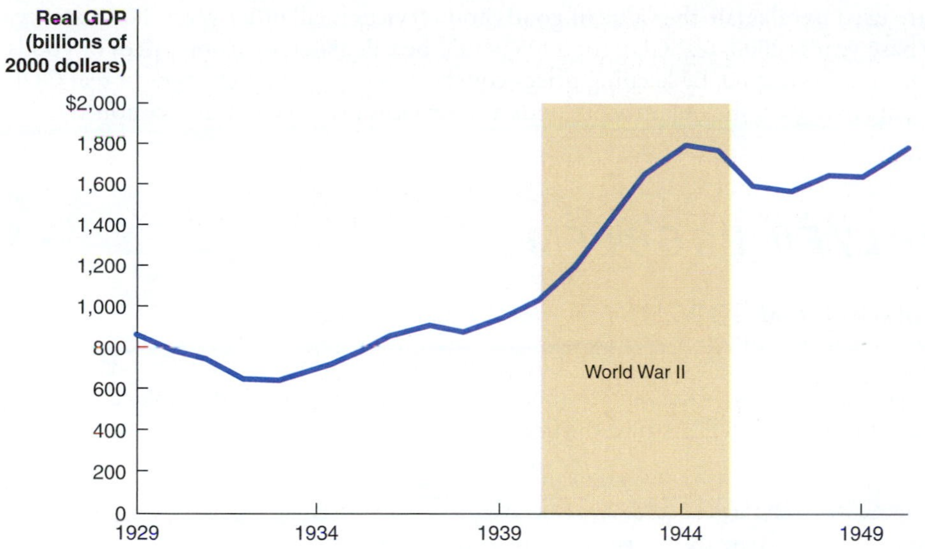

Source: Bureau of Economic Analysis.

Production of military goods soared during World War II, but production of consumption goods lagged.

Traditionally, historians have argued that World War II brought prosperity back to the U.S. economy. But did it? Economist Robert Higgs argues that if we look at the well-being of the typical person, then the World War II years were anything but prosperous. Higgs points out that increased production of tanks, ships, planes, and munitions account for most of the increase in GDP during those years. Between 1943 and 1945, more than 40 percent of the labor force was either in the military or producing war goods. As a result, between 1939 and 1944, production of consumption goods per person increased only about 2 percent, leaving the quantity of consumption goods available to the typical person in 1944 still below what it had been in 1929. With the end of the war, true prosperity did return to the U.S. economy, and by 1946 production of consumption goods per person had risen by more than 25 percent from what it had been in 1929.

World War II was a period of extraordinary sacrifice and achievement by the "greatest generation." But statistics on GDP may give a misleading indication of whether it was also a period of prosperity.

Source: Robert Higgs, "Wartime Prosperity? A Reassessment of the U.S. Economy in the 1940s," *Journal of Economic History*, Vol. 52, No. 1 (March 1992).

Real GDP versus Nominal GDP

③ **LEARNING OBJECTIVE**

Discuss the difference between real variables and nominal variables.

Because GDP is measured in value terms, we have to be careful about interpreting changes over time. To see why, consider interpreting an increase in the total value of heavy truck production from $40 billion in 2005 to $44 billion in 2006. Can we be sure—because $44 billion is 10 percent greater than $40 billion—that the number of trucks produced in 2006 was 10 percent greater than the number produced in 2005? We can draw this conclusion only if the average price of trucks did not change between 2005 and 2006. In fact, when GDP increases from one year to the next, the increase is due partly to increases in production of goods and services and partly to increases in prices. Because we are interested mainly in GDP as a measure of production, we need a way of separating the price changes from the quantity changes.

Calculating Real GDP

The Bureau of Economic Analysis separates price changes from quantity changes by calculating a measure of production called **real GDP. Nominal GDP** is calculated by summing the current values of final goods and services. Real GDP is calculated by designating a particular year as the *base year*. The prices of goods and services in the base

Real GDP The value of final goods and services evaluated at base year prices.

Nominal GDP The value of final goods and services evaluated at current year prices.

year are used to calculate the value of goods and services in all other years. For instance, if the base year is 2000, real GDP for 2005 would be calculated by using prices of goods and services from 2000. By keeping prices constant, we know that changes in real GDP represent changes in the quantity of goods and services produced in the economy.

SOLVED PROBLEM 11-2

③ LEARNING OBJECTIVE

Discuss the difference between real variables and nominal variables.

Calculating Real GDP

Suppose that a very simple economy produces only the following three final goods and services: eye examinations, pizzas, and textbooks. Use the information in the table to compute real GDP for the year 2005. Assume the base year is 2000.

	2000		2005	
PRODUCT	QUANTITY	PRICE	QUANTITY	PRICE
Eye examinations	80	$40	100	$50
Pizzas	90	11	80	10
Textbooks	15	90	20	100

Solving the Problem:

Step 1: Review the chapter material. This problem is about calculating real GDP, so you may want to review the section "Calculating Real GDP," which begins on page 343.

Step 2: Calculate the value of the three goods and services listed in the table using the quantities for 2005 and the prices for 2000. The definition on page 343 tells us that real GDP is the value of all final goods and services, evaluated at base year prices. In this case, the base year is 2000 and we are given information on the price of each product in that year.

PRODUCT	QUANTITY	PRICE	VALUE
Eye examinations	100	$40	$4,000
Pizzas	80	11	880
Textbooks	20	90	1,800

Step 3: Add up the values for the three products to find real GDP.

Real GDP for 2005 equals the sum of:

Quantity of eye examinations in 2005 × Price of eye exams in 2000 = $4,000

\+ Quantity of pizzas produced in 2005 × Price of pizzas in 2000 = $880

\+ Quantity of textbooks produced in 2005 × Price of textbooks in 2000 = $1,800

or, $6,680

Extra Credit: Notice that the quantities of each good produced in 2000 were irrelevant for calculating real GDP in 2005. Notice also that the value of $6,680 for real GDP in 2005 is lower than the value of $7,800 for nominal GDP in 2005 calculated in Solved Problem 11–1.

***YOUR TURN:* For more practice, do related problem 8 on page 353 at the end of this chapter.**

One drawback to calculating real GDP using base year prices is that, over time, prices may change relative to each other. For example, the price of cell phones may fall relative to the price of gasoline. Because this change is not reflected in the fixed prices from the base year, the estimate of real GDP is somewhat distorted. The further away the current year is from the base year, the worse the problem becomes. To make the calculation of real GDP more accurate, in 1996, the BEA switched to using *chain-weighted prices,* and now publishes statistics on real GDP in "chained (2000) dollars."

The details of calculating real GDP using chain-weighted prices are more complicated than we need to discuss here, but the basic idea is straightforward. Starting with the base year, the BEA takes an average of prices in that year and prices in the following year. It then uses this average to calculate real GDP in the year following the base year (currently the year 2000). For the next year—in other words, the year that is two years after the base year—the BEA calculates real GDP by taking an average of prices in that year and the previous year. In this way, prices in each year are "chained" to prices from the previous year, and the distortion from changes in relative prices is minimized.

Holding prices constant means that the *purchasing power* of a dollar remains the same from one year to the next. Ordinarily, the purchasing power of the dollar falls every year as price increases reduce the amount of goods and services that a dollar can buy.

Comparing Real GDP and Nominal GDP

Real GDP holds prices constant, which makes it a better measure than nominal GDP of changes in the production of goods and services from one year to the next. In fact, growth in the economy is almost always measured as growth in real GDP. If a headline in the *Wall Street Journal* states, "U.S. Economy Grew 4.3% Last Year," the article will report that real GDP increased by 4.3 percent during the previous year.

We describe real GDP as being measured in "base year dollars." For example, with a base year of 2000, nominal GDP in 2004 was $11,734 billion, and real GDP in 2004 was $10,756 billion in 2000 dollars. Because, on average, prices rise from one year to the next, real GDP is greater than nominal GDP in years before the base year and less than nominal GDP for years after the base year. In the base year, real GDP and nominal GDP are the same, because both are calculated for the base year using the same prices and quantities. Figure 11-3 shows movements in nominal GDP and real GDP between 1990 and 2004. In the 1990s, prices were, on average, lower than in 2000, so nominal GDP was lower than real GDP. In 2000, nominal and real GDP were equal. Since 2000, prices have been, on average, higher than in 2000, so nominal GDP is higher than real GDP.

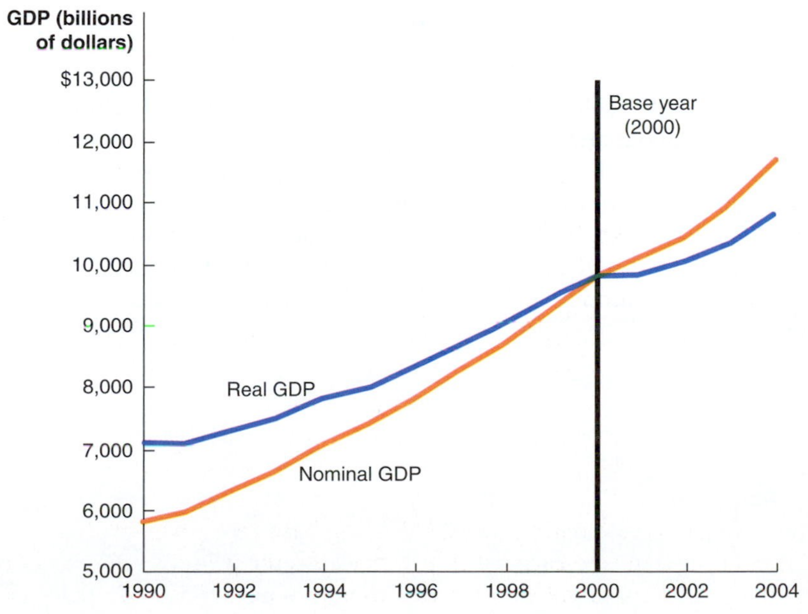

FIGURE 11-3

Nominal GDP and Real GDP, 1990–2004

Currently, the base year for calculating GDP is 2000. In the 1990s, prices were, on average, lower than in 2000, so nominal GDP was lower than real GDP. In 2000, nominal and real GDP were equal. After 2000, prices have been, on average, higher than in 2000, so nominal GDP is higher than real GDP.

Source: U.S. Bureau of Economic Analysis.

11-4 Making the Connection

Freightliner increased hiring and production in 2004 based on forecasts of GDP.

How Freightliner Uses Forecasts of GDP

As we will see in later chapters, increases and decreases in real GDP play an important role in determining the demand for the products of firms such as Freightliner that sell durable goods. Freightliner devotes significant resources to tracking and forecasting GDP because accurate forecasts of GDP help the company schedule production and decide whether or not to increase employment.

Jim Hebe, then Freightliner president and CEO, responded to the early 2001 U.S. recession by reducing sales forecasts of Class 8 trucks from 162,000 to a "disaster scenario" of 135,000. The forecast led Freightliner to lay off 1,085 workers at its Portland, Oregon, plant, reducing the number of trucks built at the plant from 74 per day to 35.

By 2002, new Freightliner president and CEO Rainer Schmüeckle was more optimistic about the economy. But he did not forecast sales increasing soon because he believed many trucking firms—his main customers—had excess capacity, meaning they had more trucks than they needed for the freight they were hauling: "Our forecast calls for gradual economic recovery in the second through the fourth quarters [of 2002], but we believe this will occur without making a major impact on the trucking business because there is still some excess capacity that needs to be worked out. Real, structural recovery will not come until the second quarter of '03."

We saw in the opening to this chapter that by 2004 managers at Freightliner were convinced that GDP would continue to increase, resulting in increased sales of heavy trucks. In early 2004, Mark Lampert, senior vice president of sales and marketing at Freightliner, predicted total sales of Class 8 trucks would rise to 245,000, an increase of more than 33 percent compared to 2003. These favorable forecasts led Freightliner to expand employment and production at its North American plants.

Sources: "Hotline," *Heavy Duty Trucking,* March 2001; Wendy Leavitt, "Freightliner's New Voice," *Fleet Owner,* March 2002; and "ITS Hosts Heavy Truck Economic Forecast," *ITS Business Daily.*

The GDP Deflator

Price level A measure of the average prices of goods and services in the economy.

GDP deflator A measure of the price level, calculated by dividing nominal GDP by real GDP, and multiplying by 100.

Economists and policymakers are interested not just in the level of total production, as measured by real GDP, but also in the *price level.* The **price level** measures the average prices of goods and services in the economy. One of the goals of economic policy is a stable price level. We can use values for nominal GDP and real GDP to compute a measure of the price level, called the *GDP deflator.* We can calculate the **GDP deflator** using this formula:

$$\text{GDP deflator} = \frac{\text{Nominal GDP}}{\text{Real GDP}} \times 100.$$

To see why the GDP deflator is a measure of the price level, think about what would happen if prices of goods and services rose while production remained the same. In that case, nominal GDP would increase, but real GDP would remain constant, so the GDP deflator would increase. In reality, both prices and production increase each year, but the more prices increase relative to the increase in production, the more nominal GDP increases relative to real GDP and the higher the value for the GDP deflator. Increases in the GDP deflator allow economists and policymakers to track increases in the price level over time.

Remember that in the base year (currently 2000) nominal GDP is equal to real GDP, so the value of the GDP price deflator will always be 100 in the base year. The following table gives the values for nominal and real GDP for 2003 and 2004:

	2003	2004
Nominal GDP	\$10,971 billion	\$11,734 billion
Real GDP	\$10,321 billion	\$10,756 billion

We can use the information from the table to calculate values for the GDP price deflator for 2003 and 2004:

FORMULA	APPLIED TO 2003	APPLIED TO 2004
$\text{GDP Deflator} = \frac{\text{Nominal GDP}}{\text{Real GDP}} \times 100$	$\left(\frac{\$10{,}971 \text{ billion}}{\$10{,}321 \text{ billion}}\right) \times 100 = 106$	$\left(\frac{\$11{,}734 \text{ billion}}{\$10{,}756 \text{ billion}}\right) \times 100 = 109$

From these values for the deflator, we can calculate that the price level increased by 2.8 percent between 2003 and 2004:

$$\left(\frac{109 - 106}{106}\right) \times 100 = 2.8\%.$$

In Chapter 12, we will see that economists and policymakers also rely on another measure of the price level, known as the consumer price index. In addition, we will discuss the strengths and weaknesses of the two measures.

Other Measures of Total Production and Total Income

4 LEARNING OBJECTIVE

Become familiar with other measures of total production and total income.

National income accounting refers to the methods the BEA uses to keep track of total production and total income in the economy. The statistical tables containing this information are called the *National Income and Product Accounts* (NIPA). Every quarter, the BEA releases NIPA tables containing data on several measures of total production and total income. We already have discussed the most important measure of total production and total income: gross domestic product (GDP). In addition to computing GDP, the Bureau of Economic Analysis computes the following five measures of production and income.

Gross National Product (GNP)

Gross domestic product is the value of final goods and services produced within the United States. Gross national product, or GNP, is the value of final goods and services produced by residents of the United States, even if the production takes place *outside* of the United States. U.S. firms have facilities in foreign countries, and foreign firms have facilities in the United States. Ford, for example, has assembly plants in the United Kingdom, and Toyota has assembly plants in the United States. GNP includes foreign production by U.S. firms but excludes U.S. production by foreign firms. For the United

States, these two numbers are almost the same, so GNP is almost the same as GDP. For example, in 2004, GDP was $11,734 billion and GNP was $11,788 billion. This difference is less than one-half of 1 percent.

For many years GNP was the main measure of total production compiled by the government and used by economists and policymakers. However, in many countries other than the United States, a significant fraction of domestic production takes place in foreign-owned facilities. For these countries, GDP will be much larger than GNP, and is a more accurate measure of the level of production within the country's borders. As a result, many countries and international agencies had long preferred using GDP to using GNP. In 1991, the United States joined these countries in using GDP as its main measure of total production.

Net National Product (NNP)

In producing goods and services, some machinery, equipment, and buildings wear out and have to be replaced. The value of this worn-out machinery, equipment, and buildings is *depreciation*. If we subtract this value from GNP, we are left with net national product, or NNP. In the NIPA tables, depreciation is referred to as the *consumption of fixed capital*.

National Income

When a consumer pays sales tax on a product, there is a difference between the amount the consumer has paid for the product and the amount that will be received as income by the people who produced the product. For instance, suppose you buy a television that is priced at $200. If the sales tax is 6 percent, you will actually pay $212, but the $12 in tax will be sent directly to the government and never show up as anyone's income. Therefore, to calculate the total income actually received by a country's residents, the BEA has to subtract the value of sales taxes from net national product. In the NIPA tables, sales taxes are referred to as *indirect business taxes*. Previously in this chapter, we stressed that the value of total production is equal to the value of total income. This point is not strictly true if by "value of total production" we mean GDP and by "value of total income" we mean national income, because national income will always be smaller than GDP. In practice, though, this distinction does not matter for most macroeconomic issues.

Personal Income

Personal income is income received by households. To calculate personal income, we subtract the earnings that corporations retain rather than pay to shareholders in the form of dividends. We also add in the payments received by households from the government in the form of *transfer payments* or interest on government bonds.

Disposable Personal Income

Disposable personal income is equal to personal income minus personal tax payments, such as the federal personal income tax. It is the best measure of the income households actually have available to spend.

Figure 11-4 shows the values of these measures of total production and total income for the year 2004 in a table and a graph.

Measure	Billions of dollars
GDP	$11,734
GNP	11,788
NNP	10,353
National Income	10,276
Personal Income	9,713
Disposable Personal Income	8,664

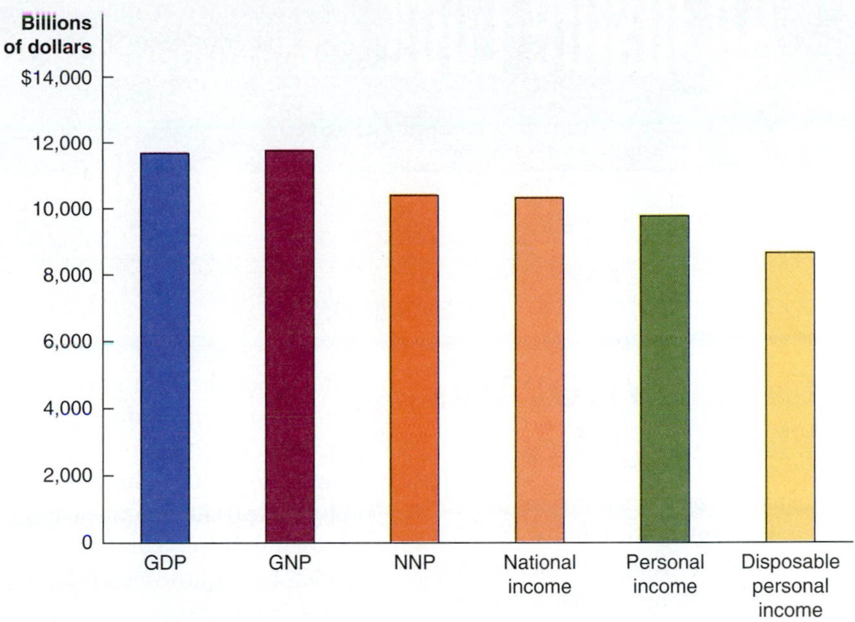

FIGURE 11-4 Measures of Total Production and Total Income, 2004

The most important measure of total production and total income is gross domestic product (GDP). As we will see in later chapters, for some purposes, the other measures of total production and total income shown in the figure turn out to be more useful than GDP. The numbers are in billions of dollars.

Conclusion

In this chapter, we have begun the study of macroeconomics by examining an important concept—how a nation's total production and income can be measured. Understanding GDP is important for understanding the business cycle and the process of long-run economic growth. In the next chapter, we discuss the issues involved in measuring two other key economic variables: the unemployment rate and the inflation rate.

Read *An Inside Look* on the next page for a discussion of fluctuations in Canadian real GDP during a recent year.

An Inside Look

Movements in Canadian GDP

WALL STREET JOURNAL, DECEMBER 23, 2004

Canadian GDP Was Flat in October

Canada's economy began the final quarter on a softer-than-expected note as the stronger Canadian dollar crimped foreign demand for fabricated products and labor disputes in the public sector and professional sports hurt services industries.

Gross domestic product, the sum of goods and services produced in the country, was steady in October from the month before, Statistics Canada said yesterday. The mean forecast of economists surveyed by Thomson IFR Bonddata was for GDP to expand 0.1%.

"For the second month in a row, growth in the Canadian economy was at a standstill in October largely due to reduced foreign demand for fabricated products and to labor strife," the statistics agency said. . . .

Industrial production, the total output of Canada's factories, mines and utilities, shrank a further 0.2% in October, after declining 0.3% in the preceding month. This was in stark contrast to the U.S where the index of industrial production rose 0.6%.

Manufacturers cut output by 0.3% in October, following a 0.2% reduction in September.

a "Foreign demand for fabricated products was reduced in the wake of a strengthening [Canadian] dollar that gained 3.3% during the month vis-à-vis the U.S. currency, reaching its highest level in 12 months," Statistics Canada said.

The weakness was widespread as only four of the 21 major manufacturing groups increased output during the month. Production of nondurable goods shrank 0.6% while output of durable products fell 0.1%.

The utilities sector's output fell 0.3% following a 0.7% gain in September. Production in the mining sector was up 0.2% after a 1.0% decline in the previous month, driven by surging oil and gas exploration and the end of a strike in iron mines that started in July.

b The construction sector shrank 0.6% after edging up 0.1% in September. Fewer housing starts pulled down residential construction by 0.5%, while nonresidential construction fell 1.2%, the seventh straight month of declines.

Overall output of goods-producing industries was down 0.2%, following a 0.1% drop in September. The services sector expanded 0.1%, the same as in September, driven by retail trade, which rose 0.9% on the back of strong motor vehicle sales.

c Two major labor disputes held back the sector. A nationwide public sector strike cut federal public administration sector production by 1.2%.

The lockout of National Hockey League players resulted in a 2.1% decline in the output of the arts and entertainment industries, Statistics Canada said.

Key Points in the Article

This article discusses the latest announcement of GDP data by Statistics Canada. Statistics Canada plays the same role in Canada that the Bureau of Economic Analysis does in the United States. Notice that Statistics Canada calculates GDP monthly, unlike in the United States, where the BEA calculates GDP quarterly. Calculating GDP entails gathering an enormous amount of information on production. The greater size of the U.S. economy, compared with the Canadian economy, would make it very costly to attempt to calculate GDP every month. Figure 1 shows movements in real GDP in Canada from October 2002 to October 2004. During several months of these two years, real GDP declined. The real GDP numbers in the figure are measured in billions of 1997 (Canadian) dollars, because Statistics Canada uses 1997 as the base year, unlike the BEA, which currently uses 2000 as the base year.

Analyzing the News

a We saw in this chapter that net exports are one component of GDP. In later chapters, we will discuss the effect of exchange rates on net exports. The exchange rate tells us how many units of foreign currency are received in exchange for a unit of domestic currency. When the exchange rate rises, exports fall because domestic goods become more expensive to foreign consumers. In this case, the exchange rate of the Canadian dollar for the U.S. dollar had risen. The result was that prices of Canadian exports to the United States—such as lumber, trucks, and small aircraft—rose, which reduced the quantity demanded. This caused a reduction in Canadian net exports, and GDP.

b Construction spending on new houses, factories, and office buildings is part of the investment component of GDP. This article indicates that both the residential (houses) and nonresidential (factories and office buildings) segments of construction spending declined, contributing to the decline in GDP.

c Government purchases are about 22 percent of GDP in Canada, as opposed to about 19 percent in the United States. The article indicates that there was a strike of public employees, which reduced government purchases. The fall in government purchases contributed to the fall in GDP.

Thinking Critically ABOUT POLICY

1. Would policymakers in the United States benefit from having monthly GDP data available to them? If so, why doesn't the U.S. Commerce Department collect GDP data on a monthly basis?
2. Exports are 37 percent of Canadian GDP, in contrast to the United States, where exports are only about 10 percent of GDP. More than 80 percent of Canadian exports are to the United States. Use these facts to explain how forecasts of U.S. real GDP could be helpful in forecasting Canadian real GDP.

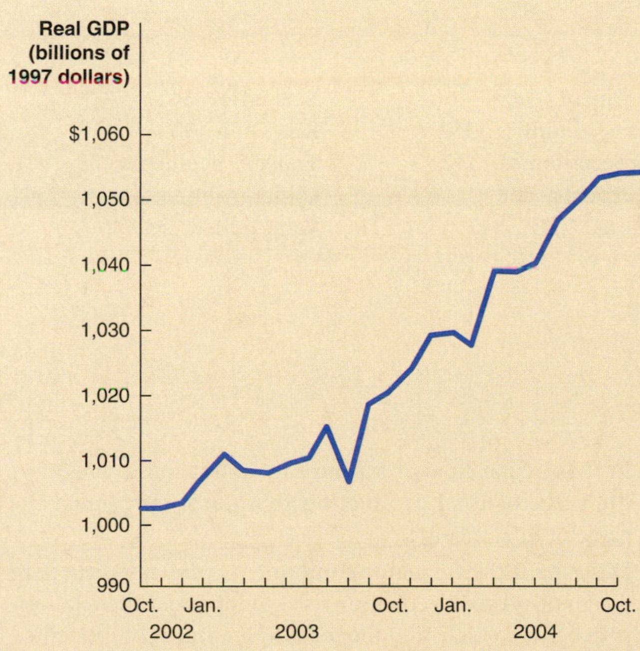

Figure 1: Monthly real GDP for Canada, October 2002 to October 2004.

Source: Statistics Canada.

SUMMARY

LEARNING OBJECTIVE ① Explain how total production is measured. Total production is measured by *gross domestic product (GDP)*, which is the value of all *final goods and services* produced in an economy during a period of time. When we measure the value of total production in the economy by calculating GDP, we are simultaneously measuring the value of total income. GDP is divided into four major categories of expenditures: consumption, investment, government purchases, and net exports. We can also calculate GDP by adding up the *value added* of every firm involved in producing final goods and services.

LEARNING OBJECTIVE ② Discuss whether GDP is a good measure of economic well-being. GDP does not include household production, which refers to goods and services people produce for themselves, nor does it include production in the *underground economy*, which consists of concealed buying and selling. The underground economy in some poorer countries may be more than half of measured GDP. GDP is not a perfect measure of well-being because it does not include the value of leisure, it is not adjusted for pollution or other negative effects of production, and it is not adjusted for changes in crime and other social problems.

LEARNING OBJECTIVE ③ Discuss the difference between real variables and nominal variables. *Nominal GDP* is the value of final goods and services evaluated at current year prices. *Real GDP* is the value of final goods and services evaluated at *base year* prices. By keeping prices constant, we know that changes in real GDP represent changes in the quantity of goods and services produced in the economy. When the price level is increasing, real GDP is greater than nominal GDP in years before the base year and less than nominal GDP for years after the base year. The *GDP deflator* is a measure of the price level, and is calculated by dividing nominal GDP by real GDP, and multiplying by 100.

LEARNING OBJECTIVE ④ Become familiar with other measures of total production and total income. The most important measure of total production and total income is gross domestic product (GDP). As we will see in later chapters, for some purposes the other measures of total production and total income shown in Figure 11-4 are actually more useful than GDP. These measures are gross national product (GNP), net national product (NNP), national income, personal income, and disposable personal income.

KEY TERMS

Business cycle 332
Consumption 336
Economic growth 332
Expansion 332
Final good or service 333
GDP deflator 346
Government purchases 337
Gross domestic product (GDP) 333
Inflation rate 332
Intermediate good or service 333
Investment 337
Macroeconomics 332
Microeconomics 332
Net exports 338
Nominal GDP 343
Price level 346
Real GDP 343
Recession 332
Transfer payments 335
Underground economy 341
Value added 339

REVIEW QUESTIONS

1. Distinguish between the topics covered by macroeconomics and the topics covered by microeconomics.
2. Why in microeconomics can we measure production in terms of quantity, but in macroeconomics we measure production in terms of market value?
3. If the U.S. Bureau of Economic Analysis added up the values of every good and service sold during the year, would the total be larger or smaller than GDP?
4. Why does the size of a country's GDP matter? How does it affect the quality of life of the country's people?
5. In the circular flow of expenditure and income, why must the value of total production in an economy equal the value of total income?
6. Describe the four major components of expenditures in GDP and write the equation used to represent the relationship between GDP and the four expenditure components.
7. Distinguish between the value of a firm's final product and the value added by the firm to the final product.
8. Why is GDP an imperfect measure of economic well-being? What types of production does GDP not measure?

Even if GDP included these types of production, why would it still be an imperfect measure of economic well-being?

9. Why does inflation make nominal GDP a poor measure of the increase in total production from one year to the next? How does the U.S. Bureau of Economic Analysis deal with the problem inflation causes with nominal GDP?
10. What is the GDP deflator and how is it calculated?
11. Under what circumstances would GDP be a better measure of total production and total income than GNP?

PROBLEMS AND APPLICATIONS

Please visit **www.prenhall.com/hubbard** *for solutions to the even-numbered problems as well as multiple-choice and true or false self-assessment quizzes.*

1. **[Related to the *Chapter Opener*]** Macroeconomic conditions affect the decisions firms and families make. Why, for example, might a college student after graduation enter the job market during an economic expansion but apply for graduate school during a recession?
2. **[Related to the *Chapter Opener*]** Recall from Chapter 3 the definitions of normal and inferior goods. During an economic expansion, would you rather be working in an industry that produces a normal good or in an industry that produces an inferior good? Why? During a recession, would you rather be working in an industry that produces a normal good or an inferior good? Why?
3. For the total value of expenditures on final goods and services to equal the total value of income generated from producing those final goods and services, all the money that a business receives from the sale of its product must be paid out as income to the owners of the factors of production. How can a business make a profit if it pays out as income all the money it receives?
4. Briefly explain whether each of the following transactions represents the purchase of a final good.
   a. The purchase of wheat from a wheat farmer by a bakery
   b. The purchase of an aircraft carrier by the federal government
   c. The purchase of French wine by a U.S. consumer
   d. The purchase of a new machine tool by the Ford Motor Company
5. Is the value of intermediate goods and services produced during the year included in GDP? For example, are computer chips produced and installed on a new PC included in GDP? Note that the question does not ask whether the computer chips are directly counted in GDP but rather whether or not their production is included in GDP.
6. Is the value of a house built in 2000 and resold in 2006 included in the GDP of 2006? Why or why not? Would the services of the real estate agent who helped sell (or buy) the house in 2006 be counted in GDP for 2006? Why or why not?
7. **[Related to *Solved Problem 11-1*]** Suppose that a simple economy produces only the following four goods and services: textbooks, hamburgers, shirts, and cotton. Assume all of the cotton is used in the production of shirts. Use the information in the following table to calculate nominal GDP for 2006.

PRODUCTION AND PRICE STATISTICS FOR 2006

PRODUCT	QUANTITY	PRICE
Textbooks	100	$60.00
Hamburgers	100	2.00
Shirts	50	25.00
Cotton	8,000	0.60

8. **[Related to *Solved Problem 11-2*]** Suppose the information in the following table is for a simple economy that produces only the following four goods and services: textbooks, hamburgers, shirts, and cotton. Assume all of the cotton is used in the production of shirts.

	2000 STATISTICS		2006 STATISTICS		2007 STATISTICS	
PRODUCT	QUANTITY	PRICE	QUANTITY	PRICE	QUANTITY	PRICE
Textbooks	90	$50.00	100	$60.00	100	$65.00
Hamburgers	75	2.00	100	2.00	120	2.25
Shirts	50	30.00	50	25.00	65	25.00
Cotton	10,000	0.80	8,000	0.60	12,000	0.70

   a. Use the information in the table to calculate real GDP for 2006 and 2007, assuming the base year is 2000.
   b. What was the growth rate of real GDP during 2007?
9. **[Related to *Don't Let This Happen To You!*]** Briefly explain whether you agree or disagree with the following statement: "In years when people buy many shares of stock, investment will be high and, therefore, so will GDP."
10. How does the value added of a business differ from the profits of a business?
11. It is reported that some state-owned firms in the former Soviet Union produced goods and services whose value was less than the value of the raw materials the firms used to

produce their goods and services. If so, what would have been the value added of these state-owned firms? Would such a firm be able to survive in a free-market economy?

12. An artist buys scrap metal from the local steel mill as a raw material for her metal sculptures. Last year she bought $5,000 worth of the scrap metal. During the year, she produced 10 metal sculptures that she sold for $800 each to the local art store. The local art store sold all of them to local art collectors at an average price of $1,000 each. For the 10 metal sculptures, what was the total value added of the artist and what was the total value added of the local art store?

13. What would you expect to happen to household production as unemployment rises during a recession? What would you expect to happen to household production as unemployment falls during an expansion? Would you therefore expect the fluctuation in actual production—GDP plus household production—to be greater or less than the fluctuation in measured GDP?

14. Which of the following are likely to increase measured GDP, and which are likely to reduce it?
    a. The fraction of women working outside the home increases.
    b. There is a sharp increase in the crime rate.
    c. Higher tax rates cause some people to hide more of the income they earn.

15. Does the fact that the typical American works less than 40 hours per week today and worked 60 hours per week in 1890 make the difference between the economic well-being of Americans today versus 1890 higher or lower than indicated by the difference in real GDP per capita today versus 1890? Explain.

16. A report of the World Bank, an international organization devoted to increasing economic growth in developing countries, includes the following statement:

    > Informal economic activities pose a particular measurement problem [in calculating GDP], especially in developing countries, where much economic activity may go unrecorded.

    What do they mean by "informal economic activities"? Why would these activities make it harder to measure GDP? Why might they make it harder to evaluate the standard of living in developing countries relative to the standard of living in the United States?
    Source: The World Bank, *World Development Indicators,* 2003, Washington, D.C.: The World Bank, p. 189.

17. Each year the United Nations publishes the Human Development Report, which provides information on the standard of living in nearly every country in the world. The Report includes data on real GDP per person, but also contains a broader measure of the standard of living called the Human Development Index (HDI). The HDI combines data on real GDP per person with data on life expectancy at birth, adult literacy, and school enrollment. The following table shows values for real GDP per person and the HDI for several countries. Prepare one list ranking countries from highest real GDP per person to lowest, and another list ranking countries from highest HDI to lowest. Briefly discuss possible reasons for any differences in the rankings of countries in your two lists. (All values in the table are for the year 2003.)

COUNTRY	REAL GDP PER PERSON	HDI
Australia	$29,632	0.955
China	5,003	0.755
Greece	19,954	0.912
Iran	6,995	0.736
Norway	37,670	0.963
Singapore	24,481	0.907
South Korea	17,971	0.901
United Arab Emirates	22,420	0.849
United States	37,562	0.944

Source: United Nations Development Programme, *Human Development Report, 2005,* New York: Oxford University Press, 2005.

18. Assuming inflation has occurred over time, what is the relationship between nominal GDP and real GDP in each of the following situations?
    a. Years after the base year
    b. In the base year
    c. Years before the base year

19. If the quantity of final goods and services produced decreased, could real GDP increase? Could nominal GDP increase? If so, how?

20. Use the data in the following table to calculate the GDP deflator for each year (values are in billions of dollars):

	NOMINAL GDP	REAL GDP
2000	$9,817	$9,817
2001	10,128	9,891
2002	10,470	10,049
2003	10,971	10,321
2004	11,734	10,756

Which year from 2001 to 2004 saw the largest percentage increase in the price level as measured by the GDP deflator? Briefly explain.

21. Suppose a country has many of its citizens temporarily working in other countries and many of its firms have facilities in other countries. Furthermore, relatively few citizens of foreign countries are working in this country and relatively few foreign firms have facilities in this country. In these circumstances, which would you expect to be larger for this country, GDP or GNP? Briefly explain.

chapter twelve

Unemployment and Inflation

Lucent Technologies Deals with Unemployment and Inflation

When we study macroeconomics, we are looking at the big picture: total production, total employment, and the price level. Of course, the big picture is determined by the decisions of millions of individual consumers and firms. When total employment in the United States declined during 2001, Lucent Technologies was one firm that contributed to the decline. In 2000, Lucent employed 175,000 workers. It began laying off large numbers of workers during 2001. By 2005, Lucent employed only 31,500 workers.

Lucent Technologies, known as the grandfather of high-technology firms, was founded in 1869. The company, originally the Western Electric Manufacturing Company, was purchased by the American Telephone and Telegraph Company (AT&T) in 1881 and renamed Bell Laboratories. Bell Labs became independent of AT&T in 1996 and took its current name, Lucent Technologies. Over the years, the company has been involved in developing many important innovations, including equipment for adding sound to motion pictures, equipment for long-distance television transmission, the transistor, the UNIX computer operating system, and Wi-Fi wireless broadband technology. Lucent's difficulties in the early 2000s were due partly to overbuilding of telecommunications infrastructure, particularly fiber-optic cables, and partly to the business cycle. We will discuss the effects of the business cycle further in later chapters. In this chapter, we will focus on measuring changes in employment and changes in the price level, or *inflation*.

Forecasts of inflation play a role in firms' wage policies. For example, in 2004 Lucent negotiated wage contracts with workers who were members of the Communications Workers of America and the International Brotherhood of Electrical Workers unions. The contracts

resulted in these workers' wages rising by a little over 16 percent over a period of seven years. To decide on an acceptable wage, both Lucent and the unions needed to forecast the inflation rate for those seven years. A higher inflation rate would make it easier for Lucent to pay any particular wage, because a higher inflation rate would allow Lucent to charge higher prices for its telecommunications equipment. A higher inflation rate would also mean that Lucent's workers could buy fewer goods and services with their wages, because prices would be higher. The contract between Lucent and its union workers increased wages by less than the increase in prices expected by the firms and the workers. Our discussion of employment and inflation in this chapter will help us understand why the negotiation between Lucent and its workers turned out as it did. *An Inside Look* on page 382 discusses the role that expectations of inflation played in a similar contract negotiation between Boeing Company and its unionized workers.

Sources: "Two Unions Ratify Contract with Lucent," *Wall Street Journal*, December 20, 2004; and "Unix's Founding Fathers," *Economist*, June 10, 2004.

LEARNING OBJECTIVES

After studying this chapter, you should be able to:

1. Define the unemployment rate and the labor force participation rate, and understand how they are computed.
2. Identify the three types of unemployment.
3. Explain what factors determine the unemployment rate.
4. Define the price level and the inflation rate, and understand how they are computed.
5. Use price indexes to adjust for the effects of inflation.
6. Distinguish between the nominal interest rate and the real interest rate.
7. Discuss the problems caused by inflation.

Unemployment and inflation are the macroeconomic problems that are most often discussed in the media and during political campaigns. For many members of the general public, the state of the economy is summarized in just two measures: the unemployment rate and the inflation rate. In the 1960s, Arthur Okun, who was chairman of the Council of Economic Advisers during President Lyndon Johnson's administration, coined the term *misery index,* which adds together the inflation rate and the unemployment rate to give a rough measure of the state of the economy. As we will see in later chapters, although inflation and unemployment are important problems, the long-run success of an economy is best judged by its ability to generate high levels of real GDP per person.

In later chapters, we will explore how the inflation rate, the unemployment rate, and the rate of growth in real GDP per person are determined. We devote this chapter to discussing how the government measures the unemployment and inflation rates. In particular, we will look closely at the statistics on unemployment and inflation the federal government issues each month.

1 LEARNING OBJECTIVE

Define the unemployment rate and the labor force participation rate, and understand how they are computed.

Measuring the Unemployment Rate and the Labor Force Participation Rate

At 8:30 A.M. on a Friday early in each month, the U.S. Department of Labor reports its estimate of the previous month's unemployment rate. If the unemployment rate is higher or lower than expected, investors are likely to change their views on the health of the economy. The result will be seen an hour later when trading begins on the New York Stock Exchange. Good news about unemployment usually causes stock prices to rise, and bad news causes stock prices to fall. The unemployment rate can also have important political implications. In most presidential elections, the incumbent president is reelected if unemployment is falling early in the election year, but is defeated if unemployment is rising. This relationship held true in 2004, when the unemployment rate was lower during the first six months of 2004 than it had been during the last six months of 2003, and incumbent George W. Bush was reelected.

The unemployment rate is a key macroeconomic statistic. But how does the Department of Labor prepare its estimates of the unemployment rate, and how accurate are these estimates? We will explore the answers to these questions in this section.

The Household Survey

Each month the U.S. Bureau of the Census conducts the *Current Population Survey,* (often referred to as the *household survey*) to collect data needed to compute the unemployment rate. The bureau interviews adults in a sample of 60,000 households, chosen to represent the U.S. population, about the employment status of everyone in the household 16 years of age and older. The Department of Labor's Bureau of Labor Statistics (BLS) uses these data to calculate the monthly unemployment rate. People are considered *employed* if they worked during the week before the survey or if they were temporarily away from their job because they were ill, on vacation, on strike, or for other reasons. People are considered *unemployed* if they did not work in the previous week, but were available for work and had actively looked for work at some time during the previous four weeks. The **labor force** is the sum of the *employed* and the *unemployed.* The **unemployment rate** is the percentage of the labor force that is unemployed.

Labor force The sum of employed and unemployed workers in the economy.

Unemployment rate The percentage of the labor force that is unemployed.

People who do not have a job and who are not actively looking for a job are *not in the labor force.* People not in the labor force according to the BLS statistics include

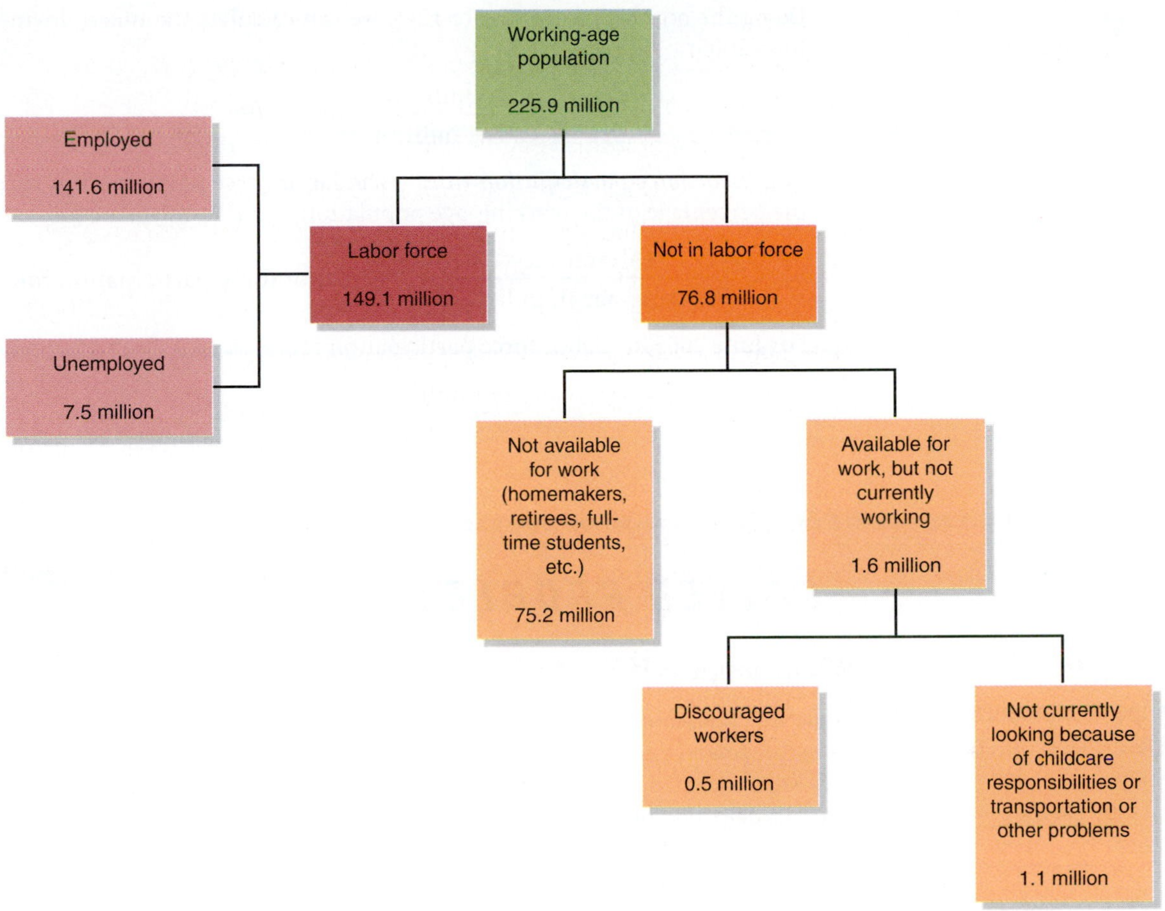

FIGURE 12-1 The Employment Status of the Civilian Working-Age Population, June 2005

In June 2005, the working-age population of the United States was 225.9 million. The working-age population is divided into those in the labor force (149.1 million) and those not in the labor force (76.8 million). The labor force is divided into the employed (141.6 million) and the unemployed (7.5 million). Those not in the labor force are divided into those not available for work (75.2 million) and those available for work (1.6 million). Finally, those available for work but not in the labor force are divided into discouraged workers (0.5 million) and those currently not working for other reasons (1.1 million).

Source: U.S. Department of Labor, "Employment Situation Summary," July 2005.

retirees, homemakers, full-time students, and people on active military service, in prison, or in mental hospitals. Also not in the labor force are people who are available for work and actively looked for a job at some point during the previous 12 months, but who have not looked during the previous four weeks. Some people have not actively looked for work lately for reasons such as transportation difficulties or child-care responsibilities. Other people who have not actively looked for work are called *discouraged workers*. **Discouraged workers** are available for work but have not looked for a job during the previous four weeks because they believe no jobs are available for them.

Discouraged workers People who are available for work but have not looked for a job during the previous four weeks because they believe no jobs are available for them.

Figure 12-1 shows the employment status of the civilian working-age population in June 2005. We can use the information in the figure to calculate two important macroeconomic indicators—the unemployment rate and the labor force participation rate.

- ***The unemployment rate.*** The unemployment rate measures the percentage of the labor force that is unemployed:

$$\frac{\text{Number of unemployed}}{\text{Labor force}} \times 100 = \text{Unemployment rate}.$$

Using the numbers from Figure 12-1, we can calculate the unemployment rate for June 2005:

$$\frac{7.5 \text{ million}}{149.1 \text{ million}} \times 100 = 5.0\%.$$

Labor force participation rate The percentage of the working-age population in the labor force.

➤ ***The labor force participation rate.*** The **labor force participation rate** measures the percentage of the working-age population that is in the labor force:

$$\frac{\text{Labor force}}{\text{Working-age population}} \times 100 = \text{Labor force participation rate.}$$

For June 2005, the labor force participation rate was:

$$\frac{149.1 \text{ million}}{225.9 \text{ million}} \times 100 = 66.0\%.$$

SOLVED PROBLEM 12-1

① LEARNING OBJECTIVE

Define the unemployment rate and the labor force participation rate, and understand how they are computed.

What Happens If You Include the Military?

In the BLS household survey, people on active military service are not included in the totals for employment, the labor force, or the working-age population. Suppose people in the military were included in these categories. How would the unemployment rate and the labor force participation rate change?

Solving the Problem:

Step 1: Review the chapter material. This problem is about calculating the unemployment rate and the labor force participation rate, so you may want to review the section "Measuring the Unemployment Rate and the Labor Force Participation Rate," which begins on page 358.

Step 2: Show that including the military decreases the measured unemployment rate. The unemployment rate is calculated as:

$$\frac{\text{Number of unemployed}}{\text{Labor force}} \times 100.$$

Including people in the military would increase the number of people counted as being in the labor force but would leave unchanged the number of people counted as unemployed. Therefore, the unemployment rate would decrease.

Step 3: Show that including the military increases the measured labor force participation rate. The labor force participation rate is calculated as:

$$\frac{\text{Labor force}}{\text{Working-age population}} \times 100.$$

Including people in the military would increase both the number of people in the labor force and the number of people in the working-age population by the same amount. This change would increase the labor force participation rate because adding the same number to both the numerator and the denominator of a fraction that is less than one increases the value of the fraction.

To see why this is true, consider the following simple example. Suppose that 100,000,000 people are in the working-age population and 50,000,000 are in the labor force, not counting people in the military. Suppose 1,000,000 people are in the military. Then, the labor force participation rate excluding the military is:

$$\frac{50,000,000}{100,000,000} \times 100 = 50\%,$$

and the labor force participation rate including the military is:

$$\frac{51,000,000}{101,000,000} \times 100 = 50.5\%.$$

***YOUR TURN:* For more practice, do related problem 4 on page 385 at the end of this chapter.**

Problems with Measuring the Unemployment Rate

Although the BLS reports the unemployment rate measured to the tenth of a percentage point, it is not a perfect measure of the current state of joblessness in the economy. One problem confronting the BLS is distinguishing between the unemployed and people who are not in the labor force. During an economic recession, for example, an increase in discouraged workers usually occurs, as people who have had trouble finding a job stop actively looking. Because these workers are not counted as unemployed, the unemployment rate as measured by the BLS may significantly understate the true degree of joblessness in the economy. The BLS also counts as employed people who hold part-time jobs even though they would prefer to hold full-time jobs. Furthermore, in a recession, counting as "employed" a part-time worker who wants to work full time tends to understate the degree of joblessness in the economy and make the employment situation appear better than it is.

Not counting discouraged workers as unemployed and counting people as employed who are working part time, although they would prefer to be working full time, has a substantial effect on the measured unemployment rate. For example, in June 2005, if the BLS counted as unemployed all people who were available for work but not actively looking for a job and all people who were in part-time jobs but wanted full-time jobs, the unemployment rate would have increased from 5.0 percent to 9.0 percent.

There are other measurement problems, however, that cause the measured unemployment rate to *overstate* the true extent of joblessness. These problems arise because the Current Population Survey does not verify the responses of people included in the survey. Some people who claim to be unemployed and actively looking for work may not be actively looking. A person might claim to be actively looking for a job to remain eligible for government payments to the unemployed. In this case, a person who is actually not in the labor force is counted as unemployed. Other people might be employed but engaged in illegal activity—such as drug dealing—or might want to conceal a legitimate job to avoid paying taxes. In this case, a person who is actually employed is counted as unemployed. These inaccurate responses to the survey cause the unemployment rate as measured by the BLS to overstate the true extent of joblessness. We can conclude that, although the unemployment rate provides some useful information about the employment situation in the country, it is far from an exact measure of joblessness in the economy.

Trends in Labor Force Participation

The labor force participation rate is important because it determines the amount of labor that will be available to the economy from a given population. The higher the labor force participation rate, the more labor will be available and the higher a country's

FIGURE 12-2

Trends in the Labor Force Participation Rates of Adult Men and Women Since 1948

The labor force participation rate of adult men has declined gradually since 1948, but the labor force participation rate of adult women has increased rapidly, leaving the overall labor force participation rate higher today than it was in 1948.

Source: U.S. Bureau of Labor Statistics.

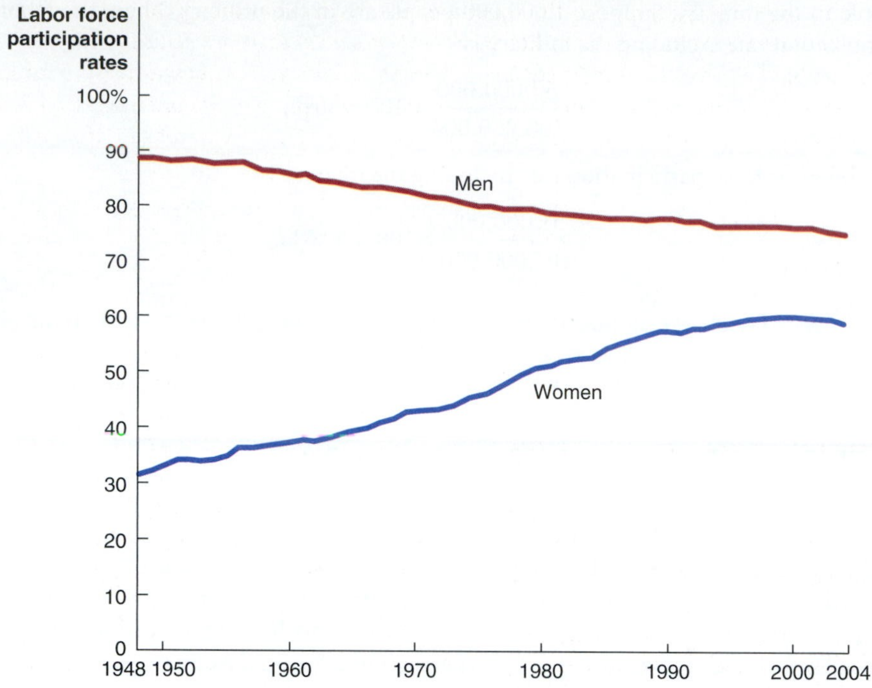

levels of GDP and GDP per person. Figure 12-2 highlights two important trends in labor force participation rates of adults aged 20 and over in the United States since 1950—the rising labor force participation rate of adult women and the falling labor force participation rate of adult men.

The labor force participation rate of adult males has fallen from 89 percent in 1948 to 76 percent in 2004. Most of this decline is due to older men retiring earlier and younger men remaining in school longer. There has also been a decline in labor force participation among males who are not in school but who are too young to retire.

12-1 Making the Connection

Why do more men seem to be adopting Kramer's lifestyle?

What Explains the Increase in "Kramers"?

Cosmo Kramer is the name of Jerry Seinfeld's next-door neighbor on the popular television comedy *Seinfeld.* One of the running jokes on the program is Kramer's ability to support himself without apparently ever holding a job. In recent years, there has been an increase in the number of men who seem to be following Kramer's lifestyle. In 1967, only 2.2 percent of men between the ages of 25 and 54 who were not in school did no paid work at all during the year. By 2002, 8 percent of men in this age category did not work. The rate of nonworking men is even higher among some groups. For example, almost 20 percent of men aged 25 to 54 who lack a high school degree do not have a job and are not looking for one.

More than half of nonworking men receive Social Security Disability Insurance. Under this program, people with disabilities receive cash payments from the federal government and receive medical benefits under the Medicaid program. In 1984, Congress passed legislation that made it easier for people with disabilities that are difficult to verify medically, such as back injuries or mental illnesses, to qualify for disability payments. In addition, the value of disability payments has increased faster than the wages of low-skilled workers. The result is that some men who in the past might have been working or actively looking for work are now being supported by disability payments and are not in the labor force.

An increasing share of nonworking men, however, are not disabled. How do nonworking men who do not receive disability payments support themselves, and how do they spend their time? Most nonworking men live with their parents, wives, or other relatives. Many of these men appear to rely on these other household members for food, clothing, and money.

A recent study by Jay Stewart of the Bureau of Labor Statistics shows that most nonworking men are not substituting nonmarket work—such as childcare or housework—for market work. Instead, nonworking men engage in leisure activities, such as sports, watching television, or sleeping during the hours freed up by not working. Stewart concludes that "the average day of a nonworking man looks very much like the average day-off of a man who works full time."

Sources: Alan Krueger, "A Growing Number of Men Are Not Working, So What Are They Doing?" *New York Times*, April 29, 2004, p. C2; and Jay Stewart, "What Do Male Nonworkers Do?" U.S. Bureau of Labor Statistics, Working Paper 371, April 2004.

The decline in labor force participation among adult men has been more than offset by a sharp increase in the labor force participation rate for adult women, which has risen from 32 percent in 1948 to 60 percent in 2004. As a result, the overall labor force participation rate has risen from 59 percent in 1948 to 68 percent in 2004. The increase in the labor force participation rate for women has several causes, including changing social attitudes due in part to the women's movement, federal legislation outlawing discrimination, increasing wages for women, and the typical family having fewer children.

Unemployment Rates for Demographic Groups

Different groups in the population can have very different unemployment rates. Figure 12-3 shows unemployment rates for different demographic groups in June 2005, when the unemployment rate for the entire population was 5.0 percent. White adults had an unemployment rate of 3.7 percent. The unemployment rate for black adults was 9.2 percent, or more than twice the rate for white adults. Teenagers have higher unemployment rates than adults. The black teenage unemployment rate of 32.4 percent was the highest for the groups shown.

How Long Are People Usually Unemployed?

The longer a person is unemployed, the greater the hardship. During the Great Depression of the 1930s, some people were unemployed for years at a time. In the modern U.S. economy, the typical unemployed person stays unemployed for a relatively brief period of time. Table 12-1 shows for June 2005 the percentage of the unemployed who had been

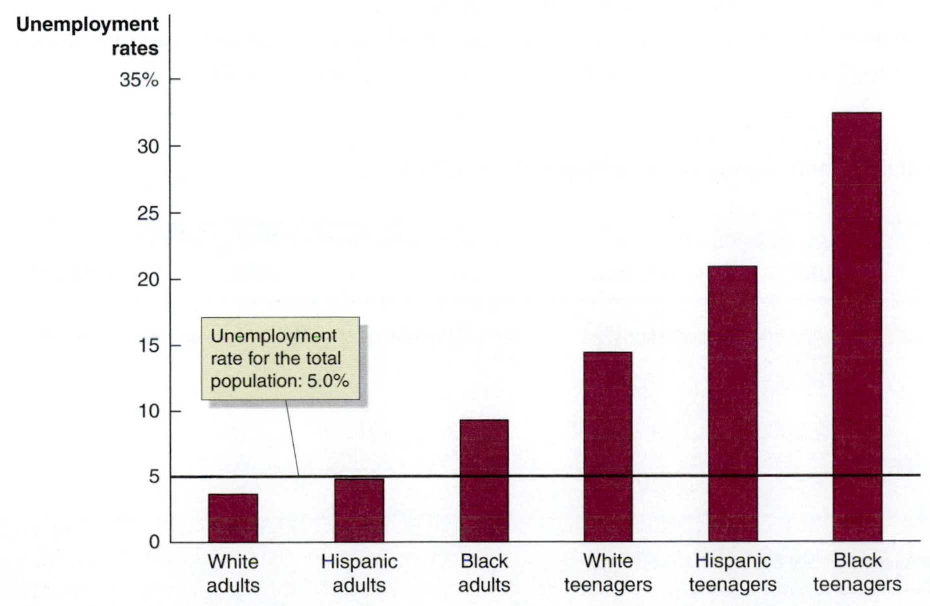

FIGURE 12-3

Unemployment Rates in the United States by Demographic Group, June 2005

The unemployment rate of black adults is more than twice that of white adults, and the unemployment rate of black teenagers is more than twice that of white teenagers. The adult unemployment rates apply to persons aged 20 and over who are in the labor force. The teenage unemployment rates apply to persons aged 16 to 19 who are in the labor force. Note that people identified as Hispanic may be of any race.

Source: U.S. Department of Labor, "Employment Situation Summary," July 2005.

TABLE 12-1

Duration of Unemployment

LENGTH OF TIME UNEMPLOYED	PERCENTAGE OF TOTAL UNEMPLOYED
Less than 5 weeks	36.2%
5 to 14 weeks	31.8
15 to 26 weeks	14.1
27 weeks or more	17.8

Source: U.S. Department of Labor, "Employment Situation Summary," July 2005.

unemployed for a given period of time. Eighty-two percent of the people unemployed in that month had been unemployed for fewer than six months. Half had been unemployed for nine weeks or less. The important conclusion is that, *except in severe recessions, the typical person who loses a job finds another one or is recalled to a previous job within a few months.*

The Establishment Survey: Another Measure of Employment

In addition to the household survey, the BLS uses the *establishment survey,* sometimes called the *payroll survey,* to measure total employment in the economy. This monthly survey samples about 300,000 business establishments. An establishment is a factory, store, or office. A small company may operate only one establishment, but large companies may operate many establishments. The establishment survey provides information on the total number of persons who are employed *and on a company payroll.* The establishment survey has three drawbacks. First, the survey does not provide information on the number of self-employed persons, because they are not on a company payroll. Second, the survey may fail to count some persons employed at newly opened firms that are not included in the survey. Third, the survey provides no information on unemployment. Despite these drawbacks, the establishment survey has the strength of being determined by actual payrolls, rather than by unverified answers, as is the case with the household survey. In recent years, some economists have come to rely more on establishment survey data than on household survey data in analyzing current labor market conditions. Some financial analysts who forecast the future state of the economy so they can better forecast stock prices have also begun to rely more on establishment survey data than on household survey data.

Table 12-2 shows household survey and establishment survey data for the months of May and June 2005. Notice that the household survey, because it includes the self-employed, gives a larger total for employment than does the establishment survey. The

TABLE 12-2 **Household and Establishment Survey Data for May and June 2005**

	HOUSEHOLD SURVEY			ESTABLISHMENT SURVEY		
	MAY	JUNE	CHANGE	MAY	JUNE	CHANGE
Employed	141,475,000	141,638,000	+163,000	133,391,000	133,537,000	+146,000
Unemployed	7,647,000	7,486,000	−161,000			
Labor Force	149,122,000	149,123,000	+1,000			
Unemployment Rate	5.1%	5.0%	−0.1%			

Source: U.S. Department of Labor, "Employment Situation Summary," July 2005.
Note: The sum of employed and unemployed may not equal labor force due to rounding.

TABLE 12-3

Establishments Creating and Eliminating Jobs, September–December 2004

	NUMBER OF ESTABLISHMENTS	NUMBER OF JOBS
ESTABLISHMENTS CREATING JOBS		
Existing establishments	1,530,000	6,365,000
New establishments	379,000	1,716,000
ESTABLISHMENTS ELIMINATING JOBS		
Continuing establishments	1,467,000	5,727,000
Closing establishments	320,000	1,485,000

Source: U.S. Bureau of Labor Statistics, "Business Employment Dynamics: Fourth Quarter 2004," August 18, 2005.

household survey provides information on the number of persons unemployed and on the number of persons in the labor force. This information is not available in the establishment survey. In both surveys, employment increased between May and June 2005, but the increase was greater in the household survey.

Job Creation and Job Destruction Over Time

One important fact about employment is not very well known: The U.S. economy creates and destroys millions of jobs every year. In 2004, for example, about 31.5 million jobs were created and about 29.4 million jobs were destroyed. This degree of job creation and destruction is what we would expect in a vibrant market system where new firms are constantly being started, some existing firms are expanding, some existing firms are contracting, and some firms are going out of business. The creation and destruction of jobs results from changes in consumer tastes, technological progress, and the success and failures of entrepreneurs in responding to the opportunities and challenges of shifting consumer tastes and technological change. The volume of job creation and job destruction helps explain why the typical person who loses a job is unemployed for a relatively brief period of time.

When the BLS announces each month the increases or decreases in the number of persons employed and unemployed, these are net *figures.* That is, the change in the number of persons employed is equal to the total number of jobs created minus the number of jobs eliminated. Take, for example, the months from September to December 2004. During that period, 8,081,000 jobs were created and 7,212,000 were eliminated, for a net increase of 869,000 jobs. Because the net change is so much smaller than the total job increases and decreases, the net change gives a misleading indication of how dynamic the U.S. job market really is.

The data in Table 12-3 reinforce the idea of how large the volume of job creation and job elimination is over a period as brief as three months. The table shows the number of establishments creating and eliminating jobs during the period between September and December 2004. During these three months, 14 percent of all private sector jobs were either created or destroyed. Fifty-six percent of establishments either eliminated jobs or added new jobs. About 379,000 new establishments opened, creating 1.72 million new jobs, and 320,000 establishments closed, eliminating 1.47 million jobs.

Types of Unemployment

(2) **LEARNING OBJECTIVE**
Identify the three types of unemployment.

Figure 12-4 illustrates that the unemployment rate follows the business cycle, rising during recessions and falling during expansions. Notice, though, that the unemployment

FIGURE 12-4

The Annual Unemployment Rate in the United States, 1950–2004

The unemployment rate rises during recessions and falls during expansion. Shaded areas mark recessions.

Source: U.S. Bureau of Labor Statistics.

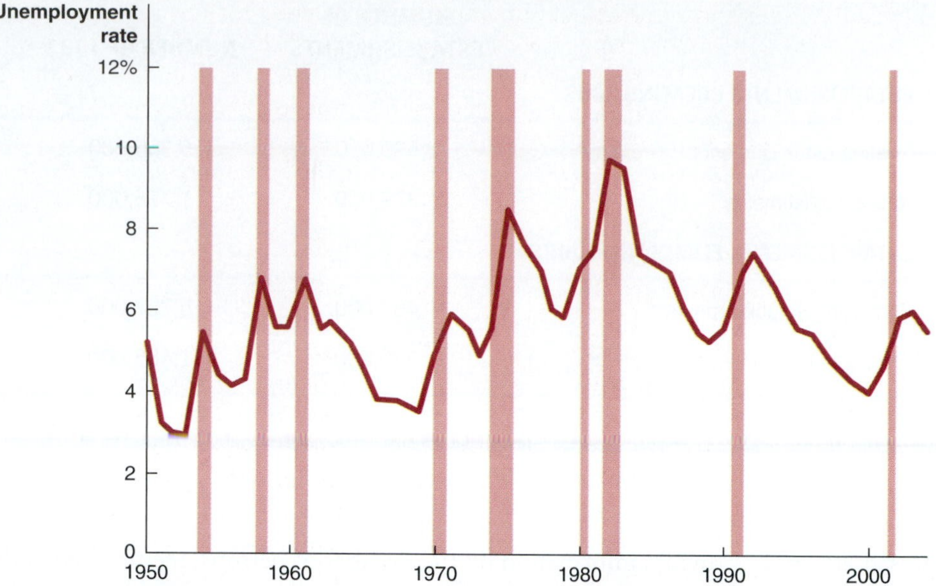

rate never falls to zero. To understand why this is true, we need to discuss the three types of unemployment:

- Frictional unemployment
- Structural unemployment
- Cyclical unemployment

Frictional Unemployment and Job Search

Frictional unemployment
Short-term unemployment arising from the process of matching workers with jobs.

Workers have different skills, interests, and abilities, and jobs have different skill requirements, working conditions, and pay levels. As a result, a new worker entering the labor force or a worker who has lost a job probably will not find an acceptable job right away. Most workers spend at least some time engaging in *job search,* just as most firms spend time searching for a new person to fill a job opening. **Frictional unemployment** is short-term unemployment that arises from the process of matching workers with jobs. Some frictional unemployment is unavoidable. As we have seen, the U.S. economy creates and destroys millions of jobs each year. The process of job search takes time, so there will always be some workers who are frictionally unemployed because they are between jobs and in the process of searching for new ones.

Some unemployment is due to seasonal factors, such as weather or fluctuations in demand during different times of the year. For example, stores located in beach resort areas reduce their hiring during the winter, just as ski resorts reduce their hiring during the summer. Department stores increase their hiring in November and December, and reduce their hiring after New Year's Day. In agricultural areas, employment increases during harvest season, and declines thereafter. Construction workers experience greater unemployment during the winter than during the summer. *Seasonal unemployment* refers to unemployment due to factors such as weather, variations in tourism, and other calendar-related events. Because seasonal unemployment can make the unemployment rate seem artificially high during some months and artificially low during other months, the BLS reports two unemployment rates each month—one that is *seasonally adjusted* and one that is not seasonally adjusted. The seasonally adjusted data eliminate the effects of seasonal unemployment. Economists and policymakers rely on the seasonally adjusted data as a more accurate measure of the current state of the labor market.

Would eliminating all frictional unemployment be good for the economy? In fact, some frictional unemployment is good for the economy because it represents workers and firms taking the time necessary to ensure a good match between the attributes of workers and the characteristics of jobs. By devoting time to job search, workers end up with jobs they find satisfying and in which they can be productive. Of course, having more productive and better satisfied workers is also in the best interest of firms.

Structural Unemployment

By 2004, computer-generated three-dimensional animation, which was used in movies such as *Shrek* and *The Incredibles,* had become much more popular than traditional hand-drawn two-dimensional animation. Many people who were highly skilled in hand-drawn animation lost their jobs at Walt Disney Pictures, Dreamworks, and other movie studios. To become employed again, many of these people either became skilled in computer-generated animation or found new occupations. In the meantime, they were unemployed. Economists consider these animators *structurally unemployed.* **Structural unemployment** arises from a persistent mismatch between the job skills or attributes of workers and the requirements of jobs. While frictional unemployment is short term, structural unemployment can last for longer periods because workers need time to learn new skills. For example, employment by U.S. auto firms dropped by more than half between the early 1980s and the early 2000s as a result of competition from foreign producers and technological change that substituted machines for workers. Many autoworkers found new jobs in other industries only after lengthy periods of retraining.

Structural unemployment Unemployment arising from a persistent mismatch between the skills and characteristics of workers and the requirements of jobs.

Some workers lack even basic skills, such as literacy, or have addictions to drugs or alcohol that make it difficult for them to perform adequately the duties of almost any job. These workers may remain structurally unemployed for years.

Cyclical Unemployment

When the economy moves into recession, many firms find their sales falling and cut back on production. As production falls, they start laying off workers. Workers who lose their jobs because of a recession are experiencing **cyclical unemployment.** For example, we saw in Chapter 11 that Freightliner laid off workers from its heavy truck plants during the recession of 2001. As the economy recovered from the recession, Freightliner began rehiring these workers. These Freightliner workers had experienced cyclical unemployment.

Cyclical unemployment Unemployment caused by a business cycle recession.

Full Employment

As the economy moves through the expansion phase of the business cycle, cyclical unemployment will eventually drop to zero. The unemployment rate will not be zero, however, because of frictional and structural unemployment. As Figure 12-4 shows, the unemployment rate in the United States is rarely below 4 percent. When the only remaining unemployment is structural and frictional unemployment, the economy is said to be at *full employment.*

Economists often think of frictional and structural unemployment as being the normal underlying level of unemployment in the economy. The fluctuations around this normal level of unemployment, which we see in Figure 12-4, are mainly due to the changes in the level of cyclical unemployment. This normal level of unemployment, which is the sum of frictional and structural unemployment, is referred to as the **natural rate of unemployment.** Economists disagree on the exact value of the natural rate of unemployment, and there is good reason to believe it varies over time. Currently, most economists estimate the natural rate to be about 5 percent. The natural rate of unemployment is also sometimes called the *full-employment rate of unemployment.*

Natural rate of unemployment The normal rate of unemployment, consisting of structural unemployment plus frictional unemployment.

12-2 Making the Connection

How can we categorize the unemployment at Lucent?

How Should We Categorize the Unemployment at Lucent Technologies?

We saw at the beginning of this chapter that Lucent Technologies experienced a sharp decline in employment in the early 2000s. Was the unemployment caused by the layoffs at Lucent frictional unemployment, structural unemployment, or cyclical unemployment? In answering this question we should acknowledge that categorizing unemployment as frictional, structural, or cyclical is useful in understanding the sources of unemployment, but it can be difficult to apply these categories in a particular case. The Bureau of Labor Statistics, for instance, provides estimates of total unemployment but does not classify it as frictional, structural, or cyclical.

Despite these difficulties, we can roughly categorize the unemployment at Lucent. We begin by considering the three basic reasons the layoffs occurred: the long-lived decline in the telecommunications products Lucent sells; the recession of 2001 that reduced the demand for Lucent's products; and the failure of Lucent managers to respond to rapid technological change in the industry. Each reason corresponds to a category of unemployment. Because the demand for the telecommunications products Lucent sells—particularly products used with fiber-optic cable networks—declined for a significant period, employment at Lucent and competing firms also declined. Between late 2000 and mid-2002, employment in the telecommunications industry declined by more than 500,000. Certain categories of employees, such as optical engineers, had difficulty finding new jobs. They were structurally unemployed because they were not able to find new jobs without learning new skills. Some of the decline in Lucent's sales was due to the recession rather than to long-term problems in the telecommunications industry. So, some of the workers who lost their jobs at Lucent were cyclically unemployed. Finally, sales and employment declined more sharply at Lucent than at some competing firms because of mistakes made by Lucent's managers. Some workers who lost their jobs at Lucent were able to find new jobs at Lucent's competitors after relatively brief job searches. These workers were frictionally unemployed.

③ **LEARNING OBJECTIVE**
Explain what factors determine the unemployment rate.

Explaining Unemployment

We have seen that some unemployment is caused by the business cycle. In later chapters, we will explore the causes of the business cycle, which will help us understand the causes of cyclical unemployment. In this section, we will look at what determines the levels of frictional and structural unemployment.

Government Policies and the Unemployment Rate

The process of job search is primarily carried out privately. Workers search for jobs by sending out resumes, registering with Internet job sites such as Monster.com, or getting job referrals from friends and relatives. Firms fill job openings by advertising in newspapers, participating in job fairs, or recruiting on college campuses. Government policy can aid these private efforts. Governments can help reduce the level of frictional unemployment by pursuing policies that help speed up the process of matching unemployed workers with unfilled jobs. Governments can help reduce structural unemployment through policies that aid the retraining of workers. For example, the federal government's Trade Adjustment Assistance program offers training to workers whose firms laid them off as a result of competition from foreign firms.

Some government policies, however, can add to the level of frictional and structural unemployment. These government policies increase the unemployment rate either by increasing the time workers devote to searching for jobs, by providing disincentives to firms to hire workers, or by keeping wages above their market level.

UNEMPLOYMENT INSURANCE AND OTHER PAYMENTS TO THE UNEMPLOYED Suppose you have been in the labor force for a few years but have just lost your job. You could probably find a low-wage job immediately if you needed to—perhaps at Wal-Mart or McDonald's. But you might decide to search for a better, higher-paying job by sending out resumes and responding to want ads and Internet job postings. Remember from Chapter 1 that the *opportunity cost* of any activity is the highest-valued alternative that you must give up to engage in that activity. In this case, the opportunity cost of continuing to search for a job is the salary you are giving up at the job you could have taken. The longer you search, the better your chances of finding a better, higher-paying job, but the longer you search, the greater the opportunity cost of the salary you are giving up by not working.

In the United States and most other industrial countries, the unemployed are eligible for *unemployment insurance payments* from the government. In the United States, these payments are equal to about half the average wage. The unemployed spend more time searching for jobs because they receive these payments. This additional time spent searching raises the unemployment rate. Does this mean that the unemployment insurance program is a bad idea? Most economists would say no. Before the unemployment insurance program was created at the end of the 1930s, unemployed workers suffered very large declines in their incomes, which led them to greatly reduce their spending. This reduced spending contributed to the severity of recessions. Unemployment insurance helps the unemployed maintain their income and spending, which lessens the personal impact of being unemployed and also helps reduce the severity of recessions.

INTERNATIONAL COMPARISONS In the United States, typical unemployed workers are eligible to receive unemployment insurance payments equal to about half their previous wage for only six months. After that, the opportunity cost of continuing to search for a job rises. In many other high-income countries, such as Canada and most of the countries of Western Europe, workers are eligible to receive unemployment payments for a year or more, and the payments may equal 70 percent to 80 percent of their previous wage. In addition, many of these countries have generous *social insurance programs* that allow unemployed adults to receive some government payments even after their eligibility for unemployment insurance has ended. In the United States, very few government programs make payments to healthy adults, with the exception of the Temporary Assistance for Needy Families program, which allows single parents to receive payments for up to five years. Because the opportunity cost of job search is lower in Canada and Western Europe, unemployed workers in those countries search longer for jobs and, therefore, the unemployment rates in those countries tend to be higher than in the United States.

Figure 12-5 shows the average yearly unemployment rate for the ten-year period from 1995 to 2004 for the United States, Canada, Japan, and several Western European countries. The United States and Japan provide unemployment insurance payments for only a short period of time, and their average unemployment rate during these years was lower than for the other countries shown. Many European countries also have laws that make it difficult for companies to fire workers. These laws create a disincentive for firms to hire workers, which also contributes to a higher unemployment rate.

MINIMUM WAGE LAWS In 1938, the federal government enacted a national minimum wage law. At first, the lowest legal wage firms could pay workers was $0.25 per hour. Over the years, Congress gradually raised the minimum wage until it reached its current level of $5.15 per hour. Some states and cities also have minimum wage laws. For example, in 2005 California has set its minimum wage at $6.75 per hour, and the minimum wage in San Francisco is $8.50 per hour. If the minimum wage is set above the market wage determined by the demand and supply of labor, the quantity of labor supplied will be greater than the quantity of labor demanded. Some workers will be unemployed who would have been employed if there were no minimum wage. As a result, the unemployment rate will be higher than it would be without a minimum wage. Economists agree that the current minimum wage is above the market wage for some workers, but they

FIGURE 12-5

Average Unemployment Rates in the United States, Canada, Japan, and Europe, 1995–2004

The unemployment rate in the United States is usually lower than the unemployment rates in most other high-income countries, partly because the United States has tougher requirements for the unemployed to receive government payments. These requirements raise the costs of searching for a better job and lower the unemployment rate.

Source: Organization for Economic Cooperation and Development.

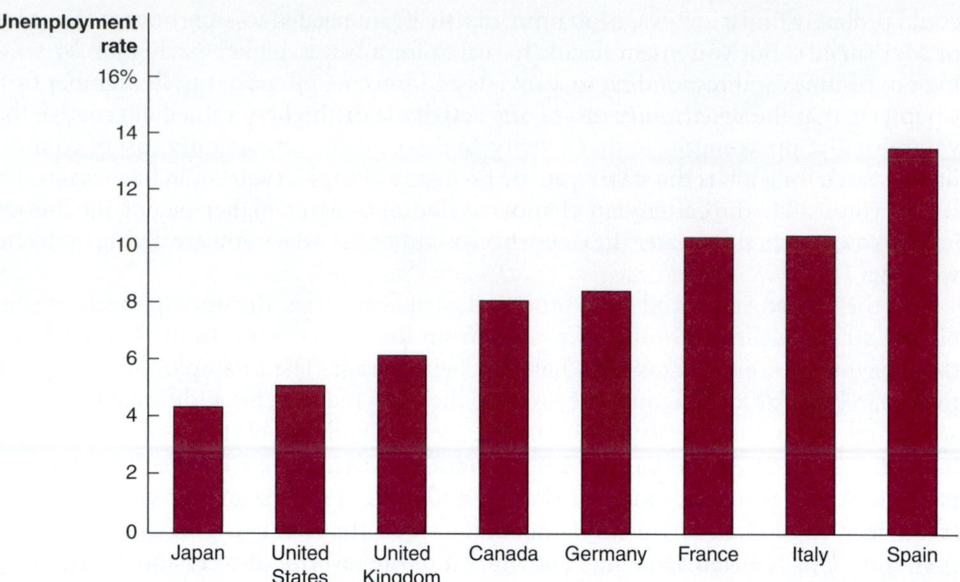

disagree on the amount of unemployment that has resulted. Because teenagers generally have relatively few job-related skills, they are the group most likely to receive the minimum wage. Studies estimate that a 10-percent increase in the minimum wage reduces teenage employment by about 2 percent. Because teenagers and others receiving the minimum wage are a relatively small part of the labor force, most economists believe that, at its present level, the effect of the minimum wage on the unemployment rate in the United States is fairly small.

Labor Unions

Labor unions are organizations of workers that bargain with employers for higher wages and better working conditions for their members. In unionized industries, the wage is usually above what otherwise would be the market wage. This above-market wage results in employers in unionized industries hiring fewer workers, but does it also increase the overall unemployment rate in the economy? Most economists would say the answer is no, because only about 9 percent of workers outside of the government sector are unionized. Although unions remain strong in a few industries, such as automobiles, steel, and telecommunications, most industries in the United States are not unionized. The result is that workers who can't find jobs in unionized industries because the wage is above its market level can find jobs in other industries.

Efficiency Wages

Efficiency wage A higher-than-market wage paid by a firm to increase worker productivity.

Many firms pay higher-than-market wages, not because the government requires them to or because they are unionized, but because they believe doing so will increase their profits. This link may seem like a paradox. Wages are the largest cost for many employers, so paying higher wages seems like a good way for firms to lower profits rather than to increase them. The key to understanding the paradox is that the level of wages can affect the level of worker productivity. Many studies have shown that workers are motivated to work harder by higher wages. An **efficiency wage** is a higher-than-market wage paid by a firm to motivate workers to be more productive. Can't firms ensure that workers work hard by supervising them? In some cases they can. For example, telemarketers can be monitored electronically to ensure they make the required number of phone calls per hour. In many business situations, however, it is much more difficult to monitor workers. Many firms must rely on workers being motivated enough to work hard. In fact, the following is the key to the efficiency wage: By paying a wage above the market wage, the firm raises the costs to workers of losing their jobs because most alternative jobs will pay only the market wage. The increase in productivity that results from paying the high wage can more than offset the cost of the wage, thereby lowering the firm's costs of production.

Because the efficiency wage is above the market wage, it results in the quantity of labor supplied being greater than the quantity of labor demanded, just as do minimum wage laws and unions. So, efficiency wages are another reason economies experience some unemployment even when cyclical unemployment is zero.

12-3 Making the Connection

Why Did Henry Ford Pay His Workers Twice as Much as Other Car Manufacturers?

In January 1914, Henry Ford announced that he would begin paying his workers $0.625 per hour, or $5.00 for an eight-hour day. Other automobile firms paid an average of only $0.29 per hour. Why would Henry Ford pay his workers more than twice as much as other firms? Ford had recently installed the first moving assembly line in his factory at Highland Park, Michigan. The moving assembly line greatly increased labor productivity, but most Ford workers hated it.

Under the old assembly system, the cars remained stationary on the factory floor and each worker had several jobs to do as he moved from one car to another. With the moving assembly line, each worker remained in the same spot all day, performing the same task—sometimes just installing a bolt or tightening a nut—over and over. Many workers found this excruciatingly boring, and many quit to take less monotonous jobs at other firms. Each time a worker quit, Ford had the expense of hiring and training a new one. These expenses became very high: Of the 15,000 workers employed by the company on December 31, 1913, only 640 had worked at Ford for more than three months.

Henry Ford claimed that paying a wage twice as high as his competitors was the finest cost-cutting move he ever made.

With the introduction of the $5-dollar-a-day wage, Ford went from having difficulty keeping workers to having long lines of men at the factory gate every morning applying for work. The *New York Times* described the situation the morning Ford first began paying the new wage: "Twelve thousand men . . . [rushed] the plant which resulted in a riot and turning of a fire hose on the crowd in weather but little different from zero [degrees] . . . . As soon as the job hunters had dried or changed their clothing they came back." Ford had begun paying an efficiency wage. According to Ford's official biographer, paying $5 per day had "improved the discipline of the workers, given them a more loyal interest in the institution, and raised their personal efficiency." Ford himself later wrote, "The payment of five dollars a day for an eight-hour day was one of the finest cost-cutting moves we ever made."

Sources: David A. Hounshell, *From the American System to Mass Production, 1800–1932,* Baltimore: The Johns Hopkins University Press, 1984, Ch. 6; Daniel M. G. Raff and Lawrence H. Summers, "Did Henry Ford Pay Efficiency Wages?" *Journal of Labor Economics,* Vol. 5, Issue 4, Part 2, October 1987, pp. S57–S86; and Alan Nevins and Frank Ernest Hill, *Ford: The Times, the Man, the Company,* New York: Scribner's, 1954, pp. 538, 550.

Measuring Inflation

LEARNING OBJECTIVE

Define the price level and the inflation rate, and understand how they are computed.

One of the facts of economic life is that the prices of most goods and services rise over time. As a result, the cost of living continually rises. In 1914, Henry Ford's $5-a-day wage seemed shockingly high. But in that year, Ford's Model T, the best-selling car in the country, sold for less than $600, the price of a man's suit was $15, the price of a ticket to a movie theater was $0.15, and the price of a box of Kellogg's Corn Flakes was $0.08. Today, when the cost of living is much higher, the minimum wage law requires firms to pay a wage of at least $5.15 per *hour,* more than Ford's highly paid workers earned in a day.

Price level A measure of the average prices of goods and services in the economy.

Inflation rate The percentage increase in the price level from one year to the next.

Knowledge of how the government's employment and unemployment statistics are compiled is important in interpreting them. The same is true of the government's statistics on the cost of living. As we saw in Chapter 11, the **price level** measures the average prices of goods and services in the economy. The **inflation rate** is the percentage increase in the price level from one year to the next. In Chapter 11, we introduced the *GDP deflator* as a measure of the price level. The GDP deflator is the broadest measure we have of the price level because it includes the price of every final good and service. But, for some purposes, it is too broad. For example, if we want to know the impact of inflation on the typical household, the GDP price deflator may be misleading because it includes the prices of products such as large electric generators and machine tools that are included in the investment component of GDP, but are not purchased by the typical household. In this chapter, we will focus on measuring the inflation rate by changes in the *consumer price index* because changes in this index come closest to measuring changes in the cost of living as experienced by the typical household. We will also briefly discuss a third measure of inflation: the *producer price index.*

The Consumer Price Index

To obtain prices of a representative group of goods and services, the Bureau of Labor Statistics (BLS) surveys 30,000 households nationwide on their spending habits. They use the results of this survey to construct a *market basket* of 211 types of goods and services purchased by the typical urban family of four. Figure 12-6 shows the goods and services in the market basket grouped into eight broad categories. Almost three-quarters of the market basket falls into the categories of housing, transportation, and food. Each month, hundreds of BLS employees visit 23,000 stores in 87 cities and record prices of the goods and services in the market basket. Each price in the consumer price index is given a weight equal to the fraction of the typical family's budget spent on that good or service. The **consumer price index (CPI)** is an average of the prices of the goods and services purchased by the typical family. One year is chosen as the base year, and the value of the CPI is set equal to 100 for that year. In any year other than the base year, the CPI is equal to the ratio of the dollar amount necessary to buy the market basket of goods in that year divided by the dollar amount necessary to buy the market basket of goods in the base year, multiplied by 100. Because the CPI measures the cost to the typical family to buy a representative basket of goods and services, it is sometimes referred to as the *cost-of-living index.*

Consumer price index (CPI) An average of the prices of the goods and services purchased by the typical urban family of four.

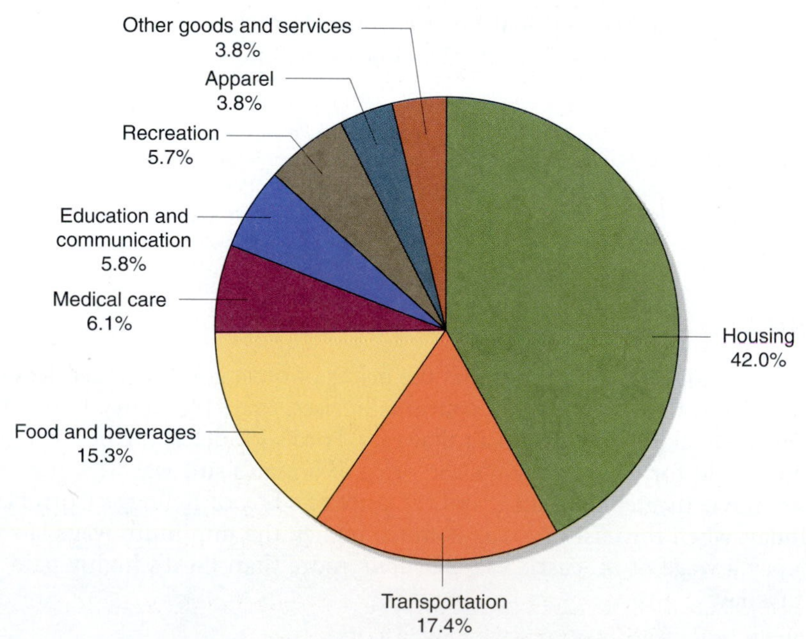

FIGURE 12-6

The CPI Market Basket, December 2004

The BLS surveys 30,000 households on their spending habits. The results are used to construct a *market basket* of goods and services purchased by the typical urban family of four. The chart shows these goods and services grouped into eight broad categories. The percentages represent the expenditure shares of the categories within the market basket. The categories of housing, transportation, and food make up about three-quarters of the market basket.

Source: Bureau of Labor Statistics.

A simple example can clarify how the consumer price index is constructed. For purposes of this example, assume the market basket has only three products: eye examinations, pizzas, and books:

	BASE YEAR (1999)			2006		2007	
PRODUCT	QUANTITY	PRICE	EXPENDITURES	PRICE	EXPENDITURES (ON BASE YEAR QUANTITIES)	PRICE	EXPENDITURES (ON BASE YEAR QUANTITIES)
Eye examinations	1	$50.00	$50.00	$100.00	$100.00	$85.00	$85.00
Pizzas	20	10.00	200.00	15.00	300.00	14.00	280.00
Books	20	25.00	500.00	25.00	500.00	27.50	550.00
Total			$750.00		$900.00		$915.00

Suppose that during the base year of 1999 a survey determines that each month the typical family purchases 1 eye examination, 20 pizzas, and 20 books. At 1999 prices, the typical family must spend $750.00 to purchase this market basket of goods and services. The CPI for every year after the base year is determined by dividing the amount necessary to purchase the market basket in that year by the amount required in the base year, multiplied by 100. Notice that the quantities of the products purchased in 2006 and 2007 are irrelevant in calculating the CPI, because *we are assuming that households buy the same market basket of products each month.* Using the numbers in the table, we can calculate the CPI for 2006 and 2007:

FORMULA	APPLIED TO 2006	APPLIED TO 2007
$\text{CPI} = \frac{\text{Expenditures in the current year}}{\text{Expenditures in the base year}} \times 100$	$\left(\frac{\$900}{\$750}\right) \times 100 = 120$	$\left(\frac{\$915}{\$750}\right) \times 100 = 122$

How do we interpret values such as 120 and 122? The first thing to recognize is that they are *index numbers,* which means they are not measured in dollars or any other units. *The CPI is intended to measure changes in the price level over time.* We can't use the CPI to tell us in an absolute sense how high the price level is, only how much it has changed over time. We measure the inflation rate as the percentage increase in the CPI from one year to the next. For our simple example, the inflation rate in 2007 would be the percentage change in the CPI from 2006 to 2007:

$$\left(\frac{122 - 120}{120}\right) \times 100 = 1.7\%.$$

Because the CPI is designed to measure the cost of living, we can also say that the cost of living increased by 1.7 percent during 2007.

Is the CPI Accurate?

The CPI is the most widely used measure of inflation. Policymakers use the CPI to track the state of the economy. Businesses use it to help set the prices of their products and the wages and salaries of their employees. Each year the federal government increases the Social Security payments made to retired workers by a percentage equal to the increase in the CPI during the previous year. In setting alimony and child support payments in divorce cases, judges will often order the payments increase each year by the inflation rate as measured by the CPI.

It is important that the CPI be as accurate as possible, but there are four biases that make changes in the CPI overstate the true inflation rate:

Don't Let This Happen To You!

Don't Miscalculate the Inflation Rate

Suppose you are given the data in the following table and are asked to calculate the inflation rate for 2004.

YEAR	CPI
2003	184
2004	189

It is tempting to avoid any calculations and simply to report that the inflation rate in 2004 was 89 percent because 189 is an 89 percent increase from 100. But 89 percent would be the wrong answer. A value for the CPI of 189 in 2004 tells us that the price level in 2004 was 89 percent higher than in the base year, but the inflation rate is the percentage increase in the price level from the previous year, *not* the percentage increase from the base year. A correct calculation of the inflation rate for 2004 is:

$$\left(\frac{189 - 184}{184}\right) \times 100 = 2.7\%.$$

YOUR TURN: **Test your understanding by doing related problems 14 and 20 on pages 386 and 387 at the end of this chapter.**

- *Substitution bias.* In constructing the CPI, the Bureau of Labor Statistics assumes that each month consumers purchase the same amount of each product in the market basket. In fact, consumers are likely to buy fewer of those products that increase most in price and more of those products that increase least in price (or fall the most in price). For instance, if apple prices rise rapidly during the month while orange prices fall, consumers will reduce their apple purchases and increase their orange purchases. Therefore, the prices of the market basket consumers actually buy will rise less than the prices of the market basket the BLS uses to compute the CPI.
- *Increase in quality bias.* Over time, most products included in the CPI improve in quality: Automobiles become more durable and side air bags become standard equipment, computers become faster and have more memory, dishwashers use less water while getting dishes cleaner, and so on. Increases in the prices of these products partly reflect their improved quality and partly are pure inflation. The BLS attempts to make adjustments so that only the pure inflation part of price increases is included in the CPI. These adjustments are difficult to make, so the recorded price increases overstate the pure inflation in some products.
- *New product bias.* For many years the Bureau of Labor Statistics updated the market basket of goods used in computing the CPI only every ten years. That meant that new products introduced between updates were not included in the market basket. For example, the 1987 update took place before cell phones were introduced. Although millions of American households used cell phones by the mid-1990s, they were not included in the CPI until the 1997 update. The prices of many products, such as cell phones, DVD players, and computers, decrease in the years immediately after they are introduced. Unless the market basket is updated frequently, these price decreases will not be included in the CPI.
- *Outlet bias.* During the mid-1990s, many consumers began to increase their purchases from discount stores such as Sam's Club. By the late 1990s, the Internet began to account for a significant fraction of sales of some products. Because the BLS continued to collect price statistics from traditional full-price retail stores, the CPI was not reflecting the prices some consumers actually paid.

Most economists believe these biases cause changes in the CPI to overstate the true inflation rate by one-half of a percentage point to one percentage point. That is, if the CPI indicates that the inflation rate was 3 percent, it is probably between 2 percent and 2.5 percent. The BLS continues to take steps to reduce the size of the bias. For example, the BLS has reduced the size of the substitution and new product biases by updating the market basket every two years, rather than every 10 years. The BLS has reduced the size of the outlet bias by conducting a point-of-purchase survey to track where consumers actually make their purchases. Finally, the BLS has used statistical methods to reduce the size of the quality bias. Prior to these changes, the size of the total bias in the CPI was probably greater than 1 percent.

The Producer Price Index

In addition to the GDP deflator and the CPI, the government also computes the **producer price index (PPI).** Like the consumer price index, the producer price index tracks the prices of a market basket of goods. But, whereas the consumer price index tracks the prices of goods and services purchased by the typical household, the producer price index tracks the prices firms receive for goods and services at all stages of production. The producer price index includes the prices of intermediate goods, such as flour, cotton, yarn, steel, and lumber, and raw materials, such as raw cotton, coal, and crude petroleum. If the prices of these goods rise, the cost to firms of producing final goods and services will rise, which may lead firms to increase the prices of goods and services purchased by consumers. Changes in the producer price index therefore can give an early warning of future movements in the consumer price index.

Producer price index (PPI) An average of the prices received by producers of goods and services at all stages of the production process.

Using Price Indexes to Adjust for the Effects of Inflation

⑤ LEARNING OBJECTIVE

Use price indexes to adjust for the effects of inflation.

The typical college student today is likely to receive a much higher salary than the student's parents did 25 or more years ago, but prices 25 years ago were, on average, much lower than prices today. Put another way, the purchasing power of a dollar was much higher 25 years ago because the prices of most goods and services were much lower. Price indexes, such as the CPI, give us a way of adjusting for the effects of inflation so that we can compare dollar values from different years. For example, suppose your mother received a salary of $20,000 in 1980. By using the consumer price index, we can calculate what $20,000 in 1980 is equivalent to in 2004. The consumer price index is 82 for 1980 and 189 for 2004. Because 189/82 = 2.3, we know that, on average, prices were more than twice as high in 2004 as in 1980. We can use this result to inflate a salary of $20,000 received in 1980 to its value in current purchasing power:

$$\text{Value in 2004 dollars} = \text{Value in 1980 dollars} \times \left(\frac{\text{CPI in 2004}}{\text{CPI in 1980}}\right)$$

$$= \$20{,}000 \times \left(\frac{189}{82}\right) = \$46{,}098.$$

Our calculation shows that if you are paid a salary of $46,098 today, you will be able to purchase roughly the same amount of goods and services that your mother could have purchased with a salary of $20,000 in 1980. Economic variables that are calculated in current year prices are referred to as *nominal variables.* The calculation we have just made used a price index to adjust a nominal variable—your mother's salary—for the effects of inflation.

For some purposes, we are interested in tracking changes in an economic variable over time, rather than in seeing what its value would be in today's dollars. In that case, to correct for the effects of inflation we can divide the nominal variable by a price index and multiply by 100 to obtain a *real variable.* The real variable will be measured in dollars of the base year for the price index. Currently, the base year for the CPI is the average of prices in the years 1982 to 1984.

SOLVED PROBLEM 12-2

(5) LEARNING OBJECTIVE

Use price indexes to adjust for the effects of inflation.

Calculating Real Average Hourly Earnings

In addition to data on employment, the BLS establishment survey gathers data on average hourly earnings of production workers. Production workers are all workers, except for managers and professionals. Average hourly earnings are the wages or salaries earned by these workers per hour. Economists closely follow average hourly earnings because they are a broad measure of the typical worker's income. Use the information in the following table to calculate real average hourly earnings for each year. What was the percentage change in real average hourly earnings between 2003 and 2004?

YEAR	NOMINAL AVERAGE HOURLY EARNINGS	CPI (1982–1984 = 100)
2002	$14.95	179.9
2003	15.35	184.0
2004	15.67	188.9

Solving the Problem:

Step 1: Review the chapter material. This problem is about using price indexes to correct for inflation, so you may want to review the section "Using Price Indexes to Adjust for the Effects of Inflation," which begins on page 385.

Step 2: Calculate real average hourly earnings for each year. To calculate real average hourly earnings for each year, divide nominal average hourly earnings by the CPI, and multiply by 100. For example, real average hourly earnings for 2002 are equal to:

$$\left(\frac{\$14.95}{179.9}\right)\times 100 = \$8.31.$$

The results for all the years:

YEAR	NOMINAL AVERAGE HOURLY EARNINGS	CPI (1982–1984 = 100)	REAL AVERAGE HOURLY EARNINGS (1982–1984 DOLLARS)
2002	$14.95	179.9	$8.31
2003	15.35	184.0	8.34
2004	15.67	188.9	8.30

Step 3: Calculate the percentage change in real average earnings from 2003 to 2004. This percentage change is equal to:

$$\left(\frac{\$8.30 - \$8.34}{\$8.34}\right)\times 100 = -0.5\%.$$

We can conclude that although nominal average hourly earnings increased between 2003 and 2004, real average hourly earnings declined.

Extra Credit: The values we have computed for real average hourly earnings are in 1982–1984 dollars. Because this period is more than 20 years ago, the values are somewhat difficult to interpret. We can convert the earnings to 2004 dollars by using the method we used earlier to calculate your mother's salary. But notice that, for purposes of calculating the *change* in the value of real average hourly earnings over time, the base year of the price index doesn't matter. The change from 2003 to 2004 would have still been −0.5 percent, no matter what the base year of the price index. If you don't see that this is true, test it by using the mother's salary method to calculate real average hourly earnings for 2003 and 2004 in 2004 dollars. Then calculate the percentage change. Unless you make an arithmetic error, you should find the answer is still −0.5 percent.

YOUR TURN: **For more practice, do related problems 15 and 16 on page 396 at the end of this chapter.**

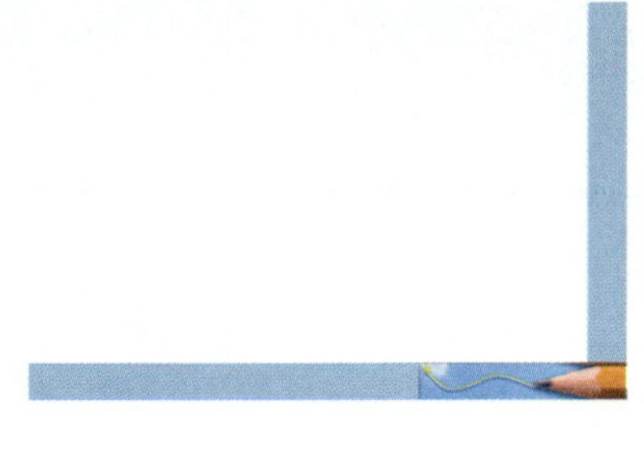

Falling Real Wages at Lucent

Nominal average hourly earnings are often referred to as the *nominal wage,* and real average hourly earnings are often referred to as the *real wage.* In a multiyear wage contract, a union knows that unless it is able to negotiate increases in nominal wages that are greater than the expected inflation rate, real wages will fall. We saw at the beginning of this chapter that the contract between Lucent and its unionized workers would result in nominal wage increases of 16 percent over a period of seven years. If the inflation rate is 3 percent per year over those seven years, the price level will have risen by about 23 percent by the end of the seventh year. With nominal wages rising 16 percent and the price level rising 23 percent, Lucent's workers will have experienced falling real wages.

Both Lucent and its unions realized that the agreement they were signing was likely to lead to falling real wages. The unions accepted the agreement because employment at telecommunications firms had declined sharply. Lucent stated that it might grant further wage increases in the later years of the contract. Lucent probably made this promise because it recognized that if output and employment in the telecommunications industry revived more quickly than expected, the firm would need to pay higher wages to attract and retain good workers.

Real versus Nominal Interest Rates

(6) **LEARNING OBJECTIVE**

Distinguish between the nominal interest rate and the real interest rate.

The difference between nominal and real values is also important when money is being borrowed and lent. As we saw in Chapter 5, the *interest rate* is the cost of borrowing funds, expressed as a percentage of the amount borrowed. If you lend someone $1,000 for one year and charge an interest rate of 6 percent, the borrower will pay back $1,060, or 6 percent more than the amount you lent. But is $1,060 that you won't receive for one year really 6 percent more than $1,000 today? Because prices will have gone up during the year, you will not be able to buy as much with $1,060 one year from now as you could with that amount today. To calculate your true return from lending the $1,000, we need to take into account the effects of inflation.

Nominal interest rate The stated interest rate on a loan.

Real interest rate The nominal interest rate minus the inflation rate.

The stated interest rate on a loan is the **nominal interest rate.** The **real interest rate** corrects the nominal interest rate for the effect of inflation and is equal to the nominal interest rate minus the inflation rate. For example, suppose you lend $1,000 for one year at an interest rate of 6 percent. Six percent is the nominal interest rate on the loan. If the inflation rate during the year is 2 percent, your real interest rate is 6 percent − 2 percent = 4 percent. If the inflation rate during the year is 4 percent, the real interest rate will be only 2 percent. Holding the nominal interest rate constant, the higher the inflation rate, the lower the real interest rate. Notice that if the inflation rate turns out to be higher than expected, borrowers pay and lenders receive a lower real interest rate than either of them expected. For example, if both you and the person to whom you lent the $1,000 expected the inflation rate to be 2 percent, you both expected the real interest rate on the loan to be 4 percent. If inflation actually turns out to be 4 percent, the real interest rate on the loan will be 2 percent: That's bad news for you but good news for your borrower.

For the economy as a whole, we can measure the nominal interest rate as the interest rate on three-month U.S. Treasury bills. U.S. Treasury bills are short-term loans investors make to the federal government. We can use inflation as measured by changes in the CPI to calculate the real interest rate on Treasury bills. Figure 12-7 shows the nominal and real interest rates for the years 1970 to 2004. Notice that when the inflation rate is low, as it was during the 1990s, the gap between the nominal and real interest rates is small. When the inflation rate is high, as it was during the 1970s, the gap between the nominal and real interest rates becomes large. In fact, a particular nominal interest rate can be associated in different periods with very different real interest rates. For example, during late 1975 the nominal interest rate was about 5.5 percent, but because the inflation rate was 7.5 percent, the real interest rate was −2 percent. In early 1991, the nominal interest rate was also 5.5 percent, but because the inflation rate was only 2.5 percent, the real interest rate was 3 percent.

This example shows that it is impossible to know whether a particular nominal interest rate is "high" or "low." It all depends on the inflation rate. *The real interest rate provides a better measure of the true cost of borrowing and the true return to lending than does the nominal interest rate.* When a firm like Lucent Technologies is deciding whether to borrow the funds to buy an investment good, such as a new factory, it will look at the real interest rate, because the real interest rate measures the true cost to the firm of borrowing.

You can also see in Figure 12-7 that the nominal interest rate is less than the real interest rate only when the inflation rate is negative. A negative inflation rate is referred to as **deflation** and occurs on the rare occasions when the price level falls. During the years shown in Figure 12-7, the price level as measured by the consumer price index declined during the second quarter of 1986 and the fourth quarter of 2001.

Deflation A decline in the price level.

FIGURE 12-7

Nominal and Real Interest Rates, 1970–2004

The real interest rate is equal to the nominal interest rate minus the inflation rate. The real interest rate provides a better measure of the true cost of borrowing and the true return to lending than does the nominal interest rate. The nominal interest rate in the figure is the interest rate on 3-month U.S. Treasury bills. The inflation rate is measured by changes in the CPI.

Source: Federal Reserve Bank of St. Louis, http://research.stlouisfed.org/fred2/.

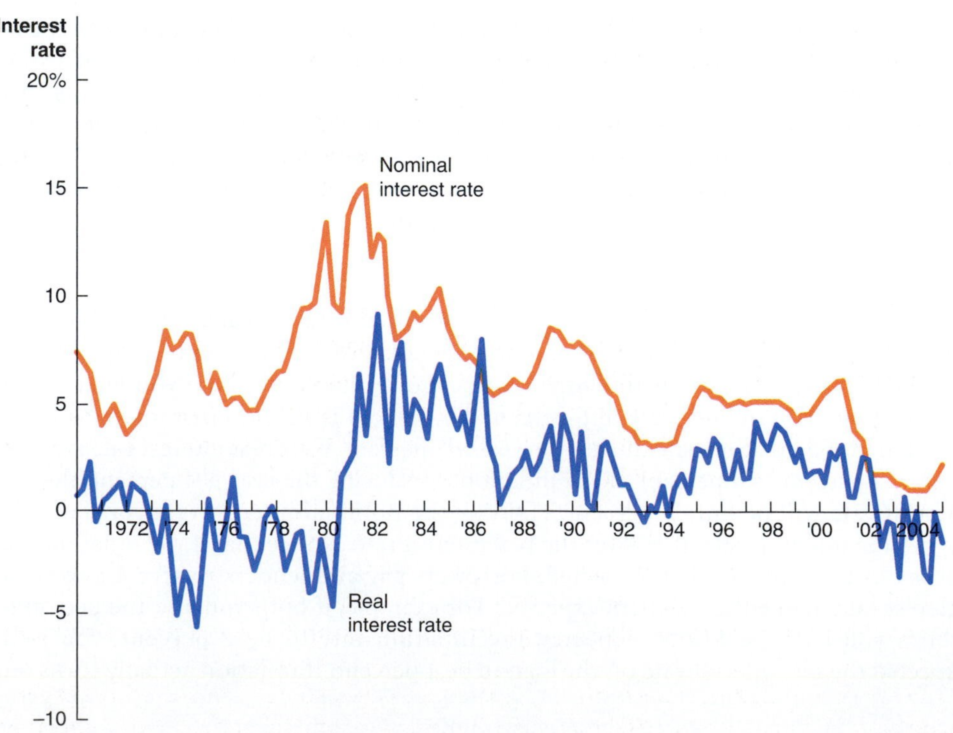

Does Inflation Impose Costs on the Economy?

LEARNING OBJECTIVE

Discuss the problems caused by inflation.

Imagine waking up tomorrow morning and finding that every price in the economy has doubled. The prices of food, gasoline, televisions, and houses have all doubled. But suppose that all wages and salaries also have doubled. Will this doubling of prices and wages matter? Think about walking into Best Buy expecting to find an iPod selling for $250. Instead, you find it selling for $500. Will you turn around and walk out? Probably not, because your salary has also increased overnight from $30,000 per year to $60,000 per year. So, the purchasing power of your salary has remained the same, and you are just as likely to buy the iPod today as you were yesterday.

This hypothetical situation makes an important point: Nominal incomes generally increase with inflation. Remember from Chapter 11 that we can think of the $250 price of the iPod as representing either the value of the product or the value of all the income generated in producing the product. The two amounts are the same whether the iPod sells for $250 or $500. When the price of the iPod rises from $250 to $500, that extra $250 ends up as income that goes to the workers at Apple, the salespeople at Best Buy, or the stockholders of Apple, just as the first $250 did.

It's tempting to think that the problem with inflation is that, as prices rise, consumers can no longer afford to buy as many goods and services, but our example shows that this is a fallacy. An expected inflation rate of 10 percent will raise the average price of goods and services by 10 percent, but it will also raise average incomes by 10 percent. Goods and services will be as affordable to the average consumer as they were before the inflation.

Inflation Affects the Distribution of Income

Why, then, do people dislike inflation? One reason is that the argument in the previous section applies to the *average* person, but not to every person. Some people will find their incomes rising faster than the rate of inflation and so their purchasing power will rise. Other people will find their incomes rising slower than the rate of inflation—or not at all—and their purchasing power will fall. People on fixed incomes are particularly likely to be hurt by inflation. If a retired worker receives a pension fixed at $2,000 per month, over time inflation will reduce the purchasing power of that payment. In that way, inflation can change the distribution of income in a way that strikes many people as being unfair.

The extent to which inflation redistributes income depends in part on whether the inflation is *anticipated*—in which case consumers, workers, and firms can see it coming and can prepare for it—or *unanticipated*—in which case they do not see it coming and do not prepare for it.

The Problem with Anticipated Inflation

Like many of life's problems, inflation is easier to manage if you see it coming. Suppose that everyone knows that the inflation rate for the next ten years will be 10 percent per year. Workers know that unless their wages go up by at least 10 percent per year, the real purchasing power of their wages will fall. Businesses will be willing to increase workers' wages enough to compensate for inflation because they know that the prices of the products they sell will increase. Lenders will realize that the loans they make will be paid back with dollars that are losing 10 percent of their value each year, so they will charge a higher interest rate to compensate them for this. Borrowers will be willing to pay these higher interest rates because they also know they are paying back these loans with dollars that are losing value. So far, there don't seem to be costs to anticipated inflation.

Even when inflation is perfectly anticipated, however, some individuals will experience a cost. Inevitably, there will be a redistribution of income, as some people's incomes fall behind even an anticipated level of inflation. In addition, firms and consumers have to hold some paper money to facilitate their buying and selling. Anyone holding paper money will find its purchasing power decreasing each year by the rate of inflation. To avoid this cost, workers and firms will try to hold as little paper money as possible, but they will have to hold some. In addition, firms that print catalogs listing the prices of their products will have to reprint them more frequently. Supermarkets and other stores that mark prices on packages or on store shelves will have to devote more time and labor to changing the marked prices. The costs to firms of changing prices are called **menu costs.** Although at moderate levels of anticipated inflation menu costs are relatively small, at very high levels of inflation, such as are experienced in some developing countries, menu costs and the costs from paper money losing value can become substantial. Finally, even anticipated inflation acts to raise the taxes paid by investors and raises the cost of capital for business investment. These effects arise because investors are taxed on the nominal payments they receive, rather than on the real payments.

Menu costs The costs to firms of changing prices.

12-4 Making the Connection

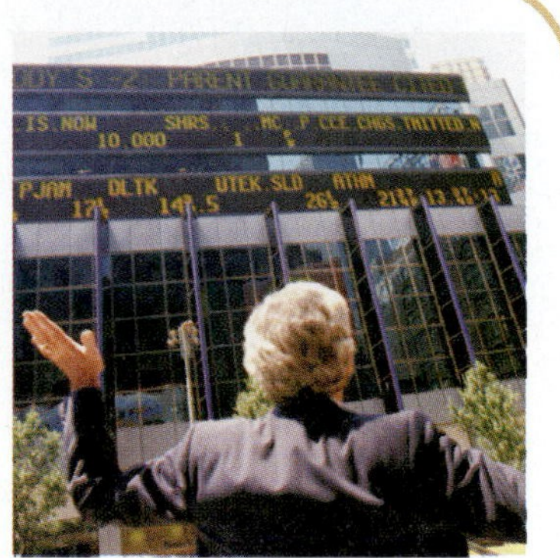

A lower inflation rate is like a tax cut for investors.

Why a Lower Inflation Rate Is Like a Tax Cut for Lucent's Bondholders

Borrowers and lenders are interested in the real interest rate, rather than the nominal interest rate. Therefore, if expected inflation increases, the nominal interest rate will rise, and if expected inflation decreases, the nominal interest rate will fall. Suppose that Lucent sells bonds to investors to raise funds to purchase investment goods. Suppose also that Lucent is willing to pay, and investors are willing to receive, a real interest rate of 4 percent. If the inflation rate is expected to be 2 percent, the nominal interest rate on Lucent's bonds must be 6 percent for the real interest rate to be 4 percent. If the inflation rate is expected to be 6 percent, the nominal rate on the bond must rise to 10 percent for the real interest rate to be 4 percent. The following table summarizes this information, assuming that the bond has a principal, or face value, of $1,000 (see Chapter 5 for a review of bonds):

PRINCIPAL	REAL INTEREST RATE	INFLATION RATE	NOMINAL INTEREST RATE
$1,000	4%	6%	10%
$1,000	4%	2%	6%

With a nominal interest rate of 6 percent, the interest payment (also known as the *coupon payment*) on newly issued bonds is $60. When the nominal interest rate rises to 10 percent, the interest payment on newly issued bonds is $100. Unfortunately for investors, the government taxes the nominal payment on bonds with no adjustment for inflation. So, even though in this case the increase in the interest payment from $60 to $100 represents only compensation for inflation, the whole $100 is subject to the income tax. The following table shows the effect of inflation on an investor's real after-tax interest payment assuming a tax rate of 25 percent:

INFLATION RATE	NOMINAL INTEREST PAYMENT	TAX PAYMENT	AFTER-TAX INTEREST PAYMENT	ADJUSTMENT FOR INFLATION	REAL AFTER-TAX INTEREST PAYMENT
6%	$100	− $25	= $75	− $60	= $15
2%	$60	− $15	= $45	− $20	= $25

The table shows that reducing the inflation rate from 6 percent to 2 percent will increase the real after-tax payment received by investors who purchase a $1,000 Lucent bond from $15 to $25. By raising the after-tax reward to investors, lower inflation rates will increase the incentive for investors to lend funds to firms. The greater the flow of funds to firms, the greater the amount of investment spending that will occur.

The Problem with Unanticipated Inflation

In any high-income economy—such as the United States—households, workers, and firms routinely enter into contracts that commit them to make or receive certain payments for years in the future. As we saw in the beginning of the chapter, Lucent Technologies signed a seven-year wage contract with two of its unions during 2004. Once signed, this contract committed Lucent to paying a specified wage for the duration of the contract. When people buy homes, they usually borrow most of the amount they need from a bank. These loans, called *mortgage loans,* commit the borrower to make a fixed monthly payment for the length of the loan. Most mortgage loans are for long periods, often as much as 30 years.

To make these long-term commitments, households, workers, and firms must forecast the rate of inflation. If a firm believes the inflation rate over the next three years will be 6 percent per year, signing a three-year contract with a union that calls for wage increases of 8 percent per year may seem reasonable because the firm may be able to raise its prices by at least the rate of inflation each year. If the firm believes that the inflation rate will be only 2 percent over the next three years, paying wage increases of 8 percent may significantly reduce its profits, or even force it out of business.

When people borrow money or banks lend money, they must forecast the inflation rate so they can calculate the real rate of interest on a loan. In 1980, banks were charging interest rates of 18 percent or more on mortgage loans. This rate seems very high compared to the roughly 6 percent charged on such loans in 2005, but the inflation rate in 1980 was more than 13 percent and was expected to remain high. In fact, the inflation rate declined unexpectedly during the early 1980s. By 1983, the inflation rate was only about 3 percent. People who borrowed money for 30 years at the high interest rates of 1980 soon found that the real interest rate on their loans was much higher than they expected.

When the actual inflation rate turns out to be very different from the expected inflation rate, some people gain and other people lose. This outcome seems unfair to most people because they are either winning or losing only because something unanticipated has happened. This apparently unfair redistribution is a key reason why people dislike unanticipated inflation.

Conclusion

Inflation and unemployment are key macroeconomic problems. Presidential elections are often won or lost on the basis of which candidate is able to convince the public that he or she can best deal with these problems. Many economists, however, would argue that, in the long run, maintaining high rates of growth of real GDP per person is the most important macroeconomic concern. Only when real GDP per person is increasing will a country's standard of living increase. We turn in the next chapter to discussing this important issue of economic growth.

Read *An Inside Look* on the next page to see how expectations of inflation affected the negotiations of a union contract between Boeing and its workers.

An Inside Look Managers and Workers at Boeing Negotiate Wages

WICHITA EAGLE, MARCH 6, 2004

Boeing Offers Unionized Workers in Wichita, Kan., Wage Increases

Boeing Wichita is offering more than 3,000 union-represented technical and professional workers wage increases of 3 percent, 2 percent and 3 percent in the next three years. The company's offer, which also includes a 2 percent signing bonus, was harshly criticized Friday by a union leader.

Negotiations between Boeing Wichita and the Society of Professional Engineering Employees in Aerospace on a three-year contract for about 3,450 Wichita technical and professional employees appear to be nearing completion. Bob Brewer, SPEEA's Midwest director, said he expects Boeing to present the union with its "last, best and final offer" sometime Tuesday or Wednesday.

a As it stands now, the union could not recommend Boeing's offer to its members when they vote on a new agreement, Brewer said. Boeing's wage offer "was very insulting and disrespectful to the employees here in Wichita," Brewer said. "That doesn't even cover the market increases and inflation."

Boeing officials called the offer a fair one and in keeping with economic realities and with the Wichita market.

b The wage proposal is "taking into consideration where we are in the latest business cycle, which has been in a downturn (and) not expected to pick up until perhaps 2006," Boeing Wichita spokesman Fred Solis said. The current contract, which expired Feb. 19, has been extended until March 19. Both sides agree there is more work to be done.

"We're still negotiating," Solis said. "We will continue looking for a solution that's fair to everybody." Talks have been tense in the past few days, Brewer said, when the two sides began talking about an economic package of benefits and wages. A large gap remains between where the offer is today and where it will have to be for the membership to accept it, Brewer said.

c "They're looking at short-term cost-cutting," Brewer said. "This isn't all about cutting costs. This is also about investing in your most valuable assets, and that is your employees."

Workers in the SPEEA bargaining unit voted last month to retain the union after an effort by some Wichita employees to decertify the unit.

Key Points in the Article

This article discusses wage contract negotiations between Boeing Company, a manufacturer of commercial and military aircraft, and workers at its Wichita, Kansas, factory. The union argues that the company's wage offer is too low because it fails to "cover the market increases and inflation." A spokesman for Boeing argues that the contract offer takes into account that the aircraft industry is still in recession.

Analyzing the News

a We saw in Solved Problem 12-2 that real earnings will increase only if nominal earnings increase faster than the price level. Therefore, not surprisingly, the expected inflation rate is important in wage negotiations. Workers hope that their real wages will increase over time. The only way their real wages can increase is if the nominal wage increases they receive are greater than increases in the cost of living. Firms can grant increases in real wages without seeing their costs rise only if they can get increased production from their workers.

b Fred Holis, the spokesman for Boeing, argues that Boeing's wage offer to its workers reflected the stage of the business cycle. That is, workers could not expect larger wage increases during a recession. As we have already seen, when economists use the phrase "business cycle," they are referring to the alternating periods of economic expansion and economic recession *in the economy as a whole.* Many firms, however, think of the business cycle in terms of the sales of their own products. Figure 1 shows Boeing's annual sales of passenger aircraft from 1979 to 2004. The shaded areas represent years in which the U.S. economy was in a business cycle recession. The figure shows that the cycle in sales of Boeing's aircraft do not follow the business cycle exactly. For example, Boeing experienced dips in sales from 1992 to 1995 and in 2002 and 2003, when the economy as a whole was expanding, and increases in sales during 1990–91 and 2001, when the economy as a whole was in recession. This pattern reflects, in part, the fact that aircraft take a long time to build, so aircraft actually shipped in one year were typically ordered in an earlier year. But sales of aircraft are also dependent on such factors as the health of the airline industry, which are not as important for the economy as a whole.

c The union representative argues that, for Boeing, paying higher wages is the equivalent of "investing in your most valuable assets . . . your employees." According to the union representative, holding down wage increases would amount to "short-term cost cutting" by the company. Such arguments are, of course, in the best interests of a union that wants the largest wage increases it can obtain for its members. But our discussion of efficiency wages indicated that sometimes it is in the best interests of firms to pay wages that are above market levels. Making the Connection 12-3 discussed Henry Ford's view that paying his workers twice what his competitors paid actually lowered his costs by causing his workers to be more productive and less likely to quit.

Thinking Critically

1. If a firm grants nominal wage increases that turn out to be greater than the actual inflation rate, will the firm's profits necessarily fall? Briefly explain.
2. For which types of occupations is it likely that paying efficiency wages will be an effective strategy for a firm?

Source: Molly McMillin, "Boeing Offers Unionized Workers in Wichita, Kan., Wage Increases," *Wichita Eagle,* March 6, 2004, p. 1.

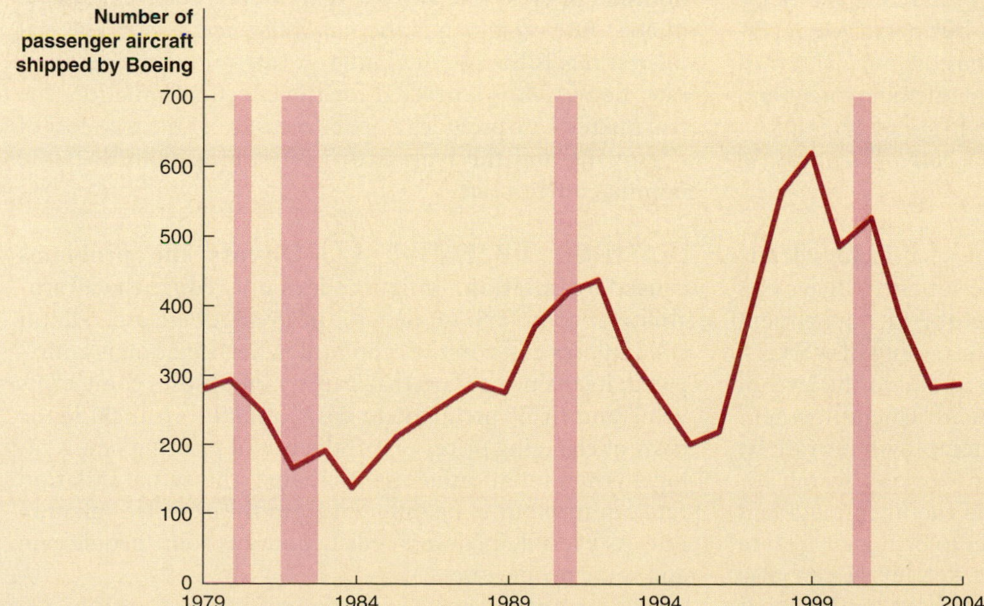

Note: The shaded areas represent years in which the U.S. economy was in a business cycle recession.

Figure 1: Cycles in Aircraft Production at Boeing.

Source: Aerospace Industries Association.

SUMMARY

LEARNING OBJECTIVE ① Define the unemployment rate and the labor force participation rate, and understand how they are computed. The U.S. Bureau of Labor Statistics uses the results of the monthly household survey to calculate the *unemployment rate* and the *labor force participation rate.* The *labor force* is the total number of people who have jobs plus the number of people who do not have jobs but are actively looking. The labor force participation rate is the percentage of the working-age population in the labor force. Since 1950, the labor force participation rate of women has been rising, while the labor force participation rate of men has been falling. White men and women have below-average unemployment rates. Teenagers and black men and women have above-average unemployment rates. The typical unemployed person finds a new job or returns to his or her previous job within a few months. Each year millions of jobs are created and destroyed in the United States.

LEARNING OBJECTIVE ② Identify the three types of unemployment. There are three types of unemployment: frictional, structural, and cyclical. *Frictional unemployment* is short-term unemployment arising from the process of matching workers with jobs. One type of frictional unemployment is *seasonal unemployment,* which refers to unemployment due to factors such as weather, variations in tourism, and other calendar-related events. *Structural unemployment* arises from a persistent mismatch between the job skills or attributes of workers and the requirements of jobs. *Cyclical unemployment* is caused by a business cycle recession. The *natural rate of unemployment* is the normal rate of unemployment, consisting of structural unemployment and frictional unemployment. The natural rate of unemployment is also sometimes called the *full-employment rate of unemployment.*

LEARNING OBJECTIVE ③ Explain what factors determine the unemployment rate. Government policies can reduce the level of frictional and structural unemployment by aiding the search for jobs and the retraining of workers. Some government policies, however, can add to the level of frictional and structural unemployment. Unemployment insurance payments can raise the unemployment rate by extending the time that unemployed workers search for jobs. Government policies have caused the unemployment rates in most other industrial countries to be higher than in the United States. Wages above market levels can also increase unemployment. Wages may be above market levels because of the minimum wage, labor unions, and *efficiency wages.*

LEARNING OBJECTIVE ④ Define the price level and the inflation rate, and understand how they are computed. The *price level* measures the average prices of goods and services. The *inflation rate* is equal to the percentage change in the price level from one year to the next. The federal government compiles statistics on three different measures of the price level: the consumer price index (CPI), the GDP price deflator, and the producer price index (PPI). The *consumer price index* is an average of the prices of goods and services purchased by the typical urban family of four. Changes in the consumer price index are the best measure of changes in the cost of living as experienced by the typical household. Biases in the construction of the CPI cause changes in it to overstate the true inflation rate by one-half of a percentage point to one percentage point. The *producer price index* is an average of prices received by producers of goods and services at all stages of production.

LEARNING OBJECTIVE ⑤ Use price indexes to adjust for the effects of inflation. Price indexes are designed to measure changes in the price level over time, not the absolute level of prices. To correct for the effects of inflation we can divide a *nominal variable* by a price index and multiply by 100 to obtain a *real variable.* The real variable will be measured in dollars of the base year for the price index.

LEARNING OBJECTIVE ⑥ Distinguish between the nominal interest rate and the real interest rate. The stated interest rate on a loan is the *nominal interest rate.* The *real interest rate* is the nominal interest rate minus the inflation rate. Because it is corrected for the effects of inflation, the real interest rate provides a better measure of the true cost of borrowing and the true return to lending than does the nominal interest rate.

LEARNING OBJECTIVE ⑦ Discuss the problems caused by inflation. Inflation does not reduce the affordability of goods and services to the average consumer, but it still imposes costs on the economy. When inflation is anticipated, its main costs are that paper money loses some of its value and firms incur menu costs. *Menu costs* include the costs of changing prices on products and printing new catalogs. When inflation is unanticipated, the actual inflation rate can turn out to be different from the expected inflation rate. As a result, income is redistributed as some people gain and some people lose.

KEY TERMS

REVIEW QUESTIONS

1. How is the unemployment rate calculated? Which groups tend to have above-average unemployment rates, and which groups tend to have below-average unemployment rates?
2. How is the labor force participation rate calculated? In the years since 1950, how have the labor force participation rates of men and women changed?
3. What is the difference between the household survey and the establishment survey? Which survey do many economists prefer for measuring changes in employment? Why?
4. If employment increases during a month, is it likely that the total number of *new* jobs created is about equal to the increase in employment? Explain.
5. What is the relationship between the natural rate of unemployment and cyclical unemployment, frictional unemployment, and structural unemployment?
6. Discuss the effect on the unemployment rate of the following:
   a. The minimum wage law
   b. Labor unions
   c. Efficiency wages
7. Briefly describe the three major measures of the price level. Which measure is used most frequently?
8. What potential biases exist in calculating the consumer price index? What steps has the Bureau of Labor Statistics taken to reduce the size of the biases?
9. If you were lending your savings, which would you prefer: a nominal interest rate of 20 percent and an inflation rate of 18 percent, or a nominal interest rate of 10 percent and an inflation rate of 5 percent? If you were a borrower, would your answer change?
10. Which is a greater problem: anticipated inflation or unanticipated inflation? Why?

PROBLEMS AND APPLICATIONS

Please visit **www.prenhall.com/hubbard** *for solutions to the even-numbered problems as well as multiple-choice and true or false self-assessment quizzes.*

1. Fill in the missing values in the table of data collected in the household survey for the year of 2000.

Working-age population	
Employment	136,891,000
Unemployment	
Unemployment rate	4.0%
Labor force	
Labor force participation rate	67.1%

2. **[Related to the *Chapter Opener*]** What would be some general reasons a firm would lay off a substantial number of workers?
3. Figure 12-2 on page 362 shows that the rapid increases in the labor force participation rate of women slowed down after 1995. Why might this slowdown have occurred? Discuss whether the labor force participation rate for women eventually might be equal to the rate for men.
4. **[Related to *Solved Problem 12-1*]** Homemakers are not included in the employment or labor force totals compiled in the Bureau of Labor Statistics household survey. They are included in the working-age population totals. Suppose

that homemakers were counted as employed and included in the labor force statistics. What would be the impact on the unemployment rate and the labor force participation rate?

5. Discuss the average amount of time the typical unemployed person in the United States has been out of work. Is the average unemployed person in Europe likely to be out of work for a shorter or a longer period of time than the average unemployed person in the United States? Why?
6. What advice for finding a job would you give someone frictionally unemployed? Someone structurally unemployed? Someone cyclically unemployed?
7. When the U.S. economy is at full employment, why isn't the unemployment rate, as measured by the Bureau of Labor Statistics, equal to zero?
8. Discuss the likely impact of each of the following on the unemployment rate:
   a. The length of time workers are eligible to receive unemployment insurance payments doubles.
   b. The minimum wage is abolished.
   c. Most U.S. workers join labor unions.
   d. More companies make information on job openings easily available on Internet job sites.
9. Why do you think the minimum wage was set at only $0.25 per hour in 1938? Wouldn't this wage have been well below the equilibrium wage?
10. An economic consultant studies the labor policies of a firm where it is difficult to monitor workers and prepares a report in which she recommends that the firm raise employee wages. At a meeting of the firm's managers to discuss the report, one manager makes the following argument: "I think the wages we are paying are fine. As long as enough people are willing to work here at the wages we are currently paying, why should we raise them?" What argument can the economic consultant make to justify her advice that the firm should increase its wages?
11. In an article on the conditions in the labor market, two business reporters remarked that the unemployment rate "typically rises months after the economy rebounds." What do they mean by the phrase "the economy rebounds"? Why would the unemployment rate be rising if the economy is rebounding?
    Source: Vince Golle and Terry Barrett, "Hiring Picks Up, Factories Expand," Bloomberg News, April 1, 2002.
12. Between December 2001 and January 2002, the total number of people employed and the unemployment rate both fell. Briefly explain how this is possible.
13. The following appeared in a *Business Week* article:

    > [The household survey for January 2002] from the Bureau of Labor Statistics showed that the labor force participation rate—the percentage of people either employed or actively job-hunting—fell by 0.8 percentage points over the past year, to 66.4%. . . . The sharp decline suggests the published unemployment rate understates the damage to the labor market."

    Why would a fall in the labor force participation rate indicate that the unemployment rate is not doing a good job reflecting labor market conditions?
14. **[Related to *Don't Let This Happen to You!*]** Briefly explain whether you agree or disagree with the following statement: "I don't believe the government price statistics. The CPI for 2004 was 189, but I know that the inflation rate couldn't have been as high as 89 percent in 2004."
15. **[Related to *Solved Problem 12-2*]** Use the information in the following table to determine the percentage changes in the U.S. and French *real* minimum wages between 1956 and 2004.

	UNITED STATES		FRANCE	
YEAR	MINIMUM WAGE (DOLLARS PER HOUR)	CPI	MINIMUM WAGE (EUROS PER HOUR)	CPI
1956	$1.00	27	0.19 euros	10
2004	5.15	189	7.61 euros	110

Does it matter for your answer that you have not been told the base year for the U.S. CPI or the French CPI? Was the percentage increase in the price level greater in the United States or in France during these years?

Source: For 1956 French data: John M. Abowd, Francis Kramarz, Thomas Lemieux, and David N. Margolis, "Minimum Wages and Youth Employment in France and the United States," in D. Blanchflower and R. Freeman, eds., *Youth Employment and Joblessness in Advanced Countries*, Chicago: University of Chicago Press, 1999, pp. 427–472 (the value for the minimum wage is given in francs; it was converted to euros at a conversion rate of 1 euro = 6.55957 francs); for 2004 French data: Insee online data bank (www.insee.fr); and for U.S. values both years: U.S. Department of Labor and U.S. Bureau of Labor Statistics.

16. **[Related to *Solved Problem 12-2*]** The Great Depression was the worst economic disaster in U.S. history in terms of declines in real GDP and increases in the unemployment rate. Use the data in the following table to calculate the percentage decline in real GDP between 1929 and 1933:

YEAR	NOMINAL GDP (BILLIONS OF DOLLARS)	GDP PRICE DEFLATOR (2000 = 100)
1929	103.6	11.9
1933	56.4	8.9

17. Consider a simple economy that produces only three products. Use the information in the following table to calculate the inflation rate for 2006 as measured by the consumer price index:

		BASE YEAR (1999)	2005	2006
PRODUCT	QUANTITY	PRICE	PRICE	PRICE
Haircuts	2	$10.00	$11.00	$16.20
Hamburgers	10	2.00	2.45	2.40
DVDs	6	15.00	15.00	14.00

18. The following table shows the top 10 films of all time through 2004, measured by box office receipts in the United States, as well as several other films farther down the list:

RANK	FILM	TOTAL BOX OFFICE RECEIPTS	YEAR RELEASED	CPI
1	*Titanic*	$600,779,824	1997	161
2	*Star Wars*	460,935,655	1977	61
3	*Shrek 2*	436,471,036	2004	189
4	*E.T. the Extra-Terrestrial*	434,949,459	1982	97
5	*Star Wars: Episode I—The Phantom Menace*	431,065,444	1999	167
6	*Spider-Man*	403,706,375	2002	180
7	*Lord of the Rings: The Return of the King*	377,019,252	2003	184
8	*Spider-Man 2*	373,377,893	2004	189
9	*The Passion of the Christ*	370,270,943	2004	189
10	*Jurassic Park*	356,784,000	1993	145
31	*Jaws*	260,000,000	1975	54
62	*Gone with the Wind*	198,655,278	1939	14
70	*Snow White and the Seven Dwarfs*	184,208,842	1937	14
110	*The Sound of Music*	163,214,286	1965	32
129	*One Hundred and One Dalmatians*	153,000,000	1961	30

The CPI in 2004 was 189. Use this information and the data in the table to calculate the box office receipts for each film in 2004 dollars. Assume that each film generated all of its box office receipts during the year it was released. Use your results to prepare a new list of the top 10 films based on their earnings in 2004 dollars. (Some of the films, such as the first *Star Wars* film, *Gone with the Wind,* and *Snow White and the Seven Dwarfs,* were re-released several times, so their receipts were actually earned during several different years, but we will ignore that complication.)

Source: IMBd online database, **www.imdb.com**.

19. The *Wall Street Journal* publishes an index of the prices of luxury homes in various cities. Here are the indexes for January 2001 and January 2002:

CITY	JANUARY 2001	JANUARY 2002
New York	113.8	120.9
San Francisco	122.4	113.3
Detroit	104.6	108.9
Boston	118.7	121.6

a. In which city did the prices of luxury homes increase the most during this year?

b. Can you determine on the basis of these numbers which city had the most expensive luxury homes in January 2002?

20. **[Related to *Don't Let This Happen to You!*]** The following appeared in an article in the Allentown *Morning Call:*

> Inflation in the Lehigh Valley during the first quarter of [the year] was less than half the national rate. . . . So, unlike much of the nation, the fear here is deflation—when prices sink so low the CPI drops below zero.

Do you agree with the reporter's definition of deflation?

21. Describing the situation in England in 1920, the historian Robert Skidelsky wrote the following:

> Who would not borrow at 4 per cent a year, with prices going up 4 per cent a *month?*

What was the real interest rate paid by borrowers in this situation? (*Hint:* What is the annual inflation rate, if the monthly inflation rate is 4 percent?)

Source: Robert Skidelsky, *John Maynard Keynes: Volume 2, The Economist as Saviour, 1920–1937,* New York: The Penguin Press, 1992, p. 39, emphasis in original.

22. During the late nineteenth century in the United States, many farmers borrowed heavily to buy land. During most of the period between 1870 and the mid-1890s, the United States experienced mild deflation: The price level declined each year. Many farmers engaged in political protests during these years and deflation was often a subject of their protests. Explain why farmers would have felt burdened by deflation.

chapter thirteen

Economic Growth, the Financial System, and Business Cycles

Growth and the Business Cycle at the Ford Motor Company

The Ford Motor Company is a little over 100 years old. In that time, its experiences have often mirrored those of the U.S. economy. Two key macroeconomic facts are that in the long run the U.S. economy has experienced economic growth and in the short run the economy has experienced a series of business cycles. Living standards in the United States have increased enormously because, in the long run, growth in the production of goods and services has been faster than growth in population. But the increase in living standards has been interrupted by periods of business cycle recession during which production of goods and services has declined. Ford has also experienced growth over the long run, but has been greatly affected by the business cycle.

Economic growth is produced by technological progress that makes possible the production of greater quantities of goods and services, and—even more importantly—the production of new and better goods and services. When the Ford Motor Company was established in 1903, personal transportation relied largely on electric street cars and horse-drawn carriages and trucks. Horse-drawn carriages and trucks were slow, unreliable, and uncomfortable. Cleaning up after the horses was itself a major problem in big cities. Ford's first cars were not a huge step forward because they were relatively slow, unreliable, difficult to repair, and expensive. In 1908, Ford introduced one of the most innovative products in business history—the Model T. Because the Model T used parts that were interchangeable, it was much easier to repair than any previous car. When Henry Ford began producing Model Ts on a moving assembly line, he increased the number of cars his workers could produce each day to such an extent that his costs fell dramatically, and he made a profit even after cutting the price as low as $250 per car.

The widespread use of automobiles has not been an unmixed blessing, of course, as shown by the toll of highway deaths and air pollution. But the speed, efficiency, and reliability of gasoline-powered cars and trucks dramatically improved transpor-

tation, greatly contributing to the economic growth of the twentieth century. The personal mobility offered by automobiles improved the quality of life for millions by, among other things, making it possible to escape from crowded apartment houses in the city to single-family homes in the suburbs that had sprung up around every major city by the 1920s.

Ford remains a major force in the U.S. economy, earning the fourth-highest revenues of any U.S. firm in 2004. In 2005, however, Ford suffered losses as an increase in gasoline prices caused fewer consumers to buy SUVs. The firm also remains vulnerable to the effects of the business cycle. Early in its history, during the recession of 1920–21 and again during the Great Depression of the 1930s, Ford came close to bankruptcy as falling sales led to large losses. More recent business cycle recessions have also hurt the firm's sales. During 2000, Ford sold 7.4 million vehicles worldwide, including almost 5 million in North America. The recession that began in 2001 cut sharply into the demand for Ford's cars. By 2003, sales had declined to 6.7 million vehicles worldwide and to just over 4 million in North America. In this chapter, we will look at long-run growth and the business cycle and why they are important for individual firms and the economy as a whole. *An Inside Look* on page 414 discusses the growth of the Chinese automobile industry.

LEARNING OBJECTIVES

After studying this chapter, you should be able to:

1. Discuss the importance of long-run economic growth.
2. Discuss the role of the financial system in facilitating long-run economic growth.
3. Explain what happens during a business cycle.

A key measure of the success of any economy is its ability to increase production of goods and services faster than the growth in population. Increasing production faster than population growth is the only way that the standard of living of the average person in a country can increase. Unfortunately, many economies around the world are not growing at all, or are growing very slowly. In many countries in sub-Saharan Africa, living standards are barely higher, or in some cases lower, than they were 50 years ago. Most people in these countries live in the same grinding poverty as their ancestors. In the United States and other developed countries, however, living standards increase during most years and are much higher than they were 50 years ago. An important macroeconomic question is why some countries grow much faster than others.

As we will see, one determinant of economic growth is the ability of firms to expand their operations, buy additional equipment, train workers, and adopt new technologies. To carry out these activities, firms must acquire funds from households, either directly through financial markets—such as the stock and bond markets—or indirectly through financial intermediaries—such as banks. Financial markets and financial intermediaries together comprise the *financial system.* In this chapter, we will present an overview of the financial system and see how funds flow from households to firms through the *market for loanable funds.*

Dating back to at least the early nineteenth century, the U.S. economy has experienced periods of expanding production and employment followed by periods of recession during which production and employment decline. As we noted in Chapter 11, these alternating periods of expansion and recession are called the **business cycle.** The business cycle is not uniform: Each period of expansion is not the same length, nor is each period of recession, but every period of expansion in American history has been followed by a period of recession, and every period of recession has been followed by a period of expansion.

Business cycle Alternating periods of economic expansion and economic recession.

In this chapter, we begin the exploration of these two key aspects of macroeconomics—the long-run growth that has steadily raised living standards in the United States and the short-run fluctuations of the business cycle.

1 LEARNING OBJECTIVE

Discuss the importance of long-run economic growth.

Long-Run Economic Growth Is the Key to Rising Living Standards

Most people in the United States, Western Europe, Japan, and other advanced countries expect that over time their standard of living will improve. They expect that year after year firms will introduce new and improved products, new prescription drugs and better surgical techniques will overcome more diseases, and their ability to afford these goods and services will increase. For most people, these are reasonable expectations.

In 1900, the United States was already enjoying the highest standard of living in the world. Yet in that year, only 3 percent of U.S. homes had electricity, and only 15 percent had indoor flush toilets. Diseases such as smallpox, typhus, dysentery, and cholera were

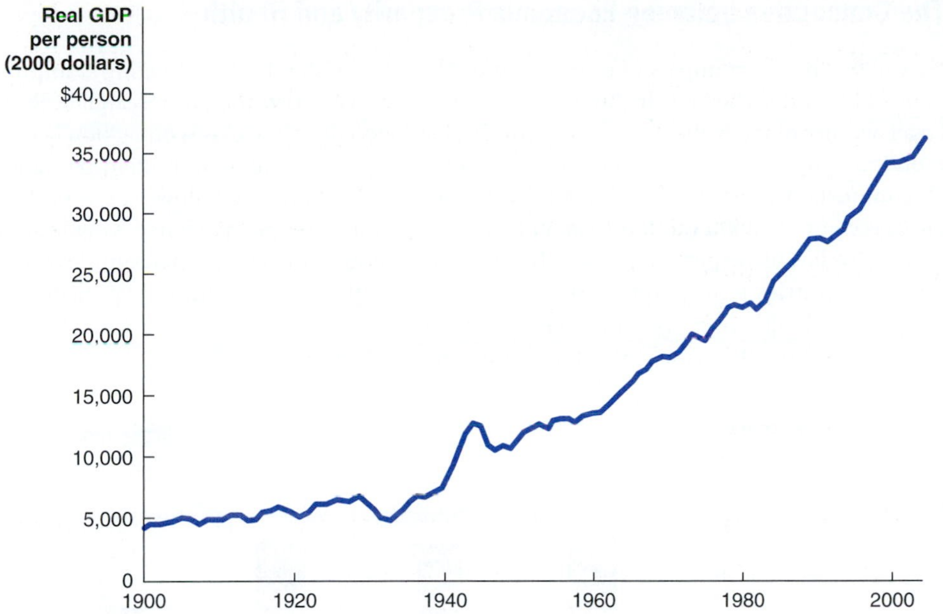

FIGURE 13-1

The Growth in Real GDP per capita, 1900–2004

Measured in 2000 dollars, real GDP per capita in the United States grew from about $4,300 in 1900 to about $37,000 in 2004. The average American in the year 2004 could buy more than eight times as many goods and services as the average American in the year 1900.

Source: Real GDP, 1900–1928: Louis Johnston and Samuel H. Williamson, "The Annual Real and Nominal GDP for the United States, 1789–Present," Economic History Services, March 2004, www.eh.net/hmit/gdp; Real GDP, 1929–2004: U.S. Bureau of Economic Analysis.

still menacing the health of Americans. In 1900, 5,000 of the 45,000 children born in Chicago died before their first birthday. In 1900, there were, of course, no televisions, radios, computers, air conditioners, or refrigerators. Many homes were heated in the winter by burning coal, which contributed to the severe pollution that fouled the air of most large cities. There were no modern appliances, so most women worked inside the home at least 80 hours per week. The typical American homemaker in 1900 baked a half ton of bread per year.

Long-run economic growth The process by which rising productivity increases the average standard of living.

The process of **long-run economic growth** brought the typical American from the standard of living of 1900 to the standard of living of today. The best measure of the standard of living is real GDP per person, which is usually referred to as *real GDP per capita*. So, we measure long-run economic growth by increases in real GDP per capita. We use real GDP rather than nominal GDP to adjust for changes in the price level over time. Figure 13-1 shows the growth in real GDP per capita in the United States from 1900 to 2004.

The values in Figure 13-1 are measured in prices of the year 2000, so they represent constant amounts of purchasing power. In 1900, real GDP per capita was about $4,300. Just over a century later, in 2004, it had risen to about $37,000, which means that the average American in 2004 could purchase more than eight times as many goods and services as the average American in 1900. Large as it is, this increase in real GDP per capita actually understates the true increase in the standard of living of Americans in 2004 compared with 1900. Many of today's goods and services were not available in 1900. For example, if you lived in 1900 and became ill with a serious infection, you would have been unable to purchase antibiotics to treat your illness no matter how high your income. You might have died from an illness for which even a very poor person in today's society could receive effective medical treatment. Of course, the quantity of goods and services that a person can buy is not a perfect measure of how happy or contented that person may be. The level of pollution, the level of crime, spiritual well-being, and many other factors ignored in calculating GDP contribute to a person's happiness. Nevertheless, economists rely heavily on comparisons of real GDP per capita because it is the best means of comparing the performance of one economy over time or the performance of different economies at any particular time.

13-1 Making the Connection

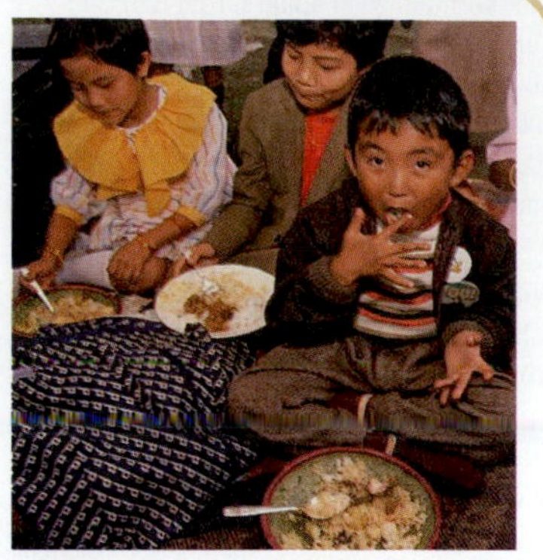

Because of technological advance, these children in India will live longer, be healthier, and work less than their parents and grandparents.

The Connection between Economic Prosperity and Health

We can see the direct impact of economic growth on living standards by looking at improvements in health in the high-income countries over the past 100 years. The research of Robert Fogel, winner of the Nobel Prize in Economics, has highlighted the close connection between economic growth, improvements in technology, and improvements in human physiology. One important measure of health is life expectancy at birth. As the following graph shows, life expectancy in 1900 was less than 50 years in the United States, the United Kingdom, and France. Today, life expectancy is nearly 80 years. Although life expectancies in the lowest-income countries remain very short, some countries that have begun to experience economic growth have seen dramatic increases in life expectancies. For example, life expectancy in India has more than doubled from 27 years in 1900 to 64 years today.

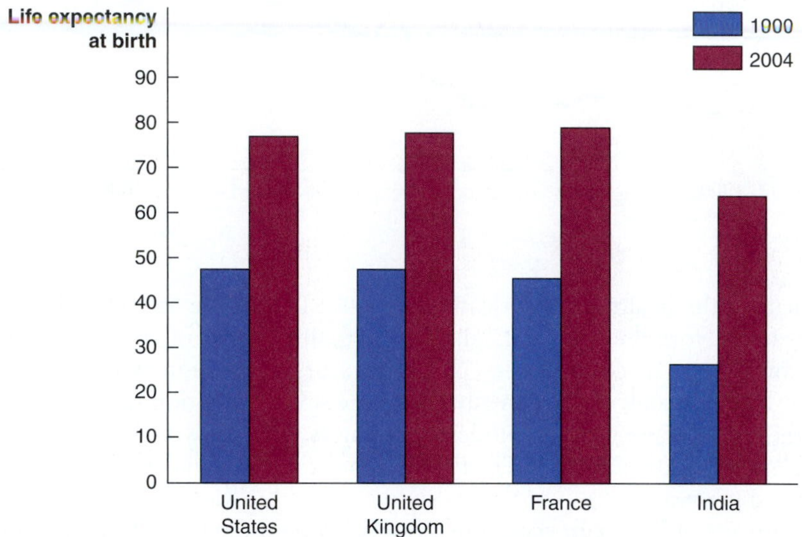

Sources: For 1900: Robert William Fogel, *The Escape from Hunger and Premature Death, 1700–2100,* New York: Cambridge University Press, 2004, p. 2; for 2004: U.S. Central Intelligence Agency, *The World Factbook 2004,* online version.

Many economists believe there is a link between health and economic growth. In the United States and Western Europe during the nineteenth century, improvements in agricultural technology and rising incomes led to dramatic improvements in the nutrition of the average person. The development of the germ theory of disease and technological progress in the purification of water in the late nineteenth century led to sharp declines in sickness from waterborne diseases. As people became taller, stronger, and less susceptible to disease, they also became more productive. Today, economists studying economic development have put increasing emphasis on the need for low-income countries to reduce disease and increase nutrition if they are to experience economic growth.

Many researchers believe that the state of human physiology will continue to improve as technology advances. In the high-income countries, life expectancy at birth is expected to rise from about 80 years today to about 90 years by the middle of the twenty-first century. Technological advance will continue to reduce the average number of hours worked per day and the number of years the average person spends in the paid workforce. Individuals spend about 10 hours per day sleeping, eating, and bathing. Their remaining "discretionary hours" are divided between paid work and leisure. The following graph is based on estimates by Robert Fogel that contrast how individuals in the United States will divide their time in 2040 compared with 1880 and 1995.

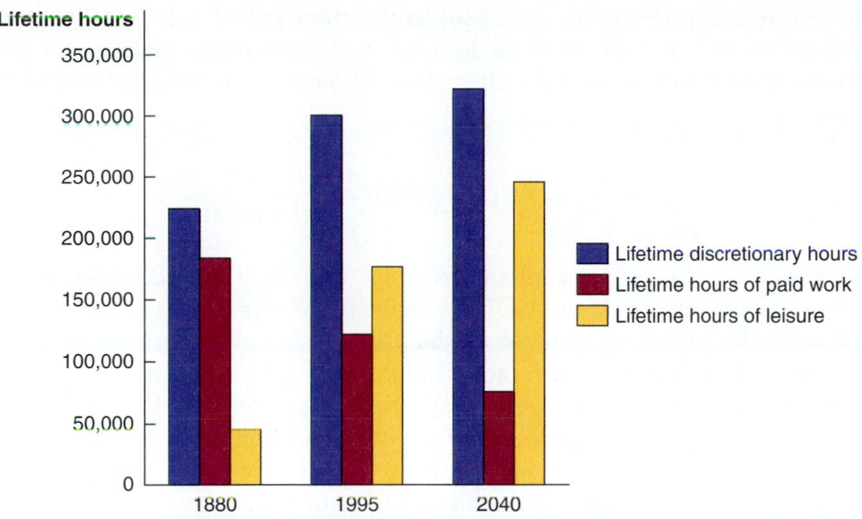

Not only will technology and economic growth allow people in the near future to live longer lives, but a much smaller fraction of those lives will need to be spent at paid work.

Source: Robert William Fogel, *The Escape from Hunger and Premature Death, 1700–2100,* New York: Cambridge University Press, 2004; second graph adapted from Table 4.2, p. 71.

Calculating Growth Rates and the Rule of 70

The growth rate of real GDP or real GDP per capita during a particular year is equal to the percentage change from the previous year. For example, measured in prices of the year 2000, real GDP equaled \$10,321 billion in 2003 and rose to \$10,756 billion in 2004. We calculate the growth of real GDP in 2004 as:

$$\frac{(\$10{,}756 \text{ bllion} - \$10{,}321 \text{ billion})}{\$10{,}321 \text{ billion}} \times 100 = 4.2\%.$$

For longer periods of time, we can use the *average annual growth rate.* For example, real GDP in the United States was \$1,777 billion in 1950 and \$10,756 billion in 2004. To find the average annual growth rate during this 54-year period, we compute the growth rate that would result in \$1,777 billion growing to \$10,756 billion over 54 years. In this case the growth rate is 3.4 percent. That is, if \$1,777 billion grows at an average rate of 3.4 percent per year, after 54 years it will have grown to \$10,756 billion.

For shorter periods of time, we get approximately the same answer by averaging the growth rate for each year. For example, real GDP in the United States grew by 1.6 percent in 2002, 2.7 percent in 2003, and 4.2 percent in 2004. So, the average annual growth rate of real GDP for the period 2002–2004 was 2.8 percent, which is the average of the three annual growth rates:

$$\frac{1.6\% + 2.7\% + 4.2\%}{3} = 2.8\%.$$

When discussing long-run economic growth, we will usually shorten "average annual growth rate" to "growth rate."

We can judge how rapidly an economic variable is growing by calculating the number of years it would take to double. For example, if real GDP per capita in a country doubles, say, every 20 years, most people in the country will experience significant increases in their standard of living over the course of their lives. If real GDP per capita doubles only every 100 years, increases in the standard of living will be too slow to notice. One easy way to calculate approximately how many years it will take real GDP per capita to double is to use the *rule of 70.* The formula for the rule of 70 is as follows:

$$\text{Number of years to double} = \frac{70}{\text{Growth rate}}.$$

For example, if real GDP per capita is growing at a rate of 5 percent per year, it will double in 70/5 = 14 years. If real GDP per capita is growing at the rate of 2 percent per year, it will take 70/2 = 35 years to double. These examples illustrate an important point: Small differences in growth rates can have large effects on how rapidly the standard of living in a country increases. Finally, notice that the rule of 70 applies not just to growth in real GDP per capita but to growth in any variable. For example, if you invest $1,000 in the stock market and your investment grows at an average annual rate of 7 percent, your investment will double to $2,000 in 10 years.

What Determines the Rate of Long-Run Growth?

Labor productivity The quantity of goods and services that can be produced by one worker or by one hour of work.

A key point to understand about economic growth is that *increases in real GDP per capita depend on increases in labor productivity.* **Labor productivity** is the quantity of goods and services that can be produced by one worker or by one hour of work. In analyzing long-run growth, economists usually measure labor productivity as output per hour of work to avoid fluctuations in the length of the workday and in the fraction of the population employed. If the quantity of goods and services consumed by the average person is to increase, the quantity of goods and services produced per hour of work must also increase. Why in 2004 was the average American able to consume more than eight times as many goods and services as the average American in 1900? Because the average American worker in 2004 was more than eight times as productive as the average American worker in 1900.

If increases in labor productivity are the key to long-run economic growth, what causes labor productivity to increase? Economists believe two key factors determine labor productivity: the quantity of capital per hour worked and the level of technology. Therefore, economic growth occurs if the quantity of capital per hour worked increases and if technological change occurs.

Capital Manufactured goods that are used to produce other goods and services.

INCREASES IN CAPITAL PER HOUR WORKED Workers today in high-income countries such as the United States have more physical capital available than workers in low-income countries or workers in the high-income countries of a hundred years ago. Recall that **capital** refers to manufactured goods that are used to produce other goods and services. Examples of capital are computers, factory buildings, machine tools, warehouses, and trucks. The total amount of physical capital available in a country is known as the country's *capital stock.*

As the capital stock per hour worked increases, worker productivity increases. A secretary with a personal computer can produce more documents per day than a secretary who has only a typewriter. A worker with a backhoe can excavate more earth than a worker who has only a shovel.

Human capital The accumulated knowledge and skills workers acquire from education and training or from their life experiences.

Human capital refers to the accumulated knowledge and skills workers acquire from education and training or from their life experiences. For example, workers with a college education generally have more skills and are more productive than workers who have only a high school degree. Increases in human capital are particularly important in stimulating economic growth.

TECHNOLOGICAL CHANGE Economic growth depends more on *technological change* than on increases in capital per hour worked. Technology refers to the processes a firm uses to turn inputs into outputs of goods and services. Technological change is an increase in the quantity of output firms can produce using a given quantity of inputs. Technological change can come from many sources. For example, a firm's managers may rearrange a factory floor or the layout of a retail store, thereby increasing production and sales. Most technological change, however, is embodied in new machinery, equipment, or software.

A very important point is that just accumulating more inputs—such as labor, capital, and natural resources—will not ensure that an economy experiences economic growth unless technological change also occurs. For example, the Soviet Union failed to maintain a high rate of economic growth, even though it continued to increase the quantity of capital available per hour worked, because it experienced very little technological change.

In implementing technological change, *entrepreneurs* are of crucial importance. Recall from Chapter 2 that an entrepreneur is someone who operates a business, bringing together the factors of production—labor, capital, and natural resources—to produce goods and services. In a market economy, entrepreneurs make the crucial decisions about whether or not to introduce new technology to produce better or lower-cost products. Entrepreneurs also decide whether to allocate the firm's resources to research and development that can result in new technologies. One of the difficulties centrally planned economies have in sustaining economic growth is that managers employed by the government are usually much slower to develop and adopt new technologies than entrepreneurs in a market system.

SOLVED PROBLEM 13-1

The Role of Technological Change in Growth

LEARNING OBJECTIVE ① Discuss the importance of long-run economic growth.

Between 1960 and 1995, real GDP per capita in Singapore grew at an average annual rate of 6.2 percent. This very rapid growth rate results in the level of real GDP per capita doubling about every 11.5 years. In 1995, Alywn Young of the University of Chicago published an article in which he argued that Singapore's growth depended more on increases in capital per hour worked, increases in the labor force participation rate, and the transfer of workers from agricultural to nonagricultural jobs than on technological change. If Young's analysis was correct, predict what was likely to happen to Singapore's growth rate in the years after 1995.

Solving the Problem:

Step 1: Review the chapter material. This problem is about the determinants of the rate of long-run growth, so you may want to review the section "What Determines the Rate of Long-Run Growth?" which begins on page 394.

Step 2: Predict what happened to the growth rate in Singapore after 1995. As countries begin to develop, they often experience an increase in the labor force participation rate, as workers who are not part of the paid labor force respond to rising wage rates. Many workers also leave the agricultural sector—where output per hour worked is often low—for the nonagricultural sector. These changes will increase real GDP per capita, but they are "one-shot" changes that eventually will come to an end, as the labor force participation rate and the fraction of the labor force outside of agriculture both approach the levels found in high-income countries. Similarly, as we already noted, increases in capital per hour worked cannot sustain high rates of economic growth, unless accompanied by technological change.

We can conclude that Singapore was unlikely to sustain its high growth rates in the years after 1995. In fact, from 1996 to 2004, the growth of real GDP per capita slowed to an average rate of 2.5 percent per year. Although this growth rate is comparable to those experienced in high-income countries, such as the United States, it leads to a doubling of real GDP per capita only every 28 years, rather than every 11.5 years.

Source: Alwyn Young, "The Tyranny of Numbers: Confronting the Statistical Realities of the East Asian Growth Experience," *Quarterly Journal of Economics*, Vol. 110, No. 3 (August 1995), pp. 641–680.

***YOUR TURN:* For more practice, do related problem 8 on page 417 at the end of this chapter.**

Finally, an additional requirement for economic growth is that the government provides secure rights to private property. As we saw in Chapter 2, a market system cannot function unless rights to private property are secure. In addition, the government can help the market work and aid economic growth by establishing an independent court system that enforces contracts between private individuals. Many economists would also say the government has a role in facilitating the development of an efficient financial system, as well as systems of education, transportation, and communication. Economist Richard Sylla of New York University has argued that every country that has experienced economic growth first experienced a "financial revolution." For example, before the United States was able to experience significant economic growth in the early nineteenth century, the country's banking and monetary systems were reformed under the guidance of Alexander Hamilton, the first Secretary of the Treasury. Without supportive government policies, long-run economic growth is unlikely.

13-2 Making the Connection

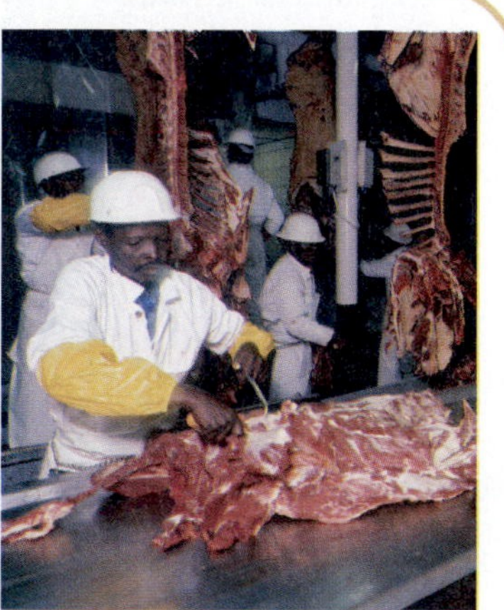

Firms like the Botswana Meat Company benefit from government policies that protect private property.

What Explains Rapid Economic Growth in Botswana?

Economic growth in much of sub-Saharan Africa has been very slow. As desperately poor as most of these countries were in 1960, some are even poorer today. Growth rates in one country in this region stand out, however, as being exceptionally rapid. The graph on the facing page shows the average annual growth rate in real GDP per capita between 1960 and 2000 for Botswana and the six most populous sub-Saharan countries. Botswana's average annual growth rate over this 40-year period was almost five times as great as that of Kenya, which was the second-fastest-growing country in the group.

What explains Botswana's rapid growth rate? Several factors have been important. Botswana avoided the civil wars that plagued other African countries during these years. The country also benefited from earnings from diamond exports. But many economists believe the pro-growth policies of its government are the most important reason for the country's success. Economists Shantayanan Devarajan of the World Bank, William Easterly of New York University, and Howard Pack of the University of Pennsylvania have summarized these policies:

> The government [of Botswana] made it clear it would protect private property rights. It was a "government of cattlemen" who were attuned to commercial interests. . . . The relative political stability and relatively low corruption also made Botswana a favorable location for investment. Botswana's relatively high level of press freedom and democracy (continuing a pre-colonial tradition that held chiefs responsible to tribal members) held the government responsible for any economic policy mistakes.

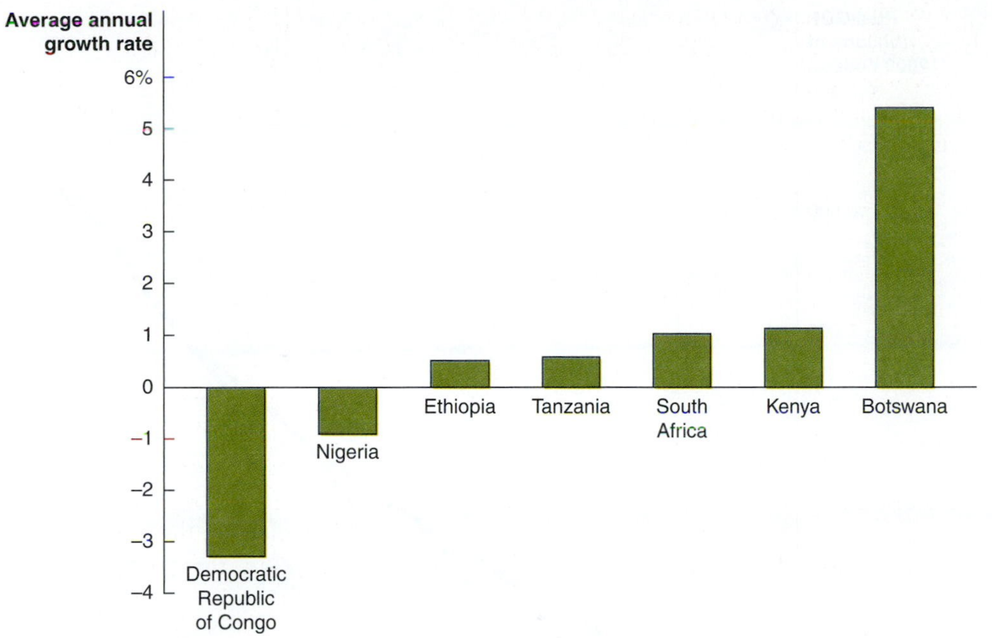

Source: Authors' calculations from data in Alan Heston, Robert Summers, and Bettina Aten, Penn World Table Version 6.1, Center for International Comparisons at the University of Pennsylvania (CICUP), October 2002.

These policies—protecting private property, avoiding political instability and corruption, and allowing press freedom and democracy—may seem a straightforward recipe for providing an environment in which economic growth can occur. Unfortunately, in practice, these are policies many countries have difficulty implementing successfully.

Source: Shantayanan Devarajan, William Easterly, and Howard Pack, "Low Investment Is Not the Constraint on African Development," *Economic Development and Cultural Change*, Vol. 51, No. 3 (April 2003), pp. 547–571.

Potential Real GDP

Because economists take a long-run perspective in discussing economic growth, the concept of *potential GDP* is useful. **Potential GDP** is the level of GDP attained when all firms are producing at capacity. Every firm has a certain capacity to produce goods and services. The capacity of a firm is *not* the maximum output the firm is capable of producing. A Ford assembly plant could operate 24 hours per day for 52 weeks per year and would be at its maximum production level. The plant's capacity, however, is measured by its production when operating on normal hours, using a normal workforce. If all firms in the economy were operating at capacity, the level of total production of final goods and services would equal potential GDP. As the labor force grows over time, new factories and office buildings are built, new machinery and equipment are installed, and technological change takes place, and potential GDP will increase.

Potential GDP The level of GDP attained when all firms are producing at capacity.

Growth in potential real GDP is estimated to be about 3.5 percent per year. In other words, each year the capacity of the economy to produce final goods and services expands by 3.5 percent. The *actual* level of GDP may increase by more or less than 3.5 percent as the economy moves through the business cycle. Figure 13-2 shows movements in actual and potential real GDP for the years since 1950. The smooth light blue line represents potential real GDP and the dark blue line represents actual real GDP.

FIGURE 13-2

Actual and Potential Real GDP

Potential real GDP increases every year as the labor force and the capital stock grow and technological change occurs. The smooth light blue line represents potential real GDP and the dark blue line represents actual real GDP. Because of the business cycle, actual real GDP has sometimes been greater than potential real GDP and sometimes less.

Sources: Potential GDP: Congressional Budget Office, "Spreadsheets for Selected Estimates and Projections," January 2005; Real GDP: Bureau of Economic Analysis.

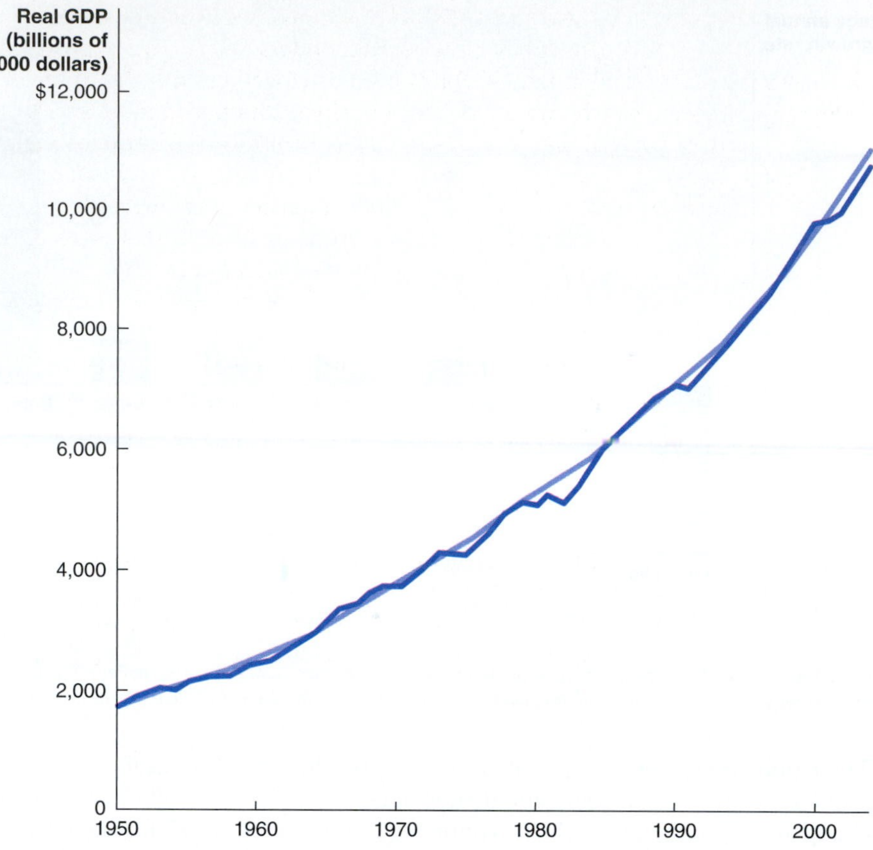

② LEARNING OBJECTIVE

Discuss the role of the financial system in facilitating long-run economic growth.

Saving, Investment, and the Financial System

The process of economic growth depends on the ability of firms to expand their operations, buy additional equipment, train workers, and adopt new technologies. Firms can finance some of these activities from *retained earnings,* which are profits that are reinvested in the firm rather than taken out of the firm and paid to the firm's owners. For many firms, retained earnings are not sufficient to finance the rapid expansion required in economies experiencing high rates of economic growth. Firms acquire funds from households, either directly through financial markets—such as the stock and bond markets—or indirectly through financial intermediaries—such as banks. Financial markets and financial intermediaries together comprise the **financial system.** Without a well-functioning financial system, economic growth is impossible because firms will be unable to expand and adopt new technologies. As we noted earlier, no country without a well-developed financial system has been able to sustain high levels of economic growth.

Financial system The system of financial markets and financial intermediaries through which firms acquire funds from households.

An Overview of the Financial System

The financial system channels funds from savers to borrowers and channels returns on the borrowed funds back to savers. Recall from Chapter 5 that in *financial markets,* such as the stock market or the bond market, firms raise funds by selling financial securities directly to savers. A financial security is a document—sometimes in electronic form—that states the terms under which funds pass from the buyer of the security—who is lending funds—to the seller. *Stocks* are financial securities that represent partial ownership of a firm. If you buy one share of stock in General Electric, you become one of millions of owners of that firm. *Bonds* are financial securities that represent promises to repay a fixed amount of funds. When General Electric sells a bond, the firm promises to pay the purchaser of the bond an interest payment each year for the term of the bond, as well as a final payment of the amount of the loan.

Financial intermediaries, such as banks, mutual funds, pension funds, and insurance companies, act as go-betweens for borrowers and lenders. When you deposit funds in your checking account, the bank may lend the funds (together with the funds of other savers) to an entrepreneur who wants to start a business. Suppose Lena wants to open a laundry. Rather than you lending money directly to Lena's Laundry, the bank acts as a go-between for you and Lena. Intermediaries pool the funds of many small savers to lend to many individual borrowers. The intermediaries pay interest to savers in exchange for the use of savers' funds and earn a profit by lending money to borrowers and charging borrowers a higher rate of interest on the loans. For example, a bank might pay you as a depositor a 3 percent rate of interest, while it lends the money to Lena's Laundry at a 6 percent rate of interest.

Banks, mutual funds, pension funds, and insurance companies also make investments in stocks and bonds on behalf of savers. For example, *mutual funds* sell shares to savers and then use the funds to buy a portfolio of stocks, bonds, mortgages, and other financial securities. Mutual funds are either closed-end or open-end funds. In closed-end mutual funds, the mutual fund company issues shares that investors may buy and sell in financial markets, like shares of stock issued by corporations. More common are open-end mutual funds, which issue shares that the mutual fund company will buy back—or redeem—at a price that reflects the underlying value of the financial securities owned by the fund. Large mutual fund companies, such as Fidelity, Vanguard, and Dreyfus, offer many alternative stock and bond funds. Some funds hold a wide range of stocks or bonds; others specialize in securities issued by a particular industry or sector, such as technology; and others invest as an index fund in a fixed market basket of securities such as shares of the Standard and Poor's 500 firms. Over the past 30 years, the role of mutual funds in the financial system has increased dramatically. By 2005, competition among hundreds of mutual fund firms gave investors thousands of funds from which to choose.

In addition to matching households that have excess funds with firms that want to borrow funds, the financial system provides three key services for savers and borrowers: risk sharing, liquidity, and information. *Risk* is the chance that the value of a financial security will change relative to what you expect. For example, you may buy a share of stock in Google at a price of $100, only to have the price fall to $20. Most individual savers are not gamblers and seek a steady return on their savings rather than erratic swings between high and low earnings. The financial system provides risk sharing by allowing savers to spread their money among many financial investments. For example, you can divide your money among a bank certificate of deposit, individual bonds, and a mutual fund.

Liquidity is the ease with which a financial security can be exchanged for money. The financial system provides the service of liquidity by providing savers with markets in which they can sell their holdings of financial securities. For example, savers can easily sell their holdings of the stocks and bonds issued by large corporations on the major stock and bond markets.

A third service that the financial system provides savers is the collection and communication of *information,* or facts about borrowers and expectations about returns on financial securities. For example, Lena's Laundry may want to borrow $10,000 from you. Finding out what Lena intends to do with the funds and how likely she is to pay you back may be costly and time-consuming. By depositing $10,000 in the bank, you are, in effect, allowing the bank to gather this information for you. Because banks specialize in gathering information on borrowers, they are able to do it faster and at a lower cost than can individual savers. The financial system plays an important role in communicating information. If you read a newspaper headline announcing that an automobile firm has invented a car with an engine that runs on water, how would you determine the effect of this discovery on the firm's profits? Financial markets do that job for you by incorporating information into the prices of stocks, bonds, and other financial securities. In this example, the expectation of higher future profits would boost the prices of the automobile firm's stock and bonds.

The Macroeconomics of Saving and Investment

As we have seen, the funds available to firms through the financial system come from saving. When firms use funds to purchase machinery, factories, and office buildings, they are engaging in investment. In this section, we explore the macroeconomics of saving and investment. A key point we will develop is that *the total value of saving in the economy must equal the total value of investment.* We saw in Chapter 11 that *national income accounting* refers to the methods the Bureau of Economic Analysis uses to keep track of total production and total income in the economy. We can use some relationships from national income accounting to understand why total saving must equal total investment.

We begin with the relationship between GDP and its components, consumption (C), investment (I), government purchases (G), and net exports (NX):

$$Y = C + I + G + NX.$$

Remember that GDP is a measure of both total production in the economy and total income.

In an *open economy,* there is interaction with other economies in terms of both trading of goods and services and borrowing and lending. All economies today are open economies, although they vary significantly in the extent of their openness. In a *closed economy,* there is no trading or borrowing and lending with other economies. For simplicity, we will develop the relationship between saving and investment for a closed economy. This allows us to focus on the most important points in a simpler framework.

In a closed economy, net exports are zero, so we can rewrite the relationship between GDP and its components as:

$$Y = C + I + G.$$

If we rearrange this relationship, we have an expression for investment in terms of the other variables:

$$I = Y - C - G.$$

This expression tells us that in a closed economy investment spending is equal to total income minus consumption spending and minus government purchases.

We can also derive an expression for total saving. *Private saving* is equal to what households retain of their income after purchasing goods and services (C) and paying taxes (T). Households receive income for supplying the factors of production to firms. This portion of household income is equal to Y. Households also receive income from government in the form of transfer payments (TR). Recall that transfer payments include Social Security payments and unemployment insurance payments. We can write an expression for private saving (S_{private}):

$$S_{\text{private}} = Y + TR - C - T.$$

The government also engages in saving. *Public saving* (S_{public}) equals the amount of tax revenue the government retains after paying for government purchases and making transfer payments to households:

$$S_{\text{public}} = T - G - TR.$$

So, total saving in the economy (S) is equal to the sum of private saving and public saving:

$$S = S_{\text{private}} + S_{\text{public}},$$

or,

$$S = (Y + TR - C - T) + (T - G - TR)$$

or,

$$S = Y - C - G.$$

The right-hand side of this expression is identical to the expression we derived earlier for investment spending. So, we can conclude that total saving must equal total investment:

$$S = I.$$

When the government spends the same amount that it collects in taxes, there is a *balanced budget.* When the government spends more than it collects in taxes, there is a *budget deficit.* In the case of a deficit, T is less than $G + TR$, which means that public saving is negative. Negative saving is also known as *dissaving.* How can public saving be negative? When the federal government runs a budget deficit, the U.S. Department of the Treasury sells Treasury bonds to borrow the money necessary to fund the gap between taxes and spending. In this case, rather than adding to the total amount of saving available to be borrowed for investment spending, the government is subtracting from it. (Notice that if households borrow more than they save, the total amount of saving will also fall.) With less saving, investment must also be lower. We can conclude that, holding constant all other factors, there is a lower level of investment spending in the economy when there is a budget deficit than when there is a balanced budget.

When the government spends less than it collects in taxes, there is a *budget surplus.* A budget surplus increases public saving and the total level of saving in the economy. A higher level of saving results in a higher level of investment spending. Therefore, holding constant all other factors, there is a higher level of investment spending in the economy when there is a budget surplus than when there is a balanced budget.

The U.S. federal government has experienced dramatic swings in the state of its budget over the past 15 years. In 1992, the federal budget deficit was $297.4 billion. This figure changed to a surplus of $189.5 billion in 2000 and back to a deficit of $406.5 billion in 2004.

The Market for Loanable Funds

We have seen that value of total saving must equal the value of total investment, but we have not yet discussed how this equality actually is brought about in the financial system. We can think of the financial system as being comprised of many markets through which funds flow from lenders to borrowers: the market for certificates of deposit at banks, the market for stocks, the market for bonds, the market for mutual fund shares, and so on. For simplicity, we can combine these markets into a single market for *loanable funds.* In the model of the **market for loanable funds,** the interaction of borrowers and lenders determines the market interest rate and the quantity of loanable funds exchanged.

Market for loanable funds The interaction of borrowers and lenders that determines the market interest rate and the quantity of loanable funds exchanged.

DEMAND AND SUPPLY IN THE LOANABLE FUNDS MARKET The demand for loanable funds is determined by the willingness of firms to borrow money to engage in new investment projects, such as building new factories or engaging in research and development of new products. In determining whether or not to borrow funds, firms compare the return they expect to make on an investment with the interest rate they must pay to borrow the necessary funds. For example, if Home Depot is considering opening several new stores and expects to earn a return of 15 percent on its investment, the investment will be profitable if it can borrow the funds at an interest rate of 10 percent but will not be profitable if the interest rate is 20 percent. In Figure 13-3, the demand for loanable funds is downward sloping because the lower the interest rate, the more investment projects firms can profitably undertake, and the greater the quantity of loanable funds they will demand.

The supply of loanable funds is determined by the willingness of households to save and by the extent of government saving or dissaving. When households save, they reduce the amount of goods and services they can consume and enjoy today. The

FIGURE 13-3

The Market for Loanable Funds

The demand for loanable funds is determined by the willingness of firms to borrow money to engage in new investment projects. The supply of loanable funds is determined by the willingness of households to save, and by the extent of government saving or dissaving. Equilibrium in the market for loanable funds determines the real interest rate and the quantity of loanable funds exchanged.

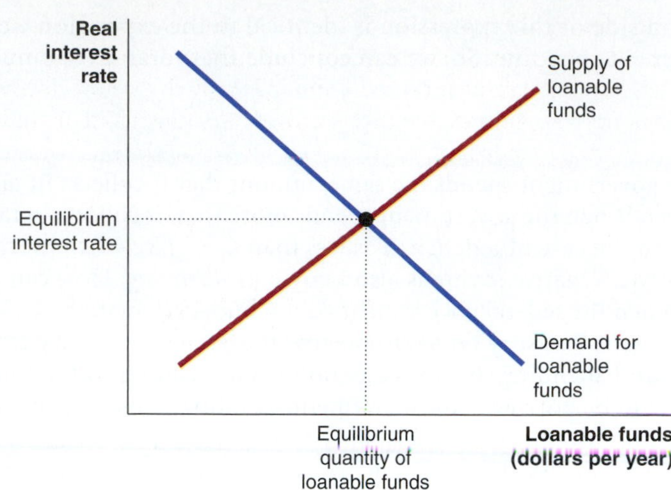

willingness of households to save rather than consume their incomes today will be determined in part by the interest rate they receive when they lend their savings. The higher the interest rate, the greater the reward to saving and the larger the amount of funds households will save. Therefore, the supply curve for loanable funds in Figure 13-3 is upward sloping to reflect the fact that the higher the interest rate, the greater the quantity of saving supplied.

In Chapter 12, we discussed the distinction between the *nominal interest rate* and the *real interest rate.* The nominal interest rate is the stated interest rate on a loan. The real interest rate corrects the nominal interest rate for the impact of inflation and is equal to the nominal interest rate minus the inflation rate. Because both borrowers and lenders are interested in the real interest rate they will receive or pay, equilibrium in the market for loanable funds determines the real interest rate rather than the nominal interest rate.

13-3 Making the Connection

Who was better for economic growth: Scrooge the saver or Scrooge the spender?

Ebenezer Scrooge: Accidental Promoter of Economic Growth?

Ebenezer Scrooge's name has become synonymous with miserliness. Before his reform at the end of Charles Dickens's *A Christmas Carol,* Scrooge is extraordinarily reluctant to spend money. Although he earns a substantial income, he lives in a cold, dark house that he refuses to heat or light properly, and he eats a meager diet of gruel because he refuses to buy more expensive food. Throughout most of the book, Dickens portrays Scrooge's behavior in an unfavorable way. Only at the end of the book, when the reformed Scrooge begins to spend lavishly on himself and others, does Dickens praise his behavior.

As economist Steven Landsburg of the University of Rochester points out, however, economically speaking it may be the pre-reform Scrooge who is more worthy of praise:

> In this whole world, there is nobody more generous than the miser—the man who *could* deplete the world's resources but chooses not to. The only difference between miserliness and philanthropy is that the philanthropist serves a favored few while the miser spreads his largess far and wide.

We can extend Landsburg's discussion to consider whether the actions of the pre-reform Scrooge or the actions of the post-reform Scrooge were more helpful to economic growth. Pre-reform Scrooge spends very little, investing most of his income in the financial markets. These funds became available for firms to borrow to build new factories and carry out research and development. Post-reform Scrooge spends much more—and saves much less. Funds that he had previously saved are now spent on food for Bob Cratchit's family and on "making merry" at Christmas. In other words, the actions of post-reform Scrooge contributed to more consumption goods being produced and fewer investment goods. We can conclude that Scrooge's reform caused economic growth to slow down—if only by a little. The larger point is, of course, that savers provide the funds that are indispensable for the investment spending that economic growth requires, and the only way to save is to not consume.

Source: Steven E. Landsburg, "What I Like About Scrooge," *Slate*, December 9, 2004.

EXPLAINING MOVEMENTS IN SAVING, INVESTMENT, AND INTEREST RATES Equilibrium in the market for loanable funds determines the quantity of loanable funds that will flow from lenders to borrowers each period. It also determines the real interest rate that lenders will receive and that borrowers must pay. We draw the demand curve for loanable funds by holding constant all factors, other than the interest rate, that affect the willingness of borrowers to demand funds. We draw the supply curve by holding constant all factors, other than the interest rate, that affect the willingness of lenders to supply funds. A shift in either the demand curve or the supply curve will change the equilibrium interest rate and the equilibrium quantity of loanable funds.

Suppose, for example, that the profitability of new investment increases due to technological change. Firms will increase their demand for loanable funds. Figure 13-4 shows the impact of an increase in demand in the market for loanable funds. As in the markets for goods and services we studied in Chapter 3, an increase in demand in the market for loanable funds shifts the demand curve to the right. In the new equilibrium, the interest rate increases from i_1 to i_2, and the equilibrium quantity of loanable funds increases from L_1 to L_2. Notice that an increase in the quantity of loanable funds means that both the quantity of saving by households and the quantity of investment by firms have increased. Increasing investment increases the capital stock and the quantity of capital per hour worked, helping to increase economic growth.

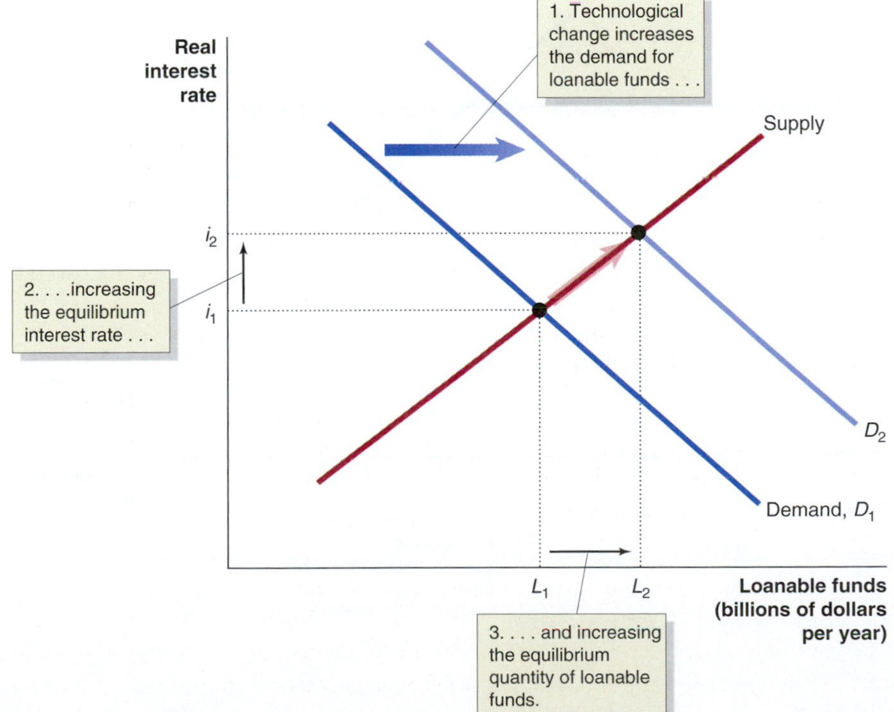

FIGURE 13-4

An Increase in the Demand for Loanable Funds

An increase in the demand for loanable funds increases the equilibrium interest rate from i_1 to i_2, and it increases the equilibrium quantity of loanable funds from L_1 to L_2. As a result, saving and investment both increase.

We can also use the market for loanable funds to examine the impact of a government budget deficit. Putting aside the effects of foreign saving, recall that if the government begins running a budget deficit, it reduces the total amount of saving in the economy. We illustrate this in Figure 13-5 by shifting the supply of loanable funds to the left. In the new equilibrium, the interest rate is higher and the equilibrium quantity of loanable funds is lower. Running a deficit has reduced the level of total saving in the economy and, by increasing the interest rate, has also reduced the level of investment spending by firms. By borrowing to finance its budget deficit, the government will have *crowded out* some firms that would otherwise have been able to borrow to finance investment. Lower investment spending means that the capital stock and the quantity of capital per hour worked will not increase as much.

A government budget surplus would have the opposite effect to a deficit. A budget surplus increases the total amount of saving in the economy, shifting the supply of loanable funds to the right. In the new equilibrium, the interest rate will be lower and the quantity of loanable funds will be higher. We can conclude that a budget surplus increases the level of saving and investment.

In practice, however, the impact of government budget deficits and surpluses on the equilibrium interest rate is relatively small. (This finding reflects in part the importance of global saving in determining the interest rate.) For example, a recent study found that increasing government borrowing by an amount equal to 1 percent of GDP would increase the equilibrium real interest rate by only about three one-hundredths of a percentage point. However, this small effect on interest rates does not imply that we can ignore the effect of deficits on economic growth. Paying off government debt in the future may require higher taxes, which can depress economic growth.

FIGURE 13-5

The Effect of a Budget Deficit on the Market for Loanable Funds

When the government begins running a budget deficit, the supply of loanable funds shifts to the left. The equilibrium interest rate increases from i_1 to i_2, and the equilibrium quantity of loanable funds falls from L_1 to L_2. As a result, saving and investment both decline.

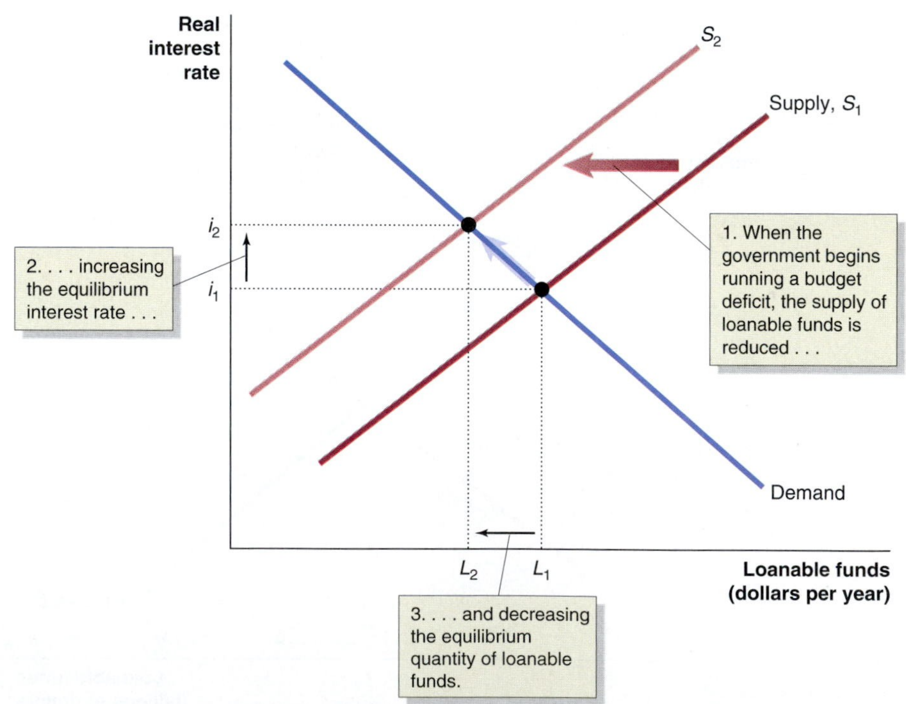

SOLVED PROBLEM 13-2

② LEARNING OBJECTIVE

Discuss the role of the financial system in facilitating long-run economic growth.

How Would a Consumption Tax Affect Saving, Investment, the Interest Rate, and Economic Growth?

Some economists and policymakers have suggested that the federal government shift from relying on an income tax to relying on a *consumption tax*. Under the income tax, households pay taxes on all income earned. Under a consumption tax, households pay taxes only on the income they spend. Households would pay taxes on saved income only if they spend the money at a later time. Use the market for loanable funds model to analyze the effect on saving, investment, the interest rate, and economic growth of switching from an income tax to a consumption tax.

Solving the Problem:

Step 1: Review the chapter material. This problem is about applying the market for loanable funds model, so you may want to review the section "Explaining Movements in Saving, Investment, and Interest Rates," which begins on page 403.

Step 2: Explain the effect of switching from an income tax to a consumption tax. Households are interested in the return they receive from saving after they have paid their taxes. For example, consider someone who puts his savings in a certificate of deposit at an interest rate of 4 percent and whose tax rate is 25 percent. Under an income tax, this person's after-tax return to saving is 3 percent $[4 \times (1 - 0.25)]$. Under a consumption tax, income that is saved is not taxed, so the return rises to 4 percent. We can conclude that moving from an income tax to a consumption tax would increase the return to saving, causing the supply of loanable funds to increase.

Step 3: Draw a graph of the market for loanable funds to illustrate your answer. The supply curve for loanable funds will shift to the right as the after-tax return to saving increases under the consumption tax. The equilibrium interest rate will fall, and the levels of saving and investment will both increase. Because investment increases, the capital stock and the quantity of capital per hour worked will grow and the rate of economic growth should increase. Note that the size of the fall in the interest rate and the increase in loanable funds shown in the graph are larger than the effects that most economists expect would actually result from the replacement of the income tax with a consumption tax.

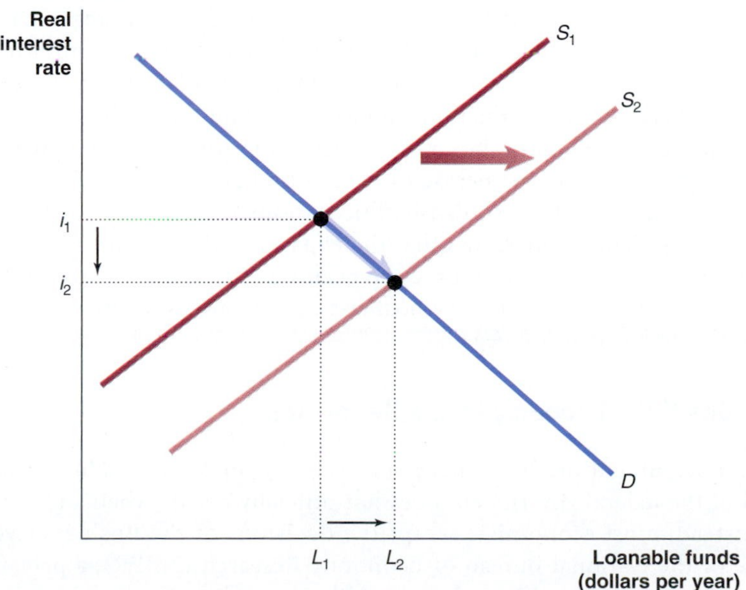

YOUR TURN: **For more practice, do related problem 18 on page 419 at the end of this chapter.**

FIGURE 13-6

Movements in Real GDP, 1998–2004

The expansion that began in 1991 continued through the late 1990s until a business cycle peak was reached in March 2001. The following recession, marked by the shaded vertical bar, was fairly short and a business cycle trough was reached in November 2001, when the next expansion began.

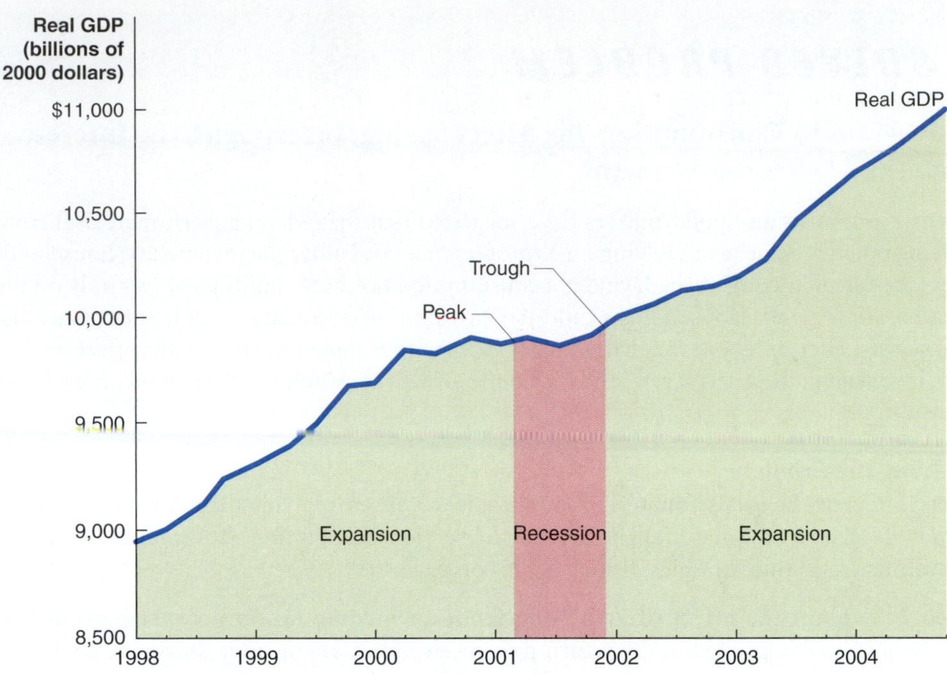

③ LEARNING OBJECTIVE

Explain what happens during a business cycle.

The Business Cycle

Figure 13-1 on page 391 showed the tremendous increase during the last century in the standard of living of the average American. But close inspection of the figure reveals that real GDP per capita did not increase every year during this century. For example, during the first half of the 1930s, real GDP per capita *fell* for several years in a row. What accounts for these fluctuations in the long-run upward trend?

Some Basic Business Cycle Definitions

The fluctuations in real GDP per capita shown in Figure 13-1 reflect the underlying fluctuations in real GDP. Dating back at least to the early nineteenth century, the U.S. economy has experienced a business cycle, consisting of alternating periods of expanding and contracting economic activity. Because real GDP is our best measure of economic activity, the business cycle is usually illustrated using movements in real GDP.

During the *expansion phase* of the business cycle, production, employment, and income are increasing. The period of expansion ends with a *business cycle peak.* Following the business cycle peak, production, employment, and income decline as the economy enters the *recession phase* of the cycle. The recession comes to an end with a *business cycle trough,* after which another period of expansion begins. Figure 13-6 illustrates the phases of the business cycle as shown by fluctuations in real GDP during the period from 1998 to 2004. The figure shows that the expansion that began in 1991 continued through the late 1990s until a business cycle peak was reached in March 2001. The following recession was fairly short and a business cycle trough was reached in November 2001, when the next expansion began.

13-4 Making the Connection

Who Decides If the Economy Is in a Recession?

The federal government produces many statistics that make it possible to monitor the economy, but the federal government does not officially decide when a recession begins or ends. Instead, most economists accept the decisions of the Business Cycle Dating Committee of the National Bureau of Economic Research (NBER), a private research group located in Cambridge, Massachusetts. Although writers for newspapers and magazines often define a recession as two consecutive quarters of declining real GDP, the

NBER has the following broader definition:

> A recession is a significant decline in activity spread across the economy, lasting more than a few months, visible in industrial production, employment, real income, and wholesale-retail trade.

The National Bureau of Economic Research determines when recessions begin and end.

The Business Cycle Dating Committee decided that the U.S. economy had reached a business cycle peak in March 2001 and a business cycle trough in November 2001.

The NBER is fairly slow in announcing business cycle dates because it takes time to gather and analyze economic statistics. Typically, the NBER will announce that the economy is in a recession only well after the recession has begun. For instance, the NBER did not announce that a recession had begun in March 2001 until nearly eight months later at the end of November. November was the same month that the NBER subsequently decided that the recession had ended, but it did not make this announcement until July 2003. Similarly, the NBER did not announce that a recession had begun in July 1990 until April 1991, one month after the recession had actually ended. Nonetheless, policymakers look to the NBER to chronicle the economy's expansions and contractions.

The following table lists the business cycle peaks and troughs identified by the NBER for the years since 1950. The length of each recession is the number of months from the peak to the following trough:

PEAK	TROUGH	LENGTH OF RECESSION
July 1953	May 1954	10 months
August 1957	April 1958	8 months
April 1960	February 1961	10 months
December 1969	November 1970	11 months
November 1973	March 1975	16 months
January 1980	July 1980	6 months
July 1981	November 1982	16 months
July 1990	March 1991	8 months
March 2001	November 2001	8 months

Source: *NBER Reporter*, Fall 2001, and NBER Web site (www.nber.org) for business cycle dates.

What Happens during a Business Cycle?

Each business cycle is different. The lengths of the expansion and recession phases and which sectors of the economy are most affected will rarely be the same in any two cycles. But most business cycles share certain characteristics, which we will discuss in this section. As the economy nears the end of an expansion, interest rates usually are rising, and the wages of workers usually are rising faster than prices. As a result of rising interest rates and rising wages, the profits of firms will be falling. Typically, toward the end of an expansion both households and firms will have substantially increased their debts. These debts are the result of the borrowing firms and households undertake to help finance their spending during the expansion.

A recession will often begin with a decline in spending by firms on capital goods, such as machinery, equipment, new factories, and new office buildings, or by households on new houses and consumer durables, such as furniture and automobiles. As spending declines, firms selling capital goods and consumer durables will find their sales declining. As sales decline, firms cut back on production and begin to lay off workers. Rising unemployment and falling profits reduce income, which leads to further declines in spending.

As the recession continues, economic conditions gradually begin to improve. The declines in spending eventually come to an end; households and firms begin to reduce their debt, thereby increasing their ability to spend; and interest rates decline, making it more likely that households and firms will borrow to finance new spending. Firms begin to increase their spending on capital goods as they anticipate the need for additional production during the next expansion. Increased spending by households on consumer durables and by businesses on capital goods will finally bring the recession to an end and begin the next expansion.

THE EFFECT OF THE BUSINESS CYCLE ON AUTOMOBILE PRODUCTION Durables are goods that are expected to last for three or more years, such as furniture, appliances, and automobiles. Consumer durables are affected more by the business cycle than are nondurables—such as food and clothing—or services—such as haircuts and medical care. During a recession, workers reduce spending if they lose their jobs, fear losing their jobs, or suffer wage cuts. Because people can often continue to use their existing furniture, appliances, or automobiles, they are more likely to postpone spending on durables than spending on other goods. Automobiles are among the most expensive products consumers buy, so consumers are very likely to postpone buying a new one during a recession.

We saw in our discussion of Ford at the beginning of this chapter that the firm's sales were significantly affected by the business cycle. Figure 13-7 shows that this is

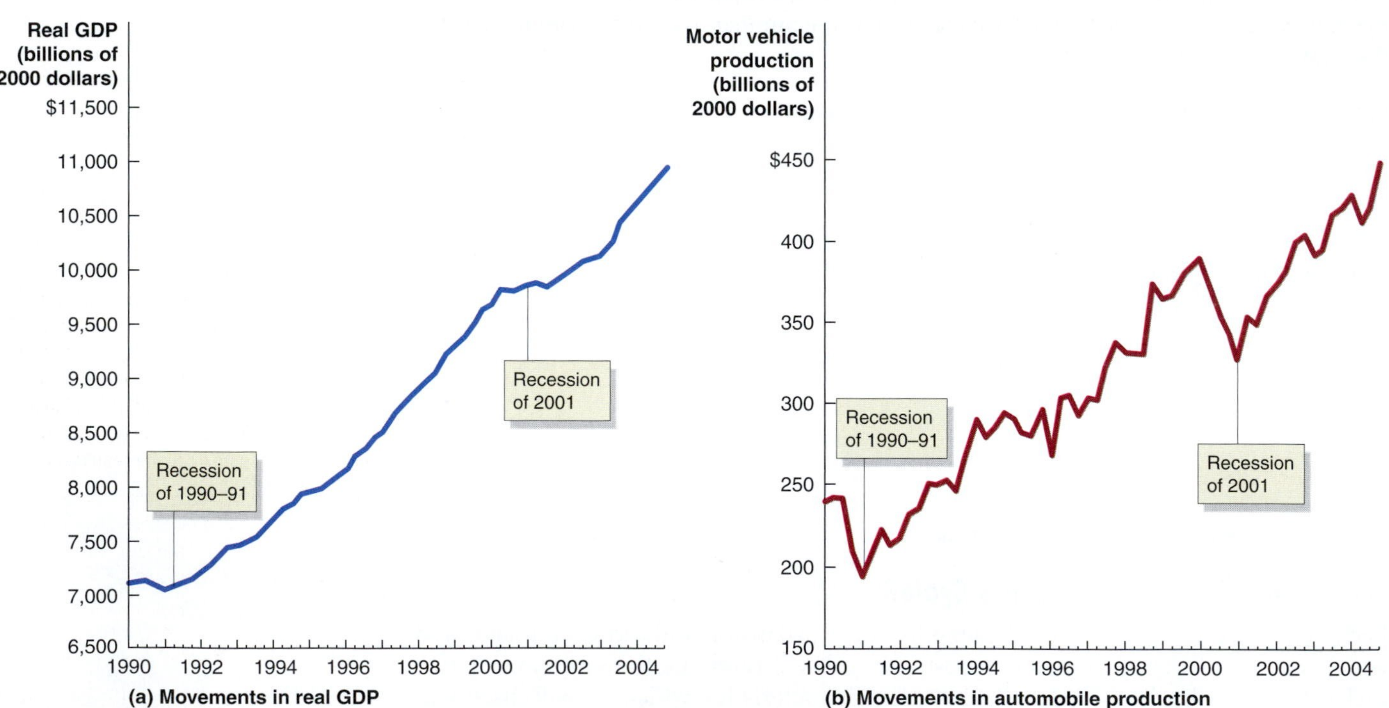

FIGURE 13-7 The Effect of the Business Cycle on Automobile Production

Panel (a) shows movements in real GDP for each quarter from the beginning of 1990 through the end of 2004. Panel (b) shows movements in the value of total motor vehicle production in the United States (in 2000 dollars) for the same period. In panel (b), the effects of the recessions are more dramatic. Real GDP declined by less than 1.5 percent during the 1990–91 recession and by less than 0.5 percent during the 2001 recession, while automobile production declined by more than 15 percent during both recessions.

Source: U.S. Bureau of Economic Analysis.

true for the automobile industry in the United States as a whole. Panel (a) shows movements in real GDP for each quarter from the beginning of 1990 through the end of 2004. We can see both the upward trend in real GDP over time and the effects of the recessions of 1990–91 and 2001. Panel (b) shows movements in the value of total motor vehicle production in the United States (in 2000 dollars) for the same period. Once again, we can see an upward trend in production over time, but now the effects of the recessions are more dramatic. Real GDP declined by less than 1.5 percent during the 1990–91 recession and by less than 0.5 percent during the 2001 recession, while automobile production declined by more than 15 percent during both recessions.

THE EFFECT OF THE BUSINESS CYCLE ON THE INFLATION RATE In Chapter 12, we saw that the *price level* measures the average prices of goods and services in the economy, and that the *inflation rate* is the percentage increase in the price level from one year to the next. An important fact about the business cycle is that during economic expansions the inflation rate usually increases, particularly near the end of the expansion, and during recessions the inflation rate usually decreases. Figure 13-8 illustrates that this was true of the recession of 2001.

As Figure 13-8 shows, toward the end of the 1991–2001 expansion, the inflation rate rose from about 1.5 percent to about 3.5 percent. The recession that began in March 2001 caused the inflation rate to fall back to below 2 percent. Figure 13-9 shows that recessions have consistently had the effect of lowering the inflation rate. In every recession since 1950, the inflation rate has been lower during the 12 months after the recession ends than it was during the 12 months before the recession began. The average decline in the inflation rate has been about 2.5 percentage points. This result is not surprising. During a business cycle expansion, spending by businesses and households is strong and producers of goods and services find it easier to raise

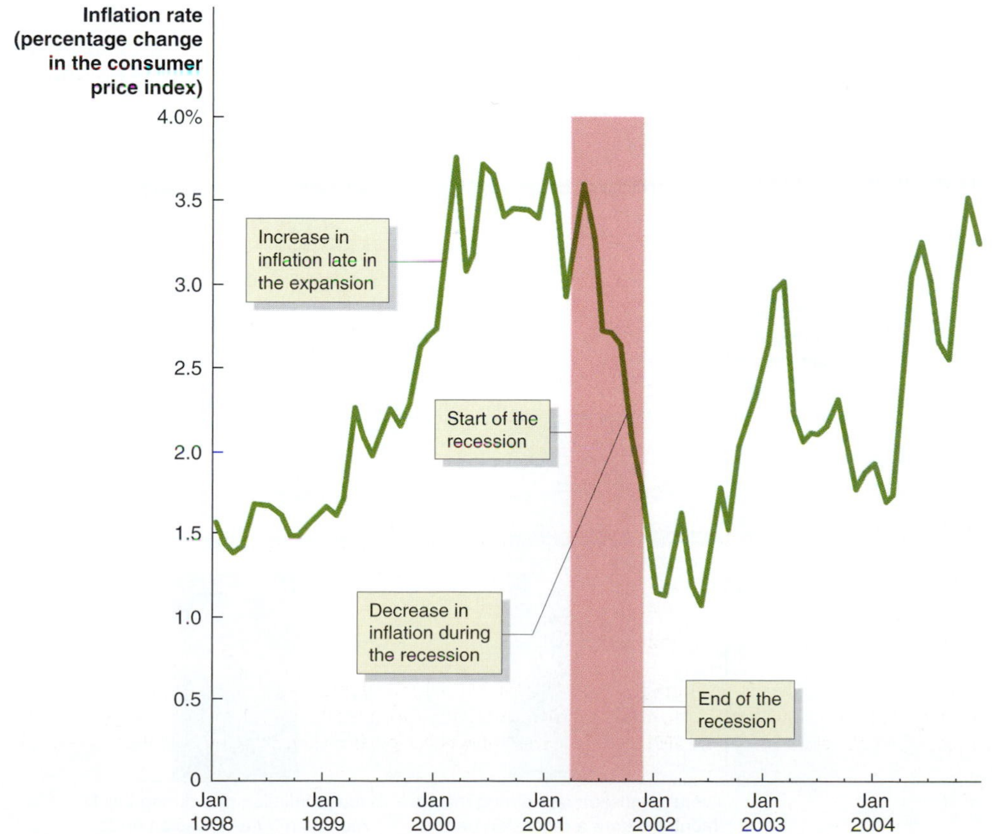

FIGURE 13-8

The Effect of the 2001 Recession on the Inflation Rate

Toward the end of the 1991–2001 expansion, the inflation rate began to rise. The recession that began in March 2001, marked by the shaded vertical bar, caused the inflation rate to fall. By the end of the recession in November 2001, the inflation rate was significantly below what it had been at the beginning of the recession.

Note: The points on the figure represent the annual inflation rate measured by the change in the CPI for the year ending in the indicated month.

Don't Let This Happen To You!

Don't Confuse the Price Level and the Inflation Rate

Do you agree with the following statement: "The consumer price index is a widely used measure of the inflation rate." The statement may sound plausible, but it is incorrect. As we saw in Chapter 12, the consumer price index is a measure of the *price level*, not of the inflation rate. We can measure the inflation rate as the *percentage change* in the consumer price index from one year to the next. In macroeconomics, it is important not to confuse the level of a variable with the change in the variable. To give another example, real GDP does not measure economic growth. Economic growth is measured by the percentage change in real GDP from one year to the next.

YOUR TURN: **Test your understanding by doing related problem 20 on page 419 at the end of this chapter.**

prices. As spending declines during a recession, firms have a more difficult time selling their goods and services and are likely to increase prices less than they otherwise might have.

THE EFFECT OF THE BUSINESS CYCLE ON THE UNEMPLOYMENT RATE Recessions cause the inflation rate to fall, but they cause the unemployment rate to increase. As firms see their sales decline, they begin to reduce production and lay off workers. Figure 13-10 shows the impact of the recession of 2001 on the unemployment rate. As the recession began in March 2001, the unemployment rate started to rise. The rate continued to rise even after the end of the recession in November 2001. This pattern is typical and is due to two factors. First, during the business cycle, discouraged workers drop out of and then return to the labor force, as we discussed in Chapter 12. When discouraged workers drop out of the labor force during a recession, they keep the measured unemployment rate from increasing as much as it would if these workers were counted as unemployed. When discouraged workers return to the labor force as the recession ends, they increase the measured unemployment rate because they are now counted as being unemployed. Second, firms continue to operate well below their capacity even after a recession has ended and production has begun to increase. As a result, at first, firms may not hire back all of the workers they have laid off and may even continue for a while to lay off more workers.

FIGURE 13-9

The Impact of Recessions on the Inflation Rate

In every recession since 1950, the inflation rate has been lower during the 12 months after the business cycle trough than it was during the 12 months before the business cycle peak. The average decline in the inflation rate has been 2.5 percentage points.

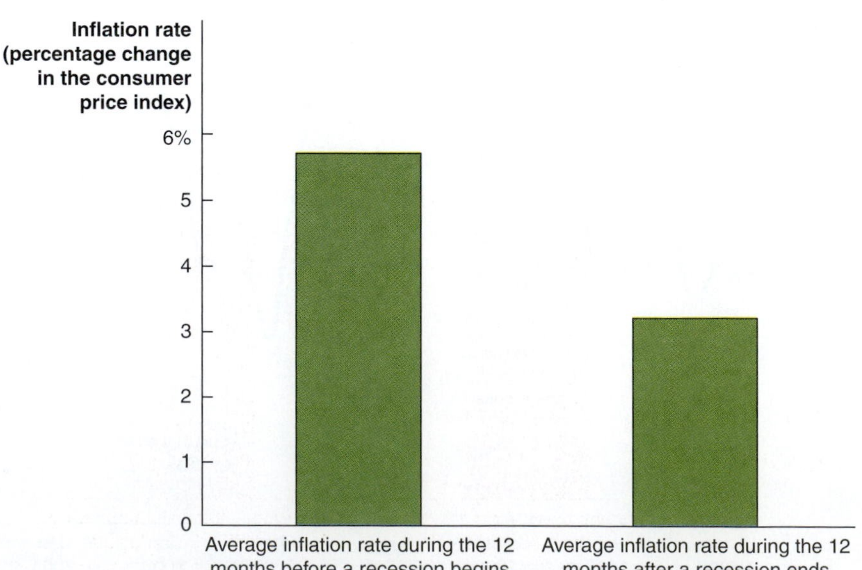

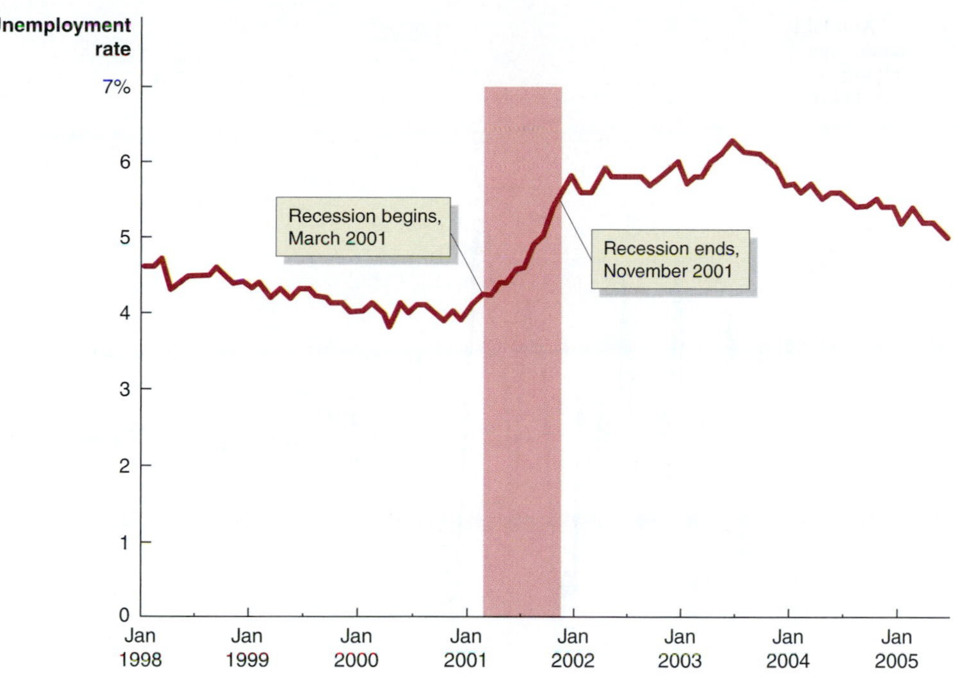

FIGURE 13-10

The Effect of the 2001 Recession on the Unemployment Rate

The reluctance of firms to hire new employees during the early stages of a recovery means that the unemployment rate usually continues to rise even after the recession has ended.

As the U.S. economy began to recover from the 2001 recession, the *Wall Street Journal* published an article giving advice to small firms on their hiring policies during the period after a recession has ended. One piece of advice was "Just because some new orders arrived, don't run out and hire a bunch of new workers." The owner of one small accounting firm suggested that during the early stages of an expansion, companies should use overtime by existing employees to meet sales, rather than hire new workers.

Figure 13-11 shows that for the recessions since 1950, the unemployment rate has risen on average by about 1.2 percentage points during the 12 months after a recession begins. So, on average, more than a million more workers have been unemployed during the 12 months after a recession begins than during the previous 12 months.

RECESSIONS HAVE BEEN MILDER AND THE ECONOMY HAS BEEN MORE STABLE SINCE 1950 Although today the U.S. economy still experiences business cycles, just as it has for at least the past 175 years, the cycles have become milder. Figure 13-12, which

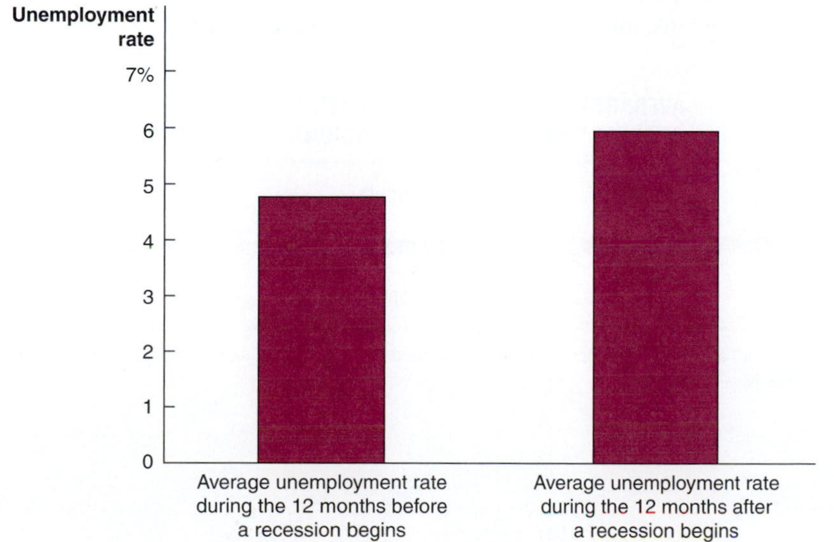

FIGURE 13-11

The Impact of Recessions on the Unemployment Rate

Unemployment rises in every recession. For the recessions since 1950, the unemployment rate rises, on average, by about 1.2 percentage points during the 12 months after a recession begins.

FIGURE 13-12

Fluctuations in Real GDP, 1900–2004

In the first half of the twentieth century, real GDP had much more severe swings than in the second half of the twentieth century.

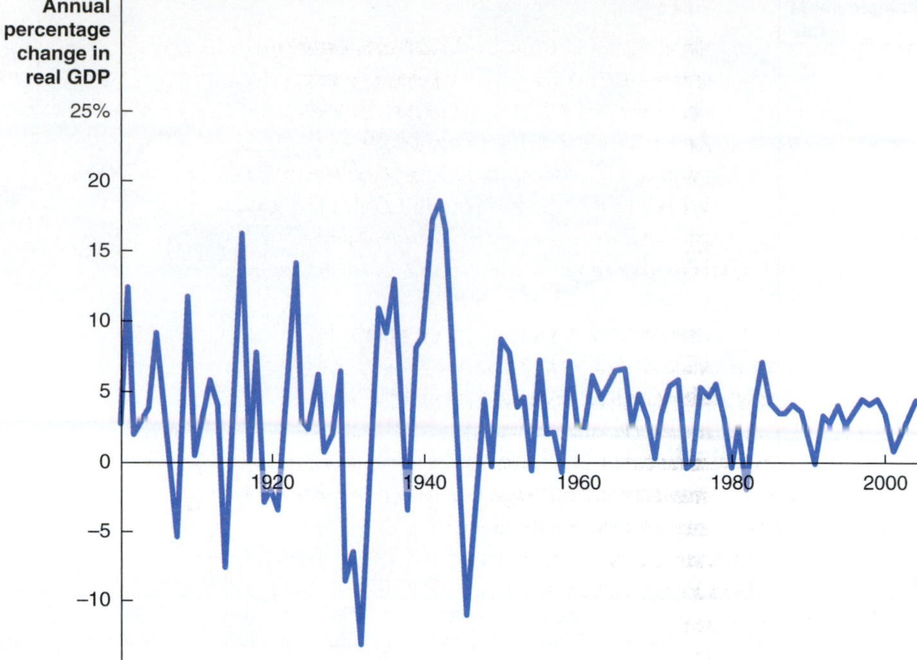

shows the year-to-year percentage changes in real GDP since 1900, illustrates a striking change in fluctuations in real GDP beginning around 1950. Before 1950, real GDP went through much greater year-to-year fluctuations than it has since that time. During the past 50 years, the U.S. economy has not experienced anything similar to the sharp fluctuations in real GDP that occurred during the early 1930s.

Another way to compare changes in the severity of business cycles over time is to look at changes in the lengths of expansions and recessions. Table 13-1 shows that in the late nineteenth century the average length of recessions was the same as the average length of expansions. During the first half of the twentieth century, the average length of expansions decreased slightly and the average length of recessions decreased significantly. As a result, expansions were about six months longer than recessions during these years. The most striking change comes after 1950, when the length of expansions has greatly increased and the length of recessions has fallen. In the second half of the twentieth century, expansions were more than five times as long as recessions. In other words, in the late nineteenth century the U.S. economy spent as much time in recession as it did in expansion. During the second half of the twentieth century, the U.S. economy experienced long expansions, interrupted by relatively short recessions.

TABLE 13-1

The Business Cycle Has Become Milder

PERIOD	AVERAGE LENGTH OF EXPANSIONS	AVERAGE LENGTH OF RECESSIONS
1870–1900	26 months	26 months
1900–1950	25 months	19 months
1950–2001	61 months	9 months

Note: The World War I and World War II periods have been omitted from the computations in the table, as has the expansion that began in November 2001.

Why Is the Economy More Stable?

Shorter recessions, longer expansions, and less severe fluctuations in real GDP have resulted in a significant improvement in the economic well-being of Americans. Economists have offered three explanations of why the economy has been more stable since 1950:

- ***The increasing importance of services and the declining importance of goods.*** As services, such as medical care or investment advice, have become a much larger fraction of GDP, there has been a corresponding decline in the production of goods. For example, at one time, manufacturing production accounted for about 40 percent of GDP, while today it accounts for about only 12 percent. Manufacturing production, particularly production of durable goods such as automobiles, fluctuates more than the production of services. Because durable goods are more expensive, during a recession households will cut back more on purchases of them than they will on purchases of services.
- ***The establishment of unemployment insurance and other government transfer programs that provide funds to the unemployed.*** Before the 1930s, programs such as unemployment insurance, which provides government payments to workers who lose their jobs, and Social Security, which provides government payments to retired and disabled workers, did not exist. These and other government programs make it possible for workers who lose their jobs during recessions to have higher incomes and, therefore, spend more than they would otherwise. This additional spending may have helped to shorten recessions.
- ***Active federal government policies to stabilize the economy.*** Before the Great Depression of the 1930s, the federal government did not attempt to end recessions or prolong expansions. Because the Great Depression was so severe, with the unemployment rate rising to more than 25 percent of the labor force and real GDP declining by almost 30 percent, public opinion began favoring attempts by the government to stabilize the economy. In the Employment Act of 1946, the federal government committed itself to "foster and promote . . . conditions under which there will be afforded useful employment to those able, willing, and seeking to work; and to promote maximum employment, production, and purchasing power." Since that time, the federal government has actively tried to end recessions and prolong expansions. Many economists believe that these government policies have played a key role in stabilizing the economy in the years since 1950. Other economists, however, argue that active policy has had little effect. This macroeconomic debate is an important one, so we will consider it further in Chapters 16 and 17 when we discuss the federal government's *monetary* and *fiscal policies.*

Conclusion

The U.S. economy remains a remarkable engine for improving the well-being of Americans. The standard of living of Americans today is much higher than it was 100 years ago. But households and firms are still subject to the ups and downs of the business cycle. In the following chapters we will continue our analysis of this basic fact of macroeconomics: Ever-increasing long-run prosperity is achieved in the context of short-run instability.

Read *An Inside Look* on the next page to learn about the growth of the Chinese automobile industry.

An Inside Look

Growth and the Chinese Automobile Industry

BUSINESSWEEK ONLINE, JUNE 6, 2005

Here Come Chinese Cars

Audacious, gutsy, and maybe a little nutty—how else to describe the push by New York auto entrepreneur Malcolm Bricklin and China's Chery Automobile Co. President Yin Tongyao to import and sell 250,000 mainland-made sport utilities, sedans, and sports coupes in the U.S. starting in 2007? After all, Chery produced only 80,000 cars in all of 2004, has near-zero brand recognition outside China, and has been sued by General Motors Corp.'s South Korean unit for allegedly ripping off the design for its best-selling QQ minicars in China—a charge Chery denies. And while Bricklin was expected to announce his first dealer on May 26, U.S. auto execs aren't exactly losing sleep over the Chery threat—not yet, anyway.

Big Three execs did take notice, however, when Honda Motor Corp. announced plans to export compact cars from China to Europe starting in June. Honda already sells about 200,000 locally built vehicles in China a year, ranging from Accord sedans to Odyssey SUVs. In April, with local partners, it began production at a new assembly plant in Guangzhou that will eventually build and export 50,000 Fit compacts a year to be sold in Europe as the Jazz. Honda won't say if it plans to send China-built cars to the U.S., but it hasn't ruled out exporting other models from China eventually.

In the global auto industry, Chery and Honda are on opposite ends of the spectrum. But they do share this: Both are betting big that the Chinese auto industry is entering a new phase that will see a shift from manufacturing only for the fast-growing local market to become an export base for the rest of the world, too. . . .

. . . China is closing the quality gap and building a base of low-cost suppliers that could eventually allow it to unleash inexpensive, well-made cars on the West. . . .

Rising Quality

a Korean cars gave Detroit fits in the late '90s by undercutting domestic small cars on price and outdoing them on quality—then moving up into other segments. Autos from China could provide more lower-cost competition for the Big Three at a time when GM and Ford Motor Co. are already reeling. . . .

How fast can the Chinese gear up? The way things are going, it won't take 20 years to match Toyota Motor Corp. quality levels, as it did for the Koreans. And with Chinese auto assembly workers earning $2 an hour—vs. $22 in Korea and nearly $60 in the U.S. for wages and benefits—it may not be long before China has the wherewithal to start selling competitively priced cars overseas. "The Chinese are probably five or six years away from being able to sell a competent low-end car," says auto analyst Maryann N. Keller.

The Chinese government is putting its heft behind the export push—subsidizing the export drive of such local players as Chery and giving the likes of Honda big incentives. Beijing also is nudging foreign auto makers to divert investment into export production so local partners can become familiar with managing foreign-exchange risk and global supply chains. . . .

b Another challenge is a bit of mind-bender: While China's labor costs are dirt cheap, the overall cost of bolting a car together there is anything but. Honda officials say the cost of making the Accord in China is still higher than in Japan or the U.S. And it costs about the same to build the Fit compact in China as it does in Japan. Honda makes money selling cars locally because prices are high. . . .

That will begin to change as higher volumes start bringing costs down. Jack Perkowski, CEO of ASMICO Technologies, which owns 13 parts factories in China, figures that will happen once the domestic market gets closer to 10 million units a year. . . .

Counter-Strategies

c For Detroit, that's a scary prospect. "Our strategy is to become competitive at the low end of the market," says GM's LaNeve. That means importing cars built by its Korean affiliate, Daewoo, to sell as Chevys, such as the $10,000 Aveo subcompact launched in fall, 2003. LaNeve wouldn't discuss GM's long-term plans. But analysts say that, under pressure from Chinese cars, the auto giant could step up exports from Korea, where quality and supplier connections are already established. Eventually, though, it might turn to its own plants in China, where it has been producing cars since 1999. . . .

In the meantime, China's auto industry is roaring into the future—building out its supplier networks and boosting quality. . . . Look out, Detroit.

Key Points in the Article

This article discusses the fast-growing Chinese automobile industry, which until recently manufactured relatively low-quality vehicles for local Chinese markets. Now the five-year-old Chinese automobile manufacturer, Chery, plans to sell 250,000 entry-level vehicles in the United States by 2007. U.S. automobile manufacturers Ford and General Motors plan to counter this credible Chinese threat with similarly priced entry-level vehicles of their own. Auto analysts predict that to keep costs low both U.S. firms will ultimately produce their vehicles in China.

Analyzing the News

a Since the late 1970s, when the Chinese government introduced market-oriented economic reforms, the Chinese economy has grown dramatically. This economic growth has spurred, in a relatively short time frame, a globally competitive Chinese automobile industry. To be sure, China remains an emerging economy, with relatively high unemployment, low labor productivity, and a low standard of living. Nonetheless, as countries develop, they tend to move from manufacturing simple goods like textiles to more complex goods like automobiles. And, in the case of China, automobile producers such as Chery have enjoyed a competitive advantage over their U.S. counterparts, because, all else equal, labor costs in China remain extremely low. This advantage is shown in Figure 1.

b Despite China's strong economic growth, the country's automobile production technologies remain relatively primitive and small-scale. Therefore, China cannot manufacture at low cost the highly sophisticated components required to produce efficient, safe, and durable automobiles. So, although labor is relatively cheap in China, the cost to manufacture an automobile is not. This competitive disadvantage will disappear in the next few years, as investment in Chinese automobile parts plants improves their efficiency and growing markets for Chinese automobiles increase the scale of parts production.

c When China does enter the U.S. automobile market, it will be at the entry or low-end level—subcompacts with a sticker price of roughly $10,000. U.S. automakers Ford and General Motors plan to counter with entry-level vehicles of their own. As the Chinese economy continues to grow, and as its network of cost-effective parts manufacturers increases, Ford and GM may determine that their least-cost option is to produce their automobiles in China. In any case, the U.S. consumer will benefit from these changes in the global automobile market, because entry-level automobile prices in the United States will fall. This pattern is shown in Figure 2, where the supply of entry-level automobiles shifts from S_1 to S_2, while the price of entry-level automobiles falls from P_1 to P_2.

Thinking Critically ABOUT POLICY

1. Suppose the Chinese government imposes restrictions on foreign direct investment in Chinese automobile parts plants. For example, suppose the Chinese government restricts U.S. firms that manufacture automobile components, from investing in and managing automobile parts plants in China. What effect would this policy have on China's automobile production costs in the next several years?
2. Suppose the U.S. government imposes an import tariff on Chinese entry-level automobiles. What effect would this policy have on the equilibrium price and quantity of entry-level automobiles sold in the United States?

Source: Brian Bremner and Kathleen Kerwin, with Dexter Roberts in Beijing, Gail Edmondson in Frankfurt, and David Kiley in New York, "Here Come Chinese Cars: Detroit Isn't Looking in the Rearview Mirror—Yet," Business Week Online, www.businessweek.com. June 6, 2005.

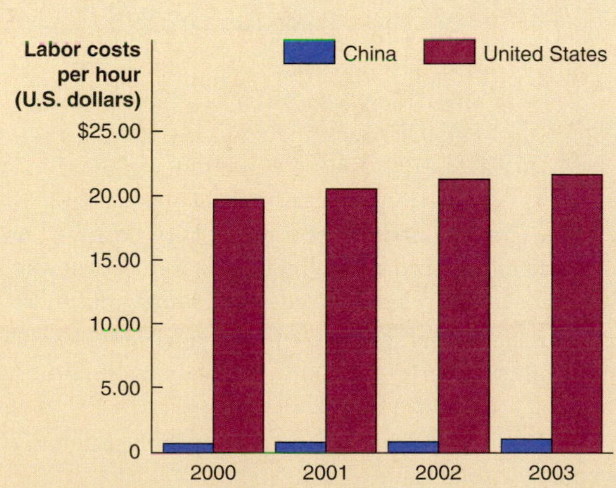

Figure 1: Labor costs per hour China v. United States
Source: The Economist Intelligence Unit.

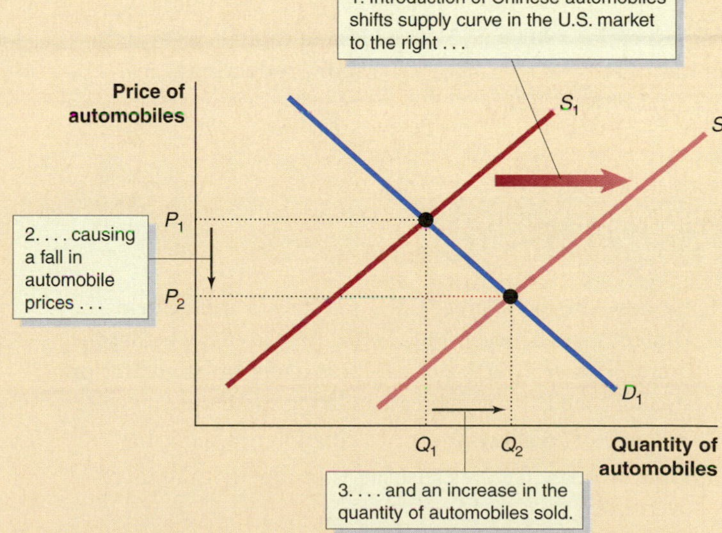

Figure 2: The introduction of Chinese automobiles causes a decrease in the price of automobiles.

SUMMARY

LEARNING OBJECTIVE ① Discuss the importance of long-run economic growth. Long-run economic growth is the process by which rising productivity increases the standard of living of the typical person. Because of economic growth, the typical American today can buy more than eight times as much as the typical American of 1900. Long-run growth is measured by increases in real GDP per capita. Increases in real GDP per capita depend on increases in *labor productivity.* Labor productivity is the quantity of goods and services that can be produced by one worker or by one hour of work. Economists believe two key factors determine labor productivity—the quantity of capital per hour worked and the level of technology. Therefore, economic growth occurs if the quantity of capital per hour worked increases and if technological change occurs.

LEARNING OBJECTIVE ② Discuss the role of the financial system in facilitating long-run economic growth. Financial markets and financial intermediaries together comprise the *financial system.* A well-functioning financial system is an important determinant of economic growth. Firms acquire funds from households, either directly through financial markets—such as the stock and bond markets—or indirectly through financial intermediaries—such as banks. The funds available to firms come from *saving.* There are two categories of saving in the economy: *private saving* by households and *public saving* by the government. The value of total saving in the economy is always equal to the value of total investment spending. In the model of the *market for loanable funds,* the interaction of borrowers and lenders determines the market interest rate and the quantity of loanable funds exchanged.

LEARNING OBJECTIVE ③ Explain what happens during a business cycle. A *business cycle* consists of alternating periods of economic expansion and contraction. During the expansion phase of a business cycle, production, employment, and income are increasing. The period of expansion ends with a business cycle peak. Following the business cycle peak, production, employment, and income decline during the recession phase of the cycle. The recession comes to an end with a business cycle trough, after which another period of expansion begins. The inflation rate usually rises near the end of a business cycle expansion and then falls during a recession. The unemployment rate declines during the later part of an expansion and increases during a recession. The unemployment rate often continues to increase even after an expansion has begun. Economists have not found a method to predict when recessions will begin and end. Recessions are difficult to predict because they have more than one cause. Recessions have been milder and the economy has been more stable since 1950.

KEY TERMS

REVIEW QUESTIONS

1. By how much did real GDP per capita increase in the United States between 1900 and 2004? Discuss whether the increase in real GDP per capita is likely to be greater or smaller than the true increase in living standards.
2. The rule of 70 allows for the calculation of what value?
3. What two key factors cause labor productivity to increase over time?
4. What supportive government policies are crucial for long-run economic growth?
5. Why is the financial system of a country important for long-run economic growth? Why is it vital for economic growth that firms have access to adequate sources of funds?
6. How does the financial system—either financial markets or financial intermediaries—provide risk sharing, liquidity, and information for savers and borrowers?
7. Briefly explain why the total value of saving in the economy must equal the total value of investment.

8. What are loanable funds? Why do businesses demand loanable funds? Why do households supply loanable funds?
9. What are the names of the following events in a business cycle?
   a. The high point of economic activity
   b. The low point of economic activity
   c. The period between the high point of economic activity and the following low point
   d. The period between the low point of economic activity and the following high point
10. Briefly describe the effect of the business cycle on the inflation rate and the unemployment rate.
11. Briefly compare the severity of recessions in the first half of the twentieth century with recessions in the second half. Do economists agree on how to explain this difference?

PROBLEMS AND APPLICATIONS

Please visit **www.prenhall.com/hubbard** *for solutions to the even-numbered problems as well as multiple-choice and true or false self-assessment quizzes.*

1. **[Related to the *Chapter Opener*]** Briefly explain whether production of each of the following goods is likely to fluctuate more or less during the business cycle than does real GDP:
   a. Ford F-150 trucks
   b. McDonald's Big Macs
   c. Kenmore refrigerators
   d. Huggies diapers
   e. Caterpillar industrial tractors
2. Briefly discuss whether you would rather live in the United States of 1900 with an income of $1,000,000 per year or the United States of 2006 with an income of $50,000 per year. Assume the incomes for both years are measured in 2000 dollars.
3. A question from Chapter 11 asked about the relationship between real GDP and the standard of living in a country. After reading about economic growth in this chapter, elaborate on the importance of growth in GDP, particularly real GDP per capita, to the quality of life of a country's citizens.
4. Use the table to answer the following questions:

YEAR	REAL GDP (BILLION OF 2000 DOLLARS)
1990	$7,113
1991	7,101
1992	7,337
1993	7,533
1994	7,836

   a. Calculate the growth rate of real GDP for each year from 1991 to 1994.
   b. Calculate the average annual growth rate of real GDP for the period from 1991 to 1994.
5. Real GDP per capita in the United States, as mentioned in the chapter, grew from about $4,300 in 1900 to about $37,000 in 2004, which represents an annual growth rate of 2.1 percent. If the United States continues to grow at this rate, how many years will it take for real GDP per capita to double?
6. The economy of China has boomed since the late 1970s, having periods of double-digit growth rates in real GDP. At a 10 percent growth rate in real GDP, how many years will it take for China's economy to double?
7. Labor productivity in the agricultural sector of the United States is more than 31 times higher than in the agricultural sector of China. What factors would cause U.S. labor productivity to be so much higher than Chinese labor productivity?
   Source: "China: Awakening Giant," Federal Reserve Bank of Dallas, *Southwest Economy*, September/October 2003, p. 2.
8. **[Related to *Solved Problem 13-1*]** Two reasons for the rapid economic growth of China over the past two to three decades have been the massive movement of workers from agriculture to manufacturing jobs and the transformation of parts of its economy into a market system. In China, labor productivity in manufacturing substantially exceeds labor productivity in agriculture, and as many as 150 million Chinese workers will move from agriculture to manufacturing over the next decade or so. In 1978, China began to transform its economy into a market system, and today nearly 40 percent of Chinese workers are employed in private firms (up from 0 percent in 1978). In the long run, which of these two factors—movement of workers from agriculture to manufacturing or transforming the economy into a market system—will be more important for China's economic growth? Briefly explain.
   Source: "China: Awakening Giant," Federal Reserve Bank of Dallas, *Southwest Economy*, September/October 2003.
9. Suppose you can receive an interest rate of 3 percent on a certificate of deposit (CD) at a bank that is charging

borrowers 7 percent on new car loans. Why might you be unwilling to loan money directly to someone who wants to borrow from you to buy a new car, even if that person offers to pay you an interest rate higher than 3 percent?

10. Consider the following data for a closed economy:
$Y = \$11$ trillion
$C = \$8$ trillion
$I = \$2$ trillion
$TR = \$1$ trillion
$T = \$3$ trillion

Use the data to calculate the following:
a. Private saving
b. Public saving
c. Government purchases
d. The government budget deficit or budget surplus

11. Consider the following data for a closed economy:
$Y = \$12$ trillion
$C = \$8$ trillion
$G = \$2$ trillion
$S_{\text{public}} = -\$0.5$ trillion
$T = \$2$ trillion

Use the data to calculate the following:
a. Private saving
b. Investment spending
c. Transfer payments
d. The government budget deficit or budget surplus

12. In problem 11, suppose that government purchases increase from \$2 trillion to \$2.5 trillion. If the values for Y and C are unchanged, what must happen to the values of S and I? Briefly explain.

13. Use the graph to answer the following questions:

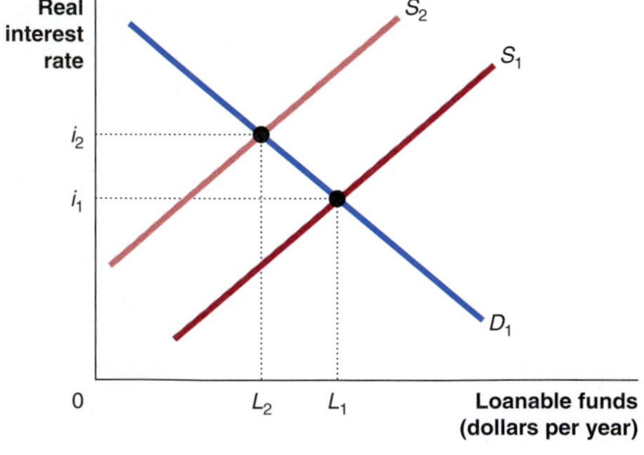

a. Does the shift from S_1 to S_2 represent an increase or decrease in the supply of loanable funds?
b. With the shift in supply, what happens to the equilibrium quantity of loanable funds?
c. With the change in the equilibrium quantity of loanable funds, what happens to the quantity of saving? What happens to the quantity of investment?

14. Use the graph to answer the following questions:

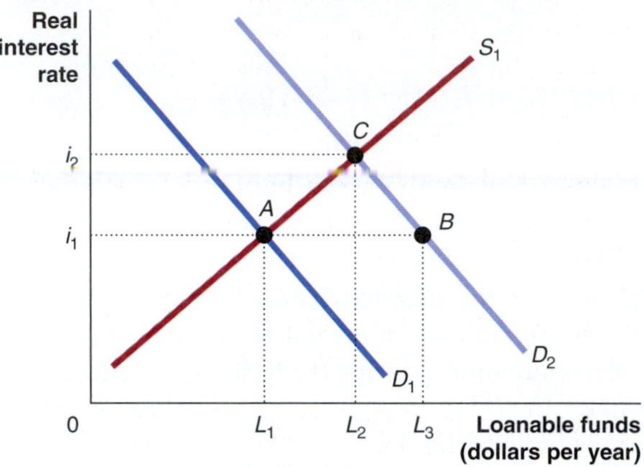

a. With the shift in the demand for loanable funds, what happens to the equilibrium real interest rate and the equilibrium quantity of loanable funds?
b. How can the equilibrium quantity of loanable funds increase when the real interest rate increases? Doesn't the quantity of loanable funds demanded decrease when the interest rate increases?
c. How much would the quantity of loanable funds demanded have increased if the interest rate had remained at i_1?
d. How much does the quantity of loanable funds supplied increase with the increase in the interest rate from i_1 to i_2?

15. Suppose the economy is currently in a recession and that economic forecasts indicate that the economy will soon enter an expansion. What is the likely effect of the expansion on the expected profitability of new investment in plant and equipment? In the market for loanable funds, graph and explain the effect of the forecast of an economic expansion, assuming borrowers and lenders believe the forecast is accurate. What happens to the equilibrium real interest rate and the quantity of loanable funds? What happens to the quantity of saving and investment?

16. Firms care about their after-tax rate of return on investment projects. In the market for loanable funds, graph and explain the effect of an increase in business taxes. (For simplicity, assume no change in the federal budget deficit or budget surplus.) What happens to the equilibrium real interest rate and the quantity of loanable funds? What will be the effect on the quantity of investment by firms and the economy's capital stock in the future?
17. Use a market for loanable funds graph to illustrate the effect of the federal budget surpluses of the late 1990s. What happens to the equilibrium real interest rate and the quantity of loanable funds? What happens to the quantity of saving and investment?
18. **[Related to *Solved Problem 13-2*]** As discussed in Chapter 12, savers are taxed on the nominal interest payments they receive rather than the real interest payments. Suppose the government shifted from taxing nominal interest payments to taxing only real interest payments. Use a market for loanable funds graph to analyze the effects of this change in tax policy. What happens to the equilibrium real interest rate and the equilibrium quantity of loanable funds? What happens to the quantity of saving and investment?
19. The National Bureau of Economic Research, a private group, is responsible for declaring when recessions begin and end. Can you think of reasons why the Bureau of Economic Analysis, part of the federal government, might not want to take on this responsibility?
20. **[Related to *Don't Let This Happen To You!*]** "GDP in 2002 was $10.4 trillion. This value is a large number. Therefore, economic growth must have been high during 2002." Briefly explain whether you agree or disagree with this statement.
21. During the later half of the 1990s, some people asserted that the business cycle was dead, meaning that we would have no more recessions. Examine this chapter's table of business cycle peaks and troughs since 1950. How many recessions has the U.S. economy experienced since the end of 1982? Since 1950, have recessions become more or less frequent? From the history of the business cycle, do you think that the U.S. economy will have another recession within the next 20 years?
22. Imagine you own a business and that during the next recession you lay off 20 percent of your workforce. Once economic activity picks up, why might you not immediately start rehiring workers?

chapter fourteen

Aggregate Demand and Aggregate Supply Analysis

Caterpillar Recovers Slowly from the 2001 Recession

Caterpillar Inc., headquartered in Peoria, Illinois, manufactures more construction and mining equipment than any company in the world. The firm has worldwide revenue of more than $30 billion, about half of which comes from sales outside of North America. About half of its 80,000 employees work outside the United States. As these figures indicate, Caterpillar competes for business around the world. In fact, Caterpillar's main competitor is the Japanese company, Komatsu, Ltd.

Caterpillar is a multinational corporation, so its sales are affected by factors that are unimportant for firms that sell only in the domestic market. Included among these factors are exchange rates, tariffs, and changing attitudes of foreign governments toward multinational corporations. In earlier chapters, we saw that the U.S. economy has experienced a business cycle, with alternating periods of expansion and recession, since at least the early nineteenth century. We also saw that recessions often will begin with a decline in investment spending as firms purchase less machinery and equipment and fewer new factories and office buildings. As investment spending declines, firms like Caterpillar that sell capital goods will find their sales declining.

In the fall of 2000, even before the recession had formally begun, Caterpillar experienced a decline in sales. The firm responded to the recession by reducing production, laying off some workers, cutting the compensation of other workers, and lowering prices. These are the typical responses of a capital goods firm to a recession. (Caterpillar was hurt less by the recession than some other capital goods firms because during the late 1990s it had diversified into areas, such as renting equipment and providing financing for equipment purchases, that are less vulnerable to the effects of a recession.) What was not typical about this recession for Caterpillar was how slow sales were to revive. Not until late in 2003—nearly two years after the recession ended—did the company experience a significant increase in sales. By the end of 2003, the number of workers Caterpillar employed in the United States was still 10 percent [illegible] what it had been at the beginning of

2001. During this period, Caterpillar's sales of construction equipment suffered from a decline in s[illegible]g by state governments on highway construction. Caterpillar also suffered from a decline in construction spending in several of its important overseas markets, as well as a longer-run decline in the worldwide mining business.

The slow recovery from the 2001 recession was not unique to Caterpillar. The manufacturing sector as a whole recovered more slowly from the 2001 recession than from any recession since World War II. Just as Caterpillar was slow to increase employment even as its sales began to revive, the level of employment in the economy as a whole was slow to regain its pre-recession level. *An Inside Look*, on page 446 discusses the recovery of the Japanese economy and its effect on Komatsu, Caterpillar's Japanese rival.

The recession of 2001 illustrates an important point about macroeconomics: All recessions share certain characteristics, but no two recessions are identical. In this chapter, we use the aggregate demand and aggregate supply model to analyze what happens during the business cycle and to understand why Caterpillar and many other U.S. companies recovered so slowly from the recession of 2001. In later chapters, we use the model to understand how the federal government can use fiscal and monetary policy to reduce the severity of the business cycle.

LEARNING OBJECTIVES

After studying this chapter, you should be able to:

(1) Discuss the determinants of aggregate demand, and distinguish between a movement along the aggregate demand curve and a shift of the curve.

(2) Discuss the determinants of aggregate supply, and distinguish between a movement along the short-run aggregate supply curve and a shift of the curve.

(3) Use the aggregate demand and aggregate supply model to illustrate the difference between short-run and long-run macroeconomic equilibrium.

(4) Use the dynamic aggregate demand and aggregate supply model to analyze macroeconomic conditions.

We saw in Chapter 13 that the U.S. economy has experienced a long-run upward trend in real gross domestic product (GDP). This upward trend has resulted in the standard of living in the United States being much higher today than it was 50 years ago. In the short run, however, real GDP fluctuates around this long-run upward trend because of the business cycle. Fluctuations in GDP lead to fluctuations in employment. These fluctuations in real GDP and employment are the most visible and dramatic part of the business cycle. During recessions, for example, we see factories close, small businesses declare bankruptcy, and workers lose their jobs. During expansions, we see new businesses open and new jobs created. In addition to these changes in output and employment, the business cycle causes changes in wages and prices. Some firms react to a decline in sales by cutting back on production, but they may also cut the prices they charge and the wages they pay, which, as we have just seen, is what Caterpillar did during the 2001 recession. Even more firms respond to a recession by raising prices and workers' wages by less than they would have otherwise. During 2002 and 2003, even though the U.S. economy was in the expansion phase of the business cycle, some firms still experienced sluggish sales and unemployment remained relatively high. By 2005, real GDP was approaching its potential level as the economy experienced sustained increases in employment.

In this chapter, we expand our story of the business cycle by developing the aggregate demand and aggregate supply model. This model will help us analyze the effects of recessions and expansions on production, employment, and prices.

1 LEARNING OBJECTIVE

Discuss the determinants of aggregate demand, and distinguish between a movement along the aggregate demand curve and a shift of the curve.

Aggregate Demand

To understand what happens during the business cycle, we need an explanation of why real GDP, the unemployment rate, and the inflation rate fluctuate. We already have seen that fluctuations in the unemployment rate are caused mainly by fluctuations in real GDP. In this chapter, we use the **aggregate demand and aggregate supply model** to explain fluctuations in real GDP and the price level. As Figure 14-1 shows, real GDP and the price level in this model are determined in the short run by the intersection of the *aggregate demand curve* and the *aggregate supply curve*. Fluctuations in real GDP and the price level are caused by shifts in the aggregate demand curve or in the aggregate supply curve.

The **aggregate demand curve (*AD*)** shows the relationship between the price level and the quantity of real GDP demanded by households, firms, and the government. The **short-run aggregate supply curve (*SRAS*)** shows the relationship in the short run between the price level and the quantity of real GDP supplied by firms. The aggregate demand and short-run aggregate supply curves in Figure 14-1 look similar to the individual market demand and supply curves we studied in Chapter 3. However, because these curves apply to the whole economy, rather than to just a single market, the aggregate demand and aggregate supply model is very different from the model of demand and supply in individual markets. Because we are dealing with the economy as a whole, we need *macroeconomic* explanations of why the aggregate demand curve is downward sloping, why the short-run aggregate supply curve is upward sloping, and why the curves shift. We begin by explaining why the aggregate demand curve is downward sloping.

Aggregate demand and aggregate supply model A model that explains short-run fluctuations in real GDP and the price level.

Aggregate demand curve (*AD*) A curve showing the relationship between the price level and the quantity of real GDP demanded by households, firms, and the government.

Short-run aggregate supply curve (*SRAS*) A curve showing the relationship in the short run between the price level and the quantity of real GDP supplied by firms.

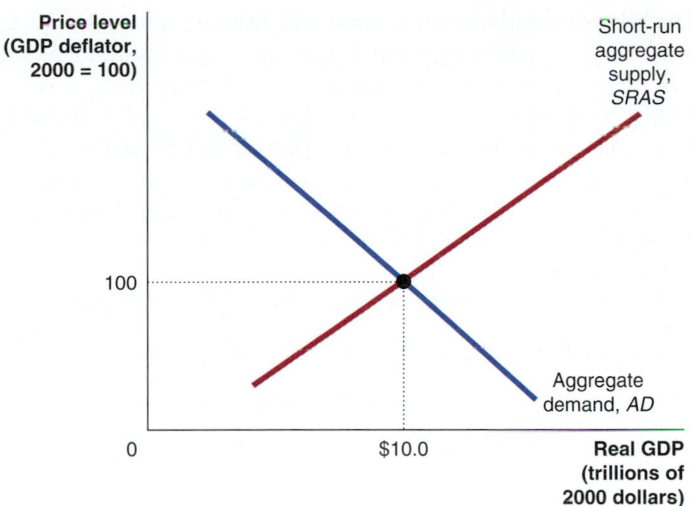

FIGURE 14-1

Aggregate Demand and Aggregate Supply

In the short run, real GDP and the price level are determined by the intersection of the aggregate demand curve and the short-run aggregate supply curve. In the figure, real GDP is measured on the horizontal axis, and the price level is measured on the vertical axis by the GDP deflator. In this example, equilibrium real GDP is $10.0 trillion and the equilibrium price level is 100.

Why Is the Aggregate Demand Curve Downward Sloping?

We saw in Chapter 11 that GDP has four components: consumption *(C)*, investment *(I)*, government purchases *(G)*, and net exports *(NX)*. If we let *Y* stand for GDP, we can write the following:

$$Y = C + I + G + NX.$$

The aggregate demand curve is downward sloping because a fall in the price level increases the quantity of real GDP demanded. To understand why this is true, we need to look at how changes in the price level affect each of the components of aggregate demand. We begin with the assumption that government purchases are determined by the policy decisions of lawmakers and are not affected by changes in the price level. We then can consider the effect of changes in the price level on each of the other three components: consumption, investment, and net exports.

THE WEALTH EFFECT: HOW A CHANGE IN THE PRICE LEVEL AFFECTS CONSUMPTION Current income is the most important variable determining the consumption of households. As income rises, consumption will rise, and as income falls, consumption will fall. But consumption also depends on household wealth. A household's wealth is the difference between the value of its assets and the value of its debts. Consider two households, both with incomes of $80,000 per year. The first household has wealth of $5 million, whereas the second household has wealth of $50,000. The first household is likely to spend more of its income than the second household. So, as total household wealth rises, consumption will rise. Some household wealth is held in cash or other *nominal assets* that lose value as the price level rises and gain value as the price level falls. For instance, if you have $10,000 in cash, a 10 percent increase in the price level will reduce the purchasing power of that cash by 10 percent. When the price level rises, the *real value* of household wealth declines, and so will consumption. When the price level falls, the real value of household wealth rises, and so will consumption. This impact of the price level on consumption is called the *wealth effect.*

THE INTEREST-RATE EFFECT: HOW A CHANGE IN THE PRICE LEVEL AFFECTS INVESTMENT When prices rise, households and firms need more money to finance buying and selling. Therefore, when the price level rises households and firms try to increase the amount of money they hold by withdrawing funds from banks, borrowing from banks, or selling financial assets, such as bonds. These actions tend to drive up the interest rate charged on bank loans and the interest rate on bonds. (In Chapter 16, we analyze in more detail the relationship between money and interest rates.) A higher interest rate raises the cost of borrowing for firms and households. As a result, firms will borrow less to build new factories or to install new machinery and equipment, and households will borrow less to buy new houses. To a smaller extent, households will also borrow less to finance spending on automobiles, furniture, and other durable goods. Consumption will therefore be reduced. A lower price level will have the reverse effect, leading to an increase in investment and—to a lesser extent—consumption. This impact of the price level on investment is known as the *interest-rate effect.*

THE INTERNATIONAL-TRADE EFFECT: HOW A CHANGE IN THE PRICE LEVEL AFFECTS NET EXPORTS *Net exports* equal spending by foreign households and firms on goods and services produced in the United States minus spending by U.S. households and firms on goods and services produced in other countries. If the price level in the United States rises relative to the price levels in other countries, U.S. exports will become relatively more expensive and foreign imports will become relatively less expensive. Some consumers in foreign countries will shift from buying U.S. products to buying domestic products, and some U.S. consumers will also shift from buying U.S. products to buying imported products. U.S. exports will fall and U.S. imports will rise, causing net exports to fall. A lower price level in the United States has the reverse effect, causing net exports to rise. This impact of the price level on net exports is known as the *international-trade effect.*

Shifts of the Aggregate Demand Curve versus Movements Along It

An important point to remember is that the aggregate demand curve tells us the relationship between the price level and the quantity of real GDP demanded, *holding everything else constant.* If the price level changes, but other variables that affect the willingness of households, firms, and the government to spend are unchanged, the economy will move up or down a stationary aggregate demand curve. If any variable changes other than the price level, the aggregate demand curve will shift. For example, if government purchases increase and the price level remains unchanged, the aggregate demand curve will shift to the right at every price level. Or, if firms become pessimistic about the future profitability of investment and cut back spending on factories and machinery, the aggregate demand curve will shift to the left.

Don't Let This Happen To You!

Be Clear Why the Aggregate Demand Curve Is Downward Sloping

The aggregate demand curve and the demand curve for a single product are both downward sloping—but for different reasons. When we draw a demand curve for a single product, such as apples, we know that it will slope downward because as the price of apples rises, apples becomes more expensive relative to other products—like oranges—and consumers buy fewer apples and more of the other products. In other words, consumers substitute other products for apples. When the overall price level rises, the prices of all domestically-produced goods and services are rising, so consumers have no other domestic products to which they can switch. The aggregate demand curve slopes downward for the reasons given on pages 433–434: A lower price level raises the real value of household wealth (which increases consumption), lowers interest rates (which increases investment and consumption), and makes U.S. exports less expensive and foreign imports more expensive (which increases net exports).

***YOUR TURN:* Test your understanding by doing related problem 4 on page 459 at the end of this chapter.**

The Variables That Shift the Aggregate Demand Curve

The variables that cause the aggregate demand curve to shift fall into three categories:

- Changes in government policies
- Changes in the expectations of households and firms
- Changes in foreign variables

CHANGES IN GOVERNMENT POLICIES As we will discuss further in Chapters 16 and 17, the federal government uses monetary policy and fiscal policy to shift the aggregate demand curve. Monetary policy involves changes in interest rates, and fiscal policy involves changes in government purchases and taxes. Lower interest rates lower the cost to firms and households of borrowing. Lower borrowing costs increase consumption and investment spending, which shifts the aggregate demand curve to the right. Higher interest rates shift the aggregate demand curve to the left. Because government purchases are one component of aggregate demand, an increase in government purchases shifts the aggregate demand curve to the right, and a decrease in government purchases shifts the aggregate demand curve to the left. An increase in personal income taxes reduces the amount of spendable income available to households. Higher personal income taxes reduce consumption spending and shift the aggregate demand curve to the left. Lower personal income taxes shift the aggregate demand curve to the right. Increases in business taxes reduce the profitability of investment spending and shift the aggregate demand curve to the left. Decreases in business taxes shift the aggregate demand curve to the right.

CHANGES IN THE EXPECTATIONS OF HOUSEHOLDS AND FIRMS If households become more optimistic about their future incomes, they are likely to increase their current consumption. This increased consumption will shift the aggregate demand curve to the right. If households become more pessimistic about their future incomes, the aggregate demand curve will shift to the left. Similarly, if firms become more optimistic about the future profitability of investment spending, the aggregate demand curve will shift to the right. If firms become more pessimistic, the aggregate demand curve will shift to the left.

CHANGES IN FOREIGN VARIABLES If firms and households in other countries buy fewer U.S. goods or if firms and households in the United States buy more foreign goods, net exports will fall and the aggregate demand curve will shift to the left. As we saw in Chapter 11, when real GDP increases, so does the income available for consumers to spend. If real GDP in the United States increases faster than real GDP in other countries, U.S. imports will increase faster than U.S. exports, and net exports will fall. This pattern occurred in the late 1990s and early 2000s. Net exports will also fall if the *exchange rate* between the dollar and foreign currencies rises, because the price in foreign currency of U.S. products sold in other countries will rise, and the dollar price of foreign products sold in the United States will fall. An increase in net exports at every price level will shift the aggregate demand curve to the right. Net exports will increase if real GDP grows more slowly in the United States than in other countries or if the value of the dollar falls against other currencies. A change in net exports that results from a change in the price level in the United States will *not* cause the aggregate demand curve to shift.

14-1 Making the Connection

The Effect of Exchange Rates on Caterpillar's Sales

As we saw at the beginning of this chapter, Caterpillar sells more than half its construction equipment and engines outside of North America. As a result, its sales are significantly affected by changes in the exchange rate between the dollar and foreign currencies. For instance, about 30 percent of Caterpillar's sales are to Europe, so changes in the exchange rate between the dollar and the euro (€)—the common currency of many European economies—can have a significant effect on sales. The following chart shows changes in the exchange rate between the dollar and the euro—expressed as the number of euros necessary to purchase one dollar—from 1999 to mid-2005.

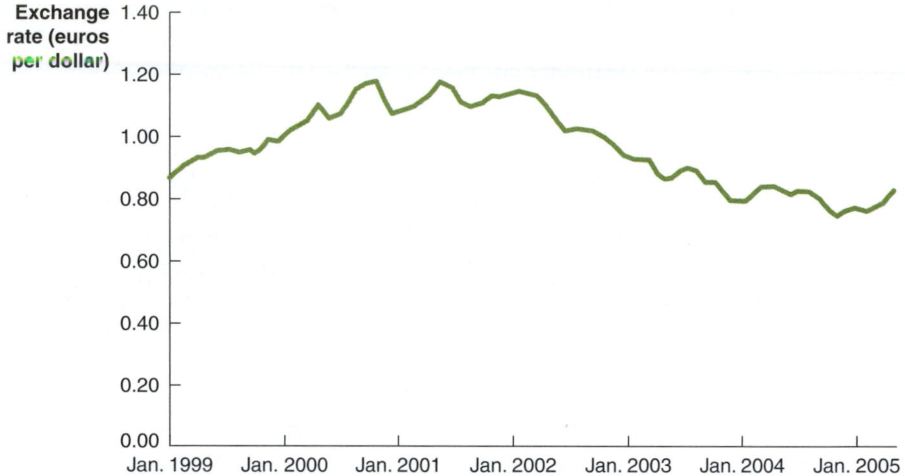

The more euros it takes to buy one dollar, the higher the euro price of Caterpillar's equipment. For example, consider a bulldozer that had a price of $100,000 in the United States. If the exchange rate was €0.86 = $1, as it was in January 1999, the equivalent price of the bulldozer in Europe would be €86,000 (= $100,000 × 0.86 euros per dollar). At the exchange rate of €1.17 = $1 in June 2001, the euro price of the bulldozer would be €117,000, or more than 35 percent higher than it had been in 1999. Not surprisingly, the rising value of the dollar during 2000 and 2001 combined with the effects of the recession to depress Caterpillar's sales. The falling value of the dollar from 2002 to 2004 combined with the economic expansion to increase Caterpillar's sales.

Because the value of the dollar rose against most currencies during 2000 and 2001, and fell against most currencies from 2002 to 2004, most U.S. exporters had experiences similar to Caterpillar's during those years.

The falling value of the dollar against the euro helped increase Caterpillar's sales from 2002 to 2004.

SOLVED PROBLEM 14-1

Movements along the Aggregate Demand Curve versus Shifts of the Aggregate Demand Curve

① LEARNING OBJECTIVE
Discuss the determinants of aggregate demand, and distinguish between a movement along the aggregate demand curve and a shift of the curve.

Suppose the current price level is 110 and the current level of real GDP is $11.2 trillion. Illustrate each of the following situations on a graph:

a. The price level rises to 115, while all other variables remain constant.

b. Firms become pessimistic and reduce their investment. Assume the price level remains constant.

Solving the Problem:

Step 1: Review the chapter material. This problem is about understanding the difference between movements along an aggregate demand curve and shifts of an aggregate demand curve, so you may want to review the section "Shifts of the Aggregate Demand Curve versus Movements Along It," which begins on page 424.

Step 2: To answer question (a), draw a graph showing a movement along the aggregate demand curve. Because there will be a movement along the aggregate demand curve, but no shift of the aggregate demand curve, your graph should look like this:

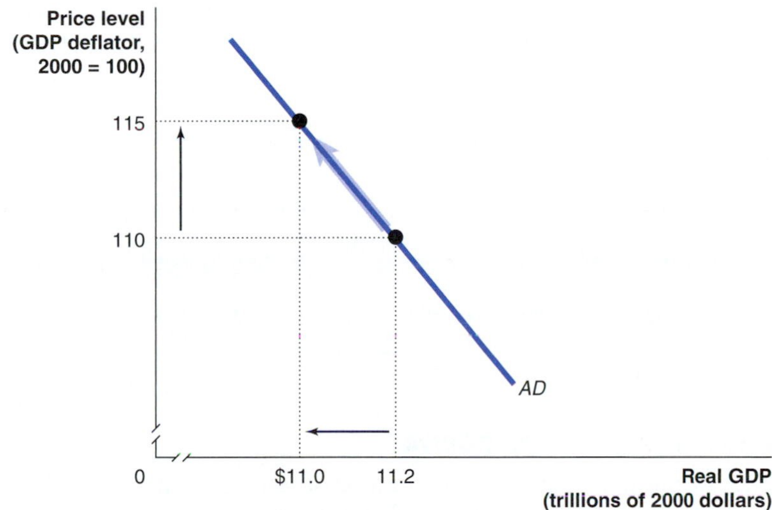

We don't have enough information to be certain what the new level of real GDP will be. We only know that it will be less than the initial level of $11.2 trillion—the graph shows the value as $11.0 trillion.

Step 3: To answer question (b), draw a graph showing a shift of the aggregate demand curve. We know that the aggregate demand curve will shift to the left, but we don't have enough information to know how far to the left it will shift. Let's assume the shift is $300 billion (or $0.3 trillion). In that case, your graph should look like this:

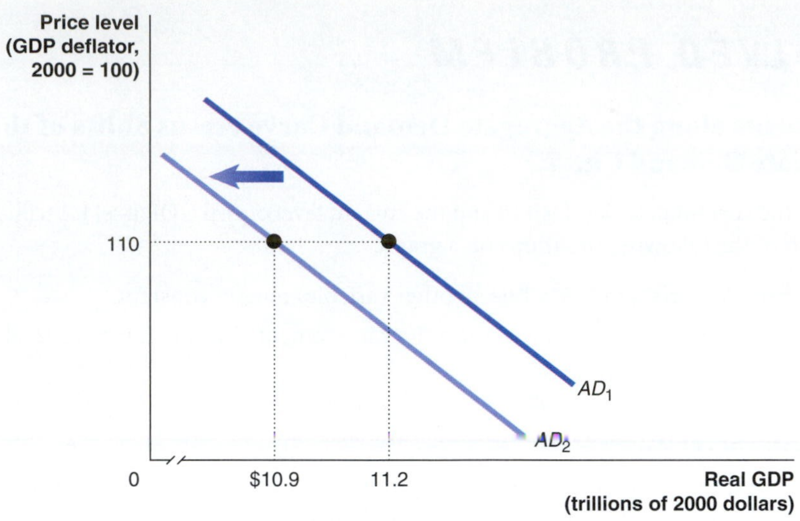

The graph shows a parallel shift in the aggregate demand curve, so that at every price level the quantity of real GDP demanded declines by $300 billion. For example, at a price level of 110, the quantity of real GDP demanded declines from $11.2 trillion to $10.9 trillion.

YOUR TURN: **For more practice, do related problem 5 on page 450 at the end of this chapter.**

Table 14-1 summarizes the most important variables that cause the aggregate demand curve to shift. It is important to notice that the table shows the shift in the aggregate demand curve that results from an increase in each of the variables. A *decrease* in these variables would cause the aggregate demand curve to shift in the opposite direction.

(2) **LEARNING OBJECTIVE**

Discuss the determinants of aggregate supply, and distinguish between a movement along the short-run aggregate supply curve and a shift of the curve.

Aggregate Supply

We just discussed the aggregate demand curve, which is one component of the aggregate demand and aggregate supply model. Now we turn to aggregate supply, which shows the effect of changes in the price level on the quantity of goods and services that firms are willing and able to supply. Because the effect of changes in the price level is very different in the short run than in the long run, we use two aggregate supply curves: one for the short run and one for the long run. We start by considering the *long-run aggregate supply curve.*

The Long-Run Aggregate Supply Curve

Long-run aggregate supply curve *(LRAS)* A curve showing the relationship in the long run between the price level and the quantity of real GDP supplied.

In Chapter 13, we saw that in the long run the level of real GDP is determined by the number of workers, the *capital stock*—including factories, office buildings, and machinery and equipment—and the available technology. Because changes in the price level do not affect the number of workers, the capital stock, or technology, *in the long run, changes in the price level do not affect the level of real GDP.* Remember that the level of real GDP in the long run is called *potential GDP* or *full-employment GDP.* At potential GDP, firms will operate at their normal level of capacity and everyone who wants a job will have one, except the structurally and frictionally unemployed. There is no reason for this normal level of capacity to change just because the price level has changed. The **long-run aggregate supply curve *(LRAS)*** is a curve showing the relationship in the long run between the price level and the quantity of real GDP supplied. As Figure 14-2 on page 430 shows, the price level was 108 in 2004 and potential real GDP was $11.0 trillion. If the price level had been 95, or if it had been 112, long-run aggregate supply would still have been a constant $11.0 trillion. Therefore, the *LRAS* is a vertical line.

TABLE 14-1

Variables That Shift the Aggregate Demand Curve

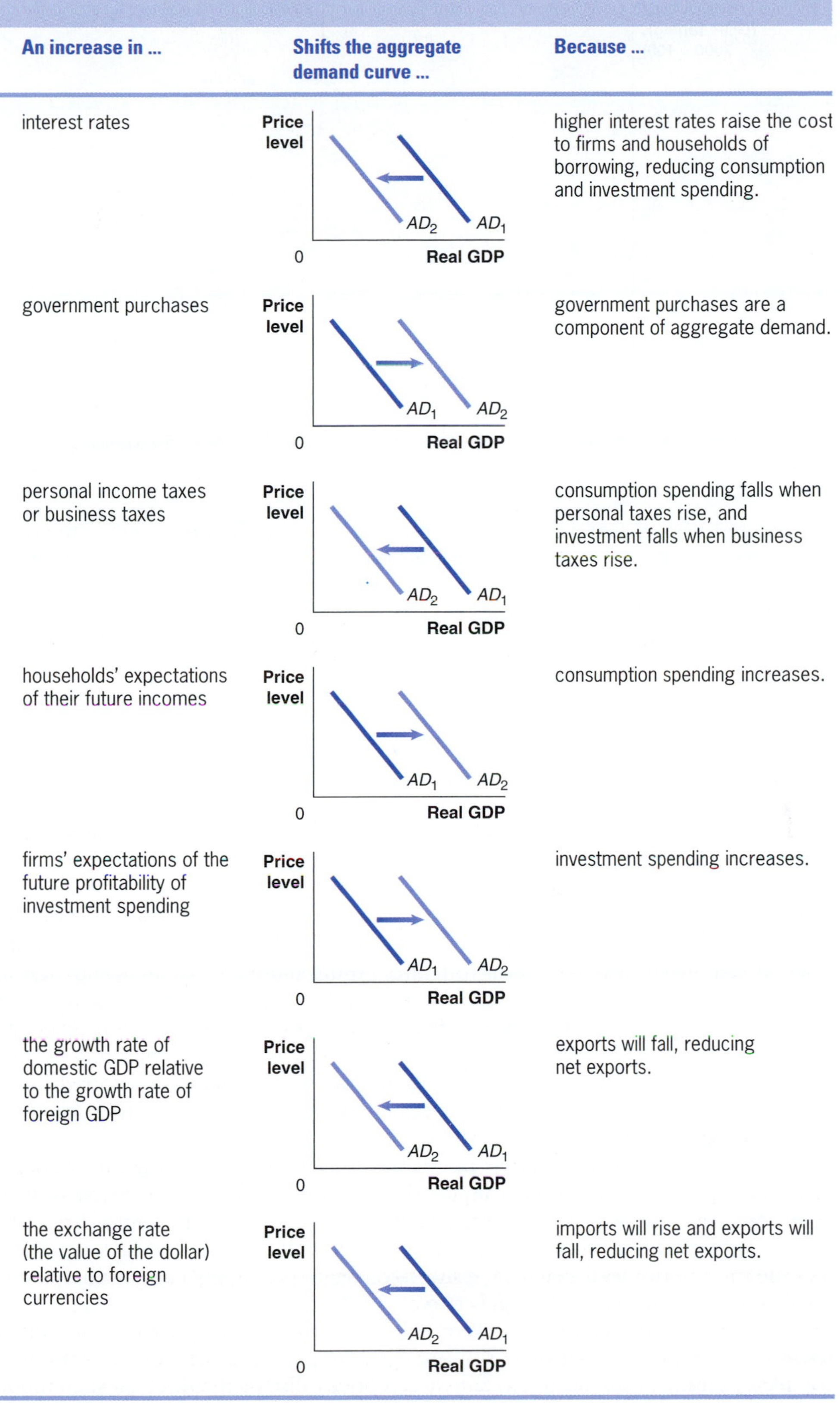

An increase in ...	Shifts the aggregate demand curve ...	Because ...
interest rates	Price level; AD_2; AD_1; 0; Real GDP	higher interest rates raise the cost to firms and households of borrowing, reducing consumption and investment spending.
government purchases	Price level; AD_1; AD_2; 0; Real GDP	government purchases are a component of aggregate demand.
personal income taxes or business taxes	Price level; AD_2; AD_1; 0; Real GDP	consumption spending falls when personal taxes rise, and investment falls when business taxes rise.
households' expectations of their future incomes	Price level; AD_1; AD_2; 0; Real GDP	consumption spending increases.
firms' expectations of the future profitability of investment spending	Price level; AD_1; AD_2; 0; Real GDP	investment spending increases.
the growth rate of domestic GDP relative to the growth rate of foreign GDP	Price level; AD_2; AD_1; 0; Real GDP	exports will fall, reducing net exports.
the exchange rate (the value of the dollar) relative to foreign currencies	Price level; AD_2; AD_1; 0; Real GDP	imports will rise and exports will fall, reducing net exports.

FIGURE 14-2

The Long-Run Aggregate Supply Curve

Changes in the price level do not affect the level of aggregate supply in the long run. Therefore, the long-run aggregate supply curve *(LRAS)* is a vertical line at the potential level of real GDP. For instance, the price level was 108 in 2004 and potential real GDP was $11.0 trillion. If the price level had been 95, or if it had been 112, long-run aggregate supply would still have been a constant $11.0 trillion. Each year the long-run aggregate supply curve shifts to the right as the number of workers in the economy increases, more machinery and equipment are accumulated, and technological change occurs.

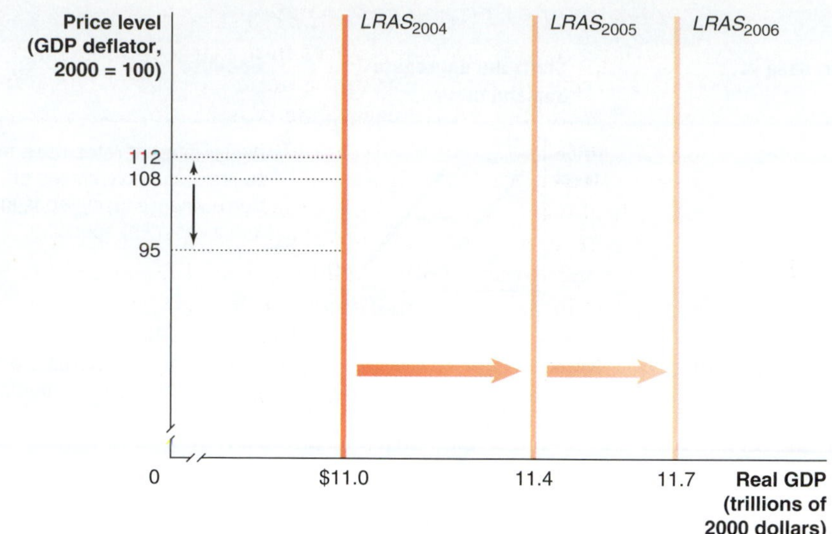

Figure 14-2 also shows that the long-run aggregate supply curve shifts to the right every year. This shift occurs because potential real GDP increases each year, as the number of workers in the economy increases, the economy accumulates more machinery and equipment, and technological change occurs. As Figure 14-2 shows, potential real GDP increased from $11.0 trillion in 2004 to $11.4 trillion in 2005 and to $11.7 trillion in 2006.

The Short-Run Aggregate Supply Curve

Although the *LRAS* is vertical, the short-run aggregate supply curve *(SRAS)* is upward sloping. The *SRAS* is upward sloping because, over the short run, as the price level increases, the quantity of goods and services firms are willing to supply will increase. The main reason firms are willing to supply more goods and services as the price level rises is that, *as prices of final goods and services rise, prices of inputs—such as the wages of workers or the price of natural resources—rise more slowly.* Profits rise when the prices of the goods and services firms sell rise more rapidly than the prices they pay for inputs. Therefore, a higher price level leads to higher profits and increases the willingness of firms to supply more goods and services. A secondary reason the *SRAS* curve slopes upward is that, as the price level rises or falls, some firms are slow to adjust their prices. A firm that is slow to raise its prices when the price level is increasing may find its sales increasing and, therefore, will increase production. A firm that is slow to reduce its prices when the price level is decreasing may find its sales falling and, therefore, will decrease production.

Why do some firms adjust prices more slowly than others, and why might the wages of workers and the prices of other inputs change more slowly than the prices of final goods and services? Most economists believe the explanation is that *some firms and workers fail to predict accurately changes in the price level.* If firms and workers could predict the future price level exactly, the short-run aggregate supply curve would be the same as the long-run aggregate supply curve.

But how does the failure of workers and firms to predict the price level accurately result in an upward-sloping short-run aggregate supply curve? Economists are not in complete agreement on this point, but we can briefly discuss the three most common explanations:

1. Contracts make some wages and prices "sticky."
2. Firms are often slow to adjust wages.
3. Menu costs make some prices sticky.

CONTRACTS MAKE SOME WAGES AND PRICES "STICKY" Prices or wages are said to be "sticky" when they do not respond quickly to changes in demand or supply. Contracts can make wages or prices sticky. For example, suppose the Ford Motor Company negotiates a three-year contract with the United Automobile Workers union at a time when demand for cars is increasing slowly. Suppose that after the contract is signed, the demand for cars starts to increase rapidly and prices of cars rise. Ford will find that producing more cars will be profitable, because it can increase car prices, while the wages it pays its workers are fixed by contract. Or a steel mill might have signed a multi-year contract to buy coal, which is used in making steel, at a time when the demand for steel is stagnant. If steel demand and steel prices begin to rise rapidly, producing additional steel will be profitable, because coal prices will remain fixed by contract. In both of these cases, rising prices lead to higher output. If these examples are representative of enough firms in the economy, a rising price level should lead to a greater quantity of goods and services supplied. In other words, the short-run aggregate supply curve will be upward sloping.

Notice, though, that if the workers at Ford or the managers of the coal companies had accurately predicted what would happen to prices, this prediction would have been reflected in the contracts, and Ford and the steel mill would not have earned greater profits when prices rose. In that case, rising prices would not have led to higher output.

FIRMS ARE OFTEN SLOW TO ADJUST WAGES We just noted that the wages of many union workers remain fixed by contract for several years. Many nonunion workers also have their wages or salaries adjusted only once a year. For instance, suppose you accept a job at a management consulting firm in June at a salary of $45,000 per year. The firm probably will not adjust your salary until the following June, even if the prices it can charge for its services later in the year are higher or lower than the firm had expected them to be when you were first hired. If firms adjust wages only slowly, a rise in the price level will increase the profitability of hiring more workers and producing more output. A fall in the price level will decrease the profitability of hiring more workers and producing more output. Once again, we have an explanation for why the short-run aggregate supply curve slopes upward.

It is worth noting that firms are often slower to *cut* wages than to increase them. Cutting wages can have a negative effect on the morale and productivity of workers and can also cause some of the firm's best workers to quit and look for jobs elsewhere.

MENU COSTS MAKE SOME PRICES STICKY Firms base their prices today partly on what they expect future prices to be. For instance, a restaurant has to decide ahead of time the prices it will charge for meals before printing menus. Many firms print catalogs that list the prices of their products. If demand for their products is higher or lower than the firms had expected, they may want to charge prices that are different from the ones printed in their menus or catalogs. Changing prices would be costly, however, because it would involve printing new menus or catalogs. The costs to firms of changing prices are called **menu costs**. To see why menu costs can lead to an upward-sloping short-run aggregate supply curve, consider the effect of an unexpected increase in the price level. In this case, firms will want to increase the prices they charge. Some firms, however, may not be willing to increase prices because of menu costs. Because of their relatively low prices, these firms will find their sales increasing, which will cause them to increase output. Once again, we have an explanation for a higher price level leading to a larger quantity of goods and services supplied.

Menu costs The costs to firms of changing prices.

Shifts of the Short-Run Aggregate Supply Curve versus Movements Along It

It is always important to remember the difference between a shift in a curve and a movement along a curve. The short-run aggregate supply curve tells us the short-run relationship between the price level and the quantity of goods and services firms are willing to supply, *holding constant all other variables that affect the willingness of firms to supply goods and services.* If the price level changes but other variables are unchanged, the economy will move up or down a stationary aggregate supply curve. If any variable other than the price level changes, the aggregate supply curve will shift.

Variables That Shift the Short-Run Aggregate Supply Curve

We now briefly discuss the five most important variables that cause the short-run aggregate supply curve to shift.

INCREASES IN THE LABOR FORCE AND IN THE CAPITAL STOCK A firm will supply more output at every price if it has more workers and more physical capital. The same is true of the economy as a whole. So, as the labor force and the capital stock grow, firms will supply more output at every price level, and the short-run aggregate supply curve will shift to the right. In Japan, the population is aging and the labor force is decreasing. Holding other variables constant, this decrease in the labor force causes the short-run aggregate supply curve in Japan to shift to the left.

TECHNOLOGICAL CHANGE As technological change takes place, the *productivity* of workers and machinery increases, which means firms can produce more goods and services with the same amount of labor and machinery. This improvement reduces the firms' costs of production and, therefore, allows them to produce more output at every price level. As a result, the short-run aggregate supply curve shifts to the right.

EXPECTED CHANGES IN THE FUTURE PRICE LEVEL If workers and firms believe that the price level is going to increase by 3 percent during the next year, they will try to adjust their wages and prices accordingly. For instance, if the United Automobile Workers union believes there will be 3 percent inflation next year, it knows that wages must rise 3 percent to preserve the purchasing power of those wages. Similar adjustments by other workers and firms will result in costs increasing throughout the economy by 3 percent. The result, shown in Figure 14-3, is that the short-run aggregate supply curve will shift to the left, so that any level of real GDP is now associated with a price level that is 3 percent higher. In general, *if workers and firms expect the price level to increase by a certain percentage, the* SRAS *curve will shift by an equivalent amount,* holding constant all other variables that affect the *SRAS* curve.

ADJUSTMENTS OF WORKERS AND FIRMS TO ERRORS IN PAST EXPECTATIONS ABOUT THE PRICE LEVEL Workers and firms sometimes make wrong predictions about the price level. As time passes, they will attempt to compensate for these errors. Suppose, for example, that the United Automobile Workers union signs a contract with Ford that contains only small wage increases because the company and the union expect only small increases in the price level. If increases in the price level turn out to be unexpectedly large, the union will take this into account when negotiating the next contract. The higher wages Ford's workers receive under the new contract will increase Ford's costs and result in Ford's needing to receive higher prices to produce the same level of output. If workers and firms across the economy are adjusting to the price level being higher than expected, the short-run aggregate supply curve will shift to the left. If they are adjusting to the price level being lower than expected, the short-run aggregate supply curve will shift to the right.

UNEXPECTED CHANGES IN THE PRICE OF AN IMPORTANT NATURAL RESOURCE An unexpected increase or decrease in the price of an important natural resource can cause firms' costs to be different from what they had expected. Oil prices can be particularly volatile. Some firms use oil in the production process. Other firms use products, such as plastics, that are made from oil. If oil prices rise unexpectedly, the costs of production will rise for these firms. Some utilities also burn oil to generate electricity, so electricity prices will rise. Rising oil prices lead to rising gasoline prices, which raise trans-

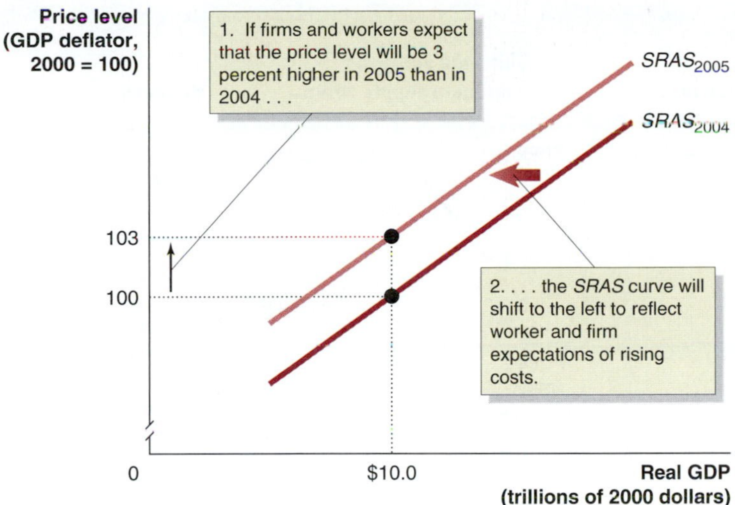

FIGURE 14-3

How Expectations of the Future Price Level Affect the Short-Run Aggregate Supply

The *SRAS* curve shifts to reflect worker and firm expectations of future prices.

1. If workers and firms expect the price level will rise by 3 percent from 100 to 103, they will adjust their wages and prices by that amount.
2. Holding constant all other variables that affect aggregate supply, the short-run aggregate supply curve will shift to the left.

If workers and firms expect the price level will be lower in the future, the short-run aggregate supply curve will shift to the right.

portation costs for many firms. Because firms face rising costs, they will only supply the same level of output at higher prices, and the short-run aggregate supply curve will shift to the left. An unexpected event that causes the short-run aggregate supply curve to shift is known as a **supply shock**. Supply shocks are often caused by an unexpected increase or decrease in the price of an important natural resource. In September 2005, the U.S. economy was hit with a different type of supply shock when hurricane Katrina slammed into the Gulf Coast region. Many people were killed, the city of New Orleans had to be evacuated, and as many as one million people in the region were forced to relocate. The Congressional Budget Office estimated that up to 400,000 jobs were temporarily lost because of the hurricane. About one-quarter of U.S. oil and natural gas output comes from the Gulf Coast, and about half of this output was disrupted by Katrina. The fall in oil production caused prices to soar, with the price of gasoline rising above $3.00 per gallon.

Supply shock An unexpected event that causes the short-run aggregate supply curve to shift.

Because the U.S. economy has experienced inflation every year since the 1930s, workers and firms always expect next year's price level to be higher than this year's price level. Holding everything else constant, this will cause the short-run aggregate supply curve to shift to the left. But everything else is not constant, because every year the U.S. labor force and the U.S. capital stock expand and changes in technology occur, which cause the short-run aggregate supply curve to shift to the right. Whether in any particular year the short-run aggregate supply curve shifts to the left or to the right depends on which of these variables has the largest impact during that year.

Table 14-2 on page 434 summarizes the most important variables that cause the short-run aggregate supply curve to shift. It is important to notice that the table shows the shift in the short-run aggregate supply curve that results from an *increase* in each of the variables. A *decrease* in these variables would cause the short-run aggregate supply curve to shift in the opposite direction.

Macroeconomic Equilibrium in the Long Run and the Short Run

(3) LEARNING OBJECTIVE

Use the aggregate demand and aggregate supply model to illustrate the difference between short-run and long-run macroeconomic equilibrium.

Now that we have discussed the components of the aggregate demand and aggregate supply model, we can use it to analyze changes in real GDP and the price level. In Figure 14-4 on page 435, we bring the aggregate demand curve, the short-run aggregate supply curve, and the long-run aggregate supply curve together in one graph, to show the *long-run macroeconomic equilibrium* for the economy. In the figure, equilibrium occurs at real GDP of $10.0 trillion and a price level of 100. Notice that in long-run equilibrium, the

TABLE 14-2

Variables That Shift the Short-Run Aggregate Supply Curve

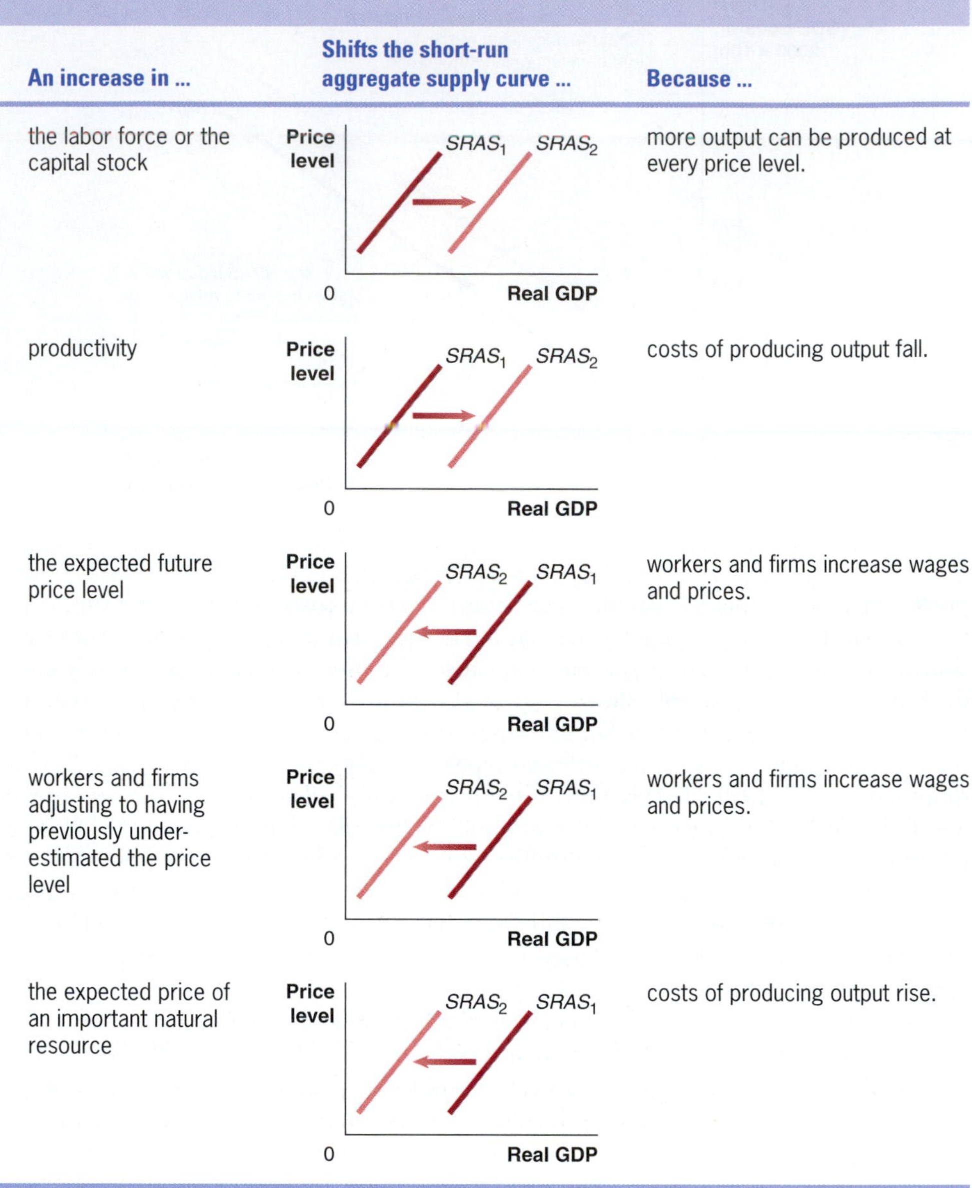

An increase in ...	Shifts the short-run aggregate supply curve ...	Because ...
the labor force or the capital stock	Price level; $SRAS_1$ → $SRAS_2$; 0; Real GDP	more output can be produced at every price level.
productivity	Price level; $SRAS_1$ → $SRAS_2$; 0; Real GDP	costs of producing output fall.
the expected future price level	Price level; $SRAS_2$ ← $SRAS_1$; 0; Real GDP	workers and firms increase wages and prices.
workers and firms adjusting to having previously under-estimated the price level	Price level; $SRAS_2$ ← $SRAS_1$; 0; Real GDP	workers and firms increase wages and prices.
the expected price of an important natural resource	Price level; $SRAS_2$ ← $SRAS_1$; 0; Real GDP	costs of producing output rise.

short-run aggregate supply curve and the aggregate demand curve intersect at a point on the long-run aggregate supply curve. Because equilibrium occurs at a point along the long-run aggregate supply curve, we know the economy is at potential real GDP: Firms will be operating at their normal level of capacity, and everyone who wants a job will have one, except the structurally and frictionally unemployed. We know, however, that the economy is often not in long-run macroeconomic equilibrium. In the following section, we discuss the economic forces that can push the economy away from long-run equilibrium.

Recessions, Expansions, and Supply Shocks

Because the full analysis of the aggregate demand and aggregate supply model can be complicated, we begin with a simplified case, using two assumptions:

1. The economy has not been experiencing any inflation. The price level is currently 100, and workers and firms expect it to remain at 100 in the future.
2. The economy is not experiencing any long-run growth. Potential real GDP is \$10.0 trillion and will remain at that level in the future.

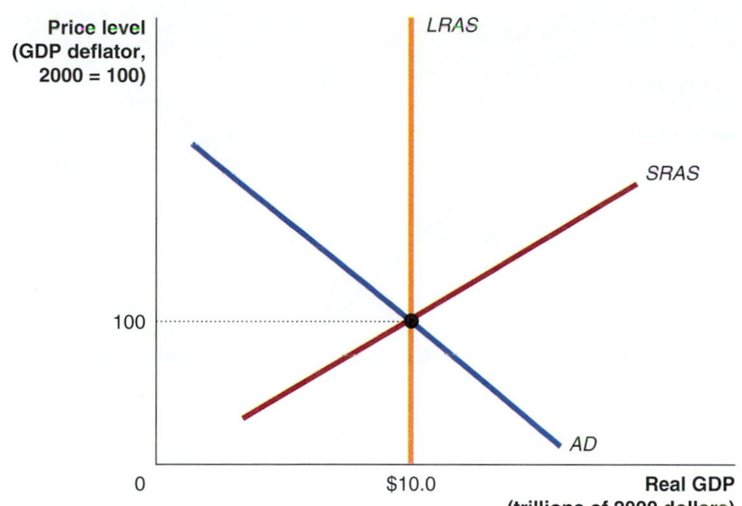

FIGURE 14-4

Long-Run Macroeconomic Equilibrium

In long-run macroeconomic equilibrium, the *AD* and *SRAS* curves intersect at a point on the *LRAS* curve. In this case, equilibrium occurs at real GDP of $10.0 trillion and a price level of 100.

These assumptions are simplifications because in reality the U.S. economy has experienced at least some inflation every year since the 1930s, and the potential real GDP also increases every year. However, the assumptions allow us to understand more easily the key ideas of the aggregate demand and aggregate supply model. In this section, we examine the short-run and long-run effects of recessions, expansions, and supply shocks.

RECESSION

The short-run effect of a decline in aggregate demand. Suppose that an outbreak of fighting in the Middle East causes firms to become pessimistic about the future profitability of new spending on factories and equipment. The decline in investment that results will shift the aggregate demand curve to the left, from AD_1 to AD_2, as shown in Figure 14-5 on page 436. The economy moves from point *A* to a new *short-run macroeconomic equilibrium* where the AD_2 curve intersects the *SRAS* curve at point *B*. In the new short-run equilibrium, real GDP has declined from $10.0 trillion to $9.8 trillion and is below its potential level. This lower level of GDP will result in declining profitability for many firms and layoffs for some workers: The economy will be in recession.

Adjustment back to potential GDP in the long run. We know that the recession will eventually end because there are forces at work that push the economy back to potential GDP in the long run. Figure 14-5 also shows how the economy moves from recession back to potential GDP. The shift from AD_1 to AD_2 initially leads to a short-run equilibrium with the price level having fallen from 100 to 98 (point *B*). Workers and firms will begin to adjust to the price level being lower than they had expected it to be. Workers will be willing to accept lower wages—because each dollar of wages is able to buy more goods and services—and firms will be willing to accept lower prices. In addition, the unemployment resulting from the recession will make workers more willing to accept lower wages, and the decline in demand will make firms more willing to accept lower prices. As a result, the *SRAS* curve will shift to the right from $SRAS_1$ to $SRAS_2$. At this point the economy will be back in long-run equilibrium (point *C*). The shift from $SRAS_1$ to $SRAS_2$ will not happen instantly. It may take the economy several years to return to potential GDP. The important conclusion is that a decline in aggregate demand causes a recession in the short run, but in the long run it causes only a decline in the price level.

Economists refer to the process of adjustment back to potential GDP just described as an *automatic mechanism* because it occurs without any actions by the government. An alternative to waiting for the automatic mechanism to end the recession is for the government to use monetary and fiscal policy to shift the *AD* curve to the right and restore potential GDP more quickly. We will discuss monetary and fiscal policy in Chapters 16 and 17. Economists debate whether or not we should wait for the automatic mechanism to end recessions, or whether it would be better to use monetary and fiscal policy.

FIGURE 14-5

The Short-Run and Long-Run Effects of Decrease in Aggregate Demand

In the short run, a decrease in aggregate demand causes a recession. In the long run, it causes only a decrease in the price level.

1. The decline in investment shifts aggregate demand from AD_1 to AD_2. Short-run equilibrium moves from potential GDP at point *A*, to recession at point *B*.
2. The price level of 98 at point *B* is lower than the price level of 100 that workers and firms had expected. As workers and firms adjust to the lower price level, prices and wages fall, and the short-run aggregate supply curve shifts from $SRAS_1$ to $SRAS_2$.
3. Equilibrium moves from point *B* back to potential GDP at point *C*, with a lower price level of 96.

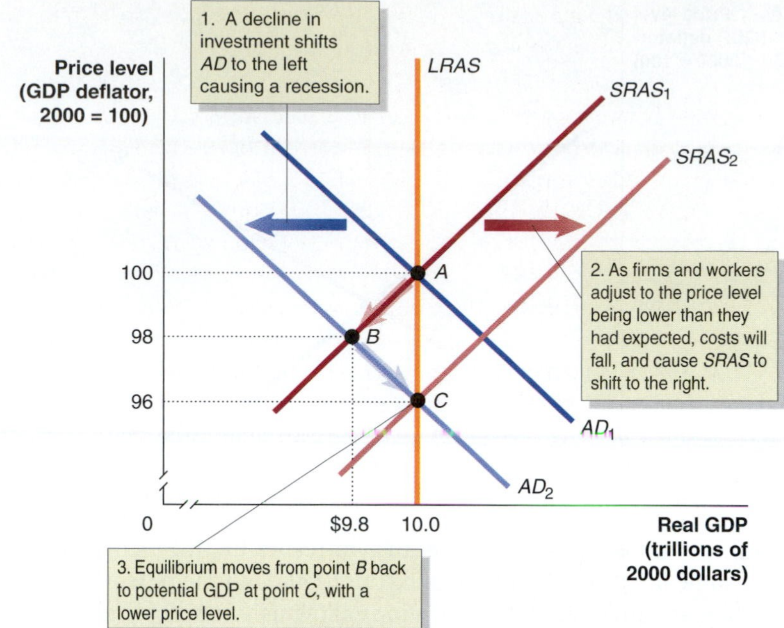

EXPANSION

The short-run effect of an increase in aggregate demand. Suppose that instead of becoming pessimistic, many firms become optimistic about the future profitability of new investment, as happened during the information technology and telecommunications booms of the late 1990s. The resulting increase in investment will shift the *AD* curve to the right, as is shown in Figure 14-6. Equilibrium moves from point *A* to point *B*. Real GDP rises from \$10.0 trillion to \$10.3 trillion, and the price level rises from 100 to 103. The economy will be above potential real GDP: Firms are operating beyond their

FIGURE 14-6

The Short-Run and Long-Run Effects of an Increase in Aggregate Demand

In the short run, an increase in aggregate demand causes an increase in real GDP. In the long run, it causes only an increase in the price level.

1. The increase in investment shifts aggregate demand from AD_1 to AD_2. Short-run equilibrium moves from potential GDP at point *A*, to beyond potential GDP at point *B*.
2. The price level of 103 at point *B* is higher than the price level of 100 that workers and firms had expected. As workers and firms adjust to the higher price level, prices and wages rise, and the short-run aggregate supply curve shifts from $SRAS_1$ to $SRAS_2$.
3. Equilibrium moves from point *B* back to potential GDP at point *C*, with a higher price level of 106.

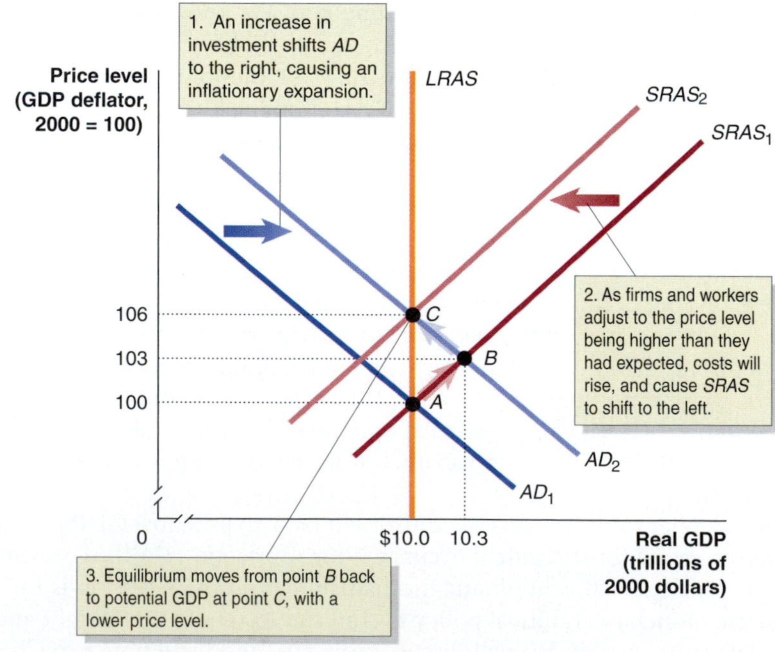

normal level of capacity, and some workers are employed who ordinarily would be structurally or frictionally unemployed, or who would not be in the labor force.

Adjustment back to potential GDP in the long run. Just as an automatic mechanism brings the economy back to potential GDP from a recession, an automatic mechanism brings the economy back from a short-run equilibrium beyond potential GDP. Figure 14-6 illustrates this mechanism. The shift from AD_1 to AD_2 initially leads to a short-run equilibrium with the price level rising from 100 to 103 (point *B*). Workers and firms will begin to adjust to the price level being higher than they had expected. Workers will push for higher wages—because each dollar of wages is able to buy fewer goods and services—and firms will charge higher prices. In addition, the low levels of unemployment resulting from the expansion will make it easier for workers to negotiate for higher wages, and the increase in demand will make it easier for firms to receive higher prices. As a result, the *SRAS* curve will shift to the left from $SRAS_1$ to $SRAS_2$. At this point, the economy will be back in long-run equilibrium. Once again, the shift from $SRAS_1$ to $SRAS_2$ will not happen instantly. The process of returning to potential GDP may stretch out for more than a year.

SUPPLY SHOCK

The short-run effect of a supply shock. Suppose oil prices increase substantially. This supply shock will increase many firms' costs and cause the *SRAS* curve to shift to the left, as is shown in panel (a) of Figure 14-7. Notice that the price level is higher in the

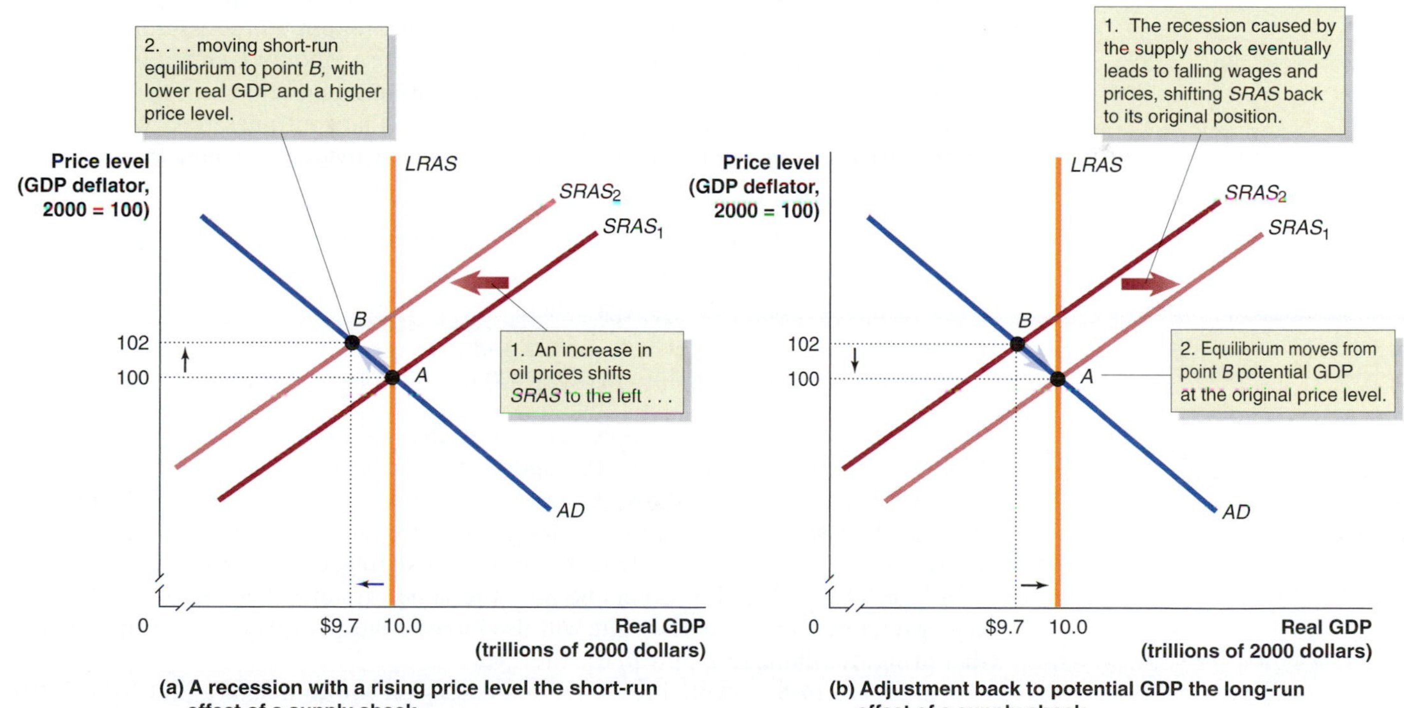

(a) A recession with a rising price level the short-run effect of a supply shock

(b) Adjustment back to potential GDP the long-run effect of a supply shock

FIGURE 14-7 The Short-Run and Long-Run Effects of a Supply Shock

Panel (a) shows that a supply shock, such as a large increase in oil prices, will cause a recession and a higher price level in the short run. The recession caused by the supply shock increases unemployment and reduces output. In panel *B*, rising unemployment and falling output result in workers being willing to accept lower wages and firms being willing to accept lower prices. The short-run aggregate supply curve shifts from $SRAS_2$ to $SRAS_1$. Equilibrium moves from point *B* back to potential GDP and the original price level at point *A*.

new short-run equilibrium (102 rather than 100) but real GDP is lower ($9.7 trillion rather than $10 trillion). This unpleasant combination of inflation and recession is called **stagflation.**

Stagflation A combination of inflation and recession, usually resulting from a supply shock.

Adjustment back to potential GDP in the long run. The recession caused by the supply shock increases unemployment and reduces output. This eventually results in workers being willing to accept lower wages and firms being willing to accept lower prices. In panel (b) of Figure 14-7, the short-run aggregate supply curve shifts from $SRAS_2$ to $SRAS_1$, moving the economy from point *B* back to point *A*. Potential GDP is regained at the original price level. It may take several years for this process to be completed. An alternative would be to use monetary and fiscal policy to shift the aggregate demand to the right. Using policy in this way would bring the economy back to potential GDP more quickly but would result in a permanently higher price level.

4 LEARNING OBJECTIVE

Use the dynamic aggregate demand and aggregate supply model to analyze macroeconomic conditions.

A Dynamic Aggregate Demand and Aggregate Supply Model

The basic aggregate demand and aggregate supply model used so far in this chapter gives us important insights into how short-run macroeconomic equilibrium is determined. Unfortunately, the model also gives us some misleading results. For instance, it incorrectly predicts that a recession caused by the aggregate demand curve shifting to the left will cause the price level to fall, which has not happened for an entire year since the 1930s. The difficulty with the basic model arises from the two assumptions we made when using it: (1) that the economy does not experience continuing inflation and (2) that the economy does not experience long-run growth. We can develop a more useful aggregate demand and aggregate supply model by dropping these assumptions. The result will be a model that takes into account that the economy is not *static,* with an unchanging level of potential real GDP and no continuing inflation, but *dynamic,* with potential real GDP that grows over time and inflation that continues every year. We can create a *dynamic aggregate demand and aggregate supply model* by making three changes to the basic model:

- Potential real GDP increases continually, shifting the long-run aggregate supply curve *(LRAS)* to the right.
- During most years, the aggregate demand curve *(AD)* will be shifting to the right.
- Except during periods when workers and firms expect high rates of inflation, the short-run aggregate supply curve *(SRAS)* will be shifting to the right.

The long-run aggregate supply curve continually shifts to the right, because over time the U.S. labor force and the U.S. capital stock will increase. Technological progress will also occur. Figure 14-8 shows the resulting increase in potential real GDP, which we illustrate by a shift to the right in the long-run aggregate supply curve from $LRAS_1$ to $LRAS_2$. The figure also shows that the short-run aggregate supply curve shifts from $SRAS_1$ to $SRAS_2$. This shift occurs because the same variables that cause the long-run aggregate supply to shift to the right, will also increase the quantity of goods and services that firms are willing to supply in the short run.

In Figure 14-8, potential real GDP increases over the course of a year from $10.0 trillion to $10.5 trillion. Assuming that no other variables that affect the *SRAS* curve have changed, the *LRAS* and *SRAS* curves will shift to the right by the same amount. But keep in mind that the *SRAS* curve is also affected by workers' and firms' expectations of future changes in the price level and by supply shocks. These variables can partially, or completely, offset the normal tendency of the *SRAS* curve to shift to the right over the course of a year.

The aggregate demand curve will usually be shifting to the right for several reasons: As population grows and incomes rise, consumption will increase over time. As the

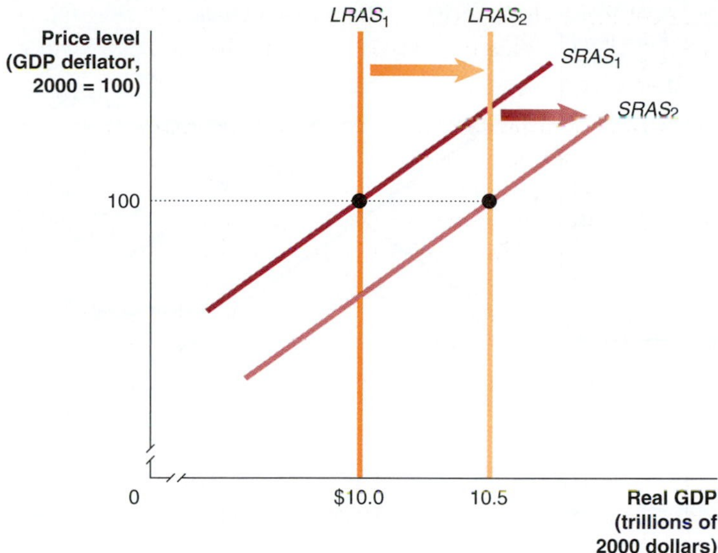

FIGURE 14-8

An Increase in Potential Real GDP

Increases in the labor force and the capital stock and technological change cause long-run aggregate supply to shift over the course of a year from $LRAS_1$ to $LRAS_2$, and cause short-run aggregate supply to shift from $SRAS_1$ to $SRAS_2$. If no other variables that affect the *SRAS* curve have changed, the *LRAS* and *SRAS* curves will shift to the right by the same amount.

economy grows, firms will expand capacity and new firms will be formed, increasing investment. An expanding population and an expanding economy require increased government services, such as more police officers and teachers, so government purchases will increase. Of course, we know that sometimes consumers, firms, and the government may cut back their expenditures. This reduced spending will result in the aggregate demand curve shifting to the right less than it normally would or, possibly, shifting to the left. As we will see, the aggregate demand curve shifting to the left will push the economy into recession, just as in the basic aggregate demand and aggregate supply model.

What Is the Usual Cause of Inflation?

The dynamic aggregate demand and aggregate supply model provides a more accurate explanation than the basic model of the source of most inflation. If total spending in the economy grows faster than total production, prices rise. Figure 14-9 illustrates this point by showing that if the *AD* curve shifts to the right by more than the *LRAS* curve, inflation results because equilibrium occurs at a higher price level, point *B*. In the new equilibrium, point *B*, the *SRAS* curve has shifted to the right by less than the *LRAS* curve because the anticipated increase in prices offsets some of the technological change and increases in the labor force and capital stock that occur during the year. Although inflation is generally the result of total spending growing faster than total production, a shift to the left of the short-run aggregate supply curve can also cause an increase in the price level, as we saw earlier in the discussion of supply shocks.

If aggregate demand increases by the same amount as short-run and long-run aggregate supply, the price level will not change. In this case, the economy experiences economic growth without inflation.

The Slow Recovery from the Recession of 2001

We can use the dynamic aggregate demand and aggregate supply model to analyze the slow recovery from the recession of 2001. The long economic expansion that began in March 1991 ended in March 2001, when a recession began. The recession was caused by a decline in aggregate demand. Several factors contributed to this decline:

- ***The end of the stock market "bubble."*** In the late 1990s, stock prices increased rapidly. Higher stock prices partly reflected higher corporate profits, but as we saw

FIGURE 14-9

Using Dynamic Aggregate Demand and Aggregate Supply to Understand Inflation

The most common cause of inflation is total spending increasing faster than total production.

1. The economy begins at point *A*, with real GDP of $10.0 trillion and a price level of 100. An increase in full-employment real GDP from $10.0 trillion to $10.5 trillion causes long-run aggregate supply to shift from $LRAS_1$ to $LRAS_2$. Aggregate demand shifts from AD_1 to AD_2.
2. Because *AD* shifts to the right by more than the *LRAS* curve, the price level in the new equilibrium rises from 100 to 104.

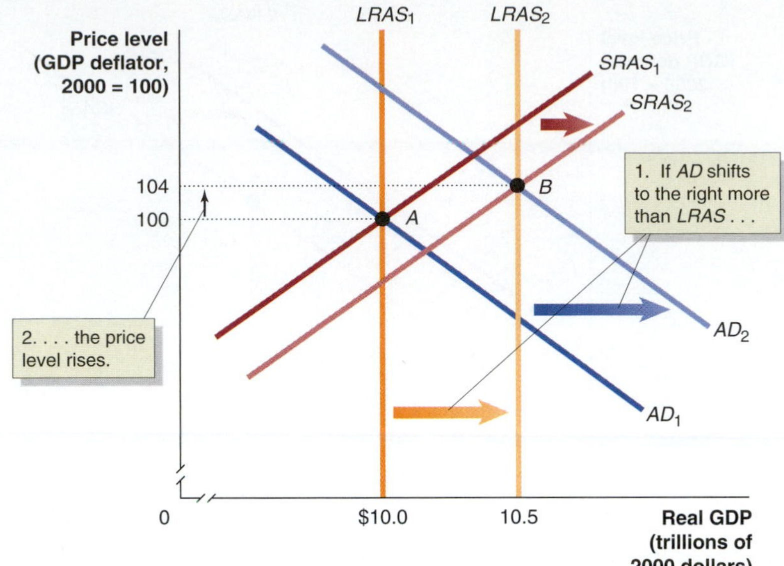

in Chapter 1, they also reflected the excessive optimism of investors about the future of dot-com companies. The increase in stock prices between 1995 and 2000 increased the wealth of U.S. households by $9 trillion. Stock prices began to fall in the spring of 2000 and eventually fell almost as far as they had risen. By 2002, the total value of stocks had declined by $7 trillion from their peak of two years before. The fall in stock prices reduced spending by households and firms. Firms that had financed investment spending by issuing new stock now had a more difficult time raising funds.

- *Excessive investment in information technology.* During the late 1990s, many firms overestimated the future profitability of investment in information technology. For example, telecommunications firms laid many more miles of fiber-optic cable than there was demand in the short run. Some firms also invested in computers and software in anticipation of the year 2000 (Y2K) problem. This problem arose from the technical difficulty many older computers had in correctly interpreting dates in years after 1999. Once older software and computers had been replaced, spending declined. Similarly, many firms had invested heavily to establish a presence on the Internet. When their Internet sales proved disappointing, the companies had more computers than they needed. For these reasons, by the spring of 2001, many companies had sharply cut back on their investment spending.
- *The terrorist attacks of September 11, 2001.* The terrorist attacks on New York and Washington, D.C., increased the level of uncertainty in the economy. Many feared further attacks would occur, and they were uncertain how the economy would respond. When firms and households face uncertainty, they often postpone spending until the uncertainty is resolved.
- *The corporate accounting scandals.* As we saw in Chapter 5, the top managers of some corporations, such as WorldCom, Tyco, and Enron, manipulated their financial statements during the stock market boom to make their corporations appear more profitable than they actually were. When these accounting manipulations were finally brought to light, some investors lost faith in the accuracy of corporate financial statements, which helped depress stock prices and added to the uncertainty in the economy.

Few economists were surprised that the long expansion of the 1990s eventually ended in recession. Although forecasting the exact date the recession would begin was

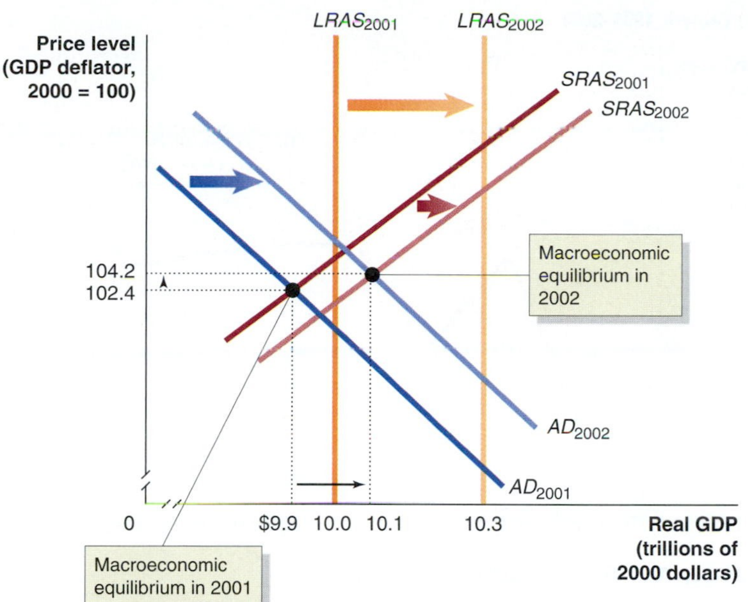

FIGURE 14-10

Using Dynamic Aggregate Demand and Aggregate Supply to Understand the Recovery from the 2001 Recession

Between 2001 and 2002, *AD* shifted to the right but not by nearly enough to offset the shift to the right of *LRAS*, which reflected the increase in potential real GDP from \$10.0 trillion to \$10.3 trillion. Although real GDP increased from \$9.9 trillion in 2001 to \$10.1 trillion in 2002, this still was far below the potential real GDP, shown by $LRAS_{2002}$. As a result, the unemployment rate rose from 4.7 percent in 2001 to 5.8 percent in 2002. Because the increase in aggregate demand was small, the price level increased only from 102.4 in 2001 to 104.2 in 2002, so the inflation rate for 2002 was only 1.8 percent.

very difficult, it was inevitable that the expansion would end, just as all previous expansions had. Some economists were surprised, however, at the weakness of the expansion that began when the recession ended in November 2001. Figure 14-10 illustrates the changes in the economy from 2001 to 2002 and shows that the economy remained well below potential GDP during 2002.

In Figure 14-10, the *AD* curve shifts to the right much less than does the *LRAS* curve. As a result, the price level increases only from 102.4 in 2001 to 104.2 in 2002, for a very low inflation rate of 1.8 percent. Real GDP increases only from \$9.9 trillion to \$10.1 trillion, which is below the potential level of \$10.3 trillion, shown by $LRAS_{2002}$. Not surprisingly, the unemployment rate actually rose from 4.7 percent in 2001 to 5.8 percent in 2002.

The increase in aggregate demand during 2002 was weak because the factors that had caused the recession continued to weigh on the economy. Stock prices did not begin to rise significantly until 2003. Many firms still did not feel the need to increase investment spending, particularly on information technology, on which they had spent heavily during the late 1990s. Uncertainty remained high as the federal government continued the war on terrorism and prepared for the invasion of Iraq. Finally, each week during 2002 seemed to bring the revelation of a new corporate accounting scandal. It is not surprising, as we saw at the beginning of this chapter, that Caterpillar and other firms were still experiencing slow sales during 2002.

Does Rising Productivity Growth Reduce Employment?

14-2 Making the Connection

We saw in Chapter 13 that growth in output per worker—labor productivity—is the key to rising living standards over the long run. But if firms can produce more output with the same number of workers, are they less likely to hire additional workers? Some observers argued that this was happening during 2002 and 2003 as productivity and real GDP rose, yet employment grew very little. The following two charts show that productivity—measured as total output of all nonfarm businesses produced per hour worked—did in fact grow very rapidly during 2002 and 2003, and that employment as measured by the Bureau of Labor Statistics' establishment survey declined.

In 2002–2003, companies like Harley-Davidson expanded output without expanding employment.

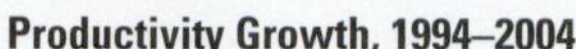

Productivity Growth, 1994–2004

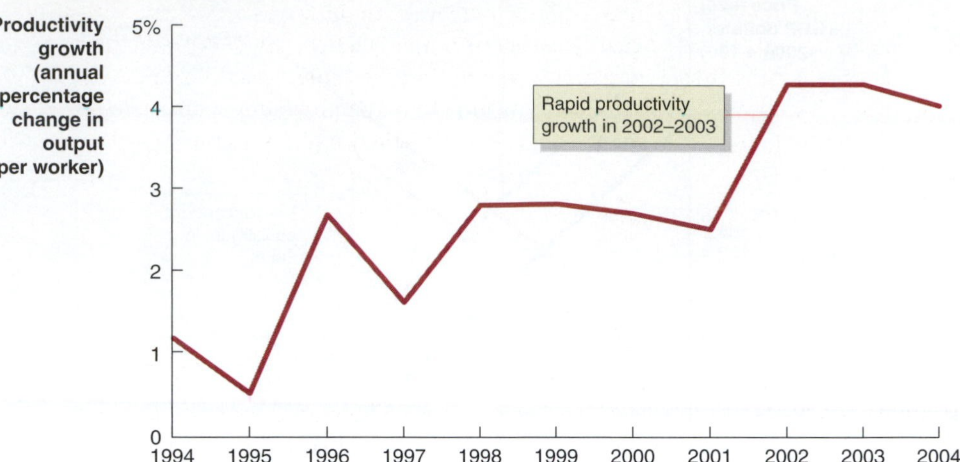

Employment, January 1994–December 2004

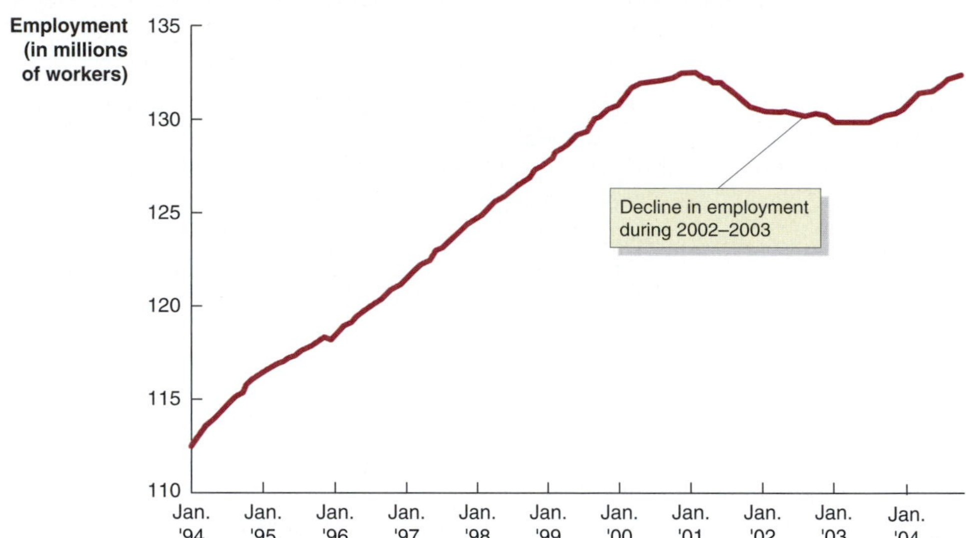

Source (both charts): Bureau of Labor Statistics; employment data from the establishment survey.

In the dynamic aggregate demand and aggregate supply model, the higher the growth of productivity during a year, the further to the right the *LRAS* and *SRAS* curves will shift. But rising productivity also leads to rising incomes, in part because rising output per worker makes it possible for firms to pay higher wages. These rising incomes raise consumption spending and allow the *AD* curve to shift to the right by enough to maintain GDP at its potential level. In 2002–2003, however, the economy was still operating below potential GDP and many firms appeared reluctant to expand employment as rapidly as typically happens during an economic recovery. In these circumstances, rising productivity made it possible for at least some firms to expand output without expanding employment. Most economists agree that rapid productivity growth probably played some role in the slow employment growth of 2002 and 2003, but the effect was only temporary. We know that over the long run, the level of employment is determined by population growth and by factors—such as the level of retirement benefits and government unemployment insurance payments—that affect the fraction of the population in the labor force. The level of employment is not determined in the long run by the rate of productivity growth. In fact, a report from the Federal Reserve Bank of Dallas noted that between 1979 and 2003 the level of productivity in the U.S. economy increased by 67 percent, while during the same period 40 million new jobs were created. That the effect of productivity growth on employment is only temporary was demonstrated in 2004, as productivity growth remained high, but employment began to increase more rapidly.

Source: Federal Reserve Bank of Dallas, *2003 Annual Report.*

The More Rapid Recovery of 2003–2004

The recovery from the recession of 2001 accelerated in the second half of 2003 and through 2004. For several reasons, aggregate demand increased more rapidly than it had during 2002 and early 2003. Low interest rates spurred spending on new houses and helped increase investment spending by firms. Tax cuts increased both consumption and investment spending. Rising stock prices contributed to increased consumption and investment spending. Finally, the value of the dollar declined against most foreign currencies, which helped exports.

Figure 14-11 shows the results of the more rapid increase in aggregate demand during 2004. In 2003, real GDP was 3.7 percent below its potential level, while the unemployment rate was 6.0 percent. The figure shows that the large shift in aggregate demand during 2004 led to an increase in real GDP from $10.3 trillion to $10.8 trillion. This level was still below potential real GDP of $11.0 trillion, but the gap had narrowed to 1.8 percent. As a result, the unemployment rate fell from 6.0 percent to 5.2 percent. The rapid increase in aggregate demand caused a rise in the inflation rate. The price level increased from 106.3 in 2003 to 109.1 in 2004, for an inflation rate of 2.6 percent. This was higher than the inflation rate of 2.0 percent during 2003.

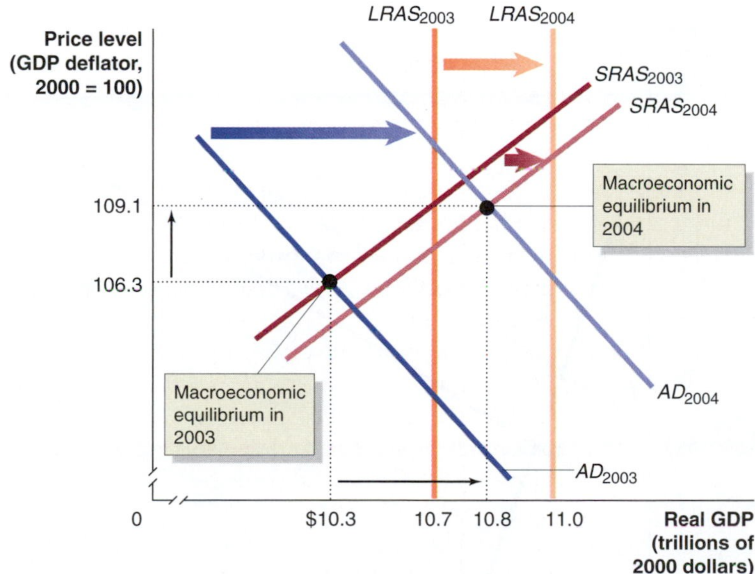

FIGURE 14-11

Using Dynamic Aggregate Demand and Aggregate Supply to Understand the More Rapid Recovery of 2003–2004

The figure shows that the large shift in aggregate demand during 2004 led to an increase in real GDP from $10.3 trillion to $10.8 trillion. This was still below the potential real GDP of $11.0 trillion, but the gap had narrowed to 1.8 percent. As a result, the unemployment rate fell from 6.0 percent to 5.2 percent. The rapid increase in aggregate demand did cause a rise in the inflation rate. The price level increased from 106.3 in 2003 to 109.1 in 2004, for an inflation rate of 2.6 percent.

SOLVED PROBLEM 14-2

(4) LEARNING OBJECTIVE

Use the dynamic aggregate demand and aggregate supply model to analyze macroeconomic conditions.

Showing the Oil Shock of 1974–1975 on a Dynamic Aggregate Demand and Aggregate Supply Graph

The 1974–1975 recession clearly illustrates how a supply shock affects the economy. Following the Arab–Israeli War of 1973, the Organization of Petroleum Exporting Countries (OPEC) increased the price of a barrel of oil from less than \$3 to more than \$10. Use this information and the statistics in the following table to draw a dynamic aggregate demand and aggregate supply graph showing macroeconomic equilibrium for 1974 and 1975. Assume that the aggregate demand curve did not shift between 1974 and 1975. Provide a brief explanation of your graph.

	ACTUAL REAL GDP	POTENTIAL REAL GDP	PRICE LEVEL
1974	\$4.32 trillion	\$4.35 trillion	34.7
1975	\$4.31 trillion	\$4.50 trillion	38.0

Source: U.S. Department of Commerce, Bureau of Economic Analysis.

Solving the Problem:

Step 1: Review the chapter material. This problem is about using the dynamic aggregate demand and aggregate supply model, so you may want to review the section "A Dynamic Aggregate Demand and Aggregate Supply Model," which begins on page 438.

Step 2: Use the information in the table to draw the graph. We need to draw five curves: *AD*, *SRAS*, and *LRAS* for both 1974 and 1975 (the *AD* curve will be the same for both years). We know that the two *LRAS* curves will be vertical lines at the values given for potential GDP in the table. Because of the large supply shock, we know that the *SRAS* curve shifted to the left. We are instructed to assume that the *AD* curve did not shift. Your graph should look like this:

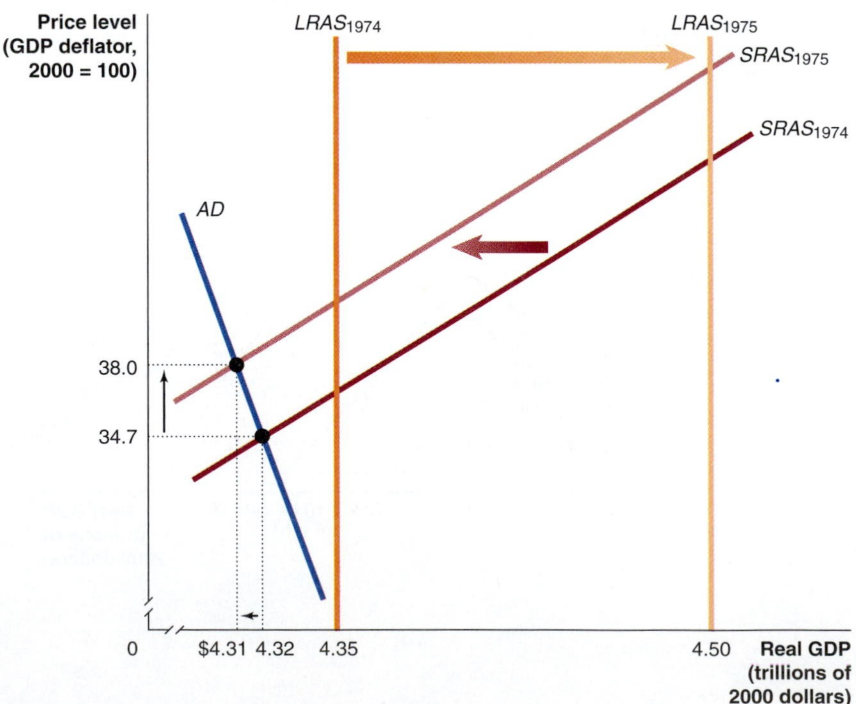

Step 3: Explain your graph. $LRAS_{1974}$ and $LRAS_{1975}$ are at the levels of potential real GDP for each year. Macroeconomic equilibrium for 1974 occurs where the *AD* curve intersects the $SRAS_{1974}$ curve, with real GDP of $4.32 trillion and a price level of 34.7. Macroeconomic equilibrium for 1975 occurs where the *AD* curve intersects the $SRAS_{1975}$ curve, with real GDP of $4.31 trillion and a price level of 38.0.

Extra Credit: As a result of the supply shock, the economy moved from an equilibrium output just below potential GDP in 1974 (the recession actually began right at the end of 1973) to an equilibrium well below potential GDP in 1975. With real GDP in 1975 about 4.2 percent below its potential level, the unemployment rate soared from 5.6 percent in 1974 to 8.5 percent in 1975.

YOUR TURN: **For more practice, do related problems 13 and 15 on pages 450–451 at the end of this chapter.**

Conclusion

Chapter 3 demonstrated the power of the microeconomic model of demand and supply in explaining how the prices and quantities of individual products are determined. This chapter showed that we need a different model to explain the behavior of the whole economy. We saw that the macroeconomic model of aggregate demand and aggregate supply explains fluctuations in real GDP and the price level.

One of the great disagreements among economists and political leaders is whether the federal government should intervene to try to reduce fluctuations in real GDP and keep the unemployment and inflation rates low. We explore this important issue in Chapters 16 and 17, but first, in the next chapter we consider the role money plays in the economy.

Read *An Inside Look* on the next page to learn how real GDP in Japan responded to increases in net exports.

An Inside Look Construction Company Komatsu Benefits from Exports to China

FINANCIAL TIMES, MARCH 2, 2004

The Recovery Is Still Fragile

a . . . Anyone would think Japan had become the world's latest tiger economy. According to official figures, gross domestic product rose 7 percent in real, deflation-adjusted terms in the fourth quarter–a rate of growth not seen since the intoxicating 1980s. The January trade surplus, swollen by shipments to China, rose almost fivefold from last year as exporters brushed aside the effects of a strengthening yen.

Moreover, the benefits of an export-led recovery are beginning to filter into the job market. Unemployment has fallen from a postwar peak of 5.5 percent in January last year to 4.9 percent in December. Corporate profits have surged, while wages have stabilized after years of decline. . . .

The Nikkei stock average, which has clawed its way back to 11,300, is 50 percent above last April's post-bubble lows. . . . Last year's talk of spiralling deflation, or an imminent collapse of the financial system under the weight of non-performing loans, now seems like absurd scaremongering. . . .

Indeed, with many reasons for caution it would be foolish to take recent headline growth figures at face value. But some things really do seem different this time around.

For a start, unlike the recoveries of the 1990s, this one has not been started by lavish government spending. Although the annual budget deficit is still running at a worrying 8 percent of GDP, the government has been paring discretionary spending and raising taxes to pay for non-discretionary items such as social security.

In the absence of government-led stimulation, companies have been taking matters into their own hands. Masamoto Yashiro, chairman of Shinsei, a rescued bank whose successful initial public offering in Tokyo last month has become symbolic of corporate revitalization, says many Japanese companies have spent several years quietly getting back into shape.

b According to Mr Yashiro, years after the bubble burst most businesses were still postponing tough decisions, convinced that asset prices would recover and that their problems would float away. Since the late 1990s, he says, prodded by the need to compete with China and by the realization that Japan's years of easy growth were over, they had been disposing of non-core businesses, shifting production abroad and paying down borrowings. Merrill Lynch estimates that, at this rate, corporate debt will be back to pre-bubble levels within two years.

. . . Japan's recovery, like those before it, leans heavily on exports. It is true about two-thirds of recent growth has been accounted for by private investment. But most economists say this is almost overwhelmingly due to capital investment by export-oriented companies.

ING calculates that as much as 80 percent of the export improvement is thanks to China, which has surpassed the US as Japan's biggest trading partner. Some of those shipments may be supplying Japanese factories in China and therefore ultimately destined for the US. In any case, Japan remains extremely vulnerable to an external shock, whether it be a slowdown in the US or in China itself. . . .

Three times a year, Komatsu, the world's second largest construction equipment maker, holds an auction for used machinery in the Japanese ports of Yokohama, Kobe and Nagoya . . .

c Komatsu's used machines–remnants from Japan's heady bubble-era building days–account for nearly half of its machines in use in China, which has a voracious appetite for goods related to infrastructure. By 2005, Komatsu's sales to China are expected to reach ¥107bn (Dollars 980m, Pounds 530m, Euros 790m), more than double the ¥45.2bn achieved in 2002.

Throughout Japan, industries including construction machinery, steel and shipbuilding, which until recently had been sitting on idle capacity, are suddenly worried that they will not be able to meet China's seemingly endless demand.

The value of Japanese goods exported to China rose 33.8 percent in January compared with the same period a year ago, while shipments to the US, until recently Japan's biggest trading partner, fell 5.4 percent. . . .

Key Points in the Article

This article discusses the strong performance of the Japanese economy at the end of 2003. It highlights the effect of increasing exports on aggregate demand. It also mentions that capital spending, or investment spending, which is another component of aggregate demand, has been increasing in Japan.

Analyzing the News

a Japanese economic growth from the late 1940s through the 1980s had been very rapid. This rapid growth had allowed Japan to make the transition to becoming an industrialized, high-income country. But during the 1990s, the growth rate of the Japanese economy slowed, and real GDP in Japan was below its potential GDP level for most of the 1990s and early 2000s. We will discuss further in Chapters 16 and 17 why this happened. A large part of the rapid growth Japan experienced during 2003 occurred due to increases in the net export component of aggregate demand. Net exports rose despite the fact that the yen was increasing in value. An increasing exchange rate will usually cause net exports to fall. In this case, however, the Chinese economy was growing so rapidly that demand for Japanese products grew despite the rising value of the yen.

b Although Japan was experiencing an "export-led recovery," investment spending was also increasing. During the 1990s and early 2000s, investment spending had grown slowly. Many corporations had borrowed heavily to finance expansion during the 1980s, and had been unwilling to consider additional investment until their debt had been reduced.

We can use the aggregate demand and aggregate supply model to analyze what happened to the Japanese economy during 2002 and 2003. Information from the article and from Japanese government statistics is used in Figure 1. The figure shows that in 2002 the economy was in short-run macroeconomic equilibrium with real GDP (measured in Japanese yen) of ¥533 trillion and a price level of 93.5. During 2003, aggregate demand, short-run aggregate supply, and long-run aggregate supply all shifted to the right. Equilibrium real GDP rose to ¥547 trillion. At the same time, the price level actually fell to 91.1. So, during 2003 the Japanese economy experienced growth in real GDP of 2.6 percent, but *deflation* of 2.6 percent. Because deflation continued several years, wages and other costs fell, which caused aggregate supply to shift to the right by more than it would have had workers and firms expected a constant price level.

c Komatsu is the second-largest manufacturer of construction equipment in the world, behind Caterpillar. Komatsu is expected to more than double its sales to China by 2005, compared with 2002. Construction companies, such as Komatsu and Caterpillar, usually do well in rapidly growing economies, particularly if economic growth is accompanied by population growth. The very slow growth of the Japanese population has been a disadvantage for Komatsu, but has been at least partially offset by the firm's access to the Chinese economy.

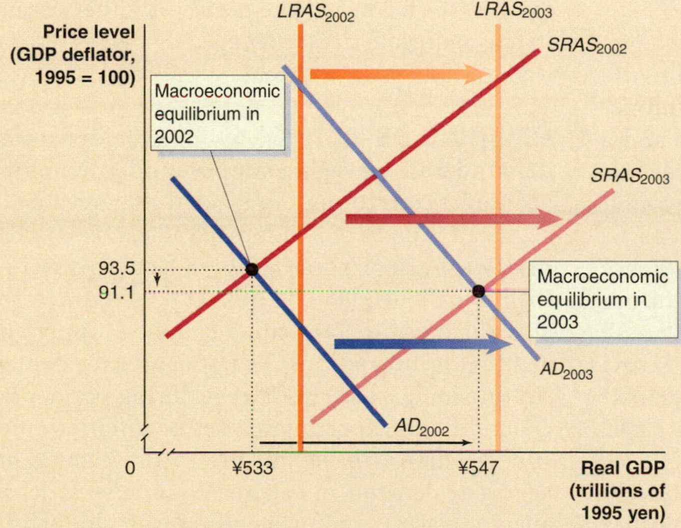

Figure 1: Japanese economic expansion during 2003.

Thinking Critically

1. Briefly explain whether investment spending is likely to increase more rapidly in a country with a rapidly growing population, or in a country with a slowly growing population. Does your answer depend on whether the country is a high-income industrial country or a low-income developing country?
2. In 2004, the value of the dollar was fixed against the Chinese yuan at a constant rate of about 8.3 yuan to the dollar. Suppose that the government of China decided to stop fixing the value of the yuan versus the dollar, and that as a result the value of the yuan rose against the dollar. Would this be good news or bad news for Caterpillar? For Komatsu?

Source: David Pilling and Mariko Sanchanta, "The Recovery Is Still Fragile," *Financial Times*, March 2, 2004. Used with permission of Financial Times.

SUMMARY

LEARNING OBJECTIVE ① Discuss the determinants of aggregate demand, and distinguish between a movement along the aggregate demand curve and a shift of the curve. The *aggregate demand and aggregate supply model* enables us to explain short-run fluctuations in real GDP and the price level. The *aggregate demand curve (AD)* shows the relationship between the price level and the quantity of real GDP demanded by households, firms, and the government. The *short-run aggregate supply curve (SRAS)* shows the relationship in the short run between the price level and the quantity of real GDP supplied by firms. The *long-run aggregate supply curve* shows the relationship in the long run between the price level and the quantity of real GDP supplied. The four components of aggregate demand are consumption *(C)*, investment *(I)*, government purchases *(G)*, and net exports *(NX)*. The aggregate demand curve is downward sloping because a decline in the price level causes consumption, investment, and net exports to increase. If the price level changes but all else remains constant, the economy will move up or down a stationary aggregate demand curve. If any variable other than the price level changes, the aggregate demand curve will shift. The variables that cause the aggregate demand curve to shift are divided into three categories: changes in government policies, changes in the expectations of households and firms, and changes in foreign variables.

LEARNING OBJECTIVE ② Discuss the determinants of aggregate supply, and distinguish between a movement along the short-run aggregate supply curve and a shift of the curve. The long-run aggregate supply curve is a vertical line because in the long run real GDP is always at its potential level and is unaffected by the price level. The short-run aggregate supply curve slopes upward because workers and firms fail to predict accurately the future price level. The three main explanations of why this failure results in an upward-sloping aggregate supply curve are: (1) contracts make wages and prices "sticky," (2) businesses often adjust wages slowly, and (3) menu costs make some prices sticky. If the price level changes but all else remains constant, the economy will move up or down a stationary aggregate supply curve. If any variable other than the price level changes, the aggregate supply curve will shift. The aggregate supply curve shifts as a result of increases in the labor force and the capital stock, technological change, expected increases or decreases in the future price level, adjustments of workers and firms to errors in past expectations about the price level, and unexpected increases or decreases in the price of an important raw material.

LEARNING OBJECTIVE ③ Use the aggregate demand and aggregate supply model to illustrate the difference between short-run and long-run macroeconomic equilibrium. In long-run macroeconomic equilibrium, the aggregate demand and short-run aggregate supply curves intersect at a point *on* the long-run aggregate supply curve. In short-run macroeconomic equilibrium, the aggregate demand and short-run aggregate supply curves often intersect at a point *off* the long-run aggregate supply curve. An automatic mechanism drives the economy to long-run equilibrium. If short-run equilibrium occurs at a point below potential real GDP, wages and prices will fall and the short-run aggregate supply curve will shift to the right until potential GDP is restored. If short-run equilibrium occurs at a point beyond potential real GDP, wages and prices will rise and the short-run aggregate supply curve will shift to the left until potential GDP is restored. Real GDP can be temporarily above or below its potential level, either because of shifts in the aggregate demand curve or because supply shocks lead to shifts in the aggregate supply curve.

LEARNING OBJECTIVE ④ Use the dynamic aggregate demand and aggregate supply model to analyze macroeconomic conditions. To make the aggregate demand and aggregate supply model more realistic, we need to make it *dynamic* by incorporating three facts that were left out of the basic model: (1) Potential real GDP increases continually, shifting the long-run aggregate supply curve to the right. (2) During most years, aggregate demand will be shifting to the right. (3) Except during periods when workers and firms expect high rates of inflation, the aggregate supply curve will be shifting to the right. The dynamic aggregate demand and aggregate supply model allows us to analyze macroeconomic conditions, including the recovery from the 2001 recession.

KEY TERMS

Aggregate demand and aggregate supply model 422
Aggregate demand curve (*AD*) 422
Long-run aggregate supply curve (*LRAS*) 428
Menu costs 431
Short-run aggregate supply curve (*SRAS*) 422
Stagflation 438
Supply shock 433

REVIEW QUESTIONS

1. Explain the three reasons the aggregate demand curve *(AD)* slopes downward.
2. What are the differences between the *AD* curve and the demand curve for an individual product, such as apples?
3. What are the variables that cause the *AD* curve to shift? For each variable, identify whether an increase in that variable will cause the *AD* curve to shift to the right or to the left.
4. Explain why the long-run aggregate supply curve *(LRAS)* is vertical.
5. What variables cause the long-run aggregate supply curve to shift? For each variable, identify whether an increase in that variable will cause the *LRAS* to shift to the right or to the left.
6. Why does the short-run aggregate supply curve *(SRAS)* slope upward?
7. What variables cause the *SRAS* curve to shift? For each variable, identify whether an increase in that variable will cause the *SRAS* curve to shift to the right or to the left.
8. What are menu costs? What is their macroeconomic significance?
9. What is a supply shock? Why might a supply shock lead to stagflation?
10. Why are the long-run effects of an increase in aggregate demand on price and output different from the short-run effects?
11. What are the key differences between the basic aggregate demand and aggregate supply model and the dynamic aggregate demand and aggregate supply model?
12. In the dynamic aggregate demand and aggregate supply model, what is the result of aggregate demand increasing faster than potential real GDP? What is the result of aggregate demand increasing slower than potential GDP?

PROBLEMS AND APPLICATIONS

Please visit **www.prenhall.com/hubbard** *for solutions to the even-numbered problems as well as multiple-choice and true or false self-assessment quizzes.*

1. Explain how each of the following events would affect the aggregate demand curve.
   a. An increase in the price level
   b. An increase in government purchases
   c. Higher state income taxes
   d. Higher interest rates
   e. Faster income growth in other countries
2. Explain how each of the following events would affect the long-run aggregate supply curve.
   a. A higher price level
   b. An increase in the labor force
   c. An increase in the quantity of capital goods
   d. Technological change occurs
3. Explain how each of the following events would affect the short-run aggregate supply curve.
   a. A higher price level
   b. An increase in what the price level is expected to be in the future
   c. The price level is currently higher than expected
   d. An unexpected increase in the price of an important raw material
   e. An increase in the labor force
4. **[Related to *Don't Let This Happen To You!*]** A student was asked to draw an aggregate demand and aggregate supply graph to illustrate the effect of an increase in aggregate supply. The student drew the following graph:

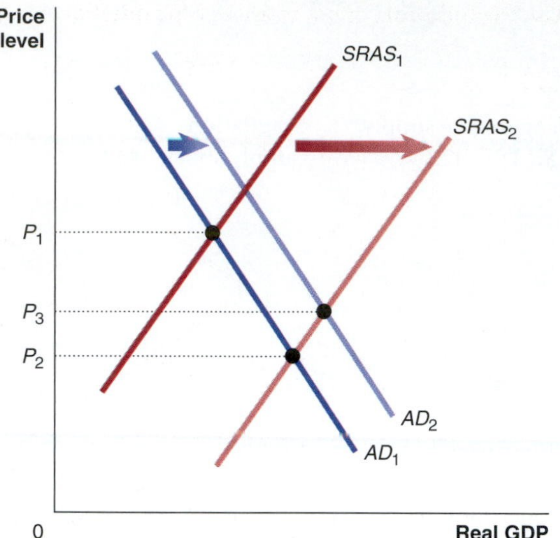

The student explained the graph as follows:

> An increase in aggregate supply causes a shift from $SRAS_1$ to $SRAS_2$. Because this shift in the aggregate supply curve results in a lower price level, consumption, investment, and net exports will increase. This change causes the aggregate demand curve to shift to the right from AD_1 to AD_2. We know that real GDP will increase, but we can't be sure whether the price level will rise or fall because that depends on whether the aggregate supply curve or the aggregate demand curve has shifted farther to the right. I assume that aggregate supply shifts out farther than aggregate demand, so I show the final price level, P_3, as being lower than the initial price level, P_1.

Explain whether you agree or disagree with the student's analysis. Be careful to explain exactly what—if anything—you find wrong with this analysis.

5. **[Related to *Solved Problem 14-1*]** Explain whether each of the following will cause a shift of the *AD* curve or a movement along the *AD* curve.
   a. Firms become more optimistic and increase their spending on machinery and equipment.
   b. The federal government increases taxes in an attempt to reduce a budget deficit.
   c. The U.S. economy experiences 4-percent inflation.
6. Suppose that workers and firms could always predict next year's price level with perfect accuracy. Briefly explain whether in these circumstances the *SRAS* curve still slopes upward.
7. Workers and firms often enter into contracts that fix prices or wages, sometimes for years at a time. If the price level turns out to be higher or lower than was expected when the contract was signed, one party to the contract will lose out. Briefly explain why, despite knowing this, workers and firms still sign long-term contracts.
8. A newspaper article published in 2004 noted, "About 50 percent of U.S. Steel's domestic production is tied up right now in long-term contracts pegged below market value price."
   a. Why would U.S. Steel have entered into contracts to sell steel below the market price? (Hint: Is it likely that these contracts were negotiated before 2004?)
   b. What impact is U.S. Steel selling steel below the current market price likely to have on its production and on the production of companies that buy its steel?

   Source: Charles Sheehan, "Happy Days Are Here Again for U.S. Steel Corp.," (Allentown, PA) *Morning Call*, November 28, 2004.
9. Suppose the price of a barrel of oil increases from $50 to $70. Use a basic aggregate demand and aggregate supply diagram to show the short-run and long-run effects on the economy.
10. Draw a basic aggregate demand and aggregate supply graph (with *LRAS* constant) showing the economy in long-run equilibrium.
    a. Now assume that there is an increase in aggregate demand. Show the resulting short-run equilibrium on your diagram. Explain how the economy adjusts back to long-run equilibrium.
    b. Now assume that there is an unexpected increase in the price of an important raw material. Show the resulting short-run equilibrium on your diagram. Explain how the economy adjusts back to long-run equilibrium.
11. Many economists believe that some wages and prices are "sticky downward," meaning that these wages and prices increase quickly when demand is increasing but decrease slowly, if at all, when demand is decreasing. Discuss the consequences of this for the automatic mechanism that brings the economy back to potential GDP after an increase in aggregate demand. Would your answer change if aggregate demand decreased rather than increased? Explain.
12. Draw a dynamic aggregate demand and aggregate supply graph showing the economy moving from potential GDP in 2006 to potential GDP in 2007, with no inflation. Your graph should contain the *AD*, *SRAS*, and *LRAS* curves for both 2006 and 2007 and should indicate the short-run macroeconomic equilibrium for each year and the directions in which the curves have shifted. Identify what must happen to have growth during 2007 without inflation.
13. **[Related to *Solved Problem 14-2*]** Consider the information in the following table for the first two years of the Great Depression (the values for real GDP are in 2000 dollars):

YEAR	ACTUAL REAL GDP	POTENTIAL REAL GDP	PRICE LEVEL
1929	$865.2 billion	$865.2 billion	12.0
1930	$790.7 billion	$895.7 billion	11.5

Source: U.S. Department of Commerce, Bureau of Economic Analysis.

a. What information in the table is different from what we would expect to happen during a recession in the past 50 years?

b. Draw a dynamic aggregate demand and aggregate supply graph to illustrate what happened during these years. Your graph should contain the *AD*, *SRAS*, and *LRAS* curves for both 1929 and 1930 and should indicate the short-run macroeconomic equilibrium for each year and the directions in which the curves have shifted.

14. Consider the data in the following table for the years 1969 and 1970 (the values for real GDP are in 2000 dollars):

YEAR	ACTUAL REAL GDP	POTENTIAL REAL GDP	UNEMPLOYMENT RATE
1969	$3.77 trillion	$3.67 trillion	3.5%
1970	$3.77 trillion	$3.80 trillion	4.9%

Source: U.S. Department of Commerce, Bureau of Economic Analysis.

a. In 1969, actual real GDP was greater than potential real GDP. Explain how this is possible.

b. Even though real GDP in 1970 was the same as real GDP in 1969, the unemployment rate increased substantially from 1969 to 1970. Why did this increase in unemployment occur?

c. Was the inflation rate in 1970 likely to have been higher or lower than the inflation rate in 1969? Does your answer depend on whether the recession was caused by a change in a component of aggregate demand or by a supply shock?

15. **[Related to *Solved Problem 14-2*]** Look again at Solved Problem 14-2 on the supply shock of 1974–1975 on pages 444–445. In the table, the price level for 1974 is given as 34.7 and the price level for 1975 is given as 38.0. The values for the price level are well below 100. Does this indicate that inflation must have been low during these years? Briefly explain.

16. Use the following graph to answer the questions:

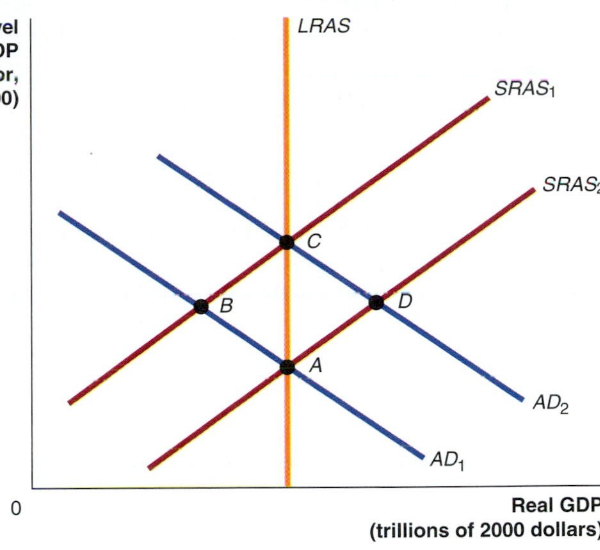

a. Which of points *A*, *B*, *C*, or *D* can represent a long-run equilibrium?

b. Suppose initially the economy is at point *A*. If aggregate demand increases from AD_1 to AD_2, which point represents the economy's short-run equilibrium? Which point represents the eventual long-run equilibrium? Briefly explain how the economy adjusts from the short-run equilibrium to the long-run equilibrium.

17. Suppose the economy moves from point *A* in year 1 to point *B* in year 2. Using the following graph, briefly explain your answers to each of the questions.

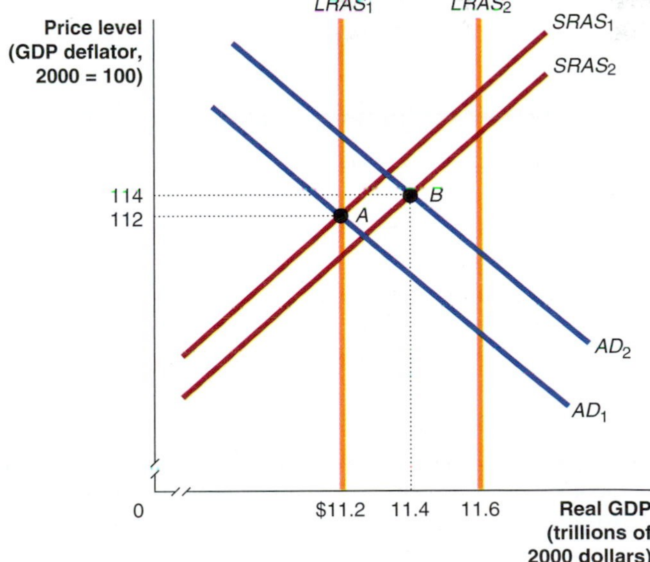

a. What is the growth rate in potential real GDP from year 1 to year 2?
b. Is the unemployment rate in year 2 higher or lower than in year 1?
c. What is the inflation rate in year 2?
d. What is the growth rate of real GDP in year 2?

18. Explain whether you agree or disagree with the following statement: "The dynamic aggregate demand and aggregate supply model predicts that a recession caused by a decline in *AD* will cause the inflation rate to fall. I know that the 2001 recession was caused by a fall in *AD*, but the inflation rate was not lower after the recession. The prices of most products were definitely higher in 2002 than they were in 2001, so the inflation rate could not have fallen."

19. An economist at the Federal Reserve Bank of St. Louis wrote the following about the recovery from the 2001 recession:

> [Since the end of the recession] real business fixed investment (BFI)—expenditures on structures, equipment and software—has declined at a 2.2 percent annual rate. By contrast, in the first four quarters of the typical recovery, real BFI *increases* a little more than 8 percent.

Why didn't investment spending increase as much as it normally does in the year following the end of the 2001 recession?
Source: Kevin L. Kliesen, "Waiting for the Investment Boom? It Might Be a While," Federal Reserve Bank of St. Louis, *National Economic Trends*, May 2003.

20. According to an article published in *Business Week* in October 2002, "The stock market plunge is weighing heavily on both businesses and consumers." Why would a decline in stock prices "weigh heavily" on businesses and consumers? What were the consequences of this for the economy?
Source: James C. Cooper and Kathleen Madigan, "Consumers: Still Some Pluses among the Minuses," *Business Week*, October 21, 2002.

21. An article in the *New York Times* in August 2003 stated the following:

> [A] cutback in business spending when the Internet and stock market bubbles burst brought on the recession of 2001 and the prolonged weakness that has existed since then.

a. What does the article mean by "business spending"?
b. What does it mean by the "Internet and stock market bubbles"?
c. Why would the bursting of these bubbles affect business spending?

Source: Louis Uchitelle and Jennifer Bayot, "Business Spending Helps to Offset Lag in Refinancing," *New York Times*, August 9, 2003.

22. The following excerpt is from an article in the *New York Times:*

> The number of Americans living below the poverty line increased by more than 1.3 million [during 2002], even though the economy technically edged out of recession during the same period.

Briefly discuss why poverty increased during 2002 even though the economy was in the expansion phase of the business cycle.
Source: Lynette Clemetson, "Census Shows Ranks of Poor Rose by 1.3 Million," *New York Times*, September 3, 2003.

23. **[Related to the *Chapter Opener*]** In the opening to this chapter, we saw that at the end of 2003, employment at Caterpillar was still 10 percent below what it had been at the beginning of 2001. Some of the employment reduction was caused by a reduction in Caterpillar's sales. But Caterpillar had also implemented new technologies that increased productivity and required fewer workers. Briefly discuss why firms might be likely to implement new technologies during a period when demand is falling, or only increasing slowly.

Macroeconomic Schools of Thought

Appendix

Macroeconomics as a separate field of economics began with the publication in 1936 of John Maynard Keynes's book, *The General Theory of Employment, Interest, and Money.* Keynes, an economist at the University of Cambridge in England, was attempting to explain the devastating Great Depression of the 1930s. Real GDP in the United States declined by more than 25 percent between 1929 and 1933 and did not return to its potential level until the United States entered World War II in 1941. The unemployment rate soared to 25 percent by 1933 and did not return to its 1929 level until 1942. Keynes developed the aggregate demand and aggregate supply model to explain these facts. The widespread acceptance during the 1930s and 1940s of Keynes's model became known as the **Keynesian revolution.**

In fact, the aggregate demand and aggregate supply model remains the most widely accepted approach to analyzing macroeconomic issues. Because the model has been modified significantly from Keynes's day, many economists who use the model today refer to themselves as *new Keynesians.* The new Keynesians emphasize the importance of the stickiness of wages and prices in explaining fluctuations in real GDP. A significant number of economists, however, dispute whether the aggregate demand and aggregate supply model, as we have discussed it in this chapter, is the best way to analyze macroeconomic issues. These alternative *schools of thought* use models that differ significantly from the standard aggregate demand and aggregate supply model. We can briefly consider each of the three major alternative models:

1. The monetarist model
2. The new classical model
3. The real business cycle model

The Monetarist Model

The monetarist model—also known as the neo-Quantity Theory of Money model—was developed beginning in the 1940s by Milton Friedman, an economist at the University of Chicago who was awarded the Nobel Prize in Economics in 1976. Friedman argued that the Keynesian approach overstates the amount of macroeconomic instability in the economy. In particular, he argued that the economy will ordinarily be at potential real GDP. In the book *A Monetary History of the United States: 1867–1960,* written with Anna Schwartz, Friedman argued that most fluctuations in real output were caused by fluctuations in the money supply, rather than by fluctuations in consumption spending or investment spending. Friedman and Schwartz argued that the severity of the Great Depression was caused by the Federal Reserve's allowing the quantity of money in the economy to fall by more than 25 percent between 1929 and 1933.

In the United States, the Federal Reserve is responsible for managing the quantity of money. As we will discuss further in Chapter 16, the Federal Reserve has typically focused more on controlling interest rates than on controlling the money supply. Friedman has argued that the Federal Reserve should change its practices and adopt a **monetary growth rule,** which is a plan for increasing the quantity of money at a fixed rate. Friedman believed that adopting a monetary growth rule would reduce fluctuations in real GDP, employment, and inflation.

Friedman's ideas, which are referred to as **monetarism,** attracted significant support during the 1970s and early 1980s, when the economy experienced high rates of unemployment and inflation. The support for monetarism declined during the late

Keynesian revolution The name given to the widespread acceptance during the 1930s and 1940s of John Maynard Keynes's macroeconomic model.

Monetary growth rule A plan for increasing the quantity of money at a fixed rate that does not respond to changes in economic conditions.

Monetarism The macroeconomic theories of Milton Friedman and his followers; particularly the idea that the quantity of money should be increased at a constant rate.

1980s and 1990s, when the unemployment and inflation rates were relatively low. We will discuss the Quantity Theory of Money, which underlies the monetarist model, in Chapter 15.

The New Classical Model

The new classical model was developed in the mid-1970s by a group of economists including Robert Lucas of the University of Chicago, Thomas Sargent of Stanford University, and Robert Barro of Harvard University. Lucas was awarded the Nobel Prize in Economics in 1995. Some of the views held by the new classical macroeconomists are similar to those held by economists before the Great Depression. Keynes referred to the economists before the Great Depression as "classical economists." Like the classical economists, the new classical macroeconomists believe that the economy normally will be at potential real GDP. They also believe that wages and prices adjust quickly to changes in demand and supply. Put another way, they believe the stickiness in wages and prices emphasized by the new Keynesians is unimportant.

Lucas argued that workers and firms have *rational expectations,* meaning that they form their expectations of the future values of economic variables, like the inflation rate, making use of all available information, including information on variables—such as changes in the quantity of money—that might affect aggregate demand. If the actual inflation rate is lower than the expected inflation rate, the actual real wage will be higher than the expected real wage. These higher real wages will lead to a recession because they will cause firms to hire fewer workers and cut back on production. As workers and firms adjust their expectations to the lower inflation rate, the real wage will decline and employment and production will expand, bringing the economy out of recession. The ideas of Lucas and his followers are referred to as the **new classical macroeconomics.** Supporters of the new classical model agree with supporters of the monetarist model that the Federal Reserve should adopt a monetary growth rule. They argue that a monetary growth rule will make it easier for workers and firms to accurately forecast the price level, thereby reducing fluctuations in real GDP.

New classical macroeconomics The macroeconomic theories of Robert Lucas and others, particularly the idea that workers and firms have rational expectations.

The Real Business Cycle Model

Beginning in the 1980s, some economists, including Finn Kydland of Carnegie Mellon University and Edward Prescott of Arizona State University (who shared the Nobel Prize in Economics in 2004), argued that Lucas was correct in assuming that workers and firms formed their expectations rationally and that wages and prices adjust quickly to supply and demand but wrong about the source of fluctuations in real GDP. They argued that fluctuations in real GDP are caused by temporary shocks to productivity. These shocks can be negative, such as a decline in the availability of oil or other raw materials, or positive, such as technological change that makes it possible to produce more output with the same quantity of inputs.

According to this school of thought, shifts in the aggregate demand curve have no impact on real GDP because the short-run aggregate supply curve is vertical. Other schools of thought all believe that the short-run aggregate supply curve is upward sloping and that only the *long-run* aggregate supply curve is vertical. Fluctuations in real GDP occur when a negative productivity shock causes the short-run aggregate supply curve to shift to the left—reducing real GDP—or a positive productivity shock causes the short-run aggregate supply curve to shift to the right—increasing real GDP. Because this model focuses on "real" factors—productivity shocks—rather than changes in the quantity of money to explain fluctuations in real GDP, it is known as the **real business cycle model.**

Real business cycle model A macroeconomic model that focuses on real, rather than monetary, causes of the business cycle.

Karl Marx: Capitalism's Severest Critic

14A-1 Making the Connection

The schools of macroeconomic thought we have discussed in this appendix are considered part of mainstream economic theory because of their acceptance of the market system as the best means of raising living standards in the long run. One quite influential critic of mainstream economic theory was Karl Marx. Marx was born in Trier, Germany, in 1818. After graduating from the University of Berlin in 1841, he began a career as a political journalist and agitator. His political activities caused him to be expelled first from Germany and then from France and Belgium. In 1849 he moved to London, where he spent the remainder of his life.

In 1867, he published the first volume of his greatest work, *Das Kapital.* Marx read closely the most prominent mainstream economists, including Adam Smith, David Ricardo, and John Stuart Mill. But Marx believed that he understood how market systems would evolve in the long run much better than those earlier authors. Marx argued that the market system would eventually be replaced by a Communist economy in which the workers would control production. He believed in the *labor theory of value,* which attributed all of the value of a good or service to the labor that was embodied in it. According to Marx, the owners of businesses—capitalists—did not earn profits by contributing anything of value to the production of goods or services. Instead, capitalists earned profits because their "monopoly of the means of production"—their ownership of factories and machinery—allowed them to exploit workers by paying them wages that were much less than the value of workers' contribution to production.

Karl Marx predicted that a final economic crisis would lead to the collapse of the market system.

Marx argued that wages of workers would be driven to levels that allowed only bare survival. He also argued that small firms would be driven out of business by larger firms, forcing owners of small firms into the working class. Eventually, control of production would be concentrated in the hands of a few firms. These few remaining firms would have difficulty selling the goods they produced to the impoverished masses. A final economic crisis would lead the working classes to rise up, seize control of the economy, and establish Communism. Marx died in 1883 without providing a detailed explanation of how the Communist economy would operate.

Marx had relatively little influence on mainstream thinking in the United States, but several political parties in Europe were guided by his ideas. In 1917, the Bolshevik party seized control of Russia and established the Soviet Union, the first Communist state. Although the Soviet Union was a vicious dictatorship under Vladimir Lenin and his successor, Joseph Stalin, its prestige rose when it avoided the macroeconomic difficulties that plagued the market economies during the 1930s. By the late 1940s, Communist parties also came to power in China, and the countries of Eastern Europe. Eventually, poor economic performance led to the collapse of the Soviet Union and its replacement by a market system. Although the Communist Party remains in power in China, the economy is evolving toward a market system. Today, only North Korea and Cuba have economies that claim to be based on the ideas of Karl Marx.

KEY TERMS

Keynesian Revolution 454
Monetarism 454
Monetary growth rule 454
New classical macroeconomics 454
Real business cycle model 454

chapter fifteen 15

Money, Banks, and the Federal Reserve System

McDonald's Money Problems in Argentina

The McDonald's Big Mac is one of the most widely available products in the world. McDonald's 30,000 restaurants in 119 countries serve 50 million customers per day. Although some McDonald's restaurants are owned by the firm, many are franchises. A *franchise* is a business with the legal right to sell a good or service in a particular area. When a firm uses franchises, local entrepreneurs are able to buy and run the stores in their area. As McDonald's began expanding to other countries in the late 1960s, it relied on the franchise system. Franchisees in other countries were able to adapt the restaurants to the tastes of local customers. For example, although all 200 McDonald's restaurants in Argentina offer Big Macs and French fries, they also offer gourmet coffees and other foods not available in the U.S. McDonald's restaurants.

In 2001, McDonald's restaurants in Argentina began to suffer from the macroeconomic problems plaguing that country. Argentina's woes centered on "money." Households and firms had begun to lose faith in the Argentine peso, the country's official money. They believed that the peso would rapidly lose its value, reducing their ability to buy goods and services. Many people converged on banks and tried to withdraw their money so they could either immediately buy goods and services or exchange Argentine pesos for U.S. dollars. To stop the outflow of money from the banking system, the government limited the amount of Argentine currency that could be withdrawn to $1,000 per account per month. This action further weakened the economy by reducing the funds households and firms had available to spend. In addition, banks became cautious about making loans, which in turn led to additional reductions in spending. An Argentine doctor was quoted as saying, "Now there's a lack of cash. . . . None of my patients can pay." Another person observed, "The chain of payments has been broken. There are millions of people forced to resort to bartering—an old sweater, anything, for goods just to survive." A cell phone dealer said, "These days, if customers want to pay us in tomatoes, I'll consider making a deal."

During the currency crisis, one Argentine province decided to issue

its own currency, which it called the *patacone*. Because the patacone was not part of Argentina's official currency, there were doubts as to how widely it would be accepted by local firms. McDonald's restaurants in the province decided to accept the new currency as payment for a meal they labeled the "Patacombo": two cheeseburgers, an order of French fries, and a soft drink.

Although the crisis in Argentina eventually passed, confidence in money remains vitally important. When you buy a DVD from a store, you get something of value. You give the store clerk dollar bills, or you might write a check with your name and the name of a bank on it or use a debit card linked to your checking account. These pieces of paper have no value in and of themselves. You and the DVD store owner consider them valuable because others consider them valuable. This confidence and trust are hallmarks of money.

Confidence and trust cannot be taken for granted. As this example from Argentina shows, when households and firms lose faith in an official money, it can harm trade and economic activity in an economy. *An Inside Look* on page 482 discusses how several Latin American countries have moved away from fixing the value of their currencies against the dollar.

Sources: Tony Smith, "Freeze Has Argentines Crying All the Way to the Bank," Associated Press, December 11, 2001, and Matt Moffett, "Unfunny Money," *Wall Street Journal*, August 21, 2001.

LEARNING OBJECTIVES

After studying this chapter, you should be able to:

1. Define money and discuss its four functions.
2. Discuss the definitions of the money supply used in the United States today.
3. Explain how banks create checking account deposits.
4. Discuss the three policy tools the Federal Reserve uses to manage the money supply.
5. Explain the quantity theory of money and use it to explain how high rates of inflation occur.

In this chapter, we will explore the role of money in the economy. We will see how the banking system creates money and what policy tools the Federal Reserve uses to manage the quantity of money. At the end of the chapter, we will explore the link between changes in the quantity of money and changes in the price level. What you learn in this chapter will serve as an important foundation to understanding monetary policy and fiscal policy, which we study in the next three chapters.

1 LEARNING OBJECTIVE

Define money and discuss its four functions.

What Is Money and Why Do We Need It?

Could an economy function without money? We know the answer to this is yes, because there are many historical examples of economies where people traded goods for other goods, rather than using money. For example, a family operating a farm on the American frontier during colonial times might trade a cow for a plow. Most economies, though, use money. What is money? The economic definition of **money** is any asset that people are generally willing to accept in exchange for goods and services or for payment of debts. Recall from Chapter 5 that an **asset** is anything of value owned by a person or a firm. There are many possible kinds of money: In West Africa, at one time cowrie shells served as money. During World War II, prisoners of war used cigarettes as money.

Money Assets that people are generally willing to accept in exchange for goods and services or for payment of debts.

Asset Anything of value owned by a person or a firm.

Barter and the Invention of Money

To understand the importance of money, let's consider further the situation in economies that do not use money. These economies, where goods and services are traded directly for other goods and services, are called *barter economies*. Barter economies have a major shortcoming. To illustrate this shortcoming, consider a farmer on the American frontier in colonial days. Suppose the farmer needs another cow and proposes to trade a spare plow to a neighbor for one of the neighbor's cows. If the neighbor does not want the plow, the trade will not happen. For a barter trade to take place between two people, each person must want what the other one has. Economists refer to this requirement as a *double coincidence of wants*. The farmer who wants the cow might eventually be able to obtain one if he first trades with some other neighbor for something the neighbor with the cow wants. However, it may take several trades before the farmer is ultimately able to trade for what the neighbor with the cow wants. Locating several trading partners and making several intermediate trades can take considerable time and energy.

The problems with barter provide an incentive to identify a product that most people will accept in exchange for what they have to trade. For example, in colonial times animal skins were very useful in making clothing. The first governor of Tennessee actually received a salary of 1,000 deerskins per year, and the secretary of the treasury received 450 otter skins per year. A good used as money that also has value independent of its use as money is called a **commodity money.** Historically, once a good became widely accepted as money, people who did not have an immediate use for it would be willing to accept it. A colonial farmer—or the governor of Tennessee—might not want a deerskin, but as long as he knew he could use the deerskin to buy other goods and services, he would be willing to accept it in exchange for what he had to sell.

Commodity money A good used as money that also has value independent of its use as money.

For hundreds of years, the cowrie shell, found on the shores of the Indian and Pacific Oceans, was widely used as money throughout Africa, Asia, and the islands of the South Pacific. The symbol representing the cowrie was adopted as the word for money in ancient China. Cowries continued to be used as money in remote areas of Asia and Africa until the mid-twentieth century.

Trading goods and services is much easier once money becomes available. People only need to sell what they have for money and then use the money to buy what they want. If the colonial family can find someone to buy their plow, they can use the money to buy the cow they want. The family with the cow will accept the money because they know they can use it to buy what they want. Families will be less likely to produce everything or nearly everything they need themselves and more likely to specialize.

Most people in modern economies are highly specialized. They do only one thing—work as a nurse, an accountant, or an engineer—and use the money they earn to buy everything else they need. As we discussed in Chapter 2, people become much more productive by specializing because they can pursue their *comparative advantage.* The high income levels in modern economies are based on the specialization that money makes possible. We can now answer the question, "Why do we need money?" *By making exchange easier, money allows for specialization and higher productivity.*

15-1 Making the Connection

Money in a World War II Prisoner-of-War Camp

R. A. Radford has described his experiences as a captured British soldier in a German prisoner-of-war camp during World War II. At first, the prisoners traded the goods they received in packages from the Red Cross or from relatives at home on a barter basis, but the usual inefficiencies of barter led the prisoners to begin using cigarettes as money. Cigarettes were included in the Red Cross packages. According to Radford, "Everyone, including non-smokers, was willing to sell for cigarettes, using them to buy at another time and place. Cigarettes became the normal currency." Even a labor market developed: "Laundrymen advertised at two cigarettes a garment. Battle-dress [uniform] was scrubbed and pressed and a pair of trousers lent for the interim period for twelve. . . . Odd tailoring and other jobs similarly had their prices."

Prisoners set up small businesses in the camp, using cigarettes for money: "There was a coffee stall owner who sold tea, coffee or cocoa at two cigarettes a cup, buying his raw materials at market prices and hiring labour to gather fuel and to stoke; he actually enjoyed the services of a chartered accountant at one stage." Even a restaurant was organized "where food and hot drinks were sold while a band . . . performed."

In January 1945, near the end of the war, the Red Cross ration of cigarettes was eliminated. Given that some of the prisoners were heavy smokers, most of the rest of the cigarette money disappeared from circulation—a disadvantage of this particular commodity money!—and the camp went back to barter trading until it was liberated by the U.S. 30th Infantry Division in April 1945.

Source: R. A. Radford, "The Economic Organization of a P.O.W. Camp," *Economica*, Vol. 12, November 1945, pp. 189–201.

During World War II, cigarettes were used as money in some prisoner-of-war camps.

The Functions of Money

Anything used as money—whether a deerskin, a cowrie seashell, or a dollar bill—should fulfill the following four functions:

- Medium of exchange
- Unit of account
- Store of value
- Standard of deferred payment

MEDIUM OF EXCHANGE Money serves as a medium of exchange when sellers are willing to accept it in exchange for goods or services. When the local supermarket accepts your $5 bill in exchange for bread and milk, the $5 bill is serving as a medium of exchange. To go back to our earlier example, with a medium of exchange, the farmer with the extra plow does not have to want a cow, and the farmer with the extra cow does not have to want a plow. Both can exchange their products for money and use the money to buy what they want. An economy is more efficient when a single good is recognized as a medium of exchange.

UNIT OF ACCOUNT In a barter system, each good has many prices. A cow may be worth two plows, 20 bushels of wheat, or six axes. Using a good as a medium of exchange confers another benefit: It reduces the need to quote many different prices in trade. Instead of having to quote the price of a single good in terms of many other goods, each good has a single price quoted in terms of the medium of exchange. This function of money gives buyers and sellers a *unit of account*, a way of measuring value in the economy in terms of money. Because the U.S. economy uses dollars as money, each good has a price in terms of dollars.

STORE OF VALUE Money allows value to be stored easily: If you do not use all your accumulated dollars to buy goods and services today, you can hold the rest to use in the future. In fact, a fisherman and a farmer would be better off holding money rather than inventories of their perishable goods. The acceptability of money in future transactions depends on its not losing value over time. Money is not the only store of value. Any asset—shares of Google stock, Treasury bonds, real estate, or Renoir paintings, for example—represents a store of value. Indeed, financial assets offer an important benefit relative to holding money because they generally pay a higher rate of interest or offer the prospect of gains in value. Other assets also have advantages relative to money because they provide services. A house, for example, offers you a place to sleep.

Why, then, would you bother to hold any money? The answer has to do with *liquidity*, or the ease with which a given asset can be converted into the medium of exchange. When money is the medium of exchange, it is the most liquid asset. You incur costs when you exchange other assets for money. When you sell bonds or shares of stock to buy a car, for example, you pay a commission to your broker. If you have to sell your house on short notice to finance an unexpected major medical expense, you pay a commission to a real estate agent and probably have to accept a lower price to exchange the house for money quickly. To avoid such costs, people are willing to hold some of their wealth in the form of money, even though other assets offer a greater return as a store of value.

STANDARD OF DEFERRED PAYMENT Money is also useful because it can serve as a standard of deferred payment in borrowing and lending. Money can facilitate exchange at a *given point in time* by providing a medium of exchange and unit of account. It can facilitate exchange *over time* by providing a store of value and a standard of deferred payment. For example, a furniture maker may be willing to sell a chair to a boat builder now in exchange for money in the future.

How important is it that money be a reliable store of value and standard of deferred payment? People care about how much food, clothing, and other goods and services their dollars will buy. The value of money depends on its purchasing power, which refers to its ability to buy goods and services. Inflation causes a decline in purchasing power because rising prices cause a given amount of money to purchase fewer goods and services. With deflation, the value of money increases because prices are falling.

You have probably heard relatives or friends exclaim, "A dollar doesn't buy what it used to!" They really mean that the purchasing power of a dollar has fallen, that a given amount of money will buy a smaller quantity of the same goods and services in the economy than it once did.

What Can Serve as Money?

Having a medium of exchange helps to make transactions easier, allowing the economy to work more smoothly. The next logical question is this: What can serve as money? That is, which assets should be used as the medium of exchange? We saw earlier that an asset must, at a minimum, be generally accepted as payment to serve as money. In practical terms, however, it must be even more.

There are five criteria that make a good suitable to use as a medium of exchange:

1. The good must be *acceptable* to (that is, usable by) most traders.
2. It should be of *standardized quality* so that any two units are identical.

3. It should be *durable* so that value is not lost by spoilage.
4. It should be *valuable* relative to its weight so that amounts large enough to be useful in trade can be easily transported.
5. The medium of exchange should be *divisible* because different goods are valued differently.

Dollar bills meet all these criteria. What determines the acceptability of dollar bills as a medium of exchange? Basically, it is through self-fulfilling expectations: You value something as money only if you believe that others will accept it from you as payment. A society's willingness to use green paper dollars as money makes them an acceptable medium of exchange. This property of acceptability is not unique to money. Your personal computer has the same keyboard organization of letters as other computer keyboards because manufacturers agreed on a standard layout. You learned to speak English because it is probably the language that most people around you speak.

COMMODITY MONEY Commodity money meets the criteria for a medium of exchange. Gold, for example, was a common form of money in the nineteenth century because it was a medium of exchange, a unit of account, a store of value, and a standard of deferred payment. But commodity money has a significant problem: Its value depends on its purity. Therefore, someone who wanted to cheat could mix impure metals with a precious metal. Unless traders trusted each other completely, they needed to check the weight and purity of the metal at each trade. In the Middle Ages, respected merchants, who were the predecessors of modern bankers, solved this problem by assaying metals and stamping them with a mark certifying weight and purity and earned a commission in the process. Unstamped (uncertified) commodity money was acceptable only at a discount. Another problem with using gold as money was that the money supply was difficult to control, because it depended partly on unpredictable discoveries of new gold fields.

FIAT MONEY It can be inefficient for an economy to rely on only gold or other precious metals for its money supply. What if you had to transport bars of gold to settle your transactions? Not only would doing so be difficult and costly, but you would also run the risk of being robbed. To get around this problem, private institutions or governments began to store gold and issue paper certificates that could be redeemed for gold. In modern economies, paper currency is generally issued by a *central bank,* which is an agency of the government, like the Federal Reserve in the United States, that regulates the money supply. Today, no government in the world issues paper currency that can be redeemed for gold. Paper currency has no value unless it is used as money and is therefore not a commodity money. Instead, paper currency is a **fiat money,** which has no value except as money. If paper currency has no value except as money, why do consumers and firms use it?

Fiat money Money, such as paper currency, that is authorized by a central bank or governmental body and that does not have to be exchanged by the central bank for gold or some other commodity money.

If you look at a the top of a U.S. dollar bill, you will see that it is actually a *Federal Reserve Note,* issued by the Federal Reserve, which is the central bank in the United States. Because U.S. dollars are fiat money, the Federal Reserve is not required to give you gold or silver for your dollar bills. Federal Reserve currency is *legal tender* in the United States, which means the federal government requires that it be accepted in payment of debts and requires that cash or checks denominated in dollars be used in payment of taxes. Despite being legal tender, without everyone's acceptance dollar bills would not be a good medium of exchange and could not serve as money. In practice, you, along with everyone else, agree to accept Federal Reserve currency as money. The key to this acceptance is that *households and firms have confidence that if they accept paper dollars in exchange for goods and services, the dollars will not lose much value during the time they hold them.* Without this confidence, dollar bills would not serve as a medium of exchange.

15-2 Making the Connection

Money without a Government? The Strange Case of the Iraqi Dinar

The value of the Iraqi dinar was rising against the U.S. dollar. This result may not seem surprising. We saw in Chapter 14 that the exchange rate, or the value of one currency in exchange for another currency, fluctuates—but this was May 2003. The Iraqi government of Saddam Hussein had collapsed the month before, following an invasion by U.S. and British forces. No new Iraqi government had been formed yet, but Iraqi paper currency with pictures of Saddam on it continued to be used in Iraq for buying and selling.

U.S. officials in Iraq had expected that once the war was over and Saddam had been forced from power, the currency with his picture on it would lose all of its value. This result had seemed inevitable once the United States had begun paying Iraqi officials in U.S. dollars. However, many Iraqis continued to use the dinar because they were familiar with that currency. As one Iraqi put it, "People trust the dinar more than the dollar. It's Iraqi." In fact, for some weeks after the invasion, increasing demand for the dinar caused its value to rise against the dollar. In early April, when U.S. troops first entered Baghdad, it took about 4,000 dinar to buy one U.S. dollar. Six weeks later, in mid-May, it took only 1,500 dinar.

Eventually, a new Iraqi government was formed, and the government ordered that dinars with Saddam's picture be replaced by a new dinar. The new dinar was printed in factories around the world, and 27 Boeing 747s filled with paper dinars were flown to Baghdad. By January 2004, two billion paper dinars in varying denominations had been distributed to banks throughout Iraq and the old Saddam dinars disappeared from circulation. That dinars issued by Saddam's government actually increased in value for a period after his government had collapsed illustrates an important fact about money: *Anything can be used as money as long as people are willing to accept it in exchange for goods and services,* even paper currency issued by a government that no longer exists.

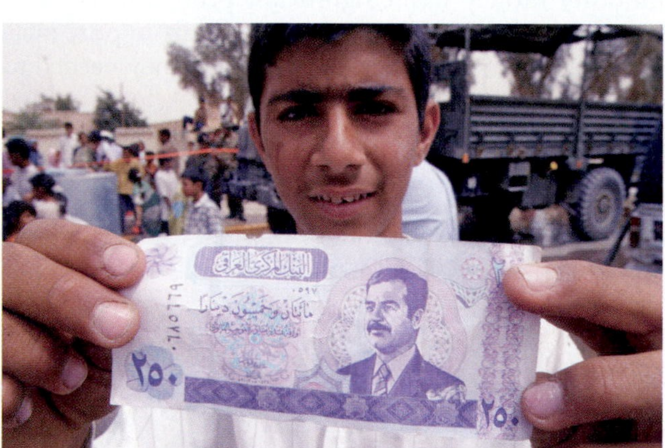

Many Iraqis continued to use currency with Saddam's picture on it, even after he was forced from power.

Sources: Edmund L. Andrews, "His Face Still Gives Fits as Saddam Dinar Soars," *New York Times,* May 18, 2003; Yaroslav Trofimov, "Saddam Hussein Is Scarce, but Not the Saddam Dinar," *Wall Street Journal,* April 24, 2003; and "A Tricky Operation," *Economist,* June 24, 2004.

② **LEARNING OBJECTIVE**

Discuss the definitions of the money supply used in the United States today.

How Do We Measure Money Today?

The definition of money as a medium of exchange depends on beliefs about whether others will use the medium in trade now and in the future. This definition offers guidance for measuring money in an economy. Interpreted literally, this definition says that money should include only those assets that obviously function as a medium of exchange: currency, checking account deposits, and traveler's checks. These assets can easily be used to buy goods and services, and thus act as a medium of exchange.

This strict interpretation is too narrow, however, as a measure of the money supply in the real world. Many other assets can be used as a medium of exchange, but they are not as liquid as a checking account deposit or cash. For example, you can convert your savings account at a bank to cash. Likewise, if you have an account at a brokerage firm, you can write checks against the value of the stocks and bonds the firm holds for you. Although these assets have restrictions on their use and there may be costs to converting them into cash, they can be considered part of the medium of exchange.

Economists have developed several different definitions of the money supply. Each definition includes a different group of assets. The definitions range from narrow to broad and are based on how liquid the assets are. The most narrow measure of money is cash. Broader measures include other assets that can be easily converted to cash, such as your checking account or savings account. In the United States, the Federal Reserve has conducted several studies of the appropriate definition of money. The job of defining the money supply has become more difficult during the past two decades as innovation in financial markets and institutions has created new substitutes for the traditional measures of the medium of exchange. During the 1980s, the Fed changed its definitions of money in response to financial innovation. Outside the United States, other central banks use similar measures. Now we will look more closely at the Fed's definitions of the money supply.

M1: The Narrowest Definition of the Money Supply

Figure 15-1 illustrates the definitions of the money supply. The narrowest definition of the money supply is called **M1.** It includes:

M1 The narrowest definition of the money supply: The sum of currency in circulation, checking account balances in banks, and holdings of traveler's checks.

1. all the paper money and coins that are in circulation—meaning what is not held by banks or the government.
2. the value of all checking account balances at banks.
3. the value of traveler's checks.

The sum of paper money and coins is called *currency.* The value of checking account balances is roughly equal to the value of currency. Holdings of traveler's checks are much smaller than currency, amounting to less than $8 billion in May 2005.

Although currency and checking account balances are roughly equal in value, checking account balances are used much more often than currency to make payments. More than 80 percent of all expenditures on goods and services are made with a check, rather than with currency. In fact, the total amount of currency in circulation—$715 billion in September 2005—is a misleading number. This amount is more than $2,300

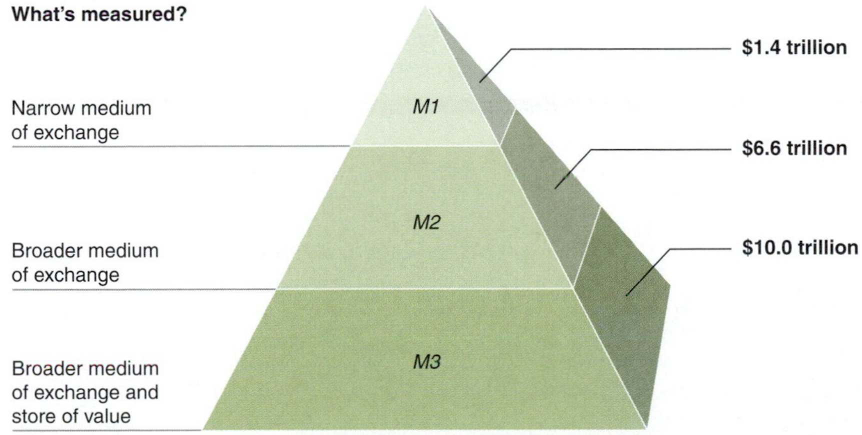

What's included?

M1	*M2*	*M3*
• Currency • Checking account balances • Traveler's checks	*M1* + • Savings account balances • Small-denomination time deposits • Money market deposit accounts in banks • Nonistitutional money market fund shares	*M2* + • Large-denomination time deposits • Institutional money market fund shares

FIGURE 15-1

Measuring the Money Supply, September 2005

The Federal Reserve uses several different measures of the money supply. In the pyramid, each measure includes the assets of the measure above it, as well as additional assets.

Source: Board of Governors of the Federal Reserve System, "Federal Reserve Statistical Release, H6," October 20, 2005.

for every man, woman, and child in the United States. If this sounds like an unrealistically large amount of currency to be held per person, it is. Economists estimate that about 60 percent of U.S. currency is actually outside the borders of the United States.

Who holds these dollars outside the United States? Foreign banks and foreign governments hold some dollars, but most are held by households and firms in countries where there is not much confidence in the local currency. When inflation rates are very high, many households and firms do not want to hold their domestic currency because it is losing its value too rapidly. The value of the U.S. dollar will be much more stable. If enough people are willing to accept dollars as well as—or instead of—domestic currency, then dollars become a second currency for the country. In some countries, such as Russia and many Latin American countries, large numbers of U.S. dollars are in circulation.

M2: A Broader Definition of Money

Before 1980, U.S. law prohibited banks from paying interest on checking account deposits. Households and firms held checking account deposits primarily to buy goods and services. M1 was, therefore, very close to the function of money as a medium of exchange. Almost all currency, checking account deposits, and traveler's checks were held with the intention of buying and selling, not to store value. People could store value and receive interest by placing funds in savings accounts in banks or by buying other financial assets, such as stocks and bonds. In 1980, the law was changed to allow banks to pay interest on certain types of checking accounts. This change reduced the difference between checking accounts and savings accounts, although people are still not allowed to write checks against their savings account balances.

M2 A broader definition of the money supply: M1 plus savings account balances, small-denomination time deposits, balances in money market deposit accounts in banks, and noninstitutional money market fund shares.

Economists began to pay closer attention to a broader definition of the money supply, **M2.** M2 includes everything that is in M1, plus savings account balances, small-denomination time deposits, such as certificates of deposit (CDs), balances in money market deposit accounts in banks, and noninstitutional money market fund shares. Small-denomination time deposits are similar to savings accounts, but the deposits are for a fixed period of time—usually from six months to several years—and withdrawals before that time are subject to a penalty. Mutual fund companies sell shares to investors and use the funds raised to buy financial assets such as stocks and bonds. Some of these mutual funds, such as Vanguard's Treasury Money Market Fund or Fidelity's Cash Reserves Fund, are called *money market mutual funds* because they invest in very short-term bonds, such as U.S. Treasury bills. The balances in these funds are included in M2.

Don't Let This Happen To You!

Don't Confuse Money with Income or Wealth

According to *Forbes* magazine, Bill Gates's wealth of $46.5 billion made him the richest person in the world in 2005. He also has a very large income, but how much money does he have? A person's *wealth* is equal to the value of his assets minus the value of any debts he has. A person's *income* is equal to his earnings during the year. Bill Gates's earnings as chairman of Microsoft and from his investments are very large. But his *money* is just equal to what he has in currency and in checking accounts. Only a small proportion of Gates's $46.5 billion in wealth is likely to be in currency or checking accounts. Most of his wealth is invested in stocks and bonds and other financial assets that are not included in the definition of money.

In everyday conversation, we often describe someone who is wealthy or who has a high income as "having a lot of money." But when economists use the word "money," they are usually referring to currency plus checking account deposits. It is important to keep straight the differences between wealth, income, and money.

Just as money and income are not the same for a person, they are not the same for the whole economy. National income in the United States was equal to $10.3 trillion in 2004. The money supply in 2004 was $1.4 trillion (using the M1 measure). There is no reason national income in a country should be equal to the country's money supply, nor will an increase in a country's money supply necessarily increase the country's national income.

YOUR TURN: **Test your understanding by doing related problem 9 on page 486 at the end of this chapter.**

There is also an M3 definition of the money supply that includes even more financial assets, including large-denomination time deposits and institutional money market mutual fund balances. Because of its relative simplicity and because it corresponds most closely to money as a medium of exchange, for the remainder of this book we will use the M1 definition of the money supply.

There are two key points about the money supply to keep in mind:

1. The money supply consists of *both* currency and balances in checking accounts and traveler's checks.
2. Because balances in checking accounts are included in the money supply, banks play an important role in the process by which the money supply increases and decreases. We will discuss this second point further in the next section.

SOLVED PROBLEM 15-1

The Definitions of M1 and M2

(2) LEARNING OBJECTIVE

Discuss the definitions of the money supply used in the United States today.

Suppose you decide to withdraw $2,000 from your checking account and use the money to buy a bank certificate of deposit (CD). Briefly explain how this will affect M1 and M2.

Solving the Problem:

Step 1: Review the chapter material. This problem is about the definitions of the money supply, so you may want to review the section "How Do We Measure Money Today?" which begins on page 462.

Step 2: Use the definitions of M1 and M2 to answer the problem. Funds in checking accounts are included in both M1 and M2. Funds in certificates of deposit are included in only M2. It is tempting to answer this problem by saying that shifting $2,000 from a checking account to a certificate of deposit reduces M1 by $2,000 and increases M2 by $2,000, but the $2,000 in your checking account was already counted in M2. So, the correct answer is that your action reduces M1 by $2,000 but leaves M2 unchanged.

YOUR TURN: **For more practice, do related problem 4 on page 486 at the end of this chapter.**

What about Credit Cards and Debit Cards?

Many people buy goods and services with credit cards, yet credit cards are not included in definitions of the money supply. The reason is that when you buy something with a credit card, you are in effect taking out a loan from the bank that issued the credit card. Only when you pay your credit card bill at the end of the month—usually with a check—is the transaction complete. In contrast, with a debit card the funds to make the purchase are taken directly from your checking account. In either case, the cards themselves do not represent money.

How Do Banks Create Money?

(3) LEARNING OBJECTIVE

Explain how banks create checking account deposits.

We have seen that the most important component of the money supply is checking accounts in banks. To understand the role money plays in the economy, we need to look more closely at how banks operate. Banks are profit-making private businesses, just like bookstores and supermarkets. Some banks are quite small, with just a few branches, and they do business in a limited area. Others are among the largest corporations in the United States, with hundreds of branches spread across many states. The key role that banks play in the economy is to accept deposits and make loans. By doing this, they create checking account deposits.

FIGURE 15-2

Balance Sheet for Wachovia Bank, December 31, 2004

The items on a bank's balance sheet of greatest economic importance are its reserves, loans, and deposits. Notice that the difference between the value of Wachovia's total assets and its total liabilities is equal to its stockholders' equity. As a consequence, the left side of the balance sheet always equals the right side.

Note: Some entries have been combined to simplify the balance sheet.

Source: Wachovia Corporation and Subsidiaries Consolidated Balance Sheets from Wachovia Corporation, *Annual Report*, 2004.

ASSETS (IN MILLIONS)		LIABILITIES AND STOCKHOLDERS' EQUITY (IN MILLIONS)	
Reserves	$34,150	Deposits	$295,053
Loans	221,083	Short-term borrowing	64,161
Deposits with other banks	4,441	Long-term debt	46,750
Securities	110,597	Other liabilities	37,216
Buildings and equipment	5,628	Total liabilities	$443,189
Other assets	117,425		
		Stockholders' equity	50,135
Total assets	$493,324	Total liabilities and stockholders' equity	$493,324

Bank Balance Sheets

To understand how banks create money, we need to briefly examine a typical bank balance sheet. Recall from Chapter 5 that on a balance sheet, a firm's assets are listed on the left and its liabilities and stockholders' equity are listed on the right. Assets are the value of anything owned by the firm, liabilities are the value of anything the firm owes, and stockholders' equity is the difference between the total value of assets and the total value of liabilities. Stockholders' equity represents the value of the firm if it had to be closed, all of its assets were sold, and all of its liabilities were paid off. A corporation's stockholders' equity is also referred to as its *net worth.*

Figure 15-2 shows the balance sheet of Wachovia Bank, which is based in Charlotte, North Carolina, and in 2005 had branches in 15 states. The key assets on a bank's balance sheet are its **reserves,** loans, and holdings of securities, such as U.S. Treasury bills. Reserves are deposits that a bank has retained, rather than loaned out or invested by, for instance, buying a U.S. Treasury bill. Banks keep reserves either physically within the bank, as *vault cash,* or on deposit with the Federal Reserve. Banks are required by law to keep as reserves 10 percent of their checking account deposits above a threshold level, which in 2005 was $47.6 million. (In 2005, the required reserve ratio was zero on a bank's first $7 million in checking account deposits, 3 percent on deposits between $7 million and $47.6 million, and 10 percent on deposits above $47.6 million.) These reserves are called **required reserves.** The minimum fraction of deposits that banks are required to keep as reserves—currently 10 percent—is called the **required reserve ratio.** We can abbreviate the required reserve ratio as *RR.* Any reserves banks hold over and above the legal requirement are called **excess reserves.** The balance sheet in Figure 15-2 shows that loans are Wachovia's largest asset, which is true of most banks.

Reserves Deposits that a bank keeps as cash in its vault or on deposit with the Federal Reserve.

Required reserves Reserves that a bank is legally required to hold, based on its checking account deposits.

Required reserve ratio The minimum fraction of deposits banks are required by law to keep as reserves.

Excess reserves Reserves that banks hold over and above the legal requirement.

Banks make *consumer loans* to households and *commercial loans* to businesses. A loan is an asset to a bank because it represents a promise by the person taking out the loan to make certain specified payments to the bank. A bank's reserves and its holdings of securities are also assets because they are things of value owned by the bank.

Don't Let This Happen To You!

Know When a Checking Account Is an Asset and When It Is a Liability

Consider the following reasoning: "How can checking account deposits be a liability to a bank? After all, they are something of value that is in the bank. Therefore, checking account deposits should be counted as a bank *asset,* rather than as a bank liability."

This statement is incorrect. The balance in a checking account represents something the bank *owes* to the owner of the account. Therefore, it is a liability to the bank, although it is an asset to the owner of the account. Similarly, your car loan is a liability to you—because it is a debt you owe to the bank—but it is an asset to the bank.

YOUR TURN: **Test your understanding by doing related problem 17 on page 487 at the end of this chapter.**

As with most banks, Wachovia's largest liability is its deposits. Deposits include checking accounts, savings accounts, and certificates of deposit. Deposits are liabilities to banks because they are owed to the households or firms that have deposited the funds. If you deposit $100 in your checking account, the bank owes you the $100 and you can ask for it back at any time.

Using T-Accounts to Show How a Bank Can Create Money

It is easier to show how banks create money using a T-account rather than a balance sheet. A T-account is a stripped-down version of a balance sheet that shows only how a transaction *changes* a bank's balance sheet. For example, suppose you deposit $1,000 in currency into an account at Wachovia Bank. This transaction raises the total deposits at Wachovia by $1,000 and also raises Wachovia's reserves by $1,000. We can show this on the following T-account:

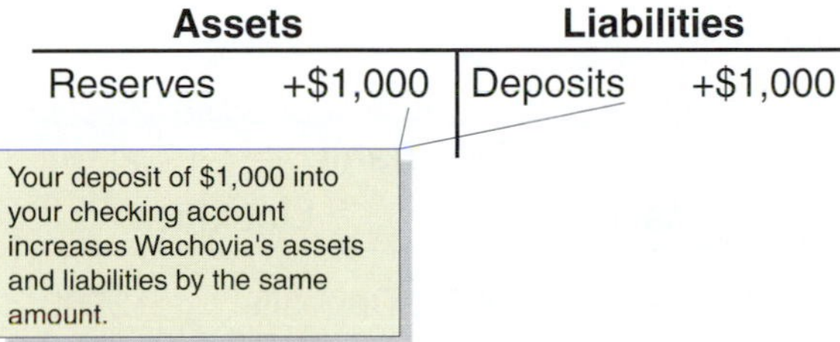

Remember that because the total value of all the entries on the right side of a balance sheet must always be equal to the total value of all the entries on the left side of a balance sheet, any transaction that increases (or decreases) one side of the balance sheet must also increase (or decrease) the other side of the balance sheet. In this case, the T-account shows that we increased both sides of the balance sheet by $1,000.

Initially, this transaction does not increase the money supply. The currency component of the money supply declines by $1,000 because the $1,000 you deposited is no longer in circulation and, therefore, is not counted in the money supply. But the decrease in currency is offset by a $1,000 increase in the checking account deposit component of the money supply.

This initial change is not the end of the story, however. Banks are required to keep 10 percent of deposits as reserves. Because banks do not earn interest on reserves, they have an incentive to loan out or buy securities with the other 90 percent. In this case, Wachovia can keep $100 as required reserves and loan out the other $900, which represents excess reserves. Suppose Wachovia loans out the $900 to someone to buy an inexpensive used car. Wachovia could give the $900 to the borrower in currency, but usually banks make loans by increasing the borrower's checking account. We can show this with another T-account:

Assets		Liabilities	
Reserves	+$1,000	Deposits	+$1,000
Loans	+$900	Deposits	+$900

1. By loaning out $900 in excess reserves. . .

2. . . .Wachovia has increased the money supply by $900.

A key point to recognize is that *by making this $900 loan, Wachovia has increased the money supply by $900.* The initial $1,000 in currency you deposited into your checking account has been turned into $1,900 in checking account deposits—a net increase in the money supply of $900.

But the story does not end here. The person who took out the $900 loan did so to buy a used car. To keep things simple, let's suppose he buys the car for exactly $900 and pays by writing a check on his account at Wachovia. The owner of the used car will now deposit the check in her bank. That bank may also be a branch of Wachovia, but in most cities there are many banks, so let's assume that the seller of the car has her account at a branch of PNC Bank. Once she deposits the check, PNC Bank will send it to Wachovia Bank to *clear* the check and collect the $900. We can show the result using T-accounts:

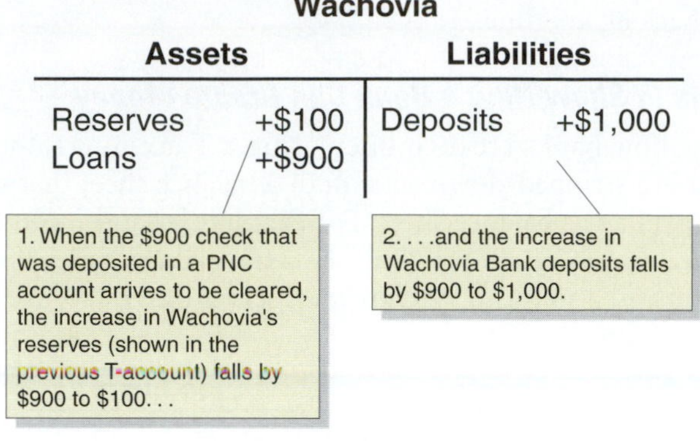

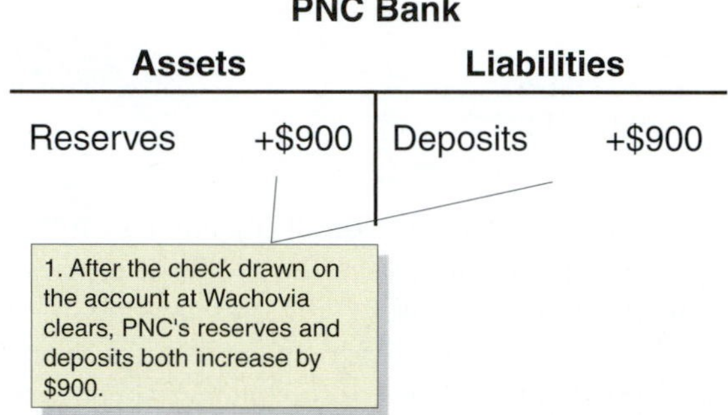

Once the car buyer's check has cleared, Wachovia has lost $900 in deposits—the amount loaned to the car buyer—and $900 in reserves—the amount it had to pay PNC when PNC sent it the car buyer's check. PNC has an increase in checking account deposits of $900—the deposit of the car seller—and an increase in reserves of $900—the amount it received from Wachovia.

PNC has 100 percent reserves against this new $900 deposit, when it only needs 10 percent reserves. It has an incentive to keep $90 as reserves and to loan out the other $810, which are excess reserves. If PNC does this, we can show the change in its balance sheet using another T-account.

PNC Bank

Assets		Liabilities	
Reserves	+$900	Deposits	+$900
Loans	+$810	Deposits	+$810

By making an $810 loan, PNC has increased both its loans and its deposits by $810.

In loaning out the $810 in excess reserves, PNC creates a new checking account deposit of $810. The initial deposit of $1,000 in currency into Wachovia Bank has now resulted in the creation of $1,000 + $900 + $810 = $2,710 in checking account deposits. The money supply has increased by $2,710 − $1,000 = $1,710.

The process is still not finished. The person who borrows the $810 will spend it by writing a check against his account. Whoever receives the $810 will deposit it in his bank, which could be a Wachovia branch or a PNC branch or a branch of some other bank. That new bank—if it's not PNC—will send the check to PNC and will receive $810 in new reserves. That new bank will have an incentive to loan out 90 percent of these reserves—keeping 10 percent to meet the legal requirement—and the process will go on. At each stage, the additional loans being made and the additional deposits being created are shrinking by 10 percent, as each bank has to withhold that amount as required reserves. We can show the total increase in checking account deposits set off by your initial deposit of $1,000:

BANK	INCREASE IN CHECKING ACCOUNT DEPOSITS	
Wachovia	$1,000	
PNC	900	(= 0.9 × $1,000)
Third Bank	810	(= 0.9 × $900)
Fourth Bank	729	(= 0.9 × $810)
•	•	
•	•	
•	•	
Total Change in Checking Account Deposits	$10,000	

The Simple Deposit Multiplier

Your initial deposit of $1,000 increased the reserves of the banking system by $1,000 and led to a total increase in checking account deposits of $10,000. The ratio of the amount of deposits created by banks to the amount of new reserves is called the **simple deposit multiplier.** In this case, the simple deposit multiplier is equal to $10,000/$1,000 = 10. Why 10? How do we know that your initial $1,000 deposit ultimately leads to a total increase in deposits of $10,000?

Simple deposit multiplier The ratio of the amount of deposits created by banks to the amount of new reserves.

There are two ways to answer this question. First, each bank in the process is keeping reserves equal to 10 percent of its deposits. For the banking system as a whole, the total increase in reserves is $1,000—the amount of your original currency deposit. Therefore, the system as a whole will end up with $10,000 in deposits, because $1,000 is 10 percent of $10,000.

A second way to answer the question is by deriving an expression for the simple deposit multiplier. The total increase in deposits equals:

$$\$1{,}000 + 0.9 \times \$1{,}000 + (0.9 \times 0.9) \times \$1{,}000 + (0.9 \times 0.9 \times 0.9) \times \$1{,}000 + \ldots$$

Or,

$$\$1{,}000 + 0.9 \times \$1{,}000 + 0.9^2 \times \$1{,}000 + 0.9^3 \times \$1{,}000 + \ldots$$

Or,

$$\$1{,}000 \times (1 + 0.9 + 0.9^2 + 0.9^3 + \ldots).$$

Mathematicians have shown that an expression like the one in the parentheses sums to:

$$\frac{1}{1-0.9}.$$

Simplifying further we have:

$$\frac{1}{0.10} = 10.$$

So,

$$\text{The total increase in deposits} = \$1{,}000 \times 10 = \$10{,}000.$$

Note that 10 is equal to 1 divided by the required reserve ratio, *RR,* which in this case is 10 percent or 0.10. This gives us another way of expressing the simple deposit multiplier:

$$\text{Simple deposit multiplier} = \frac{1}{RR}.$$

This formula makes it clear that the higher the required reserve ratio, the smaller the simple deposit multiplier. With a required reserve ratio of 10 percent, the simple deposit multiplier is 10. If the required reserve ratio were 20 percent, the simple deposit multiplier would fall to 1/0.20, or 5. We can use this formula to calculate the total increase in checking account deposits from an increase in bank reserves due to, for instance, currency being deposited in a bank:

$$\text{Change in checking account deposits} = \text{Change in bank reserves} \times \frac{1}{RR}.$$

For example, if \$100,000 in currency is deposited in a bank and the required reserve ratio is 10 percent, then:

$$\text{Change in checking account deposits} = \$100{,}000 \times \frac{1}{0.10} = \$100{,}000 \times 10 = \$1{,}000{,}000.$$

SOLVED PROBLEM 15-2

③ LEARNING OBJECTIVE

Explain how banks create checking account deposits.

Showing How Banks Create Money

Suppose you deposit \$5,000 in currency into your checking account at a branch of PNC Bank, which we will assume has no excess reserves at the time you make your deposit. Also assume that the required reserve ratio is 0.10.

a. Use a T-account to show the initial effect of this transaction on PNC's balance sheet.

b. Suppose that PNC makes the maximum loan they can from the funds you deposited. Use a T-account to show the initial effect on PNC's balance sheet from granting the loan. Also include in this T-account the transaction from question (a).

c. Now suppose that whoever took out the loan in question (b) writes a check for this amount and that the person receiving the check deposits it in Wachovia Bank. Show the effect of these transactions on the balance sheets of PNC Bank and Wachovia Bank, *after the check has been cleared.* On the T-account for PNC Bank, include the transactions from questions (a) and (b).

d. What is the maximum increase in checking account deposits that can result from your \$5,000 deposit? What is the maximum increase in the money supply? Explain.

Solving the Problem:

Step 1: Review the chapter material. This problem is about how banks create checking account deposits, so you may want to review the section "Using T-Accounts to Show How a Bank Can Create Money," which begins on page 467.

Step 2: Answer question (a) by using a T-account to show the impact of the deposit. Keeping in mind that T-accounts show only the changes in a balance sheet that result from the relevant transaction and that assets are on the left side of the account and liabilities are on the right side, we have:

PNC Bank

Assets		Liabilities	
Reserves	+$5,000	Deposits	+$5,000

Because the bank now has your $5,000 in currency in its vault, its reserves (and, therefore, its assets) have risen by $5,000. But this transaction also increases your checking account balance by $5,000. Because the bank owes you this money, the bank's liabilities have also risen by $5,000.

Step 3: Answer question (b) by using a T-account to show the impact of the loan. The problem tells you to assume that PNC Bank currently has no excess reserves and that the required reserve ratio is 10 percent. This requirement means that if the bank's checking account deposits go up by $5,000, they must keep $500 as reserves and can loan out the remaining $4,500. Remembering that new loans usually take the form of setting up, or increasing, a checking account for the borrower, we have:

PNC Bank

Assets		Liabilities	
Reserves	+$5,000	Deposits	+$5,000
Loans	+$4,500	Deposits	+$4,500

The first line of the T-account shows the transaction from question (a). The second line shows that PNC has loaned out $4,500 by increasing the checking account of the borrower by $4,500. The loan is an asset to PNC because it represents a promise by the borrower to make certain payments spelled out in the loan agreement.

Step 4: Answer question (c) by using T-accounts for PNC and Wachovia to show the impact of the check clearing. We now show the effect of the borrower having spent the $4,500 he received as a loan from PNC. The person who received the $4,500 check deposits it in her account at Wachovia. We need two T-accounts to show this:

PNC Bank

Assets		Liabilities	
Reserves	+$500	Deposits	+$5,000
Loans	+$4,500		

Wachovia Bank

Assets		Liabilities	
Reserves	+$4,500	Deposits	+$4,500

Look first at the T-account for PNC. Once Wachovia sends the check written by the borrower to PNC, PNC loses $4,500 in reserves and Wachovia gains $4,500 in reserves. The $4,500 is also deducted from the account of the borrower. PNC is now satisfied with the result. It received a $5,000 deposit in currency from you. When that money was sitting in the bank vault, it wasn't earning any interest for PNC. Now $4,500 of the $5,000 has been loaned out and is earning interest. These interest payments allow PNC to cover its costs and earn a profit, which it has to do to remain in business.

Wachovia now has an increase in deposits of $4,500, resulting from the check deposited by the contractor, and an increase in reserves of $4,500. Wachovia is in the same situation as

PNC was in question (a): It has excess reserves as a result of this transaction and a strong incentive to lend them out in order to earn some interest.

Step 5: Answer question (d) by using the simple deposit multiplier formula to calculate the maximum increase in checking account deposits and the maximum increase in the money supply. The simple deposit multiplier expression is (remember that *RR* is the required reserve ratio):

$$\text{Change in checking account deposits} = \text{Change in bank reserves} \times \frac{1}{RR}.$$

In this case, bank reserves rose by $5,000 as a result of your initial deposit and the required reserve ratio is 0.10, so

$$\text{Change in checking account deposits} = \$5{,}000 \times \frac{1}{0.10} = \$5{,}000 \times 10 = \$50{,}000.$$

Because checking account deposits are part of the money supply, it is tempting to say that the money supply has also increased by $50,000. Remember, though, that your $5,000 in currency was counted as part of the money supply while you had it, but it is not included when it is sitting in a bank vault. Therefore,

$$\text{Change in the money supply} = \text{Increase in checking account deposits} - \text{Decline in currency in circulation} = \$50{,}000 - \$5{,}000 = \$45{,}000.$$

YOUR TURN: **For more practice, do related problem 12 on page 486 at the end of the chapter.**

The story we have told about the way an increase in reserves in the banking system leads to the creation of new deposits and, therefore, an increase in the money supply has been simplified in two ways. First, we assumed that banks do not keep any excess reserves. That is, we assumed that when you deposited $1,000 in currency into your checking account at Wachovia Bank, Wachovia loaned out $900, keeping only the $100 in required reserves. In fact, banks often keep at least some excess reserves to guard against the possibility that many depositors may simultaneously make withdrawals from their accounts. The more excess reserves banks keep, the smaller the deposit multiplier. Imagine an extreme case where Wachovia keeps your entire $1,000 as reserves. If Wachovia does not loan out any of your deposit, the process described earlier of loans leading to the creation of new deposits, leading to the making of additional loans, and so on, will not take place. The $1,000 increase in reserves will lead to a total increase of $1,000 in deposits, and the deposit multiplier will be only 1, not 10.

Second, we assumed that the whole amount of every check is deposited in a bank; no one takes any of it out as currency. In reality, households and firms keep roughly constant the amount of currency they hold relative to the value of their checking account balances. So, we would expect to see people increasing the amount of currency they hold as the balances in their checking accounts rise. Once again, think of the extreme case. Suppose that when Wachovia makes the initial $900 loan to the borrower who wants to buy a used car, the seller of the car cashes the check instead of depositing it. In that case, PNC does not receive any new reserves and does not make any new loans. Once again, the $1,000 increase in your checking account at Wachovia is the only increase in deposits, and the deposit multiplier is 1.

The effect of these two factors is to reduce the real-world deposit multiplier to about 2.5. That means that a $1 increase in the reserves of the banking system results in about a $2.50 increase in deposits.

Although the story of the deposit multiplier can be complicated, the key point to bear in mind is that the most important part of the money supply is the checking account balance component. When banks make loans, they increase checking account balances, and the money supply expands. Banks make new loans whenever they gain reserves. The whole process can also work in reverse. If banks lose reserves, they reduce their outstanding loans and deposits, and the money supply contracts.

We can summarize these important conclusions:

1. Whenever banks gain reserves, they make new loans and the money supply expands.
2. Whenever banks lose reserves, they reduce their loans and the money supply contracts.

The Federal Reserve System

 **LEARNING OBJECTIVE**

Discuss the three policy tools the Federal Reserve uses to manage the money supply.

Many people are surprised to learn that banks do not keep in their vaults all of the funds that are deposited into checking accounts. In fact, in September 2005 the total amount of checking account balances in all banks in the United States was $641 billion, while total reserves were only $46 billion. The United States, like nearly all other countries, has a **fractional reserve banking system.** In a fractional reserve banking system, banks keep less than 100 percent of deposits as reserves. When people deposit money in a bank, the bank loans most of the money to someone else. What happens, though, if depositors want their money back? This would seem to be a problem because banks have loaned out most of the money and can't get it back easily.

Fractional reserve banking system A banking system in which banks keep less than 100 percent of deposits as reserves.

In practice, though, withdrawals are usually not a problem for banks. On a typical day, about as much money is deposited as is withdrawn. If a small amount more is withdrawn than deposited, banks can cover the difference from their excess reserves or by borrowing from other banks. Sometimes depositors lose confidence in a bank when they question the value of the bank's underlying assets, particularly its loans. Often, the reason for a loss of confidence is bad news, whether true or false. When many depositors simultaneously decide to withdraw their money from a bank, there is a **bank run.** If many banks experience runs at the same time, the result is a **bank panic.** It is possible for one bank to handle a run by borrowing from other banks, but if many banks simultaneously experience runs, the banking system may be in trouble.

Bank run Many depositors simultaneously decide to withdraw money from a bank.

Bank panic Many banks experiencing runs at the same time.

A *central bank*, like the Federal Reserve in the United States, can help stop a bank panic by acting as a *lender of last resort.* In acting like a lender of last resort, a central bank makes loans to banks that cannot borrow funds elsewhere. The bank can use these loans to pay off depositors. When the panic ends and the depositors put their money back in their accounts, the bank can repay the loan to the central bank.

The 2001 Bank Panic in Argentina

15-3 Making the Connection

We saw at the beginning of this chapter that Argentina suffered a bank panic in 2001. Some unusual aspects of the Argentine banking system made it very difficult for the Argentine central bank to act as a lender of last resort. As an alternative policy to stop the banking panic, the Argentine government limited the amount of Argentine currency that depositors could withdraw to $1,000 per account per month. Consumers cut back on their spending because much of the money in their bank accounts could not be withdrawn. Firms like McDonald's experienced declining sales as the country's recession worsened.

The inability of the Argentine central bank to act as a lender of last resort resulted from a decision made by the Argentine government in 1991 to fix the value of the Argentine peso relative to the U.S. dollar at one to one. This policy was meant to restore public faith in the ability of the Argentine currency to retain its value. Argentina had suffered through several periods of high inflation. In 1990, the inflation rate had been a staggering 2,300 percent. These inflationary episodes had caused the purchasing power of the currency to decline rapidly. Although the policy of fixing the value of the peso against the dollar was successful in greatly reducing inflation, it ultimately placed the banking system in an awkward situation. After 1991, Argentine banks were encouraged to take in U.S. dollar deposits and to make U.S. dollar loans, and U.S. dollars were legally recognized as a means of payment within Argentina. By 1994, 60 percent of time deposits and 50 percent of loans were in U.S. dollars.

The Argentine central bank was unable to stop the bank panic of 2001.

The Argentine central bank was allowed to issue pesos only in exchange for dollars, which limited its ability to provide pesos to banks experiencing a bank run.

By 2000, many observers had begun to doubt the ability of the Argentine government to maintain the one-to-one exchange rate. As a result, Argentine households and firms, as well as foreign investors, began moving funds out of pesos and into dollars. By late 2001, fully 80 percent of time deposits in Argentine banks were in dollars rather than in pesos. In addition, many depositors began withdrawing money from their accounts. Forty-seven of the top 50 Argentine banks experienced major withdrawals by December 2001. In January 2002, the crisis was ended when the government abandoned its commitment to the one-to-one exchange rate between the peso and the dollar and decreed that dollar deposits in banks would be converted to peso deposits at a rate of 1.4 pesos to the dollar. Although some financial stability was restored, the damage to the banking system from the crisis contributed to a decline in real GDP of 11.5 percent during 2002.

Source: Kathryn M. E. Dominguez and Linda Tesar, "International Borrowing and Macroeconomic Performance in Argentina," National Bureau of Economic Research, Working Paper 11353, May 2005.

The Organization of the Federal Reserve System

Federal Reserve System The central bank of the United States.

Bank panics lead to severe disruptions in business activity because neither households nor firms can gain access to their accounts. Not surprisingly, in the United States each banking panic in the late nineteenth and early twentieth centuries was accompanied by a recession. With the intention of putting an end to banking panics, in 1913 Congress passed the Federal Reserve Act setting up the **Federal Reserve System.** The system began operation in 1914. The Federal Reserve—often referred to as the "Fed"—is the central bank of the United States. The Fed acts as a lender of last resort to banks and as a bankers' bank, providing services such as check clearing to banks. The Fed also takes actions to control the money supply.

To aid the Fed in carrying out these functions, Congress divided the country into 12 Federal Reserve districts, as shown in Figure 15-3. Each district has its own Federal Reserve bank, which provides services to banks in that district. The real power of the Fed, however, lies in Washington, D.C., with the Board of Governors. There are seven members of the Board of Governors, all of whom are appointed by the President of the United States to 14-year, nonrenewable terms. Board members come from banking, business, and academic backgrounds. One of the seven board members is appointed chairman for a four-year, renewable term. Chairmen of the Board of Governors since World War II have come from various backgrounds, including Wall Street (William McChesney Martin), academia (Arthur Burns and Ben Bernanke), business (G. William Miller), public service (Paul Volcker), and economic forecasting (Alan Greenspan).

How the Federal Reserve Manages the Money Supply

Although Congress established the Fed to stop banking panics by acting as a lender of last resort, today an important activity for the Fed is managing the money supply. As we

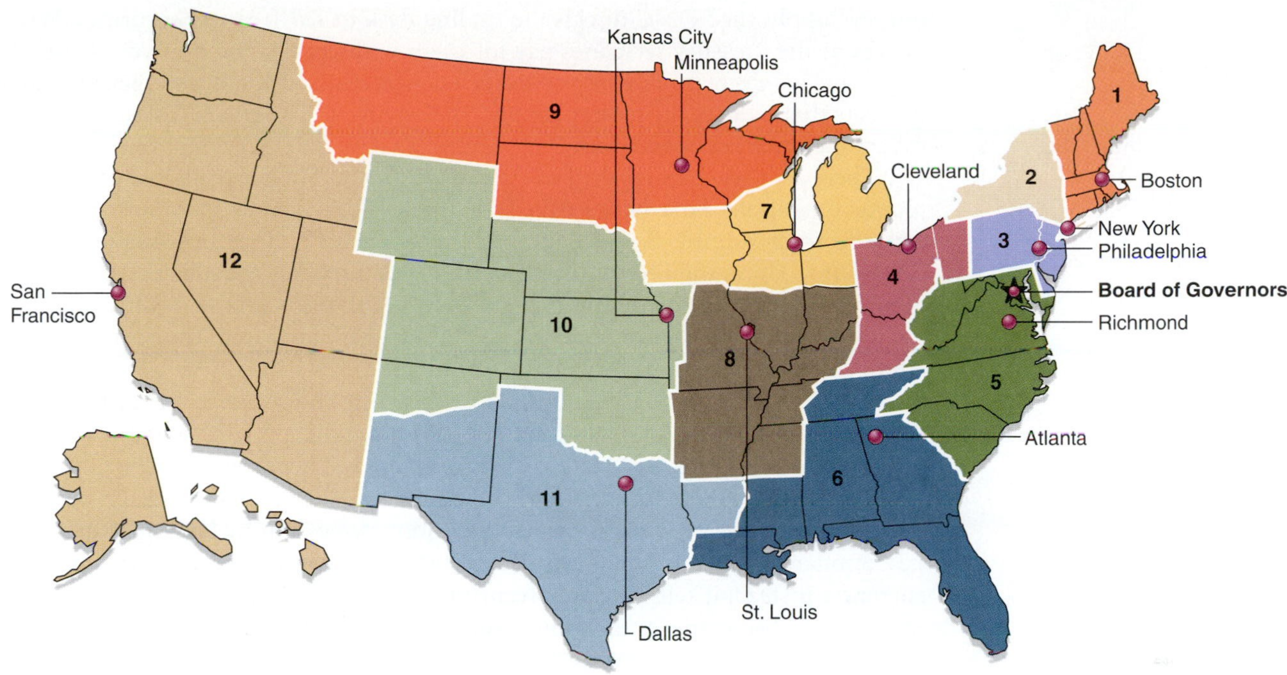

FIGURE 15-3 Federal Reserve Districts

The United States is divided into 12 Federal Reserve districts, each of which has a Federal Reserve bank. The real power within the Federal Reserve System, however, lies in Washington, D.C., with the Board of Governors.

Source: Board of Governors of the Federal Reserve System.

will discuss in more detail in Chapter 16, managing the money supply is part of **monetary policy,** which the Fed undertakes to pursue economic objectives.

Monetary policy The actions the Federal Reserve takes to manage the money supply and interest rates to pursue economic objectives.

To manage the money supply, the Fed uses three *monetary policy tools:*

1. Open market operations
2. Discount policy
3. Reserve requirements

Remember that the most important component of the money supply is checking account balances. Not surprisingly, all three of the Fed's policy tools are aimed at affecting the reserves of banks as a means of changing the volume of checking account balances.

OPEN MARKET OPERATIONS Eight times per year the **Federal Open Market Committee (FOMC)** meets in Washington, D.C., to discuss monetary policy. The committee has 12 members: the seven members of the Federal Reserve's Board of Governors, the president of the Federal Reserve Bank of New York, and four presidents from the other 11 Federal Reserve banks. These four presidents serve one-year rotating terms on the FOMC.

Federal Open Market Committee (FOMC) The Federal Reserve committee responsible for open market operations and managing the money supply.

The U.S. Treasury borrows money by selling bills, notes, and bonds. Remember that the *maturity* of a financial asset is the period of time until the purchaser receives payment of the face value or principal. Usually, bonds have face values of $1,000. Treasury bills have maturities of 1 year or less, Treasury notes have maturities of 2 years to 10 years, and Treasury bonds have maturities of 30 years. To increase the money supply, the FOMC directs the *trading desk,* located at the Federal Reserve Bank of New York to *buy* U.S. Treasury securities—most frequently bills but sometimes notes or bonds—from the public. When the sellers of the Treasury securities deposit the funds in their banks, the reserves of banks will rise. This increase in reserves will start the process of increasing loans and checking account deposits that increases the money supply. To decrease the money supply, the FOMC directs the trading desk to *sell* Treasury securities. When the buyers of the Treasury securities pay for them with checks, the reserves of their banks will fall. This decrease in reserves starts a contraction of loans and checking account deposits that reduces the money supply. The buying and selling of Treasury securities is called **open market operations.**

Open market operations The buying and selling of Treasury securities by the Federal Reserve in order to control the money supply.

There are three reasons the Fed conducts monetary policy principally through open market operations. First, because the Fed initiates open market operations, it completely controls their volume. Second, the Fed can make both large and small open market operations. Third, the Fed can implement its open market operations quickly, with no administrative delay or required changes in regulations. Many other central banks, including the European Central Bank and the Bank of Japan, also use open market operations in conducting monetary policy.

The Federal Reserve is responsible for printing the paper currency of the United States. Recall that if you look at the top of a dollar bill, you will see the words "Federal Reserve Note." When the Fed takes actions to increase the money supply, commentators will sometimes say that it is "printing more money." The main way the Fed increases the money supply, however, is not by printing more money but by buying Treasury securities. Similarly, to reduce the money supply, the Fed does not set fire to stacks of paper currency. Instead, it sells Treasury securities. We will spend more time discussing how and why the Fed manages the money supply in Chapter 16, when we discuss monetary policy.

Discount loans Loans the Federal Reserve makes to banks.

Discount rate The interest rate the Federal Reserve charges on discount loans.

DISCOUNT POLICY The loans the Fed makes to banks are called **discount loans,** and the interest rate it charges on the loans is called the **discount rate.** When a bank receives a loan from the Fed, its reserves increase by the amount of the loan. By lowering the discount rate, the Fed can encourage banks to take additional loans and thereby to increase their reserves. With more reserves, banks will make more loans to households and firms, which will increase checking account deposits and the money supply. Raising the discount rate will have the reverse effect.

The Fed doesn't control discount policy as completely as it controls open market operations, and changing discount policy is much more difficult than changing open market operations because banks must decide whether to accept discount loans. The volume of discount loans is generally small except when the Fed is actively acting as a lender of last resort, as it did, for example, in the aftermath of the U.S. stock market crash of October 1987 and the September 11, 2001, terrorist attacks. In practice, the Fed prefers to limit discount loans to helping banks that experience temporary problems with deposit withdrawals, rather than to use them to increase or decrease the money supply. Outside the United States, central banks such as the European Central Bank and the Bank of Japan use discount lending both as a monetary policy tool and as a means of mitigating financial crises.

The Fed is not called on to use discount policy to stop bank panics because of the existence of *deposit insurance.* Congress in 1933 set up the Federal Deposit Insurance Corporation (FDIC) to insure deposits in banks. Today, nearly all banks are members of FDIC, and in 2005 each deposit in these banks was insured to a limit of $100,000. Deposit insurance has largely stopped bank panics because it has reassured depositors that their deposits are safe even if their bank goes out of business.

RESERVE REQUIREMENTS When the Fed reduces the required reserve ratio, it converts required reserves into excess reserves. For example, suppose a bank has $100 million in checking account deposits and the required reserve ratio is 10 percent. The bank will be required to hold $10 million as reserves. If the Fed reduces the required reserve ratio to 8 percent, the bank will need to hold only $8 million as reserves. The Fed has converted $2 million worth of reserves from required to excess. This $2 million is now available for the bank to lend out. If the Fed *raises* the required reserve ratio from 10 percent to 12 percent, it would have the reverse effect.

The Fed changes reserve requirements much more rarely than it conducts open market operations or changes the discount rate. Because changes in reserve requirements require significant alterations in banks' holdings of loans and securities, frequent changes would be disruptive. Also, because reserves earn no interest, the use of reserve requirements to manage the money supply effectively places a tax on banks' deposit-taking and lending activities, which can be costly for the economy.

Putting It All Together: Decisions of the Nonbank Public, Banks, and the Fed

Using its three tools—open market operations, the discount rate, and reserve requirements—the Fed has substantial influence over the money supply, but that influence is not absolute. Two other actors—the nonbank public and banks—also influence the money supply in practice.

The nonbank public—households and firms—must decide how much money to hold as deposits in banks. The larger the money holdings in deposits, the greater are the reserves of banks and the more money the banking system can create. The smaller the money holdings in deposits, the lower are the reserves of banks and the less money the banking system can create. In addition, the Fed does not have absolute control over the amount bankers decide to lend. Banks create money only if they lend their reserves. If bankers retain excess reserves, they make a smaller volume of loans and create less money.

The roles of the nonbank public and banks in the money supply process do not mean that the Fed lacks meaningful control of the money supply. The Fed's staff monitors information on banks' reserves and deposits every week, and the Fed can respond quickly to shifts in behavior by depositors or banks. The Fed can therefore steer the money supply close to the level it desires.

The Quantity Theory of Money

Explain the quantity theory of money and use it to explain how high rates of inflation occur.

People have been aware of the connection between increases in the money supply and inflation for centuries. In the sixteenth century, the Spanish conquered Mexico and Peru and shipped large quantities of gold and silver back to Spain. The gold and silver were minted into coins and spent across Europe to further the political ambitions of the Spanish kings. Prices in Europe rose steadily during these years, and many observers discussed the relationship between this inflation and the flow of gold and silver into Europe from the Americas.

Connecting Money and Prices: The Quantity Equation

In the early twentieth century, Irving Fisher, an economist at Yale, formalized the connection between money and prices using the *quantity equation:*

$$M \times V = P \times Y.$$

The equation states that the money supply (M) multiplied by the **velocity of money** (V) equals the price level (P) multiplied by real output (Y). Fisher defined the velocity of money, often referred to simply as "velocity," as the average number of times each dollar of the money supply is used to purchase goods and services included in GDP. Rewriting the original equation by dividing both sides by M, we have the equation for velocity:

Velocity of money The average number of times each dollar in the money supply is used to purchase goods and services included in GDP.

$$V = \frac{P \times Y}{M}.$$

We can use M1 to measure the money supply, the GDP price deflator to measure the price level, and real GDP to measure real output. Then the value for velocity for 2004 was:

$$V = \frac{1.082 \times \$10{,}842 \text{ billion}}{\$1{,}363 \text{ billion}} = 8.6.$$

This result tells us that, on average during 2004, each dollar of M1 was spent about nine times on goods or services included in GDP.

Because velocity is *defined* to be equal to $(P \times Y)/M$, we know that the quantity equation must always hold true: The left side *must* be equal to the right side. A theory is a statement about the world that might possibly be false. Therefore, the quantity equation is not a theory. Irving Fisher turned the quantity equation into the **quantity theory of money** by asserting that velocity was constant. He argued that the average number of times a dollar is spent depends on how often people get paid, how often they do their grocery shopping, how often businesses mail bills, and other factors that do not change very often. Because this assertion may be true or false, the quantity theory of money is, in fact, a theory.

Quantity theory of money A theory of the connection between money and prices that assumes that the velocity of money is constant.

The Quantity Theory Explanation of Inflation

The quantity equation gives us a way of showing the relationship between changes in the money supply and changes in the price level, or inflation. To see this relationship more clearly, we can use a handy mathematical rule that states that an equation where variables are multiplied together is equal to an equation where the *growth rates* of these variables are *added* together. So, we can transform the quantity equation from:

$$M \times V = P \times Y$$

to:

Growth rate of the money supply + Growth rate of velocity =
Growth rate of the price level (or inflation rate) + Growth rate of real output.

This way of writing the quantity equation is more useful for investigating the effect of changes in the money supply on the inflation rate. Remember that the growth rate for any variable is just the percentage change in the variable from one year to the next. The growth rate of the price level is just the inflation rate, so we can rewrite the quantity equation to help us understand the factors that determine inflation:

Inflation rate = Growth rate of the money supply +
Growth rate of velocity – Growth rate of real output.

If Irving Fisher was correct that velocity is constant, then the growth rate of velocity will be zero. That is, if velocity is, say, always 8.6, then its percentage change from one year to the next will always be zero. This assumption allows us to rewrite the equation one last time:

Inflation rate = Growth rate of the money supply – Growth rate of real output.

This equation leads to the following predictions:

1. If the money supply grows at a faster rate than real GDP, there will be inflation.
2. If the money supply grows at a slower rate than real GDP, there will be deflation. (Recall that *deflation* is a decline in the price level.)
3. If the money supply grows at the same rate as real GDP, the price level will be stable, and there will be neither inflation nor deflation.

It turns out that Irving Fisher was wrong in asserting that the velocity of money is constant. From year to year there can be significant fluctuations in velocity. As a result, the predictions of the quantity theory of money do not hold every year, but most economists agree that the quantity theory provides a useful insight into the long-run relationship between the money supply and inflation: *In the long run, inflation results from the money supply growing at a faster rate than real GDP.*

High Rates of Inflation

Why do governments allow high rates of inflation? The quantity theory can help us to understand the reasons for high rates of inflation, such as that experienced in Argentina during the 1980s. Very high rates of inflation—in excess of hundreds or thousands of percentage points per year—are known as *hyperinflation.* Hyperinflation is caused by central banks increasing the money supply at a rate far in excess of the growth rate of real GDP. A high rate of inflation causes money to lose its value so rapidly that households and firms avoid holding it. If the inflation becomes severe enough, people stop using paper currency, so it no longer serves the important functions of money discussed previously in this chapter. Economies suffering from high inflation usually also suffer from very slow growth, if not severe recession.

Given the dire consequences that follow from high inflation, why do governments allow it by expanding the money supply so rapidly? The main reason is that governments often want to spend more than they are able to raise through taxes. Developed countries, such as the United States, can usually bridge gaps between spending and taxes by borrowing through selling bonds to the public. Developing countries often have difficulty selling bonds because the public is skeptical of their ability to pay back the money. If they are unable to sell bonds to the public, governments in developing countries will force their central banks to purchase them. As we discussed previously, when a central bank buys bonds, the money supply will increase.

High Inflation in Argentina

The link between rapid money growth and high inflation was evident in the experience of Argentina during the 1980s. Panel (a) of Figure 15-4 shows rates of growth of the money supply and the inflation rate in Argentina in the years from 1981 to 1991. Both the average annual growth rate of the money supply and the average annual inflation rate from 1981 to 1990 were greater than 750 percent. With prices rising so quickly, Argentine currency could not fulfill the normal functions of money. Not surprisingly, the Argentine economy struggled during these years, with real GDP in 1990 ending up 6 percent lower than it had been in 1981.

This weak economic performance was particularly frustrating to many people in Argentina because early in the twentieth century the country had had one of the highest standards of living in the world. In 1910, only the United States and Great Britain had higher levels of real GDP per capita. In U.S.-made films of the 1920s and 1930s, the rich foreigner was often from Argentina.

It was clear to policymakers in Argentina that the only way to bring inflation under control was to limit increases in the money supply. As we saw in Making the Connection 15-3, in 1991 the Argentine government enacted a new policy that fixed the exchange rate of the peso versus the U.S. dollar at one to one. In addition, the Argentine central bank was allowed to issue pesos only in exchange for dollars. As panel (b) in Figure 15-4 shows, the new policy greatly reduced increases in the money supply and the inflation rate (notice that the scale of panel (b) is different from the scale of panel (a), which partly disguises the fall in money growth and inflation). Economic growth also revived, with real GDP increasing at an average annual rate of almost 6 percent from 1991 to 1998. Unfortunately, though, Argentina had not come to grips with several underlying economic problems, perhaps the most important of which was the continuing gap between government expenditures and tax receipts.

By 2000, many observers expected that the Argentine government would not be able to maintain the one-to-one exchange rate between the peso and the U.S. dollar. As Argentine firms and households, along with foreign investors, began exchanging pesos

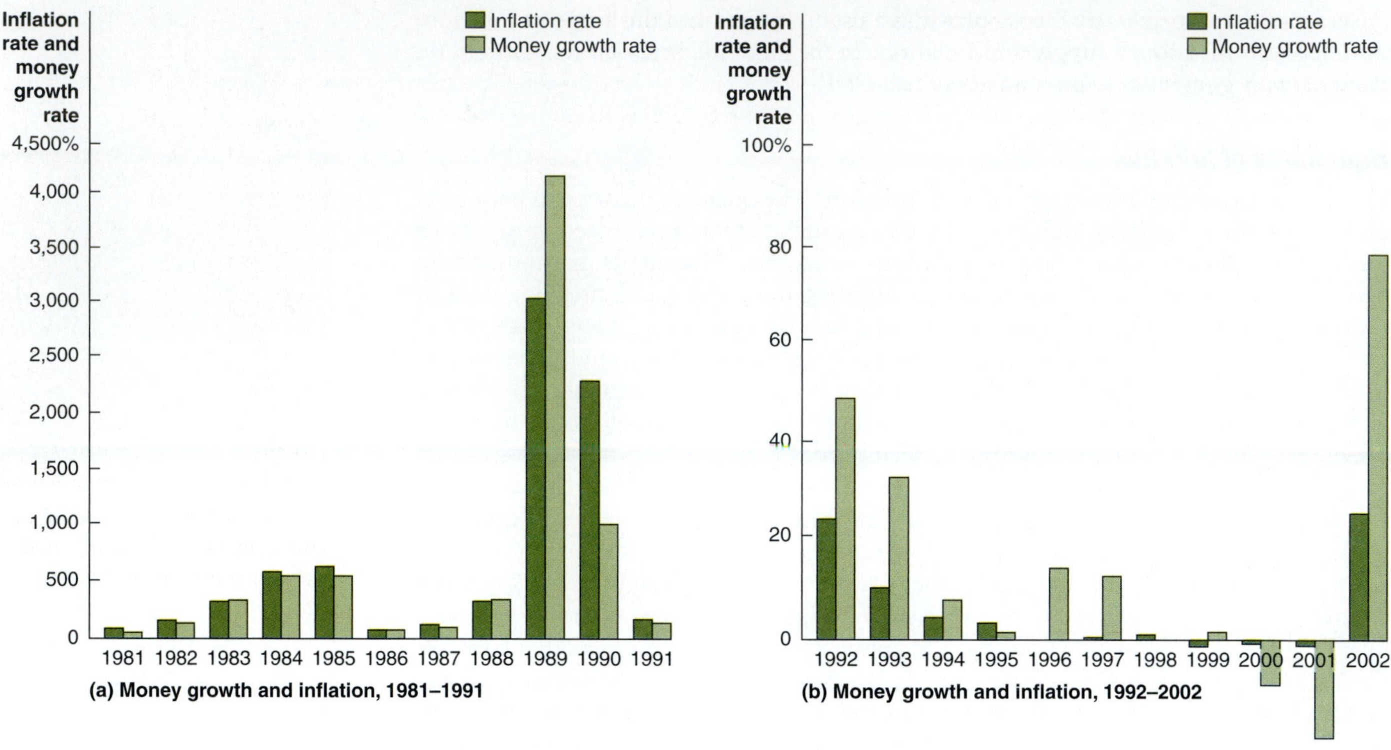

FIGURE 15-4 Money Growth and Inflation in Argentina

Panel (a) shows rates of growth of the money supply and the inflation rate in Argentina in the years from 1981 to 1991. Both the average annual growth rate of the money supply and the average annual inflation rate from 1981 to 1990 were greater than 750 percent. In 1991, the Argentine government enacted a new policy that fixed the exchange rate of the peso versus the U.S. dollar at one to one. As panel (b) shows, the new policy greatly reduced increases in the money supply and the inflation rate (notice that the scale of panel (b) is different from the scale of panel (a), which partly disguises the fall in money growth and inflation).

Source: International Monetary Fund.

for dollars, the Argentine money supply declined. The money supply declined by 9 percent in 2000 and by an additional 20 percent in 2001. Argentina experienced falling prices, or deflation, during both years, along with falling real GDP. Finally, in January 2002, the Argentine government abandoned its commitment to the one-to-one exchange rate between the peso and the dollar, and the money supply increased rapidly. During 2002, the money supply increased by nearly 80 percent and deflation was transformed to an inflation rate of 25 percent. Although the inflation rate declined over the next few years, Argentina continues to struggle to keep its money supply from growing at rates likely to result in high inflation.

15-4 Making the Connection

The German Hyperinflation of the Early 1920s

When Germany lost World War I, a revolution broke out that overthrew Kaiser Wilhelm II and installed a new government known as the Weimar Republic. In the peace treaty of 1919, the Allies—the United States, Great Britain, France, and Italy—imposed payments called *reparations* on the new German government. The reparations were meant as compensation to the Allies for the damage Germany had caused during the war. It was very difficult for the German government to use tax revenue to cover both its normal spending and the reparations.

The German government decided to pay for the difference between its spending and its tax revenues by selling bonds to the central bank, the Reichsbank. After a few years, the German government fell far behind in its reparations payment. In January 1923, the French government sent troops into the German industrial area known as the Ruhr to try to collect the payments directly. German workers in the Ruhr went on strike, and the German government decided to support them by paying their salaries. Raising the funds to do so was financed by an inflationary monetary policy—the German government sold bonds to the Reichsbank, thereby increasing the money supply.

The inflationary increase in the money supply was very large: The total number of marks—the German currency—in circulation rose from 115 million in January 1922 to 1.3 billion in January 1923 and then to 497 billion *billion* or 497,000,000,000,000,000,000 in December 1923. Just as the quantity theory predicts, the result was a staggeringly high rate of inflation. The German price index that stood at 100 in 1914 and 1,440 in January 1922 had risen to 126,160,000,000,000 in December 1923. The German mark became worthless. The German government ended the hyperinflation by (1) negotiating a new agreement with the Allies that reduced its reparations payments, (2) reducing other government expenditures and raising taxes to balance its budget, and (3) replacing the existing mark with a new mark. Each new mark was worth 1 trillion old marks. The German central bank was also limited to issuing a total of 3.2 billion new marks.

These steps were enough to bring the hyperinflation to an end—but not before the savings of anyone holding the old marks had been wiped out. Most middle-income Germans were extremely resentful of this outcome. Many historians believe that the hyperinflation greatly reduced the allegiance of many Germans to the Weimar Republic and may have helped pave the way for Hitler and the Nazis to seize power 10 years later.

Source: Thomas Sargent, "The End of Four Big Hyperinflations," in *Rational Expectations and Inflation*, New York: Harper and Row, 1986.

During the hyperinflation of the 1920s, people in Germany used paper currency to light their stoves.

Conclusion

Money plays a key role in the functioning of an economy by facilitating trade in goods and services and by making specialization possible. Without specialization, no advanced economy can prosper. Households and firms, banks, and the central bank (the Federal Reserve in the United States) are participants in the process of creating the money supply. In the next chapter, we will explore how the Federal Reserve uses monetary policy to promote its economic objectives.

An Inside Look on the next page discusses how several Latin American countries have moved away from fixing the value of their currencies against the dollar.

An Inside Look Does Using the Dollar Destabilize Latin American Countries?

WALL STREET JOURNAL, MAY 12, 2004

Latin Governments Try to Unseat the Dollar

a Once considered the bedrock of monetary stability, the U.S. dollar is losing fans among Latin American officials eager to promote their own domestic currencies. Yet recent government attempts to limit the role of the dollar contrast with the behavior of consumers who remain partial to the dollar as a dependable medium of exchange and store of value. Before governments can expect consumers to voluntarily switch allegiances, they will have to build credibility in their own currencies.

It wasn't long ago that governments saw the U.S. Federal Reserve as a legitimate and effective substitute for homegrown monetary institutions. Beginning in the late 1980s and well into the 1990s several countries set the value of their currencies at a fixed rate against the dollar.

The plan helped bring inflation under control, but a lack of accompanying structural economic policy adjustments consistent with stable money brought about the collapse of most fixed exchange rate regimes. Those countries that adopted the dollar as legal tender—Ecuador, El Salvador and Panama—have so far avoided devastating monetary crises.

b Argentina abandoned its currency peg known as "convertibility" in 2002, a painful episode that marked the end of the latest chapter in fixed exchange schemes. By then, several other countries had already adopted explicit inflation targeting as an alternative way to try to keep prices in check. Now that nine nations in the region rely on inflation targeting and the value of most currencies fluctuates in the foreign exchange market, these governments are becoming more wary of the dollar, particularly dollar borrowing on bank balance sheets.

For consumers and companies however, the dollar remains popular. Because of the trust it inspires among both borrowers and lenders, rates for commercial loans in dollars where they are available are more attractive than those on local currency lending.

The continued reliance on dollar borrowing worries officials who fret about the danger of instability if local currencies were to suddenly lose value versus the dollar. In Peru, where the dollar is widely circulated in parallel to the Peruvian sol, the government has engaged in a vocal campaign to reduce the amount of dollars in circulation.

The results have been mildly effective: During the first quarter of this year, Peru's central bank reported the amount of dollars in the banking system had dropped to 54% in 2004 from as high as 70% in 2000. . . .

c In a recent release titled "The Importance of The De-dollarization of the Banking Credit Sector," Peru's central bank states that having 74% of all bank loans denominated in dollars creates a potential currency imbalance for consumers as well as companies since most receive income denominated in soles rather than in dollars.

"The mismatch implies a currency exchange risk: if the exchange rate weakens, foreign currency liabilities rise while income doesn't. In this manner, the dollarization of the bank credit sector makes the economy vulnerable," argues the central bank. For anyone following the painful and ongoing debt cleanup of billions of dollars borrowed by Argentina's consumers and companies when the local currency was valued at parity with the dollar, the warning seems merited.

Besides Peru, other Latin American countries have conducted campaigns over the years to reduce the dollar dependency of its citizens and raise the profile of local currencies.

Mexico developed a futures market in pesos following its devaluation and financial crisis in the mid 1990s. Chile avoided the dollarization of its financial sector with the introduction of local currency deposits indexed to inflation, a measure that failed in other countries. Colombia and Uruguay have successfully issued international bonds denominated in domestic currencies.

The development of new financial instruments and markets has had an impact in some sectors, as the figures from Peru suggest. Changing the ingrained habits of individual consumers and local companies that are still partial to the U.S. currency will be a slow process. . . .

Key Points in the Article

In many Latin American countries today, businesses and households accept U.S. dollars—or Federal Reserve notes—in exchange for goods and services. The dollar's popularity in Latin America dates to the 1980s and 1990s, when local monetary policies fueled hyperinflation. Local currencies failed as mediums of exchange and stores of value, and Latin American governments had no choice but to allow their citizens to exchange goods for U.S. dollars. Today, many Latin American governments want to eliminate the U.S. dollar from local circulation because they believe these dollars threaten the stability of the region's economies.

Analyzing the News

a Fiat money is useful as long as all businesses and households accept it in exchange for goods and services. This acceptance occurs only if everyone in the economy is confident that money will not lose value over time. That is, fiat money exists because it provides two fundamental functions: it serves as a medium of exchange and a store of value. The U.S. dollar provides both of these functions in many Latin American countries. In the 1980s and 1990s, many Latin American governments accepted U.S. dollars as legal tender. They did so in response to monetary crises that occurred throughout the region. Today, Latin American governments would like businesses and households to accept only local currencies in exchange for goods and services.

b In 2002, Argentina abandoned its currency peg, which set the value of one peso equal to the value of one U.S. dollar. The result of this decision is shown in Figure 1. The value of the Argentine peso fell to roughly one third the value of a U.S. dollar. And, as the purchasing power of the peso fell, consumer price inflation in Argentina rose. This pattern is shown in Figure 2. Today, the values of many Latin American currencies are determined by demand and supply in the foreign exchange market, and Latin American central banks have low inflation rate targets to ensure that their currencies provide the functions of money described in this chapter. Inflation targeting is a monetary policy that requires a central bank to announce publicly an inflation target, and then to increase or decrease its money supply in order to hit that target. If Latin America's households and firms are confident that their central banks will have a low inflation rate target, local currencies will become the primary medium of exchange.

c In a "dollarized" economy, the value of the local currency is fixed to the value of the U.S. dollar and both currencies circulate as legal tender. Peru's central bank is concerned about the consequences of its dollarized economy. On the one hand, dollarization strengthens Peru's economy because the U.S. dollar is an excellent medium of exchange and store of value in Peru. On the other hand, dollarization threatens Peru's economy because most of Peru's businesses and households earn *soles* but owe *dollars*. If dollarization were to fail, the sol's value would fall relative to the dollar and Peru's dollar-denominated debt burden would increase in terms of soles. This currency imbalance is what caused Argentina's economy to collapse in 2002. Peru's central bankers are worried that the same could happen there.

Thinking Critically ABOUT POLICY

1. Suppose Peru's central bank announces that it will target an inflation rate of 3 percent. Now suppose Peru's economy enters a recession. Should Peru's central bank abandon its inflation target and increase the money supply to stimulate economic activity in the short run? Why or why not?
2. Why would Latin American economies tie the value of their currencies to the dollar rather than, say, the euro or the yen?

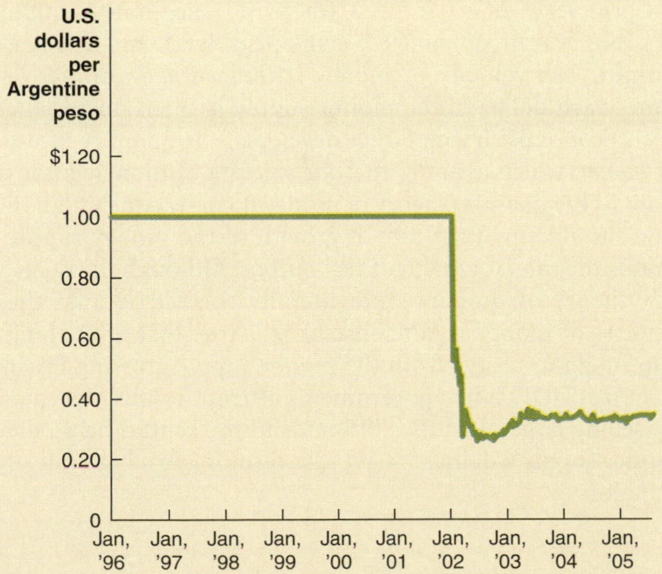

Figure 1: U.S. dollar/Argentine peso exchange rate, January 1996 to July 2005.

Source: OANDA.com.

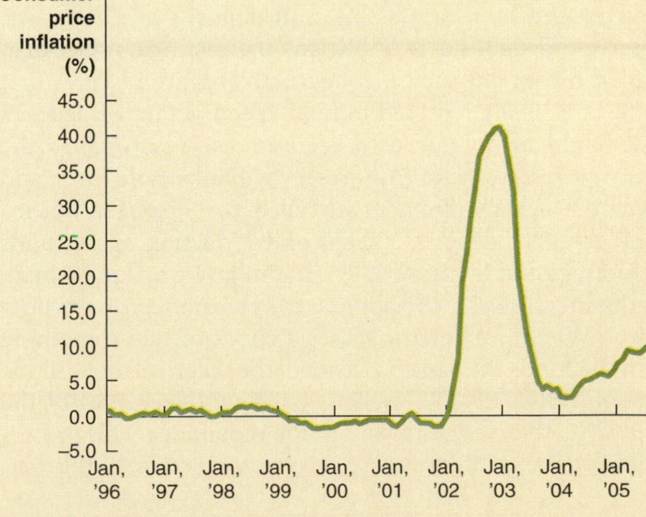

Figure 2: Greater Buenos Aires consumer price inflation, January 1996 to July 2005.

Source: National Institute of Statistics and Census, Argentina.

SUMMARY

LEARNING OBJECTIVE ① Define money and discuss its four functions. A *barter economy* is an economy that does not use money and in which people trade goods and services directly for other goods and services. Barter trade occurs only if there is a *double coincidence of wants,* where both parties to the trade want what the other one has. Because barter is inefficient, there is strong incentive to use *money,* which is anything that people are generally willing to accept in exchange for goods or services or in payment of debts. Money has four functions: a medium of exchange, a unit of account, a store of value, and a standard of deferred payment. The *gold standard* was a monetary system under which the government produced gold coins and paper currency convertible into gold. The gold standard collapsed in the early 1930s. Today no government in the world issues paper currency that can be redeemed for gold. Instead, paper currency is *fiat money,* which has no value except as money.

LEARNING OBJECTIVE ② Discuss the definitions of the money supply used in the United States today. The narrowest definition of the money supply in the United States today is M1, which includes currency, checking account balances, and traveler's checks. A broader definition of the money supply is M2, which includes everything that is in M1, plus savings accounts, small-denomination time deposits [such as certificates of deposit (CDs)], money market deposit accounts in banks, and noninstitutional money market fund shares.

LEARNING OBJECTIVE ③ Explain how banks create checking account deposits. On a bank's balance sheet, *reserves* and loans are assets, and deposits are liabilities. Reserves are deposits that the bank has retained, rather than loaned out or invested. *Required reserves* are reserves that banks are legally required to hold. The fraction of deposits that banks are required to keep as reserves is called the *required reserve ratio.* Any reserves banks hold over and above the legal requirement are called *excess reserves.* When a bank accepts a deposit, it keeps only a fraction of the funds as reserves and loans out the remainder. In making a loan, banks increase the checking account balance of the borrower. When the borrower uses a check to buy something with the funds the bank has loaned, the seller will deposit the check in his bank. The seller's bank will keep part of the deposit as reserves and loan out the remainder. This process will continue until no banks have excess reserves. In this way, the process of banks making new loans increases the volume of checking account balances and the money supply. This money creation process can be illustrated with T-accounts, which are stripped-down versions of balance sheets that show only how a transaction changes a bank's balance sheet. The *simple deposit multiplier* is the ratio of the amount of deposits created by banks to the amount of new reserves. An expression for the simple deposit multiplier is $1/RR$.

LEARNING OBJECTIVE ④ Discuss the three policy tools the Federal Reserve uses to manage the money supply. The Federal Reserve System (the "Fed") is the central bank of the United States. It was originally established in 1914 to stop banking panics, but today its main role is to control the money supply. *Monetary policy* refers to the actions the Federal Reserve takes to manage the money supply and interest rates to pursue economic objectives. The Fed's three monetary policy tools are open market operations, discount policy, and reserve requirements. *Open market operations* are the buying and selling of Treasury securities by the Federal Reserve. The loans the Fed makes to banks are called *discount loans,* and the interest rate the Fed charges on discount loans is the *discount rate.* The *Federal Open Market Committee* (FOMC) meets in Washington, D.C., eight times per year to discuss monetary policy.

LEARNING OBJECTIVE ⑤ Explain the quantity theory of money and use it to explain how high rates of inflation occur. The *quantity equation* relates the money supply to the price level: $M \times V = P \times Y$, where M is the money supply, V is the *velocity of money,* P is the price level, and Y is real output. The velocity of money is the average number of times each dollar in the money supply is spent during the year. Economist Irving Fisher developed the *quantity theory of money,* which assumes that the velocity of money is constant. If the quantity theory of money is correct, the inflation rate should equal the rate of growth of the money supply minus the rate of growth of real output. Although the quantity theory of money is not literally correct because the velocity of money is not constant, it is true that in the long run inflation results from the money supply growing faster than real GDP. When governments attempt to raise revenue by selling large quantities of bonds to the central bank, the money supply will increase rapidly, resulting in a high rate of inflation.

KEY TERMS

Asset 458
Bank panic 473
Bank run 473
Commodity money 458
Discount loans 476
Discount rate 476
Excess reserves 466
Federal Open Market Committee (FOMC) 475
Federal Reserve System 474
Fiat money 461
Fractional reserve banking system 473
M1 463
M2 464
Monetary policy 475
Money 458
Open market operations 476
Quantity theory of money 478
Required reserve ratio 466
Required reserves 466
Reserves 466
Simple deposit multiplier 469
Velocity of money 477

REVIEW QUESTIONS

1. Glyn Davies, an economist at the University of Wales, wrote: "In pure barter if the owner of an orchard, having a surplus of apples, required boots he would need to find not simply a cobbler but a cobbler who wanted to purchase apples." What do economists call the problem Davies is describing?
   Source: Glyn Davies, *A History of Money: From Ancient Times to the Present,* Cardiff: University of Wales Press, 1994.
2. What is the difference between commodity money and fiat money?
3. What are the four functions of money? Can something be considered money if it does not fulfill all four functions?
4. What is the main difference between the M1 and M2 definitions of the money supply?
5. What are the largest asset and the largest liability of the typical bank?
6. Suppose you decide to withdraw $100 in cash from your checking account. Draw a T-account showing the effect of this transaction on your bank's balance sheet.
7. Give the formula for the simple deposit multiplier. If the required reserve ratio is 20 percent, what is the maximum increase in checking account deposits that will result from an increase in bank reserves of $20,000?
8. Why did Congress decide to set up the Federal Reserve System in 1914? Today, what is the most important role of the Federal Reserve in the U.S. economy?
9. What are the policy tools the Fed uses to control the money supply? Which tool is the most important?
10. What is the quantity theory of money? How does the quantity theory explain why inflation occurs?
11. What is hyperinflation? Why do governments sometimes allow it to occur?

PROBLEMS AND APPLICATIONS

Please visit **www.prenhall.com/hubbard** *for solutions to the even-numbered problems as well as multiple-choice and true-false self-assessment quizzes.*

1. The English economist Stanley Jevons described a world tour during the 1880s by a French singer, Mademoiselle Zélie. One stop on the tour was a theater in the Society Islands, part of French Polynesia in the South Pacific. She performed for her usual fee, which was one-third of the receipts. This turned out to be three pigs, 23 turkeys, 44 chickens, 5,000 coconuts, and "considerable quantities of bananas, lemons, and oranges." She estimated that all of this would have had a value in France of 4,000 francs. According to Jevons, "as Mademoiselle could not consume any considerable portion of the receipts herself, it became necessary in the meantime to feed the pigs and poultry with the fruit." Do the goods Mademoiselle Zélie received as payment fulfill the four functions of money described in the chapter? Why or why not?
   Source: W. Stanley Jevons, *Money and the Mechanism of Exchange,* New York: D. Appleton and Company, 1889, pp. 1–2.
2. In the late 1940s, the Communists under Mao Zedong were defeating the government of China in a civil war. The paper currency issued by the Chinese government was losing much of its value and most businesses refused to accept it. At the same time, there was a paper shortage in Japan. During these years, Japan was still under military occupation by the United States, following its defeat in World War II. Some of the U.S. troops in Japan realized that they could

use dollars to buy up vast amounts of paper currency in China, ship it to Japan to be recycled into paper, and make a substantial profit. Under these circumstances, was the Chinese paper currency a commodity money or a fiat money? Briefly explain.

3. Briefly explain whether each of the following is counted in M1.
   a. The coins in your pocket
   b. The funds in your checking account
   c. The funds in your savings account
   d. The traveler's check that you have left over from a trip
   e. Your Citibank Platinum MasterCard
4. **[Related to *Solved Problem 15-1*]** Suppose you have $2,000 in currency in a shoebox in your closet. One day you decide to deposit the money in a checking account. Briefly explain how this will affect M1 and M2.
5. The paper currency of the United States is technically called "Federal Reserve Notes." The following excerpt is from the Federal Reserve Act:

   > Federal reserve notes . . . shall be redeemed in lawful money on demand at the Treasury Department of the United States, in the city of Washington, District of Columbia, or at any Federal Reserve bank.

   If you took a $20 bill to the Treasury Department or a Federal Reserve bank, with what type of "lawful money" is the government likely to redeem it?
6. The following is from a newspaper story on local, or community, banks: "Community banks . . . are awash in liabilities these days, and they couldn't be happier about it." To which "liabilities" does the story refer? Why would these banks be happy about being "awash" in these liabilities?
   Source: Christian Millman, "Bank Deposits on the Rise as People Flee the Stock Market," (Allentown, PA) *Morning Call*, August 11, 2002, pp. D1, D4.
7. The president of a local bank described deposits this way: "That's the fuel we use to be able to go out and make loans and mortgages." Briefly explain what he means.
   Source: Christian Millman, "Bank Deposits on the Rise as People Flee the Stock Market," (Allentown, PA) *Morning Call*, August 11, 2002, pp. D1, D4.
8. Suppose you decide to withdraw $100 in currency from your checking account. What is the effect on M1? Ignore any actions the bank may take as a result of your having withdrawn the $100.
9. **[Related to *Don't Let This Happen To You!*]** Briefly explain whether you agree or disagree with the following statement: "I recently read that more than half of the money issued by the government is actually held by people in foreign countries. If that's true, then the United States is less than half as wealthy as government statistics indicate."
10. "Most of the money supply of the United States is created by banks making loans." Briefly explain whether you agree or disagree with this statement.
11. Would a series of bank runs in a country decrease the total quantity of M1? Wouldn't a bank run simply move funds in a checking account to currency in circulation? How could that movement of funds decrease the quantity of money?
12. **[Related to *Solved Problem 15-2*]** Suppose you deposit $2,000 in currency into your checking account at a branch of Bank of America, which we will assume has no excess reserves at the time you make your deposit. Also assume that the required reserve ratio is 0.20.
    a. Use a T-account to show the initial impact of this transaction on Bank of America's balance sheet.
    b. Suppose that Bank of America makes the maximum loan they can from the funds you deposited. Using a T-account, show the initial impact of granting the loan on Fleet's balance sheet. Also include on this T-account the transaction from (a).
    c. Now suppose that whoever took out the loan in (b) writes a check for this amount and that the person receiving the check deposits it in a branch of Citibank. Show the effect of these transactions on the balance sheets of Bank of America and Citibank Bank, *after the check has been cleared.* [On the T-account for Bank of America, include the transactions from (a) and (b).]
    d. What is the maximum increase in checking account deposits that can result from your $2,000 deposit? What is the maximum increase in the money supply? Explain.
13. Consider the following simplified balance sheet for a bank:

Assets		Liabilities	
Reserves	$10,000	Deposits	$70,000
Loans	$66,000	Stockholders' equity	$6,000

    a. If the required reserve ratio is 10 percent, how much in excess reserves does the bank hold?
    b. What is the maximum amount by which the bank can expand its loans?
    c. If the bank makes the loans in (b), show the *immediate* impact on the bank's balance sheet.
14. Suppose that the Federal Reserve makes a $10 million discount loan to the First National Bank by increasing FNB's account at the Fed.
    a. Use a T-account to show the impact of this transaction on FNB's balance sheet. Remember that the funds a bank has on deposit at the Fed count as part of its reserves.

b. Assume that before receiving the discount loan, FNB has no excess reserves. What is the maximum amount of this $10 million that FNB can lend out?
c. What is the maximum total increase in the money supply that can result from the Fed's discount loan? Assume the required reserve ratio is 10 percent.

15. If the money supply is growing at a rate of 6 percent per year, real GDP is growing at a rate of 3 percent per year, and velocity is constant, what will the inflation rate be? If velocity is increasing 1 percent per year instead of remaining constant, what will the inflation rate be?

16. The following is from an article in the *Wall Street Journal*: Japan's "money supply is surging. If that doesn't curtail Japan's debilitating price deflation, a lot of economics textbooks may need to be rewritten."
a. What is "price deflation"?
b. If rapid increases in the money supply don't stop deflation, why will economics textbooks need to be rewritten?
c. (This is a more difficult question.) Why might price deflation in Japan be "debilitating"? *Hint:* What reaction might consumers have to price deflation?

Source: Peter Landers, "Japan Shows Vague Signs of Recovery," *Wall Street Journal,* March 5, 2002.

17. **[Related to *Don't Let This Happen To You!*]** Briefly explain whether you agree or disagree with the following statement: "Assets are things of value that people own. Liabilities are debts. Therefore, a bank will always consider a checking account deposit to be an asset, and a car loan to be a liability."

18. "Banks don't really create money, do they?" was the challenge that a retired professor of economics was known to have used in his upper division American economic history course to ascertain what his students remembered from introductory macroeconomics about the creation of money. He reported that few students were confident enough or remembered enough to reply correctly to his question. How would you reply?

19. In the 1970s, it was reported that a leader of a country proclaimed that he intended to do away with money in his country because money represents the decadence of the West (Western Europe and the United States). Historically, did money only exist in the West? What effect would the elimination of money have on the economy?

20. **[Related to the *Chapter Opener*]** During the Civil War, the Confederate States of America printed lots of its own currency—Confederate dollars—to fund the war. By the end of the war, nearly 1.5 billion paper dollars had been printed by the Confederate government. How would such a large quantity of Confederate dollars have affected the value of the Confederate currency? With the war drawing to an end, would Southerners have been as willing to use and accept Confederate dollars? How else could they have made exchanges?

Source: Textual Transcript of Confederate Currency, Federal Reserve Bank of Richmond.

chapter sixteen 16

Monetary Policy

Why Did Homebuilder Toll Brothers, Inc., Prosper during the 2001 Recession?

In March 2001, the U.S. economy moved into recession. During a typical recession, sales of new homes decline sharply as unemployment increases and incomes fall. Homebuilders are usually among the businesses hit hardest during recessions. For example, during the recession of 1974–75, spending on residential construction declined by more than 30 percent. Homebuilders fared even worse during the recessions of 1980–82, when spending on residential construction plummeted by more than 40 percent. The situation was very different during the recession of 2001, however, when spending on residential construction actually rose by 5 percent.

Founded in 1967 by Bruce and Robert Toll, Toll Brothers, Inc., is a homebuilder headquartered in Huntingdon Valley, Pennsylvania. Toll Brothers started small; on the firm's first project, Robert Toll would spend time walking around the construction site collecting discarded nails and pieces of lumber to be reused the next day. Toll Brothers expanded by buying inexpensive land and learning how to quickly obtain the approvals of local governments to build on the land. Toll Brothers specializes in building luxury homes but uses many of the techniques employed by builders of low-cost starter homes. In two factories in Pennsylvania and one in Virginia, Toll Brothers manufactures the trusses that support the roofs and the panels that form the walls of the homes it constructs. The firm employs computer-controlled machines in its factories to cut spaces for doors and windows. These practices give Toll Brothers lower costs than other builders of luxury homes, who often use carpenters and other skilled workers at construction sites to assemble wall panels and cut out doors and windows. Today, Toll Brothers builds homes in 21 states and has revenues of $6 billion, which place it among the 500 largest firms in the United States.

Still, despite its success, Toll Brothers should have experienced a

decline in sales during the recession of 2001. But look at the following excerpt from their report to shareholders for the third quarter of 2001:

> Amid continuing sluggishness in the U.S. economy, Toll Brothers once again posted record results. Thanks to hard work and efficient planning and the [housing] market's ability to weather the downturn, we have just completed the best third quarter and first nine months in our history.

The success of Toll Brothers during 2001 was not the result of good luck but rather of a policy decision made by the Federal Reserve's Federal Open Market Committee (FOMC). In early 2001, the members of the FOMC concluded that a recession was about to begin and implemented an expansionary monetary policy to keep the recession as short and mild as possible. By driving down interest rates, the Fed succeeded in heading off what some economists had predicted would be a prolonged and severe recession. *An Inside Look* on page 516 considers whether the actions taken by the Fed to stimulate spending on residential construction may have led to a "bubble" in housing prices.

Source: Shawn Tully, "Toll Brothers: The New King of the Real Estate Boom," *Fortune*, April 5, 2005.

LEARNING OBJECTIVES

After studying this chapter, you should be able to:

1. Define monetary policy and describe the Federal Reserve's monetary policy goals.
2. Describe the Federal Reserve's monetary policy targets, and explain how expansionary and contractionary monetary policies affect the interest rate.
3. Use aggregate demand and aggregate supply graphs to show the effects of monetary policy on real GDP and the price level.
4. Discuss the Fed's setting of monetary policy targets.
5. Assess the arguments for and against the independence of the Federal Reserve.

In Chapter 15, we saw that banks play an important role in creating the money supply. We also saw that the Fed manages the money supply to achieve its policy goals. As we will see in this chapter, the Fed has four policy goals: (1) price stability, (2) high employment, (3) economic growth, and (4) stability of financial markets and institutions. In this chapter, we will explore how the Federal Reserve decides which *monetary policy* actions to take to achieve its goals.

1 LEARNING OBJECTIVE
Define monetary policy and describe the Federal Reserve's monetary policy goals.

What Is Monetary Policy?

When Congress created the Federal Reserve System (the "Fed") in 1914, its main responsibility was to make discount loans to banks suffering from large withdrawals by depositors. As a result of the Great Depression of the 1930s, Congress amended the Federal Reserve Act to give the Federal Reserve's Board of Governors broader responsibility to act "so as to promote effectively the goals of maximum employment, stable prices, and moderate long-term interest rates."

Monetary policy The actions the Federal Reserve takes to manage the money supply and interest rates to pursue its economic objectives.

Since World War II, the Federal Reserve has carried out an active **monetary policy.** Monetary policy refers to the actions the Fed takes to manage the money supply and interests rates to pursue its economic objectives.

The Goals of Monetary Policy

The Fed has set four *monetary policy goals* that are intended to promote a well-functioning economy:

1. Price stability
2. High employment
3. Economic growth
4. Stability of financial markets and institutions

We briefly consider each of these goals.

PRICE STABILITY As we have seen in previous chapters, rising prices erode the value of money as a medium of exchange and a store of value. Especially after inflation rose dramatically and unexpectedly during the 1970s, policymakers in most industrial countries have set price stability as a policy goal. Figure 16-1 shows that from the early 1950s until 1968, the inflation rate remained below 4 percent per year. Inflation was above 4 percent for most of the 1970s. In early 1979, the inflation rate increased to more than 10 percent, where it remained until late 1981, when it began to rapidly fall back to the 4-percent range. Since 1992, the inflation rate has been below 4 percent. In 2004 inflation was 2.7 percent and, in the view of most economists, inflationary pressures were well contained.

The inflation rates during the years 1979–1981 were the highest the United States has ever experienced during peacetime. When Paul Volcker became chairman of the Federal Reserve's Board of Governors in August 1979, he made fighting inflation his top policy goal. Alan Greenspan, who succeeded Volcker in August 1987, and Ben Bernanke, who succeeded Greenspan in January 2006, continued to focus on inflation. Volcker, Greenspan, and Bernanke argued that if inflation is low over the long run, the Fed will have the flexibility it needs to lessen the impact of recessions. And many economists agree.

HIGH EMPLOYMENT High employment, or a low rate of unemployment, is another monetary policy goal. Unemployed workers and underused factories and office buildings reduce GDP below its potential level. Unemployment causes financial distress and decreases self-esteem for workers who lack jobs. The goal of high employment extends beyond the Fed to other branches of the federal government. At the end of World War II,

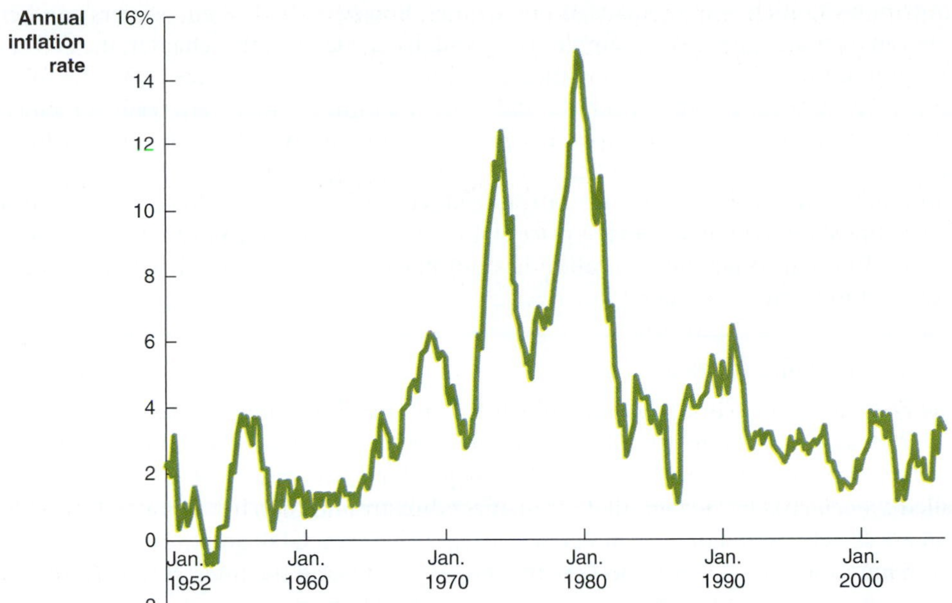

FIGURE 16-1

The Inflation Rate, 1952–2004

For most of the 1950s and 1960s, the inflation rate in the United States was 4 percent or less. During the 1970s, the inflation rate increased, peaking during 1979–1981, when it averaged more than 10 percent. Since 1992, the inflation rate has been less than 4 percent.

Note: The inflation rate is measured as the percentage increase in the consumer price index (CPI) from the same month in the previous year.

Source: Bureau of Labor Statistics.

Congress passed the Employment Act of 1946, which stated that it was the "responsibility of the Federal Government . . . to foster and promote . . . conditions under which there will be afforded useful employment, for those able, willing, and seeking to work, and to promote maximum employment, production, and purchasing power."

ECONOMIC GROWTH We discussed in Chapter 13 the importance of economic growth to raising living standards. Policy can spur economic growth by providing incentives for saving to ensure a large pool of investment funds, as well as by providing direct incentives for business investment. Policymakers aim to encourage *stable* economic growth because stable growth allows households and firms to plan accurately and encourages the long-run investment that is needed to sustain growth.

STABILITY OF FINANCIAL MARKETS AND INSTITUTIONS When financial markets and institutions are not efficient in matching savers and borrowers, resources are lost. Firms with the potential to produce goods and services valued by consumers cannot obtain the financing they need to design, develop, and market these products. Savers waste resources looking for satisfactory investments. The Fed promotes the stability of financial markets and institutions so that an efficient flow of funds from savers to borrowers will occur. The Fed's response to problems in financial markets has averted financial panics. For example, following the stock market crash of 1987 and the terrorist attacks of September 11, 2001, the Fed's willingness to rapidly increase the volume of discount loans reassured financial markets and promoted financial stability.

In the next section, we will look at how the Fed attempts to attain its monetary policy goals. Although the Fed has multiple monetary policy goals, during most periods the most important goals of monetary policy have been price stability and high employment. In the remainder of this chapter we will focus on these two goals.

The Money Market and the Fed's Choice of Targets

LEARNING OBJECTIVE

Describe the Federal Reserve's monetary policy targets, and explain how expansionary and contractionary monetary policies affect the interest rate.

The Fed's objective in setting monetary policy is to use its policy tools to achieve its monetary policy goals. Recall from Chapter 15 that the Fed's policy tools are open market operations, discount policy, and reserve requirements. Sometimes the Fed can be successful in pursuing multiple goals at the same time. For example, it can take actions that increase both employment and economic growth because steady economic growth contributes to high employment. At other times, however, the Fed encounters conflicts between its policy goals. For example, as we will discuss later in this chapter, the Fed can raise interest rates to reduce the inflation rate. But, as we saw in Chapter 14, higher interest rates typically reduce household and firm spending, which may result in slower growth. So, a policy that is intended to achieve one monetary policy goal, such as lower inflation, may have an adverse effect on another policy goal, such as economic growth. Some members of Congress have introduced legislation that would force the Fed to focus almost entirely on achieving price stability, and many economists support such a focus. Although so far this legislation has not passed Congress, the debate has gained momentum within the Federal Reserve.

Monetary Policy Targets

The Fed tries to keep both the unemployment and inflation rates low, but it can't affect either of these economic variables directly. The Fed cannot tell firms how many people to employ or what prices to charge for their products. Instead, the Fed uses variables, called *monetary policy targets*, that it can affect directly and that, in turn, affect variables that are closely related to the Fed's policy goals, such as real GDP and the price level. The two main monetary policy targets are the money supply and the interest rate. As we will see, the Fed typically uses the interest rate as its policy target.

The Demand for Money

The Fed's two monetary policy targets are related in an important way. To see this relationship, we first need to examine the demand and supply for money. Figure 16-2 shows the demand curve for money. The interest rate is on the vertical axis, and the quantity of money is on the horizontal axis. Here we are using the M1 definition of money, which equals currency in circulation plus checking account balances. Notice that the demand curve for money is downward sloping.

To understand why the demand curve for money is downward sloping, consider that households and firms have a choice between holding money or other financial assets, such as U.S. Treasury bills. Money has one very desirable characteristic: You can use it to buy goods, services, or financial assets. Money also has one undesirable characteristic: It earns either no interest or a very low rate of interest. The currency in your wallet earns no interest, and the money in your checking account earns either no interest or very little interest. Alternatives to money, such as U.S. Treasury bills, pay interest but have to be sold if you want to use the funds to buy something. When interest rates rise on financial assets such as U.S. Treasury bills, the amount of interest that households

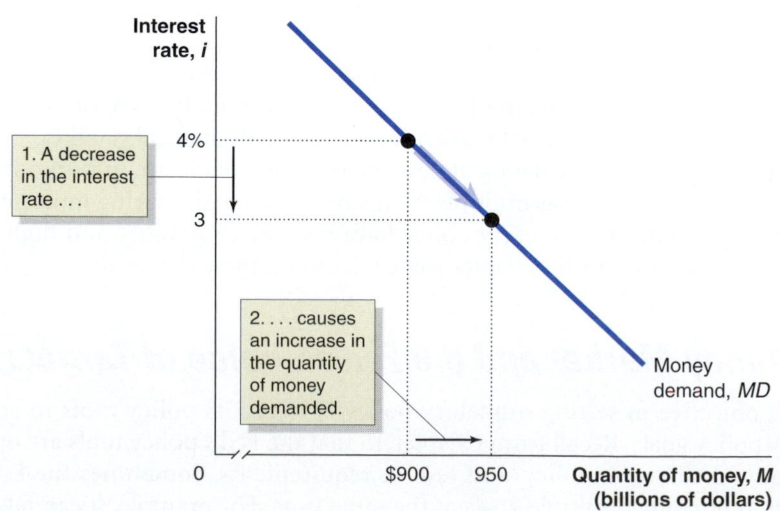

FIGURE 16-2

The Demand for Money

The money demand curve slopes downward because lower interest rates cause households and firms to switch from financial assets like U.S. Treasury bills to money. All other things being equal, a fall in the interest rate from 4 percent to 3 percent will increase the quantity of money demanded from $900 billion to $950 billion: An increase in the interest rate will decrease the quantity of money demanded.

and firms lose by holding money increases. When interest rates fall, the amount of interest households and firms lose by holding money decreases. Remember that *opportunity cost* is what you have to forgo to engage in an activity. The interest rate is the opportunity cost of holding money.

We now have an explanation for why the demand curve for money slopes downward: When interest rates on Treasury bills and other financial assets are low, the opportunity cost of holding money is low, so the quantity of money demanded by households and firms will be high; when interest rates are high, the opportunity cost of holding money will be high, so the quantity of money demanded will be low. In Figure 16-2, a decrease in interest rates from 4 percent to 3 percent causes the quantity of money demanded by households and firms to rise from $900 billion to $950 billion.

Shifts in the Money Demand Curve

We saw in Chapter 3 that the demand curve for a good is drawn holding constant all variables, other than the price, that affect the willingness of consumers to buy the good. Changes in variables other than the price cause the demand curve to shift. Similarly, the demand curve for money is drawn holding constant all variables, other than the interest rate, that affect the willingness of households and firms to hold money. Changes in variables other than the interest rate cause the demand curve to shift. The two most important variables that cause the money demand curve to shift are real GDP and the price level.

An increase in real GDP means that the amount of buying and selling of goods and services will increase. This additional buying and selling increases the demand for money as a medium of exchange, so the quantity of money households and firms want to hold increases at each interest rate. Therefore, the money demand curve will shift to the right. A decrease in real GDP decreases the quantity of money demanded at each interest rate, shifting the money demand curve to the left. A higher price level increases the quantity of money required for a given amount of buying and selling. Eighty years ago, for example, when a new car could be purchased for $500 and a salary of $30 per week was considered middle-income earnings, the quantity of money demanded by households and firms was much lower than today, even adjusting for the effect of the lower real GDP and smaller population of those years. An increase in the price level increases the quantity of money demanded at each interest rate, shifting the money demand curve to the right. A decrease in the price level decreases the quantity of money demanded at each interest rate, shifting the money demand curve to the left. Figure 16-3 illustrates shifts in the money demand curve.

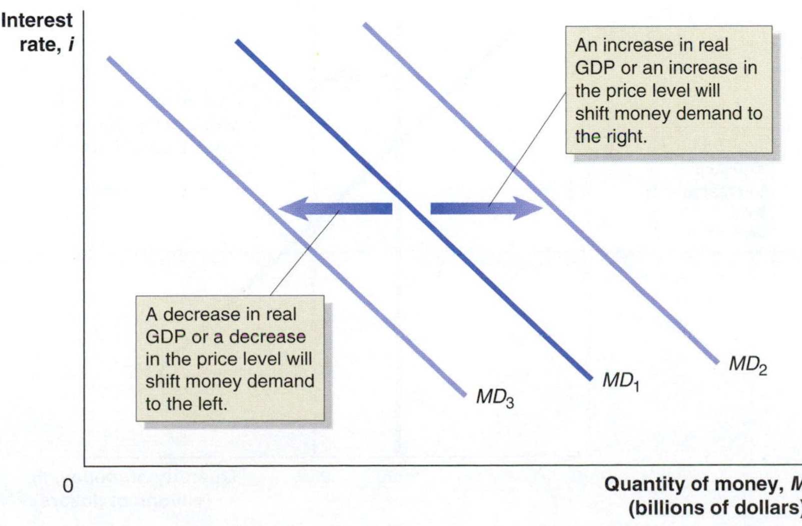

FIGURE 16-3

Shifts in the Money Demand Curve

Changes in real GDP or the price level cause the money demand curve to shift. An increase in real GDP or an increase in the price level will cause the money demand curve to shift from MD_1 to MD_2. A decrease in real GDP or a decrease in the price level will cause the money demand curve to shift from MD_1 to MD_3.

How the Fed Manages the Money Supply: A Quick Review

Having discussed money demand, we now turn to money supply. In Chapter 15, we discussed how the Federal Reserve manages the money supply. Eight times per year, the FOMC meets in Washington, D.C. If the FOMC decides to increase the money supply, it orders the trading desk at the Federal Reserve Bank of New York to purchase U.S. Treasury securities. The sellers of these Treasury securities deposit the funds they receive from the Fed in banks, which increases the banks' reserves. The banks loan out most of these reserves, which creates new checking account deposits and expands the money supply. If the FOMC decides to decrease the money supply, it orders the trading desk to sell Treasury securities, which decreases banks' reserves and contracts the money supply.

Equilibrium in the Money Market

In Figure 16-4, we include both the money demand and money supply curves. We can use this figure to see how the Fed affects both the money supply *and the interest rate.* For simplicity, we assume that the Federal Reserve is able to completely fix the money supply (although, in fact, the behavior of the public and banks can also affect the money supply). Therefore, the money supply curve is a vertical line, and changes in the interest rate have no effect on the quantity of money supplied. Just as with other markets, equilibrium in the *money market* occurs where the money demand curve crosses the money supply curve. If the Fed increases the money supply, the money supply curve will shift to the right and the equilibrium interest rate will fall. In Figure 16-4, when the Fed increases the money supply from $900 billion to $950 billion, the money supply curve shifts from MS_1 to MS_2 and the equilibrium interest rate falls from 4 percent to 3 percent.

In the money market, the adjustment from one equilibrium to another equilibrium is a little different from the adjustment in the market for a good. In Figure 16-4, the money market is initially in equilibrium with an interest rate of 4 percent and a money supply of $900 billion. When the Fed increases the money supply by $50 billion, initially households and firms will have more money than they want to hold at an interest rate of 4 percent. What do households and firms do with the extra $50 billion? They are most likely to use the money to buy short-term financial assets, such as Treasury bills. Short-term financial assets have maturities—the date when the last payment by the seller is

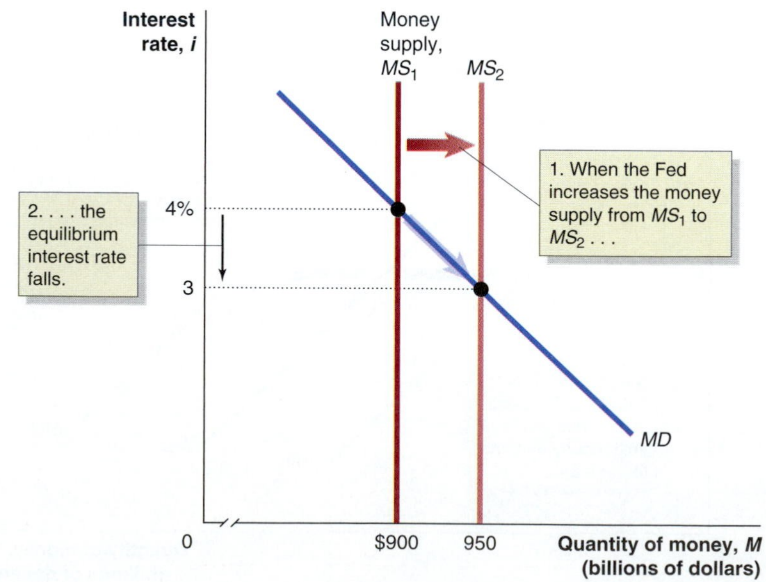

FIGURE 16-4

The Impact on the Interest Rate When the Fed Increases the Money Supply

When the Fed increases the money supply, households and firms will initially hold more money than they want, relative to other financial assets. Households and firms buy Treasury bills and other financial assets with the money they don't want to hold. This increase in demand drives up the prices of these assets and drives down their interest rates. Eventually, interest rates will fall enough that households and firms will be willing to hold the additional money the Fed has created. In the figure, an increase in the money supply from $900 billion to $950 billion causes the money supply curve to shift to the right from MS_1 to MS_2 and causes the equilibrium interest rate to fall from 4 percent to 3 percent.

made—of one year or less. By buying short-term assets, households and firms drive up their prices and drive down their interest rates.

To see why an increasing demand for Treasury bills will lower their interest rate, recall from Chapter 5 that *the prices of financial assets and their interest rates move in opposite directions.* Suppose you buy a U.S. Treasury bill today for $962 that matures in one year, at which time the Treasury will pay you $1,000. (Remember that Treasury bills are sold by the government at a price below their face value of $1,000. The difference between the price of the bill and its $1,000 face value represents the return to investors for lending their money to the Treasury.) You will earn $38 in interest on your investment of $962. The interest rate on the Treasury bill is:

$$\left(\frac{\$38}{\$962}\right) \times 100 = 4\%.$$

Now suppose that many households and firms increase their demand for Treasury bills. This increase in demand will have the same effect on Treasury bills that an increase in the demand for apples has on apples: The price will rise. Suppose the price of Treasury bills rises from $962 to $971. Now if you buy a Treasury bill you will receive only $29 in interest on your investment of $971. The interest rate on the Treasury bill is now:

$$\left(\frac{\$29}{\$971}\right) \times 100 = 3\%.$$

An increase in the price of Treasury bills has lowered the interest rate on Treasury bills.

As the interest rates on financial assets fall, the opportunity cost of holding money also falls. Households and firms move down the money demand curve. Eventually the interest rate will have fallen enough that households and firms are willing to hold the additional $50 billion worth of money the Fed has created and the money market will be back in equilibrium. To summarize: *When the Fed increases the money supply, the short-term interest rate must fall until it reaches a level at which households and firms are willing to hold the additional money.*

Figure 16-5 shows what happens when the Fed decreases the money supply. The money market is initially in equilibrium at an interest rate of 4 percent and a money supply of $900 billion. If the Fed decreases the money supply to $850 billion, households and firms will be holding less money than they would like—relative to other financial assets—at an interest rate of 4 percent. To increase their money holdings, they

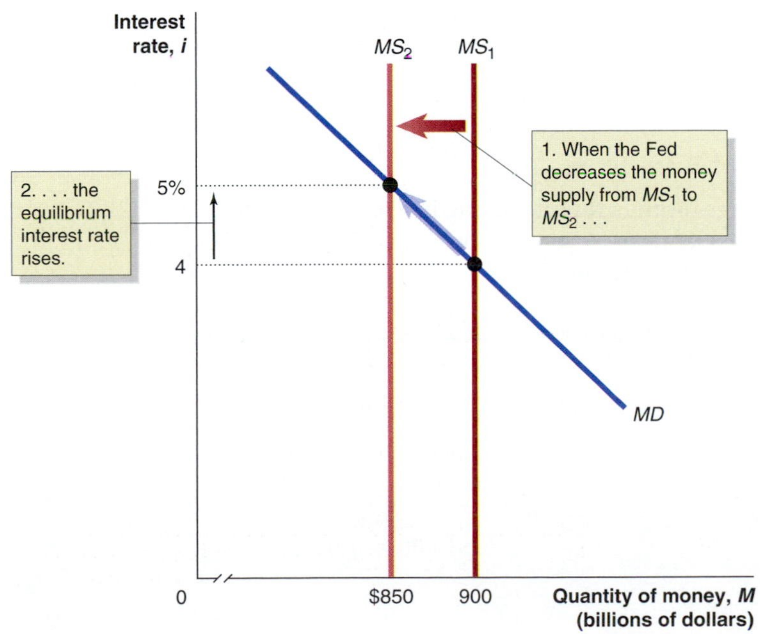

FIGURE 16-5

The Impact on Interest Rates When the Fed Decreases the Money Supply

When the Fed decreases the money supply, households and firms will initially hold less money than they want, relative to other financial assets. Households and firms will sell Treasury bills and other financial assets, reducing their prices and increasing their interest rates. Eventually, interest rates will rise to the point at which households and firms will be willing to hold the smaller amount of money that results from the Fed's actions. In the figure, a reduction in money supply from $900 billion to $850 billion causes the money supply curve to shift to the left from MS_1 to MS_2 and causes the equilibrium interest rate to rise from 4 percent to 5 percent.

will sell Treasury bills and other financial assets. The increased supply of Treasury bills for sale will decrease their prices and increase their interest rates. Rising short-term interest rates increase the opportunity cost of holding money, causing households and firms to move up the money demand curve. Equilibrium is finally restored at an interest rate of 5 percent.

SOLVED PROBLEM 16-1

② LEARNING OBJECTIVE

Describe the Federal Reserve's monetary policy targets, and explain how expansionary and contractionary monetary policies affect the interest rate.

The Relationship between Treasury Bill Prices and Their Interest Rates

What is the price of a Treasury bill that pays \$1,000 in one year, if its interest rate is 4 percent? What is the price of the Treasury bill if its interest rate is 5 percent?

Solving the Problem:

Step 1: Review the chapter material. This problem is about the relationship between Treasury bill prices and interest rates, so you may want to review the section "Equilibrium in the Money Market," which begins on page 504.

Step 2: Use the formula for calculating interest rates to determine the Treasury bill price when the interest rate is 4 percent. In this situation, the interest rate will be equal to the percentage increase from the initial purchase price of the bill to the \$1,000 buyers will receive in one year. We can set up the problem like this, where P is the purchase price of the Treasury bill:

$$\left(\frac{\$1{,}000 - P}{P}\right) \times 100 = 4.$$

Dividing both sides by 100 and multiplying both sides by P, we get:

$$\$1{,}000 - P = 0.04P,$$

or,

$$\$1{,}000 = 1.04P,$$

or,

$$\frac{\$1{,}000}{1.04} = P,$$

or, rounding to the nearest dollar,

$$P = \$962.$$

Step 3: Use the formula for calculating interest rates to determine the Treasury bill price when the interest rate is 5 percent. We can apply the same formula to find the price when the interest rate is 5 percent:

$$\left(\frac{\$1{,}000 - P}{P}\right) \times 100 = 5.$$

Once again, dividing both sides by 100 and multiplying both sides by P we get:

$$\$1{,}000 - P = 0.05P,$$

or,

$$\$1{,}000 = 1.05P,$$

or,

$$\frac{\$1{,}000}{1.05} = P,$$

or,

$$P = \$952.$$

Extra Credit: The interest rate on a Treasury bill or other financial asset is also called its *yield.* It's important to remember that prices of financial assets and their yields move in opposite directions. Consider this excerpt from the credit market column in the *Wall Street Journal:*

> The [price of the] 10-year [Treasury] note was up . . . $0.9375 per $1,000 face value. Its yield fell to 4.563% Friday, as yields move inversely to prices.

A similar reminder that the yield moves inversely to the price appears in this newspaper column every day. Any fact the *Wall Street Journal* feels is important enough to remind its readers of every day is probably worth remembering!

Source: *Wall Street Journal,* November 1, 2005, p. C1.

YOUR TURN: **For more practice, do problem 5 on page 529 at the end of this chapter.**

A Tale of Two Interest Rates

In Chapter 13, we discussed the loanable funds model of the interest rate. In that model, the equilibrium interest rate was determined by the supply and demand for loanable funds. Why do we need two models of the interest rate? The answer is that the loanable funds model is concerned with the *long-term real rate of interest,* and the money-market model is concerned with the *short-term nominal rate of interest.* The long-term real rate of interest is the interest rate that is most relevant when savers consider purchasing a long-term financial investment such as a corporate bond. It is also the rate of interest that is most relevant to firms who are borrowing to finance long-term investment projects such as new factories or office buildings, or to households who are taking out a mortgage loan to buy a new home.

When conducting monetary policy, however, the short-term nominal interest rate is the most relevant interest rate because it is the interest rate most affected by increases and decreases in the money supply. Often—but not always—there is a close connection between movements in the short-term nominal interest rate and movements in the long-term real interest rate. So, when the Fed takes actions to increase the short-term nominal interest, usually the long-term real interest rate will also increase. In other words, as we will discuss in the next section, when the interest rate on Treasury bills rises, the real interest rate on mortgage loans will also usually rise, although sometimes only after a delay.

Choosing a Monetary Policy Target

As we have seen, the Fed uses monetary policy targets to affect economic variables such as real GDP or the price level, which are closely related to the Fed's policy goals. The Fed chooses the money supply or the interest rate as its monetary policy target. As Figure 16-5 shows, the Fed is capable of affecting both. The Fed has generally focused more on the interest rate than on the money supply. After 1980, deregulation and financial innovations, including paying interest on checking accounts and the introduction of money market mutual funds, have made M1 less relevant as a measure of the medium of exchange. These developments led the Fed to rely for a time on M2, a broader measure of the money supply that had a more stable historical relationship to economic growth.

Even this relationship broke down in the early 1990s. In July 1993, then Fed Chairman Alan Greenspan informed the U.S. Congress that the Fed would cease using M1 or M2 targets to guide the conduct of monetary policy. The Fed has correspondingly increased its reliance on interest rate targets.

There are many different interest rates in the economy. For purposes of monetary policy, the Fed has targeted the interest rate known as the *federal funds rate.* In the next section, we discuss the federal funds rate before examining how targeting the interest rate can help the Fed achieve its monetary policy goals.

The Importance of the Federal Funds Rate

Recall from Chapter 15 that every bank must keep 10 percent of its checking account deposits above a certain threshold as reserves, either as currency held in the bank or as deposits with the Fed. Banks receive no interest on their reserves, so they have an incentive to invest reserves above the 10-percent minimum. Banks that need additional reserves can borrow in the *federal funds market* from banks that have reserves available. The **federal funds rate** is the interest rate banks charge on loans in the federal funds market. The loans in the federal funds market are usually very short term, often just overnight.

Federal funds rate The interest rate banks charge each other for overnight loans.

Despite the name, the federal funds rate is not set administratively by the Fed. Instead, the rate is determined by the supply of reserves relative to the demand for them. Because the Fed can increase and decrease bank reserves through open market operations, it can set a target for the federal funds rate and come very close to hitting it. The FOMC announces a target for the federal funds rate after each meeting. In Figure 16-6, the orange line shows the Fed's targets for the federal funds rate since 1995. The jagged green line represents the actual federal funds rate on a weekly basis.

The federal funds rate is not directly relevant for households and firms. No households or firms, except banks, can borrow or lend in the federal funds market. However, changes in the federal funds rate usually will result in changes in both interest rates on other short-term financial assets, such as Treasury bills, and interest rates on long-term financial assets, such as corporate bonds and mortgages. The effect of a change in the federal funds rate on long-term interest rates is usually smaller than it is on short-term interest rates and the effect may occur only after a lag in time. Although a majority of

FIGURE 16-6

Federal Funds Rate Targeting, January 1995–July 2005

The Fed does not set the federal funds rate, but its ability to increase or decrease bank reserves quickly through open market operations keeps the actual federal funds rate close to the Fed's target rate. The orange line is the Fed's target for the federal funds rate and the jagged green line represents the actual value for the federal funds rate on a weekly basis.

Source: Board of Governors of the Federal Reserve System.

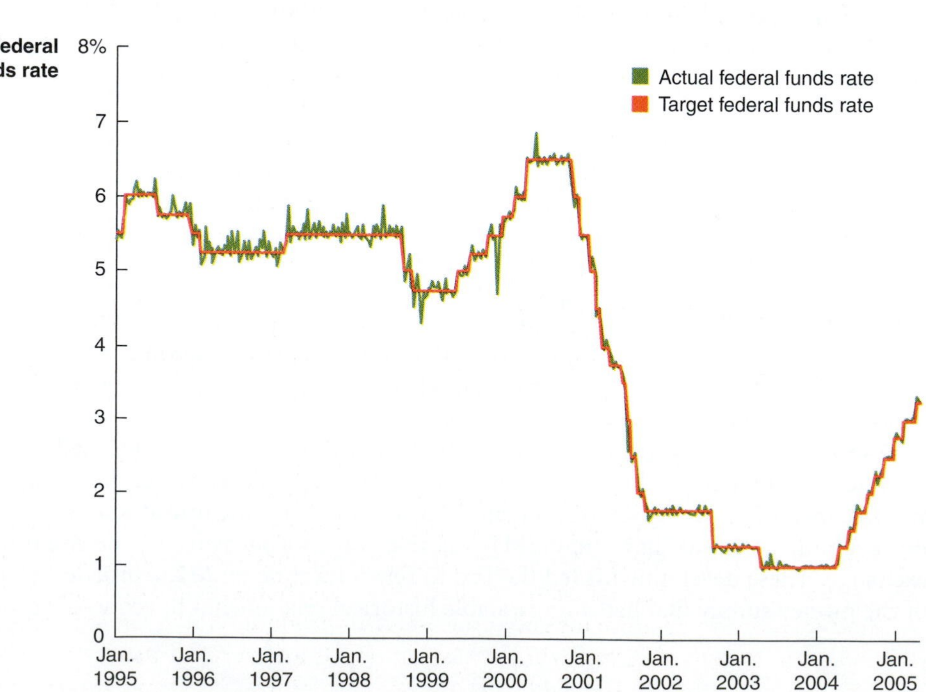

economists support the Fed's choice of the interest rate as its monetary policy target, some economists believe the Fed should concentrate on the money supply instead. We will discuss the views of these economists later in this chapter.

Monetary Policy and Economic Activity

(3) LEARNING OBJECTIVE

Use aggregate demand and aggregate supply graphs to show the effects of monetary policy on real GDP and the price level.

Remember that the Fed uses the federal funds rate as a monetary policy target because it has good control of the federal funds rate through open market operations and because it believes that changes in the federal funds rate will ultimately affect economic variables that are related to its monetary policy goals. Here it is important to consider again the distinction between the nominal interest rate and the real interest rate. Recall that we calculate the real interest rate by subtracting the inflation rate from the nominal interest rate. Ultimately, the ability of the Fed to use monetary policy to affect economic variables such as real GDP depends upon its ability to affect real interest rates, such as the real interest rates on mortgages and corporate bonds. Because the federal funds rate is a short-term nominal interest rate, the Fed sometimes has difficulty affecting long-term real interest rates. Nevertheless, for purposes of the following discussion we will assume that the Fed is able to use open market operations to affect long-term real interest rates.

How Interest Rates Affect Aggregate Demand

Changes in interest rates affect *aggregate demand,* which is the total level of spending in the economy. Recall from Chapter 14 that aggregate demand has four components: consumption, investment, government purchases, and net exports. Changes in interest rates will not affect government purchases, but they will affect the other three components of aggregate demand in the following ways:

- *Consumption.* Many households finance purchases of consumer durables, such as automobiles and furniture, by borrowing. Lower interest rates cause increased spending on durables because they lower the total cost of these goods to consumers by lowering the interest payments on loans. Higher interest rates raise the cost of these consumer durables, and households will buy fewer of them.
- *Investment.* Firms finance most of their spending on machinery, equipment, and factories out of their profits or by borrowing. Firms borrow either from the financial markets by issuing corporate bonds or from banks. Higher interest rates on corporate bonds or on bank loans make it more expensive for firms to borrow, so they will undertake fewer investment projects. Lower interest rates make it less expensive for firms to borrow, so they will undertake more investment projects. Lower interest rates can also increase investment through their impact on stock prices. As interest rates decline, stocks become a more attractive investment relative to bonds. The increase in demand for stocks raises their price. An increase in stock prices sends a signal to firms that the future profitability of investment projects has increased. By issuing additional shares of stocks, firms can acquire the funds they need to buy new factories and equipment, thereby increasing investment.

  Finally, spending by households on new homes is also part of investment. When interest rates on mortgage loans rise, the cost of buying new homes rises, and fewer new homes will be purchased. When interest rates on mortgage loans fall, more new homes will be purchased.
- *Net exports.* Recall that net exports are equal to spending by foreign households and firms on goods and services produced in the United States minus spending by U.S. households and firms on goods and services produced in other countries. The value of net exports depends partly on the exchange rate between the dollar and foreign currencies. When the value of the dollar rises, households and firms in other countries must pay more for goods and services produced in the United States, but U.S. households and firms will pay less for goods and services produced in other countries. As a result, the United States will export less and import more, so net

exports fall. When the value of the dollar falls, net exports rise. If interest rates in the United States rise relative to interest rates in other countries, investing in U.S. financial assets becomes more desirable, causing foreign investors to increase their demand for dollars, which increases the value of the dollar. As the value of the dollar increases, net exports will fall. If interest rates in the United States decline relative to interest rates in other countries, the value of the dollar will fall and net exports will rise.

16-1 Making the Connection

Was there a "bubble" in housing prices in the early 2000s?

Was There a Housing Market "Bubble" in the Early 2000s?

We have seen that low interest rates helped boost demand for housing during the 2001 recession and for several years thereafter. Lower interest rates can have a dramatic effect on the affordability of housing. For example, in 2000 the average interest rate on a new home mortgage was 7.5 percent. In 2005, the average rate was only 5.75 percent. Suppose you buy a home and need a $150,000 mortgage loan. On a 30-year mortgage with an interest rate of 7.5 percent, your monthly payment on the loan would be about $1,050. With an interest rate of 5.75 percent, your monthly payment would fall to about $875. So, it is not surprising that as interest rates fell after 2000, sales of new houses increased.

Some observers have argued that more was going on than just the normal increase in the quantity of new homes demanded due to lower interest rates; they argued that a "bubble" had formed in the housing market. As we discussed in Chapter 5, the price of any asset reflects the returns received by the owner of the asset. For example, the price of a share of stock reflects the profitability of the firm issuing the stock because the owner of a share of stock has a claim on the firm's profits and its assets. Many economists believe, however, that sometimes a stock market "bubble" can form when the prices of stocks rise above levels that can be justified by the profitability of the firms issuing the stock. This appears to have been true of many Internet stocks in the late 1990s. Bubbles end when enough investors decide stocks are overvalued and begin to sell. The resulting fall in prices can be very steep, as when the total value of stocks traded on the New York Stock Exchange declined by several trillion dollars between 2000 and 2002. Why would an investor be willing to pay more for a share of stock than would be justified by its underlying value? There are two main explanations: The investor may be caught up in the enthusiasm of the moment and, by failing to gather sufficient information, may overestimate the true value of the stock; or the investor may expect to profit from buying stock at inflated prices if the investor can sell the stock at an even higher price before the bubble bursts.

By 2004, some economists believed that a bubble was occurring in housing prices. The price of a house should reflect the value of the housing services the house provides. A measure of the value of these housing services is the rent charged for comparable houses in the area. Some economists argued that in certain housing markets the prices of houses had risen so much that monthly mortgage payments were far above the monthly rent on comparable houses. In addition, in some markets there was an increase in the number of buyers who did not intend to live in the houses they purchased but were using them as investments. Like stock investors during a stock market bubble, these housing investors were expecting to make a profit by selling houses at a higher price than they had paid for them, and they were not concerned about whether the prices of the houses were above the value of the housing services provided.

Other economists were skeptical that a bubble in housing prices actually was occurring. These economists argued that rising incomes, falling interest rates, and high rates of family formation, due in part to high levels of immigration, were sufficient to explain the increase in housing prices, and they were skeptical that investors interested in buying houses and quickly reselling them were playing an important role in the market. Unlike stocks, houses are expensive to buy and sell, which makes it difficult to make an economic profit from buying houses and quickly reselling them.

At the beginning of this chapter, we discussed the success of Robert Toll and his home building firm, Toll Brothers. Robert Toll was also skeptical that rising house prices represented a bubble. Instead, he argued that higher house prices reflected restrictions imposed by local governments on building new houses. He argued that the restrictions resulted from "NIMBY"— "Not in My Back Yard"—politics. Many existing homeowners are reluctant to see nearby farms and undeveloped land turned into new housing developments. As a result, according to Toll, "Towns don't want anything built."

In the fall of 2005, it was still unclear whether the housing price increases of the early 2000s could be sustained.

Source: Quote from Robert Toll from Shawn Tully, "Toll Brothers: The New King of the Real Estate Boom," *Fortune*, April 5, 2005.

The Effects of Monetary Policy on Real GDP and the Price Level

Figure 16-7 uses the dynamic aggregate demand and aggregate supply (*AD-AS*) model developed in Chapter 14 to illustrate how monetary policy affects real GDP and the price level. Recall from Chapter 14 that over time the U.S. labor force and U.S. capital stock will increase. Technological progress will also occur. The result will be an increase in potential real GDP, which we show by the long-run aggregate supply curve (*LRAS*) shifting to the right. These factors will also result in firms supplying more goods and services at any given price level in the short run, which we show by the short-run aggregate supply curve (*SRAS*) shifting to the right. During most years, the aggregate demand curve (*AD*) will also shift to the right, indicating that aggregate expenditure will be higher at every price level. There are several reasons why aggregate expenditure usually increase: As population grows and incomes rise, consumption will increase over time. Also, as the economy grows, firms expand capacity and new firms are established, increasing investment spending. Finally, an expanding population and an expanding economy require increased government services, such as more police officers and teachers, so government purchases will expand.

During certain periods, however, *AD* does not increase enough during the year to keep the economy at potential GDP. This slow growth in aggregate demand may be due to households and firms becoming pessimistic about the future state of the economy, leading them to cut back their spending on consumer durables, houses, and factories. Other possibilities exist, as well: The federal government might decide to balance the budget by cutting back its purchases, or recessions in other countries might cause a

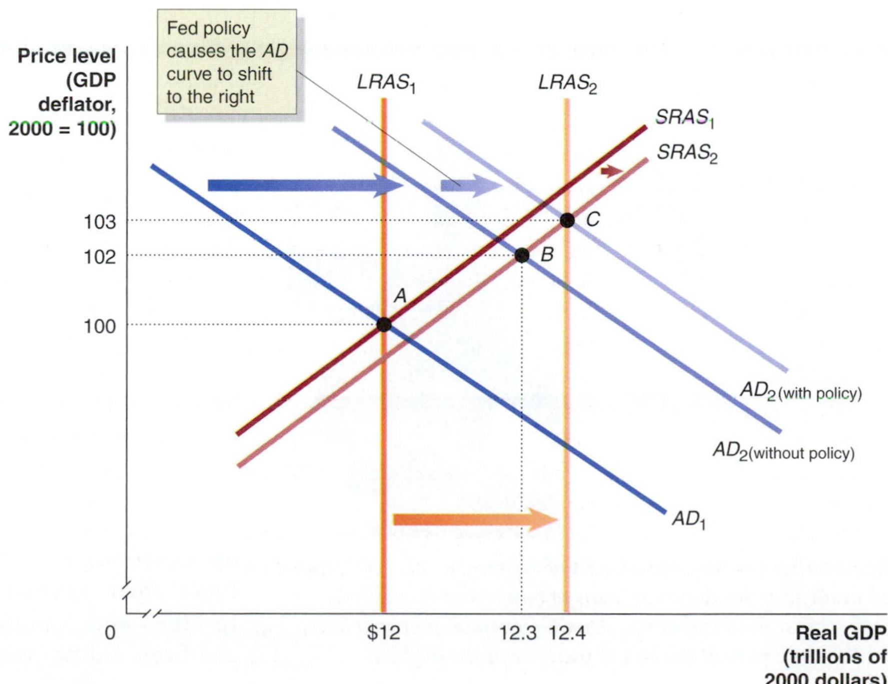

FIGURE 16-7

An Expansionary Monetary Policy

The economy begins in equilibrium at point *A*, with real GDP of $12 trillion and a price level of 100. Without monetary policy, aggregate demand will shift from AD_1 to $AD_{2(\text{without policy})}$, which is not enough to keep the economy at full employment because long-run aggregate supply has shifted from $LRAS_1$ to $LRAS_2$. The economy will be in short-run equilibrium at point *B*, with real GDP of $12.3 trillion and a price level of 102. By lowering interest rates, the Fed increases investment, consumption, and net exports sufficiently to shift aggregate demand to $AD_{2(\text{with policy})}$. The economy will be in equilibrium at point *C* with real GDP of $12.4 trillion, which is its full-employment level, and a price level of 103. The price level is higher than it would have been if the Fed had not acted to increase spending in the economy.

decline in U.S. exports. In Figure 16-7, in the first year the economy is in equilibrium at potential real GDP of $12 trillion and a price level of 100 (point *A*). In the second year *LRAS* increases to $12.4 trillion, but *AD* increases only to AD_2(without policy), which is not enough to keep the economy in macroeconomic equilibrium at potential GDP. Without the Fed intervening, the short-run equilibrium will occur at $12.3 trillion (point *B*). The $100 billion gap between this level of real GDP and potential real GDP at $LRAS_2$ means that some firms are operating at less than their normal capacity. Incomes and profits will fall, firms will begin to lay off workers, and the unemployment rate will rise.

The economists at the Federal Reserve closely monitor the economy and continually update forecasts of future levels of real GDP and prices. When these economists anticipate that aggregate demand is not growing fast enough to allow the economy to remain at full employment, they present their findings to the Federal Open Market Committee, which decides whether circumstances require a change in monetary policy. For example, suppose that the FOMC meets and considers a forecast from the staff indicating that during the following year a gap of $100 billion will open between equilibrium real GDP and potential real GDP. In other words, the situation shown in Figure 16-7 will occur. The FOMC may then decide to take action to lower interest rates to stimulate aggregate demand. The figure shows the results of a successful attempt to do this: *AD* has shifted to the right and equilibrium occurs at potential GDP (point *C*). The Fed will have successfully headed off the falling incomes and rising unemployment that otherwise would have occurred.

Expansionary monetary policy The Federal Reserve's increasing the money supply and decreasing interest rates to increase real GDP.

When the Fed increases the money supply and decreases interest rates to increase real GDP, it is engaging in **expansionary monetary policy.** Notice that in Figure 16-7 the expansionary monetary policy caused the inflation rate to be higher than it would have been. Without the expansionary policy, the price level would have risen from 100 to 102, so the inflation rate for the year would have been 2 percent. By shifting the aggregate demand curve, the expansionary policy caused the price level to increase from 102 to 103, raising the inflation rate from 2 percent to 3 percent.

16-2 Making the Connection

The Fed Responds to the Terrorist Attacks of September 11, 2001

When the Fed was founded, its main purpose was to make discount loans to banks suffering from deposit withdrawals. Today, discount loans have become relatively less important in the operations of the Fed. For example, the average weekly amount of discount loans outstanding in 2001 through September 11 was only $34 million. This volume of discount loans is very small compared with total bank reserves of more than $66 *billion.*

The day after the terrorist attacks of September 11, 2001, the Fed made massive discount loans to banks and succeeded in preventing a financial panic. Alan Greenspan, pictured here, was the chairman of the Fed at the time of the attacks.

Still, discount loans remain an effective way for the Fed to make funds quickly available to banks in an emergency. The banks can use these funds to provide cash or loans to households and firms. The day after the terrorist attacks of September 11, 2001, the Fed made massive discount loans to banks. Discount loans rose from $99 million on September 5 to $45.5 *billion* on September 12, or to 500 times their normal level. In the end, households and firms did not withdraw excessive amounts from their bank accounts following the attack, and the volume of discount loans returned to normal levels very quickly. By September 19, discount loans had fallen to $2.6 billion and by September 26, they had fallen to only $20 million. The Fed had also relied on discount loans to cushion the banking and financial systems from potential instability during the stock market crash of 1987 and the Y2K difficulties of late 1999.

Although the modern Fed concentrates on its objectives for inflation and economic growth, which it implements through open market operations, it still retains its original purpose of dealing with potential financial panics. For this purpose, discount loans are an effective tool.

Source: Federal Reserve Board of Governors, Statistical Release H.4.1, various weekly issues.

Can the Fed Eliminate Recessions?

Figure 16-7 shows an expansionary monetary policy that performs so well that no recession actually takes place. The Fed manages to shift the *AD* curve to keep the economy continually at potential GDP. In fact, however, this ideal is very difficult for the Fed to achieve. Keeping recessions shorter and milder than they would otherwise be is usually the best the Fed can do. The recession of 2001 shows the Fed performing about as well as it can in the real world. Let's review the events leading up to the 2001 recession and the actions the Fed took in response.

In the spring of 2000, stock prices began to decline. Hardest hit were the dot.coms, because online retailing failed to grow as rapidly as many Wall Street analysts had predicted. As we saw in Chapter 14, when stock prices fall, the wealth of households declines and, as a result, consumption falls. At the same time, many firms began to cut their expenditure on information technology.

On December 19, 2000, at the last FOMC meeting of the year, the committee left the target for the federal funds rate unchanged, although committee members believed the risk of recession had increased. Within a few days, increasing evidence indicated that the growth of aggregate demand was slowing, and the committee held a telephone conference meeting on January 3, 2001, four weeks before its regularly scheduled meeting. During the telephone conference, the committee decided to reduce the target for the federal funds rate from 6.5 percent to 6 percent. The committee continued to reduce the federal funds target at subsequent meetings. By December 2001, it had reduced the rate to 1.75 percent. Further decreases brought the federal funds rate to 1 percent in June 2003, the lowest it had been in more than 40 years.

Falling interest rates were not enough to head off a recession, which began in March 2001. The recession was milder than many economists had expected, despite the impact of the September 11, 2001, terrorist attacks. Real GDP declined only during two quarters in 2001, and GDP was actually higher for 2001 as a whole than it had been during 2000. We saw in Chapter 14 that the recovery from the recession was weaker than had been expected. The unemployment rate rose from 4.3 percent at the beginning of the recession to 5.6 percent at the end of the recession and to a peak of 6.3 percent in June 2003. Even at its peak, though, this was a relatively low unemployment rate compared to the more severe recessions of the post-World War II period, such as the 1981–82 recession when the unemployment rate was above 10 percent. Household purchases of consumer durables and new homes remained strong during 2001, keeping real GDP from falling too far below its potential level. Many homebuilders, like Toll Brothers, enjoyed a surprisingly good year in 2001. Although home building is usually hit hard during recessions, new home construction increased by more than 2 percent, from less than 1.57 million units in 2000 to more than 1.60 million units in 2001.

Although the Fed was able to use expansionary monetary policy successfully to reduce the severity of the 2001 recession, it was unable to entirely eliminate it. In fact, the Fed has no realistic hope of "fine-tuning" the economy to eliminate the business cycle and achieve absolute price stability.

16-3 Making the Connection

Spending on housing and other types of investment has not been high enough to bring the Japanese economy back to potential GDP.

Why Was Monetary Policy Ineffective in Japan?

Because the Japanese economy had been an amazing success story since the end of World War II, few economists predicted that it would perform as poorly as it did beginning in the early 1990s. Between 1950 and 1990, real GDP in Japan grew at an average annual rate of 6.9 percent, compared with an average annual rate of 3.5 percent in the United States. This rapid growth made the Japanese economy the second largest in the world, behind only the United States.

When the Japanese economy entered recession in 1992, most economists assumed that it would quickly recover and resume its rapid growth rate. In fact, the Japanese economy has experienced only sluggish growth since 1992. From 1992 to 2004, real GDP in Japan grew at an average annual rate of only 1.4 percent. Real GDP declined in both 1998 and 2002. During this same period, real GDP in the United States grew at an average annual rate of 3.2 percent. Since the early 1990s, Japan has also experienced significant periods of deflation—or a falling price level. Deflation can contribute to slow growth by raising real interest rates, increasing the real value of debts, and causing consumers to postpone purchases in the hope of experiencing even lower prices in the future. In the United States, the price level has not fallen for an entire year since the 1930s.

During the 1990s, the Japanese central bank, the Bank of Japan, used expansionary monetary policy to spur the economy, but the policy was unsuccessful even though interest rates were driven to very low levels. By 1999, the interest rate on overnight bank loans—the equivalent of the U.S. federal funds rate—was reduced to zero. Other interest rates were also very low. For example, the interest rate on three-month certificates of deposit in banks was only 0.2 percent. Even with these low interest rates, aggregate demand increased very slowly.

Monetary policy worked well in the United States to keep the recession of 2001 from being as severe as some economists had feared it might be. Why hasn't it worked as well in Japan? Having driven short-term interest rates to zero, it would seem that expansionary monetary policy in Japan could not go any further, but this is not quite true. Recall that the *nominal interest rate* is the stated interest rate on a loan, whereas the *real interest rate* is equal to the nominal interest rate minus the inflation rate. Although the nominal interest rate cannot go below zero, the real interest rate can be negative if the inflation rate is greater than the nominal interest rate. Some economists have argued that if the Bank of Japan increased the money supply by enough to cause a significant level of inflation, the negative real interest rate that would result might cause a substantial increase in investment spending. Furthermore, replacing deflation with inflation is likely to increase spending by reducing the real value of debts and by reducing the incentive households have to postpone spending. These sources of increased spending might be sufficient to bring the economy back to potential GDP.

The Bank of Japan, however, has been unwilling to try this approach. The leadership of the Bank of Japan believed that the Japanese economy had overheated in the late 1980s and early 1990s. The leadership believed that the deflation Japan has experienced may in fact have been beneficial in reversing previous inflationary excesses, particularly in real estate and stock prices. Although real GDP in Japan increased by more than 4 percent in 2004, consumer prices continued to decline. It was unclear in 2005 whether Japan's prolonged economic slowdown was yet over.

Using Monetary Policy to Fight Inflation

In addition to using monetary policy to reduce the severity of recessions, the Fed can also use monetary policy to keep aggregate demand from expanding so rapidly that the inflation rate begins to increase. Figure 16-8 shows the situation during 1999 and 2000, when the Fed faced this possibility. During 1999, the economy was at equilibrium beyond potential GDP, although the inflation rate for the entire year was only about 1.5 percent. By December, Alan Greenspan and other members of the FOMC were worried that aggregate demand was increasing so rapidly that the inflation rate would begin to accelerate. In fact, during the last three months of 1999, inflation had

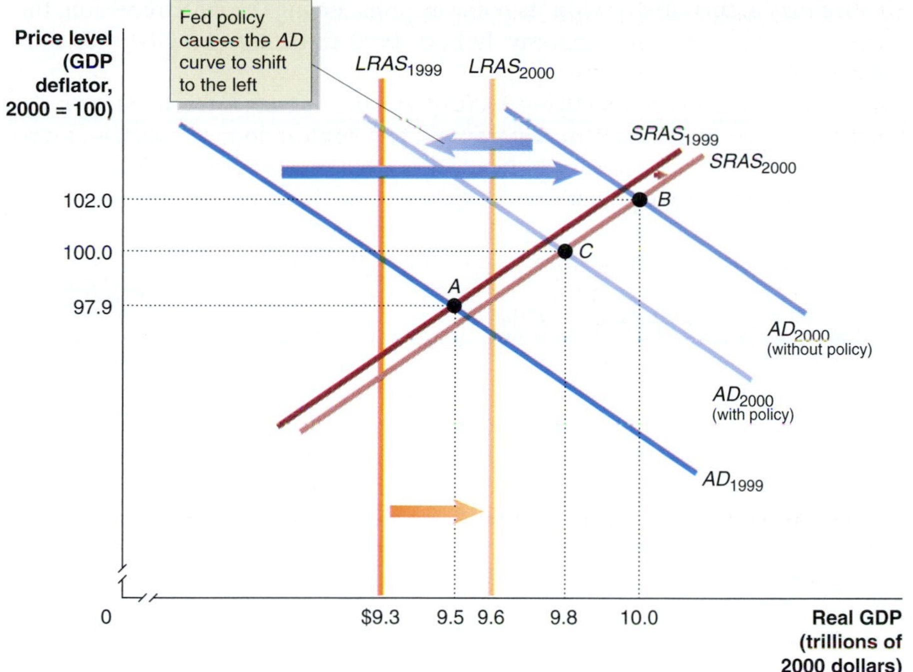

FIGURE 16-8

A Contractionary Monetary Policy in 2000

The economy began 1999 in equilibrium at point *A*, with real GDP of $9.5 trillion and a price level of 97.9. From 1999 to 2000, potential real GDP increased from $9.3 trillion to $9.6 trillion, as long-run aggregate supply increased from $LRAS_{1999}$ to $LRAS_{2000}$. The Fed raised interest rates because it believed aggregate demand was increasing too rapidly. Without the increase in interest rates, aggregate demand would have shifted from AD_{1999} to AD_{2000}(without policy), and the new short-run equilibrium would have occurred at point *B*. Real GDP would have been $10.0 trillion—$200 billion higher than it actually was—and the price level would have been 102.0. The increase in interest rates resulted in aggregate demand increasing only to AD_{2000}(with policy). Equilibrium occurred at point *C*, with real GDP of $9.8 trillion and the price level rising only to 100.0.

increased to an annual rate of about 2.5 percent. The FOMC issues a statement after each meeting that summarizes the committee's views on the current state of the economy and gives some indication of how monetary policy might change in the near future. After its meeting on December 21, 1999, the FOMC included the following remarks in its statement:

> [T]he Committee remains concerned with the possibility that over time increases in demand will continue to exceed the growth in potential supply. . . . Such trends could foster inflationary imbalances that would undermine the economy's exemplary performance. . . . At its next meeting the Committee will assess available information on the likely balance of supply and demand, conditions in financial markets, and the possible need for adjustment in the stance of policy to contain inflationary pressures.

At its next meeting on February 2, 2000, the committee raised the target for the federal funds rate from 5.5 percent to 5.75 percent. According to the minutes of the meeting:

> The Committee's decision . . . was intended to help bring the growth of aggregate demand into better alignment with the expansion of sustainable aggregate supply in an effort to avert rising inflationary pressures in the economy.

The committee raised the target for the federal funds rate twice more in following meetings until it reached 6.5 percent in May, where it remained for the rest of 2000. Although it is impossible to know exactly what would have happened during 2000 without the Fed's policy change, Figure 16-8 presents a plausible scenario. The figure shows that without the Fed's actions to increase interest rates, aggregate demand would have shifted farther to the right and equilibrium would have occurred at a level of real GDP that was even farther beyond the potential level. The price level would have risen from 97.9 in 1999 to 102.0 in 2000, meaning that the inflation rate would have been above 4 percent. Because the Fed kept aggregate demand from increasing as much as it otherwise would have, equilibrium occurred closer to potential real GDP and the price level in 2000 rose to only 100.0, keeping the inflation rate to a little over 2 percent.

Notice that in this case, as with its policy actions during the 2001 recession, the Fed was unable to "fine-tune" the economy: In both 1999 and 2000, real GDP was above its potential level.

Contractionary monetary policy The Fed's adjusting the money supply to increase interest rates to reduce inflation.

When the Fed acts as it did during 2000, increasing interest rates to reduce inflation, it is engaging in **contractionary monetary policy.** A contractionary policy is also sometimes known as a *tight* monetary policy. An expansionary policy is also sometimes known as a *loose* monetary policy.

SOLVED PROBLEM 16-2

③ LEARNING OBJECTIVE

Use aggregate demand and aggregate supply graphs to show the effects of monetary policy on real GDP and the price level.

The Effects of Monetary Policy

The hypothetical information in the table shows what the values for real GDP and the price level will be in 2011 if the Fed does *not* use monetary policy:

YEAR	POTENTIAL REAL GDP	REAL GDP	PRICE LEVEL
2010	$13.3 trillion	$13.3 trillion	140
2011	$13.7 trillion	$13.6 trillion	142

a. If the Fed wants to keep real GDP at its potential level in 2011, should it use an expansionary policy or a contractionary policy? Should the trading desk buy Treasury bills or sell them?

b. Suppose the Fed's policy is successful in keeping real GDP at its potential level in 2011. State whether each of the following will be higher or lower than if the Fed had taken no action:

i. Real GDP

ii. Potential real GDP

iii. The inflation rate

iv. The unemployment rate

c. Draw an aggregate demand and aggregate supply graph to illustrate your answer. Be sure that your graph contains *LRAS* curves for 2010 and 2011; *SRAS* curves for 2010 and 2011; *AD* curve for 2010 and for 2011, with and without monetary policy action; and equilibrium real GDP and the price level in 2011, with and without policy.

Solving the Problem:

Step 1: Review the chapter material. This problem is about the effects of monetary policy on real GDP and the price level, so you may want to review the section "The Effects of Monetary Policy on Real GDP and the Price Level," which begins on page 501.

Step 2: Answer question (a) by explaining how the Fed can keep real GDP at its potential level. The information in the table tells us that without monetary policy, the economy will be below potential real GDP in 2011. To keep real GDP at its potential level, the Fed must undertake an expansionary policy. To implement an expansionary policy, the trading desk needs to buy Treasury bills. Buying Treasury bills will increase reserves in the banking system. Banks will increase their loans, which will increase the money supply and lower the interest rate.

Step 3: Answer question (b) by explaining the effect of the Fed's policy. If the policy is successful, real GDP in 2011 will increase from the level given in the table of $13.3 trillion to its potential level of $13.7 trillion. Potential real GDP is not affected by monetary policy, so its value will not change. Because the level of real GDP will be higher, the unemployment rate will be lower than it would have been without policy. The expansionary monetary policy shifts the *AD* curve to the right, so short-run equilibrium will move up the short-run aggregate supply curve (*SRAS*) and the price level will be higher.

Step 4: Answer question (c) by drawing the graph. Your graph should look similar to Figure 16-7.

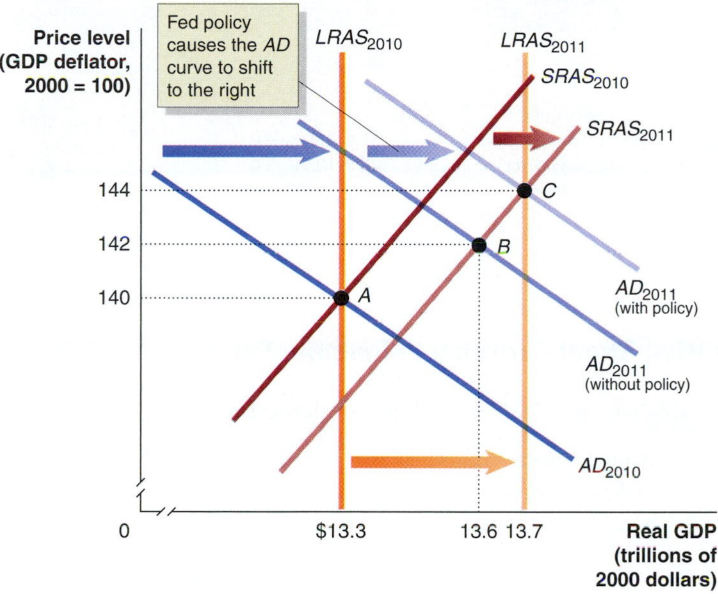

The economy starts in equilibrium in 2010 at point *A*, with the *AD* and *SRAS* curves intersecting along the *LRAS* curve. Real GDP is at its potential level of $13.3 trillion and the price level is 140. Without monetary policy, the *AD* curve shifts to AD_{2011}(without policy) and the economy is in short-run equilibrium at point *B*. Because potential real GDP has increased from $13.3 trillion to $13.7 trillion, short-run equilibrium real GDP of $13.6 trillion is below the potential level. The price level has increased from 140 to 142. With policy, the *AD* curve shifts to AD_{2011}(with policy) and the economy is in equilibrium at point *C*. Real GDP is at its potential level of $13.7 trillion. We don't have enough information to be sure of the new equilibrium price level. We do know that it will be higher than 142. The graph shows the price level rising to 144. Therefore, without policy, the inflation rate in 2011 would have been about 1.4 percent. With policy, it will be about 2.9 percent.

Extra Credit: It's important to bear in mind that in reality the Fed is unable to use monetary policy to keep real GDP exactly at its potential level, as this problem suggests. In a later section, we will discuss some of the difficulties the Fed encounters in conducting monetary policy.

YOUR TURN: **For more practice, do problem 14 on page 520 at the end of this chapter.**

A Summary of How Monetary Policy Works

Table 16-1 compares the steps involved in expansionary and contractionary monetary policies. We need to add a very important qualification to this summary. At every point we should add the phrase "relative to what would have happened without the policy." Figure 16-9 is isolating the impact of monetary policy, *holding constant all other factors affecting the variables involved.* In other words, we are invoking the *ceteris paribus condition,* discussed in Chapter 3. This point is important because, for example, a contractionary monetary policy does not cause the price level to fall. As Figure 16-8 showed, a contractionary monetary policy causes the price level *to rise by less than it would have without the policy.*

TABLE 16-1 Expansionary and Contractionary Monetary Policy

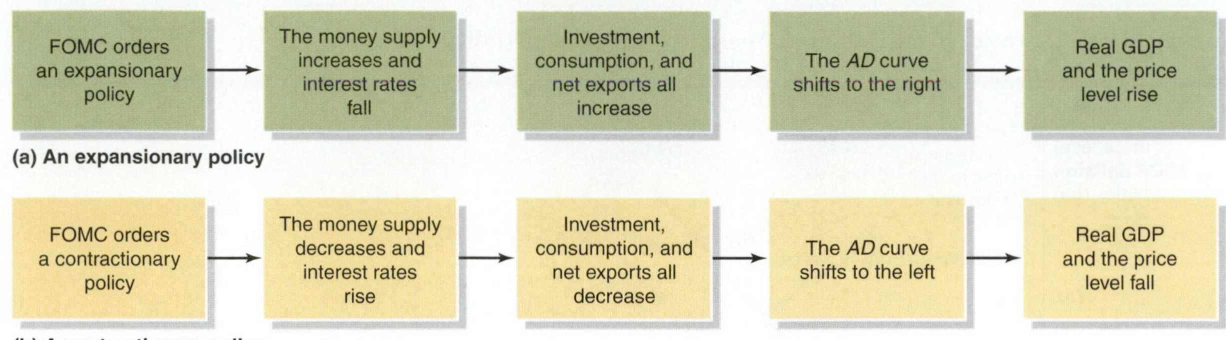

16-4 Making the Connection

Why Does Wall Street Care about Monetary Policy?

You have probably seen newspaper headlines similar to these:

"Fed Rate Cut Fuels Stock Gains"
"Stocks Fall in Anticipation of Fed Rate Increase"
"Worries of Fed Rate Increase Send Stocks Lower"

Before most meetings of the Federal Open Market Committee, newspapers report stock traders' predictions of possible Fed actions and whether those actions will cause stock prices to increase or decrease. Some Wall Street analysts are known as *Fed watchers* because they study the Fed and attempt to forecast future changes in the target for the federal funds rate. Why do changes in the federal funds rate affect the stock market? There are two main explanations. In thinking about both explanations, remember that changes in the federal funds rate usually cause changes in other interest rates.

The first reason that stock prices react to the Fed raising or lowering interest rates is because changes in interest rates affect the economy. As we have seen, lower interest rates usually result in increases in real GDP. Fundamentally, the value of a share of stock depends on the profitability of the firm that issued the stock. When real GDP is increasing, the profitability of many firms will also be increasing. Stock prices tend to rise when investors expect that the Fed will be lowering interest rates to stimulate the economy. When investors expect that the Fed will be raising interest rates to slow down an economy at risk of rising inflation, stock prices tend to fall.

The second reason that stock prices react to changes in interest rates is that changes in interest rates make it more or less attractive for people to invest in stock rather than in other financial assets. Investors look for the highest return possible on their investments, holding constant the riskiness of the investments. If the interest rates on Treasury bills, bank certificates of deposit, and corporate bonds are all low, an investment in stocks will be more attractive. When interest rates are high, an investment in stocks will be less attractive.

The stock market reacts when the Fed either raises or lowers interest rates.

Don't Let This Happen To You!

Remember That with Monetary Policy It's the Interest Rates—Not the Money—that Counts

It is tempting to think of monetary policy working like this: If the Fed wants more spending in the economy, it increases the money supply and people spend more because they now have more money. If the Fed wants less spending in the economy, it decreases the money supply and people spend less because they now have less money. In fact, that is *not* how monetary policy works. Remember the important difference between money and income: The Fed increases the money supply by buying Treasury bills. The sellers of the Treasury bills have just exchanged one asset—Treasury bills—for another asset—a check from the Fed; they have *not* increased their income. Even though the money supply is now larger, no one's income has increased, so no one's spending should be affected.

It is only when this increase in the money supply results in lower interest rates that spending is affected. When interest rates are lower, households are more likely to buy new homes and automobiles and businesses are more likely to buy new factories and computers. Lower interest rates also lead to a lower value of the dollar, which lowers the prices of exports and raises the prices of imports, thereby increasing net exports. It isn't the increase in the money supply that has brought about this additional spending; *it's the lower interest rates.* To understand how monetary policy works, and to interpret news reports about the Fed's actions, it is necessary to remember that it is the change in interest rates, not the change in the money supply, that is most important.

YOUR TURN: **Test your understanding by doing related problem 16 on page 521 at the end of this chapter.**

Can the Fed Get the Timing Right?

The Fed's ability to quickly recognize the need for a change in monetary policy is a key to its success. If the Fed is late recognizing that a recession has begun or that the inflation rate is increasing, it may not be able to implement a new policy soon enough to do much good. In fact, if the Fed implements a policy too late, it may actually destabilize the economy. To see how this can happen, consider Figure 16-9. The straight line represents the long-run growth trend in real GDP in the United States. On average, real GDP grows about 3.5 percent per year. The actual path of real GDP differs from the underlying trend because of the business cycle, which is shown by the red curving line. As we saw in Chapter 13, the actual business cycle is more irregular than the stylized cycle shown here.

Suppose that a recession begins in August 2008. Because it takes months for economic statistics to be gathered by the Commerce Department, the Census Bureau, the Bureau of Labor Statistics, and by the Fed itself, there is often a *lag*, or delay, before the Fed recognizes that a recession has begun. Then it takes time for the Fed's economists to

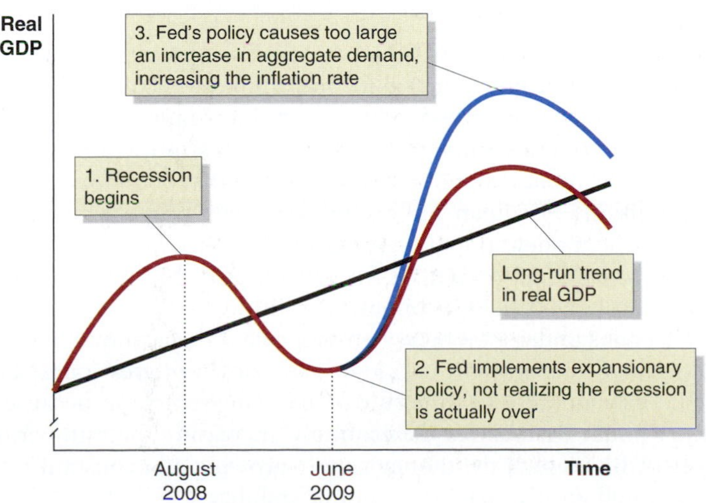

FIGURE 16-9

The Effect of a Poorly Timed Monetary Policy on the Economy

The upward-sloping straight line represents the long-run growth trend in real GDP. The red curving line represents the path real GDP takes because of the business cycle. If the Fed implements a change in monetary policy too late, real GDP will follow the blue curving line. The Fed's expansionary monetary policy has resulted in too great an increase in aggregate demand during the next expansion, which causes an increase in the inflation rate.

analyze the data. Finally, in June 2009, the FOMC concludes that the economy is in recession and begins an expansionary monetary policy. As it turns out, June 2009 is actually the trough of the recession, meaning that the recession has already ended and an expansion has begun. In these circumstances, the Fed's expansionary policy is not needed to end the recession. The increase in aggregate demand caused by the Fed's lowering interest rates is likely to push the economy beyond potential real GDP and cause a significant acceleration in inflation. Real GDP ends up following the path indicated by the curving blue line. The Fed has inadvertently engaged in a *procyclical policy.* A procyclical policy is one that increases the severity of the business cycle, as opposed to a *countercyclical policy*, which is meant to reduce the severity of the business cycle, and which is what the Fed intends to use.

It is not unusual for employment or manufacturing production to decline for a month or two in the middle of an expansion. Distinguishing these minor ups and downs from the beginning of a recession is difficult. The National Bureau of Economic Research (NBER) announces dates for the beginning and ending of recessions that are generally accepted by most economists. An indication of how difficult it is to determine when recessions begin and end is that the NBER generally makes its announcements only after a considerable delay. The NBER did not announce that a recession had begun in March 2001 until November 2001, which is the same month it later determined the recession had ended. It did not announce that a recession had begun in July 1990 until April 1991, which was one month *after* it later determined the recession had ended. Failing to react until well after a recession has begun (or ended) can be a serious problem for the Fed.

④ **LEARNING OBJECTIVE**
Discuss the Fed's setting of monetary policy targets.

A Closer Look at the Fed's Setting of Monetary Policy Targets

We have seen that the Fed, in carrying out monetary policy, changes its target for the federal funds rate depending on the state of the economy. Is using the federal funds rate as a target the best way to conduct monetary policy? If the Fed targets the federal funds rate, how should it decide what the target level should be? In this section, we consider some important issues concerning the Fed's targeting policy.

Should the Fed Target the Money Supply?

Some economists have argued that rather than using an interest rate as its monetary policy target, the Fed should use the money supply. Many of the economists who make this argument belong to a school of thought known as *monetarism.* The leader of the monetarist school is Milton Friedman, who was awarded the Nobel Prize in Economics in 1976 and who has long been critical of the Fed's ability to correctly time changes in monetary policy.

Friedman and his followers favor replacing *monetary policy* with a *monetary growth rule.* Ordinarily, we expect monetary policy to respond to changing economic conditions: When the economy is in recession, the Fed reduces interest rates, and when inflation is increasing, the Fed raises interest rates. A monetary growth rule, in contrast, is a plan for increasing the money supply at a constant rate that does not change in response to economic conditions. Friedman and his followers have proposed a monetary growth rule of increasing the money supply every year at a rate equal to the long-run growth rate of real GDP, which is 3.5 percent. If the Fed adopted this monetary growth rule, it would stick to it through changing economic conditions.

But what happens under a monetary growth rule if the economy moves into recession? Shouldn't the Fed abandon the rule to drive down interest rates? Friedman has argued that the Fed should stick to the rule even during recessions because, he believes, active monetary policy destabilizes the economy, increasing the number of recessions and their severity. By keeping the money supply growing at a constant rate, Friedman argues, the Fed would greatly increase economic stability.

Although during the 1970s some economists and politicians pressured the Federal Reserve to adopt a monetary growth rule, most of that pressure has disappeared in recent years. A key reason is that the fairly close relationship between movements in the money supply and movements in real GDP and the price level that existed before 1980 has become much weaker. Since 1980, the growth rate of M1 has been unstable. In some years it has grown more than 10 percent, while in other years it has actually fallen. Yet despite these wide fluctuations in the growth of M1, growth in real GDP has been fairly stable and inflation has remained low.

Why Doesn't the Fed Target Both the Money Supply and the Interest Rate?

Most economists believe that an interest rate is the best monetary policy target, but, as we have just seen, other economists believe the Fed should target the money supply. Why doesn't the Fed satisfy both groups by targeting both the money supply and an interest rate? The simple answer to this question is that the Fed can't target both at the same time. To see why, look at Figure 16-10, which shows the money market.

Remember that the Fed controls the money supply, but it does not control money demand. Money demand is determined by decisions of households and firms as they weigh the trade-off between the convenience of money and its low interest rate compared with other financial assets. Suppose the Fed is targeting the interest rate and decides, given conditions in the economy, that the interest rate should be 5 percent. Or, suppose the Fed is targeting the money supply and decides that the money supply should be $900 billion. Figure 16-10 shows that the Fed can bring about an interest rate of 5 percent, or a money supply of $900 billion, but it can't bring about both. The point representing an interest rate of 5 percent and a money supply of $900 billion is not on the money demand curve, so it can't represent an equilibrium in the money market. Only combinations of the interest rate and the money supply that represent equilibrium in the money market are possible.

The Fed has to choose between targeting an interest rate and targeting the money supply. For most of the period since World War II, the Fed has chosen an interest rate target.

The Taylor Rule

How does the Fed choose a target for the federal funds rate? The discussions at the meetings of the FOMC can be complex and take into account many economic variables. John Taylor of Stanford University has analyzed the factors involved in Fed decision making and developed the **Taylor rule** for federal funds rate targeting. The Taylor rule begins with an estimate of the value of the equilibrium real federal funds rate, which is the federal funds rate—adjusted for inflation—that would be consistent with real GDP being

Taylor rule A rule developed by John Taylor that links the Fed's target for the federal funds rate to economic variables.

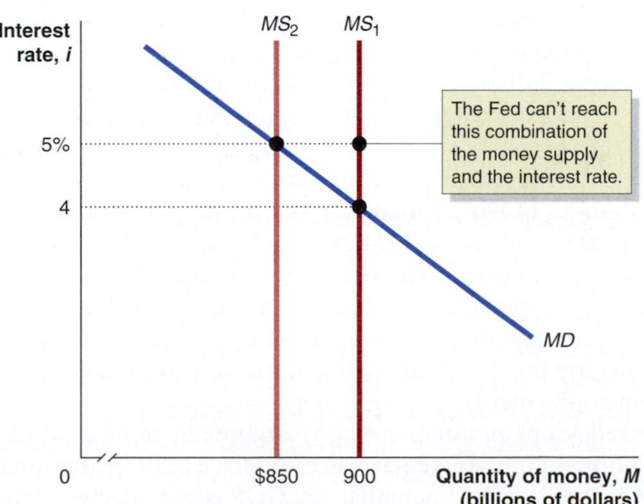

FIGURE 16-10

The Fed Can't Target Both the Money Supply and the Interest Rate

The Fed is forced to choose between using either an interest rate or the money supply as its monetary policy target. In this figure, the Fed can set a target of a money supply of $900 billion or a target of an interest rate of 5 percent, but it can't have both because only combinations of the interest rate and the money supply that represent equilibrium in the money market are possible.

equal to potential real GDP in the long run. According to the Taylor rule, the Fed should set the target for the federal funds rate so that it is equal to the sum of the inflation rate, the equilibrium real federal funds rate, and two additional terms. The first of these additional terms is the *inflation gap*—the difference between current inflation and a target rate; the second is the *output gap*—the percentage difference between real GDP and potential real GDP. The inflation gap and output gap are each given "weights" that reflect their influence on the federal funds target rate. With weights of 1/2 for both gaps, we have the following Taylor rule:

$$\text{Federal funds target rate} = \text{Current inflation rate} + \text{Real equilibrium federal funds rate} + (1/2) \times \text{Inflation gap} + (1/2) \times \text{Output gap}.$$

The presence in the Taylor rule of expressions for the inflation gap and the output gap reflect the fact that the Fed is concerned about both inflation and fluctuations in real GDP. Taylor demonstrated that if the equilibrium real federal funds rate is 2 percent, and the target rate of inflation is 2 percent, the preceding expression does a good job of explaining changes in the Fed's target for the federal funds rate. Consider an example where the inflation rate is 1 percent and real GDP is 1 percent below potential real GDP. In that case, the inflation gap is 1 percent − 2 percent = −1 percent, and the output gap is also −1 percent. Inserting these values in the Taylor rule we can calculate the predicted value for the federal funds target rate:

$$\text{Federal funds target rate} = 1\% + 2\% + ((1/2) \times -1\%) + ((1/2) \times -1\%) = 2\%.$$

The Taylor rule has accurately predicted changes in the federal funds target during the period of Alan Greenspan's leadership of the Federal Reserve. For the period of the late 1970s and early 1980s when Paul Volcker was chairman of the Federal Reserve, the Taylor rule predicts a federal funds rate target *lower* than the actual target used by the Fed. This indicates that Chairman Volcker kept the federal funds rate at an unusually high level to bring down the very high inflation rates plaguing the economy in the late 1970s and early 1980s. In contrast, using data from the chairmanship of Arthur Burns from 1970 to 1978, the Taylor rule predicts a federal funds rate target *higher* than the actual target. This indicates that Chairman Burns kept the federal funds rate at an unusually low level during these years, which can help explain why the inflation rate grew worse.

Although the Taylor rule does not account for changes in the target inflation rate or the equilibrium interest rate, many economists view the rule as a convenient way to analyze the federal funds target.

Should the Fed Target Inflation?

Inflation targeting Conducting monetary policy so as to commit the central bank to achieving a publicly announced level of inflation.

Over the past decade, many economists and central bankers, including the current Fed Chairman Ben Bernanke, have expressed significant interest in using *inflation targeting* as a framework for carrying out monetary policy. With **inflation targeting,** the central bank commits to conducting policy to achieve a publicly announced inflation target of, for example, 2 percent. Inflation targeting need not impose an inflexible rule on the central bank. The central bank would still be free, for example, to take action in case of a severe recession. Nevertheless, monetary policy goals and operations would focus on inflation and inflation forecasts. Inflation targeting has been adopted by the central banks of New Zealand (1990), Canada (1991), the United Kingdom (1992), Finland (1993), Sweden (1993), and Spain (1994). Inflation targeting has also been used in some newly industrializing countries, such as Chile, South Korea, Mexico, and South Africa, as well as in some transition economies in Eastern Europe, such as the Czech Republic, Hungary, and Poland. Experience with inflation targeting has varied, but typically the move to inflation targeting has been accompanied by lower inflation (sometimes at the cost of higher unemployment).

Should the Fed adopt an inflation target? Arguments in favor of inflation targeting focus on four points. First, as we have already discussed, in the long run real GDP returns to its potential level and potential real GDP is not affected by monetary policy.

Therefore, in the long run, the Fed can have an impact on inflation but not on real GDP. Having an explicit inflation target would draw the public's attention to this fact. Second, by announcing an inflation target, the Fed would make it easier for households and firms to form accurate expectations of future inflation, improving their planning and the efficiency of the economy. Third, an announced inflation target would help institutionalize good U.S. monetary policy. It would be less likely that abrupt changes in policy would occur as members join and leave the FOMC. Finally, an inflation target would promote accountability for the Fed by providing a yardstick against which its performance could be measured.

Inflation targeting also has opponents, who typically raise three points. First, a numerical target for inflation reduces the flexibility of monetary policy to address other policy goals. Second, inflation targeting assumes the Fed can accurately forecast future inflation rates, which is not always the case. And, finally, holding the Fed accountable only for an inflation goal may make it less likely that the Fed will achieve other important policy goals.

The Fed's performance in the 1980s, 1990s, and early 2000s has generally received high marks from economists, even without formal inflation targeting. The 1990s, for example, saw low inflation and a substantial economic expansion. Although not stated explicitly, the Fed's strategy has been to keep inflation low and stable in the long run. In addition, in recent years the Fed has acted to head off the threat of future inflation before it can become established. The Fed's strategy has much to recommend it. The Fed has been successful at building public support for the idea that low inflation is important to the efficient performance of the economy. The Fed's preemptive attacks on threatening inflation are likely to be more successful than waiting to act until actual inflation is rising. The Fed's strategy is not without risk, however. The Fed's prestige during the past two decades has been dependent on public trust in the effectiveness of Fed leadership in containing inflation, while maintaining economic growth. However, Fed leadership changes over time, which highlights what may be a need for more formal procedures to reassure both the public and elected officials about the continuity of policy. As Ben Bernanke assumed the chairmanship of the Fed in early 2006, his support for inflation targeting increased the chances the Fed would adopt such a policy.

Is the Independence of the Federal Reserve a Good Idea?

5 LEARNING OBJECTIVE

Assess the arguments for and against the independence of the Federal Reserve.

In our discussion of monetary policy, we have made no mention of Congress or the president. In fact, the Fed conducts monetary policy independently of them. The seven members of the Board of Governors are nominated by the president and confirmed by the Senate. Because members serve 14-year terms, they are insulated from political pressure. The seven members of the Board of Governors, along with five presidents of the Federal Reserve banks, make up the membership of the Federal Open Market Committee. The FOMC determines the monetary policy of the United States without the input of Congress or the president.

The Fed's political independence is reinforced by its financial independence. As we have discussed, when the FOMC wants to increase the money supply and decrease interest rates, it buys Treasury securities. To decrease the money supply and increase interest rates, it sells Treasury securities. Because a growing economy requires increases in the money supply, the Fed buys more Treasury securities than it sells. Currently the Fed owns more than $700 billion worth of Treasury securities. The interest it receives from these Treasury securities means that, unlike any other agency of the federal government, it does not have to ask Congress for the funds it needs to operate.

The Fed does not, however, have absolute independence. The U.S. Constitution contains no provision for a central bank. The authority of the Fed comes from legislation passed by Congress and signed by the president. Congress and the president are free at any time to pass new legislation to reorganize the Fed or even to abolish it. So, it is unlikely that the Fed would pursue a monetary policy that was strongly opposed by the president and a large majority in Congress. In addition, most Fed chairmen have attempted to remain in regular contact with other members of the government.

Nevertheless, the Fed is able to formulate monetary policy without taking into account the wishes of Congress and the president, unless it chooses to. Since the founding of the Fed in 1914, debate has occurred about whether or not the independence of the Fed is a good idea.

The Case for Fed Independence

The main reason to keep the Fed—or any country's central bank—independent of the rest of the government is to avoid inflation. Whenever a government is spending more than it is collecting in taxes, it must borrow the difference by selling bonds. The governments of many developing countries have difficulty finding anyone other than their central bank to buy their bonds. The more bonds the central bank buys, the faster the money supply grows and the higher the inflation rate will be. Even in developed countries, governments that control their central banks will be tempted to sell bonds to the central bank, rather than to the public.

Another fear is that if the government controls the central bank it may use that control to further its political interests. It is difficult in any democratic country for a government to be reelected at a time of high unemployment. If the government controls the central bank, it may be tempted just before an election to increase the money supply and drive down interest rates to increase production and employment. In the United States, for example, a president who had direct control over the Fed might be tempted to increase the money supply just before running for reelection, even if this led in the long run to higher inflation and accompanying economic costs.

We might expect that the more independent a country's central bank is, the lower the inflation rate in the country, and the less independent a country's central bank, the higher the inflation rate. Alberto Alesina and Lawrence Summers, economists at Harvard University, tested this idea by comparing the degree of central bank independence and the inflation rate for 16 high-income countries during the years 1955–1988. Figure 16-11 shows the results.

FIGURE 16-11

The More Independent the Central Bank, the Lower the Inflation Rate

For 16 high-income countries, the greater the degree of central bank independence from the rest of the government, the lower the inflation rate. Central bank independence is measured by an index ranging from 1 (minimum independence) to 4 (maximum independence). During these years, Germany had a high index of independence of 4 and a low average inflation rate of just over 3 percent. New Zealand had a low index of independence of 1 and a high average inflation rate of over 7 percent.

Source: Alberto Alesina and Lawrence H. Summers, "Central Bank Independence and Macroeconomic Performance: Some Comparative Evidence," *Journal of Money, Credit and Banking*, Vol. 25, No. 2, May 1993, pp. 151–162.

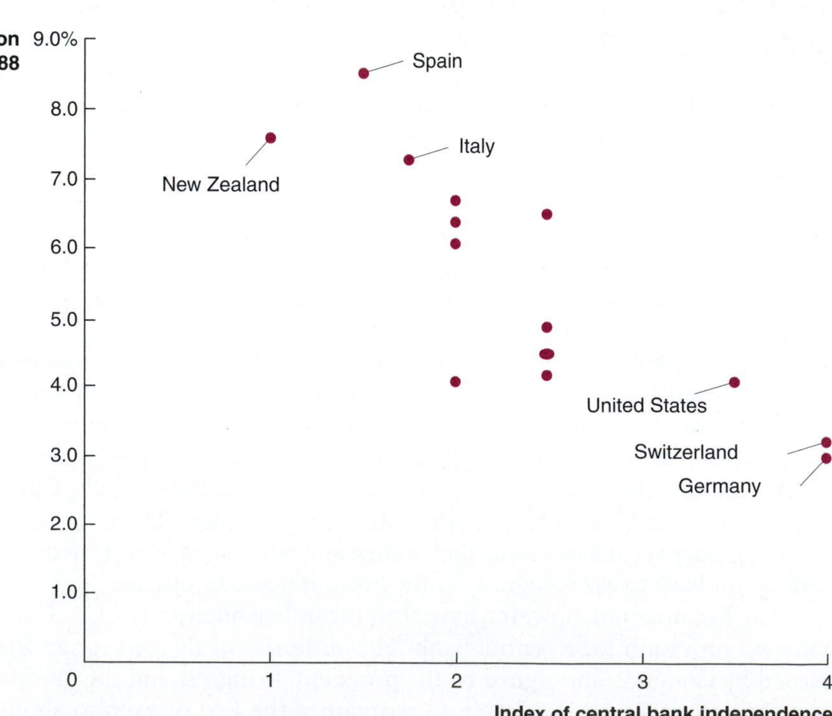

Countries with highly independent central banks, such as the United States, Switzerland, and Germany, had lower inflation rates than countries whose central banks had little independence, such New Zealand, Italy, and Spain. In the last few years, New Zealand and Canada have granted their banks more independence, at least partly to better fight inflation.

The Case against Fed Independence

In democracies, elected representatives usually decide important policy matters. In the United States, however, monetary policy is not decided by elected officials. Instead, it is decided by the unelected Federal Open Market Committee. Only rarely has anyone served on the FOMC who has ever held any elected office. The members are usually academic economists or people with careers in banking, finance, or other areas of business. Because those deciding monetary policy do not have to run for election, they are not accountable for their actions to the ultimate authorities in a democracy: the voters.

Some economists and politicians argue that the Fed should operate like other parts of the executive branch of government. Under this proposal, the members of the Board of Governors would serve only as long as the president wanted them to, as members of the president's cabinet do today. That way, if the president didn't like the current monetary policy, he would have the authority to dismiss the members of the Board of Governors and appoint others in their place. When the president ran for reelection, the voters would have an opportunity to express their approval or disapproval of his monetary policy.

The Fed's independence from the rest of the government, coupled with the Fed's decision-making process, has concentrated power in the hands of the chairman. The chairman has only 1 vote in 7 on the Board of Governors and only 1 vote in 12 on the FOMC. Nevertheless, the very strong tradition at the Fed is that the chairman plays an outsized role in setting policy.

The Fed has never set out any specific guidelines regarding when it will adopt a particular monetary policy. The Fed adopts an expansionary policy when the chairman and the FOMC decide that the economy is in danger of moving into recession. The chairman's recommendations for a policy change are based on his own experience, on the analysis prepared by the Fed's economists, and on discussions with other members of the FOMC. The Fed adopts a contractionary policy when the chairman and FOMC decide that there is a threat of rising inflation. In either case, the decision to change policy depends in part on the personal judgment of the chairman. Most economists would say that monetary policy has been successful during the years since 1979, but some economists suggest that greater transparency about the Fed's objectives would help lock in future good performance.

In periods like the 1970s, when the performance of the U.S. economy was poor, proposals to reduce the independence of the Fed gained support. On balance, though, the U.S. economy has performed well during the past 25 years, which has greatly reduced discontent with the Fed's structure. At this point, it appears unlikely that Congress would consider legislation to reduce the independence of the Fed.

Conclusion

Monetary policy is one way governments pursue goals for inflation, economic growth, and financial stability. Many journalists and politicians refer to the chairman of the Federal Reserve as second only to the president of the United States in his ability to affect the U.S. economy. Congress and the president, however, also use their power over spending and taxes to try to stabilize the economy. In the next chapter, we discuss how *fiscal policy*—changes in government spending and taxes—affect the economy.

Read *An Inside Look* on the next page for a discussion of whether the actions taken by the Fed to stimulate spending on residential construction may have led to a "bubble" in housing prices.

An Inside Look

Monetary Policy Spurs Housing Boom

WALL STREET JOURNAL, JUNE 9, 2005

In Treating U.S. After Bubble, Fed Helped Create New Threats

By many yardsticks, the Federal Reserve's response to the bursting of the stock and tech-spending bubbles in 2000 has been a remarkable success. The 2001 recession was mild and economic growth since has been brisk. Employment is up and inflation remains within the Fed's hallowed zone of price stability.

But five years after the stock market's peak, the economy faces other threatening imbalances: a potential housing bubble, rock-bottom personal saving rates and a gargantuan trade deficit. And the Fed's post-bubble prescription bears some responsibility for all three. Fed officials acknowledge as much but say the alternatives were worse.

a By slashing short-term interest rates to 45-year lows, the Fed encouraged Americans to borrow more, gave them little reward for saving and helped ignite a surge in housing prices. President Bush and Congress joined in with steep tax cuts that boosted household purchasing power. All that spending contributed to a growing U.S. economy, a steady increase in imports and—given that Americans are so eager to borrow and foreigners so eager to lend—a mountain of foreign debt.

This is pleasant for Americans as long as it lasts. But Fed officials, international financial watchdogs and private economists say it can't. At some point, American consumers must spend less, save more and rely less on foreigners' savings.

How that will happen puts the nation in uncharted territory: After treating a bubble, how does the Fed manage the side effects of its medicine?

b Faced with an asset bubble, a central bank has two choices: Prick it early or wait for it to burst and try to contain the damage. The Fed in 1929 and the Bank of Japan in 1989 tried the first route, raising interest rates in response to rapidly rising asset prices. The result in the U.S. in the 1930s was depression and deflation. In Japan it was stagnation and deflation that continues today.

In the 1990s, Mr. Greenspan chose the second route. As long as the prices of goods and services were stable, he would leave the stock market alone. When the stock bubble finally burst, the Fed cut short-term rates aggressively beginning in 2001 and then held them at a 45-year low of 1% through early 2004 until the Fed was sure the threat of deflation had receded.

Mr. Greenspan knew his strategy carried risks. But he saw far greater ones in responding timidly as the collapse of the biggest asset bubble in history wiped out more than $5 trillion in shareholder value, and terrorist attacks, war and corporate scandal rattled confidence. The economic expansion to date suggests he was right . . . The Fed is conducting a "crucial experiment" in post-bubble monetary policy, says Edward Chancellor, a financial historian. "We don't know what the outcome is yet."

c Lower interest rates normally operate through several channels. They encourage consumers to buy things on credit today instead of saving to buy the items later. They boost stock and home prices, which makes the owners of those assets wealthier and more willing to spend. They encourage businesses to borrow and invest. And they depress the dollar, boosting exports.

But after 2001, some of these channels were blocked. Businesses, burdened with a glut of unused equipment from the bubble years and cowed by geopolitical and regulatory uncertainty, didn't borrow to invest. And the dollar didn't fall initially, but rose because foreign economies were in even worse shape than the U.S.'s. This meant the economy relied disproportionately on the one channel that did respond: consumers. They bought record numbers of houses and cars, mostly on credit. They also borrowed against their houses' appreciated values, allowing them to spend more still. . . .

Key Points in the Article

When the so-called tech-spending bubble burst in 2000, the Federal Reserve responded with an expansionary monetary policy. The 2001 recession that followed was short-lived, with a relatively small decline in real gross domestic product and no deflation. Generally speaking, central banks can either prick asset price bubbles early or wait for them to burst. Economists believe that the Federal Reserve's decision to wait for the bubble to burst in 2000 has had at least three unintended consequences: a housing bubble, a low saving rate, and a large trade deficit. This is because from 2001 to 2004, as interest rates fell, households saved less, borrowed more, and purchased houses and consumer durables, many of which were imports.

Analyzing the News

a When the tech-spending bubble burst in 2000, the U.S. government resonded with both monetary and fiscal policies to increase aggregate demand. The Federal Reserve engaged in an expansionary monetary policy. As a result, the money supply increased and interest rates fell. Figure 1 illustrates the effect of the policy in the money market, where the money supply curve shifts from MS_1 to MS_2 and the interest rate falls from i_1 to i_2. The fall in the interest rate increased aggregate spending, particularly consumer durables and housing, and hence aggregate demand. Figure 2 shows that the aggregate demand curve shifted from AD_2 to AD_3. AD_2 is the economy's aggregate demand curve without an expansionary monetary policy. (For simplicity, we are ignoring the effect of an increase in real GDP on the demand for money.)

Finally, President Bush and Congress engaged in an expansionary fiscal policy. They cut taxes to increase household disposable income and hence aggregate demand.

b A central bank can either prick an asset price bubble early or wait for it to burst. Two examples of pricking a bubble are the Federal Reserve's actions just prior to the Great Depression and the Bank of Japan's actions just prior to its current decade-long recession. Although the two central banks were not entirely responsible for the severe recessions that followed their attempts to prick asset price bubbles, in both cases deflation resulted from their actions.

c Typically, a change in the interest rate affects three components of aggregate spending: consumption, investment, and net exports. However, in 2001—as interest rates fell, households saved less, borrowed more, and purchased consumer durables, many of which were imports, and houses. Indeed, many households fell further into debt as they borrowed against the rising values of their homes. By comparison, because firms had invested so heavily during the tech-spending bubble, investment spending did not increase when interest rates fell. Because foreign economies were performing less well than the U.S. economy, the dollar's exchange value did not fall very much when interest rates fell, and therefore exports did not rise.

Thinking Critically ABOUT POLICY

1. The Federal Reserve can choose either the interest rate or the money supply as its monetary policy target. Suppose business cycle fluctuations are fueled by aggregate demand shocks, only. All else equal, which of these two targeting strategies will more effectively dampen business cycle fluctuations?
2. Suppose households and firms are extremely interest rate sensitive with respect to their demand for money: For example, a very small fall in the interest rate causes households and firms to increase dramatically their quantities of money demanded; put differently, suppose the money demand curve is nearly horizontal. What does this extreme interest rate sensitivity imply about the relative effectiveness of an expansionary monetary policy?

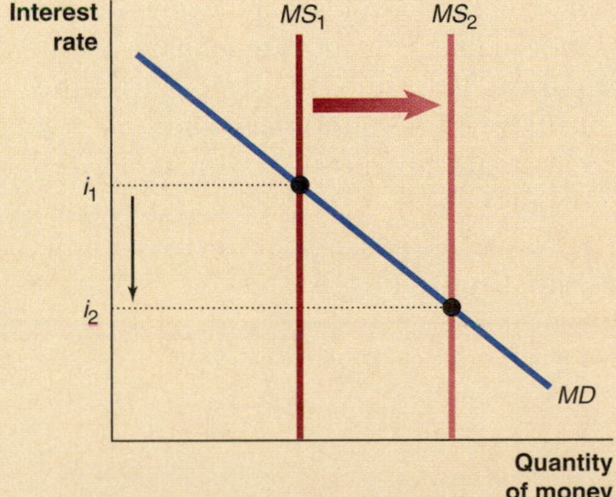

Figure 1: An increase in the money supply causes a decrease in the interest rate.

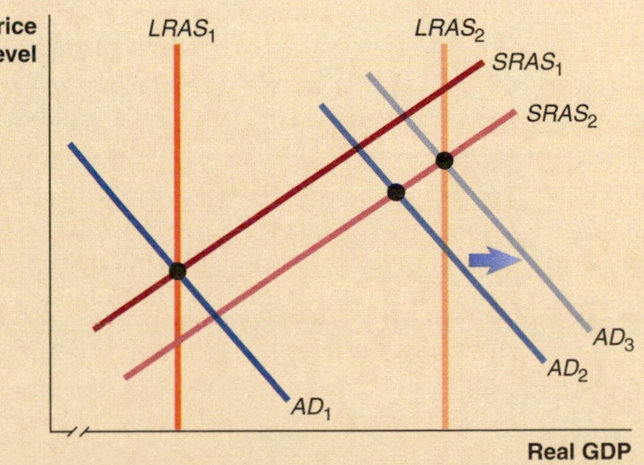

Figure 2: A decrease in the interest rate causes an increase in aggregate demand.

SUMMARY

LEARNING OBJECTIVE ① Define monetary policy and describe the Federal Reserve's monetary policy goals. *Monetary policy* is the actions the Federal Reserve takes to manage the money supply and interest rates to pursue its economic objectives. The Fed has set four *monetary policy goals* that are intended to promote a well-functioning economy: price stability, high employment, economic growth, and stability of financial markets and institutions.

LEARNING OBJECTIVE ② Describe the Federal Reserve's monetary policy targets, and explain how expansionary and contractionary monetary policies affect the interest rate. The Fed's *monetary policy targets* are economic variables that it can affect directly and that in turn affect variables such as real GDP and the price level that are closely related to the Fed's policy goals. The two main monetary policy targets are the money supply and the interest rate. The Fed has most often chosen to use the interest rate as its monetary policy target. The Federal Open Market Committee announces a target for the *federal funds rate* after each meeting. The federal funds rate is the interest rate banks charge each other for overnight loans. To fight a recession, the Fed conducts an *expansionary policy* by increasing the money supply. The increase in the money supply lowers the interest rate. To reduce the inflation rate, the Fed conducts a *contractionary policy* by adjusting the money supply to increase the interest rate. In a graphical analysis of the money market, an expansionary policy shifts the money supply curve to the right, causing a movement down the money demand curve and a new equilibrium at a lower interest rate. A contractionary policy shifts the money supply curve to the left, causing a movement up the money demand curve and a new equilibrium at a higher interest rate.

LEARNING OBJECTIVE ③ Use aggregate demand and aggregate supply graphs to show the effects of monetary policy on real GDP and the price level. An expansionary monetary policy lowers interest rates to increase consumption, investment, and net exports. This increased spending causes the aggregate demand curve (*AD*) to shift out more than it otherwise would, raising the level of real GDP and the price level. A contractionary monetary policy raises interest rates to decrease consumption, investment, and net exports. This decreased spending causes the aggregate demand curve to shift out less than it otherwise would, reducing both the level of real GDP and the inflation rate below what they would be in the absence of policy.

LEARNING OBJECTIVE ④ Discuss the Fed's setting of monetary policy targets. Some economists have argued that the Fed should use the money supply as its monetary target, rather than an interest rate. Milton Friedman and other monetarists argue that the Fed should adopt a monetary growth rule of increasing the money supply every year at a fixed rate. Support for this proposal declined after 1980 because the relationship between movements in the money supply and movements in real GDP and the price level has weakened. John Taylor has analyzed the factors involved in Fed decision making and developed the *Taylor rule* for federal funds targeting. The Taylor rule links the Fed's target for the federal funds rate to economic variables. Over the past decade, many economists and central bankers have expressed significant interest in using *inflation targeting.* Under inflation targeting, monetary policy is conducted to commit the central bank to achieving a publicly announced inflation target. A number of foreign central banks have adopted inflation targeting, but the Fed has not. The Fed's performance in the 1980s, 1990s, and early 2000s generally received high marks from economists, even without formal inflation targeting.

LEARNING OBJECTIVE ⑤ Assess the arguments for and against the independence of the Federal Reserve. The Fed conducts monetary policy without input from Congress or the president. It uses the interest it earns from purchasing U.S. Treasury bills to avoid asking Congress for the funds it needs to operate. However, the Fed's independence is not absolute because Congress and the president can pass legislation at any time to reorganize, or even abolish, it. Advocates of Fed independence argue that isolating it from political pressure allows it to choose policies in the best interest of the economy. Internationally, countries with more independent central banks tend to have lower inflation rates. Opponents of Fed independence argue that concentrating so much power in the hands of unelected officials is inconsistent with democratic principles.

KEY TERMS

REVIEW QUESTIONS

1. When Congress established the Fed in 1914, what was its main responsibility? What is its most important responsibility today? Why did this change take place?
2. What is a monetary policy target? Why does the Fed use policy targets?
3. Draw a demand and supply graph showing equilibrium in the money market. Suppose the Fed wants to lower the equilibrium interest rate. Show on the graph how the Fed would accomplish this objective.
4. Explain the effect an open market purchase has on the equilibrium interest rate.
5. What is the federal funds rate? What role does it play in monetary policy?
6. How does an increase in interest rates affect aggregate demand? Briefly discuss how each component of aggregate demand is affected.
7. If the Fed believes the economy is about to fall into recession, what actions should it take? If the Fed believes that the inflation rate is about to increase, what actions should it take?
8. What is a monetary rule, as opposed to a monetary policy? What monetary rule would Milton Friedman like the Fed to follow? Why has support for a monetary rule of the kind advocated by Friedman declined since 1980?
9. For more than 20 years, the Fed has used the federal funds rate as its monetary policy target. Why doesn't it target the money supply at the same time?
10. In what ways is the Federal Reserve more independent of the executive branch of the federal government than other agencies, like, for instance, the Environmental Protection Agency? Why did the Federal Reserve Act of 1913 give so much independence to the Fed? What arguments do economists make in favor of reducing the independence of the Fed?

PROBLEMS AND APPLICATIONS

Please visit **www.prenhall.com/hubbard** *for solutions to the even-numbered problems as well as multiple-choice and true or false self-assessment quizzes.*

1. A newspaper headline in early 2002 read, "Companies Invest as Interest Rates Are at a 40-Year Low." Explain the connection between this headline and the monetary policy pursued by the Federal Reserve during that time.
   Source: Brendan Murray, "Companies Invest as Interest Rates Are at a 40-Year Low," Bloomberg News, March 28, 2002.
2. **[Related to the *Chapter Opener*]** In an article in the *Wall Street Journal* in March 2002, Lawrence Yun, senior economist for the National Association of Realtors was quoted as saying, "In the current [2001] brief recession, the housing-market indicators were in record territories." Economists normally expect that during a recession the housing market does badly because of rising unemployment and falling incomes. Why did the housing market do so well during the 2001 recession?
   Source: Erin Schulte, "Housing's Strength Raises Another Bubble Concern," *Wall Street Journal,* March 29, 2002.
3. **[Related to the *Chapter Opener*]** An article in the *New York Times* in March 2002 reported that the housing market had been surprisingly strong during the previous year. According to the article, "In trying to explain the resilience of the housing market in the face of rising unemployment, shrinking stock portfolios and a soft economy, economists start with the Federal Reserve." Why start with the Federal Reserve in trying to explain the strength of the housing market during a recession?
   Source: Daniel Altman, "Economy's Rock: Homes, Homes, Homes," *New York Times,* March 30, 2002.
4. A "basis point" is one one-hundredth of a percentage point. If an interest rate increases by 50 basis points, it has gone up by 1/2 of a percentage point. "Monetary aggregates" are measures of the money supply, such as M1 and M2. A Federal Reserve publication from February 2002, made the following observation:

   > As the economy slipped into recession last year, the FOMC reduced its target level for the overnight federal funds rate by 475 basis points to 1.75 percent. Also during the year, growth of the monetary aggregates jumped sharply.

   a. If the target for the federal funds rate was reduced by 475 basis points to 1.75 percent, what was its original level?
   b. Is there a connection between the federal funds rate falling and the money supply increasing? Briefly explain.

   Source: Richard G. Anderson, "Interpreting Monetary Growth," *Monetary Trends,* Federal Reserve Bank of St. Louis, February 2002.
5. **[Related to *Solved Problem 16-1*]** Suppose the interest rate is 2 percent on a Treasury bill that will pay its owner $1,000 when it matures in one year.

a. What is the price of the Treasury bill?
b. Suppose that the Fed engages in open market sales resulting in the interest rate on one-year Treasury bills rising to 3 percent. What will the price of these bills be now?

6. In this chapter we depict the money supply curve as a vertical line. Is there any reason to believe the money supply curve might actually be upward sloping? (*Hint:* Think about the role of banks in the process of creating the money supply.) Draw a money demand and money supply diagram with an upward-sloping money supply curve. Suppose that households and firms decide they want to hold more money at every interest rate. Show the result on your diagram. What is the impact on the size of M1? How does this differ from the impact if the money supply curve had been a vertical line?
7. If the Federal Reserve purchases $100 million worth of U.S. Treasury bills from the public, predict what will happen to the money supply. Explain your reasoning.
8. An editorial in the *New York Times* in 2004 made the following observation about the federal funds rate:

> The Federal Reserve Board announced yesterday that it would keep its overnight interest rate where it has been for nine months—at 1 percent, its lowest level since 1958. Factor in inflation, and Alan Greenspan is essentially lending money at a loss.

What is another name for the "overnight interest rate" mentioned in this editorial? Do you agree with the author of this editorial that the Federal Reserve lends money at this interest rate? Briefly explain.
Source: "The Cost of Cheap Money," *New York Times,* March 17, 2004.

9. In December 2001, some Fed officials were worried that the U.S. economy might make only a slow recovery from the 2001 recession. An article in the *New York Times* quoted the views of these officials as follows:

> The main force inhibiting a strong comeback, Fed officials say, is the perception among businesses that the rates of return available to them from investing in new equipment remain too low given the uncertainty about demand for their products, the overall health of the economy and the risks associated with the campaign against terrorism.

How might firms' expectations that the rates of return on new investments are too low make monetary policy less effective in ending a recession?
Source: Richard W. Stevenson and Louis Uchitelle, "Fed Now Says '02 Recovery to Be Gradual," *New York Times,* December 4, 2001.

10. According to an article in the *New York Times,* an official at the Bank of Japan had the following explanation of why monetary policy was not pulling the country out of recession:

> Despite recent major increases in the money supply, he said, the money stays in banks.

Explain what the official meant by the phrase "the money stays in banks." Where does the money go if an expansionary monetary policy is successful? Why wasn't that happening in Japan?
Source: James Brooke, "Critics Say Koizumi's Economic Medicine Is a Weak Tea," *New York Times,* February 27, 2002.

11. In March 2002, an article in the *New York Times* quoted Japanese Prime Minister Junichiro Koizumi:

> I really wonder why the Japanese economy is not becoming more revitalized, why we are not seeing more economic recovery. We have been doing everything to the limit in . . . monetary policy.

Had the Bank of Japan actually been doing everything to bring the Japanese economy out of recession? (*Hint:* Review Making the Connection 16-3 on monetary policy in Japan on page 504).
Source: James Brooke, "Japan's Premier Muses on a Recovery-Proof Economy," *New York Times,* March 29, 2002.

12. Most of the countries of Western Europe use a common currency, the euro, and have a common monetary policy determined by the European Central Bank. An article in the *Economist* magazine in late 2002 argued that the European Central Bank was not pursuing an appropriate monetary policy. According to the article, when the European Central Bank was founded in the early 1990s it was:

> intended to bear down upon an inflationary threat that no longer exists. In today's Europe, the enemies are more likely to be sluggish to non-existent growth in many countries . . . [and] high unemployment.

How will the policies of a central bank differ if the main economic problem it faces is inflation rather than slow growth and unemployment?
Source: "A Hard Sell," *Economist,* October 19, 2002, p. 54.

13. William McChesney Martin, who was Federal Reserve chairman from 1951 to 1970, was once quoted as saying, "The role of the Federal Reserve is to remove the punchbowl just as the party gets going." What did he mean?
14. **[Related to *Solved Problem 16-2*]** Use the graph on the next page to answer the questions:
   a. If the Fed does not take any policy action, what will be the level of real GDP and the price level in 2008?
   b. If the Fed wants to keep real GDP at its potential level in 2008, should it use an expansionary policy or a contractionary policy? Should the trading desk be buying Treasury bills or selling them?

c. If the Fed takes no policy action, what will be the inflation rate in 2008? If the Fed uses monetary policy to keep real GDP at its full-employment level, what will be the inflation rate in 2008?

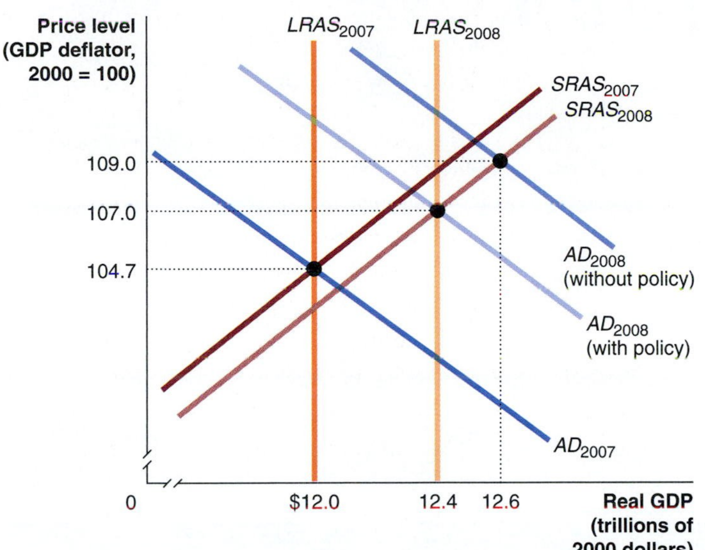

15. **[Related to *Solved Problem 16-2*]** The hypothetical information in the following table shows what the situation will be in 2011 if the Fed does *not* use monetary policy:

YEAR	POTENTIAL REAL GDP	REAL GDP	PRICE LEVEL
2010	$12.8 trillion	$12.8 trillion	140
2011	$13.3 trillion	$13.4 trillion	147

a. If the Fed wants to keep real GDP at its potential level in 2011, should it use an expansionary policy or a contractionary policy? Should the trading desk be buying T-bills or selling them?

b. If the Fed's policy is successful in keeping real GDP at its potential level in 2011, state whether each of the following will be higher, lower, or the same as it would have been if the Fed had taken no action:

i. Real GDP
ii. Potential real GDP
iii. The inflation rate
iv. The unemployment rate

c. Draw an aggregate demand and aggregate supply graph to illustrate your answer. Be sure that your graph contains *LRAS* curves for 2010 and 2011; *SRAS* curves for 2010 and 2011; *AD* curves for 2010 and for 2011, with and without monetary policy action; and equilibrium real GDP and the price level in 2011, with and without policy.

16. **[Related to *Don't Let This Happen To You!*]** Briefly explain whether you agree or disagree with the following statement: "The Fed has an easy job. Say it wants to increase real GDP by $200 billion. All it has to do is increase the money supply by that amount."

17. Some businesspeople believe that the active monetary policy of the Fed makes the economy less stable, rather than more stable. Writing in the *New York Times*, T. J. Rodgers, chief executive of Cypress Semiconductor, argued:

> There is a fundamental flaw in the Fed's operational assumption that it can know enough about the future to fine-tune the economy without continually making mistakes. Events likely to alter the economy—wars, severe winters, technology breakthroughs and so on—are not predictable. . . . Fed action is just as likely to exacerbate an economic problem as it is to mitigate it.

Do you agree with Mr. Rodgers's argument? Explain.
Source: T. J. Rodgers, "A Computer Would Do Better than the Fed," *New York Times*, April 7, 2001.

18. The following appears in a Federal Reserve publication:

> In practice, monetary policymakers do not have up-to-the-minute, reliable information about the state of the economy and prices. Information is limited because of lags in the publication of data. Also, policymakers have less-than-perfect understanding of the way the economy works, including the knowledge of when and to what extent policy actions will affect aggregate demand. The operation of the economy changes over time, and with it the response of the economy to policy measures. These limitations add to uncertainties in the policy process and make determining the appropriate setting of monetary policy . . . more difficult.

If the Fed itself admits that there are many obstacles in the way of effective monetary policy, why does it still engage in active monetary policy rather than using a monetary growth rule, as suggested by Milton Friedman and his followers?
Source: Board of Governors of the Federal Reserve System, *The Federal Reserve System: Purposes and Functions*, Washington, D.C., 1994.

19. The president of the United States appoints the comptroller of the currency and the secretary of the treasury. Until passage of the Banking Act of 1935, these officials were both members of the Board of Governors of the Federal Reserve System. How would having these two presidential appointees on the board be likely to affect monetary policy? Would it be a good idea if they were still on the board?

20. In 1975, Ronald Reagan stated that inflation "has one cause and one cause alone: government spending more than government takes in." Briefly explain whether you agree.
Source: Edward Nelson, "Budget Deficits and Interest Rates," *Monetary Trends*, Federal Reserve Bank of St. Louis, March 2004.

chapter seventeen

17

Fiscal Policy

A Boon for H&R Block

The offices of H&R Block were very busy in the spring of 2002 because millions of taxpayers were having a more difficult time than usual completing their federal income tax forms, due by April 15. Congress and the president had used the *discretionary fiscal policy* of cutting income taxes to increase household spending. Their goal was to help pull the economy out of recession. Because most taxpayers would not see the money from the tax cut until they filed their tax returns in early 2002, the federal government decided to mail out checks during the summer of 2001 for the amount each taxpayer would receive. Single taxpayers received a check for $300, and married taxpayers received a check for $600.

A new line on the tax form was meant to give taxpayers an opportunity to claim their tax cut if they had not received it the previous summer. Many taxpayers found the instructions confusing and either incorrectly claimed an additional $300 or $600 or decided they needed the help of a professional tax preparer, such as H&R Block.

In 1946, Henry Bloch started the United Business Company, which provided accounting services to small businesses. When the local office of the United States Internal Revenue Service (IRS) announced in 1955 that it would no longer provide free preparation of individual income tax forms, Henry and his brother Richard recognized an entrepreneurial opportunity. They founded a new firm, H&R Block, dedicated to preparing individual income tax returns. When the IRS announced that it would stop offering tax preparation services at its New York City offices in 1956, the Blochs decided to expand to that city by opening seven offices close to existing IRS offices. By 2005, the firm employed more than 80,000 tax preparers to prepare more than 17 million tax returns a year and earned revenue of $4.5 billion.

The tax laws have become increasingly complicated. In 1955,

when H&R Block was founded, the 1040 individual income tax form had 16 pages of instructions. In 2005, there were 191 pages of instructions. Individual tax payers in 1955 were potentially eligible for 14 credits and deductions that would reduce their tax payments. In 2005, there were 74 credits and deductions. Taxes on businesses also have become more complex over the years. In 1955, there were no business tax credits. In 2005, there were 25 business tax credits. Even Albert Einstein supposedly remarked, "The hardest thing in the world to understand is the income tax." It is not surprising that millions of Americans have given up filling out their own income tax forms, or have to rely on software such as Intuit's TurboTax or H&R Block's TaxCut.

The tax laws are complicated because Congress and the president change them repeatedly to achieve economic and social policy goals. As we will see, some changes in tax law are the result of discretionary fiscal policy and are intended to achieve macroeconomic goals of high employment, economic growth, and price stability. Other changes in tax law are intended to achieve goals such as energy conservation. *An Inside Look* on page 552 discusses the federal government's budget deficit.

LEARNING OBJECTIVES

After studying this chapter, you should be able to:

1. Define fiscal policy.
2. Explain how fiscal policy affects aggregate demand and how the government can use fiscal policy to stabilize the economy.
3. Explain how the multiplier process works with respect to fiscal policy.
4. Discuss the difficulties that can arise in implementing fiscal policy.
5. Explain how the federal budget can serve as an automatic stabilizer.
6. Discuss the long-run effects of fiscal policy.

In Chapter 16, we discussed how the Federal Reserve uses monetary policy to pursue macroeconomic policy goals, including price stability and high employment. In this chapter, we will explore how the government uses *fiscal policy,* which involves changes in taxes and government purchases, to achieve similar policy goals. As we have seen, the price level and the levels of real GDP and total employment in the economy depend in the short run on aggregate demand and short-run aggregate supply. The government can affect the levels of both aggregate demand and aggregate supply through fiscal policy. We will explore how Congress and the president decide which fiscal policy actions to take to achieve their goals. We will also discuss the disagreements among economists and policymakers over the effectiveness of fiscal policy.

① **LEARNING OBJECTIVE**

Define fiscal policy.

Fiscal Policy

Since the end of World War II, the federal government has been committed to intervening in the economy "to promote maximum employment, production, and purchasing power." As we saw in Chapter 16, the Federal Reserve closely monitors the economy and the Federal Open Market Committee meets eight times per year to decide whether to change monetary policy. Less frequently, Congress and the president also make changes in taxes and government purchases to achieve macroeconomic policy objectives, such as high employment, price stability, and high rates of economic growth. Changes in federal taxes and spending that are intended to achieve macroeconomic policy objectives are called **fiscal policy.**

Fiscal policy Changes in federal taxes and purchases that are intended to achieve macroeconomic policy objectives, such as high employment, price stability, and high rates of economic growth.

What Fiscal Policy Is and What It Isn't

In the United States, the federal, state, and local governments all have responsibility for taxing and spending. Economists restrict the term *fiscal policy* to refer only to the actions of the federal government. State and local governments will sometimes change their taxing and spending policies to aid their local economies, but these are not fiscal policy actions because they are not intended to affect the national economy. The federal government makes many decisions about taxes and spending, but not all of these decisions are fiscal policy actions because they are not intended to achieve macroeconomic policy goals. For example, a decision to cut the taxes of people who buy hybrid cars is an environmental policy action, not a fiscal policy action. Similarly, the defense and homeland security spending increases in the years after 2001 to fund the war on terrorism and the wars in Iraq and Afghanistan were part of defense and homeland security policy, not fiscal policy.

Automatic Stabilizers versus Discretionary Fiscal Policy

There is an important distinction between *automatic stabilizers* and *discretionary fiscal policy.* Some types of government spending and taxes, which automatically increase and decrease along with the business cycle, are referred to as **automatic stabilizers.** The word *automatic* refers to the fact that changes in these types of spending and taxes happen without actions by the government. For example, when the economy is expanding and employment is increasing, government spending on unemployment insurance payments to workers who have lost their jobs will automatically decrease. During a recession, as employment declines, this type of spending will automatically increase. Similarly, when the economy is expanding and incomes are rising, the amount the government collects in taxes will increase as people pay additional taxes on their higher incomes. When the economy is in recession, the amount the government collects in taxes will fall.

Automatic stabilizers Government spending and taxes that automatically increase or decrease along with the business cycle.

FIGURE 17-1

The Federal Government's Share of Total Government Expenditures, 1929–2004

Until the Great Depression of the 1930s, the majority of government spending in the United States was done at the state and local levels. Since World War II, the federal government's share of total government expenditures has been between two-thirds and three-quarters.

Source: Bureau of Economic Analysis.

With discretionary fiscal policy, the government is taking actions to change spending or taxes. The tax cuts passed by Congress in 2001 are an example of a discretionary fiscal policy action.

An Overview of Government Spending and Taxes

To provide a context for understanding fiscal policy, it is important to understand the big picture of government taxing and spending. Before the Great Depression of the 1930s, the majority of government spending took place at the state and local levels. As Figure 17-1 shows, the size of the federal government expanded significantly during the crisis of the Great Depression. Since World War II, the federal government's share of total government expenditures has been between two-thirds and three-quarters.

Economists often measure government spending relative to GDP. Remember that there is a difference between federal government *purchases* and federal government *expenditures*. When the federal government purchases an aircraft carrier or the services of an FBI agent, it receives a good or service in return. Federal government expenditures include purchases plus all other federal government spending. As Figure 17-2 shows,

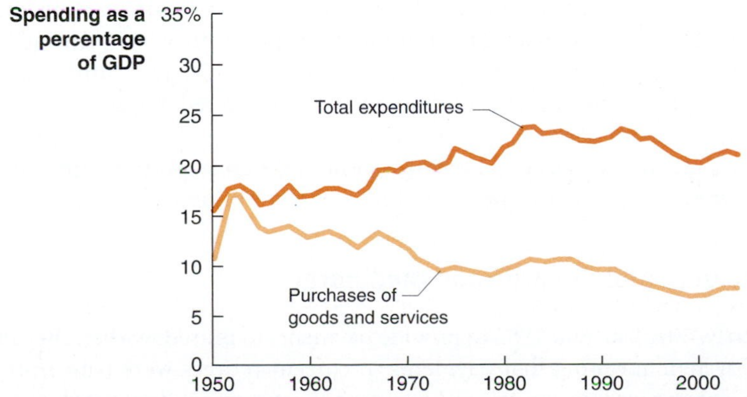

FIGURE 17-2

Federal Purchases and Federal Expenditures as a Percentage of GDP, 1950–2004

As a fraction of GDP, the federal government's *purchases* of goods and services have been declining since the Korean War in the early 1950s. Total *expenditures* by the federal government—including transfer payments—slowly rose from 1950 through the early 1990s, fell from 1992 to 2001, before rising again.

Source: Bureau of Economic Analysis.

FIGURE 17-3

Federal Government Expenditures, 2004

Federal government *purchases* can be divided into defense spending—which makes up about 20 percent of the federal budget—and spending on everything else the federal government does—from paying the salaries of FBI agents, to operating the national parks, to supporting scientific research—which makes up less than 11 percent of the budget. In addition to purchases, there are three other categories of federal government *expenditures:* interest on the national debt, grants to state and local governments, and transfer payments. Transfer payments have risen from about 25 percent of federal government expenditures in the 1960s to almost 45 percent in 2004.

Source: Bureau of Economic Analysis.

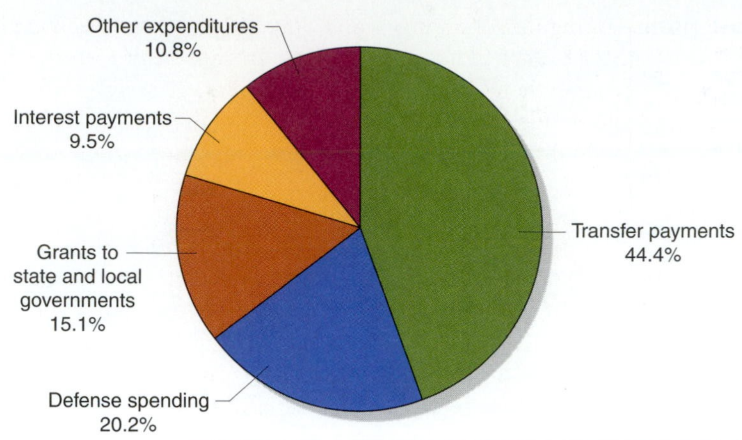

federal government *purchases* as a percentage of GDP actually have been falling since the end of the Korean War in the early 1950s. Total federal *expenditures* as a percentage of GDP rose from 1950 to the early 1990s and fell from 1992 to 2001, before rising again. The decline in expenditures between 1992 and 2001 was partly the result of the end of the Cold War between the Soviet Union and the United States, which allowed for a substantial reduction in defense spending. Real federal government spending on national defense declined from $479 billion in 1990 to $365 billion in 1998, before rising again to $485 billion in 2004 in response to the war on terrorism and the wars in Iraq and Afghanistan.

In addition to purchases, there are three other categories of federal government expenditures: *interest on the national debt, grants to state and local governments,* and *transfer payments.* Interest on the national debt represents payments to holders of the bonds the federal government has issued to borrow money. Grants to state and local governments are payments made by the federal government to support government activity at the state and local levels. For example, to help reduce crime, Congress and the Clinton administration implemented a program of grants to local governments to hire more police officers. The largest and fastest-growing category of federal expenditures is transfer payments. Some of these programs, such as Social Security and unemployment insurance, began in the 1930s. Others, such as Medicare, which provides health care to the elderly, or the Food Stamps and Temporary Assistance for Needy Families programs, which are intended to aid the poor, began in the 1960s or later.

Figure 17-3 shows that in 2004, transfer payments were almost 45 percent of federal government expenditures. In the 1960s, transfer payments had been only about 25 percent of federal government expenditures. As the U.S. population ages, federal government spending on the Social Security and Medicare programs will continue to increase, causing transfer payments to rise above 50 percent of federal government expenditures by 2010. Figure 17-3 shows that spending on most of the federal government's day-to-day activities—including running federal agencies such as the Environmental Protection Agency, the FBI, the National Park Service, and the Immigration and Naturalization Service—makes up less than 11 percent of federal government expenditures.

17-1 Making the Connection

The Future of Social Security and Medicare

Social Security, established in 1935 to provide payments to retired workers, began as a "pay-as-you-go" system, meaning that payments to current retirees were paid from taxes collected from current workers. In the early years of the program, many workers were paying into the system and there were relatively few retirees. For example, in 1940, more than 35 million workers were paying into the system, and only 222,000 were receiving benefits—a ratio of more than 150 workers to each beneficiary. In those early years, most retirees received far more in benefits than they had paid in taxes. For example, the first beneficiary was a legal secretary named Ida May Fuller. She worked for three years while the program was in place and paid total taxes of only $24.75. During her retirement, she collected $22,888.92 in benefits.

The Social Security and Medicare programs have been a great success in reducing poverty among elderly Americans, but in recent years the ability of the federal government to finance current promises has been called into doubt. After World War II, the United States experienced a "baby boom" as birth rates rose and remained high through the early 1960s. Falling birth rates after 1965 have meant long-run problems for the Social Security system, as the number of workers per retiree has continually declined. Currently there are only about three workers per retiree, and that ratio will probably decline to two workers per retiree in the coming decades. Congress has attempted to deal with this problem by raising the age to receive full benefits from 65 to 67 and by increasing payroll taxes. In 1940, the combined payroll tax paid by workers and firms was 2 percent; in 2005, it was 15.3 percent.

Under the Medicare program, which was established in 1965, the federal government provides health-care coverage to people age 65 and over. The long-term financial situation for Medicare is also a cause for concern. As Americans live longer and as new—and expensive—medical procedures are developed, the projected expenditures under the Medicare program will eventually far outstrip projected tax revenues. The federal government also faces increasing expenditures under the Medicaid program, which is administered by state governments and provides healthcare coverage to low-income people. In 2005, federal spending on Social Security, Medicare, and Medicaid was 8.4 percent of GDP. Forecasts by the Congressional Budget Office show spending on these three programs rising to 14.3 percent of GDP in 2030 and 17.7 percent of GDP by 2050. Over the coming decades, the gap between the benefits projected to be paid under the Social Security and Medicare programs and projected tax revenues is a staggering $72 *trillion.*

A lively political debate has taken place over the future of the Social Security and Medicare programs. Some economists and policymakers have proposed increasing taxes to fund future benefit payments. The tax increases needed, however, could be as much as 50 percent higher than current rates, and tax increases of that magnitude could discourage work effort, entrepreneurship, and investment, thereby slowing economic growth. There also have been proposals to slow the rate of growth of future benefits, while guaranteeing benefits to current recipients. While this strategy would avoid the need to raise taxes significantly, it would also require younger workers to save more for their retirement. Some economists and policymakers have argued for slower benefit growth for higher-income workers, while leaving future benefits unchanged for lower-income workers.

Whatever changes are ultimately made, for young people the debate over Social Security and Medicare is among the most important policy issues.

Sources: "The 2005 Annual Report of the Board of Trustees of the Federal Old-Age and Survivors Insurance and Disability Insurance Trust Funds," 109th Congress, 1st Session, House Document 109-18, April 5, 2005; Congressional Budget Office, *The Long-Term Budget Outlook,* December 2003; and the Social Security Administration Web site (www.ssa.gov).

Will the federal government be able to keep the promises made by the Social Security and Medicare programs?

Figure 17-4 shows that in 2004 the federal government raised about 40 percent of its revenue from the individual income tax. Payroll taxes to fund the Social Security and Medicare programs raised 41 percent of federal revenues. The tax on corporate profits raised about 11 percent of federal revenues. The remaining 8 percent of federal revenues were raised from sales taxes on certain products, such as cigarettes and gasoline, from tariffs on products imported from other countries, and from other sources, such as payments by companies that cut timber on federal lands.

FIGURE 17-4

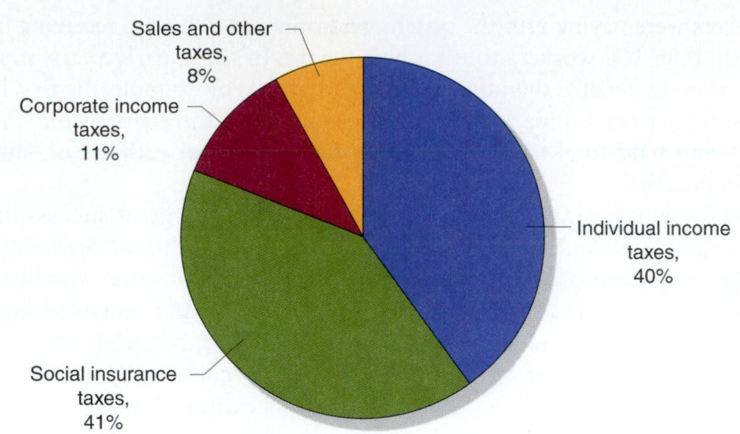

Federal Government Revenue, 2004

In 2004, the individual income tax raised about 40 percent of the federal government's revenues. The corporate income tax raised about 11 percent of revenue. Payroll taxes to fund the Social Security and Medicare programs have risen from less than 10 percent of federal government revenues in 1950 to more than 41 percent in 2004. The remaining 8 percent of revenues were raised from sales taxes, tariffs on imports, and other fees.

Note: The sales and other taxes category includes a small amount of other revenue received by the federal government.

Source: Bureau of Economic Analysis.

② **LEARNING OBJECTIVE**

Explain how fiscal policy affects aggregate demand and how the government can use fiscal policy to stabilize the economy.

Using Fiscal Policy to Influence Aggregate Demand

The federal government uses stabilization policy to offset the effects of the business cycle on the economy. We saw in Chapter 16 that the Federal Reserve carries out stabilization policy through changes in the money supply and interest rates. The government—Congress and the president—can also carry out stabilization policy through changes in government purchases and taxes. Because changes in government purchases and taxes lead to changes in aggregate demand, they can affect the level of real GDP, employment, and the price level. When the economy is in a recession, *increases* in government purchases or *decreases* in taxes will increase aggregate demand. As we have seen in Chapter 14, the inflation rate may increase when aggregate demand is increasing faster than aggregate supply. Decreasing government purchases or raising taxes can slow the growth of aggregate demand and reduce the inflation rate.

Expansionary Fiscal Policy

Expansionary fiscal policy involves increasing government purchases or decreasing taxes. An increase in government purchases will increase aggregate demand directly because government expenditures are a component of aggregate demand. A cut in taxes has an indirect effect on aggregate demand. Remember from Chapter 11 that the income households have available to spend after they have paid their taxes is called *disposable income.* If the individual income tax is cut, household disposable income will rise, and so should consumption spending. Tax cuts on business income can increase aggregate demand by increasing business investment.

Figure 17-5 shows the results of an expansionary fiscal policy. Notice that this figure is very similar to Figure 16-8 on page 505, which showed the effects of an expansionary monetary policy. The goal of both expansionary monetary policy and expansionary fiscal policy is to increase aggregate demand relative to what it would have been without the policy.

In the hypothetical situation shown in Figure 17-5, the economy begins in equilibrium at potential real GDP of \$12 trillion and a price level of 100 (point *A*). In the second year *LRAS* increases to \$12.4 trillion, but *AD* increases only to AD_2(without policy), which is not enough to keep the economy in macroeconomic equilibrium at potential GDP. Let's assume that the Fed does not react to the situation with an expansionary monetary policy. In that case, without an expansionary fiscal policy of spending increases or tax reductions, the short-run equilibrium will occur at \$12.3 trillion (point *B*). The \$100 billion gap between this level of real GDP and the potential level means that some firms are operating at less than their full capacity. Incomes

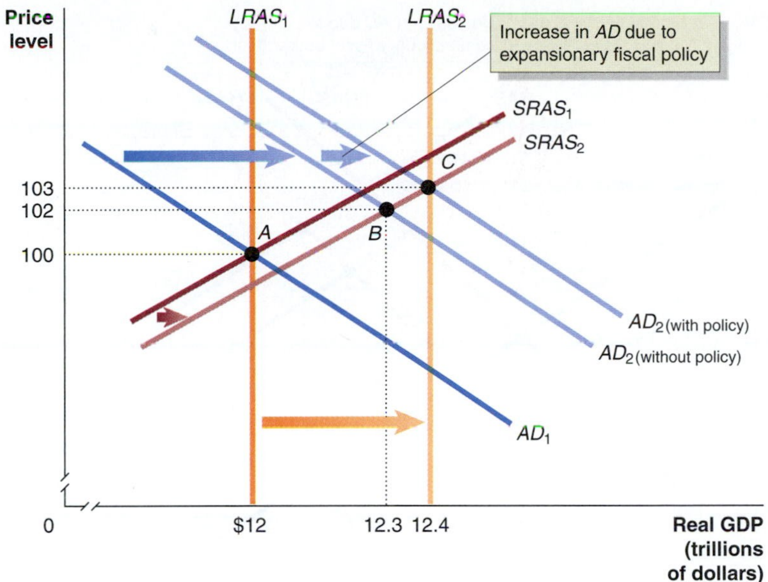

FIGURE 17-5

An Expansionary Fiscal Policy

The economy begins in equilibrium at point *A*, at potential real GDP of $12 trillion and a price level of 100. Without an expansionary policy, aggregate demand will shift from AD_1 to $AD_{2\text{(without policy)}}$, which is not enough to keep the economy at potential GDP because long-run aggregate supply has shifted from $LRAS_1$ to $LRAS_2$. The economy will be in short-run equilibrium at point *B*, with real GDP of $12.3 trillion and a price level of 102. Increasing government purchases or cutting taxes will shift aggregate demand to $AD_{2\text{(with policy)}}$. The economy will be in equilibrium at point *C* with real GDP of $12.4 trillion, which is its potential level, and a price level of 103. The price level is higher than it would have been if expansionary fiscal policy had not been used.

and profits will be falling, firms will begin to lay off workers, and the unemployment rate will rise.

Increasing government purchases or cutting taxes can shift aggregate demand to AD_2(with policy). The economy will be in equilibrium at point *C* with real GDP of $12.4 trillion, which is its potential level, and a price level of 103. The price level is higher than it would have been if expansionary fiscal policy had not been used.

Contractionary Fiscal Policy

Contractionary fiscal policy involves decreasing government purchases or increasing taxes. Policymakers use contractionary fiscal policy to reduce increases in aggregate demand that seem likely to lead to inflation. In Figure 17-6, the economy again begins at potential real GDP of $12 trillion and a price level of 100 (point *A*). Once again, *LRAS* increases to $12.4 trillion in the second year. In this scenario, the shift in aggregate to demand to AD_2(without policy) results in a short-run macroeconomic equilibrium beyond potential GDP (point *B*). If we assume, once again, that the Fed does not respond to the situation with a contractionary monetary policy, the economy will experience a rising inflation rate. Decreasing government purchases or increasing taxes can keep real GDP from moving beyond its potential level. The result, shown in Figure 17-6, is that in the new equilibrium at point *C*, the inflation rate is 3 percent, rather than 5 percent.

A Summary of How Fiscal Policy Affects Aggregate Demand

Table 17-1 summarizes how fiscal policy affects aggregate demand. Just as we did with monetary policy, we must add a very important qualification to this summary of fiscal

TABLE 17-1

Countercyclical Fiscal Policy

PROBLEM	TYPE OF POLICY	ACTIONS BY CONGRESS AND THE PRESIDENT	RESULT
Recession	Expansionary	Increase government spending or cut taxes	Real GDP and the price level rise
Rising inflation	Contractionary	Decrease government spending or raise taxes	Real GDP and the price level fall

FIGURE 17-6

A Contractionary Fiscal Policy

The economy begins in equilibrium at point *A*, with real GDP of $12 trillion and a price level of 100. Without a contractionary policy, aggregate demand will shift from AD_1 to $AD_{2(\text{without policy})}$, which results in a short-run equilibrium beyond potential GDP at point *B*, with real GDP of $12.5 trillion and a price level of 105. Decreasing government purchases or increasing taxes can shift aggregate demand to $AD_{2(\text{with policy})}$. The economy will be in equilibrium at point *C* with real GDP of $12.4 trillion, which is its potential level, and a price level of 103. The inflation rate will be 3 percent as opposed to the 5 percent it would have been without the contractionary fiscal policy.

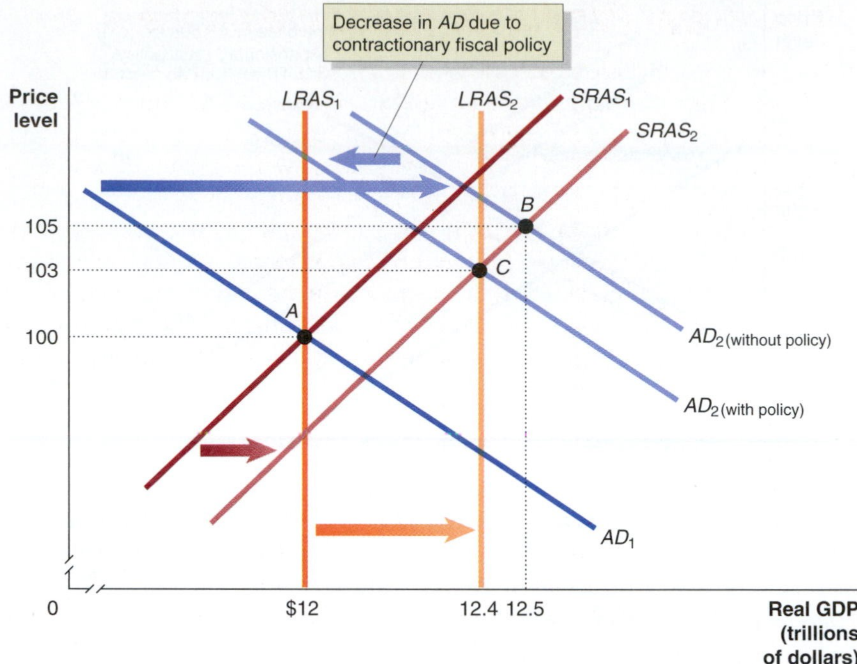

policy: The table isolates the impact of fiscal policy *by holding constant monetary policy and all other factors affecting the variables involved.* In other words, we are again invoking the *ceteris paribus* condition we discussed in Chapter 3. This point is important because, for example, a contractionary fiscal policy does not cause the price level to fall. A contractionary fiscal policy causes the price level *to rise by less than it would have without the policy,* which is the situation shown in Figure 17-6.

Don't Let This Happen To You!

Don't Confuse Fiscal Policy and Monetary Policy

If you keep in mind the definitions of *money, income,* and *spending,* the difference between monetary policy and fiscal policy will be clearer. A common mistake is to think of monetary policy as the Fed fighting recessions by increasing the money supply so people will have more money to spend, and to think of fiscal policy as Congress and the president fighting recessions by spending more money. In this view, the only difference between fiscal policy and monetary policy would be the source of the money.

To understand what's wrong with the descriptions of fiscal policy and monetary policy just given, first remember that the problem during a recession is not that there is too little *money*—currency plus checking account balances—but too little *spending.* There may be too little spending for a number of reasons. For example, households may cut back on their spending on cars and houses because they are pessimistic about the future. Firms may cut back their spending because they have lowered their estimates of the future profitability of new machinery and factories. Or the major trading partners of the United States—such as Japan and Canada—may be suffering from recessions, which cause households and firms in those countries to cut back their spending on U.S. products.

The purpose of expansionary monetary policy is to lower interest rates, which in turn increases aggregate demand. When interest rates fall, households and firms are willing to borrow more to buy cars, houses, and factories. The purpose of expansionary fiscal policy is to increase aggregate demand by either having the government directly increase its own purchases or by cutting taxes to increase household disposable income and, therefore, consumption spending.

Just as increasing or decreasing the money supply does not have any direct effect on government spending or taxes, increasing or decreasing government spending or taxes will not have any direct effect on the money supply. Fiscal policy and monetary policy have the same goals, but they have different effects on the economy.

***YOUR TURN:* Test your understanding by doing related problem 6 on page 556 at the end of this chapter.**

The Government Purchases and Tax Multipliers

③ LEARNING OBJECTIVE

Explain how the multiplier process works with respect to fiscal policy.

Suppose that during a recession the government decides to use discretionary fiscal policy to increase aggregate demand by spending $100 billion more on constructing subway systems in several cities. How much will equilibrium real GDP increase as a result of this increase in government purchases? We know that the answer is greater than $100 billion because we know the initial increase in aggregate demand will lead to additional increases in income and spending. To build the subways, the government hires private construction firms. These firms will hire more workers to carry out the new construction projects. Newly hired workers will increase their spending on cars, furniture, appliances, and other products. Sellers of these products will increase their production and hire more workers. At each step, real GDP and income will rise, thereby increasing consumption spending and aggregate demand.

Economists refer to the initial increase in government purchases as *autonomous* because it does not depend on the level of real GDP. The increases in consumption spending are *induced* by the initial increase in autonomous spending. Economists refer to the series of induced increases in consumption spending that results from an initial increase in autonomous expenditures as the **multiplier effect.**

Multiplier effect The series of induced increases in consumption spending that results from an initial increase in autonomous expenditures.

Figure 17-7 illustrates how an increase in government purchases affects the aggregate demand curve. The initial increase in government purchases causes the aggregate demand to shift to the right because total spending in the economy is now higher at every price level. The shift to the right from AD_1 to AD_2 represents the impact of the initial increase of $100 billion in government purchases. Because this initial increase in government purchases raises incomes and leads to further increases in consumption spending, the aggregate demand curve will ultimately shift further to the right to AD_3.

To understand the multiplier effect, let's start with a simplified analysis in which we assume that the price level is constant. In other words, initially we will ignore the effect of an upward-sloping *SRAS*. Figure 17-8 shows how spending and real GDP increase over a number of periods beginning with the initial increase in government purchases in the first period, holding the price level constant. The initial spending in the first period raises real GDP and total income in the economy by $100 billion. How much additional consumption spending will result from $100 billion in additional income? We know that in addition to increasing their consumption spending on domestically produced goods, households will save some of the increase in income, use some to pay income taxes, and use some to purchase imported goods, which will have no direct effect on spending and

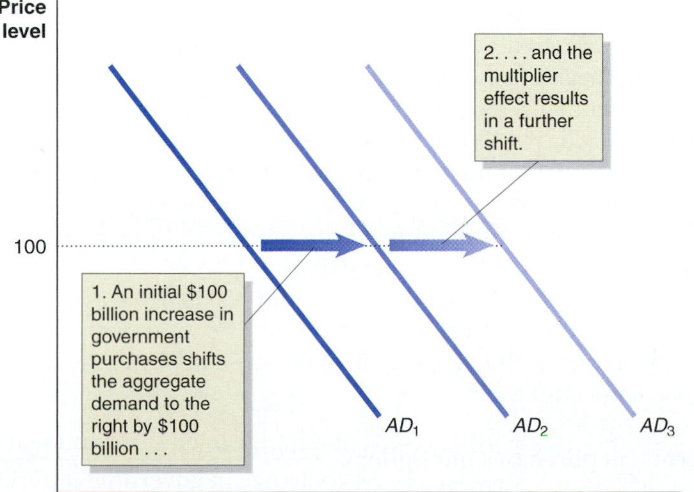

FIGURE 17-7

The Multiplier Effect and Aggregate Demand

An initial increase in government purchases of $100 billion causes the aggregate demand curve to shift to the right from AD_1 to AD_2 and represents the impact of the initial increase of $100 billion in government purchases. Because this initial increase raises incomes and leads to further increases in consumption spending, the aggregate demand curve will shift further to the right to AD_3.

Period	Additional Spending This Period	Cumulative Increase in Spending and Real GDP
1	$100 billion in government purchases	$100 billion
2	$50 billion in consumption spending	$150 billion
3	$25 billion in consumption spending	$175 billion
4	$12.5 billion in consumption spending	$187.5 billion
5	$6.25 billion in consumption spending	$193.75 billion
6	$3.125 billion in consumption spending	$196.875 billion
⋮	⋮	⋮
n	0	$200 billion

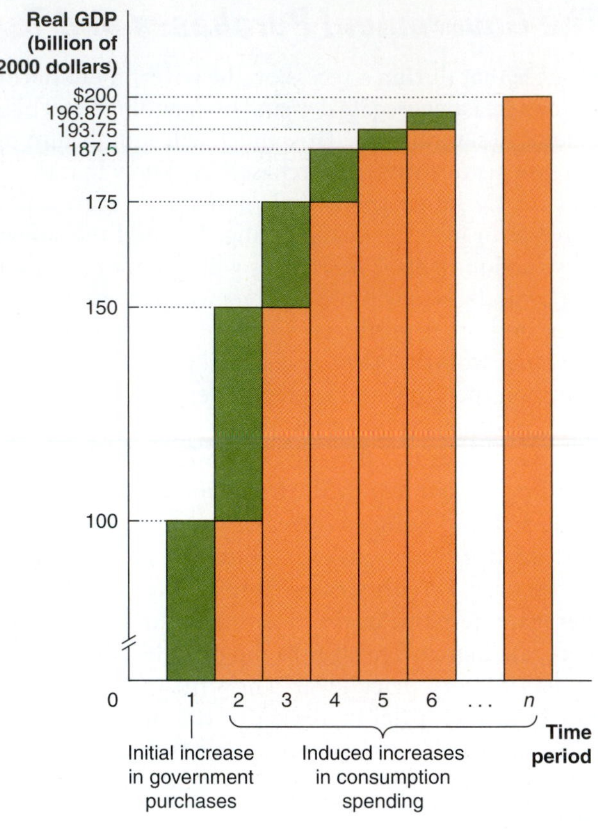

FIGURE 17-8 The Multiplier Effect of an Increase in Government Purchases

Following an initial increase in government purchases, spending and real GDP increase over a number of periods due to the multiplier effect. The new spending and increased real GDP in each period is shown in green, the level of spending from the previous period is shown in orange, so the sum of the orange and green areas represents the cumulative increase in spending and real GDP. In total, equilibrium real GDP will increase by $200 billion as a result of an initial increase of $100 billion in government purchases.

production in the U.S. economy. In Figure 17-8, we assume that in the second period households increase their consumption spending by one-half of the increase in income from the first period—or by $50 billion. This second period spending will, in turn, increase real GDP and income by an additional $50 billion. In the third period, consumption spending will increase by $25 billion, or one-half of the $50 billion increase in income from the second period.

The multiplier effect will continue through a number of periods, with the additional consumption spending in each period being half of the income increase from the previous period. Eventually, the process will be complete, although we cannot say precisely how many periods it will take, so we simply label the final period *n,* rather than giving it a specific number. In the graph in Figure 17-8, the new spending and increased real GDP in each period is shown in green, and the level of spending from the previous period is shown in orange, so the sum of the orange and green areas represents the cumulative increase in spending and real GDP.

How large will the total increase in equilibrium real GDP be as a result of the initial increase of $100 billion in government purchases? The ratio of the change in equilibrium real GDP to the initial change in government purchases is known as the *government purchases multiplier:*

$$\text{Government purchases multiplier} = \frac{\text{Change in equilibrium real GDP}}{\text{Change in government purchases}}.$$

Economists have estimated that the government purchases multiplier has a value of about 2. Therefore, an increase in government purchases of $100 billion should increase equilibrium real GDP by 2 × $100 billion = $200 billion. We show this in Figure 17-8 by having the cumulative increase in real GDP equal $200 billion.

Tax cuts also have a multiplier effect. Cutting taxes increases the disposable income of households. When household disposable income rises, so will consumption spending. These increases in consumption spending will set off further increases in real GDP and income, just as increases in government purchases do. Suppose we consider a change in taxes of a specific amount—say, a tax cut of $100 billion—with the tax *rate* remaining unchanged. The expression for this tax multiplier is:

$$\text{Tax multiplier} = \frac{\text{Change in equilibrium real GDP}}{\text{Change in taxes}}.$$

The tax multiplier is a negative number because changes in taxes and changes in real GDP move in opposite directions: An increase in taxes reduces disposable income, consumption, and real GDP, and a decrease in taxes raises disposable income, consumption, and real GDP. For example, if the tax multiplier is –1.6, a $100 billion *cut* in taxes will increase real GDP by –1.6 × –$100 billion = $160 billion. We would expect the tax multiplier to be smaller in absolute value than the government purchases multiplier. To see why, think about the difference between a $100 billion increase in government purchases and a $100 billion decrease in taxes. The whole of the $100 billion in government purchases results in an increase in aggregate demand. But some portion of a $100 billion decrease in taxes will be saved by households and not spent, and some portion will be spent on imported goods. The fraction of the tax cut that is saved or spent on imports will not increase aggregate demand. Therefore, the first period of the multiplier process will see a smaller increase in aggregate demand than occurs when there is an increase in government purchases, and the total increase in equilibrium real GDP will be smaller.

The Effect of Changes in Tax Rates

A change in tax *rates* has a more complicated effect on equilibrium real GDP than does a tax cut of a fixed amount. To begin, the value of the tax rate affects the size of the multiplier effect. The higher the tax rate, the smaller the multiplier effect. To see why, think about the size of the additional spending increases that take place in each period following an increase in government purchases. The higher the tax rate, the smaller the amount of any increase in income households have available to spend, which reduces the size of the multiplier effect. So, a cut in tax rates effects equilibrium real GDP through two channels: (1) A cut in tax rates increases the disposable income of households, which leads them to increase their consumption spending, and (2) a cut in tax rates increases the size of the multiplier effect.

Taking Into Account the Effects of Aggregate Supply

To this point, we have discussed the multiplier effect assuming that the price level was constant. We know, though, that when the *SRAS* curve is upward sloping, as the *AD* shifts to the right, the price level will rise. As a result of the rise in the price level, equilibrium real GDP will not increase by the full amount the multiplier effect indicates. Figure 17-9 illustrates how an upward-sloping *SRAS* curve affects the size of the multiplier. To keep the graph relatively simple, assume that the *SRAS* and *LRAS* curves do not shift. The economy starts at point *A*, with real GDP below its potential level. An increase in government purchases shifts the aggregate demand curve from AD_1 to AD_2. Just as in Figure 17-7, the multiplier effect causes a further shift in aggregate demand to AD_3. If the price level remained constant, real GDP would increase from $11.0 trillion at point *A* to $12.2 trillion at point *B*. However, because the *SRAS* curve is upward sloping,

FIGURE 17-9

The Multiplier Effect and Aggregate Supply

The economy is initially at point *A*. An increase in government purchases causes the aggregate demand to shift to the right from AD_1 to AD_2. The multiplier effect, results in the aggregate demand curve shifting further to the right to AD_3 (point *B*). Because of the upward-sloping supply curve, the shift in aggregate demand results in a higher price level. In the new equilibrium at point *C*, both real GDP and the price level have increased. The increase in real GDP is less than indicated by the multiplier effect with a constant price level.

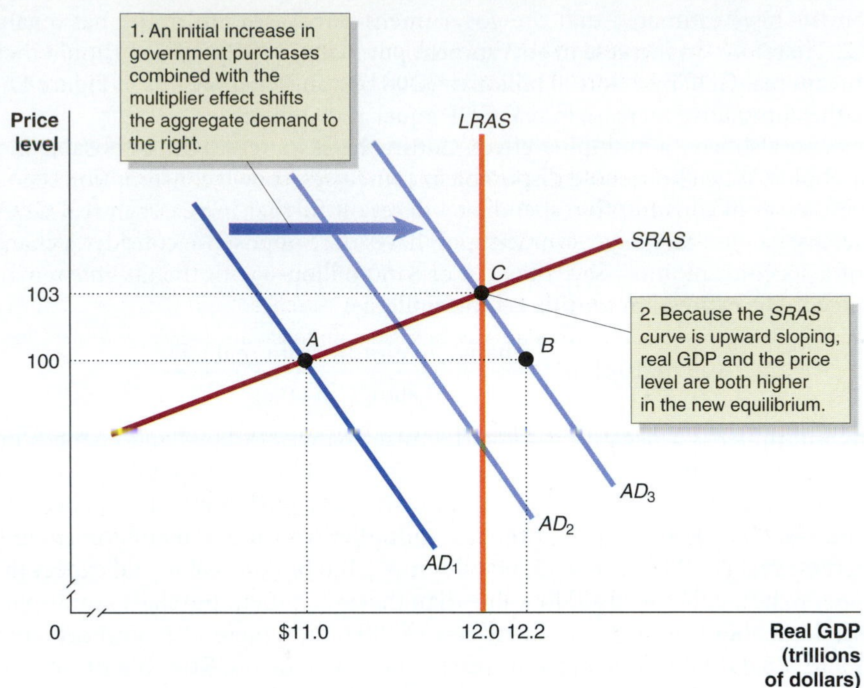

the price level rises from 100 to 103, reducing the total quantity of goods and services demanded in the economy. The new equilibrium occurs at point *C* with real GDP having risen to $12.0 trillion, or by $200 billion less than if the price level had remained unchanged. We can conclude that the actual change in real GDP resulting from an increase in government purchases or a cut in taxes will be less than indicated by the simple multiplier effect with a constant price level.

The Multipliers Work in Both Directions

Increases in government purchases and cuts in taxes have a positive multiplier effect on equilibrium real GDP. Decreases in government purchases and increases in taxes also have a multiplier effect on equilibrium real GDP, only in this case the effect is negative. For example, an increase in taxes will reduce household disposable income and consumption spending. As households buy fewer cars, furniture, refrigerators, and other products, the firms that sell these products will cut back on production and begin laying off workers. Falling incomes will lead to further reductions in consumption spending. A reduction in government spending on defense would set off a similar process of decreases in real GDP and income. The cutback would be felt first by defense contractors selling directly to the government, but then it would spread to other firms.

We look more closely at the government purchases multiplier and the tax multiplier in the Appendix to this chapter.

SOLVED PROBLEM 17-1

③ **LEARNING OBJECTIVE**

Explain how the multiplier process works with respect to fiscal policy.

Fiscal Policy Multipliers

Briefly explain whether you agree or disagree with the following statement: "Real GDP is currently $12.2 trillion, and potential real GDP is $12.5 trillion. If Congress and the president would increase government purchases by $300 billion or cut taxes by $300 billion, the economy could be brought to equilibrium at potential GDP."

Solving the Problem:

Step 1: Review the chapter material. This problem is about the multiplier process, so you may want to review the section "The Government Purchases and Tax Multipliers," which begins on page 531.

Step 2: Explain how the necessary increase in purchases or cut in taxes is less than $300 billion because of the multiplier effect. The statement is incorrect because it neglects the multiplier effect. Because of the multiplier effect, an increase in government purchases or a decrease in taxes of less than $300 billion is necessary to increase equilibrium real GDP by $300 billion. For instance, assume that the government purchases multiplier is 2 and the tax multiplier is –1.6. We can then calculate the necessary increase in government purchases as follows:

$$\text{Government purchases multiplier} = \frac{\text{Change in equilibrium real GDP}}{\text{Change in government purchases}}$$

$$2 = \frac{\$300\text{ billion}}{\text{Change in government purchases}}$$

$$\text{Change in government purchases} = \frac{\$300\text{ billion}}{2} = \$150\text{ billion.}$$

And the necessary change in taxes:

$$\text{Tax multiplier} = \frac{\text{Change in equilibrium real GDP}}{\text{Change in taxes}}$$

$$-1.6 = \frac{\$300\text{ billion}}{\text{Change in taxes}}$$

$$\text{Change in taxes} = \frac{\$300\text{ billion}}{-1.6} = -\$187.5\text{ billion.}$$

YOUR TURN: **For more practice, do related problem 3 on page 556 at the end of this chapter.**

The Limits of Using Fiscal Policy to Stabilize the Economy

(4) **LEARNING OBJECTIVE**

Discuss the difficulties that can arise in implementing fiscal policy.

Poorly timed fiscal policy, like poorly timed monetary policy, can do more harm than good. As we discussed in Chapter 16, it takes time for policymakers to collect statistics and identify changes in the economy. If the government decides to increase spending or cut taxes to fight a recession that is about to end, the effect may be to increase the inflation rate. Similarly, cutting spending or raising taxes to slow down an economy that has actually already moved into recession can make the recession longer and deeper.

Getting the timing right can be more difficult with fiscal policy than with monetary policy for two main reasons. Control over monetary policy is concentrated in the hands of the Federal Open Market Committee, which can change monetary policy at any of its meetings. By contrast, the president and a majority of the 535 members of Congress have to agree on changes in fiscal policy. Usually, the president initiates a change in fiscal policy by asking a member of Congress to introduce a *bill*, a proposed change in the law, that would increase or decrease spending or taxes. Figure 17-10 shows the many steps involved before a bill can become law.

The delays caused by the legislative process can be very long. For example, in 1962 President John F. Kennedy concluded the U.S. economy was operating below potential GDP and proposed a tax cut to stimulate aggregate demand. Congress eventually agreed to the tax cut—but not until 1964.

Once a change in fiscal policy has been approved, it takes time to implement the policy. Suppose Congress and the president agree to increase aggregate demand by

FIGURE 17-10

How a Bill Becomes Law

Fiscal policy actions require passing new laws. But the process of passing a new law can be very long and complicated, as this figure shows.

Source: *We the People: An Introduction to American Politics*, Third Edition by Benjamin Ginsberg, Theodore J. Lowi & Margaret Weir. Copyright © 2001, 1999, 1997 by W. W. Norton & Company, Inc. Used by permission of W. W. Norton & Company, Inc.

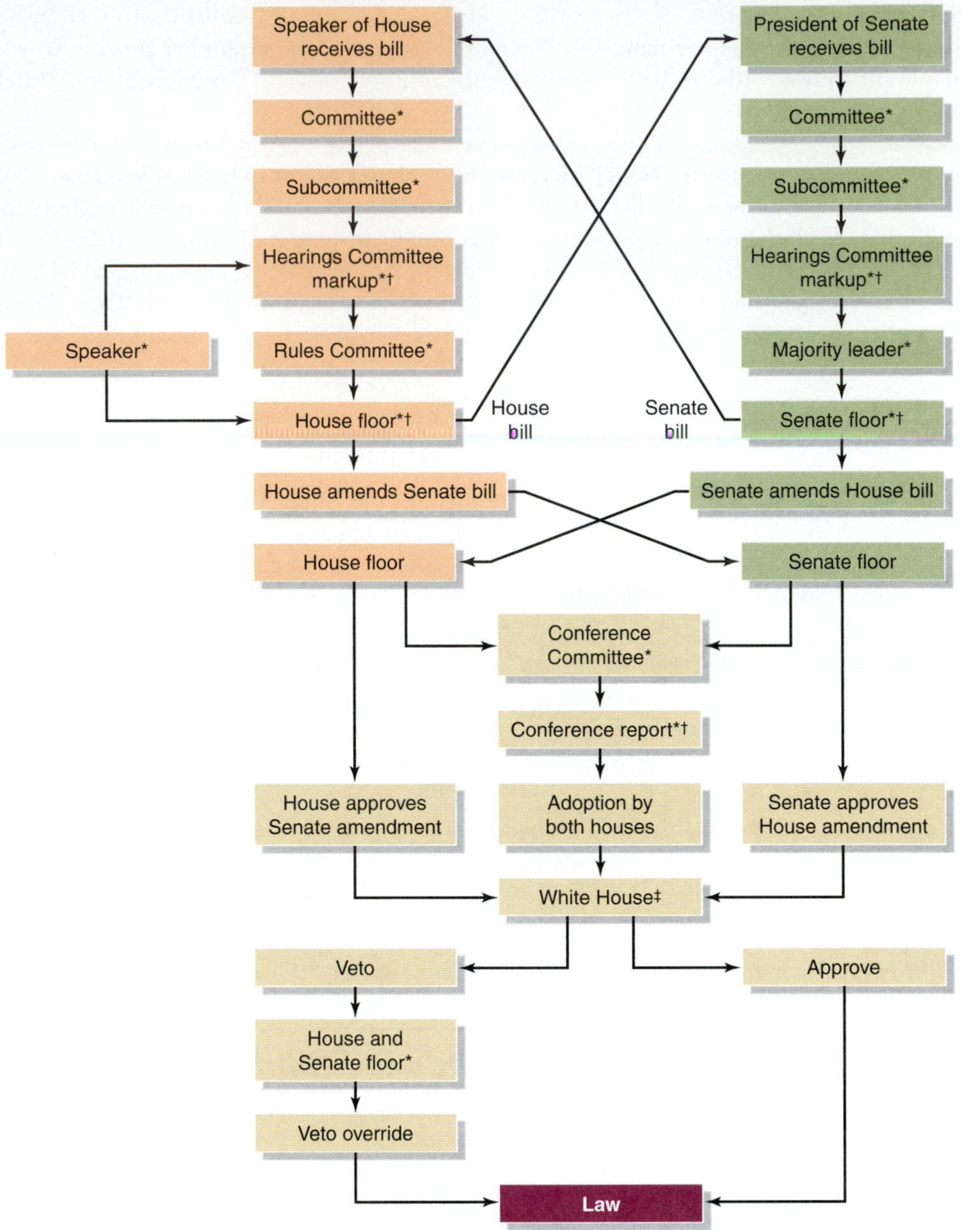

*Points at which a bill can be amended.
†Points at which a bill can die.
‡If the president neither signs nor vetoes a bill within ten days, it automatically becomes law.

spending $30 billion more on constructing subway systems in several cities. It will probably take at least several months to prepare detailed plans for the construction. Local governments will then ask for bids from private construction companies. Once the winning bidders have been selected, they will usually need several months to begin the project. Only then will significant amounts of spending actually take place. This delay may push the spending beyond the end of the recession that the spending was intended to fight.

The events of 2001 showed that it is possible to change fiscal policy in a timely manner. When President George W. Bush came into office in January 2001, he immediately proposed a tax cut. Congress passed the tax cut and the president signed it into law in early June 2001. As mentioned at the beginning of this chapter, the federal government put the tax cut into effect by mailing checks to taxpayers during the summer of 2001.

This increase in household disposable income helped increase consumption spending and contributed in part to the 2001 recession being short and relatively mild. The 2002 and 2003 tax cuts proposed by President Bush were also approved quickly. But Congress and the president use fiscal policy relatively infrequently because they are well aware of the timing problem. The Fed plays a larger role in stabilizing the economy because it can quickly change monetary policy in response to changing economic conditions.

Does Government Spending Reduce Private Spending?

In addition to the timing problem, using increases in government purchases to increase aggregate demand presents another potential problem. We have been assuming that when the federal government increases its purchases by $30 billion, the multiplier effect will cause the increase in aggregate demand to be greater than $30 billion. However, the size of the multiplier effect may be limited if the increase in government purchases causes one of the nongovernment, or private, components of aggregate expenditures—consumption, investment, or net exports—to fall. A decline in private expenditures as a result of an increase in government purchases is called **crowding out.**

Crowding out A decline in private expenditures as a result of an increase in government purchases.

Crowding Out in the Short Run

First, consider the case of a temporary increase in government purchases. Suppose the federal government decides to fight a recession by spending $30 billion more this year on subway construction. Once the $30 billion has been spent, the program will end and government spending will drop back to its previous level. As the spending takes place, income and real GDP will increase. These increases in income and real GDP will cause households and firms to increase their demand for currency and checking account balances to accommodate the increased buying and selling. Figure 17-11 shows the result, using the money market diagram introduced in Chapter 16.

At higher levels of real GDP and income, households and firms demand more money at every level of the interest rate. When the demand for money increases, the equilibrium interest rate will rise. Higher interest rates will result in a decline in each component of private expenditures. Consumption spending and investment spending will decline because households will borrow less to buy cars, furniture, and appliances, and firms will borrow less to buy factories, computers, and machine tools. Net exports will also decline because higher interest rates in the United States will attract

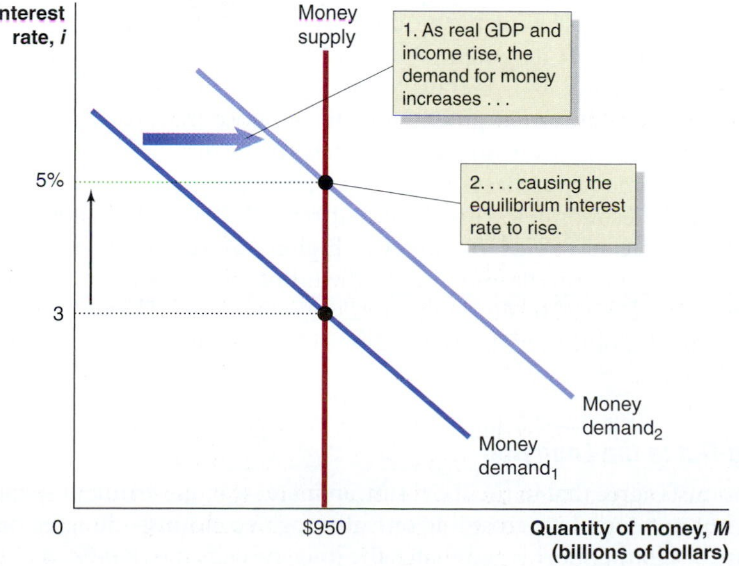

FIGURE 17-11

An Expansionary Fiscal Policy Increases Interest Rates

If the federal government increases spending, the demand for money will increase from Money demand$_1$ to Money demand$_2$ as real GDP and income rise. With the supply of money constant at $950 billion, the result is an increase in the equilibrium interest rate from 3 percent to 5 percent, which crowds out some consumption, investment, and net exports.

FIGURE 17-12

The Effect of Crowding Out in the Short Run

The economy begins at potential real GDP of $12 trillion (point *A*). In the second year, *LRAS* increases to $12.4 trillion, but *AD* fails to increase by enough to keep the economy in macroeconomic equilibrium at potential GDP. In the absence of crowding out, an increase in government purchases would shift aggregate demand to AD_2 (no crowding out) and bring the economy to equilibrium at potential real GDP of $12.4 trillion (point *B*). But the higher interest rate resulting from the increased government purchases reduces consumption, investment, and net exports, causing aggregate demand to shift only to AD_2 (crowding out). The result is a new short-run equilibrium at point *C*, with real GDP of $12.3 trillion, which is $100 billion short of potential real GDP.

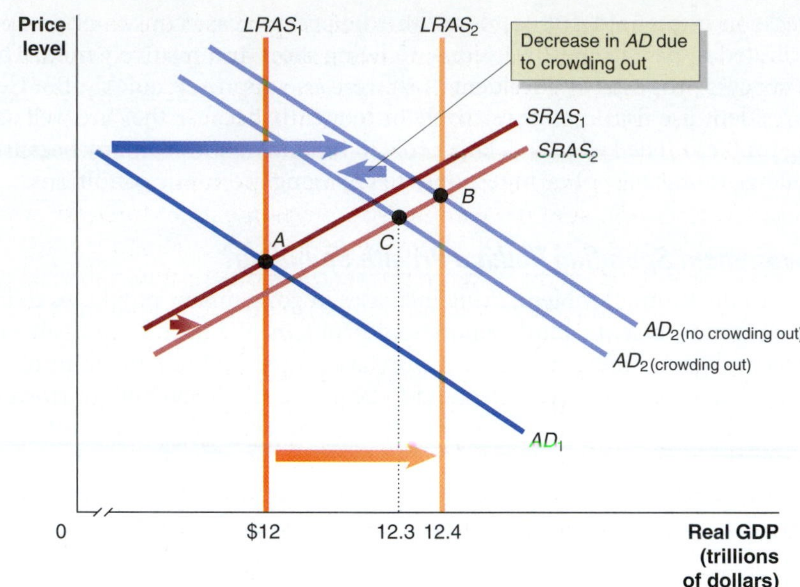

foreign investors. German, Japanese, and Canadian investors will want to exchange the currencies of their countries for U.S. dollars to invest in U.S. Treasury bills and other U.S. financial assets. This increased demand for U.S. dollars will cause an increase in the exchange rate between the dollar and other currencies. When the dollar increases in value, the prices of U.S. products in foreign countries rise—causing a reduction in U.S. exports—and the prices of foreign products in the United States fall—causing an increase in U.S. imports. Falling exports and rising imports mean that net exports are falling.

The greater the sensitivity of consumption, investment, and net exports to changes in interest rates, the more crowding out will occur. In a deep recession, many firms may be so pessimistic about the future and have so much excess capacity that investment spending falls to very low levels and is unlikely to fall much further even if interest rates rise. In this case, crowding out is unlikely to be a problem. If the economy is close to potential GDP, however, and firms are optimistic about the future, then an increase in interest rates may result in a significant decline in investment spending.

Figure 17-12 shows that crowding out may prevent an expansionary fiscal policy from meeting its goal of keeping the economy at potential GDP. The economy begins at point *A* with real GDP at its potential level of $12 trillion. In the second year, *LRAS* increases to $12.4 trillion, but *AD* fails to increase by enough to keep the economy in macroeconomic equilibrium at potential GDP. Suppose that Congress and the president decide to increase government purchases. In the absence of crowding out, the increase in government purchases would shift aggregate demand to AD_2(no crowding out) and bring the economy to equilibrium at real GDP of $12.4 trillion, which is the full-employment level (point *B*). But the higher interest rate resulting from the increased government purchases reduces consumption, investment, and net exports, causing aggregate demand to shift only to AD_2(crowding out). The result is a new short-run equilibrium at point *C*, with real GDP of $12.3 trillion, which is $100 billion short of potential GDP.

Crowding Out in the Long Run

Most economists agree that in the short run, an increase in government spending results in partial, but not complete, crowding out, although economists disagree on the extent of crowding out in the short run. What is the long-run effect of a *permanent* increase in government spending? In this case, most economists agree that the result is complete crowding out. In the long run, the decline in investment, consumption, and net exports exactly offsets the increase in government purchases, and aggregate demand remains unchanged. To understand crowding out in the long run, recall from Chapter 14 that *in the long run the economy returns to potential GDP.* Suppose that the economy is currently at potential GDP and that government purchases are 35 percent of GDP. In that case, private expenditures—the sum of consumption, investment, and net exports—will make up the other 65 percent of GDP. If government purchases are increased permanently to 37 percent of GDP, in the long run private expenditures must fall to 63 percent of GDP. There has been complete crowding out: Private expenditures have fallen by the same amount that government purchases have increased. If government spending is taking a larger share of GDP, then private spending must take a smaller share.

An expansionary fiscal policy does not have to cause complete crowding out in the short run. If the economy is below potential real GDP, it is possible for both government purchases and private expenditures to increase. But in the long run, any permanent increase in government purchases must come at the expense of private expenditures. Keep in mind, however, that it may take several, possibly many, years to arrive at this long-run outcome.

17-2 Making the Connection

Limits to Fiscal Policy: Japan in the Late 1990s

As we saw in Chapter 16, the Japanese economy did not perform well in the 1990s. From 1950 to 1990, real GDP in Japan grew at an average annual rate of 6.9 percent, but from 1992 to 2004 it grew at a rate of only 1.4 percent. Even after the Bank of Japan drove the overnight bank lending rate to 0 percent, investment spending did not increase enough to bring the Japanese economy back to potential GDP.

The Japanese government has also used fiscal policy in an attempt to stimulate the economy. Government expenditures increased from about 30 percent of GDP in 1991 to about 40 percent in 2001. Tax revenues fell from about 34 percent of GDP to about 31 percent. Many of the new spending projects involved building new bridges, roads, and airports, but some unusual spending programs were financed by grants from the central government to local governments. Kumamoto prefecture (a prefecture is similar to a U.S. state) in southern Japan hired unemployed workers to collect deer droppings, which researchers used to estimate the size of the local deer population. Shiga prefecture sent unemployed workers to mark dirty city streets on a map in its "Program to Investigate the True Condition of Litter." Together these spending increases and tax cuts resulted in large budget deficits. By the end of 2005, Japan's government debt was 160 percent of its GDP, the highest of any industrial country.

Yet fiscal policy seemed unable to bring the Japanese economy back to potential GDP. There is disagreement among economists as to why fiscal policy appears to have been ineffective in Japan. Some economists argue that fiscal policy was more effective than it seemed because without an expansionary fiscal policy, Japan would have plunged into deep recession, rather than just slow growth. During the late 1980s and early 1990s,

Fiscal policy in Japan has not been effective in expanding real GDP and reducing unemployment.

prices of many assets, particularly real estate and stocks, soared to unsustainable levels. The collapse of asset prices in the early 1990s led to reductions in consumption and investment spending that were partly offset by expansionary fiscal policy. In that sense, these economists argue, fiscal policy was at least a partial success.

Other economists argue that severe problems in the Japanese banking system made it difficult for households and firms to secure the loans necessary to finance spending. They argue that fiscal policy needed to be accompanied by reform of the banking system. Still other economists have argued that the level of investment spending in Japan is so low relative to what is needed to ensure that the economy is at potential GDP that even a very expansionary fiscal policy has not been enough to fill the gap. Finally, some economists have emphasized the wasteful nature of much of the government spending. They believe that a better-designed fiscal policy would have been more effective.

Sources: Yumiko Ono, "Japan's New Deal," *Wall Street Journal,* March 19, 2002; James Brooke, "Japan's Premier Muses on a Recovery-Proof Economy," *New York Times,* March 29, 2002; Robert H. Raashe and Daniel L. Thornton, "The Monetary/Fiscal Policy Debate: A Controlled Experiment," *Monetary Trends,* October 2001; "The Incredible Shrinking Country," *Economist,* November 11, 2004; and "Japan's Economy," *Economist,* August 22, 2005.

(5) LEARNING OBJECTIVE

Explain how the federal budget can serve as an automatic stabilizer.

Budget deficit The situation in which the government's spending is greater than its tax revenue.

Budget surplus The situation in which the government's expenditures are less than its tax revenue.

Deficits, Surpluses, and Federal Government Debt

The federal government's budget shows the relationship between its expenditures and its tax revenue. If the federal government's expenditures are greater than its revenue, a **budget deficit** results. If the federal government's expenditures are less than its tax revenue, a **budget surplus** results. As with many macroeconomic variables, it is useful to consider the size of the surplus or deficit relative to the size of the overall economy. Figure 17-13 shows that, as a percentage of GDP, the largest deficits of the twentieth century came during World Wars I and II. During major wars, massive increases in government spending are only partially offset by higher taxes, leaving large budget deficits. Figure 17-13 also shows large deficits during recessions. Government spending increases during recessions and tax revenues fall, increasing the budget deficit. The federal government entered into a long period of continuous budget deficits in 1970. From 1970 through 1997, the federal government's budget was in deficit every year. From 1998 through 2001, there were four years of budget surpluses. The recession of 2001, tax cuts, and increased government spending on homeland security and the wars in Iraq and Afghanistan all helped keep the budget in deficit in the years after 2001.

How the Federal Budget Can Serve as an Automatic Stabilizer

The federal budget deficit sometimes increases during recessions because of discretionary fiscal policy actions. Discretionary increases in spending or cuts in taxes to increase aggregate demand during a recession will increase the budget deficit. For example, the decision to cut taxes during 2001 reduced federal revenues, holding constant other factors that affect the budget. As we saw earlier, in many recessions no significant fiscal policy actions are taken. In fact, most of the increase in the federal budget deficit during recessions takes place without Congress and the president taking any action because of the effects of the *automatic stabilizers* we briefly mentioned earlier in this chapter.

Deficits occur automatically during recessions for two reasons: First, during a recession, wages and profits fall, causing government tax revenues to fall. Second, the government automatically increases its spending on transfer payments when the economy moves into recession. The government's contribution to the unemployment insurance program will increase as unemployment rises. Spending will also increase on programs to aid poor people, such as the Food Stamp, Temporary Assistance for Needy Families, and Medicaid programs. These spending increases take place without Congress and the president taking any action. Existing laws already specify who is eligible for unemploy-

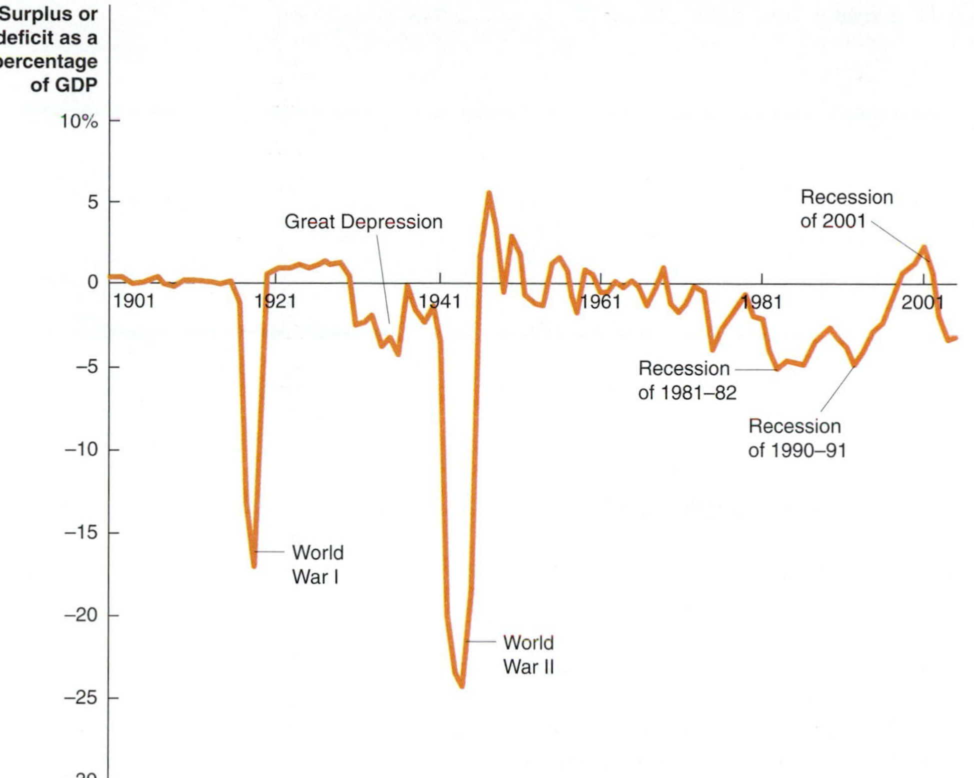

FIGURE 17-13

The Federal Budget Deficit, 1901–2004

During wars, government spending increases far more than tax revenues, increasing the budget deficit. The budget deficit also increases during recessions, as government spending increases and tax revenues fall.

Sources: *Budget of the United States Government, Fiscal Year 2003, Historical Tables,* Washington, D.C.: U.S. Government Printing Office, 2002: and Bureau of Economic Analysis.

ment insurance and these other programs. As the number of eligible persons increases during a recession, so does government spending on these programs.

Because budget deficits automatically increase during recessions and decrease during expansions, economists often look at the **cyclically adjusted budget deficit or surplus,** which can provide a more accurate measure of the effects on the economy of the government's spending and tax policies than the actual budget deficit or surplus. The cyclically adjusted budget deficit or surplus measures what the deficit or surplus would be if the economy were at potential GDP.

Cyclically adjusted budget deficit or surplus The deficit or surplus in the federal government's budget if the economy were at potential GDP.

In Figure 17-14, the federal budget is balanced at potential GDP, but it moves into surplus when GDP is above its potential level and into deficit when GDP is below its potential level. Suppose the tax code and levels of government expenditures are such that the federal budget is balanced when GDP is at its potential level of $12 trillion. If GDP is greater than $12 trillion, the increased tax revenue and the decreased transfer payments will result in a budget surplus. If GDP is less than $12 trillion, the reduced tax revenue and the increased transfer payments will result in a budget deficit.

These automatic budget surpluses and deficits can help to stabilize the economy. When the economy moves into a recession, wages and profits fall, which reduces the taxes that households and firms owe the government. In effect, households and firms have received an automatic tax cut, which keeps their spending higher than it otherwise would have been. In a recession, workers who have been laid off receive unemployment insurance payments, and households whose incomes have dropped below a certain level become eligible for food stamps and other government transfer programs. As a result of receiving this extra income, these households will spend more than they otherwise would have spent. This extra spending helps reduce the length and severity of the recession. Many economists argue that lack of an unemployment insurance system or other government transfer programs contributed to the severity of the Great Depression. During the Great Depression, workers who lost their jobs saw their wage incomes drop to zero and had to rely on their savings, what they could borrow, or what they received

FIGURE 17-14

How the Level of GDP Affects the Cyclically Adjusted Budget Deficit

Suppose the federal budget is balanced at potential real GDP of $12 trillion. If GDP is above $12 trillion, there will be a budget surplus. If GDP is below $12 trillion, there will be a budget deficit.

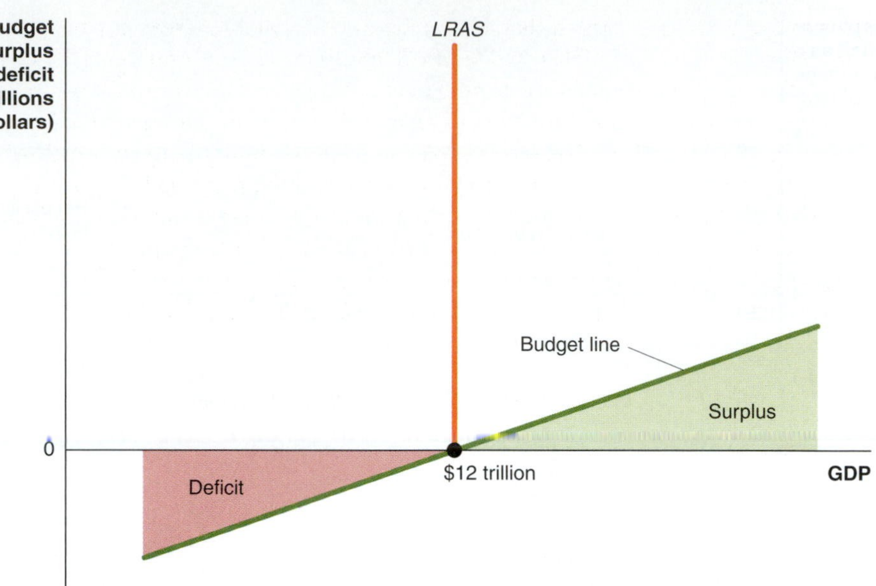

from private charities. As a result, many cut back drastically on their spending, which made the downturn worse.

When GDP increases above its potential level, households and firms have to pay more taxes to the federal government and the federal government makes fewer transfer payments. Higher taxes and lower transfer payments cause total spending to rise by less than it otherwise would have, which helps reduce the chance that the economy will experience higher inflation.

17-3 Making the Connection

Did Fiscal Policy Fail during the Great Depression?

Modern macroeconomics began during the 1930s with publication of *The General Theory of Employment, Interest, and Money* by John Maynard Keynes. One conclusion many economists drew from Keynes's book was that an expansionary fiscal policy would be necessary to pull the United States out of the Great Depression. When Franklin D. Roosevelt became president in 1933, federal government expenditures increased and there was a federal budget deficit each remaining year of the decade, except for 1937. The U.S. economy recovered very slowly, however, and did not reach potential real GDP again until the outbreak of World War II in 1941.

Although government spending increased during the Great Depression, the cyclically adjusted budget was in surplus most years.

Some economists and policymakers at the time argued that because the economy recovered slowly despite increases in government spending, fiscal policy had been ineffective. In separate studies, economists E. Cary Brown of MIT and Larry Peppers of Washington and Lee University argued that, in fact, fiscal policy had not been expansionary during the 1930s. The following table provides the data supporting the arguments of Brown and Peppers (all variables in the table are nominal, rather than real). The first column shows federal government expenditures increasing from 1933 to 1936, falling in 1937, and then increasing in 1938 and 1939. The second column shows a similar pattern, with the federal budget being in deficit each year after 1933, with the exception of 1937. The third column, though, shows that in each year after 1933 the federal government ran a cyclically adjusted budget *surplus*. Because the level of income was so low and the unemployment rate was so high during these years, tax collections were far below what they would have been if the economy had been at potential GDP. As the fourth column shows, in 1933 and again in the years 1937 to 1939, the cyclically adjusted surpluses were quite large relative to GDP.

	FEDERAL GOVERNMENT EXPENDITURES (BILLIONS OF DOLLARS)	ACTUAL FEDERAL BUDGET DEFICIT OR SURPLUS (BILLIONS OF DOLLARS)	CYCLICALLY ADJUSTED BUDGET DEFICIT OR SURPLUS (BILLIONS OF DOLLARS)	CYCLICALLY ADJUSTED BUDGET DEFICIT OR SURPLUS AS A PERCENTAGE OF GDP
1929	$2.6	$1.0	$1.24	1.20%
1930	2.7	0.2	0.81	0.89
1931	4.0	–2.1	–0.41	–0.54
1932	3.0	–1.3	0.50	0.85
1933	3.4	–0.9	1.06	1.88
1934	5.5	–2.2	0.09	0.14
1935	5.6	–1.9	0.54	0.74
1936	7.8	–3.2	0.47	0.56
1937	6.4	0.2	2.55	2.77
1938	7.3	–1.3	2.47	2.87
1939	8.4	–2.1	2.00	2.17

Although President Roosevelt did propose many new government spending programs, he had also promised during the 1932 presidential election campaign to balance the federal budget. Although he achieved a balanced budget only in 1937, his reluctance to allow the actual budget deficit to grow too large helps explain why the cyclically adjusted budget remained in surplus. Many economists today would agree with E. Cary Brown's conclusion: "Fiscal policy, then, seems to have been an unsuccessful recovery device in the 'thirties—not because it did not work, but because it was not tried."

Sources: E. Cary Brown, "Fiscal Policy in the 'Thirties: A Reappraisal," *American Economic Review*, Vol. 46, No. 5, December 1956, pp. 857–879; Larry Peppers, "Full Employment Surplus Analysis and Structural Changes," *Explorations in Economic History*, Vol. 10, Winter 1973, pp. 197–210; and Bureau of Economic Analysis.

SOLVED PROBLEM 17-2

The Effect of Economic Fluctuations on the Budget Deficit

(5) LEARNING OBJECTIVE

Explain how the federal budget can serve as an automatic stabilizer.

The federal government's budget deficit was $207.8 billion in 1983 and $185.4 billion in 1984. Someone comments, "The government must have acted during 1984 to raise taxes or cut spending or both." Do you agree? Briefly explain.

Solving the Problem:

Step 1: Review the chapter material. This problem is about the federal budget as an automatic stabilizer, so you may want to review the section "How the Federal Budget Can Serve as an Automatic Stabilizer," which begins on page 540.

Step 2: Explain how changes in the budget deficit can occur without Congress and the president acting. If Congress and the president take action to raise taxes or cut spending, the federal budget deficit will decline. But the deficit will also decline automatically when GDP increases, even if the government takes no action. When GDP increases, rising household incomes and firm profits result in higher tax revenues. Increasing GDP also usually means falling unemployment, which reduces government spending on unemployment insurance and other transfer payments. So, you should disagree with the comment. A falling deficit does not mean that the government *must* have acted to raise taxes or cut spending.

Extra Credit: Although you don't have to know it to answer the question, GDP did increase from $3.5 trillion in 1983 to $3.9 trillion in 1984.

***YOUR TURN:* For more practice, do related problem 11 on page 556 at the end of this chapter.**

Should the Federal Budget Always Be Balanced?

Although many economists believe that it is a good idea for the federal government to have a balanced budget when the economy is at potential GDP, few economists believe that the federal government should attempt to balance its budget every year. To see why economists take this view, consider what the government would have to do to keep the budget balanced during a recession, when the federal budget automatically moves into deficit. To bring the budget back into balance, the government would have to raise taxes or cut spending, but these actions would reduce aggregate demand, thereby making the recession worse. Similarly, when GDP increases above its potential level, the budget automatically moves into surplus. To eliminate this surplus, the government would have to cut taxes or increase government spending. But these actions would increase aggregate demand, thereby increasing GDP further beyond potential GDP and raising the risk of higher inflation. To balance the budget every year, the government might have to take actions that would destabilize the economy.

Some economists argue that the federal government should normally run a deficit even at potential GDP. When the federal budget is in deficit, the U.S. Treasury sells bonds to investors to raise the funds necessary to pay the government's bills. Borrowing to pay the bills is a bad policy for a household, firm, or government when the bills are for current expenses, but it is not a bad policy if the bills are for long-lived capital goods. For instance, most families pay for a new home by taking out a 15- to 30-year mortgage. Because houses last many years, it makes sense to pay for the house out of the income the family makes over a long period of time, rather than out of the income received in the year the house is bought. Businesses often borrow the funds to buy machinery, equipment, and factories by selling 30-year corporate bonds. Because these capital goods generate profits for the businesses over many years, it makes sense to pay for them over a period of years as well. By similar reasoning, when the federal government contributes to the building of a new highway, bridge, or subway, it may want to borrow funds by selling Treasury bonds. The alternative is to pay for these long-lived capital goods out of the tax revenues received in the year the goods were purchased. But that means that the taxpayers in that year have to bear the whole burden of paying for the projects even though taxpayers for many years in the future will be enjoying the benefits.

The Federal Government Debt

Every time the federal government runs a budget deficit, the Treasury must borrow funds from investors by selling Treasury securities. For simplicity, we will refer to all Treasury securities as "bonds." When the federal government runs a budget surplus, the

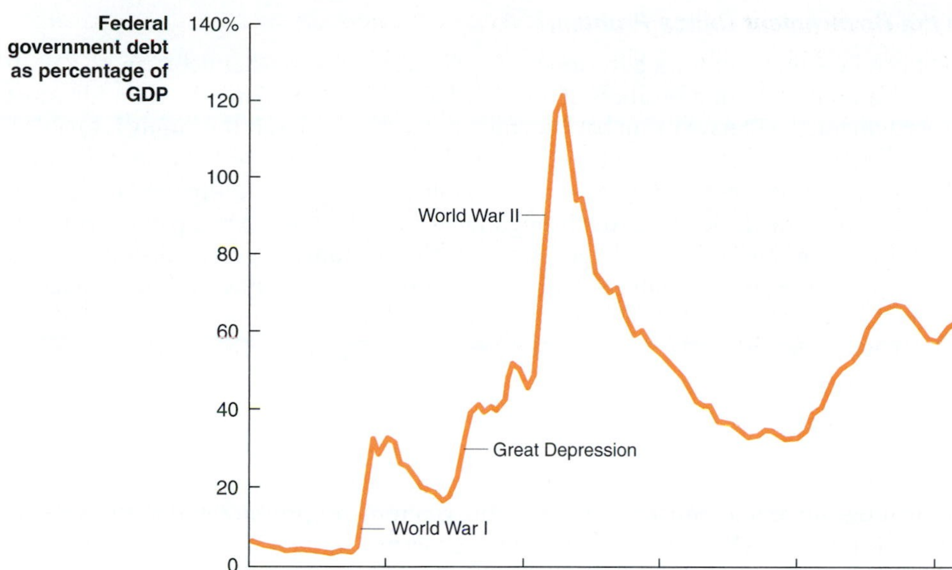

FIGURE 17-15 The Federal Government Debt, 1901–2004

The federal government debt increases whenever the federal government runs a budget deficit. The large deficits incurred during World Wars I and II, the Great Depression, and the 1980s and early 1990s increased the ratio of debt to GDP.

Sources: *Historical Statistics of the United States; Budget of the United States Government, Fiscal Year 2003, Historical Tables;* and Federal Reserve Bank of St. Louis, *National Economic Trends,* July 2005.

Treasury pays off some existing bonds. Figure 17-13 shows that there are many more years of federal budget deficits than years of federal budget surpluses. As a result, the total number of Treasury bonds has grown over the years. The total value of U.S. Treasury bonds outstanding is referred to as the *federal government debt* or, sometimes, as the *national debt.* Each year the federal budget is in deficit, the federal government debt grows. Each year the federal budget is in surplus, the debt shrinks.

Figure 17-15 shows federal government debt as a percentage of GDP over the last 100 years. The ratio of debt to GDP increased during World Wars I and II and the Great Depression, reflecting the large government budget deficits of those years. After the end of World War II, GDP grew faster than the debt until the early 1980s, which caused the ratio of debt to GDP to fall. The large budget deficits of the 1980s and early 1990s sent the debt-to-GDP ratio climbing. The budget surpluses of 1997 to 2001 caused the debt-to-GDP ratio to fall, but it rose again with the return of deficits beginning in 2002.

At the end of June 2005, the federal government debt was $7.9 trillion, but more than half of this debt was actually held by agencies of the federal government, including the Federal Reserve. In effect, the Treasury had borrowed more than half the debt from other agencies of the federal government. It may seem strange that other agencies of the federal government have purchased more than half of the bonds, or debt, issued by the Treasury. This has happened for two reasons. First, as discussed in Chapter 15, the Federal Reserve increases the money supply by buying Treasury bonds. As the economy grows, the Fed provides additional money to households and firms by adding more and more Treasury bonds to its holdings. By the end of June 2005, the Fed had accumulated about $725 billion worth of Treasury bonds. Second, the impact of the baby boom on the Social Security and Medicare systems has led the *Social Security and Medicare trust fund* to acquire more than $3.5 trillion worth of Treasury debt. Once the baby boomers retire, these bonds will be redeemed.

Is the Government Debt a Problem?

Debt can be a problem for a government for the same reasons that debt can be a problem for a household or a business. If a family has difficulty making the monthly mortgage payment, it will have to cut back spending on other things. If the family is unable to make the payments, it will have to *default* on the loan and will probably lose its house. The federal government is in no danger of defaulting on its debt. Ultimately, the government can raise the funds it needs through taxes to make the interest payments on the debt. If the debt becomes very large relative to the economy, however, the government may have to raise taxes to high levels or cut back on other types of spending to make the interest payments on the debt. Interest payments are currently about 10 percent of total federal expenditures. At this level, tax increases or significant cutbacks in other types of federal spending are not required.

In the long run, a debt that increases in size relative to GDP can pose a problem. As we discussed previously, crowding out of investment spending may occur if an increasing debt drives up interest rates. Lower investment spending means a lower capital stock in the long run and a reduced capacity of the economy to produce goods and services. This effect is somewhat offset if some of the government debt was incurred to finance improvements in *infrastructure,* such as bridges, highways, and ports, to finance education, or to finance research and development. Improvements in infrastructure, a better educated labor force, and additional research and development can add to the productive capacity of the economy.

⑥ LEARNING OBJECTIVE

Discuss the long-run effects of fiscal policy.

The Effects of Fiscal Policy in the Long Run

Some fiscal policy actions are intended to meet short-run goals of stabilizing the economy. Other fiscal policy actions are intended to have long-run effects by expanding the productive capacity of the economy and increasing the rate of economic growth. Because these policy actions primarily affect aggregate supply rather than aggregate demand, they are sometimes referred to as *supply-side economics.* Most fiscal policy actions that attempt to increase aggregate supply do so by changing taxes to increase the incentives to work, save, invest, and start a business.

The Long-Run Effects of Tax Policy

Tax wedge The difference between the pre-tax and post-tax return to an economic activity.

The difference between the pre-tax and post-tax return to an economic activity is known as the **tax wedge.** The tax wedge applies to the *marginal tax rate,* which is the fraction of each additional dollar of income that must be paid in taxes. For example, in 2005, the U.S. federal income tax has several tax brackets, which are the income ranges within which a tax rate applies. For a single taxpayer, the tax rate is 10 percent on the first $7,300 earned during a year. The tax rate rises for higher income brackets, until it reaches 35 percent on income earned above $326,450. Suppose you are paid a wage of $20 per hour. If your marginal income tax rate is 25 percent, then your after-tax wage is $15, and the tax wedge is $5. When discussing the model of demand and supply in Chapter 3, we saw that increasing the price of a good or service increases the quantity supplied. So, we would expect that reducing the tax wedge by cutting the marginal tax rate on income would result in a larger quantity of labor supplied because the after-tax wage would be higher. Similarly, we saw in Chapter 13 that a reduction in the income tax would increase the after-tax return to saving, causing an increase in the supply of loanable funds, a lower equilibrium interest rate, and an increase in investment spending. In general, economists believe that the smaller the tax wedge for any economic activity—such as working, saving, investing, or starting a business—the more of that economic activity that will occur.

We can look briefly at the effects on aggregate supply of cutting each of the following taxes:

- ***Individual income tax.*** As we have seen, reducing the marginal tax rates on individual income will reduce the tax wedge faced by workers, thereby increasing the quantity of labor supplied. Many small businesses are *sole proprietorships,* whose profits are taxed at the individual income tax rates. Therefore, cutting the individual income tax rates also raises the return to entrepreneurship, encouraging the opening of new businesses. Most households are also taxed on their returns from saving at the individual income tax rates. Reducing marginal income tax rates, therefore, also increases the return to saving.
- ***Corporate income tax.*** The federal government taxes the profits earned by corporations under the corporate income tax. In 2005, most corporations faced a marginal corporate tax rate of 35 percent. Cutting the marginal corporate income tax rate would encourage investment spending by increasing the return corporations receive from new investments in equipment, factories, and office buildings. Because innovations are often embodied in new investment goods, cutting the corporate income tax potentially can increase the pace of technological change.
- ***Taxes on dividends and capital gains.*** Corporations distribute some of their profits to shareholders in the form of payments known as *dividends.* Shareholders also may benefit from higher corporate profits by receiving *capital gains.* A capital gain is the change in the price of an asset, such as a share of stock. Rising profits usually result in rising stock prices, and capital gains to shareholders. Individuals pay taxes on both dividends and capital gains (although the tax on capital gains can be postponed if the stock is not sold). As a result, the same earnings are, in effect, taxed twice: once when corporations pay the corporate income tax on their profits, and again when the profits are received by individual investors in the form of dividends or capital gains. Economists debate the costs and benefits of a separate tax on corporate profits. With the corporate income tax remaining in place, one way to reduce the "double taxation" problem is to reduce the taxes on dividends and capital gains. These taxes were, in fact, reduced in 2003, and currently the marginal tax rates on dividends and capital gains are well below the top marginal tax rate on individual income. Lowering the tax rates on dividends and capital gains increases the supply of loanable funds from household to firms, increasing saving and investment and lowering the equilibrium real interest rate.

Tax Simplification

In addition to the potential gains from cutting individual taxes, there are also gains from tax simplification. As we saw at the beginning of the chapter, the complexity of the tax code has created a whole industry of tax preparation services, such as H&R Block. The tax code is extremely complex and is almost 3,000 pages long. The Internal Revenue Service estimates that taxpayers spend more than 6 billion hours each year filling out their tax forms. Households and firms have to deal with more than 480 tax forms to file their federal taxes. It is not surprising that there are more H&R Block offices around the country than Starbucks coffeehouses.

If the tax code were greatly simplified, the economic resources currently used by the tax preparation industry would be available to produce other goods and services. In addition to wasting resources, the complexity of the tax code may also distort the decisions taken by households and firms. For example, the tax rate on dividends has clearly affected whether corporations pay dividends. When Congress passed a reduction in the tax on dividends in 2003, many firms—including Microsoft—began paying a dividend for the first time. A simplified tax code would increase economic efficiency by reducing the number of decisions made by households and firms solely to reduce their tax payments.

17-4 Making the Connection

Should the United States simplify the tax code by moving to a flat tax?

Should the United States Adopt the "Flat Tax"?

In thinking about fundamental tax reform, some economists and policymakers have advocated simplifying the individual income tax by adopting a "flat tax." A flat tax would replace the current individual income tax system, with its many tax brackets, exemptions, and deductions, with a new system containing few, or perhaps no, deductions and exemptions and a single tax rate.

The proposal received publicity in the United States during the 2000 presidential election campaign when candidate Steve Forbes proposed the tax system be changed so that a family of four would pay no taxes on the first $36,000 of income and be taxed at a flat rate of 17 percent on income above that level. Under Forbes's proposal, corporate profits would also be taxed at a flat rate of 17 percent. The marginal tax rate of 17 percent is well below the top marginal tax rates on individual and corporate income. During the campaign Forbes declared, "The flat tax would be so simple, you could fill your tax return out on a postcard."

In 1994, Estonia became the first country to adopt a flat tax when it began imposing a single tax rate of 26 percent on individual income. As the table shows, a number of other countries in Eastern Europe have followed Estonia's lead. Although all these countries have a flat tax rate on income, they vary in the amount of annual income they allow to be exempt from the tax and on which income is taxable. For example, Estonia does not tax corporate profits directly, although it does tax dividends paid by corporations to shareholders.

COUNTRY	FLAT TAX RATE	YEAR FLAT TAX WAS INTRODUCED
Estonia	26%	1994
Lithuania	33	1994
Latvia	25	1995
Russia	13	2001
Serbia	14	2003
Ukraine	13	2004
Slovakia	19	2004
Georgia	12	2005
Romania	16	2005

Governments in Eastern Europe are attracted by the simplicity of the flat tax. It is easy for taxpayers to understand and easy for the government to administer. The result has been greater compliance with the tax code. A study of the effects of Russia's moving to a flat tax found that, before tax reform, Russians whose incomes had placed them in the two highest tax brackets had on average been reporting only 52 percent of their income to the government. In 2001, with the new single 13-percent tax bracket in place, these high-income groups on average reported 68 percent of their income to the government.

In the United States and Western Europe, proponents of the flat tax have focused on the reduction in paperwork and compliance cost and the potential increases in labor supply, saving, and investment that would result from a lower marginal tax rate. Opponents of the flat tax believe it has two key weaknesses. First, they point out that many of the provisions that make the current tax code so complex were enacted for good reasons. For example, currently taxpayers are allowed to deduct from their taxable income the interest they pay on mortgage loans. For many people, this provision of the tax code reduces the after-tax cost of owning a home, thereby aiding the government's goal of increasing home ownership. Similarly, the limited deduction for educational expenses increases the ability of many people to further their or their children's educations. The tax deduction of $2,000 in 2004 and 2005 for the purchase of hybrid cars that combine an electric motor with a gasoline-powered engine were intended to further the goal of reducing air pollution and oil consumption. These and other deductions would be eliminated under most flat tax proposals, thereby reducing the ability of the government to pursue some policy goals.

Second, opponents of the flat tax believe that it would make the distribution of income more unequal by reducing the marginal tax rate on high-income taxpayers. Because high-income taxpayers now can sometimes use the intricacies of the tax code to shelter a large fraction of their income from taxes, it is unclear whether the amount of taxes paid by high-income people actually would decrease under a flat tax.

Sources: "The Case for Flat Taxes," *Economist*, April 14, 2005; and Juan Carlos Conesa and Dirk Krueger, "On the Optimal Progressivity of the Income Tax Code," National Bureau of Economic Research, Working Paper 11044, January 2005.

The Economic Effect of Tax Reform

We can analyze the economic effects of tax reduction and simplification using the aggregate demand and aggregate supply model. Figure 17-16 shows that without tax changes the long-run aggregate supply curve will shift from $LRAS_1$ to $LRAS_2$. This shift reflects the increases in the labor force and the capital stock and the technological change that would occur even without tax reduction and simplification. As we know from our discussion of the *AD-AS* model in Chapter 14, during any year the aggregate demand and short-run aggregate supply curves will also shift. To focus on the impact of tax changes on aggregate supply, we will ignore the short-run aggregate supply curve and we will assume that the aggregate demand remains unchanged at AD_1. In this case, equilibrium moves from point *A* to point *B*, with real GDP increasing from Y_1 to Y_2, and the price level decreasing from P_1 to P_2.

If tax reduction and simplification is effective, the economy will experience increases in labor supply, saving, investment, and the formation of new firms. Economic efficiency will also be improved. Together these factors will result in an increase in the quantity of real GDP supplied at every price level. We show the effects of the tax changes in Figure 17-16 by a shift in long-run aggregate supply to $LRAS_3$. With aggregate demand remaining unchanged, the equilibrium in the economy moves from point *A* to point *C* (rather than to point *B*, which is the equilibrium without tax changes), with real GDP increasing from Y_1 to Y_3, and the price level decreasing from P_1 to P_3. An important point to notice is that compared with the equilibrium without tax changes (point *B*) the equilibrium with tax changes (point *C*) occurs at a lower price level and a higher level of real GDP. We can conclude that the tax changes have benefited the economy by increasing output and employment, while at the same time reducing the price level.

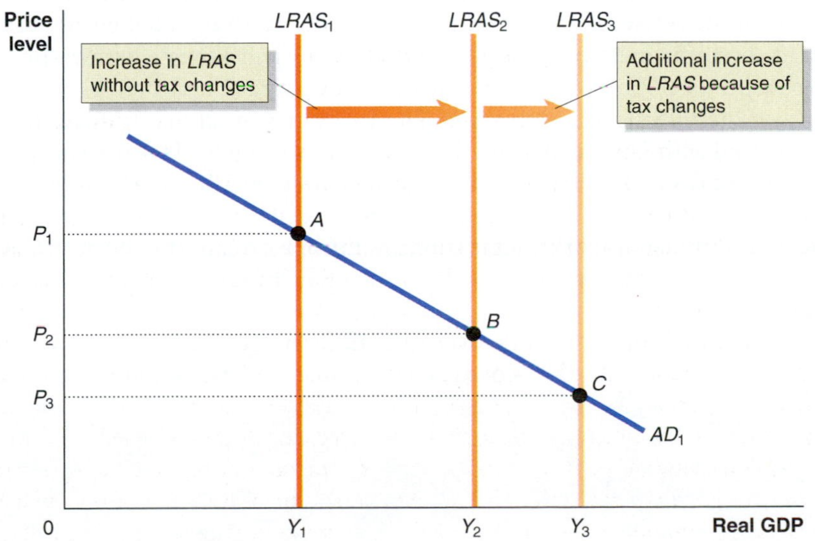

FIGURE 17-16

The Supply-Side Effects of a Tax Change

The economy's initial equilibrium is at point *A*. With no tax change, long-run aggregate supply shifts to the right from $LRAS_1$ to $LRAS_2$. Equilibrium moves to point *B*, with the price level falling from P_1 to P_2 and real GDP increasing from Y_1 to Y_2. With tax reductions and simplifications, long-run aggregate supply shifts further to the right to $LRAS_3$ and equilibrium moves to point *C*, with the price level falling to P_3 and real GDP increasing to Y_3.

Clearly our analysis is unrealistic because we ignored the changes in aggregate demand and short-run aggregate supply that will actually occur. How would a more realistic analysis differ from the simplified one in Figure 17-16? The change in real GDP would be the same because in the long run real GDP is equal to its potential level, which is represented by the long-run aggregate supply curve. The results for the price level would be different, however, because we would expect both aggregate demand and short-run aggregate supply to shift to the right. The likeliest case is that the price level would end up higher in the new equilibrium than in the original equilibrium. However, because the position of the long-run aggregate supply curve is further to the right as a result of the tax changes, the increase in the price level will be smaller—that is, the price level at point *C* is likely to be lower than at point *B*, even if it is higher than at point *A*, although—as we will discuss in the next section—not all economists would agree with this conclusion. We can conclude that a successful policy of tax reductions and simplifications will benefit the economy by increasing output and employment and, at the same time, may result in smaller increases in the price level.

How Large Are Supply-Side Effects?

Most economists would agree that there are supply-side effects to reducing taxes: Decreasing marginal income tax rates will increase the quantity of labor supplied, cutting the corporate income tax will increase investment spending, and so on. The magnitude of the effects is subject to considerable debate, however. For example, some economists argue that the increase in the quantity of labor supplied following a tax cut will be limited because many people work a number of hours set by their employers and lack the opportunity to work additional hours. Similarly, some economists believe that tax changes have only a small effect on saving and investment. In this view, saving and investment are affected much more by changes in income or changes in expectations of the future profitability of new investment due to technological change or improving macroeconomic conditions than they are by tax changes.

Economists who are skeptical of the magnitude of supply-side effects believe that tax cuts have their greatest impact on aggregate demand, rather than on aggregate supply. In their view, focusing on the impact of tax cuts on aggregate demand, while ignoring any impact on aggregate supply, yields accurate forecasts of future movements in real GDP and the price level, which indicates that the supply-side effects must be small. If tax changes have only small effects on aggregate supply, it is unlikely that they will reduce the size of price increases, as they did in the analysis in Figure 17-16.

Ultimately, the size of the supply-side effects of tax policy can be resolved only by careful studies of the effects of differences in tax rates on labor supply and saving and investment decisions. Here again, economists are not always in agreement. For example, a recent study by Nobel laureate Edward Prescott of Arizona State University concludes that the differences between the United States and Europe with respect to the average number of hours worked per week and the average number of weeks worked per year are due to differences in taxes. The lower marginal tax rates in the United States compared with Europe increase the return to working for U.S. workers and result in a larger quantity of labor supplied. But another study by Alberto Alesina and Edward Glaeser of Harvard University and Bruce Sacerdote of Dartmouth College argues that the more restrictive labor market regulations in Europe explain the shorter work weeks and longer vacations of European workers and that differences in taxes have only a small effect.

As in other areas of economics, over time differences among economists in their estimates of the supply-side effects of tax changes may narrow as additional studies are undertaken.

Conclusion

In this chapter, we have seen how the federal government uses changes in government purchases and taxes to achieve its economic policy goals. We have seen that economists debate the effectiveness of discretionary fiscal policy actions intended to stabilize the economy. In the short run, the focus of fiscal policy tends to be on its effects on aggregate demand. In the long run, changes in tax rates may also have an effect on aggregate supply. Congress and the president share responsibility for fiscal policy.

Read *An Inside Look* on the next page for a discussion of changes in the federal budget deficit.

An Inside Look

Tax Receipts Increase in 2005, but Deficit Still Looms Large

THE ECONOMIST GLOBAL AGENDA, AUGUST 16, 2005

The Not-So-Incredible Shrinking Deficit

A new forecast from the Congressional Budget Office shows America's budget deficit once again coming in lower than expected. Republicans, unsurprisingly, are rushing to claim credit for sound economic management. But the long-term outlook is still soaked in red ink....

Analysts were aghast when the Bush administration's Office of Management and Budget (OMB) projected that the fiscal year to September 2005 would bring bigger deficits still: $427 billion, according to numbers released in February. . . . Figures released by the Congressional Budget Office (CBO) in March projected a deficit of only $365 billion.

. . . In its Budget and Economic Outlook, released on Monday August 15th, the CBO's projections moved roughly into line with the administration's, forecasting a shortfall of $331 billion, or roughly 2.7% of GDP.

a Tom DeLay, the majority leader of the House of Representatives, said that the brighter budget picture "should come as no surprise" to anyone familiar with the Republican platform of cutting taxes to spur economic growth. Many voters are also prepared to give Mr. Bush the benefit of the doubt. The economy, after all, seems to be chugging along nicely. Real GDP grew at a solid 3.4% in the second quarter of 2005, an annual rate envied by most European countries. Even America's budget deficit doesn't look so bad when compared with the likes of Italy and Germany.

Democrats, of course, pooh-pooed the notion that a mere third of a trillion dollars-worth of new debt was anything to smile about. More significantly, Douglas Holtz-Eakin, the CBO's director, gave a warning that the improvement, while welcome, seemed to be largely temporary. The CBO's report attributes most of the decrease to an unexpected surge in corporate income tax receipts, thanks to double-digit growth in corporate profits since the end of the 2001 slowdown. But the boom in profits cannot be sustained over the long term, especially since much of the increase seems to stem from short-lived changes to the tax code.

Further out into the forecast period, the CBO says its outlook is largely unchanged. The deficit will shrink slowly until 2010, then drop sharply as Mr. Bush's tax cuts expire....

All of this is, of course, more art than science. The CBO itself notes that even if there are no legislative changes in levels of taxation or spending, the vagaries of economic forecasting mean that there is a 25% chance that the budget will be in balance, or show a surplus, in 2010—and a 10% chance that that year will see a budget deficit greater than 5.9% of GDP....

b But there's one prediction it is making with a high degree of confidence: Social Security and Medicare, America's old-age programs, will eat up an increasing share of federal spending and thus spell big trouble for the budget. The first "baby boomers" will be eligible for early retirement in 2008....

The CBO's forecasting period does not stretch far enough to cover the biggest shocks to come. It is not until 2017 that Social Security's outflows will begin to exceed its inflows, forcing the government to tap general tax revenues to pay benefits. Excess Social Security contributions have been masking a large portion of the budget deficit for years; without those "off-budget" surpluses, Bill Clinton would have struggled to close the deficit in his last two years in office, and last year's shortfall would have been well over half a trillion dollars.

c As they run up the national charge account, legislators can at least take comfort that the latest round of downward revisions to forecasts seems to cast further doubt on the "twin-deficit hypothesis," which argues that Mr. Bush's spendthrift ways are driving up the current-account deficit and putting the country in danger of a catastrophic revaluation of the dollar. Trade deficits have continued to soar even as budget deficits have come down, which tends to support a theory advanced by Ben Bernanke, the chairman of Mr. Bush's Council of Economic Advisers. He has suggested that a global savings glut is flooding America with cheap money, and that the government deficits may in large part have been mopping up surplus capital that would otherwise have been borrowed by America's already debt-ridden consumers....

Key Points in the Article

The U.S. federal government budget deficit for fiscal year 2005 was lower than most economists had anticipated, thanks to higher-than-expected tax receipts. Republicans attributed the higher tax receipts to President Bush's expansionary fiscal policy of 2001. Meanwhile, Democrats attributed it to a change in the corporate tax code that temporarily increased corporate profits. Nevertheless, both sides agree that the real threat to the federal budget comes shortly after 2015, when Social Security, Medicare, and Medicaid will account for over 50 percent of federal spending and tax revenues dedicated to funding these programs will no longer exceed payouts. Finally, like the federal government, the U.S. economy is also spending beyond its means; however, unlike the federal government deficit, the current account deficit continues to rise.

Analyzing the News

a Republicans and Democrats have very different views on why the federal budget deficit for fiscal year 2005 was less than most forecasters had expected, though both parties agree that higher-than-expected tax receipts had something to do with it. Republicans credit the Bush administration's tax cut of 2001. In particular, they reason that this expansionary fiscal policy increased aggregate demand and real GDP. This pattern is shown in Figure 1, where the aggregate demand curve shifts from AD_1 to AD_2; AD_1 is the economy's aggregate demand curve without an expansionary fiscal policy. Because real GDP represents income, including personal income and corporate profits, as income increases so do tax receipts.

Democrats tend to side on this issue with the Congressional Budget Office (CBO). The CBO attributes much of the decline to a one-time rise in corporate tax receipts, fueled by a change in the corporate tax code that temporarily increased corporate profits.

b Politicians and economists agree that as the U.S. population ages, Social Security, Medicare, and Medicaid will account for an increasing share of federal government expenditures. The CBO estimates that these three programs together will account for over 50 percent of federal spending by 2015. Nevertheless, Social Security and Medicare tax revenues will exceed payouts until about 2017, by which time a large portion of baby boomers will have retired. Ironically, in the meantime net revenues from these programs will add to budget surpluses and reduce budget deficits.

c The *twin-deficit hypothesis* says that federal government deficits and current account deficits are closely related: As the federal government spends beyond its means, so too does the overall economy. The recent behavior of the U.S. economy does not support this hypothesis because, while the federal budget deficit has fallen, the current account deficit has risen. According to Ben Bernanke, then chairman of the Council of Economic Advisers, the large U.S. current account deficits of the last few years were driven, in part, by foreigners' desire to save their wealth—by buying securities and opening bank accounts—in the United States. This so-called savings glut has kept U.S. interest rates low and, hence, has increased the quantity of loanable funds demanded by both the federal government and consumers.

Thinking Critically ABOUT POLICY

1. Suppose that for the U.S. economy actual real GDP is $500 billion less than potential real GDP. To eliminate this gap, the federal government conducts an expansionary fiscal policy; in particular, it increases purchases of goods and services by $200 billion. The government assumes that inflation will remain at zero for the foreseeable future and that the expenditure multiplier is 2.5. Determine the relative effectiveness of this expansionary fiscal policy if, to the surprise of the government, inflation increases as the economy approaches potential GDP.
2. Now suppose actual real GDP is $500 billion greater than potential real GDP. To eliminate this gap, the federal government conducts a contractionary fiscal policy; in particular, it increases income taxes and announces that it will lower income taxes to their original levels in one year. Assess the relative effectiveness of this contractionary fiscal policy.

Source: "The Not-So-Incredible Shrinking Deficit," *The Economist Global Agenda*, August 16, 2005. www.economist.com.

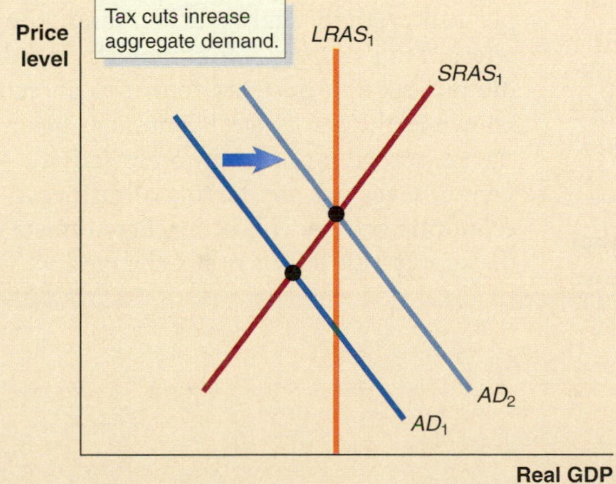

Figure 1: A decrease in taxes causes an increase in aggregate demand and real GDP.

SUMMARY

LEARNING OBJECTIVE ① Define fiscal policy. *Fiscal policy* involves changes in federal taxes and purchases that are intended to achieve macroeconomic policy objectives. Since World War II, the federal government's share of total government expenditures has been between two-thirds and three-quarters. Federal government *expenditures* as a percentage of GDP rose from 1950 to the early 1990s and fell between 1992 and 2001, before rising again. Federal government *purchases* have declined as a percentage of GDP since the end of the Korean War in the early 1950s. The largest component of federal expenditures is transfer payments. The largest source of federal government revenue is social insurance taxes, which are used to fund the Social Security and Medicare systems.

LEARNING OBJECTIVE ② Explain how fiscal policy affects aggregate demand and how the government can use fiscal policy to stabilize the economy. To fight recessions, Congress and the president can increase government purchases or cut taxes. This expansionary policy causes the aggregate demand curve *(AD)* to shift out more than it otherwise would, raising the level of real GDP and the price level. To fight rising inflation, Congress and the president can decrease government purchases or raise taxes. This contractionary policy causes the aggregate demand curve to shift out less than it otherwise would, reducing the increase in real GDP and the price level.

LEARNING OBJECTIVE ③ Explain how the multiplier process works with respect to fiscal policy. Because of the *multiplier effect,* an increase in government purchases or a cut in taxes will have a multiplied effect on equilibrium real GDP. The *government purchases multiplier* is equal to the change in equilibrium real GDP divided by the change in government purchases. The *tax multiplier* is equal to the change in equilibrium real GDP divided by the change in taxes. Increases in government purchases and cuts in taxes have a positive multiplier effect on equilibrium real GDP. Decreases in government purchases and increases in taxes have a negative multiplier effect on equilibrium real GDP.

LEARNING OBJECTIVE ④ Discuss the difficulties that can arise in implementing fiscal policy. Poorly timed fiscal policy can do more harm than good. Getting the timing right with fiscal policy can be difficult because obtaining approval from Congress for a new fiscal policy can be a very long process and because it can take months for an increase in authorized spending to actually take place. Because an increase in government purchases may lead to a higher interest rate, it may result in a decline in consumption, investment, and net exports. A decline in private expenditures as a result of an increase in government purchases is called *crowding out.* Crowding out may cause an expansionary fiscal policy to fail to meet its goal of keeping the economy at potential GDP.

LEARNING OBJECTIVE ⑤ Explain how the federal budget can serve as an automatic stabilizer. A *budget deficit* occurs when the federal government's expenditures are greater than its tax revenues. A *budget surplus* occurs when the federal government's expenditures are less than its tax revenues. The budget deficit automatically increases during recessions and decreases during expansions. The automatic movements in the federal budget help to stabilize the economy by cushioning the fall in spending during recessions and restraining the increase in spending during expansions. The federal government debt is the value of outstanding bonds issued by the U.S. Treasury. More than half of the national debt is actually owned by other federal agencies. The national debt is a problem if interest payments on it require taxes to be raised substantially or other federal expenditures to be cut.

LEARNING OBJECTIVE ⑥ Discuss the long-run effects of fiscal policy. Some fiscal policy actions are intended to have long-run effects by expanding the productive capacity of the economy and increasing the rate of economic growth. Because these policy actions primarily affect aggregate supply rather than aggregate demand, they are sometimes referred to as *supply-side economics.* The difference between the pre-tax and post-tax return to an economic activity is known as the *tax wedge.* Economists believe that the smaller the tax wedge for any economic activity—such as working, saving, investing, or starting a business—the more of that economic activity will occur. Economists debate the size of the supply-side effects of tax changes.

KEY TERMS

Automatic stabilizers 524
Budget deficit 540
Budget surplus 540
Crowding out 537
Cyclically adjusted budget deficit or surplus 541
Fiscal policy 524
Multiplier effect 531
Tax wedge 546

REVIEW QUESTIONS

1. What is fiscal policy? Who is responsible for fiscal policy?
2. What is the difference between fiscal policy and monetary policy?
3. What is the difference between federal purchases and federal expenditures? Are federal purchases higher today than they were in 1960? Are federal expenditures higher today than they were in 1960?
4. If Congress and the president decide an expansionary fiscal policy is necessary, what changes should they make in government spending or taxes? What changes should they make if they decide a contractionary fiscal policy is necessary?
5. Why does a \$1 increase in government purchases lead to more than a \$1 increase in income and spending?
6. Which can be changed more quickly: monetary policy or fiscal policy? Briefly explain.
7. What is meant by crowding out? Explain the difference between crowding out in the short run and in the long run.
8. In what ways does the federal budget serve as an automatic stabilizer for the economy?
9. What is the cyclically adjusted budget deficit or surplus? Suppose that the economy is currently at potential GDP and the federal budget is balanced. If the economy moves into recession, what will happen to the federal budget?
10. Why do most economists argue that it would not be a good idea to balance the federal budget every year?
11. What is the difference between the federal budget deficit and federal government debt?
12. In the United States, why is more than half of federal government debt actually owned by the federal government?
13. What is meant by supply-side economics?

PROBLEMS AND APPLICATIONS

Please visit **www.prenhall.com/hubbard** *for solutions to the even-numbered problems as well as multiple-choice and true or false self-assessment quizzes.*

1. Identify each of the following as (i) part of an expansionary fiscal policy, (ii) part of a contractionary fiscal policy, or (iii) not part of fiscal policy:
   a. The corporate income tax rate is increased.
   b. Defense spending is increased.
   c. Families are allowed to deduct all their expenses for day care from their federal income taxes.
   d. The individual income tax rate is decreased.
   e. The State of New Jersey builds a new highway in an attempt to expand employment in the state.
2. In *The General Theory of Employment, Interest, and Money,* John Maynard Keynes wrote this:

   > If the Treasury were to fill old bottles with banknotes, bury them at suitable depths in disused coal mines which are then filled up to the surface with town rubbish, and leave it to private enterprise . . . to dig the notes up again . . . there need be no more unemployment and, with the help of the repercussions, the real income of the community . . . would probably become a good deal greater than it is.

   Which important macroeconomic effect is Keynes discussing here? What does he mean by "repercussions"? Why does he appear unconcerned if government spending is wasteful?

3. **[Related to *Solved Problem 17-1*]** Briefly explain whether you agree or disagree with the following statement: "Real GDP is currently $12.7 trillion and full-employment real GDP is $12.5 trillion. If Congress and the president would decrease government purchases by $200 billion or increase taxes by $200 billion, the economy could be brought to equilibrium at potential GDP."

4. The following is from a message by President Hoover to Congress, dated May 5, 1932:

> I need not recount that the revenues of the Government as estimated for the next fiscal year show a decrease of about $1,700,000,000 below the fiscal year 1929, and inexorably require a broader basis of taxation and a drastic reduction of expenditures in order to balance the Budget. Nothing is more necessary at this time than balancing the Budget.

Do you think President Hoover was correct in saying that, in 1932, nothing was more necessary than balancing the federal government's budget? Explain.

5. In a column published in the *Wall Street Journal* on July 19, 2001, David Wessel wrote, "Most economic forecasters don't foresee recession this year or next." In fact, a recession had already begun in March of that year. Does this tell us anything about the difficulty of Congress and the president implementing a fiscal policy that stabilizes rather than destabilizes the economy?

Source: David Wessel, "Economic Forecasting in Three Steps," *Wall Street Journal*, July 19, 2001, p. A1.

6. **[Related to *Don't Let This Happen To You!*]** Briefly explain whether you agree with the following remark: "Real GDP is $250 billion below its full-employment level. With a multiplier of 2, if Congress and the president increase government purchases by $125 billion or the Fed increases the money supply by $125 billion, real GDP can be brought back to its full-employment level."

7. Use the graph at the top of the next column to answer the following questions:
   a. If the government does not take any policy actions, what will be the values of real GDP and the price level in 2012?
   b. If the government purchases multiplier is 2, how much will government purchases have to be increased to bring real GDP to its potential level in 2012? (Assume the multiplier value takes into account the impact of a rising price level on the multiplier effect.)
   c. If the tax multiplier is –1.6, how much will taxes have to be cut to bring real GDP to its potential level in 2012? (Again, assume the multiplier value takes into account the impact of a rising price level.)
   d. If the government takes no policy actions, what will be the inflation rate in 2012? If the government uses fiscal policy to keep real GDP at its potential level, what will be the inflation rate in 2012?

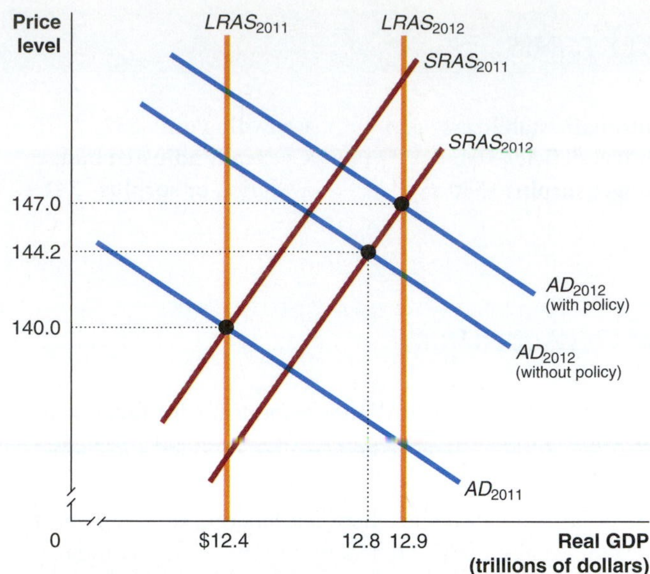

8. Figure 17-11 shows the equilibrium interest rate rising as the demand for money increases. Describe what must be happening in the market for Treasury bills.

9. Some economists argue that because increases in government spending crowd out private spending, increased government spending will reduce the long-run growth rate of real GDP.
   a. Is this most likely to happen if the private spending being crowded out is consumption spending, investment spending, or net exports? Briefly explain.
   b. In terms of its effect on the long-run growth rate of real GDP, would it matter if the additional government spending involves (i) increased spending on highways and bridges, or (ii) increased spending on the national parks? Briefly explain.

10. In his column in the *Wall Street Journal*, David Wessel wrote:

> Global financial markets, politicians, corporate executives and ordinary Americans have confidence in [the Federal Reserve Chairman's] ability to steer the U.S. economy, particularly during times of crisis.

But isn't it Congress and the president, and not the chairman of the Fed, who steer the U.S. economy? Discuss.

Source: David Wessel, "Four Hard-to-Predict Factors that Will Shape the Economy," *Wall Street Journal*, April 4, 2002.

11. **[Related to *Solved Problem 17-2*]** The federal government's budget deficit was $221.4 billion in 1990 and $269.2 billion in 1991. What does this information tell us about fiscal policy actions taken by Congress and the president during these years?

12. The following is from an article in the *Wall Street Journal:*

> The Treasury Department said it expected to borrow a net $1 billion during the April-to-June quarter—not repay a net $89 billion, as it said it would earlier this year.

Why does the Treasury Department borrow? When the Treasury "repays," who is it repaying? Why would the Treasury say it was going to repay debt and then end up borrowing?
Source: Rebecca Christie and Deborah Lagomarsino, "U.S. Debt Is Set to Rise in Quarter as Tax Receipts Come Up Short," *Wall Street Journal*, April 30, 2002.

13. The federal government calculates its budget on a fiscal year that begins each year on October 1 and ends on the following September 30. At the beginning of the 1997 fiscal year, the Congressional Budget Office (CBO) forecast that the federal budget deficit would be $127.7 billion. The actual budget deficit for fiscal 1997 was only $21.9 billion. Federal expenditures were $30.3 billion less than the CBO had forecast, and federal revenue was $75.5 billion more than the CBO had forecast.
    a. Is it likely that the economy grew faster or slower during fiscal 1997 than the CBO had expected? Explain your reasoning.
    b. Suppose that Congress and the president were committed to balancing the budget each year. Does what happened during 1997 provide any insight into difficulties they might run into in trying to balance the budget every year?

14. Paul Samuelson, an economist at MIT and a Nobel Prize winner, argued that:

> It was harmful to let a large budget surplus develop in the weak 1959–60 revival and thereby help to choke off that recovery.

Why would a large budget surplus "choke off" a recovery from economic recession? What could the federal government have done to have kept a large budget surplus from developing?
Source: Paul A. Samuelson, "Economic Policy for 1962," *American Economic Review*, Vol. 44, No. 1 (February 1962), p. 6.

15. In testifying before Congress in 2003, then Federal Reserve Chairman Alan Greenspan observed, "There is no question that if you run substantial and excessive deficits over time you are draining savings from the private sector." What did Greenspan mean by "draining savings from the private sector"? How might this be bad for the economy?
Source: Martin Crutsinger, "Greenspan Warns of Rising Deficits," *Associated Press*, July 17, 2003.

16. The following is from an article in *Business Week:*

> Although the final returns from the April tax season aren't in yet, the results so far suggest that this fiscal year's budget deficit could be as much as double the roughly $50 billion last projected by the Congressional Budget Office. But there is a silver lining: The lower tax receipts mean U.S. consumers have more money to spend.

What is likely to be happening in the economy when a CBO forecast of the federal budget deficit turns out to be too low? What effect will the "silver lining" have on the economy?

17. During 2003, China ran large government budget deficits to stimulate its economy. The *Wall Street Journal* quoted an official in China's ministry of finance as saying, "The proactive fiscal policy has brought some negative effects because it has squeezed out the private investor." What did the official mean by a "proactive fiscal policy"? Why would such a policy "squeeze out" the private investor? Does that mean the policy should not have been used?
Source: Karby Leggett and Kathy Chen, "China's Rising Debt Raises Questions about the Future," *Wall Street Journal*, January 20, 2003.

18. The following was written by a political columnist:

> Today . . . the main purpose [of government's issuing bonds] is to let craven politicians launch projects they know the public, at the moment, would rather not fully finance. The tab for these projects will not come due, probably, until after the politicians have long since departed for greener (excuse the expression) pastures.

Do you agree with this commentator's explanation for why some government spending is financed from tax receipts and other government spending is financed through borrowing, by issuing bonds? Briefly explain.
Source: Paul Carpenter, "The Bond Issue Won't Be Repaid by Park Tolls," (Allentown, PA) *Morning Call*, May 26, 2002, p. B1.

19. **[Related to the *Chapter Opener*]** It would seem that both households and businesses would benefit if the federal income tax were simpler and tax forms were easier to fill out. Why then have the tax laws become increasingly complicated?

20. Suppose a political candidate hired you to develop two arguments in favor of a flat tax. What two arguments would you advance? Alternatively, if you were hired to develop two arguments against the flat tax, what two arguments would you advance?

21. Suppose that an increase in marginal tax rates on individual income affects both aggregate demand and aggregate supply. Briefly describe the effect of the tax increase on equilibrium real GDP and the equilibrium price level. Will the changes in equilibrium real GDP and the price level be larger or smaller than they would be if the tax increase affected only aggregate demand? Briefly explain.

Appendix

A Closer Look at the Multiplier

In this chapter, we saw that changes in government purchases and changes in taxes have a multiplied effect on equilibrium real GDP. In this appendix, we will build a simple economic model of the multiplier effect. When economists forecast the effect of a change in spending or taxes, they often rely on *econometric models.* As we saw in the An econometric model is an economic model written in the form of equations, where each equation has been statistically estimated, using methods similar to those methods used in estimating demand curves as briefly described in Chapter 3.

An Expression for Equilibrium Real GDP

We can write a set of equations that includes the key macroeconomic relationships we have studied in this and previous chapters. It is important to note that in this model we will be assuming that the price level is constant. We know that this is unrealistic because an upward-sloping *SRAS* curve means that when the aggregate demand curve shifts the price level will change. Nevertheless, our model will be approximately correct when changes in the price level are small. It also serves as an introduction to more complicated models that take into account changes in the price level. For simplicity, we also start out by assuming that taxes, T, do not depend on the level of real GDP, Y. We also assume that there are no government transfer payments to households. Finally, we assume that we have a closed economy, with no imports or exports. The numbers (with the exception of the *MPC*) represent billions of dollars.

(1) $C = 1{,}000 + 0.75(Y - T)$	Consumption function
(2) $I = 1{,}500$	Planned investment function
(3) $G = 1{,}500$	Government purchases function
(4) $T = 1{,}000$	Tax function
(5) $Y = C + I + G$	Equilibrium condition

The first equation is the consumption function. The marginal propensity to consume, or *MPC*, is 0.75, and 1,000 is the level of autonomous consumption, which is the level of consumption that does not depend on income. We assume that consumption depends on disposable income, which is $Y - T$. The functions for planned investment spending, government spending, and taxes are very simple because we have assumed that these variables are not affected by GDP and, therefore, are constant. Economists who use this type of model to forecast GDP would, of course, use more realistic planned investment, government purchases, and tax functions.

Equation (5)—the equilibrium condition—states that equilibrium GDP equals the sum of consumption spending, planned investment spending, and government purchases. To calculate a value for equilibrium real GDP, we need to substitute equations (1) through (4) into equation (5). This substitution gives us the following:

$$\begin{aligned} Y &= 1{,}000 + 0.75(Y - 1{,}000) + 1{,}500 + 1{,}500 \\ &= 1{,}000 + 0.75Y - 750 + 1{,}500 + 1{,}500. \end{aligned}$$

We need to solve this equation for Y to find equilibrium GDP. The first step is to subtract $0.75Y$ from both sides of the equation:

$$Y - 0.75Y = 1{,}000 - 750 + 1{,}500 + 1{,}500.$$

Then, we solve for Y:

$$0.25Y = 3{,}250$$

or,

$$Y = \frac{3{,}250}{0.25} = 13{,}000.$$

To make this result more general, we can replace particular values with general values represented by letters:

(1) $C = \overline{C} + MPC(Y - T)$	Consumption function
(2) $I = \overline{I}$	Planned investment function
(3) $G = \overline{G}$	Government purchases function
(4) $T = \overline{T}$	Tax function
(5) $Y = C + I + G$	Equilibrium condition

The letters with "bars" represent fixed or *autonomous* values that do not depend on the values of other variables. So, $\overline{C}$ represents autonomous consumption, which had a value of 1,000 in our original example. Now, solving for equilibrium we get:

$$Y = \overline{C} + MPC(Y - \overline{T}) + \overline{I} + \overline{G}$$

or,

$$Y - MPC(Y) = \overline{C} - (MPC \times \overline{T}) + \overline{I} + \overline{G}$$

or,

$$Y(1 - MPC) = \overline{C} - (MPC \times \overline{T}) + \overline{I} + \overline{G}$$

or,

$$Y = \frac{\overline{C} - (MPC \times \overline{T}) + \overline{I} + \overline{G}}{1 - MPC}.$$

A Formula for the Government Purchases Multiplier

To find a formula for the government purchases multiplier, we need to rewrite the last equation for changes in each variable, rather than levels. Letting Δ stand for the change in a variable, we have:

$$\Delta Y = \frac{\Delta\overline{C} - (MPC \times \Delta\overline{T}) + \Delta\overline{I} + \Delta\overline{G}}{1 - MPC}.$$

If we hold constant changes in autonomous consumption spending, planned investment spending, and taxes, we can find a formula for the government purchases multiplier, which is the ratio of the change in equilibrium real GDP to the change in government purchases:

$$\Delta Y = \frac{\Delta G}{1 - MPC}$$

or,

$$\text{The government purchases multiplier} = \frac{\Delta Y}{\Delta G} = \frac{1}{1 - MPC}.$$

For an *MPC* of 0.75, the government purchases multiplier will be:

$$\frac{1}{1 - 0.75} = 4.$$

A government purchases multiplier of 4 means that an increase in government spending of $10 billion will increase equilibrium real GDP by 4 × $10 billion = $40 billion.

A Formula for the Tax Multiplier

We can also find a formula for the tax multiplier. We start again with this equation:

$$\Delta Y = \frac{\Delta \bar{C} - (MPC \times \Delta \bar{T}) + \Delta \bar{I} + \Delta \bar{G}}{1 - MPC}.$$

Now we hold constant the values of autonomous consumption spending, planned investment spending, and government purchases, but we allow the value of taxes to change:

$$\Delta Y = \frac{-MPC \times \Delta T}{1 - MPC}.$$

Or,

$$\text{The tax multiplier} = \frac{\Delta Y}{\Delta T} = \frac{-MPC}{1 - MPC}.$$

For an *MPC* of 0.75, the tax multiplier will be:

$$\frac{-0.75}{1 - 0.75} = -3.$$

The tax multiplier is a negative number because an increase in taxes causes a decrease in equilibrium real GDP and a decrease in taxes causes an increase in equilibrium real GDP. A tax multiplier of –3 means that a decrease in taxes of $10 billion will increase equilibrium real GDP by –3 × –$10 billion = $30 billion. In this chapter, we discussed the economic reasons for the tax multiplier being smaller than the government spending multiplier.

The "Balanced Budget" Multiplier

What will be the effect of equal increases (or decreases) in government purchases and taxes on equilibrium real GDP? At first, it might appear that the tax increase would exactly offset the government purchases increase, leaving real GDP unchanged. But we have just seen that the government purchases multiplier is larger (in absolute value) than the tax multiplier. We can use our formulas for the government purchases multiplier and the tax multiplier to calculate the net effect of increasing government purchases by $10 billion at the same time that taxes are increased by $10 billion:

$$\text{Increase in real GDP from the increase in government purchases} = \$10 \text{ billion} \times \frac{1}{1 - MPC}$$

$$\text{Decrease in real GDP from the increase in taxes} = \$10 \text{ billion} \times \frac{-MPC}{1 - MPC}$$

So, the combined effect equals:

$$\$10 \text{ billion} \times \left[\left(\frac{1}{1-MPC}\right)+\left(\frac{-MPC}{1-MPC}\right)\right]$$

or,

$$\$10 \text{ billion} \times \left(\frac{1-MPC}{1-MPC}\right) = \$10 \text{ billion}.$$

The balanced budget multiplier is, therefore, equal to $(1 - MPC)/(1 - MPC)$, or 1. Equal dollar increases and decreases in government purchases and in taxes lead to the same dollar increase in real GDP in the short run.

The Effects of Changes in Tax Rates on the Multiplier

We now consider the effect of a change in the tax *rate*, as opposed to a change in a fixed amount of taxes. Changing the tax rate actually changes the value of the multiplier. To see this, suppose the tax rate is 20 percent, or 0.2. In that case, an increase in household income of \$10 billion will increase *disposable income* by only \$8 billion [or, \$10 billion × (1 − 0.2)]. In general, an increase in income can be multiplied by $(1 - t)$ to find the increase in disposable income, where t is the tax rate. So, we can rewrite the consumption function as:

$$C = \overline{C} + MPC(1-t)Y.$$

We can use this expression for the consumption function to find an expression for the government purchases multiplier using the same method as we did previously:

$$\text{Government purchases multiplier} = \frac{\Delta Y}{\Delta G} = \frac{1}{1-MPC(1-t)}.$$

We can see the effect of changing the tax rate on the size of the multiplier by trying some values. First, assume that the $MPC = 0.75$ and $t = 0.2$. Then,

$$\text{Government purchases multiplier} = \frac{\Delta Y}{\Delta G} = \frac{1}{1-0.75(1-0.2)} = \frac{1}{1-0.6} = 2.5.$$

This value is smaller than the multiplier of 4 that we calculated by assuming that there was only a fixed amount of taxes (which is the same as assuming the marginal tax *rate* was zero). This multiplier is smaller because spending in each period is now reduced by the amount of taxes households must pay on any additional income they earn. We can calculate the multiplier for an MPC of 0.75 and a lower tax rate of 0.1:

$$\text{Government purchases multiplier} = \frac{\Delta Y}{\Delta G} = \frac{1}{1-0.75(1-0.1)} = \frac{1}{1-0.675} = 3.1.$$

Cutting the tax rate from 20 percent to 10 percent increased the value of the multiplier from 2.5 to 3.1.

The Multiplier in an Open Economy

Up to now, we have assumed that the economy is closed, with no imports or exports. We can consider the case of an open economy by including net exports in our analysis. Recall that net exports equal exports minus imports. Exports are determined primarily by factors, such as the exchange value of the dollar and the levels of real GDP in other countries, that we do not include in our model. So, we will assume that exports are fixed, or autonomous:

$$\text{Exports} = \overline{Exports}$$

Imports will increase as real GDP increases because households will spend some portion of an increase in income on imports. We can define the *marginal propensity to import* (*MPI*) as the fraction of an increase in income that is spent on imports. So, our expression for imports is:

$$\text{Imports} = MPI \times Y.$$

We can substitute our expressions for exports and imports into the expression we derived earlier for equilibrium real GDP:

$$Y = \overline{C} + MPC(1-t)Y + \overline{I} + \overline{G} + (\overline{Exports} - MPI \times Y),$$

where the expression $\overline{Exports} - MPI \times Y$ represents net exports. We can now find an expression for the government purchases multiplier using the same method as we did previously:

$$\text{Government purchases multiplier} = \frac{\Delta Y}{\Delta G} = \frac{1}{1-[MPC(1-t)-MPI]}.$$

We can see the effect of changing the value of the marginal propensity to import on the size of the multiplier by trying some values of key variables. First, assume $MPC = 0.75$, $t = 0.2$, and $MPI = 0.1$. Then,

$$\text{Government purchases multiplier} = \frac{\Delta Y}{\Delta G} = \frac{1}{1-(0.75(1-0.2)-0.1)} = \frac{1}{1-0.5} = 2.$$

This value is smaller than the multiplier of 2.5 that we calculated by assuming that there were no exports or imports (which is the same as assuming the marginal propensity to import was zero). This multiplier is smaller because spending in each period is now reduced by the amount of imports households buy with any additional income they earn. We can calculate the multiplier with $MPC = 0.75$, $t = 0.20$, and a higher *MPI* of 0.2:

$$\text{Government purchases multiplier} = \frac{\Delta Y}{\Delta G} = \frac{1}{1-(0.75(1-0.2)-0.2)} = \frac{1}{1-0.4} = 1.7.$$

Increasing the marginal propensity to import from 0.1 to 0.2 decreased the value of the multiplier from 2 to 1.7. We can conclude that countries with a higher marginal propensity to import will have smaller multipliers than countries with a lower marginal propensity to import.

It is always important to bear in mind that the multiplier is a short-run effect that assumes that the economy is below the level of potential real GDP. In the long run, the economy is at potential real GDP, so an increase in government purchases causes a decline in the nongovernment components of real GDP, but it leaves the level of real GDP unchanged.

The analysis in this appendix is simplified compared to what would be carried out by an economist forecasting the effects of changes in government purchases or changes in taxes on equilibrium real GDP in the short run. In particular, our assumption that the price level is constant is unrealistic. However, looking more closely at the determinants of the multiplier has helped us see more clearly some important macroeconomic relationships.

PROBLEMS AND APPLICATIONS

Please visit **www.prenhall.com/hubbard** *for solutions to the even-numbered problems as well as multiple-choice and true or false self-assessment quizzes.*

1. Assuming a fixed amount of taxes and a closed economy, calculate the value of the government purchases multiplier, the tax multiplier, and the balanced budget multiplier if the marginal propensity to consume equals 0.6.
2. Calculate the value of the government purchases multiplier if the marginal propensity to consume equals 0.8, the tax rate equals 0.25, and the marginal propensity to import equals 0.2.
3. Show on a graph the change in the aggregate demand curve resulting from an increase in government purchases if the government purchases multiplier equals 2. Now, on the same graph, show the change in the aggregate demand curve resulting from an increase in government purchases if the government purchases multiplier equals 4.
4. From an understanding of the multiplier process, explain why an increase in the tax rate would decrease the size of the government purchases multiplier. Similarly, explain why a decrease in the marginal propensity to import would increase the size of the government purchases multiplier.

chapter eighteen

Comparative Advantage, International Trade, and Exchange Rates

Sugar Quota Drives U.S. Candy Manufacturers Overseas

Trade is, simply, the act of buying or selling. Is there a difference when trade takes place within a country or when the trade is international? Within the United States, domestic trade makes it possible for consumers in Ohio to eat salmon caught in Alaska or for consumers in Montana to drive cars built in Michigan. Similarly, international trade makes it possible for consumers in the United States to drink wine from France or use DVD players from Japan. But one significant difference between domestic trade and international trade is that international trade is more controversial. At one time, nearly all the televisions, shoes, clothing, and toys consumed in the United States were also produced in the United States. Today, these goods are produced mainly by firms in other countries. This shift has benefited U.S. consumers because foreign-made goods have lower prices than the U.S.-made goods they have replaced. But at the same time, many U.S. firms that produced these goods have gone out of business and their workers have lost their jobs. Not surprisingly, opinion polls show that many Americans favor reducing international trade because they believe this would preserve jobs in the United States.

But would it? Congress enacted a sugar quota to preserve jobs in the U.S. sugar industry by reducing the quantity of sugar allowed into the United States. Several countries around the world can produce sugar at lower costs than can U.S. sugar producers. As a result the *world price* of sugar, which is the price at which sugar can be bought on the world market, is too low for U.S. sugar companies to cover their costs. The sugar quota allows U.S. companies to sell sugar domestically for a price that is about three times as high as the world price. Without the sugar quota, competition from foreign sugar producers would drive many U.S. producers out of business. But the United States also has a large candy industry, which uses many tons of sugar. So how have U.S. candy firms and their employees been affected by high sugar prices in the United States?

Life Savers used to be called the "All-American Candy." Life Savers were invented in 1912 by Clarence Crane, who wanted to develop a candy that would not melt in the heat of the summer. Because the sinking

of the cruise liner *Titanic* had been the most publicized event of the year, Crane hit on the idea of selling a hard candy in the shape of a life preserver. Today, Life Savers is no longer advertised as the all-American candy because in 2003 it moved production from Holland, Michigan, to Montreal, Canada. The six hundred workers employed at the Michigan Life Savers plant lost their jobs. The price of sugar is about 21 cents per pound in the United States, but the world price is only about 8 cents per pound. In Canada, Life Savers can be made using sugar purchased at the world price, which saves almost $9 million per year in lower sugar costs.

Life Savers is only one of several candies no longer produced in the United States. Brach's Confections, maker of Star Brites mints, closed its factory in Illinois and moved production to Argentina. Bob's Candies, the largest manufacturer of candy canes, and the Spangler Candy Company, maker of Cherry Balls, have both moved to Mexico.

Should the United States have a sugar quota? The sugar quota creates winners—U.S. sugar companies and their employees—and losers—U.S. companies that use sugar, their employees, and U.S. consumers who must pay higher prices for goods that contain sugar. In this chapter, we will explore who wins and who loses from international trade and review the political debate over whether international trade should be restricted. *An Inside Look* on page 602 discusses a recent trade agreement between the United States and Australia.

LEARNING OBJECTIVES

After studying this chapter, you should be able to:

1. Discuss the increasing importance of international trade to the United States.
2. Understand the difference between comparative advantage and absolute advantage.
3. Explain how countries gain from international trade.
4. Discuss the sources of comparative advantage.
5. Analyze the economic effects of government policies that restrict international trade.
6. Explain how exchange rates are determined and how changes in exchange rates affect the prices of imports and exports.

Markets for internationally traded goods and services can be analyzed using the tools of demand and supply that we developed in Chapter 3. We saw in Chapter 2 that trade in general—whether within a country or between countries—is based on the principle of comparative advantage. In this chapter, we look more closely at how this principle is applied to international trade. We can also use the concepts of consumer surplus, producer surplus, and deadweight loss that were developed in Chapter 4 to analyze government policies, such as the sugar quota, that interfere with trade. With this background we can return to the political debate over the desirability of international trade. In this chapter we also analyze how the exchange rate between the U.S. dollar and other currencies is determined. We begin by looking at how large a role international trade plays in the U.S. economy.

1 LEARNING OBJECTIVE

Discuss the increasing importance of international trade to the United States.

An Overview of International Trade

International trade has grown tremendously over the past 50 years. The increase in trade is the result of the falling costs of shipping products around the world, the spread of cheap and reliable communications, and changes in government policies. Businesspeople today can travel to Europe or Asia using fast, cheap, and reliable air transportation. The Internet allows managers to communicate instantaneously and at a very low cost with customers and suppliers around the world. Firms can use large container ships to send their products across the oceans at low cost. These and other improvements in transportation and communication have created a global marketplace only dreamed about by earlier generations of businesspeople.

Tariff A tax imposed by a government on imports.

Imports Goods and services bought domestically but produced in other countries.

Exports Goods and services produced domestically but sold to other countries.

In addition, over the past 50 years many governments have changed policies to facilitate international trade. For example, tariff rates have fallen. A **tariff** is a tax imposed by a government on *imports* of a good into a country. **Imports** are goods and services bought domestically but produced in other countries. In the 1930s, the United States charged an average tariff rate above 50 percent. Today, the rate is less than 2 percent. In North America, most tariffs between Canada, Mexico, and the United States were eliminated in 1994 with passage of the North American Free Trade Agreement (NAFTA). Twenty-five countries in Europe have formed the European Union, which has eliminated all tariffs among member countries, greatly increasing both imports and **exports,** which are goods and services produced domestically, but sold to other countries.

The Importance of Trade to the U.S. Economy

U.S. consumers buy increasing quantities of goods and services produced in other countries. At the same time, U.S. businesses sell increasing quantities of goods and services to consumers in other countries. Figure 18-1 shows that since 1950, both exports and imports have been steadily increasing as a fraction of U.S. gross domestic product (GDP). Recall that GDP is the value of all the goods and services produced in a country during a year. In 1950, exports and imports were both about 4 percent of GDP. In 2004, exports were about 10 percent of GDP, and imports were about 15 percent.

Not all sectors of the U.S. economy are affected equally by international trade. On the one hand, it's difficult to import or export some services, such as haircuts or appendectomies. On the other hand, a large percentage of U.S. agricultural production is exported. Each year, the United States exports about 50 percent of the wheat crop, 40 percent of the rice crop, and 20 percent of the corn crop.

Many U.S. manufacturing industries also depend on trade. About 20 percent of U.S. manufacturing jobs depend directly or indirectly on exports. In some industries, such as computers, the products these workers make are directly exported. In other industries,

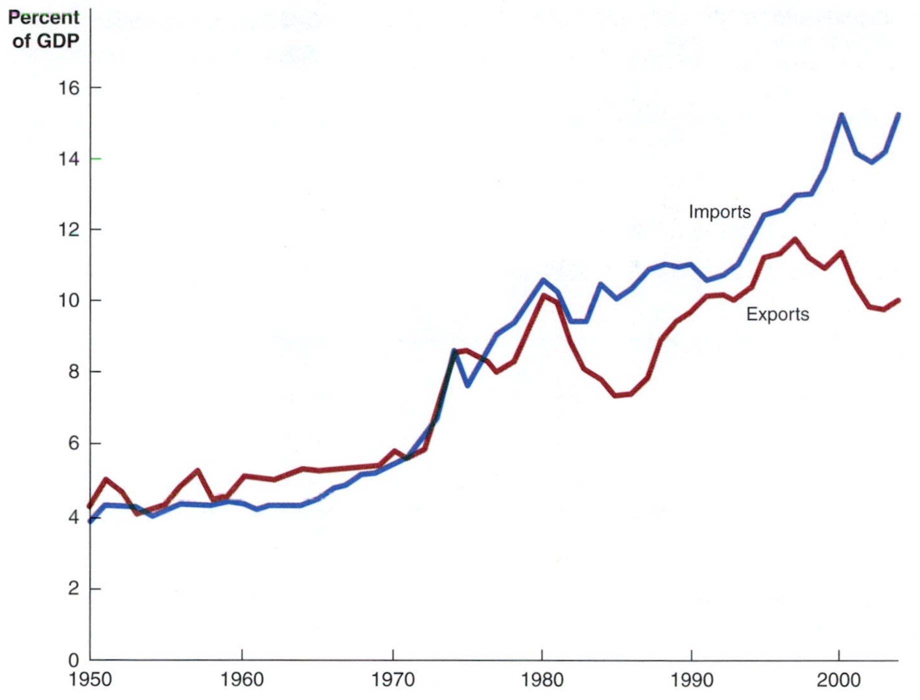

FIGURE 18-1

International Trade Is of Increasing Importance to the United States

Exports and imports of goods and services as a percentage of total production—measured by GDP—show the importance of international trade to an economy. Since 1950, both imports and exports have been steadily rising as a fraction of U.S. GDP.

Source: U.S. Department of Commerce, Bureau of Economic Analysis.

such as steel, the products are used to make other products, such as bulldozers or machine tools, that are then exported. In all, about two-thirds of U.S. manufacturing industries depend on exports for at least 10 percent of jobs.

U.S. International Trade in a World Context

The United States is the largest exporter in the world, as Figure 18-2 illustrates. Six of the other seven leading exporting countries are also large, high-income countries. The rapid growth of the Chinese economy over the past 20 years has resulted in its becoming the fifth largest exporter.

International trade remains less important to the United States than it is to most other countries. Figure 18-3 on the next page shows that imports and exports remain smaller fractions of GDP in the United States than in other countries. In some smaller countries, like Belgium, imports and exports make up more than half of GDP. Japan is the only high-income country that is less dependent on international trade than is the United States.

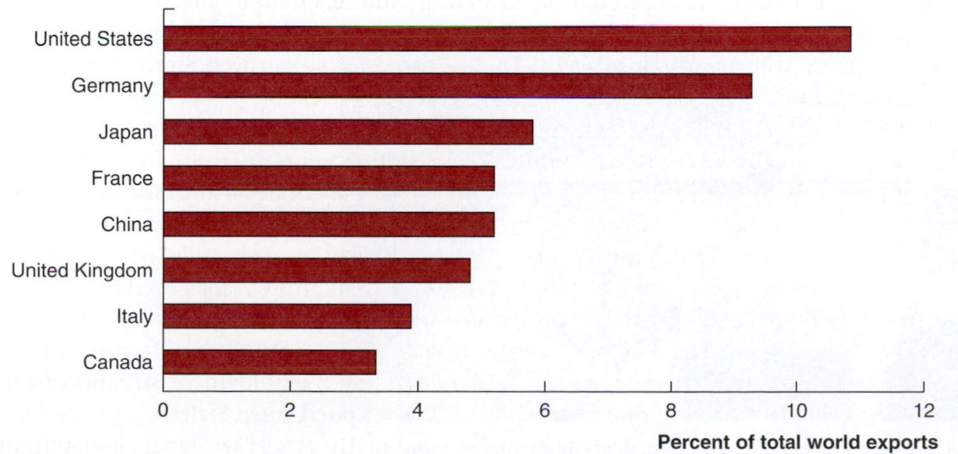

FIGURE 18-2

The Eight Leading Exporting Countries

The United States is the leading exporting country, accounting for about 11 percent of total world exports. The values are the shares of total world exports of merchandise and commercial services.

Source: World Trade Organization, *International Trade Statistics*, 2004.

FIGURE 18-3

International Trade as a Percent of GDP

International trade is still less important to the United States than to most other countries, with the significant exception of Japan.

Source: International Monetary Fund, *International Financial Statistics Yearbook*, 2004.

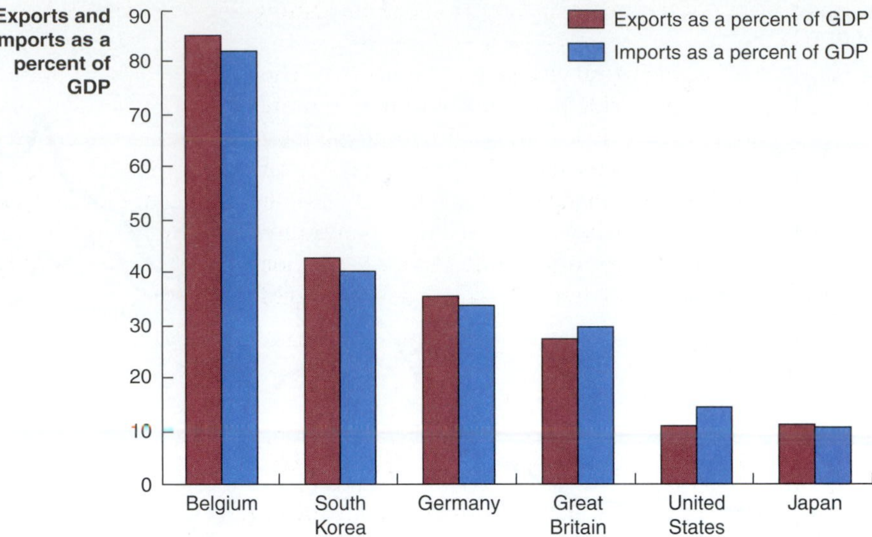

18-1 Making the Connection

Has Outsourcing Hurt the U.S. Economy?

One aspect of the increase in international trade that has been particularly controversial in recent years is *outsourcing*. Outsourcing—sometimes called "offshoring"—occurs when a domestic firm uses workers in a foreign country to produce a good or service that is then sold to domestic consumers. An example is Dell Computer using workers in Bangalore, India, to provide telephone technical support to U.S. buyers of Dell's computers. From the viewpoint of the Indian economy, this would be *insourcing*. The increase in outsourcing and insourcing reflects advances in communications and information technology that make it easier for firms to coordinate the activities of their employees in foreign countries. Outsourcing became a source of political controversy during the early 2000s as employment in the United States grew slowly following the 2001 recession. Some political commentators believed that outsourcing played a significant role in this slow employment growth.

Exact statistics are not available, but the number of jobs outsourced by U.S. companies appears to be small relative to the size of the economy. For example, a study by the U.S. Bureau of Labor Statistics indicates that during the first three months of 2004, outsourcing accounted for only 4,633 of 239,361 jobs lost at a large group of firms. The study covered only firms that employed at least 50 employees and that had eliminated at least 50 jobs, so it was not complete. It seems unlikely, however, that including smaller firms in the study would have significantly changed the results. In a market economy, new jobs are constantly being created as old jobs are destroyed. For example, during 2003, more than 30 million jobs were created and about the same number were destroyed. Some of the job creation was due to insourcing—as foreign firms increased production in the United States—and some of the job destruction was due to outsourcing—as U.S. firms moved jobs overseas. But outsourcing and insourcing are not major factors in the employment situation in the United States.

Some companies outsource technical support services to India.

How does outsourcing affect the economy? We know

that firms outsource to reduce their costs. Competition among firms ensures that lower costs are passed on to consumers in the form of lower prices. In this sense, outsourcing has an effect similar to a technological change that lowers cost. The lower prices that outsourcing makes possible are spread widely among consumers, but the costs of outsourcing are concentrated among workers who lose their jobs. Although jobs that are outsourced are lost to U.S. workers, other jobs are created in the United States to take their place. The same is true of jobs lost to technological change. Over the last 20 years, the U.S. economy has created 30 million more jobs than have been destroyed due to outsourcing, technological change, and all other causes. Nevertheless, individual workers whose jobs are lost to outsourcing may have difficulty finding jobs as desirable as the ones they have lost.

Source: U.S. Bureau of Labor Statistics, "Extended Mass Layoffs Associated with Domestic and Overseas Relocations, First Quarter 2004," June 10, 2004.

Comparative Advantage: The Basis of All Trade

Understand the difference between comparative advantage and absolute advantage.

Why have businesses around the world increasingly looked for markets in other countries? Why have consumers increasingly purchased goods and services made in other countries? People trade for one reason: Trade makes them better off. Whenever a buyer and seller agree to a sale, they must both believe they are better off—otherwise there would be no sale. This outcome must hold whether the buyer and seller live in the same city or in different countries. As we will see, governments are more likely to interfere with international trade than they are with domestic trade, but the reasons for the interference are more political than they are economic.

A Brief Review of Comparative Advantage

In Chapter 2, we discussed the key economic concept of *comparative advantage.* **Comparative advantage** is the ability of an individual, firm, or country to produce a good or service at a lower opportunity cost than other producers. Recall that **opportunity cost** is the highest-valued alternative that must be given up to engage in an activity. People specialize in those economic activities in which they have a comparative advantage. In trading, we benefit from the comparative advantage of other people (or firms or countries), and other people benefit from our comparative advantage.

Comparative advantage The ability of an individual, firm, or country to produce a good or service at a lower opportunity cost than other producers.

Opportunity cost The highest-valued alternative that must be given up to engage in an activity.

A good way to think of comparative advantage is to recall the example in Chapter 2 of you and your neighbor picking fruit. Your neighbor is better at picking both apples and cherries than you are. Why, then, doesn't your neighbor pick both types of fruit? Because the opportunity cost of picking her own apples is very high: She is a particularly skilled cherry picker, and every hour spent picking apples is an hour taken away from picking cherries. You can pick apples at a much lower opportunity cost than your neighbor, so you have a comparative advantage in picking apples. Your neighbor can pick cherries at a much lower opportunity cost than you can, so your neighbor has a comparative advantage in picking cherries. Your neighbor is better off specializing in picking cherries, and you are better off specializing in picking apples. You can then trade some of your apples for some of your neighbor's cherries and both of you will end up with more of each fruit.

Comparative Advantage in International Trade

The principle of comparative advantage can explain why people pursue different occupations. It can also explain why countries produce different goods and services. International trade involves many countries importing and exporting many different goods and services. Countries are better off if they specialize in producing the goods for which they have a comparative advantage. They can then trade for the goods for which other countries have a comparative advantage.

We can illustrate why specializing on the basis of comparative advantage makes countries better off with a simple example involving just two countries and two

TABLE 18-1

An Example of Japanese Workers Being More Productive Than American Workers

	OUTPUT PER HOUR OF WORK	
	CELL PHONES	MP3 PLAYERS
Japan	12	6
United States	2	4

products. Suppose the United States and Japan produce only cell phones and MP3 players, like Apple's iPod. Assume that each country uses only labor to produce each good, and that Japanese and U.S. cell phones and MP3 players are exactly the same. Table 18-1 shows how much each country can produce of each good with 1 hour of labor.

Notice that Japanese workers are more productive than U.S. workers in making both goods. In 1 hour of work, Japanese workers can make six times as many cell phones and one and one-half times as many MP3 players as U.S. workers. Japan has an *absolute advantage* over the United States in producing both goods. **Absolute advantage** is the ability to produce more of a good or service than competitors when using the same amount of resources. In this case, Japan can produce more of both goods using the same amount of labor as the United States.

Absolute advantage The ability to produce more of a good or service than competitors when using the same amount of resources.

It might seem at first that Japan has nothing to gain from trading with the United States because it has an absolute advantage in producing both goods. However, Japan should specialize and produce only cell phones and obtain the MP3 players it needs by exporting cell phones to the United States in exchange for MP3 players. The reason that Japan benefits from trade is that although it has an *absolute advantage* in the production of both goods, it has a *comparative advantage* only in the production of cell phones. The United States has a comparative advantage in the production of MP3 players.

If this seems contrary to common sense, think about the opportunity cost to each country of producing each good. If Japan wants to produce more MP3 players, it has to switch labor away from cell phone production. Every hour of labor switched from producing cell phones to producing MP3 players increases MP3 player production by 6 and reduces cell phone production by 12. Japan has to give up 12 cell phones for every 6 MP3 players it produces. Therefore, the opportunity cost to Japan of producing one more MP3 player is 12/6, or 2 cell phones.

If the United States switches 1 hour of labor from cell phones to MP3 players, production of cell phones falls by 2 and production of MP3 players rises by 4. Therefore, the opportunity cost to the United States of producing one more MP3 player is 2/4, or 0.5 cell phone. The United States has a lower opportunity cost of producing MP3 players and, therefore, has a comparative advantage in making this product. By similar reasoning, we can see that Japan has a comparative advantage in producing cell phones. Table 18-2 summarizes this result.

③ LEARNING OBJECTIVE

Explain how countries gain from international trade.

The Gains from Trade

Can Japan really gain from producing only cell phones and trading with the United States for MP3 players? To see that it can, assume at first that Japan and the United States do not trade with each other. A situation in which a country does not trade with other

TABLE 18-2

The Opportunity Costs of Producing Cell Phones and MP3 Players

	OPPORTUNITY COSTS	
	CELL PHONES	MP3 PLAYERS
Japan	0.5 MP3 player	2 cell phones
United States	2 MP3 players	0.5 cell phone

TABLE 18-3

Production without Trade

WITHOUT TRADE		
	PRODUCTION AND CONSUMPTION	
	CELL PHONES	MP3 PLAYERS
Japan	9,000	1,500
United States	1,500	1,000

countries is called **autarky.** Assume that in autarky each country has 1,000 hours of labor available to produce the two goods, and each country produces the quantities of the two goods shown in Table 18-3. Because there is no trade, these quantities also represent consumption of the two goods in each country.

Autarky A situation in which a country does not trade with other countries.

Increasing Consumption through Trade

Suppose now that Japan and the United States begin to trade with each other. The **terms of trade** is the ratio at which a country can trade its exports for imports from other countries. As Table 18-1 on the previous page shows, it takes twice as much labor in Japan to produce one MP3 player as to produce one cell phone. In the United States, the situation is reversed: It takes twice as much labor to produce a cell phone as it does to produce an MP3 player. For simplicity, let's assume that the terms of trade end up with Japan and the United States being willing to trade one cell phone for one MP3 player.

Terms of trade The ratio at which a country can trade its exports for imports from other countries.

Once trade has begun, the United States and Japan can exchange MP3 players for cell phones or cell phones for MP3 players. For example, if Japan specializes by using all 1,000 available hours of labor to produce cell phones, it will be able to produce 12,000. It then could export 1,500 cell phones to the United States in exchange for 1,500 MP3 players (remember we are assuming the terms of trade are one cell phone for one MP3 player). Japan ends up with 10,500 cell phones and 1,500 MP3 players. Compared with the situation before trade, Japan has the same number of MP3 players, but 1,500 more cell phones. If the United States specializes in producing MP3 players, it will be able to produce 4,000. It then could export 1,500 MP3 players to Japan in exchange for 1,500 cell phones. The United States ends up with 2,500 MP3 players and 1,500 cell phones. Compared with the situation before trade, the United States has the same number of cell phones, but 1,500 more MP3 players. Trade has allowed both countries to increase the quantities of goods consumed. Table 18-4 summarizes the gains from trade for the United States and Japan.

By trading, Japan and the United States are able to consume more than they could without trade. This outcome is possible because world production of both goods increases after trade (remember, in this example, our "world" consists of just the United States and Japan):

WORLD PRODUCTION		
	BEFORE TRADE	AFTER TRADE
Cell Phones	10,500	12,000
MP3 Players	2,500	4,000

Why does total production of cell phones and MP3 players increase when the United States specializes in producing MP3 players and Japan specializes in producing cell phones? A domestic analogy helps to answer this question: If a company shifts production from an old factory to a more efficient modern factory, its output will increase. In effect, the same thing happens in our example. Producing MP3 players in Japan and cell phones in the United States is inefficient. Shifting production to the more efficient

TABLE 18-4

The Gains from Trade for Japan and the United States

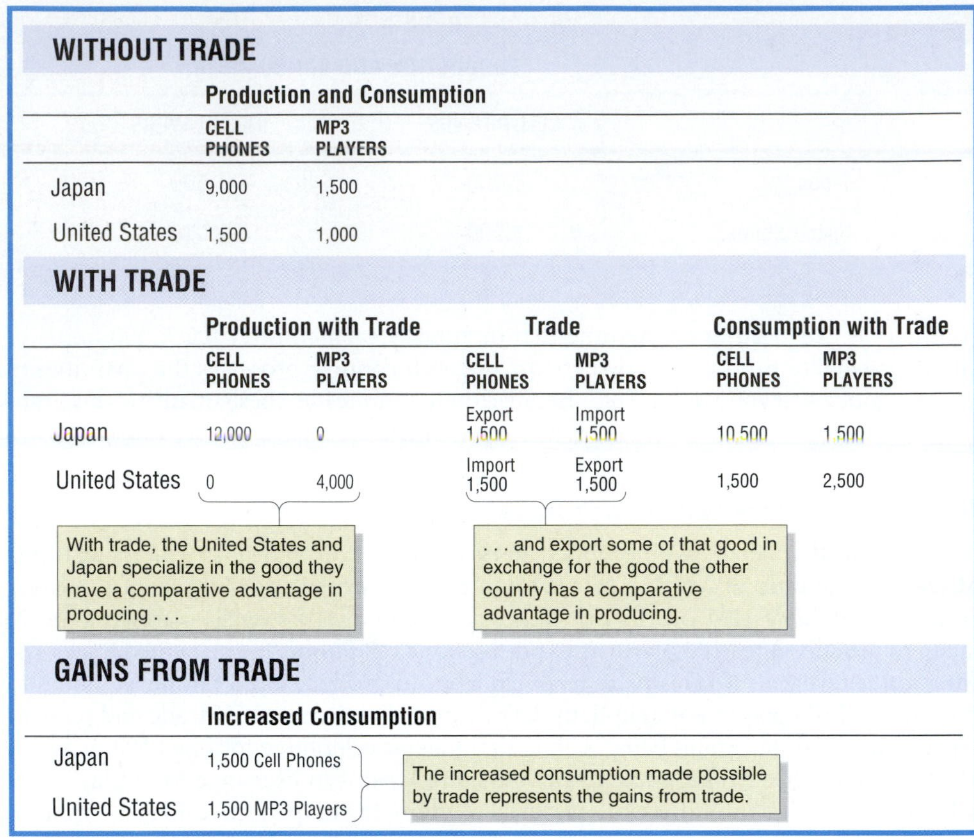

WITHOUT TRADE

	Production and Consumption	
	CELL PHONES	MP3 PLAYERS
Japan	9,000	1,500
United States	1,500	1,000

WITH TRADE

	Production with Trade		Trade		Consumption with Trade	
	CELL PHONES	MP3 PLAYERS	CELL PHONES	MP3 PLAYERS	CELL PHONES	MP3 PLAYERS
Japan	12,000	0	Export 1,500	Import 1,500	10,500	1,500
United States	0	4,000	Import 1,500	Export 1,500	1,500	2,500

With trade, the United States and Japan specialize in the good they have a comparative advantage in producing . . .

. . . and export some of that good in exchange for the good the other country has a comparative advantage in producing.

GAINS FROM TRADE

	Increased Consumption
Japan	1,500 Cell Phones
United States	1,500 MP3 Players

The increased consumption made possible by trade represents the gains from trade.

country—the one with the comparative advantage—increases total production. The key point is this: *Countries gain from specializing in producing goods in which they have a comparative advantage and trading for goods in which other countries have a comparative advantage.*

Why Don't We See Complete Specialization?

In our example of two countries producing only two products, each country specializes in producing one of the goods. In the real world, many goods and services are produced in more than one country. For example, the United States and Japan both produce automobiles. We do not see complete specialization in the real world for three main reasons:

- ***Not all goods and services are traded internationally.*** Even if, for example, Japan had a comparative advantage in the production of medical services, it would be difficult for Japan to specialize in their production and export them. There is no easy way for U.S. patients in need of appendectomies to receive them from Japanese surgeons.
- ***Production of most goods involves increasing opportunity costs.*** Recall from Chapter 2 that production of most goods involves increasing opportunity costs. As a result, when the United States devotes more workers to producing MP3 players, the opportunity cost of producing more MP3 players will increase. At some point, the opportunity cost of producing MP3 players in the United States will rise to the level of the opportunity cost of producing MP3 players in Japan. Once that happens, international trade will no longer push the United States further toward complete specialization. The same will be true of Japan: Increasing opportunity cost will cause Japan to stop short of complete specialization in producing cell phones.
- ***Tastes for products differ.*** Most products are *differentiated.* Cell phones, MP3 players, cars, and televisions—to name just a few products—come with a wide variety of

features. When buying automobiles, some people are looking for reliability and good gasoline mileage, others are looking for room to carry seven passengers, and still others want styling and high performance. So, some car buyers prefer Toyota Corollas, some prefer Ford minivans, and others prefer BMWs. As a result, Japan, the United States, and Germany may each have a comparative advantage in producing different types of automobiles.

Does Anyone Lose as a Result of International Trade?

In our cell phone and MP3 player example, consumption increases in both the United States and Japan as a result of trade. Everyone gains and no one loses. Or do they? In our example, we referred repeatedly to "Japan" or the "United States" producing cell phones or MP3 players. But countries do not produce goods—firms do. In a world without trade, there would be cell phone and MP3 player firms in both Japan and the United States. In a world with trade, there would only be Japanese cell phone firms and U.S. MP3 player firms. Japanese MP3 player firms and U.S. cell phone firms would disappear. The owners of Japanese MP3 player firms, the owners of U.S. cell phone firms, and the people who work for them are likely to do their best to convince the Japanese and U.S. governments to interfere with trade by barring imports of the competing products from the other country or by imposing high tariffs on them. Later in this chapter we will discuss government policies that restrict trade.

Where Does Comparative Advantage Come From?

(4) LEARNING OBJECTIVE

Discuss the sources of comparative advantage.

Among the main sources of comparative advantage are the following:

- ***Climate and natural resources.*** This source of comparative advantage is the most obvious. Because of geology, Saudi Arabia has a comparative advantage in the production of oil. Because of climate and soil conditions, Costa Rica has a comparative advantage in the production of bananas, and the United States has a comparative advantage in the production of wheat.
- ***Relative abundance of labor and capital.*** Some countries, such as the United States, have many highly skilled workers and a great deal of machinery. Other countries, such as China, have many unskilled workers and relatively little machinery. As a result, the United States has a comparative advantage in the production of goods that require highly skilled workers or sophisticated machinery to manufacture, such as aircraft, semiconductors, and computer software. China has a comparative advantage in the production of goods that require unskilled workers and small amounts of simple machinery, such as children's toys.
- ***Technology.*** Broadly defined, *technology* is the process firms use to turn inputs into goods and services. At any given time, firms in different countries do not all have access to the same technologies. In part, this difference reflects past investments countries have made in supporting higher education or in providing support for research and development. Some countries are strong in *product technologies,* which involve the ability to develop new products. For example, firms in the United States have pioneered the development of such products as televisions, digital computers, airliners, and many prescription drugs. Other countries are strong in *process technologies,* which involve the ability to improve the processes used to make existing products. For example, firms in Japan, such as Toyota and Nissan, succeeded by greatly improving the processes for making automobiles.
- ***External economies.*** It is difficult to explain the location of some industries on the basis of climate, natural resources, the relative abundance of labor and capital, or technology. For example, why does Southern California have a comparative advantage in making movies or Switzerland in making watches or New York in providing financial services? The answer is that once an industry becomes established in an area, firms that locate in that area gain advantages over firms located elsewhere. The

advantages include the availability of skilled workers, the opportunity to interact with other firms in the same industry, and being close to suppliers. These advantages result in lower costs to firms located in the area. Because these lower costs result from increases in the size of the industry in an area, economists refer to them as **external economies**.

External economies Reductions in a firm's costs that result from an expansion in the size of an industry.

18-2 Making the Connection

Why Is Dalton, Georgia, the Carpet-Making Capital of the World?

Factories within a 65-mile radius of Dalton, Georgia, account for 80 percent of U.S. carpet production and more than half of world carpet production. Carpet production is highly automated and relies primarily on synthetic fibers. Dalton, a small city located in rural northwest Georgia, would not seem to have any advantages in carpet production. In fact, the location of the carpet industry in Dalton was an historical accident.

In the early 1900s, Catherine Evans Whitener started making bedspreads using a method called "tufting," in which she sewed cotton yarn through the fabric and then cut the ends of the yarn so it would fluff up. These bedspreads became very popular. By the 1930s, the process was mechanized and was then applied to carpets. In the early years, the industry used cotton grown in Georgia, but today synthetic fibers, such as nylon and olefin, have largely replaced cotton and wool in carpet manufacturing.

More than 170 carpet factories are now located in the Dalton area. Supporting the carpet industry are local yarn manufacturers, machinery suppliers, and maintenance firms. Dye plants have opened solely to supply the carpet industry. Printing shops have opened whose whole business is printing tags and labels for carpets. Box factories have opened to produce cartons designed specifically for shipping carpets. The local workforce has developed highly specialized skills for running and maintaining the carpet-making machinery.

Because Catherine Evans Whitener started making bedspreads by hand in Dalton, Georgia, a hundred years ago, a multibillion-dollar carpet industry is now located there.

A company establishing a carpet factory outside the Dalton area is unable to use the suppliers or the skilled workers available to factories in Dalton. As a result, carpet factories located outside of Dalton may have higher costs than factories located in Dalton. Although there is no particular reason why the carpet industry should have originally located in Dalton, external economies gave the area a comparative advantage in carpet making once it began to grow there.

Comparative Advantage over Time: The Rise and Fall—and Rise—of the U.S. Consumer Electronics Industry

A country may develop a comparative advantage in the production of a good, then as time passes and circumstances change, the country may lose its comparative advantage in producing that good and develop a comparative advantage in producing other goods. For several decades, the United States had a comparative advantage in the production of consumer electronic goods, such as televisions, radios, and stereos. The comparative advantage of the United States in these products was based on having developed most of the underlying technology, having the most modern factories, and having a skilled and experienced workforce. Gradually, however, other countries, particularly Japan, gained access to the technology, built modern factories, and developed skilled workforces. As mentioned earlier, Japanese firms have excelled in process technologies, which involve the ability to improve the processes used to make existing products. By the 1970s and 1980s, Japanese firms were able to produce many consumer electronic goods more cheaply and with higher quality than could U.S. firms. Sony, Panasonic, and Pioneer replaced Magnavox, Zenith, and RCA as world leaders in consumer electronics.

By 2005, however, as the technology underlying consumer electronics evolved, comparative advantage began to shift again, and several U.S. firms surged ahead of their Japanese competitors. For example, Apple Computer developed the iPod; palmOne developed the Treo smartphone that has the capacity for e-mail, Web surfing, and picture taking; and Kodak developed digital cameras with EasyShare software that made it easy to organize, enhance, and share digital pictures. As pictures and music converted to digital data, process technologies became less important than the ability to design and develop new products. These new consumer electronics products required skills similar to those in computer design and software writing where the United States had long maintained a comparative advantage.

Once a country has lost its comparative advantage in producing a good, its income will be higher and its economy will be more efficient if it switches from producing the good to importing it, as the United States did when it switched from producing televisions to importing them. As we will see in the next section, however, there is often political pressure on governments to attempt to preserve industries that have lost their comparative advantage.

Government Policies That Restrict Trade

(5) LEARNING OBJECTIVE

Analyze the economic effects of government policies that restrict international trade.

Free trade Trade between countries that is without government restrictions.

Free trade, or trade between countries that is without government restrictions, makes consumers better off. We can expand on this idea using the concepts of consumer surplus and producer surplus developed in Chapter 4. Figure 18-4 shows the market for lumber in the United States assuming autarky, where the United States does not trade with other countries. The equilibrium price of lumber is \$3 per board foot and the equilibrium quantity is 1,000,000 board feet. (A board foot is a piece of lumber one inch thick and one foot wide by one foot long.) The blue area represents consumer surplus and the red area represents producer surplus.

Now suppose that the United States begins importing lumber from Canada and other countries, and that lumber is selling in these countries for \$2 per board foot. Because the world market for lumber is large, we will assume that the United States can buy as much lumber as it wants to without causing the *world price* of \$2 to rise.

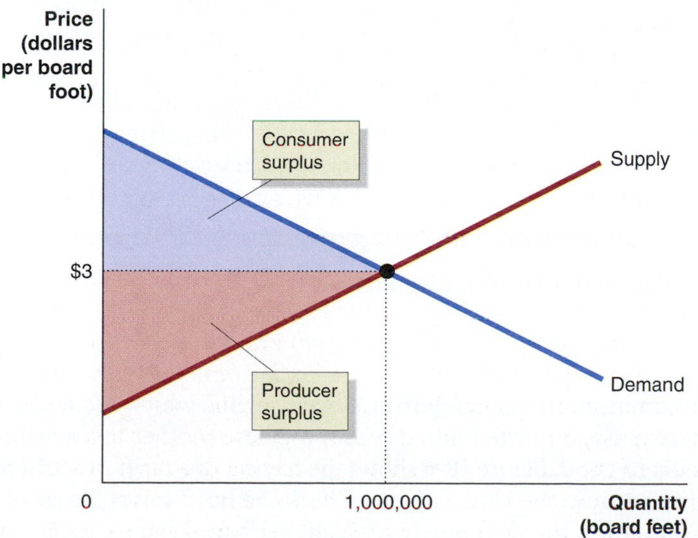

FIGURE 18-4

The U.S. Lumber Industry under Autarky

This figure shows the market for lumber in the United States assuming autarky, where the United States does not trade with other countries. The equilibrium price of lumber is \$3 per board foot and the equilibrium quantity is 1,000,000 board feet. The blue area represents consumer surplus, and the red area represents producer surplus.

FIGURE 18-5

The Effect of Imports on the U.S. Lumber Market

When imports are allowed into the United States, the price of lumber falls from \$3 to \$2. U.S. consumers increase their purchases from 1,000,000 board feet to 1,200,000 board feet. Equilibrium moves from point *F* to point *G*. U.S. producers reduce the quantity of lumber they supply from 1,000,000 board feet to 700,000 board feet. Imports equal 500,000 board feet, which is the difference between U.S. consumption and U.S. production. Consumer surplus equals the areas *A*, *B*, *C*, and *D*. Producer surplus equals the area of *E*.

	Under Autarky	With Imports
Consumer Surplus	A	$A+B+C+D$
Producer Surplus	$B+E$	E
Economic Surplus	$A+B+E$	$A+B+C+D+E$

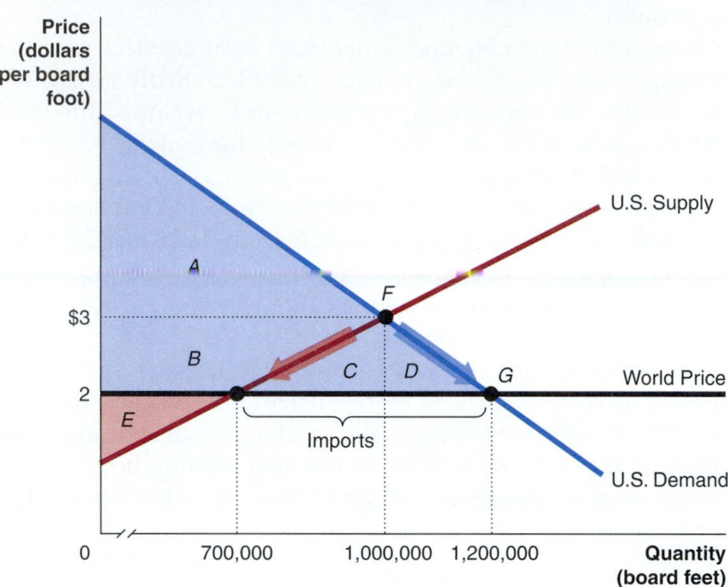

Therefore, once imports of lumber are permitted into the United States, U.S. lumber companies will not be able to sell lumber at prices higher than the world price of \$2, and the U.S. price will become equal to the world price.

Figure 18-5 shows the result of allowing imports of lumber into the United States. With the price lowered from \$3 to \$2, U.S. consumers increase their purchases from 1,000,000 board feet to 1,200,000 board feet. Equilibrium moves from point *E* to point *F*. In the new equilibrium, U.S. producers have reduced the quantity of lumber they supply from 1,000,000 board feet to 700,000 board feet. Imports will equal 500,000 board feet, which is the difference between U.S. consumption and U.S. production.

Under autarky, consumer surplus would be area *A* in Figure 18-5. With imports, the reduction in price increases consumer surplus, so it is now equal to the sum of areas *A*, *B*, *C*, and *D*. Although the lower price increases consumer surplus, it reduces producer surplus. Under autarky, producer surplus was equal to the sum of the areas *B* and *E*. With imports, producer surplus is equal to only area *E*. Recall that economic surplus equals the sum of consumer surplus and producer surplus. Moving from autarky to allowing imports increases economic surplus in the United States by an amount equal to the sum of areas *C* and *D*.

We can conclude that international trade helps consumers, but hurts firms that are less efficient than foreign competitors. As a result, these firms and their workers are often strong supporters of government policies that restrict trade. These policies usually take one of two forms:

- Tariffs
- Quotas and voluntary export restraints

Tariffs

The most common interferences with trade are tariffs, which are taxes imposed by a government on goods imported into a country. Like any other tax, a tariff will increase the cost of selling a good. Figure 18-6 shows the impact of a tariff of \$0.50 per board foot on lumber imports into the United States. The \$0.50 tariff raises the price of lumber in the United States from the world price of \$2.00 per board foot to \$2.50 per board foot.

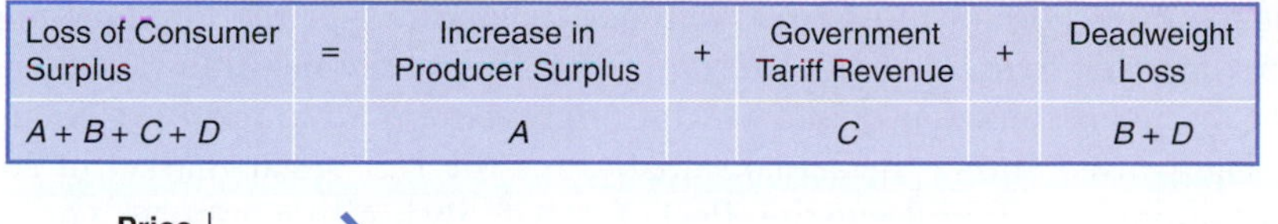

Loss of Consumer Surplus	=	Increase in Producer Surplus	+	Government Tariff Revenue	+	Deadweight Loss
$A + B + C + D$		A		C		$B + D$

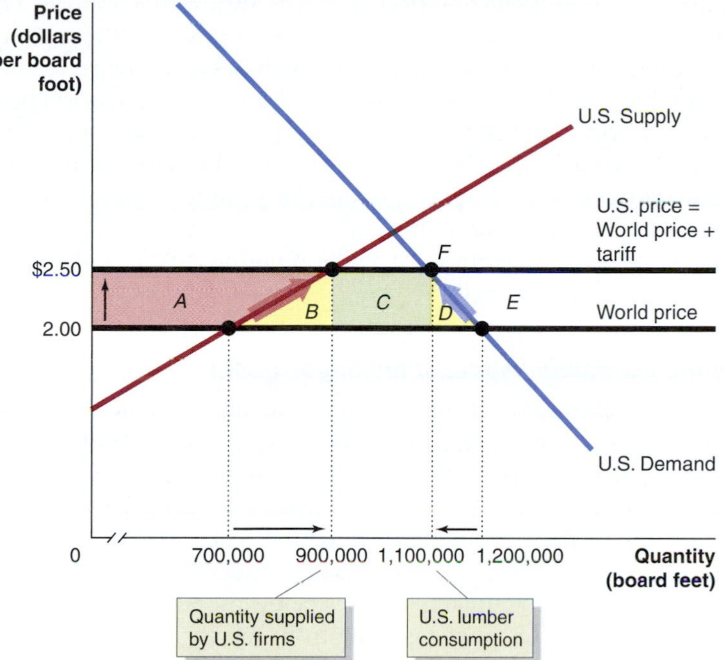

FIGURE 18-6

The Effects of a Tariff on Lumber

Without a tariff on lumber, U.S. lumber producers will sell 700,000 board feet of lumber, U.S. consumers will purchase 1,200,000 board feet, and imports will be 500,000 board feet. The U.S. price will equal the world price of \$2.00 per board foot. The \$0.50 per board foot lumber tariff raises the price of lumber in the United States to \$2.50 per board foot and U.S. producers increase the quantity they supply to 900,000 board feet. U.S. consumers reduce their purchases to 1,100,000 board feet. Equilibrium moves from point *E* to point *F*. The lumber tariff causes a loss of consumer surplus equal to the area $A + B + C + D$. The area *A* is the increase in producer surplus due to the higher price. The area *C* is the government's tariff revenue. The areas *B* and *D* represent deadweight loss.

At this higher price, U.S. lumber producers increase the quantity they supply from 700,000 board feet to 900,000 board feet. U.S. consumers, though, cut back their purchases of lumber from 1,200,000 board feet to 1,100,000 board feet. Imports decline from 500,000 board feet (1,200,000 – 700,000) to 200,000 board feet (1,100,000 – 900,000). Equilibrium moves from point *E* to point *F*.

By raising the price of lumber from \$2.00 to \$2.50, the tariff reduces consumer surplus by the sum of areas *A*, *B*, *C*, and *D*. Area *A* is the increase in producer surplus from the higher price. The government collects tariff revenue equal to the tariff of \$0.50 per board feet multiplied by the 200,000 board feet imported. Area *C* represents the government's tariff revenue. Areas *B* and *D* represent losses to U.S. consumers that are not captured by anyone. They are deadweight loss and represent the decline in economic efficiency resulting from the lumber tariff. Area *B* shows the effect on U.S. consumers of being forced to buy from U.S. producers who are less efficient than foreign producers, and area *D* shows the effect of U.S. consumers buying less lumber than they would have at the world price. As a result of the tariff, economic surplus has been reduced by the sum of areas *B* and *D*. Recall from Chapter 4 that deadweight loss represents a loss of economic efficiency.

We can conclude that the tariff succeeds in helping U.S. lumber producers, but hurts U.S. consumers and the efficiency of the U.S. economy.

Quotas and Voluntary Export Restraints

A **quota** is a numerical limit on the quantity of a good that can be imported, and it has an effect similar to a tariff. A quota is imposed by the government of the importing country. A **voluntary export restraint** is an agreement negotiated between two countries that places a numerical limit on the quantity of a good that can be imported by one country from the other country. In the early 1980s, the United States and Japan negotiated a voluntary export restraint that limited the quantity of automobiles the United States would import from Japan. Quotas and voluntary export restraints have similar economic effects.

Quota A numerical limit imposed by the government on the quantity of a good that can be imported into a country.

Voluntary export restraint An agreement negotiated between two countries that places a numerical limit on the quantity of a good that can be imported by one country from the other country.

The main purpose of most tariffs and quotas is to reduce the foreign competition faced by domestic firms. We saw an example of this at the beginning of this chapter when we discussed the sugar quota, which Congress imposed to protect U.S. sugar producers. Figure 18-7 shows the actual statistics for the U.S. sugar market in 2003. The effect of a quota is very similar to the effect of a tariff. By limiting imports, a quota forces the domestic price of a good above the world price. In this case, the sugar quota limits sugar imports to 3.5 billion pounds (shown by the bracket in Figure 18-7), forcing the U.S. price of sugar up to $0.21 per pound, or $0.13 higher than the world price. The U.S. price is above the world price because the quota keeps foreign sugar producers from selling the additional sugar in the United States that would drive the price down to the world price. At a price of $0.21 cents per pound, U.S. producers increased the quantity of sugar they supply from 1.0 billion pounds to 16.8 billion pounds, and U.S. consumers cut back their purchases of sugar from 24.3 billion pounds to 20.3 billion pounds. Equilibrium moves from point *E* to point *F*.

Measuring the Economic Impact of the Sugar Quota

Once again, we can use the concepts of consumer surplus, producer surplus, and deadweight loss to measure the economic impact of the sugar quota. Without a sugar quota, the world price of $0.08 per pound would also be the U.S. price. In Figure 18-7, consumer surplus equals the area above the $0.08 price line and below the demand curve. The sugar quota causes the U.S. price to rise to $0.21 cents and reduces consumer surplus by the area $A + B + C + D$. Without a sugar quota, producer surplus received by U.S. sugar producers would be equal to the area below the $0.08 price line and above the supply curve. The higher U.S. price resulting from the sugar quota increases the producer surplus of U.S. sugar producers by an amount equal to area *A*.

FIGURE 18-7

The Effect of the U.S. Sugar Quota

Without a sugar quota, U.S. sugar producers would have sold 1.0 billion pounds of sugar, U.S. consumers would have purchased 24.3 billion pounds of sugar, and imports would have been 23.3 billion pounds. The U.S. price would have equaled the world price of $0.08 per pound. Because the sugar quota limits imports to 3.5 billion pounds (the bracket in the graph), the price of sugar in the United States rises to $0.21 per pound and U.S. producers increase the quantity of sugar they supply to 16.8 billion pounds. U.S. consumers reduce their sugar purchases to 20.3 billion pounds. Equilibrium moves from point *E* to point *F*. The price of sugar in the United States is now $0.13 per pound higher than the world price. The sugar quota causes a loss of consumer surplus equal to the area $A + B + C + D$. The area *A* is the gain to U.S. sugar producers. The area *C* is the gain to foreign sugar producers. The areas *B* and *D* represent deadweight loss. The total loss to U.S. consumers in 2003 was $2.91 billion.

Loss of Consumer Surplus	=	Gain by U.S. Sugar Producers	+	Gain to Foreign Sugar Producers	+	Deadweight Loss
$A + B + C + D$		A		C		$B + D$
$2.91 billion	=	$1.16 billion	+	$0.46 billion	+	$1.29 billion

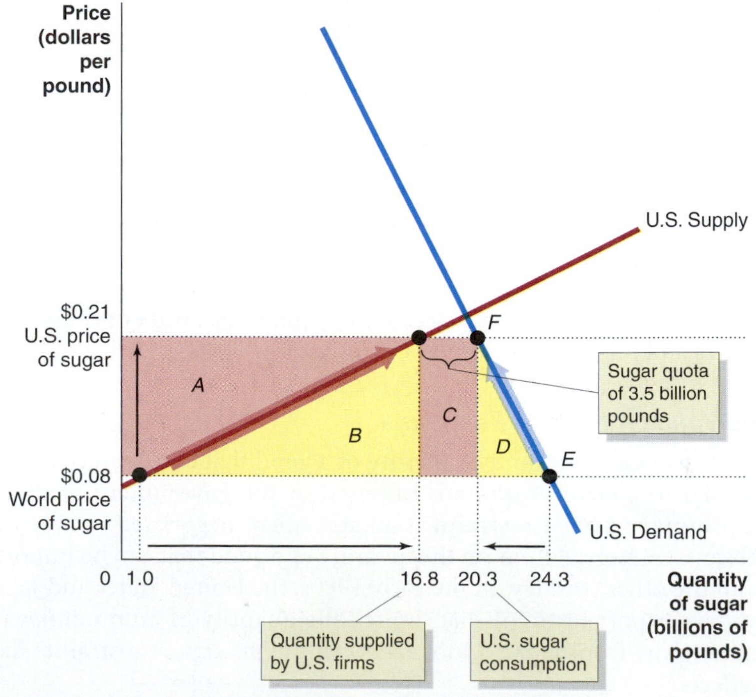

A license from the U.S. government is required to import sugar under the quota system. These import licenses are distributed to foreign producers. Therefore, foreign sugar producers who are lucky enough to have an import license also benefit from the quota because they are able to sell sugar on the U.S. market at $0.21 per pound instead of $0.08 per pound. The gain to foreign sugar producers is area *C*. Areas *A* and *C* represent transfers from U.S. consumers of sugar to U.S. and foreign producers of sugar. Areas *B* and *D* represent losses to U.S. consumers that are not captured by anyone. They are deadweight losses and represent the decline in economic efficiency resulting from the sugar quota. Area *B* shows the effect of U.S. consumers being forced to buy from U.S. producers who are less efficient than foreign producers, and area *D* shows the effect of U.S. consumers buying less sugar than they would have at the world price.

Enough information is available in the figure to calculate the dollar value of each of the four areas. The results of these calculations are shown in the table in Figure 18-7. The total loss to consumers from the sugar quota was $2.91 billion in 2003. About 40 percent of this loss, or $1.16 billion, was gained by U.S. sugar producers as increased producer surplus. About 16 percent, or $0.46 billion, was gained by foreign sugar producers as increased producer surplus, and about 44 percent, or $1.29 billion, was a deadweight loss to the U.S. economy. The U.S. International Trade Commission estimates that eliminating the sugar quota would result in the loss of about 3,000 jobs in the U.S. sugar industry. The cost to U.S. consumers of saving these jobs is equal to $2.91 billion/3,000 or about $970,000 per job. In fact, this cost is an underestimate because eliminating the sugar quota would result in new jobs being created, particularly in the candy industry. As we saw at the beginning of this chapter, U.S. candy companies have been moving factories to other countries to escape the impact of the sugar quota.

SOLVED PROBLEM 18-1

Measuring the Economic Effect of a Quota

5 LEARNING OBJECTIVE

Analyze the economic effects of government policies that restrict international trade.

Suppose that the United States currently both produces apples and imports them. The U.S. government then decides to restrict international trade in apples by imposing a quota that allows imports of only four million boxes of apples into the United States each year. The figure shows the results of imposing the quota:

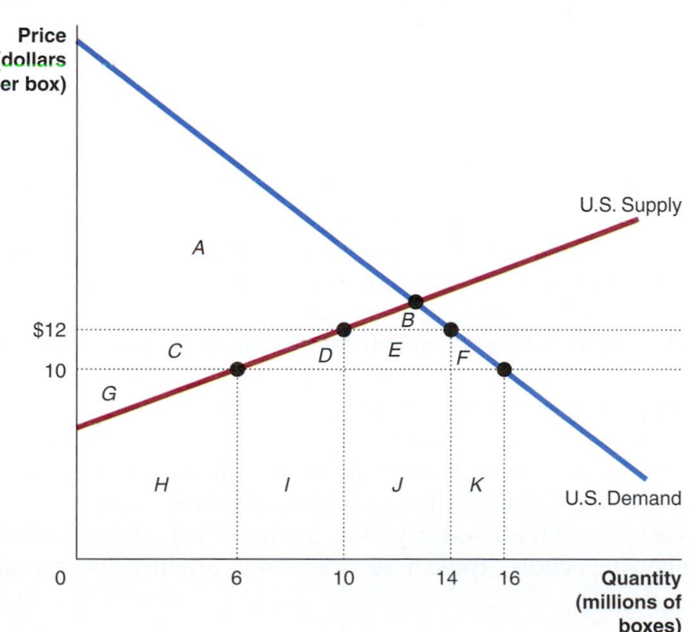

Fill in the following table using the prices, quantities, and letters in the figure:

	WITHOUT QUOTA	WITH QUOTA
World price of apples	_______	_______
U.S. price of apples	_______	_______
Quantity supplied by U.S. firms	_______	_______
Quantity demanded by U.S. consumers	_______	_______
Quantity imported	_______	_______
Area of consumer surplus	_______	_______
Area of producer surplus	_______	_______
Area of deadweight loss	_______	_______

Solving the Problem:

Step 1: Review the chapter material. This problem is about measuring the economic effects of a quota, so you may want to review the section "Quotas and Voluntary Export Restraints," which begins on page 577, and "Measuring the Economic Impact of the Sugar Quota," which begins on page 578.

Step 2: Fill in the table. After studying Figure 18-7, you should be able to fill in the table. Remember that consumer surplus is the area below the demand curve and above the market price.

	WITHOUT QUOTA	WITH QUOTA
World price of apples	\$10	\$10
U.S. price of apples	\$10	\$12
Quantity supplied by U.S. firms	6 million boxes	10 million boxes
Quantity demanded by U.S. consumers	16 million boxes	14 million boxes
Quantity imported	10 millions boxes	4 million boxes
Area of consumer surplus	$A + B + C + D + E + F$	$A + B$
Area of domestic producer surplus	G	$G + C$
Area of deadweight loss	No deadweight loss	$D + F$

YOUR TURN: **For more practice, do related problem 18 on page 597 at the end of this chapter.**

The Argument over Trade Policies and Globalization

The argument over whether the U.S. government should regulate international trade dates back to the beginning of the country. One particularly controversial attempt to restrict trade took place during the Great Depression of the 1930s. At that time the United States and other countries attempted to help domestic firms by raising tariffs on foreign imports. The United States started the process by passing the Smoot-Hawley Tariff in 1930, which raised average tariff rates to more than 50 percent. As other countries retaliated by raising their tariffs, international trade collapsed.

By the end of World War II in 1945, government officials in the United States and Europe were looking for a way to reduce tariffs and revive international trade. To help achieve this goal, they set up the General Agreement on Tariffs and Trade (GATT) in 1948. Countries that joined the GATT agreed not to impose new tariffs or import quotas. In addition, a series of *multilateral negotiations,* called *trade rounds,* took place, in which countries agreed to reduce tariffs from the very high levels of the 1930s.

In the 1940s, most international trade was in goods, and the GATT agreement covered only goods. In the following decades, trade in services and in products incorporating *intellectual property*, such as software programs and movies, grew in importance. Many GATT members pressed for a new agreement that would cover services and intellectual property, as well as goods. A new agreement was negotiated, and in January 1995 the GATT was replaced by the **World Trade Organization (WTO)**, headquartered in Geneva, Switzerland. More than 130 countries are currently members of the WTO.

World Trade Organization (WTO) An international organization that enforces international trade agreements.

During the years immediately after World War II, many low-income, or developing, countries erected high tariffs and restricted investment by foreign companies. When these policies failed to produce much economic growth, many of these countries decided during the 1980s to become more open to foreign trade and investment. This process became known as **globalization**. Most developing countries joined the WTO and began to follow its policies.

Globalization The process of countries becoming more open to foreign trade and investment.

During the 1990s, opposition to globalization began to increase. In 1999, this opposition took a violent turn at a meeting of the WTO in Seattle, Washington. The purpose of the meeting was to plan a new round of negotiations aimed at further reductions in trade barriers. A large number of protestors assembled in Seattle to meet the WTO delegates. Protests started peacefully but quickly became violent. Protesters looted stores and burned cars, and many delegates were unable to leave their hotel rooms.

Why would attempts to reduce trade barriers with the objective of increasing income around the world cause such a furious reaction? The opposition to the WTO comes from three sources. First, some opponents are specifically against the globalization process that began in the 1980s and became widespread in the 1990s. Second, other opponents have the same motivation as the supporters of tariffs in the 1930s—to erect trade barriers to protect domestic firms from foreign competition. Third, some critics of the WTO support globalization in principle but believe that the WTO favors the interests of the high-income countries at the expense of the low-income countries. Because of the importance of this issue, we will look more closely at the sources of opposition to the WTO.

ANTI-GLOBALIZATION Many of the protestors in Seattle distrust globalization. Some believe that free trade and foreign investment destroy the distinctive cultures of many countries. As developing countries began to open their economies to imports from the United States and other high-income countries, these imports of food, clothing, movies, and other goods began to replace the equivalent local products. So, a teenager in Thailand might be sitting in a McDonald's restaurant, wearing Levi's jeans and a Ralph Lauren shirt, listening to a recording by U2 on his iPod, before going to the local movie theater to watch *Spider-Man 3*. Globalization has increased the variety of products available to consumers in developing countries, but some people argue this is too high a price to pay for what they see as the damage to local cultures.

Globalization has also allowed multinational corporations to relocate factories from high-income countries to low-income countries. These new factories in Indonesia, Malaysia, Pakistan, and other countries pay much lower wages than are paid in the United States, Europe, and Japan and often do not meet the environmental or safety regulations that are imposed in high-income countries. Some factories use child labor, which is illegal in high-income countries. Some people have argued that firms with factories in developing countries should pay workers wages as high as those paid in the high-income countries. They also believe these firms should follow the health, safety, and environmental regulations that exist in the high-income countries.

The governments of most developing countries have resisted these proposals. They argue that when the currently rich countries were poor, they also lacked environmental or safety standards, and their workers were paid low wages. They argue that it is easier for rich countries to afford high wages and environmental and safety regulations than it is for poor countries. They also point out that many jobs that seem very poorly paid by high-income country standards are often better than the alternatives available to workers in low-income countries.

18-3 Making the Connection

The Unintended Consequences of Banning Goods Made with Child Labor

Would eliminating child labor in developing countries be a good thing?

In many developing countries, such as Indonesia, Thailand, and Peru, children as young as seven or eight work 10 or more hours a day. Reports of very young workers laboring long hours producing goods for export have upset many people in the high-income countries. In the United States, boycotts have been organized against stores that stock goods made in developing countries with child labor. Many people assume that if child workers in developing countries weren't working in factories making clothing, toys, and other products, they would be in school, as are children in the high-income countries.

In fact, there are usually few good alternatives to work for children in developing countries. Schooling is frequently available for only a few months each year, and even children who attend school rarely do so for more than a few years. Poor families are often unable to afford even the small costs of sending their children to school. Families may even rely on the earnings of very young children to survive, as once did poor families in the the United States, Europe, and Japan. The United States did not outlaw child labor until 1938. In developing countries, jobs producing export goods are usually better paying and less hazardous than the alternatives.

As preparations began in France for the 1998 World Cup, there were protests that Baden Sports—the main supplier of soccer balls—was purchasing the balls from suppliers in Pakistan who used child workers. France decided to ban all use of soccer balls made by child workers. Bowing to this pressure, Baden Sports moved production from Pakistan, where the balls were hand-stitched by child workers, to China, where the balls were machine-stitched by adult workers in factories. There was some criticism of the boycott of hand-stitched soccer balls at the time. In a broad study of child labor, three economists argued:

> [O]f the array of possible employment in which impoverished children might engage, soccer ball stitching is probably one of the most benign . . . [In Pakistan] children generally work alongside other family members in the home or in small workshops . . . Nor are the children exposed to toxic chemicals, hazardous tools or brutal working conditions. Rather, the only serious criticism concerns the length of the typical child stitcher's work-day and the impact on formal education.

In fact, the alternatives to soccer ball stitching for child workers in Pakistan turned out to be extremely grim. According to Keith Maskus, an economist at the University of Colorado and the World Bank, a "large proportion" of the children who lost their jobs stitching soccer balls ended up begging or in prostitution.

Sources: Drusilla K. Brown, Alan V. Deardorff, and Robert M. Stern, "U.S. Trade and Other Policy Options to Deter Foreign Exploitation of Child Labor," in Magnus Blomstrom and Linda S. Goldberg, eds., *Topics in Empirical International Economics: A Festschrift in Honor of Bob Lipsey*, Chicago: University of Chicago Press, 2001; and Tomas Larsson, *The Race to the Top: The Real Story of Globalization*, 2001, p. 48.

Protectionism The use of trade barriers to shield domestic firms from foreign competition.

"OLD-FASHIONED" PROTECTIONISM The anti-globalization argument against free trade and the WTO is relatively new. Another argument against free trade is called *protectionism* and has been around for centuries. **Protectionism** is the use of trade barriers to shield domestic firms from foreign competition. For as long as international trade has existed, governments have attempted to restrict it to protect domestic firms. As we saw with the analysis of the sugar quota, protectionism causes losses to consumers and eliminates jobs in the domestic industries that use the protected product. In addition, by reducing the ability of countries to produce according to comparative advantage, protectionism reduces incomes.

Why, then, does protectionism attract support? Protectionism is usually justified on the basis of one of the following arguments:

- ***Saving jobs.*** Supporters of protectionism argue that free trade reduces employment by driving domestic firms out of business. It is true that when more-efficient foreign firms drive less-efficient domestic firms out of business, jobs are lost, but jobs are also lost when more-efficient domestic firms drive less-efficient domestic firms out of business. These job losses are rarely permanent. In the U.S. economy, jobs are being lost and new jobs are being created continually. No economic study has ever found a connection in the long run between the total number of jobs available and the level of tariff protection for domestic industries. In addition, trade restrictions destroy jobs in some industries at the same time that they preserve jobs in others. The U.S. sugar quota may have saved jobs in the U.S. sugar industry, but, as we saw at the beginning of this chapter, it also has destroyed jobs in the U.S. candy industry.
- ***Protecting high wages.*** Some people worry that firms in the high-income countries will have to start paying much lower wages to compete with firms in the developing countries. This fear is misplaced, however, because free trade actually raises living standards by increasing economic efficiency. When a country practices protectionism and produces goods and services it could obtain more cheaply from other countries, it reduces its standard of living. The United States could ban imports of coffee and begin growing it domestically. But this would entail a very high opportunity cost because coffee could only be grown in the U.S. in greenhouses and would require large amounts of labor and equipment. The coffee would have to sell for a very high price to cover these costs. Suppose the United States did ban coffee imports: Eliminating the ban at some future time would eliminate the jobs of U.S. coffee workers, but the standard of living in the United States would rise as coffee prices declined and labor, machinery, and other resources moved out of coffee production and into production of goods and services for which the United States has a comparative advantage.
- ***Protecting infant industries.*** It is possible that firms in a country may have a comparative advantage in producing a good, but because the country begins production of the good later than other countries, its firms initially have higher costs. In producing some goods and services, substantial "learning by doing" occurs. As workers and firms produce more of the good or service, they gain experience and become more productive. Over time, costs and prices will fall. As the firms in the "infant industry" gain experience, their costs will fall and they will be able to compete successfully with foreign producers. Under free trade, however, they may not get the chance. The established foreign producers can sell the product at a lower price and drive domestic producers out of business before they gain enough experience to compete. To economists, this is the most persuasive of the protectionist arguments. It does have a significant drawback, however. Tariffs used to protect an infant industry eliminate the need for the firms in the industry to become productive enough to compete with foreign firms. After World War II, the governments of many developing countries used the "infant industry" argument to justify high tariff rates. Unfortunately, most of their infant industries never grew up and they continued for years as inefficient drains on their economies.
- ***Protecting national security.*** As already discussed, a country should not rely on other countries for goods that are critical to its military defense. For example, the United States would probably not want to import all of its jet fighter engines from

China. The definition of which goods are critical to military defense is a slippery one, however. In fact, it is rare for an industry to ask for protection without raising the issue of national security even if its products have mainly nonmilitary uses.

18-4 Making the Connection

Has NAFTA Helped or Hurt the U.S. Economy?

The North American Free Trade Agreement (NAFTA) was very controversial when it was being negotiated in the early 1990s. During the 1992 presidential campaign, independent candidate Ross Perot claimed to hear a "giant sucking sound" as jobs were pulled out of the United States and into Mexico. NAFTA went into effect in 1994 and eliminated most tariffs on products shipped between the United States, Canada, and Mexico. This policy change made it possible for each country to better pursue its comparative advantage. For example, before NAFTA the Mexican government had used tariffs to protect its domestic automobile industry, but the industry was much less efficient than the U.S. automobile industry. Once tariffs were removed, Mexican consumers could take advantage of the efficiency of the U.S. industry, and U.S. exports of motor vehicles to Mexico soared. Similarly, Canadian consumers could take advantage of lower-priced U.S. beef, and U.S. consumers could take advantage of lower-priced Canadian lumber. As we would expect, expanding trade increased consumption in all three countries. In the United States, consumption increased about $400 per year for a family of four as a result of NAFTA.

Contrary to Ross Perot's prediction, NAFTA did not lead to a loss of jobs in the United States. Between 1994, when NAFTA went into effect, and 2004, the number of jobs in the United States increased by more than 17 million. Some commentators argued that jobs in the United States could be preserved with NAFTA, but only if wages for U.S. workers declined to the much lower levels being paid Mexican workers. In fact, a study by Gordon Hanson of the University of California, San Diego, showed that the opposite occurred: wages for both U.S. and Mexican workers increased following NAFTA. In addition, the gap between U.S. wages and Mexican wages did not close.

Despite resistance to NAFTA, time proved that the U.S. economy gained jobs.

There were, of course, people in all three countries who were made worse off by NAFTA. Some firms in each country were no longer competitive once tariffs had been lowered. In the United States, government assistance helped workers who lost their jobs to retrain or relocate. Overall, most economists have concluded that NAFTA helped the U.S. economy become more efficient, thereby expanding the consumption of U.S. households.

Source: Gordon H. Hanson, "What Has Happened to Wages in Mexico Since NAFTA? Implications for Hemispheric Free Trade" in Toni Estevadeordal, Dani Rodrick, Alan Taylor Andres Velasco, eds., *FTAA and Beyond: Prospects for Integration in the Americas,* Cambridge: Harvard University Press, 2004.

Positive versus Normative Analysis (Once Again)

Economists emphasize the burden on the economy imposed by tariffs, quotas, and other government restrictions on free trade. Does it follow that these interferences are bad? Remember from Chapter 1 the distinction between *positive analysis* and *normative analysis.* Positive analysis concerns what *is.* Normative analysis concerns what *ought to be.* Measuring the impact of the sugar quota on the U.S. economy is an example of positive analysis. Asserting that the sugar quota is bad public policy and should be eliminated is normative analysis. The sugar quota—like all other interferences with trade—makes some people better off, some people worse off, and reduces total income and consumption. Whether increasing the profits of U.S. sugar companies and the number of workers they employ justifies the costs imposed on consumers and the reduction in economic efficiency is a normative question.

Most economists do not support interferences with trade, such as the sugar quota. Few people become economists if they don't believe that markets should usually be as free as possible. But the opposite view is certainly intellectually respectable. It is possible for someone to understand the costs of tariffs and quotas but still believe that tariffs and quotas are a good idea, perhaps because they believe unrestricted free trade would cause too much disruption to the economy.

The success of industries in getting the government to erect barriers to foreign competition depends partly on some members of the public knowing full well the costs of trade barriers but supporting them anyway. Two other factors are also at work:

1. The costs tariffs and quotas impose on consumers are large in total but relatively small per person. For example, the sugar quota imposes a total burden of about $3 billion per year on consumers. Spread across 295 million Americans, the burden is only about $10 per person: too little for most people to worry about, even if they know the burden exists.
2. The jobs lost to foreign competition are easy to identify, but the jobs created by foreign trade are less easy to identify.

In other words, the industries that benefit from tariffs and quotas benefit a lot—the sugar quota increases the profits of U.S. sugar producers by more than $1 billion—whereas each consumer loses relatively little. This concentration of benefits and widely spread burdens makes it easy to understand why members of Congress receive strong pressure from some industries to enact tariffs and quotas and relatively little pressure from the general public to reduce them.

The Foreign Exchange Market and Exchange Rates

6 LEARNING OBJECTIVE

Explain how exchange rates are determined and how changes in exchange rates affect the prices of imports and exports.

A firm that operates entirely within the United States will price its products in dollars and will use dollars to pay suppliers, workers, interest to bondholders, and dividends to shareholders. A multinational corporation, in contrast, may sell its product in many different countries and receive payment in many different currencies. Its suppliers and workers may also be spread around the world and may have to be paid in local currencies. Corporations may also use the international financial system to borrow in a foreign currency. During the 1990s, for example, many large firms located in East Asian countries, such as Thailand and South Korea, received dollar loans from foreign banks. When firms make extensive use of foreign currencies, they must deal with fluctuations in the exchange rate.

Exchange rate The value of one country's currency in terms of another country's currency.

The **exchange rate** is the value of one country's currency in terms of another country's currency. The exchange rate determines how many units of a foreign currency you can purchase with one dollar. For example, the exchange rate between the U.S. dollar and the Japanese yen can be expressed as ¥100 = $1. (This exchange rate can also be expressed as how many U.S. dollars are required to buy one Japanese yen: $0.01 = ¥1.) The market for foreign exchange is very active. Every day the equivalent of more than $1 trillion worth of currency is traded in the foreign exchange market. The exchange rates that result from this trading are reported each day in the business or financial sections of most newspapers.

Banks and other financial institutions around the world employ currency traders, who are linked together by computer. Rather than exchanging large amounts of paper currency, they buy and sell deposits in banks. A bank buying or selling dollars will actually be buying or selling dollar bank deposits. Dollar bank deposits exist not just in banks in the United States but also in banks around the world. Suppose that the Credit Lyonnais bank in France wishes to sell U.S. dollars and buy Japanese yen. It may exchange U.S. dollar deposits that it owns for Japanese yen deposits owned by the Deutsche Bank in Germany. Businesses and individuals usually obtain foreign currency from banks in their own country.

The market exchange rate is determined by the interaction of demand and supply, just as other prices are. Let's consider the demand for U.S. dollars in exchange for Japanese yen. There are three sources of foreign currency demand for the U.S. dollar:

1. Foreign firms and consumers who want to buy goods and services produced in the United States.
2. Foreign firms and consumers who want to invest in the United States either through foreign direct investment—buying or building factories or other facilities in the United States—or through foreign portfolio investment—buying stocks and bonds issued in the United States.
3. Currency traders who believe that the value of the dollar in the future will be greater than its value today.

Equilibrium in the Market for Foreign Exchange

Figure 18-8 shows the demand and supply of U.S. dollars for Japanese yen. Notice that as we move up the vertical axis in Figure 18-8 the value of the dollar increases relative to the value of the yen. When the exchange rate is ¥150 = $1, the dollar is worth one and a half times as much relative to the yen as when the exchange rate is ¥100 = $1. Consider, first, the demand curve for dollars in exchange for yen. The demand curve has the normal downward slope. When the value of the dollar is high, the quantity of dollars demanded will be low. A Japanese investor will be more likely to buy a $1,000 bond issued by the U.S. Treasury when the exchange rate is ¥100 = $1 and the investor pays only ¥100,000 to buy $1,000 than when the exchange rate is ¥150 = $1 and the investor must pay ¥150,000. Similarly, a Japanese firm is more likely to buy $150,000,000 worth of microchips from the Intel Corporation when the exchange rate is ¥100 = $1 and the

FIGURE 18-8

Equilibrium in the Foreign Exchange Market

When the exchange rate is ¥150 to the dollar, it is above its equilibrium level, and there will be a surplus of dollars. When the exchange rate is ¥100 to the dollar, it is below its equilibrium level, and there will be a shortage of dollars. At an exchange rate of ¥120 to the dollar, the foreign exchange market is in equilibrium.

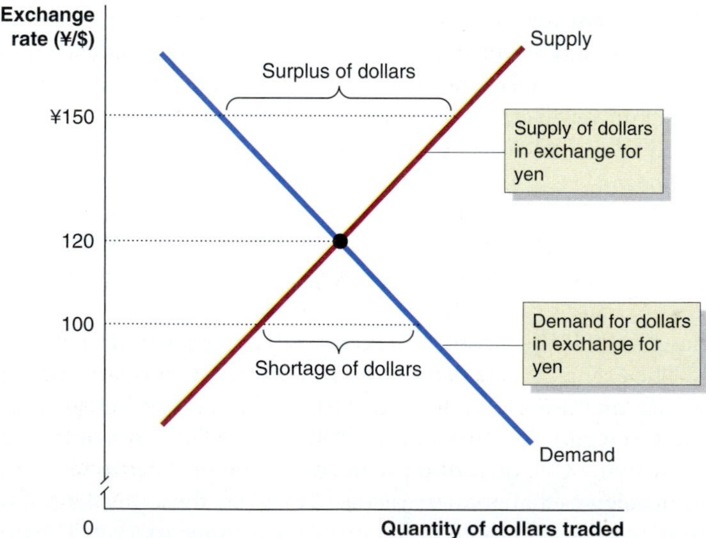

Don't Let This Happen To You!

Don't Confuse What Happens When a Currency Appreciates with What Happens When It Depreciates

One of the more confusing aspects of exchange rates is that they can be expressed in two ways. We can express the exchange rate between the dollar and the yen either as how many yen can be purchased with one dollar or as how many dollars can be purchased with one yen. That is, we can express the exchange rate as ¥100 = $1 or as $0.01 = ¥1. When a currency appreciates, it increases in value relative to another currency. When it depreciates, it decreases in value relative to another currency.

If the exchange rate changes from ¥100 = $1 to ¥120 = $1, the dollar has appreciated and the yen has depreciated because it now takes more yen to buy one dollar. If the exchange rate changes from $0.01 = ¥1 to $0.015 = ¥1, however, the dollar has depreciated and the yen has appreciated because it now takes more dollars to buy one yen. This situation can appear somewhat confusing because the exchange rate seems to have "increased" in both cases. To determine which currency has appreciated and which has depreciated, it is important to remember that an appreciation of the domestic currency means that it now takes *more* units of the foreign currency to buy one unit of the domestic currency. A depreciation of the domestic currency means it takes *fewer* units of the foreign currency to buy one unit of the domestic currency. This observation holds no matter which way we express the exchange rate.

YOUR TURN: **Test your understanding by doing related problem 19 on page 598 at the end of the chapter.**

microchips can be purchased for ¥15 billion than when the exchange rate is ¥150 = $1 and the microchips will cost ¥22.5 billion.

Consider, now, the supply curve of dollars in exchange for yen. The supply curve has the normal upward slope. When the value of the dollar is high, the quantity of dollars supplied in exchange for yen will be high. A U.S. investor will be more likely to buy a ¥200,000 bond issued by the Japanese government when the exchange rate is ¥200 = $1 and he needs to pay only $1,000 to buy ¥200,000, than when the exchange rate is ¥100 = $1 and he must pay $2,000. The owner of a U.S. electronics store is more likely to buy ¥20,000,000 worth of television sets from the Sony Corporation when the exchange rate is ¥200 = $1 and she only needs to pay $100,000 to purchase the televisions, than when the exchange rate is ¥100 = $1 and she must pay $200,000.

As in any other market, equilibrium occurs in the foreign exchange market where the quantity supplied equals the quantity demanded. In Figure 18-8, ¥120 = $1 is the equilibrium exchange rate. At exchange rates above ¥120 = $1, there will be a surplus of dollars and downward pressure on the exchange rate. The surplus and the downward pressure will not be eliminated until the exchange rate falls to ¥120 = $1. If the exchange rate is below ¥120 = $1, there will be a shortage of dollars and upward pressure on the exchange rate. The shortage and the upward pressure will not be eliminated until the exchange rate rises to ¥120 = $1. Surpluses and shortages in the foreign exchange market are eliminated very quickly because the volume of trading in major currencies such as the dollar and the yen is very large and currency traders are linked together by computer.

Currency appreciation occurs when the market value of a country's currency rises relative to the value of another country's currency. **Currency depreciation** occurs when the market value of a country's currency declines relative to the value of another country's currency.

Currency appreciation Occurs when the market value of a currency rises relative to another currency.

Currency depreciation Occurs when the market value of a currency falls relative to another currency.

How Do Shifts in Demand and Supply Affect the Exchange Rate?

Shifts in the demand and supply curves cause the equilibrium exchange rate to change. Three main factors cause the demand and supply curves in the foreign exchange market to shift:

1. Changes in the demand for U.S.-produced goods and services and changes in the demand for foreign-produced goods and services.
2. Changes in the desire to invest in the United States and changes in the desire to invest in foreign countries.
3. Changes in the expectations of currency traders about the likely future value of the dollar and the likely future value of foreign currencies.

SHIFTS IN THE DEMAND FOR FOREIGN EXCHANGE Consider first how the three factors listed above will affect the demand for U.S. dollars in exchange for Japanese yen. During an economic expansion in Japan, the incomes of Japanese households will rise and the demand by Japanese consumers and firms for U.S. goods will increase. At any given exchange rate, the demand for U.S. dollars will increase and the demand curve will shift to the right. Similarly, if interest rates in the United States rise, the desirability of investing in U.S. financial assets will increase, and the demand curve for dollars will also shift to the right. Some buyers and sellers in the foreign exchange market are **speculators**. Speculators buy and sell foreign exchange in an attempt to profit from changes in exchange rates. If a speculator becomes convinced that the value of the dollar is going to rise relative to the value of the yen, the speculator will sell yen and buy dollars. If the current exchange rate is ¥120 = $1 and the speculator is convinced that it will soon rise to ¥140 = $1, the speculator could sell ¥600,000,000 and receive $5,000,000 (¥600,000,000/¥120) in return. If the speculator is correct and the value of the dollar rises against the yen to ¥140 = $1, the speculator will be able to exchange $5,000,000 for ¥700,000,000 ($5,000,000 × ¥140), leaving a profit of ¥100,000,000.

Speculators Currency traders who buy and sell foreign exchange in an attempt to profit by changes in exchange rates.

To summarize, the demand curve for dollars shifts to the right when incomes in Japan rise, when interest rates in the United States rise, or when speculators decide that the value of the dollar will rise relative to the value of the yen.

During a recession in Japan, Japanese incomes will fall, reducing the demand for U.S.-produced goods and services, and shifting the demand curve for dollars to the left. Similarly, if interest rates in the United States fall, the desirability of investing in U.S. financial assets will decrease, and the demand curve for dollars will shift to the left. Finally, if speculators become convinced that the future value of the dollar will be lower than its current value, the demand for dollars will fall and the demand curve will shift to the left.

SHIFTS IN THE SUPPLY OF FOREIGN EXCHANGE The factors affecting the supply curve for dollars are similar to those affecting the demand curve for dollars. An economic expansion in the United States increases the incomes of Americans and increases their demand for goods and services, including goods and services made in Japan. As U.S. consumers and firms increase their spending on Japanese products, they must supply dollars in exchange for yen, which causes the supply curve for dollars to shift to the right. Similarly, an increase in interest rates in Japan will make financial investments in Japan more attractive to U.S. investors. These higher Japanese interest rates will cause the supply of dollars to shift to the right, as U.S. investors exchange dollars for yen. Finally, if speculators become convinced that the future value of the yen will be higher

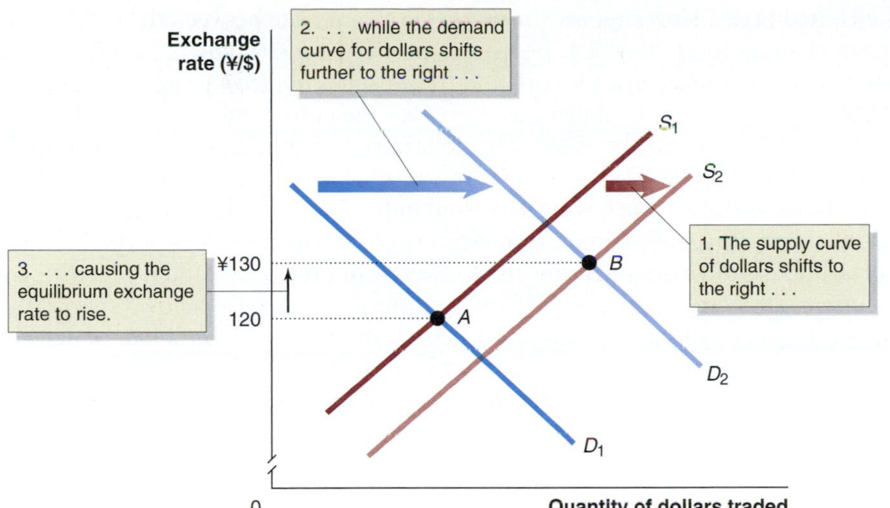

FIGURE 18-9

Shifts in the Demand and Supply Curve Resulting in a Higher Exchange Rate

An increase in the supply of dollars will decrease the equilibrium exchange rate. An increase in the demand for dollars will increase the equilibrium exchange rate, holding other factors constant. In the case shown in this figure, the demand curve and the supply curve have both shifted to the right. Because the demand curve has shifted to the right by more than the supply curve, the equilibrium exchange rate has increased from ¥120 to the dollar at point *A* to ¥130 to the dollar at point *B*.

relative to the dollar than it is today, the supply curve of dollars will shift to the right as traders attempt to exchange dollars for yen.

A recession in the United States will decrease the demand for Japanese products and cause the supply curve for dollars to shift to the left. Similarly, a decrease in interest rates in Japan will make financial investments in Japan less attractive and cause the supply curve of dollars to shift to the left. If traders become convinced that the future value of the yen will be lower relative to the dollar, the supply curve will also shift to the left.

ADJUSTMENT TO A NEW EQUILIBRIUM The factors that affect the supply and demand for currencies are constantly changing. Whether the exchange rate increases or decreases depends on the direction and size of the shifts in the demand curve and supply curve. For example, as Figure 18-9 shows, if the demand curve for dollars in exchange for Japanese yen shifts to the right by more than the supply curve does, the equilibrium exchange rate will increase.

Some Exchange Rates Are Not Determined by the Market

To this point, we have assumed that exchange rates are determined in the market. This assumption is a good one for many currencies, including the U.S. dollar, the euro, the Japanese yen, and the British pound. Some currencies, however, have *fixed exchange rates* that do not change over long periods. For example, for more than 10 years, the value of the Chinese yuan was fixed against the U.S. dollar at a rate of 8.28 yuan to the dollar. A country's central bank has to intervene in the foreign exchange market to buy and sell its currency to keep the exchange rate fixed.

How Movements in the Exchange Rate Affect Exports and Imports

When the market value of the dollar increases, the foreign currency price of U.S. exports rises and the dollar price of foreign imports falls. For example, suppose initially the market exchange rate between the U.S. dollar and the euro is $1 = €1. In that case, an Apple iPod Nano that has a price of $200 in the United States will have a price of €200 in France. A bottle of French wine that has a price of €50 in France will have a price of $50 in the United States. Now suppose the market exchange rate between the U.S. dollar and the euro changes to $1.20 = €1. Because it now takes more dollars to buy a euro, the dollar has *depreciated* against the euro and the euro has *appreciated* against the dollar.

The depreciation of the dollar has decreased the euro price of the iPod from €200 to $200/(1.20 dollars/euro) = €167. The dollar price of the French wine has risen from $50 to €50 × 1.20 dollars/euro = $60. As a result, we would expect more iPods to be sold in France and less French wine to be sold in the United States. To generalize, we can conclude that a depreciation in the domestic currency will increase exports and decrease imports, thereby increasing net exports. As we saw in previous chapters, net exports is a component of aggregate demand. If the economy is currently below potential GDP, then, holding all other factors constant, a depreciation in the domestic currency should increase net exports, aggregate demand, and real GDP.

An appreciation in the domestic currency should have the opposite effect: Exports should fall and imports should rise, which will reduce net exports, aggregate demand, and real GDP.

SOLVED PROBLEM 18-2

6 LEARNING OBJECTIVE

Explain how exchange rates are determined and how changes in exchange rates affect the prices of imports and exports.

Effect of Changing Exchange Rates on the Prices of Imports and Exports

In March 2001, the average price of goods imported into the United States from Canada fell 3.3 percent. This decline was the largest since the federal government began gathering such statistics in 1992. Is it likely that the value of the U.S. dollar appreciated or depreciated versus the Canadian dollar during this period? Is it likely that the average price in Canadian dollars of goods exported from the United States to Canada during March 2001 rose or fell?

Solving the Problem:

Step 1: Review the chapter material. This problem is about changes in the value of a currency, so you may want to review the section "How Movements in the Exchange Rate Affect Exports and Imports," which begins on page 589.

Step 2: Explain whether the value of the U.S. dollar appreciated or depreciated against the Canadian dollar. We know that if the U.S. dollar appreciates against the Canadian dollar, it will take more Canadian dollars to purchase one U.S. dollar. Equivalently, fewer U.S. dollars will be required to purchase one Canadian dollar. A Canadian consumer or business will need to pay more Canadian dollars to buy products imported from the United States: A good or service that had been selling for 100 Canadian dollars will now sell for more than 100 Canadian dollars. A U.S. consumer or business will have to pay fewer U.S. dollars to buy products imported from Canada: A good or service that had been selling for 100 U.S. dollars will now sell for fewer than 100 U.S. dollars. We can conclude that if the price of goods imported into the United States from Canada fell, the value of the U.S. dollar must have appreciated versus the Canadian dollar.

Step 3: Explain what happened to the average price in Canadian dollars of goods exported from the United States to Canada. If the U.S. dollar appreciated relative to the Canadian dollar, the average price in Canadian dollars of goods exported from the United States to Canada will have risen.

YOUR TURN: **For more practice, do related problem 24 on page 599 at the end of this chapter.**

Conclusion

There are few issues economists agree upon more than the economic benefits of free trade. However, there are few political issues as controversial as government policy toward trade. Many people who would be reluctant to see the government interfere with domestic trade are quite willing to see it interfere with international trade. The damage high tariffs inflicted on the world economy during the 1930s shows what can happen when governments around the world abandon free trade. Whether future episodes of that type can be avoided is by no means certain.

Read *An Inside Look* on the next page to learn how eliminating tariffs on wine benefits the United States and Australia.

An Inside Look The United States and Australia Reduce Trade Barriers

SAN FRANCISCO CHRONICLE, MAY 15, 2004

U.S., Australia Commerce to Leap Forward

An already close commercial and cultural relationship will grow even closer Tuesday, when the United States and Australia sign a bilateral free trade agreement that will slash tariffs, streamline investment rules and open up access to a broad spectrum of each country's markets. The free trade agreement, this country's first with a developed nation since Washington struck a free trade deal with Canada in 1988, won't take effect for months to come.

The legislatures of both nations will have to approve it before it becomes law. Australia's Parliament is expected to approve the agreement without too much fuss, while a spokesperson for the U.S. Trade Representative's office said Friday that the Bush administration plans to submit the pact to Congress "sometime this summer. We are seeing good bipartisan support for it."

Two-way trade between Washington and Canberra is already robust, with annual two-way trade of $28 billion. Australia, with a population of just 20 million, is the 13th-largest export market for the United States, while this country is Australia's top export market. Unusually, the United States, which ran a record $46 billion trade deficit with the rest of the world last month, racks up a trade surplus with Australia; the annual surplus crested at $9 billion in 2002.

a California, in particular, finds an eager Aussie market for its computers, electronic gizmos, farm produce, Hollywood movies and Silicon Valley software in Australian shops and homes. The Golden State shipped out $1.9 billion worth of goods to Australia in 2002, and ranks just behind Washington State as this country's largest exporting state to Australia.

"It's hugely positive, it's a winner for both countries," said Robert Hunt, senior investment commissioner for North America at Invest Australia, an **b** Australian federal agency. The agreement, said Hunt, who is based in Invest Australia's San Francisco office, means "the virtual elimination of tariffs, except on beef, dairy and sugar. But they are very far from being the main game. It's probably the most comprehensive agreement anywhere by any two countries."

c Even in this ambitious agreement, some sectors of the economy are off-limits to the Aussies. Notwithstanding its free-trade rhetoric, Washington shelters beef, dairy and sugar industries from foreign competition. In line with that, the proposed agreement would allow no increase in quotas for inexpensive Australian sugar and only modest increases in Aussie beef and dairy products in the huge U.S. market.

But while the free trade agreement won't change everything, it will, if enacted, be far-reaching. The rules of the game for investors, for example, will be radically revised, according to Hunt, whose agency is charged with attracting foreign direct investment. Aussie rules barring foreigners from buying more than a $37 million stake in Australian businesses would be raised to $600 million, for example, enabling Americans to buy into Australian companies and giving Aussie firms much greater access to U.S. capital.

Companies that do businesses with Australia are broadly supportive of the trade agreement. "We have a big interest in Australia, and in general, we support free trade agreements," said Johnny Ng, a spokesman for San Ramon's Chevron Texaco. The energy company is exploring for natural gas on Australia's northwest coast, where it owns 57.1 percent of a natural gas project on the northwest shelf and has a one-sixth stake in a project in the Indian Ocean called Gorgon.

Key Points in the Article

The article discusses a new trade agreement between the United States and Australia that will reduce most restrictions on trade between the two countries. Agreements, such as this one, to expand trade between two countries are known as *bilateral agreements*. The trade agreements worked out by the World Trade Organization are *multilateral agreements*. As the article predicted, both the Australian parliament and the U.S. Congress approved the agreement later in 2004. The U.S. market is the largest in the world. As the article points out, Australia exports more to the United States than to any other country, despite the great distance that separates the two countries.

Analyzing the News

a In this chapter, we have seen that expanding trade raises living standards by increasing consumption and economic efficiency. Reducing tariffs on trade between Australia and the United States will aid consumers in both countries. Figure 1 shows the U.S. market for wine following the elimination of the tariff on Australian wine (just for simplicity, we assume that there are no remaining U.S. tariffs on wine). The price of wine in the United States falls from P_1 to P_2, and equilibrium in the U.S. wine market moves from point *E* to point *F*. U.S. consumption of wine increases from Q_3 to Q_4, the quantity of wine supplied by U.S. winemakers declines from Q_2 to Q_1, and imports increase from $Q_3 - Q_2$ to $Q_4 - Q_1$. Consumer surplus increases by the sum of areas *A*, *B*, *C*, and *D*. Area *A* represents a transfer from producer surplus under the tariff to consumer surplus. Areas *B* and *D* represent the conversion of deadweight loss to consumer surplus. Area *C* represents a conversion of government tariff revenue to consumer surplus. Eliminating the tariff reduces the cost to Australian wine producers of selling their product in the United States. U.S. consumers purchase a larger quantity of Australian wine at a lower price.

b Figure 1 shows that eliminating the tariff on wine also eliminates the revenue the U.S. government had been collecting from this tariff. In high-income countries, such as Australia and the United States, governments receive most of their revenue from taxes on personal and corporate income. For example, tariff revenue in the United States for 2004 amounted to only about 1 percent of all revenue received by the federal government, but governments in low-income countries often have difficulty collecting income taxes, so they rely heavily on tariffs for revenue. In these countries, the government's need for revenue can pose a serious barrier to expanding international trade by reducing tariffs, because governments have difficulty replacing the revenues lost from tariff reductions. This was also true in the United States early in its history. In 1800, tariffs brought in 90 percent of all federal government revenue. As late as the 1950s, tariffs accounted for 14 percent of federal revenues.

c Political factors enter into most trade negotiations. In this case, for political reasons the United States was unwilling to reduce its quotas on beef, dairy products, and sugar. In this chapter, we analyzed the sugar quota's economic effect on the United States.

Thinking Critically ABOUT POLICY

1. Import quotas on sugar, beef, and dairy products save jobs for Americans working in those industries. Do you support these quotas? Why or why not?
2. In which goods mentioned in the article does the United States have a comparative advantage? In which does Australia have a comparative advantage? Explain your reasoning.

Increase in Consumer Surplus	=	Decrease in Producer Surplus	+	Decrease in Government Tariff Revenue	+	Decrease in Deadweight Loss
A + *B* + *C* + *D*		*A*		*C*		*B* + *D*

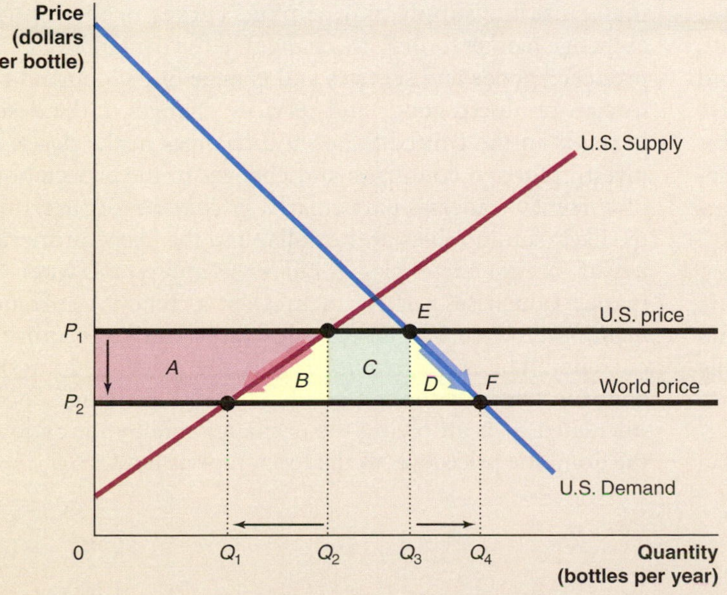

Figure 1: The market for wine in the United States after the tariff on Australian wine is eliminated.

SUMMARY

LEARNING OBJECTIVE ① Discuss the increasing importance of international trade to the United States. The quantity of goods and services the United States imports and exports has been continually increasing. Today, the United States is the leading exporting country in the world, and about 20 percent of U.S. manufacturing jobs depend upon exports.

LEARNING OBJECTIVE ② Understand the difference between comparative advantage and absolute advantage. *Comparative advantage* is the ability of an individual, business, or country to produce a good or service at the lowest opportunity cost. *Absolute advantage* is the ability to produce more of a good or service than competitors when using the same amount of resources. Countries trade on the basis of comparative advantage, not on the basis of absolute advantage.

LEARNING OBJECTIVE ③ Explain how countries gain from international trade. When a country specializes in producing goods where it has a comparative advantage and trades for the other goods it needs, the country will have a higher level of income and consumption. We do not see complete specialization in production for three reasons: Not all goods and services are traded internationally; production of most goods involves increasing opportunity costs; and tastes for products differ across countries. Although the population of a country as a whole benefits from trade, companies—and their workers—that are unable to compete with lower-cost foreign producers lose.

LEARNING OBJECTIVE ④ Discuss the sources of comparative advantage. Among the main sources of comparative advantage are these: climate and natural resources, relative abundance of labor and capital, technology, and *external economies.* A country may develop a comparative advantage in the production of a good, then as time passes and circumstances change, the country may lose its comparative advantage in producing that good and develop a comparative advantage in producing other goods.

LEARNING OBJECTIVE ⑤ Analyze the economic effects of government policies that restrict international trade. Government policies that interfere with trade usually take the form of: *tariffs, quotas,* or *voluntary export restraints.* A tariff is a tax imposed by a government on imports. A quota is a numerical limit imposed by the government on the quantity of a good that can be imported into a country. A voluntary export restraint is an agreement negotiated between two countries that places a numerical limit on the quantity of a good that can be imported by one country from the other country. The federal government's sugar quota costs U.S. consumers $2.91 billion per year, or about $970,000 per year for each job saved in the sugar industry. Saving jobs by using tariffs and quotas is often very expensive. The *World Trade Organization* (*WTO*) is an international organization that enforces international trade agreements. The WTO has promoted *globalization,* the process of countries becoming more open to foreign trade and investment. Some critics of the WTO argue that globalization has damaged local cultures around the world. Other critics oppose the WTO because they believe governments should be free to use tariffs and quotas to protect domestic industries. The WTO allows countries to use tariffs in cases of *dumping,* when an imported product is sold for a price below its cost of production. Economists can point out the burden imposed on the economy by tariffs, quotas, and other government interferences with free trade. But whether these policies should be used is a normative decision.

LEARNING OBJECTIVE ⑥ Explain how exchange rates are determined and how changes in exchange rates affect the prices of imports and exports. The exchange rate is the value of one country's currency in terms of another country's currency. The exchange rate is determined in the foreign exchange market by the demand and supply of a country's currency. Changes in the exchange rate are caused by shifts in demand or supply. The three main sets of factors that cause the supply and demand curves in the foreign exchange market to shift are changes in the demand for U.S.-produced goods and services and change in the demand for foreign-produced goods and services; changes in the desire to invest in the United States and changes in the desire to invest in foreign countries; and changes in the expectations of currency traders—particularly *speculators*—concerning the likely future values of the dollar and the likely future values of foreign currencies. A currency *appreciates* when its market value rises relative to another currency. A currency *depreciates* when its market value falls relative to another currency. The *real exchange rate* is the price of domestic goods in terms of foreign goods. The real exchange rate is calculated by multiplying the exchange rate by the ratio of the domestic price level to the foreign price level.

KEY TERMS

REVIEW QUESTIONS

1. Briefly explain whether you agree or disagree with the following statement: "International trade is more important to the U.S. economy than to most other economies."
2. What is the difference between absolute advantage and comparative advantage? Will a country always be an exporter of a good where it has an absolute advantage in production?
3. Briefly explain how international trade increases a country's consumption.
4. What is meant by a country specializing in the production of a good? Is it typical for countries to be completely specialized? Briefly explain.
5. What are the main sources of comparative advantage?
6. What is a tariff? What is a quota? Who gains and who loses when a country imposes a tariff or a quota on imports of a good?
7. What is globalization? Why are some people opposed to globalization?
8. What is protectionism? Who benefits and who loses from protectionist policies? What are the main arguments people use to justify protectionism?
9. If the exchange rate between the Japanese yen and the U.S. dollar expressed in terms of yen per dollar is ¥110 = $1, what is the exchange rate when expressed in terms of dollars per yen?
10. Suppose that the current exchange rate between the dollar and the euro is 1.1 euros per dollar. If the exchange rate changes to 1.2 euros per dollar, did the euro appreciate or depreciate against the dollar?
11. What are the three main sets of factors that cause the supply and demand curves in the foreign exchange market to shift?

PROBLEMS AND APPLICATIONS

Please visit **www.prenhall.com/hubbard** *for solutions to the even-numbered problems as well as multiple-choice and true or false self-assessment quizzes.*

1. Why do the goods that countries import and export change over time? Use the concept of comparative advantage in your answer.
2. In 1987, an economic study showed that, on average, workers in the Japanese consumer electronics industry produced less output per hour than did U.S. workers producing the same goods. Despite this fact, Japan exported large quantities of consumer electronics to the United States. Briefly explain how this is possible.
   Source: Study cited in Douglas A. Irwin, *Free Trade under Fire*, Princeton: Princeton University Press, 2002, p. 27.
3. The following table shows the hourly output per worker in two industries in Chile and Argentina:

	OUTPUT PER HOUR OF WORK	
	HATS	BEER
Chile	8	6
Argentina	1	2

   a. Explain which country has an absolute advantage in the production of hats and which country has an absolute advantage in the production of beer.
   b. Explain which country has a comparative advantage in the production of hats and which country has a comparative advantage in the production of beer.

c. Suppose that Chile and Argentina currently do not trade with each other. Each has 1,000 hours of labor to use producing hats and beer, and the countries are currently producing the amounts of each good shown in the following table:

	HATS	BEER
Chile	7,200	600
Argentina	600	800

Using this information, give a numerical example of how Chile and Argentina can both gain from trade. Assume that after trading begins, one hat can be exchanged for one barrel of beer.

4. Demonstrate how the opportunity costs of producing cell phones and MP3 players in Japan and the United States in Table 18-2 were calculated.
5. Patrick J. Buchanan, a former presidential candidate, argues in his book on the global economy that there is a flaw in David Ricardo's theory of comparative advantage:

   [C]lassical free trade theory fails the test of common sense. According to Ricardo's law of comparative advantage . . . if America makes better computers and textiles than China does, but our advantage in computers is greater than our advantage in textiles, we should (1) focus on computers, (2) let China make textiles, and (3) trade U.S. computers for Chinese textiles. . . .

   The doctrine begs a question. If Americans are more efficient than Chinese in making clothes . . . why surrender the more efficient American industry? Why shift to a reliance on a Chinese textile industry that will take years to catch up to where American factories are today?

   Do you agree with Buchanan's argument? Briefly explain.

   Source: Patrick J. Buchanan, *The Great Betrayal: How American Sovereignty and Social Justice Are Being Sacrificed to the Gods of the Global Economy*, Boston: Little, Brown, 1998, p. 66.
6. An editorial in *Business Week* argued the following:

   [President] Bush needs to send a pure and clear signal that the U.S. supports free trade on its merits. . . . That means resisting any further protectionist demands by lawmakers. It could even mean unilaterally reducing tariffs or taking down trade barriers rather than erecting new ones. Such moves would benefit U.S. consumers while giving a needed boost to struggling economies overseas.

   What does the editorial mean by "protectionist demands"? How would the unilateral elimination of U.S. trade barriers benefit both U.S. consumers and economies overseas?

   Source: "The Threat of Protectionism," *Business Week*, June 3, 2002.
7. Explain why there are advantages to a movie studio operating in Southern California, rather than in, say, Florida.
8. The United States produces beef and also imports beef from other countries.
   a. Draw a graph showing the supply and demand for beef in the United States. Assume that the United States can import as much as it wants at the world price of beef without causing the world price of beef to increase. Be sure to indicate on your diagram the quantity of beef imported.
   b. Now show on your graph the effect of the United States imposing a tariff on beef. Be sure to indicate on your diagram the quantity of beef sold by U.S. producers before and after the tariff is imposed, the quantity of beef imported before and after the tariff, and the price of beef in the United States before and after the tariff.
   c. Discuss who benefits and who loses when the U.S. imposes a tariff on beef.
9. The following excerpt is from a newspaper story on President Bill Clinton's proposals for changes in the World Trade Organization. The story was published just before the 1999 World Trade Organization meeting in Seattle that ended in rioting:

   [President Clinton] suggested that a working group on labor be created within the WTO to develop core labor standards that would become "part of every trade agreement. And ultimately I would favor a system in which sanctions would come for violating any provision of a trade agreement. . . ." But the new U.S. stand is sure to meet massive resistance from developing countries, which make up more than 100 of the 135 countries in the WTO. They are not interested in adopting tougher U.S. labor standards.

   What did President Clinton mean by "core labor standards"? Why would developing countries resist adopting these standards?
10. **[Related to the *Chapter Opener*]** Which industries are affected unfavorably by the sugar quota? Are any industries (other than the sugar industry) affected favorably by the sugar quota? (*Hint:* Think about what sugar is used for and whether substitutes exist for these uses.)
11. When Congress was considering a bill to impose quotas on imports of textiles, shoes, and other products, Milton Friedman, a Nobel Prize–winning economist, made the following comment:

> The consumer will be forced to spend several extra dollars to subsidize the producers [of these goods] by one dollar. A straight handout would be far cheaper.

Why would a quota result in consumers paying much more than domestic producers receive? Where do the other dollars go? What does Friedman mean by a "straight handout"? Why would this be cheaper than a quota?
Source: Milton Friedman, "Free Trade," *Newsweek*, August 27, 1970.

12. The European Union is an organization of more than 20 European countries. Half of the spending by the European Union consists of subsidies to farmers. These payments result in European farmers producing much more food than they otherwise would. A substantial amount of this food is exported. According to an article in the *Wall Street Journal*, Monica Shandu, a farmer in South Africa, works full-time raising sugar cane on her four-acre farm:

> Ms. Shandu was named South Africa's small-scale Cane Grower of the Year for a top-quality harvest in 2001. Yet . . . she earned only $200 after costs on that harvest. Sugar prices depressed by [European] subsidies cut her annual income by about a third.

Why would subsidies paid by European governments to European sugar farmers reduce the income of a sugar farmer in South Africa?
Source: Roger Thurow and Geoff Winestock, "Addiction to Sugar Subsidies Chokes Poor Nations' Exports," *Wall Street Journal*, September 16, 2002.

13. An economic analysis of a proposal to impose a quota on steel imports into the United States indicated that the quota would save 3,700 jobs in the steel industry but cost about 35,000 jobs in other U.S. industries. Why would a quota on steel imports cause employment to fall in other industries? Which other industries are likely to be most affected?
Source: Study cited in Douglas A. Irwin, *Free Trade Under Fire*, Princeton: Princeton University Press, 2002, p. 82.

14. Steven Landsburg, an economist at the University of Rochester, wrote the following in an article in the *New York Times:*

> Free trade is not only about the right of American consumers to buy at the cheapest possible price; it's also about the right of foreign producers to earn a living. Steelworkers in West Virginia struggle hard to make ends meet. So do steelworkers in South Korea. To protect one at the expense of the other, solely because of where they happened to be born, is a moral outrage.

How does the U.S. government protect steelworkers in West Virginia at the expense of steelworkers in South Korea? Is Landsburg making a positive or a normative statement? A few days later, Tom Redburn published an article disagreeing with Landsburg:

> It is not some evil character flaw to care more about the welfare of people nearby than about that of those far away—it's human nature. And it is morally—and economically—defensible. A society that ignores the consequences of economic disruption on those among its citizens who come out at the short end of the stick is not only heartless, it also undermines its own cohesion and adaptability.

Which of the two arguments do you find most convincing?
Source: Steven E. Landsburg, "Who Cares If the Playing Field Is Level?" *New York Times*, June 13, 2001; and Tom Redburn, "Economic View: Of Politics, Free Markets, and Tending to Society," *New York Times*, June 17, 2001.

15. Suppose China decides to pay large subsidies to any Chinese company that exports goods or services to the United States. As a result, these companies are able to sell products in the United States at far below their cost of production. In addition, China decides to bar all imports from the United States. The dollars that the United States pays to import Chinese goods are left in banks in China. Will this strategy raise or lower the standard of living in China? Will it raise or lower the standard of living in the United States? Briefly explain. Be sure to indicate your definition of "standard of living" in your answer.

16. Hal Varian, an economist at the University of California, Berkeley, has made two observations about international trade:
    1. Trade allows a country "to produce more with less."
    2. There is little doubt who wins [from trade] in the long run: consumers.

    Briefly explain whether or not you agree with either or both of these observations.
Source: Hal R. Varian, "The Mixed Bag of Productivity," *New York Times*, October 23, 2003.

17. **[Related to the *Chapter Opener*]** According to an editorial in the *New York Times*, because of the sugar quota, "Sugar growers in this country, long protected from global competition, have had a great run at the expense of just about everyone else—refineries, candy manufacturers, other food companies, individual consumers and farmers in the developing world." Briefly explain how each group mentioned in this editorial is affected by the sugar quota.
Source: "America's Sugar Daddies," *New York Times*, November 29, 2003.

18. **[Related to *Solved Problem 18-1*]** Suppose that the United States currently both produces kumquats and imports them. The U.S. government then decides to restrict international trade in kumquats by imposing a quota that allows imports of only six million pounds of kumquats

into the United States each year. The figure shows the results of imposing the quota:

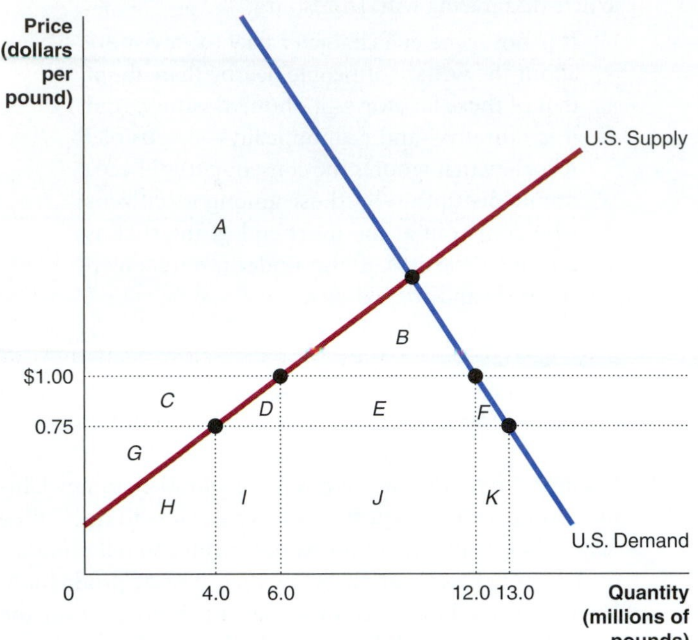

Fill in the following table using the letters in the figure:

	WITHOUT QUOTA	WITH QUOTA
World price of kumquats	______	______
U.S. price of kumquats	______	______
Quantity supplied by U.S. firms	______	______
Quantity demanded	______	______
Quantity imported	______	______
Area of consumer surplus	______	______
Area of domestic producer surplus	______	______
Area of deadweight loss	______	______

19. **[Related to *Don't Let This Happen To You!*]** If we know the exchange rate between Country A's currency and Country B's currency, and we know the exchange rate between Country B's currency and Country C's currency, then we can compute the exchange rate between Country A's currency and Country C's currency.
    a. Suppose the exchange rate between the Japanese yen and the U.S. dollar is currently ¥120 = $1 and the exchange rate between the British pound and the U.S. dollar is £0.60 = $1. What is the exchange rate between the yen and the pound?
    b. Suppose the exchange rate between the yen and dollar changes to ¥130 = $1 and the exchange rate between the pound and dollar changes to £0.50 = $1. Has the dollar appreciated or depreciated against the yen? Has the dollar appreciated or depreciated against the pound? Has the yen appreciated or depreciated against the pound?

20. Graph the demand and supply of U.S. dollars for euros and label each axis. Show graphically and explain the effect of an increase in interest rates in Europe by the European Central Bank (ECB) on the demand and supply of dollars and the resulting change in the exchange rate of euros for U.S. dollars.

21. Graph the demand and supply of U.S. dollars for euros and label each axis. Show graphically and explain the effect of an increase in U.S. government budget deficits that increase U.S. interest rates on the demand and supply of dollars and the resulting change in the exchange rate of euros for U.S. dollars.

22. Use the graph to answer the following questions:

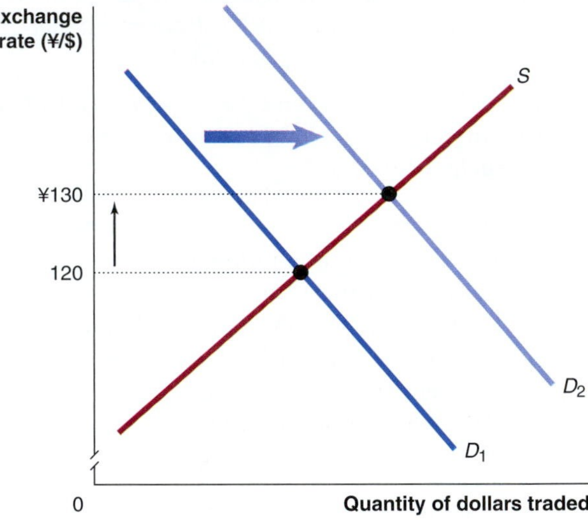

    a. Briefly explain whether the dollar appreciated or depreciated against the yen.
    b. Which of the following events could have caused the shift in demand shown in the graph?
        (i) Interest rates in the United States have declined.
        (ii) Income rises in Japan.
        (iii) Speculators begin to believe the value of the dollar will be higher in the future.

23. Beginning January 1, 2002, 12 of the 15 member countries of the European Union eliminated their own individual currencies and began using a new common currency, the euro. For a three-year period from January 1, 1999, through December 31, 2001, these 12 countries priced goods and services in terms of both their own currencies and the euro. During this period, the value of their currencies was fixed against each other and against the euro. So during this time the dollar had an exchange rate against each of these currencies and against the euro. The information in the following table shows the fixed exchange rate of four European currencies against the euro and their exchange rates against the U.S. dollar on March 2, 2001. Use this information to calculate the exchange rate between the dollar and the euro (in euros per dollar) on March 2, 2001.

CURRENCY	UNITS PER EURO (FIXED)	UNITS PER U.S. DOLLAR (AS OF MARCH 2, 2001)
German mark	1.9558	2.0938
French franc	6.5596	7.0223
Italian lira	1,936.2700	2,072.8700
Portuguese escudo	200.4820	214.6300

24. **[Related to *Solved Problem 18-2*]** When a country's currency appreciates, is this generally good news or bad news for the country's consumers? Is it generally good news or bad news for the country's businesses? Explain your reasoning.

GLOSSARY

A

Absolute advantage The ability of an individual, firm, or country to produce more of a good or service than competitors using the same amount of resources.

Accounting profit A firm's net income measured by revenue less operating expenses and taxes paid.

Aggregate demand and aggregate supply model A model that explains short-run fluctuations in real GDP and the price level.

Aggregate demand curve *(AD)* A curve showing the relationship between the price level and the quantity of real GDP demanded by households, firms, and the government.

Allocative efficiency A state of the economy in which production reflects consumer preferences; in particular, every good or service is produced up to the point where the last unit provides a marginal benefit to consumers equal to the marginal cost of producing it.

Antitrust laws Laws aimed at eliminating collusion and promoting competition among firms.

Asset Anything of value owned by a person or a firm.

Autarky A situation in which a country does not trade with other countries.

Automatic stabilizers Government spending and taxes that automatically increase or decrease along with the business cycle.

Average fixed cost *(AFC)* Fixed cost divided by the quantity of output produced.

Average product of labor The total output produced by a firm divided by the quantity of workers.

Average revenue *(AR)* Total revenue divided by the number of units sold.

Average total cost *(ATC)* Total cost divided by the quantity of output produced.

Average variable cost *(AVC)* Variable cost divided by the quantity of units produced.

B

Balance sheet A financial statement that sums up a firm's financial position on a particular day, usually the end of a quarter or a year.

Bank panic Many banks experiencing runs at the same time.

Bank run Many depositors simultaneously decide to withdraw money from a bank.

Barrier to entry Anything that keeps new firms from entering an industry in which firms are earning economic profits.

Behavioral economics The study of situations in which people act in ways that are not economically rational.

Black market Buying and selling at prices that violate government price regulations.

Bond A financial security that represents a promise to repay a fixed amount of funds.

Budget constraint The limited amount of income available to consumers to spend on goods and services.

Budget deficit The situation in which the government's spending is greater than its tax revenue.

Budget surplus The situation in which the government's expenditures are less than its tax revenue.

Business cycle Alternating periods of economic expansion and economic recession.

Business strategy Actions taken by a firm to achieve a goal, such as maximizing profits.

C

Capital Manufactured goods that are used to produce other goods and services.

Cartel A group of firms that colludes by agreeing to restrict output to increase prices and profits.

Centrally planned economy An economy in which the government decides how economic resources will be allocated.

Ceteris paribus ("all else equal") The requirement that when analyzing the relationship between two variables—such as price and quantity demanded—other variables must be held constant.

Circular-flow diagram A model that illustrates how participants in markets are linked.

Collusion An agreement among firms to charge the same price, or otherwise not to compete.

Command and control approach Government-imposed quantitative limits on the amount of pollution firms are allowed to generate, or government-required installation by firms of specific pollution control devices.

Commodity money A good used as money that also has value independent of its use as money.

Comparative advantage The ability of an individual, firm, or country to produce a good or service at a lower opportunity cost than other producers.

Competitive market equilibrium A market equilibrium with many buyers and many sellers.

Complements Goods that are used together.

Constant returns to scale Exist when a firm's long-run average costs remain unchanged as it increases output.

Consumer price index (CPI) An average of the prices of the goods and services purchased by the typical urban family of four.

Consumer surplus The difference between the highest price a consumer is willing to pay and the price the consumer actually pays.

Consumption Spending by households on goods and services, not including spending on new houses.

Contractionary monetary policy The Fed's adjusting the money supply to increase interest rates to reduce inflation.

Cooperative equilibrium An equilibrium in a game in which players cooperate to increase their mutual payoff.

Copyright A government-granted exclusive right to produce and sell a creation.

Corporate governance The way in which a corporation is structured and the impact a corporation's structure has on the firm's behavior.

Corporation A legal form of business that provides the owners with limited liability.

Coupon payment Interest payment on a bond.

Crowding out A decline in private expenditures as a result of an increase in government purchases.

Currency appreciation Occurs when the market value of a currency rises relative to another currency.

Cyclical unemployment Unemployment caused by a business cycle recession.

Cyclically adjusted budget deficit or surplus The deficit or surplus in the federal government's budget if the economy were at potential GDP.

D

Deadweight loss The reduction in economic surplus resulting from a market not being in competitive equilibrium.

Deflation A decline in the price level.

Demand curve A curve that shows the relationship between the price of a product and the quantity of the product demanded.

Demand schedule A table showing the relationship between the price of a product and the quantity of the product demanded.

Demographics The characteristics of a population with respect to age, race, and gender.

Direct finance A flow of funds from savers to firms through financial markets.

Discount loans Loans the Federal Reserve makes to banks.

Discount rate The interest rate the Federal Reserve charges on discount loans.

Discouraged workers People who are available for work but have not looked for a job during the previous four weeks because they believe no jobs are available for them.

Diseconomies of scale Exist when a firm's long-run average costs rise as it increases output.

Dividends Payments by a corporation to its shareholders.

Dominant strategy A strategy that is the best for the firm, no matter what strategy other firms use.

E

Economic efficiency A market outcome in which the marginal benefit to consumers of the last unit produced is equal to its marginal cost of production, and in which the sum of consumer surplus and producer surplus is at a maximum.

Economic growth The ability of the economy to produce increasing quantities of goods and services.

Economic loss The situation in which a firm's total revenue is less than its total cost, including all implicit costs.

Economic model Simplified versions of reality used to analyze real-world economic situations.

Economic profit A firm's revenues minus all of its costs, implicit and explicit.

Economic surplus The sum of consumer surplus and producer surplus.

Economic variable Something measurable that can have different values, such as the wages of software programmers.

Economics The study of the choices people make to attain their goals, given their scarce resources.

Economies of scale Economies of scale exist when a firm's long-run average costs fall as it increases output.

Efficiency wage A higher-than-market wage paid by a firm to increase worker productivity.

Elastic demand Demand is elastic when the percentage change in quantity demanded is greater than the percentage change in price, so the price elasticity is greater than 1 in absolute value.

Elasticity A measure of how much one economic variable responds to changes in another economic variable.

Endowment effect The tendency of people to be unwilling to sell something they already own even if they are offered a price that is greater than the price they would be willing to pay to buy the good if they didn't already own it.

Entrepreneur Someone who operates a business, bringing together the factors of production—labor, capital, and natural resources—to produce goods and services.

Equity The fair distribution of economic benefits.

Excess reserves Reserves that banks hold over and above the legal requirement.

Exchange rate The value of one country's currency in terms of another country's currency.

Expansion The period of a business cycle during which total production and total employment are increasing.

Expansion path A curve showing a firm's cost-minimizing combination of inputs for every level of output.

Expansionary monetary policy The Federal Reserve's increasing the money supply and decreasing interest rates to increase real GDP.

Explicit cost A cost that involves spending money.

Exports Goods and services produced domestically but sold to other countries.

External economies Reductions in a firm's costs that result from an expansion in the size of an industry.

Externality A benefit or cost that affects someone who is not directly involved in the production or consumption of a good or service.

F

Factor markets Markets for the factors of production, such as labor, capital, natural resources, and entrepreneurial ability.

Federal funds rate The interest rate banks charge each other for overnight loans.

Federal Open Market Committee (FOMC) The Federal Reserve committee responsible for open market operations and managing the money supply.

Federal Reserve System The central bank of the United States.

Fiat money Money, such as paper currency, that is authorized by a central bank or governmental body and that does not have to be exchanged by the central bank for gold or some other commodity money.

Final good or service A good or service purchased by a final user.

Financial system The system of financial markets and financial intermediaries through which firms acquire funds from households.

Fiscal policy Changes in federal taxes and purchases that are intended to achieve macroeconomic policy objectives, such as high employment, price stability, and high rates of economic growth.

Fixed costs Costs that remain constant as output changes.

Fractional reserve banking system A banking system in which banks keep less than 100 percent of deposits as reserves.

Free market A market with few government restrictions on how a good or service can be produced or sold, or on how a factor of production can be employed.

Free trade Trade between countries that is without government restrictions.

Frictional unemployment Short-term unemployment arising from the process of matching workers with jobs.

G

Game theory The study of how people make decisions in situations where attaining their goals depends on their interactions with others; in economics, the study of the decisions of firms in industries where the profits of each firm depend on its interactions with other firms.

GDP deflator A measure of the price level, calculated by dividing nominal GDP by real GDP, and multiplying by 100.

Globalization The process of countries becoming more open to foreign trade and investment.

Government purchases Spending by federal, state, and local governments on goods and services.

Gross domestic product (GDP) The market value of all final goods and services produced in a country during a period of time.

H

Horizontal merger A merger between firms in the same industry.

Human capital The accumulated knowledge and skills workers acquire from education and training or from their life experiences.

I

Implicit cost A nonmonetary opportunity cost.

Imports Goods and services bought domestically but produced in other countries.

Income effect The change in the quantity demanded of a good that results from the effect of a change in the good's price on consumer purchasing power.

Income statement A financial statement that sums up a firm's revenues, costs, and profit over a period of time.

Indirect finance A flow of funds from savers to borrowers through financial intermediaries, such as banks. Intermediaries raise funds from savers to lend to firms (and other borrowers).

Inelastic demand Demand is inelastic when the percentage change in quantity demanded is less than the percentage change in price, so the price elasticity is less than 1 in absolute value.

Inferior good A good for which the demand increases as income falls, and decreases as income rises.

Inflation rate The percentage increase in the price level from one year to the next.

Inflation targeting Conducting monetary policy so as to commit the central bank to achieving a publicly announced level of inflation.

Interest rate The cost of borrowing funds, usually expressed as a percentage of the amount borrowed.

Intermediate good or service A good or service that is an input into another good or service, such as a tire on a truck.

Investment Spending by firms on new factories, office buildings, machinery, and inventories, and spending by households on new houses.

Isocost line All the combinations of two inputs, such as capital and labor, that have the same total cost.

Isoquant A curve showing all the combinations of two inputs, such as capital and labor, that will produce the same level of output.

K

Keynesian revolution The name given to the widespread acceptance during the 1930s and 1940s of John Maynard Keynes's macroeconomic model.

L

Labor force The sum of employed and unemployed workers in the economy.

Labor force participation rate The percentage of the working-age population in the labor force.

Labor productivity The quantity of goods and services that can be produced by one worker or by one hour of work.

Law of demand Holding everything else constant, when the price of a product falls, the quantity demanded of the product will increase, and when the price of a product rises, the quantity demanded of the product will decrease.

Law of diminishing marginal utility Consumers experience diminishing additional satisfaction as they consume more of a good or service during a given period of time.

Law of diminishing returns The principle that, at some point, adding more of a variable input, such as labor, to the same amount of a fixed input, such as capital, will cause the marginal product of the variable input to decline.

Law of supply Holding everything else constant, increases in price cause increases in the quantity supplied, and decreases in price cause decreases in the quantity supplied.

Liability Anything owed by a person or a firm.

Limited liability The legal provision that shields owners of a corporation from losing more than they have invested in the firm.

Long run A period of time long enough to allow a firm to vary all of its inputs, to adopt new technology, and to increase or decrease the size of its physical plant.

Long-run aggregate supply curve *(LRAS)* A curve showing the relationship in the long run between the price level and the quantity of real GDP supplied.

Long-run average cost curve A curve showing the lowest cost at which the firm is able to produce a given quantity of output in the long run, when no inputs are fixed.

Long-run competitive equilibrium The situation in which the entry and exit of firms has resulted in the typical firm breaking even.

Long-run economic growth The process by which rising productivity increases the average standard of living.

Long-run supply curve A curve showing the relationship in the long run between market price and the quantity supplied.

M

M1 The narrowest definition of the money supply: The sum of currency in circulation, checking account balances in banks, and holdings of traveler's checks.

M2 A broader definition of the money supply: M1 plus savings account balances, small-denomination time deposits, balances in money market deposit accounts in banks, and noninstitutional money market fund shares.

Macroeconomics The study of the economy as a whole, including topics such as inflation, unemployment, and economic growth.

Marginal analysis Analysis that involves comparing marginal benefits and marginal costs.

Marginal benefit *(MB)* The additional benefit to a consumer from consuming one more unit of a good or service.

Marginal cost *(MC)* The change in a firm's total cost from producing one more unit of a good or service.

Marginal product of labor The additional output a firm produces as a result of hiring one more worker.

Marginal rate of technical substitution *(MRTS)* The slope of an isoquant; represents the rate at which a firm is able to substitute one input for another, while keeping the level of output constant.

Marginal revenue *(MR)* Change in total revenue from selling one more unit.

Marginal utility *(MU)* The change in total utility a person receives from consuming one additional unit of a good or service.

Market A group of buyers and sellers of a good or service and the institution or arrangement by which they come together to trade.

Market demand The demand by all the consumers of a given good or service.

Market economy An economy in which the decisions of households and firms interacting in markets allocate economic resources.

Market equilibrium A situation in which quantity demanded equals quantity supplied.

Market failure Situations in which the market fails to produce the efficient level of output.

Market for loanable funds The interaction of borrowers and lenders that determines the market interest rate and the quantity of loanable funds exchanged.

Market power The ability of a firm to charge a price greater than marginal cost.

Menu costs The costs to firms of changing prices.

Microeconomics The study of how households and firms make choices, how they interact in markets, and how the government attempts to influence their choices.

Minimum efficient scale The level of output at which all economies of scale have been exhausted.

Mixed economy An economy in which most economic decisions result from the interaction of buyers and sellers in markets, but in which the government plays a significant role in the allocation of resources.

Monetarism The macroeconomic theories of Milton Friedman and his followers; particularly the idea that the quantity of money should be increased at a constant rate.

Monetary growth rule A plan for increasing the quantity of money at a fixed rate that does not respond to changes in economic conditions.

Monetary policy The actions the Federal Reserve takes to manage the money supply and interest rates to pursue its economic objectives.

Money Assets that people are generally willing to accept in exchange for goods and services or for payment of debts.

Monopolistic competition A market structure in which barriers to entry are low, and many firms compete by selling similar, but not identical, products.

Monopoly The only seller of a good or service that does not have a close substitute.

Multiplier effect The series of induced increases in consumption spending that results from an initial increase in autonomous expenditures.

N

Nash equilibrium A situation where each firm chooses the best strategy, given the strategies chosen by other firms.

Natural monopoly A situation in which economies of scale are so large that one firm can supply the entire market at a lower average total cost than can two or more firms.

Natural rate of unemployment The normal rate of unemployment, consisting of structural unemployment plus frictional unemployment.

Net exports Exports minus imports.

Network externalities Network externalities exist when the usefulness of a product increases with the number of consumers who use it.

New classical macroeconomics The macroeconomic theories of Robert Lucas and others, particularly the idea that workers and firms have rational expectations.

Nominal GDP The value of final goods and services evaluated at current year prices.

Nominal interest rate The stated interest rate on a loan.

Noncooperative equilibrium An equilibrium in a game in which players do not cooperate but pursue their own self-interest.

Normal good A good for which the demand increases as income rises and decreases as income falls.

Normative analysis Analysis concerned with what ought to be.

O

Oligopoly A market structure in which a small number of interdependent firms compete.

Open market operations The buying and selling of Treasury securities by the Federal Reserve in order to control the money supply.

Opportunity cost The highest-valued alternative that must be given up to engage in an activity.

P

Partnership A firm owned jointly by two or more persons and not organized as a corporation.

Patent The exclusive right to a product for a period of 20 years from the date the product was invented.

Payoff matrix A table that shows the payoffs that each firm earns from every combination of strategies by the firms.

Perfectly competitive market A market that meets the conditions of (1) many buyers and sellers, (2) all firms selling identical products, and (3) no barriers to new firms entering the market.

Perfectly elastic demand Demand is perfectly elastic when a change in price results in an infinite change in quantity demanded.

Perfectly inelastic demand Demand is perfectly inelastic when a change in price results in no change in quantity demanded.

Pigovian taxes and subsidies Government taxes and subsidies intended to bring about an efficient level of output in the presence of externalities.

Positive analysis Analysis concerned with what is.

Potential GDP The level of GDP attained when all firms are producing at capacity.

Present value The value in today's dollars of funds to be paid or received in the future.

Price ceiling A legally determined maximum price that sellers may charge.

Price discrimination Charging different prices to different customers for the same product when the price differences are not due to differences in cost.

Price elasticity of demand The responsiveness of the quantity demanded to a change in price, measured by dividing the percentage change in the quantity demanded of a product by the percentage change in the product's price.

Price floor A legally determined minimum price that sellers may receive.

Price level A measure of the average prices of goods and services in the economy.

Price taker A buyer or seller that is unable to affect the market price.

Principal-agent problem A problem caused by an agent pursuing his own interests rather than the interests of the principal who hired him.

Prisoners' dilemma A game where pursuing dominant strategies results in noncooperation that leaves everyone worse off.

Private benefit The benefit received by the consumer of a good or service.

Private cost The cost borne by the producer of a good or service.

Producer price index (PPI) An average of the prices received by producers of goods and services at all stages of the production process.

Producer surplus The difference between the lowest price a firm would have been willing to accept and the price it actually receives.

Product markets Markets for goods—such as computers—and services—such as medical treatment.

Production function The relationship between the inputs employed by the firm and the maximum output it can produce with those inputs.

Production possibilities frontier A curve showing the maximum attainable combinations of two products that may be produced with available resources.

Productive efficiency The situation in which a good or service is produced at the lowest possible cost.

Profit Total revenue minus total cost.

Property rights The rights individuals or businesses have to the exclusive use of their property, including the right to buy or sell it.

Protectionism The use of trade barriers to shield domestic firms from foreign competition.

Public franchise A designation by the government that a firm is the only legal provider of a good or service.

Q

Quantity demanded The amount of a good or service that a consumer is willing and able to purchase at a given price.

Quantity supplied The amount of a good or service that a firm is willing and able to supply at a given price.

Quantity theory of money A theory of the connection between money and prices that assumes that the velocity of money is constant.

Quota A numerical limit imposed by the government on the quantity of a good that can be imported into a country.

R

Real business cycle model A macroeconomic model that focuses on real, rather than monetary, causes of the business cycle.

Real GDP The value of final goods and services evaluated at base year prices.

Real interest rate The nominal interest rate minus the inflation rate.

Recession The period of a business cycle during which total production and total employment are decreasing.

Required reserve ratio *(RR)* The minimum fraction of deposits banks are required by law to keep as reserves.

Required reserves Reserves that a bank is legally required to hold, based on its checking account deposits.

Reserves Deposits that a bank keeps as cash in its vault or on deposit with the Federal Reserve.

S

Scarcity The situation in which unlimited wants exceed the limited resources available to fulfill those wants.

Separation of ownership from control In many large corporations the top management, rather than the shareholders, control day-to-day operations.

Short run The period of time during which at least one of the firm's inputs is fixed.

Short-run aggregate supply curve *(SRAS)* A curve showing the relationship in the short run between the price level and the quantity of real GDP supplied by firms.

Shortage A situation in which the quantity demanded is greater than the quantity supplied.

Shutdown point The minimum point on a firm's average variable cost curve; if the price falls below this point, the firm shuts down production in the short run.

Simple deposit multiplier The ratio of the amount of deposits created by banks to the amount of new reserves.

Social benefit The total benefit from consuming a good, including both the private benefit and any external benefit.

Social cost The total cost of producing a good, including both the private cost and any external cost.

Sole proprietorship A firm owned by a single individual and not organized as a corporation.

Speculators Currency traders who buy and sell foreign exchange in an attempt to profit by changes in exchange rates.

Stagflation A combination of inflation and recession, usually resulting from a supply shock.

Stock A financial security that represents partial ownership of a firm.

Stockholders' equity The difference between the value of a corporation's assets and the value of its liabilities; also known as net worth.

Structural unemployment Unemployment arising from a persistent mismatch between the skills and characteristics of workers and the requirements of jobs.

Substitutes Goods and services that can be used for the same purpose.

Substitution effect The change in the quantity demanded of a good that results from a change in price making the good more or less expensive relative to other goods that are substitutes.

Sunk cost A cost that has already been paid and cannot be recovered.

Supply curve A curve that shows the relationship between the price of a product and the quantity of the product supplied.

Supply schedule A table that shows the relationship between the price of a product and the quantity of the product supplied.

Supply shock An unexpected event that causes the short-run aggregate supply curve to shift.

Surplus A situation in which the quantity supplied is greater than the quantity demanded.

T

Tariff A tax imposed by a government on a good imported into a country.

Tax wedge The difference between the pre-tax and post-tax return to an economic activity.

Taylor rule A rule developed by John Taylor that links the Fed's target for the federal funds rate to economic variables.

Technological change A change in the ability of a firm to produce a given level of output with a given quantity of inputs.

Technology The processes a firm uses to turn inputs into outputs of goods and services.

Terms of trade The ratio at which a country can trade its exports for imports from other countries.

Total cost The cost of all the inputs a firm uses in production.

Total revenue The total amount of funds received by a seller of a good or service, calculated by multiplying price per unit by number of units sold.

Trade The act of buying or selling.

Trade-off The idea that because of scarcity, producing more of one good or service means producing less of another good or service.

Transfer payments Payments by the government to individuals for which the government does not receive a good or service in return.

U

Underground economy Buying and selling of goods and services that is concealed from the government to avoid taxes or regulations or because the goods and services are illegal.

Unemployment rate The percentage of the labor force that is unemployed.

Unit-elastic demand Demand is unit-elastic when the percentage change in quantity demanded is equal to the percentage change in price, so the price elasticity is equal to 1 in absolute value.

Utility The enjoyment or satisfaction people receive from consuming goods and services.

V

Value added The market value a firm adds to a product.

Variable costs Costs that change as output changes.

Velocity of money The average number of times each dollar in the money supply is used to purchase goods and services included in GDP.

Vertical merger A merger between firms at different stages of production of a good.

Voluntary exchange The situation that occurs in markets when both the buyer and seller of a product are made better off by the transaction.

Voluntary export restraint An agreement negotiated between two countries that places a numerical limit on the quantity of a good that can be imported by one country from the other country.

World Trade Organization (WTO) An international organization that enforces international trade agreements.

COMPANY INDEX

SUBJECT INDEX

Key terms and the page on which they are defined appear in **boldface.**

D

E

N

O

CREDITS

Photo

Chapter 1, *page 3,* Michel Setboun, Corbis/Bettmann; *page 12,* Sherwin Castro/Reuters, Landov LLC.

Chapter 2, *page 33,* BMW of North America, LLC; *page 38,* AP Wide World Photos; *page 47,* Corbis/Bettmann; *page 50,* SuperStock, Inc.; *page 52,* S.I.N., Corbis/Bettmann.

Chapter 3, *page 63,* AP Wide World Photos; *page 69,* David Young-Wolff, PhotoEdit; *page 70,* Michael Newman, PhotoEdit; *page 73,* Kathleen Olson; *page 82,* AFP, Getty Images, Inc.-Agence France Presse.

Chapter 4, *page 97,* Rudi Von Briel, PhotoEdit; *page 100,* AP Wide World Photos; *page 106,* Laima Druskis, Pearson Education/PH College; *page 110,* Zefa/N. Guegan, Masterfile Corporation; *page 117,* Swift, Joe, Index Stock Imagery, Inc.

Chapter 5, *page 131,* Kim Kulish, Corbis/Bettmann; *page 133,* Ed Pritchard, Getty Images Inc.-Stone Allstock; *page 139,* Jeffrey Brown, Aurora & Quanta Productions Inc.; *page 141,* David McIntyre, Black Star.

Chapter 6, *page 163,* Corbis/Bettman; *page 173,* Duomo, Corbis/Bettmann; *page 176,* AP Wide World Photos; *page 180,* Peter Hvizdak, The Image Works; *page 186,* Myrleen Ferguson Cate, PhotoEdit.

Chapter 7, *page 201,* Yoshikazu Tsuno/AFP, Getty Images, Inc.-Agence France Presse; *page 203,* Getty Images, Inc.-Liaison; *page 204,* Stockbyte; *page 208,* AP Wide World Photos; *page 219,* Getty Images Inc.-Hulton Archive Photos; *page 235,* Walt Disney Pictures/Pixar, Picture Desk, Inc./Kobal Collection.

Chapter 8, *page 231,* AP Wide World Photos; *page 243,* Stockbyte; *page 244,* Raymond Forbes, SuperStock, Inc.; *page 253,* Richard Heinzen, SuperStock, Inc.

Chapter 9, *page 265,* Tom Stewart, Corbis/Bettmann; *page 267,* Tim Boyle, Getty Images; *page 269,* Sean Cayton, The Image Works; *page 271,* Rob Melnychuk, Getty Images, Inc.-Photodisc.; *page 288,* Joe Marquette, AP Wide World Photos.

Chapter 10, *page 309,* AP Wide World Photos; *page 316,* Mario Tama, Getty Images, Inc.-Liaison; *page 319,* Yuriko Nakao/Reuters, Corbis/Reuters America LLC; *page 321,* David Young-Wolff, PhotoEdit; *page 326,* Dreamworks/Universal/Eli Reed.

Chapter 11, *page 331,* Gary Moon; *page 338,* Diane Bondareff /Bloomberg News/Landov LLC; *page 341,* John Maier, Jr./The Image Works; *page 344,* Getty Images Inc.-Hulton Archive Photos; *page 346,* Chris Salvo/Getty Images, Inc.-Taxi.

Chapter 12, *page 357,* Tim Boyle/Getty Images, Inc. Liaison; *page 362,* NBC TV/Picture Desk, Inc./Kobal Collection; *page 368,* Tannen Maury/The Image Works; *page 371,* Image Works/Mary Evans Picture Library Ltd; *page 380,* Tom McCarthy/PhotoEdit.

Chapter 13, *page 389,* Jim West/The Image Works; *page 392,* Earl & Nazima Kowall/COR-BISNY; *page 396,* David Reed/Panos Pictures; *page 402,* Getty Images Inc.–Hulton Archive Photos; *page 408,* AP Wide World Photos.

Chapter 14, *page 421,* Caterpillar Inc.; *page 426,* Tony Freeman/PhotoEdit; *page 442,* Catherine Karnow/Woodfin Camp & Associates; *page 455,* Corbis/Bettmann.

Chapter 15, *page 457,* Larry Luxner/Luxner News, Inc.; *page 459,* Reg Speller/Getty Images Inc.–Hulton Archive Photos; *page 462,* Reuters/Russell Boyce/Corbis/Reuters America LLC; *page 474,* Alejandro Kaminetzky/Reuters/Corbis/Reuters America LLC; *page 481,* Corbis/Bettmann.

Chapter 16, *page 489,* Corbis Royalty Free; *page 500,* Corbis Royalty Free; *page 502,* Reuters/Larry Downing/Corbis/Reuters America LLC; *page 504,* Tom Wagner/Corbis/SABA Press Photos, Inc.; *page 508,* AP Wide World Photos.

Chapter 17, *page 523,* Joe Raedle/Getty Images, Inc. Liaison; *page 527,* Paddy Eckersley/ImageState/International Stock Photography Ltd.; *page 539,* Tom Wagner/Corbis/SABA Press Photos, Inc.; *page 542,* AP Wide World Photos; *page 548,* JLP/Jose L. Pelaez/CORBIS-NY.

Chapter 18, *page 565,* Burke/Triolo, Getty Images, Inc.-Brand X Pictures; *page 568,* Ron Sherman, Corbis/Bettmann; *page 574,* Corbis/Sygma *page 582,* Pallava Bagla, Corbis/Sygma; *page 584,* AP Wide World Photos.

Text

Chapter 1, *page 84:* Steve W. Martinez, "Vertical Coordination in the Pork and Broiler Industries: Implications for Pork and Chicken Products," Agricultural Economics Report No. 777, April 1999.

Chapter 4, *page 107:* Thomas Sowell, *Applied Economics: Thinking Beyond Stage One,* New York: Basic Books, 2004, page 114.

Chapter 5, *page 143:* Deborah Solomon, "WorldCom's Ex- Controller Pleads Guilty to Three Counts," *Wall Street Journal,* September 27, 2002, quoting from Myers's guilty plea; and Sharon Young, "MCI Restates 2001, 2002 Earnings, Cutting Profit by $74.4 Billion," *Wall Street Journal,* March 12, 2004.

Chapter 6, page 172: Gary S. Becker and Kevin M.Murphy, *Social Economics: Market Behavior in a Social Environment,* Cambridge: Harvard University Press, 2000, page 9; *page 175:* Richard H. Thaler, *The Winner's Curse: Paradoxes and Anomalies of Economic Life,* New York: Free Press, 1992, page 25; *page 286:* Gary Becker, "A Note on Restaurant Pricing and Other Examples of Social Influences on Prices," *Journal of Political Economy,* Vol. 99, No. 5, October 1991, pages 1109-1116; and Daniel Kahneman, Jack Knetsch, and Richard Thaler, "Fairness as a Constraint on Profit Seeking: Entitlements in the Market," *American Economic Review,* Vol. 76, No. 4, September 1986, pages 728-741; *page 178:* Daniel Kahneman and Amos Tversky, "Choices,Values, and Frames," *American Psychologist,* April 1984.

Chapter 7, *page 217:* Norihiko Shirouzu and Sebastian Moffett, "As Toyota Closes In on GM, Quality Concerns Also Grow" *Wall Street Journal,* August 4, 2004.

Chapter 8, *page 251:* Sharon M. Oster, *Modern Competitive Analysis,* Third edition, New York: Oxford University Press, 1999, page 11.

Chapter 9, *page 280:* Joseph A. Schumpeter, *Capitalism, Socialism, and Democracy,* New York: Harper & Row, 1975 (first published 1942), page 84.

Chapter 10, *page 308:* Andy Serwer, "Hot Starbucks to Go," *Fortune*, January 12, 2004; *page 401:* Peter F. Drucker, *Management: Tasks, Responsibilities, Practices*, New York: Harper & Row, 1974, pages 63-64.

Chapter 13, *page 392*: Stanley Lebergott, *The Americans: An Economic Record*, New York: W.W. Norton, 1984; Stanley Lebergott, *Pursuing Happiness: American Consumers in the Twentieth Century*, Princeton: Princeton University Press, 1993; *page 648:* Richard Sylla, "Financial Systems and Economic Modernization," *Journal of Economic History*, Vol. 62, No. 2, June 2002, pp. 277–292; *page 411*: Jeff Bailey, "Small Companies Prepare for the Good Times to Roll Again," *Wall Street Journal*, January 22, 2002.

Chapter 15, *page 458*: Jeremy Atack and Peter Passell, *A New Economic View of American History from Colonial Times to 1940*, 2nd ed., New York: W.W. Norton, 1994, pp. 81–82.

Chapter 17, *page 550*: Edward Prescott, "Why Do Americans Work So Much More Than Europeans?" Federal Reserve Bank of Minneapolis *Quarterly Review*, Vol. 28, No. 1, July 2004, pp. 2–13, and Alberto Alesina, Edward Glaeser, and Bruce Sacerdote, "Work and Leisure in the U.S. and Europe: Why So Different?" National Bureau of Economic Research,Working Paper 11278, April 2005.

Chapter 18, *page 575:* Gary McWilliams, "In Electronics, U.S. Companies Seize Momentum From Japan," *Wall Street Journal*, March 10, 2005, page A1.